Handbook of the Economics of
Risk and Uncertainty

Handbook of the Economics of
Risk and Uncertainty

VOLUME *1*

by

MARK J. MACHINA
Distinguished Professor of Economics
University of California, San Diego, CA, USA

W. KIP VISCUSI
University Distinguished Professor of Law,
Economics, and Management,
Vanderbilt University, USA

ELSEVIER

Amsterdam • Boston • Heidelberg • London • New York • Oxford
Paris • San Diego • San Francisco • Singapore • Sydney • Tokyo
North-Holland is an imprint of Elsevier

North-Holland is an imprint of Elsevier
The Boulevard, Langford Lane, Kidlington, Oxford OX5 1GB, UK
Radarweg 29, PO Box 211, 1000 AE Amsterdam, The Netherlands

First edition 2014

British Library Cataloguing in Publication Data
A catalogue record for this book is available from the British Library

Library of Congress Cataloging-in-Publication Data
A catalog record for this book is available from the Library of Congress

ISBN–13: 978-0-444-53685-3

For information on all North-Holland publications
visit our website at books.elsevier.com

Printed and bound in the UK
14 15 16 17 18   10 9 8 7 6 5 4 3 2 1

Working together
to grow libraries in
developing countries

www.elsevier.com • www.bookaid.org

CONTENTS

CONTRIBUTORS

Chapter 1
Edi Karni
Department of Economics, Johns Hopkins University, USA
Warwick School of Business, University of Warwick, UK

Chapter 2
Peter J. Hammond
Department of Economics, University of Warwick, UK

Horst Zank
Department of Economics, School of Social Sciences, University of Manchester, UK

Chapter 3
Jack Meyer
Department of Economics, Michigan State University, USA

Chapter 4
Charles A. Holt
Department of Economics, University of Virginia, USA

Susan K. Laury
Department of Economics, Georgia State University, USA

Chapter 5
Georges Dionne
HEC Montréal, Montréal, QC, Canada

Scott E. Harrington
The Wharton School, University of Pennsylvania, Philadelphia, PA, USA

Chapter 6
Benjamin E. Hermalin
University of California Berkeley, CA, USA

Chapter 7
W. Kip Viscusi
University Distinguished Professor of Law, Economics, and Management,
Vanderbilt University, USA

Chapter 8
Tomas J. Philipson
Daniel Levin Professor of Public Policy, The University of Chicago, USA

George Zanjani
AAMGA Distinguished Chair in Risk Management and Insurance,
Georgia State University, USA

Chapter 9

Thomas J. Kniesner
Claremont Graduate University, Claremont, CA, USA
Syracuse University, Syracuse, NY, USA
IZA, Bonn, Germany

John D. Leeth
Bentley University, Waltham, MA, USA

Chapter 10

Joseph E. Aldy
Assistant Professor of Public Policy, Harvard University, John F. Kennedy School of Government, USA

W. Kip Viscusi
University Distinguished Professor of Law, Economics, and Management, Vanderbilt University, USA

Chapter 11

Howard Kunreuther and Erwann Michel-Kerjan
Center for Risk Management and Decision Processes, The Wharton School, University of Pennsylvania, USA

Chapter 12

John Quiggin
School of Economics, University of Queensland, Australia

Chapter 13

Mark J. Machina
Distinguished Professor of Economics, University of California, San Diego, CA, USA
Marciano Siniscalchi
Department of Economics, Northwestern University, Evanston, IL, USA

Chapter 14

John D. Hey
Department of Economics and Related Studies, University of York, UK

Handbook of the Economics of Risk and Uncertainty

Kenneth J. Arrow
Department of Economics, Stanford, CA, USA

That the world is uncertain is an everyday observation. Any theory of action, and certainly economics is or seeks to be a theory of action, must take account of the fact that the choices have uncertain consequences. This preface is a set of musings on these issues, which are illuminated in this Handbook.

The elementary fact of uncertainty raises many questions, basic to both the logic of research and to understanding the role of uncertainty in the economic system. I will talk about three. (1) How do we describe uncertainty? (2) What is the role of information, i.e., changes in uncertainty, and how is it to be defined? (3) What are the reactions of individual economic agents and by the economy as a whole?

The predominant language in which uncertainty is described is that of probability. The concept of probability was developed for application to the evaluation of games of chance in the 16th and 17th centuries. But it was almost immediately applied to insurance and to the interpretation of actuarial tables (fire, life) already then being collected.

To determine probabilities, it is clearly necessary to know some probabilities. The axioms of probability are consistency conditions. In the context of games of chance, usually it was desired to find the probability of some event which was the union of a number of elementary events. It was usually considered that the elementary events (the upward face of a die or a card drawn from a shuffled deck) were equally probable. The argument was taken for granted by the early probability theorists. Later, more critical, scholars called this the principle of Insufficient Reason; when there is no reason to assume that one outcome is more probable than another, the probabilities may be taken as equal.

This problem, where do we start with probability judgments, remains today the chief foundational question for using probability theory as the exclusive language for characterizing uncertainty.

A key step in linking probability judgments to observed facts rather than judgments of ignorance was the statement of what later became known as the "law of large numbers" (Jacob Bernoulli, 1713). For example, in a sequence of observations in each of which an event occurs or does not occur, if the probability of occurrence is constant and if the observations are probabilistically independent, then the fraction in which the event occurs converges in probability to the true probability. This gives a justification for actuarial tables. The law of large numbers links probability judgments to observation. But it does so only for large samples, and it still depends on some prior assumptions (independence and constancy of the probability).

The law of large numbers may be regarded as the beginning of statistics, that is, the use of information to help determine probabilities. Information is the modification of probabilities through experience.

As statistics developed, its domain of application broadened. Actuarial tables broadened to finding averages in social phenomena, biology (including genetics), and economics. Another important field was the study of errors of measurement in astronomy and geodesy, a field in which regression analysis first appeared, to be later applied to biology and genetics (Francis Galton) and economics (W. Stanley Jevons).

If one looks closely at statistical practice, though, it becomes clear that probability is not the universal language of uncertainty. A typical formulation is that a probability distribution is specified but one containing unknown parameters. The aim is to estimate these parameters, e.g., the mean and variance of an error of measurement assumed to be normally distributed. The uncertainty on the parameters is not characterized, but the aim of statistics is to make some statements about them, an estimate or a test of hypothetical value. This implicit formulation was made explicit in the 20th century, with the works of R. A. Fisher and of Jerzy Neyman and Egon Pearson. However much these two parties disagreed with each other, they agreed that parameters were unknown facts, not random variables.

Of course, the question arises, how is one to choose among alternative statistical procedures? Various criteria are indeed proposed, frequently related to asymptotic behavior, following Jacob Bernoulli's lead. Others, such as Neyman's and Pearson's, give criteria analogous to the Pareto criterion familiar to economists; a procedure is inadmissible if there is another better (according to some reasonable criterion) for every set of values of the unknown parameters.

There had been a different tradition embodied in the famous Bayes' Theorem (published posthumously, 1783), expressing the probability distribution of a parameter value after making observations. But it depended, of course, on having a *prior* probability distribution of the parameter (before making the observations). What determines the prior?

Laplace (1812) embraced the Bayesian viewpoint. When dealing with probability as a parameter, he assumed a uniform distribution as the prior. This draws on the principle of insufficient reason. As Venn (1866) pointed out, this principle is not invariant to monotone transformations of the underlying parameter and so is unreasonable. Venn powerfully and influentially argued against the Bayesian viewpoint and defended what

I have taken as the standard approach of statistical practice, what is usually called the "frequentist" approach.

One frequently overlooked implication of the Bayesian viewpoint is that random sampling has no special virtue. There is always an optimal pure strategy to any Bayesian decision problem.

The situation in statistical practice is still as cloudy as ever. Though Bayesian methods have had a considerable increase in popularity, frequentism is still dominant. Further, Bayesian methods are usually used with a prior taken to be as little informative as possible, not with any prior. A common, though not universally accepted, criterion is a modern version of the principle of insufficient reason, namely, the principle of maximum entropy (Jaynes, 1968). Not any prior is considered acceptable.

The point I am trying to make is that a group of presumably very rational and informed individuals, the statisticians, do not for the most part find it possible to use a purely probabilistic account of uncertainty.

Recognition that uncertainty is not always expressed in probabilities has, of course, appeared in the literature: "uncertainty," in the term of Knight (1921) and, more fruitfully, "ambiguity," in the famous experiments of Ellsberg (1961).

I have so far talked only about the role of probabilities in describing uncertainty. Even accepting the probability description, there are problems in theorizing about the treatment of uncertainty by individuals and especially by the market.

In the early history of probability theory, the choices made by individuals were governed by the expected value of gain. A game of chance might be entered into if the expected value (net of any entry fee) was positive and rejected if negative. Nicolaus Bernoulli, a nephew of Jacob Bernoulli, proposed what has become known as the St. Petersburg game: pay an entry fee; toss a fair coin until it comes up heads; and receive 2^n ducats if this happens on the nth trial. According to the expected-value criterion, the individual would enter the game no matter how large the entry fee was.

An analysis by Daniel Bernoulli, also a nephew of Jacob Bernoulli and a cousin of Nicolaus, appeared only in 1738, published in St. Petersburg (hence the name). Daniel Bernoulli proposed that money was valued, not proportionately to its quantity but according to a "moral value" ("utility," as we would now say), which did not rise in the same proportion (i.e., was a concave increasing function). He further noted that this aversion to risk could explain why individuals at risk (shippers, in his illustration) would take out actuarially unfair insurance.

This remarkable and original study received virtually no attention from economists. Marshall refers to it in a footnote, clearly relying on a secondary source, but makes no use of it. Indeed, to my knowledge, there was no serious economic research based on the idea of risk aversion represented by a concave utility function until after 1945. Then indeed it became the standard tool for discussing portfolio selection.

But there was one important reconsideration of the St. Petersburg paradox. The mathematician, Karl Menger (1934), noted that it was not sufficient to assume risk aversion. A variant version of the paradox could be found if the utility function was unbounded. Hence, it could be concluded that the utility function whose expected value governs the choice of risks must be bounded.

There was a factor inhibiting the use of expected-utility theory among those economists of sufficient mathematical knowledge to use it. It had become recognized, following Pareto, that utility functions served only an ordinal purpose and could not be given a cardinal interpretation. Yet expected–utility theory demanded a cardinal utility. The axiomatization of choice under (probabilistic) uncertainty by von Neumann and Morgenstern (1944, though the proof did not appear until the second edition, 1947) created a dilemma for those economists, until it was gradually understood that there was no inconsistency.

Expected-utility theory thus supplied a basis for studying the supply and demand for risk-taking. But there was still the problem of integrating risk-bearing into the general equilibrium theory of economic markets. Modigliani and Miller (1958) first showed how arbitrage considerations based on the existence of securities markets can impose significant constraints on the prices of differently-levered firms.

I developed a general theory of general equilibrium under uncertainty (1953) (extended by Debreu (1959)). But there are real problems in making any use of it. The basic securities are bets on *exogenous* events. The implicit assumption is that each individual can predict the general equilibrium conditional on the occurrence of each event, a capacity which no econometrician or business analyst can seriously claim. The payments on actual risky securities are conditioned on endogenous economic events, e.g., profits derived from prices and quantities bought and sold.

There is, as is now well known, another problem with achieving an efficient allocation of risk-bearing through the market: asymmetric information. We cannot have a market for payment conditional on an event if one side of the market does not observe the event. But this point is too well known for extended comment in this brief preface.

New Frontiers Beyond Risk and Uncertainty: Ignorance, Group Decision, and Unanticipated Themes

Richard Zeckhauser
Harvard Kennedy School, Cambridge, MA, USA

What are the major challenges confronting the world today? Among the top few, many people would list recovering from the world's prolonged recession, dealing with Islamist terrorism, and coping with climate change. Yet a mere 15 years ago, none of these issues would have been a prominent concern. Big surprises in the policy sphere vividly illustrate the uncertainty of our world and the importance of strategies for coping with uncertainty. Many of the chapters in this volume point the way for policy makers. Our concern here as well will be with individuals making decisions on their own behalf.

Risk, which is a situation where probabilities are well defined, is much less important than uncertainty. Casinos, which rely on dice, cards, and mechanical devices, and insurance companies, blessed with vast stockpiles of data,[1] have good reason to think about risk. But most of us have to worry about risk only if we are foolish enough to dally at those casinos or to buy lottery cards to a significant extent. Indeed, we should now understand that many phenomena that were often defined as involving risk—notably those in the financial sphere before 2008—actually involve uncertainty. Portfolio theory built on assumed normal distributions is a beautiful edifice, but in the real financial world, tails are much fatter than normality would predict.[2] And when future prices depend on the choices of millions of human beings and on the way those humans respond to current prices and recent price movements, we are no longer in the land of martingales protected from contagions of irrationality. Herd behavior, with occasional stampedes, outperforms Brownian motion in explaining important price movements.

The medical field is another realm where risk gets vast attention. Terms such as *relative risk ratios* and *survival risk* pepper the literature. But a patient who presses a

---

[1] Actually, many insurance companies cannot do this, because changes in risk levels may affect many of their policyholders simultaneously. For example, an insurance company writing annuities based on old life tables would have gone broke given the rapid increases in life expectancy since 1900.

[2] Thus, the stock market can drop 20% in one day in October 1987, without any clear explanatory event.

physician will learn that aggregate statistics do not apply to the individual's case, that the physician and delivery institution can significantly affect risk levels, and that no data are so finely parsed as to predict individual outcomes. Uncertainty rules.

Though risky situations themselves play only a limited role, sophisticated thinking about risk has proved beneficial to decision makers ever since Daniel Bernoulli presented his solution to the St. Petersburg paradox nearly 400 years ago.[3] Utility theory is now a well-developed field that is built on an axiomatic basis, and most economists and decision theorists (EDTs) know how to make choices when confronted with lotteries that have outcomes with well-defined probabilities. (See Chapters 1–4.)

Unfortunately, the way most EDTs would counsel people to make choices is not the way most individuals do make choices. The last several decades saw major efforts in two realms chronicling the discrepancies between prescribed behavior and actual behavior. (See Chapter 14.) First, a vast number of experiments were conducted asking individuals to make choices that involve the use of marbles and urns, or their equivalents. The most famous early investigations produced the Allais and Ellsberg Paradoxes. Then, with psychologists originally taking the lead, experimental methods became a mainstay of the economics literature, most particularly when examining choices under risk and uncertainty. An array of significant heuristics and biases were identified; prospect theory was developed (Kahneman and Tversky, 1979). Second, significant analytic work was undertaken by economists to develop alternative frameworks for rational choice, frequently relaxing or altering one of the classic axioms. (See Chapters 12 and 13.) Among EDTs, there is somewhat less agreement than there was a few decades ago on how individuals should make choices, though the classical model still has overwhelming majority support. And the greater question, of what we should do if individuals' actual behavior departs from EDT-prescribed behavior, is much debated. For example, if individuals do greatly feel regret, if they find themselves to be naturally strongly ambiguity-averse, should scholars in the field wag their fingers in disapproval or incorporate these proclivities into the prescriptive model?

Let's posit that we accept utility theory, without specifying which particular strand of utility theory. Such an understanding is essential if we need to make decisions where one can only define the probabilities of outcomes on a subjective basis. The other essential is determining how to define those subjective probabilities.

---

[3]Pioneering work on probability by Blaise Pascal and Pierre Fermat a century earlier was primarily oriented to predicting distributions, not to making choices. Pascal's wager, of course, is helpful to those who take seriously the possibility of infinite negative utility, a possible outcome with, for example, the frequently employed logarithmic utility function for money. Studies of the value of statistical life—see Chapter 7—make clear that such infinite valuations make little sense, since the loss of life is a very bad outcome, much worse than the loss of money.

1 UNCERTAINTY, ALWAYS WITH US, BUT NOT ALWAYS RECOGNIZED BY ECONOMISTS

Uncertainty plays a major role at the individual scale (how to invest or what medical treatment to select) and at the societal scale (how to bolster the economy or confront terrorism). Uncertainty also plays a leading role at the middle scale, in describing and explaining market behavior. However, 50 years ago, in economists' study of economy-wide, market, and individual behavior, uncertainty did not receive much attention.

In an interesting twist, the great economists of the more distant past attended to the overwhelming role of uncertainty, and the difficulties individuals had in making decisions in uncertain contexts. Adam Smith was perhaps the first economist to recognize that individuals making real-world decisions were not only confronted with unknowable outcomes, but that, in dealing with such outcomes, the mathematical theory of probability was not helpful (Brady, 2013).

Ricardo and Keynes were extraordinarily successful speculators who understood that prices—reflections of uncertainty—could easily go awry in financial markets. I suspect that they knew then, intuitively, much that has only in recent decades become established in decision theory.

After World War II, academic economics moved into the modern era with a big extra dose of mathematical formalism; the rigor was good. But a negative side effect was that uncertainty was left by the wayside for a period. Drawing inspiration from the highly uncertain real world was not sufficient to spur the profession. It seemed that the study of economics had to wait for an appropriate theory before it could catch up. (Chapters 5–11, which focus on uncertainty, demonstrate that the discipline has caught up.)

Turn back the clock 50 years. In 1962, Stigler's classic piece on the "Economics of information" was just one year old (Stigler, 1961). Kenneth Arrow published his famed paper on "Uncertainty and the welfare economics of medical care" in 1963 (Arrow, 1963).[4] Were these symptoms of a broad movement, or mere early movers in a lagging literature? Let's examine the *American Economic Review*, the *Journal of Political Economy*, and the *Quarterly Journal of Economics* of that period. In 1962, few articles dealt with risk or uncertainty. By contrast, today's journals bristle with articles recognizing the difficulties for market participants of making choices when outcomes are not known. Table 1 below tells the story.

In 1962, a mere 5.3% of articles in these three leading journals addressed risk or uncertainty. Fifty years later, the percentage had risen to 21.8%. Our scholarly undertakings today are doing a better job of reflecting the real world.

---

[4]To be sure, Arrow and Debreu had, in the prior decade, elegantly identified the conditions for general equilibrium given uncertainty. However, as Arrow points out in this volume, the applicability was limited, since all bets were made contingent on exogenous events.

Table 1 Articles on Risk and Uncertainty in Leading Journals (*American Economic Review, Journal of Political Economy, Quarterly Journal of Economics*)*

1962

	Theoretical	Empirical	Both	Total
Neither	51	51	5	107
Risk	1	0	0	1
Uncertainty	3	2	0	5
Both	0	0	0	0
Total	55	53	5	113

2012

	Theoretical	Empirical	Both	Total
Neither	50	94	5	149
Risk	13	15	2	30
Uncertainty	9	3	1	13
Both	4	1	0	5
Total	76	113	8	197

Percentages

	1962	2012
% Articles with Risk	0.9%	15.2%
% Articles with Uncertainty	4.4%	6.6%
% Articles with Either Risk or Uncertainty	5.3%	21.8%

* Andrew Kim compiled this table. Details are available from the author.

The world was no more certain in 1962 than it is today. At that time, few macro-economists thought that the business cycle had been conquered; 40 years later, most did. (Then, the collapse of 2007–08 surprised virtually everyone, including economists.) In the 1960s, the biggest threat ever to world civilization, namely nuclear war, was a major and highly uncertain prospect. In those years, people were still starting businesses that would fail or succeed; students were deciding whether or not to invest in college educations; and folks were speculating on financial markets. There was plenty of raw material for the study of uncertainty. However, uncertainty had not yet made its grand entrance into economic theory, perhaps because the field had not yet made sufficient intellectual progress. Modern portfolio theory, a very elegant apparatus that developed from the 1950s through the 1970s, did not offer much insight into uncertainty. Portfolio theory assumed efficient markets and rational decision makers, implying that prices reflected expected values and that the world was described by normal distributions and by their godchild, Brownian motion. Black-swan events, sucker investors, and enormously successful speculators existed, but not in economists' models.

Note the contrast between blinkered economics and open-eyed physics, a field that receives a great deal of envy from economists. Several centuries ago, pioneering physicists accurately described the world of our everyday experience. More than one century ago, they started describing real-world phenomena that few of us can even contemplate, such as subatomic particles, relativity, and quantum mechanics, often at the submicroscopic or cosmic level. No doubt the empirical revolution in economics—the rush of the field to observe and explain in great detail happenings in the marketplace—helped to promote the delayed venture of the economics field into the realm of uncertainty.

This handbook documents the arrival, admittedly belated, of social-science understanding of this realm. Virtually all bases are covered in its pages. In the preceding preface, Kenneth Arrow, an economist who has contributed as much as any to our understanding of risk and uncertainty, briefly traces the path of a number of giants on whose shoulders we stand. Not surprisingly, physicists and mathematicians get as much mention in his essay as economists. The volume's theme chapters consist of fourteen essays that describe the current economic understanding of risk and uncertainty.

My preface, though following directly on Arrow, is metaphorically a back bookend. It speculates on some issues that might be added to this manual when it is updated a decade from now.

2 IGNORANCE

Economists now understand that risk is a terrific subject for gamblers, for students in high school math, and for insurance companies having data that enable them to predict the probabilities of micro outcomes with reasonable reliability.[5] But for investors, business folks, government officials, physicians, international diplomats, those in romantic pursuit, and parents of young children, indeed for almost anybody else, risk is an intriguing subject that bears little relation to the real decisions they face. Unknown outcomes confront these players every day, and the probabilities are virtually never known nor knowable. Uncertainty, not risk, is the difficulty regularly before us. That is, we can identify the states of the world, but not their probabilities.

A disturbing statistic about the present literature is in the table above: only 30% of the 2012 articles on risk and uncertainty address uncertainty.[6] Yet the distinction between risk and uncertainty was drawn more than 90 years earlier by Frank Knight in the classic *Risk, Uncertainty and Profit* (Knight, 1921). More importantly, uncertainty characterizes much more of economic activity than does risk.

I propose that there exists a third class of situation, which I call *Ignorance*, that is likely to get substantial attention in a future handbook. Ignorance arises in a situation

---

[5]A while back, this tally might (mistakenly) have included bettors on parimutuel markets. Equity markets, in effect, represent specialized versions of such markets, where there is only a single price for expected values. The behavioral finance literature, combined with such phenomena as the bubble of the late 1990s and the financial meltdown of 2008, belies the ability of such markets to reflect regularly accurate valuations.

[6]Interestingly, more than 80% of the few 1962 articles on risk and/or uncertainty addressed uncertainty.

where some potential states of the world cannot be identified. Ignorance is an important phenomenon, I would argue, ranking alongside uncertainty and above risk. Ignorance achieves its importance, not only by being widespread, but also by involving outcomes of great consequence.

Consider the societal level and the case of the United States. Among the major problems currently confronting that nation are terrorism, climate change, and an unforeseen financial collapse and the subsequent economic crisis. As the century turned, the United States basked in the knowledge that significant terrorism could not be experienced on its soil. Yet, the next year the US suffered a massive attack by an unforeseen means. Twenty-five years ago, climate change hardly registered among public concerns. Yet today it is considered by many experts to be the greatest long-term threat to the nation and the world. But our ignorance continues. Those experts, much less worried citizens, have little idea in what ways climate change will prove most consequential. And from a US national defense standpoint, the most consequential event of the past quarter century was hardly anticipated: the Soviet Union simply collapsed. The US, with thousands of experts providing guidance, proved poorly equipped to identify a significant state of the world that actually did occur.

Ignorance comes in two modes: Recognized and Unrecognized. Unrecognized means that we are venturing forth, not anticipating that something we have not even conjectured might occur. Minor developments, those of little consequence, may surprise us. Thus, we run into an old roommate while wandering in the bazaar in Marrakech or sell out the first run of our book, occurrences we thought impossible. But these are not our concern. However, major unexpected developments, those of great consequence, also happen and they are our topic. Discovering that one's wife is having an affair with one's best friend, that one's minor research idea blossoms into a grand economic insight, or that one's widow-safe investment plummets in price by 90%—these are amazing events that come out of the blue. And to the individual, they are highly consequential. They make Ignorance important to consider.

Ignorance, although it cannot be conquered, can be defended against. An attentive decision theorist cannot see into the future, but should always contemplate the possibility of consequential surprise. A decision maker should always be aware of the factor of Ignorance and should try to draw inferences about its nature from the lessons taught by history, from experiences recounted by others, from accounts given in the media, from possibilities developed in literature, etc.[7] Decision makers who anticipate Ignorance in this fashion are in a situation of Recognized Ignorance.

---

[7]Some of these ideas are developed in *Ignorance: Lessons from the Laboratory of Literature*, written jointly with English literature scholar Devjani Roy.

To assess how important is Ignorance, once Recognized, one must pay attention to consequences, c, probabilities, p, and the number of discrete events, n, about which one is ignorant. Here c is measured in absolute value; a big consequence can be positive or negative. In theory at least, one would have a prior on each of p and c. The expected consequences of Ignorance would then be computed as

$$\sum_{i=1}^{n} p_i \bullet c_i.$$

An exactly equivalent estimate would be derived by assessing the overall likelihood of a consequential surprise (the sum of the p_i values), and then multiplying that sum by the weighted average of the consequences. This latter approach might be simpler to think about. But we must admit that assessing these values given Ignorance is pushing the limits of subjective assessment. Perhaps a better term would be conjectural assessment.[8]

Figure 1 is an illustration of our Ignorance estimation involving two events, labeled A and B, of which decision makers might be ignorant. Note, when measuring consequences, an upside outcome is just as important as a downside outcome. Thus, c is measured in absolute values. The figure shows the expected consequences, with darker shading indicating greater expected consequences. Taking A and B together takes us to point S, where its consequence is the expected value of consequence given that A or B occurs. Along the rectangular hyperbola through S, or indeed along any rectangular hyperbola, expected consequences are constant.

Though this summation is exact, another way to get the same result would be to assess the overall probability of a consequential unexpected event and multiply it by the expected consequence of such an event. We believe this shortcut might be helpful in thinking about this very intractable problem. Unfortunately, numerous behavioral biases, such as overconfidence and the availability heuristic, can lead us to under- or overestimate the importance of Ignorance.[9]

The rational study of the prevalence of Ignorance, and of how to cope with Ignorance, we expect, will get considerable attention in the next *Handbook of the Economics of Risk and Uncertainty*. If so, the title should be expanded to include Ignorance.

---

[8]A further complexity would recognize uncertainty on n, which would require a summation as well over different values of n. Moreover, it would be desirable to have a joint distribution on n and the p values, since with more unimagined states, there is less density available for each one.

[9]Alas, a number of biases would also impede our ability to learn from past unexpected events. For instance, cognitive dissonance might lead us to believe that we had anticipated an event which, in fact, we had not imagined at all. See the paper cited in footnote 7.

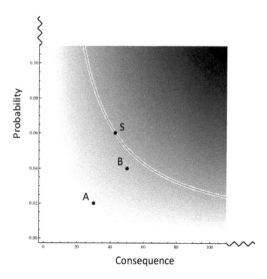

Figure 1   Expected consequences from unidentified states.

3 GROUP DECISION

A large portion of the most important decisions are made in groups. Many of those groups are informal, a family or a collection of friends. Often, the group will have some official status, such as a tenured faculty or a corporate board, but their decision processes will resemble informal decision making. A typical pattern would be a discussion, a struggle for consensus, and then a decision. A large portion of group decisions, like many individual decisions, are made under conditions of uncertainty, and often of Ignorance.

Kenneth Arrow's book, *Social Choice and Individual Values* (Arrow, 1951), launched an extensive literature on the potential for, or, more accurately, the impossibility of, effective collective decision. For decades, scholars have cherry picked axioms, starting with those of Arrow, to either barely cross into the territory of satisfactory collective decision processes or into the territory of unsatisfactory ones. This literature, however, has not yet led to many contributions that could be cited in this volume. Quite simply, despite the real-world importance of the subject, economics has made little progress in explaining how groups should or do make decisions when confronted with risk and uncertainty. Arrow's Theorem deals with the certainty case and with individuals who know their preferences. Moreover, his Independence of Irrelevant Alternatives axiom effectively rules out cardinal preferences, such as von Neumann-Morgenstern utilities, which are required for decision making under uncertainty.

However, the literature on asymmetric information is highly relevant not only to uncertainty issues (see Chapters 5 and 6), but also to group decision. Even though a group's decision may face no uncertainties, its members' preferences may be private.[10] Can those preferences be accurately elicited and still processed into an optimal decision? The Gibbard-Satterthwaite Theorem (Gibbard, 1973; Satterthwaite, 1975), an early major contribution, revealed the answer to be negative.[11] For any voting system, either voters have an incentive to vote strategically, or some other highly unattractive situation must obtain, such as dictatorship; otherwise, certain alternatives have no potential to be chosen. Here, we see the beginnings of the curse of asymmetric information in group decision processes.

Now consider a much more complex situation where uncertainty prevails about the state of the world. Moreover, individuals possess private information about the likelihood of various outcomes, and they also have their own preferences, and those preferences may be private information. This sounds like a cascade of complications piled upon a framework such as the Gibbard-Satterthwaite Theorem. Yet this is the world that surrounds us, one that we encounter when we step into a legislative body, a business negotiation, or a family meeting.

Group decisions under uncertainty, on matters large and small, pervade our lives. It seems clear that no mechanism to ensure wondrously satisfying choices across a broad range of contexts will ever emerge. But surely we can do better than the current undisciplined approaches that characterize so many group decisions. Many members of important groups could not even describe the procedures by which their groups make choices. Many groups have no routines, much less agreed-upon procedures, by which they gather assessments on possible outcomes, their probabilities, and the payoffs to participants that depend on the alternative selected and the outcome realized.[12]

Moreover, many decisions are made by multiple agents who share information but are in no sense members of a group. Exemplars would be the macroeconomists who adjust their predictions for the economy in light of the predictions made by others, and the investment banks which "learned and got reassurance" from one another as they invested heavily in mortgage-backed securities before the 2008 meltdown. When relatively orderly, such clusters of agents might be described as *decision webs*; when disorderly, as *decision tangles*. Frequently, the decisions in such clusters exert strong reciprocal externalities—as they do in research consortia—and the agents develop informal modes of cooperation. Sometimes there is a coordinating entity, equivalent to the center in economic theory models or to the owner of a shopping mall, that facilitates coordination.

---

[10]See Weyl (2013) for a recent analysis of successful group decision processes when cardinal preferences are permitted, yet information on preferences must be solicited.

[11]Zeckhauser (1973) presents a closely related negative result for voting schemes.

[12]Some groups, notably legislatures, have formal rules that discipline discussion and voting procedures. But those rules hardly require agents to provide information in the most useful form, such as separating probability assessments from preferences. And most legislatures on most issues only secure information input from a small percentage of their members.

The center's goal should be to turn tangles into webs that are effective decision-making instruments.

In short, the situation described above represents a grab bag of methods. Most methods were chosen for considerations (for example, that all votes should count equally) other than effective decision making. Many have just evolved with too little time for natural selection to work its wonders. Few have been tested to see how well they facilitate well-reasoned decisions. And none, as we remarked, is likely to produce wondrously satisfying choices.

By the time the next handbook is published, it is to be hoped, economics will have made progress on better mechanisms for making group decisions under uncertainty. This will require that theories and experimentation, and perhaps some cross-sectional analyses, to come together to upgrade our current and inadequate methods. Research on how to improve group decisions will resemble less players' efforts to improve their personal skills than a team's efforts to maximize overall performance.

The potential for effectively addressing uncertainty in group decisions will be boosted if some helpful assumptions are made. Positing that agents have common interests goes a long way. Robert Wilson's rigorous theory of syndicates (Wilson, 1968) showed that, absent common interests, side payments have great potential to help.[13] In addition, two assumptions that are commonly invoked are that there is agreement on the prior distribution of all parameters and that the search should be for a Bayesian equilibrium. The combination of side payments and these two assumptions enables group decision makers to elicit honest information on both probabilities and preferences and to decide optimally when certain reasonable conditions are met on payoff structures (Miller et al., 2007). Unfortunately, few group decisions allow for side payments, and for fewer still do the agents have common priors on all parameters. We suspect that in future studies on the theoretical potential of effective group decision under uncertainty, negative results will far outweigh the positive. No doubt, some decision processes will work on a decentralized basis, perhaps with individuals anonymously feeding in information via the Internet. Large numbers have some potential to ameliorate some problems; they tend to dampen and possibly eliminate the rewards to strategic behavior. We can hope.

Whatever technologies are developed for modes of collective decision making, we must recognize that most group decisions are still likely to fall far short of the optimum. Information will be hidden or misreported, preferences will be distorted implying that

---

[13]An extension of the Vickrey (1961) second-price auction successfully elicits honest preferences when making a public decision. Individuals vote the amount by which they prefer one alternative over another. The high total wins, and an individual whose vote changes the outcome is charged the net amount other players lose due to the change. (See subsequent work on this subject by Edward Clarke, Theodore Groves, Nicolaus Tideman, and Gordon Tullock.)

decision A will be taken when decision B would be better for all. This suggests that we should lower our aspirations and that the search should be for solid second-best performers, for doing fairly well on average.

A distinctive challenge of behavioral decision making is that individuals are concerned not only with what decision is taken, but with their standing within the group. Think of an ordinary classroom, and the potential to utilize the wisdom of crowds. The teacher asks a question. If all 25 students could work on it together, whether it be factual or conceptual, the prospects for success would be great. Consider the simplest case of multiple-choice answers. The class members could go beyond mere voting, even achieving sophisticated voting in which they changed their choices to reflect how others had voted in prior rounds until they reached an equilibrium.

A far superior strategy would milk more information, with individuals revealing why they did not pick particular alternatives and sharing whatever information they had about alternatives. Posit two very favorable conditions: 1. A big payoff, perhaps $1,000, to each for each correct answer. 2. The students would have no future connections besides the single classroom exercise. With a bit of practice, we suspect that the students would do extremely well.

However, most classrooms and most decision problems do not enjoy these two favorable conditions. Thus, individuals are concerned not only with what decision is taken, but also with their standing within the group. In an ordinary classroom, the first two students are called upon and answer alternative B. It then becomes difficult for the third cold-called student to recommend C, though that was his original choice. From what he has learned from others, he may actually think that B is the most likely correct answer, and he does not want to be embarrassed in front of the class. In this way, vast amounts of information can get suppressed. Indeed, the second student may have had little independent information suggesting that the first student, who thought B was slightly more likely than A or C could well influence the entire class to B, when there was substantial information in the class favoring C.

This problem would be compounded if the answers had political salience, or were thought to. Other-directed individuals would be hesitant to express an answer they thought others might not like. Even if there were no political sensitivities, merely the thought that there might be could lead to information suppression or distorted reports. In an agency context, concerns about the boss's views could lead to misreports if both probabilities and preferences were in play. Posit that the boss has proposed a project and asks for reactions. A loyal employee, who fully shares the boss's preferences, might be hesitant to express doubts about the project's success for fear that the boss might think he didn't like the project's goals.

No doubt, thinking along these lines has helped support the role of the secret ballot over the years. But such ballots are employed in highly specialized contexts, rarely as part of ordinary decision processes. Anonymous decision processes have advantages, but they also have grave weaknesses. For example, if we wish agents to invest to gain information, a public good, anonymous decision processes permit free riding. When both preferences and probabilities are involved, agents lose the chance to interpret shared information on the basis of: "I know where you are coming from". Might more anonymous decision processes—now much more feasible given social media—improve outcomes in some realms? Economics, now venturing strongly into becoming an experimental science, might yield some answers in the future.

4 UNANTICIPATED THEMES

Consistent with the discussion of Ignorance above, some of the greatest advances in the realms of risk and uncertainty will be in areas that we cannot currently identify. New technologies and new scientific understandings will surely develop. What do the human brain and the disembodied Internet have in common? They both have almost incomprehensible levels of information-processing capacity. The US has recently committed to a major research undertaking on the structure and functioning of the brain, recognizing that it represents an important new frontier. The Internet, a technology that hardly existed a couple of decades ago, is enabling remarkable new information-gathering, data-processing, and decision-making opportunities. Surely our improved understanding and use of super processors, as well as the steady march forward of the Internet and of those who build on it, will lead to bold discoveries of ways to deal with uncertainty.

It is worth reiterating that the economics of risk and uncertainty lost its vitality in a prison of methodology that did not admit the real world. Uncertainty pervades many important real-world phenomena that have received less attention from economics than they deserve. Their study will provide not merely improved understanding of those phenomena, but, more generally, of uncertainty.

Macroeconomics surely will have a different bent ten years from now, when its leading practitioners will have digested the lessons of the unforeseen financial meltdown and its lingering aftermath. Technological advance is a watchword on the lips of most political and business leaders, but our mastery of our expanding capabilities remains rudimentary, as does our understanding of the entrepreneurs who are impelling us forward. Venturing beyond the traditional confines of economics, how can we understand the often precipitous and unexpected social movements—the products of decisions taken by millions of individuals, and now accelerated by social media—that disrupt social mores, topple empires, and bring about religious revivals and declines? This is surely an arena where experts in uncertainty and decision making can make contributions.

5 A FINAL WORD

Uncertainty and its much more elusive cousin Ignorance make it virtually impossible for a handbook to provide a definitive statement of what is known about situations in which outcomes are unknown and unknowable. Use this handbook as a launching pad.

Recognize the role of Ignorance in life. Then help to create the breakthroughs in decision theory—those that can be hoped for and those that we cannot yet contemplate—that will make life better for all.

REFERENCES

Arrow, K.J., 1951. Social Choice and Individual Values. Yale University Press, New Haven.

Arrow, K.J., 1963. Uncertainty and the welfare economics of medical care. American Economic Review 53, 941–973.

Brady, M.E., 2013. Adam Smith's theory of probability and the roles of risk and uncertainty in economic decision making. June 30. Available at SSRN: <http://ssrn.com/abstract=2287339> or http://dx.doi.org/10.2139/ssrn.2287339.

Gibbard, A., 1973. Manipulation of voting schemes: a general result. Econometrica 41, 587–601.

Kahneman, D., Tversky A., 1979. Prospect theory: an analysis of decision under risk. Econometrica XLVII, 263–291.

Knight, F., 1921. Risk, Uncertainty and Profit. Houghton Mifflin Company, Boston.

Miller, N.H., Pratt, J.W., Zeckhauser, R.J., Johnson, S.C., 2007. Mechanism design with multidimensional, continuous types and interdependent valuations. Journal of Economic Theory 136, 476–496.

Satterthwaite, M.A., 1975. Strategy-proofness and Arrow's conditions: existence and correspondence theorems for voting procedures and social welfare functions. Journal of Economic Theory 10, 187–217.

Stigler, G.J., 1961. The economics of information. Journal of Political Economy 69, 213–225.

Vickrey, W., 1961. Counterspeculation, auctions, and competitive sealed tenders. Journal of Finance 16, 8–37.

Weyl, E.G., 2013. Quadratic vote buying. April 1. Available at SSRN: <http://ssrn.com/abstract=2003531> or http://dx.doi.org/10.2139/ssrn.2003531.

Wilson, R., 1968. Theory of syndicates. Econometrica 36, 119–132.

Zeckhauser, R., 1973. Voting systems, honest preferences, and pareto optimality. American Political Science Review 67, 934–946.

Handbook of the Economics of Risk and Uncertainty

The literature on the economics of risk and uncertainty has had a far reaching impact on our understanding of individual choice, market behavior, and public interventions to enhance market performance. This work has not only broadened the domain of economic inquiry but also has established the frameworks that are used in the design and evaluation of policies. The chapters in this Handbook provide self-contained but advanced treatments of these important topics.

Risk taking and attitudes toward risk in economics can be said to start at the level of the individual. Compared with most branches of consumer theory, theories and models of attitudes toward risk almost always have an axiomatic foundation. The most important of these, the classical model of expected utility risk preferences and probabilistic beliefs, has a well-defined analytical framework and has received dozens (if not more) axiomatic formulations. Although initiated by mathematician John von Neumann and statistician Leonard Savage, the axiomatics of the classical model has gone on to become almost exclusively the domain of economists (Chapter 1 Karni).

The field of individual attitudes toward risk and individual beliefs under uncertainty has also seen much more than its share of philosophical discussion and debate. The key axioms of the classical model — the so-called 'Independence Axiom' and 'Sure-Thing Principle' – were initially viewed as being as much an inherent feature of 'rational choice' as the principle of transitivity. However, this view has been subject to debate by both economists and philosophers (Chapter 2 Hammond and Zank). The arguments have typically centered on the implications for individual choice in situations of dynamic decisions, and when ex post decisions are, or are not, consistent with ex ante plans. An important question in this debate is whether or not agents who do not conform to the classical axioms are subject to 'Dutch book' arguments, in which they can be systematically exploited.

Starting with the foundational work of Kenneth Arrow and John Pratt, the expected utility model has gone to provide the framework for an extensive literature on individual behavior toward risk, both how risk aversion varies with an individual's wealth and how it varies across individuals (Chapter 3 Meyer). It also plays an important role in the characterization and comparison of risk in economic environments, as studied, for example, by Michael Rothschild and Joseph Stiglitz. As seen in the subsequent chapters of this volume, this work provides the basis of much of the economic analysis of individual and market behavior in the field of insurance as well in situations of incomplete information. Analysis of risk aversion also plays a central role in the evaluation of other public policy decisions involving risk.

To measure individual willingness to engage in risk-taking activities, experimental and empirical methods (Chapter 4 Holt and Laury) have operationalized the standard models of risk aversion. Researchers have developed several different methodologies for estimating individual risk aversion, including certainty equivalent pricing tasks, choices from lottery menus, and preferences revealed by investments in risky assets. In addition to developing average measures of risk aversion, several studies have identified systematic differences in risk-taking behavior, such as differences by gender and age. These risk aversion measures have in turn proven to be instrumental in predicting the effect of individual risk aversion on economic behavior, such as decisions in auctions and bargaining situations.

The properties of well-behaved markets involving different aspects of risk serve as a frequent starting point for economic analysis. Building on the pioneering work of Kenneth Arrow and others, there developed a large literature in which these theoretical insights have been applied to analysis of insurance issues. These contributions have established the framework for setting insurance rates for risks that can be addressed through financial transfers, such as property and liability risks (Chapter 5 Dionne and Harrington). The practical problems of insurance pricing that have been illuminated by economic analysis include assessments of the role of moral hazard and adverse selection, as well as the structure and appropriate degree of regulation of insurance markets. The pricing and regulation of insurance encompasses a broad range of economic considerations, including the establishment of adequate capital requirements.

A distinctive contribution of the field has been in identifying new phenomena that arise when risks are a factor. Often in the presence of risk and uncertainty, markets function quite differently than is hypothesized in idealized economic models of a riskless world. The presence of risk and uncertainty creates a potentially valuable role for information, which in turn generates a host of economic issues arising due to potential asymmetries in information, which have been explored in seminal work by George Akerlof and A. Michael Spence. The broad range of information-related topics include, among many others, the market effects of used cars that are "lemons", in which sellers know more about the quality than does the buyer, adverse selection problems in which the high risk individuals find being insured particularly attractive, and signaling phenomena in which people develop credentials to convey their underlying productivity (Chapter 6 Hermalin). Similar informational asymmetries may influence the functioning and outcomes in contracting situations.

Even in the case of risks to health, it is desirable to monetize the risks so that the value of reductions in mortality risks can be viewed in terms comparable to other expenditures. Following the insight of Thomas Schelling that the appropriate focus is on valuation of small risks of death rather than certain deaths, economists have estimated the tradeoff between risk and money in a variety of market contexts, yielding estimates of the value of a statistical life (Chapter 7 Viscusi). For several decades, many governments throughout the world have used these values to provide the basis for assessing the benefits for all major risk and environmental policies. Other studies have utilized stated preference approaches to examine the heterogeneity of the value of statistical life for outcomes such as cancer and deaths from terrorist attacks. These analyses also have found that severe health impacts reduce the marginal utility of income, which in turn has implications for optimal levels of insurance.

Many of the most challenging insurance and medical policy issues involve individual life and health, which are irreplaceable (Chapter 8 Philipson and Zanjani). The central economic challenges of insurance, such as moral hazard and adverse selection, first gained prominence in the medical care area. Economic analyses of these issues are central to the debate over the appropriate level of health insurance as well as the regulation of medical technologies and pharmaceuticals. Medical innovations, ranging from new prescription drugs to research and development for rare diseases, are often major contributors to individual health. Ensuring that new technologies are both safe and effective involves a continuing effort to strike an efficient balance between these often competing concerns.

Analyses of risk and uncertainty also have a constructive role in providing guidance with respect to how safety regulations can be structured effectively. The general task is not to achieve a zero risk society but to attain a reasonable level of risk that would be observed if markets functioned effectively or if government policies met efficiency norms. An extensive set of regulations addresses risks of products and jobs (Chapter 9 Kniesner and Leeth). Often the greatest incentives for safety are generated by market forces and by liability laws, such as the workers' compensation system. Regulations can potentially be effective, but their potential has not always been fulfilled. Economic analyses play a fundamental role in illuminating the rationale for these regulations, the benefits and costs of these efforts, and the evaluation of their performance.

The challenges posed by complex choices involving risk and uncertainty may also affect the soundness of governmental policies. Because government policies are subject to public pressures and because government officials are human, biases such as the presence of ambiguity aversion may be institutionalized in government policies, such as environmental programs. Proper application of economic analysis can overcome such biases. Another role for economic analysis is in terms of the conceptualization of very difficult policy choices. The policy issues raised by environmental uncertainties may be so far reaching that sound economic analyses can facilitate better understanding of issues that otherwise may appear intractable. For example, the risks associated with climate change have attracted considerable attention among economists as there are tremendous uncertainties regarding the extent of climate change, the societal impacts that will be generated, and the appropriate discounting of long-term environmental effects that will affect future generations (Chapter 10 Aldy and Viscusi).

Risks differ in their magnitude and their distribution in manners that alter the ability of markets to handle them effectively. Very large risks and correlated risks pose particular problems both for individuals and for insurers. Natural disasters and attacks by terrorists represent examples of such catastrophic events. Catastrophe insurance is generally quite attractive to the prospective insured, but private insurance markets may be inadequate to provide such coverage. Making sufficient levels of insurance available may entail a governmental role in insurance, perhaps coupled with policy restrictions such as zoning laws to limit risk exposures (Chapter 11 Kunreuther and Michel-Kerjan). If it is difficult to deny disaster assistance ex post, mandatory insurance may be desirable, but such requirements raise equity and affordability issues.

As a refutable hypothesis on individual behavior, the classical expected utility/subjective probability model is also subject to experimental testing (Chapter 14 Hey). The original thought experiments of Maurice Allais led to an extensive amount of experimental testing by economists, revealing that such systematic violations of the Independence Axiom indeed occur. Current experimental work largely focuses on the phenomena of ambiguity and ambiguity aversion as introduced by Daniel Ellsberg, and again, typically finds the types of violations of the Sure-Thing Principle, and of the existence of probabilistic beliefs, that he hypothesized. Psychologists, and to a growing extent economists, have also documented phenomena such as framing effects and reference point effects, which question the classical model (and most of its proposed alternatives) at a more foundational level. Although originally studied in the context of choice under uncertainty, these phenomena also extend to consumer decisions in other contexts.

Such systematic violations of the classical Independence Axiom have led to the development of a large number of alternative theories of individual risk taking (Chapter 12 Quiggin). Most (though not all) of these models retain the property of transitive preferences over risky prospects, but replace the Independence Axiom with weaker versions. Researchers have revisited much of the theory of individual attitudes toward risk, exploring which of the classical results are and are not robust, or how they differ, under such weaker hypotheses on preferences.

The systematic violations of the Sure-Thing Principle and of the existence of probabilistic beliefs have also led to a more recent but very active literature on the phenomena of ambiguity and ambiguity aversion (Chapter 13 Machina and Siniscalchi). Because of their recency, and because they must delve deeper into the nature of uncertainty, current models of ambiguity aversion are more diverse and more loosely specified than the earlier alternative models, and certainly more than the classical model. The study of how ambiguity and ambiguity aversion affects market behavior and optimal policy is just beginning and remains almost completely unexplored.

We would like to thank Kenneth Arrow and Michael Intriligator for inviting us to prepare the Handbook and for guidance on the coverage of this volume. Scott Bentley of Elsevier provided continual encouragement and support throughout this project. Kristi Anderson of Elsevier managed the incoming wave of contributions and oversaw the production of the Handbook.

Mark J. Machina & W. Kip Viscusi

CHAPTER 1

Axiomatic Foundations of Expected Utility and Subjective Probability

Edi Karni

Department of Economics, Johns Hopkins University, Baltimore, MD, USA, and Department of Economics, Warwick University, UK

Contents

Abstract

This chapter provides a critical review of the theories of decision making under risk and under uncertainty and the notion of choice-based subjective probabilities. It includes formal statements and discussions of the various models, including their analytical frameworks, the corresponding axiomatic foundations, and the representations.

Keywords

Expected Utility Theory, Subjective Expected Utility Theory, Subjective Probabilities, Incomplete Preferences, Bayesianism

JEL Classification Codes

D80, D81

1.1 INTRODUCTION

Expected utility theory consists of two main models. The first, expected utility under risk, is concerned with the evaluation of risky prospects, depicted as lotteries over an arbitrary set of outcomes, or prizes. Formally, let $X = \{x_1, \ldots, x_n\}$ be a set of outcomes

Handbook of the Economics of Risk and Uncertainty, Volume 1
ISSN 2211-7547, http://dx.doi.org/10.1016/B978-0-444-53685-3.00001-5

and denote a risky prospect by $(x_1, p_1; \ldots; x_n, p_n)$, where, for each i, p_i denotes the probability of the outcomes x_i. According to the model of expected utility under risk, risky prospects are evaluated by the formula $\Sigma_{i=1}^n u(x_i) p_i$, where u is a real-valued function on X representing the decision maker's tastes. The second expected utility under uncertainty is concerned with the evaluation of random variables, or *acts*, representing alternative courses of action, whose distributions are not included in the data. Formally, let S be a set of states of nature and denote by F the set of acts (that is, the set of all mappings from S to X). According to the model of expected utility under uncertainty, an act f is evaluated using the formula $\Sigma_{i=1}^n u(x_i) \pi(f^{-1}(x_i))$, where π is a probability measure on S representing the decision maker's beliefs regarding the likelihoods of the *events* (that is, subsets of S).[1] The foundations of these models are preference relations on the corresponding choice sets whose structures justify the use of these formulas to evaluate and choose among risky prospects or acts.

1.1.1 Decision Making in the Face of Uncertainty and Subjective Probabilities: Interpretations and Methodology

The notion that an individual's degree of belief in the truth of propositions, or the likely realization of events, is quantifiable by probabilities is as old as the idea of probability itself, dating back to the second half of the 17th century. By contrast, the idea of inferring an individual's degree of belief in the truth of propositions, or the likely realization of events, from his/her choice behavior, and quantifying these beliefs by probabilities, took shape in the early part of the twentieth century. The idea that expected utility is the criterion for evaluating, and choosing among, risky alternatives dates back to the first half of the eighteenth century, whereas the axiomatization of this criterion is a modern concept developed in the mid-twentieth century.

Subjective expected utility theory is the result of the fusion of these two developments, which took place in the 1950s. It is based on three premises: (a) that decision making is (or ought to be) a process involving the evaluation of possible outcomes associated with alternative courses of action and the assessment of their likelihoods; (b) that the evaluation of outcomes and the assessment of their likelihoods are (or ought to be) quantifiable, by utilities and subjective probabilities, respectively, the former representing the decision maker's tastes, the latter his/her beliefs; and (c) that these ingredients of the decision-making process can be inferred from observed (or prescribed) patterns of choice and are (or should be) integrated to produce a criterion of choice.

The theories of subjective probabilities and expected utility are open to alternative, not mutually exclusive, interpretations. The positive interpretation, anchored in the revealed preference methodology, presumes that actual choice behavior abides by

---

[1] The random variable f induces a partition $\mathcal{P}$ of S, whose cells are the preimages of x_i under f (that is, $\mathcal{P} = \{f^{-1}(x_i) \mid i = 1, \ldots, n\}$).

the principles underlying the expected utility criterion and that subjective probabilities can be inferred from observing this behavior. The normative interpretation presumes that the principles underlying the expected utility criterion are basic tenets of rational choice and that rational choice implies, among others, the possibility of quantifying beliefs by probabilities.

The positive interpretation is an hypothesis about choice behavior, which, like other scientific theories, has testable implications. By contrast, the normative interpretation maintains that there are principles of rational behavior sufficiently compelling to make reasonable individuals use them to guide their decisions. Moreover, according to the normative interpretation the theory may be used to educate decision makers on how to organize their thoughts and information so as to make decisions that better attain their objectives. In the same vein, the theory provides "a set of criteria by which to detect, with sufficient trouble, any inconsistencies that may be among our beliefs, and to derive from beliefs we already hold such new ones as consistency demands." (Savage, 1954, p. 20).

1.1.2 A Brief History

From the very first, circa 1660, the idea of probability assumed dual meanings: the aleatory meaning, according to which probability is a theory about the relative frequency of outcomes in repeated trials; and the epistemological meaning, according to which probability is a theory of measurement of a person's "degree of belief" in the truth of propositions, or the likelihoods he assigns to events.[2] Both the "objective" and the "subjective" probabilities, as these meanings are commonly called, played important roles in the developments that led to the formulation of modern theories of decision making under risk and under uncertainty and of the theory of statistics. From their inception, the ideas of probabilities were tied to decisions. The aleatory interpretation is associated with choosing how to play games of chance; the epistemological interpretation is prominent in Pascal's analysis of a wager on the existence of God.[3]

The formal ideas of utility and expected utility (or "moral expectations") maximization as a criterion for evaluating gambles were originally introduced by Bernoulli (1738) to resolve the difficulty with using expected value posed by the St. Petersburg paradox. Bernoulli resolved the paradox by assuming a logarithmic utility function of wealth, whose essential property was "diminishing marginal utility." Bernoulli's preoccupation with games of chance justifies his taking for granted the existence of probabilities in the aleatory, or objective, sense. Bernoulli's and later treatments of the notion of utility in the eighteenth and nineteenth centuries have a distinct cardinal flavor. By contrast, the nature of modern utility theory is ordinal (that is, the utility is a numerical representation of ordinal preferences), and its empirical content is choice behavior. Put

---

[2] See Hacking (1984) for a detailed discussion.
[3] See Devlin's (2008) review of the correspondence between Pascal and Fermat concerning the division problem and Pascal (2010).

differently, the theory of choice is based on the premise that choice is, or ought to be, governed by ordinal preference relations on the set of alternatives, called the choice set. The theory's main concern is the study of the structures of choice sets and preference relations that allow the representation of the latter by utility functions.

The theories of individual choice under risk and under uncertainty are special branches of the general theory of choice, characterized by choice sets the elements of which are courses of action whose ultimate outcomes are not known at the time the choice must be made. Expected utility theory is a special instance of the theory of choice under objective and subjective uncertainty. In expected utility theory under objective uncertainty, or risk, the probabilities are a primitive concept representing the objective uncertainty. The theory's main concern is the representation of individual attitudes toward risk. Its basic premises are that (a) because the outcomes, x_i, are mutually exclusive, the evaluation of risky prospects entails separate evaluations of the outcomes, (b) these evaluations are quantifiable by a cardinal utility, u, and (c) the utilities of the alternative outcomes are aggregated by taking their expectations with respect to the objective probabilities, $p_1, \ldots, p_n$. Expected utility theory under subjective uncertainty is based on the presumption that the preference relation is itself a fusion of two underlying relations: (a) the relation "more likely than," on events, expressing the decision maker's beliefs regarding the likelihoods of the events and (b) the relation "more desirable risk than" depicting his/her evaluation of the outcomes and risk-attitudes. The beliefs, according to this theory, are quantifiable by (subjective) probabilities, $\pi(E)$, for every event $E \subseteq S$. The subjective probabilities play a role analogous to that of objective probability under objective uncertainty, thereby reducing the problem of decision making under uncertainty to decision making under risk, and permitting risk attitudes to be quantified by a utility function.

Throughout the historical processes of their respective evolutions, the idea of representing risk attitudes via cardinal utility was predicated on the existence of objective probabilities, and the notion of subjective probabilities presumed the existence of cardinal utility representing the decision maker's risk attitudes. In the early part of the twentieth century, Ramsey (1931) and de Finetti (1937) independently formalized the concept of choice-based subjective probability. Both assumed that, when betting on the truth of propositions, or on the realization of events, individuals seek to maximize their expected utility.[4] They explored conditions under which the degree of belief of a decision maker in the truth of a proposition, or event, may be inferred from his/her betting behavior and quantified by probability.

Invoking the axiomatic approach, which takes the existence of utilities as given, and assuming that individual choice is governed by expected utility maximization,

---

[4] In the case of de Finetti, the utility function is linear. Maximizing expected utility is, hence, equivalent to maximizing expected value.

Ramsey (1931) sketched a proof of the existence of subjective probabilities. According to Ramsey, "the degree of belief is a casual property of it, which can be expressed vaguely as the extent to which we are prepared to act on it" (Ramsey, 1931, p. 170).

Taking a similar attitude, de Finetti (1937) writes that "the degree of probability attributed by an individual to a given event is revealed by the conditions under which he would be disposed to bet on that event" (de Finetti, 1937). He proposed a definition of coherent subjective probabilities based on no arbitrage opportunities. D Finetti's model is based on the notion of expected value maximizing behavior, or linear utility.

The theory of expected utility under risk received its first axiomatic characterization with the publication of von Neumann and Morgenstern's (1947) *Theory of Games and Economic Behavior*. Von Neumann and Morgenstern analyzed the strategic behavior of players in noncooperative zero-sum games in which no pure strategy equilibrium exists. In such games, the equilibrium may require the employment of mixed strategies. The interest of von Neumann and Morgenstern in the decision making of players facing opponents who use a randomizing device to determine the choice of a pure strategy justifies their modeling the uncertainty surrounding the choice of pure strategies using probabilities in the aleatory sense of relative frequency. Invoking the axiomatic approach to depict the decision maker's preference relation on the set of objective risks, von Neumann and Morgenstern identified necessary and sufficient conditions for the existence of a utility function on a set of outcomes that captures the decision maker's risk attitudes, and represented his/her choice as expected utility maximizing behavior.

Building on, and synthesizing, the ideas of de Finetti and von Neumann and Morgenstern, Savage (1954) proposed the first complete axiomatic subjective expected utility theory. In his seminal work, titled *The Foundations of Statistics*, Savage introduced a new analytical framework and provided necessary and sufficient conditions for the existence and joint uniqueness of utility and probability, as well as the characterization of individual choice in the face of uncertainty as expected utility maximizing behavior. Savage's approach is pure in the sense that the notion of probability does not appear as a primitive concept in his model.

1.1.3 Belief Updating: Bayes' Rule

In 1763 Richard Price read to the Royal Society an essay titled "Essay Towards Solving a Problem in the Doctrine of Chances." In the essay, the Reverend Bayes (1764) outlined a method, since known as Bayes' rule, for updating probabilities in light of new information. Bayes' method does not specify how the original, or prior, probabilities to be updated are determined.

Savage's (1954) theory was intended to furnish the missing ingredient — the prior probability — necessary to complete Bayes' model. The idea is to infer from the decision maker's choice behavior the prior probabilities that represent his/her beliefs and, by so doing, to provide choice-based foundations for the existence of a Bayesian prior.

In Savage's theory, new information indicates that an event that a priori is considered possible is no longer so. The application of Bayes' rule requires that the probability of the complementary event be increased to 1, and the probabilities assigned to its subevents be increased equiproportionally.

The discussion that follows highlights two aspects of this theory. The first is the presumption that Savage's subjective probabilities represent the decision maker's beliefs and, consequently, constitute an appropriate concept of the Bayesian prior. The second is that the posterior preferences of Bayesian decision makers are obtained from their prior preferences solely by the application of Bayes' rule, independently of the decision maker's particular characteristics and risk attitudes.

1.1.4 The Analytical Framework

In the theories reviewed in this chapter, analytical frameworks consist of two primitive concepts: a *choice set*, whose elements are the alternatives the decision makers can potentially choose from, and a binary relation on the choice set, having the interpretation of the decision maker's *preference relation*. Henceforth, an abstract choice set is denoted by $\mathbb{C}$ and a preference relation on $\mathbb{C}$ is denoted by $\succcurlyeq$.[5] For all $c, c' \in \mathbb{C}$, $c \succcurlyeq c'$ means that the alternative c is at least as desirable as the alternative c'. The *strict preference relation* $\succ$ and the *indifference relation* $\sim$ are the asymmetric and symmetric parts of $\succcurlyeq$. Decision makers are characterized by their preference relations. A real-valued function V on $\mathbb{C}$ is said to *represent* $\succcurlyeq$ on $\mathbb{C}$ if $V(a) \geq V(b)$ if and only if $a \succcurlyeq b$ for all $a, b \in \mathbb{C}$.

The main concern of the discussion that ensues has to do with the representations of preference relations. The nature of these representations depends on the interaction between the structure of the choice set and that of the preference relations. Throughout, the structure of the choice set reflects physical or material properties of the alternatives under consideration and is presumed to be objective, in the sense of having the same meaning for all decision makers regardless of their personal characteristics. The preference structure is depicted by a set of axioms. In the normative interpretation, these axioms are regarded as tenets of rational choice and should be judged by their normative appeal. In the positive interpretation, these axioms are principles that are supposed to govern actual choice behavior and should be evaluated by their predictive power.

1.2 EXPECTED UTILITY UNDER RISK

This section reviews the theory of decision making under risk due to the original contribution of von Neumann and Morgenstern (1947). In particular, it describes the necessary and sufficient conditions for the representation of a preference relation on risky alternatives by an expected utility functional.

---

[5] Formally, a binary relation is a subset of $\mathbb{C} \times \mathbb{C}$.

1.2.1 The Analytical Framework

Expected utility theory under risk is a special case of a more abstract choice theory in which the choice set, $\mathbb{C}$, is a convex subset of a linear space. The following examples show that distinct specifications of the objects of choice in expected utility theory under risk are but specific instances of $\mathbb{C}$.

Example 1. Let X be an arbitrary set of outcomes, and consider the set $\Delta(X)$ of all the simple distributions on X.[6] Elements of $\Delta(X)$ are referred to as *lotteries*. For any two lotteries, p and q and $\alpha \in [0, 1]$, define the convex combination $\alpha p + (1 - \alpha) q \in \Delta(X)$ by $(\alpha p + (1 - \alpha) q)(x) = \alpha p(x) + (1 - \alpha) q(x)$, for all $x \in X$. Under this definition, $\Delta(X)$ is a convex subset of the finite dimensional linear space $\mathbb{R}^n$.

Example 2. Let $M(X)$ denote the set of all the probability measures on the measure space $(X, \mathcal{X})$. For any two elements, P and Q of $M(X)$ and $\alpha \in [0, 1]$, define the convex combination $\alpha P + (1 - \alpha) Q \in M(X)$ by $(\alpha P + (1 - \alpha) Q)(T) = \alpha P(T) + (1 - \alpha) Q(T)$ for all T in the σ-algebra, $\mathcal{X}$, on X. Then $M(X)$ is a convex subset of the linear space of measures on the measurable space $(X, \mathcal{X})$.

Example 3. Let $\mathcal{F}$ denote the set of cumulative distribution functions on the real line. For any two elements F and G of $\mathcal{F}$ and $\alpha \in [0, 1]$, define the convex combination $\alpha F + (1 - \alpha) G \in \mathcal{F}$ by $(\alpha F + (1 - \alpha) G)(x) = \alpha F(x) + (1 - \alpha) G(x)$ for all $x \in \mathbb{R}$. Then $\mathcal{F}$ is a convex subset of the linear space of real-valued functions on $\mathbb{R}$.

1.2.2 The Characterization of the Preference Relations

In expected utility theory under risk, preference relations, $\succeq$ on $\mathbb{C}$, are characterized by three axioms. The first, the weak-order axiom, requires that the preference relation be complete and transitive. Completeness means that all elements of $\mathbb{C}$ are comparable in the sense that, presented with a choice between two alternatives in $\mathbb{C}$, the decision maker is (or should be) able to indicate that one alternative is at least as desirable to him as the other. In other words, the axiom rules out that the decision maker find some alternatives noncomparable and, as a result, is unable to express preferences between them. Transitivity requires that choices be consistent in the elementary sense that if an alternative a is at least as desirable as another alternative b which, in turn, is deemed at least as desirable as a third alternative c then alternative c is not (or should not be) strictly preferred over a. Formally:

(A.1)   (Weak order) $\succeq$ on $\mathbb{C}$ is *complete* (that is, for all $a, b \in \mathbb{C}$, either $a \succeq b$ or $b \succeq a$) and *transitive* (that is, for all $a, b, c \in \mathbb{C}$, $a \succeq b$ and $b \succeq c$ imply $a \succeq c$).

---

[6]A probability distribution is simple if it has finite support.

Note that the weak-order axiom does not require the use of properties of $\mathbb{C}$ that derive from its being a convex set in a linear space. This is not the case with the next two axioms.

The second axiom, the Archimedean axiom, imposes a sort of continuity on the preference relation. It requires implicitly that no alternative in $\mathbb{C}$ be infinitely more, or less, desirable than any other alternative. Specifically, let $\alpha a + (1 - \alpha) c \in \mathbb{C}$ be interpreted as a lottery that assigns the probabilities α and $(1 - \alpha)$ to the alternatives a and c, respectively. The axiom requires that, for no $a, b, c \in \mathbb{C}$ such that a is strictly preferred to b and b is strictly preferred to c, even a small chance of c makes the lottery $\alpha a + (1 - \alpha) c$ less desirable than getting b with certainty, or that even a small chance of winning a makes the lottery $\alpha a + (1 - \alpha) c$ more desirable than getting b with certainty. Formally:

(A.2) **(Archimedean)** For all $a, b, c \in \mathbb{C}$, if $a \succ b$ and $b \succ c$ then there exist $\alpha, \beta \in (0, 1)$ such that $\alpha a + (1 - \alpha) c \succ b$ and $b \succ \beta a + (1 - \beta) c$.

The third axiom, the independence axiom, imposes a form of separability on the preference relation. It requires that the comparison of any two alternatives in $\mathbb{C}$ be based on their distinct aspects (that is, the decision maker disregards all aspects that are common to the two alternatives). Let the alternatives $\alpha a + (1 - \alpha) c$ and $\alpha b + (1 - \alpha) c$, be interpreted as lotteries assigning the probabilities α to a and b, respectively, and the probability $(1 - \alpha)$ to the alternative c. Considering these two alternatives, the decision maker figures that both yield c with probability $(1 - \alpha)$, so in this respect they are the same, and that with probability α they yield, respectively, the alternatives a and b, so in this respect they are different. The axiom asserts that the preference between the alternatives $\alpha a + (1 - \alpha) c$ and $\alpha b + (1 - \alpha) c$ is the same as that between a and b. Put differently, the independence axiom requires that the preference between the lotteries a and b be the same whether they are compared directly or embedded in larger, compound, lotteries that are otherwise identical. Formally:

(A.3) **(Independence)** For all $a, b, c \in \mathbb{C}$ and $\alpha \in (0, 1], a \succcurlyeq b$ if and only if $\alpha a + (1 - \alpha) c \succcurlyeq \alpha b + (1 - \alpha) c$.

1.2.3 Representation

A real-valued function V on a linear space $\mathcal{L}$ is *affine* if $V(\alpha \ell + (1 - \alpha) \ell') = \alpha V(\ell) + (1 - \alpha) V(\ell')$, for all $\ell, \ell' \in \mathcal{L}$ and $\alpha \in [0, 1]$. It is said to be *unique up to positive affine transformation* if and only if any other real-valued, affine function $\hat{V}$ on $\mathcal{L}$ representing $\succcurlyeq$ on $\mathbb{C}$ satisfies $\hat{V}(\cdot) = \beta V(\cdot) + \gamma$, where $\beta > 0$.

The first representation theorem gives necessary and sufficient conditions for the existence of an affine representation of $\succcurlyeq$ on $\mathbb{C}$ and describes its uniqueness properties.[7]

---

[7] For a variation of this result in which $\mathbb{C}$ is a general mixture set, the Archimedean axiom is replaced by mixture continuity and the independence axiom is weakened, see Herstein and Milnor (1953).

Theorem 1.1 (von Neumann and Morgenstern). *Let $\succcurlyeq$ be a binary relation on $\mathbb{C}$. Then $\succcurlyeq$ satisfies the weak-order, Archimedean, and independence axioms if and only if there exists a real-valued, affine function, U, on $\mathbb{C}$ that represents $\succcurlyeq$. Moreover, U is unique up to a positive affine transformation.*

Clearly, any monotonic increasing (order preserving) transformation of U also represents the preference relation. However, such transformations are not necessarily affine. The uniqueness up to positive affine transformation means that the transformations under consideration preserve the affinity property of the representation.

The next theorem applies Theorem 1.1 to the set of simple probability distributions, $\Delta(X)$, in Example 1. It invokes the fact that $\Delta(X)$ is a convex set, gives necessary and sufficient conditions for existence, and the uniqueness (up to a positive affine transformation) of a utility function on the set of outcomes, X, whose expected value with respect to simple probability distributions in $\Delta(X)$ represents the preference relation on $\Delta(X)$.

Theorem 1.2 (Expected utility for simple probability measures) *Let $\succcurlyeq$ be a binary relation on $\Delta(X)$. Then $\succcurlyeq$ satisfies the weak-order, Archimedean, and independence axioms if and only if there exists a real-valued function, u, on X such that $\succcurlyeq$ is represented by:*

$$p \mapsto \sum_{x \in \{x \in X \mid p(x) > 0\}} u(x)p(x).$$

Moreover, u is unique up to a positive affine transformation.

1.2.4 Strong Continuity and Expected Utility Representation for Borel Probability Measures

The expected utility representation may be extended to more general probability measures. Doing so requires that the preference relation display stronger continuity than that captured by the Archimedean axiom.[8]

Let X be a finite dimensional Euclidean space, and let M be the set of all probability measures on $(X, \mathcal{B})$, where $\mathcal{B}$ denotes the Borel σ-algebra on X.[9] Assume that M is endowed with the topology of weak convergence.[10] Suppose that $\succcurlyeq$ is continuous in the topology of weak convergence. Formally,

(A.2') **(Continuity)** For all $P \in M$, the sets $\{Q \in M \mid Q \succcurlyeq P\}$ and $\{Q \in M \mid P \succcurlyeq Q\}$ are closed in the topology of weak convergence.

---

[8] See also Fishburn (1970).

[9] A Borel σ-algebra is the smallest σ-algebra that contains the open sets of X. Any measure μ defined on the Borel σ-algebra, $\mathcal{B}$, is called a Borel measure.

[10] The topology of weak convergence is the coarsest topology on M such that for every continuous and bounded real-valued function f on X the map $P \to \int_X f(x) dP(x)$ is continuous. In this topology, a sequence $\{P_n\}$ converges to P if $\int_X f(x) dP_n(x)$ converges to $\int_X f(x) dP(x)$ for every continuous and bounded real-valued function f on X.

Replacing the Archimedean axiom (A.2) with (A.2′) results in a stronger expected utility representation given in the following theorem. In particular, the utility function in the representation is continuous and bounded.[11]

Theorem 1.3 (Expected utility for Borel probability measures) *Let $\succcurlyeq$ be a preference relation on M. Then $\succcurlyeq$ satisfies the weak-order, continuity and independence axioms if and only if there exists a real-valued, continuous, and bounded function u on X such that $\succcurlyeq$ is represented by:*

$$P \mapsto \int_X u(x) dP(x).$$

Moreover, u is unique up to a positive affine transformation.

Let $X = \mathbb{R}$, the set of real numbers. For every $P \in M$, define the distribution function F by $F(x) = P(-\infty, x]$ for all $x \in \mathbb{R}$. Denote by $\mathcal{F}$ the set of all distribution functions so defined and let $\succcurlyeq$ be a preference relation on $\mathcal{F}$. Then, by Theorem 1.3, $\succcurlyeq$ satisfies the weak-order, continuity, and independence axioms if and only if there exists a real-valued, affine function u on X such that $\succcurlyeq$ is represented by $F \mapsto \int_{-\infty}^{\infty} u(x) dF(x)$. Moreover, u is unique up to a positive affine transformation.

1.3 EXPECTED UTILITY UNDER UNCERTAINTY AND SUBJECTIVE PROBABILITIES

This section reviews three models of decision making under uncertainty, the models of Savage (1954), Anscombe and Aumann (1963), and Wakker (1989). The models differ in the specification of the choice sets and the corresponding preference structures, but their objective is the same: the simultaneous determination of a utility function that quantifies the decision maker's tastes and a probability measure that quantifies his/her beliefs.

1.3.1 Savage's Analytical Framework

In the wake of Savage's (1954) seminal work, it is commonplace to model decision making under uncertainty by constructing a choice set using two primitive sets: a set, S, of *states of the nature* (or states, for brevity), and a set, C, whose elements are referred to as *consequences*. The choice set, F, is the set of mappings from the set of states to the set of consequences. Elements of F are referred to as *acts* and have the interpretation of courses of action.

States are resolutions of uncertainty, "a description of the world so complete that, if true and known, the consequences of every action would be known" (Arrow, 1971,

---

[11] A continuous weak order satisfying the independence axiom is representable by a continuous linear functional. Theorem 1.3 follows from Huber (1981) Lemma 2.1.

p. 45). Implicit in the definition of the state space is the notion that there is a unique *true* state. Subsets of the set of states are *events*. An event is said to *obtain* if it includes the true state.

A consequence is a description of anything that might happen to the decision maker. The set of consequences is arbitrary. A combination of an act, f, chosen by the decision maker, and a state, s, "selected" by nature determines a unique consequence, $c(f, s) \in C$.

Decision makers are characterized by preference relations, $\succcurlyeq$ on F, having the usual interpretation, namely, $f \succcurlyeq g$ means that the act f is at least as desirable as the act g.

1.3.2 The Preference Structure

Savage's (1954) subjective expected utility model postulates a preference structure that permits: (a) the numerical expression of the decision maker's valuation of the consequences by a utility function; (b) the numerical expression of the decision maker's degree of beliefs in the likelihoods of events by a finitely additive, probability measure; and (c) the evaluation of acts by the mathematical expectations of the utility of their consequences with respect to the subjective probabilities of the events in which these consequences materialize. In this model, the utility of the consequences is independent of the underlying events, and the probabilities of events are independent of the consequences assigned to these events by the acts.

The statement of Savage's postulates uses the following notation and definitions. Given an event E and acts f and h, $f_E h$ denotes the act defined by $(f_E h)(s) = f(s)$ if $s \in E$, and $(f_E h)(s) = h(s)$ otherwise. An event E is *null* if $f_E h \sim f'_E h$ for all acts f and f', otherwise it is *nonnull*. A constant act is an act that assigns the same consequence to all events. Constant acts are denoted by their values (that is, if $f(s) = x$ for all s, the constant act f is denoted by x).

The first postulate asserts that the preference relation is a weak order. Formally:

P.1 (Weak order) The preference relation is a transitive and complete binary relation on F.

The second postulate requires that the preference between acts depend solely on the consequences in the events in which the values of the two acts being compared are distinct.[12] Formally:

P.2 (Sure-Thing Principle) For all acts, $f, f', h,$ and h' and every event E, $f_E h \succcurlyeq f'_E h$ if and only if $f_E h' \succcurlyeq f'_E h'$.

The Sure-Thing Principle makes it possible to define preferences conditional on events as follows: For every event E, and all $f, f' \in F$, $f \succcurlyeq_E f'$ if $f \succcurlyeq f'$ and $f(s) = f'(s)$ for every s not in E. The third postulate asserts that, conditional on any

---

[12] The second postulate introduces separability reminiscent of that encountered in the independence axiom.

nonnull events, the ordinal ranking of consequences is independent of the conditioning events. Formally:

P.3 (Ordinal Event Independence) For every nonnull event E and all constant acts, x and y, $x \succcurlyeq y$ if and only if $x_E f \succcurlyeq y_E f$ for every act f.

In view of P.3 it is natural to refer to an act that assigns to an event E a consequence that ranks higher than the consequence it assigns to the complement of E as a *bet* on E. The fourth postulate requires that the betting preferences be independent of the specific consequences that define the bets. Formally:

P.4 (Comparative Probability) For all events E and E' and constant acts x, y, x', and y' such that $x \succ y$ and $x' \succ y'$, $x_E y \succcurlyeq x_{E'} y$ if and only if $x'_E y' \succcurlyeq x'_{E'} y'$.

Postulates P.1–P.4 imply the existence of a transitive and complete relation on the set of all events that has the interpretation of "at least as likely to obtain as," representing the decision maker's beliefs as *qualitative probability*.[13] Moreover, these postulates also imply that the decision maker's risk attitudes are event independent.

The fifth postulate renders the decision-making problem and the qualitative probability nontrivial. It requires the existence of constant acts between which the decision maker is not indifferent.

P.5 (Nondegeneracy) For some constant acts x and x', $x \succ x'$.

The sixth postulate introduces a form of continuity of the preference relation. It asserts that no consequence is either infinitely better or infinitely worse than any other consequence. Put differently, it requires that there be no consequence that, were it to replace the payoff of an act on a nonnull event, no matter how unlikely, would reverse a strict preference ordering of two acts. Formally:

P.6 (Small-Event Continuity) For all acts f, g, and h, satisfying $f \succ g$, there is a finite partition $(E_i)_{i=1}^n$ of the state space such that, for all i, $f \succ h_{E_i} g$ and $h_{E_i} f \succ g$.

A probability measure is *nonatomic* if every nonnull event may be partitioned into two non null subevents. Formally, π is a nonatomic probability measure on the set of states if for every event E and number $0 < \alpha < 1$, there is an event $E' \subset E$ such that $\pi(E') = \alpha \pi(E)$. Postulate P.6 implies that there are infinitely many states of the world and that if there exists a probability measure representing the decision maker's beliefs, it must be nonatomic. Moreover, the probability measure is defined on the set of all events, hence it is *finitely additive* (that is, for every event E, $0 \le \pi(E) \le 1$, $\pi(S) = 1$ and for any two disjoint events, E and E', $\pi(E \cup E') = \pi(E) + \pi(E')$).

---

[13] A binary relation $\succeq$ on an algebra of events, $\mathcal{A}$, in S is a *qualitative probability* if (a) $\succeq$ is complete and transitive; (b) $E \succeq \varnothing$, for all $E \in \mathcal{A}$; (c) $S \succ \varnothing$; and (d) for all $E, E', E'' \in \mathcal{A}$, if $E \cap E'' = E' \cap E'' = \varnothing$ then $E \succeq E'$ if and only if $E \cup E'' \succeq E' \cup E''$.

The seventh postulate is a monotonicity requirement asserting that if the decision maker considers an act strictly better (worse) than each of the payoffs of another act, taken as constant acts, on a given nonnull event, then the former act is conditionally strictly preferred (less preferred) than the latter. Formally:

P.7 (Dominance) For every event E and all acts f and f', if $f \succ_E f'(s)$ for all s in E then $f \succeq_E f'$ and if $f'(s) \succ_E f$ for all s in E then $f' \succeq_E f$.

Postulate P.7 is not necessary to obtain a subjective expected utility representation of *simple acts* (that is, acts with finite range). However, it is necessary if the model is to include nonsimple acts and it is sometimes regarded as a purely technical condition. However, as shown in Section 1.4, if the preference relation is incomplete, this condition has important implications for choice behavior.

1.3.3 Subjective Expected Utility Representation

Savage's (1954) theorem establishes that the properties described by the postulates P.1–P.7 are necessary and sufficient conditions for the representation of the preference relation by the expectations of a utility function on the set of consequences with respect to a probability measure on the set of all events. The utility function is unique up to a positive affine transformation, and the probability measure is unique, nonatomic, and finitely additive.

Theorem 1.4 (Savage) *Let $\succeq$ be a preference relation on F. Then $\succeq$ satisfies postulates P.1–P.7 if and only if there exists a unique, nonatomic, finitely additive probability measure π on S and a real-valued, bounded, function u on C such that $\succeq$ is represented by*

$$f \mapsto \int_S u(f(s))\, d\pi(s).$$

Moreover, u is unique up to a positive affine transformation, and $\pi(E) = 0$ if and only if E is null.

In Savage's theory the set of consequences is arbitrary. Therefore, to define quantitative probabilities on the algebra of all events the set of states must be rich in the sense that it is, at least, infinitely countable. In many applications, however, it is natural to model the decision problem using finite state spaces. For example, to model betting on the outcome of a horse race, it is natural to define a state as the order in which the horses cross the finish line, rendering the state space finite. To compensate for the loss of richness of the state space, two approaches were suggested in which the set of consequences is enriched. Anscombe and Aumann (1963) assumed that the consequences are simple lotteries on an arbitrary set of prizes. Wakker (1989) assumed that the set of consequences is a connected separable topological space. We consider these two approaches next, beginning with the model of Anscombe and Aumann (1963).

1.3.4 The Model of Anscombe and Aumann

Let S be a finite set of states, and let the set of consequences, $\Delta(X)$, be the set of lotteries on an arbitrary set of prizes, X. The choice set, H, consists of all the mappings from S to $\Delta(X)$. Elements of H are acts whose consequences are lottery tickets. The choice of an act, h, by the decision maker and a state, s, by nature entitles the decision maker to participate in the lottery $h(s)$ to determine his/her ultimate payoff, which is some element of the set X. Following Anscombe and Aumann (1963), it is useful to think about states as the possible outcomes of a horse race. An act is a bet on the outcome of a horse race whose payoffs are lottery tickets. Using this metaphor, they refer to elements of H as *horse lotteries* and elements of $\Delta(X)$ as *roulette lotteries*.

Invoking the formulation of Fishburn (1970), for any two elements, f and g, of H and $\alpha \in [0, 1]$, define the convex combination $\alpha f + (1 - \alpha) g \in H$ by $\left(\alpha f + (1 - \alpha) g\right)(s) = \alpha f(s) + (1 - \alpha) g(s)$, for all $s \in S$. Under this definition, H is a convex subset of a finite dimensional linear space.[14] To interpret this definition, consider the act $\alpha f + (1 - \alpha) g$. It is useful to think of this act as a compound lottery. The first stage is a lottery that assigns the decision maker the acts f or g, with probabilities α and $(1 - \alpha)$, respectively. Once the true state, s, is revealed, the decision maker's ultimate payoff is determined by either the lottery $f(s)$ or the lottery $g(s)$, depending on the act assigned to him in the first stage. According to this interpretation, the true state is revealed after the act is selected by the outcome of the first-stage lottery. Together, the true state, s, and the act $\alpha f + (1 - \alpha) g$ determine a lottery $\left(\alpha f + (1 - \alpha) g\right)(s)$ in $\Delta(X)$.

Consider next the lottery $\alpha f(s) + (1 - \alpha) g(s) \in \Delta(X)$. This lottery may be interpreted as a compound lottery in which the true state is revealed first and the decision maker then gets to participate in the lottery $f(s)$ or $g(s)$ according to the outcome of a second-stage lottery that assigns him $f(s)$ the probability α and $g(s)$ the probability $(1 - \alpha)$.

By definition of the choice set, these two compound lotteries are identical, implying that the decision maker is indifferent between finding out which act is assigned to him before or after the state of nature is revealed.[15] Drèze (1985) interprets this indifference as reflecting the decision maker's belief that he/she cannot affect the likelihood of the states, for if he/she could, knowing in advance the act he/she is assigned, he/she would tilt the odds in his/her favor. This opportunity is forgone if the decision maker learns which act is assigned to him only after the state has already been revealed. Hence, if a decision maker believes that he can affect the likelihood of the states, he should strictly prefer the act $\alpha f + (1 - \alpha) g$ over the act $\left(\alpha f(s) + (1 - \alpha) g(s)\right)_{s \in S}$. According to

---

[14] The linear space is $\mathbb{R}^{|S| \times n}$, $n < \infty$, where n denotes the number of elements in the supports of the roulette lotteries.
[15] Anscombe and Aumann (1963) imposed this indifference in their reversal of order axiom.

Drèze, implicit in the specification of the choice set is the assumption that the likely realization of the states is outside the control of the decision maker.[16]

Let $\succcurlyeq$ be a weak order on H satisfying the Archimedean and independence axioms. Since H is a convex subset of a linear space, application of Theorem 1.1 implies that $\succcurlyeq$ has an additively separable representation.[17]

Corollary 1.5 (State-dependent expected utility) *Let $\succcurlyeq$ be a binary relation on H, then $\succcurlyeq$ is a weak order satisfying the Archimedean and independence axioms if and only if there exists a real-valued function, w, on $\Delta(X) \times S$, affine in its first argument, such that $\succcurlyeq$ is represented by*

$$h \mapsto \sum_{s \in S} w\,(h(s)\,,\,s)\,.$$

Moreover, w is unique up to cardinal unit-comparable transformation (that is, if $\hat{w}$ represents $\succcurlyeq$ in the additive form, then $\hat{w}\,(\cdot,s) = bw\,(\cdot,s) + a(s)$, for all $s \in S$).

Presumably, the value $w\,(p, s)$ is a fusion of the decision maker's belief regarding the likelihood of the state s and his/her evaluation of the roulette lottery p. If the beliefs are independent of the payoffs, the valuations of the roulette lotteries are independent of the likelihood of the states in which they materialize, and the ex ante valuation of p equal its ex post valuation discounted by its likelihood, then $w\,(p, s)$ can be decomposed into a product $U(p)\pi(s)$, where U is a real-valued, affine function on $\Delta(X)$ and π is a probability measure on S. For such a decomposition to be well defined, the preference structure must be tightened.

To obtain the aforementioned decomposition of the function w, Anscombe and Aumann (1963) amended the von Neumann and Morgenstern model with two axioms. The first requires that the decision maker's risk attitudes (that is, his/her ranking of roulette lotteries) be independent of the state.[18] This axiom captures the essence of postulates P.3 and P.4 of Savage (1954), which assert that the preference relation exhibits state independence in both the ordinal and cardinal sense. The statement of this axiom requires the following additional notations and definitions: For all $h \in H$ and $p \in \Delta(X)$, let $h_{-s}p$ be the act obtained by replacing the s-coordinate of h, $h(s)$, with p. A state s is *null* if $h_{-s}p \sim h_{-s}q$, for all $p, q \in \Delta(X)$. A state is *nonnull* if it is not null. Formally:

(A.4) **(State independence)** For all nonnull $s, s' \in S$, and $h \in H, h_{-s}p \succcurlyeq h_{-s}q$ if and only if $h_{-s'}p \succcurlyeq h_{-s'}q$.

---

[16] Invoking the analytical framework of Anscombe and Aumann (1963), Drèze (1961, 1985) departed from their "reversal of order in compound lotteries" axiom. This axiom asserts that the decision maker is indifferent between the acts $\alpha f + (1 - \alpha)\,g$ and $\left(\alpha f(s) + (1 - \alpha)\,g(s)\right)_{s \in S}$. Drèze assume instead that decision makers may strictly prefer knowing the outcome of a lottery before the state of nature becomes known. In other words, according to Drèze, $\alpha f + (1 - \alpha)\,g \succ \left(\alpha f(s) + (1 - \alpha)\,g(s)\right)_{s \in S}$. The representation entails the maximization of subjective expected utility over a convex set of subjective probability measures.

[17] See Kreps (1988).

[18] In conjunction with the other axioms, this requirement is equivalent to the following monotonicity axiom: For all $h, h' \in H$, if $h(s) \succcurlyeq h'(s)$ for all $s \in S$, where $h(s)$ and $h'(s)$ are constant acts, then $h \succcurlyeq h'$.

The second axiom, which is analogous to Savage's P.5, requires that the decision maker not be indifferent among all acts. Formally:

(A.5) (Nontriviality) There are acts h and h' in H such that $h \succ h'$.

Preference relations that have the structure depicted by the axioms (A.1)–(A.5) have subjective expected utility representations.

Theorem 1.6 (Anscombe and Aumann) *Let $\succeq$ be a binary relation on H. Then $\succeq$ is a weak-order satisfying Archimedean, independence, state independence and nontriviality if and only if there exists a real-valued function, u, on X and a probability measure π on S such that $\succeq$ is represented by*

$$h \mapsto \sum_{s \in S} \pi(s) \sum_{x \in X} u(x)h(s)(x).$$

Moreover, u is unique up to a positive affine transformation, π is unique, and $\pi(s) = 0$ if and only if s is null.

1.3.5 Wakker's Model

Let S be a finite set of states, and let C be a connected separable topological space.[19] Elements of C are consequences and are denoted by c. The choice set, A, consists of all acts (that is, mappings from S to C). As usual, an act, a, and a state, s, determine a consequence, $c(a,s) = a(s)$. Decision makers are characterized by a preference relation, $\succeq$, on A.

Wakker (1989) assumes that a preference relation, $\succeq$, is a continuous weak order (that is, $\succeq$ on A is continuous if and only if, for all $a \in A$, the sets $\{a' \in A \mid a' \succeq a\}$ and $\{a' \in A \mid a \succeq a'\}$ are closed in the product topology on $C^{|S|}$).

To grasp the main innovation of Wakker's approach, it is useful to contrast it with the approach of Anscombe and Aumann (1963). They exploit the ordinal ranking of roulette lotteries to obtain cardinal utility representation of the "values" of the outcomes. The cardinality means that a difference between the utilities of two outcomes is a meaningful measure of the "intensity" of preference between them. Without roulette lotteries, the intensity of preferences must be gauged by other means.

Wakker measures the intensity of preferences among consequences in a given state by the compensating variations in the consequences in other states. To see how this works, for each $a \in A$, denote by $a_{-s}c$ the act obtained from a by replacing its payoff in state s, namely, the consequence $a(s)$, by the consequence c. Let s be a nonnull state and consider the following preferences among acts. The indifferences $a'_{-s}c' \sim a_{-s}c$ and $a_{-s}c'' \sim a'_{-s}c'''$ indicate that, in state s, the intensity of preference of c'' over c''' is the same as the intensity of preference of c over c', in the sense that both just compensate for the

---

[19] A topological space is connected if the only sets that are both open and closed are the empty set and the space itself, or equivalently, if the space is not the union of two nonempty disjoint open subsets. A topological space is separable if it contains a countable dense subset.

difference in the payoffs in the other states, represented by the subacts a'_{-s} and a_{-s}. The difference in the payoffs represented by the subacts a'_{-s} and a_{-s} is used as a "measuring rod" to assess the difference in values between c and c' and between c'' and c''' in state s.

Consider next another nonnull state, t, and let a''_{-t} and a'''_{-t} be subacts such that $a''_{-t}c' \sim a'''_{-t}c$. The difference in the payoffs represented by the subacts a''_{-t} and a'''_{-t} measures the difference in values between c and c' in state t. The intensity of preference of c over c' in state t is the compensating variation for the difference in the payoffs of the subacts a''_{-t} and a'''_{-t}. Using this as a measuring rod, it is possible to check whether the difference in values between c'' and c''' in state t also constitutes a compensating variation for difference in the payoffs of the subacts a''_{-t} and a'''_{-t}. If it does then we conclude that the intensity of preferences between c'' and c''' in state t is the same as that between c and c'. Since the only restriction imposed on s and t is that they be nonnull, we conclude that the intensity of preferences between consequences is state independent.

The next axiom asserts that the "intensity of preferences" as measured by compensating variations are state independent.[20] Although the axiom is stated using the weak preference relation instead of the indifference relation, the interpretation is similar—namely, that the preference relation displays no contradictory preference intensity between consequences in distinct nonnull states. Formally:

(W) (State-Independent Preference Intensity) For all $a', a'', a''' \in A, c, c', c'', c''' \in C$ and nonnull $s, t \in S$, if $a'_{-s}c' \succsim a_{-s}c$, $a_{-s}c'' \succsim a'_{-s}c'''$ and $a''_{-t}c' \succsim a'''_{-t}c$ then $a''_{-t}c'' \succsim a'''_{-t}c'''$.

State-independent preference intensity incorporates two properties of the preference relation. First, the relative ranking of acts that agree on the payoff in one state is independent of that payoff. This property, dubbed coordinate independence, is analogous to, albeit weaker than, Savage's (1954) Sure-Thing Principle. Second, the intensity of preference between consequences is independent of the state. This property is analogous to the Anscombe and Aumann (1963) state-independence axiom.

Wakker (1989) shows that a continuous weak order satisfying state-independent preference intensity admits a subjective expected utility representation.

Theorem 1.7 (Wakker) *Let $\succsim$ be a binary relation on A. Then $\succsim$ is a continuous weak-order displaying state-independent preference intensity if and only if there exists a real-valued, continuous function, u, on C and a probability measure, μ, on S such that $\succsim$ is represented by*

$$a \mapsto \sum_{s \in S} \mu(s)u(a(s)).$$

Moreover, if there are at least two nonnull states, then u is unique up to a positive affine transformation, π is unique, and $\pi(s) = 0$ if and only if s is null.

---

[20] State-independent preference intensity is equivalent to the requirement that the preference relation display no contradictory tradeoffs. For details, see Wakker (1989), in particular, Lemma IV.2.5.

1.3.6 Beliefs and Probabilities

Beginning with Ramsey (1931) and de Finetti (1937) and culminating with Savage (1954), with rare exceptions, choice-based notions of subjective probabilities are treated as an aspect of the representation of a decision maker's preference relation, that *defines* his/her degree of belief regarding the likelihood of events. In other words, while presuming to represent the decision maker's beliefs about the likelihood of events, according to this approach it is immaterial whether in fact the decision maker actually entertains such beliefs.

A different approach considers the decision maker's beliefs to be a cognitive phenomenon that feeds into the decision-making process. According to this approach, the subjective probabilities are meaningful only to the extent that they *measure* the decision maker's actual beliefs.

To highlight the difference between these two notions of subjective probability, it is convenient to think of the decision maker as a black box, which when presented with pairs of alternatives, selects the preferred alternative or express indifference between the two. Invoking this metaphor, imagine a black box into which we upload probabilities of events, utilities of consequences, and a set of commands instructing the box to select the alternative that yields the highest expected utility. Is it possible to recover the probabilities and utilities that were uploaded into the black box from the observation of its choice pattern?

To answer this question, consider the following example. Let there be two states, say 1 and 2, and upload into the box equal probabilities to each state. Suppose that acts are state-contingent monetary payoffs. Assume that for the same payoff, the utility in state 1 is twice that of state 2. Instructed to calculate expected utility, the box assigns the act that pays x_1 in state 1 and x_2 dollars in state 2 the expected utility $0.5 \times 2u(x_1) + 0.5 \times u(x_2)$, where u is the utility function uploaded into the black box. Clearly, the beliefs of the black box are represented by the uniform probability distribution on the set of states $\{1, 2\}$.

To infer the probabilities from the black box's choice behavior, apply any of the standard elicitation methods. For instance, applying the quadratic scoring rule method, we ask the black box to select the value of α, which determines a bet whose payoff is $-r\alpha^2$ in state 1 and $-r(1-\alpha)^2$ in state 2, $r > 0$. As r tends to zero the optimal value of α is an estimate of the probability of state 1. In this example, as r tends to zero, the optimal α tends to $1/3$. Clearly, this probability is not what was uploaded into the black box, and consequently does not measure the black box's beliefs. However, selecting acts so as to maximize the expected utility according to the formula $\frac{2}{3} \times u(x_1) + \frac{1}{3} \times u(x_2)$ induces choices identical to those implied by the original set of instructions. Thus, the output of the scoring rule may be taken as a definition of the black box's beliefs.

The source of the difficulty, illustrated by this example, is that the utility function and probability measure that figure in the representations in Savage's theorem and in the theorem of Anscombe and Aumann are *jointly unique* (that is, the probability is unique given the utility and the utility is unique, up to a positive affine transformations, given the probability). Thus, the uniqueness of the probabilities in the aforementioned theorems depends crucially on assigning the consequences utility values that are independent of the underlying events. In other words, the uniqueness of the probability depends on the convention that maintains constant acts are constant utility acts. This convention, however, is not implied by the axiomatic structure and, consequently, lacks testable implications for the decision maker's choice behavior. In other words, this example illustrates the fact that the subjective probability in the theories of Savage (1954), Anscombe and Aumann (1963), and all other models that invoke Savage's analytical framework, are arbitrary theoretical concepts devoid of choice-theoretic meaning. The structures of the preference relations, in particular postulates P.3 and P.4 of Savage (1954) and the state-independence axiom of Anscombe and Aumann (1963), require that the preference relation be state independent. However, neither by itself nor in conjunction with the other axioms do state-independent preferences imply that the utility function is state-independent. Put differently, state-independent preferences do not rule out that the events may affect the decision maker's well-being other than simply through their assigned consequences.[21]

In view of this discussion, it is natural to ask whether and why it is important to search for probabilities that measure the decision maker's beliefs. The answer depends on the applications of the theory one has in mind. If the model is considered to be a positive or a normative theory of decision making in the face of uncertainty, then the issue of whether the probabilities represent the decision maker's beliefs is indeed secondary. The only significance of the subjective expected utility representation is its additively separable functional form. However, as shown in Corollary 1.5, additive separability can be obtained with fewer restrictions on the structure of the underlying preferences. In the Anscombe and Aumann (1963) framework, state independence is unnecessary for the representation. Similarly, Savage's postulate P.3 is unnecessary.[22] Insisting that the preference relation exhibits state-independence renders the model inappropriate for the analysis of important decision problems, such as the demand for health and life insurance, in which the state itself may affect the decision maker's risk attitudes. Unless the subjective probabilities are a meaningful measurement of beliefs, the imposition of state-independent preferences seems unjustifiable.

Insofar as providing choice-based foundations of Bayesian statistics is concerned, which is the original motivation of Savage's (1954) work, the failure to deliver subjective probabilities that represent the decision maker's beliefs is fatal. In fact, if one does not

[21] On this point, see Schervish et al. (1990), Nau (1995), Seidenfeld et al. (1995), Karni (1996), Drèze (1961,1987).
[22] See Hill (2010).

insist that the subjective probability measure the decision maker's beliefs, it seems more convenient to interpret the additively separable representation of the preference relation as an expected utility representation with respect to a uniform prior and state-dependent utility functions.[23] Using the uniform prior for Bayesian statistical analysis seems at least as compelling as—and more practical than—using subjective probabilities obtained by an arbitrary normalization of the utility function.

A somewhat related aspect of subjective expected utility theory that is similarly unsatisfactory concerns the interpretation of null events. Ideally, an event should be designated as null, and be ascribed zero probability, if and only if the decision maker believes it to be impossible. In the models of Savage (1954) and Anscombe and Aumann (1963), however, an event is defined as null if the decision maker displays indifference among all acts whose payoffs agree on the complement of the said event. This definition does not distinguish events that the decision maker perceives as impossible from events on which all possible outcomes are equally desirable. It is possible, therefore, that events that the decision maker believes possible, or even likely, are defined as null and assigned zero probability. Imagine, for example, a passenger who is about to board a flight. Suppose that, having no relatives that he cares about, the passenger is indifferent to the size of his/her estate in the event that he dies. For such a passenger, a fatal plane crash is, by definition, a null event, and is assigned zero probability, even though he recognizes that the plane could crash. This problem renders the representation of beliefs by subjective probabilities dependent on the implicit, and unverifiable, assumption that in every event some outcomes are strictly more desirable than others. If this assumption is not warranted, the procedure may result in a misrepresentation of beliefs.

1.3.7 State-Dependent Preferences

The requirement that the (conditional) preferences be state (or event) independent imposes significant limitations on the range of applications of subjective expected utility theory. Disability insurance policies, or long-term care insurance plans, are acts whose consequences — the premia and indemnities — depend on the realization of the decision maker's state of health. In addition to affecting the decision maker's well-being — which, as the preceding discussion indicates, is not inconsistent with the subjective expected utility models — alternative states of health conceivably influence his/her risk attitudes as well as his/her ordinal ranking of the consequences. For instance, loss of ability to work may affect a decision maker's willingness to take financial risks; a leg injury may reverse his/her preferences between going hiking and attending a concert. These scenarios, which are perfectly reasonable, violate Anscombe and Aumann's (1963) state independence and Savage's (1954) postulates P.3 and P.4. Similar observations apply to the choice of life and health insurance policies.

---

[23] This is the essence of the state-dependent expected utility in Corollary 1.5.

Imposing state independence as a general characteristic of preference relations is problematic, to say the least. Moreover, as the preceding discussion shows, state independence cannot be justified as a means of defining choice-based representation of decision makers' beliefs.

To disentangle utility from subjective probabilities, or tastes from beliefs, in a meaningful way, it is necessary to observe the decision maker's response to shifts in the state probabilities. Such observations are precluded in Savage's (1954) framework. To overcome this difficulty, the literature pursued two distinct approaches to modeling state-dependent preferences and state-dependent utility functions. The first entails abandoning the revealed-preference methodology, in its strict form, and considering verbal expressions of preferences over hypothetical alternatives. The second presumes the availability of actions by which decision makers may affect the likelihoods of events. The first approach is described next. The second approach, which requires a different analytical framework, is discussed in the following section.

Unlike in the case of state-independent preferences, when the preference relations are state-dependent, it is impossible to invoke the convention that the utility function is state independent. To overcome the problem of the indeterminacy of the subjective probabilities and utilities when the preference relation is state dependent, several models based on hypothetical preferences have been proposed. Fishburn (1973), Drèze and Rustichini (1999), and Karni (2007) depart from the revealed-preference methodology, invoking instead preference relations on conditional acts (that is, preference relations over the set of acts conditional on events).

Karni and Schmeidler (1981) introduce a preference relation on hypothetical lotteries whose prizes comprise outcome–state pairs.[24] Let $\Delta (X \times S)$ denote the set of (hypothetical) lotteries on the set of outcome-state pairs, $X \times S$. Because the lotteries in $\Delta (X \times S)$ imply distinct, hence incompatible, marginal distributions on the state space, preferences among such lotteries are introspective and may be expressed only verbally. For example, a decision maker who has to choose between watching a football game in an open stadium or staying at home and watching the game on TV is supposed to be able to say how he would have chosen if the weather forecast predicted an 80% chance of showers during the game and how he would have chosen if the forecast were for 35% chance of showers during the game.

Let $\hat{\succeq}$ denote an introspective preference relation on $\Delta (X \times S)$. Assume that decision makers are capable of conceiving such hypothetical situations and evaluating them by the same cognitive processes that govern their actual decisions. Under these assumptions, the verbal expression of preferences provides information relevant for the determination of the probabilities and utilities. Specifically, suppose that the preference

---

[24] Karni (1985) provides a unified exposition of this approach and the variation due to Karni et al. (1983) described in following paragraphs.

relation, $\hat{\succcurlyeq}$, on $\Delta\left(X\times S\right)$ satisfies the axioms of expected utility and is consistent with the actual preference relation $\succcurlyeq$ on the set of acts. To grasp the meaning of consistency of the hypothetical and actual preference relations, define $\ell\in\Delta\left(X\times S\right)$ to be *nondegenerate* if $\sum_{x\in X}\ell\left(x,s\right)>0$ for all $s\in S$. Let H be the set of acts as in the model of Anscombe and Aumann (1963). Define a mapping, Ψ, from the subset of nondegenerate lotteries in $\Delta\left(X\times S\right)$ to H by: $\Psi\left(\ell\left(x,s\right)\right)=\ell\left(x,s\right)/\sum_{x\in X}\ell\left(x,s\right)$, for all $\left(x,s\right)\in X\times S$. In other words, every nondegenerate lottery in $\Delta\left(X\times S\right)$ is transformed by Ψ into an act in H by assigning to each $x\in X$ the probability of x under ℓ conditional on s.

Next recall that in Savage's analytical framework, the interpretation of a null state is ambiguous, because the definition does not distinguish between attitudes toward states that are considered impossible and events in which all outcomes are equally preferred. The availability of outcome-state lotteries makes it possible to define a state as *obviously null*, if it is null according to the usual definition and, in addition, there exist ℓ and ℓ' in $\Delta\left(X\times S\right)$ that *agree outside s* (that is, $\ell\left(x,s'\right)=\ell'\left(x,s'\right)$ for all $x\in X$ and $s'\neq s$) and $\ell\hat{\succ}\ell'$. A state is *obviously nonnull* if it is nonnull according to the usual definition.

Let $\succcurlyeq$ denote the actual preference relation on H. Intuitively, the preference relations $\succcurlyeq$ and $\hat{\succcurlyeq}$ are consistent if they are induced by the same utilities and the difference between them is due solely to the differences in the subjective probabilities. This idea is captured by the (strong) consistency axiom of Karni and Schmeidler (1981). Formally:

(KS) (Strong consistency) For all $s\in S$ and nondegenerate lotteries ℓ and ℓ' in $\Delta\left(X\times S\right)$, if $\ell\left(x,s'\right)=\ell'\left(x,s'\right)$ for all $x\in X$ and $s'\neq s$, and $\Psi\left(\ell\right)\succ\Psi\left(\ell'\right)$, then $\ell\hat{\succ}\ell'$. Moreover, if s is obviously nonnull, then, for all nondegenerate ℓ and ℓ' in $\Delta\left(X\times S\right)$ such that $\ell\left(x,s'\right)=\ell'\left(x,s'\right)$, for all $x\in X$ and $s'\neq s$, $\ell\hat{\succ}\ell'$ implies $\Psi\left(\ell\right)\succ\Psi\left(\ell'\right)$.

By the von Neumann-Morgenstern theorem, the expected utility representation of the introspective preferences, $\hat{\succcurlyeq}$, yields state-dependent utility functions, $u\left(\cdot,s\right)$, $s\in S$. Consistency implies that the same utility functions are implicit in the additive representation of the actual preferences in Corollary 1.5. This fact makes it possible to identify all of the subjective probabilities implicit in the valuation functions, $w\left(\cdot,s\right)$, in the state dependent expected utility representation. Formally, strong consistency implies that $\pi\left(s\right)=w\left(x,s\right)/u\left(x,s\right)$, $s\in S$, is independent of x. Moreover, the actual preference relation, $\succcurlyeq$ on H, has the expected utility representation, $f\mapsto\sum_{s\in S}\pi\left(s\right)\sum_{x\in X}u\left(x,s\right)f\left(s\right)\left(x\right)$, and the preference relation $\hat{\succcurlyeq}$ is represented by $\ell\mapsto\sum_{s\in S}\sum_{x\in X}u\left(x,s\right)\ell\left(x,s\right)$, where ℓ denotes a hypothetical outcome-state lottery. The function u, which is the same in both representations, is unique up to cardinal, unit-comparable transformation. Moreover, if all states are either obviously null or obviously nonnull then the probability π is unique, satisfying $\pi\left(s\right)=0$ if s is obviously null, and $\pi\left(s\right)>0$ if s is obviously nonnull.

Karni and Mongin (2000) observe that if the decision maker's beliefs are a cognitive phenomenon, quantifiable by a probability measure, then the subjective probability that figures in the representation above is the numerical expression of these beliefs. The explanation for this result is that the hypothetical lotteries incorporate distinct marginal distributions on the state space. Thus, the introspective preference relation captures the effects of shifting probabilities across states, thereby making it possible to measure the relative valuations of distinct outcomes. This aspect of the model does not exist in Savage's analytical framework.

A weaker version of this approach, based on restricting consistency to a subset of hypothetical lotteries that have the same marginal distribution on S, due to Karni et al. (1983), yields a subjective expected utility representation with state-dependent utility preferences. However, the subjective probabilities in this representation are contingent on the arbitrary choice of the marginal probabilities on the state space and are, therefore, themselves arbitrary. Consequently, the utility functions capture the decision maker's state-dependent risk attitudes but do not necessarily represent his/her evaluation of the consequences in the different states. Wakker (1987) extends the theory of Karni, Schmeidler, and Vind to include the case in which the set of consequences is a connected topological space.

Another way of defining subjective probabilities when the utilities are state dependent is to redefine the probabilities and utilities as follows: Let the state space be finite and the set of consequences be the real numbers, representing sums of money. Invoking the model of Wakker (1987), suppose that the preference relation is represented by a subjective expected utility function, $\sum_{s \in S} \pi(s) u \left(f(s), s \right)$. Suppose further that, for all $s \in S, u(\cdot, s)$, is differentiable and strictly monotonic, increasing in its first argument. Denote the derivative by $u'(\cdot, s)$ and define $\pi(s) = \hat{\pi}(s) u'(0, s) / \sum_{s \in S} \hat{\pi}(s) u'(0, s)$ and $\hat{u} \left(f(s), s \right) = u \left(f(s), s \right) / u'(0, s)$. Then the preference relation is represented by $\sum_{s \in S} \hat{\pi}(s) \hat{u} \left(f(s), s \right)$. This approach was developed by Nau (1995), who refers to $\hat{\pi}$ as risk-neutral probabilities, and by Karni and Schmeidler (1993).

Skiadas (1997) proposes a model, based on hypothetical preferences, that yields a representation with state-dependent preferences. In Skiadas' model, acts and states are primitive concepts, and preferences are defined on act–event pairs. For any such pair, the consequences (utilities) represent the decision maker's expression of his/her holistic valuation of the act. The decision maker is not supposed to know whether the given event occurred. Hence the decision maker's evaluation of the acts reflects, in part, his/her anticipated feelings, such as disappointment aversion.

1.4 BAYESIAN DECISION THEORY AND THE REPRESENTATION OF BELIEFS

The essential tenets of Bayesian decision theory are that (a) new information affects the decision maker's preferences, or choice behavior, through its effect on his/her beliefs rather than his/her tastes and (b) posterior probabilities, representing the decision maker's posterior beliefs, are obtained by updating the probabilities representing his/her prior beliefs using Bayes' rule. The critical aspect of Bayesian decision theory is, therefore, the existence and uniqueness of subjective probabilities, prior and posterior, representing the decision maker's prior and posterior beliefs that abide by Bayes' rule.

As was argued in Section 1.3.5, in decision theories invoking Savage's analytical framework, the unique representation of beliefs is predicated on a convention, that constant acts are constant utility acts, that is not implied by the preference structures. Consequently, these models do not provide choice-based foundations of Bayesian theory. A complete Bayesian decision theory anchored in the revealed preference methodology requires an alternative analytical framework, such as the one advanced in Karni (2011, 2011a) reviewed next.

1.4.1 The Analytical Framework

Let Θ be a finite set whose elements, *effects*, are physical phenomena, on which decision makers may place bets, that may or may not affect their well-being. Let A be a set whose elements, called *actions*, describe initiatives by which decision makers believe they can affect the likelihoods of ensuing effects.[25] Let B denote the set of all the real-valued mappings on Θ. Elements of B are referred to as *bets* and have the interpretation of effect-contingent monetary payoffs. Let $\bar{X}$ be a finite set of *signals* that the decision maker may receive before taking actions and choosing bets. The signals may be informative or noninformative.[26] Let X denote the set of informative signals and denote by o the noninformative signal. Hence, $\bar{X} = X \cup \{o\}$. The choice set, $\mathcal{I}$, consists of information-contingent plans, or *strategies*, for choosing actions and bets. Formally, a strategy $I \in \mathcal{I}$ is a function $I : \bar{X} \to A \times B$. Decision makers are characterized by a preference relation on $\mathcal{I}$.

The following example lends concrete meaning to the abstract terms mentioned above. Consider a resident of New Orleans facing the prospect of an approaching hurricane. The decision maker must make a plan that, contingent on the weather report, may include boarding up his/her house, moving his/her family to a shelter, and betting on the storm's damage (that is, taking out insurance on his/her property). The uncertainty is resolved once the weather forecast is obtained, the plan is put into effect, the storm passes, its path and force determined, and the ensuing damage is verified.

In this example, effects correspond to the potential material and bodily damage, and actions are the initiatives (e.g., boarding up the house, moving to a shelter) the decision maker can take to mitigate the damage. Bets are alternative insurance policies and observations are weather forecasts. The uncertainty in this example is resolved in

---

[25] A is assumed to be a connected topological space. For example, elements of A may describe levels of effort in which case A may be an interval in the real numbers.

[26] Receiving no signal is equivalent to receiving noninformative signal.

two stages. In the first stage, a weather forecast is obtained, and the action and the bet prescribed by the strategy are put into effect. In the second stage, the path and force of the hurricane are determined, the associated damage is realized, and the insurance indemnity is paid.

Consider the issue of subjective probabilities. At the point at which he/she contemplates his/her strategies, the decision maker entertains beliefs about two aspects of uncertainty. The first concerns the likelihood of alternative weather reports and, conditional on these reports, the likelihood of subsequent path-force combinations of the approaching hurricane. The second is the likelihood of the ensuing levels of damage (the effects). Clearly, the likelihoods of the latter are determined by those of the former, coupled with the actions that were taken, in the interim, by the decision maker.

As usual, a consequence depicts those aspects of the decision problem that affect the decision maker's ex post well-being. In this model, a *consequence* is a triplet (a, r, θ), representing the action, the monetary payoff of the bet, and the effect. The set of all consequences is given by the Cartesian product $C = A \times \mathbb{R} \times \Theta$.

Uncertainty in this model is resolved in two stages. In the first stage, an observation, $x \in \bar{X}$, obtains and the action and bet prescribed by each strategy for that observation are determined. In the second stage, the effect is realized and the payoff of the bet determined. Let Ω be the set of all functions from the set of actions to the set of effects (that is, $\Omega := \{\omega : A \rightarrow \Theta\}$). Elements of Ω depict the resolution of uncertainty surrounding the effects. A complete resolution of uncertainty is a function, s, from $\mathcal{I}$ to C. The *state space* is the set of all such functions, given by $S = \bar{X} \times \Omega$. Each state $s = (x, \omega)$ is an intersection of an *informational event* $\{x\} \times \Omega$ and a *material event* $\bar{X} \times \{\omega\}$. In other words, a state has two dimensions, corresponding to the two stages of the resolution of uncertainty — the purely informational dimension, x, and the material dimension, ω. Informational events do not affect the decision maker's well-being directly, whereas material events may. In general, states are abstract resolutions of uncertainty. In some situations, however, it is natural to attribute to the states concrete interpretations. In the example of the hurricane, the informational events are weather forecasts and the material events correspond to the path and force of the hurricane.

The Bayesian model requires a definition of a σ-algebra, $\mathcal{E}$, on S and a unique probability measure, P, on the measurable space $(S, \mathcal{E})$, such that (a) the conditioning of P on the noninformative signal o represents the decision maker's prior beliefs and (b) the conditioning of P on informative signals $x \in X$ represents the decision maker's posterior beliefs.

Denote by $I_{-x}(a, b)$ the strategy in which the x-coordinate of I, $I(x)$, is replaced by (a, b). The truncated strategy I_{-x} is referred to as a *substrategy*. For every given $x \in \bar{X}$, denote by $\succcurlyeq^x$ the induced preference relation on $A \times B$ defined by $(a, b) \succcurlyeq^x (a', b')$ if and only if $I_{-x}(a, b) \succcurlyeq I_{-x}(a', b')$. The induced preference relation $\succcurlyeq^o$ is referred to as the *prior* preference relation; the preference relations $\succcurlyeq^x, x \in X$, are the *posterior* preference relations. An observation, x, is *essential* if $(a, b) \succ^x (a', b')$, for some $(a, b), (a', b') \in A \times B$. Assume that all elements of $\bar{X}$ are essential.

For every $a \in A$ and $x \in \bar{X}$, define a binary relation $\succsim^x_a$ on B as follows: for all $b, b' \in B$, $b \succsim^x_a b'$ if and only if $(a, b) \succsim^x (a, b')$. An effect, θ, is said to be *nonnull given the observation–action pair* (x, a) if $(b_{-\theta}r) \succ^x_a (b_{-\theta}r')$, for some $b \in B$ and $r, r' \in \mathbb{R}$; otherwise, it is *null given the observation–action pair* (x, a). Let $\Theta(a,x)$ denote the set of nonnull effects given (x,a).

1.4.2 Preferences on Strategies and their Representation

Suppose that $\succsim$ on $\mathcal{I}$ is a continuous weak order.[27] The next axiom, coordinate independence, requires that preferences between strategies be independent of the coordinates on which they agree. It is analogous to, but weaker, than Savage's (1954) Sure-Thing Principle.[28] Formally,

(K1) **(Coordinate independence)** *For all* $x \in \bar{X}, I, I' \in \mathcal{I}$, *and* $(a, b), (a', b') \in A \times B, I_{-x}(a, b) \succsim I'_{-x}(a, b)$ *if and only if* $I_{-x}(a', b') \succsim I'_{-x}(a', b')$.

Two effects, θ and θ', are said to be *elementarily linked* if there are actions $a, a' \in A$ and observations $x, x' \in \bar{X}$ such that $\theta, \theta' \in \Theta(a, x) \cap \Theta(a', x')$. Two effects θ and θ' are said to be *linked* if there exists a sequence of effects $\theta = \theta_0, \ldots, \theta_n = \theta'$ such that θ_j and θ_{j+1} are elementarily linked, $j = 0, \ldots, n - 1$. The set of effects, Θ, is linked if every pair of its elements is linked.

The next axiom requires that the "intensity of preferences" for monetary payoffs contingent on any given effect be independent of the action and the observation. This is analogous to the assumption that the decision maker's risk attitudes are independent of the action and the observation (i.e., if the consequences were lotteries then their ordinal ranking would be action and observation independent). This axiom applies Wakker's (1989) idea that the preference relation exhibits no contradictory payoffs across states, to actions and observation. Formally,

(K2) **(Independent betting preferences)** *For all* $(a, x), (a', x') \in A \times \bar{X}, b, b', b'', b''' \in B, \theta \in \Theta(a, x) \cap \Theta(a', x')$, *and* $r, r', r'', r''' \in \mathbb{R}$, if $(b_{-\theta}r) \succsim^x_a (b'_{-\theta}r'), (b_{-\theta}r'') \succsim^x_a (b'_{-\theta}r''')$, *and* $(b''_{-\theta}r') \succsim^{x'}_{a'} (b'''_{-\theta}r)$ then $(b''_{-\theta}r'') \succsim^{x'}_{a'} (b'''_{-\theta}r''')$.

The idea behind this axiom is easier to grasp by considering a specific instance in which $(b_{-\theta}, r) \sim^x_a (b'_{-\theta}, r')$, $(b_{-\theta}r'') \sim^x_a (b'_{-\theta}r''')$ and $(b''_{-\theta}r') \sim^{x'}_{a'} (b'''_{-\theta}r)$. The first pair of indifferences indicates that, given a and x, the difference in the payoffs b and b' contingent on the effects other than θ, measures the intensity of preferences between the payoffs r and r' and r'' and r''', contingent on θ. The indifference $(b''_{-\theta}r') \sim^{x'}_{a'} (b'''_{-\theta}r)$ indicates

---

[27] Let $\mathcal{I}$ be endowed with the product topology, then $\succsim$ is continuous in this topology.
[28] See Wakker (1989) for details.

that given another action–observation pair, (a', x') the intensity of preferences between the payoffs r and r' contingent on θ is measured by the difference in the payoffs the bets b'' and b''' contingent on the effects other than θ. The axiom requires that, in this case, the difference in the payoffs b'' and b''' contingent on the effects other than θ is also a measure of the intensity of the payoffs r'' and r''' contingent on θ. Thus, the intensity of preferences between two payoffs given θ is independent of the actions and the observations.

To link the decision maker's prior and posterior probabilities the next axiom asserts that, for every $a \in A$ and $\theta \in \Theta$, the prior probability of θ given a is the sum over X of the joint probability distribution on $X \times \Theta$ conditional on θ and a. Let $I^{-o}(a, b)$ denote the strategy that assigns the action–bet pair (a, b) to every observation other than o (that is, $I^{-o}(a, b)$ is a strategy such that $I(x) = (a, b)$ for all $x \in X$). Formally;

(K.3) (Belief consistency) *For every $a \in A$, $I \in \mathcal{I}$ and $b, b' \in B$, $I_{-o}(a, b) \sim I_{-o}(a, b')$ if and only if $I^{-o}(a, b) \sim I^{-o}(a, b')$.*

The interpretation of belief consistency is as follows. The decision maker is indifferent between two strategies that agree on X and, in the event that no new information becomes available, call for the implementation of the alternative action-bet pairs (a, b) or (a, b') if and only if he is indifferent between two strategies that agree on o and call for the implementation of the same action-bet pairs (a, b) or (a, b') regardless of the observation. Put differently, given any action, the preferences on bets conditional on there being no new information are the same as those when new information may not be used to select the bet. Hence, in and of itself, information is worthless.

Bets whose payoffs completely offset the direct impact of the effects are dubbed *constant utility bets*. The present analytical framework renders this notion a choice-base phenomenon. To grasp this claim, recall that actions affect decision makers in two ways: directly through their utility cost and indirectly by altering the probabilities of the effects. Moreover, only the indirect impact depends on the observations. In the case of constant utility bets, and only in this case, the intensity of the preferences over the actions is observation independent. This means that the indirect influence of the actions is neutralized, which can happen only if the utility associated with constant utility bets is invariable across the effects. Formally,

Definition 1.8 *A bet $\bar{b} \in B$ is a constant utility bet according to $\succcurlyeq$ if, for all $I, I', I'', I''' \in \mathcal{I}$, $a, a', a'', a''' \in A$ and $x, x' \in \bar{X}$, $I_{-x}(a, \bar{b}) \sim I'_{-x}(a', \bar{b})$, $I_{-x}(a'', \bar{b}) \sim I'_{-x}(a''', \bar{b})$ and $I''_{-x'}(a, \bar{b}) \sim I'''_{-x'}(a', \bar{b})$ imply $I''_{-x'}(a'', \bar{b}) \sim I'''_{-x'}(a''', \bar{b})$ and $\cap_{(x, a) \in X \times A} \{b \in B \mid b \sim^x_a \bar{b}\} = \{\bar{b}\}$.*

As in the interpretation of independent betting preferences, think of the preferences $I_{-x}(a, \bar{b}) \sim I'_{-x}(a', \bar{b})$ and $I_{-x}(a'', \bar{b}) \sim I'_{-x}(a''', \bar{b})$ as indicating that, given $\bar{b}$ and x, the preferential difference between the substrategies I_{-x} and I'_{-x} measures the intensity of preference of a over a' and of a'' over a'''. The indifference $I''_{-x'}(a, \bar{b}) \sim I'''_{-x'}(a', \bar{b})$ implies that, given $\bar{b}$, and another observation x', the preferential difference between the substrategies $I''_{-x'}$ and $I'''_{-x'}$ is another measure of the intensity of preference of a over a'.

Then it must be true that the same difference also measures the intensity of preference of a'' over a'''. Thus, the intensity of preferences between actions is observation independent, reflecting solely the direct disutility of action. In other words, the indirect effect has been neutralized. The requirement that $\cap_{(x,a)\in X\times A}\{b \in B \mid b \sim_a^x \bar{b}\} = \{\bar{b}\}$ implicitly asserts that actions and observations affect the probabilities of the effects and that these actions and observations are sufficiently rich that $\bar{b}$ is well defined.[29]

Let $B^{cu}(\succeq)$ be a subset of all constant utility bets according to $\succeq$. In general, this set may be empty. This is the case if the range of the utilities of the monetary payoffs across effects does not overlap. Here it is assumed that $B^{cu}(\succeq)$ is nonempty. The set $B^{cu}(\succeq)$ is said to be *inclusive* if for every $(x, a) \in X \times A$ and $b \in B$ there is $\bar{b} \in B^{cu}(\succeq)$ such that $b \sim_a^x \bar{b}$.[30]

Invoking the notion of constant utility bets, the next axiom requires that the trade-offs between the actions and the substrategies be independent of the constant utility bets. Formally;

(K.4) (Trade-off independence) For all $I, I' \in \mathcal{I}$, $x \in \bar{X}$, $a, a' \in A$ and $\bar{b}, \bar{b}' \in B^{cu}(\succeq)$, $I_{-x}(a, \bar{b}) \succeq I'_{-x}(a', \bar{b})$ if and only if $I_{-x}(a, \bar{b}') \succeq I'_{-x}(a', \bar{b}')$.

Finally, the direct effect (that is, the cost) of actions, measured by the preferential difference between $\bar{b}$ and $\bar{b}'$ in $B^{cu}(\succeq)$, must be observation independent. Formally:

(K.5) (Conditional monotonicity) For all $\bar{b}, \bar{b}' \in B^{cu}(\succeq)$, $x, x' \in \bar{X}$, and $a, a' \in A$, $(a, \bar{b}) \succeq^x (a', \bar{b}')$ if and only if $(a, \bar{b}) \succeq^{x'} (a', \bar{b}')$.

The next theorem, due to Karni (2011), asserts the existence of a subjective expected utility representation of the preference relation $\succeq$ on $\mathcal{I}$ and characterizes the uniqueness properties of its constituent utilities and the probabilities. For each $I \in \mathcal{I}$, let $(a_{I(x)}, b_{I(x)})$ denote the action–bet pair corresponding to the x coordinate of I — that is, $I(x) = (a_{I(x)}, b_{I(x)})$.

Theorem 1.9 (Karni) *Let $\succeq$ be a preference relation on $\mathcal{I}$, and suppose that $B^{cu}(\succeq)$ is inclusive. Then $\succeq$ is a continuous weak order satisfying coordinate independence, independent betting preferences, belief consistency, trade-off independence, and conditional monotonicity if and only if there exist continuous, real-valued functions $\{u(\cdot, \theta) \mid \theta \in \Theta\}$ on $\mathbb{R}$, $v \in \mathbb{R}^A$, and a family, $\{\pi(\cdot, \cdot \mid a) \mid a \in A\}$, of joint probability measures on $\bar{X} \times \Theta$ such that $\succeq$ on I is represented by*

$$I \mapsto \sum_{x \in \bar{X}} \mu(x) \left[\sum_{\theta \in \Theta} \pi(\theta \mid x, a_{I(x)}) u(b_{I(x)}(\theta), \theta) + v(a_{I(x)}) \right], \tag{1.1}$$

where $\mu(x) = \sum_{\theta \in \Theta} \pi(x, \theta \mid a)$ for all $x \in \bar{X}$ is independent of a, $\pi(\theta \mid x, a) = \pi(x, \theta \mid a) / \mu(x)$ for

---

[29] To render the definition meaningful, it is assumed that, given $\bar{b}$, for all $a, a', a'', a''' \in A$ and $x, x' \in \bar{X}$ there are $I, I', I'', I''' \in \mathcal{I}$ such that the indifferences $I_{-x}(a, \bar{b}) \sim I'_{-x}(a', \bar{b})$, $I_{-x}(a'', \bar{b}) \sim I'_{-x}(a''', \bar{b})$ and $I''_{-x'}(a, \bar{b}) \sim I'''_{-x'}(a', \bar{b})$ hold.

[30] Inclusiveness of $B^{cu}(\succeq)$ simplifies the exposition.

all $(x,a) \in \bar{X} \times A$, $\pi(\theta \mid o,a) = \frac{1}{1-\mu(o)} \sum_{x \in X} \pi(x,\theta \mid a)$ for all $a \in A$, and, for every $\bar{b} \in B^{cu}(\succcurlyeq)$, $u(\bar{b}(\theta),\theta) = u(\bar{b})$, for all $\theta \in \Theta$.

Moreover, if $\{\hat{u}(\cdot,\theta) \mid \theta \in \Theta\}$, $\hat{v} \in \mathbb{R}^A$ and $\{\hat{\pi}(\cdot,\cdot \mid a) \mid a \in A\}$ is another set of utilities and a family of joint probability measures representing $\succcurlyeq$ in the sense of (1.1), then $\hat{\pi}(\cdot,\cdot \mid a) = \pi(\cdot,\cdot \mid a)$ for every $a \in A$ and there are numbers $m > 0$ and k, k' such that $\hat{u}(\cdot,\theta) = m\hat{u}(\cdot,\theta) + k$, $\theta \in \Theta$ and $\hat{v} = mv + k'$.

Although the joint probability distributions $\pi(\cdot,\cdot \mid a)$, $a \in A$ depend on the actions, the distribution μ is independent of a, consistent with the formulation of the decision problem, according to which the choice of actions is contingent on the observations. In other words, if new information becomes available, it precedes the choice of action. Consequently, the dependence of the joint probability distributions $\pi(\cdot,\cdot \mid a)$ on a captures solely the decision maker's beliefs about his/her ability to influence the likelihood of the effects by his/her choice of action.

1.4.3 Action-Dependent Subjective Probabilities on S

The family of joint probability distributions on observations and effects that figure in the representation (1.1) of the preference relation can be projected on the underlying state space to obtain a corresponding family of action-dependent, subjective probability measures. Moreover, this family of measures is the only such family that is consistent with the (unique) joint probability distributions on observations and effects. To construct the aforementioned family of probability measures partition the state space twice. First, partition the state space to *informational events*, $\mathcal{Y}$, corresponding to the observations (that is, let $\mathcal{Y} = \{\{x\} \times \Omega \mid x \in \bar{X}\}$). Second, for each action, partition the state space into *material events* corresponding to the effects. To construct the material partitions, fix $a \in A$ and, for every $\theta \in \Theta$, let $\mathcal{T}_a(\theta) := \{\omega \in \Omega \mid \omega(a) = \theta\}$. Then $\mathcal{T}_a = \{\bar{X} \times \mathcal{T}_a(\theta) \mid \theta \in \Theta\}$ is a (finite) material partition of S.

For every given action, define next a σ-algebra of events. Formally, let $\mathcal{E}_a$ be the σ-algebra on S generated by $\mathcal{Y} \wedge \mathcal{T}_a$, the join of $\mathcal{Y}$ and $\mathcal{T}_a$, whose elements are *events*.[31] Hence, events are unions of elements of $\mathcal{Y} \wedge \mathcal{T}_a$.

Consider the measurable spaces $(S, \mathcal{E}_a)$, $a \in A$. Define a probability measure η_a on $\mathcal{E}_a$ as follows: $\eta_a(E) = \sum_{x \in Z} \sum_{\theta \in \Upsilon} \pi(x,\theta \mid a)$ for every $E = Z \times \mathcal{T}_a(\Upsilon)$, where $Z \subseteq \bar{X}$, and $\mathcal{T}_a(\Upsilon) = \cup_{\theta \in \Upsilon} \mathcal{T}_a(\theta)$, $\Upsilon \subseteq \Theta$. Then, by representation (1.1), η_a is unique and the subjective probabilities, $\eta_a(E_I)$, of the informational events $E_I := \{Z \times \Omega \mid Z \subseteq \bar{X}\}$ are independent of a. Denote these probabilities by $\eta(E_I)$.

For every given a, consider the collection of material events $\mathcal{M}_a := \{\mathcal{T}_a(\Upsilon) \mid \Upsilon \subseteq \Theta\}$. By representation (1.1), the prior probability measure on $\mathcal{M}_a$ is given by $\eta_a(\mathcal{T}_a(\Upsilon) \mid o) = \sum_{\theta \in \Upsilon} \pi(\theta \mid o,a)$ and, for every $x \in X$, the posterior probability measure on $\mathcal{M}_a$ is given by $\eta_a(\mathcal{T}_a(\Upsilon) \mid x) = \sum_{\theta \in \Upsilon} \pi(\theta \mid x,a)$. Theorem 1.9 may be

---

[31] The join of two partitions is the coarsest common refinement of these partitions.

restated in terms of these probability measures as follows: Let $\succeq$ be a preference relation on $\mathcal{I}$, and suppose that $B^{cu}(\succeq)$ is inclusive. Then $\succeq$ is a continuous weak order satisfying coordinate independence, independent betting preferences, belief consistency, trade-off independence, and conditional monotonicity if and only if $\succeq$ on $\mathcal{I}$ is represented by

$$I \mapsto \sum_{x \in \bar{X}} \eta(x) \left[\sum_{\theta \in \Theta} u\left(b_{I(x)}(\theta), \theta\right) \eta_{a_{I(x)}}\left(\mathcal{T}_{a_{I(x)}}(\theta) \mid x\right) + v\left(a_{I(x)}\right) \right],$$

where the functions u on $\mathbb{R} \times \Theta$ and v on A, are as in Theorem 1.9 and, for each $a \in A$, η_a is a unique probability measure on the measurable space $(S, \mathcal{E}_a)$, such that $\eta_a(\{x\} \times \Omega) = \eta_{a'}(\{x\} \times \Omega) = \eta(x)$, for all $a, a' \in A$ and $x \in \bar{X}$.

The existence of a unique collection of measure spaces $\{(S, \mathcal{E}_a, \eta_a) \mid a \in A\}$ is sufficiently rich to allow action-dependent probabilities to be defined for every event that matters to the decision maker, for all conceivable choices among strategies he might be called upon to make. Hence, from the viewpoint of Bayesian decision theory, the family of action-dependent subjective probability measures is complete in the sense of being well defined for every conceivable decision problem that can be formulated in this framework. However, there is no guarantee that these subjective probability measures are mutually consistent. Karni (2011a) provides necessary and sufficient conditions for the existence of a unique probability space that supports all these action-dependent measures in the sense that $\eta_a(E)$ coincides with this measure for every $a \in A$ and $E \in \mathcal{E}_a$.

1.5 EXPECTED UTILITY THEORY WITH INCOMPLETE PREFERENCES

Perhaps the least satisfactory aspect of decision theory in general and expected utility theories under risk and under uncertainty in particular, is the presumption that decision makers can always express preferences, or choose between alternatives in a coherent manner. Von Neumann and Morgenstern expressed doubts concerning this aspect of the theory. "It is conceivable — and may even in a way be more realistic — to allow for cases where the individual is neither able to state which of two alternatives he prefers nor that they are equally desirable" (von Neumann and Morgenstern, 1947, p. 19). Aumann goes even further, writing "Of all the axioms of utility theory, the completeness axiom is perhaps the most questionable. Like others of the axioms, it is inaccurate as a description of real life; but unlike them, we find it hard to accept even from a normative viewpoint" (Aumann, 1962, p. 446). The obvious way to address this issue while maintaining the other aspects of the theory of rational choice is to relax the assumption that the preference relations are complete.

1.5.1 Expected Multi-Utility Representation Under Risk

Aumann (1962) was the first to model expected utility under risk without the completeness axiom.[32] Invoking the algebraic approach, Shapley and Baucells (1998) characterized in complete expected utility preferences over risky prospects whose domain is lotteries. They showed that relaxing the completeness axiom while maintaining the other aspects of the theory, one risky prospect, or lottery, is weakly preferred over another only if its expected utility is greater for a set of von Neumann–Morgenstern utility functions. Dubra et al. (2004) used the topological approach to obtain an analogous result for incomplete expected utility preferences over risky prospects whose domain is a compact metric space. Formally, let X be an arbitrary compact metric space whose elements are outcomes, and denote by $\mathcal{P}(X)$ the set of all Borel probability measures on X.

Theorem 1.10 (Dubra, Maccheroni and Ok) *A reflexive and transitive binary relation, $\succcurlyeq$ on $\mathcal{P}(X)$, satisfying the independence axiom and weak continuity[33] if and only if there exists a convex set $\mathcal{U}$ of real-valued, continuous functions on X such that for all $P, Q \in \mathcal{P}(X)$,*

$$P \succcurlyeq Q \Leftrightarrow \int_X u(x)dP(x) \geq \int_X u(x)\,dQ(x) \text{ for all } u \in \mathcal{U}. \tag{1.2}$$

Let $\langle \mathcal{U} \rangle$ be the closure of the convex cone generated by all the functions in $\mathcal{U}$ and all the constant functions on X. Dubra et al. (2004) show that if $\mathcal{U}$ in (1.2) consists of bounded functions, then it is unique in the sense that if $\mathcal{V}$ is another nonempty set of continuous and bounded real-valued functions on X representing the preference relation $\succcurlyeq$ as in (1.2), then $\langle \mathcal{U} \rangle = \langle \mathcal{V} \rangle$.

The interpretation of the expected multi-utility representation under risk is that the preference relation is incomplete because the decision maker does not have a clear sense of his/her tastes or, more precisely, his/her risk attitudes. The range of risk attitudes that the decision maker might entertain is represented by the utility functions in $\mathcal{U}$, which makes it impossible for him/her to compare risky prospects that are ranked differently by different elements of $\mathcal{U}$.

1.5.2 Expected Multi-Utility Representation Under Uncertainty

Under uncertainty, the inability of a decision maker to compare all acts may reflect his/her lack of a clear sense of his/her risk attitudes, his/her lack of ability to arrive at precise assessment of the likelihoods of events, or both. The incompleteness of preferences in this case entails multi-prior expected multi-utility representations. In the context

---

[32] See discussion of Aumann's contribution in Dubra et al. (2004).

[33] Weak continuity requires that, for any convergent sequences (P_n) and (Q_n) in $\mathcal{P}(X)$, $P_n \succcurlyeq Q_n$ for all n implies that $\lim_{n \to \infty} P_n \succcurlyeq \lim_{n \to \infty} Q_n$.

of Anscombe and Aumann's (1963) analytical framework, one act, f, is preferred over another act, g, if and only if there is a nonempty set, Φ, of pairs, (π, U), consisting of a probability measure, π, on the set of states, S, and real-valued affine function, U on $\Delta(X)$, such that

$$\sum_{s \in S} \pi(s) U\big(f(s)\big) \geq \sum_{s \in S} \pi(s) U\big(g(s)\big), \text{ for all } (\pi, U) \in \Phi. \tag{1.3}$$

The issue of incomplete preferences in the context of decision making under uncertainty was first addressed by Bewley (2002).[34] The incompleteness of the preference relation in Bewley's model is due solely to the incompleteness of beliefs. In terms of representation (1.3), Bewley's work corresponds to $\Phi = \Pi \times \{U\}$, where Π is a closed convex set of probability measures on the set of states and U is a real-valued affine function on $\Delta(X)$.

Seidenfeld et al. (1995), Nau (2006) and Ok et al. (2012) study the representation of preference relations that accommodate incompleteness of both beliefs and tastes. Seidenfeld et al. (1995) axiomatize the case in which the representation entails $\Phi = \{(\pi, U)\}$. Ok et al. (2012) axiomatize a preference structure in which the source of incompleteness is either beliefs or tastes, but not both.[35] Galaabaatar and Karni (2013) axiomatize incompleteness in both beliefs and tastes, providing necessary and sufficient conditions for multi-prior expected multi-utility representations of preferences. They obtain Bewley's Knightian uncertainty and expected multi-utility representation with complete beliefs as special cases. Because this contribution is more satisfactory from the axiomatic point of view (that is, its simplicity and transparency), it is reviewed below.

Consider a strict preference relation, $\succ$ on H. The set H is said to be $\succ$ -bounded if it includes best and worst elements (that is, there exist h^M and h^m in H such that $h^M \succ h \succ h^m$, for all $h \in H - \{h^M, h^m\}$).[36] For every $h \in H$, let $B(h) := \{f \in H \mid f \succ h\}$ and $W(h) := \{f \in H \mid h \succ f\}$ denote the upper and lower contour sets of h, respectively. The relation $\succ$ is convex if the upper contour set is convex.

Since the main interest here is the representation of incomplete preferences, instead of the weak-order axiom, assume the following weaker requirement:

(A.1') (**Strict partial order**) The preference relation $\succ$ is transitive and irreflexive.

Let $\succ$ be a binary relation on H. Then, analogous to Corollary 1.5, H is $\succ$ -bounded strict partial order satisfying the Archimedean and independence axioms if and only if

---

[34] Bewley's original work first appeared in 1986 as a Cowles Foundation Discussion Paper no. 807.

[35] In terms of representation (1.3), Ok et al. (2012) consider the cases in which $\Phi = \Pi \times \{U\}$ or $\Phi = \{\pi\} \times \mathcal{U}$.

[36] The difference between the preference structure above and that of expected utility theory is that the induced relation $\neg\big(f \succ g\big)$ is reflexive but not necessarily transitive (it is not necessarily a preorder). Moreover, it is not necessarily complete. Thus, $\neg\big(f \succ g\big)$ and $\neg\big(g \succ f\big)$, do not imply that f and g are indifferent (i.e., equivalent), rather they may be *noncomparable*. If f and g are noncomparable, we write $f \bowtie g$.

there exists a nonempty, convex, and closed set $\mathcal{W}$ of real-valued functions, w, on $X \times S$, such that

$$\sum_{s \in S} \sum_{x \in X} h^M(x,s) w(x,s) > \sum_{s \in S} \sum_{x \in X} h(x,s) w(x,s) > \sum_{s \in S} \sum_{x \in X} h^m(x,s) w(x,s)$$

for all $h \in H - \{h^M, h^m\}$ and $w \in \mathcal{W}$, and for all $h, h' \in H, h \succ h'$ if and only if

$$\sum_{s \in S} \sum_{x \in X} h(x,s) w(x,s) > \sum_{s \in S} \sum_{x \in X} h'(x,s) w(x,s) \quad \text{for all } w \in \mathcal{W}. \tag{1.4}$$

To state the uniqueness properties of the representation, the following notations and definitions are needed. Let δ_s be the vector in $\mathbb{R}^{|X| \cdot |S|}$ such that $\delta_s(t,x) = 0$ for all $x \in X$ if $t \neq s$ and $\delta_s(t,x) = 1$ for all $x \in X$ if $t = s$. Let $D = \{\theta \delta_s \mid s \in S, \theta \in \mathbb{R}\}$. Let $\mathcal{U}$ be a set of real-valued functions on $\mathbb{R}^{|X| \cdot |S|}$. Fix $x^0 \in X$, and for each $u \in \mathcal{U}$ define a real-valued function, $\hat{u}$, on $\mathbb{R}^{|X| \cdot |S|}$ by $\hat{u}(x,s) = u(x,s) - u(x^0,s)$ for all $x \in X$ and $s \in S$. Let $\widehat{\mathcal{U}}$ be the normalized set of functions corresponding to $\mathcal{U}$ (that is, $\widehat{\mathcal{U}} = \{\hat{u} \mid u \in \mathcal{U}\}$). We denote by $\langle \widehat{\mathcal{U}} \rangle$ the closure of the convex cone in $\mathbb{R}^{|X| \cdot |S|}$ generated by all the functions in $\widehat{\mathcal{U}}$ and D. With this in mind, the uniqueness of the representation requires that if $\mathcal{W}'$ be another set of real-valued, affine functions on H that represents $\succ$ in the sense of (4), then $\langle \widehat{\mathcal{W}'} \rangle = \langle \widehat{\mathcal{W}} \rangle$.

This representation is not the most parsimonious, as the set $\mathcal{W}$ includes functions that are redundant (that is, their removal does not affect the representation). Henceforth, consider a subset of essential functions, $\mathcal{W}^o \subset \mathcal{W}$, that is sufficient for the representation. Define the sets of essential component functions $\mathcal{W}_s^o := \{w(\cdot, s) \mid w \in \mathcal{W}^o\}$, $s \in S$.

As in the state-dependent expected utility representation, decomposing the functions $w(p,s)$ into subjective probabilities and utilities requires tightening the structure of the preferences. To state the next axiom, which is a special case of Savage's (1954) postulate P.7, the following notation is useful. For each $f \in H$ and every $s \in S$, let f^s denote the constant act whose payoff is $f(s)$ in every state (that is, $f^s(s') = f(s)$ for all $s' \in S$). The axiom requires that if an act, g, is strictly preferred over every constant act, f^s, obtained from the act f, then g is strictly preferred over f. Formally,

(A.6) (Dominance) For all $f, g \in H$, if $g \succ f^s$ for every $s \in S$, then $g \succ f$.

Galaabataar and Karni (2013) show that a preference relation is a strict partial order satisfying Archimedean, independence, and dominance if and only if there is a nonempty convex set of affine utility functions on $\Delta(X)$ and, corresponding to each utility function, a convex set of probability measures on S such that, when presented with a choice between two acts, the decision maker prefers the act that yields a higher expected utility according to every utility function and every probability measure in the corresponding set.

Let the set of probability–utility pairs that figure in the representation be $\Phi := \{(\pi, U) \mid U \in \mathcal{U},\ \pi \in \Pi^U\}$. Each $(\pi, U) \in \Phi$ defines a hyperplane $w := \pi \cdot U$. Denote by $\mathcal{W}$ the set of all these hyperplanes, and define $\langle \Phi \rangle = \langle \mathcal{W} \rangle$.

Theorem 1.11 (Galaabaatar and Karni) *Let $\succ$ be a binary relation on H. Then H is $\succ$-bounded and $\succ$ is nonempty bounded strict partial order satisfying the Archimedean, independence, and dominance axioms if and only if there exists a nonempty, and convex set, $\mathcal{U}$, of real-valued, affine functions on $\Delta(X)$, and closed and convex sets Π^U, $U \in \mathcal{U}$, of probability measures on S such that, for all $h \in H$ and $(\pi, U) \in \Phi$,*

$$\sum_{s \in S} \pi(s) U(h^M(s)) > \sum_{s \in S} \pi(s) U(h(s)) > \sum_{s \in S} \pi(s) U(h^m(s))$$

and for all $h, h' \in H$,

$$h \succ h' \Leftrightarrow \sum_{s \in S} \pi(s) U(h(s)) > \sum_{s \in S} \pi(s) U(h'(s)) \text{ for all } (\pi, U) \in \Phi, \tag{1.5}$$

where $\Phi = \{(\pi, U) \mid U \in \mathcal{U},\ \pi \in \Pi^U\}$. Moreover, if $\Phi' = \{(\pi', V) \mid V \in \mathcal{V},\ \pi' \in \Pi'^V\}$ is another set of real-valued, affine functions on $\Delta(X)$ and sets of probability measures on S that represent $\succ$ in the sense of (1.5), then $\langle \Phi' \rangle = \langle \Phi \rangle$ and $\pi(s) > 0$ for all s.

1.5.2.1 Special Cases

Galaabaatar and Karni (2013) analyze three special cases. The first involves complete separation of beliefs from tastes (that is, $\Phi = \mathcal{M} \times \mathcal{U}$, where $\mathcal{M}$ is a nonempty convex set of probability measures on S, and $\mathcal{U}$ is a nonempty, closed, and convex set of real-valued, affine functions on $\Delta(X)$).

To grasp the next result, recall that one of the features of Anscombe and Aumann's (1963) model is the possibility it affords for transforming uncertainty into risk by comparing acts to their reduction to lotteries under alternative measures on $\Delta(S)$. In particular, there is a subjective probability measure, α^* on S, that governs the decision-maker's choice. In fact, every act, f, is indifferent to the constant act f^{α^*} obtained by the reduction of the compound lottery represented by (f, α^*).[37] It is, therefore, natural to think of an act as a tacit compound lottery in which the probabilities that figure in the first stage are the subjective probabilities that govern choice behavior. When the set of subjective probabilities that govern choice behavior is not a singleton, an act f corresponds to a set of implicit compound lotteries, each of which is induced by a (subjective) probability measure. The set of measures represents the decision maker's indeterminate

---

[37] For each act–probability pair $(f, \alpha) \in H \times \Delta(S)$, we denote by f^α the constant act defined by $f^\alpha(s) = \Sigma_{s' \in S} \alpha_{s'} f(s')$ for all $s \in S$.

beliefs. If, in addition, the reduction of compound lotteries assumption is imposed, then (f, α) is equivalent to its reduction, f^a.

The next axiom asserts that $g \succ f$ is sufficient for the reduction of (g, α) to be preferred over the reduction of (f, α) for all α in the aforementioned set of measures. Formally:

(A.7) (Belief consistency) For all $f, g \in H, g \succ f$ implies $g^\alpha \succ f^\alpha$ for all $\alpha \in \Delta(S)$ such that $f' \succ h^p$ implies $\neg(h^p \succ (f')^\alpha)$ (for any $p \in \Delta(X), f' \in H$).

The next theorem characterizes the "product representation." For a set of functions, $\mathcal{U}$ on X, we denote by $\langle \mathcal{U} \rangle$ the closure of the convex cone in $\mathbb{R}^{|X|}$ generated by all the functions in $\mathcal{U}$ and all the constant functions on X.

Theorem 1.12 (Galaabaatar and Karni) *Let $\succ$ be a binary relation on H, then H is $\succ$-bounded and $\succ$ nonempty bounded strict partial order satisfying the Archimedean, independence dominance and belief consistency axioms if and only if there exist nonempty sets, $\mathcal{U}$ and $\mathcal{M}$, of real-valued, affine functions on $\Delta(X)$ and probability measures on S, respectively, such that, for all $h \in H$ and $(\pi, U) \in \mathcal{M} \times \mathcal{U}$,*

$$\sum_{s \in S} \pi(s)U(h^M(s)) > \sum_{s \in S} \pi(s)U(h(s)) > \sum_{s \in S} \pi(s)U(h^m(s))$$

and for all $h, h' \in H, h \succ h'$ if and only if

$$\sum_{s \in S} \pi(s)U(h(s)) > \sum_{s \in S} \pi(s)U(h'(s)) \text{ for all } (\pi, U) \in \mathcal{M} \times \mathcal{U}.$$

Moreover, if $\mathcal{V}$ and $\mathcal{M}'$ are another pair of sets of real-valued functions on X and probability measures on S that represent $\succ$ in the above sense, then $\langle \mathcal{U} \rangle = \langle \mathcal{V} \rangle$ and $cl(conv(\mathcal{M})) = cl(conv(\mathcal{M}'))$, where $cl(conv(\mathcal{M}))$ is the closure of the convex hull of $\mathcal{M}$. In addition, $\pi(s) > 0$ for all $s \in S$ and $\pi \in \mathcal{M}$.

The model of Knightian uncertainty requires a formal definition of complete tastes. To provide such a definition, it is assumed that the conditional on the state the strict partial orders induced by $\succ$ on H exhibits negative transitivity.[38] Formally:

(A.8) (Conditional negative transitivity) For all $s \in S$, $\succ_s$ is negatively transitive.

Define the weak conditional preference relation, $\succsim_s$ on $\Delta(X)$ as follows: For all $p, q \in \Delta(X)$, $p \succsim_s q$ if $\neg(q \succ_s p)$. Then $\succsim_s$ is complete and transitive.[39] Let $\succ^c$ be the restriction of $\succ$ to the subset of constant acts, H^c, in H. Then $\succ^c = \succ_s$ for all $s \in S$. Define $\succsim^c$ on H^c as follows: For all $p, q \in H^c$, $p \succsim^c q$ if $\neg(q \succ p)$. Then $\succsim^c = \succsim_s$ for all $s \in S$.

---

[38] A strict partial order, $\succ$ on a set D, is said to exhibit negative transitivity if for all $x, y, z \in D, \neg(x \succ y)$ and $\neg(y \succ z)$ imply $\neg(x \succ z)$.

[39] See Kreps' (1988) proposition (2.4).

Conditional negative transitivity implies that the weak preference relation $\succsim^c$ on H^c is complete.[40]

The Galaabaatar and Karni (2013) version of Knightian uncertainty can be stated as follows:

Theorem 1.13 (Knightian uncertainty) *Let $\succ$ be a binary relation on H. Then H is $\succ$-bounded, and $\succ$ is nonempty, strict partial order satisfying the Archimedean, independence, dominance, and conditional negative transitivity if and only if there exists a nonempty set, $\mathcal{M}$, of probability measures on S and a real-valued, affine function U on $\Delta(X)$ such that*

$$\sum_{s \in S} U\left(h^M(s)\right) \pi(s) > \sum_{s \in S} U\left(h(s)\right) \pi(s) > \sum_{s \in S} U\left(h^m(s)\right) \pi(s)$$

for all $h \in H$ and $\pi \in \mathcal{M}$, and for all $h, h' \in H$, $h \succ h'$ if and only if $\sum_{s \in S} U(h(s)) \pi(s) > \sum_{s \in S} U(h'(s)) \pi(s)$ for all $\pi \in \mathcal{M}$. Moreover, U is unique up to a positive affine transformation, the closed convex hull of $\mathcal{M}$ is unique, and for all $\pi \in \mathcal{M}$, $\pi(s) > 0$ for any s.

The dual of Knightian uncertainty is the case in which the incompleteness of the decision-maker's preferences is due solely to the incompleteness of his/her tastes. To define the notion of coherent beliefs, denote by h^p the constant act in H whose payoff is p for every $s \in S$. For each event E, $pEq \in H$ is the act whose payoff is p for all $s \in E$ and q for all $s \in S - E$. Denote by $p\alpha q$ the constant act whose payoff, in every state, is $\alpha p + (1 - \alpha) q$. A *bet* on an event E is the act pEq, whose payoffs satisfy $p \succ q$.

A decision maker who prefers the constant act $p\alpha q$ to the bet pEq is presumed to believe that α exceeds the likelihood of E. A preference relation $\succ$ on H is said to exhibit *coherent beliefs*, if for all events E and $p, q, p', q' \in \Delta(X)$ such that $h^p \succ h^q$ and $h^{p'} \succ h^{q'}$, $p\alpha q \succ pEq$ if and only if $p'\alpha q' \succ p'Eq'$, and $pEq \succ p\alpha q$ if and only if $p'Eq' \succ p'\alpha q'$. It is noteworthy that a decision maker whose preference relation satisfies strict partial order, Archimedean, independence, and dominance exhibits coherent beliefs.

Belief completeness is captured by the following axiom:

(A.9) (Complete beliefs) For all events E and $\alpha \in [0, 1]$, either $p^M \alpha p^m \succ p^M E p^m$ or $p^M E p^m \succ p^M \alpha' p^m$ for all $\alpha > \alpha'$.

If the beliefs are complete, then the incompleteness of the preference relation on H is due entirely to the incompleteness of tastes.

The next theorem is the subjective expected multi-utility version of the Anscombe–Aumann (1963) model corresponding to the situation in which the decision-maker's beliefs are complete.

Theorem 1.14 (Subjective expected multi-utility) *Let $\succ$ be a binary relation on H. Then H is $\succ$-bounded and $\succ$ is a nonempty strict partial order satisfying the Archimedean,*

---

[40] This is the assumption of Bewley (2002).

independence, dominance, and complete beliefs if and only if there exists a nonempty set, $\mathcal{U}$, of real-valued, affine functions on $\Delta(X)$ and a probability measure π on S such that

$$\sum_{s \in S} U\left(h^M(s)\right) \pi(s) > \sum_{s \in S} U\left(h(s)\right) \pi(s) > \sum_{s \in S} U\left(h^m(s)\right) \pi(s), \tag{1.6}$$

for all $h \in H$ and $U \in \mathcal{U}$ and for all $h, h' \in H$, $h \succ h'$ if and only if $\sum_{s \in S} U(h(s)) \pi(s) > \sum_{s \in S} U\left(h'(s)\right) \pi(s)$ for all $U \in \mathcal{U}$. Moreover, if $\mathcal{V}$ is another set of real-valued, affine functions on $\Delta(X)$ that represent $\succ$ in the above sense then $\langle \mathcal{V} \rangle = \langle \mathcal{U} \rangle$. The probability measure, π, is unique and $\pi(s) > 0$ if and only if s is nonnull.

1.6 CONCLUSION

For more than half a century, expected utility theory has been the paradigmatic model of decision making under risk and under uncertainty. The expected utility model acquired its dominant position because it is founded on normatively compelling principles, and its representation has an appealing functional form. The functional form captures two subroutines that are presumed to be activated when decision makers must choose among alternative courses of action — tastes for the consequences and beliefs regarding their likely realizations — and integrates them to obtain a decision criterion. In addition to providing analytical tools for the study of decision making under uncertainty, the theory was also intended to furnish choice-based foundations of the prior probabilities in Bayesian statistics.

This chapter reviewed the main models that formalized these ideas, emphasizing the interaction among the structure of the choice sets and the axiomatic structure of the preference relations. In addition, the chapter includes a critical evaluation of the expected utility models and a discussion of alternative developments intended to address some of their perceived shortcomings.

Almost from the start, doubts were raised about the descriptive validity of the central tenets of expected utility theory — the independence axiom in the case of decision making under risk and the Sure-Thing Principle in the case of decision making under uncertainty. The weight of the experimental evidence, suggesting that decision makers violate the independence axiom and the Sure-Thing Principle in a systematic manner, inspired the developments of alternative models that depart from these axioms. The development and study of these nonexpected utility theories have been the main concern of decision theory during the last quarter of century and led to the development of an array of interesting and challenging ideas and models. These developments are treated in other chapters in this handbook.

ACKNOWLEDGMENTS

I am grateful to John Quiggin, David Schmeidler, Peter Wakker, and the editors for their useful comments and suggestions on an earlier draft of this chapter.

REFERENCES

Anscombe, F.J., Aumann, R.J., 1963. A definition of subjective probability. Annals of Mathematical Statistics 43, 199–205.

Arrow, K.J., 1971. Essays in the Theory of Risk Bearing. Markham Publishing Co., Chicago.

Aumann, Robert J., 1962. Utility theory without the completeness axiom. Econometrica 30, 445–462.

Bayes, T., 1764. Essay towards solving a problem in the doctrine of chances. Philosophical Transactions of the Royal Society of London.

Bernoulli, D., 1738. Specimen theoriae novae de mensura sortis. Commentarii Academiae Scientiatatum Imperalas Petropolitanae 5, 175–192 (Translated as "Exposition of a New Theory on the Measurement of Risk." Econometrica 22 (1954): 23–26).

Bewley, T.F., 2002. Knightian decision theory: part I. Decision in Economics and Finance 25, 79–110 (This article appeared as Cowles Foundation discussion paper no. 807, in (1986).).

de Finetti, B., 1937. La prévision: Ses lois logiques, ses sources subjectives. Annals de l'Institute Henri Poincare 7, 1–68 (English translation, by H.E. Kyburg, appears in H.E. Kyburg and H.E. Smokler (Eds.) (1964) Studies in Subjective Probabilities. John Wiley and Sons, New York.).

Devlin, K., 2008. The Unfinished Game. Basic Books, New York.

Drèze, J.H., 1961. Les fondements logiques de l'utilit é cardinale et de la probabilité subjective. La D écision. Colloques Internationaux de CNRS.

Drèze, J.H., 1985. Decision theory with moral hazard and state-dependent preferences. In: Essays on Economic Decisions under Uncertainty. Cambridge University Press, Cambridge.

Drèze, J.H., Rustichini, A., 1999. Moral hazard and conditional preferences. Journal of Mathematical Economics 31, 159–181.

Dubra, J., Maccheroni, F., Ok, E.A., 2004. Expected utility theory without the completeness axiom. Journal of Economic Theory 115, 118–133.

Fishburn, P.C., 1970. Utility Theory for Decision Making. Wiley, New York.

Fishburn, P.C., 1973. A mixture-set axiomatization of conditional subjective expected utility. Econometrica 41, 1–25.

Galaabataar, T., Karni, E., 2013. Subjective expected utility with incomplete preferences. Econometrica 81, 255–284.

Hacking, I., 1984. The Emergence of Probabilities. Cambridge University Press, Cambridge.

Herstein, I.N., Milnor, J., 1953. An axiomatic approach to measurable utility. Econometrica 21, 291–297.

Hill, B., 2010. An additively separable representation in the savage framework. Journal of Economic Theory 145, 2044–2054.

Huber, P.J., 1981. Robust Statistics. John Wiley and Sons, New York.

Karni, E., 1985. Decision Making under Uncertainty: The Case of State-Dependent Preferences. Harvard University Press, Cambridge, MA.

Karni, E., 1996. Probabilities and beliefs. Journal of Risk and Uncertainty 13, 249–262.

Karni, E., 2007. A foundations of Bayesian theory. Journal of Economic Theory 132, 167–188.

Karni, E., 2011. Bayesian decision making and the representation of beliefs. Economic Theory 48, 125–146.

Karni, E., 2011a. Subjective probabilities on a state space. American Economic Journal – Microeconomics 3, 172–185.

Karni, E., Mongin, P., 2000. On the determination of subjective probability by choice. Management Science 46, 233–248.

Karni, E., Schmeidler, D., 1981. An expected utility theory for state-dependent preferences. Working paper 48–80, Foerder Institute for Economic Research, Tel Aviv University.

Karni, E., Schmeidler, D., 1993. On the uniqueness of subjective probabilities. Economic Theory 3, 267–277.

Karni, E., Schmeidler, D., Vind, K., 1983. On state-dependent preferences and subjective probabilities. Econometrica 51, 1021–1031.

Kreps, D.M., 1988. Notes on the Theory of Choice. Westview Press, Boulder.

Nau, R.F., 1995. Coherent decision analysis with inseparable probabilities and utilities. Journal of Risk and Uncertainty 10, 71–91.

Nau, R.F., 2006. The shape of incomplete preferences. Annals of Statistics 34, 2430–2448.

Ok, E.A., Ortoleva, P., Riella, G., 2012. Incomplete preferences under uncertainty: indecisiveness in beliefs vs. tastes. Econometrica 80, 1791–1808.

Pascal, B., 2010. Pensées De Pascal Sur La Religion: Et Sur Quelques Autres Sujets (1867). Kessinger Publishing, LLC original work published 1670.

Ramsey, F.P., 1931. Truth and Probability. In: Braithwaite, R.B., Plumpton, F. (Eds.), The Foundations of Mathematics and Other Logical Essays. K. Paul, Trench, Truber and Co., London.

Savage, L.J., 1954. The Foundations of Statistics. John Wiley and Sons, New York.

Schervish, M.J., Seidenfeld, T., Kadane, J.B., 1990. State-dependent utilities. Journal of the American Statistical Association 85, 840–847.

Seidenfeld, T., Schervish, M.J., Kadane, J.B., 1995. A representation of partially ordered preferences. Annals of Statistics 23, 2168–2217.

Shapley, L.S., Baucells, M.J., 1998. Multiperson utility. Games and Economic Behavior 62, 329–347.

Skiadas, C., 1997. Subjective probability under additive aggregation of conditional preferences. Journal of Economic Theory 76, 242–271.

von Neumann, J., Morgenstern, O., 1947. Theory of Games and Economic Behavior. Princeton University Press, Princeton.

Wakker, P.P., 1987. Subjective probabilities for state-dependent continuous utility. Mathematical Social Sciences 14, 289–298.

Wakker, P.P., 1989. Additive Representations of Preferences. Kluwer Academic Publishers, Dordrecht.

CHAPTER 2

Rationality and Dynamic Consistency Under Risk and Uncertainty

Peter J. Hammond[a] and Horst Zank[b]

[a]Department of Economics, University of Warwick, UK
[b]Department of Economics, School of Social Sciences, University of Manchester, UK

Contents

Abstract

For choice with deterministic consequences, the standard rationality hypothesis is ordinality, i.e., maximization of a weak preference ordering. For choice under risk (resp. uncertainty), preferences are assumed to be represented by the objectively (resp. subjectively) expected value of a von Neumann-Morgenstern utility function. For choice under risk, this implies a key independence axiom; under uncertainty, it implies some version of Savage's sure-thing principle. This chapter investigates the extent to which ordinality, independence, and the sure thing principle can be derived from more fundamental axioms concerning behavior in decision trees. Following Cubitt (1996), these principles include dynamic consistency, separability, and reduction of sequential choice, which can be derived in turn from one consequentialist hypothesis applied to continuation subtrees as well as entire decision trees. Examples of behavior violating these principles are also reviewed, as are possible explanations of why such violations are often observed in experiments.

Keywords

Expected utility, Consequentialism, Independence axiom, Consistent planning, Rationality, Dynamic consistency, Subjective probability, Sure-Thing principle

JEL Classification Codes

D01, D03, D81, D91, C72

Handbook of the Economics of Risk and Uncertainty, Volume 1
ISSN 2211-7547, http://dx.doi.org/10.1016/B978-0-444-53685-3.00002-7

2.1 INTRODUCTION AND OUTLINE

2.1.1 Purpose of Chapter

The main subject of this chapter is single person decision theory, especially the normative principles of decision making under risk and uncertainty. We will pay particular attention to principles of "rationality" such as:

1. the existence of a preference ordering;
2. when discussing the choice of risky consequences, the representation of preferences by the expected value of a von Neumann–Morgenstern utility function;
3. when discussing the choice of uncertain consequences, the use of subjective or personal probabilities attached to unknown states of the world.

We will review rather thoroughly some arguments for (and against) the first two of these rationality principles for both behavior and consistent planning. As for the third principle, space permits us only to sketch some arguments very briefly.

The arguments we will consider involve "consequentialism" and some closely related axioms put forward by, in particular, Hammond (1977, 1983, 1988a,b, 1989, 1998a,b), McClennen (1986), Seidenfeld (1988), Machina (1989), Cubitt (1996), and Steele (2010). The main issue we will focus on is whether standard principles of rational choice in a static framework, like those enunciated above, can be derived as implications of some possibly more basic hypotheses intended to describe properties of behavior and plans in a dynamic framework that includes single-person games in extensive form, more commonly referred to as decision trees.[1]

An important implication of our analysis will be that it enables a comparison between:

1. the parsimonious *normative* or *prescriptive* approach to decision theory embodied in just one potent consequentialist principle, whose appeal is that it can be used to derive important familiar axioms such as ordinality, independence, and the sure-thing principle;
2. the *positive* or *descriptive* approach, where a factorized set of many principles is used in order that violations of the expected utility principle can be more fully analyzed and their psychological properties better understood.

Indeed, when assessing a descriptive decision theory, it is important to see which of its aspects fail empirically. We also note that, in experiments involving subjects such as rats, pigeons, primates, or very young children, it is hard to observe much beyond their actual behavior; for humans with sufficient ability to communicate verbally, however, we can ask their intentions, motivations, plans, etc. At least in principle, a theory of rational behavior can therefore be expanded in order to accommodate such additional information, especially any possible mismatch between planned and realized consequences. In particular, the theory should recognize that behavior could be irrational because it is the result of irrational planning, or because behavior departs from rational plans.

---

[1] We do not discuss Karni and Schmeidler's (1991) contrasting approach, which considers sequential decisions within an "atemporal" framework involving compound lotteries rather than decision trees. They motivate this with the example of ascending bid auctions, where decisions presumably succeed each other rather swiftly. See also Volij (1994).

2.1.2 The Expected Utility (or EU) Hypothesis

The famous St. Petersburg paradox relies on the *risk-neutrality* hypothesis requiring one lottery to be preferred to another if its expected (monetary) value is greater. The paradox originated in a 1713 letter by Nicolas Bernoulli to Pierre Raymond de Montmort. It considers a lottery with an infinite sequence of prizes equal to 2^n monetary units, for $n = 1, 2, \ldots$. The nth prize is assumed to occur with probability 2^{-n}, for $n = 1, 2, \ldots$. The lottery lacks an expected value because the sum $\sum_{n=1}^{\infty} 2^{-n} 2^n$ evidently diverges to $+\infty$.

The more general *expected utility* (or EU) hypothesis, however, is that one lottery is preferred to another iff the expected *utility* of its prizes is higher. This hypothesis appeared in Cramer's (1728) suggestion to Daniel Bernoulli (1738) for resolving the St. Petersburg paradox by using either $v(w) = \min\{w, 2^{24}\}$ or $v(w) = \sqrt{w}$ as a utility function of wealth w, for $w \geq 0$. For either of these two utility functions, a routine exercise shows that the expected utility $\sum_{n=1}^{\infty} 2^{-n} v(2^n)$ converges to a finite value.

For over 200 years thereafter the EU hypothesis was rarely used and poorly understood. The situation began to change only after the publication of von Neumann and Morgenstern's (1944, 1953) treatise. Even this, however, makes little use of the distinction between expected monetary payoffs and expected utility that was later clarified in the theory of risk aversion due to Arrow (1965) and Pratt (1964). In an appendix to their treatise, von Neumann and Morgenstern did make the first attempt to formulate a preference based axiom system that would justify expected utility, with expected payoff as a special case.[2]

Fishburn and Wakker (1995) carefully discuss the incompleteness of von Neumann and Morgenstern's attempt to axiomatize the EU hypothesis. This is because, as Dalkey (1949), Marschak (1950), Nash (1950), and Malinvaud (1952) soon pointed out, von Neumann and Morgenstern had left implicit a key "independence" axiom. Perhaps more to the point, the quick succession of papers by Marschak (1950), Arrow (1951a), Samuelson (1952), and Herstein and Milnor (1953) rapidly reduced von Neumann and Morgenstern's unnecessarily complicated axiom system. Finally, the process of refining these axioms reached a much more satisfactory culmination in Jensen (1967), who based expected utility on just the three principles of *ordering*, *independence*, and *continuity*—see also Fishburn (1970).[3]

Meanwhile, the EU framework rapidly became the dominant model for choice under risk in economics, finance, insurance, game theory, and beyond.

2.1.3 Paradoxes

The EU hypothesis implies some rather restrictive additive separability conditions. Indeed, nonadditive utility functions are rather obviously generic within the space of all possible utility functions. Thus, as Samuelson (1983, pp. 503–518) in particular

---

[2] See Leonard (1995) for some of the relevant history, including a possible explanation (footnote 21 on p. 753) of why this appendix was changed for the second edition.

[3] The chapter in this *Handbook* by Karni sets out these principles as axioms, but uses "weak order" to describe what we call the ordering principle, and "Archimedean" to describe one version of our continuity principle.

emphasized in his discussion, the expected utility "dogma" was seen as determining a special case, unlikely to be empirically justified.

Even while the axioms of EU theory were still being developed, its descriptive accuracy came under severe challenge. This was largely due to the results of one ingenious experiment that Allais (1953) designed. The experiment involved subjects who typically reported preferences in clear violation of the key independence property which had only recently been properly formulated. This property rightly came to be seen as typically inconsistent with observed behavior, especially in a laboratory setting. Even more damaging for the EU hypothesis, Allais's results for the case of risky consequences were then supplemented by Ellsberg (1961) for the case when risk was combined with uncertainty.[4]

These and later examples due to Allais (1979), Kahneman and Tversky (1979) and others were all used to question not only the descriptive accuracy but also the prescriptive relevance of the EU model. Indeed, these "paradoxes" ignited a fruitful debate over what rationality means, especially in the face of risk and uncertainty. This chapter is intended in part to contribute to that debate.

2.1.4 Non-Expected Utility

Dropping the contentious independence axiom allowed the development of *"non-expected" utility* theories of behavior under both risk and uncertainty, such as those surveyed by Starmer (2000), as well as later chapters in this *Handbook*. In experimental studies to date, the predictions of this theory do indeed accord much better with the available data, if only because non-expected utility typically allows many more free parameters than expected utility does.

The motivation for "non-expected" utility theory, however, is precisely to provide a more accurate descriptive model. Many authors may have claimed that, because non-expected utility is descriptively more accurate, that makes it somehow prescriptively more appealing. This argument, however, strikes as philosophically suspect, not least because it crosses the fact/value divide that some philosophers refer to as Hume's Law.

Furthermore, independence is only one of Jensen's three axioms for EU. The two other ordering and continuity axioms have remained largely unquestioned, even though they actually remain as key postulates for non-expected as well as expected utility theory. In this chapter we propose to focus on normative or prescriptive decision theory, treating both ordering and independence as axioms that should be justified. If we neglect continuity, it is only because it is really a technical topological axiom of a kind which makes it hard to observe when the axiom is violated.

---

[4] Ellsberg regarded his example as contradicting Savage's sure-thing postulate. Yet it might be more accurate to regard it as contradicting Anscombe and Aumann's (1963) extension of that postulate, which was not even published until two years after Ellsberg (1961).

2.1.5 Chapter Outline

Following this introduction, the first part of the chapter provides some essential background regarding the theory of rational choice in static settings. The two Sections 2.2 and 2.3 are intended to remind the reader of the standard "static" approach to rational planning that is encountered in most microeconomics textbooks. In this approach, following von Neumann's (1928) definition of a game in normal form, the decision maker is typically assumed to choose a planned course of action once and for all. Section 2.2 focuses on the case when actions have deterministic consequences; Section 2.3 allows actions to have risky consequences described by lotteries over the consequence domain. For each of these two cases we also briefly review some of the experimental tests of the usual ordinality and independence conditions that standard economic theory imposes as postulates in these settings.

The heart of the chapter consists of Sections 2.4 and 2.5, which together introduce the dynamic considerations that arise whenever the decision maker is confronted by a nontrivial decision tree. These two sections survey the main attempts to provide axiom systems specific to decision trees that can be used to justify the usual rationality postulates in static settings, which were considered in Sections 2.2 and 2.3. As with those sections, we divide the discussion between decision trees with consequences that are:

1. purely deterministic, which are used in Section 2.4 to offer a possible justification for the ordinality principle (of making choices that maximize a complete and transitive preference ordering);
2. risky, which are used in Section 2.5 to offer a possible justification for a version of the contentious independence axiom that distinguishes expected from non-expected utility theory;[5]
3. uncertain, which are used in Section 2.6 to offer a possible justification for Savage's sure-thing principle that plays a large role in the theory of subjective probability.

Apart from one particular "consequentialist invariance" postulate developing earlier work by the first author, we will focus on Cubitt's (1996) "factorization" of this postulate into the following set of five axioms, which together are logically equivalent to consequentialist invariance:

1. dynamic consistency, discussed in Sections 2.4.3.2, 2.5.1.4 and 2.6.4.4;
2. separability, discussed in Sections 2.4.3.3, 2.5.1.5 and 2.6.4.5;
3. reduction of compound lotteries, discussed in Section 2.5.1.3, and the closely related reduction of compound events, discussed in Section 2.6.4.3;
4. invariance to the timing of risk or uncertainty, discussed in Sections 2.5.1.6 and 2.6.4.6;
5. reduction of sequential choice, discussed in Section 2.4.3.4.

---

[5] Because we refrain from discussing any continuity issues, we cannot even attempt to offer a compelling justification for the existence of a utility function.

Actually, following Cubitt's (1996) own suggestion, we even factorize the axioms further by introducing two distinct versions of dynamic consistency, as well as two distinct versions of separability, which respectively apply at decision and chance nodes of the relevant decision tree. We confirm that a relevant subset of our version of these axioms, when applied in a very restricted domain of decision trees that contain no more than two decision nodes, implies ordinal choice; furthermore, in the case of trees with risky or uncertain consequences, the same axioms imply the contentious vNM independence axiom or the sure-thing principle, even when decision trees with at most one decision node and at most two chance or event nodes are considered.

To establish logical equivalence with consequentialist invariance, in Section 2.4.5 we formulate this condition in a way that applies to general decision trees. This sets the stage for one elementary result establishing that consequentialist invariance implies our versions of all Cubitt's axioms that are relevant in the different cases. Closing the logical circle, however, requires demonstrating that Cubitt's axioms imply consequentialist invariance, which is rather more challenging. One obstacle is that Cubitt's axioms apply to plans, whereas consequentialist invariance applies to the realized consequences of behavior. Nevertheless, given any preference ordering on a consequence domain, in Section 2.4.6 on "ordinal dynamic programming" we are able to construct a behavior rule that:

1. at every decision node of every finite tree with consequences in that domain, prescribes a nonempty set of moves to an immediately succeeding node;
2. determines a consequence choice function satisfying consequentialist invariance, with the property that the chosen consequences maximize the given preference ordering.

Then in Section 2.5, where we allow decision trees with chance nodes and risky consequences, we are able to establish that, given any preference ordering on a lottery consequence domain that satisfies vNM independence, the same two properties hold. A similar result is shown in Section 2.6, where we allow decision trees with event nodes and uncertain consequences.

Logic alone dictates that, among the several normatively appealing dynamic choice principles enunciated in Cubitt (1996), those that imply the ordinality and independence properties must share the same descriptive shortcomings as the EU hypothesis. It took until the late 1990s, however, before the first experiments were carried out that tested these dynamic choice principles systematically. A major justification of Cubitt's choice of axioms is that, when subjects in experiments are observed to violate either ordinality, or independence, or perhaps even both, seeing which of his larger axiom set is violated can help shed light on possible psychological or other explanations of the "anomalous" behavior. With this in mind, the latter parts of Sections 2.4 and 2.5 briefly review some of the experiments which have set out to test the axioms that underlie this dynamic approach to rationality, rather than the static theory discussed in Sections 2.2 and 2.3.

2.2 STATIC RATIONALITY WITH DETERMINISTIC CONSEQUENCES

2.2.1 Preferences in Consumer Theory

In standard economics, especially consumer demand theory in microeconomics, the "ordinalist revolution" of the 1930s (see Cooter and Rappoport, 1984) saw rationality being defined as choosing, within a feasible set determined by conditions such as a budget constraint and nonnegativity conditions, a consumption bundle $\mathbf{x} = (x_g)_{g \in G}$ in a finite-dimensional Euclidean commodity space $\mathbb{R}^G$ which maximizes a (complete and transitive) preference ordering $\succsim$ on $\mathbb{R}^G$. Typically it is assumed that $\succsim$ also satisfies the monotonicity property requiring more of any good to be preferred to less, at least weakly. Moreover, it is often also assumed that the upper contour set $\{\mathbf{x} \in \mathbb{R}^G \mid \mathbf{x} \succsim \bar{\mathbf{x}}\}$ is convex, for each fixed $\bar{\mathbf{x}} \in \mathbb{R}^G$.

A little more restrictively, behavior should maximize a utility function $\mathbf{x} \rightarrow U(\mathbf{x})$ mapping $\mathbb{R}^G$ into $\mathbb{R}$ that is strictly increasing, or at least nondecreasing, in the consumption quantity x_g of each good $g \in G$. In that case behavior will be unchanged whenever the utility function to be maximized is replaced by any other that is "ordinally equivalent" in the sense of representing the same preference ordering—i.e, by any new utility function $\mathbf{x} \mapsto \tilde{U}(\mathbf{x}) = \phi(U(\mathbf{x}))$ that results from applying a strictly increasing transformation $U \mapsto \phi(U)$ to the old utility function U.

2.2.2 Consequence Choice Functions

Later developments in decision theory extended this preference-based approach from consumer theory, where the objects of preference are consumption bundles, to completely general choice settings, where the objects of preference are abstract consequences belonging to an arbitrary domain. As Arrow (1951b, p. 404) writes:[6]

> The point of view will be that of a theory of choice, as it is usually conceived of. The general picture of such a theory is the following: There is a set of conceivable actions which an individual could take, each of which leads to certain consequences. … Among the actions actually available, then, that action is chosen whose consequences are preferred to those of any other available action.

This is a rather clear statement of the doctrine for which Anscombe (1958) introduced the neologism "consequentialism" in her forceful critique. The idea, of course, is much older.

From now on, we consider an arbitrary domain Y of consequence choices that are relevant to the decision maker. For each non-empty finite *feasible set* $F \subseteq Y$, let $C(F) \subseteq F$ denote the corresponding *choice set* of consequences deemed suitable, even "rational," choices from the set F.

---

[6] We remark that Arrow went on to invoke the existence of a preference ordering over consequences. One advantage of using consequentialist invariance as a basic rationality principle is that it allows ordinality to be derived as a logical implication rather than assumed as a questionable postulate.

Definition 2.1   A *choice function* on Y is a mapping $F \mapsto C(F)$ which is defined on the domain $\mathcal{F}(Y)$ of all nonempty finite subsets of Y, and satisfies $C(F) \subseteq F$ for all finite $F \in \mathcal{F}(Y)$. We focus on the important special case when the choice function $F \mapsto C(F)$ is *decisive* in the sense that $C(F) \neq \emptyset$ whenever F is non-empty and finite.

2.2.3 Base Preference Relations

Given the choice function $F \mapsto C(F)$, we can define the associated *base relation* $\succsim^C$ as the unique binary *weak preference* relation on Y satisfying

$$a \succsim^C b \iff a \in C(\{a, b\}) \tag{2.1}$$

for all $a, b \in Y$. Thus, $a \succsim^C b$ just in case the decision maker, when required to choose between a and b with no other consequences possible, is willing to choose a.

Note that, assuming the choice function $F \mapsto C(F)$ is indeed decisive, especially when F is a pair set $\{a, b\}$, it follows that the base relation $\succsim^C$ is *complete* in the sense that, for all $a, b \in Y$, either $a \succsim^C b$, or $b \succsim^C a$, or both. Indeed, given any pair $a, b \in Y$, decisiveness allows one to distinguish between three separate cases:

1. $C(\{a, b\}) = \{a\}$, in which case we say that a is *strictly preferred* to b and write $a \succ^C b$;
2. $C(\{a, b\}) = \{b\}$, in which case we say that a is *strictly dispreferred* to b and write $a \prec^C b$;
3. $C(\{a, b\}) = \{a, b\}$, in which case we say that a and b are *indifferent* and write $a \sim^C b$.

2.2.4 Arrow's Conditions for Ordinality

Definition 2.2   The choice function $F \mapsto C(F)$ is said to be *ordinal* when

$$C(F) = \{a \in F \mid b \in F \implies a \succsim^C b\}. \tag{2.2}$$

That is, the set $C(F)$ consists of all consequences $a \in F$ that are "optimal" in the sense of being weakly preferred to any alternative $b \in F$ according to the base relation $\succsim^C$ which is derived from choice among pairs. In order to simplify (2.2), we make the innocuous postulate that the relation $\succsim^C$ is *reflexive* in the sense that $a \succsim^C a$ for all $a \in Y$.[7]

The base relation $\succsim^C$ is *transitive* just in case, for all $a, b, c \in Y$, it is true that $a \succsim^C b$ and $b \succsim^C c$ jointly imply that $a \succsim^C c$.

Arrow (1959) characterized ordinal choice functions as those that satisfy the condition

$$[G \subset F \subseteq Y \text{ and } C(F) \cap G \neq \emptyset] \implies C(F) \cap G = C(G) \tag{2.3}$$

---

[7] If the base relation $\succsim^C$ were not reflexive, we could change equation (2.2) to $C(F) = \{a \in F \mid b \in F \setminus \{a\} \implies a \succsim^C b\}$. But as noted by Mas-Colell et al. (1995, p. 6 footnote 2), amongst others, it really loses no generality to assume that $\succsim^C$ is reflexive, in which case this change to equation (2.2) is irrelevant.

that he called (C5). It is useful to break this single condition into two parts:

Contraction Consistency

$$[G \subset F \subseteq Y \text{ and } C(F) \cap G \neq \emptyset] \Longrightarrow C(F) \cap G \subseteq C(G) \qquad (2.4)$$

Expansion Consistency

$$[G \subset F \subseteq Y \text{ and } C(F) \cap G \neq \emptyset] \Longrightarrow C(G) \subseteq C(F) \cap G \qquad (2.5)$$

as discussed by Bordes (1976) and Sen (1977), who call these two conditions α and β^- respectively.[8]

By considering the case when the subset $G \subseteq F$ is the pair $\{a, b\}$, we obtain the following "pairwise" variations of the contraction and expansion consistency conditions (2.4) and (2.5), respectively. First, the choice function $F \mapsto C(F)$ satisfies the principle of *pairwise contraction consistency* if, for any finite non-empty feasible set $F \subset Y$ one has

$$[a \in C(F) \text{ and } b \in F] \Longrightarrow a \succsim^C b. \qquad (2.6)$$

Second, the choice function $F \mapsto C(F)$ satisfies the principle of *pairwise expansion consistency* if, for any finite non-empty feasible set $F \subset Y$, one has

$$\left[b \in C(F) \text{ and } a \in F \text{ with } a \succsim^C b \right] \Longrightarrow a \in C(F). \qquad (2.7)$$

Theorem 2.1   *Provided the choice function $F \mapsto C(F)$ is decisive, the following three conditions are equivalent:*

(a) *C satisfies both contraction consistency and expansion consistency;*
(b) *C satisfies both pairwise contraction consistency and pairwise expansion consistency;*
(c) *C is ordinal, and the base relation $\succsim^C$ is transitive.*

Proof   (c) $\Longrightarrow$ (a): Routine arguments show that, if C is ordinal (i.e., satisfies (2.2)) and if also the base relation $\succsim^C$ is transitive, then C must satisfy both conditions (2.4) and (2.5). (a) $\Longrightarrow$ (b): This is an obvious implication of definitions (2.4) and (2.5) when one puts $G = \{a, b\}$.
(b) $\Longrightarrow$ (c): Suppose first that $a \in F$ and that $a \succsim^C b$ for all $b \in F$. Because C is decisive, there exists $a^* \in C(F)$. Then $a \succsim^C a^*$ and so the definition (2.7) of pairwise expansion consistency implies that $a \in C(F)$. On the other hand, if $a \in C(F)$ and $b \in F$, then the definition (2.6) of pairwise contraction consistency immediately implies that $a \succsim^C b$. It follows that (2.2) is satisfied, so C is ordinal.

Next, suppose that $a, b, c \in Y$ satisfy $a \succsim^C b$ and $b \succsim^C c$. Define F as the triple $\{a, b, c\}$. By the hypothesis that C is decisive, there are three logically possible cases, not necessarily disjoint:

---

[8] The contraction consistency condition was first propounded by Chernoff (1954); sometimes it is referred to as "Chernoff's choice axiom."

1. $a \in C(F)$: Here pairwise contraction consistency implies directly that, because $c \in F$, so $a \succsim^C c$.
2. $b \in C(F)$: Here, because $a \succsim^C b$, pairwise expansion consistency implies that $a \in C(F)$. But then case 1 applies and so $a \succsim^C c$.
3. $c \in C(F)$: Here, because $b \succsim^C c$, pairwise expansion consistency implies that $b \in C(F)$. But then case 2 applies and so $a \succsim^C c$.

Hence $a \succsim^C c$ in every case, and so the relation $\succsim^C$ is transitive.   □

2.2.5 Experimental Tests of Ordinality

2.2.5.1 Background

Many early experimental studies of economic behavior focused on the ordinality property and questioned the existence of coherent or stable preferences as such. This subsection summarizes a few puzzling empirical phenomena that emerged. We recall some of this older literature first and give references to further survey papers. Where time is involved, it is typically through consideration of timed consequences, which will be considered in Section 2.4.7.1. Where time plays a more crucial role by allowing the decision maker to face successive choices in a nontrivial decision tree, we defer our discussion till Section 2.5.5.

2.2.5.2 Two-Dimensional Choice Problems

The problem of choosing a single real number, when more is better than less, is not very interesting. So we consider choice among options whose consequences differ in more than one characteristic or attribute. For example, many experiments involve risky consequences in the form of a binary lottery where one prize is 0. That still leaves two dimensions: (i) a positive monetary prize; (ii) the probability of winning that prize. In marketing, the products, such as cars, drinks, or other goods, typically differ in both quality and affordability, with the latter often measured as the inverse of price.

Accordingly, we start by considering choice problems where the consequences are represented by points in the two-dimensional space $\mathbb{R}^2$. We will be interested in the *dominance relation* $>_D$ defined on $\mathbb{R}^2$ by

$$(a_1, a_2) >_D (b_1, b_2) \iff a_1 > b_1 \text{ and } a_2 > b_2. \tag{2.8}$$

We typically assume that choice involves *undominated* options—i.e., for every nonempty finite set $F \subseteq Y$, one has $y^* \in C(F)$ only if $y \in F$ and there is no *dominant* alternative $y \in F$ such that $y >_D y^*$. We do *not* assume, however, that $C(F)$ includes every undominated option in F.

2.2.5.3 The Attraction Effect

In Section 2.2.4 it was shown that the ordinality principle of rational choice holds if and only if choice behavior satisfies both contraction and expansion consistency. These two properties were challenged by Huber et al. (1982) in an early example of choice inconsistency. Their example involves an original feasible set $G = \{c, t\}$, where c is called the competitor and t is called the target. It is presumed that neither of these two dominates the other.

Consider now expanding the set G by appending a third "decoy" alternative d that is strictly dominated by alternative t. The feasible set expands to become $F=\{c, t, d\}$.

In the experiments that Huber et al. (1982) reported in this setting, a majority of subjects' choices were observed to satisfy $C(G)=\{c\}$ and $C(F)=\{t\}$. Clearly $G \subset F$ and $C(F) \cap G = \{t\} \neq \emptyset$, yet

1. $\{c\} = C(G) \not\subseteq C(F) \cap G = \{t\}$, so expansion consistency is violated;
2. $\{t\} = C(F) \cap G \not\subseteq C(G) = \{c\}$, so contraction consistency is also violated.

Huber et al. (1982) propose an "attraction effect" as a potential explanation for such behavior. Because t dominates d, it appears superior not only to d, but more generally; in particular, t also seems superior to c, which neither dominates nor is dominated by either t or d. In contrast, when d is unavailable in the original choice between c or t, this reason to perceive t as superior disappears, allowing c to be chosen.

2.2.5.4 The Compromise Effect

A related "compromise effect" was discussed by Simonson (1989). As before, the example starts with the feasible set $G=\{c, t\}$, where neither c nor t dominates the other. But now the third option f that is appended to G is assumed to be dominated by both c and t in an attribute for which c dominates t. Assuming this is attribute 1 in our two-dimensional model, this means that $c_1 > t_1 > f_1$. To make the example interesting, we assume that $c_2 < t_2 < f_2$. This ordering of the attributes of the different options can make t appear as a good compromise between c and f when t is feasible. This can explain why $C(\{c, t, f\}) = \{t\}$ may be observed even though originally one had $C(G) = \{c\}$.

2.2.5.5 Attempted Explanations

Such compromise or attraction effects preclude ordinal choice. One strand of subsequent literature seeks to explain such incoherent choice behavior and other related phenomena by means of more sophisticated psychological models (see, e.g., Tsetsos et al., 2010). Another strand of the literature appeals to heuristics such as Tversky's (1972) lexicographic procedure (see also Gigerenzer et al., 1999) or other boundedly rational choice procedures (see Manzini and Mariotti, 2007, and the references therein).

2.3 STATIC RATIONALITY WITH RISKY CONSEQUENCES

2.3.1 The Mixture Space of Risky Roulette Lotteries

The EU hypothesis offers a normative principle for decision problems where the consequences y in an arbitrary domain Y are risky. Formally, this means that the objects of choice are as in the following:

Definition 2.3 A *consequence lottery* λ attaches to each consequence $y \in Y$ a specified "objective" probability $\lambda(y) \geq 0$, where:

1. $\lambda(\gamma) > 0$ if $\gamma \in$ supp λ for some finite *support* set supp $\lambda \subseteq Y$;
2. $\sum_{\gamma \in Y} \lambda(\gamma) = \sum_{\gamma \in \mathrm{supp}\lambda} \lambda(\gamma) = 1$.

Let $\mathcal{L}$ or $\Delta(Y)$ denote the set of all such "roulette" lotteries.[9] Given any two lotteries $\lambda, \mu \in \Delta(Y)$, for each number $\alpha \in [0, 1] \subset \mathbb{R}$ there exists a *mixture* $\alpha\lambda + (1 - \alpha)$ of the two lotteries defined by

$$[\alpha\lambda + (1-\alpha)\mu](\gamma) := \alpha\lambda(\gamma) + (1-\alpha)\mu(\gamma) \quad \text{for all } \gamma \in Y \tag{2.9}$$

which evidently also belongs to $\Delta(Y)$. This property of *closure under mixing* makes the set $\Delta(Y)$ of consequence lotteries a *mixture space* (see Herstein and Milnor, 1953).

For each $\gamma \in Y$, let δ_γ denote the unique *degenerate lottery* that satisfies $\delta_\gamma(\gamma) = 1$. Note that any $\lambda \in \Delta(Y)$ can be expressed in the form $\lambda = \sum_{\gamma \in Y} \lambda(\gamma)\,\delta_\gamma$. It follows that $\Delta(Y)$ is trivially isomorphic to the convex hull of the collection of degenerate lotteries $\delta_\gamma (\gamma \in Y)$, regarded as unit vectors in the real linear space spanned by these points. Indeed, each degenerate lottery δ_γ is an extreme point of the convex set $\Delta(Y)$.

We remark finally that, because of part (1) in Definition 2.3, the *expectation* $\mathbb{E}_\lambda f$ of any function $Y \ni \gamma \mapsto f(\gamma) \in \mathbb{R}$ w.r.t. any lottery $\lambda \in \Delta(Y)$ is well defined as the sum

$$\mathbb{E}_\lambda f := \sum_{\gamma \in Y} \lambda(\gamma)f(\gamma) = \sum_{\gamma \in \mathrm{supp}\lambda} \lambda(\gamma)f(\gamma) \tag{2.10}$$

of finitely many nonzero terms.

Moreover, let $\mathcal{L}^*(Y)$ denote the entire linear space spanned by the set $\{\delta_\gamma \mid \gamma \in Y\}$ of all degenerate lotteries on Y. Then for any fixed $f : Y \to \mathbb{R}$, the mapping $\mathcal{L}^*(Y) \ni \lambda \mapsto \mathbb{E}_\lambda f$ is still well defined by (2.10), and is obviously linear in λ. Its restriction to the domain $\Delta(Y)$ of lotteries then satisfies the *mixture preservation* property that

$$\mathbb{E}_{\alpha\lambda+(1-\alpha)\mu} f = \alpha\mathbb{E}_\lambda f + (1-\alpha)\mathbb{E}_\mu f \tag{2.11}$$

whenever $\lambda, \mu \in \Delta(Y)$ and $\alpha \in [0, 1] \subset \mathbb{R}$.

2.3.2 The Expected Utility Hypothesis

In recent decades it has become commonplace for economists to extend the expected utility (or EU) hypothesis for wealth, as discussed in Section 2.1.2, to an arbitrary consequence domain Y, and to the set $\Delta(Y)$ of consequence roulette lotteries on Y.

Definition 2.4 A *utility* function $V : \mathcal{L} \to \mathbb{R}$ is said to *represent* the preference relation $\succsim$ on $\mathcal{L} = \Delta(Y)$ just in case, for any pair of lotteries $\lambda, \mu \in \mathcal{L}$, one has

---

[9] Following Anscombe and Aumann (1963), we use the term "roulette" lottery when each outcome occurs with a probability which is presumed to be objectively specified. This is in contrast to a "horse" lottery whose outcomes depend on an unknown state of the nature. This corresponds to one possible interpretation of Knight's (1921) famous distinction between risk, with objective probabilities, and uncertainty where, if probabilities exist at all, they are subjective—or perhaps better, following Savage (1954), "personal."

$$\lambda \succsim \mu \iff V(\lambda) \geq V(\mu). \tag{2.12}$$

The *EU hypothesis* postulates the existence of a (complete and transitive) preference ordering $\succsim$ on $\Delta(Y)$ that is represented by the *expected value*

$$V(\lambda) := \mathbb{E}_\lambda v := \sum_{y \in Y} \lambda(y)\, v(y) \tag{2.13}$$

of a *von Neumann–Morgenstern utility function* (or NMUF) $v : Y \to \mathbb{R}$.

Combining (2.12) and (2.13), it is evident that the EU hypothesis entails

$$\lambda \succsim \mu \iff \mathbb{E}_\lambda v \geq \mathbb{E}_\mu v \iff V(\lambda) - V(\mu) = \sum_{y \in Y} [\lambda(y) - \mu(y)]\, v(y) \geq 0.$$
$$\tag{2.14}$$

2.3.3 Implications of the Expected Utility Hypothesis

2.3.3.1 Utility Transformations

A *strictly increasing affine transformation* of utility is a mapping $v \mapsto \alpha + \rho v$, where α and ρ are real constants, with $\rho > 0$. If any such transformation is applied to the original NMUF $y \mapsto v(y)$, thereby producing another new NMUF $y \mapsto \tilde{v}(y) \equiv \alpha + \rho v(y)$ that is "cardinally equivalent," then expected utility maximizing behavior will be the same regardless of whether one uses the old or the new NMUF.

2.3.3.2 Von Neumann–Morgenstern Independence

The following independence condition is the one that von Neumann and Morgenstern neglected to state. Nevertheless, it is often given their name because it is a key ingredient for their axiomatic justification of the EU hypothesis.

Definition 2.5 The preference ordering $\succsim$ on $\Delta(Y)$ satisfies the (vNM) *independence* principle provided that, for all lottery triples $\lambda, \mu, v \in \Delta(Y)$ and all scalars $\alpha \in (0,1] \subset \mathbb{R}$, we have

$$\lambda \succsim \mu \iff \alpha\lambda + (1-\alpha)v \succsim \alpha\mu + (1-\alpha)v \tag{2.15}$$

In particular, independence requires the preference between the two lotteries $\alpha\lambda + (1-\alpha)v$ and $\alpha\mu + (1-\alpha)v$ to be independent of the risky component v that is common to the two lotteries.

Theorem 2.2 *If the EU hypothesis holds, then the preference ordering $\succsim$ on $\Delta(Y)$ satisfies (2.15) for all $\lambda, \mu, v \in \Delta(Y)$ and all $\alpha \in (0,1]$.*

Proof Modifying (2.14) appropriately, we see that

$$V(\alpha\lambda + (1-\alpha)v) - V(\alpha\mu + (1-\alpha)v)$$
$$= \alpha \sum_{y \in Y} [\lambda(y) - \mu(y)]\, v(y) = \alpha[V(\lambda) - V(\mu)]$$

So, because $\alpha > 0$, the equivalence (2.15) follows from (2.12) and (2.13).   □

2.3.3.3 Archimedean Continuity

Definition 2.6   The preference ordering $\succsim$ on $\Delta(Y)$ satisfies the *Archimedean continuity* principle[10] provided that, for all lottery triples $\lambda, \mu, \nu \in \Delta(Y)$ where $\lambda \succ \nu \succ \mu$, there exist scalars $\alpha', \alpha'' \in (0, 1)$ such that

$$\alpha'\lambda + (1 - \alpha')\mu \succ \nu \succ \alpha''\lambda + (1 - \alpha'')\mu. \tag{2.16}$$

Theorem 2.3   *If the EU hypothesis holds, then the preference ordering $\succsim$ on $\Delta(Y)$ satisfies (2.16) for all $\lambda, \mu, \nu \in \Delta(Y)$.*

Proof   Consider any lottery triple $\lambda, \mu, \nu \in \Delta(Y)$ where $\lambda \succ \nu \succ \mu$, and so $V(\lambda) > V(\nu) > V(\mu)$. Because the mapping $\lambda \mapsto V(\lambda)$ defined by (2.13) is continuous in the probabilities $\lambda(y)$ of the different consequences $y \in Y$, there must exist scalars $\alpha', \alpha'' \in (0, 1)$, with α' close to 1 and α'' close to 0, such that

$$\alpha' V(\lambda) + (1 - \alpha')V(\mu) > V(\nu) > \alpha'' V(\lambda) + (1 - \alpha'')V(\mu). \tag{2.17}$$

Because V satisfies mixture preservation, this implies that

$$V(\alpha'\lambda + (1 - \alpha')\mu) > V(\nu) > V(\alpha''\lambda + (1 - \alpha'')\mu)$$

and so (2.16) must hold.   □

2.3.4 Jensen's Three Axioms

Jensen's (1967) three axioms can be stated as follows:
Ordering: The binary relation $\succsim$ on $\Delta(Y)$ is an *ordering*—i.e., it satisfies the following three properties:
1. for all $\lambda \in \Delta(Y)$, one has $\lambda \succsim \lambda$ (so $\succsim$ is *reflexive*);
2. for all $\lambda, \mu \in \Delta(Y)$, one has $\lambda \succsim \mu$, or $\mu \succsim \lambda$, or both (so $\succsim$ is *complete*);
3. for all $\lambda, \mu, \nu \in \Delta(Y)$, if $\lambda \succsim \mu$ and $\mu \succsim \nu$, then $\lambda \succsim \nu$ (so $\succsim$ is *transitive*).
Independence: For all $\lambda, \mu, \nu \in \Delta(Y)$ and $\alpha \in (0, 1)$, one has

$$\alpha\lambda + (1 - \alpha)\nu \succsim \alpha\mu + (1 - \alpha)\nu \iff \lambda \succsim \mu.$$

Continuity: For all $\lambda, \mu, \nu \in \Delta(Y)$ with $\lambda \succ \mu$ and $\mu \succ \nu$, the two sets

$$\{\alpha \in [0, 1] \mid \alpha\lambda + (1 - \alpha)\nu \succsim \mu\} \text{ and } \{\alpha \in [0, 1] \mid \alpha\lambda + (1 - \alpha)\nu \precsim \mu\}$$

of mixtures of λ and ν which are weakly preferred (resp. dispreferred) to μ are both closed.

The following important characterization theorem states that Jensen's three axioms are not only necessary, but also sufficient, for EU to hold for preferences on the mixture space $\Delta(Y)$.

---

[10]The principle is also often referred to as *Jensen continuity* (cf. Jensen, 1967).

Theorem 2.4   *Assume that $\succsim$ is an arbitrary binary preference relation on the set $\mathcal{L} := \Delta(Y)$ of simple roulette lotteries over consequences in the domain Y. The following two statements are equivalent:*

(i) The preference relation $\succsim$ on $\Delta(Y)$ is represented by the expected value of each von Neumann–Morgenstern utility function $Y \ni \gamma \mapsto v(\gamma)$ in a cardinal equivalence class. Moreover, this equivalence class is unique except in the trivial case where $\succsim$ induces at most two indifference classes among the set δ_γ ($\gamma \in Y$) of degenerate lotteries.

(ii) The preference relation $\succsim$ on $\Delta(Y)$ satisfies Jensen's three axioms of ordering, independence and continuity.

Proof   See elsewhere in this *Handbook*, or else consult Hammond (1998a).   □

2.3.5 Experimental Tests

2.3.5.1 *Preference Reversal under Risk*

Consider the often discussed case when the consequence domain Y consists of real numbers γ representing monetary amounts, and more money is preferred to less. In this case, assuming there is a continuous preference ordering $\succsim$ over $\Delta(Y)$ the *certainty equivalent* of any lottery $\lambda \in \Delta(Y)$ is defined as the unique $\gamma(\lambda) \in \mathbb{R}$ such that λ is indifferent to the degenerate lottery $\delta_{\gamma(\lambda)}$. Note that uniqueness is assured because with more money always being preferred to less, one always has $\delta_{\gamma'} \succ \delta_{\gamma''} \iff \gamma' > \gamma''$.

Starting with Lichtenstein and Slovic (1971), several experimenters have asked subjects to report their certainty equivalents for different lotteries, and have then noticed a "preference reversal phenomenon" (see also Grether and Plott, 1979; Tversky et al., 1990; List, 2002; Butler and Loomes, 2007; for a review see Seidl, 2002). This phenomenon occurs when there are two lotteries $\lambda, \mu \in \Delta(Y)$ such that the subject claims that $\lambda \succ \mu$, and yet the same subject's reported certainty equivalents satisfy $\gamma(\lambda) < \gamma(\mu)$. For example, the lottery λ might offer a high probability of winning a moderate monetary prize, which is often preferred to a lottery μ that offers a moderate probability of winning a high monetary prize. Yet often the elicited certainty equivalent of λ is lower than that of μ. The opposite reversal is also observed, but less often.

If all these claims made by a typical subject were valid, one would of course have the preference cycle

$$\lambda \succ \mu \sim \delta_{\gamma(\mu)} \succ \delta_{\gamma(\lambda)} \sim \lambda$$

which contradicts ordinality. Such reversals may indicate that preferences are context dependent in a way that makes the elicited certainty equivalents induce a ranking which differs from preferences (Tversky et al., 1988). This is still an area of active research (Loomes et al., 2010; Plott and Zeiler, 2005; Isoni et al., 2011).

2.3.5.2 *The Allais Paradox*

Preference reversal calls into question the existence of a single preference ordering that explains statements regarding both preference and certainty equivalents. We now move

on to a test of the independence condition, based on the following challenge for decision theorists originally issued by Allais (1953, p. 527):[11]

1. Do you prefer situation A to situation B?

 SITUATION A: The certainty of receiving 100 million.

$$\textbf{SITUATION B} \begin{cases} 10 \text{ chances out of 100 of winning 500 million.} \\ 89 \text{ chances out of 100 of winning 100 million.} \\ 1 \text{ chance out of 100 of winning nothing.} \end{cases}$$

2. Do you prefer situation C to situation D?

$$\textbf{SITUATION C} \begin{cases} 11 \text{ chances out of 100 of winning 100 million.} \\ 89 \text{ chances out of 100 of winning nothing.} \end{cases}$$

$$\textbf{SITUATION D} \begin{cases} 10 \text{ chances out of 100 of winning 500 million.} \\ 90 \text{ chances out of 100 of winning nothing.} \end{cases}$$

He reports the results of an informal survey as follows:

*Now, and precisely for the majority of very prudent people, …whom common opinion considers
very rational, the observed responses are A > B, C < D.*

Thus did Allais's subjects (and many others since) express their unwillingness to move
from A to B by giving up a 0.11 chance of winning 100 million in exchange for the same
chance of a winning a lottery ticket offering a conditional probability $\frac{10}{11}$ of winning 500
million, but a conditional probability $\frac{1}{11}$ of not winning anything. In preferring D to C,
however, they are willing to have the probability of winning any prize fall from 0.11 to
0.10 provided that the size of that prize rises from 100 million to 500 million.

The preference domain here is $\Delta(Y)$, which consists of lotteries over the consequence domain

$$Y = \{a, b, c\} = \{5, 1, 0\} \cdot 10^8$$

of monetary prizes. We recall the notation δ_y for the degenerate lottery which yields y
with probability 1. Then Allais's two lottery comparisons A vs. B and C vs. D can be
expressed in the form

---

[11] The translation from the French original is our own. The monetary unit was the old French franc, whose exchange
rate during 1953 was about 350 to the US dollar. So these were large hypothetical gambles.

$$\lambda_A = \delta_b \qquad\qquad \text{vs.} \quad \lambda_B = (1-\alpha)\delta_b + \alpha\mu$$
$$\lambda_C = (1-\alpha)\delta_c + \alpha\delta_b \quad \text{vs.} \quad \lambda_D = (1-\alpha)\delta_c + \alpha\mu \tag{2.18}$$

respectively, where $\alpha := 0.11$ and $\mu := (1-\alpha')\delta_a + \alpha'\delta_c$ with $\alpha' := \frac{1}{11}$. Now the independence axiom gives the chain of logical equivalences

$$\lambda_D \succ \lambda_C \Longleftrightarrow \mu \succ \delta_b \Longleftrightarrow \lambda_B \succ (1-\alpha)\delta_b + \alpha\delta_b = \delta_b = \lambda_A \tag{2.19}$$

which violates the preferences $\lambda_A \succ \lambda_B$ and $\lambda_D \succ \lambda_C$ that Allais reports.[12]

2.3.5.3 The Common Consequence Effect
The Allais paradox is a particular instance of the *common consequence effect* concerning three lotteries $\lambda, \mu, \nu \in \Delta(Y)$, and the observation that, given $\alpha \in (0,1)$ sufficiently small, a decision maker's preferences often seem to satisfy:

1. when the "common consequence" ν is sufficiently close to λ, where the left-hand lottery collapses to just λ, then

$$\alpha\lambda + (1-\alpha)\nu \succ \alpha\mu + (1-\alpha)\nu \tag{2.20}$$

which would imply $\lambda \succ \mu$ if the independence axiom were satisfied;

2. when ν is sufficiently worse than λ, then

$$\alpha\lambda + (1-\alpha)\nu \prec \alpha\mu + (1-\alpha)\nu \tag{2.21}$$

which would imply $\lambda \prec \mu$ if the independence axiom were satisfied. These preferences are of course entirely consistent with (2.18) provided that we take $\lambda = \delta_b$ and either $\nu = \delta_b$ in case (2.20) or $\nu = \delta_c$ in case (2.21).

The common consequence effect occurs when the first pair of lotteries being compared involve mixtures sharing a common good consequence that gets replaced by a common bad consequence in forming the second pair of lotteries being compared. Machina (1989) interprets this as violating a separate principle that he calls "replacement separability."

2.3.5.4 The Common Ratio Effect
Like the Allais paradox of Section 2.3.5.2, the common ratio effect involves three distinct consequences $a, b, c \in Y$ such that preferences over the corresponding degenerate lotteries satisfy $\delta_a \succ \delta_b \succ \delta_c$. Given any two constants $p, q \in (0,1)$, consider the following two choices between pairs of alternative lotteries:

---

[12] Allais (1953) regards this as violating "Savage's postulate," though he also writes of "Samuelson's substitutability principle," which seems more accurate.

$$\lambda := \delta_b \qquad\qquad \text{vs.} \quad \mu := p\delta_a + (1-p)\delta_c$$
$$\lambda' := q\delta_b + (1-q)\delta_c \quad \text{vs.} \quad \mu' := qp\delta_a + (1-qp)\delta_c \tag{2.22}$$

Note that the Allais paradox is a special case where the consequences a, b, c are three monetary prizes respectively equal to 500 million, 100 million, and 0 old French francs, whereas the numerical mixture weights are $p = \frac{10}{11} = 0.90909\ldots$ and $q = 0.11$ (implying that $pq = 0.1$).

The example owes its name to the existence of a *common ratio*

$$q = \lambda'(b)/\lambda(b) = \mu'(a)/\mu(a) \tag{2.23}$$

between the probabilities of the most favorable two outcomes. Note too that

$$\lambda' = q\lambda + (1-q)\delta_c \quad \text{and} \quad \mu' = q\mu + (1-q)\delta_c. \tag{2.24}$$

In particular, the common ratio q is the weight attached to both lotteries λ and μ in forming the respective mixtures λ' and μ' of λ and μ with δ_c.

Of course the vNM independence axiom implies that

$$\lambda \succ \mu \iff q\lambda + (1-q)\delta_c \succ q\mu + (1-q)\delta_c \iff \lambda' \succ \mu'.$$

So the preferences $\lambda \succ \mu$ and $\mu' \succ \lambda'$ that many of Allais's subjects reported do contradict the vNM independence axiom.

The common ratio effect occurs when different lotteries are mixed with a common bad consequence. Machina (1989) interprets this as violating a principle that he calls "mixture separability."

2.4 DYNAMIC RATIONALITY WITH DETERMINISTIC CONSEQUENCES

2.4.1 Dynamic Inconsistency

Strotz (1956) started his famous article on inconsistent dynamic choice with the following quotation from Homer's Odyssey:

> *but you must bind me hard and fast, so that I cannot stir from the spot where you will stand me …and if I beg you to release me, you must tighten and add to my bonds.*

Thus does Strotz (1956) recognize that, going back to the mists of time before Homer's *Odyssey* was ever set down in writing, humanity has recognized the important distinction between: (i) the intention to make a sequence of successive rational decisions; (ii) actually carrying out those plans. Using contemporary language, Strotz (1956) began to explore what would happen if an intertemporal utility maximizing agent could experience changing tastes.

Indeed, when decision makers can re-evaluate their plans, changing preferences typically lead to *dynamic inconsistency* in the sense that the eventually chosen course of action deviates from the one that was originally planned. Consistency, on the other hand, requires choices at later stages to conform with those that were planned at earlier stages. Later, the logical link between consistent planning and Selten's (1965) "subgame perfect equilibrium" refinement of Nash equilibrium in game theory also became readily apparent.

2.4.1.1 Naïve Behavior

When considering games with one player, economists have followed Strotz (1956) and Pollak (1968) in describing choice as "naïve" or "myopic" if the agent, faced with a succession of several decisions to make, simply maximizes a current objective function at each stage, without heeding how that objective may change in the future. In particular, the naïve decision maker's actual choices at later stages of any decision tree differ from earlier planned choices.

2.4.1.2 Sophisticated Behavior

By contrast, the sophisticated decision maker works backward through the overall decision problem, as in the subgame perfect equilibrium of an extensive form game (Selten, 1965) with a different player each period, whose payoffs match the decision maker's variable preferences. This subgame perfect equilibrium outcome coincides with the result of applying backward induction outcome to a game of perfect information of the kind investigated by Farquharson (1969), Moulin (1979), and many successors. Like dynamic programming, backward induction starts in the last period, where an optimal choice is made myopically. In all subsequent induction steps, which apply to earlier stages of the decision problem, a choice is identified so that an optimal plan of action results for both the current and all following periods. The backward recursion process concludes with an optimal plan of action for the whole problem, starting with the first decision.

Strotz (1956, p. 173) described this problem as follows:

"Since precommitment is not always a feasible solution to the problem of intertemporal conflict, the man with insight into his future unreliability may adopt a different strategy and reject any plan which he will not follow through. His problem is then to find the best plan among those that he will actually be following."

And Pollak (1968, p. 203) as follows:

"A sophisticated individual, recognizing his inability to precommit his future behaviour beyond the next decision point, would adopt a strategy of consistent planning and choose the best plan among those he will actually follow."

Issues such as the existence and characterization of optimal sophisticated plans, or of non-empty valued choice functions, were discussed for growth models by, amongst others, Phelps and Pollak (1968), Pollak (1968), Peleg and Yaari (1973), Inagaki (1970), and, for an approach to "Rawlsian" just savings rules, by Dasgupta (1974).[13]

Another issue is whether any ordinal intertemporal utility function could represent the result of optimal sophisticated planning. In fact, in the microeconomic context of demand theory, Blackorby et al. (1973) showed how a consumer with changing preferences would generally have demand functions that violate the usual Slutsky conditions for rationality. Then Hammond (1976) showed how the "potential addict" example, already suggested by Strotz (1956) and analyzed in Section 2.4.2, would lead to choices that violate the ordering principle. Indeed, naïve choice is ordinal if sophisticated choice is ordinal, and both these hold if naïve and sophisticated choice coincide, which in turn holds if there is no "essential inconsistency" of the kind that characterizes the "potential addict" example.

2.4.1.3 Commitment Devices

Similar ideas emerged in what most macroeconomists now like to call the "time (in) consistency" problem, especially in the work that follows Kydland and Prescott (1977) in distinguishing between successive policy choices that follow a fixed rule from those that exhibit discretion in adapting to circumstances. Indeed, Kydland and Prescott typically presume that, like Odysseus alerted to the dangers presented by the Sirens, it is worth investing in some sort of commitment device which can prevent any departures from the original plan that the agent may be tempted to make—see also McClennen (1990) among philosophers and Klein (1990) among legal scholars.

2.4.2 Example: A Strict Preference Cycle and the Potential Addict

2.4.2.1 Three Decision Trees

The first example concerns choice under certainty when there is a strict preference cycle. Specifically, suppose that a, b, c are three different consequences in the domain Y. Consider the choice function $F \mapsto C(F)$ defined on $\mathcal{F}(Y)$, the family of non-empty subsets of Y. Suppose that $F \mapsto C(F)$ induces a base relation $\succsim^C$ on Y for which there is a *strict preference cycle* on the triple $Z := \{a, b, c\}$—i.e., $a \succ^C b, b \succ^C c$, and $c \succ^C a$. This will be true, of course, if and only if the choice function $F \mapsto C(F)$ applied to pair sets $F \subset S$ satisfies

$$C(\{a, b\}) = \{a\}, \quad C(\{b, c\}) = \{b\}, \quad \text{and} \quad C(\{a, c\}) = \{c\}. \qquad (2.25)$$

Suppose too that $C(\{a, b, c\}) = \{b\}$, because b is deemed to be the "best" of the three consequences in S.

---

[13] One of the main motivations for the use of infinite-horizon planning in Hammond (1973) was to avoid the inconsistencies that would arise in any finite-horizon planning approach.

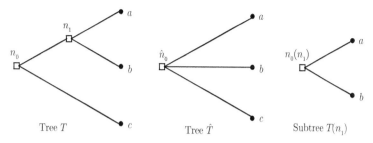

Figure 2.1 Three decision trees associated with a strict preference cycle.

Consider now the triple of decision trees in Figure 2.1, each of which starts with an initial node that is also a decision node, indicated by a square. Furthermore, in each tree the terminal nodes are indicated by dots and labelled by their respective consequences a, b, c.

Of these three trees, the leftmost tree T has a second decision node n_1. The decision at node n_0 is therefore:

either to move down, leading directly to the terminal node whose consequence is c;

or to move up, leading to the decision node n_1 and the later choice between the two terminal nodes whose consequences are a and b respectively.

2.4.2.2 A Potential Addict

The "potential addict" example of Hammond (1976) involves the particular decision tree T in Figure 2.1, with the three respective consequences in the set $Z = \{a, b, c\}$ interpreted as follows:

a is **addiction**, which is the worst *ex ante* of the three possible consequences in S;

b is **bliss**, which is the best *ex ante* of the three possible consequences in S, allowing the decisionmaker to enjoy some of the pleasures of addiction without experiencing any long-lasting harm;

c results from the **commitment** to avoid any possibility of addiction, thus denying oneself all the benefits of b, as well as sparing oneself all the costs of a.

After reaching the second decision node n_1 of tree T, however, the decision maker has become addicted. This implies that preferences change *ex post* so that a becomes strictly preferred to b.

The presumed potential addict's preferences $a \succ^C b, b \succ^C c$, and $c \succ^C a$ are those of an agent who prefers addiction to bliss after becoming addicted, but prefers bliss to commitment and commitment to addiction. A naïve agent plans b but gets diverted to a, whereas a sophisticated agent plans c and realizes that plan.

The potential addict example, with its changing preferences and even a strict preference cycle, will be ruled out by the following axioms that are inspired by Cubitt (1996).

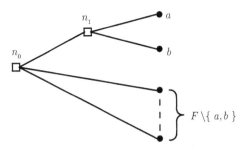

Figure 2.2 Decision tree $T_{F, a, b}$ illustrating ordinality.

2.4.3 Axioms for Ordinality

2.4.3.1 A General Tree with Two Decision Nodes

The potential addict example is a particular case of a special kind of decision tree, of the form shown in Figure 2.2. The single lower branch in the leftmost tree of Figure 2.1, whose consequence is c, has been replaced in the decision tree $T_{F,a,b}$ of Figure 2.2 by an arbitrary finite set of branches, each with its own separate consequence in the set $F \setminus \{a, b\}$. Here $F \subseteq Y$ is an arbitrary finite set of consequences that includes both a and b as distinct members, and has at least one other distinct member besides.

At each of the two decision nodes n_0 and n_1 of the decision tree $T_{F, a, b}$, we will be especially interested in the *feasible sets of consequences* after reaching that decision node, which are evidently $F(T_{F,a,b}, n_0) = F$ and $F(T_{F,a,b}, n_1) = \{a, b\}$ respectively. We will also represent plans at those two nodes by the two *planned consequence sets*[14]

$$\Psi(T_{F,a,b}, n_0) \subseteq F(T_{F,a,b}, n_0) = F \text{ and } \Psi(T_{F,a,b}, n_1) \subseteq F(T_{F,a,b}, n_1) = \{a, b\}$$

Another piece of useful notation is

$$N_{+1}(T_{F,a,b}, n_0) = \{n_1\} \cup (F \setminus \{a, b\}) \quad \text{and} \quad N_{+1}(T_{F,a,b}, n_1) = \{a, b\}$$

for the sets of nodes that *immediately succeed* the two decision nodes n_0 and n_1 respectively in the tree $T_{F,a,b}$.

Finally, given the planned consequence set $\Psi(T_{F,a,b}, n_0)$ at n_0, let

$$\psi(T_{F,a,b}, n_0) := \{n' \in N_{+1}(T_{F,a,b}, n_0) \mid \Psi(T_{F,a,b}, n_0) \cap F(T_{F,a,b}, n') \neq \emptyset\}$$

be the *planned move set* at node n_0; it represents those nodes in $N_{+1}(T_{F,a,b}, n_0)$ which the decision maker must be willing to go to in order not to rule out any consequence in $\Psi(T_{F,a,b}, n_0)$.

---

[14] Cubitt (1996) defines a plan as a chosen set of terminal nodes. Because we identify each terminal node with the consequence that is obtained there, it loses no generality to define $\Psi(T_{F,a,b}, n)$ as a subset of the feasible set of consequences $F(T_{F,a,b}, n)$.

The following definition applies to general decision trees T.

Definition 2.7   Given any node n of any finite decision tree T, let:

1. $N_{+1}(T, n)$ denote the set of nodes that immediately succeed n in T;

2. $F(T, n)$ denote the feasible set of consequences given that node n has been reached in decision tree T;

3. $\Psi(T, n) \subseteq F(T, n)$ denote the planned consequence set at node n.

When n is a terminal node leading to the consequence $y \in Y$, then

$$N_{+1}(T, n) = \emptyset \quad \text{and} \quad F(T, n) = \{y\}. \tag{2.26}$$

2.4.3.2 Dynamic Consistency at a Decision Node

Whenever the decision maker at node n_0 of tree $T_{F, a, b}$ plans to achieve a consequence a or b in $F(T_{F,a,b}, n_1)$, this entails arriving at node n_1. In fact one must have $n_1 \in \psi(T_{F,a,b}, n_0)$. Then "dynamic consistency at n_0" requires the plan at n_1 to involve choosing all the consequences that were both planned at n_0 and are still feasible at n_1. These are precisely the consequences in $\Psi(T_{F,a,b}, n_0) \cap F(T_{F,a,b}, n_1)$. Thus dynamic consistency at n_0 is satisfied if and only if $\Psi(T_{F,a,b}, n_0) = \Psi(T, n_0) \cap F(T_{F,a,b}, n_1)$ whenever $\Psi(T_{F,a,b}, n_0) \cap F(T_{F,a,b}, n_1) \neq \emptyset$.

More generally:

Definition 2.8   Let n be any decision node of any decision tree T, with $N_{+1}(T, n)$ as the set of immediately succeeding nodes. Then there is *dynamic consistency at the decision node* n provided that, whenever the planned consequence sets $\Psi(T, n)$ and $\Psi(T, n')$ at nodes n and $n' \in N_{+1}(T, n)$ satisfy $\Psi(T, n) \cap F(T, n') \neq \emptyset$, then $\Psi(T, n') = \Psi(T, n) \cap F(T, n')$.

2.4.3.3 Separability after a Decision Node

The next condition requires the "continuation subtree" $T(n_1)$ of $T_{F, a, b}$ that starts at node n_1 to be treated as if it were a full decision tree. Formally:

Definition 2.9   Let $T(n_1)$ denote the *continuation subtree* of tree T, which is the subtree whose initial node is n_1 and whose other nodes are a, b, the two successors of n_1 in tree T. The planned set $\Psi(T, n_1)$ of consequences at node n_1 satisfies *separability* provided that it equals the planned set $\Psi(T(n_1), n_1)$ of consequences at the initial node n_1 of the continuation subtree $T(n_1)$.

2.4.3.4 Reduction of Sequential Choice

The next condition requires that, given a decision tree that allows a sequence of choices at its two decision nodes, transforming that tree to its "reduced form" with just one decision node has no effect on the planned set of consequences. Formally:

Definition 2.10   Let $\hat{T}_F$ be the *reduced form* of the tree $T_{F, a, b}$, defined so that its initial node $\hat{n}_0$ is the only decision node, and also so that the feasible sets of consequences are the same, with $F(T, n_0) = F(\hat{T}_F, \hat{n}_0) = F$. Then reduction of sequential choice requires that the planned sets of consequences satisfy $\Psi(T, n_0) = \Psi(\hat{T}_F, \hat{n}_0)$.

2.4.4 Ordinality

Theorem 2.5   *Suppose that, given any finite feasible set $F \subseteq Y$ consisting of at least 3 consequences, as well as any pair of consequences c the planned consequence sets $\Psi(T, n_0)$ and $\Psi(T, n_1)$ in the decision tree $T_{F, a, b}$ of Figure 2.2 satisfy dynamic consistency, separability, and reduction of sequential choice.*
Let $\mathcal{F}(Y) \ni F \mapsto C(F) := \Psi(\hat{T}_F, \hat{n}_0)$ be the consequence choice function defined on the domain $\mathcal{F}(Y)$ of all non-empty finite subsets of Y whose value is the planned consequence set in the reduced form decision tree $\hat{T}_F$ with one decision node $\hat{n}_0$ such that $F(\hat{T}_F, \hat{n}_0) = F$.
Let $\succsim$ denote the binary relation defined on Y by the requirement that $a \succsim b \iff a \in C(\{a, b\})$ for each pair a, b $\in$ Y. Then:

1. the relation $\succsim$ is complete and transitive;

2. $C(F) = C^{\succsim}(F) := \{a \in F \mid b \in F \implies a \succsim b\}$ for each $F \in \mathcal{F}(Y)$.

Proof   Because $\Psi(\tilde{T}, \tilde{n}_0) \neq \emptyset$ for any tree $\tilde{T}$ with $F(\tilde{T}, \tilde{n}_0) = \{a, b\}$, the definition of $\succsim$ implies that the relation is complete.

Given any triple (F, a, b) with $F \in \mathcal{F}(Y)$, $a \in C(F)$ and $b \in F$, construct the decision tree $T_{F, a, b}$ shown in Figure 2.2. Then $F(T, n_0) = F = F(\hat{T}_F, \hat{n}_0)$, where $\hat{T}_F$ is the reduced form of F with $\hat{n}_0$ as its only decision node. By reduction of sequential choice, it follows that $C(F) = \Psi(\hat{T}, \hat{n}_0) = \Psi(T, n_0)$. In particular, because $a \in C(F)$ by hypothesis, and also $a \in F(T, n_1)$ by construction of the tree T, it follows that

$$a \in C(F) \implies a \in \Psi(T, n_0) \cap F(T, n_1). \tag{2.27}$$

From dynamic consistency and then separability, it follows that

$$\Psi(T, n_0) \cap F(T, n_1) = \Psi(T, n_1) = \Psi(T(n_1), n_1). \tag{2.28}$$

Because $T(n_1)$ is a reduced form decision tree, the definition of $F \mapsto C(F)$ implies that

$$\Psi(T(n_1), n_1) = C(F(T(n_1), n_1)) = C(\{a, b\}). \tag{2.29}$$

Combining (2.27), (2.28), and (2.29), we see that $a \in C(F) \implies a \succsim b$. Since this is true whenever $a, b \in F \subseteq Y$ where F is finite, it follows that the consequence choice function $F \mapsto C(F)$ satisfies binary contraction consistency.

Next, suppose that not only $a \in C(F)$, but also $b \succsim a$. The above construction shows that in the tree $T_{F, a, b}$ shown in Figure 2.2, one has

$$b \in C(\{a, b\}) = C(F(T(n_1), n_1) = \Psi(T, n_1) = \Psi(T, n_0) \cap F(T, n_1)$$

and so

$$b \in \Psi(T, n_0) = C(F(T, n_0)) = C(F).$$

It follows that the consequence choice function $F \mapsto C(F)$ satisfies binary expansion consistency.

We have proved that $F \mapsto C(F)$ satisfies both binary contraction consistency and binary expansion consistency. It follows from Theorem 2.1 that the choice function $F \mapsto C(F)$ is ordinal and its base relation $\succsim$ is transitive. $\qquad\square$

2.4.5 Consequentialist Invariance

2.4.5.1 Behavior and Its Consequences

Definition 2.11   In the decision tree $T_{F, a, b}$ of Figure 2.2, for each of the two decision nodes $n \in \{n_0, n_1\}$, let:

1. $N_{+1}(T, n)$ denote the set of *immediately succeeding nodes* of node n in decision tree T; evidently $N_{+1}(T, n_0) = \{n_1\} \cup (F \setminus \{a, b\})$ and $N_{+1}(T, n_1) = \{a, b\}$;
2. $\beta(T, n) \subseteq N_{+1}(T, n)$ denote the non-empty *behavior set* of moves that it would be acceptable for the decision maker to make at node n;
3. $\Phi(T, n) \subseteq F(T, n)$ denote the *consequence choice set* induced by behavior $\beta(T, n')$ at all nodes n' of the continuation subtree $T(n)$ whose initial node is n.

Instead of the planned consequences $\Psi(T, n)$ of reaching node n in decision tree T, the "consequentialist" approach focuses on the consequence choice set $\Phi(T, n)$ generated by the behavior $\beta(T, n)$. This set can be found by backward induction, otherwise known as "folding back" (Raiffa, 1968; Sarin and Wakker, 1994) or even "rolling back" (LaValle and Wapman, 1986). The idea is, for each node $n' \in N_{+1}(T, n)$, to fold back the corresponding continuation subtree $T(n')$ into the single node n', and attach to it the consequence choice set $\Phi(T, n') \subseteq F(T, n')$ that applies after reaching node n'. Along with the feasible sets $F(T, n)$, the consequence choice sets $\Phi(T, n)$ are constructed by backward recursion, based on the respective equations

$$F(T, n) = \bigcup\nolimits_{n' \in N_{+1}(T, n)} F(T, n') \text{ and } \Phi(T, n) = \bigcup\nolimits_{n' \in \beta(T(n), n)} \Phi(T, n').$$

(2.30)

The second equation states that, for any $y \in F(T, n)$ to be a possible consequence of behavior starting from node n in tree T, there must be a node $n' \in \beta(T(n), n)$ such that $y \in \Phi(T, n')$.

Especially noteworthy here is that definition (2.30), in order to determine each consequence choice set $\Phi(T, n)$ generated by behavior in the tree T, depends on behavior only at the *initial node of the continuation subtree* $T(n)$. This relates to the old English adage "don't cross your bridges before you come to them," as cited by Savage (1954) in particular. That is, behavior at node n is undetermined until node n itself is reached and the "bridge" one needs to cross is to one of the immediately succeeding nodes $n' \in N_{+1}(T, n) = N_{+1}(T(n), n)$. As will be seen, definition (2.30) obviates the need to assume that behavior satisfies the dynamic consistency requirement $\beta(T, n) = \beta(T(n), n)$. It is one important feature that distinguishes actual from planned behavior.

2.4.5.2 Consequentialist Invariance and Its Implications
The following definition is deliberately very general because in future sections we will want to apply it in several different contexts that allow decision trees with chance or event nodes as well as, in some cases, more than two decision nodes.

Definition 2.12 A *behavior rule* is a mapping $(T, n) \mapsto \beta(T, n)$ defined at every decision node n of all decision trees T in a specified domain $\mathcal{T}$, and satisfying $\emptyset \neq \beta(T, n) \subseteq N_{+1}(T, n)$. A behavior rule satisfies *consequentialist invariance* provided that, whenever $n, \tilde{n}$ are decision nodes of the respective trees $T, \tilde{T} \in \mathcal{T}$ at which the respective feasible sets satisfy $F(T, n) = F(\tilde{T}, \tilde{n})$, the corresponding consequence choice sets satisfy $\Phi(T, n) = \Phi(\tilde{T}, \tilde{n})$.

The following result demonstrates that, when applied to the particular decision tree $T_{F,a,b}$ shown in Figure 2.2, consequentialist invariance implies that the consequence choice sets $\Phi(T_{F,a,b}, n)$ satisfy the three assumptions on the planned consequence sets $\Psi(T_{F,a,b}, n)$ that were imposed in Section 2.4.3.

Theorem 2.6 *Given the decision tree $T_{F,a,b}$ shown in Figure 2.2, suppose that behavior $\beta(T_{F,a,b}, n)$ and its consequence choice sets $\Phi(T_{F,a,b}, n)$ at the two decision nodes $n \in \{n_0, n_1\}$ satisfy consequentialist invariance. Then the consequence choice sets $\Phi(T_{F,a,b}, n)$ also satisfy dynamic consistency at the decision node n_0, separability after the decision node n_0, and reduction of sequential choice.*

Proof   Suppose that $\Phi(T, n_0) \cap F(T, n_1) \neq \emptyset$. Because of (2.30), this is only possible if $n_1 \in \beta(T, n_0)$, in which case (2.30) implies that $\Phi(T, n_1) \subseteq \Phi(T, n_0)$. In particular, $\Phi(T, n_1) = \Phi(T, n_0) \cap F(T, n_1)$, as required for dynamic consistency.

Equation (2.30) also implies that $\Phi(T(n_1), n_1) = \Phi(T, n_1) = \beta(T, n_1)$, as required for separability.

Finally, the reduced form $\hat{T}_F$ of the tree $T_{F,a,b}$ obviously has the property that $F(T, n_0) = F(\hat{T}_F, \hat{n}_0) = F$. Hence consequentialist invariance implies that $\Phi(T, n_0) = \Phi(\hat{T}_F, \hat{n}_0)$, as required for reduction of sequential choice. $\square$

2.4.6 Ordinal Dynamic Programming

So far we have shown that if our versions of Cubitt's axioms (dynamic consistency at a decision node, separability after a decision node, and reduction of sequential choice) hold only in each tree $T_{F,a,b}$, this is enough to ensure that the planned choice sets must maximize a preference ordering. We have also shown that if consequentialist invariance holds in each tree $T_{F,a,b}$, then our versions of Cubitt's axioms are implied. To close the logical circle we now establish the following result, which is inspired by Sobel's (1975) work on "ordinal dynamic programming". The result is stated and proved for a general finite decision tree.

Theorem 2.7   *Let $\succsim$ be any preference ordering on Y. Let $C^{\succsim}$ denote the ordinal choice function on the domain $\mathcal{F}(Y)$ of non-empty finite subsets of Y that is induced by $\succsim$. Then there exists a behavior rule $(T, n) \mapsto \beta(T, n)$ defined on the domain $\mathcal{T}(Y)$ of all finite decision trees with consequences in Y with the property that the induced consequence choice sets, which are calculated by folding back rule (2.30), satisfy consequentialist invariance with*

$$\Psi(T, n) = C^{\succsim}(F(T, n)) \tag{2.31}$$

at every node n of every tree T in $\mathcal{T}(Y)$.

Proof   Given any decision node n of any tree T in $\mathcal{T}(Y)$, construct the set

$$\beta(T, n) := \{ n' \in N_{+1}(T, n) \mid C^{\succsim}(F(T, n)) \cap F(T, n') \neq \emptyset \} \tag{2.32}$$

of moves at n allowing some consequence in the choice set $C^{\succsim}(F(T, n))$ to be reached. Because the choice function $F \mapsto C^{\succsim}(F)$ is ordinal on the domain $\mathcal{F}(Y)$, Theorem 2.1 implies that it must satisfy both expansion and contraction consistency. Hence

$$n' \in \beta(T, n) \iff C^{\succsim}(F(T, n)) \cap F(T, n') \neq \emptyset$$
$$\iff C^{\succsim}(F(T, n')) = C^{\succsim}(F(T, n)) \cap F(T, n').$$

But this implies the chain of equalities

$$\bigcup_{n' \in \beta(T,n)} C^{\succsim}(F(T, n')) = \bigcup_{n' \in \beta(T,n)} [C^{\succsim}(F(T, n)) \cap F(T, n')]$$
$$= \bigcup_{n' \in N_{+1}(T,n)} [C^{\succsim}(F(T, n)) \cap F(T, n')]$$
$$= C^{\succsim}(F(T, n)) \cap \left[\bigcup_{n' \in N_{+1}(T,n)} F(T, n') \right]$$
$$= C^{\succsim}(F(T, n)) \cap F(T, n) = C^{\succsim}(F(T, n))$$

from which the equality

$$C^{\succsim}(F(T, n)) = \bigcup_{n' \in \beta(T,n)} C^{\succsim}(F(T, n')) \tag{2.33}$$

follows trivially.

We now prove by backward induction that (2.31) holds at every node n of T. At any terminal node n with a consequence $y \in Y$ one has

$$\Psi(T, n) = F(T, n) = C^{\succsim}(F(T, n)) = \{y\}$$

so (2.31) holds trivially.

As the induction hypothesis, suppose that $\Psi(T, n') = C^{\succsim}(F(T, n'))$ for every $n' \in N_{+1}(T, n)$. Now, rule (2.30) states that $\Psi(T, n) = \cup_{n' \in \beta(T,n)} \Psi(T, n')$. Together with (2.33) and the induction hypothesis, this implies that

$$\Psi(T, n) = \bigcup_{n' \in \beta(T,n)} \Psi(T, n') = \bigcup_{n' \in \beta(T,n)} C^{\succsim}(F(T, n')) = C^{\succsim}(F(T, n)).$$

This proves the relevant backward induction step, so (2.31) holds for all nodes n in tree T.

$\square$

2.4.7 Time Inconsistency and Hyperbolic Discounting

2.4.7.1 Timed Consequences and Discounting

Following Samuelson (1937), Koopmans (1960), and many others the early literature on discounting future utilities typically considers an entire *consumption stream* $\mathbf{c}$ in the form of a function $T \ni t \mapsto c(t) \in \mathbb{R}_+$, where (just in this section) $T \subseteq \mathbb{R}_+$ is the relevant *time domain*. Sometimes time was discrete, in which case a typical intertemporal utility function would take the form $\sum_{t \in T} D_t u(c_t)$, where $c \mapsto u(c)$ is a *time-independent* util-ity function, and D_t denotes a *discount factor* which is assumed to decrease with time. Sometimes time was continuous, in which case T would become an interval and the sum would be replaced with an integral of the form $\int_T D(t)u(c(t))dt$. A special case of some importance arose with *exponential discounting*, implying that $D(t) = d^t$ for some constant $d \in (0, 1)$ in the discrete time case, and that $D(t) = e^{-\delta t}$ for some negative constant δ in the continuous time case. Strotz's (1956) work in particular considered the possible dynamic inconsistency of choice in the continuous time framework, especially when nonexponential discounting was combined with a particular kind of stationarity that required the plan chosen at any time $s > 0$ to maximize $\int_s^\infty D(t - s)u(c(t))dt$ so that future utility was effectively discounted back to the date at which the plan was made, rather than to a fixed time like 0.

The experimental literature has focused on simpler decision problems where, instead of entire consumption streams, the objects of choice are *timed consequences* of the form $(t, y) \in \mathbb{R}_+ \times Y$, where t denotes the time at which the consequence $y \in Y$ is experi-enced. Following Fishburn and Rubinstein (1982), it is usually assumed that preferences over timed consequences are represented by just one term $D(t) u(y)$ of the intertemporal sum, with time t treated as part of the chosen consequence.

In case $Y = \mathbb{R}_+$ and one assumes that there is complete indifference over the timing of the 0 consequence, then one can impose the convenient normalization $u(0) = 0$. In this setting Fishburn and Rubinstein (1982) have provided further results concerning what transformations of the two functions $t \mapsto D(t)$ and $\gamma \mapsto u(\gamma)$ leave invariant the preferences over timed consequences that are represented by the function $(t, \gamma) \mapsto D(t)u(\gamma)$.

2.4.7.2 Experimental Tests of Exponential Discounting

A parsimonious special case occurs when there is the exponential discounting, meaning that $D(t) = d^t$ as with preferences for intertemporal consumption streams. Following Strotz's (1956) insight, exponential discounting is a necessary and sufficient condition for consistency between the planned choices today, at time 0, and future choices at time s when the objective over pairs (t, γ) with $t \geq s$ shifts to $D(t - s)u(\gamma)$.

One of the first experimental tests of exponential discounting was reported in Thaler (1981). Subjects' stated preferences for timed consequences in the near future were compared with their preferences when these timed consequences were shifted out into the far future. For example, the preferences compared were between: (i) one apple today vs. two apples tomorrow; (ii) one apple in a year from now vs. two apples in a year and a day from now. Many people state a preference in situation (i) for one apple today, but in situation (ii) they state a preference for two apples in a year and a day from now, which is inconsistent with exponential discounting. Such preferences are usually attributed to decreasing impatience. They also suggest that subjects fail to foresee that in one year from now situation (ii) will have become situation (i). This allows them liable to violate their originally stated preferences by preferring one apple as soon as possible to two apples one day later. It also makes them have inconsistent preferences like Strotz's naïve planners.

2.4.7.3 Hyperbolic Discounting and Beyond

The literature on time preferences received particular attention in Akerlof's (1991) lecture on the naïve planner's propensity to procrastinate.[15] Many theoretical models of naïve planning that followed have extended the exponential discounting model. Laibson (1997, 1998) studies economic applications of the "hyperbolic" discounting model that had earlier been suggested by psychologists (Ainslie, 1992). For example, Phelps and Pollak (1968) had proposed "quasi-hyperbolic discounting" in discrete time with $D_0 = 1$ and $D_t = bd^t$, for an additional parameter $b \in (0, 1)$. Such quasi-hyperbolic discounting implies that there is more impatience in determining preferences between successive pairs $(0, \gamma)$, $(1, \gamma')$ than corresponding pairs (t, γ), $(t + 1, \gamma')$ at later times, but there is constant impatience otherwise. A more general form of *hyperbolic discounting* that implies decreasing impatience at all times comes from taking $D(t) = (1 + dt)^{-b/d}$ with parameters $d \geq 0$ and $b > 0$. As d approaches 0, this form of discounting approaches exponential discounting.

---

[15] We do not refrain from remarking that the link between procrastination and naïve plans was briefly discussed in Hammond (1973).

More recent works on applications of time preferences include Barro (1999), O'Donoghue and Rabin (1999a,b, 2001), Harris and Laibson (2001), as well as Krusell and Smith (2003). Bernheim and Rangel (2007) further explore the policy relevance of "nonconstant" discounting models; Hayashi (2003) along with Bleichrodt et al. (2009) provide extensions to non-hyperbolic discounting. These works have been motivated and complemented by the many experimental studies of the dynamic consistency of time preferences, which have been surveyed by Loewenstein and Prelec (1992) and by Frederick et al. (2002). Overall these studies provide plenty of evidence to support the hypothesis that discounting is often not exponential.

2.5 DYNAMIC RATIONALITY WITH RISKY CONSEQUENCES

2.5.1 Axioms for Independence

2.5.1.1 A Family of Simple Trees with Risky Consequences

We are going to introduce a parametric family of decision trees, with the idea of using some simple relationships between them in order to explore the implications of a set of axioms inspired by Cubitt (1996). Especially interesting will be a condition that is related to the vNM independence condition (2.15) in Section 2.3.3.2.

The parameters are precisely those involved in the statement of the vNM independence condition. Specifically, they consist of a variable triple of lotteries $\lambda, \mu, \nu \in \Delta(Y)$, together with a variable probability $\alpha \in (0, 1)$ of moving "up" rather than "down." For each value of the parameter vector $(\lambda, \mu, \nu; \alpha)$ there will be four closely related trees $\bar{T}_{\lambda,\mu,\nu;\alpha}, T'_{\lambda,\mu,\nu;\alpha}, \bar{T}_{\lambda,\mu,\nu;\alpha}(n_1)$, and $\hat{T}_{\lambda,\mu,\nu;\alpha}$. Often we will simplify notation by omitting the parameter vector $(\lambda, \mu, \nu; \alpha)$ when this creates no ambiguity.

Following the notation that was introduced in Section 2.4.3.1 for decision trees with deterministic consequences:

Definition 2.13   In each of the four decision trees T of Figures 2.3 and 2.4, and for each of the nodes n of T, let:

1. $N_{+1}(T, n)$ denote the set of nodes that immediately succeed n in the tree T;

2. $F(T, n) \subset \Delta(Y)$ denote the *feasible set* of consequences given that node n has been reached in decision tree T;

3. $\Psi(T, n) \subseteq F(T, n)$ denote the *planned set* of consequences at node n.[16]

---

[16]Cubitt (1996) restricts the definition of planned sets to *decision* nodes. We do not, for two reasons. First, it seems perfectly reasonable that wholly rational decision makers should be able to report their plans even when they are not about to make a decision. Second, we could in any case adopt Cubitt's device in trees like $\bar{T}_{\lambda,\mu,\nu;\alpha}$ of introducing immediately before the original initial node n_0 an extra "dummy" decision node n_{dummy} whose only immediate successor is n_0. Then the plans that we are attaching to chance (and event) nodes in our framework could be attached instead to an extra dummy decision node that precedes each chance (or event) node.

2.5.1.2 Folding Back Feasible Sets

The feasible sets $F(T, n)$ at some nodes of the trees in Figures 2.3 and 2.4 are obvious. Specifically,

$$F(\bar{T}_{\lambda,\mu,\nu;\alpha}, n_1) = F(\bar{T}_{\lambda,\mu,\nu;\alpha}(n_1), n_1) = \{\lambda, \mu\}$$

$$\text{and} \quad F(\hat{T}_{\lambda,\mu,\nu;\alpha}, \hat{n}_0) = \{\alpha\lambda + (1-\alpha)\nu, \alpha\mu + (1-\alpha)\nu\} \qquad (2.34)$$

$$= \alpha\{\lambda, \mu\} + (1-\alpha)\{\nu\}$$

where the last equality follows from an obvious definition of the mixture of the two sets of lotteries $\{\lambda, \mu\}$ and $\{\nu\}$, which are subsets of $\Delta(Y)$. Furthermore, invoking the first equation in (2.30) at the decision node n_0' of $T_{\lambda,\mu,\nu;\alpha}'$ yields

$$F(T_{\lambda,\mu,\nu;\alpha}', n_0') = F(T_{\lambda,\mu,\nu;\alpha}', n_1') \cup F(T_{\lambda,\mu,\nu;\alpha}', n_2'). \qquad (2.35)$$

At the chance nodes n_0 of $\bar{T}_{\lambda,\mu,\nu;\alpha}$ and n_1', n_2' of $T_{\lambda,\mu,\nu;\alpha}'$, however, and indeed for any decision node n of any finite decision tree T, we invoke:

Definition 2.14 Let n be any chance node of a decision tree T. For each immediately succeeding node $n' \in N_{+1}(T, n)$ of n in T, let $\pi(n'|n)$ denote the specified *conditional probability* of reaching each immediately succeeding node $n' \in N_{+1}(T, n)$ of n in T. The feasible set $F(T, n)$ at n satisfies the *folding back rule* provided it is given by the corresponding mixture

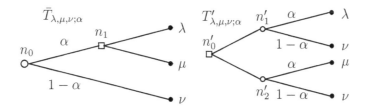

Figure 2.3 The decision tree $\bar{T}_{\lambda,\mu,\nu;\alpha}$ and the variation $T_{\lambda,\mu,\nu;\alpha}'$.

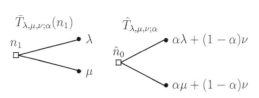

Figure 2.4 The continuation $\bar{T}_{\lambda,\mu,\nu;\alpha}(n_1)$ and the reduction $\hat{T}_{\lambda,\mu,\nu;\alpha}$.

$$F(T, n) = \sum_{n' \in N_{+1}(T, n)} \pi(n'|n) F(T, n') \tag{2.36}$$

of the immediately succeeding feasible sets $F(T, n')$.

Applying (2.36) at the three different chance nodes in the two decision trees of Figure 2.3 yields

$$
\begin{aligned}
F(\bar{T}_{\lambda,\mu,\nu;\alpha}, n_0) &= \alpha F(\bar{T}_{\lambda,\mu,\nu;\alpha}, n_1) + (1 - \alpha)\{\nu\} \\
&= \alpha\{\lambda, \mu\} + (1 - \alpha)\{\nu\}
\end{aligned}
$$

$$\text{as well as} \quad F(T'_{\lambda,\mu,\nu;\alpha}, n'_1) = \alpha\{\lambda\} + (1 - \alpha)\{\nu\} \tag{2.37}$$

$$\text{and} \quad F(T'_{\lambda,\mu,\nu;\alpha}, n'_2) = \alpha\{\mu\} + (1 - \alpha)\{\nu\}.$$

Along with (2.34) and (2.35), this implies that

$$F(\bar{T}_{\lambda,\mu,\nu;\alpha}, n_0) = F(T'_{\lambda,\mu,\nu;\alpha}, n'_0) = F(\hat{T}_{\lambda,\mu,\nu;\alpha}, \hat{n}_0) = \alpha\{\lambda, \mu\} + (1 - \alpha)\{\nu\}. \tag{2.38}$$

We note in passing that rule (2.36) for folding back feasible sets is really no more than an implication of the laws of probability, together with the obvious requirement that the random moves at different chance nodes of any decision tree should be stochastically independent. After all, any possible source of dependence between different random moves should be modelled somewhere within the tree itself.

2.5.1.3 Reduction of Compound Lotteries

Our first substantive assumption on planning involves the planned consequence sets in two of the decision trees in Figures 2.3 and 2.4. Note that $\hat{T}$ is a reduction of T' in the sense that the only difference is that there is an extra step at node n'_1 in resolving the lotteries; this makes no difference to the two feasible sets $F(T', n'_0)$ and $F(\hat{T}, \hat{n}_0)$, which by (2.38) are both equal to $\alpha\{\lambda, \mu\} + (1 - \alpha)\{\nu\}$.

Definition 2.15   The planned consequence sets $\Psi(T', n'_0)$ and $\Psi(\hat{T}, \hat{n}_0)$ at the initial nodes n'_0 and $\hat{n}_0$ of the two trees $T' = T'_{\lambda,\mu,\nu;\alpha}$ and $\hat{T} = \hat{T}_{\lambda,\mu,\nu;\alpha}$ shown in Figures 2.3 and 2.4 satisfy *reduction of compound lotteries* provided they are equal.

2.5.1.4 Dynamic Consistency at a Chance Node

Consider again the decision tree $\bar{T} = \bar{T}_{\lambda,\mu,\nu;\alpha}$ shown in Figure 2.3. Whatever the planned consequence set at node n_0 may be, it entails arriving at node n_1 with probability $\alpha > 0$, and also anticipating that a specific non-empty subset $\Psi(\bar{T}, n_1) \subseteq \{\lambda, \mu\}$ will be selected at that node. Now, there is an obvious bijection $j : F(\bar{T}, n_1) \to F(\bar{T}, n_0)$ whereby

$$\lambda \mapsto j(\lambda) = \alpha\lambda + (1 - \alpha)\nu \quad \text{and} \quad \mu \mapsto j(\mu) = \alpha\mu + (1 - \alpha)\nu. \tag{2.39}$$

The following dynamic consistency condition requires this bijection to induce a correspondence between the two planned consequence sets $\Psi(\bar{T}, n_1)$ and $\Psi(\bar{T}, n_0)$. Formally:

Definition 2.16   The planned consequence sets $\Psi(\bar{T}, n_0)$ and $\Psi(\bar{T}, n_1)$ at the two nonterminal nodes of the tree $\bar{T} = \bar{T}_{\lambda,\mu,\nu;\alpha}$ of Figure 2.3 are *dynamically consistent at node n_0* provided that

$$
\begin{aligned}
\lambda \in \Psi(\bar{T}, n_1) &\Longleftrightarrow \alpha\lambda + (1-\alpha)\nu \in \Psi(\bar{T}, n_0) \\
\text{and} \quad \mu \in \Psi(\bar{T}, n_1) &\Longleftrightarrow \alpha\mu + (1-\alpha)\nu \in \Psi(\bar{T}, n_0)
\end{aligned}
\tag{2.40}
$$

or equivalently, provided that $\Psi(\bar{T}, n_0) = \alpha\Psi(\bar{T}, n_1) + (1-\alpha)\{\nu\}$.

2.5.1.5 Separability after a Chance Node
As in Section 2.4.3.3, separability requires the "continuation subtree" $\bar{T}(n_1)$ of tree $\bar{T} = \bar{T}_{\lambda,\mu,\nu;\alpha}$ that starts at node n_1 to be treated as if it were a full decision tree. The difference from Section 2.4.3.3 is that there the preceding node was a decision node; here it is a chance node.

Here is a formal definition for an arbitrary finite tree T of separability at a chance node n of T.

Definition 2.17   Given any decision tree T, the planned consequence set $\Psi(T, n)$ at a chance node satisfies *separability after the chance node n* provided that it equals the planned consequence set $\Psi(T(n), n)$ at the initial node n of the continuation subtree $T(n)$.

2.5.1.6 Timing Invariance with Risk
Consider once again the two decision trees $\bar{T} = \bar{T}_{\lambda,\mu,\nu;\alpha}$ and $T' = T'_{\lambda,\mu,\nu;\alpha}$ shown in Figure 2.3. We have already noted in (2.38) that the two feasible sets $F(\bar{T}, n_0)$ and $F(T', n'_0)$ at the initial nodes must be equal. The only difference between these two trees is that in $\bar{T}$, the lottery that picks "up" with probability α and "down" with probability $1-\alpha$ precedes the decision node, whereas in T' this timing is reversed. Our last condition, which we state only for two trees like those in Figure 2.3, requires the planned consequence set to be invariant to this timing reversal. Formally:

Definition 2.18   Given the two decision trees $\bar{T} = \bar{T}_{\lambda,\mu,\nu;\alpha}$ and $T' = T'_{\lambda,\mu,\nu;\alpha}$ shown in Figure 2.3, which differ only in the timing of the decision and chance nodes, say that there is *timing invariance* provided that the two planned consequence sets $\Psi(\bar{T}, n_0)$ and $\Psi(T', n'_0)$ are identical.

2.5.2 An Independence Condition
The following Lemma establishes a useful condition precursor of the vNM independence axiom:

Lemma 2.8   *Given any three lotteries $\lambda, \mu, \nu \in \Delta(Y)$ (not necessarily distinct) and any scalar $\alpha \in (0,1)$, consider the four decision trees $\bar{T} = \bar{T}_{\lambda,\mu,\nu;\alpha}$, $T' = T'_{\lambda,\mu,\nu;\alpha}$, $\bar{T}(n_1) = \bar{T}_{\lambda,\mu,\nu;\alpha}(n_1)$, and $\hat{T} = \hat{T}_{\lambda,\mu,\nu;\alpha}$ as shown in Figures 2.3 and 2.4. Suppose that the planned consequence sets $\Psi(T,n)$ at the non-terminal nodes of these trees satisfy reduction of compound lotteries, dynamic consistency at a chance node, separability after a chance node, and timing invariance. Then the two planned consequence sets $\Psi(\hat{T}, \hat{n}_0)$ and $\Psi(\bar{T}(n_1), n_1)$ satisfy*

$$\Psi(\hat{T}, \hat{n}_0) = \alpha \Psi(\bar{T}(n_1), n_1) + (1-\alpha)\{\nu\}. \tag{2.41}$$

Proof   Applying successively reduction of compound lotteries, timing invariance, dynamic consistency at a chance node, then separability after a chance node, we obtain the chain of equalities

$$\begin{aligned}
\Psi(\hat{T}, \hat{n}_0) = \Psi(T', n'_0) = \Psi(\bar{T}, n_0) &= \alpha \Psi(\bar{T}, n_1) + (1-\alpha)\{\nu\} \\
&= \alpha \Psi(\bar{T}(n_1), n_1) + (1-\alpha)\{\nu\}
\end{aligned} \tag{2.42}$$

from which (2.41) follows trivially.   □

The following Theorem establishes that our versions of Cubitt's (1996) axioms are sufficient for ordinality and independence.

Theorem 2.9   *Suppose that:*

1. the hypotheses of Theorem 2.5 are satisfied whenever $F \subset \Delta(Y)$ is a feasible set consisting of at least 3 distinct lotteries;

2. the hypotheses of Lemma 2.8 are satisfied.
Then there exists a preference ordering $\succsim$ on $\Delta(Y)$ satisfying the vNM independence axiom with the property that, in every reduced form finite decision tree $\hat{T}$ whose terminal nodes have consequences in $\Delta(Y)$, the planned consequence set satisfies

$$\Psi(\hat{T}, \hat{n}_0) = C^{\succsim}(F(\hat{T}, \hat{n}_0)) \tag{2.43}$$

where $\mathcal{F}(\Delta(Y)) \ni F \mapsto C^{\succsim}(F)$ is the ordinal choice function on non-empty finite subsets $F \subset \Delta(Y)$ that is generated by the ordering $\succsim$.

Proof   By Theorem 2.5 applied to the domain $\Delta(Y)$ instead of the domain Y, the ordering $\succsim$ exists on $\Delta(Y)$ and (2.43) is satisfied.

Given any three lotteries $\lambda, \mu, \nu \in \Delta(Y)$ and any scalar $\alpha \in (0,1)$, Lemma 2.8 implies that for the two decision trees $\bar{T}(n_1) = \bar{T}_{\lambda,\mu,\nu;\alpha}(n_1)$ and $\hat{T} = \hat{T}_{\lambda,\mu,\nu;\alpha}$ shown in Figure 2.4, one has

$$F(\bar{T}(n_1), n_1) = \{\lambda, \mu\} \quad \text{and} \quad F(\hat{T}, \hat{n}_0) = \alpha F(\bar{T}(n_1), n_1) + (1-\alpha)\{\nu\}.$$

By definition of the ordering $\succsim$, it follows that

$$\lambda \in \Psi(\bar{T}(n_1), n_1) \Longleftrightarrow \lambda \succsim \mu \quad \text{and}$$

$$\alpha\lambda + (1-\alpha)\nu \in \Psi(\hat{T}, \hat{n}_0) \Longleftrightarrow \alpha\lambda + (1-\alpha)\nu \succsim \alpha\mu + (1-\alpha)\nu. \tag{2.44}$$

But equation (2.41) implies that

$$\lambda \in \Psi(T(n_1), n_1) \Longleftrightarrow \alpha\lambda + (1 - \alpha)\nu \in \Psi(\hat{T}, \hat{n}_0).$$

Combining this with (2.44) yields

$$\lambda \succsim \mu \Longleftrightarrow \alpha\lambda + (1 - \alpha)\nu \succsim \alpha\mu + (1 - \alpha)\nu$$

which is precisely the vNM independence axiom.   □

2.5.3 Behavior and Its Consequences

2.5.3.1 Folding Back at a Decision Node

We begin by recalling the notation of Section 2.4.5.1 where, at any decision node n of any tree T, one has:

1. a set $N_{+1}(T, n)$ of immediately succeeding nodes in the decision tree T;
2. a non-empty behavior set $\beta(T, n) \subseteq N_{+1}(T, n)$;
3. a feasible consequence set $F(T, n) \subset \Delta(Y)$;
4. a consequence choice set $\Phi(T, n) \subseteq F(T, n)$ induced by behavior $\beta(T, n')$ at all nodes n' of the continuation subtree $T(n)$ whose initial node is n.

As in Section 2.4.5.1, we assume that at any decision node n of any decision tree T, the feasible set $F(T, n)$ and the consequence choice set $\Phi(T, n)$ satisfy the folding back rule (2.30), reproduced here for convenience:

$$F(T, n) = \bigcup_{n' \in N_{+1}(T,n)} F(T, n') \text{ and } \Phi(T, n) = \bigcup_{n' \in \beta(T(n),n)} \Phi(T, n').$$

2.5.3.2 Folding Back at a Chance Node

At the chance node n_0 of the first tree $\bar{T} = \bar{T}_{\lambda,\mu,\nu;\alpha}$ that is shown in Figure 2.3, we naturally assume that the random move to one of the two succeeding nodes in $N_{+1}(\bar{T}, n) = \{n_1, \nu\}$ is stochastically independent of both the two lotteries λ, ν at the terminal nodes succeeding n_1. This implies that a commitment to choose up at node n_1 results in the consequence lottery $\alpha\lambda + (1 - \alpha)\nu$ back at n_0, whereas a commitment to choose down at node n_1 results in the consequence lottery $\alpha\mu + (1 - \alpha)\nu$ back at n_0. Hence

$$F(\bar{T}, n_0) = \{\alpha\lambda + (1 - \alpha)\nu, \alpha\mu + (1 - \alpha)\nu\} = \alpha F(\bar{T}, n_1) + (1 - \alpha)\{\nu\}.$$
$$(2.45)$$

Furthermore, by a similar argument,

$$\lambda \in \beta(\bar{T}, n_1) \Longleftrightarrow \lambda \in \Phi(\bar{T}, n_1) \Longleftrightarrow \alpha\lambda + (1 - \alpha)\nu \in \Phi(\bar{T}, n_0)$$
$$\mu \in \beta(\bar{T}, n_1) \Longleftrightarrow \mu \in \Phi(\bar{T}, n_1) \Longleftrightarrow \alpha\mu + (1 - \alpha)\nu \in \Phi(\bar{T}, n_0) \qquad (2.46)$$

which obviously implies that

$$\Phi(\bar{T}, n_0) = \alpha\Phi(\bar{T}, n_1) + (1 - \alpha)\{\nu\}. \qquad (2.47)$$

Equations (2.45) and (2.47) are special cases of the more general folding back rules

$$F(T, n) = \sum_{n' \in N_{+1}(n)} \pi(n'|n) F(T, n')$$
$$\Phi(T, n) = \sum_{n' \in N_{+1}(n)} \pi(n'|n) \Phi(T, n') \qquad (2.48)$$

that apply in a general decision tree T to the feasible set and consequence choice set at any chance node n where the probabilities of reaching each immediately succeeding node $n' \in N_{+1}(n)$ are specified to be $\pi(n'|n)$.

2.5.3.3 Implications of Consequentialist Invariance

The following result demonstrates that consequentialist invariance as defined in Section 2.4.5.1 implies that the consequence choice sets $\Phi(T, n)$ satisfy the axioms for independence that were imposed in Section 2.5.1.

Theorem 2.10   *Given the four decision trees shown in Figures 2.3 and 2.4, suppose that behavior $\beta(T, n)$ and the consequence choice sets $\Phi(T, n)$ at all the nodes n of these trees satisfy consequentialist invariance. Then the consequence choice sets $\Phi(T, n)$ also satisfy reduction of compound lotteries, dynamic consistency at the chance node n_0, separability after the chance node n_0, and timing invariance.*

Proof   First, because $F(T', n_0') = F(\hat{T}, \hat{n}_0) = \alpha\{\lambda, \mu\} + (1 - \alpha)\{\nu\}$, consequentialist invariance implies that $\Phi(T', n_0') = \Phi(\hat{T}, \hat{n}_0)$, so these two sets satisfy reduction of compound lotteries.

Second, the folding back rule (2.47) is identical to the equation $\Phi(\bar{T}, n_0) = \alpha\Phi(\bar{T}, n_1) + (1 - \alpha)\{\nu\}$ in Definition 2.16, so dynamic consistency at the chance node n_0 is satisfied.

Third, because $F(\bar{T}, n_1) = F(\bar{T}(n_1), n_1) = \{\lambda, \mu\}$, consequentialist invariance implies that $\Phi(\bar{T}, n_1) = \Phi(\bar{T}(n_1), n_1)$, which is the condition for separability after the chance node n_0.

Finally, because $F(\bar{T}, n_0) = F(T', n_0') = \alpha\{\lambda, \mu\} + (1 - \alpha)\{\nu\}$, consequentialist invariance implies that $\Phi(\bar{T}, n_0) = \Phi(T', n_0')$, which is the condition for timing invariance.

$\square$

2.5.4 Ordinal Dynamic Programming with Risky Consequences

The main result of this section extends the ordinal dynamic programming result in Theorem 2.7 of Section 2.4.6 to allow for chance as well as decision nodes.

Theorem 2.11   *Let $\succsim$ be any preference ordering on $\Delta(Y)$ that satisfies vNM independence. Let $C^{\succsim}$ denote the ordinal choice function on the domain $\mathcal{F}(\Delta(Y))$ of non-empty finite subsets of $\Delta(Y)$ that is induced by $\succsim$. Then there exists a behavior rule $(T, n) \mapsto \beta(T, n)$ defined on the domain $\mathcal{T}(\Delta(Y))$ of all finite decision trees with consequences in $\Delta(Y)$ having the property that the induced consequence choice sets, which are calculated by applying the folding back rules (2.30) and (2.48), satisfy consequentialist invariance with*

$$\Psi(T, n) = C^{\succsim}(F(T, n)) \tag{2.49}$$

at every node n of every tree T in $\mathcal{T}(\Delta(Y))$.

Proof   Given any decision node n of any tree T in $\mathcal{T}(\Delta(Y))$, construct the set

$$\beta(T, n) := \{n' \in N_{+1}(T, n) \mid C^{\succsim}(F(T, n)) \cap F(T, n') \neq \varnothing\} \tag{2.50}$$

as in the proof of Theorem 2.7. We now prove by backward induction that (2.49) holds at every node n of T.

First, at any terminal node n with a consequence $\lambda \in \Delta(Y)$ one has

$$\Psi(T, n) = F(T, n) = C^{\succsim}(F(T, n)) = \{\lambda\}$$

so (2.49) holds trivially.

As the induction hypothesis, suppose that $\Psi(T, n') = C^{\succsim}(F(T, n'))$ for every $n' \in N_{+1}(T, n)$. There are two cases to consider.

Case 1 occurs when n is a decision node of T. Then, as in the proof of Theorem 2.7, the construction (2.50) implies (2.33) which, when combined with the folding back rule (2.30) and the induction hypothesis, implies that

$$\Psi(T, n) = \bigcup_{n' \in \beta(T, n)} \Psi(T, n') = \bigcup_{n' \in \beta(T, n)} C^{\succsim}(F(T, n')) = C^{\succsim}(F(T, n)).$$

This confirms the backward induction step at any decision node n in tree T.

Case 2 occurs when n is a chance node of T.

First, suppose that $\lambda \in \Psi(T, n)$, and consider any $\mu \in F(T, n)$. Then the rolling back rules imply that, given any $n' \in N_{+1}(n)$, there exist $\lambda(n') \in \Psi(T, n')$ and $\mu(n') \in F(T, n')$ satisfying

$$\lambda = \sum_{n' \in N_{+1}(n)} \pi(n'|n)\,\lambda(n') \quad \text{and} \quad \mu = \sum_{n' \in N_{+1}(n)} \pi(n'|n)\,\mu(n'). \tag{2.51}$$

By the induction hypothesis, for all $n' \in N_{+1}(n)$ one has $\lambda(n') \in C^{\succsim}(F(T, n'))$, so $\lambda(n') \succsim \mu(n')$. But then, because $\succsim$ is transitive, repeated application of the vNM independence condition can be used to show that $\lambda \succsim \mu$. Because this is true for all $\mu \in F(T, n)$, it follows that $\lambda \in C^{\succsim}(F(T, n))$. We have therefore proved that $\Psi(T, n) \subseteq C^{\succsim}(F(T, n))$.

Second, suppose $\lambda \in C^{\succsim}(F(T, n))$. Because $\lambda \in F(T, n)$, folding back implies that for all $n' \in N_{+1}(n)$ there exists $\lambda(n') \in F(T, n')$ such that $\lambda = \sum_{n' \in N_{+1}(n)} \pi(n'|n) \lambda(n')$. Consider now any fixed $\bar{n} \in N_{+1}(n)$. Because $\lambda \in C^{\succsim}(F(T, n))$, for any $\mu \in F(T, \bar{n})$ it must be true that

$$\lambda = \pi(\bar{n}|n) \lambda(\bar{n}) + \sum_{n' \in N_{+1}(n) \setminus \{\bar{n}\}} \pi(n'|n) \lambda(n')$$

$$\succsim \pi(\bar{n}|n) \mu + \sum_{n' \in N_{+1}(n) \setminus \{\bar{n}\}} \pi(n'|n) \lambda(n').$$

Because $\pi(\bar{n}|n) > 0$, the vNM independence condition then implies that $\lambda(\bar{n}) \succsim \mu$. This is true for all $\mu \in F(T, \bar{n})$, implying that $\lambda(\bar{n}) \in C^{\succsim}(F(T, \bar{n}))$, and so $\lambda(\bar{n}) \in \Phi(T, \bar{n})$ by the induction hypothesis. Since this is true for all $\bar{n} \in N_{+1}(n)$, one has

$$\lambda = \sum_{n' \in N_{+1}(n)} \pi(n'|n) \lambda(n') \in \sum_{n' \in N_{+1}(n)} \pi(n'|n) \Phi(T, n')$$

and so $\lambda \in \Phi(T, n)$ because of the rolling back rule. We have therefore proved that $C^{\succsim}(F(T, n)) \subseteq \Psi(T, n)$. Together with the result of the previous paragraph, this confirms that $\Psi(T, n) = C^{\succsim}(F(T, n))$ and so completes the final induction step.   □

2.5.5 Timing and Nonlinear Expectations

Halevy (2008) notices a parallel between observed preferences in examples like the Allais paradox we described in Section 2.3.5.2 and preferences for *timed consequences* $(t, y) \in \mathbb{R}_+ \times Y$ of the kind considered in Section 2.4.7.1 (see also Quiggin and Horowitz, 1995; Ebert and Prelec, 2007). The connection seems to arise because, in contrast to sure consequences in the near future, delayed consequences are perceived as inherently risky (Dasgupta and Maskin, 2005). As such, nonlinear probability transformations like those which some writers such as Kahneman and Tversky (1979) and Tversky and Kahneman (1992) applied to explain Allais-like behavior can also adjust discount factors in order to help explain choice of timed outcomes (Epper et al., 2011; Baucells and Heukamp, 2012).

Some recent experiments explicitly look at time preferences for *timed risky consequences* of the form $(t, \lambda) \in \mathbb{R}_+ \times \Delta(Y)$. The findings of Noussair and Wu (2006) and Abdellaoui et al. (2011) suggest that people become more risk tolerant as the risk they face is delayed—i.e., as the time when that risk is resolved recedes further into the future. This hints at the possibility that preferences for delayed risky consequences may conform better to the EU hypothesis than do the preferences for immediate risky consequences that most previous experiments have been designed to elicit. Investigating this further may shed light on the relationship between time preferences and standard preferences over risky consequences, as well as on the potential effect on choices over risky consequences of decreasing impatience and other timing related phenomena.

2.5.6 Experimental Tests

2.5.6.1 Potential Challenges for Dynamic Choice Experiments

Designing and implementing dynamic choice experiments is complex and challenging. It demands a lot of creativity to avoid introducing biases which may obscure the interpretation of the findings. We highlight a few difficulties here.

One major problem is that risk-taking behavior may change as a decision tree unfolds. Static choice may be influenced by numerous empirically well documented phenomena such as regret or disappointment, reference points and loss aversion, optimism and pessimism, or attitudes to ambiguity. All of these may arise in dynamic choice. These phenomena may themselves be affected in addition by real-time delays in resolving risk. Design of dynamic choice experiments to control for these features is therefore necessary.

Another potential difficulty results from the fact that real people make errors. Observing a single contradictory choice need not imply that the subject was violating a choice principle intentionally. To allow for errors like this requires running studies where some choice problems are repeated.

Yet such repetitions introduce new difficulties. The subject's preferences may change during the course of the experiment. With repeated or multiple decision tasks there are additional complications when financial incentives are provided. Indeed, if participants in a study are paid for each choice they make, income effects may lead to biases. On the other hand, if participants are paid at the end of the experiment based on just a small randomly chosen subset of all the decisions they make during the experiment, this means that participants are in fact facing one large dynamic choice problem instead of many small independent problems. For further discussion of the incentives one can provide to participants in dynamic choice experiments, see Cubitt et al. (1998).

Notwithstanding these and other significant difficulties, there have been sufficient advances in experimental design to allow a useful body of results to emerge during the last two decades. We summarize the main findings of the few studies we are aware of next focusing mainly on Cubitt (1996)'s factorized properties leading to the independence property.

2.5.6.2 Experimental Diagnosis of the Common Ratio Effect

One of the empirically most frequently documented descriptive findings in static choice is that people are extremely sensitive to probabilities near the two end points of the probability interval [0, 1] (Wakker, 1994, 2001, 2010). A typical experimental finding is that for good consequences small probabilities are overweighted, but for bad consequences they are underweighted. These observations hint at the possibility of finding subtle explanations for systematic violations of the independence axiom in particular choice problems. Naturally, such findings can inform the design of dynamic choice problems intended to test separately each of Cubitt's (1996) "factorized" dynamic choice principles.

Now, there is a large body of experimental evidence on static Allais paradoxes (see Camerer (1995) and Starmer (2000) for summaries), which also involve decision problems with small probabilities. So it is not surprising that a dynamic version of the choice problem involving the common ratio effect has often been used to study potential violations of those dynamic choice principles.

Cubitt et al. (1998) used a between-subject design to test for possible systematic variations in the frequency with which a consequence like λ is chosen in decision problems such as those shown in Figures 2.3 and 2.4. In their study, 451 subjects were divided into six groups, each subject facing a single decision problem which was played out for real. Cubitt et al. (1998) report violations of timing invariance. No violations were observed for the other dynamic choice principles (dynamic consistency after a chance node, separability after a chance node, and reduction of compound lotteries).

Busemeyer et al. (2000) also tested separability and dynamic consistency after chance nodes. They designed decision problems related to a tree with several successive decision nodes, at each of which there was a choice between: (i) ending the choice process at once and finishing with a deterministic payoff; (ii) continuing to the next decision node. At the final decision node the choice is between a safe consequence and a 50 : 50 lottery. Busemeyer et al. (2000) used a within-subject design to test the dynamic consistency condition by comparing stated plans at the initial node with the choices actually made when the final decision node was reached. They also tested the separability condition by comparing: (i) the isolated choice in a "pruned off" problem that starts at the terminal decision node of the original problem; (ii) the actual choices of those subjects who had started at the initial node of the original problem and decided to follow the path to the final decision node. Overall, taking into account errors in choice (i.e., different choices when the same decision problem is presented again), Busemeyer et al. (2000) found statistically significant violations of dynamic consistency, but no statistically significant violation of separability.

Cubitt and Sugden (2001) also used multistage decision problems. In their experiment, subjects who started with a monetary balance m had to choose between obtaining $3^k m$ if they were lucky enough to survive k chance events, or 0 otherwise. The survival probabilities were set at $(7 - k)/(7 - k + 1)$ for $k = 1, 2, \ldots, 6$. In a between-subject design, subjects were allocated randomly to one of three conditions and paid according to a single decision that they make. In the first multistage condition subjects had to decide, prior to the first four chance events being resolved, whether they would like to continue or not with one (i.e., $k = 5$) or two (i.e., $k = 6$) subsequent chance events. By contrast, in the second condition, subjects had to take the same decision only after they knew they had survived the first four chance events. In the third condition, subjects were endowed with $3^4 m$ and were then asked if they would choose none, one (i.e., $k = 5$) or two (i.e., $k = 6$) subsequent chance events (as if they had survived a series of four chance events). Comparing the choice frequencies across the first two different conditions revealed that neither of the two hypotheses of dynamic consistency or separability could be rejected. The third treatment, however, led to significantly different choice probabilities. One possible explanation is that participants may have perceived the endowment of 3^4m as "house money" (Thaler and Johnson, 1990), making them more risk seeking than if they had earned this amount in previous lotteries, or otherwise. Without this house money effect, the data could be interpreted as supporting a reversed common ratio effect (see Cubitt and Sugden, 2001, p. 121).

The previous studies provide some evidence that dynamic consistency is violated in dynamic choice problems. It seems that in multiple stage problems the number of chance nodes that subjects face matters because it affects their willingness to be exposed to additional chance events. Motivated by this observation, Johnson and Busemeyer (2001) replicated the study of Busemeyer et al. (2000) and added additional controls to analyze the data for the effect of the number of chance nodes (which they call the *length of planning horizon* in their study). Their data gives evidence against dynamic consistency, with the effect becoming stronger as the number of chance nodes increases.

In a recent study, Cubitt et al. (2012) tested separability by designing dynamic choice problems with a variable number of chance nodes preceding a decision node. They implemented a between-subject design and paid each participant the outcome of the single task that they answered. They collected data from three treatments. In one treatment subjects faced a decision problem similar to T' in Figure 2.3 that starts with a decision node. In a second treatment subjects faced a decision like that in $\bar{T}$ in Figure 2.3 where risk is resolved before a decision node like n_1 at which the subjects could either leave the experiment with nothing or else face the continuation subtree $\bar{T}(n_1)$ in Figure 2.4. In their third treatment the decision tree $\bar{T}$ was lengthened by adding five extra chance nodes before the decision node, at all of which the right chance move had to occur before subjects could reach $\bar{T}(n_1)$. According to their data, no evidence was found that separability is violated. This indicates that the history of how one arrives at the decision problem $\bar{T}(n_1)$, including the number of chance nodes one has passed through, appears not to affect subsequent choice behavior.

2.5.6.3 Evidence for Naïve, Sophisticated, or Resolute Choice

According to McClennen (1990) there are decision makers who, faced with decision trees like the potential addict example shown in Figure 2.1 of Section 2.4.2, are neither naïve nor sophisticated. Instead, these individuals are *resolute* in planning b at n_0 and resisting the revised preference for a instead of b that becomes apparent at n_1.

With this possibility in mind, Hey and Paradiso (2006) conducted an experimental study whose aim was to find out which of the following descriptions best fitted the behavior of subjects with non-EU preferences in a dynamic choice setting. They could be:

- *naïve* in not predicting their own changes of preference, but instead planning at each decision node according to what may be their changed preferences;
- *resolute* in determining a plan which they then implement regardless of whether their preferences have changed;
- *sophisticated* in anticipating their own future behavior and using backward induction to determine their plans and decisions;
- *myopic* in entirely overlooking the existence of any future decision nodes.

Their experiment used a within-subject design to obtain information about how participants value strategically equivalent dynamic choice problems. They implemented a second-price sealed-bid auction mechanism combined with a random lottery incentive scheme. The advantage of this method is that it provides information about the strength of their preference for facing a particular problem. They study decision problems similar to those of Cubitt et al. (1998). They found that the majority, 56%, of people valued the three problems roughly equally, hence had preferences in agreement with EU. The residual fraction had non-EU preferences and violated a dynamic choice principle:

- 20% of the participants were resolute in that they both violated dynamic consistency and valued the opportunity to precommit to their decision prior before uncertainty was resolved;
- 18% were sophisticated planners who achieve dynamic consistency by using backward induction to reach their decision;
- only 6% were naïve in both violating dynamic consistency and valued the opportunity to change their original decision after uncertainty was resolved.

Hey and Lotito (2009) extended this earlier study by combining decisions in four dynamic choice problems with valuations. They added several other features to their design to account for errors in choice.[17] They find that 44% of the subjects have preferences that agree with EU theory. A further 30% of the subjects seem naïve and 24% seem resolute. Only 2% appear to be sophisticated decision makers.

From these and other recent studies it appears that the majority of participants either do not violate EU theory or have preferences close to its predictions. Further, among the non-EU maximizers a large fraction is resolute, violating dynamic consistency because they prefer to stick to originally planned actions. Naïve planners, who also violate dynamic consistency, are a small group. Similarly, very few non-EU participants are sophisticated and, in anticipating potential dynamic inconsistency of behavior, apply backward induction.

---

[17] Hey and Lotito use deception in their incentive mechanism to a limited number of participants that end up being paid while extracting useful information from many participants (see their footnote 18, p. 13). Further, two of their decision trees include stochastically dominated alternatives, which may bias subjects towards particular choices.

2.5.6.4 *Summary of Experimental Evidence*

The few studies reviewed in the last two subsections indicate that dynamic consistency of planned behavior is frequently violated, but apparently not by the majority of subjects. Separability does not seem to be violated. The study by Barkan and Busemeyer (2003) discusses the potential role of reference points as causes for violations of dynamic consistency through changes in risk attitudes. A further review of experimental evidence and a discussion on future directions in modeling dynamic choice is provided in Cubitt et al. (2004). Nebout and Dubois (2011) indicate that the parameters used in the experiments seem to have significant influence on the frequency of violations of the vNM independence axiom and that these frequencies are related to the frequencies of dynamic consistency violations.

The only study of separability and dynamic consistency at event nodes that we are aware of is Dominiak et al. (2012). They also report frequent violations of dynamic consistency and few of separability. We hope that our extension of Cubitt's factorized approach, with its distinction between dynamic choice principles at decision and chance (or event) nodes, will be helpful for designing further experimental tests beyond the theoretical discussion provided here.

2.6 DYNAMIC RATIONALITY WITH UNCERTAIN CONSEQUENCES

2.6.1 The Ellsberg Paradox

The following famous example is due to Ellsberg (1961). An urn conceals 90 balls, of which exactly 30 are known to be red, whereas the remaining 60 must be either black or yellow, but in unknown proportions. Apart from their colors, the balls are otherwise entirely identical, so that each ball has exactly the same 1/90 chance of being drawn at random from the urn. Before the ball is drawn, the decision maker is offered the choice between two different lottery pairs or "acts."

Act/Event	Red	Black	Yellow
L_1	$100	$0	$0
L_2	$0	$100	$0
L_3	$100	$0	$100
L_4	$0	$100	$100

Each of the four lotteries has a prize of either $100 or $0, depending on the color of the randomly drawn ball, as indicated in the table. Subjects were asked to make choices:

(i) between lotteries L_1 and L_2; (ii) between lotteries L_3 and L_4. Typical reported preferences are $L_1 \succ L_2$ and $L_4 \succ L_3$. It would seem that the typical subject prefers the known probability $\frac{1}{3}$ of winning \$ 100 when L_1 is chosen to the unknown probability of winning \$100 when L_2 is chosen, but also prefers the known probability $\frac{1}{3}$ of not winning \$100 when L_4 is chosen to the unknown probability of not winning \$100 when L_3 is chosen.

Following Raiffa's (1961) suggestion, consider the two mixed lotteries

$$L' = \tfrac{1}{2}L_1 + \tfrac{1}{2}L_4 \quad \text{and} \quad L'' = \tfrac{1}{2}L_2 + \tfrac{1}{2}L_3.$$

Whatever color ball is drawn from the urn, the results of both L' and L'' are exactly the same: there is a roulette lottery with a probability $\frac{1}{2}$ of winning \$100, and a probability $\frac{1}{2}$ of winning \$0. This suggests that L' and L'' should be indifferent. Yet the reported preferences $L_1 \succ L_2$ and $L_4 \succ L_3$ also suggests that L' offers a better lottery, either L_1 or L_4, with probability 1 compared to L'', which offers either L_2 or L_3.

Indeed, the preferences $L_1 \succ L_2$ and $L_4 \succ L_3$ not only contradict the subjective version of the EU hypothesis; they also exclude a form of "probabilistic sophistication" (cf. Machina and Schmeidler, 1992) whereby one attaches subjective probabilities p and q to the events of drawing a yellow and black respectively.

These subjective probabilities may come from a more basic hypothesis concerning b, the unknown number of black balls, with $60 - b$ as the number of yellow balls. Suppose that for each $b \in \{0, 1, 2, \ldots, 59, 60\}$ there is a subjective probability P_b that there will be b black balls in the urn. In this case the probability that the one ball drawn at random is black will be $p = \sum_{b=0}^{60} P_b b/90$, and that it is yellow will be $q = \sum_{b=0}^{60} P_b (60 - b)/90$, with $p + q = \sum_{b=0}^{60} P_b(60/90) = \frac{2}{3}$ of course.

Assume that the decision maker prefers a higher to a lower probability of winning the \$100 prize. Given that the probability of red is supposed to be $\frac{1}{3}$, the preference $L_1 \succ L_2$ implies that $\frac{1}{3} > p$, whereas the preference $L_4 \succ L_3$ implies that $p + q > \frac{1}{3} + q$, or equivalently that $p > \frac{1}{3}$, which is an obvious contradiction. So the decision maker cannot be probabilistically sophisticated in this way.

2.6.2 States of the World, Events, Uncertain Consequences, and Preferences

Let S be a non-empty finite set of uncertain *states of the world* s, like the color of a ball drawn from an urn in Ellsberg's example. An *event* E is a non-empty subset of S.

For each $s \in S$, assume there is a state-contingent *consequence domain* Y_s. Then, for each event $E \subseteq S$, the Cartesian product space $Y^E := \prod_{s \in E} Y_s$, or equivalently the space of mappings $E \ni s \mapsto y_s \in Y_s$, is the domain of *contingent consequences* conditional upon the event E.[18] Each point $\gamma^E := \langle \gamma_s \rangle_{s \in E} \in Y^E$ then represents a pattern of uncertain consequences, given that E is known to occur. By definition, the event S is always known to occur.

In dynamic decision problems, it is important to keep track of what event is known to the decision maker at each stage. The relevant version of the ordinality hypothesis, in fact, is that for each event $E \subseteq S$, there is a *conditional preference ordering* $\succsim^E$ given E defined on the domain Y^E. Thus, we shall need to consider the whole family $\succsim^E (\emptyset \neq E \subseteq S)$ of conditional preference orderings as E varies over all possible events in S.

2.6.3 The Sure-Thing Principle

One of Savage's (1954) main axioms is the following:[19]

Definition 2.19   The family $\succsim^E$ ($\emptyset \neq E \subseteq S$) of conditional preference orderings satisfies the *sure-thing principle* (or STP) provided that whenever the two non-empty events $E, E' \subseteq S$ are disjoint, and whenever $a^E, b^E \in Y^E, c^{E'} \in Y^{E'}$, then the preference relation between $(a^E, c^{E' \setminus E})$ and $(b^E, c^{E' \setminus E})$ in $Y^{E \cup E'} = Y^E \times Y^{E' \setminus E}$ satisfies

$$(a^E, c^{E'}) \succsim^{E \cup E'} (b^E, c^{E'}) \iff a^E \succsim^E b^E. \tag{2.52}$$

The rest of this section is devoted to providing an axiomatic foundation for this principle that is similar to those we have already provided for both ordinality and vNM independence.

2.6.4 Axioms for the Sure-Thing Principle

2.6.4.1 A Family of Simple Trees with Uncertain Consequences

As in Sections 2.4.3 and 2.5.1, we are again going to introduce a parametric family of decision trees. This time our goal is to develop variations of Cubitt's (1996) axioms that apply to choice under uncertainty, and which together imply Savage's sure-thing principle.

The parameters we use are a pair of disjoint events $E, E' \subseteq S$, and a triple of contingent consequences $a^E, b^E \in Y^E, c^{E'} \in Y^{E'}$, as in the statement of STP. For each value of the parameter vector $(E, E'; a^E, b^E, c^{E'})$ there will again be four closely related trees

$$\bar{T}_{E,E';a^E,b^E,c^{E'}}, \quad T'_{E,E';a^E,b^E,c^{E'}}, \quad \check{T}_{E,E';a^E,b^E,c^{E'}}(n_1), \quad \text{and} \quad \hat{T}_{E,E';a^E,b^E,c^{E'}}.$$

---

[18] This choice reveals a preference for Debreu's (1959) terminology, in connection with contingent consumption vectors, over Savage's (1954), who uses the term *act* instead.

[19] Technically, we have simplified Savage's axiom by excluding "null events" E (relative to S) with the property that $(a^E, c^{S \setminus E}) \sim^S (b^E, c^{S \setminus E})$ for all $a^E, b^E \in Y^E$. One logical implication of the consequentialist approach is that an event E can be null only if $a^E \sim^E b^E$ for all $a^E, b^E \in Y^E$. In Hammond (1998b) the axiom we have stated here is called STP*, in contrast to Savage's which is called STP.

The four trees are illustrated in Figures 2.5 and 2.6. Rather than chance nodes, the three nodes n_0, n_1' and n_2' marked by diamonds are *event nodes* at which "Nature" makes a move, and the decision maker discovers which of the two disjoint events E or E' has occurred. Each terminal node of each tree has been marked by a contingent consequence in the appropriate domain, Y^E or $Y^{E'}$, depending on what happened at the previous event node.

The trees can be used to illustrate Ellsberg's example for the special case when one ignores the information that 30 of the 90 balls in the urn are red. To do so, take the events $E := \{red, black\}$ and $E' := \{yellow\}$, along with contingent consequences $a^E = (100, 0)$, $b^E = (0, 100)$, and then $c^{E'}$ either 0 in the case when the choice is between L_1 and L_2, or 100 in the other case when the choice is between L_3 and L_4.

2.6.4.2 Preliminaries

Because of the need to keep track of what states $s \in S$ are possible, we must adapt the notation that was introduced in Section 2.4.3.1 for decision trees with deterministic consequences, and in Section 2.5.1.1 for decision trees with risky consequences.

Definition 2.20 In each of the four decision trees T of Figures 2.5 and 2.6, and for each of the nodes n of T, let:

1. $N_{+1}(T, n)$ denote the set of nodes that immediately succeed n in the tree T;

2. $E(T, n) \subset S$ denote the event containing those states $s \in S$ that are possible after reaching node n in the tree T;

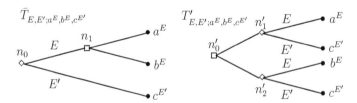

Figure 2.5 The decision tree $\bar{T}_{E,E';a^E,b^E,c^{E'}}$ and the variation $T'_{E,E';a^E,b^E,c^{E'}}$.

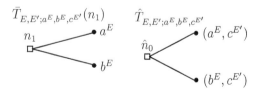

Figure 2.6 The continuation $\bar{T}_{E,E';a^E,b^E,c^{E'}}(n_1)$ and the reduction $\hat{T}_{E,E';a^E,b^E,c^{E'}}$.

3. $F(T, n) \subset Y^{E(T,n)}$ denote the *feasible set* of contingent consequences given that node n has been reached in decision tree T;

4. $\Psi(T, n) \subseteq F(T, n)$ denote the *planned set* contingent of consequences at node n.

Note that, in the four trees $\bar{T}, T', \bar{T}(n_1)$ and $\hat{T}$ of Figures 2.5 and 2.6, the relevant values of $E(T, n)$ and of $F(T, n)$ are obvious at the terminal nodes because they correspond to the contingent consequences; at the different non-terminal nodes of these trees, however, they are given:

1. at the node n_1 of trees $\bar{T}$ and $\bar{T}(n_1)$, by

$$E(\bar{T}, n_1) = E(\bar{T}(n_1), n_1) = E \text{ and } F(\bar{T}, n_1) = F(\bar{T}(n_1), n_1) = \{a^E, b^E\}$$

2. at all the other nonterminal nodes, by $E(T, n) = E \cup E'$, and

$$F(T', n_1') = \{(a^E, c^{E'})\}; F(T', n_2') = \{(b^E, c^{E'})\}$$

$$F(\bar{T}, n_0) = F(\bar{T}, n_1) \times \{c^{E'}\} = \{a^E, b^E\} \times \{c^{E'}\} = \{(a^E, c^{E'}), (b^E, c^{E'})\}$$

$$F(T', n_0') = F(T', n_1') \cup F(T', n_2') = \{(a^E, c^{E'}), (b^E, c^{E'})\}$$

Note that at any event node, the feasible sets all satisfy the equality

$$F(T, n) = \prod_{n' \in N_{+1}(n)} F(T, n') \tag{2.53}$$

whose right-hand side is the Cartesian product. This is the general rule for folding back the feasible sets at an event node. Of course, we still have the folding back rule $F(T, n) = \cup_{n' \in N_{+1}(n)} F(T, n')$ when n is a decision node.

2.6.4.3 Reduction of Compound Events

The two trees $T' = T'_{E,E';a^E,b^E,c^{E'}}$ in Figure 2.5 and $\hat{T} = \hat{T}_{E,E';a^E,b^E,c^{E'}}$ in Figure 2.6 both start with a decision node. In $\hat{T}$ a move at the initial decision node $\hat{n}_0$ leads directly to one of the two contingent consequences $(a^E, c^{E'})$ or $(b^E, c^{E'})$; in T' a move at the initial decision node n_0' leads instead to one of the two immediately succeeding event nodes n_1' or n_2'. But at both these event nodes Nature makes a move resulting in either the event E or the event E'. In either case, when the consequences of this move by Nature are folded back in the obvious way, the final result is again one of the two contingent consequences $(a^E, c^{E'})$ or $(b^E, c^{E'})$.

The following axiom requires that, because the differences between T' and $\hat{T}$ are essentially irrelevant, there should be no difference in the planned consequence sets $\Psi(T', n_0')$ and $\Psi(\hat{T}, \hat{n}_0)$.

Definition 2.21 Given the two decision trees $T' = T'_{E,E';a^E,b^E,c^{E'}}$ in Figure 2.5 and $\hat{T} = \hat{T}_{E,E';a^E,b^E,c^{E'}}$ in Figure 2.6, say that *reduction of compound events* is satisfied provided that the two planned consequence sets $\Psi(T', n_0')$ and $\Psi(\hat{T}, \hat{n}_0)$ coincide.

2.6.4.4 Dynamic Consistency at an Event Node

Consider again the decision tree $\bar{T}$ shown in Figure 2.5. Regardless of what is planned at node n_0, the decision maker will be taken to decision node n_1 in case the event E occurs, as opposed to E'. It should also be anticipated that a specific non-empty subset $\Psi(\bar{T}, n_1) \subseteq \{a^E, b^E\}$ will be selected at that node.

With $c^{E'}$ fixed, we now require the bijection $y^E \leftrightarrow (y^E, c^{E'})$ between the two sets $F(\bar{T}, n_1)$ and $F(\bar{T}, n_0)$ to induce a correspondence between the two planned consequence sets $\Psi(\bar{T}, n_1)$ and $\Psi(\bar{T}, n_0)$. Formally:

Definition 2.22 The planned consequence sets $\Psi(\bar{T}, n_0)$ and $\Psi(\bar{T}, n_1)$ at the two non-terminal nodes of the tree $\bar{T} = \bar{T}_{E,E';a^E,b^E,c^{E'}}$ of Figure 2.5 are *dynamically consistent at event node n_0* provided that

$$a^E \in \Psi(\bar{T}, n_1) \Longleftrightarrow (a^E, c^{E'}) \in \Psi(\bar{T}, n_0)$$
$$\text{and} \quad b^E \in \Psi(\bar{T}, n_1) \Longleftrightarrow (b^E, c^{E'}) \in \Psi(\bar{T}, n_0) \tag{2.54}$$

or equivalently, provided that $\Psi(\bar{T}, n_0) = \Psi(\bar{T}, n_1) \times \{c^{E'}\}$.

2.6.4.5 Separability after an Event Node

As in Sections 2.4.3.3 and 2.5.1.5, separability requires the "continuation subtree" $\bar{T}(n_1)$ of tree $\bar{T} = \bar{T}_{E,E';a^E,b^E,c^{E'}}$ that starts at node n_1 to be treated as if it were a full decision tree. The difference from before is that here the preceding node is an event node.

Here is a formal definition for an arbitrary finite tree T of separability at an event node n of T.

Definition 2.23 Given any decision tree T, the planned consequence set $\Psi(T, n)$ at a chance node satisfies *separability after the event node n* provided that it equals the planned consequence set $\Psi(T(n), n)$ at the initial node n of the continuation subtree $T(n)$.

2.6.4.6 Timing Invariance with Uncertainty

Consider once again the two decision trees $\bar{T} = \bar{T}_{E,E';a^E,b^E,c^{E'}}$ and $T' = T'_{E,E';a^E,b^E,c^{E'}}$ shown in Figure 2.5. The calculations in Section 2.6.4.2 already imply that the sets

$F(\bar{T}, n_0)$ and $F(T', n_0')$ must be equal. The only difference between these two trees is that in $\bar{T}$, the move by Nature that picks "up" in event E and "down" in event E' precedes the decision node, whereas this timing is reversed in T'. We introduce the following counterpart of the timing reversal condition stated in Section 2.5.1.6.

Definition 2.24   Given the two decision trees $\bar{T} = \bar{T}_{E,E';a^E,b^E,c^{E'}}$ and $T' = T'_{E,E';a^E,b^E,c^{E'}}$ shown in Figure 2.5, which differ only in the timing of the decision and event nodes, say that there is *timing invariance under uncertainty* provided that the two planned consequence sets $\Psi(\bar{T}, n_0)$ and $\Psi(T', n_0')$ coincide.

2.6.5 A Precursor of the Sure-Thing Principle

We now have the following useful result:

Lemma 2.12   *Given any pair of disjoint events $E, E' \subseteq S$, and any triple of contingent consequences $a^E, b^E \in Y^E$, $c^{E'} \in Y^{E'}$, consider the four decision trees $\bar{T}_{E,E';a^E,b^E,c^{E'}}$, $T'_{E,E';a^E,b^E,c^{E'}}$, $\bar{T}_{E,E';a^E,b^E,c^{E'}}(n_1)$, and $\hat{T}_{E,E';a^E,b^E,c^{E'}}$ as shown in Figures 2.5 and 2.6. Suppose that the planned consequence sets $\Psi(T, n)$ at all the nonterminal nodes n of each tree T among these four satisfy: (i) reduction of compound events; (ii) dynamic consistency at an event node; (iii) separability after an event node; (iv) timing invariance under uncertainty. Then the two planned consequence sets $\Psi(\hat{T}, \hat{n}_0)$ and $\Psi(\bar{T}(n_1), n_1)$ in the reduced trees $\hat{T}$ and $\bar{T}(n_1)$ of Figure 2.6 satisfy*

$$\Psi(\hat{T}, \hat{n}_0) = \Psi(\bar{T}(n_1), n_1) \times \{c^{E'}\}. \tag{2.55}$$

Proof   Applying the four conditions (i)–(iv) one after another yields successively each equality in the chain

$$\Psi(\hat{T}, \hat{n}_0) = \Psi(T', n_0') = \Psi(\bar{T}, n_0) = \Psi(\bar{T}, n_1) \times \{c^{E'}\}$$
$$= \Psi(\bar{T}(n_1), n_1) \times \{c^{E'}\} \tag{2.56}$$

from which (2.55) follows trivially.   □

We can now show that appropriate versions of the three axioms introduced in Sections 2.4.3.2–2.4.3.4 as well as here are sufficient for ordinality and a strengthened version of Savage's sure-thing principle.

Theorem 2.13   *Suppose that:*

1. *for each event $E \subset S$, the hypotheses of Theorem 2.5 are satisfied whenever $F \subset Y^E$ is a feasible set consisting of at least 3 distinct contingent consequences;*

2. *the hypotheses of Lemma 2.12 are satisfied.*
Then there exists a family $\succsim^E$ ($\emptyset \neq E \subseteq S$) of conditional preference orderings on the respective domains Y^E which satisfy the sure-thing principle, and also have the property that, in every reduced form finite decision tree $\hat{T}$ whose terminal nodes have consequences in Y^E, the planned consequence set satisfies

$$\Psi(\hat{T}, \hat{n}_0) = C^{\succsim^E}(F(\hat{T}, \hat{n}_0)) \tag{2.57}$$

where $\mathcal{F}(Y^E) \ni F \mapsto C^{\succsim^E}(F)$ is the ordinal choice function on non-empty finite subsets $F \subset Y^E$ that is generated by the ordering $\succsim^E$.

Proof For each event $E \subseteq S$, applying Theorem 2.5 to the domain Y^E instead of Y implies that the ordering $\succsim^E$ exists on Y^E and (2.57) is satisfied.

Given any two disjoint events $E, E' \subseteq S$ and any $a^E, b^E \in Y^E$, $c^{E'} \in Y^{E'}$, applying Lemma 2.12 implies that for the two decision trees $\bar{T}(n_1) = \bar{T}_{\lambda,\mu,\nu;\alpha}(n_1)$ and $\hat{T} = \hat{T}_{\lambda,\mu,\nu;\alpha}$ shown in Figure 2.4, one has

$$F(\bar{T}(n_1), n_1) = \{a^E, b^E\} \quad \text{and} \quad F(\hat{T}, \hat{n}_0) = F(\bar{T}(n_1), n_1) \times \{c^{E'}\}.$$

By definition of each ordering $\succsim^E$, it follows that

$$\begin{aligned}
a^E \in \Psi(\bar{T}(n_1), n_1) &\Longleftrightarrow a^E \succsim^E b^E \quad \text{and} \\
(a^E, c^{E'}) \in \Psi(\hat{T}, \hat{n}_0) &\Longleftrightarrow (a^E, c^{E'}) \succsim^{E \cup E'} (b^E, c^{E'}).
\end{aligned} \tag{2.58}$$

But equation (2.55) implies that

$$a^E \in \Psi(T(n_1), n_1) \Longleftrightarrow (a^E, c^{E'}) \in \Psi(\hat{T}, \hat{n}_0).$$

Combining this with (2.58) yields

$$a^E \succsim^E b^E \Longleftrightarrow (a^E, c^{E'}) \succsim^{E \cup E'} (b^E, c^{E'})$$

which is precisely the STP axiom as stated in (2.52). □

2.6.6 Behavior and Its Uncertain Consequences

2.6.6.1 Folding Back at Decision and Event Nodes

We begin by recalling the notation of Section 2.4.5.1, and introducing some new notation to recognize the unfolding of events as one passes through an event node. So at any decision node n of any tree T, one has:

1. a set $N_{+1}(T, n)$ of immediately succeeding nodes in the decision tree T;
2. a non-empty behavior set $\beta(T, n) \subseteq N_{+1}(T, n)$;
3. a non-empty set $E(T, n) \subset S$ of possible states;
4. a feasible consequence set $F(T, n) \subseteq Y^{E(T,n)}$;
5. a consequence choice set $\Phi(T, n) \subseteq F(T, n)$ induced by behavior $\beta(T, n')$ at all nodes n' of the continuation subtree $T(n)$ whose initial node is n.

As in Section 2.4.5.1, we assume that at any decision node n of any decision tree T, the feasible set $F(T, n)$ and the consequence choice set $\Phi(T, n)$ satisfy the folding back rule (2.30), reproduced below for convenience:

$$F(T, n) = \bigcup_{n' \in N_{+1}(T,n)} F(T, n') \text{ and } \Phi(T, n) = \bigcup_{n' \in \beta(T(n),n)} \Phi(T, n').$$

The folding back rules at an event node n of any decision tree T allowing uncertainty include an extra rule for the sets $E(T, n)$ of possible states. They take the form

$$F(T, n) = \prod_{n' \in N_{+1}(T,n)} F(T, n')$$

$$\Phi(T, n) = \prod_{n' \in \beta(T(n),n)} \Phi(T, n') \tag{2.59}$$

$$\text{and} \quad E(T, n) = \bigcup_{n' \in N_{+1}(T,n)} E(T, n').$$

The third equation reflects the fact that Nature's move at the event node n generates a partition of the set of states $E(T, n)$ into the collection $\{E(T, n') \mid n' \in N_{+1}(T, n)\}$. In the first two equations, the left-hand side is a subset of $Y^{E(T,n)} := \prod_{n' \in N_{+1}(T,n)} Y^{E(T,n')}$, so matches the right-hand side as one would expect.

2.6.6.2 Implications of Consequentialist Invariance

The following result demonstrates that consequentialist invariance as defined in Section 2.4.5.1 implies that the consequence choice sets $\Phi(T, n)$ satisfy our axioms for the sure-thing principle.

Theorem 2.14 *Given the four decision trees shown in Figures 2.5 and 2.6, suppose that behavior $\beta(T, n)$ and the consequence choice sets $\Phi(T, n)$ at all the nodes n of these trees satisfy consequentialist invariance. Then the consequence choice sets $\Phi(T, n)$ also satisfy reduction of compound events, dynamic consistency at the event node n_0, separability after the event node n_0, and timing invariance under uncertainty.*

Proof As in Section 2.6.4.2, one has $F(T', n_0') = F(\hat{T}, \hat{n}_0) = \{a^E, b^E\} \times \{c^{E'}\}$. Consequentialist invariance then implies that $\Phi(T', n_0') = \Psi(\hat{T}, \hat{n}_0)$, which is the condition for the consequence choice sets to satisfy reduction of compound events.

The relevant second folding back rule in (2.59) is identical to the equation $\Phi(\bar{T}, n_0) = \Phi(\bar{T}, n_1) \times \{c^E\}$ in Definition 2.22, so dynamic consistency at the event node n_0 is satisfied.

Next, because $F(\bar{T}, n_1) = F(\bar{T}(n_1), n_1) = \{a^E, b^E\}$, consequentialist invariance implies that $\Phi(\bar{T}, n_1) = \Phi(\bar{T}(n_1), n_1)$, which is the condition for separability after the event node n_0.

Finally, because $F(\bar{T}, n_0) = F(T', n_0') = \{a^E, b^E\} \times \{c^{E'}\}$, consequentialist invariance implies that $\Phi(\bar{T}, n_0) = \Phi(T', n_0')$, which is the condition for timing invariance under uncertainty.   □

2.6.7 Ordinal Dynamic Programming under Uncertainty

Let $\mathcal{T}(S; Y^S)$ denote the domain of all finite decision trees T with decision and event nodes for which there exists some event $E \subset S$ such that the initial set of states is $E(T, n_0) = E$, and also $F(T, n) \subset Y^{E(T,n)}$ at every node of T.

The ordinal dynamic programming result stated as Theorem 2.11 of Section 2.5.4 for the case when decisions have risky consequences has the following counterpart for decisions under uncertainty, when the decision tree has event rather than chance nodes.

Theorem 2.15 *Let $\succsim^E$ ($\emptyset \neq E \subseteq S$) be any family of conditional preference orderings on the respective domains Y^E that satisfy the sure-thing principle. For each event $E \subseteq S$, let $C^{\succsim^E}$ denote the ordinal choice function on the domain $\mathcal{F}(Y^E)$ of non-empty finite subsets of Y^E that is induced by $\succsim^E$. Then there exists a behavior rule $(T, n) \mapsto \beta(T, n)$ defined on the domain $\mathcal{T}(S; Y^S)$ having the property that the induced consequence choice sets, which are calculated by applying the folding back rules (2.30) and (2.59), satisfy consequentialist invariance with*

$$\Psi(T, n) = C^{\succsim^{E(T,n))}}(F(T, n)) \tag{2.60}$$

at every node n of every tree T in $\mathcal{T}(S; Y^S)$.

Proof   See Hammond (1998b) for a proof of a comparable result in a more complicated setting that combines risk with uncertainty.   □

2.6.7.1 Experimental Tests: Ellsberg and Beyond

The vNM independence axiom has been tested experimentally very often; despite Ellsberg's early example, the sure-thing principle has been tested much more rarely, especially in a dynamic setting.

A summary of early empirical evidence for and against the sure-thing principle appeared in Camerer and Weber (1992). They identify two kinds of experimental study. The first kind, represented by Dominiak et al. (2012), sticks quite closely to Ellsberg's (1961) original example. The second kind of study focuses on phenomena related to attitudes towards "ambiguity," following a more modern interpretation of the Ellsberg example. A prominent example is the work of Baillon et al. (2011) on Machina's (2009) extension of that famous example. Other works on ambiguity are too numerous to discuss here, and are anyway covered elsewhere in this *Handbook*.

REFERENCES

Abdellaoui, M., Diecidue, E., Öncüler, A., 2011. Risk preferences at different time periods: an experimental investigation. Management Science 57, 975–987.

Ainslie, G.W., 1992. Picoeconomics. Cambridge University Press, Cambridge.

Akerlof, G.A., 1991. Procrastination and obedience. American Economic Review, Papers and Proceedings 81, 1–19.

Allais, M., 1953. Le comportement de l'homme rationnel devant le risque: critique des postulats et axiomes de l'école Américaine. Econometrica 21, 503–546.

Allais, M., 1979. The so-called Allais paradox and rational decisions under uncertainty. In: Allais, M., Hagen, O. (Eds.), Expected Utility Hypotheses and the Allais Paradox. Reidel, Dordrecht.

Anscombe, F.J., Aumann, R.J., 1963. A definition of subjective probability. Annals of Mathematical Statistics 34, 199–205.

Anscombe, G.E.M., 1958. Modern moral philosophy. Philosophy 33, 1–19.

Arrow, K.J., 1951a. Alternative approaches to the theory of choice in risk-taking situations. Econometrica 19, 404–437.

Arrow, K.J., 1951b. Social Choice and Individual Values. John Wiley, New York (2nd edn 1963).

Arrow, K.J., 1959. Rational choice functions and orderings. Economica 26, 121–127.

Arrow, K.J., 1965. The theory of risk aversion. In: Aspects of the Theory of Risk Bearing. Yrjo Jahnssonin Saatio, Helsinki. Reprinted in: Essays in the Theory of Risk Bearing (1971, pp. 90–109). Markham Publ. Co., Chicago.

Baillon, A., L'Haridon, O., Placido, L., 2011. Ambiguity models and the Machina paradoxes. American Economic Review 101, 1547–1560.

Barkan, R., Busemeyer, J.R., 2003. Modeling dynamic inconsistency with a changing reference point. Journal of Behavioral Decision Making 16, 235–255.

Barro, R.J., 1999. Ramsey meets Laibson in the neoclassical growth model. Quarterly Journal of Economics 114, 1125–1152.

Baucells, M., Heukamp, F., 2012. Probability and time tradeoff. Management Science 58, 831–842.

Bernheim, B.D., Rangel, A., 2007. Behavioral public economics: welfare and policy analysis with non-standard decision-makers. In: Diamond, P., Vartiainen, H. (Eds.), Behavioral Economics and its Applications. Princeton University Press, Princeton.

Bernoulli, D., 1738. Specimen theoriae novae de mensura sortis. In: Commentarii Academiae Scientiarum Imperialis Petropolitanae; translated by Sommer, L. (1954) as Exposition of a new theory on the measurement of risk. Econometrica 22, 23–36.

Blackorby, C., Nissen, D., Primont, D., Russell, R.R., 1973. Consistent intertemporal decision making. Review of Economic Studies 40, 239–248.

Bleichrodt, H., Rohde, K.I.M., Wakker, P.P., 2009. Non-hyperbolic time inconsistency. Games and Economic Behavior 66, 27–38.

Bordes, G., 1976. Consistency, rationality, and collective choice. Review of Economic Studies 43, 451–457.

Busemeyer, J.R., Weg, E., Barkan, R., Li, X., Ma, Z., 2000. Dynamic and consequential consistency of choices between paths of decision trees. Journal of Experimental Psychology: General 129, 530–545.

Butler, D.J., Loomes, G.C., 2007. Imprecision as an account of the preference reversal phenomenon. American Economic Review 97, 277–297.

Camerer, C., 1995. Individual decision making. In: Kagel, J., Roth, A.E. (Eds.), Handbook of Experimental Economics. Princeton University Press, Princeton.

Camerer, C., Weber, M., 1992. Recent developments in modelling preferences: uncertainty and ambiguity. Journal of Risk and Uncertainty 5, 325370.

Chernoff, H., 1954. Rational selection of decision functions. Econometrica 22, 423–443.

Cooter, R., Rappoport, P., 1984. Were the ordinalists wrong about welfare economics? Journal of Economic Literature 22, 507–530.

Cramer, G., 1728. Letter to Nicholas Bernoulli; extracts printed in Bernoulli (1738).

Cubitt, R.P., 1996. Rational dynamic choice and expected utility theory. Oxford Economic Papers 48, 1–19.

Cubitt, R.P., Ruiz-Martos, M., Starmer, C., 2012. Are bygones bygones? Theory and Decision 73, 185–202.

Cubitt, R.P., Starmer, C., Sugden, R., 1998. Dynamic choice and the common ratio effect: an experimental investigation. Economic Journal 108, 1362–1380.

Cubitt, R.P., Starmer, C., Sugden, R., 2004. Dynamic decisions under uncertainty: some recent evidence from economics and psychology. In: Brocas, I., Carrillo, J.D. (Eds.), The Psychology of Economic Decisions, vol. II. Oxford University Press.

Cubitt, R.P., Sugden, R., 2001. Dynamic decision making under uncertainty: an experimental investigation of choices between accumulator gambles. Journal of Risk and Uncertainty 22, 103–128.

Dalkey, N.C., 1949. A numerical scale for partially ordered utilities. RAND Corporation, Santa Monica, CA. RM-296.

Dasgupta, P., 1974. On some alternative criteria for justice between generations. Journal of Public Economics 3, 405–423.

Dasgupta, P., Maskin, E., 2005. Uncertainty and hyperbolic discounting. American Economic Review 95, 1290–1299.

Debreu, G., 1959. Theory of Value: An Axiomatic Analysis of Economic Equilibrium. Yale University Press, New Haven and London.

Dominiak, A., Dürsch, P., Lefort, J.-P., 2012. A dynamic Ellsberg urn experiment. Games and Economic Behavior 75, 625–638.

Ebert, J., Prelec, D., 2007. The fragility of time: time-insensitivity and valuation of the near and far future. Management Science 53, 1423–1438.

Ellsberg, D., 1961. Risk, ambiguity and the Savage axioms. Quarterly Journal of Economics 75, 643–669.

Epper, T., Fehr-Duda, H., Bruhin, A., 2011. Viewing the future through a warped lens: why uncertainty generates hyperbolic discounting. Journal of Risk and Uncertainty 43, 169–203.

Farquharson, R., 1969. Theory of Voting. Blackwell, Oxford.

Fishburn, P.C., 1970. Utility Theory for Decision Making. John Wiley and Sons, New York.

Fishburn, P.C., Rubinstein, A., 1982. Time preference. International Economic Review 23, 677–694.

Fishburn, P.C., Wakker, P.P., 1995. The invention of the independence condition for preferences. Management Science 41, 1130–1144.

Frederick, S., Loewenstein, G., O'Donoghue, T., 2002. Time discounting and time preference: a critical review. Journal of Economic Literature 40, 351–401.

Gigerenzer, G., Todd, P.M., The ABC Research Group, 1999. Simple Heuristics That Make Us Smart. Oxford University Press, New York.

Grether, D.M., Plott, C.R., 1979. Economic theory of choice and the preference reversal phenomenon. American Economic Review 69, 623–639.

Halevy, Y., 2008. Strotz meets Allais: diminishing impatience and certainty effect. American Economic Review 98, 1145–1162.

Hammond, P.J., 1973. Consistent Planning and Intertemporal Welfare Economics. Ph.D. dissertation, University of Cambridge.

Hammond, P.J., 1976. Changing tastes and coherent dynamic choice. Review of Economic Studies 43, 159–173.

Hammond, P.J., 1977. Dynamic restrictions on metastatic choice. Economica 44, 337–350.

Hammond, P.J., 1983. Ex-post optimality as a dynamically consistent objective for collective choice under uncertainty. In: Pattanaik, P.K., Salles, M. (Eds.), Social Choice and Welfare. North-Holland.

Hammond, P.J., 1988a. Consequentialist foundations for expected utility. Theory and Decision 25, 25–78.

Hammond, P.J., 1988b. Orderly decision theory: a comment on Professor Seidenfeld. Economics and Philosophy 4, 292–297.

Hammond, P.J., 1989. Consistent plans, consequentialism, and expected utility. Econometrica 57, 1445–1449.

Hammond, P.J., 1998a. Objective expected utility: a consequentialist perspective. In: S. Barberà, S., Hammond, P.J., Seidl, C. (Eds.), Handbook of Utility Theory Volume I: Principles. Kluwer, Dordrecht, The Netherlands.

Hammond, P.J., 1998b. Subjective expected utility. In: Barberà, S., Hammond, P.J., Seidl, C. (Eds.), Handbook of Utility Theory Volume I: Principles. Kluwer, Dordrecht, The Netherlands.

Harris, C.J., Laibson, D.I., 2001. Dynamic choices of hyperbolic consumers. Econometrica 69, 935–957.

Hayashi, T., 2003. Quasi-stationary cardinal utility and present bias. Journal of Economic Theory 112, 343–352.

Herstein, I.N., Milnor, J., 1953. An axiomatic approach to measurable utility. Econometrica 21, 291–297.

Hey, J.D., Lotito, G., 2009. Naive, resolute or sophisticated? A study of dynamic decision making. Journal of Risk and Uncertainty 38, 1–25.

Hey, J.D., Paradiso, M., 2006. Preferences over temporal frames in dynamic decision problems: an experimental investigation. The Manchester School 74, 123–137.

Huber, J., Payne, J.W., Puto, C., 1982. Adding asymmetrically dominated alternatives: violations of regularity and the similarity hypothesis. Journal of Consumer Research 9, 90–98.

Inagaki, M., 1970. Optimal Economic Growth: Shifting Finite versus Infinite Time Horizon. North-Holland, Amsterdam.

Isoni, A., Loomes, G., Sugden, R., 2011. The willingness to pay—willingness to accept gap, the 'endowment effect', subject misconceptions, and experimental procedures for eliciting valuations: comment. American Economic Review 101, 991–1011.

Jensen, N.E., 1967. An introduction to Bernoullian utility theory, I: utility functions. Swedish Journal of Economics 69, 163–183.

Johnson, J.G., Busemeyer, J.R., 2001. Multiple-stage decision-making: the effect of planning horizon length on dynamic consistency. Theory and Decision 51, 217–246.

Kahneman, D., Tversky, A., 1979. Prospect theory: an analysis of decision under risk. Econometrica 47, 263–291.

Karni, E., Schmeidler, D., 1991. Atemporal dynamic consistency and expected utility. Journal of Economic Theory 54, 401–408.

Klein, D.B., 1990. The microfoundations of rules vs. discretion. Constitutional Political Economy 1, 1–19.

Knight, F.H., 1921. Risk, Uncertainty, and Profit. Hart, Schaffner & Marx, Houghton Mifflin Company, Boston, MA.

Koopmans, T.C., 1960. Stationary ordinal utility and impatience. Econometrica 28, 287–309.

Krusell, P., Smith Jr., A.A., 2003. Consumption-savings decisions with quasi-geometric discounting. Econometrica 71, 365–375.

Kydland, F.E., Prescott, E.C., 1977. Rules rather than discretion: the inconsistency of optimal plans. Journal of Political Economy 85, 473–492.

Laibson, D.I., 1997. Golden eggs and hyperbolic discounting. Quarterly Journal of Economics 112, 443–477.

Laibson, D.I., 1998. Life-cycle consumption and hyperbolic discounting. European Economic Review 42, 861–871.

LaValle, I.H., Wapman, K.R., 1986. Rolling back decision trees requires the independence axiom! Management Science 32, 382–385.

Leonard, R.J., 1995. From parlor games to social science: von Neumann, Morgenstern, and the creation of game theory 1928–1944. Journal of Economic Literature 33, 730–761.

Lichtenstein, S., Slovic, P., 1971. Reversals of preference between bids and choices in gambling decisions. Journal of Experimental Psychology 89, 46–55.

List, J.A., 2002. Preference reversals of a different kind: the more is less phenomenon. American Economic Review 92, 1636–1643.

Loewenstein, G.F., Prelec, D., 1992. Anomalies in intertemporal choice: evidence and an interpretation. Quarterly Journal of Economics 107, 573–597.

Loomes, G., Starmer, C., Sugden, R., 2010. Preference reversals and disparities between willingness to pay and willingness to accept in repeated markets. Journal of Economic Psychology 31, 374–387.

Machina, M.J., 1989. Dynamic consistency and non-expected utility models of choice under uncertainty. Journal of Economic Literature 27, 1622–1688.

Machina, M.J., 2009. Risk, ambiguity, and the rank-dependence axioms. American Economic Review 99, 385–392.

Machina, M.J., Schmeidler, D., 1992. A more robust definition of subjective probability. Econometrica 60, 745–780.

Malinvaud, E., 1952. Note on von Neumann–Morgenstern's strong independence axiom. Econometrica 20, 679.

Manzini, P., Mariotti, M., 2007. Sequentially rationalizable choice. American Economic Review 97, 1824–1839.

Marschak, J.A., 1950. Rational behavior, uncertain prospects, and measurable utility. Econometrica 18, 111–141.

Mas-Colell, A., Whinston, M.W., Green, J.R., 1995. Microeconomic Theory. Oxford University Press.

McClennen, E.F., 1986. Prisoner's dilemma and resolute choice. In: Campbell, R., Sowden, L. (Eds.), Paradoxes of Rationality and Cooperation. University of British Columbia Press, Vancouver.

McClennen, E.F., 1990. Rationality and Dynamic Choice: Foundational Explorations. Cambridge University Press, Cambridge.

Moulin, H., 1979. Dominance solvable voting schemes. Econometrica 47, 1337–1351.

Nash, J.F., 1950. The bargaining problem. Econometrica 18, 155–162.

Nebout, A., Dubois, D., 2011. When Allais meets Ulysses: dynamic axioms and the common ratio effect. Research Paper 2011–02, LAMETA Working Paper Series, University of Montpellier. <http://www.asfee.fr/sites/default/files/201102asfee.pdf>.

Noussair, C., Wu, P., 2006. Risk tolerance in the present and the future: an experimental study. Managerial and Decision Economics 27, 401–412.

O'Donoghue, T., Rabin, M., 1999a. Doing it now or later. American Economic Review 89, 103–124.

O'Donoghue, T., Rabin, M., 1999b. Incentives for procrastinators. Quarterly Journal of Economics 114, 769–816.

O'Donoghue, T., Rabin, M., 2001. Choice and procrastination. Quarterly Journal of Economics 116, 121–160.

Peleg, B., Yaari, M.E., 1973. On the existence of a consistent course of action when tastes are changing. Review of Economic Studies 40, 391–401.

Phelps, E.S., Pollak, R.A., 1968. On second-best national saving and game-equilibrium growth. Review of Economic Studies 35, 185–199.

Plott, C.R., Zeiler, K., 2005. The willingness to pay–willingness to accept gap, the 'endowment effect', subject misconceptions, and experimental procedures for eliciting valuations. American Economic Review 95, 530–545.

Pollak, R.A., 1968. Consistent planning. Review of Economic Studies 35, 201–208.

Pratt, J.W., 1964. Risk aversion in the small and in the large. Econometrica 32, 122–136.

Quiggin, J., Horowitz, J., 1995. Time and risk. Journal of Risk And Uncertainty 10, 37–55.

Raiffa, H., 1961. Risk, ambiguity, and the Savage axioms: comment. Quarterly Journal of Economics 75, 690–694.

Raiffa, H., 1968. Decision Analysis: Introductory Lectures on Choice Under Uncertainty. Addison-Wesley, Reading, MA, USA.

Samuelson, P.A., 1937. A note on measurement of utility. Review of Economic Studies 4, 155–161.

Samuelson, P.A., 1952. Probability, utility, and the independence axiom. Econometrica 20, 670–678.

Samuelson, P.A., 1983. Foundations of Economic Analysis. Harvard University Press (Enlarged Edtion).

Sarin, R., Wakker, P.P., 1994. Folding back in decision trees. Management Science 40, 625–628.

Savage, L.J., 1954. The Foundations of Statistics. Wiley, New York, USA.

Seidl, C., 2002. Preference reversal. Journal of Economic Surveys 16, 621–655.

Seidenfeld, T., 1988. Decision theory without 'independence' or without 'ordering': what is the difference?. Economics and Philosophy 4, 267–290.

Selten, R., 1965. Spieltheoretische Behandlung eines Oligopolmodells mit Nachfrageträgheit. Zeitschrift für die gesamte Staatswissenschaft 12, 201–324.

Sen, A.K., 1977. Social choice theory: a re-examination. Econometrica 45, 53–89.

Simonson, I., 1989. Choice based on reasons: the case of attraction and compromise effects. Journal of Consumer Research 16, 158–174.

Sobel, M.J., 1975. Ordinal dynamic programming. Management Science 21, 967–975.

Starmer, C., 2000. Developments in non-expected utility theory: the hunt for a descriptive theory of choice under risk. Journal of Economic Literature 38, 332–382.

Steele, K.S., 2010. What are the minimal requirements of rational choice? Arguments from the sequential-decision setting. Theory and Decision 68, 463–487.

Strotz, R.H., 1956. Myopia and inconsistency in dynamic utility maximization. Review of Economic Studies 23, 165–180.

Thaler, R.H., 1981. Some empirical evidence on dynamic inconsistency. Economics Letters 8, 201–207.

Thaler, R.H., Johnson, E.J., 1990. Gambling with the house money and trying to break even: the effects of prior outcomes on risky choice. Management Science 36, 643–660.

Tsetsos, K., Usher, M., Chater, N., 2010. Preference reversals in multiattribute choice. Psychological Review 117, 1275–1293.

Tversky, A., 1972. Choice by elimination. Journal of Mathematical Psychology 9, 341–367.

Tversky, A., Kahneman, D., 1992. Advances in prospect theory: cumulative representation of uncertainty. Journal of Risk and Uncertainty 5, 297–323.

Tversky, A., Sattath, S., Slovic, P., 1988. Contingent weighting in judgment and choice. Psychological Review 95, 371–384.

Tversky, A., Slovic, P., Kahneman, D., 1990. The causes of preference reversal. American Economic Review 80, 204–217.

Volij, O., 1994. Dynamic consistency, consequentialism and reduction of compound lotteries. Economics Letters 46, 121–129.

von Neumann, J., 1928. Zur Theorie der Gesellschaftsspiele. Mathematische Annalen 100, 295–320. translated as On the theory of games of strategy in: Luce, R.D., Tucker, A.W., (Eds.), 1959. Contributions to the Theory of Games, vol IV. Princeton University Press, Princeton.

von Neumann, J., Morgenstern, O., 1944. Theory of Games and Economic Behavior. Princeton University Press, Princeton (3rd edn. 1953).

Wakker, P.P., 1994. Separating marginal utility and probabilistic risk aversion. Theory and Decision 36, 1–44.

Wakker, P.P., 2001. Testing and characterizing properties of nonadditive measures through violations of the sure-thing principle. Econometrica 69, 1039–1059.

Wakker, P.P., 2010. Prospect Theory: For Risk and Ambiguity. Cambridge University Press, Cambridge, UK.

CHAPTER 3

The Theory of Risk and Risk Aversion

Jack Meyer
Department of Economics, Michigan State University, USA

Contents

Abstract

Risk and risk aversion are important concepts when modeling how to choose from or rank a set of random variables. This chapter reviews and summarizes the definitions and related findings concerning risk aversion and risk in both a mean-variance and an expected utility decision model context.

Keywords

Risk Aversion, Increases in Risk, Stochastic Dominance

JEL Classification Codes

D81

3.1 INTRODUCTION

Risk and risk aversion have been recognized and included in the scientific discussion of decision making under uncertainty for hundreds of years. The St. Petersburg Paradox presented by mathematician Daniel Bernoulli (1954) in 1738 is often mentioned when first introducing the topic. Bernoulli identifies a gamble that most persons would pay only a small sum to be allowed to participate in, but whose expected value is infinite. Bernoulli suggests diminishing marginal utility as a reason why this is the case.

Bernoulli describes the following gamble. Suppose a person receives an outcome of size 2 if flipping a fair coin results in heads on the first toss. The gamble ends if this occurs. Should a tail occur on the first toss, the gamble continues. When the coin is flipped a second time, if heads is observed, the payment is increased to 4, and the gamble ends. Should a tail occur on each of the first two tosses, the gamble continues

Handbook of the Economics of Risk and Uncertainty, Volume 1
ISSN 2211-7547, http://dx.doi.org/10.1016/B978-0-444-53685-3.00003-9

to a third toss, with the payoff and the continuation decision following this same pattern. The gamble continues until heads is first observed. The payment is 2^n when heads is first observed on the nth toss. The probability of heads occurring first on the nth toss of a fair coin is $\{1/2\}^n$. Thus, the expected value of this gamble is given by $\sum_{i=1}^{\infty}(2^i)(\frac{1}{2^i})$ which is not finite.

The paradox that Bernoulli is pointing out is that most persons are unwilling to pay more than a modest sum to participate in this gamble even though the expected value from participating in the gamble is infinite. Clearly, then, using only the expected value to rank gambles is not enough. Bernoulli uses the St. Petersburg Paradox to suggest that the gain in utility from additions to wealth diminishes as a person is wealthier. In fact he suggests that the utility function could be represented by the logarithmic function. Since this function is concave, this solution to the St. Petersburg Paradox has been pointed to as the first representation of risk aversion in an expected utility decision model.

The focus in this chapter is on how risk aversion and risk are represented in various decision models. The emphasis is overwhelmingly on the expected utility decision model discussed in Sections 3.3 to 3.5. The mean-variance decision model is also discussed, first in Section 3.2 and then again briefly at the end in Section 3.6.

3.2 THE MEAN-VARIANCE APPROACH TO RISK AND RISK AVERSION

3.2.1 Introduction

One of the primary alternatives to the expected utility decision model in applied economic analysis is the mean-variance decision model (M-V). In this model the risk associated with a random variable is measured by the variance.[1] The typical notation is to use μ to represent the mean or expected outcome from a random variable, and to use σ or σ^2 to represent the standard deviation, or variance, respectively. Any random variable for which σ is strictly greater than 0 is said to be risky. Only a degenerate random variable, one where μ occurs with certainty, is without risk.

Variance and aversion to variance have been used to represent risk and risk aversion for many years and continue to be used extensively especially in disciplines other than economics. Researchers in statistics regularly determine the minimum variance unbiased estimator of a parameter. Those in finance calculate and use the covariance of an asset's return with the market portfolio as a way to measure the portion of an asset's risk that cannot be eliminated by diversification. The price of risk is often given as the gain in expected return from assuming an additional unit of standard deviation. While economics uses the M-V decision model less often than it did before the expected utility decision model was fully developed, the M-V model is still employed in some areas and

---

[1] More often, the positive square root of this variance, the standard deviation, is used so that the unit of measure for risk and the unit of measure for the mean value are the same.

for certain questions. The version of the M-V decision model described in the following sections draws heavily on the writings of Markowitz (1952, 1959) and Tobin (1958).

3.2.2 The M-V Decision Model

The critical and powerful assumption that is made in the M-V decision model is that preferences over random variables can be represented by a utility or ranking function denoted $V(\sigma, \mu)$ that depends only on the mean and standard deviation of the possible outcomes. This ranking function represents an ordinal ranking of random variables, and thus the function $V(\sigma, \mu)$ is unique up to a positive monotonic transformation. The ordering over random variables represented by $V(\sigma, \mu)$ is complete; that is, all pairs of random variables can be ranked as one better than the other, or the decision maker is indifferent between the two random variables. The focus in this M-V decision model is on just two moments of the probability distributions. All other moments and other properties of these probability distributions such as the median, the skewness, the kurtosis, or the smallest possible outcome play no separate role in the ranking of random variables.

It is usual in economic analysis to model decisions so that higher values for the outcome variable are preferred to lower values. This is clearly the case for decisions where the outcome is wealth, or profit, or consumption, or return on an investment. This preference for higher values is reflected in the assumption that $V_\mu > 0$ for all values of σ and μ. Risk aversion is exhibited when lower standard deviation or variance is preferred to higher standard deviation or variance; that is, when $V_\sigma < 0$ for all σ and μ. Risk loving behavior is represented when $V_\sigma > 0$ for all σ and μ, and risk neutrality, not caring about risk, is characterized by $V_\sigma = 0$ for all σ and μ. Each of these three types of risk preference places a requirement on the partial derivative V_σ for all σ and μ. Thus, the definitions leave open the possibility that preferences can display risk aversion for some σ and μ, and be risk loving for other values; that is the M-V decision model allows for decision makers who are neither risk averse nor risk loving nor risk neutral, but instead display each of these preferences toward risk at different values for σ and μ.

A frequently used form for an M-V utility function is $V(\sigma, \mu) = \mu - \lambda \cdot \sigma^2$ although there are others that are employed. For this particular form, $\lambda > 0$ characterizes the decision maker as risk averse. This form and others that are used are selected to ensure that $V(\sigma, \mu)$ is a quasiconcave function. This implies that maximization of $V(\sigma, \mu)$ subject to choosing from a linear opportunity set in (σ, μ) space typically yields an interior solution. It is most common to place σ on the horizontal axis and μ on the vertical axis when graphing indifference curves for these utility functions. Figure 3.1 illustrates typical indifference curves in (σ, μ) space labeled as I_1 and I_2.

One of the positive features of the M-V decision model is that it is very simple and lends itself to two-dimensional graphical analysis and illustration. Opportunity or choice sets are sets of points in two-space, with (σ, μ) denoting the coordinates. For

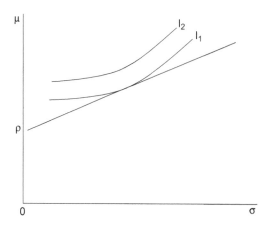

Figure 3.1 Typical indifference curves in (σ, μ) space, labeled as I_1 and I_2.

example, in the one risky and one riskless asset portfolio model with unit initial wealth, and where ρ is the riskless return and σ_r and μ_r are the risk and expected return for the risky asset, the opportunity set in (σ, μ) space is a straight line with vertical intercept $(0, \rho)$ and slope equal to $\frac{\mu_r - \rho}{\sigma_r}$. This is also illustrated in Figure 3.1. The value of this slope is referred to as the price of risk in the M-V decision model. This price of risk represents the extra expected return over the risk-free return that is earned by assuming an additional unit of risk as measured by the standard deviation of return. The opportunity set in this portfolio decision is a weakly convex set, and for most economic decision models, assumptions are made so the opportunity set in (σ, μ) space is a convex set. Because of its simplicity and because of its ability to take covariances of assets into account, the M-V decision model is often one of the first models used when beginning the discussion of a particular decision under uncertainty.

The M-V model is particularly well suited for and difficult to replace when modeling decisions where forming portfolios of assets or activities is possible, and where the fundamental decision being examined is which portfolio would be chosen by the decision maker. This point was emphasized by Markowitz (1959) who titled his book *Portfolio Selection*. The ability to deal with portfolio questions continues to be an important positive property of the M-V decision model. Because of the role that portfolios play in that model, the M-V decision model is at the heart of the well-known Capital Asset Pricing Model (CAPM) developed by Sharpe (1964), Lintner (1965) and Mossin (1966).

3.2.3 M-V Model Weaknesses

The M-V decision model has been replaced by the expected utility (EU) decision model in theoretical economic analysis of most decision problems, especially those where the selection of an optimal portfolio is not one of the decisions of interest. Fundamental weaknesses of the M-V model lead many to use the EU model instead. One weakness is that in the M-V decision model, all alternatives with the same mean and variance are necessarily ranked the same. This implies, for instance, that alternatives with positively skewed outcomes are ranked the same as ones which are negatively skewed as long as the mean and variance of the two are the same. For example, alternative A: obtaining -1 with probability .9999 and 9999 with probability .0001 is ranked the same as alternative B: obtaining -9999 with probability .0001 and 1 with probability .9999. These two alternatives each have the same mean value, 0, and the same variance, 9999, and therefore all M-V decision makers must be indifferent between A and B when preferences are represented by $V(\sigma, \mu)$. There is much evidence indicating that these two alternatives are not ranked the same by many decision makers, and that decision makers vary in their preference for such skewness. This same example also illustrates the fact that the size of the worst possible outcome is not important in the M-V ranking of alternatives. For many decision makers, the possibility of losing 9999 in gamble B makes it much worse than gamble A where the maximum loss is only 1 and this preference cannot be represented using an M-V utility function $V(\sigma, \mu)$.

Another important negative property of the M-V decision model was pointed out by Borch (1969), who shows that indifference curves in (σ, μ) space are not consistent with preferring higher outcomes. The following example illustrates a general calculation presented by Borch. Suppose a decision maker is indifferent between two points, $(\sigma_A, \mu_A) = (1, 1)$ and $(\sigma_B, \mu_B) = (2, 2)$. Two gambles A and B can be constructed with these values for σ and μ such that indifference between the two gambles is not possible when decision makers prefer higher outcomes. For this particular choice of (σ_A, μ_A) and (σ_B, μ_B), the constructed gamble A has outcomes 0 or 2 which are equally likely, while gamble B yields either 0 and 4 with equal probability. These two gambles satisfy $(\sigma_A, \mu_A) = (1, 1)$ and $(\sigma_B, \mu_B) = (2, 2)$, yet any person who prefers larger outcomes to smaller ones must strictly prefer gamble B to gamble A. It is not possible that $(1, 1)$ and $(2, 2)$ lie on the same indifference curve if these two random variables are to be ranked.

Borch gives a general procedure that allows such an example to be constructed for any two points claimed to be on an indifference curve in (σ, μ) space. Using terminology not available at the time Borch was writing, Borch shows that for any two points on an indifference curve for utility function $V(\sigma, \mu)$, two random variables can be constructed with the appropriate values for σ and μ, where one dominates the other in the first degree. First degree stochastic dominance is discussed in Section 3.5.2.

The M-V decision model exhibits the negative properties just mentioned. The EU decision model on the other hand is more flexible and can represent decision makers who exhibit preference for, or aversion to, skewness, or those who focus intensely on the worst outcomes, or those who always prefer larger outcomes. In general, by choosing the form for the utility function appropriately, EU risk preferences can be made to reflect preference for, or avoidance of, virtually any property or attribute of a probability distribution or random variable that may be important to the decision maker. In the last section of this chapter, Section 3.6, the M-V model is again discussed very briefly. The focus in that discussion is on the question of when do the M-V and EU decision models coincide. The EU model is discussed next.

3.3 THE EXPECTED UTILITY APPROACH

Determining the ranking function for random variables in the expected utility (EU) decision model is a two-step process. First, a utility function u(x), whose domain is the set of possible outcomes that the random variables can yield, is determined. Various properties of this utility function represent the risk preferences of the specific decision maker. The second step in the expected utility ranking procedure calculates the expectation of this utility function u(x). This expectation, expected utility, is the function used to represent the ranking of random variables. Common notation for continuously distributed random variables is to let F(x) denote the cumulative distribution function (CDF) associated with a particular random variable. The expected utility or ranking number attached to that random variable is given by:

$$U(F(x)) = E_F u(x) = \int_a^b u(x)dF(x)$$

where the support of the random variable is assumed to lie in the interval [a, b]. Alternatively, for discrete random variables $f(x_i)$ is used to denote the probability function indicating the likelihood of outcome x_i, where $i = 1, 2,..., n$. The expected utility is then given by

$$U(f(x_i)) = Eu(x) = \sum_{i=1}^n u(x_i) \cdot f(x_i).$$

The magnitude of this ranking number, $U(F(x))$ or $U(f(x_i))$, is then compared with a similar number for another CDF G(x) or another probability function $g(x_i)$

$$U(G(x)) = E_G u(x) = \int_a^b u(x)dG(x)$$

$$U(g(x_i)) = Eu(x) = \sum_{i=1}^n u(x_i) \cdot g(x_i)$$

to choose between or rank the two random variables represented by CDFs F(x) and G(x) or probability functions $f(x_i)$ and $g(x_i)$.

As with the M-V ranking of random variables, this ranking provided by EU is an ordinal one; thus U(F) or U(f) is unique to a positive monotonic transformation. The von-Neumann-Morgenstern (N-M) utility function u(x), however, is unique to a positive linear transformation. This property results from the fact that the computing of expected utility is a process that is linear in probabilities. The fact that $u(x)$ is unique to a positive linear transformation does not imply that $u(x)$ represents a cardinal ranking over outcomes x, nor that $U(F)$ represents a cardinal ranking. Early in the discussion of the expected utility decision model there was confusion concerning these ordinality/cardinality issues. Alchian (1953), Baumol (1958) and Luce and Raiffa (1957) each discuss this point.

A number of papers present sets of axioms or assumptions concerning preferences for random variables that are necessary and sufficient for the existence of a N-M utility function $u(x)$ with which expected utility is computed. Herstein and Milnor (1953), Friedman and Savage (1948) and Arrow (1965) are examples. Other chapters in this handbook discuss the EU assumptions more fully so only an informal presentation is given here. Luce and Raiffa provide a particularly easy-to-follow proof of the basic representation theorem, and a brief presentation of the logic of their argument is given next. The Luce and Raiffa proof is proof by construction. Their analysis demonstrates the existence of the N-M utility function $u(x)$ and how one uses it to rank random variables by giving a step-by-step procedure for constructing $u(x)$.

Suppose outcomes $x_1, x_2, \ldots x_n$ are possible. These outcomes can be elements of real number space, vectors representing bundles of goods, or even unrelated objects such as tickets to a Detroit Tigers baseball game or a cheese enchilada dinner at Jose's restaurant. To determine a N-M utility function for calculating EU, several assumptions are made. First, it is assumed that these outcomes can be ordered so that x_1 is the most preferred, x_n is the least preferred, and x_i is preferred or indifferent to x_j for $i \leq j$. Once this ordering of outcomes has occurred, the next assumption is that for each outcome x_i one can find a probability u_i such that a particular gamble $\tilde{x}_i$ which is indifferent to x_i can be formulated. This gamble $\tilde{x}_i$ has only two possible outcomes, x_1 and x_n, and yields the most preferred outcome x_1 with probability u_i and the least preferred outcome x_n with probability $(1 - u_i)$. Obviously $u_i = 1$ for outcome x_1, and $u_i = 0$ for outcome x_n, and u_i is between zero and one for all other outcomes. This assumption is a continuity assumption.

Having constructed a gamble $\tilde{x}_i$ that is indifferent to x_i, the important substitution assumption is that it is possible to replace x_i with $\tilde{x}_i$ wherever x_i occurs as a possible outcome in a gamble. Doing this for all x_i and assuming the usual rules of probability allows any gamble to be reduced to one that has only x_1 and x_n as possible outcomes. For example, let $(p_1, p_2, \ldots p_n)$ and $(q_1, q_2, \ldots q_n)$ represent two gambles over outcomes $x_1, x_2, \ldots x_n$. In each of these gambles, replace outcomes x_2 to x_{n-1} by $\tilde{x}_2$ to $\tilde{x}_{n-1}$. Doing this yields two equivalent gambles with only x_1 and x_n as possibilities. Moreover, the probability of receiving the most preferred outcome x_1 is $\sum_{i=1}^{n} u_i \cdot p_i$ for the first gamble and $\sum_{i=1}^{n} u_i \cdot q_i$ for the second. With only two possible outcomes, the gamble with the highest probability of obtaining the most preferred outcome is best. Thus, the term $\sum_{i=1}^{n} u_i \cdot p_i$ can be used to represent the ranking of gambles. This of course is the expected utility for that gamble when function $u(x_i) = u_i$ is chosen to be the N-M utility function.

The expected utility decision model, although available in its modern axiomatic form since the work of von Neumann and Morgenstern (1944), did not dominate and replace the M-V decision model in economic analysis until the 1960s.[2] Important papers and books by Arrow (1965), Pratt (1964), Rothschild and Stiglitz (1970), Hadar and Russell (1969), Hanoch and Levy (1969) and many others led to this transition. Arrow and Pratt present definitions and measures of risk aversion, while Rothschild and Stiglitz define increases in risk and mean preserving spreads to replace the use of variance as a measure of risk. Hadar and Russell and Hanoch and Levy define first and second degree stochastic dominance. The focus of the discussion of the EU decision model in this chapter is on defining and measuring risk aversion and risk, and begins with a definition of risk aversion, and the well-known Arrow-Pratt (A-P) measure of absolute risk aversion.

3.4 RISK AVERSION

3.4.1 Introduction

A decision maker is said to be *risk averse* if that person starting from a position of certainty rejects the addition of any fair gamble to that certain starting position.[3] Adding a fair gamble to a nonrandom starting position yields a gamble whose mean value is the same as the initial nonrandom starting value. Thus, a certain starting position is converted to a random one with the same mean. Risk aversion is always avoiding such a change. This simple and basic definition is used to characterize risk aversion in virtually every decision model that ranks random variables. In the M-V model just discussed, the assumption that $V_\sigma < 0$ for all σ and μ ensures that all fair gambles are rejected and that the decision maker is risk averse. In the EU decision model, risk aversion is equivalent to the concavity of the N-M utility function $u(x)$ used to compute expected utility.

Consider any gamble $\tilde{z}$ with outcomes x and y, where x and y occur with probabilities p and $1 - p$, respectively. The mean value of this gamble is $\mu = p \cdot x + (1 - p) \cdot y$, and the utility from μ is given by $u(\mu)$. The expected utility from the gamble is $[p \cdot u(x) + (1 - p)u(y)] = Eu(\tilde{z})$. For functions $u(z)$ that are concave, $u(p \cdot x + (1 - p) \cdot y) \geq [p \cdot u(x) + (1 - p)u(y)]$. This property of concave functions is illustrated in Figure 3.2 and is a form of Jensen's inequality which indicates directly that $Eu(\tilde{z}) \leq u(\mu)$ for all concave functions $u(z)$. All risk averse persons prefer to receive the mean value of a gamble, rather than participate in the gamble itself. If the utility function were convex rather than concave, the argument just given and the use of Jensen's inequality is

---

[2] There were earlier important papers including a paper by Friedman and Savage (1948).
[3] A fair gamble is any gamble whose mean value is zero.

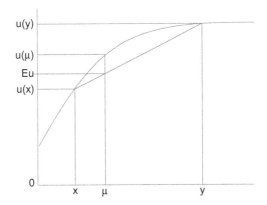

Figure 3.2 Illustration that $Eu(\tilde{z}) \leq u(\mu)$ for all concave functions u(z).

reversed. For the linear or risk neutral utility function, $Eu(\tilde{z}) = u(\mu)$ for all random variables. Since u(z) is unique to a positive linear transformation, the most often used utility function to represent risk neutrality is the identity function u(z) = z. Risk neutral decision makers choose among random variables on the basis of $E[\tilde{z}] = \mu$, their mean values. Thus, the M-V and EU decision models are the same in this regard. Also like the M-V model, the EU decision model allows for decision makers who are neither risk averse, nor risk loving, nor risk neutral; that is the utility function u(z) can be neither concave, convex, nor linear for all z.

3.4.2 Measuring Risk Aversion Locally

Arrow and Pratt (A-P) not only identify risk aversion with concavity of the N-M utility function u(x), they also provide a way to measure the degree of concavity, and hence the strength or intensity of risk aversion. A-P give two related measures and both are extensively used in current day economic analysis. Most of the material discussed here focuses on the A-P measure of absolute risk aversion, denoted $A_u(x)$. The relative risk aversion measure, $R_u(x)$, is briefly discussed after $A_u(x)$ is carefully described.

Definition 3.1: The absolute risk aversion measure $A_u(x)$ for N-M utility function u(x) is

$$A_u(x) = \frac{-u''(x)}{u'(x)}.$$

Two things concerning $A_u(x)$ are worth noting at the outset. First, absolute risk aversion is defined for outcomes in single dimension real number space. The risk aversion measure is a univariate function. Arrow and Pratt refer to the outcome variable x as wealth. Thus, even though the expected utility ranking of random variables allows outcomes to be vectors or dissimilar objects, this univariate measure of risk aversion does not. Second, $A_u(x)$ is uniquely associated with a given set of risk preferences; that is, $u(x)$, or any positive linear transformation of $u(x)$, each lead to exactly the same measure of absolute risk aversion. The process of differentiation and forming a ratio of derivatives eliminates the arbitrary constants associated with N-M utility functions. Thus, no matter which of the functions $A + B \cdot u(x)$ for $B > 0$ is used to represent the risk preferences of a decision maker, the A-P absolute risk aversion measure for that decision maker is a single function independent of such affine transformations.

In a variety of settings involving small risks, both Arrow and Pratt show that a decision maker's reaction to a risk is proportional to the product of this absolute risk aversion measure $A_u(x)$ and the size of the risk. For instance, the *risk premium*, $\pi(x)$, is defined as the amount a decision maker starting with nonrandom wealth x would discount the mean value of a random variable in order to sell that random variable. Letting $\tilde{z}$ represent a random variable with mean μ_z, the risk premium $\pi(x)$ when starting with nonrandom wealth x for random variable $\tilde{z}$ is defined by:

$$u(x + \mu_z - \pi(x)) = Eu(x + \tilde{z}).$$

It is common to restrict attention to variables $\tilde{z}$ whose mean value is zero which allows this expression to be written as:

$$u(x - \pi_z(x)) = Eu(x + \tilde{z}).$$

This definition for the risk premium $\pi(x)$ holds for all $\tilde{z}$ no matter the size of the possible outcomes that can occur for gamble $\tilde{z}$. For small $\tilde{z}$, however, Arrow and Pratt use Taylor Series approximations to show that $\pi(x)$ is approximated by

$$\pi(x) \approx (1/2) \cdot A_u(x) \cdot \sigma_z^2.$$

Putting this mathematical statement into words, the decision maker's reaction to risk, $\pi(x)$, is proportional to the product of the measure of risk aversion $A_u(x)$, and the measure of risk σ_z^2.

For random variables whose outcomes are negative, the *insurance premium*, $i(x)$, can be considered instead. Here, $i(x)$ represents the amount above the expected loss for a random variable that the decision maker would pay to be fully insured against that risk. When $\mu_z = 0$, $i(x)$ and $\pi(x)$ are the same, and in general, $i(x) = \pi(x) + \mu_z$.

A-P also present a related finding concerning a quite different reaction to risk called the probability premium, denoted $\phi(x,h)$. The *probability premium* is defined to be the deviation from 1/2 that is needed to induce a decision maker to accept a gamble with two possible outcomes that are equal in size, but opposite in sign. The notation used is that an amount h is either added to or subtracted from current wealth which is nonrandom value x. Formally, the equation that defines the probability premium $\phi(x, h)$ is:

$$u(x) = [.5 + \phi(x, h)]u(x + h) + [.5 - \phi(x, h)]u(x - h).$$

Again this definition for φ(x,h) holds for all values for h. For small h, Arrow and Pratt use a quadratic Taylor Series approximation to u(x+h) and u(x−h) and show that the probability premium is approximately given by:

$$\phi(x, h) \approx (1/2) \cdot A_u(x) \cdot h.$$

As with the risk premium, the form of this result is that the decision maker's reaction to risk, φ(x,h), is proportional to the product of the strength or intensity of risk aversion $A_u(x)$, and the size of the risk, in this case measured by h.

3.4.3 A-P Global Risk Aversion

The local and approximate findings discussed in Section 3.4.1 lend considerable intuitive appeal to $A_u(x)$ as a measure of the intensity of risk aversion. These findings are greatly enhanced, however, by global or in the large results that do not rely on the assumptions that the gambles being considered are small. These global results, stated next, are the primary justification for using $A_u(x)$ as an intensity measure for risk aversion in the EU decision model. The global results take on a different form than do the local results, and involve the comparison of the risk aversion levels of two decision makers with utility functions u(x) and v(x). The theorem given below defines u(x) as *at least as risk averse* as v(x) for all x using the condition $A_u(x) \geq A_v(x)$ for all x. The theorem and the discussion that follows also provide several other ways to characterize the A-P more risk averse partial order over decision makers.

Theorem 3.1: *The followiwng statements are equivalent.*

(1) u(x) is at least as risk averse as v(x).
(2) $A_u(x) \geq A_v(x)$ for all (x).
(3) $u(x) = \theta(v(x))$ where $\theta'(\cdot) \geq 0$ and $\theta''(\cdot) \leq 0$.
(4) $\pi_u(x) \geq \pi_v(x)$ for all x and all gambles $\tilde{z}$.
(5) $\phi_u(x, h) \geq \phi_v(x, h)$ for all x and all h.

The first two of these statements give Arrow and Pratt's definition of more risk averse. The third is a mathematical characterization indicating that u(x) is more risk averse than v(x) if and only if u(x) can be written as an increasing and concave transformation of v(x). An alternate mathematical characterization that is sometimes useful involves marginal utility functions rather than utility functions and is:

(6) $u'(x) = \delta'(x) \cdot v'(x)$ where $\delta'(x) \geq 0$ and $\delta''(x) \leq 0$.
The characterization given in (6) implies that $A_u(x) = A_v(x) + A_\delta(x)$, where $A_\delta(x) = \frac{-\delta''(x)}{\delta'(x)} \geq 0.$

Characterizations (4) and (5) extend the local results concerning the risk and probability premiums to risks which are no longer assumed to be small. A more risk averse person always has a larger risk and probability premium. A rewriting of characterization (4) allows the condition on risk premiums to be stated for certainty equivalents instead. The *certainty equivalent* (CE) for a gamble is defined to be that amount which, when obtained for certain, provides the same expected utility as the gamble. Letting CE_u and CE_v denote the certainty equivalents for person's with utility functions $u(x)$ and $v(x)$ respectively,

(7) $u(x + CE_u) = Eu(x + \tilde{z})$ and $v(x + CE_v) = Ev(x + \tilde{z})$ imply $CE_u \leq CE_v$ for all x and all $\tilde{z}$.

It is the case that the reactions to risk in the form of the risk premium or probability premium each involve a variable which is *constructed* to allow measurement of the intensity of risk aversion. It is also possible to consider other reactions to risk that involve choices made by the decision maker in response to risk. In many decision settings, the choice of a parameter is also a way to define or characterize the Pratt and Arrow absolute risk aversion measure. Pratt and Arrow provide this discussion for the investment choice made in the single risky and riskless asset portfolio model.[4] The literature contains many similar findings in other decision contexts.

Consider a decision maker who can allocate current nonrandom wealth between a risky and riskless asset. Let $\tilde{r}$ denote final wealth and $\widetilde{W} = \alpha \cdot \tilde{r} + (W_0 - \alpha) \cdot \rho$, where $\tilde{r}$ is the random return on the risky asset, ρ is the nonrandom return on the riskless asset, W_0 is initial nonrandom wealth, and α is the amount of initial wealth allocated to the risky asset. Pratt and Arrow show that $A_u(x) \geq A_v(x)$ for all x is equivalent to $\alpha_u \leq \alpha_v$ for all initial wealth levels and all risky assets. That is, A-P show that the more risk averse decision maker, when risk aversion is measured by $A_u(x)$, reacts to a risk in a portfolio decision setting by investing more of wealth in the riskless asset and less in the risky asset. This finding is given below as characterization (8).

(8) $\alpha_u \leq \alpha_v$ for all $W_0, \tilde{r}$ and ρ.

Similar results have been demonstrated in many other decision settings by researchers other than Arrow or Pratt. For example, Sandmo (1971) shows that for a competitive firm that chooses its output level when facing a random output price, more risk averse firms, those with a larger $A_u(x)$, choose a smaller output level. Similarly, when purchasing coinsurance, Smith (1968) and Mossin (1968) show that one consumer is more risk averse than another as measured by $A_u(x)$ if and only if that consumer chooses a higher

---

[4] Portfolio decisions involving a single risky asset can be dealt with in an EU decision model. It is the case of multiple risky assets that M-V analysis is more tractable than is EU analysis.

degree of coinsurance than does the less risk averse consumer. These and other such findings in a wide variety of decision settings lend considerable support for using $A_u(x)$, the A-P measure of absolute risk aversion, both as a measure of the intensity or strength of risk aversion, and as a way to compare risk aversion levels across decision makers.

There are some technical matters concerning $A_u(x)$ that are of interest. These stem from analysis presented by Pratt (1964) showing how $u(x)$ can be obtained from $A_u(x)$ using a three step procedure. In the first step, $[-A_u(x)] = \frac{u''(x)}{u'(x)}$ is integrated to obtain $\ln[u'(x)] + c_1$, where c_1 is the constant of integration. In step two, the result from step one is used as the exponent for base e. This yields $u'(x) \cdot e^{c_1}$. Finally in step three, the result from step two is integrated giving the final outcome of the three steps as $u(x) \cdot e^{c_1} + c_2$. This three step procedure indicates how one can find the $u(x)$ that leads to a particular $A_u(x)$. The process, however, is not as easy to carry out as it is to describe because the integration involved may not lead to a closed form solution.

This three step process can be carried out in principle as long as one assumes that either $u'(x) > 0$ or $u'(x) < 0$ for all x so that $A_u(x)$ never involves division by zero and is everywhere defined. Of course, in economic analysis $u'(x) > 0$ is the common assumption. As a practical matter, however, the integration of $[-A_u(x)]$ in step one, or integrating $[u'(x) \cdot e^{c_1}]$ in step three may not lead to a solution in closed form. As a consequence, some EU risk preferences can be represented by $A_u(x)$, but one cannot write down either the $u'(x)$ or $u(x)$ associated with those risk preferences. It is also the case that there are EU risk preferences that can be represented by a marginal utility function $u'(x)$, and the corresponding $u(x)$ is not of closed form. These things can be important to keep in mind when choosing functional forms to represent the risk preferences of decision makers in more applied settings. Many functional form choices exist for $A_u(x)$, fewer for $u'(x)$, and fewer forms yet for $u(x)$. Saha (1993), Conniffe (2007a,b) and Meyer (2010) provide additional discussion of these issues. The next section discusses the two primary forms for $u(x)$ considered in the literature.

3.4.4 Constant and Decreasing Absolute Risk Aversion

The findings presented in Sections 3.4.1 and 3.4.2 support using the magnitude of the A-P measure of absolute risk aversion to measure the intensity of risk aversion and using $A_u(x)$ to compare the risk aversion levels of decision makers. There are a number of other topics concerning risk aversion that can be discussed. This section focuses on one of the more important ones involving *decreasing absolute risk aversion* (DARA). As part of this discussion, the two most commonly employed functional forms for $u(x)$ are presented, and a general class of utility functions, the hyperbolic absolute risk averse (HARA) class, is defined.

To determine functional forms for utility functions that display DARA, starting with those where $A_u(x)$ is a constant is useful. These *constant absolute risk averse* (CARA) utility functions take the form

$$u(x) = -e^{-cx}$$

where $A_u(x) = c$ is the measure of absolute risk aversion. Decision makers who are constant absolute risk averse have risk and probability premiums that do not depend on the initial wealth.

At the very beginning of their discussion of measuring risk aversion both Arrow and Pratt conjecture that the slope of the absolute risk aversion measure is negative. The assumption that $A_u'(x) \leq 0$ is referred to as *decreasing absolute risk aversion* with acronym DARA. This assumption can be defended in many ways, but most support for the assumption in the economics literature comes from showing that the assumption leads to sensible predictions in a variety of models. A sample of these comparative static predictions is given in Section 3.4.5.

DARA is the assumption that, as the initial starting point for a decision maker becomes larger, the reaction to a risk of fixed size falls. For instance, if a decision maker begins with a larger amount of wealth, the risk premium or probability premium associated with a fixed gamble $\tilde{z}$ is smaller. Similarly, a decision maker with more wealth to invest will allocate more to the risky asset. Each of these statements assumes that the size of the risk itself is unchanged, and thus under DARA an increase in the starting position causes the decision maker to evaluate the alternatives using utility values from a less risk averse portion of the utility function. More formally, the following theorem is similar to one found in Pratt's work.

Theorem 3.2: *The following statements are equivalent.*

(1) $A_u(x)$ is decreasing for all x.

(2) $\pi(x)$ is decreasing for all x and all gambles $\tilde{z}$.

(3) $\phi(x, h)$ is decreasing in x for all x and all h.

(4) $\alpha(W_0)$ is increasing in W_0 for all W_0, $\tilde{r}$ and ρ.

To determine which utility functions exhibit DARA, the following explicit writing out of $A_u'(x)$ is used:

$$A_u'(x) = \frac{-u'''(x) \cdot u'(x) + (u''(x))^2}{(u'(x))^2}.$$

This expression makes a number of things quite obvious. First, it is the case that $u'''(x) \geq 0$ is a necessary, but not sufficient condition for $A_u'(x)$ to be negative. The assumption that $u'''(x) \geq 0$ is referred to as *prudence*, thus it is the case that DARA implies prudence. Prudence is discussed again in Section 3.4.7. Also, since $u'''(x) = 0$ under quadratic utility, a quadratic utility function does not display DARA, but is *increasing absolute risk averse* instead. This property of a quadratic function is often mentioned as a negative feature and an argument against using quadratic functions as N-M utility functions. Quadratic utility functions also display the even worse feature that they must eventually have a negative slope.

A form for $A_u(x)$ that exhibits DARA, and that is commonly used, is $A_u(x) = \frac{\alpha}{x}$ for $\alpha > 0$. This family of risk aversion measures, indexed by α, has the feature that $A_u(x)$ is always decreasing, but does not become zero for any finite value for x. These $A_u(x)$ represent risk preferences for which the reaction to a given risk diminishes as the starting position is increased, but risk aversion never disappears. The form for the utility function leading to these absolute risk aversion measures is

$$u(x) = \frac{x^{1-\alpha}}{1 - \alpha} \text{ for all } \alpha \neq 1$$
$$u(x) = \ln \ x \text{ for } \alpha = 1.$$

These risk preferences and this particular functional form for utility also display *constant relative risk aversion* (CRRA) discussed next.

3.4.5 Relative Risk Aversion

In addition to defining and supporting the use of the absolute risk aversion measure $A_u(x)$, Arrow and Pratt also define *relative or proportional risk aversion*. This relative risk aversion measure, $R_u(x)$, differs from $A_u(x)$ in the way it measure the intensity of risk aversion, but $A_u(x)$ and $R_u(x)$ *do not* yield different partial orders over decision makers in terms of their levels of risk aversion. That is, $R_u(x) \geq R_v(x)$ for all $x > 0$ is equivalent to $A_u(x) \geq A_v(x)$ for all $x > 0$. When measuring the intensity of risk aversion, $R_u(x)$ uses the reaction to risk measured as a proportion of the initial wealth rather than as an absolute value. $R_u(x)$ is defined by

$$R_u(x) = \frac{-x \cdot u''(x)}{u'(x)} = x \cdot A_u(x).$$

$R(x)$ is supported as a measure of the intensity of risk aversion using arguments similar to those that are used for $A(x)$. For instance, the proportional risk premium, $\pi^*(x)$, defined to be $\frac{\pi(x)}{x}$, can be related to the size of $R_u(x)$ and σ_z^2 using the same Taylor's series approximation as was employed earlier for $\pi(x)$. Doing this gives

$$\pi^*(x) \approx (1/2) \cdot R_u(x) \cdot \sigma_z^2.$$

Relative risk aversion is only sensibly defined when $x > 0$ is assumed. This implies that in portfolio decisions, for instance, the random outcome x is selected to be return[5]

---

[5] The return is equal to one plus the rate of return. In the typical portfolio model, final wealth $W = \alpha \cdot \tilde{r} + (W_0 - \alpha) \cdot \rho$ where W_0 is initial wealth and α is the amount invested in the risky asset. In this formulation, both $\tilde{r}$ and ρ are returns to the risky and riskless assets respectively. These variables represent the gain or loss to the investment plus the return of the amount initially invested. If losses are limited to the amount invested, then the random return $\tilde{r}$ cannot be smaller than zero. Rate of return gives the change in the initial investment expressed as a percentage change and can be negative.

rather than rate of return so that $x > 0$ is an acceptable restriction. Relative risk aversion is the elasticity of marginal utility, $u'(x)$, and thus is unit free.

$$R_u(x) = \frac{-d(u'(x))/u'(x)}{dx/x}.$$

Being unit free is a valuable property for a risk aversion measure when comparing findings concerning the magnitude of risk aversion across various studies where different units of measure for x are employed.

A theorem similar to Theorem 3.1 follows immediately.

Theorem 3.3: *The following statements are equivalent.*

(1) u(x) is at least as risk averse as v(x).

(2) $R_u(x) \geq R_v(x)$ for all $x > 0$.

(3) $u(x) = \theta(v(x))$ where $\theta'(\cdot) \geq 0$ and $\theta''(\cdot) \leq 0$.

(4) $\pi_u^*(x) \geq \pi_v^*(x)$ for all x and all gambles $\tilde{z}$.

As noted earlier, Arrow and Pratt conjecture that $A_u(x)$ is likely to be a decreasing function. They also argue that $R_u(x)$ is likely to be an increasing function. This assumption is referred to as *increasing relative risk aversion* (IRRA). $R_u(x)$ is a constant, $R_u(x) = \alpha$, for the family of utility functions where $A_u(x) = \frac{\alpha}{x}$ for $\alpha > 0$ that was just discussed. Analysis since Pratt and Arrow lends considerable support for the assumption of DARA, especially when the outcome variable is wealth, but the findings are mixed concerning IRRA for wealth or for any other outcome variable. In fact, when the outcome variable is consumption rather than wealth, the opposite finding is often claimed for $R_u(x)$; that is, $R_u(x)$ is often estimated to display *decreasing relative risk aversion* (DRRA) when x represents consumption. A decreasing $R_u(x)$ implies an even more steeply decreasing $A_u(x)$. Habit formation utility is a good example of such a DRRA utility function for consumption. Constantinides (1990), and Campbell and Cochrane (1999) use such habit formation utility functions. Meyer and Meyer (2005, 2006) provide a comprehensive review of this topic and literature.

The two families of utility functions discussed so far are special cases of a more general family termed the *hyperbolic absolute risk averse* (HARA) family. Members of this general family of utility functions have the characteristic that *risk tolerance*, $T_u(x) = \frac{1}{A_u(x)}$, is a linear function of x. A general form for a HARA form utility function is

$$u(x) = \frac{(\gamma)}{(1-\gamma)} \left(\frac{x}{\gamma} + \eta \right)^{(1-\gamma)}.$$

From this utility function one can easily determine that $T_u(x) = \frac{x}{\gamma} + \eta$ and $A_u(x) = \frac{\gamma}{x+\gamma\cdot\eta}$. Letting γ go to infinity allows the CARA family of risk aversion measures with risk aversion measure $1/\eta$ to be obtained. The CRRA class of utility functions results from choosing $\eta = 0$. Gollier (2001) provides a more detailed discussion of special cases of the HARA family. A modified version of his notation was used here.

3.4.6 Comparative Statics Using Risk Aversion Measures

The derivatives of risk aversion, measured by either $A_u'(x)$ or $R_u'(x)$, are important factors in determining how the choice made by a decision maker changes as the starting wealth changes. This is true in most decision models where expected utility is maximized. Two of the best-known results are presented next to illustrate the comparative statics of risk aversion, and how these comparative static findings are demonstrated. The two examples also illustrate the difference between and the absolute and relative risk aversion intensity measures.

First consider a perfectly competitive firm choosing output level x to maximize expected utility from profit given by $\tilde{\pi} = \tilde{p} \cdot x - c(x) - B$. In this model, which follows Sandmo's (1970) notation, output price $\tilde{p}$ is random with CDF F(p) with support in [a, b], c(x) is the total variable cost function for the firm and B is total fixed cost. The firm chooses output level x to maximize

$$\int_a^b u(\pi)dF(p).$$

The first order condition for this maximization is:

$$\int_a^b u'(\pi)(p - c'(x))dF(p) = 0.$$

The second order condition is satisfied when the firm is risk averse and variable costs are convex. Now consider what happens when fixed cost B changes. This change is a downward shifting or reduction of the starting point for the decision maker, equivalent to a reduction in initial wealth. Differentiating the first order expression with respect to B gives

$$\int_a^b -u''(\pi)(p - c'(x))dF(p).$$

This expression can be rewritten so that the absolute risk aversion measure and the first order expression each are present in the expression

$$\int_a^b A_u(\pi)[u'(\pi)(p - c'(x))]dF(p).$$

Integrating by parts one time gives

$$\int_a^s -A_u'(\pi) \cdot \int_a^s u'(\pi)(p - c'(x))dF(p)ds.$$

Using the first order condition, it is the case that $\int_a^s u'(\pi)(p - c'(x))dF(p) \leq 0$ for all s, and therefore if $A_u'(\pi)$ is assumed to be negative (positive), this expression is negative (positive). This shows that when B is increased, a firm always decreases its choice of output level if $A_u'(\pi) \leq 0$. The assumption of DARA implies that increased fixed costs cause firms to reduce output. The logic is quite simple. DARA combined with an increase in B implies that the firm is evaluating its output decision assuming lower profit levels and hence using a more risk averse portion of its N-M utility function $u(\pi)$. Since the conclusion reverses when $A_u(\pi)$ is an increasing function instead, this result is considered to be support for the DARA assumption. Much of the comparative static analysis in EU decision models follows this general pattern and involves proofs using a similar methodology.

A second example illustrates the comparative static effect of $R_u(x)$ in the important and often examined single risky and riskless asset portfolio problem. Let the final outcome variable be wealth given by

$$\widetilde{W} = W_0(\alpha \cdot \tilde{r} + (1 - \alpha)\rho)$$

where W_0 is nonrandom initial wealth, and $\tilde{r}$ is the random return from investing in the risky asset. The CDF for $\tilde{r}$ is denoted $F(r)$ whose support is in some interval $[0, b]$ and ρ is the nonrandom return from the riskless asset. In this version of the portfolio decision, α is the *proportion* of wealth invested in the risky asset. $\tilde{r} > 0$ and $\rho > 0$ and α in $[0, 1]$ are assumed so that $\widetilde{W} > 0$. This model differs from that used in Section 3.4.2 when discussing characterization (8) of more risk averse in that α is now a proportion of initial wealth rather than an absolute amount. This change implies that W_0 and the random parameter $\tilde{r}$ are multiplied by one another rather than added together. The investor is assumed to maximize $Eu(W)$ which is given below.

$$\int_0^b u(W)dF(r)$$

The first order condition for this maximization is

$$\int_0^b u'(W)W_0(r - \rho)dF(r) = 0.$$

The second order condition is satisfied if the investor is risk averse. Now the shifting of the starting point is increasing the initial wealth W_0. Differentiating the first order expression with respect to W_0 yields

$$\int_0^b u''(W)W(r - \rho)dF(r)$$

which can be rewritten as

$$\int_0^b -R_u'(W)u'(W)(r - \rho)dF(r).$$

As in the previous example, integrating this expression by parts can be used to show that if $R(W)$ is increasing (constant, decreasing), the proportion of initial wealth allocated to the risky asset decreases (stays the same, increases) as initial wealth increases.

These two detailed examples are each special cases of a general decision model where the decision maker chooses a variable α to maximize expected utility from $z(\alpha, \tilde{x}, \beta)$. In this notation $\tilde{x}$ is a random parameter with CDF $F(x)$ with support in the interval $[a, b]$, and β represents nonrandom parameters, possibly more than one, and α represents a decision variable. A variety of questions can be posed within this framework. One can ask how α changes as a parameter β changes, including the starting wealth the parameter just discussed in the two detailed examples. Other parameters, including the random parameter $\tilde{x}$ can also be changed and the analysis follows a similar methodology. Kraus (1979) and Katz (1981) ask how does α change as $\tilde{x}$ becomes riskier in a specific way. The general model they pose omits the notation for the nonrandom β since these parameters are held constant in their analysis. The literature contains far more comparative static analyses of both general and specific decisions than can be discussed further here.

Other measures of risk aversion that preserve the partial order over decision makers have been suggested. These are often defined because an assumption concerning the new risk aversion measure is particularly well suited for a particular comparative statics question. One such measure is proposed by Menezes and Hanson (1970). Using their notation, the measure of *partial relative risk aversion* is given by

$$P_u(t; w) = \frac{-t \cdot u''(t + w)}{u'(t + w)} = t \cdot A_u(t + w).$$

This measure is a partial measure of relative risk aversion in that the variable multiplying $A_u(t + w)$ is not the whole argument of $A_u(\cdot)$, but only a portion of it. This measure proves to be particularly useful for comparative static analysis when the initial wealth is kept fixed, but the scale of the risk is altered. Like $R_u(x)$, this partial relative risk aversion measure does not define a different ordering over decision makers in terms of risk aversion. The main reason for defining either relative risk aversion or partial relative risk aversion is to allow a convenient interpretation of a particular assumption concerning risk preferences. It is easier to interpret the statement that R(x) is a constant than it is to interpret the statement that A(x) takes the form $A(x) = \frac{\alpha}{x}$ even though these are equivalent statements.

3.4.7 Ross's Strongly More Risk Averse Order

For a number of important decisions, it is the case that the assumption that $A_u(x) \geq A_v(x)$ for all x is not sufficient to predict how one decision maker chooses differently than another. This is especially true in decision models where there is more than one source of randomness. Ross (1981) proposes a different definition of increased risk aversion, shows that his definition implies that of Arrow and Pratt, and uses the term *strongly more risk averse* to describe the order over decision makers his definition yields. Ross then shows that when one decision maker is strongly more risk averse than another, comparative static predictions that are ambiguous under the assumption that $A_u(x) \geq A_v(x)$, for all x, become determinate. Formally, Ross provides the following definition of when a decision maker with utility function u(x) is *strongly more risk averse* than another with utility function v(x).

Definition 3.2: u(x) is strongly more risk averse than v(x) if there exists a $\lambda > 0$ such that

$$\frac{u''(x)}{v''(x)} \geq \lambda \geq \frac{u'(y)}{v'(y)} \quad \text{for all x and y.}$$

To understand where the Ross order is most applicable and the additional requirements this stronger order imposes, recall that Arrow and Pratt define the risk premium for a decision maker starting with nonrandom wealth x and associated with gamble $\tilde{z}$ whose mean value is zero, using the equation

$$u(x - \pi) = \mathrm{E}u(x + \tilde{z}).$$

For this $\pi(x)$, Theorem 3.1 indicates that $A_u(x) \geq A_v(x)$ for all x is necessary and sufficient for $\pi_u(x) \geq \pi_v(x)$ for all x and all gambles $\tilde{z}$. What is important to note is that in this definition of $\pi(x)$, the starting point or initial wealth x is not a random variable.

Ross considers a very similar risk premium, a fixed amount to be subtracted from the decision maker's initial wealth, but allows the initial wealth to be a random variable $\tilde{x}$ rather than requiring it to be nonrandom. Since both $\tilde{z}$ and $\tilde{x}$ are random, Ross assumes that $\mathrm{E}[\tilde{z}|x] = 0$ for all x. This replaces the assumption that $\mathrm{E}[\tilde{z}] = 0$ made by Arrow and Pratt. Formally, the Ross risk premium is the amount the mean value of $\tilde{z}$ is discounted in order to sell it when the decision maker begins with random wealth $\tilde{x}$. This is the same terminology as used to describe the Arrow and Pratt risk premium $\pi(x)$. The difference is that the initial wealth is no longer assumed to be certain. Formally, π is defined by the equation

$$Eu(\tilde{x} - \pi) = Eu(\tilde{x} + \tilde{z}).$$

Ross shows that a stronger definition of more risk averse is required to determine when $\pi_u \geq \pi_v$ for all random initial wealth positions, $\tilde{x}$, and all gambles $\tilde{z}$ satisfying $E[\tilde{z}|x] = 0$. He shows that the following three statements are equivalent ways to define when a decision maker with utility function $u(x)$ is strongly more risk averse than another with utility function $v(x)$.

Theorem 3.4: *The following three conditions are equivalent.*

(1)   There exists a $\lambda > 0$ such that $\frac{u''(x)}{v''(x)} \geq \lambda \geq \frac{u'(y)}{v'(y)}$ for all x and y.

(2)   There exists a $\lambda > 0$ and a function $\phi(x)$ with $\phi'(x) \leq 0$ and $\phi''(x) \leq 0$ such that $u(x) = \lambda \cdot v(x) + \phi(x)$ for all x.

(3)   For all random $\tilde{x}$ and $\tilde{z}$ such that $E(\tilde{z}|x) = 0$, $Eu(\tilde{x} + \tilde{z}) = Eu(\tilde{x} - \pi_u)$ and $Ev(\tilde{x} + \tilde{z}) = Ev(\tilde{x} - \pi_v)$ imply that $\pi_u \geq \pi_v$.

The Ross definition of strongly more risk averse differs from other alternatives to absolute risk aversion such as relative or proportional risk aversion in that it provides a different and stronger partial order over decision makers in terms of their risk aversion levels.

With the stronger risk aversion order, Ross is able to extend many theorems to more general settings. For instance, consider a portfolio decision with two assets where both assets are risky and yield a random return. If the return on the first asset is denoted $\tilde{x}$ and the return on the second $\tilde{y}$, then the portfolio allocation decision is to choose α to maximize expected utility from

$$\widetilde{W} = W_0(\alpha \cdot \tilde{y} + (1 - \alpha)\tilde{x}) = W_0(\tilde{x} + \alpha(\tilde{y} - \tilde{x})).$$

Letting $\tilde{z} = (\tilde{y} - \tilde{x})$ and assuming that $E(\tilde{z}|x) \geq 0$ for all x so that the second asset has return $\tilde{y}$ which is both larger and riskier than $\tilde{z}$ Ross shows that when $u(W)$ is strongly more risk averse than $v(W)$, then $\alpha_u \leq \alpha_v$ for all such $\tilde{y}$ and $\tilde{x}$. That is, the strongly more risk averse decision maker chooses to include more of the less risky asset and less of the more risky asset in the two asset portfolio. Many other models can be generalized to include multiple random variables and a random starting point and yet comparative static findings can be obtained if the strongly more risk averse assumption is made.

The Ross fixed risk premium was generalized to a random risk premium by Machina and Neilson (1987) who use this to provide an additional characterization of Ross's strongly more risk averse order. Pratt (1990) points out several negative and overly strong aspects of the Ross order. In addition, because the strongly more risk averse order allows a random starting point, higher order measures of risk aversion use the Ross methodology in their formulation. Modica and Scarsini (2005), Jindapon and Neilson (2007) and Denuit and Eeckhoudt (2010a,b) use this feature to discuss higher order measures of risk aversion.

3.4.8 Other Risk Aversion Terms and Measures

Rather than additional conditions on the first and second derivatives of u(x), other contributions to the discussion of risk aversion add conditions that restrict the sign of higher order derivatives of u(x). These conditions provide another way to strengthen the requirement that $A_u(x) \geq A_v(x)$ for all x so that additional comparative static findings can be obtained. Ekern (1980) does this in a very general fashion defining *nth degree risk aversion* as follows.

Definition 3.3: Decision maker with utility function u(x) is *n*th degree risk averse if $(-1)^{n-1} \cdot u^{(n)}(x) > 0$ for all x.

In this notation, $u^{(n)}$ denotes the nth derivative of u(x). Ekern uses this definition and a related one concerning *n*th degree risk increases to show that G(x) has more *n*th degree risk than F(x) if and only if every *n*th degree risk averse decision maker prefers F(x) to G(x). This is discussed more completely in Section 3.5.4, where the measurement of higher order risk and risk increases is discussed, and higher order stochastic dominance is defined.

At least two of the higher order derivatives of u(x) have been used to define additional terms that describe risk preferences of decision makers. Kimball (1990) focuses on the sign of $u'''(x)$. He notes that when $u'''(x) \geq 0$, marginal utility is convex and many of the Arrow and Pratt derivations for u(x) can be reapplied and interpreted for $u'(x)$ instead. The sign of $u'''(x)$ and $P(x) = \frac{-u'''(x)}{u''(x)}$ are used to define and measure the intensity of *prudence*.

Definition 3.4: A decision maker with utility function u(x) is prudent if $u'''(x) \geq 0$ for all x.

As mentioned when discussing DARA, being prudent is a necessary but not sufficient condition for a decision maker to be decreasingly absolute risk averse. Kimball shows that this weaker restriction, prudence, is sufficient to generate interesting comparative static predictions in several decision settings. The initial discussion of prudence focuses on the effect of the introduction of randomness in the amount available to spend in the second period of a two period consumption model. The question is whether this future randomness increases or decreases saving from the first period to the second. Kimball shows that prudent decision makers, those with $u'''(x) \geq 0$ for all x, save more as a result of the introduction of risk into the amount available in the second period. In another paper, Kimball (1993) also defined *temperance* using the sign of the fourth order derivative of u(x). He also defines *standard risk aversion* as the property that both $A_u(x)$ and $P_u(x)$ are decreasing functions. There is still considerable discussion concerning the correct way to measure the intensity of prudence or temperance. Eeckhoudt and Schlesinger (2006) use the combining or separating of two simple "bads," a reduction in initial wealth or the addition of a zero mean random variable, to further characterize prudence and temperance and other higher order derivatives of u(x). Others using the signs of higher order derivatives of u(x) include Menezes et al. (1980) who use the sign of the third derivative when defining *downside risk aversion*. Those adding to this discussion include Crainich and Eeckhoudt (2008), Keenan and Snow (2002, 2009) and Liu and Meyer (2012).

As was mentioned at the outset, the A-P risk aversion measure $A_u(x)$ assumes that the N-M utility function u(x) has a single argument rather than a vector of arguments. At the same time, there is nothing in the axioms of expected utility that disallow outcome variables that are vectors. The discussion here of measuring risk aversion concludes with a brief review of the findings concerning extending measures of risk aversion to vector valued outcomes.

An initial discussion of this topic occurs in the two period consumption model where utility is assumed to take the form $u(c_1, c_2)$. For this decision model, the assumption is that first period consumption is a choice variable and is nonrandom, with second period consumption resulting from the return on the saving from the first period plus additional resources made available in the second period. It is typical to assume that either the return on saving or the additional resources that arrive in the second period is a random variable. Thus, in this model, c_1 is chosen first and is not random, and c_2 is random because its value is partially determined by random return on saving or random endowment in the second period. Typical notation is for W_1 and W_2 to represent the endowment in periods one and two respectively. The amount consumed in period one, c_1, is chosen and the residual, $(W_1 - c_1)$ is saved for second period consumption. Second period consumption is given by $c_2 = W_2 + (W_1 - c_1) \cdot r$. To introduce randomness, either W_2 or r, but not both, is assumed to be random. In this two period consumption model, since only c_2 is random, the ratio $\frac{-u_{22}}{u_2}$ can be used as a measure of absolute risk aversion. This measure has many of the same general properties as the A-P measure $A_u(x)$. Sandmo (1970) and Leland (1968) use such a measure and present results in the two period consumption model.

For the more general case, where utility is a function of a vector of outcome variables, Kihlstrom and Mirman (1974) present a thorough discussion and draw a quite negative conclusion. Using an example, they show that it is not possible to disentangle preferences for bundles of goods in settings without randomness from preferences for risk. Thus, they settle on a general definition of more risk averse that is similar to characterization (3) from Theorem 3.1 and listed below for convenience.

(3) $u(x) = \theta(v(x))$ where $\theta'(\cdot) \geq 0$ and $\theta''(\cdot) \leq 0$.

Kihlstrom and Mirman propose exactly this same condition as the definition of $u(\vec{x})$ being more risk averse than $v(\vec{x})$ with the interpretation that $\vec{x}$ can be a vector of dimension higher than one.

Definition 3.5: For $\vec{x}$ in R^n, utility function $u(\vec{x})$ is at least as risk averse as utility function $v(\vec{x})$ if there exist a $\theta(\cdot)$ such that $\theta'(\cdot) \geq 0$ and $\theta''(\cdot) \leq 0$ and $u(\vec{x}) = \theta(v(\vec{x}))$.

To compare the risk aversion of decision makers using this definition requires that the decision makers display exactly the same ordinal preferences in settings without randomness. This severely limits the applicability of the definition yet a replacement has not been proposed.

3.5 INCREASES IN RISK AND STOCHASTIC DOMINANCE

3.5.1 Introduction

Soon after Arrow and Pratt defined and supported $A_u(x)$ as a useful measure of risk aversion, the attention of researchers shifted to the other half of the expected utility calculation, how to categorize and describe the random variable or CDF representing the likelihood of the various possible outcomes that could occur. Two different but related questions are discussed. The more general question asks what are the necessary and sufficient conditions for one random variable or CDF to be preferred or indifferent to another by all decision makers with risk preferences restricted to some particular set? That is, what are the necessary and sufficient conditions for $F(x)$ to be preferred or indifferent to $G(x)$ for all EU decision makers with N-M utility function in some set Ω? First degree, second degree and other forms of stochastic dominance are discussed using this general framework. Hadar and Russell (1969) and Hanoch and Levy (1969) are early contributors in this area. The second question is more narrowly focused and is directly related to the question of defining or measuring risk aversion. This question asks when is one random variable or CDF riskier than another? Rothschild and Stiglitz (1970) provide an answer in the form of a definition of increasing risk. The discussion begins with first degree stochastic dominance.

3.5.2 First Degree Stochastic Dominance

Hadar and Russell (1969) and Hanoch and Levy (1969) each provide what are now known as first and second degree stochastic dominance conditions, and use these conditions to define one random variable stochastically dominating another in the first and second degree. These conditions use CDFs to represent random variables and place restrictions on $[G(x) - F(x)]$. These conditions could also be written as restrictions on the random variables themselves. Because of its simple nature *first degree stochastic dominance* is reviewed first and the discussion of second degree dominance is deferred to Section 3.5.3 following the presentation of the definition of increasing risk.

Definition 3.6: $F(x)$ dominates $G(x)$ in the first degree if $G(x) \geq F(x)$ for all x.

This definition is formulated without making the assumption that the decision maker maximizes EU. That is, first degree stochastic dominance (FSD) is defined outside of the expected utility decision model context. The implications in an EU decision model, however, provide an interpretation for FSD and support for the definition.

Theorem 3.5: F(x) dominates G(x) in the first degree if and only if F(x) is preferred or indifferent to G(x) by all EU decision makers with N-M utility functions satisfying $u'(x) \geq 0$ for all x.

First degree stochastic dominance can be thought as the extension of the concept of "larger" as it applies to real numbers. FSD is "larger" for random variables whose outcomes are real numbers. Random variables can become larger in at least two distinct ways. Without changing the likelihoods, the outcomes themselves can be increased, or alternatively, without changing the outcomes, the likelihood of the larger outcomes can be increased and the likelihood for the smaller outcomes decreased. Each of these changes increases the size of a random variable and is represented by a first degree stochastic dominant increase as given in Definition 3.6. Theorem 3.5 indicates that all decision makers who prefer larger outcomes, that is, those with $u'(x) \geq 0$, agree unanimously that this restriction, $G(x) \geq F(x)$ for all x, captures their preference for larger outcomes and larger random variables. The proof of Theorem 3.5 is quite simple and involves integration by parts and steps similar to the comparative static analysis discussed in Section 3.4.5. FSD yields a partial order over CDFs. It only provides a ranking for random variables whose CDFs do not cross.

3.5.3 Increases in Risk

Rothschild and Stiglitz (1970) (R-S) present a definition of what it means for one random variable to be riskier than another. In fact, they present three distinct definitions and then show that the three seemingly different definitions of one random variable being riskier than another are equivalent. As is the case for the Arrow and Pratt measure of risk aversion, the result of this analysis is a single definition of increasing risk with multiple ways to characterize the definition. The R-S definition only applies to random variables whose mean values are the same. The R-S definition of increasing risk is different from variance, but does imply that the riskier random variable has higher variance.

The first definition of one random variable being riskier than another that R-S propose is one that involves the addition of "noise" to an existing random variable, and is similar to definitions used in the literature concerned with the analysis of signals. Random variable $\tilde{y}$ is defined to be riskier than $\tilde{x}$ when $\tilde{y}$ is obtained from $\tilde{x}$ by adding noise.

Definition 3.7A: $\tilde{y}$ is riskier than $\tilde{x}$ if $\tilde{y}$ is equal in distribution to $\tilde{x} + \tilde{z}$, where $E(\tilde{z}|x) = 0$.

It is important to notice that the added noise, $\tilde{z}$, is uncorrelated with $\tilde{x}$ and since it has zero mean for each x, the mean of $\tilde{z}$ is zero. This implies that $\tilde{y}$ and $\tilde{x}$ have the same mean. It need not be the case that $\tilde{z}$ is independent of $\tilde{x}$.

The second definition of $\tilde{y}$ riskier than $\tilde{x}$ is based on the most basic concept of risk aversion in EU decision models, namely the concavity of u(x). Random variable $\tilde{y}$ is said to be riskier than $\tilde{x}$ if $\tilde{x}$ is preferred or indifferent to $\tilde{y}$ by all decision makers with concave utility functions, those who are risk averse. No assumption is made concerning the sign of u'(x). In the formal statement of this definition, random variables $\tilde{y}$ and $\tilde{x}$ are represented by CDFs G(x) and F(x), respectively. This second definition argues that one can define an increase in risk as a change in a random variable that reduces expected utility for all risk averse persons, those who avoid risk.

Definition 3.7B: $\tilde{y}$ is riskier than $\tilde{x}$ if $\int_a^b u(x)dF(x) \geq \int_a^b u(x)dG(x)$ for all concave u(x).

In stating this definition, the assumption is made that the supports of the random variables lie in a bounded interval. Rothschild and Stiglitz assume that this bounded interval is [0, 1].

The third R-S definition of increasing risk introduces and defines a term that is important in its own right. This term has become part of an economist's vocabulary. This third definition indicates that $\tilde{y}$ is riskier than $\tilde{x}$ if the probability or density function for $\tilde{y}$ has "more weight in the tails" than that for $\tilde{x}$. To make "more weight in the tails" precise, R-S define a *mean preserving spread*, and this term is now in common usage.

A mean preserving spread (MPS) is a taking of probability mass from its current location in the distribution of probability, and redistributing that mass to locations to the right and to the left of the original location. This redistribution is carried out in such a way as to preserve the mean of the random variable. Probability mass is taken from center of the initial distribution, where "center" can be anywhere that probability mass is currently distributed, and this mass is redistributed to both lower and higher outcomes, keeping the mean outcome fixed. When such a MPS is carried out, R-S argue that it is natural to think of the new random variable as riskier than the original. A formal definition of a mean preserving spread for a discrete random variable is provided by Rothschild and Stiglitz. A definition for continuously distributed random variables is given here. The notation follows that of Diamond and Stiglitz (1974) and Meyer (1975).

Assume that random variable $\tilde{x}$ has probability density function f(x). Define as a mean preserving spread the function s(x).

Definition 3.7C: $\tilde{y}$ is riskier than $\tilde{x}$ if $\int_a^s [G(x) - F(x)]dx \geq 0$ for all s in [a, b] and $\int_a^b [G(x) - F(x)]dx = 0$.

The conditions on [G(x) − F(x)] specified in this third definition provide useful test conditions that can be readily applied to any pair of CDFs and have become the most common way to specify when one random variable is riskier than another.

R-S show that these three quite different definitions are actually one and demonstrate the following theorem.

Definition 3.8 s(x) is a mean preserving spread if

i) $\int_a^b s(x)dx = 0$.

ii) $\int_a^b x - s(x)dx = 0$.

iii) s(x) changes sign twice from positive to negative back to positive.

iv) $f(x) + s(x) \geq 0$ for all x.

The first and fourth conditions together ensure that when s(x) is added to f(x), the result is a density function g(x). Condition ii) makes the change mean preserving. Condition iii) indicates that when s(x) is added to f(x), probability mass is shifted from its current location, where s(x) is negative, and some of this mass is moved to the left and some to the right. This occurs when s(x) is positive. A typical mean preserving spread is given in Figure 3.3. A single mean preserving spread leads to CDFs that cross exactly one time and the riskier CDF is positive first. The mean preserving condition implies that the area above the horizontal axis is the same size as that below the axis. This is illustrated in Figure 3.4.

Assuming that the definition of increased risk is transitive and therefore a sequence of mean preserving spreads also leads to a riskier random variable, R-S determine the

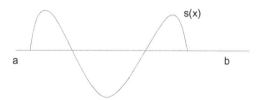

Figure 3.3 A typical mean preserving spread for density functions.

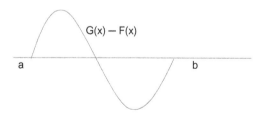

Figure 3.4 A typical mean preserving spread for cumulative distribution functions.

conditions on CDFs F(x) and G(x) for G(x) to be obtainable from F(x) by a sequence of MPSs. These conditions involve partial integrals of [G(x) − F(x)] and are the formal statement of the third definition of an increase in risk.

Theorem 3.6: *The following statements are equivalent.*

(1) $\tilde{y}$ is equal in distribution to $\tilde{x} + \tilde{z}$, where $E(\tilde{z}|x) = 0$.

(2) $\int_a^b u(x)dF(x) \geq \int_a^b u(x)dG(x)$ for every concave u(x).

(3) $\int_a^s [G(x) - F(x)]dx \geq 0$ for all s in [a, b] and $\int_a^b [G(x) - F(x)]dx = 0$.

The R-S definition of increasing risk has been accepted and used for more than forty years. No serious alternative has arisen in that time to replace it. This definition leads to a partial rather than complete order over random variables in terms of riskiness. The order is partial in two different senses. First, only the riskiness of random variables with the same mean can be compared. Second, even for random variables with the same mean, it is very possible that neither is riskier than the other. Attempts have been made to extend the definition to random variables whose means are different. Diamond and Stiglitz do this defining a mean utility preserving spread, replacing condition ii) in Definition 3.8 with

$$\text{ii)}^* \int_a^b u(x) \cdot s(x)dx = 0$$

which is the mean utility preserving condition. Meyer (1975) shows that this yields an order that is complete for all random variables whose cumulative distribution functions cross a finite number of times, but that this complete order is equivalent to the max–min order which ranks random variables according to the size of the worst possible outcome.

The R-S definition of increasing risk is an ordinal concept. None of the three characterizations is used to measure the size of the risk associated with a random variable. This is in contrast to variance, which orders random variables completely in terms of riskiness, and also gives a numerical measure of the size of the risk. Aumann and Serrano (2008) use the reciprocal of the absolute risk aversion measure of the CARA decision maker who is just indifferent between taking and rejecting a gamble as a measure of the size of the riskiness of that gamble. They specifically examine gambles with a positive mean value and a positive probability that negative outcomes occur. For these gambles, they show that their measure of riskiness has several desirable properties, and compare it with other attempts to determine an index of riskiness. The Aumann and Serrano index provides a measure of riskiness that is an alternative to variance as a measure of riskiness. Finally, as with the measure of absolute risk aversion, the definition of increased riskiness is for random variables whose outcomes are single dimension rather than vectors.

There is an extensive literature that uses the R-S definition of increasing risk (Rothschild and Stiglitz, 1971). Comparative statics analysis in a variety of decision models has examined the effects of R-S increases in risk on choices made, and on the welfare of the decision maker. It is often the case that analysis of these comparative static questions does not yield a determinate conclusion that applies to all R-S increases in risk, and therefore further restrictions on the change in riskiness have been proposed. Sandmo (1971) discusses risk increases that change $\tilde{x}$ by defining $\tilde{y} = \alpha + \theta \cdot \tilde{x}$ where α and θ are chosen so that the mean is not changed. $\theta > 1$ implies that risk has increased. Meyer and Ormiston (1985) generalize this, defining *strong increases in risk*. Others, including Black and Bulkley (1989) and Kihlstrom et al. (1981), add to this literature. The literature was summarized and a very general result presented by Gollier (1995). A review of these refinements is beyond the scope of this chapter. A summary can be found in Gollier (1995) and Gollier and Pratt (1996).

3.5.4 Second Degree Stochastic Dominance

Definition 3.7B is in the form of a *stochastic dominance* finding. That is, that definition provides an answer to a question of the form: what are necessary and sufficient conditions for one random variable to be preferred or indifferent to another by all decision makers in a specified group of decision makers? Rothschild and Stiglitz answer this question for the group of decision makers that include all those who are risk averse. *Second degree stochastic dominance* adds the restriction that the utility function must also satisfy $u'(x) \geq 0$ for all x; that is, second degree stochastic dominance considers all decision makers whose utility functions satisfy both $u'(x) \geq 0$ and $u''(x) \leq 0$ for all x. The conditions for unanimous preference of one random variable over another for this group of decision makers define the well-known second degree stochastic dominance condition. Hadar and Russell (1969) and Hanoch and Levy (1969) each provide the definition. Like first degree stochastic dominance and the second R-S definition, these conditions use CDFs to represent random variables and place restrictions on $[G(x) - F(x)]$.

Second degree stochastic dominance (SSD) is related to the R-S definition of an increase in risk. SSD differs from the definition of increasing risk because in addition to concavity of u(x), $u'(x) \geq 0$ is also assumed. With this smaller set of decision makers, the equal means condition of the R-S definition of an increase in risk is no longer necessary, and therefore the condition that $\int_a^b [G(x) - F(x)]dx = 0$ is not part of the SSD definition.

Definition 3.9: F(x) dominates G(x) in the second degree if $\int_a^s [G(x) - F(x)]dx \geq 0$ for all s in [a, b].

As with FSD, the implications in an EU decision model provide support for the definition.

Theorem 3.7: F(x) *dominates* G(x) *in the second degree if and only if* F(x) *is preferred or indifferent to* G(x) *by all EU decision makers with N-M utility functions satisfying* $u'(x) \geq 0$ *and* $u''(x) \leq 0$ *for all* x.

One random variable can dominate another in the second degree because it is larger, less risky, or as a result of a combination of these two reasons. It is the case that when F(x) dominates G(x) in SSD that $\mu_F \geq \mu_G$.

3.5.5 Other Forms of Stochastic Dominance

A number of other forms of stochastic dominance have also been defined. Some have further restricted the set of decision makers under consideration by imposing sign conditions on higher order derivatives of u(x). Along with *n*th degree risk aversion discussed briefly in Section 3.4.7, Ekern also provides a definition of an *n*th degree risk increase and demonstrates a general stochastic dominance theorem. Definition 3.3 from Section 3.4.7 is repeated for convenience.

Definition 3.3: Decision maker with utility function u(x) is *n*th degree risk averse if $(-1)^{n-1} \cdot u^{(n)}(x) > 0$ for all x.

Definition 3.10: G(x) has more *n*th degree risk than F(x) if $G^{(n)}(x) \geq F^{(n)}(x)$ for all x in [a, b] and $G^{(k)}(b) = F^{(k)}(b)$. These statements hold for k = 1, 2, ..., n.

$F^{(k)}(x)$ denotes the kth cumulative probability distribution; that is, let $F^{(1)}(x)$ denote F(x), and higher order cumulative functions are defined by $F^{(k)}(x) = \int_a^x F^{(k-1)}(s)ds$, k = 2, 3,.... The relationship between Definitions 3.3 and 3.10 is also provided by Ekern who demonstrates the following theorem.

Theorem 3.8: *G(x) has more nth degree risk than F(x) if and only if every nth degree risk averse decision maker prefers F(x) to G(x).*

This theorem contains the FSD result, Theorem 3.5, and a portion of the R–S increasing risk definition, Theorem 3.6, as special cases. Each of those findings restricts the sign of only one derivative of u(x) as does Definition 3.3. If one restricts the sign of each of the first n derivatives of u(x) rather than just the nth, then the following theorem results. Theorem 3.9 contains both Theorems 3.5 and 3.7 as special cases. This theorem also contains the *third degree stochastic dominance* result that was presented by Whitmore (1970).

Theorem 3.9: F(x) *stochastically dominates* G(x) *in the nth degree; that is* $G^{(n)}(x) \geq F^{(n)}(x)$ *for all* x *in* [a, b] *and* $G^{(k)}(b) \geq F^{(k)}(b)$ *for* k = 1, 2, ..., n *if and only if every decision maker who is kth degree risk averse for* k = 1, 2, ..., n *prefers* F(x) *to* G(x).

Other forms of stochastic dominance have imposed restriction on $A_u(x)$. DARA stochastic dominance, for instance, considers decision makers for whom $u'(x) \geq 0$, $u''(x) \leq 0$ and $A_u'(x) \leq 0$. The necessary and sufficient conditions for DARA stochastic dominance have not been characterized in a simple way. It is known, however, that DARA and third degree stochastic dominance are equivalent when the means of $F(x)$ and $G(x)$ are equal to one another. Fishburn and Vickson (1978) and Liu and Meyer (2012) demonstrate this.

Diamond and Stiglitz (1974) when defining *mean utility preserving spreads* and Meyer (1977) when defining *stochastic dominance with respect to a function* consider sets of decision makers defined by a lower bound on $A_u(x)$ that need not be zero; that is, all decision makers who are more risk averse than a reference decision maker where the reference decision maker need not be the risk neutral one. The following theorem provides a stochastic dominance condition for such sets of decision makers.

Theorem 3.10: $F(x)$ *is preferred or indifferent to* $G(x)$ *by all EU decision makers with N-M utility functions satisfying* $u'(x) \geq 0$ *and* $A_u(x) \geq A_v(x)$ *if and only if* $\int_a^s [G(x) - F(x)]v'(x)dx \geq 0$ *for all s in* $[a, b]$.

Fishburn (1974) discusses extending the concept of stochastic dominance to more than a pair-wise comparison. His work focuses on the case of two sets of random variables with CDFs $\{F_1(x), F_2(x), \ldots F_n(x)\}$ and $\{G_1(x), G_2(x), \ldots G_n(x)\}$, respectively. For FSD the following theorem applies. A similar result holds for SSD.

Theorem 3.11: *For each* $u(x)$ *with* $u'(x) \geq 0$, *there exists an* i, $i = 1, 2, \ldots$ n, *such that* $F_i(x)$ *is preferred or indifferent to* $G_i(x)$ *if and only if* $\sum_{i=1}^n \lambda_i F_i(x)$ *dominates* $\sum_{i=1}^n \lambda_i G_i(x)$ *in FSD for some* $(\lambda_1, \lambda_2, \ldots \lambda_n)$ *such that* $\lambda_i \geq 0$ *and* $\sum_{i=1}^n \lambda_i = 1$.

3.6 MEAN VARIANCE ANALYSIS AND EXPECTED UTILITY

Now that the EU decision model has been reviewed, the discussion returns briefly to the M-V decision model and the important question of when are these two decision models equivalent to one another in the way that they rank the random variables in the choice set. That is, when can an EU ranking of alternatives $F(x)$ and $G(x)$ be represented equivalently with a ranking function $V(\sigma, \mu)$? Many have addressed this question, especially during the time period when the two decision models were each considered to be an interesting alternative in theoretical economic modeling of risky decisions. A very good summary of this literature is given by Baron (1977) and a portion of the material here comes from that paper.

The main and simple answer to this equivalence question is that if there are no restrictions placed on the set of random variables to be ranked, it is necessary and sufficient that the N-M utility function $u(x)$ be a quadratic function. Baron attributes this result to Markowitz (1959). If one adds the Borch requirement, discussed in section 3.2.2, that the utility function represent preferences where more is preferred to less, then even with quadratic utility functions the random variables that can be ranked have supports that are severely restricted. To see this assume that u(x) takes the form $u(x) = x + c \cdot x^2$ for $c < 0$. For this quadratic utility function, the maximum outcome possible must be less than $\frac{1}{-2c}$ for $u'(x)$ to be nonnegative. Therefore if risk aversion is allowed, so that $c > 0$, the random variables being ranked must have supports that lie in intervals truncated on the right by $\frac{1}{-2c}$. This makes it difficult to model wide ranges of risk aversion.

All other answers to the equivalence question restrict the set of random variables to be ranked at the outset. When the choice set is restricted to normally distributed random variables, Chipman (1973) provides a very complete and detailed discussion. With the normality assumption, the utility function must be bounded for expected utility to be finite. Also, the M-V utility function over *variance* and mean $T(\sigma^2, \mu)$ satisfies a particular differential equation given by

$$2\frac{\partial T}{\partial \sigma^2} = \frac{\partial^2 T}{\partial \mu^2}.$$

Also for normally distributed random variables, Freund (1956) shows that the EU ranking function U(F) can be reduced to a simple $V(\sigma, \mu)$ whenever the N-M utility functions u(x) are of the CARA form. That is, Freund shows if $u(x) = -e^{-cx}$ and $\tilde{x}$ is normally distributed, the EU ranking function U(F) can be reduced to the M-V utility function $V(\sigma, \mu) = \mu - \lambda \cdot \sigma^2$, a commonly used and simple functional form for $V(\sigma, \mu)$.

More recently Sinn (1983) and Meyer (1987) show that when the set of random variables to be ranked is restricted to include only alternatives which are location and scale transformations of one another, that is elements from the same location and scale family, then an EU ranking of these alternatives can be represented by $V(\sigma, \mu)$.

Definition 3.11: Random variables $\{x_1, x_2, x_n, ...\}$ are in the same location and scale family if for each x_i and x_j it is the case that $x_i =_d a + b \cdot x_j$ where $b > 0$.

It is typical to choose to focus on a particular element x^* from the location and scale family whose mean equals zero and variance equals one. For this x^*, each $x_i =_d \mu_i + \sigma_i \cdot x^*$. Here, μ_i and σ_i are the mean and standard deviation of x_i.

The set of all normally distributed random variables is a location and scale family as is the set of all uniformly distributed random variables. There is an infinity of such families. Location and scale families of random variables can be generated by picking any random variable with mean zero and variance equal to one as x^* and then forming the remaining elements of the family with mean μ_i and standard deviation σ_i using the equation $x_i =_d \mu_i + \sigma_i \cdot x^*$ to generate those random variables. Obviously only a few such families have been named.

When the set of random variables to be ranked are from a location and scale family, the M-V ranking function $V(\sigma, \mu)$ and the slope of indifference curves in (σ, μ) space, $S(\sigma, \mu)$, have several interesting properties. Among the more important of these properties are:

Property 1: $V(\sigma, \mu)$ *is concave if* $u(x)$ *is concave.*

Property 2: $S_u(\sigma, \mu) \geq S_v(\sigma, \mu)$ *for all* (σ, μ) *if* $u(x)$ *is more risk averse than* $v(x)$.

Property 3: $\frac{\partial S}{\partial \mu} \leq 0$ *if* $u(x)$ *is decreasingly absolute risk averse.*

One reason why focusing on random variables from a location and scale family is a worthwhile exercise is that for decision models with only one random variable, and whose outcome variable is linear in that random variable, all possible random outcome variables automatically form a location and scale family. For instance in the single risky asset portfolio choice model where the outcome variable $\widetilde{W} = W_0(\alpha \cdot \tilde{r} + (1 - \alpha)\rho)$, all possible $\widetilde{W}$ that can be formed by choosing different values for α, or when the parameters ρ or W_0 are varied, are a location and scale family of random alternatives. Thus, this model and many others like it can be analyzed using either the M-V or EU decision model framework.

ACKNOWLEDGMENT

Helpful comments from the editors and Liqun Liu are gratefully acknowledged.

REFERENCES

Alchian, A., 1953. The meaning of utility measurement. American Economic Review 43, 26–50.

Arrow, K.J., 1965. Aspects of the Theory of Risk Bearing. Yrjö Jahnssonin Säätiö, Helsinki.

Aumann, R.J., Serrano, R., 2008. An economic index of riskiness. Journal of Politcal Economy 116, 810–836.

Baron, D.P., 1977. On the utility theoretic foundations of meanvariance analysis. Journal of Finance 32, 1683–1697.

Baumol, W., 1958. The cardinal utility which is ordinal. Economic Journal 68, 665–672.

Bernoulli, D., 1954. Exposition of a new theory on the measurement of risk. Econometrica 22, 23–36.

Black, J.M., Bulkley, G., 1989. A ratio criterion for signing the effect of an increase in uncertainty. International Economic Review 30, 119–130.

Borch, K., 1969. A not on uncertainty and indifference curves. Review of Economic Studies 36, 1–4.

Campbell, J.Y., Cochrane, J.H., 1999. By force of habit: a consumption-based explanation of aggregate stock market behavior. Journal of Political Economy 107, 205–251.

Chipman, J.S., 1973. The ordering of portfolios in terms of mean and variance. The Review of Economic Studies 40, 167–190.

Conniffe, D., 2007a. The generalized extreme value distribution as utility function. The Economic and Social Review 38, 275–288.

Conniffe, D., 2007b. The flexible three parameter utility function. Annals of Economics and Finance 8, 57–63.

Constantinides, G.M., 1990. Habit formation: a resolution of the equity premium puzzle. Journal of Political Economy 98, 519–543.

Crainich, D., Eeckhoudt, L., 2008. On the intensity of downside risk aversion. Journal of Risk and Uncertainty 36, 267–276.

Denuit, M., Eeckhoudt, L., 2010a. A general index of absolute risk attitude. Management Science 56, 712–715.

Denuit, M., Eeckhoudt, L., 2010b. Stronger measures of higher-order risk attitudes. Journal of Economic Theory 145, 2027–2036.

Diamond, P.A., Stiglitz, J.E., 1974. Increases in risk and in risk aversion. Journal of Economic Theory 8, 337–360.

Eeckhoudt, L., Schlesinger, H., 2006. Putting risk in its proper place. American Economic Review 96, 280–289.

Ekern, S., 1980. Increasing Nth degree risk. Economics Letters 6, 329–333.

Fishburn, P., 1974. Convex stochastic dominance with continuous distribution functions. Journal of Economic Theory 7, 143–158.

Fishburn, P., Vickson, R.G., 1978. Theoretical foundations of stochastic dominance. In: Whitmore, G.A., Findlay, M.C. (Eds.), Stochastic Dominance: An Approach to Decision Making Under Risk. Lexington, Toronto.

Freund, R.J., 1956. The introduction of risk into a programming model. Econometrica 24, 253–263.

Friedman, M., Savage, L.J., 1948. Utility analysis of choices involving risk. Journal of Political Economy 56, 279–304.

Gollier, C., 1995. The comparative statics of changes in risk revisited. Journal of Economic Theory 66, 522–536.

Gollier, C., 2001. The Economics of Risk and Time. MIT Press, Cambridge MA.

Gollier, C., Pratt, J.W., 1996. Risk vulnerability and the tempering effect of background risk. Econometrica 64, 1109–1124.

Hadar, J., Russell, W., 1969. Rules for ordering uncertain prospects. American Economic Review 59, 25–34.

Hanoch, G., Levy, H., 1969. Efficiency analysis of choices involving risk. Review of Economic Studies 36, 335–346.

Herstein, I.N., Milnor, J., 1953. An axiomatic approach to measurable utility. Econometrica 21, 291–297.

Jindapon, P., Neilson, W.S., 2007. Higher-order generalizations of Arrow-Pratt and ross risk aversion: a comparative statics approach. Journal of Economic Theory 136, 719–728.

Katz, E., 1981. A note on the comparative statics theorem for choice under risk. Journal of Economic Theory 25, 318–319.

Keenan, D., Snow, A., 2002. Greater downside risk aversion. Journal of Risk and Uncertainty 24, 267–277.

Keenan, D., Snow, A., 2009. Greater downside risk aversion in the large. Journal of Economic Theory 144, 1092–1101.

Kihlstrom, R.E., Mirman, L.J., 1974. Risk aversion with many commodities. Journal of Economic Theory 8, 361–388.

Kihlstrom, R.E., Romer, David, Williams, Steve, 1981. Risk aversion with random initial wealth. Econometrica 49, 911–920.

Kimball, M.S., 1990. Precautionary saving in the small and in the large. Econometrica 58, 53–73.

Kimball, M.S., 1993. Standard risk aversion. Econometrica 61, 589–611.

Kraus, M., 1979. A comparative statics theorem for choice under risk. Journal of Economic Theory 21, 510–517.

Leland, H., 1968. Saving and uncertainty: the precautionary demand for saving. Quarterly Journal of Economics 82, 465–473.

Lintner, J., 1965. The valuation of risk assets and the selection of risky investments in stock portfolios and capital budgets. Review of Economics and Statistics 47, 13–37.

Liu, L., Meyer, J., 2012. Decreasing absolute risk aversion, prudence and increased downside risk aversion. Journal of Risk and Uncertainty 44, 243–260.

Luce, R. Duncan, Raiffa, Howard, 1957. Games and Decisions: Introduction and Critical Survey. Wiley, New York.

Machina, M.J., Neilson, W.S., 1987. The ross characterization of risk aversion: strengthening and extension. Econometrica 55, 1139–1149.

Markowitz, H., 1952. Portfolio selection. Journal of Finance 7, 77–91.

Markowitz, H., 1959. Portfolio Selection. Yale University Press, New Haven.

Menezes, C., Geiss, C., Tressler, J., 1980. Increasing downside risk. American Economic Review 70, 921–932.

Menezes, C.F., Hanson, D.L., 1970. On the theory of risk aversion. International Economic Review 11, 481–487.

Meyer, J., 1975. Increasing risk. Journal of Economic Theory 11, 119–132.

Meyer, J., 1977. Stochastic dominance with respect to a function. International Economic Review 18, 477–487.

Meyer, J., 1987. Two moment decision models and expected utility maximization. American Economic Review 77, 421–430.

Meyer, J., 2010. Representing risk preferences in expected utility based decision models. Annals of Operations Research 76, 179–190.

Meyer, J., Meyer, D.J., 2005. Habit formation, the equity premium puzzle and risk preferences in multi-period consumption models. Journal of Monetary Economics 52, 1497–1515.

Meyer, J., Meyer, D.J., 2006. Measuring risk aversion. Foundations and Trends in Microeconomics 2, 107–203.

Meyer, J., Ormiston, M., 1985. Strong increases in risk and their comparative statics. International Economic Review 26, 425–437.

Modica, S., Scarsini, M., 2005. A note on comparative downside risk aversion. Journal of Economic Theory 122, 267–271.

Mossin, J., 1966. Equilibrium in a capital asset market. Econometrica 34, 768–783.

Mossin, J., 1968. Aspects of rational insurance purchasing. Journal of Political Economy 76, 553–568.

Pratt, J.W., 1964. Risk aversion in the small and in the large. Econometrica 32, 122–136.

Pratt, J.W., 1990. The logic of partial-risk aversion: paradox lost. Journal of Risk and Uncertainty 3, 105–113.

Ross, S.A., 1981. Some stronger measures of risk aversion. Econometrica 49, 621–638.

Rothschild, M., Stiglitz, J.E., 1970. Increasing risk I: a definition. Journal of Economic Theory 2, 225–243.

Rothschild, M., Stiglitz, J.E., 1971. Increasing risk II: its consequences. Journal of Economic Theory 3, 66–84.

Saha, A., 1993. Expo-power utility: a flexible form for absolute and relative risk aversion. American Journal of Agricultural Economics 75, 905–913.

Sandmo, A., 1970. The effect of uncertainty on saving decisions. Review of Economic Studies. 37, 353–360.

Sandmo, A., 1971. On the theory of the competitive firm under price uncertainty. American Economic Review 61, 65–73.

Sharpe, W.F., 1964. Capital asset prices: a theory of market equilibrium under conditions of risk. Journal of Finance 19, 425–442.

Sinn, H.W., 1983. Economic Decisions under Uncertainty. North-Holland, Amsterdam.

Smith, V., 1968. Optimal insurance coverage. Journal of Political Economy 68, 68–77.

Tobin, J., 1958. Liquidity preference as a behavior toward risk. Review of Economic Studies 25, 65–86.

von Neumann, J., Morgenstern, O., 1944. Theory of Games and Economic Behavior. Princeton University Press.

Whitmore, G.A., 1970. Third-degree stochastic dominance. American Economic Review 60, 457–459.

CHAPTER 4

Assessment and Estimation of Risk Preferences

Charles A. Holt[a] and Susan K. Laury[b]

[a]Department of Economics, University of Virginia, USA
[b]Department of Economics, Georgia State University, USA

Contents

Abstract

This chapter surveys the rapidly growing literature in which risk preferences are measured and manipulated in laboratory and field experiments. The most commonly used measurement instruments are: an *investment task* for allocations between a safe and risky asset, a *choice menu task* for eliciting probability indifference points, and a *pricing task* for eliciting certainty equivalents of a lottery. These methods are compared in a manner that will help the practitioner decide which one to use, and how to deal with methodological issues associated with incentives, stakes, and the structure of choice menus. Applications involve using inferred risk preferences to document demographic effects, e.g. gender, and to explain the effects of risk aversion on observed behavior in economic in settings, e.g. bargaining, auctions, and contests. Some suggestions for evaluating the separate effects of utility curvature and probability weighting are provided.

Keywords

Risk Aversion, Risk Preference, Elicitation, Probability Weighting, Framing Effects, Incentive Effects, House Money Effects, Loss Aversion, Gender, Demographics, Certainty Equivalents, Probability Equivalents, Auctions, Bargaining, Contests, Asset Integration, Heuristics

JEL Classification Codes

D81, C91, C92, C93

Handbook of the Economics of Risk and Uncertainty, Volume 1
ISSN 2211-7547, http://dx.doi.org/10.1016/B978-0-444-53685-3.00004-0

4.1 INTRODUCTION

A primary advantage of experimentation in economics is the ability to *induce or manipulate* payoff structures with specific theoretical predictions. The calculation of optimal decisions for individuals or game-theoretic predictions for groups, however, requires assumptions about aspects of preferences that are beyond the direct control of the experimenter, e.g. other-regarding preferences or risk aversion. Notions of risk and risk aversion pervade many areas of economics, especially insurance, contract theory, finance, and business cycle theory (post 2008), and obtaining measures of risk aversion is important for interpreting observed data patterns. This survey deals with the large literature on experimental methods for measurement of attitudes toward risk.

4.1.1 Background and Early Insights Based on Introspection and Informal Surveys

The earliest thinking about risk aversion may be Daniel Bernoulli's (1738) paper, which even predates the birth of economics and psychology as distinct fields of inquiry. Bernoulli's point was that the maximization of the expected value of monetary payoffs is not a reasonable description of actual behavior because it takes no account of risks associated with small probabilities and low payoffs. He considered a lottery in which a fair coin is flipped repeatedly, with no payoff made until "heads" is first obtained. The possible money payoff starts at 2 and is doubled, 4, 8, etc., after each "tails" is observed. The expected value of this lottery is $(1/2)2 + (1/4)4 \ldots + (1/2^n)2^n + \ldots$, which is an infinite sum of ones. The Bernoulli paradox is that people would not be willing to pay large amounts of money in exchange for a random lottery with an infinite expected value. His resolution was to suggest that the utility function is nonlinear, with a concave shape that underweights high payoffs.

Milton Friedman, who had been working on decision theoretic and statistical issues during World War II, returned to this issue in collaboration with Leonard Savage, one of the founders of decision theory. Their 1948 paper argued that the von Neumann–Morgenstern utility function for wealth should contain both convex and concave segments to explain why some people simultaneously purchase insurance and lottery tickets for large gains (Friedman and Savage, 1948).

Harry Markowitz, who studied under both Friedman and Savage at Chicago, had always been fascinated with the trade-off between risk and return. His 1952 *Journal of Finance* (1952a) paper on portfolio theory formalized the decision theory behind the construction of a portfolio based on a trade-off between expected return and risk (measured by variance). Although this paper was the primary basis for a Nobel Prize forty years later, there was another more relevant paper that Markowitz published in the same year in the *Journal of Political Economy*. The earliest stirrings of experimental economics were emerging in those years, and Markowitz (1952b) devised a *structured* series of binary lottery choices with scaled payoffs for both gains and losses. For example, one question that he would pose to his friends and colleagues was whether a person would rather owe a penny for sure or have a 1/10 chance of owing a dime (most people were risk averse, preferring the sure loss of a penny). These losses were scaled up by a factor of 10 or more, e.g. to dimes and dollars, for subsequent questions. He found that people switched from risk aversion to risk preference for large losses, e.g. preferring a 1/10 chance of losing \$10,000 to a sure loss of \$1,000. The opposite pattern was observed for gains above "customary wealth." In particular, people tended to take small, fair gambles, e.g. they preferred a 1/10 chance of \$10 to a sure \$1. But risk aversion was prevalent for large gambles; everyone preferred a sure million dollars to a 1/10 chance of ten million. Markowitz concluded that the utility function had to have convex segments in order to explain the risk-seeking responses that he was encountering for small gains or large losses from the present wealth position. His paper contains a graph of a utility function (Figure 5, p. 154) with several convex and concave segments, positioned around the origin ("o") at present wealth. He concluded that utility should be a function of gains and losses *from this level*, not a function of final wealth as implied by "asset integration." Even more remarkable was the fact that Markowitz's informal questions also turned up a strong hint of loss aversion:

> *"Generally people avoid symmetric bets. This suggests that the curve falls faster to the left of the origin than it rises to the right of the origin. (i.e., U(X) > |U(−X)|, X > 0.)" (Markowitz, 1952b, p. 154).*

His utility graphs were explicitly constructed to be monotonic but bounded, in order to avoid the Bernoulli paradox. This tradition of considering a reference point that is affected by present or customary wealth levels has been followed by psychologists and experimental economists ever since.

The next key development was the Kahneman and Tversky (1979) paper on prospect theory. This paper was motivated by experimental evidence for gains and losses and high and low probability levels. In addition, they added a third element, the replacement of probabilities with weights (as proposed by Edwards, 1962), to the Markowitz insights about reference points and risk seeking in the loss domain. Another key component of prospect theory is the notion of "loss aversion," which they modeled as a kink in the utility function at the reference point, in contrast to the inflection point at the origin in the Markowitz graph. Kahneman and Tversky's paper is one of the most widely cited papers in the economics literature, and it was a primary impetus for Kahneman's 2003 Nobel Prize.

This survey is focused on more recent work, mostly in experimental economics, which builds upon and refines the deep insights provided from the Bernoulli–Friedman–Savage–Markowitz–Kahneman–Tversky tradition, using real financial incentives instead of the hypothetical payoff questions that were generally used in previous work.

Of course, there is a rich empirical econometric literature on behavior in insurance and financial markets in which estimates of risk aversion play a role. In contrast, the focus here is on measuring risk aversion directly, or alternatively, on making qualitative inferences about changes in levels of risk aversion (or preference) that result from changes in laboratory treatment variables and demographic characteristics.

4.1.2 Overview

Most of the papers that will be discussed here follow Markowitz in the sense of working with a set of related lottery choice tasks, or a set of choices that correspond to alternative investment portfolios. Section 4.2 will introduce these alternative approaches. The use of menus of related questions or options brings up issues of presentation, framing, and treatment-order effects. The possibility of using financial incentives also raises a number of considerations, e.g. controlling for wealth effects. These and other procedural issues are addressed in Section 4.3. The fourth section surveys the wide variety of treatments that have been used in risk aversion experiments, e.g. group versus individual decisions, gains versus losses, and biological treatments. Section 4.5, in contrast, pertains to factors that cannot be manipulated during an experiment, e.g. demographic effects of gender, age, income, cognitive ability, culture, etc. This is followed in Section 4.6 by a discussion of economic applications in the lab and in the field, based on selected examples in which risk aversion measures were elicited and used to obtain a deeper perspective on otherwise perplexing behavioral patterns, e.g. in tournaments and contests, bargaining, laboratory financial markets, and simple games. The final sections provide a summary of the main findings and their implications, both for theoretical work on decision theory and for practitioners interested in eliciting risk aversion in laboratory and field settings.

4.2. ASSESSMENT APPROACHES

Risk aversion can be inferred from choices between two alternatives, e.g. a sure payoff of $3 or a risky payoff that provides a 0.8 chance of $4 ($0 otherwise). A single choice like this can be used to separate individuals into two risk preference categories. Interval estimates can be refined by providing subjects with choices among more than two alternatives, or by letting subjects make multiple choices in a structured list. This section begins with a review of some results based on sets of binary choices, and then introduces the three main approaches that have been used to provide more structure for the elicitation of risk preferences. All three are motivated by the common intellectual framework that was outlined in the introduction, although key differences emerge.

1) The *investment portfolio* approach bases risk aversion inferences on a single choice that is made among alternative gambles, which typically correspond to different divisions of investment funds between safe and risky assets. Here, more risk aversion corresponds to investing less of one's stake in the risky asset.

2) The *lottery choice menu* approach is built around a structured list of distinct binary choices between safe and risky gambles, with risk aversion being inferred from the total number of safe choices, or the point at which a subject switches between the safe and risky gambles.

3) The *pricing task* approach involves the elicitation of a certainty equivalent money amount, e.g. by using Becker et al. (1964) procedures for obtaining a buying or selling price for a gamble. In this case, risk aversion is inferred from the difference between the expected value of the gamble and the elicited certainty equivalent value (no difference corresponds to risk neutrality).

The lines of division between these alternative approaches are not as sharp as would first appear. For example, binary choices in a menu list can be thought of as pairs of alternative investment portfolios. Alternatively, it is possible (and usually desirable) to elicit a certainty equivalent for a gamble using a menu (of choices between the gamble and a list of alternative money amounts) instead of asking the subject to provide a price and using random procedures to generate a bid or ask price from the other side of the market.

4.2.1 Binary Choices

In a choice between a sure \$3 and a 0.8 chance of \$4, Kahneman and Tversky (1979) report that 80% of subjects selected the safe outcome, which indicates some risk aversion, since the safe payoff of \$3 is below the expected payoff of $0.8(\$4) = \$3.20$ for the risky option. A choice like this puts a lower bound on risk aversion, depending on what measure you want to use. For a utility function $u(x)$, a common measure is proportional to the ratio of the first and second derivatives: $r = -xu''(x)/u'(x)$. For example, if $u(x) = x^{1-r}/(1-r)$, then relative risk aversion is given by a constant r for all values of x, and hence this utility exhibits "constant relative risk aversion" (CRRA). If a person with this utility function prefers a sure \$3 to a 0.8 chance of \$4, it can be shown that $r > 0.22$. In contrast, only 8% of the subjects in the study chose the sure outcome when payoffs were transformed into losses. The intuition is that "… certainty increases the aversiveness of losses as well as the desirability of gains" (Kahneman and Tversky, 1979, p. 269). Another way in which the choice between a sure \$3 and a 0.8 chance of \$4 can be altered is to scale down each of the gain probabilities to a quarter of the original levels, so probabilities of 1 and 0.8 would become 0.25 and 0.20, respectively. Thus the choice would be between a 0.25 chance of \$3 (\$0 otherwise) and a 0.2 chance of \$4 (\$0 otherwise). Since all original probabilities have been multiplied by 0.25, the expected utility for each of these prospects has been scaled down by the same proportion, so the sign of the expected utility difference is unchanged. The implication is that an expected-utility maximizer who selects the sure \$3 in the first choice task would be predicted to select the 0.25 chance of \$3 in the second task. This "Allais paradox" (Allais, 1953) prediction is contradicted in Kahneman and Tversky's experiment with hypothetical payoffs, and in subsequent experiments with real financial incentives (e.g., de Palma et al., 2008).

Anomalies are sometimes explained in terms of nonlinear perceptions of probabilities, which are generally thought to involve overweighting probabilities near 0 and underweighting probabilities near 1. In the choice between a sure $3 and a 0.8 chance of $4, for example, some underweighting of the 0.8 for the second option could enhance the likelihood of the safe choice. Next consider a person who chooses a 0.05 chance of $100 over a sure $10. Such a person exhibits risk-seeking behavior, but this could be due to a tendency to overweight the low probability of the high gain, instead of being caused by convexity of the utility function, which is the usual way that risk preference is modeled in an expected utility framework. Of course, another possibility is that behavior is best modeled by nonlinearities in both the probability and utility dimensions. Laboratory experiments with more structured sets of alternatives can shed light on these issues. For example, we will review experiments in which subjects make risk-averse choices in some settings with a downside risk, with a small probability of a low payoff, but the same subjects exhibit risk seeking in settings with upside risk, in which there is a small probability of a high payoff.

Simple introspection, however, suggests that probability weighting might not be the whole story. The overweighting of low probabilities, for example, would exacerbate the Bernoulli paradox, which is based on a series of probabilities that converge zero. Or in the Markowitz tradition, try asking people whether they would prefer a million dollars over a fair coin flip on getting two million or nothing. Here there are no small probabilities, so overweighting of low probabilities is not an issue. What you will find is that most people essentially discount the marginal benefit of the second million, in comparison with the lifestyle changes that would result from becoming an instant millionaire. This hypothetical example, of course, does not rule out pessimism effects or other nonexpected utility factors, but it does suggest why economists have been especially interested in experiments with high payoff stakes, which are discussed next. We will review experiments in which scaled-up payoffs, holding probabilities constant, produce sharp increases in risk aversion. Later, in the section on Implications for Theory, we will discuss recent advances in using structured sets of choices to disentangle the separate effects of utility curvature and probability weighting.

4.2.2 Investment Menus: A Single Choice Among Alternative Portfolios

Binswanger's (1981) classic paper was one of the first to use choices with high cash payoffs to elicit measures of risk aversion. The impact of this paper was enhanced by a careful theoretical and econometric analysis, and the use of very high stakes that were possible to implement in the rural Bangladesh setting: "Unlike most of the studies to date in psychology and economics, this experiment used payoffs that were both real and large to induce participants to reveal their preferences. Indeed, the highest expected payoff for a single decision exceeded the average monthly income of an unskilled worker." (Binswanger, 1981, p. 867) The subjects were farmers who were given a range

Table 4.1 The Binswanger (1981) Menu of Alternative Gambles Arrayed by Risk

Choice Alternative	Equally Likely Payoffs	Gamble Structure	CRRA Midpoint	Category Description	Choice Percentage* (0.5× scale)
Gamble 5	0 or 200	0 + 0.5 chance of 200	≤ 0	Neutral to Preferred	19%
Gamble 4	10 or 190	10 + 0.5 chance of 180	0.17	Slight to Neutral	15%
Gamble 3	30 or 150	30 + 0.5 chance of 120	0.51	Moderate	20%
Gamble 2	40 or 120	40 + 0.5 chance of 80	1.9	Intermediate	29%
Gamble 1	45 or 95	45 + 0.5 chance of 50	3.6	Severe Aversion	6%
Gamble 0	50	50	≥ 7.5	Extreme Aversion	2%

In addition, 10% of the choices were for Gamble 2 (payoffs of 35 or 125) or Gamble 3* (payoffs of 20 or 160), which are mean-preserving spreads of gambles 2 and 3.

of alternative gambles to choose between, with differing degrees of risk. One gamble offered a sure payoff of 50 for each outcome of a coin flip (Gamble 0 in Table 4.1), which is analogous to putting all of one's money into a safe asset. Other options offered higher ("good luck") and lower ("bad luck") outcomes, with the most extreme choice providing a payoff of either 0 or 200, corresponding to putting all cash into a risky asset. The choices were structured so that people with lower levels of risk aversion would select options with higher expected values and a large range between the maximum and minimum payoffs. In addition, several of the options were "inefficient" in that they provided mean preserving spreads of other options, i.e., more risk but no more in the way of expected return, which could only be selected by risk-seeking individuals.

The choice alternatives provided to the villagers involved two possible payoffs, as shown in the Equally Likely Payoffs column of Table 4.1 (the dominated options are not shown). Notice that the options in the upper rows of the table offer a higher expected payoff and a large range from the maximum to minimum payoff. For example, the top row corresponds to a risky portfolio that pays 0 or 200 with equal probability, and the bottom row is analogous to leaving an initial stake of 50 in a safe asset. Even though the choices were presented and explained in a relatively neutral frame, it turns out that each option can be thought of as an alternative portfolio. Gamble 1 in the second to last row is analogous to taking $5 out of the $50 stake and putting it in an investment that yields 50 with probability 0.5, zero otherwise. If the investment yields nothing, one is left with $45 (the starting $50 stake minus the $5 investment); if the investment yields $50, one is left with $95 (the starting $50 stake minus the $5 investment plus $50 return on the investment). This is shown in column 3 of Table 4.1. This highly attractive option is presumably designed to prevent a pileup of choices at the safe endpoint. Similarly, Gamble 2 involves taking $10 out of the stake of $50 in order to obtain a 0.5 chance of $80. The return to the risky asset diminishes more sharply at the top of the table, which would tend to prevent boundary effects. (An alternative approach, with a constant rate of return for the risky asset, will be considered below.)

Binswanger calculated a range of risk aversion coefficients for those who would choose each gamble, and the midpoints of this range are provided in the column for constant relative risk aversion (CRRA), along with category descriptions in the adjacent column. A "neutral to preferred" person would choose the riskiest portfolio in the top row, and a person with "extreme aversion" (CRRA > 7.5) would choose the safe position in the bottom row.

Binswanger began the experiment by visiting villages and presenting a choice menu with low cash payoffs. Then he returned to the same villages after time intervals that were at least two weeks apart, with all cash payoffs being scaled up by a factor of 10 in each successive visit. The choice percentages for the $1\times$ (0.5 rupee) scale are shown in the right side column of Table 4.1. Notice that about a third of the responses are in the top two rows, which include the slight-to-neutral and neutral-to-preferred categories, so that the other two-thirds are clearly risk averse even for this low payoff scale. The most salient aspect of this study, however, is the observation of higher levels of implied risk aversion as all payoffs are scaled up in successive visits. For example, a $100\times$ increase in payoffs from 0.5 rupees to 50 rupees caused the percentage in the risk "neutral to preferred" category in the top row of Table 4.1 to fall from 19% to 2%. Conversely, this $100\times$ payoff increase doubled the percentage (from 20% to 40%) in the "moderate" risk aversion category (constant relative risk aversion $=0.51$, or square root utility). Note that a multiplicative scale factor applied to a money payoff x will factor out of the constant relative risk aversion (CRRA) utility function $u(x)=(x)^{1-r}/(1-r)$, so differences in expected utilities are unaffected by payoff scale changes when relative risk aversion is constant. The observed increases in implied relative risk aversion at higher payoff scales, therefore, led Binswanger to reject the hypothesis that risk aversion is constant over a wide range of payoff scales. Payoff scale effects and order effects due to sequencing some decisions after others are considered in more detail in Section 4.4. For purposes of making comparisons, we will occasionally follow Binswanger's practice of reporting implied levels of constant relative risk aversion, even though these measures would not be expected to stay the same for large changes in payoff scale.

From a financial decision-making point of view, a natural perspective is to use an investment allocation between safe and risky assets to infer risk aversion, although as noted, Binswanger's portfolio alternatives were presented in a neutral framework. In contrast, Gneezy and Potters (1997) present subjects with an explicit investment decision, where the rate of return for the risky asset is *independent* of the amount invested.

This presentation is intuitive and easy for subjects to understand. Specifically, subjects were given an endowment of \$2 that could be divided between a safe asset (returning the amount invested) and a risky asset that provided a $\{2/3\}$ chance of a \$1 loss and a $\{1/3\}$ chance of a \$2.50 return. Since $(\{2/3\})\star(-1) + (\{1/3\})\star(2.5) > 1$, each dollar invested in the risky asset provides an expected net gain, so a risk neutral or seeking person would invest everything in the risky asset, but a person who is sufficiently risk averse would prefer to leave all money in the safe asset. Gneezy and Potters used the average amount invested in the safe asset as a measure of risk aversion, an approach that has been followed in a number of subsequent papers.

The purpose of this classic experiment was to manipulate the salience of losses by changing the frequency with which feedback is provided. The intuition is that the probability of a loss is diminished by simultaneously announcing a number of independent realizations of returns for the risky asset in a manner that permits gains to cover losses. In the high-frequency treatment, subjects played the rounds one by one, i.e. they made asset allocations and were informed about the payout for the risky asset after each decision, so that the probability of a loss is $\{2/3\}$ for each round. In contrast, subjects played three rounds at a time in the low-frequency treatment, with the investment decision forced to be the same in all three rounds. This treatment is *not* equivalent to scaling up payoffs by 3, since the realizations for the risky asset are independent across rounds, which tends to "average out" gains and losses. Since a single gain of \$2.50 is higher than two losses of \$1.00, the only way to obtain an overall loss is for all three outcomes to be losses. Thus a loss occurs with probability $(\{2/3\})^3$, or about 0.30, which is much lower than the 0.67 probability of a loss in a single round. The salience of a recent gain or loss may have a disproportionate effect on decisions, and such "recency effects" have been observed in other contexts. This effect can be thought of as "myopic loss aversion," which would tend to make people more risk averse (less prone to invest in the risky asset) in the high frequency treatment in which a loss, if it occurs, is observed prior to the next decision. As predicted, the percentage of endowment invested in the risky asset increased (from about 50% to 67%) as the feedback frequency was reduced.

The investment portfolio approach was also used by Eckel and Grossman (2002) in their seminal study of gender effects on risk and loss aversion. Recall that subjects in the Gneezy and Potters experiment could divide an initial endowment between safe and risky assets in an essentially continuous manner. In contrast, Eckel and Grossman present subjects with a discrete set of five possible gambles, which correspond to investing various proportions in the risky asset. The "all safe" portfolio in the bottom row of Table 4.2 corresponds to leaving an initial stake of \$16 in a safe asset. The "more safe" option in the second-to-last row is analogous to taking \$4 out of the safe account (leaving only \$12 there) in order to obtain a 0.5 chance of a tripled return ($\$4 \times 3 = \$12$), zero otherwise, so the payoff outcome for both accounts would be \$12 (remaining stake) with probability 0.5 and \$24 (stake plus gain) with probability 0.5, as shown in the equally

Table 4.2 Eckel and Grossman Gambles with a Portfolio Choice Interpretation

Portfolio	Equally Likely Payoffs	Investment Allocation and Gamble Structure	CRRA Range	Male Choice Rate*	Female Choice Rate*
All risky	**$0** or $48	0.5 chance of 3×$16	< 0.2	0.35	0.14
More risky	**$4** or $40	$4 + 0.5 chance of 3×$12	0.2 – 0.38	0.23	0.18
Equal split	$8 or $32	$8 + 0.5 chance of 3×$8	0.38 – 0.67	0.24	0.42
More safe	$12 or $24	$12 + 0.5 chance of 3×$4	0.67 – 2	0.16	0.19
All safe	$16	$16	> 2	0.02	0.08

*Combined data for gain and loss frames.

likely payoffs column. As one moves up from one row to the next higher one, higher amounts are taken out of the safe asset and put into an asset that either triples the investment or fails completely. The top row corresponds to investing the entire $16 in a risky asset, which yields either $3 \times \$16 = \$48$ or $0 with equal probability. Since each outcome in the second column is equally likely, the expected payoff for each gamble is the average of the two numbers in the Payoffs column. It is apparent that a person who is risk neutral or risk seeking would invest all in the risky asset (top row), which has the highest expected payoff. Eckel and Grossman (2002) do not provide subjects with explicit investment terminology, which may (or may not) make the task less transparent, but which has the distinct advantage of avoiding the focal "equal split" terminology seen in the middle row.[1] For purposes of comparison, we have added the CRRA column that shows the range of values for a coefficient of constant relative risk aversion that would correspond to each choice. This task does not permit one to distinguish between risk neutrality and risk seeking, since all people in these categories would select the gamble in the top row with the highest expected value.[2]

---

[1] In a subsequent paper, Eckel and Grossman (2008b) compare an explicit investment frame with a neutral frame in an experiment with the same investment game payoff structure, and they conclude that the frame has relatively minor effects on the overall pattern of decisions.

[2] Following Binswanger's approach, the addition of a mean preserving spread of the most risky gamble would make it possible to distinguish risk preferring behavior from risk neutrality. For example, a row could be added to the top of Table 4.2 with payoffs of −$6 or $54, which would have the same expected value ($24) as the "all risky" gamble, but which has higher variance. This is the approach taken in a number of subsequent papers that use the investment approach to consider a range of interesting effects of risk aversion: Eckel and Grossman (2008b), Barr and Genicot (2008), Ball et al. (2010), Eckel et al. (2012), Arya et al. (forthcoming), and Leonard et al. (2013).

The Eckel and Grossman treatment involves shifting all payoffs down by $6. This shift produces possible losses for gambles with pretransformation payoffs of $4 and $0 in the top two rows, which have been shown in boldface font in the second column. Wealth effects were controlled by having subjects fill out an initial survey in both treatments, with no payment in the first treatment and with a $6 payment for the loss treatment. Loss aversion is typically modeled as a kink in the utility function that pulls utilities down to the left of the reference point. In this context, with 0 as a reference point, loss aversion would be predicted to result in more choices of portfolios that do not offer the possibility of a loss even after the downward shift in payoffs, i.e. portfolios in the bottom three rows. However, there was no significant difference between the choice data for the two treatments in a between-subjects design, so the table only shows combined data for both treatments, separated by gender in the final two columns. The modal decision for the 104 male subjects was the all-risky portfolio in the top row, whereas the modal decision for the 96 females was the equal split. Eckel and Grossman concluded that the observed gender differences are statistically and economically significant in this environment. Loss and gender effects are considered in more detail in Sections 4.4 and 4.5.

4.2.3 Structured Menus of Binary Choices

Wallach and Kogan (1959, 1961) use a structured choice menu based on a set of 12 hypothetical scenarios where one option is relatively safe in the sense of being low variance, and another involves a significant risk, for example an operation that might result in a cure or death. For each scenario, the questions elicit a probability of success for the risky option that make the person indifferent. For example, one scenario begins with a paragraph about the patient's current condition and a risky operation that could improve the condition if it succeeds. This scenario is followed by an instruction (Wallach and Kogan, 1964, pp. 256–57):

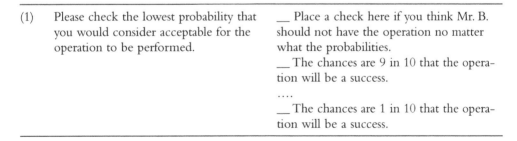

(1)   Please check the lowest probability that you would consider acceptable for the operation to be performed.

__ Place a check here if you think Mr. B. should not have the operation no matter what the probabilities.
__ The chances are 9 in 10 that the operation will be a success.
….
__ The chances are 1 in 10 that the operation will be a success.

By checking one of these rows, the respondent indicates an approximate indifference point between not having the operation and the probability selected. The selection of a row determines an integer between 1 and 10; the sum of the scores for all 10 scenarios is between 12 and 120, which provides a measure of risk aversion. This procedure, known as the Choice Dilemmas instrument, was later used by Sherman (1972), which contains results from one of the first dissertations in experimental economics.[3]

Murnighan et al. (1988) pioneered a menu-based approach using money payoffs that also elicits a point of probability indifference between safe and risky options, as part of a study of bilateral bargaining. They provided subjects with a list of choices between a sure payoff, e.g. $5, and a random prospect, e.g. a 60% chance of $10 and a 40% chance of $4. Here the lottery offers a much higher expected payoff of $7.60, without much downside risk, so only an extremely risk averse person would choose the safe $5. Then by reducing the chance of getting the high payoff in subsequent rows and counting the number of rows in which the safe $5 is selected, one obtains a measure of risk aversion.

The crossover point from risky to safe determines a "probability equivalent," analogous to the measure obtained in the Wallach and Kogan instrument.

(2)	Option A	Option B
	$5 with probability 1(same in all rows)	p chances in 10 of $10 and $1-p$ chances in 10 of $4 (where p starts at 6 and is reduced in subsequent rows)

In order to control for wealth and portfolio effects, only one of the rows in the table is selected at random *ex post* to determine the subject's earnings, which would either be $5 if that amount was selected or a randomly determined payoff if the lottery was selected. This measure was used to divide subjects into more and less risk-averse categories, and the subsequent bargaining task involved pairs of people from the same risk preference category. As indicated in the applications in Section 4.6, the effects of inferred risk aversion were in the predicted direction, but the unpredicted effects were even stronger than the predicted effects, due to factors such as the prominence of 50/50 splits and focal points.

Millner and Pratt (1991) used the Murnighan, Roth, and Schoumaker choice menu to classify subjects as being more or less risk averse. The choice menu involved 20 paired choices between a sure $12 and a gamble with possible payoffs of $18 or $8, where the probability of the high payoff was reduced by 5% increments, from 98% in the top row to 93% in the second row of the choice menu table, and so on continuing to 3% in the 20th row at the bottom. It can be shown that a risk neutral person would prefer the sure $12 when the probability of the high $18 payoff falls below 0.4, which implies 8

---

[3] Wallach and Kogan (1964) also had subjects play a "dice game" that involved choosing between pairs of safe and risky options with small gains and losses. All of the safe and risky options involved zero expected values, so that the risky option had a higher variance. They used 66 pairs of choices that spanned all combinations of 4 win probability levels ({1/9}, {1/4}, {1/2}, and {3/4}) and three payoff levels. The responses were used to calculate several indices that measured the tendency to choose the option with the highest possible gain, the highest variance, etc. These measures of risk seeking were generally significantly negatively correlated with the risk aversion index obtained from the hypothetical scenarios.

choices of the sure outcome. More risk-averse individuals would select the sure payoff more than 8 times. If there is a unique crossover row, then the number of rows where the safe option is selected implies a range of coefficients of constant relative risk aversion. In their study, the median subject selected the sure outcome in 12 rows. According to our calculations for a person with a single crossover at the observed median number of safe choices (12), the implied range of CRRA is: $1.8 < r < 2.3$. This range is quite high relative to other measures for payoffs of this magnitude, which might be due to the attraction of the certain payoff on one side of each row.

The benefit of a structured menu of binary choices is that it provides interval estimates of risk aversion, although this was not done in the studies just cited. By having both choices in each row be nondegenerate lotteries, one can also avoid the "certainty effect" (the overweighting of certainty) outlined by Kahneman and Tversky (1979). Another advantage of having lotteries for both options is that this controls for a difference in complexity, the time required to determine the payoff, or a preference for playing or avoiding the lottery, independent of the probabilities involved. These were some of the motivations for the Holt and Laury (2002) choice menu shown in Table 4.3 below. Each row of the table presented a choice between a safer gamble, labeled "Option A" and a more risky gamble, labeled "Option B." The gambles were explained in terms

Table 4.3 Holt and Laury Binary Choice Menu ($1 \times$ Scale)

	Lottery S	Lottery R	EV of S − EV of R	Choice Pattern CRRA Range	Choice Rate
1	1/10 of $2.00, 9/10 of $1.60	1/10 of $3.85, 9/10 of $0.10	$1.17	*SRRRRRRRRR* $-1.71 < r < -0.95$	0.01
2	2/10 of $2.00, 8/10 of $1.60	2/10 of $3.85, 8/10 of $0.10	$0.83	**SS**RRRRRRRR $-0.95 < r < -0.49$	0.01
3	3/10 of $2.00, 7/10 of $1.60	3/10 of $3.85, 7/10 of $0.10	$0.50	**SSS**RRRRRRR $-0.49 < r < -0.15$	0.06
4	4/10 of $2.00, 6/10 of $1.60	4/10 of $3.85, 6/10 of $0.10	$0.16	**SSSS**RRRRRR $-0.15 < r < 0.15$	0.26
5	5/10 of $2.00, 5/10 of $1.60	5/10 of $3.85, 5/10 of $0.10	−$0.18	**SSSSS**RRRRR $0.15 < r < 0.41$	0.26
6	6/10 of $2.00, 4/10 of $1.60	6/10 of $3.85, 4/10 of $0.10	−$0.51	**SSSSSS**RRRR $0.41 < r < 0.68$	0.23
7	7/10 of $2.00, 3/10 of $1.60	7/10 of $3.85, 3/10 of $0.10	−$0.85	**SSSSSSS**RRR $0.68 < r < 0.97$	0.13
8	8/10 of $2.00, 2/10 of $1.60	8/10 of $3.85, 2/10 of $0.10	−$1.18	**SSSSSSSS**RR $0.97 < r < 1.37$	0.03
9	9/10 of $2.00, 1/10 of $1.00	9/10 of $3.85, 1/10 of $0.10	−$1.52	**SSSSSSSSS**R $1.37 < r$	0.01
10	10/10 of $2.00, 0/10 of $1.60	10/10 of $3.85, 0/10 of $0.10	−$1.85	**SSSSSSSSSS** (dominated)	

of how throws of a ten-sided die would determine the payoff. For example, the option labeled "Lottery S" in the top row of Table 4.3 would have been presented to subjects in neutral terms as:

Option A:	
(3)	$2.00 if throw of die is 1
	$1.60 if throw of die is 2–10

The choices for all 10 rows were done with pen and paper, after which the throw of a 10-sided die would be used to select a single row for payoff purposes. The subject's choice for that row then would be played out with a second die throw to determine whether the payoff was high or low. Since both options involved a throw of a 10-sided die, subjects (who were visually separated) were not able to infer other's choices by listening. The instructions are archived: http://people.virginia.edu/~cah2k/highdata.pdf.[4]

The seemingly arbitrary payoffs used in the payoff table ($1.60 or $2.00 for the safe option and $3.85 or $0.10 for the risky option) were selected to make expected value calculations less obvious. There are, of course, pros and cons of taking this approach. Providing calculations can prevent arithmetic errors, but people who are taught expected value in class may see this as the correct approach, creating a bias towards risk neutrality.[5] The expected value difference between the safe and risky gambles is shown in the EV column of Table 4.3; this was not shown to subjects. This difference is positive in the top 4 rows, so a risk-neutral person would choose Lottery S in those rows, as indicated by the choice pattern **SSSS**RRRRRR. Coming down the table, the probability of the higher payoff for each option increases by 0.10 (one increment in the throw of the 10-sided die). These discrete increments were designed to avoid rounding problems, e.g. 49% may be rounded to 50%, in an "editing" process. We wanted a relatively small number of choices that would fit on a single page, with a sure thing at the top or bottom to serve as a rationality test. The choice in the bottom row of Table 4.3, for example, involves a choice between a sure $2.00 and a sure $3.85. Therefore, the CRRA range is listed as "dominated" for someone who chooses all safe choices (the SSSSSSSSSS pattern). It is important to note that the CRRA ranges shown, which were

---

[4] See Holt and Laury (2002) for a full description of the procedural details, including a probability-equivalent "trainer" choice menu with a different set of payoff numbers ($3.00 for the safe option in all rows, and $6.00 or $1.00 for the risky option with changing probabilities). The purpose of this trainer was to provide subjects with a clear understanding of the process making choices for all rows and then having one row selected at random for the payoff, using a 10-sided die to play out the relevant gamble.

[5] Colin Camerer once remarked in a conference presentation that he no longer poses Allais paradox questions to MBA students in class, since they are so prone to rely on expected value calculations, which would prevent violations of expected utility from being observed.

used in the design phase for this instrument, were not provided to subjects. The provision of these ranges is meant to provide an overall perspective on observed choice patterns, and it does not imply that subjects exhibit constant relative risk aversion or that risk aversion effects are primarily due to utility curvature effects (to the exclusion of probability weighting effects).

Payoffs were chosen to provide ranges of relative risk aversion levels that we anticipated would be relevant on the basis of intuition and prior studies. We wanted to position the risk-neutral category near the middle row of the table (row 4), to minimize the boundary effects and to ensure that anticipated moderate levels of risk aversion would involve nonboundary numbers of safe choices in the 5–7 range.[6] Our hope was that providing the structured menu of choices, with easier choices at either end, would tend to reduce noise. The random selection of a row on which to base payoffs is intended to avoid wealth effects.

This basic menu structure can be easily manipulated to scale payoffs up without altering the ranges of constant relative risk aversion implied by each choice pattern, which are provided in Table 4.3. Each session began with a 1× (low real) menu, and the choice proportions for this initial task are shown in the right column of Table 4.3. Notice that about a third of the participants exhibited risk seeking or risk neutrality, with the remainder exhibiting risk aversion.[7] This initial task (with a scale of 1×) was followed by a high hypothetical choice (with scales of 20×, 50×, or 90×, depending on the session), which in turn was followed by a high real choice (with a scale that matched the previous high hypothetical choice), and finished with a "return to baseline" low real (1×) choice. The highest payoff in the 90× treatment was over $300, for a decision task that took less than 20 minutes.[8] These manipulations will be discussed in the Methodology and Treatment sections that follow, but it is useful to summarize the main results here: subjects were generally risk averse, even for low (1×) payoffs. Moreover, there was no significant difference between the amounts of risk aversion observed with low real (1×) and low hypothetical payoffs. Scaling up real payoffs resulted in sharp increases in observed levels of risk aversion, which suggests the danger of assuming a model of constant relative risk aversion. In contrast, scaling up

---

[6] In Laury and Holt (2008) we put the "degenerate" choice between the two sure payoffs in the top row (and deleted the bottom row choice between two sure high payoffs) so that the crossover row was moved to row 5 in the middle. This change was made because the latter study involved losses, with the possibility of more crossovers in the risk-seeking region.

[7] There is no easy way to compare payoff scales with the Binswanger (1981) study, so the similarity between the proportions of risk averse subjects and others in the right-hand columns in Tables 4.1 and 4.3 is probably a coincidence.

[8] Professor Ron Cummings had first approached us in the spring of 2000 with a generous offer to accompany him on a trip to run some experiments at the University of Central Florida in Orlando and at the University of Miami. He stressed that there was no binding budget constraint, so we worked out a lottery-choice design with a wide range of payoff scales. The day before we left, Cummings went into the Dean's office and requested $10,000, *in small bills*, for the trip. Cummings and Laury divided up the bags of cash prior to the flight to Miami, where screenings and detentions could be triggered by high cash amounts in carry-on bags.

hypothetical had little or no effect on overall decision patterns. Models with increasing relative risk aversion will be considered in Section 4.7.

4.2.4 Price Based Assessments of a Certainty Equivalent

In addition to the investment method (a single choice among a structured set of alternative portfolios) and the choice menu method (structured binary choices), there is a third approach to risk elicitation that is based on finding a subject's certainty equivalent money value of a gamble. Harrison (1986) first used the Becker et al. (1964) method to determine certainty equivalents for a set of gambles with a range of "win" probabilities associated with the high payoff outcome. This "BDM" method was structured so that subjects were asked to provide a "selling price" for a gamble. Then a "buying price" would be randomly generated. If the buying price is above the subject's selling price, then the subject receives a money amount equal to the buying price; otherwise the subject retains the gamble, which is played out to determine the earnings. Since the amount received from a sale is not the posted selling price, it is a dominant strategy for subjects to post selling prices that equal their certainty-equivalent money values for the gamble. To see the intuition, think of a descending price auction in which the proposed selling price is lowered continuously until a bid is obtained, and the seller would receive an amount of money for the gamble that is equal to that bid. Thus a seller should "stay active" unless the proposed selling price falls below their own "keep value," so the exit point reveals the seller's value. There is no continuous time element in the Becker-DeGroot-Marshak procedure, but the same intuition applies, and the optimal selling price to post is one's actual value.[9]

For a risk-neutral person, this certainty equivalent should equal the expected value of the lottery, which would allow one to test the hypothesis of risk neutrality. Each subject was presented with a sequence of gambles with the same pair of high and low payoffs, but with varying probabilities associated with the high payoff. For each subject, Harrison regressed the expected value of the gamble on the elicited certainty equivalent "selling price" and higher order (e.g. squared) values of the selling price. As noted above, the elicited value for the gamble should equal its expected value if the person is risk neutral, and Harrison presented tests that reject this null hypothesis for most subjects. The actual regression coefficients, however, were not reported.[10]

Becker-DeGroot-Marshak procedures to elicit certainty equivalents for lotteries were also used by Kachelmeier and Shehata (1992). Their study was, in part, motivated by a desire to investigate the effects of high payoffs. The primary Kachelmeier and

---

[9] The intuition is basically the same as that for an English (ascending bid) auction, in which bidders should stay active in the bidding as long as the current high bid does not exceed their own values, so that bids reveal values. The intuition, however, is not correct if subjects' preferences do not obey the axioms of expected utility theory (Karni and Safra, 1987).

[10] See Millner et al. (1988) for a discussion of the econometric restrictions implied by risk neutrality, i.e. that the slope of a regression of the expected value on the certainty equivalent be 1.

Shehata treatment was run in the People's Republic of China, which (in those days) facilitated the use of extremely high payoffs that resulted in earnings at about three times the normal monthly wage for a single two-hour session. The authors were aware that Binswanger (1981, p. 396) preferred to offer subjects a menu of choices because he feared that they would not understand the notion of a certainty equivalent, but this consideration was felt to be less important given the higher education level of the Chinese subjects. Unlike Binswanger, who used 50/50 lotteries, Kachelmeier and Shehata consider prospects with varying probabilities of the high payoff, which allows them to consider the risk preferences for low probability gains with high values. The paper has a rich variety of design elements and interesting results, but the focus here is on the difference between BDM methods that elicit a selling price for an endowed lottery and analogous BDM methods that elicit a buying price for a lottery that can be purchased.

The basic BDM price elicitation method used for the Chinese subjects involved asking for a *minimum selling price* for a lottery that specified a probability p of a gain G, with a $1 - p$ chance of 0. Then a random number was generated by letting subjects draw a card from a deck of 100, with all increments of $G/100$ represented. The card drawn corresponds to a buy price, and the subject would earn the amount of the card drawn if it exceeded the subject's own sell price. Otherwise, the $(G; p)$ lottery was played out to determine the person's earnings. Some groups of subjects did 25 rounds of this procedure, with differing levels of p, followed by 25 rounds in which the prize amounts were increased by a factor of 10. The general pattern was for subjects to exhibit *risk preference*, i.e. certainty equivalents (selling prices) that were higher than expected values, a result that is not consistent with the observation of risk aversion in most previous studies.[11] This risk preference was diminished or eliminated when payoffs were increased, which is consistent with the increasing relative risk aversion reported earlier by Binswanger. Thinking about this result stimulated us to ask Harrison for the certainty equivalent values for his prior experiment. It turns out that the average selling price (over all subjects) was greater than or equal to the expected value for all gambles considered, and hence the implication is that Harrison's subjects also exhibited *risk-seeking* behavior.[12]

The paradoxical finding of risk preference in BDM tasks can be explained by a "response mode effect" that showed up in a subsequent experiment that Kachelmeier and Shehata ran in Canada. This experiment involved 25 rounds with low payoffs and selling prices, as in China, but the final 2 rounds involved a high payoff round with selling prices (round 26) and with buying prices (round 27). The results of these two rounds

---

[11] The other salient pattern of the Kachelmeier and Shehata data was higher risk preference for gambles involving low probabilities of gain, which could be explained by an overweighting of the low gain probabilities.

[12] Harrison (1990) also notes that the risk-seeking behavior inferred from BDM tasks in his experiment is inconsistent with the risk aversion that other investigators had inferred from measures of "over bidding" in first-price private-value auctions.

were not revealed until decisions had been made for both. In the buying price round, subjects were asked to state a maximum willingness to pay for the lottery (a 50% chance of $20), and if a random draw turned out to be less than the buy price then the subject would purchase the lottery for the amount of the random draw. This change in response mode had a dramatic effect. The average certainty equivalent in the selling price mode was about $11 for a lottery with an expected value of $10, which would seem to indicate mild risk preference, consistent with the Chinese results. In contrast, the average certainty equivalent for the same lottery was only about half as large, about $5.50, in the buying price mode, indicating strong risk aversion.[13] In a discussion of which method might be preferred, the authors conclude that the selling price mode might be more biased due to the "endowment effect" that artificially enhances the perceived value of the lottery being sold (p. 1133). At this point, it is an open question whether the other primary finding, higher risk preference for low probability gains, is caused or exaggerated by the response mode. In any case, the take-away, which experimental economists of all people should not forget, is that if you desire to elicit a high value for a lottery, ask for a selling price, and if you desire to elicit a low value, ask for a buying price. This simple and intuitive response-mode bias is only partially mitigated by using financial incentives.

A number of seemingly anomalous results in the literature can be explained by this response mode bias. In a paper entitled "Just Who Are You Calling Risk Averse?", for example, Isaac and James (2000) measure risk aversion for the same subjects in two ways. Risk preferences are inferred from bidding against (computer simulated) others in first-price, private-value auctions, and risk preferences are also inferred from BDM selling prices for lotteries. Only a few of the subjects who seem to be risk averse in the auction also provide certainty equivalent BDM selling prices that are below the expected value of the lottery. The general tendency to "overprice" the lottery relative to expected value indicated risk preference in this BDM task, which is of course not surprising given the response mode bias reported by Kachelmeier and Shehata. More perplexing, perhaps, is that relative rankings of risk aversion are reversed between the bidding-based and BDM selling-price-based measures of risk aversion. (Stability of risk preferences across tasks and frames is discussed further in Section 4.4.)

One way to avoid the response mode bias is to ask for a monetary amount (not referred to as a selling price), after explaining the use of a random number B (not referred to as a bid) used to determine whether or not the subject gets to play out the lottery or receive the number B. Holt and Smith (2009) take this approach in a similar setting, eliciting a subjective probability instead of a certainty equivalent value. The down side, of course, is that the Becker-DeGroot-Marshak method, a complex

---

[13] In studies that elicit values of environmental goods, it is not uncommon for willingness to pay (WTP) values to be about half as large as willingness to accept (WTA) values.

procedure to begin with, is even more confusing without market terminology. A better way to avoid the response mode bias associated with asking for a selling price is to provide subjects with a list of choices between the lottery and specific sure payoff alternatives, which are essentially prices, one of which will later be selected at random. This "multiple price list" format was used by Tversky and Kahneman (1992) with hypothetical payoffs, and by Fehr-Duda et al. (2006), Abdellaoui et al. (2011), and Dohmen et al. (2005, 2011) with cash payoffs. In the latter paper, for example, the lottery involved a 0.5 chance of 300, otherwise 0. This high payoff was diluted by only paying subjects with a 1/7 probability. The menu consisted of 20 rows, with the same lottery listed on the right side of each row, and with sure money payments on the left, 0, 10, 20, … 190, which bracketed the expected value of 150.

(4)	Option A	Option B
	0 with probability 1 (with prices of 10, 20, … 190 in subsequent rows)	5 chances in 10 of 300 and 5 chances in 10 of 0 (same in all rows)

For low payment amounts in the upper rows, most subjects will prefer the lottery, and the crossover point determines the certainty equivalent. About 78% of the subjects crossed over at values below 150, indicating risk aversion; 13% of the subjects were approximately risk neutral, and only 9% were risk seeking, with elicited certainty equivalents that exceeded 150, which was the expected value of the lottery. Thus, the neutral choice menu structure of this value elicitation task seems to have avoided the bias associated with a BDM selling price.[14] One potential problem with the approach is the fact that about half of the responses were at focal points of 10, 50, 100, 150, and 190 (see Dohmen et al., 2005, Figure 5c). Another potential problem with this certainty equivalent approach is that only a single and very simple expected value calculation is required to determine a price cutoff that might have considerable attraction for someone who has been taught to calculate expected values. Sprenger (2010) reports an experiment in which "virtual risk neutrality" is obtained with a price-based certainty

---

[14] Holt and Smith (2012) use a choice menu version of the BDM task to elicit a subjective probability in a Bayes' rule experiment, and they conclude that the choice menu provides more accurate probabilities than the BDM price task, even when it is stripped of potentially biased (willingness to pay or willingness to accept) terminology. The Holt and Smith choice menu uses synchronized, identical payoffs for an "event lottery" and a "dice lottery" with specified probabilities, so that the crossover point of indifference in the choice menu identifies the person's subjective probability of the event. Since there are only two possible money payoffs in the menu, there is no role for risk aversion, so there is no need to use "outside" estimates of risk aversion to de-bias the elicited beliefs. A somewhat more complex alternative is to use a menu of lottery choices for which there are more than two possible money payoffs to elicit beliefs, and then rely on a separate task to estimate a parametric measure of risk aversion (e.g. CRRA), controlling for demographic variables. The estimated level of risk aversion is then used to de-bias the elicited beliefs, as is done in Fiore et al. (2009) and in Antoniou et al. (2012). This two-stage recursive approach could add some extra "noise" associated with risk aversion measurement.

equivalent choice menu analogous to (4), whereas subjects who received the probability equivalent menu analogous to (2) were three to four times more likely to exhibit risk aversion. These differences were also apparent in a separate experiment using a within-subjects design.[15] Given these sharp differences, it would be very imprecise to refer to all of these menu-based procedures as "multiple price lists," and we will reserve the multiple price list term for the certainty equivalent elicitation procedure where one side of the menu really is a list of prices.

4.2.5 Comparison of Alternative Elicitation Methods

The main features of the three commonly used methods for eliciting risk preferences with financial incentives are shown in Table 4.4. A fourth option, not shown, would be to use a scale or menu of choices based on hypothetical scenarios (Wallach and Kogan, 1959), or a general question about a person's overall willingness to take risk (Dohmen et al., 2005, 2011).

First, consider the *investment task* listed in the top row of Table 4.4. The continuous nature of the Gneezy and Potters version of this task convexifies the set of feasible decisions.[16] This investment task is typically simplified by using integer dollar payoff numbers and 0.5 probabilities that may mitigate the effects of extreme probability weighting. Risk aversion is measured or inferred from the amount invested in the risky asset, and the subject's payoff is the randomly determined outcome of the selected investment. The declining structure of marginal returns to the risky asset used by Binswanger could be useful in avoiding data spikes at a corner, which are sometimes observed. Next consider the *probability choice menu* listed in the second row. This method may involve changing payoff probabilities for both the safe and risky options, in order to induce a single cross-over, so that risk aversion can be inferred from the number of rows in which the safe option was selected. The subject's payoff is determined by picking one of the rows at random and playing out the option selected for that row. Of course, the safe option could be a fixed money amount that is the same for all rows, so that the crossover point determines a probability equivalent of that fixed payoff.[17] The *pricing task* listed in the

---

[15] In a pilot experiment with 60 subjects at the University of Virginia done with a menu-based certainty equivalent procedure, about 30% of the men provided exact expected values, correct to the penny. In contrast, such calculation-based responses were only observed for about 10% of the women. In a second pilot with 24 subjects that used the probability equivalent approach, only one subject tended to provide probabilities that exactly equated expected values. Finding a probability equivalent for a truly risk neutral person involves solving an equation, which is apparently more trouble for subjects than just multiplying two numbers together to obtain an expected value.

[16] Convexification is an approach that has been followed in some recent work on eliciting time preferences (Andreoni and Sprenger, 2012a, 2012b).

[17] Another variation is to let the safe option be a nondegenerate *lottery* that stays the same in all rows, and then change the probabilities for the risky option in subsequent rows, so that the crossover point determines an "uncertainty equivalent" between the fixed lottery and the equivalent risky lottery with an appropriate probability mix. Andreoni and Sprenger (2010) use elicited uncertainty equivalents to identify "interior" cases where violations of expected utility theory are minimal and boundary cases where deviations are more systematic.

Table 4.4 Alternative Methods of Eliciting Risk Aversion Measures

Investment Task	Continuous or discrete choices for alternative divisions of money between a value-preserving asset and a risky asset.
Probability Choice Menu	A structured set of binary choices between safe and risky options, which can involve changing probabilities of the high payoff for only one side (as with probability equivalent elicitation) or for both sides (as with the procedure used by Holt and Laury, for example).
Pricing Task	Elicitation of a money value for a risky option, using incentive-compatible BDM selling price mechanisms, or a set of binary choices between the risky option and possible monetary values (a "price list") that avoids the use of buy/sell terminology.

third row of the table can be implemented with BDM selling price terminology and a randomly determined bid, a context that may facilitate understanding but that generates a clear bias toward a high value for the lottery, which would seem to indicate risk seeking. Our preferred approach for the elicitation of a certainty equivalent is to use neutral terminology for the BDM procedure, or to use a list of choices between the lottery, e.g. on the right side of (4), and sure money payments that correspond to price bids, one of which is selected at random to determine whether the subject receives the bid or keeps the lottery. This lottery is then played out to determine the subject's payoff. Risk aversion or preference is inferred by comparing the certainty equivalent with the expected payoff of the lottery, e.g. a certainty equivalent that is below the expected payoff indicates risk aversion.

The term "multiple price list" is sometimes used to refer to any table with binary choices in each row. For the certainty equivalent elicitation in equation (4), for example, the sure payoffs on the left side can be thought of as prices, and the crossover point determines the certainty equivalent. However, applying the "multiple price list" terminology to the Probability Choice Menus described in the second row of Table 4.4 is a bit confusing since the probabilities, not prices, are changing from row to row. As noted above, these quite different approaches may have sharply different properties. Therefore, using the same "multiple price list" terminology for all of these approaches may be misleading.

4.3 METHODOLOGICAL ISSUES

The most salient feature of the Binswanger (1981) and Holt and Laury (2002) results is that increases in the scale of monetary payoffs produce a clear pattern of increased levels of risk aversion.[18] On the other hand, risk aversion is common with low payoffs: about

---

[18] Even in the high stakes Kachelmeier and Shehata (1992) paper where BDM selling prices are above expected values, a 20× increase in payoffs reduces the amount of risk seeking implied by ratios of selling prices to expected values.

two-thirds of the subjects in the low payoff treatment for Binswanger (1981) and Holt and Laury (2002) are classified as risk averse, and only 20–25% are in the risk-neutral category, with the remainder of about 10% being in a clearly risk seeking category.[19] The methodological implication is that if you are looking for qualitative results, then low payoffs may be fine. A good example would be the Murnighan et al. (1988) and Millner and Pratt (1991) papers that use (probability equivalent) risk aversion measures with low stakes to categorize and sort players, in order to see how differences in risk aversion affect behavior in bargaining and rent-seeking games respectively. Alternatively, the researcher might consider a general "willingness to take risk" question as proposed by Dohmen et al. (2011). However, if the goal is to obtain a *quantitative* measure or even a rough guess of how behavior in high-stakes economics decisions might be influenced by risk aversion, then there is a strong argument for running a test with some scaled-up payoffs. We will return to the issue of payoff scale effects in the next section, but first it is useful to survey the various methodological considerations that arise from using risk elicitation mechanisms.

Even a single lottery choice task raises important methodological issues, e.g. whether to use real or hypothetical incentives, whether to present probabilities in a numerical or graphical manner, and whether or not to frame choices in terms of a specific context, e.g. as an investment. More complex approaches with menus of choices raise other issues, e.g. sequence effects, framing effects due to menu structure, and wealth/portfolio effects that may arise if payments are made for multiple decisions. It is often the case that the solution of one methodological concern may raise another. For example, one way to avoid wealth effects is to select a single decision at random, *ex post*, for actual payment. With a large number of decisions, however, this random selection procedure might dilute the effects of financial incentives. Another example involves exposing the *same group* of subjects to different treatments, e.g. gains versus losses, in order to control for individual differences. This "within subjects" approach, however, may introduce biases due to "sequence effects" in which behavior in one treatment is affected by experience in the previous treatment. There is no single best approach that works for all situations, and it may even make sense to use several approaches, such as a within-subjects design to control for individual variations, complemented with a between-subjects design in which each subject is exposed to a single treatment that prevents sequence effects. This section summarizes results of experiments designed to shed light on these and other methodological questions.

4.3.1 Incentive Effects: Real vs. Hypothetical Payoffs

One issue that is closely related to scale effects is whether to use monetary payoffs at all, since it is possible to scale up hypothetical payoffs to any desired level without worrying

---

[19] As noted in subsequent sections, risk-seeking behavior is predominant for some particular demographic groups, e.g. young children.

about the cost of the experiment. Most laboratory studies in economics involve actual monetary payments, reflecting the general view that there is less "noise" in behavior when real incentives are used. An alternative approach would be to use low payoffs with experienced subjects who will be less confused by the procedures. For example, Smith and Walker (1993) consider the effects of experience in a previous session involving first-price sealed bid auctions, and they estimate that this experience is comparable to a 20× increase in payoffs in terms of reductions in random variations abound predictions. A second issue is whether financial incentives affect average measures, as opposed to the effect of reductions in noise. Camerer and Hogarth (1999) compiled an extensive study of experiments done with and without financial incentives, and found that actual payments made a difference in average performance measures in some contexts, e.g. recall tasks when effort is required, and not in others, e.g. tasks involving judgment biases. For the experiments involving choices between gambles, incentives resulted in more risk aversion in eight studies, less risk aversion in two studies, and no difference in three studies. Even with monetary incentives, the payoff scale used in most laboratory experiments tends to be small relative to risky decisions made by consumers and firms, as noted by Kahneman and Tversky (1979, p. 265):

> "Experimental studies typically involve contrived gambles for small stakes, and a large number of repetitions of very similar problems. These features of laboratory gambling complicate the interpretation of the results and restrict their generality. By default, the method of hypothetical choices emerges as the simplest procedure by which a large number of theoretical questions can be investigated. The use of the method relies on the assumption that people often know how they would behave in actual situations of choice, and on the further assumption that the subjects have no special reason to disguise their true preferences."

The perspective that subjects may take hypothetical payoffs seriously is supported by Binswanger's (1981) study, discussed in the previous section, in which payoff scales were increased by a factor of 10 in each subsequent treatment. Scaling real money payoffs up (from 1× to 10× to 100×) resulted in sharp increases in implied risk aversion. However, the final treatment, with a 1000× payoff scale, was only done with hypothetical payoffs. Yet it resulted in even further increases in "intermediate" to "severe" levels of risk aversion, with corresponding declines in choices categorized as implying "slight-to-neutral" and "moderate" levels of risk aversion. In a footnote, Binswanger (1981, p. 869) notes: "It appears that toward the end of a prolonged game sequence, individuals do reveal preferences in hypothetical games that are consistent with their actual game behaviour." For example, it could be the case that participants who had enjoyed actual high payoffs in previous trials could better imagine how they would behave even if stakes are hypothetical.

Kachelmeier and Shehata (1992) also report comparisons of real and hypothetical payoff conditions, although the hypothetical treatment was done with a different subject pool (in Canada instead of China). For the Chinese subjects, a scaling up of payoffs by a factor of 10 produced more risk aversion (or more precisely, less risk seeking) for the BDM selling-price procedure. In contrast, the Canadian subjects showed little or no effect of scaling up hypothetical payoffs, which suggests the importance of using real cash payoffs.

The issue of whether or not it is appropriate to study high-stakes situations with high hypothetical payoffs was, at this point, unclear. In our 2002 paper, we reported within-subjects comparisons using scaled versions of the choice menu in Table 4.3, with either real cash or hypothetical payoffs. As noted in the previous section, most subjects were risk averse even for low stakes gambles, but we observed dramatic increases in risk aversion as financial payoffs are scaled up. In contrast, the scaling up of hypothetical payoffs did not increase the implied risk aversion measures above levels observed for our low (1×) real payoffs. The rough correspondence between behavior in the low real (1×) and the high hypothetical (20×, 50×, 90×) incentive structures matches the claims made by Kahneman and Tversky.[20] But this conformity between low real and high hypothetical payoffs does not imply that financial incentives are unnecessary, given that we do observe large increases in risk aversion as real payoffs are scaled up.

4.3.2 Order Effects: Between-Subjects and Within-Subjects Designs

Harrison et al. (2005) pointed out that Holt and Laury (2002) may have introduced sequence effects by using a within-subjects design in which the low real payoff choice always preceded the high payoff choices. To support this conjecture, Harrison et al. (2005) reported a new experiment in which half of the subjects made decisions for a 10× menu by itself, and half made decisions for a 10× menu after making an earlier decision for a 1× menu. They observed an increase in inferred risk aversion for those who did the 10× treatment second (6.7 safe choices on average, versus 5.7 safe choices for those who only did the 10× treatment, and hence did it first). Such a sequence effect could explain why Holt and Laury observed more risk aversion with high real payoffs (done after high hypothetical payoffs).[21]

The potential confusion of treatment and sequence effects is a valid point. One way to deal with it could be to do the treatments in alternating order as a rough control for sequence effects, while maintaining the advantage of a between-subjects design.[22]

---

[20] The average numbers of safe choices across all 10 decisions for the 20×, 50×, and 90× hypothetical payoff treatments are: 4.9, 5.1, and 5.3, as compared with 5.2 safe choices for the 1× real payoff treatment. These differences are not economically or statistically different.

[21] It could not, however, explain why scaling up real payoffs done second from 20× to 50× to 90× raised the observed levels of risk aversion (from 6.0 to 6.8 to 7.2 safe choices) as this was done between subjects.

[22] This solution was precluded by the Holt–Laury practice of asking subjects in the high real treatment to agree to give up the payment from the low real choice before making a choice for the high real menu.

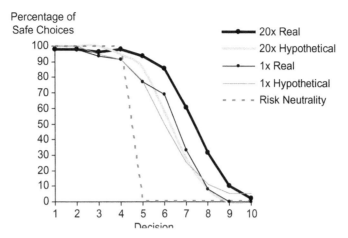

Figure 4.1 Percentages of safe choices by decision row in a between-subjects experiment with no order effects (Holt and Laury, 2005).

Another approach is to compare real and hypothetical payoffs using a between-subjects design in which each participant makes a single decision, either low hypothetical, low real, high hypothetical, or high real. Holt and Laury (2005) used this latter approach, and they find (as in Holt and Laury, 2002) scaling up real payoffs from $1\times$ to $20\times$ raises risk aversion significantly (from 5.7 safe choices to 6.7 safe choices). In contrast, raising hypothetical payoffs from $1\times$ to $20\times$ has no significant effect (from 5.6 safe choices to 5.7 safe choices).

The sharp difference between high real and high hypothetical payoffs is apparent in Figure. 4.1, which plots the percentage of safe choices for each row of the decision menu. The risk neutral prediction (dashed line) involves 100% safe choices for the decisions 1–4, and then 0% after that. The dark line for the $20\times$ real treatment shows higher percentages of safe choices than for the other treatments, with vertical distances of 20–30 percentage points for decisions 5–8 where most of the switching occurs. Notice that the lines for the two hypothetical treatments (lines with no dots) are quite close to each other and to the line for the low real treatment. In addition, all four data average lines are well to the right of the dashed-line prediction for risk neutrality. This exchange illustrates how one experiment can raise issues that are resolved by subsequent experiments, and how different design approaches (between- and within-subjects) can provide complementary perspectives on the same behavioral patterns.

Even if the primary payoff-scale conclusions of the Holt and Laury (2002) study are not altered after order effects are removed, the takeaway is the researchers should be careful about order effects, e.g. by rotating or randomizing treatment orders or by using a between-subjects design as a check. Andersen et al. (2006) used a randomized treatment order for four treatments in a laboratory study involving Danish subjects.

They used a random effects interval regression model to estimate the marginal effects of a treatment being 2nd, 3rd, or 4th. The coefficients for being 2nd or 3rd were small and insignificant, but the marginal effect of being in the 4th order was to raise the estimated coefficient of relative risk aversion by 0.14, with a standard error of 0.05. However, order effects are not present in a second laboratory experiment with US subjects and some procedural differences; see Andersen et al. (2006, Table 7).

4.3.3 Framing Effects and the Structure of Choice Menus

The structure of the Holt–Laury choice menu in Table 4.3 has the crossover point for risk neutrality occurring after decision 4. As can be seen from Figure 4.1, most of the crossovers occur for decisions 5–7, away from the endpoints of 1 and 10. Glenn Harrison, in a series of papers with various coauthors, investigates the effects of the location of the crossover point relative to the middle of the table. Recall that the probability of the high payoff is incremented by 0.1 in each successive row as one comes down the payoff menu used by Holt and Laury (Table 4.3 above). The crossover point can be moved down by using smaller increments at the top than at the bottom, and vice versa. In particular, Harrison et al. (2007a) moved the crossover down in a *skewLO* treatment with probabilities of (0.1, 0.2, 0.3, 0.5, 0.7, and 1) for the high payoff, which was designed to elicit lower risk aversion. Conversely, the *skewHI* treatment used probabilities of (0.3, 0.5, 0.7, 0.8, 0.9, and 1), which was designed to elicit higher risk aversion, i.e. crossovers at higher probabilities of the high payoff. As a control, they used a symmetric menu with 10 rows and 0.1 probability increments. The study was done with a random sample of Danish citizens. The estimated coefficient of constant relative risk aversion for the symmetric choice menu with 10 rows was 0.67 (weighted to reflect the demographic characteristics of the Danish population).[23] The expected framing effects were observed with the asymmetric menus: *skewLO* reduced the estimated coefficient of constant relative risk aversion to 0.43, and *skewHI* increased the estimated coefficient to 0.91. These differences do not change the authors' overall conclusion that the Danish population is risk averse and that the hypothesis of risk neutrality can be rejected. In a parallel laboratory study, also done in Denmark, Andersen et al. (2006) find that the *skewLO* treatment has a significant downward effect, but that the *skewHI* treatment has no effect. The authors note that although there are framing effects, they can be estimated and controlled for. Finally, in a field study with coin dealers in the US, the only skew treatment with a significant effect was in the opposite of the predicted direction. The authors conjectured that "the frame may have appeared to be skewed to the subjects, leading them to overreact to avoid responding to the frame" (Harrison et al., 2007b).

---

[23] This estimate is roughly comparable to the estimates that Holt and Laury (2002) obtained for their high-stakes treatments, although an exact comparison of stakes with the Harrison, Lau, and Rutström paper is tricky given that only 1 in 10 subjects in the field experiment were selected for payment (see their discussion in footnote 16, p. 353).

A somewhat stronger framing effect has been documented by Bosch-Domenech and Silvestre (2012), who show that the levels of risk aversion implied by observed crossover points can be manipulated by removing rows from the choice menu in Table 4.3. The removal of the top three rows that correspond to risk-seeking behavior (those with high payoff probabilities of 0.1, 0.2, and 0.3) does not have much of an effect on the binary choices in the remaining rows. In contrast, the elimination of rows 8–10 at the bottom of the menu table tends to yield a higher proportion of risky choices in some of the remaining rows, which would produce lower estimates of risk aversion. The authors show that comparable framing effects are not significant if a price list is used to elicit the certainty equivalent value of a lottery. See (4) in Section 4.2.4 for an example of a table-based method of eliciting a certainty equivalent. When one option is a sure payoff and the other is a 50/50 split between two "evenly spaced" numbers like 5 and 15, then it is easy for subjects to anchor on expected value differences, which are near 0 in the middle, and then adjust for risk, so framing changes at the top and bottom of the table could have less of an effect. In general, our conjecture is that choice menus with easy-to-calculate expected values would be less prone to framing manipulations, but this does not mean that such measures are recommended. For example, a certainty equivalent based method that produces "virtual risk neutrality," as reported by Sprenger (2010), would not be subject to framing effects but would not be useful for categorizing subjects as being more or less risk averse for purposes of studying their behavior in other tasks.

One possibility is that subjects view the endpoints of a table as boundaries on what would be a reasonable decision, which could increase the attractiveness of decisions in the middle (Andersen et al., 2006). With probability-elicitation tasks, Andersen et al. observe that 0 and 1 are natural endpoints to use. Note, however, that subjects must make a choice in each row of a choice menu, but they might infer that rows with "obvious" choices have been deleted, which create experimenter demand effects that alter choices in other rows. In any case, the implication of the framing experiments is that the *quantitative* numerical measures of risk obtained from choice lists should be interpreted with caution or corrected with proper econometric adjustments, although qualitative conclusions like overall risk aversion or payoff scale effects are probably unaffected. An understanding of framing effects is very important for psychological studies of perception, and for others who need to spot biases in procedures. Most economics experiments, in contrast, involve attempts to select a neutral frame and then changing an economic variable of interest. Of course, if you are comparing results of *different* studies that use different frames, then an appreciation of framing affects is essential in evaluating differences in results.

The 0 and 1 boundaries for the choice menu in Table 4.3 seem natural, but the associated payoff amounts can be manipulated to move the risk neutral crossover point, which is between 0.4 and 0.5 in Holt and Laury (2002) and between 0.5 and 0.6 in

Laury and Holt (2008). A comparison of differences in results between papers that have different crossover points, like the two papers just mentioned, would require a careful consideration of framing effects. And obviously, it would be a mistake to run an experiment in which the risk neutral crossover is near a boundary, e.g. between rows 1 and 2, and then reach a conclusion that subjects are risk averse.

One aspect of choice menus is that some subjects do not exhibit a single crossover. Murnighan et al. (1988) and others since have discarded data with multiple crossovers. Alternatively, Holt and Laury (2002) determined a cut-point that equalizes the number of "wrong" choices on each side. Andersen et al. (2006) simply force a single crossing point from safe to risky options as one comes down the basic Holt/Laury choice menu.[24] They conclude that forcing a single crossover point has no significant effect on average levels of implied risk aversion in a laboratory experiment, although it does, by construction, reduce "noise" and eliminate violations of monotonicity. They also discuss presenting the 10 decision rows in a random order and reject the idea because it would make the cognitive task more difficult and, hence, would tend to increase response "noise." We agree with this assessment. Notice that it would be complicated to enforce a single crossover with randomly ordered binary choices.

Andersen et al. (2006) also propose and evaluate the use of a second-stage choice menu in which the interval of possible preferred crossover points determined by a given switch point in the initial stage can be split up into a more refined set of choices. For example, if a subject selects the safe option in row 4 and the risky option in row 5, then the actual preferred crossover point could be somewhere between a 0.4 and 0.5 probabilities for the high payoff. The second stage decision could break up this range of probabilities into smaller increments. Andersen et al. (2006) report that the use of the second (fine-interval) stage may have caused an increase in measured risk aversion in their experiment with Danish subjects, but that the use of the second stage had no significant effect on overall risk aversion estimates in a second study using US subjects. If the primary focus is on qualitative differences and treatment effects, then existing evidence would suggest that imposing a single crossing may be a good way to get better data, but usefulness of a second stage (fine-grid) is not clear.[25]

One design issue is whether to make payments for the decisions in all rows of a choice menu or to pick one row at random and use the decision from that row to determine earnings. The prevailing practice, beginning with Murnighan et al. (1988), is to use one decision, selected at random *ex post*. This procedure, which is intended

---

[24] This is easily done, even with hand-run tasks, either by asking subjects to select a single crossover point (e.g. Wallach and Kogan, 1959) or by asking them to reconsider when they first select multiple points.

[25] Holt and Smith (2012) use a simple choice menu to elicit event probabilities, with software that imposes a single crossing and a second-stage fine grid. The combination of the single crossing and the fine grid have the effect of avoiding the need to report a range of probability assessments. This precision is especially useful for the study of Bayesian probability assessments, where the choice of a specific probability, e.g. 0.33, might indicate a correct Bayesian choice or a specific bias.

to obtain independent binary choices, may not be valid if subjects' preferences do not conform to the independence axiom of expected utility theory (Holt, 1986). But paying for all decisions is likely to raise more problems, including cost and major wealth effects. In addition, there may be "hedging" or "portfolio effects" in which choices for one decision are perceived to balance the risks of another, a type of behavior that has been observed in a different context (Blanco et al., 2010). Laury (2012) reports an experiment with a standard lottery choice menu that addresses the incentive effects of a random payment procedure, by comparing three treatments: 1) make a payment for one randomly selected decision, 2) make payments for all 10 decisions, and 3) increase stakes by a factor of 10 and only pay for 1 randomly selected decision. There was no significant difference between behavior in the "pay-one" and "pay-all" treatments, and both yielded the same average number of safe choices (5.2). In contrast, scaling up the payoffs by a factor of 10 (with one decision selected at random to be paid) causes a statistically significant increase in risk aversion as measured by the number of safe choices made.

Another payment method that can be used to save on costs, especially with high stakes, is to only pay a fraction of subjects for their choices. Others are paid nothing or just a show-up fee. Laury et al. (2012) elicited risk aversion with the 90x payoff scale taken from Holt and Laury (2002). The only difference was that subjects made 20 decisions, with probabilities changing in 5% increments, instead of 10 decisions with 10% probability increments. After the binding payment decision was determined, there was a 10% chance that any given subject would be paid for that decision. The observed numbers of safe choices with this 10% payout probability were significantly lower than what was observed in the original Holt and Laury study for the same scale and a 100% payout probability. The take-away is that these papers have not raised concerns about the popular procedure of paying for one randomly selected decision, but that only paying a fraction of subjects does seem to dilute incentives.

4.3.4 Software and Implementation

All of these elicitation procedures can be implemented with paper record sheets and dice, which has its advantages, not the least of which is speed in getting started and making changes. Our feeling is that using dice was important for establishing credibility for very high stakes experiments, e.g. Holt and Laury (2002). Today most researchers use a computer interface, e.g. programmed with *z-tree* or something else, since this permits easy data recording, uniform instructions, forcing single crossovers if desired, and tracking of things like decision times. One advantage of a web-based interface is that subjects from various remote locations can participate. Computerized interfaces make it possible to present choices in an intuitive manner. For example, Choi et al. (2007) provide subjects with a two-dimensional budget constraint in which the mouse can be used to make investment portfolio decisions.

A major advantage of computerized procedures is the ease of running classroom demonstrations. For example, the administrator page of the Veconlab site (http://veconlab.econ.virginia.edu/admin.htm) has a link to the "Decisions" menu, which in turn has links to several separate programs, e.g. the Gneezy Potters continuous "Investment Game," the Holt-Laury "Lottery Choice Menu," and a program called "Value Elicitation" that implements either a menu-based certainty equivalent price list task or a menu-based probability equivalent task. All of the programs have many setup options in terms of payoffs, rounds, probability ranges, etc., and the instructions adapt automatically to the setup choices made. The Value Elicitation program, for example, has the option to implement a second stage of refined choices and to force single crossovers. Students log in by replacing "admin" with "login" in the link given above, or by just a Google search for "veconlab login." Students can use wireless laptops, cell phone browsers, or comparable devices, and it is fine to let pairs of students share laptops. Alternatively, the instructor can set up the experiment in advance and have students log in and make decisions from home in the evening, since these programs do not have interactive elements.

It is important to note that risk aversion elicitation tasks are frequently used in field studies, sometimes with subjects who are not literate. Researchers have devised clever ways of dealing with field conditions. One team, for example, implemented a Holt-Laury menu by putting colored beads on pairs of sticks, where the color determines the payoff, so the string of beads on a stick reveals the probability associated with the choice of that stick. One stick from each pair is selected and the beads from the chosen stick are placed in a cup. With ten choices corresponding to ten rows of a choice menu, there would be ten cups with beads, one of which would be selected at random in the end to be used for the final drawing of a colored bead and the corresponding payoff.

4.4 TREATMENT EFFECTS

This section covers the effects of changes in treatment parameters that are under the direct control of the experimenter, although some demographic effects will also be mentioned. Ever since Markowitz's (1952b) initial reports of different responses to lottery choice questions in gain and loss domains, both economists and psychologists have been quite interested in documenting these behavioral differences. Then we go on to consider other treatments that are relevant for understanding decision-making under risk: group decision-making versus individuals, stability of risk preferences, and biological treatments. A complete review of the literature is beyond the scope of this chapter; we choose instead to focus on representative studies for each of these treatment effects.

4.4.1 Gains Versus Losses and House Money Effects

Characterizing the effect of losses on risk preferences is difficult because behavior appears to be even more sensitive to elicitation method, and thus there is no "typical" result from changing the decision-making domain from gains to losses. Some studies show a higher proportion of risk-seeking behavior under losses, others show a higher proportion of risk-averse behavior. The contradictory evidence exists even when confining attention to studies that use real cash payoffs. The story is further complicated by methodological issues associated with endowing subjects with an initial stake in settings that involve potential losses.

The seminal study comparing risk preferences over gains and losses is Kahneman and Tversky (1979). While their paper addresses a wide range of lottery choice anomalies, one of their most widely cited results concerns Prospect Theory's "reflection effect"—that replacing all positive payoffs by negatives (reflection around zero) will reverse the pattern of choices. For example, a choice between a certain payoff of 3,000 and an 80 percent chance of earning 4,000 is replaced by a certain loss of 3,000 and an 80 percent chance of losing 4,000. In their study, subjects were presented with a series of binary choice lotteries. Each subject completed no more than 12 choices, with the presentation order varied between subjects. Their data showed strong support for reflection—specifically a reversal of choices that imply risk aversion over gains to risk seeking over losses. In some treatments, including the example above, this can be attributed to a certainty effect (certain outcomes are subjectively overweighted relative to outcomes that are not certain). They concluded that "certainty increases the aversiveness of losses as well as the desirability of gains" (Kahneman and Tversky, 1979, p. 269). Nevertheless, high rates of reflection were also observed when both outcomes were uncertain.

Additional evidence in favor of this reflection effect is reported in Tversky and Kahneman (1992), at least when small probabilities of gains and losses are avoided. Tversky and Kahneman report data that support Cumulative Prospect Theory's fourfold pattern of risk preference that implies a reversal of risk preference for small probability gains or losses. They observe that subjects are risk averse over moderate-to-large probability gains, and risk seeking for small probability gains. This pattern is reversed in the loss domain: subjects are risk averse for small probability losses and risk seeking for moderate-to-large probability losses. It's important to note, however, that all payoffs reported in Kahneman and Tversky (1979) and Tversky and Kahneman (1992) were hypothetical. Other studies have considered the question of consistency of risk preferences over gains and losses using real payments.

Of course, inducing real monetary losses in the lab is complicated. In general, it is difficult to require subjects to put their own money at risk. We begin with a brief digression here into the methodological issues associated with inducing losses in the lab, including earned or unearned endowment (house money). One issue is the nature of the "reference point" from which gains and losses are perceived. For example, if a subject's reference point is a zero payoff, then what we attempt to induce as losses may be viewed as a smaller gain. For example, endowing a person with a $30 initial payment and inducing a loss of $20 may instead be viewed as a $10 gain relative to the zero reference point. The problem is that an unexpected or unearned endowment of house money may not change the relevant reference point. In contrast, many subjects may arrive at the lab expecting to earn a reasonable amount, e.g. $30, and if this is the reference point, a $10 payoff outcome may be viewed as a loss of $20 from the reference point. Markowitz argued that current wealth was a major determinant of the reference point, and he did not need to worry about payoff expectations since his choice menu questions pertained to hypothetical payoffs. Kahneman and Tversky recognized that reference points would be responsive to a range of psychological factors.

Bosch-Domenech and Silvestre (2010) argue that even if subjects earn the money, it may be viewed as house money. They attempt to avoid this problem by separating the earnings and loss tasks by a period of several months (and a semester break) so that subjects are more likely to integrate their initial earnings into their background wealth and consumption. When subjects returned for the second session they paid any small losses on the spot and any large losses (up to 90 euros) within several days. Bosch-Domenech and Silvestre (2006) presented subjects with a series of binary choices in which they held the probability constant for a given subject, but changed the (real monetary) payoffs. Each subject made up to seven choices between a lottery and its expected value, with the size of the lottery varying from 3 euros to as much as 90 euros, with payment based on one choice selected at random after all had been made. They varied (between subjects) whether the subject faced a chance of winning or losing money. The probability of winning (losing) the money, either 0.2 or 0.8, was also varied between subjects. As in Bosch-Domenech and Silvestre (2010), subjects in the loss treatments earned their endowment (30, 45, 60, or 90 euros) based on their score on a quiz several months before participating in the lottery-choice experiment.[26]

Unlike the four-fold pattern described by Tversky and Kahneman (1992), Bosch-Domenech and Silvestre (2006) find higher rates of risk seeking behavior under losses than gains both at low and high probabilities. Moreover, they find some consistency in behavior across gains and losses that are not predicted by Cumulative Prospect Theory. Increasing the probability of the bad outcome increases risk-seeking behavior under both gains and losses. Most participants exhibit risk-seeking behavior for small monetary stakes (independent of the choice probabilities and whether facing gains or losses), and most display risk-averse behavior for large monetary stakes (again, independent of choice probabilities and whether facing gains or losses).

Harbaugh et al. (2002) also used a menu of binary choices to study Prospect Theory's four-fold pattern over gains and losses, but held constant for a subject the (real) monetary

---

[26] They limited the potential loss that a subject faced to be no more than their earned endowment, so subjects who earned less than 90 euros would not choose any lottery with a potential loss more than their starting endowment. As a consequence, some subjects made fewer than seven lottery choices.

payment (both the starting endowment and the potential gain or loss) and instead varied the probability of either winning or losing money in the experiment. The probability of a gain or loss ranged from .02 to .98. All subjects completed 14 decisions, with one chosen randomly for payment. The authors were particularly interested in how choice patterns varied across age groups. They used child participants (some as young as five years old), teenagers, college students, and nonstudent adults (up to age 64). All subjects were given their starting endowments by the experimenter (it was not earned), and the size of the endowment, gains, and losses varied by populations. In all cases the gain or loss was set to be 80 percent of the starting endowment. Child participants were paid in "tokens" that could be converted into purchases of toys, games, and art supplies at a "store" set up by the experimenters.

Aggregating across all subjects, Harbaugh et al. (2002) observe a pattern of behavior that is the opposite of that predicted by Prospect Theory: they observe that more subjects choose a gamble over its expected value (indicating at least some degree of risk seeking) as the probability of a gain increases, but fewer choose the gamble as the probability of a loss increases. Thus, across all age groups they find evidence of risk preference for high-probability gains (over 60 percent of subjects chose the gamble when the probability of winning is 80 or 98 percent), but at least moderate risk aversion for high probability losses (fewer than 50 percent of subjects choose the gamble when the loss probability is 80 or 98 percent). This is also inconsistent with Bosch-Domenech and Silvestre (2006), who found higher rates of risk seeking for losses than for gains at both high and low probabilities. In contrast, Harbaugh et al. (2002) observed increased risk seeking only for low probabilities of gains and losses. Disaggregating the data by age, Harbaugh et al. (2002) find support for Prospect Theory's four-fold pattern only among the oldest participants. The youngest subjects (those aged 5–8) generally choose the gamble when faced with either gains or losses with low or high probability. The modal response pattern for older children (aged 9–13) is the opposite of that predicted by the four-fold pattern: choosing the gamble for high-probability gains and low-probability losses, but otherwise choosing its expected value.

Laury and Holt (2008) focused on whether individual risk attitudes switch from risk averse under gains to risk seeking under losses, depending on the size of the stakes and whether payments were real or hypothetical. They used a binary choice menu in which the monetary payments were held constant across choice, with the probability of winning or losing changing among choices as one moves from row to row in the menu. Unlike either Bosch-Domenech and Silvestre (2006) or Harbaugh et al. (2002), subjects in the Laury and Holt experiment had to choose between two gambles (as opposed to a gamble and its expected value). The basic design was like that described in Holt and Laury (2002), where the probability of the high-payoff outcome varied in 10 percent increments from 0 to 90 percent. Each subject completed two lottery choice tasks: a menu of choices that involved only gains and a second identical menu of choices with all positive earnings replaced by their negative.[27] Subjects earned their starting balance by participating in another, unrelated, experiment prior to the lottery choice part of the experiment. Subjects were told their initial earnings, but did not actually receive any earnings until the end of the session. The size of payoffs (baseline payoffs were several dollars, and high payoffs were 15 times the baseline level) and whether the stakes were real or hypothetical was varied between subjects. We observed reflection as the modal outcome only when payments were both low and hypothetical. In all other treatments (low real, and high payments both real and hypothetical) risk aversion under both gains and losses is the modal outcome.[28]

Even a cursory review of the literature makes it clear that there is no consistent pattern of results in experimental studies of risk preferences over losses, whether one focuses on the degree of risk aversion or the responsiveness of risk attitude to changes between gains and losses, payoff scale, and probability of gain or loss. This may be explained, in part, if elicited risk preferences are highly sensitive to the procedure used to elicit them. Harbaugh et al. (2010) provide convincing evidence that this may, in fact, be the case. They report a within-subjects analysis of lottery choices for gains and losses (with probabilities of the gain or loss set equal to 0.1, 0.4, and 0.8). They directly compare behavior using a choice-based approach, in which subjects choose between the lottery and its expected value, and a price-based approach, in which the subject must specify a maximum willingness to pay to either play the lottery over gains (or avoid the lottery over losses). Thus they are able to test the prevalence of both reflection of choices between gains and losses and Prospect Theory's four-fold pattern under the choice- and price-based elicitation procedures. When subjects specify a maximum willingness to pay, 34 percent of subjects exhibit the full four-fold pattern: when probabilities are low, subjects are risk seeking for gains but risk averse for losses; when probabilities are high, subjects are risk averse for gains but risk seeking for losses. However, when subjects choose between the lottery and its expected value, only six percent of subjects make choices consistent with the four-fold pattern. In the choice-task, the modal pattern is reflection, but in the opposite direction as that predicted by Prospect Theory.

One useful perspective on risk preference is that it is affected by several conceptually distinct factors, curvature of utility in gain and loss domains, the nature of reference points that separate perceived gains and losses, and by nonlinear perceptions of probabilities. The potentially offsetting effects of these components and their apparent sensitivity to procedure present a difficult problem that would benefit from a better understanding of how to decompose and distinguish the different factors that affect risk preferences. We will return to this topic in the Implications for Theory section.

---

[27] Results were not determined until after all choice tasks were completed. The two tasks were separated by a neutral (matching pennies) game task, and the order of presentation of gains and losses was varied across sessions.

[28] Under high real payments, an approximately equal number of subjects are risk neutral and averse over losses, but very few subjects are risk loving for losses.

4.4.2 Groups Versus Individuals

Many risky decisions are made by groups rather than individuals. The laboratory provides an ideal platform for direct comparisons of individual risk attitudes with the preferences implied by group decisions for analogous tasks. Of particular interest is whether group decisions are more consistent with the average (or median) of individual preferences, whether more extreme risk preferences (either the most risk averse or the most risk seeking) dominate the group decision, or whether group decisions tend to be more or less consistent with risk neutral behavior that has an easy mathematical "justification."

One hypothesis that was prominent in the social psychology literature is that group choices are characterized by "risky shift." For example, Stoner (1961) found in experiments using hypothetical choices that groups tend to make decisions that involve higher levels of risk than the decisions that would be made by the individuals in the group. This prediction has been generalized to "choice shift" (Davis et al., 1992), stating that group decisions are simply more extreme than those of the individuals. If the individuals are risk averse, the group choice tends to be even more risk averse than that of the individuals. And if individuals are risk seeking, the group choice tends to be even more risk seeking that that of the individuals.

Evidence from experiments that use real incentives over the past decade has largely shown that differences exist between groups and individuals in risky situations, but that these differences are more complex than simply a difference in average behavior. The complexity stems in part from the variation in elicitation method used, e.g. choice between risky prospects or a pricing task involving choices between a lottery and alternative money payments. Another relevant factor seems to be the manner in which group decisions are made, e.g. unstructured discussion, a single group vote with the outcome based on majority rule, or iterative voting until unanimity is reached. Another methodological issue that arises is whether to use a between-subjects design, which allows for a relatively straightforward analysis of whether group choices differ significantly from individual decisions, or a within-subjects design, which allows one to study how individual preferences combine to form the group choice, or conversely how group discussion may affect subsequent individual decision-making.

Shupp and Williams (2008) elicited each subject's maximum willingness to pay ("WTP") for a chance to win $20 ($60 in the group treatment, to be divided equally among each member of the three-person group).[29] Each made choices in nine gambles, where the probability of winning $20 varied from 10 percent to 90 percent (in equal increments of 10 percent). Subjects made nine choices with one randomly chosen to count for payment. In the gamble chosen, the stated willingness to pay was compared to a randomly drawn price between $0 and $19.99. If the WTP exceeded the random price, the gamble was "purchased" at the random price and the gamble was then played

---

[29] Each subject was endowed with $20 at the start of the experiment ($60 for each three-person group).

out. They implemented both a between-subjects treatment, and a within-subjects treatment (choices were made in the individual treatment before being told about the subsequent group treatment).

Group decisions were made via unstructured (and unmonitored) discussion. Groups had up to 20 minutes to come to a unanimous decision about the maximum willingness to pay for each of the nine gambles. If any group was unable to come to a unanimous decision within 20 minutes, each person would submit a WTP and the group choice would be the average of the three submitted bids. All groups reached a unanimous agreement, and so this was never implemented.

In both the within-subjects and between-subjects treatments, the variance of group decisions was lower than the variance of individual decisions. Also, choices of both individuals and groups tended to be closer to the risk-neutral prediction (willingness to pay equal to expected value of the gamble) as the probability of winning the gamble increased. As Shupp and Williams point out, the expected (monetary) loss from submitting a WTP that is different than expected value is higher as the probability of winning increases. Thus, one interpretation of this observation is that this is consistent with a bounded rationality explanation: deviations decrease as the expected loss from doing so increases.

Perhaps more interesting is the impact of the probability of winning on the difference between group and individual behavior. In the highest-risk gambles (those where the probability of winning is no greater than 40 percent), groups are more risk averse than individuals in both the within- and between-subjects treatments. In contrast, for the lowest-risk gambles (with a high probability of winning) groups are significantly *less* risk averse than individuals in the between-subjects treatment. No significant difference between group and individual willingness to pay is observed in these gambles for the within-subjects treatment, which could be due to some persistence of order effects.

Further support for the interaction between the riskiness of a lottery and the difference between group and individual decision-making can be found in Baker et al. (2008) and Masclet et al. (2009). Both studies use a Holt-Laury style structured choice menu with real payments. As in Shupp and Williams, Baker et al. (2008) compared choices in both within- and between-subjects treatments, and used an unstructured 20-minute conversation period for group decision-making. If unanimous agreement was not obtained in any decision after 20 minutes, then majority rule would be used to determine the group choice (such disagreements were not observed). Subjects in the within-subject treatment made two decisions as an individual: one before and one after the group decision. Thus Baker et al. could study how individual preferences relate to group decisions as well as studying the impact of group decision-making on subsequent individual decisions. It turned out to be the case that there was a significant, positive effect of the group decision on participants' subsequent individual decisions.

Baker et al. find lower variance of group choices than for individuals (where the observation is the total number of "safe" lottery choices). In the between-subjects sessions, they find no significant difference in the mean number of safe choices made by individuals and groups, and the observed medians are identical. However, they find a significant interaction between the probability of a good outcome (in this case, winning the higher monetary value in the lottery) and the difference between group and individual decisions. For high-risk lotteries (where the probability of winning the higher monetary payment is between 10 and 30 percent) all groups choose the safe lottery consistent with either risk-neutral or risk-averse behavior, compared with only 80 to 90 percent of individuals. Anyone choosing the risky lottery at these probabilities would be classified as risk seeking; thus groups appear more risk averse than individuals for the highest-risk lotteries. For the lowest-risk lotteries (probability of the better outcome of 80 to 90 percent), individuals are more apt to choose the safe lottery and thus act more risk averse than groups in these situations. This interaction effect also exists between the first individual decision and the group decision in the within-subjects treatment. All three major findings of the Baker et al. paper (lower variance for groups, interactions with win probabilities, and more risk aversion for groups in the highest risk lotteries) are consistent with the findings reported by Shupp and Williams.

Masclet et al. (2009) also compared choices of individuals and three-person groups. They presented subjects with the same ten lotteries used in Holt and Laury (2002) with a $20\times$ payoff scale using euros instead of dollars. The risky lottery's outcomes were 77 euros or 2 euros and the safe lottery's outcome was 40 or 32 euros. However, instead of presenting them to subjects in order of increasing probability of the better outcome (and all at once), they presented them to subjects in a random order and one at a time (in a series of ten "periods"). In their group treatment, subjects were assigned to an anonymous three-person group, with group composition randomly reassigned after each period. At the start of the period, each subject submitted (via computer) a vote for the safe or risky lottery outcome. If the vote was unanimous, this outcome was the group's choice. If the vote was not unanimous, the result of the vote was reported to each of the three group members and they voted again. This continued for up to five total votes (or until a unanimous vote was obtained). If the fifth vote was not unanimous, then group's choice was randomly determined. Subjects made choices as both an individual and a group (with the order of treatment reversed between sessions).[30] Masclet et al. observed a similar interaction to that reported earlier between the probability of the good outcome and the difference between individual and group behavior. Specifically, in high-risk lotteries (low probability of the better outcome) groups were

---

[30] Masclet et al. (2009) also implemented a "choice" treatment in which, at the start of each period, subjects submitted a maximum willingness to pay to make the decision on their own; the top three bidders played alone and the remaining 15 made decisions via group vote. Bids were generally low (about 45 percent of subjects bid nothing), with higher bids for those who were less risk averse or whose group did not reach a unanimous vote in the previous round(s).

more risk averse than individuals. Overall, groups were more likely to choose the safe outcome than individuals. This is largely because those choosing the risky option were more likely to change their vote if they were in the minority.

The general conclusion of this work is that groups exhibit less variation than individuals in risky choices, and that groups tend to be more risk averse, especially in high risk lotteries. A partial exception to this pattern is provided by Harrison et al. (2013), who combined features of the Baker et al. and Masclet et al. experimental designs. They utilized a Holt-Laury style menu in which subjects were presented with ten choices between safe and risky lotteries in ascending order of the probability of obtaining the higher payoff. While they used voting to arrive at a group decision, the group choice was based on a single majority vote of anonymous three-person groups.[31] All sessions were conducted in Colombia, and 70 percent of the subjects were male. Subjects were cash-motivated, but each subject had a 10 percent probability of being paid their experiment earnings. They found no significant difference between group and individual choices. They do not report any test of interactions between the probability of the better outcome and the difference between group and individual choices, so it is not clear whether this finding from other studies is present in their data.

4.4.3 Stability of Risk Preferences Across Domains

Most experiments measure the risk preference of a subject at a single point in time and in a single context. In some cases (including many of those cited in this chapter), what interests the researcher is simply a measure of risk aversion or individual characteristics that affect the degree of risk aversion. However, in other situations risk aversion is elicited to predict or explain behavior in another (often related) environment. For example, Andersen et al. (2008) demonstrate that one obtains biased estimates of discount rates if the curvature of the utility function is ignored. They propose a two-stage approach to measure discount rates. They elicit choices in a Holt-Laury risk preference experiment, and also choices in a standard discount rate elicitation task.[32] They obtain a curvature-adjusted discount rate estimate using a dual estimation procedure in which they use the risk-preference choices to measure the curvature of the utility function and then use the discount rate choices to estimate a curvature-adjusted discount rate.

This raises the question of whether risk preferences that are elicited in one context (for example, using a lottery choice menu) have predictive power for choices made in another context (for example, decisions about smoking or asset market purchases).

---

[31] Harrison et al. (2013) were also interested in the interaction of altruistic preferences on individual votes for a group-choice over risks prospects; thus they also implemented a dictator task in addition to those described here.

[32] Subjects complete a series of choices between receiving payment at two (distinct) future dates. The amount to be paid at the earlier payment date is held constant, and the payment at the later date increases across decision rows. (For example, the subject may choose between $200 in 3 weeks and $205 in 12 weeks in one decision; the choice may be between $200 in 3 weeks and $210 in 12 weeks in another decision). The amount of additional payment required for the subject to postpone payment until the later time period allows the researcher to estimate an implied discount rate for the subject.

Taken as a whole, the evidence suggests that one should be cautious about using a risk aversion estimate obtained in one context to make inferences about behavior in another (unrelated) context. It is not altogether surprising that estimates of the coefficient of risk aversion differ across elicitation methods, but it is troubling that the rank-order of subjects in terms of their risk aversion coefficient differs across elicitation methods (Deck et al., 2010a; Dave et al., 2010; Isaac and James, 2000).

A nice example of this research is an experiment conducted by Deck et al. (2010a) that tests for consistency of risk preference across four measurement tasks, and also with a survey that elicits attitudes toward risk (measured as likelihood of engaging in risky behaviors) in six domains: social, recreational, health and safety, gambling, ethical, and investment. They are able to conduct a within-subjects comparison of behavior across risk-elicitation tasks, and also to see whether choices in any of these tasks are consistent with self-reported information on risk-taking behavior. The four choice tasks were:

- A lottery choice menu (Holt and Laury, 2002) in which the monetary payments are fixed, but the probability of winning the better outcome varies among lotteries.
- A "spinner" investment task (Eckel and Grossman, 2002) in which a subject selects which one of six lotteries to play. Each lottery involves a 50% chance of winning one of two (positive) payoffs. The lotteries are shown as divided circles, with the outcome determined based upon where a virtual spinner stops. In this task, the probabilities are fixed (50 percent chance of winning either outcome) but the payoffs associated with each lottery vary. The choice of lottery is used to infer the degree of risk aversion.
- A "Deal or No Deal" task (Deck et al., 2008), which is based on the popular game show. Subjects are presented with 12 "cases," given to them virtually via a computer interface. Each case is associated with a different amount of money between $0.01 and $100 that is randomly assigned to each case. In the initial stage of the game, the subject must choose whether to accept $2.99 and stop playing, or choose a case to open. Once a case is opened, the amount of money in the case is taken out of the game. The subject must then decide whether to accept a different sum of money, which is based on the money left in the remaining cases, or to open another case. This continues until the subject decides to stop playing (and accept the offered sum) or until only one case remains, in which event the subject receives the money in the remaining case.
- A Balloon Task in which a subject inflates a virtual balloon. The value of the balloon starts at $2 and increases as it inflates (by $2 per inflation), and at any time the subject can stop the task and take the current value of the balloon. If the balloon bursts, the subject receives $1. The number of times the balloon can be inflated before it bursts is determined by a random draw of an integer between 0 and 24.

The first two tasks are static in the sense that a subject makes a single decision (which of six lotteries to play in the spinner task) or a series of decisions (whether to play the safe or risky lottery in each of row of the lottery choice menu) with the outcome determined after all decisions are made. The second two tasks are more dynamic in the sense that subjects make a decision, then receive feedback (the dollar amount in the case is revealed in the Deal or No Deal task, or the subject sees whether the balloon bursts in the Balloon task). Therefore, Deck et al. expected to find choices in the last two tasks more associated with a propensity to take gambling risks and the first two tasks more associated with the propensity to take financial risks. These propensities are measured by the subjects' responses to the survey.

Like other previous studies, Deck et al. find little evidence of correlation of risk attitude between decision-making tasks. There is significant, but weak, correlation between the first two tasks (correlation coefficient of 0.27) and between the second two tasks (correlation coefficient of 0.21). Moreover there is little evidence that behavior in any of these choice tasks explains self-reported propensities to take naturally occurring risks.

In a follow-up study, Deck et al. (2010b) consider the effect of framing on the consistency of choices under uncertainty. They present subjects with two equivalent decision-making tasks, each based on lottery choice menu (as in Holt and Laury, 2002). Their Financial Task Frame is the usual presentation of the decision-making task: a choice between a relatively safe lottery and a risky lottery, with payment amounts held constant and the probability of winning the higher outcome increasing across decision-making rows. Their Gambling Task Frame uses the same payoffs and probabilities, but the subject is asked to "place a bet" and the computer screen is designed to resemble a casino-gambling environment. Each subject completed both decision-making tasks (presented in alternating order) and a survey that elicited the subject's propensity to engage in naturally occurring risk-taking activities. The authors found that changing the frame affects choices (with fewer safe choices being made in the gambling frame). Moreover, one's self-reported propensity to take financial risks has a significant, negative effect on the difference between choices in the Financial and Gambling frames. This indicates that one's likelihood of taking financial risks has more of an effect on choices in the Gambling frame. Taken as a whole, this research "further calls into question the appropriateness of attempts to model risk as simply dependent upon payoffs and probabilities" (Deck et al., 2010b).

4.4.4 Biological Manipulations of Risk Preferences

Given evidence that risk attitudes may not be stable across domains or presentation frame, it is also of interest how biological factors may affect risk attitudes. Inherent traits (such as gender) are discussed elsewhere in this paper. In this section we consider two factors (hormonal levels and sleep deprivation) that may be measured or manipulated and studied in the lab.

Buser (2012) studies how menstrual cycle and hormonal contraceptives affect women's decisions about whether to compete. Subjects in his experiment also participate in a risk elicitation task in which they make a series of choices between a sure payment and a lottery with a 50-percent chance of winning one of two non-negative outcomes.

For example, in one decision, the subject must choose between 8 euros for sure and a lottery with equally likely payoffs of either 12 or 6 euros. In another the subject must choose between 8 euros for sure and a lottery with payoffs of 24 or 0 euros (with a 50 percent chance of each payoff). As in other structured elicitation measures, the point at which the subject switches between the sure payoff and the risky lottery is used to infer the degree of risk aversion. Buser finds no significant effect of either menstrual cycle phase or hormonal contraceptives on risk-taking behavior. However, he finds that women who take oral contraceptives are more risk averse than others during the 21-day period in which they take oral contraceptives. He speculates that an increase in sample size would cause this difference to be significant.

Chen et al. (2013) compare bidding behavior of men and women in laboratory first- and second-price auctions. The Bayesian Nash Equilibrium bidding strategy in a first-price auction is sensitive to one's risk attitude, but not in a second-price auction. In some sessions they also directly elicit risk attitude using a Holt-Laury type lottery choice task. They find that women bid significantly higher than men in the first-price auction, but not the second (and they bid higher throughout their menstrual cycle); however, risk attitude as measured by the Holt-Laury task does not account for this gender gap. They do not, however, report any evidence on how risk attitude itself varies across the menstrual cycle.

In another domain, McKenna et al. (2007) present an interesting experiment that explores the effects of one night of full sleep deprivation on attitude toward risk (and ambiguity). They use a lottery-choice task that involves a series of choices between two lotteries; the lotteries have equal expected payoffs, but different variances in payoffs. For example, in one lottery-choice task, the subject must choose between Lottery 1: {2/3} chance of winning $20 and a {1/3} chance of winning $0; and Lottery 2: {1/3} chance of winning $37, {1/3} chance of winning $2, and a {1/3} chance of winning $1. The control group experienced a night of normal sleep between two sets of lottery-choice tasks; the treatment group experienced no sleep (total sleep deprivation) between the two sets of tasks. For the control group there was no sequence effect: the before- and after-measures of risk preference did not differ. In contrast, the treatment group exhibited less risk aversion for gains and also less risk seeking for losses. They did not, however, reach a conclusion about the underlying mechanism that appears to reduce the risk-sensitivity of sleep-deprived individuals.

4.5 DEMOGRAPHIC PATTERNS

Attitudes toward risk can be thought of as bundles of cognitive and emotional reactions to distinct aspects of risky choices. Summary measures of risk aversion are useful for the big picture, but progress toward a deeper understanding of the aversion and attraction of risk might be obtained by looking at demographic effects. Unfortunately, the story behind demographic effects is somewhat mixed.

One tricky aspect of the analysis is that factors such as wealth and education may be affected by risk aversion, especially for nonstudent subjects. Binswanger's (1981) classic paper deals with these issues by estimating a three-equation model in which risk aversion, schooling, and wealth are endogenous. The model also includes a measure of inherited wealth (market value of inherited land).[33] The only variable that was significant in the risk aversion equation was a "luck" variable, defined on the basis of how often the high payoff outcome had been obtained in prior decisions (recall that Binswanger visited the same villages at discrete time intervals). Variables that were not significant include: age, gender, cast rank, and the predicted values of schooling and net assets.

4.5.1 Representative Surveys

Field experiments like Binswanger's are appealing for the study of demographic effects, since they have a wider geographic and demographic focus than is the case in the typical laboratory study in which subjects are not selected to be representative. For example, consider the original Holt and Laury (2002) experiment, which included about sixty MBA students, thirty business school faculty, and over 100 undergraduates from three universities. There was a slight tendency for people with higher incomes to be less risk averse. The women were more risk averse than men in the low-payoff condition shown in Table 4.3, but this gender effect disappeared for higher payoff scales. There was no white/nonwhite difference, but Hispanics in the sample were a little less risk averse. It is not appropriate, however, to make broad inferences about demographic effects from a single study using a sample of students and faculty at three universities. For example, the Hispanic effect could be due to the fact that most of the Hispanic subjects were MBA students in Miami, many of whom were from families that emigrated from Cuba, which was probably a very risky life-style change.

In contrast, Harrison et al. (2007a) used the Holt-Laury procedure to estimate risk preferences for a large *representative sample* of adults in Denmark, using high payoffs comparable to scaling the payoffs in Table 4.3. (The payoffs were about eight times higher, but only one person in ten was actually paid.) One advantage of a field experiment with careful sampling is that it may be possible to make inferences about the effects of social policies for the whole country. The overall conclusion of this study is that the Danes are risk averse, with a relative risk aversion measure of about 0.67.[34] Most

---

[33] Binswanger's careful distinction between endogenous and exogenous variables sets a high standard that probably deserves more attention than it has received. A notable exception is Dohmen et al. (2011) who use parent's education as an exogenous variable.

[34] Individual measures of risk aversion in the field experiment tended to be relatively stable when the experiment was repeated with a subsample at a later date. Individual responses did change, but changes were typically small and non-systematic, with several exceptions. For example, students tended to exhibit less stability. Changes in risk aversion were unrelated to measured changes in background conditions, with one intuitive exception; those who had become more favorable about their overall economic situation tended to become more risk preferring.

demographic variables had no significant effect, with the exception that middle-aged and educated people tended to be less risk averse. There was no gender effect, which is consistent with the Holt and Laury (2002) high-payoff results and with the Laury and Holt (2008) study of the effects of gains and losses, with both low and high payoffs. The Harrison et al. field experiment was complemented with a laboratory experiment with Danish students, Andersen et al. (2006), which also used a Holt-Laury choice menu. The only demographic effect that was significant was the "lives alone" variable, which, intuitively, produced more risk seeking (but might be better modeled as being endogenous and potentially affected by other factors like income).[35] Again, there was no significant gender effect. Another somewhat broad-based study that did not find a gender effect is the Harbaugh et al. (2002) experiment that used both children and adults, for low and high probability gains and losses.

Many empirical studies of risk aversion, however, do indeed find a gender effect, with women being more risk averse, especially for survey-type questionnaires of a willingness to take risk (see the discussion in Eckel and Grossman, 2008a). For example, Dohmen et al. (2005, 2011) conducted a large representative survey of Germans and validated it with a field experiment using cash incentives for a subsample of respondents. The survey assessed risk attitudes with an 11-point question about willingness-to-take-risks "in general." The main finding is that the people surveyed are generally risk averse in a manner that is relatively stable but may vary across contexts. The main demographic results are that men are more willing to take risks, as are people who are taller, younger, and have parents with more education. The survey was followed by an experiment involving a subsample of respondents who participated in the certainty-equivalent elicitation task described in Section 4.2. The structure was analogous to that shown in (4), but with payoffs in euros and a 1/7 chance of being paid. The incentivized elicitation measures of risk aversion are strongly correlated with the general willingness-to-take-risks measure, although the latter provided the best overall predictor of self-reported risky behaviors in terms of driving, smoking, investing, self-employment, athletics, etc. The results of the incentivized elicitation measure were not broken down by gender, but a subsequent analysis of the data done by Nelson (2012) indicates only marginal significance of a gender effect for one test ($p = 0.07$). In regressions with the same data, but with the addition of a measure of cognitive ability, being female is not significantly related to a willingness to take risk as measured in the experiment (Dohmen et al., 2010, Table 3). Cognitive ability is significantly correlated with the measured willingness to take risk, as is age (but age squared has a significant negative coefficient).

---

[35] In another paper, Andersen et al. (2010) report no significant difference between the mean estimate of risk aversion obtained in a laboratory experiment with Danish students and a field experiment using a representative sample from the Danish population. They do, however, note different demographic effects between samples that they point out calls into question whether this observation would be robust to the use of a different student sample.

Risk preference and other behavioral tendencies such as trust and time preference are widely estimated in field experiments. Cardenas et al. (2008) survey this fast-growing literature and take note of the substantial overlap in inferred measures of risk aversion between studies done in different areas. They conclude: "Overall, there does not seem to be much support for the idea that poor people in developing countries are more risk averse than richer people in developed countries."

4.5.2 A Second Look at Gender Effects and Other Factors

As Harrison et al. (2007a, p. 361) note : "The absence of an effect from sex is noteworthy, since it has been intensively studied using related experimental and survey methods, and has even been the focus of theorizing about the role of evolution in forming preferences." The quote was followed by a footnote that summarized a surprising number of no-effect results to date, most of which are listed in the previous subsection. In contrast, the Croson and Gneezy (2009) survey of gender differences in preferences has a table with 10 studies, all but one of which indicate that women are more risk averse. "We find that women are indeed more risk averse than men" (Croson and Gneezy, 2009, p. 448). This issue obviously merits a closer look.

The weakest evidence for gender differences comes from studies that use variations of the Holt-Laury choice menu. The original Holt and Laury (2002), the one exception noted by Croson and Geneezy, observed slightly more risk aversion for low stakes but not for high stakes. But using similar measures obtained in an experimental study of bank runs, Porter (2011) reports a midpoint CRRA estimate of 0.25 for men and 0.36 for women, which is both economically and statistically significant (p-value$= 0.00$). Another strong gender effect is reported by He et al. (2012) using cohabitating Chinese student couples discussed in the previous section. In particular, men were significantly less risk averse than couples, which are less risk averse than women. So the gender results go both ways. There are, however, a number of recent studies using the Holt-Laury procedure that show no gender effect, e.g. Chakravarty et al. (2011) using students in India. In addition to making decisions for themselves, the subjects in this study made a decision that affected earnings for another subject, and they were significantly less risk averse with the other person's money. Another example is the Galarza (2009) study done with rural subjects in Peru, which produced a large number of multiple crossings and irrational choices of the safe option in the bottom row of the choice menu. The only significant demographic variable was a measure of skilled education, which was correlated with a willingness to take risk, even after the irrational decisions were removed.

One way to understand differences is to look at underlying biological markers. Schipper (2011) uses a Holt-Laury menu to measure risk aversion for gains and losses, along with salivary measures of various hormones for 200 subjects. Overall, risk aversion is negatively correlated with testosterone and positively correlated with cortisol (associated with stress) for gains only. However, risk aversion is positively correlated with being female for losses only.

The strongest evidence for gender differences comes from the investment-based elicitation approach, described in Section 4.2, in which an initial monetary stake is divided between a value-preserving safe investment and a risky investment, e.g. with Eckel and Grossman (2002). In contrast with Binswanger's study of agricultural villagers in (then) Bangladesh, the gender difference observed by Eckel and Grossman with U.S. student subjects was quite sharp. The modal choice for men was the all-risky option at the top of Table 4.2 above, whereas the modal choice for women corresponded to an equal split between the safe and risk assets. Eckel and Grossman (2008b) report a comparison of neutral and explicit investment framing of this same gamble structure. The effect of the investment frame on the average number of the gamble selected is not economically significant, but the strong gender difference is present in both frames.

A recent field experiment by Dave et al. (2010) used 881 Canadian residents, with ages ranging from 18 to 44 and consisting of high school students and adults. All participants made decisions in a standard Holt-Laury menu from Table 4.3, scaled up for $20\times$ payoffs (in Canadian dollars). The same subjects also made a portfolio choice for the Eckel Grossman setup from Table 4.2, but with payoffs scaled up to be comparable to the Holt-Laury task (and with a dominated high-variance option added to separate out risk-seeking individuals, as was done earlier by Binswanger). Each task was used to estimate a coefficient of constant relative risk aversion for each subject. The Holt-Laury method yielded slightly but significantly higher estimates of relative risk aversion (by about 0.15). Women were found to be significantly more risk averse than men, but this gender effect is about twice as large in the regressions involving the Eckel Grossman (discrete investment game) task as with the Holt-Laury choice menu task. The age and income variables were not significant.

Similarly strong gender effects are observed in continuous investment games, in which an initial stake can be divided between a value-preserving safe asset and a risky asset that yields a gain of g times the amount invested, with probability p, and 0 otherwise. These games are structured so that $gp > 1$. Therefore both risk-neutral and risk-seeking subjects should invest the full stake. Charness and Gneezy (2012) summarize results from 10 investment games that are special cases of this exact structure, done under an array of different payoff conditions, different subject pools, and overall objectives. In all but one of the studies, male subjects invest more than females. The one exception was Gneezy et al. (2009), which was the only one that involved non-Western subjects (villagers in Tanzania and India).

Finally, we consider results obtained from using the third common elicitation method, based on estimating a certainty equivalent with a list of alternative money amounts, but without the BDM selling price terminology. Akay et al. (2012) elicit certainty equivalents in this manner for rural peasants in Ethiopia. Ninety-two subjects were randomly selected from a longer list of households, and the procedures were explained in terms of dice and colored balls, since about a third of the participants were illiterate. Risk aversion was inferred from the "crossover" decision. In general, the peasants were quite risk averse, with about half of the Ethopian subjects selecting the lowest feasible certainty equivalent, a decision that was only observed for 1% of the student subjects in a control done at a university in the Netherlands. Among the Ethiopians, the only demographic variable that was significant was poor health, which was correlated with risk aversion. No gender effect was observed with this list-based pricing task. In contrast, Fehr-Duda et al. (2006) do find gender differences using a similar (certainty equivalent elicitation) approach for an experiment done in Zurich. They estimate a rank-dependent utility model separately for men and women, and conclude that utility functions are similar and not highly curved, but that women are less sensitive to probability changes and tend to underweight the higher probabilities associated with the higher of two payoffs. A difference in probability perceptions is potentially very important, but it cannot be the whole story behind gender differences, since all of the commonly used risk aversion assessment methods are sensitive to the degrees of nonlinear probability weighting that are typically estimated. We will consider the effects of probability weighting in the Implications for Theory section that follows.

To summarize, there is mixed evidence for gender effects coming from studies using the Holt-Laury choice menu and certainty equivalent pricing tasks. In contrast, there is uniformly strong evidence for gender effects based on results of investment games (with the exception of Binswanger's original study, which involved non-Western subjects). The stronger evidence for gender differences in risk aversion provided by investment task experiments is a problem for other elicitation approaches if, in fact, there is a strong gender effect on risk taking behavior. For a skeptical review based on an analysis of 26 large scale experiments, see Nelson (2012), who argues that gender effects are generally overstated in both the primary literature and in the secondary (survey paper) literature.

In trying to make sense of observed differences between elicitation methods, we were influenced by Fehr et al. (2011), which offers some additional observations about gender differences in probability weighting. Women are found to respond to their moods, e.g. they weight the probabilities of the higher payoff less optimistically when they are not in a good mood, and vice versa. In contrast, the authors report that probability weights for men are less responsive to mood states, in part because the use of mechanical criteria, such as the application of expected value calculations, tends to insulate men against the effects of changing emotions. In their study, about 40% of the male subjects report using expected value as a decision criterion, whereas only a "negligible number" of women report this behavior.

A differential reliance on mathematical calculations could explain the lower incidence of gender differences found with the Holt-Laury type choice menus, which were designed to make it harder to calculate and equate expected values in one's head. In contrast, the intentional simplicity of investment game incentives would facilitate the use of mental expected payoff calculations. In the Holt-Laury menu, the probabilities are generally different from 0.5 and the payoff amounts are not evenly spaced integers, which makes mental expected value calculations more tedious. But investment games and certainty equivalent pricing tasks with 0.5 probabilities and simple payoffs are designed to be as simple as possible, as noted by Eckel and Grossman (2002) for example. In such simple contexts, a tendency for men to use expected value calculations could explain observed gender differences. For example, the modal choice for males of the all-risky gamble at the top of Table 4.2 can be justified by taking the averages of the two equally likely payoffs for each gamble. Similarly, in a continuous-choice investment game of the type surveyed by Charness and Gneezy (2012), the risky asset has a higher expected payoff as long as the payoff probability times the multiplicative gain factor is greater than 1, and expected payoff is maximized by putting the entire stake into the risky asset. Choices in this type of investment task also tend to exhibit gender differences in which most of the men invest all in the risky asset and women tend to invest about half.[36] Finally, note that gender differences based on numeracy might not arise in rural areas of Ethiopia or Bangladesh, for example, where many are illiterate and incentives may not even be presented in numerical formats. One possibility is that the main gender effect really is a difference between educated males in developed economies and everybody else.

4.5.3 Age effects

The evidence from large representative surveys summarized above is that a willingness to take risks may peak among middle-aged people. This pattern was observed by Harrison et al. (2007a), using the Holt-Laury choice menu on a random sample of Danish citizens, as described above. The Dohmen et al. (2005, 2011) survey of Germans found a similar quadratic pattern in the effect of age on willingness to take risk.

   Albert and Duffy (2012) also report a lower willingness to take risk among older adults in their sample. They measure risk preferences with a $10\times$ payoff scale applied to the choice menu in Table 4.3 above, where the safe option involves either $16 or $20, and the risky option involves payoffs of $38.50 or $1. The task was done twice: first as a trainer (no payment) and then for cash payoffs. The young adults were recruited from doctors' offices or preschool programs and were all mothers with young children. Older

---

[36] For example, Charness and Gneezy (2010), (Appendix Table A1, treatment T1) lists choice data for 18 men and 9 women. Ten of the men invested 100% in the risky asset, and only one woman did so. The median decision for this treatment was 100 for men and 60 for women. Over all 8 treatments, 51 of the 59 choices that involved investing all in the risky asset were made by men. A similar pattern is reported by Ball et al. (2010, Figure 1) for a discrete investment menu similar to Table 4.2 above, but with a mean-preserving spread option added at the top. The modal choice for men was the gamble with the highest expected payoff (but not the one with the extra risk), and the modal choice for women was the gamble that corresponded to a split between safe and risky investments, analogous to the "equal split" row in Table 4.2.

adults were already participants in research studies of "health and function." Those with test scores indicating dementia or "major depressive disorder" were excluded. The average age for the young adults was 39, all were female, all had completed high school, with an average of 17 years of education. The average age for the older adults was 71, 82% were female, 82% had completed high school, with an average of 13 years of education. The main finding for age was that the young adults in this study were less risk averse. Restricting attention only to those who completed high school, the average number of safe choices was 5.5 for young adults and 6.8 for older adults. It is interesting to note that there is little difference between the proportions of subjects who are either risk seeking or risk neutral across the two groups (about 11% for each group). The overall gender difference that does arise is due to the fact that older adults who are risk averse are more so than is the case for the younger adults.

4.6 APPLICATIONS: UNDERSTANDING BEHAVIOR IN RISKY ENVIRONMENTS

In most cases, it makes sense to begin a theoretical analysis with minimal assumptions, e.g. risk neutrality, in order to derive a benchmark prediction. If observed behavior deviates from predictions, the next step is to add the most salient omitted factor. This section presents a series of applications from different areas of economics in which the inclusion of risk aversion helps clarify seemingly anomalous behavior. The focus is on cases where elicited measures of risk aversion do (or sometimes do not) provide a good signal of other behavior observed for the same subjects in laboratory or field settings.

4.6.1 Bargaining

Murnighan et al. (1988) point out that differences in risk aversion have predictable effects on bargaining success that are common for a surprisingly broad class of bargaining models, including all standard axiomatic bargaining models and the strategic Rubinstein bargaining model. The Murnighan et al. (1988) study is seminal in that it is the first paper to use individual measures of risk aversion to deconstruct economic behavior in a subsequent experiment. In particular, they considered unstructured, continuous-time bargaining games in which disagreement point payoffs may be affected by risk aversion. As mentioned in Section 4.2, they first measured risk aversion with a special form of a lottery choice menu in which the safe option in each row is a sure amount, e.g. $5, and the risky option is a random payoff, e.g. $10 or $4, with specified probabilities. The probability of the high payoff starts high and is reduced in subsequent rows, which should result in a crossover point to the safe option. Risk aversion was measured by the number of safe choices (participants with multiple crossovers were excluded from subsequent bargaining games). This procedure was used to select the eight subjects in the session with the highest degree of risk aversion (the largest numbers of safe choices). Each of these subjects was paired with one of the eight subjects with the fewest safe choices. In this manner, the authors were able to evaluate the extent to which differences in risk aversion affected bargaining behavior. The average number of safe choices (from the 21 rows) made by the risk-averse group was about 15, and the average number of safe choices for the less risk-averse group was about 5.

In the bargaining games that Murnighan, Roth, and Schoumaker considered, risk aversion affects a person's disagreement point. In one of their games, continuous-time unstructured bargaining was over the division of 100 tickets for a lottery that pays $10 if you win and $2 otherwise. If the pair failed to agree on the division of lottery tickets in the specified time interval, they each received a fixed amount, $5. In this particular bargaining game, a more risk-averse person would require a higher fraction of lottery tickets to be equivalent to the fixed disagreement payment of $5, so the more risk-averse person's disagreement point *in the bargaining process over lottery tickets* would involve a higher number of tickets. In theory, the bargaining process should provide each person with a number of tickets that exceeds that person's disagreement point, a prediction that is consistent with a wide variety of strategic and axiomatic bargaining models. This is an interesting case where being risk averse, which implies a higher disagreement point in the number of lottery tickets, is advantageous. The reverse situation, where risk aversion is disadvantageous, is a game in which both of the lottery payoff amounts are higher than the exogenous disagreement payoff. The effects of differences in risk aversion were in the predicted directions, i.e. with more tickets going to the more risk-averse person in the treatment where that person had a higher disagreement point, and with more tickets going to the less risk-averse person in the other treatment in which risk aversion is disadvantageous. These predicted treatment effects, however, were generally smaller than the unpredicted effects of focal points and equal splits.

4.6.2 Auctions

The possible effect of risk aversion in auctions is surely the most controversial application to be considered in this section. The intuition is simple, i.e. that a high bid in a pay-as-bid auction is "safe" in the sense that it increases the probability of winning, but at a cost of lower profit contingent on winning. For example, risk aversion has been suggested as an explanation of the tendency for subjects to bid above Nash predictions for risk neutral bidders in private value pay-as-bid auctions, although a number of other plausible explanations have also been offered. The sometimes heated exchanges about risk aversion in auctions could be the topic of a separate survey paper, so our coverage will be illustrative of this kind of exchange, not exhaustive or definitive.

A number of papers have reported bidding patterns in experiments that line up nicely with predictions based on risk aversion, especially with small numbers of bidders or private value structures for which the predicted effects of risk aversion are stronger, e.g. Goeree et al. (2002).[37] In other more competitive settings, however, risk neutrality seems to work fine. For example, the *risk-neutral* Nash bid function for a private-value, pay-as-bid auction with 12 bidders and 6 prizes produces a curved array of theoretical predictions that looks more like a fitted quadratic regression line when plotted in the same graph with observed data averages (Holt and Liao, 2012).

Here we consider a simple auction for distinct items, e.g. condos, for which different people may have strong but differing preferences. One way to auction these items would be to sell them in a preannounced sequence. An alternative "right-to-choose" auction lets the bidders select their preferred item in an order determined by the bid rank, with a payment that can be either based on the winning bid or on the highest rejected bid. Revenue equivalence holds for a Nash equilibrium calculated under simple assumptions that include private values and risk neutrality, but the presence of risk aversion would yield higher sales revenues in the right-to-choose auction. These "bidders' choice auctions" can create competition across different goods for which the market would otherwise be thin, and the fear of not obtaining one's preferred good may cause risk-averse bidders to bid more aggressively.

This revenue enhancement associated with right-to-choose auctions was observed in an experiment conducted by Goeree et al. (2004), who attributed the difference to risk aversion. The magnitude of the implied common coefficient of constant relative risk aversion (CRRA) parameter is of a plausible magnitude, but the authors did not obtain separate measures of risk aversion. On the other hand, Eliaz et al. (2008) use a different variant of a right-to-choose auction in which risk aversion should lower bids instead of raising them. They also observe higher revenues with the right-to-choose auction, and they conclude that risk aversion, if it has an effect at all, cannot be the only cause of the difference. This type of frustratingly inconclusive exchange is typical of this literature, and one way to resolve issues might be to obtain individual estimates of risk aversion for each bidder.

Alevy et al. (2010) used a variant of a binary choice menu procedure to measure risk aversion for farm owners in Peru, who then bid in auctions for four distinct types of irrigation rights in a "framed field experiment" (real cash, real water rights that had been previously purchased by the research team, but artificially constructed auction procedures). The risk aversion elicitation was done once with cash payoffs and once with payoffs in irrigation water volume, with alternating orders and a standard random selection to determine payoffs. Measures of time preference were also obtained. The right-to-choose auction involved four distinct irrigation sources and was done in four phases, with a highest-rejected-bid payment mechanism. This format generated significantly higher bids and revenues than the baseline sequential auction procedure, as predicted by theory with risk aversion.

---

[37] In this study, the fit was so good that our colleague, Charlie Plott, was unable to distinguish the bar graph of theoretical predictions (with logit errors) from the actual data averages (he guessed incorrectly).

The authors also report regressions of bids on a set of variables that include a dummy for the right-to-choose auction, and its coefficient is positive, large in magnitude, and highly significant. Then the inclusion of the risk aversion measure into the same regression caused the coefficient on the auction format to fall from about 48 to about 5 and to lose significance. Risk aversion is, as predicted, positively correlated with individual bidding behavior in the right-to-choose format ($p = 0.028$ for the variable that interacts this auction format with risk aversion). As the authors note, one way in which direct elicitation of risk helps in this study is that it does not require a risk aversion homogeneity assumption of the type that is typically used to derive predictions for theoretical models. (Recall that heterogeneity in risk postures is apparent in all of the data display columns for the tables in Section 4.2.) While this regression-based analysis is suggestive, it is important to keep in mind that bidding behavior in auctions might be affected by many other factors that are not modeled in the standard Nash analysis of auctions, e.g. joy of winning balanced by anticipated regret from losing, or an overweighting of low probabilities of winning. The striking thing about risk aversion relative to these other alternatives, however, is that *individuals* with higher measured risk aversion in this study tend to bid higher in the bidder's choice auction. It's not just that the *averages* are above the risk-neutral prediction, which could be due to risk aversion or a number of other factors listed above. In any case, the effect of risk aversion on bidding in auctions is a controversial topic, and the example presented here is intended to show how direct estimates of risk aversion may help clarify some of the issues.

4.6.3 Contests and Rent Seeking

Many lobbying activities are modeled as contests in which the competitors for a prize make costly effort decisions, with the prize awarded on a winner-take-all basis. For example, the effort might be the amount spent on lobbying effort directed toward securing a protected market position, e.g. a license. The focus of studies of such contests is typically on the extent to which effort costs of all participants tends to "dissipate" the rent associated with the prize. The most common modeling assumption in winner-take-all contests is that the probability of obtaining the prize is the ratio of one's own effort to the sum of all players' efforts. Thus the expected payoff is the value of the prize times the probability of winning, minus the cost of effort, which is incurred whether or not the prize is obtained. If there are N risk neutral contestants for a prize with a known money value of V, and if effort is measured in dollar expenditures on lobbying, then it can be shown that the Nash equilibrium is for each person to spend an amount $V(N-1)/N^2$ on effort. For example, if $V = 120$ and $N = 4$, the Nash effort for risk neutral players is $3 \star 120/16 = 22.5$. Notice that as the number of competitors gets large, the predicted effort expenditure for each of the N players converges to V/N, so all rent is dissipated in the limit.

In this type of "all-pay, winner-take-all" contest, a high effort is risky, since it is like a "bid" that must be paid whether or not it is a winning bid. This observation is the intuition behind the standard result from theoretical papers on contest games, which is that an increase in risk aversion will *lower* bids. Contests provide an especially interesting application for our purposes, since the standard result from contest experiments is that of *overbidding*, not underbidding as implied by risk aversion. The Sheremeta (2013) survey of contest experiments lists 30 studies with the same general structure described above, and, of these, 28 studies report overbidding that is statistically significant. The effect is also economically significant, since the median rate of overbidding relative to the risk-neutral Nash prediction is 72%. In some cases, the rate of overbidding is so high that earnings are negative on average. Obviously, the prevalent and severe overbidding in contests must be caused by something other than risk aversion. But this is where direct elicitation of risk preferences is helpful.

Price and Sheremeta (2011) ran an experiment with $V = 120$ and with random matchings in groups of 4. Each person was given an endowment of 120 at the start of each round, and the bid was required to be between 0 and 120. One way to think about the strategic situation is that each person receives a stake of 120 that can be left in a safe, value-preserving account or invested in an asset with a payoff probability that depends on the amounts invested by others. The endowment, which exceeds the Nash prediction of 22.5, has no effect on predicted behavior. The average observed bid (about 42) was more than double the Nash prediction. More interesting for our purposes, individuals with higher levels of risk aversion tended to bid *lower*, although this effect was not present in a second treatment in which there was a much looser upper limit on individual effort in each contest. In both cases, risk aversion was measured with a choice menu that was similar to the one used by Millner and Pratt (1991) 30 years earlier in their seminal contest experiment procedure. The menu involved a fixed amount $1 in each row on the safe side, and a gamble offering $3 or $0, with the probability of the high payoff declining in subsequent rows, so that the number of safe ($1) choices can be used as a measure of risk aversion. Millner and Pratt had also observed that those with higher measured risk aversion tended to exert less effort in their (continuous time) contest experiment. Sheremeta's (2013) survey cites several other papers, e.g. Sheremeta and Zhang (2010), with similar conclusions about risk aversion effects in contest experiments.

To summarize, Sheremeta (2013) provides experimental evidence to support several plausible explanations of the salient feature of behavior in contest experiments: extreme "overbidding" relative to risk neutral Nash predictions. Even though the predicted effect of introducing risk aversion is to reduce bids, it is striking that subjects with higher direct measures of risk aversion tend to submit lower bids. In this sense, risk aversion does not explain the average bid deviations, but it does seem to explain some of the heterogeneity.

4.7. IMPLICATIONS FOR THEORY

This section considers some implications of this research for theoretical modeling. This discussion provides an opportunity to introduce an alternative approach to the measurement of risk preferences, based on econometric estimates that use a wide range of lottery or portfolio choices, e.g. Hey and Orme (1994), Holt and Laury (2002) who used a Luce power function error specification, and Choi et al. (2007). See Harrison and Rutström (2008) for a very careful description of maximum likelihood estimation of risk aversion and other parameters under different specifications of the error term.

4.7.1 Functional Forms, Curvature, and Risk Aversion

The clearest implication of constant relative risk aversion (CRRA), with $u(x) = x^{1-r}$, is that scaling up all payoffs proportionally will not affect risk preference, since the scale parameter would factor out of the power function and cancel out in all expected utility comparisons. This implication is contradicted by the sharp increases in risk aversion that Binswanger (1981), Holt and Laury (2002, 2005), and others report for high-stakes treatments, using both within and between-subjects designs. The increases in risk aversion, however, are not as severe as would be observed with constant absolute risk aversion (CARA). To see this, consider the CARA utility function $u(x) = (1 - e^{-\alpha x})/\alpha$ for which absolute risk aversion $-u''(x)/u'(x) = \alpha$. A twenty-fold increase in all payoffs that replaces x with $20x$ in this function is analogous to leaving payoffs unchanged and increasing risk aversion to 20α. It can be shown that a value of absolute risk aversion that fits the 1x data in Figure 4.1 would, at 20α, imply much more risk aversion than is observed for the $20\times$ payoff treatment in Figure 4.1. This observation led Holt and Laury (2002) to consider an "expo-power" utility function proposed by Saha (1993), which is a composition of the exponential (constant absolute risk aversion) function and the power (constant relative risk aversion) function: $u(x) = \frac{1 - e^{-\alpha x^{1-r}}}{\alpha}$. This reduces to a power function as $\alpha \to 0$, and it reduces to the CARA function as $r \to 0$. For positive values of both parameters, the function exhibits increasing relative risk aversion and decreasing absolute risk aversion, as desired.

Holt and Laury (2002) report estimates of $\alpha = 0.029$ (0.0025) and $r = 0.27$ (0.17), with standard errors in parentheses, using a power function probabilistic choice model associated with Luce (1959), instead of the usual exponential (logit) form. These estimates provide inverse S-shaped prediction patterns that track the outward shift in the observed proportions of safe choices in a figure that is analogous to Figure 4.1. The nice feature of this formulation is that the expo-power function can "explain" choice patterns for payoff treatments that range from 1x to 90x in the experiment. In other words, the combined effects of the increasing relative risk aversion and decreasing absolute aversion provide an explanation for the observed increases in the proportions of safe choices in observed as payoffs are scaled up. But it would be a mistake to extrapolate these predictions very far outside of the range of payoff scales considered, since additional adjustments would likely be necessary to account for nonlinearities.

4.7.2 Probability Weighting and Risk Aversion

One of the key implications of prospect theory is that risk preference can be sensitive to low probabilities, as was documented by Cohen et al. (1985). The intuition is simple. Suppose a normally risk averse subject is presented with a small, e.g. 0.1, chance of obtaining a large payoff, e.g. $100. If this low probability is overweighted, then the subject could exhibit risk preference, which is what Markowitz (1952b) observed in his informal survey. A dramatic example of this "upside risk" effect is provided by a recent paper by Comeig et al. (2013), who ran an experiment with a number of paired choices, in which the risky option always had an expected value that was $0.80 higher than the safe option. They find that subjects are quite risk averse when choosing between a safe option and an option with "downside risk" of a very low payoff. But when the same subjects face a choice between a safe option and an option with a lot of upside risk, they become much more likely to select the risky option, even though the expected value difference is held constant. With downside risk, women in the sample were much more likely to choose the safe option in each pair. In contrast, the gender differences were much smaller with upside risk. This result suggests a role for probability weighting, but that cannot be the whole story, since a scaling up of all payoffs by a factor of 5 (which does not affect probabilities and their weights) resulted in a higher proportion of choices of the safe option.

When probability weighting was incorporated into the original version of prospect theory in 1979, all probabilities were weighted with a function $W(p)$ that is increasing from 0 to 1 as the probability goes from 0 to 1, but with overweighting of low probabilities, as shown by the curved lines in Figure 4.2. The solid line function shows the Prelec (1998) function: $W(p) = \exp(-(-\ln(p)^w)$ for $w > 0$. Note that if the weighting parameter $w = 1$, then the minus signs cancel and $W(p) = p$, so the function includes expected utility as a special case. Kahneman and Tversky used a weighting function that is a ratio of powers: $W(p) = \frac{p^w}{[p^w + (1-p)^w]^{(1/w)}}$ for $w > 0$, which reduces to $W(p) = p$ when $w = 1$. Note that these alternative forms have the same shapes, and indeed they essentially overlap as drawn with a weighting parameter of 0.7 that is typical of many estimates. There is a literature on which functional form is best, but Figure 4.2 suggests that it may not matter.

Even at the time of the first prospect theory paper, it was known that any nonlinear weighting of probabilities could yield violations of stochastic dominance (Handa, 1977). The insight of rank dependent utility (Quiggin, 1982) is that stochastic dominance is based on comparisons of cumulative distributions, so the fix is to apply the weight to the inverse cumulative distribution (not to the probability density) in order to preserve

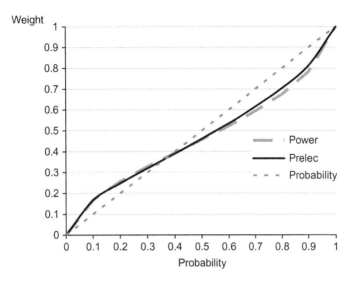

Figure 4.2 Power and Prelec probability weighting functions for $w = 0.7$.

stochastic dominance. With only two events, as is the case for the gambles used in the Holt-Laury menu for example, this procedure is equivalent to applying the weighting function $W(p)$ to the probability of the higher payoff and to weight the utility of the lower payoff with the residual $1 - W(p)$.

The effects of probability weighting may not matter much in investment tasks that use probabilities of 0.5, since the weights of $W(0.5)$ and $1 - W(0.5)$ may be close to the probabilities, as is approximately the case for the functions shown in Figure 4.2. Similarly, for a risk neutral person, the crossover point for the Holt-Laury menu in Table 4.3 would be in row 4, where the high payoff probabilities of 0.4 would not be affected. But most subjects are somewhat risk averse and cross over in lower rows. The key insight is to notice that the underweighting in Figure 4.2 is greatest for probabilities in the range from 0.5 to 0.7, which would mean that the high payoffs in rows 5 to 7 of the Holt-Laury choice menu in Table 4.1 would be underweighted. The overweighting would have little effect on the attractiveness of the safe option, since the high and low payoffs of $2.00 and $1.60 are relatively close. But the reduced "attraction" of the highest $3.85 payoff would mean that people would be less prone to switch from the safe to the risky gamble in those rows, which increases the risk aversion. To summarize, observed risk aversion in this setting, and in other commonly used settings, may be due to a mixture of probability weighting and utility curvature considerations.

This intuition from the previous paragraph is confirmed by a joint estimation of risk aversion and probability weighting parameters. Using a probabilistic choice framework, Comeig et al. (2013) find that the gender differences are largely in utility curvature for the expo-power function, not for the probability weighting parameter. For women, these curvature parameter estimates are $\alpha = 0.04$, $r = 0.39$ and the probability weighting parameter estimate is $w = 0.66$ for women, all of which are significantly different from 0 at conventional levels. The estimates for men are $\alpha = 0.02$, $r = 0.18$ and $w = 0.67$, which suggests that men are less risk averse in terms of the expo-power parameters. The estimates for the weighting parameter are close together and are close to other estimates that are typically near 0.7. The expo-power function was needed to accommodate the wide range of payoffs, since as noted above, the data included a high payoff (5×) scale treatment. The resulting predictions for proportions of safe choices track the observed higher risk aversion for females with downside risk, the tendency for both genders to take more upside risk, and the tendency for everyone to be more risk averse with high stakes.

The take-away is that many (but not all) anomalous differences in propensities to make risky decisions may be cleared up by using functional forms that permit one to estimate the effects of payoff scale and risk profiles on observed behavior. What is surprising is not how well these probability weighting models tend to work well in some contexts, but rather, the fact that they are typically not even mentioned in the standard (and somewhat thick) textbooks used in most doctoral microeconomic theory classes. But with individual choice data, which is known to be riddled with anomalies and context effects, general theoretical solutions have to be viewed as tenuous.

Econometric estimates of specialized models, however, are not convenient for the kinds of simple risk preference assessments that are desired for most laboratory and field applications. Moreover, to be useful, such estimates have to be done for individual subjects who make limited numbers of decisions, which limits the number of parameters that can be used. A simple procedure for obtaining individual estimates can be derived for the Prelec weighting function and the standard model of constant relative risk aversion. To simplify the calculations, utility is normalized so that the utility of the low payoff L is 0: $u(x) = (x - L)^{1-r}/1 - r$. Consider a person who is presented with a high payoff H, a low payoff L, and a choice menu that elicits a probability equivalent of a sure payment of V. A risk neutral person would cross over at a probability that equates with the expected values: $V = pH + (1-p)L$, which would be $p^* = (V-L)/(H-L)$. With rank-dependent utility, the equation would be: $u(V) = w(p)u(H)$, since the term for $u(L)$ is 0. By substituting the formula for the normalized utility function and for the Prelec weighting function, $W(p) = \exp(-(-\ln(p)^w))$, we obtain an equation that can be simplified by taking natural logs of both sides twice, to get:

$$\ln(\ln(1/p)) = \alpha + \beta\ \ln(\ln(1/p^*))$$

where $\alpha = \ln(1-r)/w$ and $\beta = 1/w$. The data are obtained by giving subjects several alternative values of the certain payoff V and eliciting a probability equivalent for each.

This simple linear regression can be run in any spreadsheet program, which can provide intercept and coefficient values that produce estimates of the probability weighting and risk aversion parameters: $w = 1/\beta$ and $r = 1 - \exp(\alpha/\beta)/w$. To illustrate how this works, data were obtained for 24 subjects using the Veconlab Value Elicitation program discussed above in Section 4.3, with the probability equivalent setup option and choice menus with 20 rows, a single crossover requirement, and a second (more precise) stage. The elicitation task consisted of 5 rounds with $H = \$7.50$, $L = \$0.50$, and $V = \$2$, $\$3$, $\$4$, $\$5$, or $\$6$, presented in random order, with one round selected *ex post* at random for payment. Four of the 24 responses were not useful, e.g. people who made the same p choice in all rounds. For the other 20, the median estimates were $r = 0.54$ and $w = 1.06$, indicating moderate risk aversion and no systematic probability weighting. Four of the subjects tended to overweight low probabilities, with $w < 0.85$, but eight of them tended to underweight low probabilities with $w > 1.15$. Only 2 out of 20 subjects were risk seeking or risk neutral, and the median levels of risk aversion were slightly higher for women ($r = 0.59$) than for men ($r = 0.45$). This work is very preliminary, but it does indicate some promise for a method that offers subject-by-subject breakdowns of curvature and weighting parameters.

An alternative to econometric estimation would be to add choice menus that permit one to assess probability weighting effects. Tanaka et al. (2010) offer a promising start in this direction, with choice menus that allow one to distinguish probability weighting, utility curvature, and loss aversion.

4.7.3 Frugal Heuristics

There is a strand of literature that emphasizes the *process* of decision making for boundedly rational people. The hope is that a deeper understanding is achieved from a study of how decisions are made, not just of what decisions are made. Much of this literature is inspired by the Allais Paradox and other anomalies that raise doubts about rationality-based models. The main idea is that people rely on simple rules of thumb or "heuristics" when faced with complex decisions. The work on risk aversion surveyed here can be used to assess some of these theories.

Binswanger (1981) explicitly considers whether various heuristics or "safety rules" that were being discussed at the time were superior to utility of gain/loss explanations of the data he observed. For example, a rule that prescribes the maximum of the minimum gain (as long as its probability exceeds a perception threshold) would require that all subjects select the safe option in Binswanger's investment choice list, which provides equal payoffs of 50 and 50 for both coin flips. This prediction is rejected by the data. Other heuristic rules, including one with a lexicographic structure, are also considered.

The best known process model of choice under uncertainty is Rubinstein's (1988) "similarity theory," which is based on comparison of the similarity of gambles in probability and payoff dimensions. The formal presentation of that theory, however, is based on risky prospects that have the same minimum payoff of 0, which is not directly applicable to the types of binary choices found in most risk preference elicitation mechanisms. Another lexicographic heuristic (which is strikingly similar in spirit to similarity theory and to the theories that Binswanger tested 25 years earlier) is the "priority heuristic" of Brandstätter et al. (2006). They note that a choice between gambles with two payoffs may involve comparisons of the high payoff in each, the lower payoff in each, or the probability of the high payoff. The model stipulates that the comparisons are made, one dimension at a time, until a difference of sufficient magnitude is noted, and that difference determines which lottery is selected in a lexicographic manner. After reviewing experimental evidence, the authors conclude that the priority order is: 1) minimum gain, 2) probability of minimum gain, and 3) maximum gain. In particular, the first comparison dominates if the minimum gain for one option differs from that of the other by 1/10 of the maximum gain. This heuristic is shown to explain a wide range of choice anomalies, including the Allais Paradox. For the Holt-Laury menu in Table 4.3, the safe option offers the highest minimum gain in all rows, by an amount that exceeds the 1/10 threshold, so this would be the choice predicted by the priority heuristic. This prediction is clearly contradicted by the data.

Our view is that the heuristics provide useful ways of thinking about perplexing deviations from optimal decisions in special situations, but they are "over sold" when they are presented as being general models of decision making. Any model with a lexicographic structure that begins with a probability comparison, for example, would fail if one of the payoffs is set to be extremely high, e.g. at a million dollars. What is interesting is that these models fail even in low stakes lottery choice menus.

4.7.4 Asset Integration

As noted in the introduction, Markowitz first conjectured that utility should be modeled as a function of "present wealth" or, in the case of recent windfall gains and losses, of "customary wealth." This conjecture is considered in Binswanger (1981). His econometric analysis involved estimation of a two-stage least-squares regression in which wealth and schooling are assumed to be endogenous and possibly affected by risk aversion. The "luck" variable, based on the frequency with which a participant had obtained a high payoff in prior rounds, enters the risk aversion equation but not the wealth or schooling equations. The log of net assets has a small (negative) effect on risk aversion, but Binswanger estimates that the effect of a change in the monetary gain (M) is 100 times larger than the net effect of a change in net assets (w), which contradicts the asset integration formulation $U(w + M)$ in which these two effects should be the same. He concludes: "The major finding with respect to the utility-based models is that the assumption of asset integration is inconsistent with the experimental evidence reported, as well as with experimental evidence involving hypothetical questions reported by Kahneman and Tversky (1979)" (p. 888). A similar conclusion is reached by Kachelmeier and Shehata (1992) who made cash payments in all rounds. They report no significant effects of wealth accumulation on elicited risk preferences and conclude that wealth effects are not pronounced. It is worth noting that this conclusion is based on an additional assumption that *future earnings* are not fully anticipated when earnings are accumulated in a series of rounds.

A more nuanced conclusion is reached by Andersen et al. (2013). They use confidential demographic and wealth data for Danish subjects who participated in an earlier risk elicitation experiment to estimate a model in which utility is a nonlinear (CES) function of both wealth and income, which permits "partial asset integration." Although their wealth measures exclude some important elements, like cash on hand, the estimation results provide clear evidence that assets are partially integrated into the observed risky decisions made by subjects in the experiment.

One important product of this analysis is the light it sheds on the "calibration" critique raised by Rabin (2000) and others before and since. If wealth is fully integrated with income (both enter additively as an argument in utility), then Rabin constructs an example where small amounts of risk aversion over a wide range of initial wealth levels would imply an absurd amount of risk aversion at a high initial wealth. For example, a person who declines a bet with a 0.5 chance of losing $100 and a 0.5 chance of gaining $110 exhibits some risk aversion. A person who declines this bet *for all levels of initial wealth* between $100 and $300,000 would, at an initial wealth of $290,000, decline a bet that either loses $2,000 or gains $12,000,000, each with probability one half. This implausible prediction is based on full asset integration. Cox and Sadiraj (2006) show that the implications of small stakes risk aversion are not necessarily implausible when assets are only partially integrated. Andersen et al. (2013) put this issue to rest by showing that, for their estimates of partial asset integration, the implied behavior for high stakes gambles at high wealth levels is not ridiculous.

4.8 SUMMARY OF MAIN FINDINGS AND UNRESOLVED ISSUES

Murnighan et al. (1988, p.102) stress the importance of risk aversion in the analysis of bargaining, and they go on to say that it is "one of the most powerful explanatory hypotheses in a number of other areas of economics (e.g., in explanations of investment behavior, futures markets, and insurance)." Risk aversion is only one of many possible confounding factors that may cause behavior in laboratory and field experiments to deviate from theoretical predictions, and therefore direct measures of risk aversion have an important role to play. Even when observed deviations from risk-neutral Nash predictions are in the opposite direction of what is predicted by risk aversion, e.g. in winner-take-all contest games, it can be the case that observed heterogeneity at the individual level is explained by differences in risk aversion. This section will summarize what has been learned from efforts to measure risk aversion, and what remains to be resolved.

The historical perspective provided in the introduction to this survey reveals a rich tradition that began a full half century before our 2002 paper. The story begins with a structured set of binary choices devised by Markowitz (1952b) for both gains and losses and for different payoff scales. Markowitz concluded that utility must have a mix of convex (risk-seeking) and concave (risk averse) segments, both above and below a reference point based on "present" or "customary" wealth. He also observed a reluctance of people to take fair gambles with balanced (hypothetical) gains and losses, and he concluded that utility falls more sharply with losses than it rises with gains, a notion that was later termed "loss aversion." Psychologists Kahneman and Tversky picked up on the Markowitz insights and mixed in probability weighting from the psychology literature, to obtain a rich theory of behavior over a range of probability and payoff conditions. The theory was supported with subsequent experiments in which certainty equivalents of risky prospects were elicited by presenting subjects with structured choices between the prospect and alternative money amounts, which serve as "prices." Risk aversion is inferred if the elicited *certainty equivalent* price is lower than the expected value of the lottery.

An alternative to this price-based procedure is to hold the safe money payment option constant and vary the probabilities associated with the risky gamble. In menu form, subjects choose between a fixed money payoff, e.g. $8, and gambles with increasing probabilities of the high payoff, e.g. $20. Here the crossover row, where the subject is indifferent between the monetary amount and the gamble, determines a *probability equivalent*. This approach was used by Murnighan et al. (1988) who presented subjects with a menu and subsequently used the subject's decision for one randomly selected row to determine payoffs. The Holt-Laury (2002) procedure is similar, except that the fixed money amount is replaced by a "safe" lottery with two payoff amounts that are closer together than the payoffs for the "risky" lottery.

A reliable measurement instrument for lab or field situations has to be simple enough to explain, sometimes to subjects who are not even literate. But too much simplicity can also be a drawback if it facilitates a simple decision, e.g. based on an expected value calculation. For example, suppose a person is presented with a single gamble, e.g. a 0.2 chance of $7, and asked for a certainty equivalent crossover point. An obvious calculation is to multiply the two numbers to obtain the expected value of $1.40, which would indicate risk neutrality. In our experience with student subjects, precise mathematical answers that seem to imply risk neutrality are much more common for male than female subjects, who may rely more on intuition. In contrast, a probability-based choice menu with changing safe and risky prospects in each row is much less likely to induce responses that conform to simple mathematical calculations. Such probability-based choice menus can be presented to illiterate subjects using colored beads on pairs of sticks (Doerr et al., 2013), although color may blur the effects of payoff differences.

Another major development is the classic Binswanger (1981) paper that used very high stakes to evaluate risk aversion among farmers, by presenting them with a range of alternative investment portfolios, ordered by increasing risk. Similar investment games have been used ever since, both in continuous (Gneezy and Potters, 1997) and discrete (Eckel and Grossman, 2002) frameworks. The original Binswanger formulation has a nice feature: the returns for investments in the risky asset are diminishing as more is invested in this asset, which tends to prevent "pile-ups" of data at the extreme points, a pattern that is commonly observed for men in investment tasks with a more linear structure, e.g. where the amount invested in the risky option is tripled. Simple linear structures, however, are easier to explain to subjects, especially when there is a continuum of mixtures between the safe and risky assets.

To summarize, the main approaches used to measure risk preference involve 1) a *pricing task* based on a list of binary choices between a single risky prospect and various monetary amounts, with a crossover certainty equivalent price that can be used to infer risk aversion, 2) a structured *choice menu* that lists binary choices between risky prospects with changing probabilities, for which the point of probability indifference is used to infer risk aversion, and 3) an *investment task* in which subjects make a single choice among alternative asset allocations between safe and risky investments, with risk aversion indicated by lower allocations to the risky asset.

In addition to the three main approaches listed above, economists have devised many other clever ways to make inferences about risk preferences, e.g. providing subjects with an array of choices and using econometric methods to estimate risk aversion and other parameters, as surveyed in Harrison and Rutström (2008). For example, the previous section suggests a simple approach based on log transformations of elicited probability equivalents, for which the intercept and slope of a linear regression determine a probability weighting parameter and a coefficient of relative risk aversion for each subject. Such parametric estimates are useful for theoretical analysis, but an alternative, less theoretical, approach is to present subjects with opportunities to self-report behavioral tendencies associated with risky or safe behaviors. This survey-based approach has been used to derive measures of risk aversion that have good stability and predictive properties. It is worth emphasizing that risk aversion inferred from any of the above procedures may be due to a mix of utility curvature and probability weighting elements.

All of these approaches have been used extensively to document the finding that people are generally risk averse, although a minority of participants exhibit risk seeking or risk neutral behavior. There is generally more risk seeking for small probabilities of attractive gains ("upside risk") than for small probabilities of very low payoffs ("downside risk"). Less progress has been made in the loss domain, where procedural issues associated with losses are difficult, but not impossible, to deal with. As was first conjectured by Markowitz (1952b) and confirmed by Binswanger (1981) in the field, risk aversion increases sharply with scaled-up payoffs for gains, which refutes the simple model of constant relative risk aversion. It is worth noting that even though standard elicitation techniques provide ranges of constant relative risk aversion associated with each alternative decision, the techniques themselves do not rely on an assumption of constant relative risk aversion. Indeed, results of payoff scale treatments have been used to suggest new functional forms with properties that are consistent with observed data patterns, e.g. increasing relative risk aversion and decreasing absolute risk aversion. Estimates of an "expo power utility" function with these properties are reported in Holt and Laury (2002) and Harrison and Rutström (2008), for example.

Experiments with high-stakes gambles have addressed the issue of what is the appropriate argument of utility, wealth plus income, just income, or some mix. Experimental evidence is clearly inconsistent with full asset integration (Binswanger, 1981). More recently, estimates of models with partial asset integration in Andersen et al. (2013) have provided a constructive solution to the "calibration critiques" that small stakes risk aversion over a wide range of initial wealth levels implies implausible amounts of risk aversion for some high-stakes gambles (assuming that wealth and income are perfect substitutes).

There were, of course, some bumps along the way. For example, if subjects are asked to report a "selling price" for a lottery, the resulting high prices that are generally selected would seem to indicate a love of risk, even though the Becker-DeGroot-Marschak mechanism being used is incentive compatible in that it provides an incentive for subjects to reveal true certainty equivalents for the lottery. This is just an example of the well-known "willingness-to-pay, willingness-to-accept bias" which can be reversed by asking for a buying price. (Low elicited buy prices for a lottery would seem to indicate extreme risk aversion.) All of this can be avoided by using market-neutral terminology or providing subjects with a list of binary choices between a lottery and monetary values that span a relevant range.

In the decade since 2002, the use of simple measures of risk aversion in laboratory and field experiments has become commonplace, in some cases the norm rather than the exception. Many unresolved issues remain. There is not a generally accepted way of using a simple choice menu to untangle the possible effects of utility curvature and probability weighting, although econometric analysis has provided clear insights in some cases. But if risk aversion combines aspects of curvature and probability weighting, which many believe to be the case, then a good measure should be sensitive to both. The evidence for demographic correlates of risk aversion is surprisingly weak, with gender and occasionally age being the only factors that are reliably correlated with risk aversion in many studies. Gender effects seem to be stronger when risk aversion is measured by investment tasks, where the modal decision for men tends to be full investment in the risky asset, whereas women are more diversified. In the laboratory, there are many other unmodeled factors besides risk aversion that may pull decisions away from theoretical predictions, e.g. the joy of winning in a contest. The section on applications is, therefore, focused on selected studies in which elicited measures of risk aversion for individual subjects are correlated with their decisions. The literature on risk aversion measurement and associated applications is rapidly growing, and there are still a lot of exciting areas to be explored.

ACKNOWLEDGMENTS

This research was funded in part by NSF/NSCC grants 0904795 and 0904798. We would like to thank Dan Lee, Allison Oldham, Sarah Tulman, and Sijia Yang for research assistance. In addition, we would like to thank Sean Sullivan, Mike Schreck, Michael LaForest, Beatrice Boulu-Reshef, and Irene Comeig for helpful comments on earlier drafts.

REFERENCES

Abdellaoui, M., Driouchi, A., L'Haridon, O., 2011. Risk aversion elicitation: reconciling tractability and bias minimization. Theory and Decision 71, 63–80.

Akay, A., Martinsson, P., Medhin, H., Trautmann, S., 2012. Attitudes Toward Uncertainty Among the Poor: Evidence from Rural Ethiopia. Environment for Development Discussion Paper 10–04.

Albert, S.M., Duffy, J., 2012. Differences in risk aversion between young and older adults. Neuroscience and Neuroeconomics 1, 3–9.

Alevy, J.E., Cristi, O., Melo, O., 2010. Right-to-choose auctions: a field study of water markets in the Limari Valley of Chile. Agricultural and Resource Economics Review 39, 213–226.

Allais, M., 1953. Le comportement de l'homme rationnel devant le risque, Critique des postulates et axiomes de l'ecole Americaine. Econometrica 21, 503–546.

Andersen, S., Harrison, G., Lau, M., Rutström, E., 2006. Elicitation using multiple price list formats. Experimental Economics 9, 383–405.

Andersen, S., Harrison, G., Lau, M., Rutström, E., 2008. Eliciting risk and time preferences. Econometrica 76, 583–618.

Andersen, S., Harrison, G., Lau, M., Rutström, E., 2010. Preference heterogeneity in experiments: comparing the field and the laboratory. Journal of Economic Behavior and Organization 73, 209–224.

Andersen, S., Cox, J. C., Harrison, G., Lau, M., Rutström, E., Sadiraj, V., 2013. Asset Integration and Attitudes to Risk: Theory and Evidence. Georgia State University, CEAR Working Paper.

Andreoni, J., Sprenger, C., 2010. Uncertainty Equivalents: Testing the Limits of the Independence Axiom. Working Paper, UC San Diego.

Andreoni, J., Sprenger, C., 2012a. Estimating time preferences from convex budgets. American Economic Review 102, 3333–3356.

Andreoni, J., Sprenger, C., 2012b. Risk preferences are not time preferences. American Economic Review 102, 3357–3376.

Antoniou, C., Harrision, G.W., Lau, M., Read, D., 2012. Subjective Bayesian Beliefs. Working Paper, Georgia State University.

Arya, S., Eckel, C., Wichman, C., forthcoming. Anatomy of the credit score: the impact of impulsivity, risk, time preference and trustworthiness. Journal of Economic Behavior and Organization.

Baker, R.J., Laury, S.K., Williams, A.W., 2008. Comparing small-group and individual behavior in lottery-choice experiments. Southern Economic Journal 75, 367–382.

Ball, S.B., Eckel, C.C., Heracleous, M., 2010. Risk preferences and physical prowess: is the weaker sex more risk averse, or do we just think so? Journal of Risk and Uncertainty 41, 167–193.

Barr, A., Genicot, G., 2008. Risk sharing, commitment, and information: an experimental analysis. Journal of the European Economic Association 6, 1151–1185.

Becker, G.M., DeGroot, Morris H., Marschak, J., 1964. Measuring utility by a single-response sequential method. Behavioral Science 9, 226–232. July.

Bernoulli, D., 1738. Specimen theoriae novae de mensura sortis (exposition on a new theory on the measurement of risk. Comentarii Academiae Scientiarum Imperialis Petropolitanae 5, 175–192. translated by L. Sommer in Econometrica, 1954, 22, 23–36.

Binswanger, H.P., 1981. Attitudes toward Risk: theoretical implications of an experiment in rural India. Economic Journal 91, 867–890.

Blanco, M., Engelmann, D., Koch, A.K., Normann, H.T., 2010. Belief elicitation in experiments: is there a hedging problem? Experimental Economics 13, 412–438.

Bosch-Domenech, A., Silvestre, J., 2006. Reflections on gains and losses: A $2 \times 2 \times 7$ experiment. Journal of Risk and Uncertainty 33, 217–235.

Bosch-Domenech, A., Silvestre, J., 2010. Averting risk in the face of large losses: Bernoulli vs. Tversky and Kahneman. Economics Letters 107, 180–182.

Bosch-Domenech, A., Silvestre, J., 2012. Measuring risk aversion with Lists: a new bias. Theory and Decision, 1–32.

Brandstätter, E., Gigerenzer, G., Hertwig, R., 2006. The Priority Heuristic: Choices without Tradeoffs. Psychological Review 113, 409–432.

Buser, T., 2012. The impact of the menstrual cycle and hormonal contraceptives on competitiveness. Journal of Economic Behavior and Organization 83, 1–10.

Camerer, C., Hogarth, R.M., 1999. The effects of financial incentives in experiments: a review and capital-labor-production framework. Journal of Risk and Uncertainty 19, 7–42.

Cardenas, J.C., Carpenter, J., 2008. Behavioural development economics: lessons from field labs in the developing world. Journal of Development Studies 44, 311–338.

Chakravarty, S., Harrison, G.W., Haruvy, E.E., Rutstrom, E.E., 2011. Are you risk averse over other people's money? Southern Economic Journal 77, 901–913.

Charness, G., Gneezy, U., 2010. Portfolio choice and risk attitudes: an experiment. Economic Inquiry 48, 133–146.

Charness, G., Gneezy, U., 2012. Strong evidence for gender differences in risk taking. Journal of Economic Behavior and Organization 83, 50–58.

Chen, Yan, Katuscak, Peter, Ozdenoren, Emre, 2013. Why can't a woman bid more like a man? Games and Economic Behavior 77, 181–213.

Choi, S., Fisman, R., Gale, D., Kariv, S., 2007. Consistency and heterogeneity of individual behavior under uncertainty. American Economic Review 97, 1921–1938.

Cohen, M., Jaffrey, J.Y., Said, T., 1985. Individual behavior under risk and under uncertainty: an experimental study. Theory and Decision 18, 203–228.

Comeig, I., Holt, C.A., Jaramillo, A., 2013. Dealing with Risk. Working Paper presented at the ESA meetings in Tucson.

Cox, J.C., Sadiraj, V., 2006. Small- and large-stakes risk aversion: implications of concavity calibration for decision theory. Games and Economic Behavior 56, 45–60.

Croson, R., Gneezy, U., 2009. Gender differences in preferences. Journal of Economic Literature 47, 1–27.

Dave, C., Eckel, C., Johnson, C., Rojas, C., 2010. Eliciting risk preferences: when is simple better? Journal of Risk and Uncertainty 41, 219–243.

Davis, J.H., Kameda, T., Stasson, M.F., 1992. Group risk taking: selected topics. In: Yates, J.F. (Ed.), Risk-Taking Behavior. John Wiley & Sons, New York, pp. 163–181.

de Palma, A., Ben-Akiva, M., Brownstone, D., Holt, C., Magnac, T., McFadden, D., Moffatt, P., Picard, N., Train, K., Wakker, P., Walker, J., 2008. Risk, uncertainty, and discrete choice models. Marketing Letters 8, 269–285.

Deck, C., Lee, J., Reyes, J., 2008. Risk attitudes in large stake gambles: evidence from a game show. Applied Economics 40, 41–52.

Deck, C., Lee, J., Reyes, J., 2010a. Measuring Risk Aversion on Multiple Tasks: Can Domain Specific Risk Attitudes Explain Apparently Inconsistent Behavior? Discussion Paper, U. of Arkansas.

Deck, C., Lee, J., Reyes, J., 2010b. Personality and the Consistency of Risk Taking Behavior. Discussion Paper, U. of Arkansas.

Doerr, U., Mahmoud, T., Schmidt, U., 2013. Overconfidence and Risk Taking of Ethiopian Farmers. Discussion Paper, University of Kiel.

Dohmen, T, Falk, A., Huffman, D., Sunde, U., Schupp, J., Wagner, G., 2005. Individual Risk Attitudes: New Evidence from a Large, Representative, Experimentally-Validated Survey. Institute for the Study of Labor Discussion Paper 1730.

Dohmen, T., Falk, A., Huffman, D., Sunde, U., 2010. Are risk aversion and impatience related to cognitive ability? American Economic Review 100, 1238–1260.

Dohmen, T., Falk, A., Huffman, D., Sunde, U., Schupp, J., Wagner, G., 2011. Individual risk attitudes: measurement, determinants, and behavioral consequences. Journal of European Economic Association 9, 522–550.

Eckel, C.C., Grossman, P.J., 2002. Sex differences and statistical stereotyping in attitudes towards financial risks. Evolution and Human Behavior 23, 281–295.

Eckel, C.C., Grossman, P.J., 2008a. Men, women, and risk aversion: experimental evidence. In: Plott, C., Smith, V. (Eds.), Handbook of Experimental Economic Results, vol. 1, pp. 1061–1073.

Eckel, C.C., Grossman, P.J., 2008b. Forecasting risk attitudes: an experimental study using actual and forecast gamble choices. Journal of Economic Behavior and Organization 68, 1–17.

Eckel, C.C., Grossman, P.J., Johnson, C.A., de Oliveira, A.C.M., Rojas, C., Wilson, R., 2012. School environment and risk preferences: experimental evidence. Journal of Risk and Uncertainty 45, 265–292.

Edwards, W., 1962. Subjective Probabilities Inferred from Decisions. Psychological Review 69, 109–135.

Eliaz, K., Offerman, T., Schotter, A., 2008. Creating competition out of thin air: an experimental study of right-to-choose auctions. Games and Economic Behavior 62, 383–416.

Fehr, H., Epper, T., Bruhin, A., Schubert, R., 2011. Risk and rationality: the effects of mood and decision rules on probability weighting. Journal of Economic Behavior and Organization 78, 14–24.

Fehr-Duda, H., de Gennaro, M., Schubert, R., 2006. Gender, financial risk, and probability weights. Theory and Decision 60, 283–313.

Fiore, S.M., Harrison, G.W., Hughes, C.E., Rutström, E.E., 2009. Virtual experiments and environmental policy. Journal of Environmental Economics and Management 57, 65–86.

Friedman, M., Savage, L., 1948. The utility analysis of choices involving risk. Journal of Political Economy 56, 279–304.

Galarza, F.B., 2009. Choices Under Risk in Rural Peru. Department of Agricultural and Applied Economics, University of Wisconsin, Staff Paper No. 542.

Gneezy, U., Potters, J., 1997. An experiment on risk taking and evaluation periods. Quarterly Journal of Economics 112, 631–645.

Gneezy, U., Leonard, K.L., List, J.A., 2009. Gender differences in competition: evidence from a matrilineal and a patriarchal society. Econometrica 77, 1637–1664.

Goeree, J.K., Holt, C.A., Palfrey, T.R., 2002. Quantal response equilibrium and overbidding in private-value auctions. Journal of Economic Theory 104, 247–272.

Goeree, J.K., Plott, C.R., Wooders, J., 2004. Bidders' choice auctions: raising revenue through right to choose auction. Journal of the European Economic Association 2, 504–515.

Handa, J., 1977. Risk, probabilities, and a new theory of cardinal utility. Journal of Political Economy 85, 97–122.

Harbaugh, W.T., Krause, K., Vesterlund, L., 2002. Risk attitudes of children and adults: choices over small and large probability gains and losses. Experimental Economics, 553–584.

Harbaugh, W.T., Krause, K., Vesterlund, L., 2010. The fourfold pattern of risk attitudes in choice and pricing tasks. Economic Journal 120, 595–611.

Harrison, G.W., 1986. An experimental test for risk aversion. Economics Letters 21, 7–11.

Harrison, G.W., 1990. Risk attitudes in first price auction experiments: a Bayesian analysis. Review of Economics and Statistics 72, 541–546.

Harrison, G.W., Johnson, E., McInnes, M.M., Rutström, E., 2005. Risk aversion and incentive effects: comment. American Economic Review 95, 897–901.

Harrison, G.W., Rutström, E.E., 2008. Risk aversion in the laboratory. In: Cox, J.C., Harrison, G.W. (Eds.), Risk Aversion in Experiments, Research in Experimental Economics, vol. 12. Emerald, Bingley UK, pp. 41–197.

Harrison, G.W., Lau, M.I., Rutström, E.E., 2007a. Estimating risk attitudes in Denmark: A field experiment. Scandinavian Journal of Economics 109, 341–368.

Harrison, G.W., List, J.A., Towe, C., 2007b. Naturally occurring preferences and exogenous laboratory experiments: a case study of risk aversion. Econometrica 75, 433–458.

Harrison, G.W., Lau, M.I., Rutström, E., Tarazona-Gómez, M., 2013. Preferences over social risk. Oxford Economic Papers 65, 25–46.

He, H., Martinsson, P., Sutter, M., 2012. Group decision making under risk: an experiment with student couples. Economics Letters 117, 691–693.

Hey, J.D., Orme, C., 1994. Investigating generalizations of expected utility theory using experimental data. Econometrica 62, 1291–1326.

Holt, C.A., 1986. Preference reversals and the independence axiom. American Economic Review 76, 508–515.

Holt, C.A., Laury, S.K., 2002. Risk aversion and incentive effects. American Economic Review 92, 1644–1655.

Holt, C.A., Laury, S.K., 2005. Risk aversion and incentive effects: new data without order effects. American Economic Review 95, 902–912.

Holt, C.A., Liao, E.Z., 2012. The Pursuit of Revenue Reduction: An Experimental Analysis of the Shanghai License Plate Auction. Discussion Paper, University of Virginia.

Holt, C.A., Smith, A., 2009. An update on Bayesian updating. Journal of Economic Behavior and Organization 69, 125–134.

Holt, C.A., Smith, A., 2012. Belief Elicitation with a Synchronized Lottery Choice Menu. Working Paper, University of Virginia.

Isaac, R.M., James, D., 2000. Just who are you calling risk averse? Journal of Risk and Uncertainty 22, 177–187.

Kachelmeier, S.J., Shehata, M., 1992. Examining risk preferences under high monetary incentives: experimental evidence from the people's republic of China. American Economic Review 82, 1120–1141.

Kahneman, D., Tversky, A., 1979. Prospect theory: an analysis of decision under risk. Econometrica 47, 263–291.

Karni, E., Safra, Z., 1987. 'Preference Reversal' and the observability of preferences by experimental methods. Econometrica 55, 675–685.

Laury, S.K., 2012. Pay One or Pay All: Random Selection of One Choice for Payment. Discussion Paper, Andrew Young School, Georgia State University.

Laury, S.K., Holt, C.A., 2008. Further reflections on the refection effect. In: Cox, J., Harrison, G. (Eds.), Research in Experimental Economics, vol. 12. Emerald Group Publishing, Bingley, UK, pp. 405–440.

Laury, S.K., McInness, M.M., Swarthout, J.T., 2012. Avoiding the curves: direct elicitation of time preferences. Journal of Risk and Uncertainty 44, 181–217.

Leonard, T., Shuval, K., de Oliveira, A., Skinner, C., Eckel, C., Murdoch, J.C., 2013. Health behavior and behavioral economics: economic preferences and physical activity stages of change in a low-income African American community. American Journal of Health Promotion 27, 211–221.

Luce, Duncan., 1959. Individual Choice Behavior. John Wiley & Sons, New York.

Markowitz, H., 1952a. Portfolio Selection. Journal of Finance 7, 77–91.

Markowitz, H., 1952b. The utility of wealth. Journal of Political Economy 60, 150–158.

Masclet, D., Colombier, N., Denant-Boemont, L., Loheac, Y., 2009. Group and individual risk preferences: a lottery choice experiment with self-employed workers and salaried workers. Journal of Economic Behavior and Organization 70, 470–484.

McKenna, B.S., Dickinson, D.L., Orff, H.J., Drummond, D.P.A., 2007. The effects of one night of sleep deprivation on known-risk and ambiguous-risk decisions. Journal of Sleep Research 16, 245–252.

Millner, E.L., Pratt, M.D., 1991. Risk aversion and rent-seeking: an extension and some experimental evidence. Public Choice 69, 81–92.

Millner, E.L., Pratt, M.D., Reiley, R.J., 1988. A re-examination of harrison's experimental test for risk aversion. Economics Letters 27, 317–319.

Murnighan, J.K., Roth, A.E., Schoumaker, F., 1988. Risk aversion in bargaining: an experimental study. Journal of Risk and Uncertainty 1, 101–124.

Nelson, J., 2012. Are Women Really More Risk Averse Than Men? Institute of New Economic Thinking Note 012.

Porter, T.K., 2011. Stuffing the Mattress: An Experiment on Risk and Bank Runs. Senior Thesis, College of William and Mary.

Prelec, D., 1998. The probability weighting function. Econometrica 66, 497–527.

Price, C.R., Sheremeta, R.M., 2011. Endowment effects in contests. Economics Letters 111, 217–219.

Quiggin, J., 1982. A theory of anticipated utility. Journal of Economic Behavior and Organization 3, 323–343.

Rabin, M., 2000. Risk aversion and expected utility theory: a calibration theorem. Econometrica 68, 1281–1292.

Rubinstein, A., 1988. Similarity and decision making under risk (is there a utility theory resolution to the Allais paradox?). Journal of Economic Theory 46, 145–153.

Saha, A., 1993. Expo-power utility: a 'Flexible' form for absolute and relative risk aversion. American Journal of Agricultural Economics 75, 905–913.

Schipper, B.C., 2011. Sex Hormones and Choice Under Risk. Discussion Paper, University of California, Irvine.

Sheremeta, R.M., 2013. Overbidding and heterogeneous behavior in contest experiments. Journal of Economic Surveys.

Sheremeta, R.M., Zhang, J., 2010. Can groups solve the problem of over-bidding in contests? Social Choice and Welfare 35, 175–197.

Sherman, R., 1972. Oligopoly. Lexington Books, Lexington, MA.

Shupp, R.S., Williams, A.W., 2008. Risk preference differentials of small groups and individuals. Economic Journal 118, 258–283.

Smith, V.L., Walker, J., 1993. Monetary rewards and decision costs in experimental economics. Economic Inquiry 31, 245–261.

Sprenger, C., 2010. An Endowment Effect for Risk: Experimental Tests of Stochastic Reference Points. Discussion Paper, UC San Diego.

Stoner, J. A. F., 1961. A Comparison of Individual and Group Decisions Involving Risk. Unpublished master's thesis, MIT School of Industrial Management.

Tanaka, T., Camerer, C., Nguyen, Q., 2010. Risk and time preferences: experimental and household data from vietnam. American Economic Review 100, 557–571.

Tversky, A., Kahneman, D., 1992. Advances in prospect theory: cumulative representation of uncertainty. Journal of Risk and Uncertainty 5, 297–323.

Wallach, M., Kogan, N., 1959. Sex differences and judgment processes. Journal of Personality 27, 555–564.

Wallach, M., Kogan, N., 1961. Aspects of judgment and decision making: interrelationships and changes with age. Behavioral Science, 22–36.

Wallach, M., Kogan, N., 1964. Risk Taking: A Study in Cognition and Personality. Holt, Rinehart, and Winston, Oxford, UK.

CHAPTER 5

Insurance and Insurance Markets

Georges Dionne[a] and Scott E. Harrington[b]

[a]HEC Montréal, Montreal, QC, Canada
[b] The Wharton School, University of Pennsylvania, Philadelphia, PA, USA

Contents

Abstract

Kenneth Arrow and Karl Borch published several important articles in the early 1960s that can be viewed as the beginning of modern economic analysis of insurance activity. This chapter reviews the main theoretical and empirical contributions in insurance economics since that time. The review begins with the role of utility, risk, and risk aversion in the insurance literature and summarizes work on the demand for insurance, insurance and resource allocation, moral hazard, and adverse selection. It then turns to financial pricing models of insurance and to analyses of price volatility and underwriting cycles; insurance price regulation; insurance company capital adequacy and capital regulation; the development of insurance securitization and insurance-linked securities; and the efficiency, distribution, organizational form, and governance of insurance organizations.

Keywords

Insurance, Insurance Market, Risk Sharing, Moral Hazard, Adverse Selection, Demand for Insurance, Financial Pricing of Insurance, Price Volatility, Insurance Regulation, Capital Regulation, Securitization, Insurance-Linked Security, Organization Form, Governance of Insurance Firms

JEL Classification Codes

D80, D81, D82, G22, G30

Handbook of the Economics of Risk and Uncertainty, Volume 1
ISSN 2211-7547, http://dx.doi.org/10.1016/B978-0-444-53685-3.00005-2

5.1 INTRODUCTION

Although the prevalence of risk in economic activity has always been recognized (Green, 1984), deterministic models dominated economic explanations of observed phenomena for many years. As a result, the economics of insurance has a relatively short history. In early work that formally introduced risk and uncertainty in economic analysis (von Neumann and Morgenstern, 1947; Friedman and Savage, 1948; Allais, 1953a; Arrow, 1953; Debreu, 1953), insurance was viewed either as a contingent good or was discussed in relation to gambling. Before 1960, economic literature was largely void of analyses of the nature of insurance markets or of the economic behavior of individual agents in these markets.[1]

During the early 1960s, Kenneth Arrow and Karl Borch published several important articles (Arrow, 1963, 1965; Borch, 1960, 1961, 1962) that can be viewed as the beginning of modern economic analysis of insurance activity.[2] Arrow was a leader in the development of insurance economics, and more generally, in the development of the economics of uncertainty, information, and communication. Arrow (1965) presented a framework of analysis that explains the role of different institutional arrangements for risk-shifting, such as insurance markets, stock markets, implicit contracts, cost-plus contracts, and futures markets. All of these institutions transfer risk to parties with comparative advantage in risk bearing. In the usual insurance example, risk averse individuals confronted with risk are willing to pay a fixed price to a less risk averse or more diversified insurer who offers to bear the risk at that price. Since both parties agree to the contract, they are both better off.

Risk is seldom completely shifted in any market. Arrow (1963) discussed three of the main reasons that risk shifting is limited: moral hazard, adverse selection, and transaction costs. Arrow (1965) emphasized the problem of moral hazard and suggested that coinsurance arrangements in insurance contracts can be explained by this information problem.[3] Arrow (1963) showed, in absence of asymmetric information, that full insurance above a deductible is optimal when the premium contains a fixed-percentage loading. Raviv (1979) proved that convex insurance costs and risk aversion on the part of the insurer are explanations for coinsurance above a deductible in absence of asymmetric information. These last two results were extended by Blazenko (1985), Gollier (1987a) and others. Gollier (2013) offers an extensive review of this literature.

Borch (1960, 1961, 1962) also made significant contributions to the theory of optimal insurance. He developed necessary and sufficient conditions for Pareto optimal

---

[1] Borch (1990, Chapter 1) reviews brief discussions of insurance contained in the works of Adam Smith and Alfred Marshall, as well as the role of uncertainty in Austrian economics.

[2] Arrow (1963) is reprinted in Diamond and Rothschild (1978) and Borch (1960, 1961) are reprinted in Borch (1990).

[3] In the insurance economics literature, coinsurance refers to a contract in which the insurer pays a fixed proportion of any claim amount.

exchange in risk pooling arrangements. He also showed, in a general framework, how risk aversion affects the optimal coverage (or optimal shares) of participants in the pool. Although his formal analysis was in terms of reinsurance contracts, it was shown by Moffet (1979) that the same result applies for contracts between policyholders and direct insurers. Borch's formulation of risk exchange influenced the development of principal-agent models (Wilson, 1968; Ross, 1973; Holmstrom, 1979; Shavell, 1979a), and it has led to many other applications in the insurance literature.[4] More generally, Borch made many contributions to the application of expected utility theory to insurance and influenced the development of portfolio theory and its applicability to the insurance industry. Finally, Borch's contributions established some important links between actuarial science and insurance economics (Loubergé, 2013).[5]

The remainder of this chapter reviews the main developments of insurance economics subsequent to the pathbreaking work of Arrow and Borch. The remaining sections include contributions related to insurance economics that cover the following subjects: (1) utility, risk, and risk aversion in the insurance literature, (2) the demand for insurance, (3) insurance and resource allocation (in which we include Borch, 1962, and Arrow, 1965), (4) moral hazard, (5) adverse selection, (6) financial pricing models of insurance, (7) price volatility and underwriting cycles, (8) price regulation, (9) capital adequacy and capital regulation, (10) securitization and insurance-linked securities, and (11) efficiency, distribution, organizational form, and governance.

The selection of articles was based on several criteria including the significance of the contribution, the representativeness of the work, and the desire to include empirical as well as theoretical articles. We do not attempt to cover the wide variety of applications of insurance economics in the areas of health insurance, life insurance and annuities, social insurance, and in the law and economics literature. Instead, we review significant applications and include several articles dealing with property-liability insurance, and, to a lesser extent, life insurance. However, our discussion helps to illustrate issues, concepts, and methods that are applicable in many areas of insurance.[6]

5.2 UTILITY, RISK, AND RISK AVERSION IN THE INSURANCE LITERATURE

5.2.1 The Expected Utility Model

Although the theory of decision making under uncertainty has frequently been criticized since its formal introduction by von Neumann and Morgenstern (1947), it remains the workforce in the study of optimal insurance decisions. The linear expected utility model remains the standard paradigm used to formally analyze economic

---

[4] See Lemaire (1990) for a survey of these applications.
[5] See Boyle (1990) for a survey of Borch's scholarly contributions.
[6] Compare, for example, the surveys of health insurance by McGuire (2012) and Morrisey (2013).

behavior under uncertainty and to derive applications in many fields such as insurance (Drèze, 1974; Schoemaker, 1982; see also the recent survey of Karni, 2013). With objective probabilities, three basic axioms are necessary to obtain the von Neumann–Morgenstern theorem: weak order, independence, and continuity. Given these three axioms (and some other technical assumptions), insurance policy A will be chosen over policy B if and only if $E_A U > E_B U$ (where $E_i U$ is the linear expected utility associated with policy i). With subjective probabilities, additional axioms must be introduced in order to obtain a unique subjective probability measure over the set of states and a utility function that is unique up to a positive linear transformation.[7]

Linearity in probabilities is directly associated with the independence axiom (Machina, 1987; as well the survey by Quiggin, 2013). This axiom has been challenged by many researchers, starting with Allais (1953b) who presented a now-classic example that violates linearity in probabilities (and thus the independence axiom). Nonetheless, a large number of fundamental results in insurance economics have been derived from the linear expected utility model. For contributions using nonlinear models, see Karni (1992) and Machina (2013). The classical expected utility model remains, however, the most useful model for insurance analysis.

5.2.2 Measures of Risk Aversion

The Arrow–Pratt measures of absolute and relative risk aversion (Arrow, 1965; Pratt, 1964) are commonly used in analyses of insurance decisions.[8] They measure both the intensity of an individual's preference to avoid risk, and variation in this intensity as a function of wealth. They are very important to compare optimal insurance contracting by different risk averse individuals and to analyze insurance demand. They also explain the intensity of self-insurance, self-protection and precaution. Given a von Neumann–Morgenstern utility function of wealth, $U(W)$ with $U'(W) > 0$ and $U''(W) < 0$ for risk aversion, these measures of risk aversion are useful in calculating the certainty equivalent of a risky situation and the corresponding risk premium Π^U. The risk premium can be interpreted as the largest sum of money a risk averse decision maker with a given utility function is willing to pay above the expected loss (actuarially fair premium) to avoid a given risk. Insurers must evaluate this risk premium when they set the total insurance premium. Moreover, an insured with utility function U is said to be more risk averse than another insured with utility function V if and only if $\Pi^U \geq \Pi^V$ when both face

---

[7] See Anscombe and Aumann (1963) on subjective probabilities. See Machina (1987) for an analysis of the limitations of the linear expected utility model. See Drèze (1987) for an analysis of the foundations of the linear expected utility model in presence of moral hazard. For analyses of the foundations and economic implications of linear state-dependent preferences, see Karni (1985), Drèze (1987), Karni (1990), and Viscusi and Evans (1990).

[8] A concept of partial risk aversion also has been defined by Menezes and Hanson (1970) and Zeckhauser and Keeler (1970). See Dionne (1984) for an application to insurance economics and Briys and Eeckhoudt (1985) for other applications and a discussion of the relationships between the three measures of risk aversion.

the same risky situation and have identical nonrandom initial wealth.[9] Finally, the absolute measure of risk aversion corresponding to a given utility function $(-U''/U')$ is said to be non-increasing in wealth, W, if and only if, in the same risky situation, $\Pi^U(W_1) \geq \Pi^U(W_2)$ for $W_1 \leq W_2$. A necessary condition for decreasing absolute risk aversion is that $U'''(W) > 0$.[10] As we will see later, these concepts are very useful to study the properties of insurance demand and other forms of protection.

5.2.3 Measures of Risk

Another important concept in the analysis of optimal insurance behavior is the measurement of risk. Let X and Y be two random variables with respective distribution functions F_X and F_Y. F_X is a mean preserving spread of F_Y (Rothschild and Stiglitz, 1970) if $E(X) = E(Y)$ and $E_X U < E_Y U$ (where $E_i U$ is the linear expected utility associated with the random variable i). Insurance contracts with actuarially fair premiums can be interpreted in terms of a mean preserving spread since they reduce the spread of the loss distribution without affecting the mean. For example, full insurance (i.e., a contract that pays the full amount of loss) corresponds to a global decrease in risk since it implies the comparison of a risky situation with a nonrisky one (Meyer and Ormiston, 1989).

In some cases, Rothschild and Stiglitz's definition of increasing risk is too general to generate nonambiguous comparative statics results on insurance demand and other optimal decisions under uncertainty (Rothschild and Stiglitz, 1971; Meyer and Ormiston, 1985; Laffont, 1989). When this is the case, a particular definition of an increase in risk can be defined by imposing restrictions on the distribution functions representing the initial and final random variables in order to compare the optimal values of decision variables for each distribution function. Alarie et al. (1992) show how this methodology can be applied to the optimal choice of insurance coverage. Several types of increases in risk that represent particular cases of mean preserving spreads are analyzed in the literature, including a strong increase in risk (Meyer and Ormiston, 1985), a "squeeze of the distribution" (Eeckhoudt and Hansen, 1980), "tail dominance" (Eeckhoudt and Hansen, 1984), a relatively strong increase in risk (Black and Bulkley, 1989) and a relative weak increase in risk (Dionne et al., 1993). Meyer and Ormiston (1989) generalized another definition of increasing risk: the "stretching of a density around a constant mean" (Sandmo, 1970). This approach, which they characterized as involving "deterministic transformations of random variables", also represents a particular type of mean preserving spread. It has been applied to many economic decision problems, such as optimal output choice by a risk averse firm under uncertainty (Sandmo, 1971; Leland, 1972),

---

[9] See Ross (1981), Kihlstrom et al. (1981), and Doherty et al. (1987) for analyses of risk aversion with random independent initial wealth and Dionne and Li (2013) for the introduction of random dependent initial wealth.

[10] An equivalent condition is that $-U'''/U'' > 0$ where $-U'''/U''$ is absolute "prudence" (Kimball, 1990). Prudence measures how an individual's preferences affect optimal values of decision variables such as savings. A more prudent agent should save more to protect future consumption following an increase in future income risk.

optimal saving under uncertainty (Sandmo, 1970), optimal portfolio choice (Meyer and Ormiston, 1989; Laffont, 1989), and optimal insurance decisions (Alarie et al., 1992). See Eeckhoudt and Gollier (2013) for a general analysis of restrictions on the utility function to obtain intuitive results on insurance demand following changes in insurable risk and background risk.

5.3 DEMAND FOR INSURANCE[11]

5.3.1 Basic Models of Coinsurance and Deductible Choice

Mossin (1968) and Smith (1968) propose a simple model of insurance demand in which a risk averse decision maker has a random wealth (W) equal to W_0-L where W_0 is nonstochastic initial wealth and L is a random insurable loss with a given distribution function. To illustrate this model, first assume that the individual can buy coverage $\alpha L (0 \leq \alpha \leq 1)$ for a premium α P where $P \equiv \lambda E(L)$, α is the rate of insurance coverage (the coinsurance rate), $\lambda (\lambda \geq 1)$ is the premium loading factor, and $E(L)$ is the expected loss. It can be shown that the optimal insurance coverage is such that $0 \leq \alpha^\star \leq 1$ for a premium P where $\overline{P} \geq P \geq E(L)$ and $\overline{P} = \bar{\lambda} E(L)$ solves:

$$E\left[U(W_0 - L + \alpha^*(L - \bar{\lambda} E(L)))\right] = EU(W_0 - L)$$

and where U is a von Neumann–Morgenstern utility function ($U'(\cdot) > 0$, $U''(\cdot) < 0$). $EU(W_0 - L)$ is the level of expected utility corresponding to no insurance. Hence, when the premium loading factor exceeds one but is less than $\bar{\lambda}$, partial coverage ($0 < \alpha^\star < 1$) is demanded. The optimal coverage is obtained by maximizing $E[U(W_0 - L + \alpha (L - \lambda E(L)))]$ over α and the constraint that $0 \leq \alpha \leq 1$. One can verify that the solution of this problem corresponds to a global maximum under risk aversion.

When $\lambda = 1$, $\alpha^\star$ is equal to one and the maximum premium that a risk averse individual is willing to pay above the actuarially fair value of full insurance is the Arrow–Pratt risk premium (Π^U). This premium solves:

$$U(W - E(L) - \Pi^U) = EU(W_0 - L).$$

A more risk averse individual with utility function V such that $V = k(U)$, $k' > 0$, and $k'' < 0$ (Pratt, 1964) will accept to pay a risk premium Π^V greater than Π^U. Finally, when $\lambda > \bar{\lambda}$, a risk averse individual does not buy any insurance.

---

[11] In this section, we limit discussion to the case where insurance premiums are exogenously determined. The general case is considered in the next section.

Another important result in Mossin (1968) is that insurance coverage is an inferior good if the insured has decreasing absolute risk aversion. Under this assumption, there are two opposite effects on the demand for insurance when the loading factor (λ) or the price of insurance increases: a negative substitution effect and a positive wealth effect. Hoy and Robson (1981) propose an explicit theoretical condition under which insurance is a Giffen good for the class of constant relative risk aversion functions. Briys et al. (1989) generalize their analysis and provide a necessary and sufficient condition for insurance not to be a Giffen good. This condition bounds the variation of absolute risk aversion so that the wealth effect is always dominated by the substitution effect.

The demand for insurance can also be affected by the level of risk. Alarie et al. (1992) present sufficient conditions to obtain the intuitive result that a risk averse insured will increase his demand for insurance (coinsurance α) when a mean preserving increase in risk is introduced in the initial loss distribution. Finally, the level of $\alpha^{\star}$ can be affected by the level of risk aversion. As discussed by Schlesinger (2013), an increase in risk aversion will lead to an increase in coinsurance, at all levels of wealth.

Another form of partial insurance is a policy with a deductible (Mossin, 1968; Gould, 1969; Pashigian et al., 1966; Schlesinger, 1981). Extending the above model, consider a general indemnity function $I(L)$ and premium $P = \lambda \int I(L) f(L) dL$ where $\lambda (\geq 1)$ is again a proportional loading factor. It can be shown under the constraint $I(L) \geq 0$ for all L, that, for every $P \leq \overline{P}$:

$$I^{*}(L) = \begin{cases} L - D^{*} & \text{if } L - D^{*} \geq 0 \\ 0 & \text{if } L - D^{*} < 0 \end{cases}$$

where $D^{\star} \geq 0$ is the optimal deductible and $\overline{P} = \overline{\lambda} E(I(L))$. Since an insured bears some risk with the optimal contract it is reasonable to expect that a more risk averse insured would prefer a policy with a smaller deductible and higher premium. This result is proved by Schlesinger (1981) for the standard $EU(W)$ model. Moreover, under decreasing absolute risk aversion, $dD^{\star}/dW_0 > 0$ (Mossin, 1968). It is possible to infer the degree of risk aversion of insurance buyers by observing their choices of deductibles (Drèze, 1981; Cohen and Einav, 2007). All these results are obtained under the assumption the insurer is not exposed to any solvency risk. With solvency risk the above results do not in general hold (Doherty and Schlesinger, 1990). For example, full insurance coverage is no more optimal when $\lambda = 1$. Moreover, an increase in risk aversion does not necessarily lead to a higher level of insurance coverage. Consequently, insurance is not necessarily an inferior good under solvency risk.

5.3.2 Optimal Coverage with Random Initial Wealth

If W_0 is an uninsurable random variable rather than fixed, the optimal level of coverage ($\alpha^{\star\star}$) depends on the statistical relationship between W_0 and L. Let us suppose that W_0

and L are independent random variables. This case is often described as the independent background risk case. One can show that, if $U(W)$ is quadratic or corresponds to constant absolute risk aversion, the presence of a random W_0 does not affect the optimal level of insurance chosen.

If we assume that the correlation coefficient is a sufficient measure of the dependence between W_0 and L, Doherty and Schlesinger (1983b) show that the Mossin (1968) and Smith (1968) result on the optimal coinsurance rate ($\alpha^\star$) with fixed W_0 is qualitatively similar to the case in which W_0 and L are independent random variables $\alpha^{\star\star}$. That is, $\alpha^{\star\star} = 1$ when the premium is actuarially fair and $\alpha^{\star\star} < 1$ when $\lambda > 1$. Moreover, Eeckhoudt and Kimball (1992) show that $\alpha^{\star\star} \neq \alpha^\star$ when $\lambda > 1$. Specifically, they show that $\alpha^{\star\star} > \alpha^\star$ under standard risk aversion (decreasing risk aversion and decreasing prudence). This result was proved for independent risks. They also analyze optimal deductibles and show, under the same conditions, that $0 < D^{\star\star} < D^\star$ where $D^{\star\star}$ is the optimal deductible when W_0 and L are independent random variables and $D^\star$ is the optimal deductible with fixed W_0. Hence, with independent risks, more coverage is demanded than with fixed wealth in both coinsurance and deductible contracts, under standard risk aversion and nonactuarial insurance pricing.

It was mentioned above that a more risk averse individual with utility V is willing to pay a higher risk premium for full insurance than a less risk averse individual with utility U when W_0 is not random. This result also holds when W_0 and L are independent random variables. For example, Kihlstrom et al. (1981) show that a more risk averse individual with utility V is willing to pay a higher premium than an individual with utility U if the absolute risk aversion for either individual for realized levels of W_0 is non-increasing in wealth.

If W_0 and L are negatively (positively) correlated, high losses are likely to accompany low (high) values of W_0. Doherty and Schlesinger (1983b) show in the case of a two-state marginal distribution that $\alpha^{\star\star} > 1 (< 1)$ when actuarially fair insurance is available for L. They also analyzed non-actuarially fair insurance prices. More details and more general results are outlined in Schlesinger and Doherty (1985).[12] Eeckhoudt and Kimball (1992) show, in presence of a positive relationship between W and L, that decreasing absolute risk aversion and decreasing absolute prudence are sufficient to guarantee that the presence of a background risk increases the optimal insurance coverage against L. To obtain this result, a simple positive correlation between L and W is not sufficient. The authors use the stronger assumption that "the distribution of background risk conditional upon a given level of insurable loss deteriorates in the sense of third-order stochastic dominance as the amount of insurable loss increases" (p. 246). In conclusion, there is no general measure of dependency that can yield general results on

---

[12] See also Doherty and Schlesinger (1983a), Schulenburg (1986), Turnbull (1983), Eeckhoudt and Kimball (1992) and Lévy-Garboua and Montmarquette (1990).

insurance demand in presence of dependent risk. Aboudi and Thon (1995) and Hong et al. (2011) propose some orderings such as expectation dependence to obtain intuitive results (see also Li, 2011, and Dionne and Li, 2012, for more general discussions on expectation dependence and Schlesinger, 2013, for a longer discussion on the effect of dependent risk on insurance demand).

5.3.3 Insurance, Portfolio Choice, and Saving

Mayers and Smith (1983) and Doherty (1984) analyze the individual demand for insurance as a special case of a general portfolio choice model. They introduce nonmarketable assets (such as human capital) and other indivisible assets (such as houses) in a capital asset pricing model to simultaneously determine the demand for insurance contracts and the demand for other assets in the individual portfolio.[13] Mayers and Smith (1983) propose a sufficient condition for a separation theorem between insurance decisions and other portfolio decisions. Their condition is that the losses of a particular type are orthogonal to the insured's gross human capital, the payoff of all marketable assets, and the losses of other insurable events. This is a strong condition and their analysis suggests that portfolio and insurance decisions are generally interdependent. Consequently, full insurance is not necessarily optimal even when insurance is available at actuarially fair prices. This result is similar to that obtained by Doherty and Schlesinger (1983) for dependent risks.

Moffet (1975, 1977) and Dionne and Eeckhoudt (1984) provide joint analyses of the saving (consumption) and insurance decisions in a two-period model. Dionne and Eeckhoudt (1984) generalize Moffet's results and show that, under decreasing temporal risk aversion, savings and insurance are pure substitutes in the Hicksian sense. Moreover, in their two-decision-variable model, insurance is not necessarily an inferior good. They also present two conditions under which a separation theorem holds between insurance and saving decisions:[14] Actuarially fair insurance premiums or constant temporal risk aversion. The conditions differ from those of Mayers and Smith (1983) in their portfolio model of insurance decisions without consumption. This difference can be explained by the fact that Mayers and Smith consider a menu of risky assets while Dionne and Eeckhoudt (1984) consider only one risky asset. The latter study, which used a more general utility function than Mayers and Smith, is actually more closely related to the consumption-portfolio model developed by Sandmo (1969).

Briys (1988) extends these studies by jointly analyzing insurance, consumption, and portfolio decisions in a framework similar to that defined by Merton (1971). The individual's optimal insurance choice is explicitly derived for the class of isoelastic utility

---

[13] See Kahane and Kroll (1985) and Smith and Buser (1987) for extensions of these models.

[14] See Drèze and Modigliani (1972) for another sufficient condition on utility to obtain separation between consumption, portfolio, and insurance decisions.

functions. Not surprisingly, the properties of optimal insurance coverage are much more difficult to characterize than in models where insurance is studied in isolation or in the presence of either consumption or portfolio choice alone.

5.3.4 Self-Insurance and Self-Protection

Returning to the case of a single random variable L, market insurance can be analyzed in relation to other risk-mitigation activities. Ehrlich and Becker (1972) introduced the concepts of self-insurance and self-protection. Self-insurance refers to actions (y) that reduce the size (severity) of loss (i.e., $L'(y) < 0$ with $L''(y) > 0$) while self-protection refers to actions (x) that reduce the probability $p(x)$ (frequency) of accidents $(p'(x) < 0$ with $p''(x) > 0)$ in a two-state environment. Ehrlich and Becker gave conditions under which self-insurance and market insurance are substitutes and conditions under which self-protection and market insurance are complements. In both cases, self-protection and self-insurance activities were assumed to be observable by insurers.[15]

While Ehrlich and Becker (1972) focus on the interaction between market insurance and activities involving either self-insurance or self-protection, they do not study in detail interactions between self-insurance and self-protection with and without the existence of market insurance. Boyer and Dionne (1983, 1989a) and Chang and Ehrlich (1985) present propositions concerning the choices among all three activities. When full insurance is not available, risk aversion affects the optimal choice of self-insurance and self-protection. While it seems intuitive that increased risk aversion should induce a risk averse decision maker to choose a higher level of both activities, Dionne and Eeckhoudt (1985) show, in a model with two states of the world, that this is not always the case: more risk averse individuals may undertake less self-protection.[16] Briys and Schlesinger (1990) document that self-insurance corresponds to a mean preserving contraction in the sense of Rothschild and Stiglitz (1970) while self-protection does not necessarily reduce the risk situation. Chiu (2005) did a further step by showing that a mean-preserving increase in self-protection is a special case of a combination of an increase in downside risk and a mean-preserving contraction. This introduces the role of prudence in the comparative static analysis of self-protection. In fact, Dionne and Li (2011) maintain that a risk averse individual will produce more self-protection than a risk neutral individual if $p(x) < 1/2$ and if prudence is lower than an upper bound. This upper bound can be interpreted as the skewness of the loss distribution per amount of loss for risk averse agents with decreasing prudence. Dachraoui et al. (2004) and Chiu (2005) show

---

[15] See Winter (2013) for an analysis of self-protection and self-insurance under asymmetric information. We will come back on this issue in the moral hazard section of this chapter.

[16] See Hiebert (1989), Briys and Schlesinger (1990), Jullien et al. (1999), Dachraoui et al. (2004), and Dionne and Li (2011) for extensions of their analysis. A recent literature review on this subject is presented in Courbage et al. (2013).

how self-insurance and self-protection are related to willingness to pay (Drèze, 1962; Jones-Lee, 1974) for reducing the amount of loss or the loss probability, respectively.

5.3.5 Precaution

Precaution differs from protection in many ways. Courbage et al. (2013) propose this analytical difference: protection is a static concept while precaution is dynamic, in the sense that precaution evolves with the observation of more information. In fact, in practice, precaution activities are implemented because decision makers do not have enough information to implement self-protection, self-insurance and insurance decisions. When precaution decisions are made, this is generally because decision makers suspect a potential risk but cannot attribute a probability to this risk nor an evaluation of the amount of loss. Precaution has been associated with the irreversibility effect (Henry, 1974; Arrow and Fischer, 1974; Epstein, 1980; Gollier et al., 2000).

Although the analysis of Epstein (1980) did provide a strong reference framework to analyze how new information over time would improve precaution decision making, there are not clear results in the literature on how risk averse individuals make decisions about precaution. One explanation offered by Courbage et al. (2013) is that the Blackwell notion of better information used in this literature is too general to obtain clear conclusions. More research is necessary on this important concept because our societies face many situations where the scientific knowledge is not developed enough to make informed decisions even if some decisions must be made in the short run. Climate changes and associated hurricanes are evident examples; pandemics are other examples. The precautionary principle is a concept that may help to improve research in that direction (Gollier et al., 2000).

5.3.6 State Dependent Utility

The previous analyses have implicitly assumed that all commodities subject to loss can be valued in relevant markets. Examples of such insurable commodities include buildings and automobiles. For these commodities, an accident primarily produces monetary losses and insurance contracts offer compensation to replace them in whole or in part. However, there are other commodities for which market substitutes are imperfect or do not exist. Examples include good health, the life of a child, and family heirlooms. For these "commodities," an accident generates more losses than monetary losses: it has a nonmonetary component (such as "pain and suffering"). Nonmonetary losses can be introduced in a two-state model (I for no-accident and II for an accident) by using state-dependent utility functions (Cook and Graham, 1977; Karni, 1985). Without a monetary loss, an accident is assumed to reduce utility if $U^I(W) > U^{II}(W)$ for all W (where $U^i(W), i=I,II$, is the utility in state i). With a monetary loss $(L>0)$, $U^{II}(W_0) - U^{II}(W_0 - L)$ measures the disutility of the monetary loss in the accident state and $U^I(W_0) - U^{II}(W_0)$ measures the disutility of the nonmonetary loss from state I to state II.

Marginal utility of wealth also depends on the state of the world. Three cases are usually considered: (1) $U_W^I = U_W^{II}$ for all W; (2) $U_W^I > U_W^{II}$ for all W; and (3) $U_W^I < U_W^{II}$ for all W where U_W^i denotes $\partial U^i / \partial W$. It can be shown that $\alpha^{* \geq (<)} 1$ for a policy with an actuarially fair premium as long as $U_W^{II \geq (<)} U_W^I$ for all W. That is, the individual will buy more (less) insurance than under state independent preferences when the marginal utility of wealth is greater (less) in the accident state than in the no-accident state for all W. Karni (1985) shows how an increase in risk aversion affects optimal insurance coverage when preferences are state-dependent, but the extension of measures of risk aversion to this case is not straightforward (Dionne and Ingabire, 2001).

5.3.7 Corporate Demand for Insurance and Enterprise Risk Management

Portfolio decisions have implications for the demand of insurance by corporations. When corporations are owned by shareholders who can reduce their investment risk at low cost through diversification of their own portfolios, risk aversion by owners is insufficient to generate corporate demand for insurance. Specifically, if shareholders can costlessly eliminate the risk of corporate losses in their own portfolios through portfolio diversification, the purchase of insurance by corporations can only increase shareholder wealth if it increases expected net cash flows by an amount that exceeds any loading in insurance premiums.[17] Mayers and Smith (1982) analyze the corporate demand for insurance in the perspective of modern finance theory (also see Main, 1982; Mayers and Smith, 1990; MacMinn and Garven, 2013). Market imperfection can explain corporate demand for insurance. They discuss how solvency costs; risk aversion by stakeholders such as managers, employees, customers, and suppliers; efficiencies in claims administration by insurers; and a number of other factors such as taxes or investment financing in imperfect capital markets can all provide an incentive for the purchase of insurance (or risk hedging) even when shareholders can costlessly eliminate risk through portfolio diversification. In a later study, Mayers and Smith (1987) consider the possible ability of insurance to increase shareholder wealth by mitigating the underinvestment problem that was originally analyzed by Myers (1977). This literature is now related to that of firms' risk management (Stulz, 1990; Tufano, 1996; Cummins et al, 2000; Dionne and Triki, 2013; Hoyt and Liebenberg, 2011; Campello et al, 2011).

Although perfect markets finance theory provides little rationale for widely held firms to expend resources to hedge unsystematic risk, various market imperfections create opportunities for such firms to maximize market value through hedging. The principal market imperfections that motivate corporate hedging are corporate income taxation (Smith and Stulz, 1985; Graham and Smith, 1999; Graham and Rogers, 2002),

---

[17] This statement also holds if insurable risk has an undiversifiable (i.e., market) component, since insurers have no comparative advantage in bearing market risk (see Main, 1982).

financial distress costs (Smith and Stulz, 1985), investment opportunity costs (Froot et al., 1993; Froot and Stein, 1998), information asymmetries (DeMarzo and Duffie, 1991), and corporate governance considerations (Dionne and Triki, 2013). Firms also engage in hedging for non-value-maximizing reasons such as managerial risk aversion (Stulz, 1990; Tufano, 1996).

In recent years the literature on corporate risk management has begun to emphasize unified management of all major risks confronting organizations through a process of "enterprise risk management." In principle, enterprise risk management has the potential to increase value by considering correlations among distinct risks and focusing more attention on firms' aggregate exposure to loss, thus reducing, for example, redundancies in hedging and insurance coverage (e.g., Harrington and Niehaus, 2002). Another important question relates to the value of risk management to the shareholders' wealth.[18]

5.4 INSURANCE AND RESOURCE ALLOCATION

Allais (1953a) and Arrow (1953) proposed general equilibrium models of resource allocation in the presence of uncertainty at a meeting on the subject in Paris during 1952. Debreu (1953) extended Arrow's (1953) contribution to a general framework of resource allocation under uncertainty.[19] In this framework, physical goods are redefined as functions of states of the world and a consumption plan specifies the quantity of each good consumed in each state. Preferences among consumption plans reflect tastes, subjective beliefs about the likelihoods of states of the world, and attitudes towards risk.[20] However, beliefs and attitudes towards risk do not affect producer behavior since for given contingent prices, there is no uncertainty about the present value of production plans. The existence of a competitive equilibrium that entails a Pareto optimal allocation of goods and services can be demonstrated for this economy.

Insurance markets can be viewed as markets for contingent goods. Borch (1962) proposed the first formal model of optimal insurance contracts. He presented a very elegant comparison between a general model of reinsurance and the Arrow–Debreu model with pure contingent goods and contingent prices for every state of the world. As noted earlier, Borch's insurance model can be reinterpreted in terms of standard insurance contracts. Two of his major contributions were to provide conditions for

---

[18] Hoyt and Liebenberg (2011) obtain a positive relation between firm value and enterprise risk management for US insurers. Cummins et al. (2009) argue that risk management and financial intermediation are two activities that may be used by insurers to improve efficiency, where efficiency is gauged by the capacity to reduce the costs of providing insurance. They measure insurer efficiency by estimating an econometric cost frontier. Because risk management and financial intermediation are key activities for insurers, they treat these activities as endogenous. Their econometric results suggest that risk management significantly increases the efficiency of U.S. property/casualty insurance industry.

[19] This paper became a chapter in Debreu (1959).

[20] In the Arrow-Debreu world each agent has incomplete information about states of nature (uncertainty) but all agents share the same information (Radner, 1968). The latter assumption rules out moral hazard and adverse selection problems.

Pareto optimal exchange of risk and to show how risk aversion by insurers can explain partial coverage. Arrow (1965) used the same argument to introduce some element of coinsurance in optimal insurance contracts. Moreover, Arrow (1963) showed that if a risk neutral insurer offers a policy with a premium equal to the expected indemnity plus a proportional loading then the optimal contract provides full coverage of losses above a deductible. These forms of partial insurance limit the possibilities of risk shifting between economic agents (Arrow, 1965).

Raviv (1979) extended these results and showed that a Pareto optimal contract involves both a deductible and coinsurance of losses above the deductible.[21] He also showed that the optimal contract does not have a deductible if the administrative cost of providing insurance does not depend on the amount of coverage. Coinsurance was explained either by insurer risk aversion or convexity of insurer costs. Conditions for an optimal contract with an upper limit of coverage also were presented. All these results were obtained under the constraint that insurance coverage be nonnegative.[22]

Kihlstrom and Roth (1982) studied the nature of negotiated insurance contracts in a noncompetitive context in which there is bargaining over the amount and price of coverage. They showed that a risk neutral insurer obtains a higher expected income when bargaining against a more risk averse insured and that the competitive equilibrium allocation is not affected by the insured's risk aversion. Many of their results are represented in an Edgeworth Box diagram.

5.5 MORAL HAZARD IN INSURANCE MARKETS

The concept of moral hazard was introduced in the economics literature by Arrow (1963) and Pauly (1968) (see also Kihlstrom and Pauly, 1971; and Spence and Zeckhauser, 1971).[23] Two types of moral hazard have been defined according to the timing of an individual's actions in relation to the realization of the state of nature. They are identified as *ex ante* and *ex post* moral hazard. In the first case the action is taken before the realization of the state of nature while in the second case the action is taken after.

5.5.1 *Ex Ante* Moral Hazard

Pauly (1974), Marshall (1976a), Holmstrom (1979), and Shavell (1979a,b) consider the case in which the occurrence of an accident (or the output of the consumption good) can be observed by the insurer and where neither the insured's actions nor the states of nature are observed.[24] Under this structure of asymmetric information, the provision of

---

[21] Also see Arrow (1974), Bühlmann and Jewell (1979), Gerber (1978), Gollier (1987b), and Marshall (1992).

[22] See Gollier (1987a) for an extensive analysis of this constraint and Gollier (1992) for a review of optimal insurance contracting.

[23] See Rowell and Connelly (2012) for a historical analysis of the origin of moral hazard.

[24] The *ex ante* actions can affect event probabilities, event severity, or both (see Winter, 2013, for more details).

insurance reduces (in general) the incentive of risk averse individuals to take care compared to the case of full information. Thus, there is a trade-off between risk sharing and incentives for prevention when the insured (or the agent) is risk averse.

Shavell (1979b) used a simple two-state model where the individual faces either a known positive loss or no loss with probabilities that depend on effort (care or prevention) to show that partial insurance coverage is optimal in the presence of moral hazard.[25] He emphasized that the type of care has a major impact on the optimal solution. As the cost of care decreases from high levels to lower levels, partial coverage becomes desirable. In other words, when the cost of care is very high, partial coverage has no effect on prevention and reduces protection. Another important result is that moral hazard alone cannot eliminate the gains of trade in insurance markets when an appropriate pricing rule is implemented by the insurer (i.e., moral hazard reduces but does not eliminate the benefits of insurance). These results were obtained assuming that the insurer has no information on an individual's level of care. In the second part of the paper, Shavell showed that moral hazard problems are reduced (but not eliminated) when actions are partially observable by the insurer (also see Holmstrom, 1979).

Shavell's two-state model did not permit a detailed characterization (security design) of insurance contracts. More than two states are necessary to derive conditions under which deductibles, coinsurance, and coverage limits are optimal under moral hazard (see Holmstrom, 1979, and Winter, 2013, for detailed analysis). For example, when prevention affects only the accident probability (and not the conditional loss distribution), a fixed deductible is optimal. However, when prevention affects the conditional distribution of losses, the coassurance coverage becomes necessary in order to introduce more prevention against high losses.

Moral hazard in insurance can be analyzed within a general principal-agent framework (Ross, 1973; Holmstrom, 1979; Grossman and Hart, 1983; Salanié, 1997; Laffont and Martimort, 2002; Bolton and Dewatripont, 2005). However, certain conditions must be imposed to generate predictions and obtain optimality when using the first-order approach. First, the action of the agent cannot affect the support of the distribution of outcomes, a condition naturally met in the two-state model (Shavell 1979). The other two conditions concern the use of a first-order condition to replace the incentive compatibility constraint. The first-order approach is valid if it identifies the global optimal solution. Mirrlees (1975) and Rogerson (1985a) proposed two sufficient conditions for the first-order approach to be valid when corner solutions are ruled out: (1) the distribution function must be a convex function of effort (CDFC) and (2) the likelihood ratio has to be monotone (MLRP condition). If the distribution function satisfies the above conditions, optimal insurance coverage will be decreasing in the size of loss since large losses signal

---

[25] Also see Pauly (1974) for a similar model. See Dionne (1982) for a model with state-dependent preferences. It is shown that moral hazard is still an important problem when preferences are not limited to monetary losses. Viauroux (2013) extends the principal-agent model to introduce taxes.

low effort levels to a Bayesian principal. Jewitt (1988) questioned the intuitive economic justification of these two conditions and showed that they can be violated by reasonable examples. Specifically, he showed that most of the distributions commonly used in statistics are not convex.[26] He then supplied an alternative set of conditions including restrictions on the agent's utility function to validate the first-order approach (see Winter, 2013, and Arnott, 1992, for further discussion on insurance applications).

Grossman and Hart (1983) proposed a method to replace the first-order approach. They also showed that the two conditions proposed by Mirrlees and Rogerson are sufficient to obtain monotonicity of the optimal incentive scheme. They analyzed the principal problem without using the first-order approach and consequently did not need any restriction on the agent's utility function or on the distribution function. As Grossman and Hart noted, many of their results were limited to a risk-neutral principal. This restriction is reasonable for many insurance problems.[27]

Long-term contracts between principals and agents can increase welfare in the presence of moral hazard (Rogerson, 1985b; Radner, 1981; Rubinstein and Yaari, 1983; Henriet and Rochet, 1986). In multiperiod insurance models, an individual's past experience eventually gives a good approximation of care. Hence insurers use the individual's past experience to determine premiums and to increase incentives for exercising care. For example, Boyer and Dionne (1989b) show empirically how past demerit points approximate drivers' effort. In automobile insurance, insurers use the bonus–malus scheme to obtain more incentives for safe driving (see Dionne et al, 2013, for a recent survey of empirical studies on asymmetric information models in the literature on road safety and automobile insurance).

Moral hazard may alter the nature of competitive equilibrium by, for example, introducing nonconvexities in indifference curves. A competitive equilibrium may not exist, and when it does, insurance markets for some risks may fail to exist. More importantly, neither the first nor second theorem of welfare economics holds under moral hazard. Since market prices will not reflect social opportunity costs, theory suggests that governmental intervention in some insurance markets possibly could improve welfare if government has superior information (Arnott and Stiglitz, 1990; Arnott, 1992).

Moral hazard also can affect standard analyses of government responses to externalities. An important example involves liability rules and compulsory insurance.[28] With strict liability and risk averse victims and injurers, Shavell (1982) showed with perfect information that both first-party and liability insurance produce an efficient allocation of risk between parties in a model of unilateral accidents (with pecuniary losses only).

---

[26] See LiCalzi and Spaeter (2003) for an extension of this research.

[27] See Dye (1986) and Mookherjee and Png (1989) for recent applications of Grossman and Hart's model.

[28] See Harrington and Danzon (2000a) for a survey on the demand and supply of liability insurance and Shavell (2004) for a comprehensive review of the economic analysis of law. For a recent comparison of strict liability and a negligence rule for risk-incentives trade-off, see Fagart and Fluet (2009).

When insurers cannot observe defendants' care, moral hazard results in a trade-off between care and risk sharing (as in the case of first-party coverage). Shavell (1982) noted that if the government has no better information than insurers, its intervention in liability insurance does not improve welfare. This conclusion assumes that defendants were not judgment proof (i.e., they had sufficient assets to fully satisfy a judgment). Otherwise, their incentives to purchase liability insurance are reduced (Keeton and Kwerel, 1984; Shavell, 1986). Under strict liability, Shavell (1986) obtained that if insurers cannot observe care, insureds buy partial insurance and the level of care is not optimal. He also showed that making liability insurance compulsory under these conditions need not restore efficient incentives. In fact, compulsory insurance could reduce care, and it is even possible that prohibiting insurance coverage could improve the level of care.

The level of activity or risk exposure must also be considered in the analysis. Liability rules affect not only the level of care but also the level of activity. For example, negligence rule may continue to implement the social level of prevention, but it induces injurers to inflate their level of activity (miles driven) (see Shavell, 2004, for a complete coverage of different liabilities rules in presence of insurance).

Litigation is important in insurance economics. Litigation procedures and their costs affect the legal system's capacity to obtain appropriate incentives and compensations. A question analyzed by Shavell (2004) is the following: Why should insurers be motivated to influence litigation? First, they receive the insurance compensation paid to the victims. Moreover, defendants may own liability insurance policies and insurers may have incentives to defeat plaintiffs. There may be conflicts of interest between the insurers and their clients. For example, the plaintiff's insurer may be more willing to settle than the plaintiff and the defendant's insurer may be less willing to settle than the defendant. As observed by Shavell (2004), "insurance generally reduces incentives to spend at trial" (p. 440) because insurers bear legal costs and often make litigation decisions. But this is not necessarily inefficient. Some forms of insurance contracts may be jointly beneficial in terms of litigation.

Finally, point-record driver's licenses may complement insurance incentive schemes for road safety, particularly when fines for traffic violations are bounded. Bounded fines exist for different reasons: 1) many offenders are judgment proof and are unable to pay optimal fines; 2) many drivers are expected to escape from paying tickets issued by the authorities when fines are very high; 3) society thinks it is unfair that rich and reckless drivers will pay high fines and continue to drive dangerously (Shavell, 1987a,b). However, fines do reinforce the effectiveness of the point-record mechanism by providing normal drivers with more incentives (Bourgeon and Picard, 2007). For a recent comparison of strict liability and a negligence rule for risk-incentives trade-off, see Fagart and Fluet (2009). See Dionne et al. (2011) for a comparative analysis of different incentive schemes for safe driving under moral hazard. See also Abbring et al. (2003, 2008) for empirical analyses of the presence of moral hazard in automobile insurance markets, and Chiappori and Salanié

(2013) and Dionne et al. (2013) for surveys and drop for a survey of empirical research on asymmetric information problems in insurance markets.

5.5.2 *Ex Post* Moral Hazard

The second type of moral hazard was first suggested by Spence and Zeckhauser (1971) who showed that an optimal contract between a principal and agent depends on the principal's ability to monitor the state of nature, the *ex ante* action taken by the agent, and the nature of the accident. The previous discussion of *ex ante* moral hazard assumed that the principal knew the nature of the accident. Marshall (1976b), Dionne (1984), and Townsend (1979) investigated the case in which the nature of an accident is not perfectly observable by the principal. Townsend (1979) considered the case in which the nature of the accident is known by the agent and verification is costly to the principal. One interpretation of such costly verification problem is auditing. He shows that a deductible contract can be optimal under certain circumstances since it reduces the cost of audit.

Mookherjee and Png (1989) extended the Grossman and Hart (1983) model to consider optimal contracts in the presence of both *ex ante* and *ex post* moral hazard. In their model, the agent takes an unobservable action that affects accident probabilities and then reports his realized accident to the principal. The principal may audit the report at a cost. Their main result is that random audits reduce expected auditing costs without distorting the incentives of the agent provided that wealth of the agent is strictly positive in all states of the world. Their results apply when falsification is costless and verification is costly. Lacker and Weinbery (1989) showed that partial insurance can be optimal if the nature of an accident can be falsified by the agent, but only at a cost.[29]

Insurance fraud (Derrig, 2002) is directly related to *ex post* moral hazard. The economic analysis of insurance fraud is not limited to illegal activities. The notion of fraud covers "unnecessary, unwanted, and opportunistic manipulations" (Derrig, 2002) of the insurance system. It results from asymmetric information in the claiming behavior. The recent literature on the economic analysis of insurance fraud is divided into two main approaches: that related to the costly state verification analysis of moral hazard and that related to the costly state falsification. Under costly state verification, the insurer can verify the nature of the claim at a cost. Claims verification can be deterministic or random and can be conditioned on signals received by insurers. Under costly state falsification, the insured uses resources for modifying his claim (as for a build-up). Picard (2013) proposes a general theoretical model that relates the main contributions in this literature (Picard, 1996; Crocker and Morgan, 1997; Bond and Crocker, 1997; Picard, 2000; Fagart and Picard, 1999).

---

[29] See Dionne and St-Michel (1991) for an empirical measure of the second type of moral hazard in the workers' compensation market and the recent survey of Butler et al. (2013).

A general conclusion from Picard's survey (2013) is that insurance fraud affects the design of insurance contracts. In some cases, a deductible can be optimal but usually some degrees of coinsurance are necessary, particularly when policyholders can manipulate audit costs or falsify claims. Another issue is related to the insurers' incentives of reducing insurance fraud. There is a free riding issue in competitive markets: Individual insurers may simply increase their premiums following an increase in *ex post* average losses. Some authors have suggested the development of common agencies to develop common data sets and models of fraud detection (Derrig, 2002). Finally, services providers' (garage owner, doctor, lawyer...) payoffs are also affected by the insurance coverage of the service cost they provide. Preventing collusion between insured and service provider is still an open question in the literature. See Dionne and Gagné (2001, 2002), Dionne et al (2009) and Dionne and Wang (2013), for recent empirical analyses of insurance fraud in different insurance markets.

5.6 ADVERSE SELECTION IN INSURANCE MARKETS

Adverse selection occurs in insurance markets when the insurer cannot observe an individual's risk at the time policies are issued and the individual has superior information about his or her risk. Akerlof (1970) proposed that if insurers have imperfect information about differences in risk for prospective insureds, then some insurance markets may fail to exist and others may be inefficient. Studies have analyzed the ability of partial insurance coverage, experience rating, and risk categorization to reduce the negative effects of adverse selection.[30] Others have considered the effect of adverse selection on economic welfare and market equilibrium.

5.6.1 Partial Insurance and Sorting

Partial insurance coverage can result from two types of insurance pricing: "price only" policies (Pauly, 1974) and "price-quantity" policies (Rothschild and Stiglitz, 1976; Stiglitz, 1977). In the first case, insurers charge a uniform premium rate per unit of coverage to all applicants. Pauly's model ruled out price-quantity competition by assuming that insurers could not observe the total amount of coverage purchased by a client. In Rothschild and Stiglitz (1976), insurers offer a menu of policies with different prices and quantities so that different risks choose different insurance contracts. These strategies have been studied for single vs. multi-period contracts, for competition vs. monopoly, and, when assuming competition, for several different equilibrium concepts.[31]

---

[30] We only consider models in which uninformed agents move first (screening): uninformed insurers offer contracts and consumers choose contracts given their accident probability. Stiglitz and Weiss (1984) analyzed differences between screening and signaling models.

[31] See Cooper and Hayes (1987), Crocker and Snow (1985), and Cresta (1984) for an introduction to these models and Dionne et al. (2013) for a survey on adverse selection in insurance contracts.

In a single period model with competition, Rothschild and Stiglitz (1976) show that a pooling equilibrium cannot exist if a Nash definition of equilibrium is adopted (i.e., if each firm assumes that competitors' contract offers are independent of its own offer). Conditions under which "separating" contracts reveal information about insured risk were then studied by the authors. A major result is that when firms offer a menu of policies with different prices and quantities, policyholders may be induced to reveal hidden information.[32] They showed that a separating Nash equilibrium can exist in which high risk and low risk buyers purchase separate contracts. This separating equilibrium is characterized by zero profits for each contract, by partial insurance coverage for low risk buyers, and by full insurance for the high risk buyers. Another characteristic of their definition of Nash equilibrium under adverse selection is that no contract outside the equilibrium can make a positive profit with a risk type. However, when there exist relatively few high risk persons in the market, they showed that neither a separating nor a pooling equilibrium exists.

Other equilibrium concepts that eliminate the nonexistence problem have been proposed. Wilson (1977), Miyazaki (1977), and Spence (1978) considered the case in which firms anticipate that other insurers' policies that become unprofitable as a result of new offerings will be withdrawn.[33] A Wilson-Mijasaki-Spence (WMS) equilibrium is a pair of contracts in which profits on low-risk contracts offset losses on high-risk contracts. A WMS equilibrium exists regardless of the number of high-risk persons in the market. If a Nash equilibrium exists, it coincides with the WMS equilibrium.[34] Finally, a WMS equilibrium is always second best efficient.

Dahlby (1983) provided some empirical evidence of adverse selection in the Canadian automobile insurance market. He suggests that his empirical results are consistent with the WMS model with cross-subsidization between individuals in each class of risk. However, Riley (1983) argues that Dahlby's results were also consistent with Wilson's (1977) anticipatory equilibrium and Riley's (1979) reactive equilibrium. Cross-subsidization is not feasible in either of these models. More recently, Chiappori and Salanié (2000) and Dionne et al. (2001) proposed a test for the presence of residual asymmetric information in insurance markets. Their test cannot separate moral hazard from adverse selection because both information problems predict a positive correlation

---

[32] A similar analysis was provided by Stiglitz (1977) for the monopoly case. In his model there is always a separating equilibrium and the monopolist extracts all surplus subject to self-selection constraints.

[33] The anticipatory concept of equilibrium was introduced by Wilson (1977). Miyazaki (1977) (for the labor market) and Spence (1978) (for the insurance market) extended Wilson's model to the case in which each firm could break even by offering a portfolio of contracts. Riley (1979) and Grossman (1979) proposed other non-Nash equilibrium concepts. (See Crocker and Snow (1985) for a review of alternative equilibrium concepts.)

[34] Each of these models either explicitly or implicitly assumes that insurers could enforce the requirement that their customers would buy coverage from only one insurer. Hellwig (1988) considered a model with endogenous sharing of information about customers' purchases and obtained an equilibrium with a reactive element that is similar to Wilson's (1977) anticipatory equilibrium.

between individual risk type and realized accidents. The separation of the two problems can be obtained by applying a causality test where contract choice predicts risks (moral hazard) and risks predict contracts choices (adverse selection). Dionne et al. (2013) propose such a test.[35]

5.6.2 Experience Rating

Experience rating can be viewed as either a substitute or a complement to both risk categorization and sorting contracts with self-selection constraints when adverse selection is present.[36] One polar case is when infinite length contracts yield the same solution as with full information. In this case, *ex ante* risk categorization is useless. The other polar case is when costless risk categorization permits full observation of an individual risk so that information on past experience is irrelevant. While experience rating, risk categorization, and sorting contracts are used simultaneously in most markets, economic analysis to date has considered the three mechanisms independently (see Dionne et al., 2013, for a more detailed review).

Dionne (1983), Dionne and Lasserre (1985), and Cooper and Hayes (1987) extend Stiglitz, monopoly model (1977) to multiperiod contracts. Dionne (1983) considers infinite length contracts without discounting while Cooper and Hayes (1987) mainly deals with a finite horizon model (without discounting). While findings in both cases suggest that experience rating induces sorting or risk disclosure, the analyses differ in many respects. In Dionne (1983), a simple statistical review strategy is proposed along with risk announcement in the first period. The insurer offers a buyer full coverage at the full information price unless the observed average loss is greater than the true expected loss plus a statistical margin of error. Otherwise, full coverage is offered at a premium that includes a penalty. Both elements—announcement of risk and penalties—are necessary to obtain the same solution as with full information. They have the same role as the self-selection constraint and the premium adjustment mechanism of Cooper and Hayes (1987). In their model, the premium adjustment mechanism serves to relax the self-selection constraints and to increase the monopolist's profits. Finally, in both articles the monopolist commits to the terms of the contract.[37]

Cooper and Hayes (1987) also extend the Rothschild and Stiglitz (1976) model to two periods assuming that a Nash separating equilibrium exists. When consumers are assumed to be bound to a two-period contract, they obtain the same result as for the monopoly case. When the assumption that consumers sign a binding two-period

[35] For other empirical tests of asymmetric information with dynamic data, see Abbring et al. (2003, 2008) and Dionne et al. (2011).

[36] See Dahlby (1992), Dionne and Lasserre (1987), and Dionne and Vanasse (1992) for analyses of experience rating when moral hazard and adverse selection are present simultaneously.

[37] See Hosios and Peters (1989) for an analysis of contracts without any commitment by a monopolist in a finite-horizon environment.

contract is relaxed, they show that competition in the second period limits but does not eliminate the use of experience rating. In both cases, the insurer is assumed to be committed to its experience rating contract.

Nilssen (2000) analyzes experience rating contracts without commitment by insurers in a competitive market. His results differ from those of Cooper and Hayes and are quite similar to those of Kunreuther and Pauly (1985), who assume that insurers sell price-only policies (Pauly, 1974) rather than price-quantity policies. Another important assumption in Kunreuther and Pauly's model is myopic behavior by insureds, whereas firms could have foresight. With foresight, firms suffer losses in early periods, and make profits in later periods, whereas in the Cooper-Hayes (1987) model, they make profits in the initial period and losses in subsequent periods. D'arcy and Doherty (1990) provide some empirical evidence that is consistent with Kunreuther and Pauly's model while Dionne and Doherty (1994) consider the semi-commitment model. Dionne and Doherty (1994) do not reject the presence of adverse selection.

5.6.3 Risk Categorization[38]

In most types of insurance, insurers classify risks using many variables. In auto insurance, for example, empirical evidence indicates that driver age and sex are significantly related to accident probabilities (Dionne and Vanasse, 1992). In particular, evidence suggests that young male drivers (less than age 25) have much higher accident probabilities than the average driver. Since age and sex can be observed at very low cost, competition will force insurers to charge higher premiums to young males. Categorization using particular variables is prohibited in many markets, and the efficiency of categorization is an important policy issue.

Is statistical classification efficient in the presence of asymmetric information and adverse selection? Crocker and Snow (1985, 1986, 2013), (also see Hoy, 1982; and Rea, 1987, 1992) show that costless imperfect categorization always enhances efficiency when efficiency is defined as in Harris and Townsend (1981): second-best efficiency given the self-selection constraints imposed by asymmetric information. However, if classification is costly, the efficiency implications were ambiguous. More recently, Rothschild (2011) showed that categorical pricing bans are inefficient even when categorization is costly. Crocker and Snow (1986) also consider the existence of a balanced-budget tax-subsidy policy that provides private incentives to use risk categorization. With appropriate taxes, they show that no agent would lose from classification. In their 1986 article, the results were obtained using a WMS equilibrium, but a tax system also may sustain an efficient allocation with a Nash equilibrium. Their results can also be applied to a Wilson (1977) anticipatory equilibrium, or to a Riley (1979) reactive equilibrium (see Crocker and

---

[38] We limit our discussion to exogenous categorization of risks. See Bond and Crocker (1991) for an analysis of endogenous categorization of risks.

Snow, 1985). These results suggest that prohibiting statistical discrimination will impose efficiency losses in insurance markets (e.g., age and sex classification in auto insurance). Browne and Kamiya (2012) show that a policy requiring insurance buyers to take an underwriting test can provide full coverage when perfect classification is possible or when there is no residual asymmetric information in insurers' risk classes.

5.6.4 Multidimensional Adverse Selection

The recent literature on adverse selection added other dimensions than risk to the asymmetric information between insurer and insured. For example, Villeneuve (2003) and Smart (2000) consider differences in risk aversion that are not observable by the insurer. Wambach (2000) incorporates heterogeneity in initial wealth. Snow (2009) shows that profitable contracts obtained in the above contributions cannot be sustained as a Nash equilibrium when insurers offer menus of contracts. Other extensions analyze insurance contracting with multiple risks (Fluet and Pannequin, 1997; Crocker and Snow, 2011).

5.6.5 Participating Contracts and Adverse Selection

Participating contracts is a form of mutualization where individuals' premiums are functions of individual and collective loss experience of the insurance pool. In a recent paper, Picard (2009) shows that allowing insurers to offer participating policies in addition to nonparticipating ones guarantees the existence of an equilibrium in the Rothschild and Stiglitz (1976) environment. The presence of participating contracts dissuades other insurers to offer contracts to low-risk individuals only as an alternative. Picard (2009) shows that when there is no Rothschild and Stiglitz (1976) pooling equilibrium, equilibrium with cross-subsidized participating contracts exists.

Other papers in the literature that suggest the coexistence of stock and mutual contracts are related to aggregate risk (Doherty and Dionne, 1993), adverse selection (Ligon and Thistle, 2005), and insolvency of stock insurers (Rees et al., 1999; Fagart et al., 2002).

5.7 FINANCIAL MODELS OF INSURANCE PRICES

Basic financial theory predicts that in long-run equilibrium, competitively determined insurance premiums, commonly known as *fair premiums*, will equal the risk-adjusted discounted value of expected cash outflows for claims, sales expenses, income taxes, and any other costs, including the tax and agency costs of capital. A large literature has considered the technical details in the context of specific financial pricing models.

5.7.1 Basic CAPM and Related Models

Early work on financial pricing of insurance examines the implications of the Capital Asset Pricing Model (CAPM). Biger and Kahane (1978) show in that context and the absence of taxes that equilibrium insurance underwriting profit margins were a linear function of the riskless rate of interest and the systematic risk (beta) of underwriting. They also provide estimates of underwriting betas using accounting data for different lines of insurance (also see Cummins and Harrington, 1985, and more recently, Cummins and Phillips, 2005). Fairley (1979) develops a similar model and shows that with income taxes fair premiums increase with the tax rate and the amount of financial capital invested to support the sale of insurance. Kraus and Ross (1982) consider application of arbitrage pricing theory to insurance pricing using both discrete and continuous time models. Myers and Cohn (1986) propose a discounted cash flow model that would leave insurance company owners indifferent between selling policies and operating as an investment company. Key variables affecting equilibrium premiums again include tax rates on investment income, the amount of capital invested, and the required compensation to owners for risk bearing.

5.7.2 Option-Based Models

The financial pricing literature next advanced to analyzing the effects on fair premiums of limited liability and the insurer's resulting default put. Doherty and Garven (1986) (also see Cummins, 1988) analyze fair premiums with limited liability using discrete time options pricing theory under conditions in which stochastic investment returns and claim costs can be valued using risk neutral valuation, showing numerically that premiums increase and default risk declines as invested capital increases.[39] A number of studies subsequently provided empirical evidence consistent with this intuitive prediction (Sommer, 1996; Phillips et al., 1998; Phillips et al., 2006).[40]

5.7.3 Pricing with Multiple Lines of Business

The early pricing studies essentially model prices for a company writing a single line of business. In a multiline context, a key question is whether differences in risk and capital across lines of business imply differences in prices across lines for a given level of the default put. Phillips et al. (1998) extend option pricing methods to a multiline context assuming no frictional costs, such as tax and agency costs, of holding capital. They assume that in the event of default, the excess of liabilities over assets would be allocated among policyholders in proportion to their *ex ante* expected claims. Under this assumption, the ratio of expected default costs to expected claims is constant across lines of business, implying a constant ratio of premiums to expected claims. As a result,

---

[39] Borch (1974) obtains a qualitatively similar result assuming limited liability and expected utility maximization by insurers.

[40] Bauer et al. (2013) provide an overview of more rigorous theoretical models that consider insurance prices with frictionless securities markets and no arbitrage opportunities, incomplete markets for insurance, varying degrees to which insurance risk is diversifiable, and possible dependencies between insurance and financial markets.

their model implies that it is not necessary to allocate an insurer's capital across lines of business to determine prices.

Other studies consider by-line pricing and capital allocation in the presence of frictional costs of holding capital. In this case, the question arises as to whether the frictional costs must be allocated across lines of business to determine line-specific prices. Myers and Read (2001) (also see Merton and Perold, 1993) analyze a linear capital allocation rule implied by an Euler equation for the insurer's default risk (the default put value). They derive the marginal capital increase needed from an increase in a particular source of risk to maintain a constant overall risk level. The resulting marginal changes satisfy an "adding up" property: the sum of the marginal values over different sources of risk (lines of business) equals the firm's total capital. Subsequent work questions the risk measure chosen by Myers and Read and proposes a variety of alternative risk measures and conceptual frameworks for determining unique capital allocations (see, for example, Sherris, 2006; Grundl and Schmeiser, 2007; Zanjani, 2010; Ibragimov et al., 2010 and the review by Bauer and Zanjani, 2013). In related work, Froot and Stein (1998) and Froot (2007) consider pricing, capital allocation, capital budgeting, and risk management decisions for financial institutions in general and insurers/reinsurers in particular.

The necessity and details of capital allocation notwithstanding, a key implication of the literature on multiline pricing is that frictional costs of holding capital will require higher prices for riskier lines of business. Particular attention has been paid to prices of catastrophe coverage. Zanjani (2002b), for example, develops a model in which prices are high for capital intensive lines of business, such as catastrophe coverage. Harrington and Niehaus (2003) explore in detail the tax costs of capital that arise from double taxation of investment income from capital and illustrate that the effects on premiums can be very large for catastrophe risk, where expected claim costs are low in relation to the amount of capital needed to achieve a low level of default risk.[41] Phillips et al. (2006) provide evidence that by-line insurance prices reflect capital allocations and default risk.

5.8 PRICE VOLATILITY AND UNDERWRITING CYCLES

Abstracting from technical details, financial pricing models imply that fair premiums and loss ratios (ratios of incurred losses to premiums) should vary over time in relation to the fundamental determinants of prices.[42] The "fundamentals" include predicted claim costs and underwriting expenses, riskless interest rates and any systematic risk of claim costs and associated market risk premia that affect the discount rate for expected claim costs, and the tax and agency costs of holding capital to bond an insurer's promise to pay claims. Not surprisingly, there is abundant evidence that changes in claim costs, which should be

---

[41] Froot (2001) and Froot and O'Connell (1997) provide empirical evidence of high prices for catastrophe coverage and consider alternative explanations.

[42] This and the following sections draw from Harrington et al. (2013).

highly correlated with insurer forecasts when policies are priced, explain much of the time series variation in premiums. Examples include studies of premium growth in automobile insurance (Cummins and Tennyson, 1992) and medical malpractice insurance (Danzon, 1985; Neale et al., 2009). Numerous studies also provide evidence, albeit sometimes weak, of the predicted inverse relationship between interest rates and loss ratios or combined ratios (e.g, Smith, 1989; Choi and Thistle, 2000; Harrington et al., 2008; Jawad et al., 2009). Other evidence and popular wisdom regarding insurance underwriting cycles are more difficult to reconcile with plausible changes in pricing fundamentals.

5.8.1 Aggregate Time Series Studies

Because data on average premiums per exposure generally are not available to researchers, most empirical analyses of price volatility in insurance markets use data on loss ratios or "combined" ratios (loss ratios plus administrative expense ratios) to control for scale effects and abstract in part from the effects of changes in claim cost forecasts over time. Many studies document empirical regularities in underwriting results that are not easily reconciled with plausible changes in pricing fundamentals. Several studies using U.S. data through the 1980s provide evidence that loss ratios and reported underwriting profit margins (e.g., one minus the combined ratio) exhibited second-order autoregression, implying a cyclical period of about six years (Venezian, 1985; Cummins and Outreville, 1987; Doherty and Kang, 1988). Analysis also suggests cyclical underwriting results in other countries (Cummins and Outreville, 1987; Leng and Meier, 2006; Meier, 2006a,b; Meier and Outreville, 2006). Other studies suggest that underwriting results remain cyclical after controlling for the expected effects of changes in interest rates (Fields and Venezian, 1989; Smith, 1989; also see Winter, 1991a). Cummins and Outreville (1987) show conditions under which accounting and regulatory lags could generate a cycle in reported underwriting margins and present suggestive empirical results. Doherty and Kang (1988) argue that cyclical patterns in underwriting results reflect slow but presumably rational adjustment of premiums to changes in expected claim costs and interest rates.

5.8.2 Unit Roots and Cointegration Analyses

Early time series studies paid little attention to stationarity assumptions. Later work more carefully considers whether underwriting margins are stationary and, if not, whether they are cointegrated with macroeconomic factors. Assuming nonstationarity, Haley (1993, 1995) presents evidence that underwriting profit margins are negatively cointegrated with interest rates in the long run. Results for error correction models indicate a short-run relation between interest rates and underwriting margins. Grace and Hotchkiss (1995) provide evidence of cointegration between quarterly combined ratios and short-term interest rates, the consumer price index, and real GDP. Choi et al. (2002) provide evidence that underwriting profit margins are cointegrated with annual Treasury bond yields, but not with the ratio of capital to assets.

Harrington and Yu (2003) conduct extensive unit root tests of the series typically analyzed in underwriting cycle research, presenting evidence largely consistent with stationarity (absence of a unit root). In contrast, Leng (2006) presents evidence that combined ratios are nonstationary and subject to structural breaks.[43] Jawad et al. (2009) provide evidence that premiums are cointegrated with interest rates using nonlinear cointegration techniques. Lazar and Denuit (2012) analyze the dynamic relationship between U.S. property-casualty premiums, losses, GDP, and interest rates using both single equation and vector cointegration analyses. The results suggest long-term equilibrium between premiums, losses, and the general economy, and that premiums adjust quickly to long-term equilibrium.

5.8.3 Capital Shocks and Capacity Constraints

Economic models of premium volatility have generally focused on the potential effects of industry-wide shocks to capital. These capital shock models basically assume that industry supply depends on the amount of insurer capital and that industry supply is upward sloping in the short run because the stock of capital is costly to increase due to the costs of raising new capital.[44] These features imply that shocks to capital (e.g., from catastrophes or unexpected changes in liability claim costs) affect the price and quantity of insurance supplied in the short run. Holding industry demand fixed, a backward shift in the supply curve due to a capital shock causes price to increase and quantity to decrease, which roughly describes "hard" insurance markets. Soft markets—low prices and high availability—either are not addressed by these models or are explained by periods of excess capital that is not paid out to shareholders because of capital exit costs.

Theoretical contributions to the literature on the relationship between premium volatility and insurer capital include Winter (1991a,b, 1994), Gron (1994b), Cagle and Harrington (1995), Doherty and Garven (1995), and Cummins and Danzon (1997). All of the models incorporate the idea that insolvency risk depends on the amount of insurer capital because of uncertainty in claim costs and/or investment returns. Some models explicitly or implicitly assume that in the long run insurers choose capital levels to equate the marginal costs and benefits of additional capital.[45] Others assume that

---

[43] Note that it is not clear why insurance underwriting margins would be nonstationary apart from structural breaks. A unit root would imply that shocks to ratios of insurance losses and expenses to premiums or GDP would be permanent after controlling for trend, and there is no obvious reason that shocks would be permanent.

[44] All of the capital shock models are built on the assumption that external capital is costlier than internal capital, often justified with the logic of Myers and Majluf (1984). Capital shock models were motivated in significant part by the hard market in U.S. general liability insurance in the mid-1980s. A related line of work considers the effects of subsequent tort liability reforms (e.g., Born and Viscusi, 1994).

[45] Cagle and Harrington (1995) examine the extent to which the cost of a capital shock may be passed on to consumers in the form of higher prices. In their model, insurers choose an optimal level of capital based on the cost of holding capital and the benefits of protecting franchise value. They derive comparative statics for the upper bound effect on price of a shock to capital, assuming that demand is perfectly inelastic and that additional capital cannot be raised, and show that prices will not increase enough to fully offset shocks.

insurer capital must satisfy a regulatory constraint on the probability of insolvency. Most models are static, with dynamic aspects of the market explained by periodic exogenous shocks. An exception is Winter (1994), which models the dynamics of the insurance market in a discrete time equilibrium model.

In empirical tests, Winter (1994) regresses an "economic loss ratio" (which discounts reported losses) on interest rates and the lagged values of insurer capital relative to its previous five-year average. Consistent with the prediction that higher prices (lower expected loss ratios) occur when capital is low, the coefficients on the lagged capital variables are positive and statistically significant in most of his specifications.[46] Gron (1994b) obtains results with similar implications with different underwriting performance measures. Gron (1994a) examines aggregate time series data on underwriting profit margins for auto physical damage, auto liability, homeowners' multiple peril, and other liability insurance. The evidence suggests that margins are negatively related to deviations of relative capacity (capital to GDP) from its normal level, which again is consistent with the notion that prices increase when capacity (insurer capital) is reduced.

Other capital shock models consider the potential for heterogeneous responses among firms. Doherty and Garven (1995) consider the effects of interest rate changes, which can influence capital by changing the value of assets and liabilities. They predict that interest rate changes will cause firm-specific capital shocks, as well as alter the long run equilibrium price of insurance. They use insurer panel data to estimate the sensitivity of insurer underwriting returns to interest rate changes. The results provide some evidence that return sensitivity is related to surplus duration.

Cummins and Danzon (1997) consider an insurer that enters a period with existing liabilities and a stock of capital and chooses the amount of new capital to raise and the price for new policies. Demand for coverage depends both on price and quality (insolvency risk). The benefit of additional capital is increased by the demand for new policies. The cost of additional capital is that the old policyholders (existing liabilities) experience reduced insolvency risk, while not paying additional premiums.[47] Among other predictions, Cummins and Danzon show that prices could fall if a capital shock increases insolvency risk. They estimate a two-equation system using insurer level data, where price depends on lagged capital and additions to capital depend on the change in price. Their results indicate that insurers with more capital charge higher prices and that price is inversely related to deviations of capital from normal levels.

Froot and O'Connell (1997) test the extent to which shocks in one insurance market influence pricing in other markets. They present evidence that catastrophe

---

[46] During the 1980s, however, the correlation between insurer capital and the economic loss ratio was negative. Winter argues that the 1980s can be explained in part by the omission of reinsurance capacity in his capital variables, a factor which also may have influenced the results of Cummins and Danzon (1997, see below).

[47] Gron and Winton (2001) provide a related analysis of the resulting risk overhang and market behavior.

reinsurance prices change across the board in response to shocks caused by specific types of catastrophes (e.g., a hurricane) or by catastrophes in specific regions (also see the discussion in Froot, 2001). Weiss and Chung (2004) provide evidence that reinsurance prices are negatively related to worldwide relative capacity.

5.8.4 Price Cutting in Soft Markets

The traditional view of underwriting cycles by insurance industry analysts is that supply expands when expectations of profits are favorable, that competition then drives prices down to the point where underwriting losses deplete capital, and that supply ultimately contracts in response to unfavorable profit expectations or to avert financial collapse. Price increases then replenish capital until price-cutting ensues again. The traditional explanation of supply contractions is largely consistent with shock models. The principle puzzle is why competition in soft markets would cause insurers to cut prices to the point where premiums and anticipated investment income are insufficient to finance optimal forecasts of claim costs and ensure a low probability of default.[48]

Some authors suggest that a tendency towards inadequate prices might arise from differences in insurer expectations concerning the magnitude of future loss costs, from differences in insurer solvency incentives, or both.[49] Harrington and Danzon (1994) develop and test hypotheses based on this intuition and the literature on optimal bidding and moral hazard within the framework of alleged underpricing of U.S. commercial general liability insurance during the early 1980s. In their analysis, some firms may price below cost because of moral hazard, which results from limited liability and risk-insensitive guaranty programs. Others may price below cost due to heterogeneous information concerning future claim costs, which results in low loss forecasts relative to optimal forecasts accompanied by winners' curse effects. In response to underpricing by some firms, other firms may cut prices to preserve market share and thus avoid loss of quasi-rents from investments in tangible and intangible capital. Harrington and Danzon use cross-firm data from the early 1980s on premiums growth and loss forecast revisions for accidents in a given year to test whether moral hazard and/or heterogeneous information contributed to differences in general liability insurance prices and premium growth rates among firms. Their results provide some evidence consistent with their moral hazard hypothesis.[50]

---

[48] Similarly, popular explanations of "cash flow underwriting" usually imply that insurers reduce rates too much in response to increases in interest rates. Winter's model implies that hard markets that follow large shocks tend to be preceded by periods of excess capacity and soft prices. However, capital shocks should be unpredictable. Neither Winter's model nor other shock stories can readily explain any second-order autoregression in underwriting results.

[49] Winter (1988, 1991a) mentions the possibility of heterogeneous information and winner's curse effects.

[50] Harrington (2004c) presents evidence that higher firm-level premium growth for general liability insurance during the 1992–2001 soft market was reliably associated with higher loss forecast revisions, as would be expected if low-priced firms captured market share and ultimately experienced relatively high reported losses. Harrington et al. (2008) provide similar evidence using firm-level data for the U.S. medical malpractice insurance soft market during 1994–1999.

5.9 PRICE REGULATION

Insurance markets generally are subject to substantial government regulation and supervision encompassing licensing of insurers and agents and brokers, solvency and capital standards, rates and policy forms (contract language), sales and claim practices, and requirements to issue coverage.[51] A large literature has considered the effects of price regulation in insurance markets, especially in U.S. property/casualty insurance, where rates for many lines of insurance in many states are subject to regulatory prior approval; whereas other states allow rates to be used without prior regulatory approval.[52] Most states had prior approval regulation during the 1950s and 1960s, when rate regulation often encouraged insurers to use rates developed collectively by rating bureaus within the framework of the limited exemption from U.S. antitrust law for the "business of insurance" (Joskow, 1973). A trend towards deregulation began in the late 1960s and continued, albeit sporadically, through the 1990s (see Harrington, 2000).

Rate regulation can affect an insurer's average rate level in a given period. It also can affect rate differentials between groups of consumers by imposing limits on rates for particular groups through residual market mechanisms and/or by restricting risk classification.[53] Research on rate regulation in the United States has generally focused on politically sensitive lines of business, in particular automobile and workers' compensation insurance, and more recently homeowners' insurance in catastrophe-prone regions. These lines have been subject to more restrictive rate regulation in many states, and they periodically have experienced large residual markets in some states, in significant part due to restrictive rate regulation.

Many studies compare loss ratios, most often for automobile insurance, in states with and without prior approval regulation to provide evidence of whether prior approval affects average rate levels in relation to claim costs.[54] Hypotheses considered include that regulation raises rates due to capture by industry, that regulation persistently reduces rates due to consumer pressure, or that on average rate regulation will have little effect in competitively structured insurance markets. Some analyses indicate that regulation in some states and periods resulted in higher auto insurance loss ratios in states with prior approval rate regulation (e.g., during the mid-to-late 1970s and early 1980s; Harrington, 1987; Grabowski et al., 1989) and that a significant number of insurers exited the auto insurance market in such states.

On the other hand, and consistent with an inherent inability of prior approval regulation to reduce insurance rates persistently without harmful effects on availability and

---

[51] See Klein (2012, 2013) for overviews in the context of current issues.

[52] Harrington (2000) provides historical background; Harrington (1984) surveys early work.

[53] Involuntary markets, which are important mainly in auto, workers' compensation, and medical malpractice insurance, include mechanisms such as assigned risk plans and joint underwriting associations. They require joint provision of coverage by insurers at a regulated rate.

[54] Cummins (2002) and the studies therein consider this issue and other effects of rate regulation.

quality, studies generally have found no persistent difference over time between average loss ratios in states with and without prior approval regulation. Harrington (2002), for example, analyzes automobile insurance loss ratios, residual market shares, and volatility of premium growth rates by type of rate regulation with annual state-level data during 1972–1998. Conditioning on several factors that could affect loss ratios, the average loss ratio in prior approval states was only slightly larger than in other states, with the difference primarily attributable to the 1970s and at most weakly significant in a statistical sense.

Other studies document larger residual markets in automobile insurance in states with prior approval regulation (Ippolito, 1979; Grabowski et al., 1989; Harrington, 2002), with some degree of cross-subsidy flowing from voluntary markets to higher risk buyers in residual markets. Harrington and Danzon (2000b) and Danzon and Harrington (2001) consider the incentive effects of regulatory-induced cross-subsidies to higher risk employers in workers' compensation insurance residual markets. They provide evidence that higher subsidies are associated with greater growth in loss costs and increases in the proportion of employers that self-insure. Using annual, state-level panel data during 1980–1998, Weiss et al. (2010) provide evidence that rate regulation that suppresses premiums is associated with higher average loss costs and claim frequency for automobile insurance. Comparing Massachusetts and other states and towns within Massachusetts, Derrig and Tennyson (2011) provide evidence that regulatory-induced cross-subsidies to high risk drivers are likewise associated with higher automobile insurance loss costs.

Another avenue of inquiry is whether delays in the rate approval process under prior approval rate regulation could influence or even cause cyclical fluctuations in underwriting results (Cummins and Outreville, 1987). A number of studies analyze whether rate regulation affects cyclical movements in statewide loss ratios (e.g., Outreville, 1990; Tennyson, 1993). Such studies generally obtain mixed results concerning whether regulatory lag amplifies volatility in underwriting results.

5.10 CAPITAL ADEQUACY AND REGULATION

5.10.1 Optimal Capital Decisions

The theory of insurers' optimal capital decisions focuses on the trade-off between the benefits and cost of holding additional capital. The primary benefits include higher prices from risk sensitive policyholders and/or reducing the likelihood of financial distress, including the potential loss of franchise value. The primary costs include tax and agency costs. Building on the work of Borch (1982; also see DeFinetti, 1957), Munch and Smallwood (1982; also see Munch and Smallwood, 1980) and Finsinger and Pauly (1984) model insurer capital decisions in the presence of costly financial distress assuming that insurers maximize value to shareholders, that policyholder demand is inelastic with respect to default risk, that investing financial capital to support insurance operations is costly, and that firms cannot add capital after claims are realized. In the event of insolvency, Munch and Smallwood (1982) assume a loss of goodwill. Finsinger and Pauly (1984) assume loss of an entry cost that otherwise would allow the firm to continue operating (also see Tapiero et al., 1978). In both models firms will commit capital *ex ante* to reduce the likelihood of insolvency.[55]

Doherty and Tinic (1981), Doherty (1989, 2000), and Tapiero et al. (1986) consider insurers' capital decisions when demand for coverage is sensitive to insolvency risk. Garven (1987) analyzes insolvency risk within an agency cost framework in which shareholders, managers, sales personnel, and policyholders have different incentives regarding insolvency risk. Cagle and Harrington (1995) consider a static trade-off model of capital decisions when insurers are exposed to loss of franchise value for the cases of risk sensitive and risk insensitive policyholder demand. Froot (2007) models capital decisions with risk sensitive demand, tax costs of holding capital, and adjustment costs if capital is raised following losses.

5.10.2 Market Discipline

The scope of market discipline provided by policyholders and capital markets is a key element affecting capital decisions in many models. Factors affecting overall market discipline include (1) potential loss of franchise value, which arises from insurers' upfront investments in infrastructure and distribution, underwriting expertise and information, and reputation; (2) the risk sensitivity of demand, which depends on the ability of policyholders or their representatives to assess insolvency risk, the scope of any government guarantees of insurers' obligations, and the scope of the judgment proof problem, where some buyers may rationally seek low prices regardless of insolvency risk; (3) the risk sensitivity of insurance intermediaries (agents and brokers), who are exposed to increased costs or reduced revenues from insurer financial distress; and (4) risk sensitive debt-holders, which provide debt finance primarily at the insurance holding company level (Harrington, 2004b; also see Zanjani, 2002a).

A variety of studies provide empirical evidence on market discipline. Consistent with risk sensitive demand, studies that employ measures of property/casualty insurers' premiums in relation to realized claim costs as proxies for the price of coverage have found that prices are negatively correlated to insolvency risk (Sommer, 1996; Phillips et al., 1998; Phillips et al., 2006). Zanjani (2002a) provides evidence that life insurance policy termination rates are greater for insurers with lower A.M. Best financial strength ratings, although terminations are not related to rating changes. Epermanis and Harrington (2006) estimate abnormal premium growth surrounding changes in A.M. Best financial strength ratings for a large panel of property/casualty insurers during 1992–1999. They report evidence of significant premium declines in the year of

---

[55] The literature on capital decisions by banks contains similar results (e.g., Herring and Vankudre, 1987).

and the year following rating downgrades. Consistent with greater risk sensitivity of demand for customers with more sophistication and less guaranty fund protection, premium declines were concentrated among commercial insurance. Premium declines were greater for firms with low pre-downgrade ratings, and especially pronounced for firms falling below an A-rating, a traditional industry benchmark for many corporate buyers. Eling and Schmit (2012) conduct similar tests for German insurers and obtain qualitatively similar results, although the responses to rating changes appear smaller in magnitude than in the United States.

The extent to which partial state government guarantees of U.S. insurers' obligations dull policyholders' incentives and/or induce excessive risk taking from moral hazard has been explored in a number of studies that exploit cross-state variation in insurance guaranty fund characteristics or adoption dates to test whether guarantees have increased risk taking. Lee et al. (1997) provide evidence that asset risk increased for stock property/casualty insurers following the introduction of guaranty funds (also see Lee and Smith, 1999, and Downs and Sommer, 1999). Brewer et al. (1997) provide evidence that life insurer asset risk is greater in states where guaranty fund assessments against surviving insurers are offset against state premium taxes and thus borne by taxpayers, which may reduce financially strong insurers' incentives to press for efficient regulatory monitoring.[56]

Many studies and numerous anecdotes for particular insolvencies document unusually large premium growth prior to the insolvencies of some property/casualty insurers (e.g., A.M. Best Company, 1991; Bohn and Hall, 1999; also see Harrington and Danzon, 1994), which could in some cases be plausibly related to underpricing and excessive risk taking.[57] The 1990–1991 insolvencies of First Executive Corporation, First Capital Corporation, and Mutual Benefit Life in the United States suggest some degree of *ex ante* excessive risk taking, but the evidence is not sharp. Mutual Benefit ended up meeting virtually all of its obligations. Both First Executive and First Capital might have remained viable without regulatory intervention despite the temporary collapse of the junk bond market, and their experience demonstrated that demand was risk sensitive: as more bad news surfaced, more policyholders withdrew their funds (DeAngelo et al., 1995, 1996). Consistent with market discipline by equity holders, Fenn and Cole (1994) and Brewer and Jackson (2002) provide evidence that life insurer stock price declines during the high-yield bond and commercial real estate market slumps of 1989–1991 were concentrated among firms with problem assets.

---

[56] A few papers have analyzed the design of state guaranty funds, including their *ex post* assessment feature (see, e.g., Bernier and Mahfoudhi, 2010).

[57] On the other hand, Epermanis and Harrington (2006) found no evidence of excessive risk taking in the form of rapid commercial or personal lines premium growth following downgrades of A− or low-rated insurers.

5.10.3 Solvency Regulation and Capital Requirements

There are three main strands of literature on insurance company insolvencies and solvency regulation: (1) analyses (generally descriptive) of the causes of insolvencies; (2) insolvency prediction models, including those that incorporate information from regulatory solvency monitoring systems and risk-based capital requirements; and (3) the design and performance of regulatory risk-based capital (RBC) requirements.

Cummins and Phillips (2009) provide a representative, descriptive summary of the causes of U.S. insurer insolvencies and a hierarchy for understanding those causes (also see A.M. Best Company, 1991). Pinches and Trieschmann (1973) provide an early analysis of the ability of financial data to predict U.S. property/casualty insurer insolvencies. Cummins et al. (1995) analyze the ability of National Association of Insurance Commissioners (NAIC) RBC requirements (developed in the early 1990s) to predict insolvency of U.S. property/casualty insurers. Grace and Harrington (1998) and Cummins et al. (1999) compare the predictive ability of RBC requirements and the NAIC FAST system of solvency audit ratios. Grace et al. (1998) evaluate the predictive ability of the NAIC's FAST ratios for life insurer insolvencies. The evidence from these studies generally indicates that NAIC RBC ratios lack predictive power compared with models that include other metrics. Cummins et al. (1999) also provide evidence that cash flow simulation models significantly enhance predictive accuracy. Pottier and Sommer (2002) compare the predictive ability of NAIC FAST ratios, RBC ratios, and A.M. Best capital adequacy ratios and ratings for property/casualty insurer insolvencies and find that the A.M. best metrics have greater predictive power than the NAIC ratios.

Cummins et al. (1994) provide an early conceptual evaluation of the NAIC's RBC requirements. More recent work contrasts the NAIC RBC standards and capital standards in the E.U.'s forthcoming Solvency II regime (and in some cases other countries; Eling et al., 2007; Eling and Holzmuller, 2008; Holzmuller, 2009; Cummins and Phillips, 2009). The NAIC system is a deterministic and formulaic approach that combines fixed weights on a variety of risk measures based on statutory accounting to obtain a required RBC amount. The Solvency II regime, patterned to a great extent after the Basel II (and III) regime for banks, determines required capital using market-based valuation and Value-at-Risk (VaR) models, and it encourages firms to use internal capital models. Cummins and Phillips (2009; also see Holzmuller, 2009) recommend adoption of market valuation, stochastic risk modeling, and internal capital models in the United States.[58]

Harrington (2004a) considers the optimal stringency of capital standards in relation to the degree of market discipline when imperfect information concerning capital adequacy results in costly Type 1 and 2 errors from any system of capital standards

---

[58] Klein (2012) discusses insurance regulatory modernization initiatives in the United States in the context of challenges posed by Solvency II.

(i.e., failing to constrain some inadequately capitalized insurers and inefficiently distorting the decisions of some adequately capitalized insurers). His model predicts that cost minimizing capital standards will be less stringent the greater is the proportion of insurers that would be adequately capitalized without regulation. An implication is that optimal capital standards should not bind most insurers in a market characterized by strong market discipline. He therefore argues that the U.S. RBC system, where most insurers hold significantly more capital that the required minimums (Harrington, 2004a; Cummins and Phillips, 2009), is consistent with strong market discipline in U.S. insurance markets.[59]

5.10.4 Systemic Risk

The 2007–2009 financial crisis in general and the 2008 collapse of American International Group (AIG) in particular stimulated substantial research and analysis of the extent to which insurance involves systemic risk. Those events also led to the adoption in the United States of regulation requiring the identification of systemically important financial institutions ("SIFIs"), including insurance entities, and heightened regulatory standards for such entities.[60]

Although there is no uniform definition, the term "systemic risk" generally is used broadly to encompass the risk of any large, macroeconomic shock that affects financial stability and the risk arising from extensive interdependencies or "interconnectedness" among firms, with an attendant risk of contagion and significant economic spillovers on the real economy. Cummins and Weiss (2013b), for example, define systemic risk as "the risk that an event will trigger a loss of economic value or confidence in a substantial segment of the financial system that is serious enough to have significant adverse effects on the real economy with a high probability." They suggest that primary indicators of systemic risk at the firm level include size (volume of exposures), interconnectedness, and a lack of substitutability for a firm's services.[61]

There is a distinction between the risk of common shocks to the economy, such as widespread reductions in housing prices or large changes in interest rates or foreign

---

[59] De Haan and Kakes (2010) document that the vast majority of Dutch insurers hold much more capital than required by the E.U.'s pre-Solvency II rules.

[60] Similarly, the International Association of Insurance Supervisors and the Financial Stability Board are in the process of identifying global systemically important insurers. The systemic risk issue for insurance received some attention prior to the financial crisis. Harrington (2004a), for example, contrasts systemic risk among property/casualty insurers, life insurers, reinsurers, and banks.

[61] Section 113 of the 2010 U.S. Dodd-Frank Act authorizes the newly created Financial Stability Oversight Council (FSOC) to designate a nonbank financial company as systemically significant and subject to enhanced supervision by the Federal Reserve if "material financial distress at the nonbank financial company" or "the nature, scope, size, scale, concentration, interconnectedness, or mix of the activities of the nonbank financial company could pose a threat to the financial stability of the United States." The FSOC identified six broad risk categories for determining systemic importance: size, lack of substitutes for the firm's services and products, interconnectedness with other financial firms, leverage, liquidity risk and maturity mismatch, and existing regulatory scrutiny.

exchange, which have the potential to directly harm large numbers of people and firms, and financial risk that arises from interconnectedness and contagion.[62] However, it often is difficult to sort out any contagion effects from the effects of common shocks, and broad definitions of systemic risk encompass both sources of risk. Harrington (2009) discusses uncertainty about whether AIG's credit default swaps and securities lending presented significant risk of contagion and the extent to which an AIG bankruptcy would have had significant adverse effects beyond its counterparties, or the extent to which its counterparties had hedged or otherwise reduced their exposure to AIG.[63]

Analyses generally conclude that the core activities of insurers pose little systemic risk, especially compared with banking, in part because many insurers hold relatively large amounts of capital in relation to their liabilities and have relatively little exposure to short-term liabilities, reducing their vulnerability to shocks (Swiss Re, 2003; Harrington, 2004a; Geneva Association, 2010, 2012; Grace, 2010; Cummins and Weiss, 2013b). Based on a detailed review and analysis, for example, Cummins and Weiss (2013b) conclude that "the core activities of U.S. insurers do not pose systemic risk." They also conclude, however, that "life insurers are vulnerable to intra-sector crises" and that "both property-casualty and life insurers are vulnerable to reinsurance crises arising from counterparty credit risk."

Research on financial institutions' stock prices provides evidence of interconnectedness among insurers and other financial firms and develops new metrics for measuring systemic risk with stock price data. Billio et al. (2012), for example, use principal components analysis and Granger causality tests to analyze stock returns for insurers, banks, securities brokers, and hedge funds during 1994–2008. They find evidence of causal relationships between the sectors during 2001–2008 but not 1994–2000, and they identify several insurers as systemically important.[64] Acharya et al. (2010) develop a measure of systemic risk (systemic or marginal expected shortfall) to reflect a firm's tendency to lose value when the overall market suffers large losses. Their analysis of stock returns for insurers and other financial firms during 2006–2008 suggests that insurance firms were the least systemically risky. Insurers with the largest systemic risk measures had significant activity in credit derivatives and financial guarantees. Cummins and Weiss (2013b) conclude that the Billio et al. and Acharya et al. studies strongly suggest that insurance

---

[62] There are at least four sources of potential contagion that could contribute to systemic risk (e.g., Kaufman, 1994), including: (1) asset price contagion ("fire sales"); (2) counterparty contagion; (3) information-based contagion (the revelation of financial problems at some institutions creates uncertainty about the value of others); and (4) irrational contagion (investors and/or customers withdraw funds without regard to risk). Ellul et al. (2011) provide evidence of regulatory induced fire sales of downgraded corporate bonds by life insurers.

[63] Without intervention by the U.S. government, many more of AIG's insurance customers might have terminated or declined to renew their policies, but that by itself would not imply contagion, or that those customers would be significantly harmed.

[64] Chen et al. (2012) use Granger causality tests to examine interconnectedness between banks and insurers using data on credit default swap spreads.

firms can be a source of systemic risk from noncore activities and that interconnectedness among financial firms goes beyond exposure to common shocks.

5.11 SECURITIZATION AND INSURANCE-LINKED SECURITIES

Innovations in hybrid reinsurance–financial products and insurance-linked securities (ILS) represent a major development in insurance and reinsurance markets during the past two decades. Hybrid products and structures include finite risk reinsurance (which smooth financial results over multiple years with limited risk transfer), retrospective excess of loss coverage (protection against adverse loss development after events have occurred), loss portfolio transfers (transfers of entire blocks of claim liabilities), multiple trigger products (protection, for example, against the simultaneous occurrence of an insurance event and a financial market event), industry loss warranties (multiple trigger products combing industry and indemnity triggers), and side cars (reinsurance companies established by institutional investors to provide coverage to a single insurer or reinsurer sponsor). ILS products include contingent capital arrangements (which allow an insurer to raise capital at predetermined terms following a specified event), catastrophe futures and options (providing payoffs dependent on a specified index or trigger), and catastrophe bonds (bondholders receive less than full repayment of principal and/or interest if specified catastrophe losses occur).

Many of these innovations offer the potential for more efficient risk transfer through reduced moral hazard and adverse selection, improved diversification, reduced frictional costs of risk transfer, and/or enhanced capital market opportunities for investors. Cummins and Barrieu (2013; also see Cummins and Weiss, 2009; and Cummins and Trainar, 2009) provide a detailed review of hybrid and ILS product features, markets, and research. This section provides an overview of selected research on catastrophe futures/options and catastrophe (cat) bonds.

5.11.1 Catastrophe Futures, Options, and Basis Risk

Early research on catastrophe derivatives coincided with Hurricane Andrew and the introduction by the Chicago Board of Trade of catastrophe futures contracts in 1992 (replaced by catastrophe options in 1994, which in turn were withdrawn in 2000). D'Arcy and France (1992), Cox and Schwebach (1992), and Niehaus and Mann (1992) identify potential benefits of insurance derivatives compared with reinsurance, including possibly lower transaction costs and reduced counterparty risk, and they discuss the trade-off between moral hazard and basis risk, possible regulatory barriers, and potential hedging strategies. Harrington et al. (1995) consider the potential benefits of catastrophe futures and options compared with reinsurance or holding additional equity capital, and they provide evidence of potential hedging effectiveness by analyzing national loss ratios for alternative lines of business.

Harrington and Niehaus (1999) analyze the relationship between U.S. insurers' loss ratios, state-level catastrophe losses, and industry loss ratios in different geographic areas. The results suggest that basis risk with state-specific catastrophe derivatives would likely be manageable for many insurers, in particular for homeowners' insurance. Cummins et al. (2004) analyze basis risk for catastrophe loss indexes for insurers writing windstorm insurance in Florida using exposure level data and simulated losses from a catastrophe modeling firm. The results suggest significant basis risk for smaller insurers.

Doherty (1997, 2000) emphasizes differences in basis risk associated with different types of triggers in ILS contracts. Contracts with indemnity triggers, which link payoffs to a specific insurer or reinsurer's losses, minimize basis risk, but they aggravate moral hazard. Contracts with nonindemnity triggers (e.g., tied to an industry index) reduce moral hazard but increase basis risk. Doherty and Richter (2002) consider whether optimal hedging could involve a combination of indemnity and industry-based triggers.

5.11.2 Cat Bonds

While catastrophe futures and options have failed to gain market traction, the market for cat bonds appears viable and could be poised for additional growth. The basic structure of a cat bond involves the issuer (e.g., a reinsurer) issuing bonds through a fully collateralized special purpose vehicle, with the bonds providing the issuer an embedded call option that is triggered by a defined catastrophe event (see Cummins and Loubergé, 2009; and Cummins and Barrieu, 2013, for details). A variety of different triggers are used, including industry loss triggers, indemnity triggers, and parametric triggers based on physical severity levels. As a result of the embedded option, full repayment of principal and/or interest is contingent on whether the defined event occurs during the life of the bond. The resulting transfer of catastrophe risk to the bondholders provides investors with a "pure play" in the underlying risk, and it can achieve the tax advantages of debt vs. equity finance. Cat bonds with nonindemnity triggers also might reduce the adverse effects of asymmetric information (Finken and Laux, 2009). On the other hand, Lakdawalla and Zanjani (2012) explain that full collateralization of cat bonds "abandons the reinsurance principle of economizing on collateral through diversification of risk transfer."

Research on the magnitude of cat bonds spreads over LIBOR and comparisons to catastrophe reinsurance prices identify two puzzles (Froot and O'Connell, 2008; Cummins and Mahul, 2008; Cummins and Barrieu, 2013). First, cat bond spreads are very high on average compared to those that might be expected given that cat bond returns should have little correlation with market returns. Second, cat bond spreads appear to mimic reinsurance rate changes in soft and hard markets. Dieckmann (2008) analyzes a habit and consumption-based asset pricing model in which cat bond losses tend to occur when catastrophe losses reduce consumption, thus increasing cat bond risk and possibly helping to explain large spreads even though catastrophe losses are small relative to aggregate consumption.

5.12 INSURER EFFICIENCY, DISTRIBUTION, ORGANIZATIONAL FORM, AND CORPORATE GOVERNANCE

5.12.1 Efficiency Studies

Joskow's (1973) seminal analysis of the U.S. property/casualty insurance industry considered market concentration and barriers to entry, estimated returns to scale, analyzed direct writer (exclusive agency/salaried employee) and independent agency (multiple insurer representation) distribution systems. Joskow estimated simple models of insurer operating expense ratios, concluding that the industry was characterized by constant returns to scale. Following Joskow, other early studies estimated insurers' cost functions with cross-sectional accounting data (e.g., Doherty, 1981; Johnson et al., 1981). Analysis of insurers' operating efficiency then shifted to more elaborate models estimated with stochastic frontier analysis (SFA) and/or data envelope analysis (DEA).

Cummins and Weiss (2013a) review insurance efficiency studies in property/casualty and life insurance in nearly 20 countries. They identify 53 studies during the period 2000–2011, in addition to 21 studies considered earlier by Cummins and Weiss (2000). A majority of the 74 studies employ DEA as the primary methodology. Thirty-one studies were published during 2008–2011. Twenty studies focus on the effects of organizational form or corporate governance on estimated efficiency; 12 focus on the general level of efficiency over time; 12 focus on market structure, and 5 focus on economies of scale and scope. About two-thirds of the studies use loss, benefit, or claim-based measures of output, with 11 using premiums. The number and diversity of insurance efficiency studies obviates any high-level summary. Some specific studies dealing with distribution and organizational form are noted below.

5.12.2 Insurance Distribution

Insurance markets exhibit a wide variety of distribution methods across lines of business and countries. Hilliard et al. (2013) review the distribution literature, including studies of the economic rationales for different distributions systems, insurer relationships with and compensation of agents and brokers, and regulation of distribution. They also provide background information on the prevalence of alternative distribution methods in different lines of business in the Unites States and other countries. The literature generally focuses on differences between direct writing systems, where insurers primarily rely on exclusive agents, employee sales forces, or telephone/mail/internet systems, versus independent agency and brokerage systems, where intermediaries have relationships with multiple insurers.

Numerous studies compare insurers' costs for different distribution methods, especially for direct writing versus independent agents and brokers in U.S. property/casualty insurance. Joskow (1973) provided early evidence that expense ratios were lower for direct writers than for independent agency insurers. Cummins and VanDerhei (1979) estimate more elaborate models of insurers' expenses using pooled cross-section and time-series data. The results again indicate significantly lower expense ratios for direct writers. Later analyses by Barrese and Nelson (1992) and Regan (1999) obtain similar results with richer measures of distribution type and data for more lines of business.

Joskow (1973) argued that differences in operating costs between direct writers and independent agency insurers could not be explained by differences in service. He suggested that prior approval rate regulation had discouraged price cuts by direct writers, that difficulty in raising capital and obtaining consumer recognition slowed their expansion, and that it would be costly for independent agency insurers to become direct writers. He argued that direct writers behaved as oligopolists subject to short-run capacity constraints and that constrained profit maximization involved selection of risks with lower than average expected claim costs. Smallwood (1975) also suggested barriers to insurers switching to direct writer distribution. He argued that independent agency insurers were more vulnerable to adverse selection, and he developed a formal model of insurer risk selection (which did not consider asymmetric information).

Cummins and VanDerhei (1979) assume that lower operating expenses for direct writers provide prima facie evidence of superior efficiency. On the other hand, based on stochastic frontier analysis of cost and profit efficiency for alternative distribution systems, Berger et al. (1997) provide evidence that while insurers with independent agents and brokers were less cost efficient than direct writers, there was no difference in profit efficiency. They interpret their overall results as consistent with higher costs being attributable to higher quality for independent agency and brokerage insurers.

Other work considers whether higher costs of independent agency and brokerage systems are associated with specific dimensions of service quality. Etgar (1976) provides evidence that independent agents are significantly more likely to assist policyholders in claims settlement than exclusive agents. Barrese et al. (1995) present evidence using data on consumer complaints to regulators in five states that insurers using independent agents receive fewer complaints. More recently, Eckardt and Rathke-Doppner (2010) provide evidence that independent agents in Germany provide better service quality, while exclusive agents provide a broader array of services.

Regarding insurers' choice of distribution systems and co-existence of multiple systems, Marvel (1982) posits that direct writing helps internalize the benefits to the firm of advertising and promotion, implying that direct writing will be more prevalent when such activities are more important in generating sales. Grossman and Hart (1986) predict that ownership of customer lists by the insurer or intermediary will be allocated to the party for which ownership is most likely to promote investments that maximize value and that agents will be allocated ownership when agent services are a more important determinant of value than insurers' investments in brand formation. Sass and Gisser (1989) consider how direct writing depends on sufficient density of customers to offer agents greater volume potential at lower commission rates, and they provide evidence that market size and customer density are positively related to direct writer market shares.

Regan and Tennyson (1996) argue that independent agency systems provide greater incentives for agents to exert effort in risk selection. The reason is that independent agents' have the ability to capture more profits from such efforts in view of their ability to influence consumers' choices among competing firms. They predict that independent agency systems enhance efficiency when they have unverifiable, subjective information that is important to underwriting. Using state level data on market shares of direct writers during 1980–1987, they provide evidence that direct writer market shares are lower in states where exposures are more heterogeneous and complex.

Kim et al. (1996) posit that independent agents and brokers will be used when agent monitoring of insurers is important to consumers and that such monitoring is more important for stockholder owned than mutual insurers. Using U.S. insurer level data for 1981, they provide evidence that direct writing is positively related to mutual ownership. Regan (1997) further considers transactions cost explanations of distribution choice and provides evidence with insurer level data that direct writing is positively related to insurers' investments in advertising and technology and mutual ownership.[65] Regan and Tzeng (1999) consider endogenous choice of distribution and organizational form and provide evidence that product complexity is more closely related to distribution choice than organizational form.

Cummins and Doherty (2006) provide detailed analysis of the economics of distribution and the forms of commission-based compensation in the U.S. commercial property/casualty insurance. Their work was motivated by allegations in 2004 by then New York Attorney General Elliot Spitzer that certain insurers and brokers had used contingent commissions to enforce anticompetitive pricing and market allocation schemes. They stress the role of independent agents and brokers in matching policyholders with insurers that have capabilities of meeting their needs. They explain how contingent commissions, which make compensation to agents and brokers contingent on the volume, profitability, and/or persistency of business placed with an insurer, can help align insurer and intermediary interests, in part by reducing informational asymmetries between insurers and buyers and associated adverse selection.

A few studies have begun to explore the use and effects of internet technology on insurance distribution and market outcomes. Brown and Goolsbee (2002) provide evidence that internet comparison shopping in the United States significantly reduced term life insurance prices. Using data on internet investment and organizational characteristics for a sample of insurers, Forman and Gron (2011) provide evidence that direct writing speeds adoption of consumer internet applications that complement existing distribution.

---

[65] Posey and Tennyson (1998) model the influence of search costs on distribution system choice, predicting that low production and search costs will be associated with direct writing. They provide suggestive empirical evidence.

5.12.3 Alternative Organizational Forms

In addition to significant variation in distribution methods, insurance markets are characterized by a variety of organizational forms, including stockholder ownership, mutual ownership, reciprocals, and Lloyds associations. Mayers and Smith (2013) describe the main types and survey the literature on choice of organization form, with an emphasis on the ability of alternative forms to reduce contracting costs associated with potential incentive conflicts among owners (residual claimants), managers, and policyholders.

Mayers and Smith (1981) consider the ability of alternative forms of ownership to minimize the cost of incentive conflicts (also see Fama and Jensen, 1983).[66] They predict that mutuals will specialize in lines of insurance where managers have limited discretion to pursue their own interests at the expense of owners, whereas Lloyds associations should have greater penetration in lines where managers have the most discretion. Mayers and Smith (1988) discuss further the management discretion hypothesis, and they develop and test hypotheses concerning product specialization and geographic concentration across ownership types (also see Mayers and Smith, 1986). They obtain some evidence consistent with the prediction, for example, that mutuals specialize in lines with low managerial discretion.

Mayers and Smith (1990) analyze reinsurance purchases for U.S. property/casualty insurers (also see Mayers and Smith, 1982), providing evidence that Lloyds organizations reinsure the most and that stock insurers reinsure less than mutuals. Lamm-Tennant and Starks (1993) provide evidence that stockholder owned insurers write more business than mutuals in lines of business with greater underwriting risk. The authors interpret that result as consistent with the managerial discretion hypothesis (lower risk lines involve less managerial discretion). Kleffner and Doherty (1996) find that stock insurers write more earthquake insurance than mutuals, but they interpret the result as consistent with stock insurers having superior access to capital following potentially large losses. Harrington and Niehaus (2002) provide evidence using U.S. property/casualty insurance data that mutual insurers hold more capital compared with stock insurers and adjust capital more slowly to target levels, interpreting these findings to mutuals' greater costs of obtaining capital after adverse loss experience. Zanjani (2007) discusses the role of mutual firms' inferior access to capital in his historical analysis of organizational form in life insurance.

A variety of studies have analyzed within-firm changes in organizational form. Mayers and Smith (1986) analyze the effects of insurer conversion from stock to mutual ownership on returns to stockholders, premium volume and persistence, product mix, and management turnover, concluding on average that such conversions were efficiency

---

[66] Hansmann (1985), on the other hand, provided detailed discussion of the possible role of mutual ownership in reducing conflicts between owners and policyholders over the level of insurer default risk. He also considered the possible ability of mutual ownership to facilitate risk selection during the formative years of U.S. insurance markets.

enhancing. Mayers and Smith (2002) provide evidence that mutual-to-stock conversions of property/casualty insurers were in large part motivated by the desire to achieve greater access to capital. Viswanathan and Cummins (2003) provide evidence that capital and liquidity constraints contributed to U.S. mutual insurer conversions to stock ownership for both property/casualty and life/health insurers (also see McNamara and Rhee, 1992). Erhemjamts and Phillips (2012) provide evidence that U.S. life insurer mutual-to-stock conversions were likewise motivated by access to capital concerns.

Cummins et al. (1999) use DEA methods to analyze the relative efficiency of stock and mutual insurers. They provide evidence that stock and mutual firms have distinct production and cost frontiers, consistent with their having distinct technologies.[67] Erhemjamts and Leverty (2010) use DEA methods to provide evidence that greater estimated cost efficiency for U.S. stock life insurers than mutual life insurers during 1995–2004 contributed to mutual-to-stock conversions, along with access to capital concerns.

5.12.4 Corporate Governance

Corporate governance is a new research topic in the insurance literature. It was motivated by corporate scandals around the world and the recent crisis in financial markets. Resources expropriations by well-paid executives and their risk-taking behavior motivated many studies on corporate governance in financial markets.

Boubakri (2013) offers a survey of the literature on the nature of corporate governance in the insurance industry. This new subject was covered extensively in a special issue of the *Journal of Risk and Insurance* in 2011. The focus is on several corporate governance mechanisms such as the composition of the Board of Directors, CEO compensation, and ownership structure. The impact of such mechanisms on insurers' performance and risk taking is also discussed. Several avenues of future research are identified.

5.13 CONCLUSIONS

The theoretical literature on insurance has advanced enormously since the early work of Arrow and Borch. Models of optimal insurance and insurance demand by individuals have become highly refined, including detailed analysis of the influences of transaction costs, moral hazard, asymmetric information, uninsurable background risk, state dependent utility, and other issues. The theory of insurance and resource allocation also exhibits considerable sophistication. Substantial progress has likewise been made on modeling the demand for insurance and hedging by corporations. As is typically the case, empirical work has in many instances lagged theoretical developments, in large part

---

[67] Cummins and Rubio-Misas (2006) obtain results with similar implications for Spanish insurers. Bikker and Gorter (2011) conduct cost-efficiency analysis of Dutch stock and mutual non-life insurers.

due to limitations associated with available data. The increased availability of micro data, however, has led to significant progress, and it bodes well for further empirical work.

While less mature than theoretical work on demand and market equilibrium, significant theoretical literatures also have evolved to increase our understanding of insurance supply, including pricing, capital decisions, regulation, efficiency, distribution, and organizational form. Significant progress has been made in empirical work to test hypotheses generated by theoretical work on supply-related issues and on asymmetric information. Increasing availability of data again bodes well for future empirical work to test extant theories and new theoretical developments. Additional innovations in theoretical and empirical work also can be expected on the growing markets for insurance-lined securities and their effects on primary insurance and reinsurance markets. The overall evolution of the broad literature on insurance and insurance markets suggests continued progress in achieving a fuller understanding of existing arrangements and future developments in the years ahead.

ACKNOWLEDGMENTS

Comments on an earlier version by L. Eeckhoudt, C. Gollier, M. Machina, and K. Viscusi were very useful.

REFERENCES

A.M. Best Company, 1991. Best's Insolvency Study, A.M. Best Co.
Abbring, J., Chiappori, P.A., Pinquet, J., 2003. Moral hazard and dynamic insurance data. Journal of the European Economic Association 1, 767–820.
Abbring, J., Chiappori, P.A., Zavadil, T., 2008. Better Safe than Sorry? Ex Ante and Ex Post Moral Hazard in Dynamic Insurance Data. Mimeo, Columbia University.
Aboudi, R., Thon, D., 1995. Second-degree stochastic dominance decisions and random initial wealth with applications to the economics of insurance. Journal of Risk and Insurance 62, 30–49.
Acharya, V.V, Pedersen, L.H., Philippon, T., Richardson, M., 2010. Measuring Systemic Risk. Working Paper, Federal Reserve Bank of Cleveland, Cleveland, Ohio.
Akerlof, G.A., 1970. The market for 'lemons': quality uncertainty and the market mechanism. Quarterly Journal of Economics 84, 488–500.
Alarie, Y., Dionne, G., Eeckhoudt, L., 1992. Increases in risk and demand for insurance. In: Dionne, G. (Ed.), Contributions to Insurance Economics. Kluwer Academic Publishers, The Netherlands.
Allais, M., 1953a. Généralisation des théories de l'équilibre économique général et du rendement social au cas du risque. Econométrie, 81–110. CNRS, Paris.
Allais, M., 1953b. Le comportement de l'homme rationnel devant le risque, critique des postulats et axiomes de l'École américaine. Econometrica 21, 503–546.
Anscombe, F.J., Aumann, R.J., 1963. A definition of subjective probability. Mathematical Statistics 43, 199–205.
Arnott, R., 1992. Moral hazard and competitive insurance markets. In: Dionne, G. (Ed.), Contributions to Insurance Economics. Kluwer Academic Publishers.
Arnott, R., Stiglitz, J.E., 1990. The welfare economics of moral hazard. In: Louberge, H. (Ed.), Risk, Information and Insurance: Essays in the Memory of Karl Borch. Kluwer Academie Publishers.
Arrow, K.J., 1953. Le rôle des valeurs boursières pour la répartition la meilleure des risques. Économétrie. CNRS, Paris, pp. 41–47 (Translated as The Role of Securities in the Optimal Allocation of Risk-Bearing. Review of Economic Studies 31, 1964, 91–96.).

Arrow, K.J., 1963. Uncertainty and the welfare economics of medical care. American Economic Review 53, 941–969.

Arrow, K.J., 1965. Insurance, Risk and Resource Allocation. In: Aspects of the Theory of Risk-Bearing. Yrjö Jahnsson Foundation, Helsinki, pp. 134–143 (Reprinted in Arrow, K.J., 1971. Essays in the Theory of Risk Bearing. Elsevier Publishing Company Inc.).

Arrow, K.J., 1974. Optimal insurance and generalized deductibles. Scandinavian Actuarial Journal 1, 1–42.

Arrow, K.J., Fischer, A.C., 1974. Environmental preservation, uncertainty and irreversibility. Quarterly Journal of Economics 88, 312–319.

Barrese, J., Doerpinghaus, H.I., Nelson, J.M., 1995. Do independent agent insurers provide superior service? The insurance marketing puzzle. Journal of Risk and Insurance 62, 297–308.

Barrese, J., Nelson, J.M., 1992. Independent and exclusive agency insurers: a reexamination of the cost differential. Journal of Risk and Insurance 59, 375–397.

Barrieu, P., Loubergé, H., 2009. Hybrid cat bonds. Journal of Risk and Insurance 76, 547–578.

Bauer, D., Phillips, R.D., Zanjani, G., 2013. Financial pricing of insurance. In: Dionne, G. (Ed.), The Handbook of Insurance, second ed. Springer, New York.

Bauer, D., Zanjani, G., 2013. Capital allocation and its discontents. In: Dionne, G. (Ed.), The Handbook of Insurance, second ed. Springer, New York.

Berger, A.N., Cummins, J.D., Weiss, M.A., 1997. The coexistence of multiple distribution systems for financial services: the case of property-liability insurance. Journal of Business 70, 515–546.

Bernier, G., Mahfoudhi, R.M., 2010. On the economics of postassessments in insurance guaranty funds: a stakeholders' perspective. Journal of Risk and Insurance 77, 857–892.

Biger, N., Kahane, Y., 1978. Risk considerations in insurance ratemaking. Journal of Risk and Insurance 45, 121–132.

Bikker, J.A., Gorter, J., 2011. Restructuring of the Dutch non-life insurance industry: consolidation, organizational form, and focus. Journal of Risk and Insurance 78, 163–184.

Billio, M., Getmansky, M., Lo, A.W., Pelizzon, L., 2012. Econometric measures of connectedness and systemic risk in the finance and insurance sectors. Journal of Financial Economics 104, 535–559.

Black, J.M., Bulkley, G., 1989. A ratio criterion for signing the effects of an increase in uncertainty. International Economic Review 30, 119–130.

Blazenko, G., 1985. The design of an optimal insurance policy: note. American Economic Review 75, 253–255.

Bohn, J., Hall, B., 1999. The moral hazard of insuring the insurers. In: Froot, K. (Ed.), The Financing of Catastrophe Risk. University of Chicago Press, Chicago, IL.

Bolton, P., Dewatripont, M., 2005. Contract Theory. MIT Press, Cambridge, MA. p. 724.

Bond, E.W., Crocker, K.J., 1991. Smoking, skydiving, and knitting: the endogenous categorization of risks in insurance markets with asymmetric information. Journal of Political Economy 99, 177–200.

Bond, E., Crocker, K.J., 1997. Hardball and the soft touch: the economics of optimal insurance contracts with costly state verification and endogenous monitoring costs. Journal of Public Economics 63, 239–264.

Borch, K., 1960. The safety loading of reinsurance premiums. Skandinavisk Aktuarietidskrift, 163–184.

Borch, K., 1961. The utility concept applied to the theory of insurance. Astin Bulletin 1, 245–255.

Borch, K., 1962. Equilibrium in a reinsurance market. Econometrica 30, 424–444.

Borch, K., 1974. Capital markets and the supervision of insurance companies. Journal of Risk and Insurance 41, 397–405.

Borch, K., 1982. Optimal strategies in a game of economic survival. Naval Research Logistics Quarterly 29, 19–27.

Borch, K., 1990. Economics of Insurance. Amsterdam, North Holland.

Born, P., Viscusi, W.K., 1994. Insurance market responses to the 1980s liability reforms: an analysis of firm-level data. Journal of Risk and Insurance 61, 192–208.

Boubakri, N., 2013. Corporate governance in the insurance industry: a synthesis. In: Dionne, G. (Ed.), The Handbook of Insurance, second ed. Springer, New York.

Bourgeon, J.M., Picard, P., 2007. Point-Record driving license and road safety: an economic approach. Journal of Public Economics 91, 235–258.

Boyer, M., Dionne, G., 1983. Variations in the probability and magnitude of loss: their impact on risk. Canadian Journal of Economics 16, 411–419.

Boyer, M., Dionne, G., 1989a. More on insurance, protection and risk. Canadian Journal of Economics 22, 202–205.

Boyer, M., Dionne, G., 1989b. An empirical analysis of moral hazard and experience rating. Review of Economics and Statistics 71, 128–134.

Boyle, P.B., 1990. Karl Borch's research contributions to insurance. Journal of Risk and Insurance 57, 307–320.

Brewer, E., Jackson, W., 2002. Intra-Industry Contagion and the Competitive Effects of Financial Distress Announcements: Evidence from Commercial Banks and Insurance Companies. Federal Reserve Bank of Chicago Working Paper No. 2002–23.

Brewer, E., Mondschean, T., Strahan, P., 1997. The role of monitoring in reducing the moral hazard problem associated with government guarantees: evidence from the life insurance industry. Journal of Risk and Insurance 64, 302–322.

Briys, E., 1988. On the theory of rational insurance purchasing in a continuous time model. Geneva Papers on Risk and Insurance 13, 165–177.

Briys, E., Eeckhoudt, L., 1985. Relative risk aversion in comparative statics: comment. American Economic Review 75, 284–286.

Briys, E., Dionne, G., Eeckhoudt, L., 1989. More on insurance as a Giffen good. Journal of Risk and Uncertainty 2, 420–425.

Briys, E., Schlesinger, H., 1990. Risk aversion and the propensities for self-insurance and self-protection. Southern Economic Journal 57, 458–467.

Brown, J.R., Goolsbee, A., 2002. Does the Internet make markets more competitive? Evidence from the life insurance industry. Journal of Political Economy 110, 481–507.

Browne, M.J., Kamiya, S., 2012. A theory of the demand for underwriting. Journal of Risk and Insurance 79, 335–349.

Bühlmann, H., Jewell, H., 1979. Optimal risk exchanges. Astin Bulletin 10, 243–262.

Butler, R.J., Gardner, H.H., Kleinman, N.L., 2013. Workers' compensation: occupational injury insurance's influence on the workplace. In: Dionne, G. (Ed.), The Handbook of Insurance, second ed. Springer, New York.

Cagle, J., Harrington, S.E., 1995. Insurance supply with capacity constraints and endogenous insolvency risk. Journal of Risk and Uncertainty 11, 219–232.

Campello, M., Lin, Y., Ma, C., Zou, H., 2011. The real and financial implications of corporate hedging. Journal of Finance 66, 1615–1647.

Chang, Y.M., Ehrlich, I., 1985. Insurance, protection from risk and risk bearing. Canadian Journal of Economics 18, 574–587.

Chen, H., Cummins, J.D., Viswanathan, K.S., Weiss, M.A., 2012. Systemic risk and the inter-connectedness between banks and insurers: an econometric analysis. Journal of Risk and Insurance, http://dx.doi.org/10.1111/j.1539-6975.2012.01503.x.

Chiappori, P.A., Salanié, B., 2000. Testing for asymmetric information in insurance markets. Journal of Political Economy 108, 56–78.

Chiappori, P.A., Salanié, B., 2013. Asymmetric information in insurance markets: predictions and tests. In: Dionne, G. (Ed.), The Handbook of Insurance, second ed. Springer, New York.

Chiu, W.H., 2005. Degree of downside risk aversion and self-protection. Insurance: Mathematics and Economics 36, 93–101.

Choi, S., Thistle, P., 2000. Capacity constraints and the dynamics of underwriting profits. Economic Inquiry 38, 442–457.

Choi, S., Hardigree, D., Thistle, P., 2002. The property/liability insurance cycle: a comparison of alternative models. Southern Economic Journal 68, 530–548.

Cohen, A., Einav, L., 2007. Estimating risk preferences from deductible choice. American Economic Review 97, 745–788.

Cook, P.J., Graham, D.A., 1977. The demand for insurance protection: the case of irreplaceable commodities. Quarterly Journal of Economics 91, 143–156.

Cooper, R., Hayes, B., 1987. Multi-period insurance contracts. International Journal of Industrial Organization 5, 211–231.

Courbage, C., Rey, B., Treich, N., 2013. Prevention and precaution. In: Dionne, G. (Ed.), The Handbook of Insurance, second ed. Springer, New York.

Cox, S.H., Schwebach, R.G., 1992. Insurance futures and hedging insurance price risk. Journal of Risk and Insurance 59, 628–644.

Cresta, J.P., 1984. Théorie des Marchés d'Assurance, Collection "Approfondissement de la connaissance économique". Economica, Paris.

Crocker, K.J., Morgan, J., 1997. Is honesty the best policy? Curtailing insurance fraud through optimal incentive contracts. Journal of Political Economy 106, 355–375.

Crocker, K.J., Snow, A., 1985. The efficiency of competitive equilibria in insurance markets with adverse selection. Journal of Public Economics 26, 207–219.

Crocker, K.J., Snow, A., 1986. The efficiency effects of categorical discrimination in the insurance industry. Journal of Political Economy 94, 321–344.

Crocker, K.J., Snow, A., 2011. Multidimensional screening in insurance markets with adverse selection. Journal of Risk and Insurance 78, 287–307.

Crocker, K.J., Snow, A., 2013. The theory of risk classification. In: Dionne, G. (Ed.), The Handbook of Insurance, second ed. Springer, New York.

Cummins, J.D., 1988. Risk-based premiums for insurance guaranty funds. Journal of Finance 43, 823–839.

Cummins, J.D. (Ed.), 2002. Deregulating Property-Liability Insurance. AEI-Brookings Joint Center for Regulatory Studies.

Cummins, J.D., Barrieu, P., 2013. Innovations in insurance markets: hybrid and securitized risk-transfer solutions. In: Dionne, G. (Ed.), The Handbook of Insurance, second ed. Springer, New York.

Cummins, J.D., Danzon, P.M., 1997. Price, financial quality, and capital flows in insurance markets. Journal of Financial Intermediation 6, 3–38.

Cummins, J.D., Dionne, G., Gagné, R., Nouira, A., 2009. Efficiency of insurance firms with endogenous risk management and financial intermediation activities. Journal of Productivity Analysis 32, 145–159.

Cummins, J.D., Doherty, N.A., 2006. The economics of insurance intermediaries. Journal of Risk and Insurance 73, 359–396.

Cummins, J.D., Grace, M.F., Phillips, R.D., 1999. Regulatory solvency prediction in property-liability insurance: risk-based capital, audit ratios, and cash flow simulation. Journal of Risk and Insurance 66, 417–458.

Cummins, J.D., Harrington, S.E., 1985. Property-liability insurance rate regulation: estimation of underwriting betas using quarterly profit data. Journal of Risk and Insurance 52, 16–43.

Cummins, J.D., Harrington, S.E., Niehaus, G., 1994. An economic overview of risk-based capital requirements for the property-liability insurance industry. Journal of Insurance Regulation 11, 427–447.

Cummins, J.D., Harrington, S.E., Klein, R.W., 1995. Insolvency experience, risk-based capital, and prompt corrective action in property-liability insurance. Journal of Banking and Finance 19, 511–527.

Cummins, J.D., Lalonde, D., Phillips, R.D., 2004. The basis risk of index-linked catastrophic loss securities. Journal of Financial Economics 71, 77–111.

Cummins, J.D., Mahul, O., 2008. Catastrophe Risk Financing in Developing Countries: Principles for Public Intervention. The World Bank, Washington, DC.

Cummins, J.D., Outreville, J.F., 1987. An international analysis of underwriting cycles in property-liability insurance. Journal of Risk and Insurance 54, 246–262.

Cummins, J.D., Phillips, R.D., Smith, S.D., 2000. Financial risk management in the insurance industry. In: Dionne, G. (Ed.), Handbook of Insurance. Kluwer Academic Publishers, Boston, pp. 565–591.

Cummins, J.D., Phillips, R.D., 2005. Estimating the cost of equity capital for property liability insurers. Journal of Risk and Insurance 72, 441–478.

Cummins, J.D., Phillips, R.D., 2009. Capital adequacy and insurance risk-based capital systems. Journal of Insurance Regulation, 26–72.

Cummins, J.D., Rubio-Misas, M., 2006. Deregulation, consolidation, and efficiency: evidence from the Spanish insurance industry. Journal of Money, Credit, and Banking 38, 323–355.

Cummins, J.D., Tennyson, S., 1992. Controlling automobile insurance costs. Journal of Economic Perspectives 6, 95–115.

Cummins, J.D., Trainar, P., 2009. Securitization, insurance, and reinsurance. Journal of Risk and Insurance 76, 463–492.

Cummins, J.D., VanDerhei, J., 1979. A note on the relative efficiency of property-liability insurance distribution systems. Bell Journal of Economics 10, 709–719.

Cummins, J.D., Weiss, M.A., 2000. Analyzing firm performance in the insurance industry using frontier efficiency and productivity methods. In: Dionne, G. (Ed.), The Handbook of Insurance. Kluwer Academic Publishers., pp. 767–829.

Cummins, J.D., Weiss, M.A., 2009. Convergence of insurance and financial markets: hybrid and securitized risk transfer solutions. Journal of Risk and Insurance 76, 493–545.

Cummins, J.D., Weiss, M.A., 2013a. Analyzing firm performance in the insurance industry using frontier efficiency and productivity methods. In: Dionne, G. (Ed.), The Handbook of Insurance, second ed. Springer, New York.

Cummins, J.D., Weiss, M.A., 2013b. Systemic risk and the insurance industry. In: Dionne, G. (Ed.), The Handbook of Insurance, second ed. Springer, New York.

Cummins, J.D., Weiss, M.A., Zi, H., 1999. Organizational form and efficiency: the coexistence of stock and mutual property-liability insurers. Management Science 45, 1254–1269.

Dachraoui, K., Dionne, G., Eeckhoudt, L., Godfroid, P., 2004. Comparative mixed risk aversion: definition and application to self-protection and willingness to pay. Journal of Risk and Uncertainty 29, 261–276.

Dahlby, B., 1983. Adverse selection and statistical discrimination: an analysis of Canadian automobile insurance. Journal of Public Economics 20, 121–131.

Dahlby, B., 1992. Testing for asymmetric information in Canadian automobile insurance. In: Dionne, G. (Ed.), Contributions to Insurance Economics. Kluwer Academic Publishers, The Netherlands.

DeAngelo, H., DeAngelo, L., Gilson, S., 1995. The collapse of first executive corporation: junk bonds, adverse publicity, and the 'run on the bank' phenomenon. Journal of Financial Economics 36, 287–336.

DeAngelo, H., DeAngelo, L., Gilson, S., 1996. Perceptions and the politics of finance: junk bonds the regulatory seizure of first capital life. Journal of Financial Economics 41, 475–512.

Danzon, P.M., 1985. Medical Malpractice: Theory, Evidence and Public Policy. Harvard University Press, Cambridge, MA.

Danzon, P.M., Harrington, S.E., 2001. Workers' compensation rate regulation: how price controls increase costs. Journal of Law and Economics 44, 1–36.

D'Arcy, S.P., Doherty, N., 1990. Adverse selection, private information and lowballing in insurance markets. Journal of Business 63, 145–163.

D'Arcy, S.P., France, V.G., 1992. Catastrophe futures: a better hedge for insurers. Journal of Risk and Insurance 59, 575–600.

De Haan, L., Kakes, J., 2010. Are non-risk based capital requirements for insurance companies binding? Journal of Banking and Finance 34, 1618–1627.

Debreu, G., 1953. Une économie de l'incertain. Miméo. Électricité de France.

Debreu, G., 1959. Theory of Value. Wiley, New York.

Definetti, B., 1957. Su una Impostazione Altenativa delta Teoria Collettiva del Rischio. Transactions of the XV International Congress of Actuaries 2, 433–443.

DeMarzo, P., Duffie, D., 1991. Corporate financial hedging with proprietary information. Journal of Economic Theory 53, 261–286.

Derrig, R.A., 2002. Insurance Fraud. Journal of Risk and Insurance 69, 271–287.

Derrig, R.A., Tennyson, S., 2011. The impact of rate regulation on claims: evidence from Massachusetts automobile insurance. Risk Management and Insurance Review 14, 173–199.

Diamond, P.A., Rothschild, M., 1978. Uncertainty in Economics: Readings and Exercises. Academic Press, New York.

Dieckmann, S., 2008. By Force of Nature: Explaining the Yield Spread on Catastrophe Bonds. Working Paper, Wharton School, University of Pennsylvania, Philadelphia, PA.

Dionne, G., 1982. Moral hazard and state-dependent utility function. Journal of Risk and Insurance 49, 405–423.

Dionne, G., 1983. Adverse selection and repeated insurance contracts. Geneva Papers on Risk and Insurance 8, 316–333.

Dionne, G., 1984. Search and insurance. International Economic Review 25, 357–367.

Dionne, G., Doherty, N., 1994. Adverse selection, commitment and renegotiation: extension to and evidence from insurance markets. Journal of Political Economy 102, 209–235.

Dionne, G., Eeckhoudt, L., 1984. Insurance and saving: some further results. Insurance: Mathematics and Economics 3, 101–110.

Dionne, G., Eeckhoudt, L., 1985. Self insurance, self protection and increased risk aversion. Economics Letters 17, 39–42.

Dionne, G., Eeckhoudt, L., Gollier, C., 1993. Increases in risk and optimal portfolio. International Economic Review 34, 309–320.

Dionne, G., Fombaron, N., Doherty, N., 2013. Adverse selection in insurance contracting. In: Dionne, G. (Ed.), The Handbook of Insurance, second ed. Springer, New York.

Dionne, G., Gagné, R., 2001. Deductible contracts against fraudulent claims: evidence from automobile insurance. Review of Economics and Statistics 83, 290–301.

Dionne, G., Gagné, R., 2002. Replacement cost endorsement and opportunistic fraud in automobile insurance. Journal of Risk and Uncertainty 24, 213–230.

Dionne, G., Gouriéroux, C., Vanasse, C., 2001. Testing for evidence of adverse selection in the automobile insurance market: a comment. Journal of Political Economy 109, 444–453.

Dionne, G., Giuliano, F., Picard, P., 2009. Optimal auditing with scoring: theory and application to insurance fraud. Management Science 55, 58–70.

Dionne, G., Ingabire, M.G., 2001. Diffidence theorem, state-dependent preferences, and DARA. Geneva Papers on Risk and Insurance Theory 26, 139–154.

Dionne, G., Lasserre, P., 1985. Adverse selection, repeated insurance contracts and announcement strategy. Review of Economic Studies 52, 719–723.

Dionne, G., Lasserre, P., 1987. Dealing with Moral Hazard and Adverse Selection Simultaneously. Working Paper, University of Pennsylvania.

Dionne, G., Li, J., 2011. The impact of prudence on optimal prevention revisited. Economics Letters 113, 147–149.

Dionne, G., and Li, J., 2012. When can expected utility handle first-order risk aversion? http://dx.doi.org/10.2139/ssrn.2197741.

Dionne, G., Li, J., 2013. Comparative Ross risk aversion in the presence of mean dependent risks. Journal of Mathematical Economics, http://dx.doi.org/10.1016/j.jmateco.2013.08.001.

Dionne, G., Michaud, P.C., Dahchour, M., 2013a. Separating moral hazard from adverse selection and learning in automobile insurance: longitudinal evidence from France. Journal of the European Economic Association 11, 897–917.

Dionne, G., Michaud, P.C., Pinquet, J., 2013b. A review of recent theoretical and empirical analyses of asymmetric information in road safety and automobile insurance. Research in Transportation Economics 43, 85–97.

Dionne, G., Pinquet, J., Maurice, M., Vanasse, C., 2011. Incentive mechanisms for safe driving: a comparative analysis with dynamic data. Review of Economics and Statistics 93, 218–227.

Dionne, G., St-Michel, P., 1991. Moral hazard and workers' compensation. Review of Economics and Statistics 73, 236–244.

Dionne, G., Triki, T., 2013. On risk management determinants: what really matters? European Journal of Finance 19, 145–164.

Dionne, G., Vanasse, C., 1992. Automobile insurance ratemaking in the presence of asymmetrical information. Journal of Applied Econometrics 7, 149–165.

Dionne, G., Wang, K., 2013. Does insurance fraud in automobile theft insurance fluctuate with the business cycle? Journal of Risk and Uncertainty 47, 67–92.

Doherty, N., 1981. The measurement of output and economies of scale in property-liability insurance. Journal of Risk and Insurance 48, 390–402.

Doherty, N., 1984. Portfolio efficient insurance buying strategies. Journal of Risk and Insurance 51, 205–224.

Doherty, N., 1989. On the capital structure of insurance firms. In: Cummins, J.D., Derrig, R.A. (Eds.), Financial Models of Insurer Solvency. Kluwer Academic Publishers, The Netherlands.

Doherty, N., 1997. Innovations in managing catastrophe risk. Journal of Risk and Insurance 64, 713–718.

Doherty, N.A., 2000. Innovation in corporate risk management: the case of catastrophe risk. In: Dionne, G. (Ed.), The Handbook of Insurance. Kluwer Academic Publishers, Boston.

Doherty, N., Dionne, G., 1993. Insurance with undiversifiable risk: contract structure and organizational form of insurance firms. Journal of Risk and Uncertainty 6, 187–203.

Doherty, N., Garven, J.R., 1986. Price regulation in property/liability insurance: a contingent claims approach. Journal of Finance 41, 1031–1050.

Doherty, N.A., Garven, J.R., 1995. Insurance cycles: Interest rates and the capacity constraint model. Journal of Business 68, 383–404.

Doherty, N., Kang, R.B., 1988. Price instability for a financial intermediary: interest rates and insurance price cycles. Journal of Banking and Finance 12, 191–214.

Doherty, N., Loubergé, H., Schlesinger, H., 1987. Additive and multiplicative risk premiums. Scandinavian Actuarial Journal 13, 41–49.

Doherty, N.A., Richter, A., 2002. Moral hazard, basis risk, and gap insurance. Journal of Risk and Insurance 69, 9–24.

Doherty, N., Schlesinger, H., 1983a. The optimal deductible for an insurance policy when initial wealth is random. Journal of Business 56, 555–565.

Doherty, N., Schlesinger, H., 1983b. Optimal insurance in incomplete markets. Journal of Political Economy 91, 1045–1054.

Doherty, N., Schlesinger, H., 1990. Rational insurance purchasing: considerations of contract non-performance. Quarterly Journal of Economics 105, 243–253.

Doherty, N.A., Tinic, S., 1981. A note on reinsurance under conditions of capital market equilibrium. Journal of Finance 48, 949–953.

Downs, D.H., Sommer, D.W., 1999. Monitoring, ownership, and risk-taking: the impact of guaranty funds. Journal of Risk and Insurance 66, 477–497.

Drèze, J., 1962. L'utilité sociale d'une vie humaine. Revue Française de Recherche Opérationnelle 6, 93–118.

Drèze, J., 1974. Axiomatic theories of choice, cardinal utility and subjective probability: a review. In: Drèze, J. (Ed.), Allocation under Uncertainty: Equilibrium and Optimality. Wiley. Reprinted in Diamond and Rothschild (1978).

Drèze, J., 1981. Inferring risk tolerance from deductibles in insurance contracts. Geneva Papers on Risk and Insurance 20, 48–52.

Drèze, J., 1987. Decision theory with moral hazard and state-dependent preferences. In: Drèze, J., (Ed.), Essays on Economic Decisions under Uncertainty. Cambridge University Press.

Drèze, J., Modigliani, F., 1972. Consumption decisions under uncertainty. Journal of Economic Theory 5, 308–335.

Dye, R.A., 1986. Optimal monitoring policies in agencies. Rand Journal of Economics 17, 339–350.

Eckardt, M., Rathke-Doppner, S., 2010. The quality of insurance intermediary services—empirical evidence for Germany. Journal of Risk and Insurance 77, 667–701.

Eeckhoudt, L., Gollier, C., 2013. The effects of changes in risk on risk taking: A survey. In: Dionne, G. (Ed.), The Handbook of Insurance, second ed. Springer, New York.

Eeckhoudt, L., Hansen, P., 1980. Minimum and maximum prices, uncertainty and the theory of the competitive firm. American Economic Review 70, 1064–1068.

Eeckhoudt, L., Hansen, P., 1984. Mean-Preserving Changes in Risk with Tail-Dominance. Working paper 8413, Département de sciences économiques, Université de Montréal.

Eeckhoudt, L., Kimball, M., 1992. Background risk, prudence and the demand for insurance. In: Dionne, G. (Ed.), Contributions to Insurance Economics. Kluwer Academic Publishers, The Netherlands.

Ehrlich, J., Becker, G., 1972. Market insurance, self-insurance and self-protection. Journal of Political Economy 80, 623–648.

Eling, M., 2012. What do we know about market discipline in insurance? Risk Management and Insurance Review 15, 185–223.

Eling, M., Holzmuller, I., 2008. An overview and comparison of risk-based capital standards. Journal of Insurance Regulation 26, 31–60.

Eling, M., Schmeiser, H., Schmit, J.T., 2007. The Solvency II process: overview and critical analysis. Risk Management and Insurance Review 10, 69–85.

Eling, M., Schmit, J.T., 2012. Is there market discipline in the European insurance industry? An analysis of the German insurance market. Geneva Risk and Insurance Review 37, 180–207.

Ellul, A., Jotikasthira, C., Lundblad, C.T., 2011. Regulatory pressure and fire sales in the corporate bond market. Journal of Financial Economics 101, 596–620.

Epermanis, K., Harrington, S.E., 2006. Market discipline in property/casualty insurance: evidence from premium growth surrounding changes in financial strength ratings. Journal of Money, Credit, and Banking 38, 1515–1544.

Epstein, L.S., 1980. Decision-making and the temporal resolution of uncertainty. International Economic Review 21, 269–284.

Erhemjamts, K.C., Leverty, J.T., 2010. The demise of the mutual organizational form: an investigation of the life insurance industry. Journal of Money, Credit, and Banking 42, 1011–1036.

Erhemjamts, K.C., Phillips, R.D., 2012. Form over matter: differences in the incentives to convert using full versus partial demutualization in the U.S. life insurance industry. Journal of Risk and Insurance 79, 305–334.

Etgar, M., 1976. Service performance of insurance distributors. Journal of Risk and Insurance 43, 487–499.

Fagart, M.C., Fluet, C., 2009. Liability insurance under the negligence rule. Rand Journal of Economics 40, 486–509.

Fagart, M.C., Fombaron, N., Jeleva, M., 2002. Risk mutualization and competition in insurance markets. Geneva Risk and Insurance Review 27, 115–141.

Fagart, M., Picard, P., 1999. Optimal insurance under random auditing. Geneva Papers on Risk and Insurance Theory 29, 29–54.

Fairley, W., 1979. Investment income and profit margins in property-liability insurance: theory and empirical results. Bell Journal of Economics 10, 192–210.

Fama, E.F., Jensen, M.C., 1983. Separation of ownership and control. Journal of Law and Economics 26, 301–325.

Fenn, G., Cole, R., 1994. Announcements of asset-quality problems and contagion effects in the life insurance industry. Journal of Financial Economics 35, 181–198.

Fields, J., Venezian, E., 1989. Profit cycles in property-liability insurance: a disaggregated approach. Journal of Risk and Insurance 56, 312–319.

Finken, S., Laux, C., 2009. Cat bonds and reinsurance: the competitive effect of information-insensitive triggers. Journal of Risk and Insurance 76, 579–605.

Finsinger, J., Pauly, M.V., 1984. Reserve levels and reserve requirements for profit-maximizing insurance firms. In: Bamberg, G., Spremann, K. (Eds.), Risk and Capital. Springer-Verlag, pp 160–180.

Fluet, C., Pannequin, F., 1997. Complete versus incomplete insurance contracts under adverse selection with multiple risks. Geneva Papers on Risk and Insurance Theory 22, 81–101.

Forman, C., Gron, A., 2011. Vertical integration and information technology investment in the insurance industry. Journal of Law, Economics, and Organization 27, 180–218.

Friedman, M., Savage, L.J., 1948. The utility analysis of choices involving risk. Journal of Political Economy 56, 279–304.

Froot, K.A., 2001. The market for catastrophe risk: a clinical examination. Journal of Financial Economics 60, 529–571.

Froot, K.A., 2007. Risk management, capital budgeting and capital structure policy for insurers and reinsurers. Journal of Risk and Insurance 74, 273–299.

Froot, K.A., O'Connell, P., 1997. The Pricing of U.S. Catastrophe Reinsurance. Working Paper 6043, National Bureau of Economic Research.

Froot, K.A., O'Connell, P., 2008. On the pricing of intermediated risks: theory and application to catastrophe reinsurance. Journal of Banking and Finance 32, 69–85.

Froot, K.A., Scharfstein, D., Stein, J.C., 1993. Risk management: coordinating corporate investment and financing policies. Journal of Finance 48, 1629–1658.

Froot, K.A., Stein, J.C., 1998. Risk management, capital budgeting, and capital structure policy for financial institutions: an integrated approach. Journal of Financial Economics 47, 55–82.

Garven, J.R., 1987. On the application of finance theory to the insurance firm. Journal of Financial Services Research 1, 57–76.

Geneva Association, 2010. Systemic Risk in Insurance: An Analysis of Insurance and Financial Stability. Geneva, Switzerland.

Geneva Association, 2012. Insurance and Resolution in Light of the Systemic Risk Debate. Geneva, Switzerland.

Gerber, H., 1978. Pareto-optimal risk exchanges and related decision problems. Astin Bulletin 10, 25–33.

Gollier, C., 1987a. The design of optimal insurance contracts without the nonnegativity constraint on claims. Journal of Risk and Insurance 54, 314–324.

Gollier, C., 1987b. Pareto-optimal risk sharing with fixed costs per claim. Scandinavian Actuarial Journal 13, 62–73.

Gollier, C., 1992. Economic theory of risk exchanges: a review. In: Dionne, G. (Ed.), Contributions to Insurance Economics. Kluwer Academic Publishers, The Netherlands.

Gollier, C., 2013. The economics of optimal insurance design. In: Dionne, G. (Ed.), The Handbook of Insurance, second ed. Springer, New York.

Gollier, C., Jullien, B., Treich, N., 2000. Scientific progress and irreversibility: an economic interpretation of the precautionary principle. Journal of Public Economics 75, 229–253.

Gould, J.P., 1969. The expected utility hypothesis and the selection of optimal deductibles for a given insurance policy. Journal of Business 42, 143–151.

Grabowski, H., Viscusi, W.K., Evans, W.N., 1989. Price and availability tradeoffs of automobile insurance regulation. Journal of Risk and Insurance 56, 275–299.

Grace, M.F., 2010. The Insurance Industry and Systemic Risk: Evidence and Discussion. Working Paper, Georgia State University.

Grace, M.F., Harrington, S.E., 1998. Risk-based capital and solvency screening in property-liability insurance: hypotheses and empirical tests. Journal of Risk and Insurance 65, 213–243.

Grace, M.F., Harrington, S.E., Klein, , 1998. Identifying troubled life insurers: an analysis of the NAIC FAST system. Journal of Insurance Regulation 16, 249–290.

Grace, M.F., Hotchkiss, J., 1995. External impacts on the property-liability insurance cycle. Journal of Risk and Insurance 62, 738–754.

Graham, J., Rogers, D., 2002. Do firms hedge in response to tax incentives? Journal of Finance 57, 815–839.

Graham, J., Smith Jr., C., 1999. Tax incentives to hedge. Journal of Finance 54, 2241–2262.

Green, M.R., 1984. Insurance. In: The New Encyclopedia Britannica, 15th ed., vol. 9. Encyclopaedia Britannica, pp. 645–658.

Gron, A., 1994a. Capacity constraints and cycles in property-casualty insurance markets. RAND Journal of Economics 25, 110–127.

Gron, A., 1994b. Evidence of capacity constraints in insurance markets. Journal of Law and Economics 37, 349–377.

Gron, A., Winton, A., 2001. Risk overhang and market behavior. Journal of Business 74, 591–612.

Grossman, H.I., 1979. Adverse selection, dissembling and competitive equilibrium. Bell Journal of Economics 10, 330–343.

Grossman, S., Hart, O.D., 1983. An analysis of the principal-agent problem. Econometrica 51, 7–45.

Grundl, H., Schmeiser, H., 2007. Capital allocation for insurance companies: what good is it? Journal of Risk and Insurance 74, 301–317.

Haley, J., 1993. A cointegration analysis of the relationship between underwriting margins and interest rates: 1930–1989. Journal of Risk and Insurance 60, 480–493.

Haley, J., 1995. A by-line cointegration analysis of underwriting margins and interest rates in the property-liability insurance industry. Journal of Risk and Insurance 62, 755–763.

Hansmann, H., 1985. The organization of insurance companies: mutual versus stock. Journal of Law, Economics, and Organization 1, 125–153.

Harrington, S.E., 1984. The impact of rate regulation on prices and underwriting results in the property-liability insurance industry: a survey. Journal of Risk and Insurance 51, 577–617.

Harrington, S.E., 1987. A note on the impact of auto insurance rate regulation. Review of Economics and Statistics 69, 166–170.

Harrington, S.E., 2000. Insurance rate regulation in the 20th century. Journal of Insurance Regulation 19, 204–218.

Harrington, S.E., 2002. Effects of prior approval regulation in automobile insurance. In: Cummins, J.D. (Ed.), Deregulating Property-Liability Insurance. AEI-Brookings Joint Center for Regulatory Studies.

Harrington, S.E., 2004a. Capital adequacy in insurance and reinsurance. In: Scott, H. (Ed.), Capital Adequacy Beyond Basel: Banking, Securities, and Insurance. Oxford University Press.

Harrington, S.E., 2004b. Market discipline in insurance and reinsurance. In: Borio, C. et al. (Eds.), Market Discipline: The Evidence across Countries and Industries. MIT Press.

Harrington, S.E., 2004c. Tort liability, insurance rates, and the insurance cycle. In: Herring, R., Litan, R. (Eds.), Brookings-Wharton Papers on Financial Services: 2004. Brookings Institution Press.

Harrington, S.E., 2009. The financial crisis, systemic risk, and the future of insurance regulation. Journal of Risk and Insurance 76, 785–819.

Harrington, S.E., Danzon, P.M., 1994. Price cutting in liability insurance markets. Journal of Business 67, 511–538.

Harrington, S.E., Danzon, P.M., 2000a. The economics of liability insurance. In: Dionne, G. (Ed.), Handbook of Insurance. Kluwer Academic Publishers.

Harrington, S.E., Danzon, P.M., 2000b. Rate regulation, safety incentives, and loss growth in workers' compensation insurance. Journal of Business 73, 569–595.

Harrington, S.E., Danzon, P.M., Epstein, A.J., 2008. 'Crises' in medical malpractice insurance: evidence of excessive price-cutting in the preceding soft market. Journal of Banking and Finance 32, 157–169.

Harrington, S.E., Mann, S.V., Niehaus, G., 1995. Insurer capital structure decisions and the viability of insurance derivatives. Journal of Risk and Insurance 62, 483–508.

Harrington, S.E., Niehaus, G., 1999. Basis risk with PCS catastrophe insurance derivative contracts. Journal of Risk and Insurance 66, 49–82.

Harrington, S.E., Niehaus, G., 2002. Enterprise risk management: the case of united grain growers. Journal of Applied Corporate Finance 14, 71–80.

Harrington, S.E., Niehaus, G., 2003. Capital, corporate income taxes, and catastrophe insurance. Journal of Financial Intermediation 12, 365–389.

Harrington, S.E., Niehaus, G., Yu, T., 2013. Insurance price volatility and underwriting cycles. In: Dionne,, The Handbook of Insurance, second ed. Springer, New York.

Harrington, S.E., Yu, T., 2003. Do property/casualty insurance underwriting margins have unit roots? Journal of Risk and Insurance 70, 715–734.

Harris, M., Townsend, R.M., 1981. Resource allocation under asymmetric information. Econometrica 49, 33–64.

Hellwig, M., 1988. A note of the specification of interfirm communication in insurance markets with adverse selection. Journal of Economic Theory 46, 154–163.

Henriet, D., Rochet, J.C., 1986. La logique des systèmes bonus-malus en assurance automobile: une approche théorique. Annales d'Économie et de Statistique, 133–152.

Henry, C., 1974. Investment decisions under uncertainty: the irreversibility effect. American Economic Review 64, 1006–1012.

Herring, R.J., Vankudre, P., 1987. Growth opportunities and risk-taking by financial intermediaries. Journal of Finance 42, 583–600.

Hiebert, L.D., 1989. Optimal loss reduction and risk aversion. Journal of Risk and Insurance 56, 300–306.

Hilliard, J.I., Regan, L., Tennyson, S., 2013. Insurance distribution. In: Dionne, G. (Ed.), The Handbook of Insurance, second ed. Springer, New York.

Holmstrom, B., 1979. Moral hazard and observability. Bell Journal of Economics 10, 74–91.

Holzmuller, I., 2009. The United States RBC standards, solvency II and the SWISS solvency test: a comparative assessment. The Geneva Papers 34, 56–77.

Hong, K.H., Lew, K.O., MacMinn, R., Brockett, P., 2011. Mossin's theorem given random initial wealth. Journal of Risk and Insurance 78, 309–324.

Hosios, A.J., Peters, M., 1989. Repeated insurance contracts with adverse selection and limited commitment. Quarterly Journal of Economics 104, 229–253.

Hoy, M., 1982. Categorizing risks in the insurance industry. Quarterly Journal of Economics 97, 321–336.

Hoy, M., Robson, R.J., 1981. Insurance as a Giffen good. Economics Letters 8, 47–51.

Hoyt, R.E., Liebenberg, A.P., 2011. The value of enterprise risk management. Journal of Risk and Insurance. 78, 795–822.

Ibragimov, R., Jaffee, D., Walden, J., 2010. Pricing and capital allocation for multiline insurance firms. Journal of Risk and Insurance 77, 551–578.

Ippolito, R., 1979. The effects of price regulation in the automobile insurance industry. Journal of Law and Economics 22, 55–89.

Jawad, F., Bruneau, C., Sghaier, N., 2009. Nonlinear cointegration relationships between non-life insurance premiums and financial markets. Journal of Risk and Insurance 76, 753–783.

Jewitt, I., 1988. Justifying the first-order approach to principal-agent problems. Econometrica 56, 1177–1190.

Johnson, J., Flanigan, G., Weisbart, S.N., 1981. Returns to scale in the property and liability insurance industry. Journal of Risk and Insurance 48, 18–45.

Jones-Lee, M.W., 1974. The value of changes in the probability of death or injury. Journal of Political Economy 82, 835–849.

Joskow, P.J., 1973. Cartels, competition and regulation in the property-liability insurance industry. Bell Journal of Economics and Management Science 4, 327–427.

Jullien, B., Salanié, B., Salanié, F., 1999. Should more risk-averse agents exert more effort? Geneva Papers on Risk and Insurance Theory 24, 19–28.

Kahane, Y., Kroll, Y., 1985. Optimal insurance coverage in situations of pure and speculative risk and the risk free asset. Insurance Mathematics and Economics 4, 191–199.

Karni, E., 1985. Decision Making Under Uncertainty. Harvard University Press, Cambridge, MA.

Karni, E., 1990. A Definition of Subjective Probabilities with State-Dependent Preferences. Working paper # 247, Johns Hopkins University.

Karni, E., 1992. Optimal insurance: a non-expected utility analysis. In: Dionne, G. (Ed.), Contributions to Insurance Economics. Kluwer Academic Publishers, The Netherlands.

Karni, E., 2013. Survey on Expected Utility (Chapter 2 in this Handbook).

Kaufman, G., 1994. Bank contagion: a review of theory and evidence. Journal of Financial Services Research, 123–150.

Keeton, W.R., Kwerel, E., 1984. Externalities in automobile insurance and the uninsured driver problem. Journal of Law and Economics 27, 149–180.

Kihlstrom, R.E., Pauly, M., 1971. The role of insurance in the allocation of risk. American Economic Review 61, 371–379.

Kihlstrom, R.E., Romer, D., Williams, S., 1981. Risk aversion with random initial wealth. Econometrica 49, 911–920.

Kihlstrom, R.E., Roth, A.E., 1982. Risk aversion and the negotiation of insurance contracts. Journal of Risk and Insurance 49, 372–387.

Kim, W.J., Mayers, D., Smith, C.W., 1996. On the choice of insurance distribution systems. Journal of Risk and Insurance 63, 207–227.

Kimball, M., 1990. Precautionary saving in the small and in the large. Econometrica 58, 53–73.

Kleffner, A.E., Doherty, N.A., 1996. Costly risk and the supply of catastrophic insurance. Journal of Risk and Insurance 63, 657–671.

Klein, R.W., 2012. Insurance Regulation and Challenge of Solvency II: Modernizing the System of U.S. Solvency Regulation. National Association of Mutual Insurance Companies.

Klein, R.W., 2013. Insurance market regulation: catastrophe risk, competition and systemic risk. In: Dionne, G. (Ed.), The Handbook of Insurance, second ed. Springer, New York.

Kraus, A., Ross, S.A., 1982. The determinants of fair profits for the property-liability insurance firm. Journal of Finance 37, 1015–1030.

Kunreuther, H., Pauly, M.V., 1985. Market equilibrium with private knowledge: an insurance example. Journal of Public Economics 26, 269–288.

Lacker, J.M., Weinbery, J.A., 1989. Optimal contracts under costly state falsification. Journal of Political Economy 97, 1343–1363.

Laffont, J.J., 1989. The Economics of Uncertainty and Information. MIT Press, Cambridge, MA.

Laffont, J.J., Martimort, D., 2002. The Theory of Incentives: The Principal Agent Model. Princeton University Press.

Lakdawalla, D., Zanjani, G., 2012. Catastrophe bonds, reinsurance, and the optimal collateralization of risk transfer. Journal of Risk and Insurance 79, 449–476.

Lamm-Tennant, J., Starks, L.T., 1993. Stock versus mutual ownership structures: the risk implications. Journal of Business 66, 29–46.

Lazar, D., Denuit, M., 2012. Multivariate analysis of premium dynamics in P&L insurance. Journal of Risk and Insurance 79, 431–448.

Lee, S.J., Mayers, D., Smith Jr., C.W., 1997. Guaranty finds and risk-taking behavior: evidence for the insurance industry. Journal of Financial Economics 44, 3–24.

Lee, S.J., Smith, C.W., 1999. Property/casualty insurance guaranty funds and insurer vulnerability to misfortune. Journal of Banking and Finance 23, 1437–1456.

Leland, H.E., 1972. Theory of the firm facing uncertain demand. American Economic Review 62, 278–291.

Lemaire, J., 1990. Borch's theorem: a historical survey of applications. In: Loubergé, H. (Ed.), Risk. Kluwer Academic Publishers, Information and Insurance, pp. 15–37.

Leng, C., 2006. Stationarity and stability of underwriting profits in property-liability insurance: parts I and II. Journal of Risk Finance 7, 38–63.

Leng, C., Meier, U.B., 2006. Analysis of multinational underwriting cycles in property-liability insurance. Journal of Risk Finance 7, 146–159.

Lévy-Garboua, L., Montmarquette, C., 1990. The Demand for Insurance against More than One Risk, with an Application to Social Insurance. Mimeo, Economics Department, Université de Montréal.

Li, J., 2011. The demand for a risky asset in the presence of a background risk. Journal of Economic Theory 146, 372–391.

LiCalzi, M., Spaeter, M., 2003. Distributions for the first-order approach to principal-agent problems. Economic Theory 21, 167–173.

Ligon, J.A., Thistle, P.D., 2005. The Formation of mutual insurers in markets with adverse selection. Journal of Business 78, 529–555.

Loubergé, H., 2013. Developments in risk and insurance economics: the past 40 years. In: Dionne, G. (Ed.), Handbook of Insurance, second ed. Springer, New York.

MacMinn, R., Garven, J., 2013. On the demand for corporate insurance. In: Dionne, G. (Ed.), Handbook of Insurance, second ed. Springer, New York.

Machina, M.J., 1987. Choice under uncertainty: problems solved and unsolved. Journal of Economic Perspectives 1, 121–154.

Machina, M.J., 2013. Non-expected utility and the robustness of the classical insurance paradigm. In: Dionne, G. (Ed.), Handbook of Insurance, second ed. Springer, New York.

Main, B., 1982. Business insurance and large, widely-held corporations. Geneva Papers on Risk and Insurance 7, 237–247.

Marshall, J.M., 1976a. Moral hazard. American Economic Review 66, 880–890.

Marshall, J.M., 1976b. Moral Hazard. Working Paper no 18, University of California, Santa Barbara.

Marshall, J.M., 1992. Optimum insurance with deviant beliefs. In: Dionne, G. (Ed.), Contributions to Insurance Economics. Kluwer Academic Publishers, The Netherlands.

Marvel, H.P., 1982. Exclusive dealing. Journal of Law and Economics 25, 1–25.

Mayers, D., Smith, C.W., 1981. Contractual provisions, organizational structure, and conflict control in insurance markets. Journal of Business 54, 407–434.

Mayers, D., Smith, C.W., 1982. On the corporate demand for insurance. Journal of Business, 281–296.

Mayers, D., Smith, C.W., 1983. The interdependence of individual portfolio decisions and the demand for insurance. Journal of Political Economy 91, 304–311.

Mayers, D., Smith, C.W., 1986. Ownership structure and control: the mutualization of stock life insurance companies. Journal of Financial Economics 16, 73–98.

Mayers, D., Smith, C.W., 1987. Corporate insurance and the underinvestment problem. Journal of Risk and Insurance 54, 45–54.

Mayers, D., Smith, C.W., 1988. Ownership structure across lines of property-casualty insurance. Journal of Law and Economics 31, 351–378.

Mayers, D., Smith, C.W., 1990. On the corporate demand for insurance: evidence from the reinsurance market. Journal of Business 63, 19–40.

Mayers, D., Smith, C.W., 2002. Ownership structure and control: property-casualty insurer conversion to stock charter. Journal of Financial Services Research 21, 117–144.

Mayers, D., Smith, C.W., 2013. On the choice of organizational form: theory and evidence from the insurance industry. In: Dionne, G. (Ed.), Handbook of Insurance, second ed. Springer, New York.

McGuire, T.G., 2012. Demand for Health Insurance. In: Pauly, M.V., McGuire, T.G., Barros, P.P. (Eds.), Handbook of Health Economics, vol. 2. North-Holland.

McNamara, M.J., Rhee, S.G., 1992. Ownership structure and performance: the demutualization of life insurers. Journal of Risk and Insurance 59, 221–238.

Meier, U.B., 2006a. Multi-national underwriting cycles in property-liability insurance: part I—some theory and empirical results. Journal of Risk Finance 7, 64–82.

Meier, U.B., 2006b. Multi-national underwriting cycles in property-liability insurance: part II—model extensions and further empirical results. Journal of Risk Finance 7, 83–97.

Meier, U.B., Outreville, J.-F., 2006. Business cycles in insurance and reinsurance: the case of France, Germany and Switzerland. Journal of Risk Finance 7, 160–176.

Menezes, C., Hanson, D., 1970. On the theory of risk aversion. International Economic Review 2, 481–487.

Merton, R.C., 1971. Optimum consumption and portfolio rules in a continuous-time model. Journal of Economic Theory 3, 373–413.

Merton, R., Perold, A., 1993. Theory of risk capital in financial firms. Journal of Applied Corporate Finance 6, 16–32.

Meyer, J., Ormiston, M., 1985. Strong increases in risk and their comparative statics. International Economic Review 17, 425–437.

Meyer, J., Ormiston, M., 1989. Deterministic transformations of random variables and the comparative statics of risks. Journal of Risk and Uncertainty 2, 179–188.

Mirrlees, J., 1975. The theory of moral hazard and unobservable behavior—part I. Mimeo, Nuffield College, Oxford.

Miyazaki, H., 1977. The rat race and internal labor markets. Bell Journal of Economics 8, 394–418.

Moffet, D., 1975. Risk bearing and consumption theory. Astin Bulletin 8, 342–358.

Moffet, D., 1977. Optimal deductible and consumption theory. Journal of Risk and Insurance 44, 669–683.

Moffet, D., 1979. The risk sharing problem. Geneva Papers on Risk and Insurance 11, 5–13.

Mookherjee, D., Png, I., 1989. Optimal auditing insurance and redistribution. Quarterly Journal of Economics 104, 205–228.

Morrisey, M., 2013. Health insurance in the United States. In: Dionne, G. (Ed.), Handbook of Insurance, second ed. Springer, New York.

Mossin, J., 1968. Aspects of rational insurance purchasing. Journal of Political Economy 79, 553–568.

Munch, P., Smallwood, D.E., 1980. Solvency regulation in the property-liability insurance industry: empirical evidence. Bell Journal of Economics 11, 261–282.

Munch, P., Smallwood, D.E., 1982. Theory of solvency regulation in the property and casualty insurance industry. In: Fromm, G. (Ed.), Studies in Public Regulation. MIT Press.

Myers, S., 1977. Determinants of corporate borrowing. Journal of Financial Economics 5, 147–175.

Myers, S.C., Cohn, R.A., 1986. A discounted cash flow approach to property-liability insurance rate regulation. In: Cummins, J.D., Harrington, S.E. (Eds.), Fair Rate of Return in Property-Liability Insurance. Kluwer-Nijhoff Publishing.

Myers, S.C., Majluf, N., 1984. Corporate financing and investment decisions when firms have information that investors do not. Journal of Financial Economics 11, 187–221.

Myers, S.C., Read, J.A., 2001. Capital allocation for insurance companies. Journal of Risk and Insurance 68, 545–580.

Neale, F.R., Eastman, K., Peterson Drake, P., 2009. Dynamics of the market for medical malpractice insurance. Journal of Risk and Insurance 76, 221–247.

Niehaus, G., Mann, S.V., 1992. The trading of underwriting risk: an analysis of insurance futures contracts and reinsurance. Journal of Risk and Insurance 59, 601–627.

Nilssen, T., 2000. Consumer lock-in with asymmetric information. International Journal of Industrial Organization 19 (4), 641–666.

Outreville, J.-F., 1990. Underwriting cycles and rate regulation in automobile insurance markets. Journal of Insurance Regulation 8, 274–286.

Pashigian, B., Schkade, L., Menefee, G., 1966. The selection of an optimal deductible for a given insurance policy. Journal of Business 39, 35–44.

Pauly, M.V., 1968. The economics of moral hazard: comment. American Economic Review 58, 531–536.

Pauly, M.V., 1974. Overinsurance and public provision of insurance: the role of moral hazard and adverse selection. Quarterly Journal of Economics 88, 44–62.

Phillips, R.D., Cummins, J.D., Allen, F., 1998. Financial pricing of insurance in the multiple line insurance company. Journal of Risk and Insurance 65, 597–636.

Phillips, R.D., Cummins, J.D., Lin, Y., 2006. Capital Allocation and the Pricing of Financially Intermediated Risks: An Empirical Investigation. Working Paper, Wharton Financial Institutions Center.

Picard, P., 1996. Auditing claims in insurance market with fraud: the credibility issue. Journal of Public Economics 63, 27–56.

Picard, P., 2000. On the design of optimal insurance contracts under manipulation of audit cost. International Economic Review 41, 1049–1071.

Picard, P., 2009. Participating Insurance Contracts and the Rothschild-Stiglitz Equilibrium Puzzle. Working Paper, ECORE.

Picard, P., 2013. Economic analysis of insurance fraud. In: Dionne, G. (Ed.), Handbook of Insurance, second ed. Springer, New York.

Pinches, G.E., Trieschmann, J.S., 1973. A multivariate model for predicting financially distressed property-liability insurers. Journal of Risk and Insurance 40, 327–338.

Posey, L.L., Tennyson, S., 1998. The coexistence of distribution systems under price search: theory and some evidence from insurance. Journal of Economic Behavior and Organization 35, 95–115.

Pottier, S.W., Sommer, D.W., 2002. The effectiveness of public and private sector summary risk measures in predicting insurer insolvencies. Journal of Financial Services Research 21, 101–116.

Pratt, J.W., 1964. Risk aversion in the small and in the large. Econometrica 32, 122–136.

Quiggin, J., 2013. Survey on Non-Expected Utility Models (Chapter 14 in this Handbook).

Radner, R., 1968. Competitive equilibrium under uncertainty. Econometrica 36, 31–58.

Radner, R., 1981. Monitoring cooperative agreements in a repeated principal-agent relationship. Econometrica 49, 1127–1148.

Raviv, A., 1979. The design of an optimal insurance policy. American Economic Review 69, 84–96.

Rea, S.A., 1987. The market response to the elimination of sex-based annuities. Southern Economic Journal 54, 55–63.

Rea, S.A., 1992. Insurance classifications and social welfare. In: Dionne, G. (Ed.), Contributions to Insurance Economics. Kluwer Academic Publishers, The Netherlands.

Rees, R., Gravelle, H., Wambach, A., 1999. Regulation of insurance markets. The Geneva Papers on Risk and Insurance Theory 24, 55–68.

Regan, L., 1997. Vertical integration in the property-liability insurance industry: a transaction cost approach. Journal of Risk and Insurance 64, 41–62.

Regan, L., 1999. Expense ratios across insurance distribution systems: an analysis by lines of business. Risk Management and Insurance Review 2, 44–59.

Regan, L., Tennyson, S., 1996. Agent discretion and the choice of insurance marketing system. Journal of Law and Economics 39, 637.

Regan, L., Tzeng, L.Y., 1999. Organizational form in the property-liability insurance industry. Journal of Risk and Insurance 66, 253–273.

Riley, J.G., 1979. Informational equilibrium. Econometrica 47, 331–359.

Riley, J.G., 1983. Adverse selection and statistical discrimination: further comments. Journal of Public Economics 20, 131–137.

Rogerson, W.P., 1985a. The first-order approach to principal-agent problems. Econometrica 53, 1357–1367.

Rogerson, W.P., 1985b. Repeated moral hazard. Econometrica 53, 69–76.

Ross, S., 1973. The economic theory of agency: the principal's problem. American Economic Review 63, 134–139.

Ross, S., 1981. Some stronger measures of risk aversion in the small and in the large with applications. Econometrica 49, 621–638.

Rothschild, C., 2011. The efficiency of categorical discrimination in insurance markets. Journal of Risk and Insurance 78, 267–285.

Rothschild, M., Stiglitz, J.E., 1970. Increasing risk, I: a definition. Journal of Economic Theory 2, 225–243.

Rothschild, M., Stiglitz, J., 1971. Increasing risk, II: its economic consequences. Journal of Economic Theory 3, 66–84.

Rothschild, M., Stiglitz, J., 1976. Equilibrium in competitive insurance markets: an essay on the economics of imperfect information. Quarterly Journal of Economics 90, 629–650. Reprinted in G. Dionne and S. Harrington (Eds.), Foundations of Insurance Economics – Readings in Economics and Finance, Kluwer Academic Publishers, 1992..

Rowell, D., Connelly, L.B., 2012. A history of the term 'moral hazard'. Journal of Risk and Insurance 79, 1051–1075.

Rubinstein, A., Yaari, M.E., 1983. Repeated insurance contracts and moral hazard. Journal of Economic Theory 30, 74–97.

Salanié, B., 1997. The Economics of Contracts: A Primer. MIT Press, Cambridge, MA.

Sandmo, A., 1969. Capital risk, consumption and portfolio choice. Econometrica 37, 568–599.

Sandmo, A., 1970. The effect of uncertainty on saving decisions. Review of Economic Studies 37, 353–360.

Sandmo, A., 1971. On the theory of the competitive firms under price uncertainty. American Economic Review 61, 65–73.

Sass, T.R., Gisser, M., 1989. Agency cost, firm size, and exclusive dealing. Journal of Law and Economics 32, 381–400.

Schlesinger, H., 1981. The optimal level of deductibility in insurance contracts. Journal of Risk and Insurance 48, 465–481.

Schlesinger, H., 2013. The theory of insurance demand. In: Dionne, G. (Ed.), The Handbook of Insurance, second ed. Springer, New York.

Schlesinger, H., Doherty, N., 1985. Incomplete markets for insurance: an overview. Journal of Risk and Insurance 52, 402–423.

Schoemaker, P.J., 1982. The expected utility model: its variants, evidence and limitations. Journal of Economic Literature 20, 529–563.

Schulenburg, J.M., 1986. Optimal insurance purchasing in the presence of compulsory insurance and insurable risks. Geneva Papers on Risk and Insurance 38, 5–16.

Shavell, S., 1979a. Risk-sharing and incentives in the principal and agent relationship. Bell Journal of Economics 10, 55–73.

Shavell, S., 1979b. On moral hazard and insurance. Quarterly Journal of Economics 93, 541–562.

Shavell, S., 1982. On liability and insurance. Bell Journal of Economics 13, 120–132.

Shavell, S., 1986. The judgment proof problem. International Review of Law and Economics 6, 45–58.

Shavell, S., 1987a. The optimal use of nonmonetary sanctions as a deterrent. American Economic Review 77, 584–592.

Shavell, S., 1987b. Economic Analysis of Accident Law. Harvard University Press, Cambridge.

Shavell, S., 2004. Foundations of economic analysis of law. Belknap Press of Harvard University., 737.

Sherris, M., 2006. Solvency, capital allocation, and fair rate of return in insurance. Journal of Risk and Insurance 73, 71–96.

Smallwood, D., 1975. Regulation, and product quality in the automobile insurance industry. In: Phillips, Almarin. (Ed.), Promoting Competition in Regulated Markets. The Brooking Institution.

Smart, M., 2000. Competitive insurance markets with two unobservables. International Economic Review 41, 153–169.

Smith, C., Stulz, R., 1985. The determinants of firms' hedging policies. Journal of Financial and Quantitative Analysis 20, 391–405.

Smith, M.L., 1989. Investment returns and yields to holders of insurance. Journal of Business 62, 81–98.

Smith, M.L., Buser, S.A., 1987. Risk aversion, insurance costs and optimal property-liability coverages. Journal of Risk and Insurance 54, 225–245.

Smith, V., 1968. Optimal insurance coverage. Journal of Political Economy 79, 68–77.

Snow, A., 2009. On the possibility of profitable self-selection contracts in competitive insurance markets. Journal of Risk and Insurance 76, 249–259.

Sommer, D., 1996. The impact of firm risk on property-liability insurance prices. Journal of Risk and Insurance 63, 501–514.

Spence, M., 1978. Product differentiation and performance in insurance markets. Journal of Public Economics 10, 427–447.

Spence, M., Zeckhauser, R., 1971. Insurance, information and individual action. American Economic Review 61, 380–387.

Stiglitz, J.E., 1977. Monopoly, non-linear pricing and imperfect information: the insurance market. Review of Economic Studies 44, 407–430.

Stiglitz, J.E., Weiss, A., 1984. Sorting Out the Differences Between Screening and Signaling Models. Mimeo, Princeton University.

Stulz, R., 1990. Managerial discretion and optimal financing policies. Journal of Financial Economics 26, 3–28.

Swiss Re, 2003. Reinsurance—A Systemic Risk? Sigma No. 5.

Tapiero, C.S., Kahane, Y., Jacques, L., 1986. Insurance premiums and default risk in mutual insurance. Scandinavian Actuarial Journal, 82–97.

Tapiero, C.S., Zuckerman, D., Kahane, Y., 1978. Regulation of an insurance firm with a compound poisson claim process. In: Kahane, Y. (Ed.), New Frontiers in Insurance. Papirus Press.

Tennyson, S.L., 1993. Regulatory lag in automobile insurance. Journal of Risk and Insurance 60, 36–58.

Townsend, R., 1979. Optimal contracts and competitive contracts with costly state verification. Journal of Economic Theory 22, 265–293.

Tufano, P., 1996. Who manages risk? An empirical examination of risk management practices in the gold mining industry. Journal of Finance 51, 1097–1137.

Turnbull, S., 1983. Additional aspects of rational insurance purchasing. Journal of Business 56, 217–229.

Venezian, E.C., 1985. Ratemaking methods and profit cycles in property and liability insurance. Journal of Risk and Insurance 52, 477–500.

Viauroux, C., 2013. Tax sharing in insurance markets: a useful parametrization. Mimeo, University of Maryland. Journal of Risk and Insurance. http://dx.doi.org/10.1111/j.1539-6975.2013.01528.x

Villeneuve, B., 2003. Concurrence et Antisélection Multidimensionnelle en Assurance. Annales d'Economie et Statistiques 69, 119–142.

Viscusi, W.K., Evans, W.N., 1990. Utility functions that depend on health status: estimates and economic implications. American Economic Review 80, 353–374.

Viswanathan, K., Cummins, J.D., 2003. Ownership structure changes in the insurance industry: an analysis of demutualization. Journal of Risk and Insurance 70, 401–437.

Von Neumann, J., Morgenstern, O., 1947. Theory of Games and Economic Behavior. Princeton University Press.

Wambach, A., 2000. Introducing heterogeneity in the rothschild-stiglitz model. Journal of Risk and Insurance 67, 579–591.

Weiss, M.A., Chung, J.-H., 2004. U.S. reinsurance prices, financial quality, and global capacity. Journal of Risk and Insurance 71, 437–467.

Weiss, M.A., Tennyson, S., Regan, L., 2010. The effects of regulated premium subsidies on insurance costs: an empirical analysis of automobile insurance. Journal of Risk and Insurance 77, 597–624.

Wilson, C., 1977. A model of insurance markets with incomplete information. Journal of Economic Theory 12, 167–207.

Wilson, R., 1968. The theory of syndicates. Econometrica 36, 113–132.

Winter, R.A., 1988. The liability crisis and the dynamics of competitive insurance markets. Yale Journal on Regulation 5, 455–499.

Winter, R.A., 1991a. The liability insurance market. Journal of Economic Perspectives 5, 15–136.

Winter, R.A., 1991b. Solvency regulation and the insurance cycle. Economic Inquiry 29, 458–471.

Winter, R.A., 1994. The dynamics of competitive insurance markets. Journal of Financial Intermediation 3, 379–415.

Winter, R.A., 2013. Optimal insurance under moral hazard. In: Dionne, G. (Ed.), The Handbook of Insurance, second ed. Springer, New York.

Zanjani, G., 2002a. Market Discipline and Government Guarantees in Life Insurance. Working Paper, Federal Reserve Bank of New York.

Zanjani, G., 2002b. Pricing and capital allocation in catastrophe insurance. Journal of Financial Economics 65, 283–305.

Zanjani, G., 2007. Regulation, capital, and the evolution of organizational form in U.S. life insurance. American Economic Review, 973–983.

Zanjani, G., 2010. An economic approach to capital allocation. Journal of Risk and Insurance 77, 523–549.

Zeckhauser, R., Keeler, E., 1970. Another type of risk aversion. Econometrica 38, 661–665.

CHAPTER 6

Uncertainty and Imperfect Information in Markets

Benjamin E. Hermalin
University of California Berkeley, CA, USA

Contents

Abstract

This chapter deals with uncertainty and incomplete information in markets. It first considers situations in which the contract proposer is the ignorant party with the problem of designing a mechanism that induces the counter party, who is exogenously endowed with his information, to reveal that information in such a way that maximizes the contract proposer's expected payoff. In contrast to settings of symmetric information, inefficiencies will tend to arise in equilibrium. Also considered is the situation when each side of the transaction is endowed with his or her own payoff-relevant information. Here the focus is on whether and how a social planner could design a contract to achieve efficiency. The following section assumes it is the contract proposer who is endowed with the payoff-relevant information. The quintessential example of this is a seller who knows the quality of the good she seeks to sell. Because she cannot commit fully to not deceive her counter party, inefficiencies arise. The last section examines the problems that arise if the asymmetry of information arises endogenously, because one party's prior-to-trade actions provide him or her payoff-relevant information.

Keywords

Tariff Construction, Economic Mechanism, Revelation Principle, Spence-Mirrlees Condition, Direct Revelation Mechanism, Linear Pricing, Insurance Theory, Economic Trade Theory, Information Asymmetry

Handbook of the Economics of Risk and Uncertainty, Volume1
ISSN 2211-7547, http://dx.doi.org/10.1016/B978-0-444-53685-3.00006-4

6.1 INTRODUCTION

Almost every market transaction is plagued by one party, at least, being ignorant of pertinent information. In some instances, both parties are ignorant of the same thing: neither farmer nor commercial granary know what the weather will be over the coming season when agreeing to a futures contract. In many instances, however, while one party is ignorant, the other knows the relevant information (or at least has better information): you know your willingness to pay for items in a shop, but the shopkeeper does not; you know the reliability of the used car you are selling, a potential buyer does not; and so on.

Although instances of common ignorance are not without interest—they, for example, are critical to understanding insurance and financial markets—such markets can often be analyzed using "textbook" methods once the situation is reformulated in terms of state-contingent commodities (see, e.g., Section 6.2.2.1 *infra*).[1] What are arguably of greater interest are settings in which ignorance (or, equivalently, knowledge) is asymmetric between the parties: one party has better information about payoff-relevant factors than the other. Those settings are the focus of this chapter.

Asymmetry of information can arise in many ways and at various points in a bilateral relationship. Some examples:

1. one party can simply be endowed with better information than the other prior to any transaction (e.g., a used-car seller has experienced her car's reliability);
2. a party takes a payoff-relevant action, unobservable to her counter party, prior to any transaction (e.g., a seller knows the quality of materials used in the manufacture of the product she sells);
3. after entering into a relationship, a party acquires better information (e.g., a contractor learns how easy a job will be once on it);
4. after entering into a relationship, a party takes a payoff-relevant action, unobservable to his counter party (e.g., an insured knows what precautions he takes to avoid a loss).

Asymmetry of information can also be relevant in *multilateral* settings (e.g., an auction with many privately informed bidders). A complete treatment of all settings in which asymmetric information matters would entail a sizable volume in itself. Hence, of necessity, this chapter will be more tightly focused: for the most part, attention is limited to bilateral settings in which asymmetries of information exist prior to any transactions. The chapter will, thus, have little to say about scenarios **3.** and **4.** (i.e.,

---

[1] Chapter 19 of Mas-Colell et al. (1995) provides a good introduction to state-contingent commodities and markets for their trade. See also Huang and Litzenberger (1988).

situations of hidden-information agency and moral hazard, respectively).[2] The next subsection briefly discusses some other areas of the literature that are being ignored, along with citations for readers interested in those areas.

Beyond that next subsection, the rest of the chapter is divided as follows: Section 6.2 considers situations in which the contract proposer is the ignorant party. Her problem is to design a *mechanism* that induces her counter party, who is exogenously endowed with his information, to reveal that information in such a way that maximizes the contract proposer's expected payoff. The quintessential example of this is an uninformed seller designing a profit-maximizing price discrimination scheme. As will become clear, to induce the informed party to reveal his information, the uninformed contract proposer will need to leave him some surplus (an information rent). Because she cannot, therefore, capture all the surplus, the contract proposer will not have appropriate incentives to maximize surplus (welfare). Hence, in contrast to settings of symmetric information, inefficiencies will tend to arise in equilibrium. Section 6.3 considers the situation when each side of the transaction is endowed with his or her own payoff-relevant information. Unlike the preceding section, the focus will be on whether and how a social planner could design a contract to achieve efficiency.[3] Section 6.4 assumes it is the contract proposer who is endowed with the payoff-relevant information. The quintessential example of this is a seller who knows the quality of the good she seeks to sell. Because she cannot commit fully to not deceive her counter party, inefficiencies arise. Section 6.5 turns to the problems that arise if the asymmetry of information arises *endogenously*, because one party's prior-to-trade actions provide him or her payoff-relevant information.

6.1.1 What's Not in this Chapter
6.1.1.1 Competition Among Sellers
Among the topics not being covered are models in which multiple sellers compete by offering contracts to buyers.

If price competition within an oligopoly is sufficiently fierce, then there is little scope for price discrimination. It is, for instance, readily shown that if the standard Bertrand equilibrium would hold if sellers were limited to linear pricing, then it continues to hold even if their strategy spaces encompass complicated tariffs. On the other hand, if competition is less fierce—as, say, is true of Hotelling competition—then

---

[2] Hidden-information agency is similar, in terms of methods, to the mechanism-design analysis of Section 6.2.1 *infra*. This is especially true if the agent is free to quit after learning the payoff-relevant information because, then, the contract will have to satisfy individual-rationality constraints similar to those that arise in that section. Classic articles on moral hazard—also known as *hidden-action agency*—are Holmstrom (1979); Shavell (1979); and Grossman and Hart (1983). Good textbook treatments can be found in Chapter 4 of Bolton and Dewatripont (2005) and Chapters 4 and 5 of Laffont and Martimort (2002). For a web-based resource see Caillaud and Hermalin (2000).

[3] If, in contrast, one side had the ability to design the contract, subject only to the other's acceptance of it, then the problem would be little different than the analysis of Section 6.2.

equilibria can exist in which sellers engage in price discrimination. The topic of price discrimination in oligopolistic settings is, however, a chapter in itself, as the excellent surveys by Armstrong (2006b) and Stole (2007) attest. The interested reader would do well to start his or her study there.

Insurance markets with multiple insurers are particularly complex markets to analyze. Under the most natural formulation of competition and using standard notions of equilibrium, such markets can even fail to have equilibria (the well-known Rothschild and Stiglitz, 1976, non-existence result). Although modifying the models or the equilibrium concept can avoid non-existence (see, e.g., Wilson, 1977; or Hellwig, 1987), such modifications are not always appealing.

Many of those modifications can, in a sense, be seen as expanding the space of potential contracts that insurers can offer. Implicitly or explicitly, insurers are allowed to make offers that are contingent on the offers of other insurers. Unfortunately, the economic modeling of competition in contracts (offers) is not well developed and the results highly sensitive to the extent to which competitors can make their offers contingent on those of others. As an illustration, extend the basic Bertrand model of price competition as follows. Suppose each firm could make the offer:

1. If my rivals all make the same offer as me (i.e., an offer with these points **1.** and **2.**), then I am offering to sell my product at price equal to the monopoly price; but

2. if any rival makes a different offer, then I am offering to sell my product at price equal to marginal cost.

Clearly, a best response to all rivals offering the above is to do so yourself: if you don't, then you can make at most zero profit, because your rivals would, then, be pricing at marginal cost; but if you make that offer, then you get a fraction of the monopoly profit, which is a positive amount. To be sure, one can legitimately object to such an equilibrium as being unrealistic (at least with a large number of sellers), possibly illegal under relevant antitrust statutes, or dependent on an implausible level of commitment by sellers to their offers.[4] But as a matter of game theory per se, this is a perfectly legitimate equilibrium. Given the unsettled nature of modeling competition in contracts and the almost anything-goes results of many of such models—to say nothing of the limited space afforded this chapter—I have chosen not to consider competition among sellers. The reader interested in competing contract offers is well advised to begin with Katz (1991, 2006).

6.1.1.2 Externalities Across Buyers

Although many of the models analyzed below are readily extended to allow for multiple buyers, such extensions are predicated on there being no direct or indirect externalities across buyers.

---

[4] On the other hand, it is claimed that retailers' guaranteed-low-price policies are essentially offers of this nature. See, for instance, Edlin (1997) and cites therein.

In particular, an extension to multiple buyers can be complicated if the seller's production technology does not exhibit constant marginal costs.[5] Related complications arise if there are many potential buyers for a single item (e.g., the seller has a unique piece of art to sell). A common way of selling such an item is an auction. The literature on auctions is vast and arguably goes beyond a survey chapter itself—to say nothing of being a portion of a survey chapter; consequently, this chapter does not consider auctions. For the interested reader, there are a number of excellent books on the topic (consider, e.g., Krishna, 2002; Klemperer, 2004; and Milgrom, 2004).

With multiple buyers there is also the possibility that the actions of one buyer can convey information about other buyers. By exploiting such correlation, the seller can extract more of the buyers' surplus. This has, for example, been considered in a pair of articles by Crémer and McLean (1985, 1988).[6] That topic is not covered in this chapter.

A growing area of research has been on so-called *two-sided markets*, such as telecommunications, payment cards, and singles bars.[7] In such markets, one actor—the platform—provides a service that facilitates the interaction of two other actors (or classes of actors). A payment-card network, for instance, facilitates the exchanges of consumers and merchants. In its pricing, a platform often needs to contend with two externalities that exist between the two sides: a transaction externality and a membership externality. The former is the benefit a user on one side (e.g., a merchant) derives when a user on the other (e.g., a consumer) chooses to transact with it. The latter is the benefit a user on one side (e.g., a man in a stereotypical singles bar) derives from having more options on the other side (e.g., more women at the bar). In designing the tariffs it offers, the platform needs to be mindful of these externalities.[8] Although an interesting topic, the limited space afforded here precludes further discussion.

6.1.1.3 Incomplete Contracts and Contract Renegotiation

As noted, the focus here is when buyer and seller (the contractual parties) possess different information. Starting with Grossman and Hart (1986), a literature has arisen that studies the consequences of asymmetric information not between the contractual parties, but between those parties and some third party (e.g., a judge) that enforces the contract between the contractual parties. In particular, the contractual parties know payoff-relevant information that the third party does not (in the literature, such information is described as "observable, but unverifiable"). Although this kind of informational

---

[5] See Crémer and Riordan (1987) for an extension when the seller's cost function is not linear.

[6] There has been related work in hidden-information agency settings with multiple agents. See, for instance, Demougin and Garvie (1991) and McAfee and Reny (1992).

[7] For recent surveys of the two-sided markets literature see Rochet and Tirole (2006) or Rysman (2009).

[8] For instance, a platform, which can utilize two-part tariffs and which confronts a transaction externality, will wish to set the prices of the transactions to sum to less than the cost of facilitating the transaction (see, e.g., Hermalin and Katz, 2004, for details). For an analysis of membership externalities, see Armstrong (2006a).

asymmetry has proved to be of great importance, it is not covered here. For a partial survey of the literature, see Hermalin et al. (2007), especially Section 4.

When payoff-relevant information is observable to the contractual parties, but unverifiable (unobservable to a third-party contract enforcer), the resulting contracts are often described as *incomplete*. As Grossman and Hart (1986) observed, one way the contractual parties will respond to contractual incompleteness is to renegotiate their contracts should the contractual parties learn the observable-but-unverifiable information after writing their initial contract, but before its full execution. There is a large literature on contract renegotiation (see Hermalin et al., 2007, for a partial survey). Among the debates in that literature is whether the contractual parties can commit to a renegotiation mechanism or must continue to renegotiate as long as there is "money on the table" (for a brief introduction to the "money-on-the-table" problem see Section 6.3.3 *infra*). This touches more generally on the problem of the parties committing to a contract that will prove *ex post* inefficient: if the parties come to understand that there is money to be had, it seems natural to imagine that they will seek to pick it up by, if necessary, renegotiating their contract. The problem is that the anticipation of such a lack of commitment can have adverse effects *ex ante*: it can be in the parties's interest to commit to leaving some money on the table, at least off the equilibrium path, in order to provide themselves appropriate incentives *ex ante*.[9]

Dealing with the money-on-the-table problem has proved difficult because of the general difficulty of satisfactorily modeling bargaining given asymmetric information. For further discussion see Section 6.3.3. It is that difficulty—in addition to the overall length constraint on the chapter—that has led me to omit a more detailed discussion of the topic.

6.1.1.4 Hard Information

This chapter is essentially limited to what is known as *soft* information: although the informed party can make claims about what s/he knows, those claims are cheap talk insofar as her/his counter party cannot verify such claims. That is, the informed party can lie. The literature has also considered *hard* information: if the informed party chooses to reveal her/his information, then the counter party can verify it. As an example, a seller's information about the reliability of her car is soft, but her information about its repair history is hard to the extent she can provide receipts from her mechanic for work done. Although hard information cannot be misstated, it can be concealed: unless the informed party reveals it, the uninformed party still does not know what it is (e.g., a used-car seller can hide receipts from her mechanic).

---

[9] Such issues arise, for instance, in the bilateral investment literature (e.g., Demski and Sappington, 1991; Nöldeke and Schmidt, 1995, 1998; and Edlin and Hermalin, 2000). Another important example, having to do with hidden-action agency, is Fudenberg and Tirole (1990).

In some instances, the *existence* of hard information is the informed party's private information (e.g., the seller knows what receipts she has) and in others it is commonly known (e.g., a college graduate can produce a transcript). When existence is commonly known, it may be difficult for the informed party to conceal her/his hard information due to the unraveling argument of Grossman (1981): the uninformed party's expectation of the information conditional on concealment is necessarily less than the true value for some informed players; hence, those players, who are presumably concealing, would, in fact, do better to reveal. Extending this logic, only someone with the worst information would be willing to conceal.[10] When the existence of information is uncertainty, then concealment may occur in equilibrium.[11]

6.1.1.5 Signal Jamming

In some situations, the parties may initially be symmetrically informed, but actions of one may hamper the ability of the other to learn new information. A sizable literature of such *signal-jamming* models exists.[12] For instance, suppose one party wishes to infer the value of a payoff-relevant parameter that is known to have been drawn from a specific distribution. A signal, s, that is informative of that parameter will be generated, but one party may only see $s + x$, where x is an action taken by the other party to distort the signal. For example, as in Holmstrom (1999), a manager's efforts affect a firm's revenues, which are a signal of his ability (the payoff-relevant parameter). In some situations, such signal-jamming efforts can be welfare enhancing (as suggested by Fama, 1980, and as evidenced in some models in Holmstrom, 1999); in others they can be welfare reducing (as in Fudenberg and Tirole, 1986; Stein, 1989; or other models in Holmstrom, 1999).

6.2 EXOGENOUS ASYMMETRIES OF INFORMATION AT TIME OF CONTRACTING: INFORMED BUYER

To start, consider a situation in which one party proposes a contract to another. The offer is take-it-or-leave-it (TIOLI): the offer's recipient can accept, in which case the contract is binding on both parties; or he can reject, in which case there is no further

---

[10] As a simple model, suppose the informed party's (his) hard information is $\theta \in [0, 1]$ and the uninformed party's (her) prior belief is it's distributed uniformly on that interval. Suppose her best-response action to her posterior belief is $a = \mathbb{E}\{\theta\}$ and that is worth $v(a)$ to the informed party, $v(\cdot)$ strictly increasing. Suppose there were an equilibrium in which the informed party conceals if $\theta \leq \bar{\theta}$ and he reveals otherwise. Because the uninformed party's best response would be $\bar{\theta}/2$ if information was not revealed, the informed party would do better to reveal than to conceal if $\theta > \bar{\theta}/2$. This can be consistent with the purported equilibrium only if $\bar{\theta} = 0$; that is, if all reveal.

[11] To extend the example of the previous footnote: suppose that informed party acquires the hard information with probability 1/2. It is readily seen that an equilibrium exists in which those who acquire the information reveal if $\theta > 1/3$ and otherwise conceal. The uninformed party's estimate of θ given no information is revealed is 1/3.

[12] The term "signal jamming" appears to be due to Fudenberg and Tirole (1986). There are some earlier examples of the phenomenon in the literature, though (see, e.g., Holmstrom, 1999—the original version of which appears in 1982).

negotiation and the parties receive their default (no-trade) payoffs. In many market settings, the contract offeror is a seller and the recipient a buyer. For the sake of brevity, let's employ the names seller and buyer, with the understanding that much of what follows is more general (e.g., the contract proposer could be an employer and the recipient an employee).

A prominent example is the basic monopoly model, the one taught in introductory economics. To be sure, as typically taught, the model presumes many buyers, but the number of buyers is (essentially) irrelevant for the conclusions reached. In that model, the seller offers the buyer the opportunity to buy the quantity he wishes, x, in exchange for paying the seller $T(x)$, where the function $T : \mathbb{R}_+ \to \mathbb{R}_+$ is stipulated in the offer. For example, in the most basic monopoly model, the function T is a *linear tariff*: if the buyer announces (buys) x, he pays the seller px, where the rate (price) p is quoted in units of currency per unit of the good. Of course, as one learns in more advanced economics courses, the tariff needn't be linear. Depending on the various informational and other constraints she faces, the seller can derive greater profit by engaging in *price discrimination* via a *nonlinear* tariff.

The design of the tariff is, in part, a function of the informational asymmetry that exists between seller and buyer. In particular, the buyer is assumed to have been endowed with payoff-relevant information—his *type*, β. The buyer's type is typically his private information. It is, however, common knowledge that his type is drawn from a known type space, B, according to a specific distribution. In some instances, such as simple monopoly pricing, this may be all that the seller knows. In other instances, such as third-degree price discrimination, the seller is somewhat better informed, having observed some signal that is informative about the buyer's type.[13]

As an example, the buyer may wish to purchase, at most, one unit of the seller's product. The buyer's payoff if he does is $\beta - p$. If he doesn't (there's no trade), his payoff is zero. Suppose that his type space is $B = [0, 1]$ and β is drawn by "Nature" from that space according to a known distribution $1 - D$ (the reason for writing it in this unusual manner will become clear shortly). Assume this is all the seller knows. The seller's payoff is p if she sells a unit (for convenience, normalize her costs to zero) and it is 0 otherwise. Suppose the seller offers the contract "one unit for p." The buyer does better buying than not buying if $\beta - p \geq 0$. The probability that a seller who quotes a price of p makes a sale is, therefore, $\Pr\{\beta \geq p\}$; that is, it equals the survival function of the buyer's type evaluated at p. Hence, the expected quantity sold is $D(p)$. Observe this survival function is equivalent to what, in introductory economics, would be called a demand function.[14]

---

[13] This chapter omits a discussion of third-degree price discrimination—the interested reader is directed to Varian (1989) or Tirole (1988, Section 3.2).

[14] It can be shown that any well-behaved demand function is proportional to a survival function, where "well-behaved" means finite demand at zero price, zero demand at an infinite price, and demand is everywhere non-increasing in price. The proportionality factor is just demand at zero price.

The seller will choose p to maximize her expected payoff, $pD(p)$. For instance, if the buyer's type is distributed uniformly, then the seller chooses p to solve

$$\max_{p} p(1 - p).$$

The solution is readily seen to be $p^* = 1/2$. In short, the seller would make the buyer the TIOLI offer "one unit at price $1/2$."[15]

Although somewhat trivial, this example reveals a basic point about efficiency when contracting occurs in the shadow of asymmetric information. Welfare is β if trade occurs, but zero if it doesn't. Because $\beta \geq 0 = \text{cost}$, welfare is maximized if trade always occurs. The seller, however, sets a price of $1/2$: trade thus occurs with probability $1/2$. This is the standard result that linear pricing by a monopolist tends to yield too little trade. Observe this inefficiency is the result of (i) asymmetry of information and (ii) the bargaining game assumed: if the seller knew β—information were symmetric—then she would offer a type-β buyer "one unit at price β." Because $\beta - \beta \geq 0$, the buyer would accept. Trade would always occur and maximum welfare, thus, achieved. Alternatively, if the buyer were to make a TIOLI offer to the seller, then welfare would also be maximized: the buyer would offer "one unit at price equal cost (i.e., 0)." Because $0 \geq 0$, the seller would accept. Trade would be certain to occur and welfare thus maximized.

These observations generalize: consider a contract $\langle x, t \rangle$, where $x \in \mathcal{X}$ is an allocation and $t \in \mathbb{R}$ a monetary transfer. Let the seller's payoff be $t - c(x)$ and the buyer's $u(x, \beta) - t$, where $c : \mathcal{X} \to \mathbb{R}$ and $u : \mathcal{X} \times B \to \mathbb{R}$. Let x_0 be the "no trade" allocation; that is, if no agreement is reached, then the allocation is x_0. Assume $x_0 \in \mathcal{X}$: among the feasible contracts is one that replicates no trade.

Proposition 6.1. *Consider the model set forth above. One player's (e.g., the buyer's) payoff is type dependent, but the other's (e.g., the seller's) is not. The player with the type-dependent payoff knows his type. Assume that for all types, there is a welfare-maximizing allocation.[16] Then if one party gets to offer a contract on a take-it-or-leave-it basis and s/he knows the type when doing so, then welfare will be a maximum for all values of type in equilibrium.*

Proof: Because the offeror could always offer the no-trade allocation and zero transfer, there is no loss of generality in assuming the offeror's contract is accepted in equilibrium. If the seller makes the offer, she does best to offer

$$\arg\max_{x \in \mathcal{X}, t \in \mathbb{R}} t - c(x)$$

---

[15] If the bargaining is other than seller makes a TIOLI offer, then the outcome would be different. In particular, a key assumption is that the seller can commit to never make the buyer a subsequent offer should he reject the seller's initial offer. The literature on the Coase conjecture (Coase, 1972) explores what happens if the seller is unable to so commit. See, for example, Gul et al. (1986). See also the discussion in Section 6.3.3 *infra*.

[16] That is, using the notation introduced above, assume the program $\max_{x \in \mathcal{X}} u(x, \beta) - c(x)$ has a solution for all $\beta \in B$.

subject to

$$u(x, \beta) - t \geq u(x_0, \beta). \tag{6.2.1}$$

For any x, if the buyer's participation (offer-acceptance) constraint (6.2.1) did not bind, then the seller could raise t slightly, keeping x fixed, and do better. Hence, in equilibrium, (6.2.1) must bind. The seller's choice of x therefore solves

$$\max_{x \in \mathcal{X}} u(x, \beta) - c(x) - u(x_0, \beta). \tag{6.2.2}$$

Because (6.2.2) is welfare less a constant, the result follows.

The analysis when the buyer makes the offer is similar and, thus, omitted for the sake of brevity. ∎

What, in fact, is *not* general is the conclusion that giving the bargaining power to the uninformed player (i.e., the seller) leads to inefficiency. To see this, return to the simple example, maintaining all assumptions except, now, let $B = [1, 2]$. Because the seller can guarantee herself a profit of 1 by quoting a price of 1, it would be irrational of her to quote either a price less than 1 or greater than 2 (the latter because it would mean no sale). Hence, the seller's pricing problem can be written as

$$\max_{p \in [1,2]} p(2 - p).$$

The solution is $p^* = 1$. At that price, all types of buyer will buy—welfare is maximized.

The astute reader will, at this point, object that efficiency has been shown only under the assumption that the seller is restricted to linear pricing. What, one may ask, if the seller were unconstrained in her choice of contract? To answer this, we need to derive the profit-maximizing tariff for the seller, the topic of the next subsection. Anticipating that analysis, however, it will prove—*for this example*—that linear pricing is the profit-maximizing tariff and, thus, the seller's ignorance of the buyer's type need not always lead to inefficiency.

6.2.1 Tariff Construction via Mechanism Design

Now consider a mechanism-design approach to tariff construction. Payoffs are as above. The buyer's type, β, is fixed exogenously and is his private information. The seller knows the distribution from which β was drawn. Denote that distribution by F and its support by B. The structure of the game is common knowledge.

6.2.1.1 Mechanism Design: A Crash Course

There are numerous texts that cover mechanism design.[17] Consequently, the discussion here will be brief.

---

[17] A partial list is Gibbons (1992); Salanié (1997); Laffont and Martimort (2002); and Bolton and Dewatripont (2005). See also Chapters 13 and 23 of Mas-Colell et al. (1995).

Call an allocation-transfer pair, (x, t), a *contractual outcome*. The set of all such outcomes is $\mathcal{X} \times \mathbb{R}$. Let $\Delta(\mathcal{X} \times \mathbb{R})$ denote the set of all possible probability distributions over outcomes.

Definition. A *mechanism* is a game form, $\langle \mathcal{M}, \mathcal{N}, \sigma \rangle$, to be played by the parties. The set $\mathcal{M}$ is the informed player's (*e.g.*, the buyer's) strategy set, the set $\mathcal{N}$ the uninformed player's (*e.g.*, the seller's) strategy set, and σ maps any pair of strategies, (m, n), to a probability distribution over contractual outcomes; that is, $\sigma : \mathcal{M} \times \mathcal{N} \rightarrow \Delta(\mathcal{X} \times \mathbb{R})$. Observe that any conceivable contract can be viewed as a mechanism. For example, linear pricing is the mechanism in which $\mathcal{M} = \mathcal{X} \subseteq \mathbb{R}_+$, $\mathcal{N} = \emptyset$, and $\sigma: m \mapsto (m, pm)$.[18]

Let $\mathbb{E}_{\sigma(m,n)}\{\cdot\}$ denote expectation with respect to the random vector (x, t) when it is distributed $\sigma(m,n)$. Define

$$U\left(\sigma\left(m, n\right), \beta\right) = \mathbb{E}_{\sigma(m,n)}\left\{u(x, \beta) - t\right\} \; ;$$

that is, $U\left(\sigma\left(m, n\right), \beta\right)$ is the informed player's expected payoff if he is type β, he plays m, and the uninformed player plays n.

A mechanism is *direct* if $\mathcal{M} = B$; that is, if the informed player's action is an announcement of type. It is a *direct-revelation mechanism* if, *in equilibrium*, the informed player announces his type truthfully. For truth-telling to be an equilibrium strategy, it must be a best response to the informed player's type and his expectation of the uninformed player's action n:[19]

$$U\left(\sigma\left(\beta, n\right), \beta\right) \geq U\left(\sigma\left(\beta', n\right), \beta\right) \; \forall \beta' \in B \, . \tag{6.2.3}$$

The *uninformed* player seeks to design a mechanism that will, in equilibrium, maximize her expected payoff. Doing so entails choosing $\mathcal{M}, \mathcal{N}$, and σ. The classes of spaces and outcome functions are incomprehensibly large. How can the optimal mechanism be found within them? Fortunately, a simple, yet subtle, result—the *Revelation Principle*—allows us to limit attention to direct-revelation mechanisms.

Proposition 6.2   (The Revelation Principle). [20] *For any general mechanism* $\langle \mathcal{M}, \mathcal{N}, \sigma \rangle$ *and associated Bayesian Nash equilibrium, there exists a direct-revelation mechanism*

---

[18] If one wished to get technical, one could write that σ maps m to the distribution that assigns all weight to the outcome (m, pm).

[19] Hence, the equilibrium concept is Bayesian Nash. In other situations, different equilibrium concepts, such as solution in dominant strategies or perfect Bayesian equilibrium, are relevant. The discussion here, including the Revelation Principle, extends to other equilibrium concepts.

[20] The Revelation Principle is often attributed to Myerson (1979), although Gibbard (1973) and Green and Laffont (1977) could be identified as earlier derivations. Suffice it to say that the Revelation Principle has been independently derived a number of times and was a well-known result before it received its name. Proposition 6.2 states the Revelation Principle for a situation with one informed player. Extending the Revelation Principle to many informed players is straightforward. Further, as observed in footnote 19, the Revelation Principle holds under different solution concepts.

such that the associated truthful Bayesian Nash equilibrium generates the same distribution over outcomes in equilibrium as the general mechanism.

Proof: A Bayesian Nash equilibrium of the game $\langle \mathcal{M}, \mathcal{N}, \sigma \rangle$ is a pair of strategies $(m(\cdot), n)$, $m(\cdot)$ a mapping from the type space to $\mathcal{M}$.[21] Consider the direct mechanism: $\hat{\sigma}(\cdot) = \sigma(m(\cdot), n)$. The claim is that $\hat{\sigma}(\cdot)$ induces truth-telling (is a direct-revelation mechanism). To see this, suppose not. Then there must exist a type β that does better to lie—announce some $\beta' \neq \beta$; that is, formally, there must exist β and $\beta' \neq \beta$ such that

$$U(\hat{\sigma}(\beta'), \beta) > U(\hat{\sigma}(\beta), \beta).$$

Using the definition of $\hat{\sigma}(\cdot)$, this means, however, that

$$U(\sigma(m(\beta'), n), \beta) > U(\sigma(m(\beta), n), \beta).$$

But if that expression is true, then the informed player prefers to play $m(\beta')$ instead of $m(\beta)$ in the *original* mechanism. This contradicts the assumption that $m(\cdot)$ is an equilibrium best response to n in the original game. It follows, *reductio ad absurdum*, that $\hat{\sigma}$ induces truth-telling.

Moreover, because $\hat{\sigma}(\beta) = \sigma(m(\beta), n)$, the same distribution over outcomes is implemented in equilibrium.   ∎

An intuitive way to grasp the Revelation Principle is to imagine that, before he plays some general mechanism, the informed player could delegate his play to some trustworthy third party. Suppose the third party knew the agent's equilibrium strategy—the mapping $m : B \to \mathcal{M}$—so the informed player need only reveal his type to the third party with the understanding that the third party should choose the appropriate action, $m(\beta)$. But, because this third party can be "incorporated" into the design of the mechanism, there is no loss of generality in restricting attention to direct-revelation mechanisms.

6.2.1.2 The Standard Assumptions

So far, the seller's cost has been assumed to be independent of the buyer's type. This can be relaxed—let $c(x, \beta)$ denote her cost from now on.[22] Welfare is now

$$w(x, \beta) = u(x, \beta) - c(x, \beta).$$

To derive the seller's profit-maximizing mechanism, certain assumptions are necessary to make the problem tractable. The following are standard.

---

[21] Observe that the informed player's strategy can be conditioned on β, which he knows, while the uninformed player's cannot be (since she is ignorant of β).

[22] With this change in assumptions, Proposition 6.1 no longer holds if the buyer makes a TIOLI offer to the seller unless the seller knows the buyer's type.

Assumption 1   (Spence-Mirrlees Condition). There exist complete orders $\succ_\beta$ and $\succ_x$ on B and $\mathcal{X}$, respectively, such that the implication

$$u(x, \beta') - t \geq u(x', \beta') - t' \implies u(x, \beta) - t > u(x', \beta) - t' \qquad (6.2.4)$$

is valid whenever $\beta \succ_\beta \beta'$ and $x \succ_x x'$.

Assumption 2   (Trade is Desirable). If β is not the infimum of B under the complete order $\succ_\beta$, then there exists an $x \in \mathcal{X}$ such that $w(x, \beta) > w(x_0, \beta)$.

Assumption 3   (Too Much of a Good Thing). Either (i) the set of possible allocations is bounded or (ii) for all $\beta \in B$ there exists an $\bar{x}(\beta) \in \mathcal{X}$ such that $x \succ_x \bar{x}(\beta)$ implies $w(x, \beta) < w(\bar{x}(\beta), \beta)$.

Assumption 4   (No Countervailing Incentives). There exists a constant u_R such that, for all $\beta \in B$, $u(x_0, \beta) = u_R$.

Assumption 5   (Minimum Element). The no-trade allocation x_0 is the minimum element of $\mathcal{X}$ under the complete order $\succ_x$.

The requirement of complete orders on the type space, B, and allocation space, $\mathcal{X}$, means little further loss of generality from treating each as a subset of the real line, $\mathbb{R}$. Henceforth, assume $B \subseteq \mathbb{R}$ and $\mathcal{X} \subseteq \mathbb{R}$. In general, expanding the analysis to allow for a (meaningful) multidimensional allocation space is difficult because of the issues involved in capturing how the buyer's willingness to make trade-offs among the dimensions (including payment) varies with his type. The reader interested in multidimensional allocation spaces should consult Rochet and Choné (1998).[23]

Given that $B \subseteq \mathbb{R}$ and $\mathcal{X} \subseteq \mathbb{R}$, it is meaningful to say β is a higher type than β' if $\beta > \beta'$. Similarly, the allocation x is greater than allocation x' if $x > x'$.

The Spence-Mirrlees condition (Assumption 1) says that if a lower type prefers the outcome (x, t) to (x', t'), $x > x'$, then a higher type will strictly prefer (x, t) to (x', t'). The Spence-Mirrlees condition has other interpretations. For instance, suppose $x > x'$ and $\beta > \beta'$. By choosing t and t' so that

$$u(x, \beta') - u(x', \beta') = t - t',$$

it follows, from (6.2.4), that

$$u(x, \beta) - u(x', \beta) > u(x, \beta') - u(x', \beta'); \qquad (6.2.5)$$

---

[23] Armstrong and Rochet (1999) and Basov (2010) are also useful references for those interested in multidimensional screening problems.

in other words, the Spence-Mirrlees condition implies $u(\cdot,\cdot)$ exhibits increasing differences. As is well known, increasing indifferences is equivalent to the condition that the marginal utility of allocation increase with type. If

$$u(x, \beta') - t \geq u(x', \beta') - t',$$

then

$$u(x, \beta') - u(x', \beta') \geq t - t';$$

hence, (6.2.5) implies (6.2.4). These arguments establish:

Proposition 6.3.   *The following are equivalent:*
(i) The Spence-Mirrlees condition holds.
(ii) The function $u(\cdot,\cdot)$ exhibits strictly increasing differences.
(iii) The marginal utility of allocation is greater for a higher type than a lower type.[24]

In light of Proposition 6.3, the following is immediate.

Corollary 6.1.   *Suppose $\mathcal{X}$ and B are intervals in $\mathbb{R}$. If the cross-partial derivative of $u(\cdot,\cdot)$ exists everywhere on $\mathcal{X} \times B$, then the Spence-Mirrlees condition holds if*

$$\frac{\partial^2 u(x, \beta)}{\partial \beta \partial x} > 0. \tag{6.2.6}$$

Corollary 6.1 explains why the Spence-Mirrlees condition is sometimes referred to as the cross-partial condition.

Assumptions 2 and 3 ensure that trade is desirable with all types except, possibly, the lowest and trade never involves allocating an infinite amount. Assumption 4 says that all types of buyer enjoy the same utility, u_R, if there isn't trade. The value u_R is called the *reservation utility*. In many contexts, a common reservation utility is a reasonable assumption. For instance, if x denotes the amount of a good the buyer obtains, with $x_0 = 0$, then there is no obvious reason why different types would enjoy different levels of utility when they don't purchase. On the other hand, in other situations of contractual screening (e.g., an uninformed principal seeks to hire an informed agent and higher agent types have better alternatives *vis-à-vis* working for the principal than lower agent types), this assumption is less innocuous. Relaxing Assumption 4 requires a more

---

[24] If we think of a buyer's indifference curve in allocation-transfer (x–t space), its marginal rate of substitution is minus the marginal utility of allocation divided by the marginal utility of paying an additional dollar. The latter is -1; hence the marginal rate of substitution (MRS) equals the marginal utility of allocation. Given Spence-Mirrlees, a higher type has a greater MRS than a lower type. In other words, a higher type's indifference through a given point is steeper than a lower type's. Hence, an indifference curve for a higher type can cross that of a lower type at most once. This discussion explains why the Spence-Mirrlees condition is often referred to as a single-crossing condition.

extensive analysis than fits within this chapter. The reader interested in such models—in particular, so-called models of *countervailing incentives* in which $u(x_0,\cdot)$ is increasing in type—should consult Lewis and Sappington (1989) and Maggi and Rodriguez-Clare (1995), among other articles.

Assumption 5 reflects that the buyer is acquiring something more than what he would have absent trade. It is a natural assumption in contractual screening settings more generally (e.g., no trade could constitute zero hours worked when an uninformed principal seeks to hire an informed agent).

6.2.1.3 Characterizing Mechanisms

The Revelation Principle (Proposition 6.2) implies no loss of generality in restricting attention to direct-revelation mechanisms: the buyer's announcement of his type, β, maps to $(x(\beta), t(\beta))$ and, in equilibrium, the buyer announces truthfully. Because $(x(\beta), t(\beta))$ could equal $(x_0, 0)$, the no-trade allocation and "transfer," there is no loss of generality in assuming that all types participate in equilibrium. These equilibrium conditions can be written as

$$u\left(x(\beta), \beta\right) - t(\beta) \geq u_R \quad \text{for all } \beta \in B \tag{IR}$$

and

$$u\left(x(\beta), \beta\right) - t(\beta) \geq u\left(x(\beta'), \beta\right) - t(\beta') \quad \text{for all } \beta, \beta' \in B. \tag{IC}$$

Condition (IR) is the requirement that all types participate. It is known in the literature as a participation or individual rationality (hence, IR) constraint. Condition (IC) is the requirement of truth telling in equilibrium. It is known in the literature as a truth-telling or incentive compatibility (hence, IC) constraint.

A well-known "trick" in mechanism design is to work with equilibrium utilities rather than directly with transfers. Observe a type-β buyer's equilibrium utility is

$$v(\beta) = u\left(x(\beta), \beta\right) - t(\beta). \tag{6.2.7}$$

By adding and subtracting $u\left(x(\beta'), \beta'\right)$ from the righthand side of (IC) and using (6.2.7), the IC constraint can be rewritten as

$$v(\beta) \geq v(\beta') + u\left(x(\beta'), \beta\right) - u\left(x(\beta'), \beta'\right) \quad \text{for all } \beta, \beta' \in B. \tag{IC'}$$

Consider two types, β and β', $\beta > \beta'$. The relevant IC constraints must hold between these two (i.e., β cannot do better to announce he's β' and *vice versa*):

$$v(\beta) \geq v(\beta') + u\left(x(\beta'), \beta\right) - u\left(x(\beta'), \beta'\right) \quad \text{and} \tag{6.2.8}$$

$$v(\beta') \geq v(\beta) + u\left(x(\beta), \beta'\right) - u\left(x(\beta), \beta\right) . \tag{6.2.9}$$

(This line of argumentation is known as a *revealed-preference argument*.) Expressions (6.2.8) and (6.2.9) together imply

$$u\left(x(\beta), \beta\right) - u\left(x(\beta), \beta'\right) \geq v(\beta) - v(\beta') \geq u\left(x(\beta'), \beta\right) - u\left(x(\beta'), \beta'\right) .$$

$$\tag{6.2.10}$$

Ignoring the middle term for the moment and recalling that the Spence-Mirrlees condition implies $u(\cdot,\cdot)$ exhibits increasing differences (Proposition 6.3), we have

Lemma 6.1 *A necessary condition for a mechanism to be a direct-revelation mechanism (i.e., to induce truthful announcements in equilibrium) is that the allocation be nondecreasing with type (i.e., $x(\beta) \geq x(\beta')$ if $\beta > \beta'$).*

Recall that *if* the seller knew the buyer's type, her problem would be to choose x and t to maximize

$$t - c(x, \beta) \text{ subject to } u(x, \beta) - t \geq u_R .$$

As argued in the proof of Proposition 6.1, the constraint must bind. So if there were no asymmetry of information, the buyer would enjoy no rent (in equilibrium he would get just his reservation utility). With asymmetric information, that conclusion need no longer hold—some buyer types may earn a rent (have equilibrium utilities greater than their reservation utility). Because such a rent is due to the asymmetry of information, it is called an *information rent*. The following lemma is key to determining which types earn a rent and which don't.[25]

Lemma 6.2 *Consider a direct-revelation mechanism such that $\beta' \in B$ is induced to buy; that is, such that $x(\beta') > x_0$. Then any higher-type buyer, $\beta \in B$, will also be induced to buy under this mechanism (i.e., $x(\beta) > x_0$) and will enjoy a greater equilibrium utility (i.e., $v(\beta) > v(\beta')$).* An immediate corollary given the IR constraint is:

Corollary 6.2 *Consider a direct-revelation mechanism such that $\beta' \in B$ is induced to buy. Then any higher-type buyer, $\beta \in B$, must earn an information rent in equilibrium under this mechanism.* In other words, all types that trade, except possibly the lowest type who trades, capture an information rent in equilibrium.

What about the lowest type to trade? If the seller has designed the mechanism to maximize her expected payoff, then that buyer earns no rent:

Lemma 6.3 *Consider a direct-revelation mechanism that maximizes the seller's expected payoff and assume a positive measure of types purchase in equilibrium. If, under this mechanism,*

---

[25] The proof of this lemma can be found in the Appendix. As a rule, proofs not given in the text can be found in the Appendix.

$\tilde{\beta}$ *is the lowest buyer type to buy (formally,* $x(\beta) > x_0$, *for all* $\beta > \tilde{\beta}$; $x(\tilde{\beta}) \geq x_0$; *and* $x(\beta') = x_0$ *for all* $\beta' < \tilde{\beta}$)), *then the type-*$\tilde{\beta}$ *buyer captures no rent (i.e.,* $v(\tilde{\beta}) = u_R$).

Further characterization of mechanisms is facilitated by—but not really dependent on—deciding whether the type space is discrete or continuous.

A Discrete Type Space. The type space is discrete if B is denumerable; that is, it can be put in a one-to-one mapping with an index set (set of consecutive integers), $\mathbb{Z}_B$. Let the type to which $n \in \mathbb{Z}_B$ maps be denoted β_n. The mapping is increasing. There is, thus, no type between β_n and β_{n+1} for any n and $n + 1 \in \mathbb{Z}_B$. Call β_n and β_{n+1} *adjacent types.*

Because the index set is arbitrary, we can renormalize it in whatever way is convenient. In particular, adopt, for the moment, the convention that β_1 is the lowest type to purchase in equilibrium (i.e., $x(\beta_1) > x_0$ and $x(\beta) = x_0$ for all $\beta < \beta_1$). Because the seller offers the mechanism on a TIOLI basis, we can restrict attention to mechanisms that maximize the seller's expected payoff; hence, from Lemma 6.3, $v(\beta_1) = u_R$.

For all $n \in \mathbb{Z}_B$ (except the minimum n should it exist), define the *rent function* as

$$R_n(x) = u(x, \beta_n) - u(x, \beta_{n-1}) \,.$$

To understand this name, observe, from (6.2.8), that

$$v(\beta_n) \geq v(\beta_{n-1}) + R_n\left(x(\beta_{n-1})\right) \,. \tag{6.2.11}$$

Expression (6.2.11) is sometimes called the *downward adjacent IC constraint* (see, e.g., Caillaud and Hermalin, 1993). Observe

$$v(\beta_2) \geq v(\beta_1) + R_2\left(x(\beta_1)\right) = u_R + R_2\left(x(\beta_1)\right) \,,$$

$$v(\beta_3) \geq v(\beta_2) + R_3\left(x(\beta_2)\right) \geq u_R + \sum_{j=2}^{3} R_j\left(x(\beta_{j-1})\right) \,,$$

and, so on; hence,

$$v(\beta_n) \geq u_R + \sum_{j=2}^{n} R_j\left(x(\beta_{j-1})\right) \,. \tag{6.2.12}$$

One can, thus, describe $R_n\left(x(\beta_{n-1})\right)$ as the contribution to the type-β_n buyer's information rent necessary to keep him from mimicking his adjacent downward neighbor. (Admittedly, this would be clearer if (6.2.12) were an equality; fortunately, as shown below, it is under the seller's optimal mechanism.)

Recall $v(\beta) = u(x(\beta), \beta) - t(\beta)$. Hence, (6.2.12) implies

$$t(\beta_n) \leq u\left(x(\beta_n), \beta_n\right) - u_R - \sum_{j=2}^{n} R_j\left(x(\beta_{j-1})\right) \,. \tag{6.2.13}$$

There are no countervailing incentives, so $R_j(x_0) \equiv 0$. By assumption $x(\beta_j) = x_0$ for $j <$ 1. So, the inequality in (6.2.13) is not reversed if $\sum_{j \leq 1} R_j\left(x(\beta_{j-1})\right)$ is subtracted from the RHS of (6.2.13). This demonstrates the necessity of

$$t(\beta_n) \leq u(x(\beta_n), \beta_n) - u_R - \sum_{j \leq n} R_j(x(\beta_{j-1})) . \tag{6.2.14}$$

The seller maximizes her revenue by having $t(\cdot)$ be as large as possible, which means, for any allocation profile $x(\cdot)$, she cannot do better than to have transfer function $t(\cdot)$ defined so that the inequality in (6.2.14) binds.

So far, only the necessary conditions for a direct-revelation mechanism have been characterized. Fortunately, for purposes of calculating such mechanisms, these conditions are sufficient too:

Proposition 6.4. *Suppose the type space is discrete. A mechanism $\langle x(\cdot), t(\cdot)\rangle$ in which $x(\cdot)$ is nondecreasing and $t(\cdot)$ is given by*

$$t(\beta_n) = u\left(x(\beta_n), \beta_n\right) - u_R - \sum_{j \leq n} R_j\left(x(\beta_{j-1})\right) \tag{6.2.15}$$

is a direct-revelation mechanism.

Proof: Consider an arbitrary type β_n. We wish to show he participates and won't lie about his type.

Increasing differences (Spence-Mirrlees) implies $R_n(x) \geq 0$ for all $x \geq x_0$. Hence, (6.2.15) implies

$$u\left(x(\beta_n), \beta_n\right) - t(\beta_n) = u_R + \sum_{j \leq n} R_j\left(x(\beta_{j-1})\right) \geq u_R ;$$

that is, all types participate. Increasing differences also implies that $R_n(\cdot)$ is an increasing function.

Consider $n < m$. The goal is to show that a β_n-type buyer doesn't wish to pretend to be a β_m-type buyer. His utility were he to do so is

$$u\left(x(\beta_m), \beta_n\right) - t(\beta_m)$$

$$= u\left(x(\beta_m), \beta_n\right) - u\left(x(\beta_m), \beta_m\right) + u_R + \sum_{j \leq n} R_j\left(x(\beta_{j-1})\right) + \sum_{j=n+1}^{m} R_j\left(x(\beta_{j-1})\right)$$

$$= u\left(x(\beta_m), \beta_n\right) - u\left(x(\beta_m), \beta_m\right) + v(\beta_n) + \sum_{j=n+1}^{m} R_j\left(x(\beta_{j-1})\right)$$

$$= v(\beta_n) - \sum_{j=n+1}^{m}\left(R_j\left(x(\beta_m)\right) - R_j\left(x(\beta_{j-1})\right)\right) \leq v(\beta_n) , \tag{6.2.16}$$

where the first two equalities follow from (6.2.15) and the third because

$$u\left(x(\beta_m),\beta_m\right) - u\left(x(\beta_m),\beta_n\right) = \sum_{j=n+1}^{m} R_j\left(x(\beta_m)\right).$$

The inequality in (6.2.16) follows because x(·) is nondecreasing and Rj(·) is an increasing function.

The proof for the case $n>m$ is in the Appendix.   ∎

A Continuous Type Space. The other common assumption is the type space is an interval $(\underline{\beta},\bar{\beta}) \in \mathbb{R}$. Assume—primarily to avoid technical complications—that both limits are finite. To facilitate working with this space, take the buyer's utility, $u(\cdot,\cdot)$, to be twice continuously differentiable in both arguments. Assume for any $x \in \mathcal{X}$ that $\partial u(x,\hat{\beta})/\partial\beta$ is bounded above for all $\hat{\beta} \in B$.

There is now no well-defined notion of adjacent types. However, an obvious calculus-based analogue to the rent function is the partial derivative

$$\frac{\partial u\left(x(\beta),\beta\right)}{\partial\beta}.$$

The corresponding analogue to the sum of rent functions (e.g., as appears in (6.2.15) above) is the integral:

$$\int_{\underline{\beta}}^{\beta} \frac{\partial u\left(x(z),z\right)}{\partial\beta} dz.$$

(Because z appears twice in that expression, it is readily seen that the integral is *not* a simple antiderivative of the partial derivative.) Further reasoning by analogy suggests that the seller's optimal direct-revelation mechanism is characterized by a nondecreasing allocation profile $x(\cdot)$ and transfer function

$$t(\beta) = u\left(x(\beta),\beta\right) - u_R - \int_{\underline{\beta}}^{\beta} \frac{\partial u\left(x(z),z\right)}{\partial\beta} dz. \tag{6.2.17}$$

This conclusion is, in fact, correct:

Proposition 6.5 *Suppose the type space is a continuous bounded interval in $\mathbb{R}$, that the buyer's utility function is twice continuously differentiable in both arguments, and the partial derivative with respect to type is bounded above. A mechanism $\langle x(\cdot),t(\cdot)\rangle$ is a direct-revelation mechanism if and only if $x(\cdot)$ is nondecreasing and*

$$t(\beta) = u\left(x(\beta),\beta\right) - \tau - \int_{\underline{\beta}}^{\beta} \frac{\partial u\left(x(z),z\right)}{\partial\beta} dz, \tag{6.2.18}$$

where $\tau \geq u_R$ is a constant.

Given a nondecreasing allocation profile, $x(\cdot)$, the seller can choose any $t(\cdot)$ satisfying (6.2.18) to implement it. She does better the greater is $t(\cdot)$, so it follows she wants τ as small as possible; that is, equal to u_R. Hence, as claimed, her expected-payoff-maximizing mechanism has a transfer function satisfying (6.2.17).

6.2.1.4 The Equilibrium Mechanism and Tariff

Consider, now, the question of the seller's choice of mechanism to offer.

Two additional points before proceeding. First, it follows from the economic definition of cost that $c(x_0,\beta) \equiv 0 \; \forall \beta$. Second, for the case of a discrete type space, "match" the continuous-space case by assuming the space is bounded above and below. Given the denumerability of the space, this is equivalent to assuming it has a finite number of elements, N. Using the ability to renormalize the index function, let the lowest type be β_1.

Given mechanism $\langle x(\cdot), t(\cdot) \rangle$, the seller's expected payoff is

$$\mathbb{E}\left\{ t(\beta) - c\left(x(\beta), \beta\right) \right\}.$$

In light of Proposition 6.4 or 6.5, as appropriate, there is no loss in limiting the seller to nondecreasing allocation profiles $x(\cdot)$ and transfer functions given by (6.2.15) or (6.2.17), as appropriate. Hence, her choice of mechanism is the program

$$\max_{x(\cdot)} \mathbb{E}\left\{ \left(u\left(x(\beta), \beta\right) - \int_{\{z \in B \mid z \leq \beta\}} R(z)dz - c\left(x(\beta), \beta\right)\right) \right\} - u_R$$

$$\equiv \max_{x(\cdot)} \mathbb{E}\left\{ \left(w\left(x(\beta), \beta\right) - \int_{\{z \in B \mid z \leq \beta\}} R(z)dz \right) \right\} - u_R$$

$$(6.2.19)$$

subject to $x(\cdot)$'s being nondecreasing; where $R(\beta)$ is the rent function (equal to $R_n\left(x(\beta_{n-1})\right)$ in the discrete case and equal to $\partial u\left(x(\beta), \beta\right) / \partial \beta$ in the continuous case) and $\int_{\{z \in B \mid z \leq \beta\}}$ is to be read as the appropriate summation notation in the discrete case.

Going forward let $f(\cdot)$ denote the density function implied by the distribution function $F(\cdot)$.[26] When B is a discrete space, it is often convenient to write f_n for $f(\beta_n)$ and *vice versa*. In the discrete case, there is no loss of generality in assuming that $f_n > 0$ for all n (to assume otherwise would be equivalent to assuming that type β_n simply didn't exist—drop that type and reindex). The analogous assumption in the continuous case, $f(\beta) > 0$ for all $\beta \in (\underline{\beta}, \bar{\beta})$, is less general, but standard. Make both assumptions.

---

[26] Observe, in the continuous-space case, this essentially implies the distribution function is differentiable (i.e., a density function is defined for all $\beta \in B$). This assumption is readily relaxed; the added complexity, though, of doing so makes such a generalization too costly relative to its benefit to include in this chapter.

Two useful facts are captured in the following lemma:

Lemma 6.4.

$$\sum_{n=1}^{N}\left(\sum_{k=2}^{n}R_k\left(x(\beta_{k-1})\right)\right)f_n = \sum_{n=1}^{N-1}R_{n+1}\left(x(\beta_n)\right)\left(1-F(\beta_n)\right)$$

and

$$\int_{\underline{\beta}}^{\bar{\beta}}\left(\int_{\underline{\beta}}^{\beta}\frac{\partial u\left(x(z),z\right)}{\partial\beta}dz\right)f(\beta)d\beta = \int_{\underline{\beta}}^{\bar{\beta}}\frac{\partial u\left(x(\beta),\beta\right)}{\partial\beta}\left(1-F(\beta)\right)d\beta.$$

From the lemma, (6.2.19) becomes, in the discrete case:

$$\max_{x(\cdot)}\sum_{n=1}^{N-1}\left(w\left(x(\beta_n),\beta_n\right)f_n - R_{n+1}\left(x(\beta_n)\right)\left(1-F(\beta_n)\right)\right) + w\left(x(\beta_N),\beta_N\right)f_N - u_R$$

$$= \max_{x(\cdot)}\sum_{n=1}^{N}\left(w\left(x(\beta_n),\beta_n\right) - \frac{1-F(\beta_n)}{f_n}R_{n+1}\left(x(\beta_n)\right)\right)f_n - u_R, \tag{6.2.20}$$

where the fact that $1-F(\beta_N)\equiv 0$ (the probability of drawing a type higher than the greatest is zero) permits the inclusion of the undefined term $R_{N+1}(x(\beta_N))$. Similarly, in the continuous case, (6.2.19) becomes

$$\max_{x(\cdot)}\int_{\underline{\beta}}^{\bar{\beta}}\left(w\left(x(\beta),\beta\right) - \frac{1-F(\beta)}{f(\beta)}\frac{\partial u\left(x(\beta),\beta\right)}{\partial\beta}\right)f(\beta)d\beta - u_R. \tag{6.2.21}$$

In both cases, underscoring the great similarity between them, the principal chooses an allocation profile to maximize

$$\mathbb{E}\left\{w\left(x(\beta),\beta\right) - \frac{1-F}{f}R\right\} - u_R$$

subject to $x(\cdot)$'s being nondecreasing. The expression inside the curly brackets—welfare generated by trade with a β-type buyer less a term reflecting the contribution the allocation $x(\beta)$ has on the information rents of types higher than β—is often referred to as *virtual surplus* (less often, virtual welfare). The information rent component reflects the inability of the seller to fully capture all the welfare generated by trade because she cannot escape "paying" an information rent to certain types. The ratio $(1-F)/f$ is the multiplicative inverse of the hazard rate of the distribution of types.[27]

---

[27] In statistics, the ratio $(1-F)/f$ is known as the Mills ratio. That term is not widely used in economics, however.

Were it not for the constraint that the allocation profile be nondecreasing, the solution to the principal's mechanism-design problem could be found by point-wise optimization; that is, for each β, the optimal $x(\beta)$ would maximize the virtual surplus; that is, be the solution to

$$\max_{x \in \mathcal{X}} w(x, \beta) - \frac{1 - F(\beta)}{f(\beta)} R(x, \beta), \tag{6.2.22}$$

where $R(\cdot, \cdot)$ is the relevant rent function (i.e., $R(x, \beta_n) = R_{n+1}(x)$ in the discrete case; and $R(x, \beta) = \partial u(x, \beta)/\partial \beta$ in the continuous case). Of course, if solving (6.2.22) for each β yields a profile that is nondecreasing, then we've solved the seller's problem—in such a case, the constraint on the allocation profile is simply not binding. In what follows, attention is limited to situations in which the nondecreasing-allocation condition is not binding.[28]

Let $\Omega(x, \beta)$ denote virtual surplus (i.e., the expression to be maximized in (6.2.22)). By the usual comparative statics, if $\Omega(\cdot, \cdot)$ exhibits increasing differences, then the x that solves (6.2.22) is necessarily nondecreasing in β and the constraint on the allocation profile can be ignored. This observation motivates the following series of assumptions.

Assumption 6. The welfare function (i.e., $w(x, \beta) = u(x, \beta) - c(x, \beta)$) exhibits increasing differences.

Observe Assumption 6 is implied by the Spence-Mirrlees condition (Proposition 6.3) if cost is invariant with respect to buyer type (an assumption true of most price-discrimination models).

Given Assumption 6, virtual surplus will exhibit increasing differences if, for $\beta > \beta'$ and $x > x'$,

$$\frac{1 - F(\beta)}{f(\beta)} \left(R(x, \beta) - R(x', \beta) \right) < \frac{1 - F(\beta')}{f(\beta')} \left(R(x, \beta') - R(x', \beta') \right). \tag{6.2.23}$$

This observation motivates:

Assumption 7   (Monotone Hazard Rate Property). The hazard rate associated with distribution of buyer types is nondecreasing in type.

Assumption 8. The rent function exhibits *nonincreasing* differences.

As the discussion shows, one can conclude:

---

[28] For many problems of interest in economics, the nondecreasing-allocation condition does not bind, which is why I'm limiting attention to that case here. For the interested reader, let me briefly note that when the condition binds, the seller's optimal mechanism-design problem becomes an optimal-control problem. In particular, if $X(\cdot)$ is the schedule implied by solving (6.2.22) for each β and it is *not* nondecreasing, then the actual allocation schedule is a flattening—or, as it is typically described *ironing*—out of the hills and valleys in $X(\cdot)$ to achieve a nondecreasing allocation profile. Section 2.3.3.3 of Bolton and Dewatripont (2005) provides details on ironing.

Lemma 6.5.   *Given Assumptions 6–8, virtual surplus exhibits increasing differences.*

As noted, Assumption 6 is, in many instances, implied by the Spence-Mirrlees condition. Because many common distributions (including the normal, uniform, and exponential) exhibit the monotone hazard rate property (MHRP), Assumption 7 is typically also seen as innocuous. Only Assumption 8 is difficult to justify as generally true because it does not correspond to any obvious *economic* principle (although it does not necessarily contradict any either). On the other hand, Assumptions 6–8 are merely sufficient conditions; it is possible that virtual surplus could exhibit increasing differences even if one or more of these assumptions fail.

Provided point-wise optimization is valid, the fact that there is zero probability of drawing a type greater than the highest type means

$$x(\beta_N) = \arg\max_{x \in \mathcal{X}} w(x, \beta_N) \text{ and } x(\bar{\beta}) = \arg\max_{x \in \mathcal{X}} w(x, \bar{\beta})$$

for the discrete and continuous cases, respectively. This result is often described as *no distortion at the top*.

Proposition 6.6   (No distortion at the top). *Assume the seller can solve her mechanism-design problem via point-wise optimization (assume, e.g., Assumptions 6–8). Then the allocation provided the highest type is the welfare-maximizing allocation given that type.*

On the other hand, if (i) $\beta \in B$ is not the highest type and (ii) all functions are differentiable, then

$$\frac{\partial \Omega(x, \beta)}{\partial x} = \frac{\partial w(x, \beta)}{\partial x} - \frac{1 - F(\beta)}{f(\beta)} \frac{\partial R(x, \beta)}{\partial x} < \frac{\partial w(x, \beta)}{\partial x}, \qquad (6.2.24)$$

where the inequality follows because $\partial R(x, \beta)/\partial x > 0$ by Spence-Mirrlees. Consequently, if point-wise optimization is valid and $x(\beta)$ is an *interior* solution to (6.2.22), then $x(\beta)$ does *not* maximize welfare given that type. This is sometimes referred to as *distortion at the bottom*, which is slightly misleading insofar as this distortion affects *all* types other than the highest. Expression (6.2.24) also tells us the direction of the distortion: the type-β buyer will be allocated less than the welfare-maximizing amount given his type. To summarize:

Proposition 6.7.   *Assume the seller can solve her mechanism-design problem via point-wise optimization (assume, e.g., Assumptions 6–8). Assume all functions are differentiable.*[29] *Consider a type other than the highest. If his allocation is an interior maximizer of virtual surplus, then his allocation is not welfare maximizing and is less than the welfare-maximizing amount.*

---

[29] It should be clear that analogous results can be derived when the functions aren't differentiable. The value of such an extension is too small to justify its inclusion here.

Intuitively, allocating more to a low-type buyer costs the seller insofar as it raises the information rent she must "pay" all higher types (equivalently, reduces what she can charge all higher types). Hence, she distorts the allocation to any type, but the highest, as she balances the gains from trade with that type against the forgone revenue from higher types.

6.2.1.5 Examples

Linear Pricing. Recall the example, given at the beginning of this section, in which the buyer seeks at most one unit of the good and his benefit from the good is β, where $\beta \in [\underline{\beta}, \bar{\beta}], \underline{\beta} \geq 0$ and the distribution of types is uniform. At its most general, an allocation, $x(\beta)$, is a probability of the good in question ending up in the buyer's hands. Hence, $\mathcal{X} = [0, 1]$, with $x_0 = 0$ (the buyer only gets the good if trade). Earlier, it was assumed that $c(x, \beta) \equiv 0$; let's generalize that slightly by assuming $c(x, \beta) \equiv xc \geq 0, c$ a constant. Note $u(x, \beta) = x\beta$. The cross-partial derivative of that is 1; given $1 > 0$, the Spence-Mirrlees condition is met, as is Assumption 6. It is readily verified that Assumptions 2–5 are satisfied. The uniform distribution satisfies MHRP. Observe $R(x, \beta) = \partial u(x, \beta)/\partial \beta = x$, which trivially satisfies nonincreasing differences. Hence, the optimal mechanism can be found by point-wise maximization of virtual surplus:

$$\max_{x \in [0,1]} x\beta - xc - \underbrace{(\bar{\beta} - \beta) x}_{\frac{1-F}{f}}.$$

It follows that $x(\beta) = 1$ if $2\beta \geq \bar{\beta} + c$ and $x(\beta) = 0$ otherwise. Observe if $\underline{\beta} \geq (\bar{\beta} + c)/2$, then the profit-maximizing mechanism entails trade with all types; this validates the claim made earlier that the seller's ignorance of the buyer's type need not necessarily result in inefficiency. Of course this particular problem is special insofar as maximizing virtual surplus here always yields a corner solution and, hence, Proposition 6.7 does not apply. It was also claimed earlier that linear pricing is the profit-maximizing tariff. To confirm this, let $\tilde{\beta} = \max\{\underline{\beta}, (\bar{\beta} + c)/2\}$. Type $\tilde{\beta}$ is the lowest type to buy. Clearly $u_R = 0$. From Lemma 6.3, $u_R = v(\tilde{\beta})$. The latter quantity is $\tilde{\beta} - t(\tilde{\beta})$. Hence, $t(\tilde{\beta}) = \tilde{\beta}$.[30] Given $x(\beta) = x(\tilde{\beta}) = 1$ for all $\beta > \tilde{\beta}$, the IC constraint implies $t(\beta) = t(\tilde{\beta})$. So the tariff is $T(x) = \tilde{\beta}$ if $x > 0$ and $T(x) = 0$ if $x = 0$; that is, it is linear pricing with a price $p = \tilde{\beta}$.

---

[30] Of course, we can derive $t(\cdot)$ directly from (6.2.17):

$$t(\beta) = x(\beta)\beta - \int_{\underline{\beta}}^{\beta} x(z)dz = \begin{cases} \beta - \beta + \tilde{\beta} = \tilde{\beta}, & \text{if } \beta \geq \tilde{\beta} \\ 0 - 0 = 0, & \text{if } \beta < \tilde{\beta} \end{cases}.$$

Second-degree Price Discrimination via Quality Distortion.[31] Many goods can be obtained in one of many versions or classes. This is true, for example, of software (business vs. home editions), travel (first vs. economy class), theater (orchestra vs. balcony seating), etc. In such cases, the seller is using quality differences to discriminate across buyers. To have a sense of this, suppose there are two types of buyer, β_1 and β_2, $\beta_2 > \beta_1 > 1$. Let not receiving the good correspond to quality $x_0 \equiv 1$ and assume that $\mathcal{X} = [1, \infty)$. Let $u(x, \beta) = \beta \log(x)$ and $c(x) = x - 1$. Assumptions 1–5 are readily verified. The validity of pointwise optimization will be shown directly. Observe

$$x(\beta_1) = \arg\max_{x \in \mathcal{X}} \beta_1 \log(x) - (x - 1) - \frac{1 - f_1}{f_1} \log(x) \text{ and} \qquad (6.2.25)$$

$$x(\beta_2) = \arg\max_{x \in \mathcal{X}} \beta_2 \log(x) - (x - 1). \qquad (6.2.26)$$

Hence, $x(\beta_2) = \beta_2$ and

$$x(\beta_1) = \begin{cases} 1, \text{ if } f_1 \leq \frac{1}{\beta_1} \\ \frac{f_1(\beta_1 + 1) - 1}{f_1}, \text{ otherwise} \end{cases}.$$

The solution, $x(\cdot)$, is nondecreasing, so pointwise optimization is valid. Note if low types are too small a proportion of the population, then the seller prefers to exclude them altogether (sometimes referred to as *shutting out the low types*). Hence, observing a seller offering a single version does not mean that she has ignored the possibility of price discrimination: she could have simply chosen to shut out the low types. In some settings, the set $\mathcal{X}$ of possible qualities may be limited by technology (it could even be binary—an air traveler, e.g., can be required to stay over Saturday night or not). Again the seller solves (6.2.25) and (6.2.26), but perhaps without being able to use calculus.

   Second-degree Price Discrimination via Quantity Discounts. A familiar phenomenon is quantity discounts: the price ratio of a larger package to a smaller is less than their size ratio. To understand such pricing, suppose a buyer's benefit from x mobile-phone minutes is $\beta\gamma \log(x + 1)$, $\gamma > 0$ a known constant. Assume a constant marginal cost of supplying minutes, $c \in (0, 1)$. Assume β is distributed uniformly on $[0, 1]$. The various assumptions are readily verified for this example. Virtual surplus is

$$\beta\gamma \log(x + 1) - cx - \underbrace{(1 - \beta)}_{\frac{1-F}{f}} \underbrace{\gamma \log(x + 1)}_{\partial u/\partial \beta}.$$

---

[31] In the usual labeling of price discrimination (i.e., first, second, and third degree), discrimination in which the consumer must be induced to reveal his preferences is called second-degree discrimination. Such discrimination is, as seen, equivalent to tariff construction via mechanism design.

The derivative of virtual surplus is

$$\frac{(2\beta - 1)\gamma - c(1 + x)}{1 + x} .$$

It immediately follows that

$$x(\beta) = \begin{cases} 0, & \text{if } \beta \leq \frac{\gamma + c}{2\gamma} \\ \frac{(2\beta - 1)\gamma - c}{c}, & \text{otherwise} \end{cases} .$$

Observe some low types are shut out. The transfer function is, from (6.2.17),

$$t(\beta) = \beta\gamma \log(x(\beta) + 1) - \int_0^\beta \gamma \log(x(z) + 1)\, dz$$

$$= \begin{cases} 0, & \text{if } \beta \leq \frac{\gamma + c}{2\gamma} \\ \frac{\gamma}{2}\left(2\beta - 1 + \log\left(\frac{\gamma(2\beta - 1)}{c}\right)\right) - \frac{c}{2}, & \text{otherwise} \end{cases} .$$

Observe the transfer can be reexpressed as a traditional tariff:[32,33]

$$T(x) = \frac{1}{2}\left(cx + \gamma \log(x + 1)\right) . \tag{6.2.27}$$

It is readily verified that there are quantity discounts (e.g., $2T(x) > T(2x)$).

6.2.2 The Monopoly Provision of Insurance

The analysis of the previous subsection covers a wide variety of trading situations and, via suitable redefinition of variables, an even wider array of contractual situations, but

---

[32] That a deterministic direct-revelation mechanism can always be reexpressed as a standard tariff is a general result known in the literature as the *taxation principle* (Rochet, 1985, attributes the name "taxation principle" to Roger Guesnerie). Formally if $x(B)$ is the set of allocations feasible under a direct-revelation mechanism and if it is possible to penalize the buyer sufficiently so that he would never choose an $x \notin x(B) \cup \{x_0\}$, then an equilibrium outcome under any deterministic direct-revelation mechanism defined by $\beta \mapsto x(\beta), t(\beta)$, is also an equilibrium outcome of the game in which the seller allows the buyer to choose the allocation, x, in exchange for payment $T(x)$, where $T(\cdot)$ is defined by

$$T(x) = \begin{cases} 0, & \text{if } x = x_0 \\ t(\beta), & \text{if } \beta \in x^{-1}(x) \text{ (i.e., such that } x = x(\beta) \text{ for some } \beta \in B) \\ \text{buyer pays large penalty,} & \text{if } x \notin x(B) \cup \{x_0\} \end{cases} .$$

[33] An alternative method of designing the profit-maximizing tariff to engage in price discrimination via quantity discounts is the so-called *demand profile* approach. This approach is particularly useful if the seller has access to actual data (e.g., of the sort generated by grocery store checkout scanners). See Wilson (1993) for details.

it does not cover all situations of interest. In particular, because the analysis exploits the buyer's quasi-linear utility, it is not suited to situations in which quasi-linear utility is a poor assumption. One such situation is an insurance market, where attitudes toward risk are of primary importance.

Suppose, now, the buyer's utility in a given state is $u(\gamma_i)$, where γ_i is his income in state i and $u(\cdot) : \mathbb{R} \to \mathbb{R}$ is an increasing function (people prefer greater incomes to smaller incomes). A buyer's type is, now, his distribution over states. As an example, a buyer could have income γ_H when healthy and γ_I when injured, where $\gamma_H > \gamma_I$ because of lost wages, the need to pay for medical care, and so forth. His type, β, is his probability of injury.

Assume the buyer is risk averse: $u(\cdot)$ is strictly concave. Let $\mathbb{E}$ be the relevant expectation operator over income. Given a nondegenerate distribution over income, Jensen's inequality implies:

$$\mathbb{E}\left\{u(\gamma)\right\} < u\left(\mathbb{E}\{\gamma\}\right) . \tag{6.2.28}$$

Because $u(\cdot)$ is monotone, it is invertible. Define the *certainty equivalence* by

$$\gamma_{ce} = u^{-1}\left(\mathbb{E}\left\{u(\gamma)\right\}\right) .$$

In words, if the buyer received γ_{ce} for certain (i.e., in all states), then his utility would be equal to his expected utility given the relevant distribution over income. Expression (6.2.28) implies $\gamma_{ce} < \mathbb{E}\{\gamma\}$.

6.2.2.1 The Basics of Insurance

Consider a risk-neutral seller (i.e., a party for whom the utility from a transfer of t is just t). As a benchmark, suppose the buyer's type were known to the seller prior to trade. The seller could offer to insure the buyer via a contract in which the buyer agreed to transfer his income in each state to the seller and the seller agreed to transfer a fixed $\hat{\gamma}$ to the buyer in each state.[34] Hence, the buyer's utility would be $u(\hat{\gamma})$ with certainty and the seller's expected utility would be $\mathbb{E}\{\gamma\} - \hat{\gamma}$ (normalize the seller's no-trade income to zero). Provided $\hat{\gamma} \geq \gamma_{ce}$, the buyer does at least as well trading as he would not trading. Provided $\mathbb{E}\{\gamma\} \geq \hat{\gamma}$, the seller does at least as well trading as she would not trading. Because the interval $\left(\gamma_{ce}, \mathbb{E}\{\gamma\}\right)$ is nonempty, there exist values for $\hat{\gamma}$ such that each side does at least weakly better to trade than not.

---

[34] Obviously this contract can be replicated by one stated in the more familiar terms of premia and benefits. See footnote 37 *infra*.

The last paragraph established that gains to trade exist. It didn't, though, establish that *full* insurance—a constant income for the risk-averse party across all states—is optimal. That full insurance is optimal is, however, readily shown.[35]

Proposition 6.8. *Let there be a discrete set of states. An insurance contract between risk-neutral and risk-averse parties that does not fully insure the risk-averse party is strictly Pareto dominated by one that does.*

Proof: Let there be N states, indexed by n. Let π_n denote the probability of state n occurring. Because otherwise state n does not really exist, we may take $\pi_n > 0$ for all n. Let y_n denote the risk-averse party's income in state n. An insurance contract, $\mathbf{Y} = \langle Y_1, \ldots, Y_N \rangle$, yields the risk-averse party a payoff of Y_n in state n and the risk-neutral party a payoff of $y_n - Y_n$. Suppose $\mathbf{Y}$ were such that $Y_n \neq Y_m$ for some n and m. The buyer's expected utility is

$$\sum_{n=1}^{N} \pi_n u(Y_n) \equiv \bar{U} .$$

If $\mathbf{Y}$ is not strictly Pareto dominated, then it must be a solution to the program

$$\max_{X_1,\ldots,X_N} \sum_{n=1}^{N} \pi_n(y_n - X_n) \text{ subject to } \sum_{n=1}^{N} \pi_n u(X_n) = \bar{U} . \tag{6.2.29}$$

Let λ denote the Lagrange multiplier on the constraint. The Lagrangian is

$$\sum_{n=1}^{N} \pi_n \left(y_n - X_n + \lambda u(X_n) \right) - \lambda \bar{U} .$$

The corresponding first-order condition is

$$-1 + \lambda u'(X_n) = 0 \ \forall n . \tag{6.2.30}$$

Because $u'(\cdot)$ is strictly monotone, it follows that a necessary condition for a contract to solve (6.2.29) is $X_1 = \cdots = X_N$. By assumption, $\mathbf{Y}$ does not satisfy this and is, thus, strictly dominated by the solution to (6.2.29). ∎

Expression (6.2.30), the condition for a Pareto-optimal insurance contract, is sometimes referred to as the Borch (1968) sharing rule. In terms of economics, the Pareto-optimal contract must be one in which the ratio of the insurer's marginal utility of income to

---

[35] The analysis here assumes a discrete set of states. The extension to a continuum of states is straightforward, but slightly more involved because of issues of measurability and the irrelevance of sets of states of measure zero. Because the economic intuition is the same, the extension is omitted for the sake of brevity.

the insured's marginal utility of income is a constant across all states.[36] This makes sense: if the ratios varied, then income could be transferred across states in a way that made both parties better.

6.2.2.2 Adverse Selection

Now return to the situation in which there are multiple buyer types and the seller is ignorant of the buyer's type at the time of contracting.

Although the analysis could be done for more than two income states, limiting attention to two is with little loss because, to make the analysis tractable, a sufficiently strong order condition—essentially a variation of the Spence-Mirrlees condition—needs to be assumed. Given such an assumption, there is little further loss of generality in limiting attention to two states. Doing so also permits a graphical analysis. Call the two states healthy (H) and injured (I).

Assume that a buyer's injury probability, β, is the sole dimension of variation. Regardless of type, a buyer has income γ_H if healthy and γ_I if injured, $\gamma_H > \gamma_I$. A type-β buyer's expected income is $\bar{\gamma}(\beta) = (1 - \beta)\gamma_H + \beta\gamma_I$. Let

$$\gamma_{ce}(\beta) = u^{-1}\left((1 - \beta)u(\gamma_H) + \beta u(\gamma_I)\right)$$

denote his certainty equivalence. Note $\gamma_{ce}(\cdot)$ is a decreasing function.

From Proposition 6.8, the seller, if she knew the buyer's type, would maximize her expected payoff by offering full insurance at the level $\gamma_{ce}(\beta)$. When she doesn't know type, she cannot offer type-specific full insurance to multiple types: if $\beta' < \beta$, then, because $\gamma_{ce}(\cdot)$ is a decreasing function, type β would do better to sign the type-β' contract. This potential for higher-risk insureds to pretend to be lower-risk insureds is known in the insurance literature as the problem of *adverse selection*. The seller's response to this adverse selection will be to offer a menu of insurance contracts, not all of which will provide full insurance.

The Revelation Principle (Proposition 6.2) still applies, so one can view the seller as designing a direct-revelation mechanism in which a buyer's announcement of type, β, maps to a contract $\langle Y_I(\beta), Y_H(\beta) \rangle$; that is, one in which the buyer transfers his income in state n, γ_n, to the seller in exchange for $Y_n(\beta)$.[37]

---

[36] The rule generalizes to a mutual insurance arrangement between two risk-averse parties. Replace $\gamma_n - X_n$ in (6.2.29) with $\psi(\gamma_n - X_n)$, where $\psi(\cdot)$ is strictly increasing and strictly concave. Solving the new (6.2.29) would yield the following analogue of (6.2.30):

$$-\psi'(\gamma_n - X_n) + \lambda u'(X_n) = 0 \; \forall n \implies \frac{\psi'(\gamma_n - X_n)}{u'(X_n)} = \lambda \; \forall n.$$

[37] Observe we can readily reexpress this contract in the familiar form of a premium, t, the buyer pays in both states and a benefit, b, he receives in the insured-against state (e.g., injury):

$$t = \gamma_H - Y_H \text{ and } b = \gamma_H - Y_H + Y_I - \gamma_I.$$

Working directly with income is simpler, though.

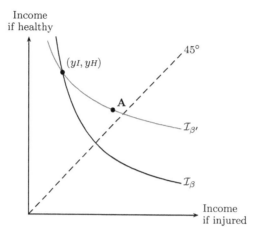

Figure 6.1 Illustration of Spence-Mirrlees condition. An indifference curve, $\mathcal{I}_\beta$, for a high-risk type, β, and one, $\mathcal{I}_{\beta'}$, for a low-risk type, β', through the uninsured point, (y_I, y_H), are shown. Because the low-risk type prefers (weakly) the partial-insurance contract **A** to no insurance, the high-risk type strictly prefers the contract **A** to no insurance.

As earlier, a Spence-Mirrlees condition holds:

Lemma 6.6   (Spence-Mirrlees). Suppose $\beta > \beta'$ and $Y_I > Y_I'$. Then if a β'-type buyer prefers $\langle Y_I, Y_H \rangle$ to $\langle Y_I', Y_H' \rangle$, a β-type buyer strictly prefers $\langle Y_I, Y_H \rangle$.

Figure 6.1 illustrates Lemma 6.6. Note it also illustrates why the Spence-Mirrlees condition is known as a single-crossing condition.

Figure 6.1 also demonstrates that, in equilibrium, if the seller sells a lower-risk type (e.g., β') a policy (contract) with some amount of insurance, then the higher-risk type (e.g., β) could achieve strictly greater expected utility buying that policy than going without any insurance. For example, as shown, type β' is willing to buy **A** if offered and type β would enjoy strictly greater expected utility under **A** than if he went without any insurance. Consequently, it must be that if the seller serves lower-risk types in equilibrium, then higher-risk types earn an information rent, a result similar to Corollary 6.2. This establishes:

Proposition 6.9.   *If a lower-risk type purchases an insurance contract in equilibrium, then all higher-risk types earn an information rent in equilibrium.*

Figure 6.2 illustrates the tradeoffs faced by the seller. Suppose there are only two types, β_h and β_l—high and low risk types, respectively. Suppose the seller offered a full-insurance contract, denoted **F**, acceptable to the low-risk type. The high-risk would also purchase this contract and enjoy a considerable information rent. Suppose, instead, the seller moved along the low-risk type's indifference curve (the curve labeled $\mathcal{I}_{\beta_\ell}$) and offered a contract with less than full insurance (e.g., contract **D**). For a contract **D** near **F**, the efficiency loss from doing this would be second order given **F** is an optimum.

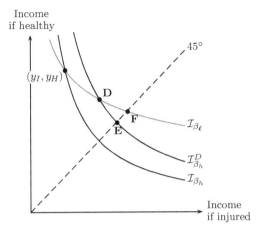

Figure 6.2 Illustration of distortion of low-risk type's contract to reduce information rent of high-risk type. Indifference curve $\mathcal{I}_{\beta_h}^D$ is the high-risk type's indifference curve through the contract **D** offered the low-risk type.

But by doing this, the seller could offer the high-risk type a full-insurance contract that gave him a smaller information rent (e.g., contract **E**). Reducing the information rent represents a first-order gain for the seller. Because the efficiency loss is second order, while the rent-reduction benefit is first order, moving away from offering just **F** is in the seller's interest. The expected profit-maximizing choices of **D** and **E** depend on the relative proportions of high and low-risk types in the population. The greater the proportion of high-risk types, the closer **D** will be to the no-insurance point (y_I, y_H). Reminiscent of Proposition 6.7 above, there is distortion at the bottom—to reduce the information rent of the high-risk type, the low-risk type is offered less than full insurance.

6.3 TWO-SIDED ASYMMETRIC INFORMATION

Now, consider a setting in which both buyer and seller have private information relevant to trade.

A key issue in the study of trading mechanisms is the point at which the buyer and seller become committed to play the mechanism. Figure 6.3 illustrates the three possible points. The first is *before* they learn their types. This corresponds to a situation in which there is symmetric uncertainty about how much the good or goods will cost to supply and the benefit it or they will yield. Such a situation arises when yet-to-be-realized market conditions will affect cost and benefit. Whether or not a party wishes to participate depends on his or her *expectation* of his or her type. When the participation decision is made prior to learning type, the situation is one of *ex ante* individual rationality.

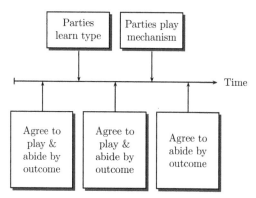

Figure 6.3 Possible points of commitment.

The second point at which commitment could occur is *after* the parties learn their types, but before they play the mechanism. This is a situation in which either (i) contracting occurs after the parties learn their types or (ii) they learn their types after contracting, but can exit the relation without penalty before playing the mechanism. Interpretation (i) applies when a buyer and seller, who know their types, meet and seek to trade. Interpretation (ii) could be reasonable given certain aspects of real-life legal systems. For instance, courts may allow parties to walk away from contracts if they can prove that a change in circumstances makes the contract commercially impractical (e.g., cost proves to be higher than expected) or purpose has been frustrated (e.g., the buyer's benefit has significantly fallen).[38] The participation constraint at this point is known as interim individual rationality.

Finally, it might be possible for the parties to refuse to accept the results of the mechanism: the corresponding constraint that they accept the results is known as *ex post* individual rationality. In the literature, it is typically assumed that a mechanism (contract) will be enforced by some third party, which means the mechanism is *ex post* individually rational because neither party is willing to suffer the punishment the third party would impose for noncompliance. In reality, there are limits to enforcement. In such cases, those limits would be relevant to the design of the mechanism.

Another issue is whether the mechanism is *balanced*: transfers among the parties to the mechanism or contract always sum to zero. If a mechanism is *unbalanced*, then either an outside source must be providing funds if the sum of transfers is positive or the parties must be committed to ridding themselves of excess funds if the sum is negative. For most buyer–seller relations, it is unreasonable to imagine there is a third party willing

---

[38] An illustration of frustration of purpose is the case *Krell v. Henry*, in which the benefit of renting an apartment to watch a coronation parade was vastly reduced by the postponement of the coronation (Hermalin et al., 2007, p. 95).

to subsidize their trading. Similarly, it is unreasonable to imagine that the parties will actually rid themselves of excess funds ("burn money"). Should the mechanism call for them to rid themselves of excess funds, the parties will presumably renegotiate their agreement and divide the excess funds among themselves. In essence, one can think of burning money as violating a collective *ex post* rationality constraint.

That noted, one can, however, imagine a few trading relations in which unbalanced mechanisms could be reasonable. If buyer and seller are different divisions of the same firm, then headquarters could be willing to subsidize trade or vacuum up excess funds if need be.

6.3.1 Trade Subject to Ex Ante Individual Rationality

To begin, assume that the relevant participation constraint is *ex ante* individual rationality; that is, each party's *expected* payoff must exceed his or her no-trade payoff. In line with the previous analysis, normalize the no-trade payoff to zero for each party.

6.3.1.1 Single-Unit Exchange

Suppose the parties will exchange at most a single unit. At the time of contracting, both buyer and seller know that the buyer's value for the unit, b, will be drawn from $[0, \infty)$ according to the distribution F. Similarly, they both know that the seller's cost (equivalently, her value for the unit), c, will be drawn from $[0, \infty)$ according to the distribution G. Assume b and c are independent random variables. Once drawn, the buyer's value is his private information and likewise the seller's cost is her private information.

As before, a mechanism is an allocation rule $x : \mathbb{R}_+^2 \to [0, 1]$ and transfer rule. Limit attention to balanced mechanisms, so the amount the buyer pays is necessarily the seller's payment. Let $p : \mathbb{R}_+^2 \to \mathbb{R}$ denote the seller's payment as a function of the buyer and seller's announcements.

Welfare is maximized provided trade occurs if and only if $b \geq c$. A mechanism is efficient therefore if

$$x(b, c) = \begin{cases} 0, & \text{if } b < c \\ 1, & \text{if } b \geq c \end{cases}.$$

A bit of intuition facilitates the mechanism-design problem. To wit, if the seller has been induced to reveal her cost, c, truthfully, then we only need the buyer, if exchange is to be efficient, to announce—having heard the seller's announced c—whether he wants the good, provided the mechanism is such that he wants it if and only if $b \geq c$. Buyer rationality implies he will do so if his payment to the seller is exactly c greater if he says he wants the good than if he says he doesn't. The issue then, at least with respect to truthful revelation, is to induce the seller to announce c truthfully.

Notice that the mechanism is such that one party's announcement follows—and can be conditioned on—the announcement of another party. Such mechanisms are known as *sequential mechanisms* for obvious reasons.[39]

The buyer would behave efficiently if his payment were simply c if he buys. Linear pricing would not, however, induce truthful revelation from the seller: were the payment just c, then the seller would announce the $\hat{c}$ that solved

$$\max_{\hat{c}} \hat{c}\left(1 - F(\hat{c})\right) + cF(\hat{c}) \quad \text{equivalently} \quad \max_{\hat{c}}(\hat{c} - c)\left(1 - F(\hat{c})\right) . \qquad (6.3.1)$$

Lemma 6.7. *Unless her cost exceeds the buyer's maximum value, the seller would not announce her price truthfully if her payment were just her announced cost.*

Proof: By assumption, there exists a $c' > c$ such that $1 - F(c') > 0$. Clearly, either expression in (6.3.1) is strictly greater if $\hat{c} = c'$ than if $\hat{c} = c$. ∎

Because, in a sequential mechanism, the buyer chooses whether to buy or not given the seller's announcement, we can write the payment as $p(x, c)$. Efficiency, as well as incentive compatibility for the buyer, requires that

$$b - p(1, c) \geq -p(0, c)$$

for all $b \geq c$ and

$$b - p(1, c) \leq -p(0, c)$$

for all $b < c$. This requirement can be met if and only if

$$c - p(1, c) = -p(0, c) ,$$

from which it follows that $p(\cdot, \cdot)$ must be of the form

$$p(x, c) = xc + T(c) ,$$

where $T(c)$ depends only on the seller's announcement and is independent of the buyer's purchase decision. If the seller claims her cost is $\hat{c}$ when it is truly c, then her expected profit (utility) is

$$\hat{c}\left(1 - F(\hat{c})\right) + cF(\hat{c}) + T(\hat{c}) , \quad \text{alternatively} \quad (\hat{c} - c)\left(1 - F(\hat{c})\right) + T(\hat{c}) . \qquad (6.3.2)$$

The first expression in (6.3.2) applies if c is the seller's value from consuming the item herself if no sale occurs, while the second applies if she only expends c if trade occurs

---

[39] Crémer and Riordan (1985) was among the first use of sequential mechanisms (sometimes called *sequential-announcement mechanisms*) and consequently such mechanisms are sometimes referred to as Crémer-Riordan mechanisms.

(e.g., in the latter case, c is the cost of manufacture). But since the same $\hat{c}$ will maximize either—see (6.3.1) above—the analysis applies to either alternative. (There is no "magic" here: the equivalence simply follows from the concept of opportunity cost.)

For convenience, consider the second alternative. Take any two types c and c', $c > c'$. By the Revelation Principle, attention can be limited to mechanisms that induce the seller's truthful revelation. A standard revealed-preference argument implies

$$T(c) \geq (c' - c)\left(1 - F(c')\right) + T(c') \quad \text{and} \quad T(c') \geq (c - c')\left(1 - F(c)\right) + T(c) .$$

Combining these expressions yields

$$1 - F(c') \geq -\frac{T(c) - T(c')}{c - c'} \geq 1 - F(c) .$$

This suggests—via integration—the following:[40]

$$T(c) = T(0) - \int_0^c \left(1 - F(z)\right) dz . \tag{6.3.3}$$

Remark 1. Recognize that the argument to this point does *not* establish that it is sufficient to limit attention to mechanisms in which $T(\cdot)$ is given by (6.3.3). Consequently, if this mechanism failed to maximize welfare, then one couldn't conclude that no mechanism would. Fortunately, as will be seen shortly, this mechanism does maximize welfare.

Remark 2. The expression $\int_0^c \left(1 - F(z)\right) dz$ has an economic interpretation. Recall the survival function, $1 - F(\cdot)$, is equivalent to a demand curve. The area beneath a demand curve between two prices p' and p is the amount by which consumer benefit is reduced if the price is raised from p' to p. Recall the effective price faced by the buyer is the seller's announced cost $\hat{c}$ (the $T(\hat{c})$ component is sunk from the buyer's perspective). If the seller announces $\hat{c} > c$, the latter being her true cost, then she reduces consumer benefit by $\int_c^{\hat{c}} \left(1 - F(z)\right) dz$. But this is $T(c) - T(\hat{c})$; that is, she reduces her transfer by exactly the amount she reduces the consumer's benefit. This causes her to internalize the externality that her announcement has on the buyer.

The mechanism is incentive compatible for the seller if the seller solves

$$\max_{\hat{c}} (\hat{c} - c)\left(1 - F(\hat{c})\right) + T(\hat{c}) \tag{6.3.4}$$

by choosing $\hat{c} = c$ for all c. To see that is her choice, suppose it were not. Then there would exist a c and $\hat{c}$ such that

---

[40] The mechanism derived here was originally derived in Hermalin and Katz (1993), where it was referred to as a *fill-in-the-price mechanism*.

$$(\hat{c} - c)\left(1 - F(\hat{c})\right) + T(\hat{c}) > T(c).$$

Suppose $\hat{c} > c$, then this last expression implies

$$1 - F(\hat{c}) > \frac{1}{\hat{c} - c} \int_c^{\hat{c}} (1 - F(z)) \, dz = 1 - F(\tilde{c}) \tag{6.3.5}$$

where $\tilde{c} \in (c, \hat{c})$. (Such a $\tilde{c}$ exists by the mean-value theorem.) Survival functions are nonincreasing, hence (6.3.5) is impossible. *Reductio ad absurdum*, the seller wouldn't prefer to announce $\hat{c}$ rather than c. A similar argument reveals that there is no $\hat{c} < c$ that the seller would rather announce than c.

To summarize to this point: the sequential mechanism in which the seller announces her cost, c, and the buyer then decides to buy or not, with the buyer's payment being $p(x, c) = xc + T(c)$, with $T(\cdot)$ given by (6.3.3), induces the seller to announce her cost truthfully in equilibrium and induces the buyer to buy if and only if his valuation, b, exceeds the seller's cost. The one remaining issue is can $T(0)$ be set so as to satisfy *ex ante* IR for both buyer and seller? The seller and buyer's respective expected utilities under this mechanism are

$$U_S = \int_0^\infty T(c) dG(c) = T(0) - \int_0^\infty \left(\int_0^c (1 - F(b)) \, db \right) dG(c)$$

and

$$U_B = \int_0^\infty \left(-T(c) + \int_c^\infty (b - c) dF(b) \right) dG(c)$$
$$= -U_S + \int_0^\infty \int_c^\infty (b - c) dF(b) dG(c). \tag{6.3.6}$$

Set

$$T(0) = \int_0^\infty \left(\int_0^c (1 - F(b)) \, db \right) dG(c), \tag{6.3.7}$$

making U_S zero; IR for the seller is satisfied. Plugging that into (6.3.6) reveals $U_B \geq 0$, so the buyer's IR is also satisfied. To conclude:

Proposition 6.10. *Assume a buyer and seller wish to exchange a single unit of a good efficiently. Assume, too, that the parties can enter into a contract prior to learning their valuation and cost. Then a mechanism exists that achieves first-best efficiency and is ex ante individually* *rational for both parties. An example of such a mechanism is one in which the seller announces her cost, c, and the buyer subsequently decides to purchase (x = 1) or not (x = 0), with the buyer's payment to the seller equal to xc + T(c), where T(·) is defined by expressions (6.3.3) and (6.3.7).*

6.3.1.2 Multi-Unit Exchange

Now consider the exchange of multiple units of a good. Assume the buyer's utility is $U(x, \beta) - t$ and the seller's $t - C(x, \gamma)$, where β and γ are the buyer and seller's types, respectively; and, as before, x and t are units of the good and a monetary transfer, respectively. Assume that U and C are twice continuously differentiable in both arguments. Assume β and γ are independent random variables distributed, respectively, $F:[\beta_L, \beta_H] \to [0, 1]$ and $G:[\gamma_L, \gamma_H] \to [0, 1]$.

Welfare is

$$W(x, \beta, \gamma) = U(x, \beta) - C(x, \gamma).$$

Assume, for all β and γ, that $U(\cdot, \beta)$ is a concave function (buyer's marginal benefit is nonincreasing) and $C(\cdot, \gamma)$ a convex function (nonincreasing returns to scale), with one function at least strictly so. Hence, $W(\cdot, \beta, \gamma)$ is strictly concave for all β and γ. There is, thus, a unique welfare maximizing amount of trade, $x^*(\beta, \gamma)$, for all β and γ. To insure interior maxima assume:

- $\partial U(0, \beta)/\partial x > 0$ (marginal benefit at 0 is positive) for all $\beta > \beta_L$;
- $\partial C(0, \gamma)/\partial x = 0$ (marginal cost at 0 is 0) for all $\gamma < \gamma_H$;
- For all β and γ, there exists a finite $\bar{x}(\beta, \gamma)$ such that $x > \bar{x}(\beta, \gamma)$ implies $\partial W(x, \beta, \gamma)/\partial x < 0$ (infinite trade is never desirable).

As in the previous subsection, the goal is an efficient sequential mechanism. To "mix things up," let the buyer be the one to announce first. The objective is for the seller to respond to the buyer's announcement, $\hat{\beta}$, by truthfully revealing her type, γ; that is, the solution to

$$\max_{\hat{\gamma}} p(\hat{\beta}, \hat{\gamma}) - C\left(x(\hat{\beta}, \hat{\gamma}), \gamma\right) \tag{6.3.8}$$

needs to be $\hat{\gamma} = \gamma$ for all γ and $\hat{\beta}$. This can be achieved by defining

$$x(\beta, \gamma) = x^*(\beta, \gamma) \text{ and } p(\beta, \gamma) = U\left(x^*(\beta, \gamma), \beta\right) - \tau(\beta) \tag{6.3.9}$$

(the role of $\tau : [\beta_L, \beta_H] \to \mathbb{R}$ will be made clear below). To verify (6.3.9) induces truth-telling by the seller, observe (6.3.8) is equivalent to

$$\max_{x \in x^*\left(\hat{\beta}, [\gamma_L, \gamma_H]\right)} U(x, \hat{\beta}) - C(x, \gamma), \tag{6.3.10}$$

where $x^* \left(\hat{\beta}, [\gamma_L, \gamma_H] \right)$ is the *image* of $x^*(\hat{\beta}, \cdot)$.[41] Because $x^*(\hat{\beta}, \gamma)$ is the unconstrained maximizer of (6.3.10) and it's in $x^* \left(\hat{\beta}, [\gamma_L, \gamma_H] \right)$, a best response for the seller is to announce her type truthfully.

The additional function, $\tau(\cdot)$, is necessary to induce truth-telling by the buyer. The buyer's expected utility in equilibrium is

$$\tau(\hat{\beta}) + \int_{\gamma_L}^{\gamma_H} \left(U \left(x^*(\hat{\beta}, \gamma), \beta \right) - U \left(x^*(\hat{\beta}, \gamma), \hat{\beta} \right) \right) dG(\gamma),$$

if his type is β but he announces $\hat{\beta}$. His utility is $\tau(\beta)$ if he tells the truth. Consider $\beta > \beta'$. By revealed preference:

$$\tau(\beta) \geq \tau(\beta') + \int_{\gamma_L}^{\gamma_H} \left(U \left(x^*(\beta', \gamma), \beta \right) - U \left(x^*(\beta', \gamma), \beta' \right) \right) dG(\gamma) \text{ and}$$

$$\tau(\beta') \geq \tau(\beta) + \int_{\gamma_L}^{\gamma_H} \left(U \left(x^*(\beta, \gamma), \beta' \right) - U \left(x^*(\beta, \gamma), \beta \right) \right) dG(\gamma).$$

Rearranging,

$$\int_{\gamma_L}^{\gamma_H} \frac{U \left(x^*(\beta, \gamma), \beta' \right) - U \left(x^*(\beta, \gamma), \beta \right)}{\beta - \beta'} dG(\gamma) \geq \frac{\tau(\beta) - \tau(\beta')}{\beta - \beta'}$$

$$\geq \int_{\gamma_L}^{\gamma_H} \frac{U \left(x^*(\beta', \gamma), \beta \right) - U \left(x^*(\beta', \gamma), \beta' \right)}{\beta - \beta'} dG(\gamma)$$

Via the implicit function theorem, it is readily shown that x^* is continuous in each of its arguments. One can, therefore, take the limit of the outer expressions as $\beta' \to \beta$. This yields[42]

$$\tau'(\beta) = \int_{\gamma_L}^{\gamma_H} \frac{\partial U \left(x^*(\beta, \gamma), \beta \right)}{\partial \beta} dG(\gamma).$$

Consequently,

$$\tau(\beta) = \tau(0) + \int_{\gamma_L}^{\gamma_H} \int_{\beta_L}^{\beta} \frac{\partial U \left(x^*(z, \gamma), z \right)}{\partial \beta} dz dG(\gamma). \tag{6.3.11}$$

[41] Recall that the *image* of a function is the set of all values the function can take.
[42] Because the question is the sufficiency of the mechanism, there is no loss in assuming $\tau(\cdot)$ differentiable provided an efficient mechanism is derived.

We want to simplify (6.3.11). To that end, observe the envelope theorem entails

$$\frac{d}{d\beta} W\left(x^*(\beta,\gamma),\beta,\gamma\right) \equiv \frac{\partial U\left(x^*(\beta,\gamma),\beta\right)}{\partial\beta}.$$

Consequently, (6.3.11) can be rewritten as

$$\tau(\beta) = \tau(0) + \int_{\gamma_L}^{\gamma_H} \left(W\left(x^*(\beta,\gamma),\beta,\gamma\right) - W\left(x^*(\beta_L,\gamma),\beta_L,\gamma\right)\right) dG(\gamma)$$

$$= \xi(0) + \int_{\gamma_L}^{\gamma_H} W\left(x^*(\beta,\gamma),\beta,\gamma\right) dG(\gamma).$$

(6.3.12)

It remains to be verified that this mechanism induces truth-telling. Consider $\hat{\beta} \neq \beta$, the latter being the buyer's true type. Is

$$\tau(\beta) \geq \tau(\hat{\beta}) + \int_{\gamma_L}^{\gamma_H} \left(U\left(x^*(\hat{\beta},\gamma),\beta\right) - U\left(x^*(\hat{\beta},\gamma),\hat{\beta}\right)\right) dG(\gamma)?$$

Suppose it weren't. Substituting for $\tau(\cdot)$ yields:

$$\int_{\gamma_L}^{\gamma_H} W\left(x^*(\beta,\gamma),\beta,\gamma\right) dG(\gamma) < \int_{\gamma_L}^{\gamma_H} \left(U\left(x^*(\hat{\beta},\gamma),\beta\right) - C\left(x^*(\hat{\beta},\gamma),\gamma\right)\right) dG(\gamma)$$

$$= \int_{\gamma_L}^{\gamma_H} W\left(x^*(\hat{\beta},\gamma),\beta,\gamma\right) dG(\gamma).$$

But this is a contradiction because $x^*(\beta,\gamma)$ maximizes $W(x,\beta,\gamma)$. *Reductio ad absurdum*, the supposition is false and the mechanism induces truth-telling.

The intuition for why the mechanism works can be seen from (6.3.9): the buyer's expected payment is

$$\int_{\gamma_L}^{\gamma_H} p(\hat{\beta},\gamma) dG(\gamma) = \int_{\gamma_L}^{\gamma_H} C(x^*(\hat{\beta},\gamma),\gamma) dG(\gamma) - \xi(0);$$

that is, he pays the expected cost of providing what would be the welfare-maximizing quantity were his type $\hat{\beta}$. Consequently, he maximizes actual expected welfare if he tells the truth, but fails to do so if he lies. Effectively, the buyer is made to face the social planner's optimization problem and, so, made to maximize welfare.

Finally, it needs to be verified that a $\tau(0)$ exists such that both buyer and seller are willing to participate. To that end, let

$$\tau(0) = \int_{\gamma_L}^{\gamma_H} \left(W\left(x^*(\beta_L, \gamma), \beta_L, \gamma\right) - \int_{\beta_L}^{\beta_H} W\left(x^*(\beta, \gamma), \beta, \gamma\right) dF(\beta) \right) dG(\gamma).$$

$$(6.3.13)$$

It is readily seen that the seller's expected utility is positive—there are, in expectation, positive gains to trade and these expected gains to trade equal the sum of the buyer's and seller's expected utilities. To summarize:

Proposition 6.11. *Assume buyer and seller wish to exchange the welfare-maximizing quantity of some good, where the welfare-maximizing quantity depends on their types. Assume, too, that the parties can enter into a contract prior to learning their types. Then a mechanism exists that achieves first-best efficiency and is ex ante individually rational for both parties. An example of such a mechanism is given by expressions* (6.3.9), (6.3.12), *and* (6.3.13).

6.3.2 Trade Subject to Interim Individual Rationality

Suppose, now, a mechanism must satisfy interim individual rationality. Recall, this means that each party must wish to play the mechanism *knowing* his or her type. The no-trade payoffs continue to be zero for each party.

Limit attention to single-unit exchange. The result will prove to be that *no* balanced mechanism yields welfare-maximizing exchange for all buyer and seller types, a finding due originally to Myerson and Satterthwaite (1983).

At the time of contracting, both buyer and seller know the buyer's value for the unit, b, was drawn from $[0, \bar{b}]$ according to the distribution F. Only the buyer knows what value was drawn. Similarly, they both know the seller's cost (equivalently, value for the unit), c, was drawn from $[\underline{c}, \bar{c}]$ according to the distribution G. Only the seller knows what cost was drawn. Assume b and c are independent random variables. Assume both distributions F and G are differentiable. Let their derivatives (density functions) be denoted by f and g, respectively. Assume full support, so that $f(b) > 0$ for all $b \in [0, \bar{b}]$ and $g(c) > 0$ for all $c \in [\underline{c}, \bar{c}]$. Because trade is never efficient if $\underline{c} \geq \bar{b}$, assume $\bar{b} > \underline{c}$. Given c is a cost, $c \geq 0$; hence, $\bar{c} > 0$.

As before, a mechanism is an allocation rule $x : \mathbb{R}_+^2 \to [0, 1]$ and a transfer rule $p : \mathbb{R}_+^2 \to \mathbb{R}$.

Efficiency requires trade occur if and only if $b \geq c$. A mechanism is efficient, therefore, if and only if it satisfies

$$x(b, c) = \begin{cases} 0, & \text{if } b < c \\ 1, & \text{if } b \geq c \end{cases}.$$

To determine whether an efficient balanced mechanism exists, one either needs to derive a mechanism that works (the strategy employed in the previous subsection) or characterize the entire set of mechanisms and show no element of that set works (the strategy to be pursued here). From the Revelation Principle, attention can be limited to direct-revelation mechanisms. The first step is to characterize the set of balanced direct-revelation mechanisms; that is, mechanisms in which truth-telling by one party is a best response to truth-telling by the other and vice versa.

Define

$$\xi_B(b) = \int_{\underline{c}}^{\bar{c}} x(b,c)g(c)\,dc \ \text{ and } \ \xi_S(c) = \int_0^{\bar{b}} x(b,c)f(b)\,db \,.$$

The quantity $\xi_i(\theta)$ is the probability of trade given party i's announced type, θ, and truth-telling by the other party. Similarly, define

$$\rho_B(b) = \int_{\underline{c}}^{\bar{c}} p(b,c)g(c)\,dc \ \text{ and } \ \rho_S(c) = \int_0^{\bar{b}} p(b,c)f(b)\,db \,.$$

The quantity $\rho_i(\theta)$ is the expected payment given party i's announced type and truth-telling by the other party.

Let $u(b)$ and $\pi(c)$ be, respectively, the buyer and seller's expected utilities if they announce their types truthfully in equilibrium. Hence,

$$u(b) = b\xi_B(b) - \rho_B(b) \text{ and} \tag{6.3.14}$$

$$\pi(c) = \rho_S(c) - c\xi_S(c) \,. \tag{6.3.15}$$

A mechanism induces truth-telling and satisfies interim IR if and only if, for all $b, b' \in [0, \bar{b}]$ and all $c, c' \in [0, \bar{c}]$, we have

$$u(b) \geq b\xi_B(b') - \rho_B(b') \,, \tag{IC$_B$}$$

$$\pi(c) \geq \rho_S(c') - c\xi_S(c') \,, \tag{IC$_S$}$$

$$u(b) \geq 0 \,, \text{ and} \tag{IR$_B$}$$

$$\pi(c) \geq 0 \,. \tag{IR$_S$}$$

By revealed preference:

$$u(b) \geq u(b') + \xi_B(b')(b - b') \text{ and}$$
$$u(b') \geq u(b) + \xi_B(b)(b' - b) \,.$$

Combining these expressions yields:

$$\xi_B(b)(b - b') \geq u(b) - u(b') \geq \xi_B(b')(b - b') . \qquad (6.3.16)$$

A similar revealed-preference argument yields:

$$\xi_S(c')(c - c') \geq \pi(c') - \pi(c) \geq \xi_S(c)(c - c') . \qquad (6.3.17)$$

Suppose $b > b'$. It follows from (6.3.16) that $\xi_B(b) \geq \xi_B(b')$—a necessary condition for the mechanism to be incentive compatible is that the probability of trade be nondecreasing in the buyer's type. Similarly, suppose $c > c'$. It follows from (6.3.17) that a necessary condition for the mechanism to be incentive compatible is that the probability of trade be nonincreasing in the seller's cost.

The functions $u(\cdot)$ and $\pi(\cdot)$ are absolutely continuous.[43] It follows that they are differentiable almost everywhere. Where their derivatives exist, taking limits reveals that

$$u'(b) = \xi_B(b) \text{ and } \pi'(c) = -\xi_S(c) .$$

Finally, because $u(\cdot)$ and $\pi(\cdot)$ are absolutely continuous, they can be expressed as the indefinite integral of their derivative (Yeh, 2006, Theorem 13.17, p. 283):

$$u(b) = u(0) + \int_0^b \xi_B(z)dz \text{ and} \qquad (6.3.18)$$

$$\pi(c) = \pi(\bar{c}) + \int_c^{\bar{c}} \xi_S(z)dz . \qquad (6.3.19)$$

Because probabilities are non-negative, (6.3.18) implies that $u(b) \geq 0$ if $u(0) \geq 0$. Likewise, (6.3.19) implies that $\pi(c) \geq 0$ if $\pi(\bar{c}) \geq 0$. This analysis yields:

Lemma 6.8. *If a mechanism is incentive compatible, then (i) the buyer's perceived probability of trade given his value (i.e., $\xi_B(\cdot)$) is nondecreasing in his value; (ii) the seller's perceived probability of trade given her cost (i.e., $\xi_S(\cdot)$) is nonincreasing in her cost; (iii) the buyer's equilibrium expected utility conditional on his value is given by (6.3.18); and (iv) the seller's equilibrium expected utility conditional on her cost is given by (6.3.19). Moreover, necessary and sufficient*

---

[43] Proof: Because ξ is a probability, it is less than one. Hence, for all b, b', c, and c', it follows from (6.3.16) and (6.3.17), respectively, that $|u(b) - u(b')| < |b - b'|$ and $|\pi(c) - \pi(c')| < |c - c'|$. The functions $u(\cdot)$ and $\pi(\cdot)$ thus satisfy the Lipschitz condition. The result follows because all Lipschitzian functions are absolutely continuous (see, e.g., van Tiel, 1984, p. 5).

conditions for the mechanism to be interim individually rational are that the buyer with the lowest value wish to participate and the seller with the highest cost wish to participate (i.e., $u(0) \geq 0$ and $\pi(\bar{c}) \geq 0$).

What about sufficiency with respect to incentive compatibility? Suppose a mechanism satisfies conditions (i)–(iv) of Lemma 6.8. Suppose the mechanism were not IC for the buyer, then there would exist b and b' such that

$$u(b) < u(b') + \xi_B(b')(b - b').\tag{6.3.20}$$

Substituting for $u(\cdot)$ and canceling like terms, this last expression implies

$$\int_{b'}^{b} \xi_B(z)\,dz < \xi_B(b')(b - b')\tag{6.3.21}$$

if $b > b'$ or

$$\int_{b}^{b'} \xi_B(z)\,dz > \xi_B(b')(b' - b)\tag{6.3.22}$$

if $b < b'$. By the intermediate value theorem, (6.3.21) and (6.3.22) imply

$$\xi_B(\tilde{b})(b - b') < \xi_B(b')(b - b') \text{ and}\tag{6.3.23}$$

$$\xi_B(\tilde{b})(b' - b) > \xi_B(b')(b' - b),\tag{6.3.24}$$

respectively, where $\tilde{b} \in \left(\min\{b', b\}, \max\{b', b\}\right)$. But expression (6.3.23) implies $\xi_B(\tilde{b}) < \xi_B(b')$, which contradicts the fact that $\xi_B(\cdot)$ is nondecreasing (recall (6.3.23) is the relevant expression if $b' < b$ and, thus, $b' < \tilde{b}$). Similarly, (6.3.24) leads to a contradiction. Given that (6.3.20) leads to a contradiction, it follows that it cannot hold and, thus, that the mechanism cannot fail to be IC. This establishes that conditions (i) and (iii) of Lemma 6.8 are sufficient for a mechanism to induce truth-telling by the buyer. A similar analysis holds for the seller. To summarize:

Lemma 6.9.   *If a mechanism is such that (i) the buyer's perceived probability of trade given his value (i.e., $\xi_B(\cdot)$) is nondecreasing in his value; (ii) the seller's perceived probability of trade given her cost (i.e., $\xi_S(\cdot)$) is nonincreasing in her cost; (iii) the buyer's equilibrium expected utility conditional on his value is given by (6.3.18); and (iv) the seller's equilibrium expected utility conditional on her cost is given by (6.3.19), then the mechanism is a direct-revelation mechanism.*

The following can now be shown:

Proposition 6.12   (Myerson-Satterthwaite). *No balanced interim individually rational mechanism exists that achieves the first best in a setting in which a single unit is potentially to be exchanged and the buyer's value and seller's cost are continuously distributed with full support over overlapping intervals.*

Given that an efficient mechanism doesn't exist, the next question is what is the *second*-best mechanism? To answer, it is helpful to restate the interim IR constraint: Lemma 6.9 implies a necessary condition for interim IR is that $u(0) + \pi(\bar{c}) \geq 0$. This condition is also *sufficient*. Why? Well, if one component, say $u(0)$, were negative, the other must be positive; moreover, $-u(0)$ in surplus can be shifted from the seller to the buyer to obtain new constants of integration:

$$\tilde{u}(0) = 0 \text{ and } \tilde{\pi}(\bar{c}) = \pi(\bar{c}) - u(0) \geq 0.$$

(Recall the constants of integration are arbitrary.) Next, the mechanism is balanced, so

$$\int_0^{\bar{b}} \rho_B(b) f(b)\, db = \int_{\underline{c}}^{\bar{c}} \rho_S(c) g(c)\, dc.$$

Expressions (6.3.14), (6.3.15), (6.3.18), and (6.3.19) imply

$$\rho_B(b) = b\xi_B(b) - u(0) - \int_0^b \xi_B(z)\, dz \text{ and } \rho_S(c) = c\xi_S(c) + \pi(\bar{c}) + \int_c^{\bar{c}} \xi_S(z)\, dz.$$

Hence,

$$-u(0) + \int_0^{\bar{b}} \left(b\xi_B(b) - \int_0^b \xi_B(z)\, dz \right) f(b)\, db$$
$$= \pi(\bar{c}) + \int_{\underline{c}}^{\bar{c}} \left(c\xi_S(c) + \int_c^{\bar{c}} \xi_S(z)\, dz \right) g(c)\, dc. \tag{6.3.25}$$

From (6.3.25), a mechanism satisfies interim IR if and only if

$$\int_0^{\bar{b}} \left(b\xi_B(b) - \int_0^b \xi_B(z)\, dz \right) f(b)\, db - \int_{\underline{c}}^{\bar{c}} \left(c\xi_S(c) + \int_c^{\bar{c}} \xi_S(z)\, dz \right) g(c)\, dc \geq 0.$$

From the definitions of $\xi_B(\cdot)$ and $\xi_S(\cdot)$, the LHS of this last expression equals

$$\int_0^{\bar{b}} \left(b \int_{\underline{c}}^{\bar{c}} x(b, c) g(c)\, dc - \int_0^b \int_{\underline{c}}^{\bar{c}} x(z, c) g(c)\, dc\, dz \right) f(b)\, db$$
$$- \int_{\underline{c}}^{\bar{c}} \left(c \int_0^{\bar{b}} x(b, c) f(b)\, db + \int_c^{\bar{c}} \int_0^{\bar{b}} x(b, z) f(b)\, db\, dz \right) g(c)\, dc.$$

In turn, this equals

$$\int_0^{\bar{b}} \int_{\underline{c}}^{\bar{c}} (b-c)x(b,c)f(b)g(c)db\,dc + \int_0^{\bar{b}} \int_0^{b} \int_{\underline{c}}^{\bar{c}} x(z,c)g(c)dc\,dz \times \left(-f(b)db\right)$$

$$- \int_{\underline{c}}^{\bar{c}} \int_{c}^{\bar{c}} \int_0^{\bar{b}} x(b,z)f(b)db\,dz \times g(c)dc$$

$$= \int_0^{\bar{b}} \int_{\underline{c}}^{\bar{c}} (b-c)x(b,c)f(b)g(c)db\,dc - \int_0^{\bar{b}} (1-F(b)) \int_{\underline{c}}^{\bar{c}} x(b,c)g(c)dc\,db$$

$$- \int_{\underline{c}}^{\bar{c}} G(c) \int_0^{\bar{b}} x(b,c)f(b)db\,dc$$

$$= \int_0^{\bar{b}} \int_{\underline{c}}^{\bar{c}} \left(\left(b - \frac{1-F(b)}{f(b)}\right) - \left(c + \frac{G(c)}{g(c)}\right) \right) x(b,c)f(b)g(c)dc\,db,$$

$$(6.3.26)$$

where the first equality follows via integration by parts. To summarize the analysis to this point:

Lemma 6.10. *A necessary and sufficient condition for a direct-revelation mechanism to be interim individually rational is that expression (6.3.26) be non-negative.*

The second-best problem can now be stated:

$$\max_{x(\cdot,\cdot)} \int_0^{\bar{b}} \int_{\underline{c}}^{\bar{c}} (b-c)x(b,c)f(b)g(c)dc\,db$$

subject to the constraints that (6.3.26) be non-negative, $\int_{\underline{c}}^{\bar{c}} x(b,c)g(c)dc$ be nondecreasing in b, and $\int_0^{\bar{b}} x(b,c)f(b)db$ be nonincreasing in c. In light of Proposition 6.12, the constraint that expression (6.3.26) be non-negative is binding. Let $\lambda > 0$ be the Lagrange multiplier on that constraint. As is often done in such problems, proceed by ignoring the monotonicity constraints on $\xi_B(\cdot)$ and $\xi_S(\cdot)$ and hope that the solution ends up satisfying them. The Lagrangean is

$$\int_0^{\bar{b}} \int_{\underline{c}}^{\bar{c}} (b-c)x(b,c)f(b)g(c)dc\,db$$

$$+\lambda \int_0^{\bar{b}} \int_{\underline{c}}^{\bar{c}} \left(\left(b - \frac{1-F(b)}{f(b)}\right) - \left(c + \frac{G(c)}{g(c)}\right) \right) x(b,c)f(b)g(c)dc\,db$$

$$\propto \int_0^{\bar{b}} \int_{\underline{c}}^{\bar{c}} \left(\left(b - \frac{\lambda}{1+\lambda} \frac{1-F(b)}{f(b)}\right) - \left(c + \frac{\lambda}{1+\lambda} \frac{G(c)}{g(c)}\right) \right) x(b,c)f(b)g(c)dc\,db,$$

where $\propto$ denotes "proportional to"; that is, the last line is the Lagrangean up to a positive multiplicative constant. Since such a constant is irrelevant to the solution, the optimal $x(\cdot,\cdot)$ maximizes that last line. The obvious solution is to set $x(b, c) = 1$ when

$$b - \frac{\lambda}{1+\lambda}\frac{1-F(b)}{f(b)} \geq c + \frac{\lambda}{1+\lambda}\frac{G(c)}{g(c)} \tag{6.3.27}$$

and to set $x(b, c) = 0$ otherwise.

Does the solution given by condition (6.3.27) yield $\xi_B(\cdot)$ and $\xi_S(\cdot)$ that satisfy the monotonicity constraints?

Lemma 6.11.   *A sufficient condition for the monotonicity conditions on $\xi_B(\cdot)$ and $\xi_S(\cdot)$ to be satisfied is that $x(\cdot, c)$ be a nondecreasing function for all c and that $x(b, \cdot)$ be a nonincreasing function for all b.*

In light of Lemma 6.11, it remains to check if (6.3.27) yields an $x(\cdot,\cdot)$ that is nondecreasing in its first argument and nonincreasing in its second. This will hold if the LHS of (6.3.27) is nondecreasing in b and the RHS is nondecreasing in c.

Lemma 6.12.   *If*

$$b - \frac{1-F(b)}{f(b)} \quad \text{and} \quad c + \frac{G(c)}{g(c)} \tag{6.3.28}$$

are nonincreasing in b and c, respectively, then the allocation rule satisfying (6.3.27) satisfies the monotonicity conditions on $\xi_B(\cdot)$ and $\xi_S(\cdot)$.

Corollary 6.3.   *If $F(\cdot)$ satisfies the monotone hazard rate property (MHRP) and $G(\cdot)$ the monotone reverse hazard rate property (the latter property being that the reverse hazard rate be nonincreasing),[44] then the allocation rule satisfying (6.3.27) satisfies the monotonicity conditions on $\xi_B(\cdot)$ and $\xi_S(\cdot)$.*

As shown in the proofs given in the appendix, the key to the analysis is the expressions

$$V_B(b,\sigma) = b - \sigma\frac{1-F(b)}{f(b)} \quad \text{and} \quad V_C(c,\sigma) = c + \sigma\frac{G(c)}{g(c)}.$$

These are similar to the virtual surplus function encountered in the previous section (consider, e.g., expression (6.2.22) and surrounding discussion). We can view them,

---

[44] The *reverse* hazard rate is the density function divided by the distribution function.

respectively, as the *virtual benefit function* and *virtual cost function*. As with the virtual surplus function, these functions differ from the true benefit (*b*) and true cost (*c*) because of the information rents the parties get: the cost of inducing truthful revelation is that high-benefit buyers and low-cost sellers must be left some amount of information rent. The need to satisfy *interim* IR prevents the mechanism designer from recapturing these rents, in expectation, via *ex ante* noncontingent transfers. The consequence is distortion in the allocation of the good.

Summarizing the analysis to this point:

Proposition 6.13.   *Consider a setting in which a single unit is potentially to be exchanged, the buyer's value and seller's cost are continuously distributed with full support over overlapping intervals, and the mechanism must satisfy interim individual rationality. Assume, given $\sigma = 1$, the virtual benefit function is increasing in the buyer's valuation and the virtual cost function is increasing in the seller's cost. Then there exists a second-best direct-revelation mechanism. Moreover, there exists a $\sigma \in (0,1)$ such that this second-best mechanism utilizes an allocation rule such that there is exchange if virtual benefit exceeds virtual cost and no exchange otherwise (i.e., there is exchange if $V_B(b,\sigma) \geq V_C(c,\sigma)$ and no exchange otherwise).*

As an example, suppose that b is distributed uniformly on $[0, \bar{b}]$ and c is distributed uniformly on $[0, \bar{c}]$ (note, here, $\underline{c} = 0$). Assume $\bar{c} \geq \bar{b}$. The uniform satisfies both MHRP and the monotone reverse hazard rate property. Consequently,

$$V_B(b,\sigma) = b - \sigma(\bar{b} - b) \quad \text{and} \quad V_C(c,\sigma) = c + \sigma c.$$

The allocation rule, given σ, is

$$x(b,c) = \begin{cases} 0, & \text{if } (1+\sigma)b - \sigma\bar{b} < (1+\sigma)c \\ 1, & \text{if } (1+\sigma)b - \sigma\bar{b} \geq (1+\sigma)c \end{cases}.$$

Interim IR binds; hence, (6.3.26) entails

$$0 = \int_0^{\bar{b}} \int_0^{\bar{c}} \left(V_B(b,1) - V_C(c,1)\right) x(b,c) \left(\bar{b}\bar{c}\right)^{-1} dc\, db$$

$$= \int_0^{\bar{b}} \int_0^{\bar{c}} (2b - \bar{b} - 2c)x(b,c) \left(\bar{b}\bar{c}\right)^{-1} dc\, db \tag{6.3.29}$$

Note that $x(b,c) = 0$ if

$$b \leq \frac{\sigma}{1+\sigma}\bar{b} \equiv \zeta.$$

It is also 0 if

$$c > b - \frac{\sigma}{1 + \sigma} \bar{b} = b - \zeta .$$

It is otherwise equal to 1. Knowing this, rewrite (6.3.29) as

$$0 = \int_{\zeta}^{\bar{b}} \int_{0}^{b - \zeta} (2b - \bar{b} - 2c) \left(\bar{b}\bar{c} \right)^{-1} dc \, db = \frac{(4\zeta - \bar{b})(\bar{b} - \zeta)^2}{6\bar{b}\bar{c}} = \frac{\bar{b}^2(1 - 3\sigma)}{6\bar{c}(1 + \sigma)^3} .$$

It follows that $\sigma = 1/3$. Observe

$$V_B \left(b, \frac{1}{3} \right) - V_C \left(c, \frac{1}{3} \right) = \frac{4}{3} b - \frac{4}{3} c - \frac{1}{3} \bar{b} .$$

Hence, in this example, the second-best mechanism employs the allocation rule:

$$x(b, c) = \begin{cases} 0, & \text{if } b < c + \bar{b}/4 \\ 1, & \text{if } b \geq c + \bar{b}/4 \end{cases} .$$

In words, exchange occurs if and only if the buyer's valuation exceeds the seller's cost by at least one-quarter of the buyer's maximum valuation. Figure 6.4 illustrates for the case in which $\bar{b} = \bar{c}$ ("should" in the figure means if the first best is to be achieved).[45]

6.3.3 The Money-on-the-Table Problem

From Proposition 6.13, the best outcome when subject to interim IR is exchange whenever $V_B(b, \sigma) \geq V_C(c, \sigma)$. Unless $\sigma = 0$, there exist values of b and c such that $b > c$, but $V_B(b, \sigma) < V_C(c, \sigma)$. Given that $\sigma = 0$ is impossible (Myerson-Satterthwaite), the following arises with positive probability: exchange should occur ($b > c$), but is blocked by the second-best mechanism. Moreover, if buyer and seller hear each other's announcement, then they know that an efficient exchange could have occurred but didn't. Assuming the possibility of exchanging the good has not vanished, the parties are confronted with a situation in which abiding by the mechanism means "leaving money on the table"; that is, there is surplus to be realized—and presumably split between the parties—if only they can go back and trade.

---

[45] For more on how much the second-best mechanism loses *vis-à-vis* the first-best solution see Williams (1987). See also Larsen (2012) for an empirical analysis that suggests that, at least in some contexts, real-life mechanisms are not too inefficient *vis-à-vis* the first-best ideal.

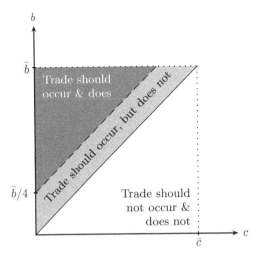

Figure 6.4 Welfare loss due to interim individual rationality constraint.

As a rule, it is difficult to see parties walking away and leaving money on the table. Presumably, after hearing that $b > c$, but exchange is not to occur, one party would approach the other and propose exchange at some price between b and c (e.g., $p = (b+c)/2$). This is fine if the parties are naïve; that is, somehow they failed to anticipate the possibility of such future bargaining and, thus, announced their types truthfully as intended under the mechanism. We should not, though, expect such naïveté. Rather, each would anticipate that money wouldn't be left on the table. But, then, each would have incentive to lie about his or her type.

To see that lying would occur—formally, that truth-telling is no longer an equilibrium—suppose the buyer will tell the truth and consider whether the seller also wishes to tell the truth. To make the problem concrete, suppose that, if $b > c$ but no exchange occurs under the mechanism, then the price splits the difference; that is, $p = (b+c)/2$. The seller's optimization problem is

$$\max_{\hat{c}} \rho_S(\hat{c}) - c \left(1 - F\left(V_B^{-1}(V_C(\hat{c}, \sigma), \sigma) \right) \right)$$
$$+ \frac{b^E + \hat{c} - 2c}{2} \left(F\left(V_B^{-1}(V_C(\hat{c}, \sigma), \sigma) \right) - F(\hat{c}) \right),$$

where V_B^{-1} is defined by $V_B\left(V_B^{-1}(x, \sigma), \sigma \right) \equiv x$, b^E is the expected value of b given $b \in \left(\hat{c}, V_B^{-1}\left(V_C(\hat{c}, \sigma), \sigma \right) \right)$, and the first line of that last expression would be the seller's payoff if there were no play beyond the end of the mechanism.[46] The derivative of the first line with respect to $\hat{c}$ is zero evaluated at $\hat{c} = c$ (the mechanism induces truth-telling). The derivative of the second line is

$$F\left(V_B^{-1}(V_C(\hat{c},\sigma),\sigma)\right) - F(\hat{c})$$

$$+ \frac{b^E + \hat{c} - 2c}{2} \left(f\left(V_B^{-1}(V_C(\hat{c},\sigma),\sigma)\right) \frac{\partial V_B^{-1}}{\partial V_C} \frac{\partial V_C}{\partial c} - f(\hat{c}) \right).$$

Generically, there is no reason to expect that expression to be zero at $\hat{c} = c$; in other words, the potential for later bargaining will cause the seller to deviate from truth-telling.

What should be made of this? The answer is that one should be suspicious of the mechanism of Proposition 6.13 unless there is good reason to believe the parties are committed to playing the mechanism as given (i.e., not negotiating if exchange does not occur, but $b > c$). One good reason would be if there is literally one point in time at which the good can be exchanged (it is, e.g., highly perishable and negotiations to pick up the money left on the table would conclude only after the good has perished). A second is that the one or both parties wish to develop a reputation for never negotiating after the play of the mechanism:[47] because the mechanism is second best, it could be in the interest of one or both parties to develop a reputation for fully committing to the mechanism to avoid a third-best outcome. In general, these reasons are likely to be the exception, not the rule;[48] hence, another solution is necessary.

Unhappily, the current state of economic theory is weak with respect to the modeling of bargaining between two asymmetrically informed parties. One reason is that such games are highly sensitive to the extensive form that is assumed. For example, a game in which one player repeatedly makes offers and the other merely says yes or no can have quite a different outcome than a game in which the players alternate making offers. Nevertheless, some such bargaining game is played and one should expect that it ends with trade if $b > c$ and no trade otherwise.[49]

---

[46] Note that V_B^{-1} exists if we assume $V_B(\cdot, \sigma)$ is increasing. Stronger versions of the assumptions in Lemma 6.12 or Corollary 6.3 would be sufficient for this property to hold.

[47] Such reputations could be realistic in some settings. For instance, some divorce lawyers, referred to as "bombers," have developed a reputation for making take-it-or-leave-it offers in pretrial settlement talks; that is, they are committed to never negotiate beyond putting their initial demands on the table. (Lest the reader worry that the author obtained this knowledge through painful personal experience, he did not—he learned this by talking to divorce lawyers in a social setting.)

[48] Larsen (2012) can be seen as evidence in favor of this claim. He shows the parties don't commit to a mechanism (an auction) and post-mechanism bargaining occurs.

[49] This assumes no frictions. If the parties had to pay a fixed amount per round of bargaining, then they might cease bargaining without agreeing to trade even if $b > c$.

As an example of such a game, suppose that the seller makes repeated offers to the buyer until the buyer accepts or the seller concludes $c > b$.[50] Each round of bargaining takes a unit of time and both parties discount at a rate $\delta \in (0,1)$ per unit of time. Assume that $\bar{b} = 1$ and F is the uniform distribution. Let $p_t(c)$ be the price offered by a seller of cost c at time t. The objective is an equilibrium in which $p_1(c) \neq p_1(c')$ for $c \neq c'$; that is, after the seller's first offer, the buyer knows, in equilibrium, the seller's cost. That is, the game from that point on is a game of one-sided asymmetric information.

Consider the following renormalization. Define $\omega = \max\{b - c, 0\}$. Given c, one can think of ω as distributed uniformly on $[0, 1 - c]$ because the mass at 0 is irrelevant (no exchange should occur there). Let $m = p - c$ denote the seller's markup. The goal will be an equilibrium in which the parties play linear strategies: a buyer who hasn't yet bought buys if $\omega \geq \alpha m$ and, if ω is the highest renormalized type who hasn't purchased prior to the current period, the seller sets her markup (price less cost) $m = \gamma\omega$.

Proposition 6.14.   *Assume the buyer's valuation is uniformly distributed. Then there exists a subgame-perfect equilibrium in which the parties play linear strategies.*

As shown in the proof of Proposition 6.14, $\gamma < 1$; hence, $m_t = (1 - c)\gamma^t$ tends to 0 as $t \to \infty$. In words, the markup approaches zero, which means the seller's price approaches her cost. Consequently, eventually all buyers for whom $b > c$ will buy. The equilibrium of this bargaining game is, thus, such that no money gets left on the table.

Although money is not left on the table, this does not mean that the first best is achieved. In fact, it isn't because, with positive probability, welfare-enhancing exchange (i.e., when $b > c$) is delayed. Indeed, this was known: Proposition 6.12 (Myerson-Satterthwaite) rules out the first best. Arguments about money left on the table don't change that conclusion: if there were some bargaining game that achieved the first best—achieved efficient trade immediately and at no bargaining cost—then, by the Revelation Principle, that game would be replicable by a direct-revelation mechanism, but Proposition 6.12 establishes that is impossible. In other words, the true importance of Proposition 6.12 is it implies that, for any procedure in which exchange is guaranteed to happen (eventually) if $b > c$, there must be costs that cause the buyer and seller's collective welfare to be less than the first-best level, at least with positive probability.

6.4 EXOGENOUS ASYMMETRIES OF INFORMATION AT TIME OF CONTRACTING: INFORMED SELLER

Now consider the situation of a contract proposer endowed with payoff-relevant information that her counter party does not know. In keeping with Section 6.2's naming convention, call the contract proposer the seller and the counter party the buyer

---

[50] The following discussion also serves as a demonstration of the Coase (1972) conjecture. For a more general approach, see Gul et al. (1986).

(although, again, the techniques and insights developed here have wider applicability). As in that earlier section, the contract offer is made on a take-it-or-leave-it (TIOLI) basis.

As before, call the informed party's information her type. Denote it by γ and assume it is an element of Γ. Let $G : \Gamma \to [0, 1]$ be the distribution function by which "Nature" chooses γ. While γ is the informed party's (here, seller's) private information, Γ and $G(\cdot)$ are common knowledge.

6.4.1 The Lemons Model

The classic informed-seller model is Akerlof's (1970) "lemons model": the seller's type (i.e., γ) describes the quality of the good or service she is offering. For example, as in Akerlof, 1970's original paper, the seller knows the quality of the used car she is offering, whereas the buyer does not.[51] It is further assumed that the buyer cannot simply observe quality prior to trade: he only learns quality once he has taken possession or received the service. Because of this feature, these models are often called *experience-good models*.

Although quality could be multidimensional, it is standard to assume either that it is unidimensional or buyer and seller have a common complete preference order over the elements of Γ, the seller's type space.[52] Consequently, there is no further loss in treating Γ as a subset of $\mathbb{R}$. To avoid pathological cases, assume $\Gamma \subseteq (\underline{\gamma}, \bar{\gamma})$, both limits finite. As a convention, $\gamma > \gamma'$ is understood to mean that type γ is higher quality than γ'. Assume the buyer and seller's payoffs are, respectively,

$$U_B = x\big(u(\gamma) - p\big) \text{ and } U_S = xp + (1 - x)\gamma,$$

where $x \in \{0, 1\}$ denotes the amount of trade, p is payment in case of trade, and $u : \Gamma \to \mathbb{R}$ is an increasing function.[53] Trade would never be efficient if $u(\gamma) < \gamma$ for all $\gamma \in \Gamma$; hence, assume there exists a $\Gamma^* \subseteq \Gamma$, $G(\Gamma^*) > 0$, such that $u(\gamma) > \gamma$ if $\gamma \in \Gamma^*$.

In the basic lemons model, the buyer plays a pure-strategy response: his strategy is an $x : \mathbb{R} \to \{0, 1\}$—a mapping from prices into purchase decisions. Observe that, for $p > p'$ such that $x(p) = x(p') = 1$, there can be no equilibrium in which the seller quotes

---

[51] A low-quality car is colloquially known as a "lemon," hence the title of Akerlof's, 1970 original article.

[52] The analyses of multidimensional signaling in Quinzii and Rochet (1985) and Engers (1987) are two notable exceptions.

[53] Note there is no gain in generality from assuming

$$U_S = xp + (1 - x)v(\gamma),$$

$v : \Gamma \to \mathbb{R}$ increasing, because one could simply renormalize the type space and the buyer's utility: $\tilde{\Gamma} = v(\Gamma)$ and $\tilde{u}(\tilde{\gamma}) \mapsto u\left(v^{-1}(\tilde{\gamma})\right)$. Given the notion of opportunity cost, an equivalent analysis is possible assuming

$$U_S = xp - c(\gamma),$$

where $c : \Gamma \to \mathbb{R}$, an increasing function, is the cost of supplying a product of quality γ.

price p': in any equilibrium in which trade may occur, there is a single price, $\hat{p}$, offered by seller types who wish to trade.

The rationality of the seller is assumed to be common knowledge. The buyer can thus infer from a price quote of p that $\gamma \not> p$. If there is an equilibrium in which the buyer accepts $\hat{p}$, it follows the buyer must believe that the seller is playing the strategy[54]

$$p(\gamma) = \begin{cases} \hat{p}, & \text{if } \gamma \leq \hat{p} \\ \infty, & \text{if } \gamma > \hat{p} \end{cases}.$$

Buying, $x(\hat{p}) = 1$, is a best response if and only if

$$\mathbb{E}\left\{u(\gamma)|\gamma \leq \hat{p}\right\} \geq \hat{p}; \tag{6.4.1}$$

that is, if and only if the buyer's expected utility exceeds $\hat{p}$ conditional on knowing quality is no greater than $\hat{p}$. To conclude: there is an equilibrium with trade if and only if condition (6.4.1) has a solution.

As an example, suppose that $u(\gamma) = m\gamma + b$, $\Gamma = [0, 1]$, and $G(\cdot)$ is the uniform distribution. It is readily shown that

$$\mathbb{E}\left\{u(\gamma)|\gamma \leq \hat{p}\right\} = \begin{cases} b + \frac{m\hat{p}}{2}, & \text{if } \hat{p} \leq 1 \\ b + \frac{m}{2}, & \text{if } \hat{p} > 1 \end{cases}.$$

For instance, suppose that $b=0$ and $m=3/2$. Condition (6.4.1) is satisfied only for $\hat{p} = 0$; hence, the probability of trade is zero. This is, however, inefficient because $u(\gamma) > \gamma$ for all $\gamma > 0$ (i.e., $\Gamma^* = (0, 1]$). For these parameters, the *lemons problem* is severe: asymmetric information destroys the market.

Consider different parameters: $b=1/8$ and $m=3/2$. Condition (6.4.1) is now satisfied for all $\hat{p} \leq 1/2$. There is, thus, an equilibrium in which types $\gamma \leq 1/2$ offer to sell at price 1/2, other types make no offer, and the buyer purchases if offered the product at price 1/2.[55] Trade occurs 50% of the time rather than never, so this is a more efficient

---

[54] A price of ∞ is equivalent to not making an offer.
[55] Formally, a perfect Bayesian equilibrium is seller and buyer, respectively, play strategies

$$p(\gamma) = \begin{cases} 1/2, & \text{if } \gamma \leq 1/2 \\ \infty, & \text{if } \gamma > 1/2 \end{cases} \quad \text{and} \quad x(p) = \begin{cases} 1, & \text{if } p = 1/2 \\ 0, & \text{if } p \neq 1/2 \end{cases};$$

and the buyer believes types $\gamma \leq 1/2$ offer at price 1/2, types $\gamma > 1/2$ make no offer, and any other price offer was made by type 0.

outcome than under the initial set of parameters; but it is still inefficient *vis-à-vis* the symmetric-information ideal.

The analysis to this point is premised on the buyer's playing pure strategies only. Are there mixed-strategy equilibria? To explore this, suppose $\Gamma = \{\gamma_L, \gamma_H\}$, $\gamma_H > \gamma_L$, and let $g = G(\gamma_L) \in (0,1)$. Define $u_i = u(\gamma_i)$. If $u_i \leq \gamma_i$ both i, there are no gains to trade. If $u_L > \gamma_L$, but $u_H \leq \gamma_H$, there is an efficient pure-strategy equilibrium in which $\hat{p} = u_L$. Hence, the only case of interest is $u_H > \gamma_H$. Moreover, to truly be interesting, it must be that

$$g u_L + (1 - g) u_H < \gamma_H, \tag{6.4.2}$$

as otherwise there is a pure-strategy equilibrium in which both seller types sell.

Suppose that there is an equilibrium in which trade occurs with positive probability at *two* prices p_h and p_ℓ, $p_h > p_\ell$. For p_ℓ to be offered, it must be that $x(p_h) < x(p_\ell)$, where, now, $x : \mathbb{R} \to [0, 1]$. Let $U_j = \mathbb{E}\{u(\gamma) | p = p_j\}$; that is, U_j is the buyer's expectation of his utility upon being offered the product at price p_j, where the expectation is calculated given the seller's equilibrium strategy. Because $0 < x(p_h) < 1$, the buyer mixes over accepting or rejecting in response to p_h; hence, $U_h - p_h = 0$.

What if the γ_H-type seller offers p_h and the γ_L-type offers p_ℓ in equilibrium (i.e., the seller does not mix)? Buyer rationality implies $p_\ell \leq u_L$ and his mixing implies $p_h = u_H$. Suppose p_ℓ in fact equals u_L and suppose $x(p_\ell) = 1$. Given earlier assumptions and condition (6.4.2), for this to be an equilibrium, it is necessary that

$$u_L \geq x(u_H) u_H + (1 - x(u_H)) \gamma_L \tag{6.4.3}$$

(i.e., the γ_L-type seller must prefer to offer the product at $p = u_L$ than at $p = u_H$). Expression (6.4.3) holds if and only if $u_L > \gamma_L$. Assuming that condition, (6.4.3) can be solved for $x(u_H)$:

$$x(u_H) \leq \frac{u_L - \gamma_L}{u_H - \gamma_L}. \tag{6.4.4}$$

In this context, efficiency entails maximizing the probability of trade; hence, the most efficiency equilibrium is the one in which (6.4.4) holds as equality. To summarize:

Proposition 6.15. *For the two-type model considered here, there is an equilibrium in which the low-quality seller (γ_L) offers the product at price u_L, the high-quality seller (γ_H) offers it at price u_H, the buyer accepts a price of u_L or less with certainty, mixes over accepting a price of u_H with probability equal to the RHS of expression (6.4.4), and rejects all other offers. The buyer believes an offer at price u_H comes from the high-quality seller and he believes any other offer is from the low-quality seller.*

As an example, suppose $\gamma_L = 1$, $\gamma_H = 3$, $u(\gamma) = \gamma + 1$, and $g = 3/5$. Limiting both buyer and seller to pure strategies, the equilibrium is one with a price of 2 and expected welfare of 36/15. In contrast, under the Proposition 6.15 equilibrium, the prices are 2 and 4, the buyer accepts an offer of 4 with probability 1/3, and expected welfare is 38/15. In other words, the lemons problem proves less severe than might originally have been thought once account is taken of the possibility that the buyer can mix.

6.4.1.1 Credence Goods

A phenomenon related to experience goods is the following: a buyer knows he has a problem (e.g., with his car, of a medical nature, etc.), but not its cause. He seeks treatment from the seller (an expert, such as a mechanic or physician), who can diagnosis the cause and administer a treatment. The buyer knows if the the problem has been fixed or not, but not whether the diagnosis and treatment regime were correct. This is relevant insofar as long as the seller corrects the problem, she can claim a more severe diagnosis (e.g., engine needs replacing) even when the truth is less severe (e.g., just the carburetor needs replacing) and provide the more expensive treatment (e.g., replace the engine rather than just the carburetor). Models that explore such situations are known as *credence-good* models.[56]

One issue in such models is whether the buyer has recourse if promised one treatment but receives another. For instance, suppose, based on his mechanic's diagnosis, the buyer agrees to a new engine (rather than just a new carburetor). When the buyer picks his car up, it runs well (i.e., he knows the problem has been fixed). Question: does he know if the engine inside his car is new (as the mechanic claims) or is it his old engine with just a new carburetor (the mechanic has cheated him)? If the answer is he knows (and can obtain recourse in case of fraud), then we have one kind of credence-good model. If he doesn't, then we have the other. Call the two scenarios verifiable and unverifiable treatment, respectively. Here, attention is limited to the verifiable-treatment scenario. For an analysis of the unverifiable-treatment scenario see Fong (2005).

As a basic model, suppose the buyer's gross benefit if his problem is corrected is $\bar{v}$. Without loss, we can and will normalize $\bar{v} = 0$. If his problem goes *uncorrected* and it is of type (severity) $\sigma, \sigma \in \{L,H\}$ (low and high severity, respectively), then his gross benefit is $-\ell_\sigma$; that is, he loses ℓ_σ if his problem is not fixed. Assume

$$0 \leq \ell_L \leq \ell_H,$$

with at least one inequality strict.[57] The seller's cost of treatment is c_σ, where $c_H > c_L$. Let $q = \Pr\{\sigma = L\}$. Assume $0 < q < 1$. This probability is common knowledge, but only the seller can determine actual severity.

---

[56] Darby and Karni (1973) are often credited with introducing the notion of credence goods into the literature. For a relatively recent treatment, as well as citations to earlier literature, see Fong (2005).

[57] The case $\ell_L = 0$ corresponds to a situation in which the problem quickly clears up without treatment. The case $\ell_L = \ell_H$ corresponds to one in which the problem (e.g., car doesn't run) has the same effect on the buyer's wellbeing regardless of cause.

The extent of possible fraud by the seller is limited given the assumption of verifiable treatment. Specifically, assume that the treatment for the more severe problem cures the less severe problem (e.g., replacing the entire engine "fixes" a broken carburetor), but the opposite is not true (e.g., changing a broken carburetor is not a fix when the entire engine must be replaced).

If the buyer had to pay for treatment prior to receiving a diagnosis, the most he would pay is

$$\bar{p} = q\ell_L + (1 - q)\ell_H .$$

If $\bar{p} \geq c_H$ and $\ell_\sigma \geq c_\sigma$ for both σ, then efficiency will result: the seller offers to fix any problem for $\bar{p}$ and the buyer accepts the offer. The seller has the appropriate incentive to employ the correct treatment and it is efficient for problems of both severity levels to be treated. Issues arise if $\bar{p} < c_H$ or if $\ell_\sigma < c_\sigma$ for one σ.

Cost to correct severe problem exceeds average benefit of repair. Suppose that $\bar{p} < c_H$, but $\ell_\sigma \geq c_\sigma$ for both σ. It is, thus, efficient to fix both problems, but the seller is unwilling to fix the severe problem if she is paid only $\bar{p}$.[58] Observe, $\ell_L < c_H$ given $\bar{p} < c_H$. If

$$\ell_H - c_H \leq \ell_L - c_L \qquad (6.4.5)$$

(i.e., the social benefit of fixing the more severe problem does not exceed that of fixing the less severe problem), then efficiency can be attained using two prices: $p_\sigma = \ell_\sigma$, $\sigma \in \{L, H\}$. In other words, the seller offers to fix a problem of severity σ for price p_σ. Because, given (6.4.5), her *margin* is greater on fixing the low-severity problem than on fixing the high-severity one and she cannot fraudulently use the low-severity treatment for the high-severity problem, the seller will behave honestly.[59]

---

[58] The assumption is the seller can quit if fixing a problem at a quoted price would cause her a loss; that is, an *ex post* IR constraint is in effect for the seller.

[59] Observe this conclusion relies on the verifiability of treatment. Were treatment unverifiable and $p_H > p_L$, then the seller would always have an incentive to claim $\sigma = H$. As Fong (2005) shows, the solution in this case would be similar to Proposition 6.15: the buyer agrees to treatment with certainty if the diagnosis is $\sigma = L$ and pays p_L, but agrees to treatment with probability

$$\frac{p_L - c_L}{p_H - c_L}$$

and pays p_H if the diagnosis is $\sigma = H$. The seller who faces a buyer with a severe ($\sigma = H$) problem never lies and a seller who faces a buyer with a minor problem ($\sigma = L$) states her diagnosis honestly with probability

$$\frac{p_H - \ell_L}{\ell_H - \ell_L} . \qquad (\bigstar)$$

It is readily verified this is an equilibrium for a given (p_L, p_H) pair of announced prices. It can be shown that the price pair (l_L, l_H) maximizes the seller's expected profit. Given ($\bigstar$) this means that the seller is always honest in equilibrium (but the buyer still mixes because he is indifferent about obtaining treatment or not). Because of the mixing, the equilibrium is inefficient. See Fong, 2005 for further details.

If (6.4.5) does not hold, then the seller would have an incentive to behave fraudulently were $p_\sigma = \ell_\sigma$ for both σ. Anticipating such fraud, the buyer infers he will pay
p_H regardless of his true problem. This exceeds $\bar{p}$, so the buyer would not do business
with the seller. Nonetheless, there remains a two-price solution that achieves efficiency:
to wit, let m_σ be the seller's margin on fixing problem σ given her quoted prices (i.e.,
$m_\sigma = p_\sigma - c_\sigma$). As we've seen, seller honesty requires that $m_L \geq m_H$. In choosing her
prices, the seller seeks to solve:

$$\max_{m_L, m_H} qm_L + (1-q)m_H \tag{6.4.6}$$

subject to

$$m_L \geq m_H, \tag{Seller IC}$$

$$q\left(\ell_L - \underbrace{(m_L + c_L)}_{p_L}\right) + (1-q)\left(\ell_H - \underbrace{(m_H + c_H)}_{p_H}\right) \geq 0, \tag{Buyer IR}$$

and

$$m_H \geq 0 \tag{Seller IR}$$

(given the seller's IC condition, the additional condition that $m_L \geq 0$ is superfluous and,
so, can be ignored). Let S denote expected surplus from trade:

$$S = q(\ell_L - c_L) + (1-q)(\ell_H - c_H).$$

It is readily seen that the solution to the seller's linear-programming problem is any pair
(m_L, m_H), $m_L \geq m_H$ and $m_H \geq 0$ on the line

$$S = qm_L + (1-q)m_H. \tag{6.4.7}$$

In other words, there is an efficient outcome if the seller commits to her prices prior
to learning the buyer's actual problem and the buyer commits to pay those prices prior
to learning the seller's diagnosis. Reflecting her bargaining power, the seller captures all
surplus in expectation.

Unlike the earlier analysis of the market for lemons, efficiency is achieved here. This
is because, here, prices are set *before* the seller learns her type. As such, the comparison
between the two analyses reflects a general point: inefficiencies due to asymmetric

information are more pronounced if the asymmetry information predates the parties' ability to write contracts than if it arises after such contracting.[60]

In many situations, the buyer is allowed to walk away after receiving a diagnosis. In such situations, the program (6.4.6) would also need to satisfy *ex post* IR constraints for the buyer:

$$\ell_L - (m_L + c_L) \geq 0 \text{ and}$$

(IR–L)

$$\ell_H - (m_H + c_H) \geq 0.$$

(IR–H)

Because (6.4.5) does not hold, the *ex post* constraint (IR–L) is binding. To see this, observe the smallest value of m_L that satisfies the program (6.4.6) as originally given is

$$m_L = m_H = S.$$

Substituting that into the LHS of (IR–L) yields

$$(1 - q)\left(\left(\ell_L - c_L\right) - \left(\ell_H - c_H\right)\right),$$

(6.4.8)

which is negative given (6.4.5) does not hold. Given (IR–L) is binding, it follows that

$$m_L = \ell_L - c_L; \text{ equivalently that } p_L = \ell_L.$$

It will also be that $m_H = m_L$, hence

$$p_H = \ell_L + (c_H - c_L) < \ell_H,$$

where the inequality follows because (6.4.5) does not hold. Observe, now, that although full efficiency is still achieved, the seller no longer captures all the surplus generated: the need to provide the seller strong enough incentives to make an honest diagnosis conflicts with the need to keep the buyer from walking away.

If

$$\ell_H - c_H < 0,$$

(6.4.9)

then efficiency will also attain: either $\ell_L < c_L$, in which case the market should not exist and won't; or $\ell_L \geq c_L$ and the market should exist for fixing the less-severe problem

---

[60] See Hermalin and Katz (1993) and Hermalin et al. (2007, §§2–3) for further development of this point.

only and it will exist (the seller promises to fix any problem she diagnoses as L at price ℓ_L).

The remaining case when $\bar{p} < c_H$ is

$$\ell_H - c_H \geq 0 > \ell_L - c_L : \qquad (6.4.10)$$

efficiency dictates that only the more severe problem be treated. The previous logic continues to apply: for the seller to have an incentive to make an honest diagnosis, $m_L \geq m_H$. Here, given no market for fixing less severe problems, $m_L = 0$; hence, efficiency is achievable only if $p_H = c_H$. In other words, in this case, the seller announces she won't fix L problems, but will fix H problems at cost, c_H. In this case, the incentive problem is so severe that it results in all surplus going to the buyer.

Cost to correct severe problem less than average benefit of repair. Now suppose that $\bar{p} \geq c_H$. Suppose $\ell_\sigma < c_\sigma$ for one σ, so it is inefficient to fix all problems. If (6.4.9) holds, then an efficient equilibrium exists: rather than quote a price of $\bar{p}$ and offer to fix all problems, the seller does better to quote a price of $p_L = \ell_L$ and offer to fix only L problems. To see this, observe

$$\bar{p} - \left(qc_L + (1-q)c_H\right) = q\left(\ell_L - c_L\right) + (1-q)\left(\ell_H - c_H\right) < q\left(\ell_L - c_L\right),$$
$$(6.4.11)$$

where the first term is expected profit from offering to fix all problems and the last is expected profit from offering to fix L problems only.

Finally, suppose $\bar{p} \geq c_H$, but $\ell_L < c_L$. It is now impossible to provide the seller incentives to diagnosis honestly (absent setting $p_H = c_H$, which the seller wouldn't do). In this scenario, the seller offers to fix all problems and fixes all problems even though it is inefficient to fix the L problems.

6.4.2 Signaling

The welfare loss due to the lemons problem is essentially borne by high-quality (high-γ) sellers. This is immediate in the two-type case leading up to Proposition 6.15: the low-quality seller is always able to sell her product—a rational buyer is willing to pay up to $u(\gamma_L)$ regardless of his beliefs about the seller's quality since, for any beliefs, $\mathbb{E}\{u(\gamma)\} \geq u(\gamma_L)$—the low-quality seller is sure to receive at least what she would have under symmetric information. It is the high-quality seller who is at risk of not realizing the profit, $u(\gamma_H) - \gamma_H$, she would have were the setting one of symmetric information.

This insight suggests that were there a way for a high-quality seller to prove who she was, she would do so provided it were not too expensive. In some instances, such proof is direct—the seller, for example, employs a reliable rating agency to certify publicly that her product is high quality. In other instances, the proof is more indirect—the high-quality seller undertakes an action that is worthwhile for her if it convinces the buyer she's high quality, but would not be worthwhile for a low-quality seller even if it misled the buyer into believing she was high quality. An example of such indirect proof would be a seller who offers a warranty with her product: if repair costs are high enough, then it could be too costly for a low-quality seller to offer a warranty, even if it misled the buyer, but not so costly for a high-quality seller. Hence, a buyer would accurately infer that a seller offering a warranty is high quality. In the language of information economics, such indirect proof is known as a *signal*.

6.4.2.1 A Brief Review of Signaling

Spence (1973) was the first analysis of the use of signals or *signaling*. In that original paper, the seller was an employee and quality was her ability. The buyer—potential employer—could not directly observe a would-be employee's ability, but he could observe the employee's educational attainment. The key assumption of the model was that the marginal cost of obtaining an additional level of attainment (e.g., year in school) was always less for high-ability employees than for low-ability employees. Hence, by obtaining enough education, a high-ability employee could signal her ability to the potential employer.

Since Spence's seminal work, signaling models have been utilized to explore a wide variety of economic and other social phenomena. The topic is, thus, of great importance. On the other hand, due to its importance, there are now many excellent texts that cover signaling (see, e.g., Fudenberg and Tirole, 1991; Gibbons, 1992; Mas-Colell et al., 1995). Consequently, despite its importance, the treatment here will be brief.

A signaling game is one between an informed party, who plays first, and an uninformed party, who responds. In keeping with this chapter's nomenclature, call the former party the seller and the latter the buyer, although the analysis applies more generally. The seller has utility $V(a, x, \gamma)$, where $a \in \mathcal{A}$ is the seller's action, $x \in \mathcal{X}$ is the buyer's response, and $\gamma \in \Gamma$ is the seller's type. In the typical buyer–seller relation, $\mathcal{X} = \{0, 1\}$ —the buyer rejects or accepts the seller's offer, respectively. In that relation, $\mathcal{A}$ might be a two-dimensional space consisting of a price and signaling action (e.g., a warranty). As before, γ could be a measure of quality. The buyer's utility is $U(a, x, \gamma)$. A pure strategy for the seller is a mapping $a : \Gamma \to \mathcal{A}$. A pure strategy for the buyer is a mapping $x : \mathcal{A} \to \mathcal{X}$. Mixed strategies are the usual extension of pure strategies. An outcome is *separating* if $\gamma \neq \gamma'$ implies $a(\gamma) \neq a(\gamma')$ for any $\gamma, \gamma\prime \in \Gamma$; that is, an outcome is separating if different seller types choose different actions. An outcome is *pooling* if $a(\gamma) = a(\gamma')$ for all $\gamma, \gamma' \in \Gamma$; that is, it is pooling if all types choose the same action. Various hybrid outcomes are also possible (e.g., one type plays a with certainty, while another mixes between a and a').

Although not normally characterized as a signaling game, the treatment of the lemons problem in the previous subsection nonetheless fits the structure of a signaling game. In particular, the equilibrium of Proposition 6.15 is a separating equilibrium: the two types offer different prices (i.e., $a(\gamma_L)=p_\ell = u_L$ and $a(\gamma_H)=p_h=u_H$). For the same game, if (6.4.2) were instead reversed, then a pooling equilibrium would exist in which both types offered

$$\hat{p} = g u_L + (1-g) u_H$$

(i.e., $a(\gamma_L) = a(\gamma_H) = \hat{p}$). Returning to the assumption that (6.4.2) holds, one can construct a hybrid (partial-separating) equilibrium in which the high-quality type offers p_h only, but the low-quality type mixes between p_ℓ and p_h.

As just indicated, signaling games often admit multiple solutions (equilibria). For example, under the assumptions underlying Proposition 6.15, another equilibrium is

$$p(\gamma) = \begin{cases} u_L, & \text{if } \gamma = \gamma_L \\ \infty, & \text{if } \gamma = \gamma_H \end{cases}; \quad x(p) = \begin{cases} 1, & \text{if } p \le u_L \\ 0, & \text{if } p > u_L \end{cases};$$

and the buyer believes all offers come from the low-quality type. This is because the standard solution concept for such games, perfect Bayesian equilibrium (PBE), does not tie down the uninformed player's beliefs in response to an out-of-equilibrium move by the informed player.[61] In particular, it is possible to construct equilibria that are supported by what the uninformed player "threatens" to believe in response to out-of-equilibrium play. To reduce the set of equilibria—in particular, to eliminate equilibria supported by "unreasonable" out-of-equilibrium beliefs—various equilibrium refinements can be employed (see, e.g., Fudenberg and Tirole, 1991, especially Chapter 11, for an introduction to refinements). A prominent refinement is the "Intuitive Criterion" of Cho and Kreps (1987).

To help illustrate the issue further, as well as provide a basic understanding of the Intuitive Criterion, consider the signaling game in Figure 6.5, which is based on Cho and Kreps's famous beer and quiche game. The game starts at the chance node in the middle, where Nature determines whether the seller is low quality or high quality. The probability she selects low quality is g. The seller moves next (hollow decision node), deciding whether to offer a warranty, but charge a high price; or to offer no warranty, but charge a low price. The buyer moves last (filled-in decision node), deciding whether to buy or not. The game, then, ends with payoffs as indicated; the first number in each pair is the seller's payoff and the second the buyer's. The seller knows Nature's move; that is, she knows the quality of what she's selling. The buyer does not—he only observes what he is offered. That the buyer is ignorant of the seller's type is indicated

---

[61] In contrast, the uninformed's beliefs following a move or action that can occur in equilibrium must be consistent with Bayes Law given the distribution of types and the informed player's equilibrium strategy.

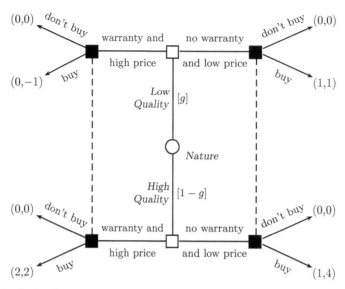

Figure 6.5 A simple signaling game.

by the dashed lines connecting his decision nodes, which indicate they are in the same information set for the buyer.

The game has two equilibria: (1) a low-quality seller offers no warranty and a low price, a high-quality seller a warranty and a high price, and the buyer accepts both offers; and (2) both seller types offer no warranty and the low price, the buyer accepts that offer, but will reject the warranty-and-high-price offer. Equilibrium (1) is separating and equilibrium (2) is pooling. The pooling equilibrium is supported by the buyer's believing that the out-of-equilibrium play of an offer of a warranty and high price indicates he is facing the *low*-quality seller with a probability, $\hat{g}$, in excess of 2/3. Given such a belief, his rejecting that offer is rational (i.e., $-1\hat{g} + 2(1 - \hat{g}) < 0$).

The second equilibrium is a valid PBE, but nonetheless strikes most observers as unreasonable. No matter what response offering a warranty and high price triggered in the buyer, a low-quality seller is better off playing her equilibrium strategy of no warranty and low price; that is, a low-quality seller has no incentive whatsoever to deviate. The same is not true of a high-quality seller: if the buyer bought in response to the deviation of a warranty and high price, then a high-quality seller is better off—she gets 2 instead of 1. Given this, it seems unreasonable to postulate $\hat{g} > 2/3$; indeed, $\hat{g} = 0$ seems most sensible. As Cho and Kreps (1987) observe, one can even imagine the seller helping the buyer to make such a forward induction: if the parties expected the second PBE to be played, a high-quality seller could make the following speech to accompany a deviating offer of a warranty and high price.

*Dear buyer, I know you were expecting an offer of no warranty and a low price. Instead, I'm offer-
ing you a warranty, but a higher price. What should you make of this innovation? If I were a low-
quality seller—which I am assuredly not—I would have absolutely no reason to make this offer:
even if you accepted, I would be worse off than I would be in the equilibrium you thought we were
playing. On the other hand, if you accept my offer, then, because I'm truly high quality, I am better off. Hence, because only a high-quality seller could have a motive to make this offer, it is only
reasonable of you to believe that I am high quality.*

This reasoning can be formalized: assume Γ is finite with N elements. Let Δ^N be the
N-dimensional unit simplex (i.e., the subset of vectors in $\mathbb{R}^N_+$ whose elements sum to
1). Let $\mathcal{X}(a)$ be the set of responses available to the uninformed player (e.g., buyer) if the
informed player (e.g., seller) takes action $a \in \mathcal{A}$ (it could be—as in Figure 6.5 and many
games of interest—that $\mathcal{X}(a) = \mathcal{X}$ for all a; the formulation $\mathcal{X}(a)$ simply permits a more
general analysis). As a second generalization, it may be that an informed player's action
space depends on her type; let $\Gamma(a)$ denote the types that have $a \in \mathcal{A}$ in their action
space. Let $\mu : \Gamma \to \Delta^N$ denote beliefs over types; that is, μ is a density function over Γ.
Define

$$\mathrm{br}(\mu, a) = \arg\max_{x \in \mathcal{X}(a)} \sum_{\gamma \in \Gamma} U(a, x, \gamma)\mu(\gamma).$$

In words, $\mathrm{br}(\mu, a)$ are the uninformed player's best responses, given belief μ, to action a
by the informed player. If $\widehat{\Gamma} \subseteq \Gamma$, define

$$\mathrm{BR}(\widehat{\Gamma}, a) = \bigcup_{\{u \mid \mu(\widehat{\Gamma})=1\}} \mathrm{br}(\mu, a);$$

that is, $\mathrm{BR}(\widehat{\Gamma}, a)$ are actions for the uninformed player that are best responses to the
informed player's action a for some beliefs provided those beliefs assign all weight to
types in the subset $\widehat{\Gamma}$. For example, in the Figure 6.5 game, if $\widehat{\Gamma} = \{\gamma_H\}$—$\gamma_H$ again
denoting the high-quality type—then

$$\mathrm{BR}(\widehat{\Gamma}, \text{warranty \& high price}) = \{\text{buy}\},$$

because if the buyer assigns no weight to the low-quality type, his best response to that
offer is to buy. In contrast, if $\widehat{\Gamma} = \Gamma$, then

$$\mathrm{BR}(\widehat{\Gamma}, \text{warranty \& high price}) = \{\text{buy, don't buy}\},$$

because there are beliefs (e.g., $\mu(\gamma_H) \leq 1/3$) such that not buying is a best response
and there are beliefs (e.g., $\mu(\gamma_H) \geq 1/3$) such that buying is a best response. Finally, let

$V^*(\gamma)$ denote the payoff to a type-γ informed player in the equilibrium under analysis. The Intuitive Criterion can now be formally given:

Definition   (Intuitive Criterion). Consider an equilibrium. For each out-of-equilibrium action of the informed player, a, let

$$\Gamma^0 = \left\{ \gamma \in \Gamma(a) \mid V^*(\gamma) > \max_{x \in \mathrm{BR}(\Gamma(a),\, a)} V(a, x, \gamma) \right\}.$$

If there is a type $\gamma' \in \Gamma(a) \backslash \Gamma^0$ such that

$$V^*(\gamma') < \min_{x \in \mathrm{BR}(\Gamma(a) \backslash \Gamma^0, a)} V(a, x, \gamma'), \tag{6.4.12}$$

then the equilibrium fails the Intuitive Criterion.

The set Γ^0 are types who do better in the equilibrium in question than they could reasonably hope to do by deviating to a. For example, in the pooling PBE of Figure 6.5, if a is warranty and high price, then $\Gamma^0 = \{\gamma_L\}$ (i.e., the set contains only the low-quality type). Types in Γ^0 have no incentive to play the deviation a. In contrast, if there is a type γ' not in Γ^0 who has the ability to play a (i.e., $\gamma' \in \Gamma(a) \backslash \Gamma^0$) and that type would do better than its equilibrium payoff playing a, even if that triggered the worst response, from its perspective, from the uninformed player given he believes no type in Γ^0 played a (i.e., condition (6.4.12) holds), then the equilibrium is unreasonable (not "intuitive") and should be rejected.

The pooling equilibrium of Figure 6.5 fails the Intuitive Criterion: there is a type, namely the high-quality seller, in $\Gamma(a) \backslash \Gamma^0$ whose equilibrium payoff, 1, is less than the worst she would receive if the buyer, recognizing the low-quality seller would not offer a warranty and high price, plays his best response to the offer of a warranty and high price (which is to buy, yielding the high-quality seller a payoff of 2). The separating equilibrium trivially passes the Intuitive Criterion because there is no out-of-equilibrium action (offer).

6.4.2.2 *Application of Signaling to Trading Relations*

Consider, as an initial model, a seller who can take a public action $s \in \mathcal{S}$ prior to trade. For instance, the seller could be a website designer and s is a measure of the quality of her own website. Let her utility be $xp - c(s, \gamma)$, where p is the payment she may receive from the buyer, $\gamma \in \Gamma \subset \mathbb{R}$ is her type, and $c : \mathcal{S} \times \Gamma \to \mathbb{R}_+$. Assume the cost function induces a *common* complete ordering, $\succ$, over $\mathcal{S}$, where $s \succ s'$ if and only if $c(s, \gamma) > c(s', \gamma)$ for all $\gamma \in \Gamma$ (e.g., $\succ$ denotes "better design" and a better-designed site costs all types of website designers more than a worse-designed site). To avoid issues of countervailing incentives, assume there is a minimum element, $s_0 \in \mathcal{S}$, such that $c(s_0, \gamma) < c(s, \gamma)$ for all γ and $s \in \mathcal{S} \backslash \{s_0\}$ and, moreover,

$$c(s_0, \gamma) = c(s_0, \gamma')$$ (6.4.13)

for all $\gamma, \gamma' \in \Gamma$. There is no loss of generality in normalizing the common value $c(s_0, \gamma)$ to zero and that normalization is made henceforth.

The buyer's utility if he buys is $\gamma - p$ and 0 if he does not. Observe that s does not enter his utility function directly; hence, this is a model of *wasteful signaling* insofar as (first-best) efficiency dictates $s \equiv s_0$.

A critical assumption is that the seller's utility satisfies the Spence-Mirrlees condition. To wit, if $s \succ s'$ and $\gamma > \gamma'$, then

$$c(s, \gamma) - c(s', \gamma) < c(s, \gamma') - c(s', \gamma');$$ (6.4.14)

that is, a higher-quality type of seller finds it less costly to raise the value of the signal than does a lower-quality type. Letting $s' = s_0$, conditions (6.4.13) and (6.4.14) together imply that if $\gamma > \gamma'$ and $s \neq s_0$, then

$$c(s, \gamma) < c(s, \gamma');$$ (6.4.15)

that is, a higher type has a lower cost of signaling than does a lower type.

The timing is that the seller chooses s, which the buyer observes, and then she makes a TIOLI price offer.

Assume there is a lowest type, $\underline{\gamma} \geq 0$. Observe that type can guarantee herself a payoff of $\underline{\gamma}$: following any play by the seller, the worst belief possible—from the seller's perspective—is that the seller's quality is $\underline{\gamma}$. So if $\underline{\gamma}$-type seller chooses s_0 and price $\underline{\gamma}$, the buyer has no reason to reject. It follows that in a *separating* equilibrium, the $\underline{\gamma}$-type seller's payoff is $\underline{\gamma}$: because the seller's type is revealed in equilibrium, the buyer will rationally never pay more than $\underline{\gamma}$. It further follows that such a seller must play s_0 in a separating equilibrium. This is a general result: the worst-type seller gets the same payoff in a separating equilibrium as she would have under symmetric information. This underscores that it is not the worst type that is harmed by asymmetric information.

Suppose there are two types, $\Gamma = \{\underline{\gamma}, \bar{\gamma}\}$, and two signals, $\mathcal{S} = \{s_0, s_1\}$. Let $G : \Gamma \to [0, 1]$ again denote the distribution "Nature" uses when determining the seller's type. Let $g = G(\underline{\gamma})$. Define

$$\gamma_P = g\underline{\gamma} + (1-g)\bar{\gamma};$$

that is, γ_P is the expected value of γ given the prior distribution. A pooling PBE is $a(\gamma) = (s_0, \gamma_P)$ for both γ (i.e., each type chooses signal s_0 and prices at γ_P); the buyer's belief is $\mu = (g, 1-g)$ (i.e., the prior) regardless of the seller's action; and the buyer accepts all $p \leq \gamma_P$, but rejects all $p > \gamma_P$. Does this PBE satisfy the Intuitive Criterion? Consider the out-of-equilibrium action $\bar{a} = (s_1, \bar{\gamma})$. If

$$\gamma_P > \bar{\gamma} - c(s_1, \bar{\gamma}), \tag{6.4.16}$$

then (6.4.15) implies $\Gamma^0 = \Gamma$, so $\Gamma(\bar{a}) \backslash \Gamma^0 = \emptyset$, which means the Intuitive Criterion is satisfied. If (6.4.16) is an equality, then (6.4.15) implies $\Gamma^0 = \{\bar{\gamma}\}$. But if (6.4.16) is an equality, then (6.4.12) doesn't hold, so the Intuitive Criterion is again satisfied. To summarize to this point:

Lemma 6.13.   *For the two-type-two-signal game of the previous paragraph, the pooling equilibrium described above satisfies the Intuitive Criterion if*

$$\bar{\gamma} - c(s_1, \bar{\gamma}) \leq \gamma_P. \tag{6.4.17}$$

What if (6.4.17) does not hold? Observe, given the Spence-Mirrlees condition (6.4.14), there must therefore be a $\tilde{p} \in (\gamma_P, \bar{\gamma})$ such that

$$\tilde{p} - c(s_1, \underline{\gamma}) < \gamma_P < \tilde{p} - c(s_1, \bar{\gamma}). \tag{6.4.18}$$

Consider the out-of-equilibrium action $\widetilde{a} = (s_1, \tilde{p})$. Expression (6.4.18) entails $\Gamma^0 = \{\underline{\gamma}\}$ and $\Gamma(\widetilde{a}) \backslash \Gamma^0 = \{\bar{\gamma}\}$. Given that $\tilde{p} < \bar{\gamma}$, $\mathrm{BR}\left(\Gamma(\widetilde{a}) \backslash \Gamma^0\right) = \{1\}$ (i.e., the only possible best response for the buyer is to accept). It follows that (6.4.12) holds; that is, the pooling PBE fails the Intuitive Criterion when (6.4.17) doesn't hold. To summarize:

Lemma 6.14.   *For the two-type-two-signal game described above, the pooling equilibrium described there satisfies the Intuitive Criterion if and only if condition (6.4.17) holds.*

Next consider separating PBE. From the discussion above, $a(\underline{\gamma}) = (s_0, \underline{\gamma})$. Clearly if the equilibrium is separating, the high-quality seller must choose signal s_1. Let her action be $a(\bar{\gamma}) = (s_1, p)$. A necessary condition for this to constitute an equilibrium is that neither type can wish to mimic the other:

$$\underline{\gamma} \geq p - c(s_1, \underline{\gamma}) \text{ and} \tag{6.4.19}$$

$$p - c(s_1, \bar{\gamma}) \geq \underline{\gamma}. \tag{6.4.20}$$

Combining these conditions, a necessary condition is that

$$p \in [\underline{\gamma} + c(s_1, \bar{\gamma}), \underline{\gamma} + c(s_1, \underline{\gamma})] \equiv \mathcal{P}_S.$$

Given that the buyer will never accept a $p > \bar{\gamma}$, it follows from (6.4.20) that a necessary condition for a separating PBE to exist is that

$$\bar{\gamma} - \underline{\gamma} \geq c(s_1, \bar{\gamma}) \,. \tag{6.4.21}$$

Because (6.4.17) can be rewritten as

$$(\bar{\gamma} - \underline{\gamma})g \leq c(s_1, \bar{\gamma}) \,,$$

it follows that if (6.4.21) doesn't hold, then a pooling PBE satisfying the Intuitive Criterion exists. Define

$$\mathcal{P}^* = \{p | p \leq \bar{\gamma}\} \cap \mathcal{P}_S \,.$$

If (6.4.21) holds, then $\mathcal{P}^*$ is non-empty; that is, there exists as least one p that satisfies (6.4.19) and (6.4.20), which is acceptable to the buyer. The following is a separating PBE: a low-quality seller plays $(s_0, \underline{\gamma})$ and a high-quality seller plays $(s_1, \bar{p}), \bar{p} \in \mathcal{P}^*$; the buyer believes $s = s_0$ or $p > \bar{p}$ means the seller is low quality and that $s = s_1$ and $p \leq \bar{p}$ means the seller is high quality; and the buyer accepts $p \leq \underline{\gamma}$ if $s = s_0$, he accepts $p \leq \bar{p}$ if $s = s_1$, and he otherwise rejects the seller's offer.

Because a separating equilibrium can be constructed for any $\bar{p} \in \mathcal{P}^*$, it follows that there is a continuum of such equilibria if $\mathcal{P}^*$ contains more than a single element. Only one, however, satisfies the Intuitive Criterion. Define $p^* = \max \mathcal{P}^*$. By construction

$$p^* = \min\left\{ \bar{\gamma}, \underline{\gamma} + c(s_1, \underline{\gamma}) \right\} \,. \tag{6.4.22}$$

Consider some $\bar{p} \in \mathcal{P}^*, \bar{p} < p^*$, and the separating PBE in which $\bar{p}$ is the high-quality seller's price offer. Observe there exists a $\widetilde{p} \in (\bar{p}, p^*)$. Consider the out-of-equilibrium action $\widetilde{a} = (s_1, \widetilde{p})$. Given (6.4.22),

$$\underline{\gamma} > \widetilde{p} - c(s_1, \underline{\gamma}) \,.$$

It follows that $\Gamma^0 = \{\underline{\gamma}\}$. Because $\widetilde{p} < \bar{\gamma}$, $\mathrm{BR}\left(\Gamma(\widetilde{a}) \backslash \Gamma^0\right) = \{1\}$. Because $\widetilde{p} > \bar{p}$, it follows that (6.4.12) holds; that is, the PBE fails the Intuitive Criterion. To summarize:

Proposition 6.16. *Consider the two-type-two-signal game described above. If the difference in quality, $\bar{\gamma} - \underline{\gamma}$, does not exceed $c(s_1, \bar{\gamma})/g$, then a pooling equilibrium in which both types choose the lower-cost signal, s_0, and price at average quality, γ_P, exists and satisfies the Intuitive Criterion. If the difference in quality is not less than $c(s_1, \bar{\gamma})$, then separating equilibria exist; the unique separating equilibrium to satisfy the Intuitive Criterion is the one in which the low-quality seller chooses the lower-cost signal and prices at $\underline{\gamma}$ and the high-quality seller chooses the higher-cost signal, s_1, and prices at p^* as given by (6.4.22).*

As an extension of this model, expand the space of possible signals to $[s_0, \infty)$. The set Γ remains $\{\underline{\gamma}, \bar{\gamma}\}$. Assume $c(\cdot, \gamma)$ is a continuous function for both γs, with $\lim_{s \to \infty} c(s, \bar{\gamma}) = \infty$. As will be seen, a consequence of these changes is that there is only one PBE that satisfies the Intuitive Criterion.

Lemma 6.15.   *In a PBE, the low-quality seller plays, with positive probability, at most one signal that is not the lowest signal, s_0 , and only if the high-quality seller also plays that signal with positive probability.*

Lemma 6.16.   *A PBE in which the low-quality seller sends a signal other than the lowest signal does not satisfy the Intuitive Criterion.*

The logic used in the proof of Lemma 6.16 (see Appendix) can be extended to prove:

Lemma 6.17.   *A pooling equilibrium in which both seller types send signal s_0 does not satisfy the Intuitive Criterion.*

Lemma 6.16 and the last lemma together establish that the only PBE that could satisfy the Intuitive Criterion are separating equilibria. Among the separating PBE, only one satisfies the Intuitive Criterion:

Proposition 6.17.   *Consider the signaling game described above in which there are two types and a continuum of signals with a continuous and unbounded cost-of-signaling function. Then the only PBE of that game that survives the Intuitive Criterion is the least-cost separating equilibrium.[62] (i) the low-quality seller chooses the lowest signal, s_0, and charges a price equal to her quality, $\underline{\gamma}$; (ii) the high-quality seller chooses the signal s^*, the unique solution to*

$$\bar{\gamma} - \underline{\gamma} = c(s^*, \underline{\gamma}), \tag{6.4.23}$$

and charges a price equal to her quality, $\bar{\gamma}$; (iii) the buyer believes any signal less than s^* is sent by a low-quality seller and any signal s^* or greater is sent by a high-quality seller; and (iv) the buyer accepts an offer if and only if it yields him a non-negative payoff given his beliefs.

To take stock: Proposition 6.17 establishes that when the seller can incur a continuum of signaling costs, the only "reasonable" equilibrium is a separating one in which the low-quality seller admits who she is (doesn't signal) and sets a price equal to the buyer's value for a low-quality product; and in which the high-quality seller signals just enough to be convincing—the minimum signal that the low-quality seller would be unwilling to mimic—and sets a price equal to the buyer's value for a high-quality product. Because the high-quality seller chooses the smallest effective signal, the equilibrium is known as *least-cost separating*.

---

[62] This separating equilibrium is also known as the Riley equilibrium from Riley (1979).

This logic can be extended to a setting in which there are N quality levels, $\{\gamma_0, \ldots, \gamma_{N-1}\} = \Gamma$. Assume the same payoffs as before and maintain the Spence-Mirrlees condition. Then, in a least-cost separating equilibrium, the γ_n-type seller plays (s_n^*, γ_n), where $s_0^* = s_0$ and $s_n^*, n > 0$, is defined recursively as the solution to

$$c(s_n^*, \gamma_{n-1}) = \gamma_n - \gamma_{n-1} + c(s_{n-1}^*, \gamma_{n-1}).$$

A Continuum of Types. To conclude this subsection, suppose that $\Gamma = [\underline{\gamma}, \bar{\gamma}] \subset \mathbb{R}_+$ (i.e., Γ is an interval). Maintain the same payoffs, but assume now that $c(\cdot,\cdot)$ is twice differentiable in each argument. The Spence-Mirrlees condition can now be given by

$$\frac{\partial^2 c(s, \gamma)}{\partial \gamma \partial s} < 0; \tag{6.4.24}$$

that is, the marginal cost of the signal is falling in the seller's type. The goal is to derive a separating equilibrium in which a γ-type seller plays $(s(\gamma), \gamma)$, where $s(\cdot)$ is a differentiable function.

Because all $s \in s([\underline{\gamma}, \bar{\gamma}])$ are potentially played in equilibrium, a necessary condition is

$$\gamma \in \arg\max_{\gamma' \in \Gamma} \gamma' - c\left(s(\gamma'), \gamma\right) \tag{6.4.25}$$

for all γ. All functions are differentiable, so consider replacing (6.4.25) with the first-order condition

$$0 = 1 - \frac{\partial c\left(s(\gamma), \gamma\right)}{\partial s} s'(\gamma) \tag{6.4.26}$$

for all γ. Because $\partial c / \partial s > 0$, (6.4.26) implies $s(\cdot)$ is strictly increasing—higher types signal more than lower types. In addition, recall the lowest-quality type doesn't signal at all in a separating PBE:

$$s(\underline{\gamma}) = s_0. \tag{6.4.27}$$

It follows that a function $s^*(\cdot)$ that solves the differential equation (6.4.26) given initial condition (6.4.27) is part of a separating PBE provided (6.4.26), with $s(\gamma) = s^*(\gamma)$, is a *sufficient* condition for a maximum. That it is follows from the Spence-Mirrlees condition:

$$1 - \frac{\partial c\left(s^*(\gamma'), \gamma\right)}{\partial s} \underbrace{\left(\frac{\partial c\left(s^*(\gamma'), \gamma'\right)}{\partial s}\right)^{-1}}_{=s^{*\prime}(\gamma')} \tag{6.4.28}$$

is negative for all $\gamma' > \gamma$ and positive for all $\gamma' < \gamma$.

As an example, suppose $s_0 = 0$ and $c(s, \gamma) = s^2/\gamma$. Expression (6.4.26) implies

$$\gamma = 2s(\gamma)s'(\gamma).$$

The class of solutions to this differential equation is $s(\gamma) = \sqrt{\gamma^2 - k}/\sqrt{2}$, k a constant. Expression (6.4.27) implies $k = \underline{\gamma}^2$; that is,

$$s^*(\gamma) = \frac{\sqrt{\gamma^2 - \underline{\gamma}^2}}{\sqrt{2}}.$$

For more on signaling games with a continuum of types, see Mailath (1987).

6.4.3 Experience Goods and Seller Reputation

Buyers often frequent the same seller repeatedly. If the quality of the seller's good is constant, then buyers will learn its quality over time through experience. Beyond issues of getting buyers to try the product in the first place—which resemble the issues of the one-shot analysis considered so far—such settings are straightforward and, thus, of little independent interest. A more interesting setting is one in which the quality of the seller's good varies over time; as might occur if there are variations across batches (e.g., random fluctuations in chemical processes) or the product is agricultural (e.g., variation across vintages of a given vineyard's wine).[63] In such settings, a seller may be able to develop a reputation for truthfully revealing quality.

Let $\gamma_t \in \Gamma$ denote the quality of the seller's good in period t. The set of possible qualities, Γ, is time invariant, but realized quality can vary period to period. To keep the analysis straightforward, assume each period's quality is independently drawn from the same distribution, $G : \Gamma \to [0, 1]$. Assume the unit cost of producing a quality-γ good is $c(\gamma)$.[64]

Assume the per-period payoffs of the buyer and seller, respectively, to be

$$U_B = x(\gamma - p) \text{ and } U_S = x\left(p - c(\gamma)\right),$$

---

[63] Quality is here determined exogenously. This is what distinguishes the analysis in this section from that of models of seller reputation with *endogenous* quality, such as those of Klein and Leffler (1981) and Shapiro (1982); see Section 6.5.1 *infra*.

[64] A natural assumption, given that quality is exogenous, is that unit cost is invariant with respect to quality. On the other hand, recalling that what is relevant is opportunity cost, it is also plausible that $c(\cdot)$ is an increasing function (e.g., rather than selling its grapes as wine under its own label, a vineyard can sell the grapes to another winery or it can sell the wine under a generic label, with the return from such activity being $c(\gamma)$).

where $x \in \{0, 1\}$ again indicates trade.[65]

6.4.3.1 A Basic Model

Suppose that $\Gamma = \{\gamma_L, \gamma_H\}$, $\gamma_L < \gamma_H$, and define $g = G(\gamma_L)$. Let $c(\gamma) = \hat{c}$ for both γ. Assume, critically, that at least some trade is desirable: $\gamma_H > \hat{c}$. For convenience, consider pure-strategy equilibria only. In a one-shot game, there are two possibilities: if

$$\gamma_P = g\gamma_L + (1-g)\gamma_H \geq \hat{c}, \tag{6.4.29}$$

then an equilibrium exists in which both types of seller set $p = \gamma_P$ and the buyer purchases; or, if the inequality in (6.4.29) does not hold, then the seller sets $p > \gamma_P$ and the buyer does not purchase in equilibrium (there is no market).

Now suppose that the game is repeated infinitely. Let $\delta \in (0, 1)$ be the seller's discount factor. Consider the following strategy for the buyer to play in any given period:

- if the seller has never lied, believe the seller's announcement of her type and buy if the price she quotes does not exceed her announced type; but
- if the seller has ever lied, disregard the seller's announcement of her type and buy if the price she quotes does not exceed γ_P.

Clearly if the seller has never lied and her type is γ_H, her best response to the buyer's strategy is to announce her type as γ_H and set $p = \gamma_H$. What if her type is γ_L? If she tells the truth, then the expected present discounted value (PDV) of her payoffs is

$$(\gamma_L - \hat{c})^+ + \sum_{t=1}^{\infty} \delta^t \left(g(\gamma_L - \hat{c})^+ + (1-g)(\gamma_H - \hat{c}) \right)$$
$$= (\gamma_L - \hat{c})^+ + \frac{\delta}{1-\delta} \left(g(\gamma_L - \hat{c})^+ + (1-g)(\gamma_H - \hat{c}) \right), \tag{6.4.30}$$

where $(z)^+ = z$ if $z \geq 0$ and equals 0 if $z < 0$. If she lies, then the expected PDV of her payoffs is

$$\gamma_H - \hat{c} + \sum_{t=1}^{\infty} \delta^t(\gamma_P - \hat{c})^+ = \gamma_H - \hat{c} + \frac{\delta}{1-\delta}(\gamma_P - \hat{c})^+. \tag{6.4.31}$$

---

[65] Given the assumption of quasi-linear utility, there is no further loss of generality in letting γ denote the buyer's utility from a good of quality γ (recall footnote 53 *supra*). Given the opportunity-cost definition of cost, the seller's utility could equivalently be written

$$U_S = xp + (1-x)c(\gamma).$$

Suppose $\gamma_P \geq \hat{c}$ (i.e., trade will incur in the equilibrium of the one-shot game). From (6.4.29), if $\gamma_L \geq \hat{c}$, then (6.4.30) is less than (6.4.31): a low-quality seller will lie. Hence, there is no equilibrium in which the seller is truthful. Note, the condition under which this holds, $\gamma_L \geq \hat{c}$, means the one-shot equilibrium is efficient—trade should always occurs and does. There is no efficiency loss from being unable to support truth-telling in equilibrium.

Continue to suppose $\gamma_P \geq \hat{c}$, but now assume $\gamma_L < \hat{c}$: trade will always occur in the one-shot equilibrium, but it is inefficient with a low-quality seller. Straightforward algebra reveals that (6.4.30) is at least (6.4.31) provided:

$$\delta \geq \frac{\gamma_H - \hat{c}}{(\gamma_H - \hat{c}) - g(\gamma_L - \hat{c})} . \tag{6.4.32}$$

In other words, if the seller is sufficiently patient (has a discount factor greater than the RHS of (6.4.32)), then her best response to the buyer's strategy is to always tell the truth (here, seek to sell if and only if she has high quality to offer). Given she is telling the truth, the buyer's strategy is clearly a best response for him—this is an equilibrium. Observe that the RHS of (6.4.32) is decreasing in g—the greater the likelihood of low quality, the easier it is to sustain an efficient equilibrium.[66]

Finally, suppose $\gamma_P < \hat{c}$; that is, trade never occurs in the equilibrium of the one-shot game, which is inefficient. Necessarily, $\gamma_L < \hat{c}$. Straightforward algebra reveals that (6.4.30) is at least (6.4.31) provided:

$$\delta \geq \frac{1}{2 - g} . \tag{6.4.33}$$

For the same reasons just given, if (6.4.33) holds, then an equilibrium exists in which the seller tells the truth (i.e., seeks to sell if and only if she has high quality to offer). Observe that the RHS of (6.4.33) is decreasing in g—the less likely low quality is, the easier it is to sustain an efficient equilibrium.[67]

As is the rule with repeated games, the feasibility of sustaining a desired outcome (here, efficient trade) is easier the worse the punishment for deviating. Here, a deviating seller is effectively punishing herself (regardless of equilibria, the buyer's expected surplus is always zero). Put slightly differently, the issue is whether a current seller sufficiently internalizes the externality that her lying imposes on her future selves who will have a high-quality product. The punishment that deters dishonesty is losing the future

---

[66] Given that $\gamma_P \geq \hat{c}$, it must be that $g \leq (\gamma_H - \hat{c})/(\gamma_H - \gamma_L)$.
[67] Given that $\gamma_P < \hat{c}$, it follows $g > (\gamma_H - \hat{c})/(\gamma_H - \gamma_L)$.

gains from efficient trade. Hence, when the one-shot equilibrium is already efficient, there is no scope for sustaining truthful revelation. When the one-shot equilibrium is inefficient (i.e., $\gamma_L < \hat{c}$), efficiency gains arise from the use of valuable information. It follows that the more valuable is the information, the more feasible an efficient outcome is (i.e., the lower the cutoff δ below which efficiency is not sustainable). From the analysis of (6.4.32) and (6.4.33), efficient trade in a repeated context (given $\gamma_L < \hat{c}$) is most feasible (the δ cutoff is smallest) when

$$g = \frac{\gamma_H - \hat{c}}{\gamma_H - \gamma_L} \ . \tag{6.4.34}$$

Straightforward algebra shows that when g takes that value, $\gamma_P = \hat{c}$; that is, absent information revelation, the seller is indifferent between selling and not selling. This reflects a general result: information is most valuable when, absent the information, the decision maker is indifferent between alternative decisions (see Proposition 6.19 *infra*). To summarize:

Proposition 6.18. *A seller's type (quality) varies independently period to period. If trade would be efficient in a one-shot game despite the buyer's ignorance of quality, then there is no equilibrium of a repeated game with truthful revelation of type. If trade would be inefficient with positive probability in a one-shot game, then an equilibrium with truthful revelation exists in a repeated game if the seller is sufficiently patient (has a high enough discount factor, δ). It is easier to sustain such an equilibrium (i.e., δ can be lower) the more valuable is information about type.*

6.4.3.2 An Aside: The Value of Information

It was noted that information is most valuable when the decision maker would otherwise be indifferent between different actions in the absence of that information. This subsection establishes that insight more formally.

A decision maker can make one of two decisions: d_0 or d_1. Given there are only two possible decisions, there is no loss of generality in assuming two possible states, s_0 and s_1.[68] Assume that decision d_i is best for the decision maker in state s_i. Formally, let her payoff if she makes decision d_i in state s_j be $U(d_i|s_j)$. The assumption d_i is best given s_i means $U(d_i|s_i) > U(d_i|s_j)$ for any i and j, $i \neq j$. Define

$$L(d_j|s_i) = U(d_i|s_i) - U(d_j|s_i)$$

as the loss from choosing d_j in state s_i. Let q_i denote the probability that the true state is s_i.

---

[68] If there are more than two states, we can view the state space as partitioned into two: the set of states in which one decision is optimal and the set of states in which the other decision is optimal. Relabel these two sets (events) as the relevant states.

Absent information as to the state, the decision maker decides d^*, where

$$d^* = \arg\max_{d \in \{d_0, d_1\}} q_0 U(d|s_0) + q_1 U(d|s_1).$$

The value of information, V, is the difference between the decision maker's expected payoff if she makes her decision with information about the state and her expected payoff if she makes it in ignorance:

$$V = \left(q_0 U(d_0|s_0) + q_1 U(d_1|s_1)\right) - \left(q_0 U(d^*|s_0) + q_1 U(d^*|s_1)\right).$$

Without loss of generality, suppose $d^* = d_i$. Algebra reveals

$$V = (1 - q_i)L(d_i|s_{-i});$$

hence, the value of information is decreasing in the probability of the state in which d_i is the correct action and increasing in the loss from choosing d_i in state s_{-i}. The probability q_i cannot be too low *ceteris paribus*, because otherwise d^* would no longer be d_i. Similarly, $L(d_i|s_j)$ cannot be too great *ceteris paribus*, because otherwise $d^* \neq d_i$. These insights yield

Proposition 6.19. *Consider a binary decision problem. Holding constant all other parameters, the value of information is greatest when the probabilities of the two states are such that the decision maker would be indifferent between her two alternatives in the absence of information. Similarly, holding constant all other parameters, the value of information is greatest when the losses from making the wrong decision are such that the decision maker would be indifferent between her two alternatives in the absence of information.*

6.4.3.3 Seller Reputation with Signaling

Return to the model of Section 6.4.3.1. Suppose, now, though the seller can signal: specifically, at cost $C(s, \gamma)$, she can send signal s. Assume $C : [0, \infty) \times \{\gamma_L, \gamma_H\}$ satisfies the Spence-Mirrlees condition:

$$\frac{\partial C(s, \gamma_H)}{\partial s} < \frac{\partial C(s, \gamma_L)}{\partial s}.$$

For example, s could be the number of positive reviews or tests the seller can produce.[69] Consistent with the usual notion of cost, $C(0, \gamma) = 0$ and $\partial C(s, \gamma)/\partial s > 0$ for both γ. Assume, for all $k \in \mathbb{R}$, that an $s \in \mathbb{R}$ exists such that $k = C(s, \gamma_L)$.

---

[69] Consider γ to be the *average* quality of the product in a given period and assume all parties are risk neutral. Suppose reviews or tests are *hard information*: the seller can suppress those she does not like, but if she reports a review or test it must be accurate. A seller with higher average quality (i.e., a greater γ) will find it easier *ceteris paribus* to generate s favorable reports or reviews than will a seller with lower average quality.

Define s^* as the value of s that solves

$$\max\{0, \gamma_L - \hat{c}\} = \gamma_H - \hat{c} - C(s, \gamma_L).$$ (6.4.35)

It is readily shown that the assumptions given imply that s^* exists and is unique. The Spence-Mirrlees condition and (6.4.35) ensure that

$$\gamma_H - \hat{c} - C(s^*, \gamma_H) > \max\{0, \gamma_L - \hat{c}\};$$

hence, a high-type seller would prefer to send signal s^* than to shutdown or be seen as a low-quality seller. It is readily seen that the one-shot game satisfies the conditions of Proposition 6.17. Consequently, the only reasonable PBE of the one-shot game is the least-cost separating equilibrium in which a low-quality seller either does not sell (if $\gamma_L < \hat{c}$) or sells without signaling (if $\gamma_L \geq \hat{c}$), while a high-quality seller sells at price γ_H and transmits signal s^*.

Consider, now, an infinitely repeated version of this game.[70] Again $\delta \in (0, 1)$ denotes the seller's discount factor. The goal is to determine conditions such that an equilibrium exists in which the seller announces her type truthfully *without* signaling. To that end, consider the following strategy for the buyer:

- if the seller has never lied, believe the seller's announcement of her type and buy if the price she quotes does not exceed her announced type; but
- if the seller has ever lied, disregard the seller's announcement of her type. Believe her type that period is γ_H if she sends a signal s^* or greater and believe her type is γ_L otherwise. Buy if the price she quotes does not exceed the quality her signal indicates.

In other words, if the seller ever lies, then the game reverts to infinite repetition of the one-shot game with play defined by the sole PBE that satisfies the Intuitive Criterion of Cho and Kreps (1987).

As in Section 6.4.3.1, a high-quality seller has no incentive to lie about her type. The issue is whether a low-quality type would lie. Her payoff from telling the truth is

$$(\gamma_L - \hat{c})^+ + \sum_{t=1}^{\infty} \delta^t \left(g(\gamma_L - \hat{c})^+ + (1-g)(\gamma_H - \hat{c})\right)$$
$$= (\gamma_L - \hat{c})^+ + \frac{\delta}{1-\delta}\left(g(\gamma_L - \hat{c})^+ + (1-g)(\gamma_H - \hat{c})\right).$$ (6.4.36)

[70] Mester (1992) considers a finitely repeated game of signaling in which the signaler's type is correlated across periods (in contrast to here, where it is independently drawn each period).

Her payoff from lying is

$$\gamma_H - \hat{c} + \sum_{t=1}^{\infty} \delta^t \left(g(\gamma_L - \hat{c})^+ + (1-g)\left(\gamma_H - \hat{c} - C(s^*, \gamma_H)\right)\right)$$

$$= \gamma_H - \hat{c} + \frac{\delta}{1-\delta} \left(g(\gamma_L - \hat{c})^+ + (1-g)\left(\gamma_H - \hat{c} - C(s^*, \gamma_H)\right)\right) .$$

(6.4.37)

Truth-telling dominates lying (i.e., (6.4.37) does not exceed (6.4.36)) if

$$\frac{\delta}{1-\delta}(1-g)C(s^*, \gamma_H) \geq \gamma_H - \hat{c} - (\gamma_L - \hat{c})^+ ;$$

(6.4.38)

that is, should the expected discounted cost of future signaling (if her reputation for truth-telling be lost) exceed the one-period gain from fooling the buyer, then the seller's best response is to tell the truth every period. Given she will tell the truth, the buyer is also playing a best response and we have an equilibrium.

The fraction $\frac{\delta}{1-\delta}$ is increasing in δ. It follows, therefore, from (6.4.38) that the greater the likelihood the seller is high type or the greater the cost of signaling, the lower is the cutoff value of δ for which truth-telling can be sustained. To summarize:

Proposition 6.20. *A seller's type (quality) varies independently period to period. Suppose the seller has access to a costly signal and the cost of signaling function satisfies the Spence-Mirrlees condition. An equilibrium of the repeated game exists in which there is no signaling in equilibrium, but rather the seller simply announces her type truthfully each period if the seller is sufficiently patient (has a high enough discount factor, δ). It is easier to sustain such an equilibrium (i.e., δ can be lower) the more likely the seller is to be the high type or the greater the high type's cost of signaling.*

In Proposition 6.18, a truth-telling equilibrium did not exist if trade was efficient in the one-shot game. Here, trade is efficient in the one-shot game insofar as it occurs if and only if $\gamma \geq \hat{c}$. But the one-shot game here is never wholly efficient because the high-type seller engages in costly signaling. If $\gamma_L \geq \hat{c}$, then this signaling is completely wasteful from a welfare perspective. If $\gamma_L < \hat{c}$, then signaling enhances efficiency insofar as it ensures trading efficiency, but the first-best is nevertheless not achieved.

In this model, as opposed to the one of Section 6.4.3.1, what deters a low-quality seller from lying is the knowledge that her future selves will have to pay signaling costs in the future. The effectiveness of this deterrent is increasing in both the amount of those costs and the likelihood that they will have to be paid. This is why, in contrast to the result in Proposition 6.18, the ease of sustaining a truth-telling equilibrium is monotonically increasing in the probability of the high quality.

A final question is what if (6.4.38) does not hold: does this imply the equilibrium is infinite repetition of the equilibrium of the one-shot game (i.e., the seller sends signal s^* when she is high quality)? To answer this, we need to ask if there could be an equilibrium of the repeated game with only some signaling. Specifically, we seek an equilibrium of the following sort: when high type, the seller announces her type as γ_H and sends signal $\hat{s} \in (0, s^*)$; when low type, she announces her types as γ_L and sends no signal. The buyer believes the seller's announcement if accompanied by the appropriate signal, provided he's never been lied to. If he's been lied to, then the game reverts to infinite repetition of the one-shot equilibrium. As before, the issue is whether a low-type seller's payoff from truth telling,

$$(\gamma_L - \hat{c})^+ + \frac{\delta}{1 - \delta} \left(g(\gamma_L - \hat{c})^+ + (1 - g)\left(\gamma_H - \hat{c} - C(\hat{s}, \gamma_H)\right)\right), \quad (6.4.39)$$

exceeds her payoff from lying,

$$\gamma_H - \hat{c} - C(\hat{s}, \gamma_L) + \frac{\delta}{1 - \delta}\left(g(\gamma_L - \hat{c})^+ + (1 - g)\left(\gamma_H - \hat{c} - C(s^*, \gamma_H)\right)\right). \quad (6.4.40)$$

Expression (6.4.39) exceeds (6.4.40) if

$$\frac{\delta}{1 - \delta}(1 - g)\left(C(s^*, \gamma_H) - C(\hat{s}, \gamma_H)\right) \geq (\gamma_H - \hat{c}) - (\gamma_L - \hat{c})^+ - C(\hat{s}, \gamma_L)$$
$$= C(s^*, \gamma_L) - C(\hat{s}, \gamma_L), \quad (6.4.41)$$

where the equality follows because s^* is the least-cost level of signaling in the equilibrium of the one-shot game. Observe that (6.4.41) reduces to (6.4.38) if $\hat{s} = 0$. Given Spence-Mirrlees, if (6.4.41) holds for $\hat{s}$ it must hold for all $\hat{s}' \in (\hat{s}, s^*]$. Consequently, if, as conjectured, (6.4.38) does not hold, then (6.4.41) fails to hold for all $\hat{s} \in (0, s^*)$. To conclude:

Proposition 6.21.   *Given the signaling game of this section, the equilibrium of the infinitely repeated game is either one with honest announcements of type and no signaling or it is simply infinite repetition of the equilibrium of the one-shot game.*[71]

---

[71] This result is, in part, due to the signal's not being directly productive. In a game in which signaling is partially productive, equilibria with honest announcements and limited signaling are possible. See Hermalin (2007) for an example.

6.5 ENDOGENOUS ASYMMETRIES OF INFORMATION AT TIME OF CONTRACTING

To this point, the parties have been endowed with private information. In many situations, their private information arises because of actions they take; that is, it is *endogenous*. For instance, a seller's decisions about materials, production methods, and the like could determine the quality of her product. As a second example, a buyer could make investments in complementary assets that affect his utility from purchasing the seller's product (e.g., a buyer's utility from buying a new DVD player could depend on the number of DVDs previously acquired).

Suppose that private information is the consequence of actions. These actions—typically investments—fall into two broad categories: selfish and cooperative (to use the terminology of Che and Hausch, 1999). Selfish actions directly affect the actor's payoff from trade. Cooperative actions directly affect the payoffs of the actor's trading partner. For instance, a seller's investment in the quality of her product is cooperative, while a buyer's acquisition of complementary assets is selfish. Given the focus here on situations in which the seller possesses all the bargaining power (makes TIOLI offers), only three possibilities are of interest:[72] cooperative action by the seller, cooperative action by the buyer, and selfish action by the buyer. Selfish actions by the seller are not of interest because the seller's (contract proposer's) private information about her own payoffs generally do not create distortions.

6.5.1 Cooperative Seller Actions

Suppose the seller takes an action, $q \in \mathcal{Q}$, that affects the buyer's payoff should trade occur. In a buyer-seller relationship, a natural interpretation is that q affects or is the quality of the seller's product.

Consider a basic model: the buyer wants at most one unit, $\mathcal{Q} = [\underline{q}, \infty), \underline{q} > 0$, and the payoffs of seller and buyer are

$$U_S = x\left(p - c(q)\right) \text{ and } U_B = x(q - p),$$

respectively; where $x \in \{0, 1\}$ indicates whether trade occurs, p is price, and $c : \mathcal{Q} \to \mathbb{R}_+$. Critically, assume the seller's cost is increasing in the quality of the good she produces: $q > q' \Rightarrow c(q) > c(q')$. Assume there exist $q \in \mathcal{Q}$ such that $q > c(q)$ (i.e., trade is efficient for some quality levels), but that there exists a finite $\bar{q}$ such that $q < c(q)$ for all $q > \bar{q}$ (i.e., too much quality is inefficient to produce).

---

[72] Recall, in this chapter, that "seller" and "buyer" are shorthand for contract proposer and contract recipient, respectively.

If the buyer could observe the seller's choice of q, then the seller would do best to choose p and q to solve

$$\max_{p,q} p - c(q)$$

subject to

$$q - p \geq 0 .$$

It was earlier established that the buyer's participation constraint binds (see Proposition 6.1), so substituting the constraint the problem is

$$\max_{q} q - c(q) . \tag{6.5.1}$$

In other words, were the buyer able to observe quality, the seller would have an incentive to choose a quality that maximizes welfare: efficiency would attain.

If the buyer cannot observe quality, then one of two possibilities arises: if $\underline{q} \geq c(\underline{q})$, the seller offers a product of that quality and sets a price of $p = \underline{q}$; or, if $\underline{q} < c(\underline{q})$, then there is no market. To understand these conclusions, observe that if $\hat{p}$ is the maximum price the buyer will accept, then, anticipating a sale at $\hat{p}$, the seller's choice of quality is

$$\max_{q} \hat{p} - c(q) .$$

The sole solution is $q = \underline{q}$. Hence, the highest quality the buyer can expect is $\underline{q}$. If trade is to occur, the largest price he will accept is $p = \underline{q}$. Knowing this, the seller either shuts down if $\underline{q} < c(\underline{q})$ (she cannot make a profit at that price); or she charges $p = \underline{q}$ and provides the lowest possible quality. Unless $\underline{q}$ is a solution to (6.5.1), the outcome is inefficient. To summarize:

Proposition 6.22. *Suppose the quality of an experience good is endogenous, with higher quality costing the seller more. Then the equilibrium of the one-shot game is inefficient unless minimum quality is welfare maximizing.*

6.5.1.1 Seller Reputation Models

A better outcome than the Proposition 6.22 outcome can attain in an infinitely repeated game if the seller is sufficiently patient.[73] To wit, suppose q^* is a solution to (6.5.1). To make the problem of interest, assume $\underline{q}$ is not a solution. Define

$$\underline{\pi} = \max \left\{ 0, \underline{q} - c(\underline{q}) \right\} ;$$

---

[73] This analysis is along the lines of that in Klein and Leffler (1981). A difference is that Klein and Leffler, 1981 allow for multiple sellers to enter the market and compete. This enriches the analysis, but does not matter for the points being made here.

that is, $\underline{\pi}$ is the seller's profit in the equilibrium of the one-shot game. Observe that repetition of the one-shot game means the seller is free to change her quality each period if she wishes.

Observe that if the buyer believes quality will be $\underline{q}$, then the seller's best response is either shutdown ($\underline{q} < c(\underline{q})$) or offer quality $\underline{q}$ at price $\underline{q}$. Hence, even in the infinitely repeated game, there is a subgame-perfect equilibrium in which the seller's per-period payoff is $\underline{\pi}$.

Consider the following strategy for the buyer:

- if the seller has never provided quality less than q^*, then believe she is offering quality q^* this period; and buy if and only if the price she charges does not exceed q^*;
- but if the seller has ever provided quality less than q^*, then believe she is offering quality $\underline{q}$ if she offers to sell; and buy if and only if the price she charges does not exceed $\underline{q}$.

If the buyer is expecting quality q^*, then the seller's best deviation from offering quality q^* remains $\underline{q}$. Hence, offering quality q^* and charging price q^* is the seller's best response to the buyer's strategy if

$$\sum_{t=0}^{\infty} \delta^t \left(q^* - c(q^*) \right) \geq q^* - c(\underline{q}) + \sum_{t=1}^{\infty} \delta^t \underline{\pi} \,,$$

where $\delta \in (0, 1)$ is again the seller's discount factor. Straightforward algebra reveals that condition holds provided

$$\delta \geq \frac{c(q^*) - c(\underline{q})}{q^* - \underline{\pi} - c(\underline{q})} \,. \tag{6.5.2}$$

If the seller's discount factor satisfies condition (6.5.2), then there is an equilibrium in which welfare-maximizing quality is provided. That and readily done comparative statics yield:

Proposition 6.23.   *Consider an infinitely repeated game in which the seller chooses quality each period. If the seller is sufficiently patient (as defined by condition (6.5.2)), then an equilibrium exists in which the welfare-maximizing level of quality is provided each period. Such an equilibrium is supported for a larger set of discount factors the smaller is the cost difference between producing welfare-maximizing quality and producing minimal quality ceteris paribus.*

The last part of the proposition follows because what tempts the seller to cheat on quality is the cost savings from producing minimal quality versus higher quality: the smaller the temptation, the easier it is to sustain an equilibrium with honest provision of high quality.

If $\underline{q} \geq c(\underline{q})$, then (6.5.2) becomes

$$\delta \geq \frac{c(q^*) - c(\underline{q})}{q^* - \underline{q}} \,. \tag{6.5.3}$$

If $c(\cdot)$ is a strictly convex function, then the RHS of expression (6.5.3) is increasing in q^*.[74] Hence, if the seller's discount factor is less than the RHS of (6.5.3), then there may exist a $\hat{q} \in (\underline{q}, q^*)$ such that

$$\frac{c(\hat{q}) - c(\underline{q})}{\hat{q} - \underline{q}} = \delta \,. \tag{6.5.4}$$

It follows, from now familiar logic, that if (6.5.4) holds, then there is an equilibrium of the infinitely repeated game in which the seller supplies quality $\hat{q}$. Given the assumed convexity of $c(\cdot)$ and the optimality of q^*, it must be that supplying $\hat{q}$ is welfare superior to supplying minimum quality. To summarize:

Proposition 6.24. *Assume an infinitely repeated game in which the seller chooses quality each period. Assume the cost-of-quality function, $c(\cdot)$, is strictly convex and the production of minimum quality, $\underline{q}$, is welfare superior to shutting down (i.e., $\underline{q} \geq c(\underline{q})$). Then there is an equilibrium of the repeated game in which quality greater than minimal quality is supplied provided the seller is sufficiently patient; that is, provided her discount factor δ satisfies*[75]

$$\delta > \lim_{q \downarrow \underline{q}} \frac{c(q) - c(\underline{q})}{q - \underline{q}} \,. \tag{6.5.5}$$

---

[74] Proof: Let $q' > q > \underline{q}$. Convexity entails

$$c(q) < \frac{q' - q}{q' - \underline{q}} c(\underline{q}) + \frac{q - \underline{q}}{q' - \underline{q}} c(q')$$

Subtracting $c(\underline{q})$ from both sides yields

$$c(q) - c(\underline{q}) < \frac{q - \underline{q}}{q' - \underline{q}} c(q') - c(\underline{q}) \,.$$

The claim follows.

[75] Because $c(\cdot)$ is convex, the limit in (6.5.5) (the right derivative) exists. See van Tiel (1984, Theorem 1.6).

6.5.1.2 One-Time Quality Choice with Consumer Learning

Suppose that the seller chooses quality, q, once and for all at time 0.[76] The cost of producing a unit of quality q remains $c(q)$. Assume that the seller will potentially trade with the buyer in T periods (where T could be infinity). Once the buyer has experienced the good, he knows for sure what its quality will be in future periods. To keep the analysis straightforward, assume trading minimal quality yields nonnegative surplus (i.e., assume $\underline{q} \geq c(\underline{q})$).

To construct an equilibrium, suppose that the seller plays a pure strategy with respect to her choice of quality. In equilibrium, the buyer must correctly anticipate this.[77] Let q^e be the quality he anticipates the seller will choose. Hence, if the buyer has not yet purchased, he will buy if the seller offers the good at price q^e or less and won't purchase otherwise.[78] Once the buyer has purchased, he knows quality for sure and the seller can, therefore, charge him price equal to actual quality, q. Because $q^e \geq \underline{q} \geq c(\underline{q})$, the seller can have no reason to avoid a sale in the initial period, 0. Hence, if her actual choice is q, her discounted profit is

$$
\Pi = q^e - c(q) + \sum_{t=1}^{T-1} \delta^t \left(q - c(q) \right) = q^e + \frac{1}{1-\delta} \left((\delta - \delta^T)q - (1 - \delta^T)c(q) \right).
$$

Maximizing Π is equivalent to maximizing

$$
\max_q \frac{\delta - \delta^T}{1 - \delta^T} q - c(q). \tag{6.5.6}
$$

Because $\delta < 1$, $\frac{\delta-\delta^T}{1-\delta^T} < 1$. Hence, the solution to (6.5.6) cannot exceed the minimum level of quality that maximizes welfare. Under standard assumptions—$c(\cdot)$ is strictly convex and everywhere differentiable—the solution to (6.5.6)—call it q^{SB}—is strictly less than the, then, unique welfare-maximizing quality, q^*. Observe that if $T=1$—this is just the one-period game—then $q^{SB} = \underline{q}$, as is to be expected. In equilibrium, the buyer must correctly anticipate the seller's quality choice; that is, $q^e = q^{SB}$. To summarize:

Proposition 6.25.   *Suppose buyer and seller potentially trade in T periods ($1 \leq T \leq \infty$), but the seller sets quality for all time prior to the initial period of trade. Suppose trade is welfare*

---

[76] The analysis in this section is similar in spirit to that in Section 2 of Shapiro (1982).

[77] The notion that the buyer—consumers more generally—can engage in such game-theoretic reasoning separates the analysis here from some of the analysis in Shapiro (1982) and from Shapiro (1983) (as well as some earlier literature), in which the buyer's estimation of quality follows a more exogenously given path. The analysis below leading up to Proposition 6.26 illustrates how the analysis changes with less rational consumers.

[78] Given his beliefs, the buyer anticipates no gain from experimenting.

superior to no trade even at minimal quality (i.e., $\underline{q} \geq c(\underline{q})$). Then there is an equilibrium in which the seller sets the same price every period, which equals the quality of the good, and there is trade in every period. The quality of the good solves the program (6.5.6) and is never greater than any welfare-maximizing quality. It is strictly less for all T if $c(\cdot)$ is strictly convex and everywhere differentiable.

Continuing to assume $c(\cdot)$ differentiable and strictly convex, the following is readily shown:

Corollary 6.4. *Maintain the assumptions of Proposition 6.25. Assume, in addition, that $c(\cdot)$ is everywhere differentiable and strictly convex. Let q^{SB} be the solution to the program (6.5.6); that is, equilibrium quality and price. Then*

(i) $q^{SB} = \underline{q}$ (minimal quality) if $\frac{\delta - \delta^T}{1 - \delta^T} \leq c'(\underline{q})$;

(ii) $q^{SB} > \underline{q}$ if $\frac{\delta - \delta^T}{1 - \delta^T} > c'(\underline{q})$; and

(iii) q^{SB} is nondecreasing in the number of periods, T, and strictly increasing at T if $\frac{\delta - \delta^T}{1 - \delta^T} > c'(\underline{q})$.

The last result follows because $\frac{\delta - \delta^T}{1 - \delta^T}$ is increasing in T. Because the limit of that ratio is strictly less than 1 as $T \to \infty$, maximum welfare will not attain even if there are infinite periods of trade.

A prediction of Corollary 6.4 is that consumers will expect higher quality from a product they anticipate a manufacturer selling for a long time than from a product they anticipate will be sold for a short time.

Proposition 6.25 might strike one as odd insofar as there is no deception on the equilibrium path—the buyer always "knows" the quality he will receive and the seller provides him that quality—yet somehow welfare is not maximized. The reason it is not maximized is that the seller cannot *commit* not to cheat the buyer. In particular, the seller's discounted profit, Π, is the sum of discounted total surplus plus a payment that is independent of any choice she makes (q^e) less a cost that does depend on what she does (the first $c(q)$ term in the expression for Π). If she chose $q = q^*$, then she would maximize the sum of the discounted surplus. Since that is a maximum, lowering q slightly from that level would represent a second-order loss. But she would enjoy a first-order gain by lowering her initial period cost. It follows, therefore, that she cannot be expected to choose the welfare-maximizing level of quality.

In some of the original literature in this area (e.g., Shapiro, 1982, 1983), the buyer was less sophisticated than modeled above. As an example, suppose that the buyer's estimate of quality after consumption at time $t-1$, given a prior estimate of q_{t-1}^e and actual quality q, is

$$q_t^e = \lambda q + (1 - \lambda)q_{t-1}^e, \qquad (6.5.7)$$

where $\lambda \in [0, 1]$. A $\lambda = 0$ represents no learning and a $\lambda = 1$ represents immediate learning. Assuming the buyer has bought in all periods $0, \ldots, t-1$, solving the recursive expression (6.5.7) reveals his estimate of quality at the beginning of period t is

$$q_t^e = \left(1 - (1 - \lambda)^t\right) q + (1 - \lambda)^t q_0^e, \tag{6.5.8}$$

where q_0^e is his estimate prior to any exchange.

For the sake of brevity, limit attention to $c(\cdot)$ strictly convex and everywhere differentiable.

Assume the seller knows q_0^e. Because even selling minimal quality is weakly profitable, the seller will wish to sell in every period and her price in each period will be q_t^e. The seller's choice of q solves:

$$\max_q \sum_{t=0}^{T-1} \delta^t (q_t^e - c(q)) \equiv \max_q q_0^e \frac{1 - \delta^T (1 - \lambda)^T}{1 - \delta + \delta\lambda}$$

$$+ q \frac{\delta\lambda + \delta^T (1 - \delta)(1 - \lambda)^T - \delta^T (1 - \delta(1 - \lambda))}{(1 - \delta)(1 - \delta(1 - \lambda))}$$

$$- c(q) \frac{1 - \delta^T}{(1 - \delta)(1 - \delta(1 - \lambda))}.$$

That program is equivalent to

$$\max_q q \underbrace{\frac{\delta\lambda + \delta^T (1 - \delta)(1 - \lambda)^T - \delta^T (1 - \delta(1 - \lambda))}{1 - \delta^T}}_{R(\delta, \lambda, T)} - c(q). \tag{6.5.9}$$

It is readily shown that $\partial R(\delta, \lambda, T)/\partial T > 0$ and $\lim_{T \to \infty} R(\delta, \lambda, T) = \delta\lambda < 1$. Consequently, (6.5.9) implies the seller will choose a quality level less than the welfare-maximizing quantity.

Let $\hat{q}(\lambda)$ denote the solution to (6.5.9). Observe that if $\lambda = 1$ (learning is immediate), then

$$R(\delta, 1, T) = \frac{\delta - \delta^T}{1 - \delta^T}.$$

The program (6.5.9) thus reduces to the program (6.5.6) if $\lambda = 1$; hence, $\hat{q}(1) = q^{SB}$. Because $R(\delta, \lambda, T) < \delta\lambda$, it follows that as $\lambda \downarrow 0$ (the buyer ceases to learn), $R(\delta, \lambda, T) \to 0$, which implies $\hat{q}(0) = \underline{q}$: if the buyer never learns, then the seller will cheat him by providing minimal quality. Finally, observe

$$\frac{\partial R(\delta, \lambda, T)}{\partial \lambda} \propto \frac{1 - \delta^T}{1 - \delta} - T\delta^{T-1}(1 - \lambda)^{T-1} \geq \frac{1 - \delta^T}{1 - \delta} - T\delta^{T-1}.$$

The rightmost term is positive for $T = 1$. For $T \geq 2$, the rightmost term is the difference between the slope of the chord between (δ, δ^T) and $(1, 1^T)$ and the derivative of δ^T at δ. Because the power function is a convex function for powers greater than 1, the slope of the chord must exceed the derivative; that is, the rightmost term is positive. It follows, therefore, that $\partial R/\partial \lambda > 0$, which in turn entails that the quicker the buyer is at learning true quality, the greater will be the quality the seller provides (assuming quality is not a corner solution, $\underline{q}$). In other words, $\hat{q}(\lambda)$ is nondecreasing in λ and strictly increasing at any point at which $\hat{q}(\lambda) > \underline{q}$. To summarize:

Proposition 6.26.   *Consider the model of gradual buyer learning just articulated. If learning is immediate (i.e., $\lambda = 1$), then the equilibrium is identical to the one of Proposition 6.25 with respect to the seller's choice of quality (i.e., she will choose q^{SB}). If the buyer never learns, the seller will provide minimal quality (i.e., $\underline{q}$). Finally, the faster the buyer's rate of learning (i.e., λ), the weakly greater will be the seller's choice of quality.*

From expression (6.5.9), it follows that the seller's choice of quality is independent of the buyer's initial expectation, q_0^e. In particular, even if the buyer correctly anticipates the seller's quality initially in equilibrium, $\hat{q}(\lambda) < q^{SB}$ if $\lambda < 1$. In other words, the possibility that the buyer will not immediately detect that the seller has provided quality other than what he expected puts a downward pressure on quality. In essence, the ability to fool the buyer (at least in a limited fashion for a limited time), further erodes the seller's ability to commit to high quality.

Observe for any λ (including $\lambda = 1$), the seller would do better if she could commit to the welfare-maximizing level of quality, q^*. To the extent that warranties or similar measures provide such commitment, the seller would have an incentive to offer them.

6.5.2 Semi-Cooperative Seller Actions

The selfish–cooperative dichotomy set forth above can, in some contexts, be too stark. Consider a scenario where the seller is a homebuilder. Again, she chooses the quality of the house—perhaps through the quality of the materials she uses. Assume, critically, however, that she (i) incurs the costs *prior* to sale and (ii) has, as an alternative to sale, living in the house herself. That is, the seller's action is cooperative if sale occurs, but selfish if it does not.[79] Sale is, however, always welfare superior to no sale.

---

[79] The analysis in this section draws heavily from Hermalin (2013).

To study such a scenario, let the payoffs of seller and buyer be, respectively,

$$U_S = x(t - q) + (1 - x)b_S(q) - q \text{ and } U_B = x\big(b_B(q) - t\big) \,,$$

where $x \in \{0, 1\}$ indicates the amount of trade, $t \in \mathbb{R}$ is payment in the event of sale, and $b_i : \mathbb{R}_+ \to \mathbb{R}$ is party i's benefit (possibly expected) from possession of a good of quality q. Observe, as a normalization, the cost of supplying quality q is, now, just q.

Some assumptions on the benefit functions:

- The functions $b_i(\cdot)$ are twice continuously differentiable, strictly increasing, and strictly concave functions (i.e., there is a positive, but diminishing, marginal benefit to increased quality).
- For all $q > 0$, $b_B(q) > b_S(q)$ (i.e., trade is strictly welfare superior, at least if the seller has chosen positive quality).
- Zero quality is not privately optimal for the seller if she is certain to retain possession: $b_S'(0) > 1$.
- Infinite quality is not optimal: there exists a $\bar{q} < \infty$ such that $b_B'(q) < 1$ if $q > \bar{q}$.

In light of these assumptions, a unique welfare-maximizing quality, q^*, exists (i.e., q^* maximizes $b_B(q) - q$). If trade were impossible (i.e., autarky held), then the seller would choose quality to maximize

$$b_S(q) - q \,. \tag{6.5.10}$$

The earlier given assumptions ensure that program has a unique interior solution: call it $\hat{q}$. To eliminate a case of minor interest, assume[80]

$$b_B(0) < b_S(\hat{q}) - \hat{q} \,; \tag{6.5.11}$$

that is, maximum welfare under autarky exceeds welfare given trade but zero quality.

As is common in settings such as these (see, e.g., Gul, 2001, for a discussion), no pure-strategy equilibrium exists:

Proposition 6.27.   *No pure-strategy equilibrium exists.*
Proof: Suppose, to the contrary, the seller played a pure-strategy of q. Suppose $q > 0$. In equilibrium, the buyer must correctly anticipate the seller's action. Hence, he is willing to pay up to $b_B(q)$ for the good. As the seller has the bargaining power, that is the price she will set. However, knowing she can receive a price of $b_B(q)$ regardless of the

---

[80] See Hermalin (2013) for an analysis with this case included.

quality she actually chooses, the seller would do better to deviate to 0 quality ($b_B(q) - q$ < $b_B(q)$ if $q>0$). Suppose $q=0$. The seller can then obtain only $b_B(0)$ for the good. But given (6.5.11), the seller would do better to invest $\hat{q}$ and keep the good for herself. The result follows *reductio ad absurdum*.   ■

Because welfare maximization requires the seller to choose q^* with certainty and trade to occur with certainty, Proposition 6.27 implies that the first-best outcome is unattainable in equilibrium.

What about the second best? As demonstrated by Proposition 6.27, there is a trade-off between trading efficiently and providing the seller investment incentives. The second-best welfare-maximization program can be written as

$$\max_{x,q,t} xb_B(q) + (1 - x)b_S(q) - q \tag{6.5.12}$$

subject to

$$q \in \arg\max_{q} xt + (1 - x)b_S(q) - q, \tag{6.5.13}$$

$$b_B(q) \geq t, \text{ and} \tag{6.5.14}$$

$$xt + (1 - x)b_S(q) - q \geq b_S(\hat{q}) - \hat{q}. \tag{6.5.15}$$

Constraint (6.5.13) is the requirement that the choice of q be incentive compatible for the seller. Constraints (6.5.14) and (6.5.15) are, respectively, the buyer and seller's participation (IR) constraints.

The previously given assumptions imply that the program in (6.5.13) is globally concave in q with an interior solution. Hence, that constraint can be replaced with the corresponding first-order condition:

$$(1 - x)b'_S(q) - 1 = 0.$$

This, in turn, defines the probability of trade as

$$x = 1 - \frac{1}{b'_S(q)}. \tag{6.5.16}$$

Note that $x = 0$ if $q = \hat{q}$. Because marginal benefit is decreasing in quality, it follows that $q \in [0, \hat{q}]$. Substituting that back into (6.5.12) makes the program:

$$\max_{q \in [0,\hat{q}]} \left(1 - \frac{1}{b'_S(q)}\right) b_B(q) + \frac{1}{b'_S(q)} b_S(q) - q. \tag{6.5.17}$$

Because the domain is compact and the function to be maximized continuous, the program must have at least one solution. Let $\mathcal{M}$ equal the maximized value of (6.5.17). Let $\mathcal{Q}_{\mathcal{M}}$ denote the set of maximizers of (6.5.17). A second-best level of quality is, therefore, $q^{SB} \in \mathcal{Q}_{\mathcal{M}}$.

This analysis has ignored the participation constraints, expressions (6.5.14) and (6.5.15). There is no loss in having done so: given q^{SB} is played, these will hold for a range of transfers, including $t = b_B(q^{SB})$.

The next proposition finds that the second-best solution is supportable as an equilibrium:

Proposition 6.28. *A perfect Bayesian equilibrium exists in which the second best is achieved.[81] Specifically, it is an equilibrium for the seller to choose a second-best quality (an q^{SB}) with certainty and offer the good to the buyer at price $b_B(q^{SB})$. The buyer plays the mixed strategy in which he accepts the seller's offer with probability x,*

$$ x = 1 - \frac{1}{b'_S(q^{SB})} . $$

The buyer believes a price less than $b_B(q^{SB})$ means the seller has chosen quality 0; a price of $b_B(q^{SB})$ means the seller has chosen quality q^{SB}; and a price greater than $b_B(q^{SB})$ means the seller has chosen a quality no greater than q^{SB}.

Because of the buyer's playing of a mixed strategy, the seller may retain ownership and that possibility gives her an incentive to provide quality. Hence, it is possible to have an equilibrium in which quality is provided. The problem—and the reason the first best cannot be attained—is that the final allocation may prove to be inefficient: the good may remain in the seller's hands. This reflects the fundamental trade-off in this situation: the seller's incentives to provide quality are greatest when she is certain to retain ownership, but her retention of ownership is inefficient; conversely, if trade is certain, she has no incentive to provide quality. The second-best solution balances these competing tensions.

6.5.3 Cooperative Buyer Actions

Suppose that prior to trade, the buyer can make an investment, $I \in \mathcal{I} \subseteq \mathbb{R}_+$, that affects the seller's cost. Assume $0 \in \mathcal{I}$ (i.e., the buyer can choose not to invest). One interpretation is that by investing I, the buyer facilitates delivery by the seller. Another

---

[81] As Hermalin (2013) notes, this equilibrium is not unique. The outcome (level of quality and probability of trade) of this PBE can, however, be part of an essentially unique equilibrium if the contract space is expanded to allow the seller to make TIOLI offers of mechanisms. See Hermalin (fourthcoming) for details.

interpretation is that the investment lowers the seller's cost of customizing her product for the buyer. Assume that the parties may trade $x \in [0, \bar{x}], \bar{x} \leq \infty$ units.[82] Let the pay-offs be

$$U_S = t - c(x, I) \text{ and } U_B = b(x) - t - I ,$$

respectively, for seller and buyer, where $t \in \mathbb{R}$ is a transfer between them (possibly contingent on x), $b : \mathbb{R}_+ \to \mathbb{R}$ is an increasing function, and $c : \mathbb{R}_+ \times \mathcal{I} \to \mathbb{R}_+$ is increasing in its first argument and decreasing in its second. Assume, for all $I > 0$, a positive and finite quantity solves

$$\max_{x \in [0, \bar{x}]} b(x) - c(x, I) .$$

Denote the solution to that equation by $x^*(I)$.

The welfare-maximizing level of investment solves

$$\max_{I \in \mathcal{I}} b\left(x^*(I)\right) - c\left(x^*(I), I\right) - I . \tag{6.5.18}$$

Assume the program has a unique, finite, and positive solution. Denote it as I^*.

Suppose the seller believes the buyer has invested I^e. Her best response is to offer the buyer $x^*(I^e)$ units for a total payment of $b\left(x^*(I^e)\right)$. Anticipating this, the buyer understands his choice of investment as the program

$$\max_{I \in \mathcal{I}} b(x^*(I^e)) - \underbrace{b\left(x^*(I^e)\right)}_{t} - I \equiv \max_{I \in \mathcal{I}} -I . \tag{6.5.19}$$

The obvious solution is $I = 0$. Because the seller appropriates the benefit of his investment, the buyer has no incentive to invest. In other words, a *holdup problem* arises.[83]

Could a better outcome be obtained by allowing the buyer to play mixed strategies? The answer is no: suppose the buyer played a mixed strategy over his investments. The seller can, at no cost, induce the buyer to reveal his investments by offering the mechanism $\langle x^*(I), t(I) = b(x^*(I)) \rangle$. Since, regardless of what he announces, the buyer always

---

[82] The analysis here also encompasses the case in which there is, at most, one unit to trade. In this case $\bar{x} = 1$ and x denotes the probability of trade. The benefit function would be $b(x) = xv$, v a constant, and the cost function $xC(I)$.

[83] A holdup problem arises when the party making an investment cannot fully capture its benefit because some portion of that benefit is being captured by another party. Williamson (1976) is often credited as introducing the holdup problem into the literature.

gets surplus zero, he has no incentive to lie and can be presumed to tell the truth in equilibrium.[84] But, as just seen, if he gains no surplus, he has no incentive to invest.

To conclude:

Proposition 6.29. *If the buyer's actions (e.g., investments) are purely cooperative, then there is no equilibrium in which he takes an action other than the one that is least costly to him (e.g., he makes no investment) when the seller has all the bargaining power (makes TIOLI offers).*

6.5.3.1 Buyer Investment in an Infinitely Repeated Game

As has become evident, infinitely repeated play often yields a better outcome than the one-shot game. Unlike earlier analyses in this chapter, here both buyer and seller must be induced to cooperate: the buyer must invest and the seller cannot gouge him.[85]

Let δ be the common discount factor. Define

$$U_S^0 = b\left(x^*(0)\right) - c\left(x^*(0), 0\right).$$

The quantity U_S^0 is the seller's payoff should the parties revert to repetition of the equilibrium of the one-shot game. Given he has no bargaining power, the buyer's payoff under such reversion is 0.

Suppose the timing within each period is the buyer chooses his investment for that period, which the seller cannot observe. The seller makes an offer $\langle x, t \rangle$. The buyer accepts or rejects it. If he accepts, then there is trade. Because of this trade, the seller will know her costs, from which she learns what the buyer's investment was. Let the parties wish to support an outcome in which the buyer invests $\hat{I} > 0$ each period, the seller offers $\langle x^*(\hat{I}), \hat{t} \rangle$ each period, and the buyer accepts that offer. If either player deviates from that, then each expects future play to revert to infinite repetition of the one-shot equilibrium and plays accordingly.[86]

Given the threat of reversion, buyer rationality dictates he accepts an offer $\langle x, t \rangle$—even if not $\langle x^*(\hat{I}), \hat{t} \rangle$—provided

$$b(x) - t \geq 0.$$

---

[84] Although the fact that he obtains zero surplus might suggest consideration of allowing the buyer to mix over accepting the seller's offer, that cannot represent an equilibrium: the seller can trivially induce truth telling and acceptance by offering $\langle x^*(I), b\left(x^*(I)\right) - \varepsilon \rangle$, $\varepsilon > 0$ but arbitrarily small.

[85] In its logic, the analysis here is similar to the analysis of followers paying a leader tribute in Hermalin (2007), among other literatures (including the literature on relational contracting; see MacLeod, 2007, for a survey).

[86] To be complete, certain subtle issues can arise when parties deviate in terms of offers, but not actions. See, for example, Halac (2012).

As noted, the buyer must be given incentives to invest and the seller incentives not to overcharge. These conditions are, respectively, equivalent to[87]

$$b(x^*(\hat{I})) - \hat{t} - \hat{I} \geq (1 - \delta)(b(x^*(\hat{I})) - \hat{t}) \text{ and} \qquad (6.5.20)$$

$$\hat{t} - c(x^*(\hat{I}), \hat{I}) \geq (1 - \delta)(b(x^*(\hat{I})) - c(x^*(\hat{I}), \hat{I})) + \delta U_S^0 . \qquad (6.5.21)$$

Taking the limit as $\delta \to 1$, (6.5.20) and (6.5.21) imply

$$b\left(x^*(\hat{I})\right) - c\left(x^*(\hat{I}), \hat{I}\right) - \hat{I} \geq U_S^0 . \qquad (6.5.22)$$

By definition (6.5.22) holds—indeed is a strict inequality—if $\hat{I} = I^*$. By continuity, it follows that if the parties are sufficiently patient (δ is large enough), then an equilibrium of the repeated game exists in which the buyer invests. Observe, critically, that such an equilibrium requires that the seller not capture all the surplus—she must leave the buyer with some.[88]

6.5.4 Semi-Cooperative Buyer Actions

As noted in Section 6.5.2, the selfish–cooperative dichotomy is sometimes too stark. Suppose a buyer can produce the relevant good himself or buy it from the seller. In either scenario, assume an investment by the buyer reduces production costs (e.g., the buyer needs a service performed—which he can do himself or have provided by the seller—and the cost of the service is reduced for either by the buyer's preparatory investment). As in Section 6.5.2, sale is welfare superior to no sale (i.e., the seller is the more efficient provider).

To study this situation, let the payoffs of seller and buyer be, respectively,

$$U_S = x\left(t - c_S(I)\right) \text{ and } U_B = b - xt - (1 - x)c_B(I) - I ,$$

---

[87] Observe

$$\sum_{\tau=0}^{\infty} \delta^\tau w \geq \gamma + \sum_{\tau=1}^{\infty} \delta^\tau z \iff \frac{1}{1 - \delta} w \geq \gamma + \frac{\delta}{1 - \delta} z .$$

The claimed equivalence follows immediately.

[88] Expression (6.5.20) is equivalent to

$$\hat{I} \leq \delta \left(b\left(x^*(\hat{I})\right) - \hat{t}\right) ;$$

the cost of investing today must not exceed the present discounted value of consumer surplus tomorrow.

where $x \in [0, 1]$ denotes the probability of trade, $t \in \mathbb{R}$ is payment in the event of trade, b is the inherent benefit the buyer obtains from the good or service, and $c_i : \mathbb{R}_+ \to \mathbb{R}_+$ is party i's cost of providing the good or service as a function of the buyer's preparatory investment, I. As the parameter b has no bearing on the analysis to follow, there is no loss in setting it to 0.[89]

Some assumptions on the cost functions:

- The functions $c_i(\cdot)$ are twice continuously differentiable, strictly decreasing, and strictly convex functions (i.e., there is a positive, but diminishing, marginal *benefit* to greater preparatory investment).
- For all $I > 0$, $c_B(I) > c_S(I)$ (i.e., trade is strictly welfare superior to no trade, at least if the buyer has invested).
- Zero investment is not privately optimal for the buyer if no trade is certain: $c'_B(0) < -1$.
- Infinite investment is not optimal: there exists an $\bar{I} < \infty$ such that $c'_S(I) > -1$ if $I > \bar{I}$.

These assumptions imply a unique interior welfare-maximizing investment level, I^*, exists (i.e., I^* maximizes $-c_S(I) - I$). If there were autarky, the buyer would invest to maximize

$$-c_B(I) - I . \tag{6.5.23}$$

The assumptions just given ensure that program has a unique interior solution: call it $\hat{I}$. To eliminate a case of minor interest, assume[90]

$$-c_S(0) < -c_B(\hat{I}) - \hat{I} ; \tag{6.5.24}$$

that is, maximum welfare under autarky exceeds welfare given trade but zero investment.

For the same reasons as in Section 6.5.2, no pure-strategy equilibrium exists:

Proposition 6.30. *No pure-strategy equilibrium exists. Moreover, there is no equilibrium in which the buyer invests a given amount as a pure strategy.*

Because welfare maximization requires the buyer invest I^* and trade always occur, this last proposition establishes that the first-best outcome is unattainable in equilibrium. Moreover, to avoid holdup, the buyer is compelled to mix over different investment levels.

The analysis is facilitated by working with the buyer's production cost, C, if no trade occurs: Define $C = c_B(I)$. Because $c_B(\cdot)$ is strictly monotone, it is invertible. Define $\iota(\cdot)$ as

---

[89] The model set forth in this section yields the same results as would the model of Section 6.5.2 if the buyer possessed all the bargaining power in that model.

[90] Again, see Hermalin (2013) for an analysis with this case included.

the inverse; that is, $\iota(c_B(I)) \equiv I$ for all I. Earlier given assumptions entail that $\iota(\cdot)$ is strictly decreasing, strictly concave, and twice continuously differentiable. The analysis proceeds by acting as if the buyer chooses his cost should trade not occur, C.

Recall the seller does not observe the buyer's investment; that is, C is the buyer's private information. It can, thus, be considered to be the buyer's type. Let $\mathcal{C} \equiv [\underline{C}, \bar{C}]$ denote his type space. As will become evident,

$$\mathcal{C} \subseteq \left[c_B(\hat{I}), c_B(0) \right] ;$$

that is, the buyer will never invest more than the autarky level, $\hat{I}$. To economize on notation, let $\hat{C} = c_B(\hat{I})$ and $C^0 = c_B(0)$.

Assuming the buyer has played a mixed strategy in terms of his investment, the seller's problem of what contract to offer is a mechanism-design problem, akin to those considered in Section 6.2.1. A mechanism is, here, a pair $\langle x(\cdot), \tau(\cdot) \rangle$, where $x : \mathcal{C} \to [0, 1]$ is a probability of trade and $\tau : \mathcal{C} \to \mathbb{R}$ is the seller's payment. (By the Revelation Principle—Proposition 6.2—there is no loss of generality in restricting attention to direct-revelation mechanisms.)

Let

$$U(C) = - (1 - x(C)) \, C - \tau(C) \tag{6.5.25}$$

denote the buyer's utility if he truthfully announces his type. Note (i) at the time the mechanism is being played, the buyer's investment is sunk; and (ii) consistent with the approach in Section 6.2.1, what the buyer pays the seller is contingent on his announcement only (i.e., it does not depend on whether trade actually occurs).

As preliminaries to studying such mechanisms, we have:

Lemma 6.18.   *Given an incentive-compatible mechanism, $x(\cdot)$ is non-decreasing and $U(\cdot)$ is a convex function.*

We can now characterize incentive-compatible mechanisms:

Proposition 6.31.   *Necessary conditions for a mechanism to be incentive compatible (induce truth-telling by the buyer) are (i) that the probability of trade, $x(\cdot)$, be nondecreasing in the buyer's cost and (ii) that the buyer's utility as a function of his type be given by*

$$U(C) = \underline{U} - \int_{\underline{C}}^{C} (1 - x(z)) \, dz , \tag{6.5.26}$$

where $\underline{U}$ is a constant.

Moreover, any mechanism in which $x(\cdot)$ is nondecreasing and expression (6.5.26) holds is incentive compatible (i.e., conditions (i) and (ii) are also sufficient).

Anticipating the mechanism the seller will offer him, the buyer is willing to invest $\iota(C)$ if and only if it maximizes $U(C) - \iota(C)$. It follows:

Proposition 6.32.   *If $\iota(C) > 0$ is a level of investment chosen by the buyer with positive probability in equilibrium, then the subsequent probability of trade given that investment is $1 + \iota'(C)$.*
A corollary is

Corollary 6.5.   *There is no equilibrium in which the buyer invests more than his autarky level of investment, $\hat{I}$.*

We seek to construct an equilibrium. To that end, suppose the buyer mixes over $\mathcal{C}$ according to the distribution function $F : \mathcal{C} \to [0, 1]$. To facilitate the analysis take F to be differentiable on $(\underline{C}, \bar{C})$, with derivative (density) $f(C)$. The possibility that there is a "mass" at $\bar{C}$ is permitted: defining $\Sigma(\cdot)$ as the corresponding survival function, it may be that $\Sigma(\bar{C}) > 0$.[91] Take $f(C) > 0$ for all $C \in [\underline{C}, \bar{C})$, $\hat{C} \leq \underline{C} < \bar{C} \leq C^0$. Of course, these properties will need to be verified.

The first-order condition for maximizing $U(C) - \iota(C)$ (expression (A.23) in the Appendix) holds for any $C < C^0$ that the buyer chooses with positive probability (i.e., such that $f(C) > 0$). Moreover, because the buyer could invest $\hat{I}$ and refuse to trade, his equilibrium utility cannot be less than $-\hat{C} - \iota(\hat{C})$. Hence,

$$U(C) - \iota(C) = \underline{U} - \iota(\underline{C}) \geq -\hat{C} - \iota(\hat{C})$$

for all $C \in [\underline{C}, \bar{C})$, where use has been made of both (6.5.26) and Proposition 6.32. Because the seller makes a TIOLI offer, this constraint is binding.

The seller chose $x(\cdot)$ and $\underline{U}$ to maximize her expected profit:

$$\left(\tau(\bar{C}) - x(\bar{C}) c_S \left(\iota(\bar{C}) \right) \right) \Sigma(\bar{C}) + \int_{\underline{C}}^{\bar{C}} \left(\tau(C) - x(C) c_S \left(\iota(C) \right) \right) f(C) dC .$$

$$(6.5.27)$$

Using (6.5.25), (6.5.26), and defining $\sigma(C) = -f(C)$ (hence, $\sigma(C) = \Sigma'(C)$), this last expression can be rewritten as

---

[91] Here,

$$\Sigma(C) \equiv 1 - \int_{\underline{C}}^{C} f(z) dz .$$

$$-\underline{U} - \left(x(\bar{C}) c_S \left(\iota(\bar{C}) \right) + \left(1 - x(\bar{C}) \right) \bar{C} - \int_{\underline{C}}^{\bar{C}} (1 - x(z))\, dz \right) \Sigma(\bar{C})$$

$$+ \int_{\underline{C}}^{\bar{C}} \left(x(C) c_S \left(\iota(C) \right) + (1 - x(C))\, C - \int_{\underline{C}}^{C} (1 - x(z))\, dz \right) \sigma(C) dC.$$

$$(6.5.28)$$

Integration by parts permits rewriting that expression as

$$- \underline{U} - \left(x(\bar{C}) c_S \left(\iota(\bar{C}) \right) + \left(1 - x(\bar{C}) \right) \bar{C} \right) \Sigma(\bar{C})$$

$$+ \int_{\underline{C}}^{\bar{C}} \left(x(C) c_S \left(\iota(C) \right) + (1 - x(C))\, C + (1 - x(C)) \frac{\Sigma(C)}{\sigma(C)} \right) \sigma(C) dC.$$

$$(6.5.29)$$

From Proposition 6.32, if the buyer plays $C < \bar{C} \leq C^0$ with positive probability, then $x(C)$ must equal $1 + \iota'(C)$. Differentiating, pointwise, the seller's expected profit (i.e., expression (6.5.29)) with respect to $x(C)$ reveals that consistency with Proposition 6.32 and seller optimization is met if and only if

$$\frac{\Sigma(C)}{\sigma(C)} = c_S \left(\iota(C) \right) - C \qquad (6.5.30)$$

for $C < \bar{C} \leq C^0$, because, then, the seller is indifferent as to her choice of $x(\cdot)$ and might as well choose $x(\cdot)$ to be consistent with the buyer's mixing (i.e., such that $x(\cdot) = 1 + \iota'(\cdot)$).

Using (6.5.30), expression (6.5.29) can be rewritten as

$$-\underline{U} - \left(x(\bar{C}) c_S \left(\iota(\bar{C}) \right) + \left(1 - x(\bar{C}) \right) \bar{C} \right) \Sigma(\bar{C}) + \int_{\underline{C}}^{\bar{C}} (C\sigma(C) + \Sigma(C))\, dC$$

$$= -\underline{U} - \underline{C} + \left(\bar{C} - c_s \left(\iota(\bar{C}) \right) \right) x(\bar{C}) \Sigma(\bar{C})$$

$$= -\underline{C} - \iota(\underline{C}) - \left(-\hat{C} - \iota(\hat{C}) \right) + \left(\bar{C} - c_s \left(\iota(\bar{C}) \right) \right) x(\bar{C}) \Sigma(\bar{C}),$$

$$(6.5.31)$$

where the last equality follows because the buyer's participation constraint binds. Because $\hat{C}$ maximizes $-C - \iota(C)$, (6.5.31) cannot exceed

$$\left(\bar{C} - c_s \left(\iota(\bar{C}) \right) \right) x(\bar{C}) \Sigma(\bar{C}).$$

At the same time, the seller could deviate from offering the mechanism by simply offering to sell at price $\bar{C}$, which would net her expected profit

$$\left(\bar{C} - c_s\left(\iota(\bar{C})\right)\right) \Sigma(\bar{C}).$$

From (6.5.31), it follows she will do so unless $\underline{C} = \hat{C}$ and, if $\Sigma(\bar{C}) > 0, x(\bar{C}) = 1$. The following can now be established:

Proposition 6.33.   *There exists a subgame-perfect equilibrium in which the seller makes the buyer a TIOLI offer in which the buyer plays a mixed strategy whereby he chooses $C \in [\hat{C}, C^0]$ according to the distribution function*

$$F(C) = 1 - \exp\left(\int_{\hat{C}}^{C} \frac{1}{c_S(\iota(z)) - z} dz\right) \tag{6.5.32}$$

and seller offers the mechanism $\langle x(\cdot), \tau(\cdot)\rangle$ such that

$$x(C) = \begin{cases} 1 + \iota'(C), & \text{if } C < C^0 \\ 1, & \text{if } C = C^0 \end{cases}$$

and

$$\tau(C) = \hat{C} + \iota(\hat{C}) - \iota(C) - (1 - x(C))C. \tag{6.5.33}$$

Because the buyer is playing a nondegenerate mixed strategy, the equilibrium of Proposition 6.33 is not even second best insofar as the buyer is, with positive probability, making investments that are welfare inferior to the second-best investment level. If, contrary to the maintained assumption, he had the bargaining power, then there is an equilibrium in which he invests at the second-best level with certainty (the equilibrium would be similar to the one in Proposition 6.28). In other words, the holdup problem that arises when the noninvesting party has the bargaining power further exacerbates a situation already made imperfect by asymmetric information. To reduce the degree to which he is held up, the buyer must mix—otherwise he would be vulnerable to being held up completely—and this undermines his incentive to choose the right level of investment.[92]

---

[92] Note, critically, this distortion does not mean he "underinvests": his average investment can actually be higher when he doesn't have the bargaining power than when he does. See Hermalin (2013) for details.

6.5.5 Selfish Buyer Actions

We now turn to wholly selfish actions by the buyer. As a somewhat general framework suppose that the timing of the game between buyer and seller is the following:

- Buyer sinks an investment $I \in \mathbb{R}_+$. This affects his benefit, $b \in \mathbb{R}_+$, should he obtain a unit of some good, asset, or service from the seller. The buyer is assumed to want at most one unit.
- The seller observes a signal, s, that may contain information about b.
- The seller makes a TIOLI offer to sell one unit at price p.
- After observing b and s, the buyer decides whether to buy or not.

The payoffs to buyer and seller are, respectively,

$$U_B = x(b - p) - I \text{ and } U_S = xp \,,$$

where $x \in \{0, 1\}$ is the amount of trade. Note, for convenience, the seller's cost has been normalized to zero.

6.5.5.1 No Asymmetric Information

Suppose that the seller's signal, s, is just b; that is, there is no asymmetry of information. The seller will obviously set $p = s$ (equivalently, $p = b$) in equilibrium. The buyer will buy in equilibrium. Hence, his equilibrium payoff is $-I$. He maximizes this by choosing $I = 0$. In this case, holdup destroys all investment incentives:

Proposition 6.34. *If the seller can observe the buyer's benefit, then the buyer will invest nothing in equilibrium.*

To the extent positive investment is welfare superior to no investment (i.e., if $0 \notin \arg\max_I \mathbb{E}\{b|I\} - I$), this outcome is undesirable.

6.5.5.2 Deterministic Return

Suppose there is a function $B : \mathbb{R}_+ \rightarrow \mathbb{R}_+$ such that an investment of I returns a benefit $b = B(I)$. Assume, primarily to make the problem interesting and straightforward, that $B(\cdot)$ is twice differentiable, strictly increasing (benefit increases with investment), and strictly concave (diminishing returns to investment). In addition, assume there is a finite $I^* > 0$ such that $B'(I^*) = 1$. Observe that I^* is the unique welfare-maximizing level of investment.

Unlike the previous subsection assume the seller does not observe b. Nor does she observe I (which, here, would be equivalent to observing b). In fact, let her signal, s, be pure noise (or, equivalently, assume she observes nothing).

For reasons similar to those explored above (see, e.g., Proposition 6.30), there is no equilibrium in which the buyer invests a positive amount as a pure strategy:

Proposition 6.35.   *There is no equilibrium in which the buyer invests a positive amount as a pure strategy.*

Proof: Suppose not. Then, in equilibrium, the seller would set $p = B(I)$, where I is the buyer's pure-strategy investment level. The buyer's equilibrium payoff would, thus, be $-I < 0$. Given the buyer can secure a payoff of 0 by not investing at all, it follows this is not an equilibrium. The result follows *reductio ad absurdum*. ∎

As Gul (2001) observed, the equilibrium in a game such as this depends critically on whether $B(0) = 0$ or $B(0) > 0$.[93] In the former case, trade is worthless unless the buyer invests; in that latter, it has value even when there is no investment.

Lemma 6.19.   *Suppose $B(0) = 0$ (trade is worthless absent buyer investment). Then there is an equilibrium in which $I = 0$ and the seller charges some price p, $p > B(I^*)$.*

Note, critically, that what sustains the Lemma 6.19 equilibrium is the willingness of the seller to charge an exorbitant price. That willingness goes away if $B(0) > 0$ (trade is valuable even absent investment). Knowing that the buyer will always accept $B(0)$ regardless of how much he has invested, the seller can ensure herself a positive profit by offering $p = B(0)$.

Lemma 6.20.   *Suppose trade is valuable even absent investment (i.e., $B(0) > 0$). Then, in equilibrium, neither the buyer nor the seller plays a pure strategy.*

To analyze the mixed strategies played in equilibrium, it is easier to treat the buyer as choosing a benefit, b, and, thus, making investment $B^{-1}(b)$. For convenience, denote $B^{-1}(\cdot)$ by $\iota(\cdot)$. The seller's strategy is a distribution function, G, over prices and the buyer's strategy is a distribution function, F, over benefits. Let p_ℓ and p_h be the lowest and highest prices the seller might play (technically, $p_\ell = \sup\{p \,|\, G(p) = 0\}$ and $p_h = \inf\{p \,|\, G(p) = 1\}$). Let b_ℓ and b_h be the lowest and highest benefits the buyer might play (they have analogous technical definitions). Some initial observations:

- By construction, $b_\ell \geq B(0)$ (no negative investment).
- From Lemma 6.20, $p_h > p_\ell$ and $b_h > b_\ell$. Let $\mathcal{B}^+$ denote the set of $b > B(0)$ played by the buyer with positive probability. Note that set is nonempty by Lemma 6.20.
- The seller can guarantee herself a profit of b_ℓ by playing $p = b_\ell$. Hence, $p_\ell \geq b_\ell$.
- The buyer's utility, u_B, from playing b_ℓ is $-\iota(b_\ell)$:

$$u_B = \max\{0, b_\ell - p\} - \iota(b_\ell) = -\iota(b_\ell),$$

where the second equality follows from the previous bullet point.
- Hence, $b_\ell = B(0)$.

Note that the last bullet point means the buyer's equilibrium expected payoff is zero.

---

[93] Technically, whether $B(0)$ equals or exceeds the seller's cost of production.

Lemma 6.21. *In equilibrium, $p_l = B(0)$.*

An immediate corollary is that the seller's expected profit in equilibrium is $B(0)$.

Lemma 6.22. *In equilibrium, $b_h = B(I^*)$ if $p_h \leq B(I^*)$.*

Consider the following strategies for the seller and buyer, respectively:

$$G(p) = G(B(0)) + \int_{B(0)}^{p} g(z)dz \text{ and } F(b) = 1 - \int_{b}^{b_h} f(z)dz. \qquad (6.5.34)$$

Because the buyer's expected utility given any b he plays is zero, we have

$$bG(B(0)) + \int_{B(0)}^{b} (b - p)g(p)dp - \iota(b) \equiv 0. \qquad (6.5.35)$$

Since that is an identity, differentiating implies

$$G(b) - \iota'(b) = 0.$$

Hence, the strategy for the seller is

$$G(p) = \iota'(p). \qquad (6.5.36)$$

Because $\iota(\cdot)$ is convex and $\iota'(B(I^*)) = 1$, this strategy requires $p_h = B(I^*)$. Similarly, the seller's expected profit given any p she plays is $B(0)$; hence,

$$p(1 - F(p)) \equiv B(0).$$

It follows that

$$F(p) = 1 - \frac{B(0)}{p};$$

in other words, the strategy for the buyer is

$$F(b) = \begin{cases} 1 - \frac{B(0)}{b}, & \text{if } b < b_h \\ 1, & \text{if } b = b_h \end{cases}. \qquad (6.5.37)$$

Expression (6.5.37) does not directly pin down b_h. But given $p_h = B(I^*)$, it follows from Lemma 6.22 that $b_h = B(I^*)$. To summarize:[94]

---

[94] This proposition is essentially Proposition 1 of Gul (2001).

Proposition 6.36. *An equilibrium is the seller mixes over price in the interval* $[B(0), B(I^*)]$ *according to the distribution*

$$G(p) = \iota'(B(0)) + \int_{B(0)}^{p} \iota''(z)dz$$

and the buyer mixes over benefit in the interval $[B(0), B(I^*)]$ *according to the distribution*

$$F(b) = \begin{cases} 1 - \frac{B(0)}{b}, & \text{if } b < B(I^*) \\ 1, & \text{if } b = B(I^*) \end{cases} . \tag{6.5.38}$$

Proof: As the analysis in the text shows, the parties are indifferent over all actions in $[B(0), B(I^*)]$. As established in the proof of Lemma 6.22 any $b > B(I^*)$ is dominated for the buyer if $p_h = B(I^*)$. That proof also established that any $p > b_h$ is dominated for the seller. ∎

Observe that as $B(0) \downarrow 0$, the buyer's strategy, expression (6.5.38), converges to his *not* investing with probability 1. This suggests a link between this proposition and Lemma 6.19. Indeed, when $B(0) = 0$, there is no equilibrium in which the buyer invests with positive probability.[95]

Proposition 6.37. *If* $B(0) = 0$, *then the buyer's expected level of investment is zero in equilibrium.*

6.5.5.3 Stochastic Return

Suppose now that the buyer's benefit b is stochastic, with a distribution that depends on his investment, I. Denote the survival function for this conditional distribution by $D(\cdot|I)$; that is, the probability of the buyer's benefit equaling or exceeding b is $D(b|I)$. The use of the letter "D" is not accidental. Let the set of possible b be $[0, \bar{b})$, where $0 < \bar{b} \le \infty$.

Assume D is twice differentiable in each argument. Using integration by parts, it follows, for a given $\underline{b}$, that

$$\mathbb{E}\left\{\max\{b - \underline{b}, 0\}\right\} = \int_{\underline{b}}^{\bar{b}} (b - \underline{b})\left(-\frac{\partial D(b|I)}{\partial b}\right) db = \int_{\underline{b}}^{\bar{b}} D(b|I)db.$$

Further assume: the buyer gets no benefit with certainty absent investment (i.e., $D(0|0) = 0$) and there is a finite positive level of investment that maximizes welfare (i.e., there is an $I^* \in (0, \infty)$ that maximizes $\int_0^{\bar{b}} D(b|I)db - I$).

---

[95] This is essentially Proposition 4 of Hermalin and Katz (2009).

Two possibilities will be considered here about what the seller knows prior to trade: (i) the seller observes the buyer's investment, but not his benefit; or (ii) the seller observes neither the buyer's investment nor his his benefit. In terms of earlier introduced notation, case (i) corresponds to $s = I$ and case (ii) corresponds to s being pure noise.[96]

In case (ii), a degenerate equilibrium exists along the lines of the Lemma 6.19 equilibrium in which the buyer does not invest because he anticipates the seller will offer an exorbitant price and because she believes the buyer has not invested, the seller may as well charge such an exorbitant price given $D(0|0) = 0$.

Our interest here, though, is nondegenerate equilibria. To see that there are functions that support nondegenerate equilibria, suppose $\bar{b} = \infty$ and

$$D(b|I) = \exp\left(-\frac{\alpha b}{\sqrt{I}}\right), \tag{6.5.39}$$

where α is constant. In case (i), the seller chooses p to maximize

$$pD(p|I) = p\exp\left(-\frac{\alpha p}{\sqrt{I}}\right),$$

the solution to which is $p(I) = \sqrt{I}/\alpha$. Anticipating this response, the buyer chooses I to maximize

$$\int_{p(I)}^{\infty} D(b|I)\,db - I = \frac{\sqrt{I}}{\alpha e} - I,$$

where $e = \exp(1)$, the base of the natural logarithm. The solution to the maximization problem is

$$\hat{I} = \frac{1}{4\alpha^2 e^2}. \tag{6.5.40}$$

In case (ii), if the seller anticipates the buyer has chosen $\widetilde{I}$, then she will play $p(\widetilde{I})$. To have an equilibrium, $\widetilde{I}$ must in fact be a best response for the buyer to $p(\widetilde{I})$. It will be if

$$\widetilde{I} \in \arg\max_{I} \int_{p(\widetilde{I})}^{\infty} D(b|I)\,db - I \,;$$

---

[96] Hermalin and Katz (2009) consider the case in which s is an imperfect, but informative, signal of b; that is, there is some joint distribution of s and b given I. See Hermalin and Katz, 2009 for details.

equivalently if $\widetilde{I}$ is a solution to the first-order condition

$$0 = -1 + \frac{p(\widetilde{I}) \exp\left(-p(\widetilde{I})\alpha/\sqrt{I}\right)}{2I} + \frac{\exp\left(-p(\widetilde{I})\alpha/\sqrt{I}\right)}{2\alpha\sqrt{I}}$$

$$= -1 + \frac{\sqrt{\widetilde{I}} \exp\left(-\sqrt{\widetilde{I}/I}\right)}{2I\alpha} + \frac{\exp\left(-\sqrt{\widetilde{I}/I}\right)}{2\alpha\sqrt{I}}.$$

The solution is

$$\widetilde{I} = \frac{1}{\alpha^2 e^2}. \tag{6.5.41}$$

Comparing the two equilibria for this example—expressions (6.5.40) and (6.5.41)—we see that, when the seller can observe the buyer's investment (case (i)), the buyer invests less in equilibrium than when the seller cannot observe it (case (ii)). At first blush this might seem a general phenomenon: being able to observe the buyer's investment allows the seller to better holdup the buyer, correspondingly reducing the buyer's incentives to invest. This logic, although tempting, proves to be incomplete. As Hermalin and Katz (2009) show, the result depends on the properties of the demand function, D: in particular, the buyer invests less when his investment is observable if the buyer's demand becomes less price elastic the greater is his investment.[97]

The welfare consequences of observable investment are also less than clear cut. Although Hermalin and Katz, 2009 provide conditions under which welfare is greater with unobservable investment than with observable investment, that cannot be seen as a general result. What is a general result is that the buyer actually does better when his investment is observable than when it is not:

Proposition 6.38.   *The buyer's equilibrium expected utility is at least as great when the seller can observe his investment than when she cannot.*
Proof: Define

$$U(p, I) = \int_p^\infty D(b|I)db.$$

---

[97] For this example, elasticity is $p\alpha/\sqrt{I}$, which is clearly decreasing in I.

Suppose the buyer's investment is observable. Then the buyer can "pick" the price he faces in the sense that he knows an investment of I will result in a price of $p(I)$. By revealed preference:

$$U\left(p(\hat{I}),\hat{I}\right) - \hat{I} \geq U\left(p(\widetilde{I}),\widetilde{I}\right) - \widetilde{I}, \tag{6.5.42}$$

where $\hat{I}$ and $\widetilde{I}$ are as defined above. But the RHS of (6.5.42) is the buyer's expected utility in equilibrium when investment is unobservable. ∎

Intuitively, when investment is observable, the buyer becomes the Stackelberg leader of the game. This result illustrates a very general point: consider, as in case (ii), a game in which the second mover does not observe the first mover's action. If that game has an equilibrium in which the first mover plays a pure strategy, then the first mover would necessarily be better off in equilibrium in the variant of that game in which the second mover can observe the first mover's action.[98]

6.6 FINAL THOUGHTS

As the introduction sought to make clear, the economics of asymmetric information is a vast topic. A complete survey, even if that were a feasible task, would necessarily yield a massive tome. This chapter has, of necessity, had to consider a narrow subset of literature: attention has been limited to buyer–seller relations and, then, largely to those involving a single buyer and a single seller, in which the asymmetry of information between them arises prior to their establishing a trading relationship.[99]

Much of the literature surveyed in this chapter, especially in Sections 6.2–6.4, although novel when I began my career, has become part of the established literature. More recent literature has, as hinted at in Section 6.5, involved asymmetries that arise endogenously.[100] This topic remains an area of active research.

With respect to ongoing and future research, a key issue is the modeling of bargaining. This chapter has focused almost exclusively on take-it-or-leave-it (TIOLI) bargaining. Assuming that bargaining vastly simplifies matters. In some contexts, however, it is unrealistic. Hence, despite the complications of non-TIOLI bargaining, allowing for such bargaining is an important area of exploration.

Related to the issue of bargaining is the "money on the table" problem (recall, e.g., Section 6.3.3 *supra*): many mechanisms require the parties to commit to honor *ex*

---

[98] This is true even if in the unobservable-action version the second mover plays a mixed strategy in equilibrium: think of U in expression (6.5.42) as expected payoff given the mixed strategy $p(\cdot)$.

[99] As observed previously, however, many of the techniques considered are more broadly applicable.

[100] In addition to some of the articles cited above in this regard, the reader is also directed to González (2004) and Lau (2008).

post inefficient outcomes (possibly only off the equilibrium path). But if it is common knowledge that an outcome is inefficient and there is no impediment to renegotiation, then it is unreasonable to expect the parties will not take action to remedy the situation. Anticipation of such action would, in many cases, undermine the original mechanism, creating some doubt as to whether such mechanisms are good predictors of actual behavior. This, thus, represents an important area of research.[101]

Beyond the suggestions for future work contained in this section and also made earlier, I hope the reader has been motivated to ask his or her own questions about alternative assumptions or possible extensions. At the very least, I hope this chapter has provided the reader a good foundation from which to do his or her own research.

APPENDIX

Proof of Lemma 6.2: The IR constraint for β' and the Spence-Mirrlees condition imply

$$u\left(x(\beta'),\beta\right) - t(\beta') > u(x_0,\beta) - 0 = u_R;$$

hence, β must do better to buy than not buy. The Spence-Mirrlees condition also implies strictly increasing differences (Proposition 6.3):

$$u\left(x(\beta'),\beta\right) - u\left(x(\beta'),\beta'\right) > u(x_0,\beta) - u(x_0,\beta') = 0.$$

That $v(\beta) > v(\beta')$ then follows from (6.2.10).   ∎

Proof of Lemma 6.3: Suppose not. Let $\langle x(\cdot), t(\cdot) \rangle$ be the seller's expected-payoff-maximizing mechanism. Consider a new mechanism $\langle x(\cdot), \tilde{t}(\cdot) \rangle$, where

$$\tilde{t}(\beta) = t(\beta) + v(\tilde{\beta}) - u_R$$

for all $\beta \geq \tilde{\beta}$ and $\tilde{t}(\beta) = t(\beta) = 0$ for $\beta < \tilde{\beta}$. Using (IC), it is readily verified that if type β participates, he does best to purchase the same $x(\beta)$ as he would have under the original mechanism. By design, $\tilde{\beta}$ is still willing to purchase. From Lemma 6.2,

---

$$u\left(x(\beta), \beta\right) - t(\beta) > v(\tilde{\beta}) \implies u\left(x(\beta), \beta\right) - \tilde{t}(\beta) > u_R .$$

So all types $\beta > \tilde{\beta}$ who participated under the original mechanism participate under the new mechanism. (Clearly those types that "participated" by purchasing nothing continue to participate in the same way.) Given the buyer's true type, the seller incurs, in equilibrium, the same cost as she would have under the original mechanism (i.e., $c(x(\beta), \beta)$ remains unchanged), but her transfer is strictly greater under the new mechanism; this contradicts the supposition that the original mechanism maximized her expected payoff. The result follows *reductio ad absurdum*. ∎

Proof of Proposition 6.4   (completion): Consider $n > m$. A chain of reasoning similar to that in the main text provides:

$$u(x(\beta_m), \beta_n) - t(\beta_m)$$

$$= u(x(\beta_m), \beta_n) - u(x(\beta_m), \beta_m) + u_R + \sum_{j \leq n} R_j(x(\beta_{j-1})) - \sum_{j=m+1}^{n} R_j(x(\beta_{j-1}))$$

$$= u(x(\beta_m), \beta_n) - u(x(\beta_m), \beta_m) + v(\beta_n) - \sum_{j=m+1}^{n} R_j\left(x(\beta_{j-1})\right)$$

$$= v(\beta_n) - \sum_{j=n+1}^{m} \left(R_j\left(x(\beta_{j-1})\right) - R_j\left(x(\beta_m)\right)\right) \leq v(\beta_n)$$

(note, in this case,

$$u(x(\beta_m), \beta_n) - u(x(\beta_m), \beta_m) = \sum_{j=m+1}^{n} R_j(x(\beta_m))$$

and $x(\beta_{j-1}) \geq x(\beta_m)$ for $j \geq m+1$). ∎

Proof of Proposition 6.5: Lemma 6.1 established the necessity of $x(\cdot)$ being nondecreasing.
    Using the fundamental theorem of calculus, (6.2.10) can be rewritten as

$$\int_{\beta'}^{\beta} \frac{\partial u(x(\beta), z)}{\partial \beta} \, dz \geq v(\beta) - v(\beta') \geq \int_{\beta'}^{\beta} \frac{\partial u(x(\beta'), z)}{\partial \beta} \, dz . \qquad (A.1)$$

The function $v(\cdot)$ is absolutely continuous.[102] An absolutely continuous function has a derivative almost everywhere (see, e.g., Royden, 1968, p. 109). Dividing (A.1) through by $\beta - \beta'$ (recall this is positive) and taking the limit as $\beta' \to \beta$, it follows the derivative of $v(\cdot)$ is given by

$$\frac{dv(\beta)}{d\beta} = \frac{\partial u\,(x(\beta), \beta)}{\partial \beta}$$

almost everywhere. An absolutely continuous function is the integral of its derivative (see, e.g., Yeh, 2006, p. 283), hence

$$v(\beta) = v(\underline{\beta}) + \int_{\underline{\beta}}^{\beta} \frac{\partial u\,(x(z), z)}{\partial \beta}\, dz\,. \tag{A.2}$$

---

[102] **Proof:** The function $\partial u(x(\bar{\beta}), \cdot)/\partial \beta$ is continuous and bounded, it thus has a finite maximum, M, and a maximizer β_M. By Spence-Mirrlees,

$$M = \frac{\partial u(x(\bar{\beta}), \beta_M)}{\partial \beta} \geq \frac{\partial u(x(\bar{\beta}), \beta')}{\partial \beta} > \frac{\partial u(x(\beta), \beta')}{\partial \beta}\,,$$

for any β and $\beta' \in B$. Pick any $\varepsilon > 0$ and let $\delta = \varepsilon/M$. Consider any finite non-overlapping collection of intervals $\big((\beta'_i, \beta_i)\big)_{i=1}^{I}$ such that

$$\sum_{i=1}^{I}(\beta_i - \beta'_i) < \delta\,.$$

The conclusion follows if

$$\sum_{i=1}^{I} |v(\beta_i) - v(\beta'_i)| < \varepsilon$$

(see, e.g., Royden, 1968, p. 108). Because $v(\cdot)$ is nondecreasing (Lemma 6.2), the absolute value can be ignored (i.e., $|v(\beta_i) - v(\beta'_i)|$ can be replaced with just $v(\beta_i) - v(\beta'_i)$). From (A.1) and the intermediate value theorem, there is some $\hat{\beta}_i \in (\beta'_i, \beta_i)$ such that

$$M(\beta_i - \beta'_i) \geq \frac{\partial u(x(\beta_i), \hat{\beta}_i)}{\partial \beta}(\beta_i - \beta'_i) = \int_{\beta'_i}^{\beta_i} \frac{\partial u(x(\beta_i), z)}{\partial \beta}\, dz \geq v(\beta_i) - v(\beta'_i)\,.$$

Summing over i yields

$$\varepsilon = M\delta > M \sum_{i=1}^{I}(\beta_i - \beta'_i) \geq \sum_{i=1}^{I} v(\beta_i) - v(\beta'_i)\,.$$

Because $v(\beta) = u(x(\beta),\beta) - t(\beta)$, (A.2) implies

$$t(\beta) = u\left(x(\beta), \beta\right) - v(\underline{\beta}) - \int_{\underline{\beta}}^{\beta} \frac{\partial u\left(x(z), z\right)}{\partial \beta} \, dz \, . \tag{A.3}$$

Setting $\tau = v(\underline{\beta})$, the necessity of (6.2.18) follows.

The logic for establishing sufficiency is similar to that in the proof of Proposition 6.4; hence, I will be brief. The proof of participation is the same. To establish incentive compatibility, one needs to show that a β-type buyer won't pretend to be a β'-type buyer. His utility were he to do so is

$$u\left(x(\beta'), \beta\right) - t(\beta')$$

$$= u\left(x(\beta'), \beta\right) - u\left(x(\beta'), \beta'\right) + \tau + \int_{\underline{\beta}}^{\beta} \frac{\partial u\left(x(z), z\right)}{\partial \beta} \, dz - \int_{\beta'}^{\beta} \frac{\partial u\left(x(z), z\right)}{\partial \beta} \, dz$$

$$= u\left(x(\beta'), \beta\right) - u\left(x(\beta'), \beta'\right) + v(\underline{\beta}) - \int_{\beta'}^{\beta} \frac{\partial u\left(x(z), z\right)}{\partial \beta} \, dz$$

$$= v(\beta) - \int_{\beta'}^{\beta} \left(\frac{\partial u\left(x(z), z\right)}{\partial \beta} - \frac{\partial u\left(x(\beta'), z\right)}{\partial \beta} \right) dz \le v(\beta) \, , \tag{A.4}$$

where the first two equalities follow from (6.2.18) and the last from the fundamental theorem of calculus. That the integral in the last line is positive follows from Spence-Mirrlees because $x(\cdot)$ is nondecreasing: the integrand is positive if $\beta > \beta'$ and integration is in the positive direction; it is negative if $\beta < \beta'$ and integration is in the negative direction. ■

Proof of Lemma 6.4: Observe

$$\sum_{n=1}^{N} \left(\sum_{k=2}^{n} R_k\left(x(\beta_{k-1})\right) \right) f_n = \sum_{n=1}^{N} \left(\sum_{k=1}^{n-1} R_{k+1}\left(x(\beta_k)\right) \right) f_n$$

$$= \sum_{n=1}^{N-1} \left(R_{n+1}\left(x(\beta_n)\right) \sum_{k=n+1}^{N} f_n \right) = \sum_{n=1}^{N-1} R_{n+1}\left(x(\beta_n)\right) \left(1 - F(\beta_n)\right)$$

(note $\sum_{k=1}^{0} \equiv 0$).

Observe, via integration by parts, that

$$\int_{\underline{\beta}}^{\bar{\beta}} \left(\int_{\underline{\beta}}^{\beta} \frac{\partial u\,(x(z), z)}{\partial \beta}\, dz \right) f(\beta) d\beta$$

$$= -\left(1 - F(\beta)\right) \int_{\underline{\beta}}^{\beta} \frac{\partial u\,(x(z), z)}{\partial \beta}\, dz \Bigg|_{\underline{\beta}}^{\bar{\beta}} + \int_{\underline{\beta}}^{\bar{\beta}} \frac{\partial u\,(x(\beta), \beta)}{\partial \beta}\, \left(1 - F(\beta)\right) d\beta$$

$$= \int_{\underline{\beta}}^{\bar{\beta}} \frac{\partial u\,(x(\beta), \beta)}{\partial \beta}\, \left(1 - F(\beta)\right) d\beta \,. \quad \blacksquare$$

Proof of Lemma 6.6: The result is immediate if $Y_H \geq Y_H'$, so suppose $Y_H < Y_H'$. By assumption,

$$\beta' u(Y_I) + (1 - \beta')u(Y_H) \geq \beta' u(Y_I') + (1 - \beta')u(Y_H') \,.$$

Hence,

$$\beta' \left(\left(u(Y_I) - u(Y_I')\right) + \left(u(Y_H') - u(Y_H)\right) \right) \geq u(Y_H') - u(Y_H) \,.$$

Because $\beta > \beta'$, it follows that

$$\beta \left(\left(u(Y_I) - u(Y_I')\right) + \left(u(Y_H') - u(Y_H)\right) \right) > u(Y_H') - u(Y_H) \,;$$

and, thus, that $\beta u(Y_I) + (1 - \beta)u(Y_H) > \beta u(Y_I') + (1 - \beta)u(Y_H')$. $\quad \blacksquare$

Proof of Proposition 6.12: Suppose such a mechanism existed. Because it is efficient $x(b, c) = 1$ if $b \geq c$ and $= 0$ otherwise. Hence, from (6.3.18),

$$u(b) = u(0) + \int_0^b \underbrace{\int_{\underline{c}}^{\bar{c}} x(z, c)g(c)dc}_{=\xi_B(z)}\, dz = u(0) + \int_0^b \int_{\underline{c}}^{z} g(c)dcdz$$

$$= u(0) + \int_{\underline{c}}^{b} G(z)dz \,, \tag{A.5}$$

where the second equality follows because $x(b, c) = 1$ for $c \leq b$ and $= 0$ for $c > b$. A similar analysis reveals

$$\pi(c) = \pi(\bar{c}) + \int_c^{\bar{b}} (1 - F(z)) \, dz .$$ (A.6)

Realized surplus is $b - c$ if $b \geq c$ and 0 otherwise. Hence, ex ante expected surplus is

$$
\begin{aligned}
S^* &= \int_0^{\bar{b}} \left(\int_{\underline{c}}^b (b - c) g(c) \, dc \right) f(b) \, db \\
&= \int_0^{\bar{b}} \underbrace{\left((b - b) G(b) - (b - 0) G(0) + \int_{\underline{c}}^b G(c) \, dc \right)}_{\text{integration by parts}} f(b) \, db \\
&= \int_0^{\bar{b}} \int_{\underline{c}}^b G(c) \, dc f(b) \, db.
\end{aligned}
$$ (A.7)

If the mechanism is balanced, then $S^* = \mathbb{E}_b \{u(b)\} + \mathbb{E}_c \{\pi(c)\}$. But, from (A.5),

$$\mathbb{E}_b \{u(b)\} = \int_0^{\bar{b}} \left(u(0) + \int_{\underline{c}}^b G(z) \, dz \right) f(b) \, db = u(0) + S^* ,$$ (A.8)

where the last equality follows from (A.7). The mechanism can, thus, be balanced only if $u(0) = 0$ and $\mathbb{E}_c \{\pi(c)\} = 0$; but, from (A.6), $\mathbb{E}_c \{\pi(c)\} > 0$. Reductio ad absurdum, *no* balanced, efficient, and interim IR mechanism can exist. ∎

Proof of Lemma 6.11: Consider $b > b'$. Then, for all $c, x(b, c) \geq x(b', c)$. Hence,

$$0 \leq \int_{\underline{c}}^{\bar{c}} \left(x(b, c) - x(b', c) \right) g(c) \, dc = \xi_B(b) - \xi_B(b') .$$

So $\xi_B(\cdot)$ is nondecreasing as desired. The proof for $\xi_S(\cdot)$ is similar. ∎

Proof of Lemma 6.12 and Corollary 3: Consider the functions:

$$V_B(b, \sigma) = b - \sigma \frac{1 - F(b)}{f(b)} \quad \text{and} \quad V_C(c, \sigma) = c + \sigma \frac{G(c)}{g(c)} .$$ (A.9)

The premise of the lemma is that $V_B(\cdot,1)$ and $V_C(\cdot,1)$ are nondecreasing functions. Observe, given the discussion preceding the statement of the lemma, that one needs to show

$$V_B\left(\cdot, \frac{\lambda}{1+\lambda}\right) \quad \text{and} \quad V_C\left(\cdot, \frac{\lambda}{1+\lambda}\right)$$

are nondecreasing functions. Note $\lambda/(1+\lambda) \in (0, 1)$. We have

$$\frac{\partial^2 V_B(b,\sigma)}{\partial\sigma\,\partial b} = -\frac{d}{db}\left(\frac{1-F(b)}{f(b)}\right) \quad \text{and} \quad \frac{\partial^2 V_C(c,\sigma)}{\partial\sigma\,\partial c} = \frac{d}{dc}\left(\frac{G(c)}{g(c)}\right). \quad (A.10)$$

If the expressions in (A.10) are non-negative, then

$$0 < 1 = \frac{\partial V_B(b,0)}{\partial b} \le \frac{\partial V_B(b,\sigma)}{\partial b}$$

(and similarly for V_C) for all $\sigma \ge 0$. So the result would follow. If the expressions in (A.10) are negative, then

$$0 \le \frac{\partial V_B(b,1)}{\partial b} \le \frac{\partial V_B(b,\sigma)}{\partial b}$$

(and similarly for V_C) for all $\sigma \le 1$ (where the first inequality follows by assumption). This proves the lemma.

The corollary follows because, given the assumptions of the corollary, $V_B(\cdot,1)$ and $V_C(\cdot,1)$ are nondecreasing functions. ∎

Proof of Proposition 6.14: Suppose that $p_1(c) \ne p_1(c')$ for $c \ne c'$ (this is verified below). Assume the buyer's belief upon seeing $p_1(c)$ is the seller's type is c with probability 1. If $p_1 \ne p_1(c)$ for any c, assume the buyer believes that $c = \underline{c}$. Suppose the buyer is playing a linear strategy. The objective is to show that a linear strategy is the seller's best response regardless of c. Consider an arbitrary period t. Assume all normalized types greater than ω_t have purchased by t. The expected present value of the seller's profit discounted back to t is

$$(1-c)\Pi_t = (\omega_t - \alpha m_t)m_t + \sum_{\tau=t+1}^{\infty} \delta^{\tau-t}(\alpha m_{\tau-1} - \alpha m_\tau)m_\tau,$$

where the scaling $(1 - c)$ reflects that ω is distributed uniformly on $[0, 1 - c]$. Maximizing Π_t with respect to $m_t, m_{t+1}, \ldots$ yields the first-order conditions:

$$\omega_t - 2\alpha m_t + \delta\alpha m_{t+1} = 0$$

$$\vdots$$

$$\delta^\tau \left(\alpha m_{t+\tau-1} - 2\alpha m_{t+\tau} + \delta\alpha m_{t+\tau+1} \right) = 0$$

$$\vdots$$

Solving this system of difference equations yields:

$$m_{t+\tau} = \frac{\omega}{\alpha} \left(\frac{1 - \sqrt{1 - \delta}}{\delta} \right)^{\tau+1} = \left(\frac{1 - \sqrt{1 - \delta}}{\alpha\delta} \right) \times \underbrace{\alpha m_{t+\tau-1}}_{=\omega_{t+\tau-1}} \qquad (A.11)$$

if $\tau \geq 1$ and

$$m_t = \left(\frac{1 - \sqrt{1 - \delta}}{\alpha\delta} \right) \omega_t . \qquad (A.12)$$

So a linear rule is, indeed, a best response for the seller regardless of her cost. The linear rule has

$$\gamma = \frac{1 - \sqrt{1 - \delta}}{\alpha\delta} .$$

Next, verify that the buyer wishes to follow a linear rule in response to the seller's linear rule: let b be the indifferent type at time t, then we have

$$b - p_t = \delta(b - p_{t+1}) \iff \omega - m_t = \delta(\omega - \gamma\omega) ,$$

where the equivalence follows by adding and subtracting c on the LHS and recognizing that $p_{t+1} = m_{t+1} + c = \gamma\omega + c$. Solving:

$$\omega = \frac{1}{1 - \delta + \delta\gamma} m_t .$$

So we also have a linear rule for the buyer with

$$\alpha = \frac{1}{1 - \delta + \delta\gamma} \,.$$

We can solve our linear rules:

$$\gamma = \frac{-(1 - \delta) + \sqrt{1 - \delta}}{\delta} \quad \text{and} \quad \alpha = \frac{1}{\sqrt{1 - \delta}} \,.$$

Note, critically, that neither γ nor α depend on c. Finally, observe that

$$p_1(c) = m_1(c) + c = \gamma(1 - c) + c = \gamma + (1 - \gamma)c \,,$$

so $p_1(c) \neq p_1(c')$ if $c \neq c'$. ∎

Proof of Lemma 6.15: First, suppose, contrary to the lemma, that there are at least two distinct pairs the $\underline{\gamma}$ type plays that do not include s_0: (s, p) and (s', p'). The order is arbitrary, hence one is free to assume $s_0 < s < s'$. Given the $\underline{\gamma}$ type plays the two pairs with positive probability (mixes):

$$xp - c(s, \underline{\gamma}) = x'p' - c(s', \underline{\gamma}) \,,$$

where x and x' are the equilibrium probabilities the buyer accepts the seller's offer. Spence-Mirrlees (i.e., expression (6.4.14)) implies:

$$xp - c(s, \bar{\gamma}) < x'p' - c(s', \bar{\gamma}) \,.$$

Consequently, the $\bar{\gamma}$ type never offers (s,p) in equilibrium. The buyer must, therefore, believe the seller is low quality upon seeing (s,p). Because $s > s_0$, seller rationality dictates that $x > 0$; so buyer rationality dictates $p \leq \underline{\gamma}$. But the $\underline{\gamma}$ type can guarantee herself a payoff $\underline{\gamma}$ by playing $(s_0, \underline{\gamma})$. The chain

$$\underline{\gamma} \geq x\underline{\gamma} - c(s_0, \underline{\gamma}) \geq xp - c(s_0, \underline{\gamma}) > xp - c(s, \underline{\gamma})$$

indicates that (s,p) is strictly dominated for the low-quality type, which contradicts that she plays it with positive probability. The first part of the lemma follows *reductio ad absurdum*.

We just saw that an action (s,p), $s > s_0$, not played by the high-quality type is strictly dominated for the low-quality type, which proves the lemma's second part. ∎

Proof of Lemma 6.16: Given the previous lemma, there is at most one such signal, $s > s_0$, that the low-quality seller could send. Let π be the expected *payment* sellers who play that signal get. Because $s > s_0$, seller rationality dictates that $\pi > 0$, which entails buyer acceptance with strictly positive probability. It must be that $\pi < \bar{\gamma}$. To see this, note the buyer never accepts a price greater than $\bar{\gamma}$; hence, $\pi \not> \bar{\gamma}$. If $\pi = \bar{\gamma}$, then the buyer always accepts when faced with $(s, \bar{\gamma})$. Hence, the only price that would be rational for the seller to offer given signal s is $p = \bar{\gamma}$. But, by supposition, the $\underline{\gamma}$ plays the signal s with positive probability; hence, the buyer's Bayesian beliefs dictate that $\mathbb{E}\{\gamma|s\} < \bar{\gamma}$ and so the buyer should not accept $p = \bar{\gamma}$. *Reductio ad absurdum*, $\pi < \bar{\gamma}$ follows. Define $\hat{s}$ by

$$\bar{\gamma} - c(\hat{s}, \underline{\gamma}) = \pi - c(s, \underline{\gamma});$$

that is, a low-quality seller would be indifferent between playing signal $\hat{s}$ in exchange for receiving $\bar{\gamma}$ for sure and playing s in exchange for receiving expected payment π. That such a $\hat{s}$ exists follows because $c(\cdot, \underline{\gamma})$ is unbounded and continuous. Because $\pi < \bar{\gamma}$, it follows that $\hat{s} > s$. Spence-Mirrlees (6.4.14) entails

$$\bar{\gamma} - c(\hat{s}, \bar{\gamma}) > \pi - c(s, \bar{\gamma}).$$

These last two expressions imply that there exists $\delta > 0$ such that

$$\bar{\gamma} - \delta - c(\hat{s}, \underline{\gamma}) < \pi - c(s, \underline{\gamma}) \quad \text{and} \tag{A.13}$$

$$\bar{\gamma} - \delta - c(\hat{s}, \bar{\gamma}) > \pi - c(s, \bar{\gamma}). \tag{A.14}$$

Consider the deviation $(\hat{s}, \bar{\gamma} - \delta)$:[103] expressions (A.13) and (A.14) imply that $\Gamma^0 = \{\underline{\gamma}\}$. But as

$$\Gamma\left((\hat{s}, \bar{\gamma} - \delta)\right) \backslash \Gamma^0 = \{\bar{\gamma}\},$$
$$\mathrm{BR}\left(\Gamma\left((\hat{s}, \bar{\gamma} - \delta)\right) \backslash \Gamma^0, (\hat{s}, \bar{\gamma} - \delta)\right) = \{1\},$$

which, given (A.14), means (6.4.12) holds. As claimed, the equilibrium fails the Intuitive Criterion. ∎

---

[103] This must be a deviation—out-of-equilibrium play—because otherwise (A.14) implies the high-quality seller would never play s.

Proof of Proposition 6.17: It needs to be shown that (a) this is an equilibrium; (b) it satisfies the Intuitive Criterion; and (c) in light of the earlier lemmas, no other *separating* PBE satisfies the Intuitive Criterion.

With respect to (a): the buyer's beliefs and strategy are obviously consistent with a PBE. Consequently, a seller's expected payment, π, is at most $\underline{\gamma}$ if $s < s^*$ and at most $\bar{\gamma}$ if $s \geq s^*$. A low-quality seller will not wish to deviate:

$$\underline{\gamma} > \underline{\gamma} - c(s, \underline{\gamma}) \tag{A.15}$$

for all $s > s_0$ and, by (6.4.23),

$$\underline{\gamma} = \bar{\gamma} - c(s^*, \underline{\gamma}) \geq \bar{\gamma} - c(s, \underline{\gamma})$$

for all $s \geq s^*$. Nor will a high-quality seller:

$$\underline{\gamma} - c(s, \bar{\gamma}) \leq \underline{\gamma} < \bar{\gamma} - c(s^*, \bar{\gamma}) \tag{A.16}$$

for all $s < s^*$, where the second inequality follows from (6.4.14) (i.e., Spence-Mirrlees) and (6.4.23), and

$$\bar{\gamma} - c(s, \bar{\gamma}) \leq \bar{\gamma} - c(s^*, \bar{\gamma}) \tag{A.17}$$

for all $s \geq s^*$.

With respect to (b), $\Gamma^0 = \Gamma$ if $p \notin (\underline{\gamma}, \bar{\gamma}]$ or $s \geq s^*$, in which case the Intuitive Criterion holds trivially. Consider $s \in (s_0, s^*)$ and $p \in (\underline{\gamma}, \bar{\gamma}]$. If $\underline{\gamma} > p - c(s, \underline{\gamma})$, then, given $\underline{\gamma} = \bar{\gamma} - c(s^*, \underline{\gamma})$, Spence-Mirrlees implies

$$\bar{\gamma} - c(s^*, \bar{\gamma}) > p - c(s, \bar{\gamma}) \, ;$$

in other words, $\underline{\gamma} \in \Gamma^0$ implies $\bar{\gamma} \in \Gamma^0$. Hence, $\Gamma(a)\backslash\Gamma^0$ can equal $\emptyset$, $\{\underline{\gamma}\}$, or Γ. If the first, the Intuitive Criterion holds trivially. If the latter two,

$$\min_{x\in\mathrm{BR}\left(\Gamma(a)\backslash\Gamma^0,a\right)} V(a, x, \underline{\gamma}) \leq \underline{\gamma} - c(s, \underline{\gamma}) < \underline{\gamma} \, ;$$

hence, (6.4.12) could not hold given (A.15) and (A.16); that is, the Intuitive Criterion is satisfied.

Turning to (c): in a separating PBE, the γ type plays $(s_0, \underline{\gamma})$ and the buyer accepts all $p \leq \underline{\gamma}$. Let $(\bar{s}, \bar{p})$ be an action of the $\bar{\gamma}$ type that she plays with positive probability in a separating PBE.

Claim. *In a separating PBE that satisfies the Intuitive Criterion, $\bar{p} = \bar{\gamma}$ and the buyer must accept the high-quality seller's price offer with probability one.*

Proof of Claim: Suppose not. The parties' rationality rules out an equilibrium in which $\bar{p} > \bar{\gamma}$. Let π be the expected payment the seller receives if she plays $(\bar{s}, \bar{p})$. By supposition, $\pi < \bar{\gamma}$. There exists a $\delta > 0$ such that

$$\bar{\gamma} - c(\bar{s} + \delta, \underline{\gamma}) = \pi - c(\bar{s}, \underline{\gamma}). \tag{A.18}$$

By Spence-Mirrlees,

$$\bar{\gamma} - c(\bar{s} + \delta, \bar{\gamma}) > \pi - c(\bar{s}, \bar{\gamma}).$$

Hence, there exists an $\varepsilon > 0$ such that

$$\bar{\gamma} - \varepsilon - c(\bar{s} + \delta, \bar{\gamma}) > \pi - c(\bar{s}, \bar{\gamma}). \tag{A.19}$$

It follows from (A.18) and the definition of equilibrium that

$$\underline{\gamma} \geq \pi - c(\bar{s}, \underline{\gamma}) > \bar{\gamma} - \varepsilon - c(\bar{s} + \delta, \underline{\gamma}). \tag{A.20}$$

Expressions (A.19) and (A.20) reveal that the deviation $(\bar{s} + \delta, \bar{\gamma} - \varepsilon)$ is such that the PBE fails the Intuitive Criterion. ∎

In light of the claim, there is no PBE satisfying the Intuitive Criterion such that $\bar{s} < s^*$. Consider $\bar{s} > s^*$. Define

$$\varepsilon = \frac{1}{2}\left(c(\bar{s}, \bar{\gamma}) - c(s^*, \bar{\gamma}) \right).$$

Note $\varepsilon > 0$. In light of the claim, definition of ε, and condition (6.4.23):

$$\underline{\gamma} > \bar{\gamma} - \varepsilon - c(s^*, \underline{\gamma}) \text{ and } \bar{\gamma} - c(\bar{s}, \bar{\gamma}) < \bar{\gamma} - \varepsilon - c(s^*, \bar{\gamma}),$$

where the terms on the left of the inequalities are the relevant payoffs under the PBE. Considering the deviation $(s^*, \bar{\gamma} - \varepsilon)$, it is readily seen that these last two inequalities mean the PBE fails the Intuitive Criterion. ∎

Proof of Proposition 6.28: Given his beliefs, the buyer is indifferent between accepting and rejecting an offer at price $b_B(q^{\text{SB}})$. He is, thus, willing to mix. Given the probabilities with which the buyer mixes, it is a best response for the seller to choose quality q^{SB} if she intends to offer the good at price $b_B(q^{\text{SB}})$. All that remains is to verify that the seller does not wish to deviate with respect to investment *and* price given the buyer's beliefs. Given that $b_B(\cdot)$ is increasing, the buyer, given his beliefs, will reject any price greater than $b_B(q^{\text{SB}})$ or in the interval $(b_B(0), b_B(q^{\text{SB}}))$. Because the seller's expected payoff is $\mathcal{M}$ on the purported equilibrium path, she cannot do strictly better under autarky; that is, she has no incentive to induce the buyer to reject her offer. Finally, setting a price of $b_B(0)$ cannot be a profitable deviation for the seller given

$$b_B(0) - q < \mathcal{M}$$

for all q. ∎

Proof of Proposition 6.30: Given the seller makes a TIOLI offer, if the buyer invests a given amount, I, as a pure-strategy, the seller's best response is to offer trade at price

$$t = c_B(I) \geq c_S(I).$$

But Proposition 6.29 rules out a pure-strategy equilibrium in which the buyer invests a positive amount and trade is certain to occur. There is thus no equilibrium in which the buyer plays $I > 0$ as a pure strategy. If the buyer doesn't invest, then trade would occur. But from (6.5.24), the buyer would do better to deviate, invest $\hat{I}$, and not trade. ∎

Proof of Lemma 6.18: A revealed-preference argument yields:

$$U(C) \geq -\left(1 - x(C')\right)C - \tau(C') = U(C') - \left(1 - x(C')\right)(C - C') \text{ and}$$
$$U(C') \geq -(1 - x(C))C' - \tau(C) = U(C) - (1 - x(C))(C' - C).$$
$$\text{(A.21)}$$

Hence,

$$(1 - x(C))(C' - C) \geq U(C) - U(C') \geq \left(1 - x(C')\right)(C' - C). \quad \text{(A.22)}$$

Without loss take $C' > C$, then $x(C') \geq x(C)$ if (A.22) holds.

Pick C and $C' \in \mathcal{C}$ and a $\lambda \in (0, 1)$. Define $C_\lambda = \lambda C + (1-\lambda)C'$. Revealed preference implies:

$$\lambda U(C) \geq \lambda U(C_\lambda) - \lambda\,(1 - x(C_\lambda))\,(C - C_\lambda) \text{ and}$$
$$(1 - \lambda)U(C') \geq (1 - \lambda)U(C_\lambda) - (1 - \lambda)\,(1 - x(C_\lambda))\,(C' - C_\lambda).$$

Add those two expressions:

$$\lambda U(C) + (1 - \lambda)U(C') \geq U(C_\lambda) - (1 - x(C_\lambda))\underbrace{\left(\lambda C + (1 - \lambda)C' - C_\lambda\right)}_{=0}.$$

The convexity of $U(\cdot)$ follows. ∎

Proof of Proposition 6.31: The necessity of condition (i) follows immediately from Lemma 6.18. Convex functions are absolutely continuous (see, e.g., van Tiel, 1984, p. 5). As noted earlier (see proof of Proposition 6.5), an absolutely continuous function has a derivative almost everywhere and, moreover, is the integral of its derivative. Hence, dividing (A.22) through by $C'-C$ and taking the limit as $C' \to C$ reveals that $U'(C) = -(1-x(C))$ almost everywhere. Expression (6.5.26) follows.

To establish sufficiency, suppose the buyer's type is C and consider any $C' < C$. We wish to verify (A.21):

$$U(C) - U(C') = \int_C^{C'} (1 - x(z))\,dz \geq \int_C^{C'} \left(1 - x(C')\right)dz = \left(1 - x(C')\right)(C' - C),$$

where the inequality follows because $x(\cdot)$ is nondecreasing. Expression (A.21) follows. The case $C' < C$ is proved similarly and, so, omitted for the sake of brevity. ∎

Proof of Proposition 6.32: By supposition, the buyer chooses C with positive probability in equilibrium, hence $C \in \mathcal{C}$. Consequently, C must satisfy the first-order condition

$$0 = U'(C) - \iota'(C) = -(1 - x(C)) - \iota'(C). \tag{A.23}$$

The result follows. ∎

Proof of Proposition 6.33: Expression (6.5.32) solves the differential equation (6.5.30). By assumption, $c_s(\iota(C)) < C$ for all $C < C^0$. So, if $\bar{C} < C^0$, then the integral in (6.5.32) exceeds $-\infty$, implying $\Sigma(\bar{C}) > 0$. That, in turn, would entail $x(\bar{C}) = 1$, but that is inconsistent with Proposition 6.32 when $\bar{C} < C^0$. *Reductio ad absurdum*, $\bar{C} = C^0$.

Expression (6.5.33) follows from Proposition 6.31 because $1-x(C)=-\iota'(C)$. The remaining steps were established in the text that preceded the statement of the proposition. ∎

Proof of Lemma 6.19: If the buyer has not invested, he will reject all offers at positive prices. Hence, the seller cannot expect to earn more than zero from any price offer. Given this, p is a best response for her. Expecting a price of p, the buyer would accept the offer only if he has invested $I > I^*$. In that case, his payoff would be

$$B(I) - I - p < B(I) - I - B(I^*) + I^* < 0,$$

where the second inequality follows because $I^* = \arg\max_z B(z) - z$. The buyer would not deviate to an $I > I^*$. Because he won't buy if $I \leq I^*$, he prefers not investing to investing an $I \in (0, I^*]$. So not investing and rejecting is a best response for the buyer. ∎

Proof of Lemma 6.20: From Proposition 6.35, there is no equilibrium in which the buyer invests a positive amount as a pure strategy. Suppose, then, he invests 0 as a pure strategy in equilibrium. The seller's unique best response is $p=B(0)$. But if the seller would play $p=B(0)$ as a pure strategy, the buyer's best response is I^*: because $B(I^*) - I^* > B(0) - 0$, $B(I^*) > B(0)$ (the buyer will buy if he invested) and his overall utility is positive (i.e., $B(I^*) - I^* - B(0) > 0$). *Reductio ad absurdum*, there is no equilibrium in which the buyer plays a pure strategy.

Suppose the seller played a pure strategy of p. Because the seller can secure herself $B(0)$, the buyer must accept an offer of p with positive probability; that is, he must play an I such that $B(I) \geq p$ and $B(I) - I - p \geq 0$. Note that if the second condition holds, the first automatically holds; hence, the buyer must be playing investment levels that maximize

$$B(I) - I - p.$$

But there is a unique maximizer, I^*; that is, the buyer can only play I^* as a best response to p. But this contradicts the first half of the proof, which established he doesn't play a pure strategy in equilibrium. *Reductio ad absurdum*, there is no equilibrium in which the seller plays a pure strategy. ∎

Proof of Lemma 6.21: Suppose not. Observe then that buyer rationality rules out his playing any $b \in (B(0), p_\ell)$. Let $\underline{b} = \inf \mathcal{B}^+$. Observe $\underline{b}$ must strictly exceed p_ℓ:

$$0 \leq \mathbb{E}_G \left\{ \max\{0, \underline{b} - p\} \right\} - \iota(\underline{b}) \leq \underline{b} - p_\ell - \iota(\underline{b}) < \underline{b} - p_\ell,$$

where the last inequality follows because $\iota(\underline{b}) > 0$. The seller's expected profit from playing p_ℓ is

$$\left(1 - F(\underline{b})\right) p_\ell < \left(1 - F(\underline{b})\right) \underline{b} \,.$$

But this means the seller would do better to deviate to $\underline{b}$, a contradiction. ∎

Proof of Lemma 6.22: There is no equilibrium in which $p_h > b_h$, since otherwise the seller's profit is zero from p_h whereas she gets a profit of $B(0)$ by playing p_ℓ. So the buyer's payoff if he plays b_h is

$$u_B = b_h - \iota(b_h) - \mathbb{E}\{p\}. \tag{A.24}$$

If $b_h < B(I^*)$, the buyer would do better to deviate to $B(I^*)$. Hence, $b_h \geq B(I^*)$. Suppose $b_h > B(I^*)$. Given $p_h \leq B(I^*)$, then (A.24) remains a valid expression for the buyer's expected payoff with b_h replaced by any $b \in [B(I^*), b_h]$. But since such a b enhances the buyer's expected payoff, it follows the buyer would deviate if $b_h > B(I^*)$. ∎

Proof of Proposition 6.37: Proposition 6.35 rules out an equilibrium in which the buyer invests a positive amount as a pure strategy.

Suppose, contrary to the proposition, that the buyer invests a positive amount in expectation. There must exist a $\hat{b} > 0$ such that $1 - F(\hat{b}) > 0$. It follows that the seller can guarantee herself an expected profit of

$$\hat{\pi} \equiv \left(1 - F(\hat{b})\right) \hat{b} > 0 \,.$$

Hence, $p_\ell \geq \hat{\pi}$. Buyer rationality dictates that

$$b - \iota(b) - p_\ell \geq 0$$

for any $b > 0$ he is willing to play with positive probability. It follows that $\underline{b} = \inf \mathcal{B}^+ > p_\ell$. But then, as shown in the proof of Lemma 6.21, the seller could increase her profit by charging $\underline{b}$ rather than p_ℓ; hence, p_ℓ isn't the infimum of prices the seller charges. *Reductio ad absurdum*, the buyer cannot invest a positive amount in expectation. ∎

ACKNOWLEDGMENT

The author gratefully acknowledges the financial support of the Thomas and Alison Schneider Distinguished Professorship in Finance.

REFERENCES

Akerlof, G.A., 1970. The market for 'lemons': qualitative uncertainty and the market mechanism. Quarterly Journal of Economics 84, 488–500.

Armstrong, M., 2006a. Competition in two-sided markets. RAND Journal of Economics 37, 668–691.

Armstrong, M., 2006b. Recent developments in the economics of price discrimination. In: Blundell, R., Newey, W.K., Persson, T. (Eds.), Advances in Economics and Econometrics: Theory and Applications, vol II. Cambridge University Press, Cambridge, UK.

Armstrong, M., Rochet, J.-C., 1999. Multi-dimensional screening: A user's guide. European Economic Review 43, 959–979.

Basov, S., 2010. Multidimensional Screening. Springer-Verlag, Berlin.

Beaudry, P., Poitevin, M., 1993. Signalling and renegotiation in contractual relationships. Econometrica 61, 745–782.

Beaudry, P., Poitevin, M., 1995. Competitive Screening in financial markets when borrowers can recontract. Review of Economic Studies 62, 401–423.

Bolton, P., Dewatripont, M., 2005. Contract Theory. MIT Press, Cambridge, MA.

Borch, K.H., 1968. The Economics of Uncertainty. Princeton University Press, Princeton, NJ.

Caillaud, B., Hermalin, B.E., 1993. The use of an agent in a signalling model. Journal of Economic Theory 60, 83–113.

Caillaud, B., Hermalin, B.E., 2000. Hidden Actions and Incentives. Unpublished Manuscript. <http://faculty.haas.berkeley.edu/hermalin/#WP>.

Che, Y.-K., Hausch, D.B., 1999. Cooperative investments and the value of contracting. American Economic Review 89, 125–147.

Cho, I.-K., Kreps, D., 1987. Signaling games and stable equilibria. Quarterly Journal of Economics 102, 179–222.

Coase, R.H., 1972. Durability and monopoly. Journal of Law and Economics 15, 143–149.

Crémer, J., McLean, R.P., 1985. Optimal selling strategies under uncertainty for a discriminating monopolist when demands are interdependent. Econometrica 53, 345–361.

Crémer, J., Riordan, M.H., 1985. A sequential solution to the public goods problem. Econometrica 53, 77–84.

Crémer, J., Riordan, M.H., 1987. On governing multilateral transactions with bilateral contracts. RAND Journal of Economics 18, 436–451.

Crémer, J., McLean, R.P., 1988. Full extraction of the surplus in Bayesian and dominant strategy auctions. Econometrica 56, 1247–1257.

Darby, M.R., Karni, E., 1973. Free competition and the optimal amount of fraud. Journal of Law and Economics 16, 67–88.

Demougin, D.M., Garvie, D.A., 1991. Contractual design with correlated information under limited liability. RAND Journal of Economics 22, 477–489.

Demski, J.S., Sappington, D.E.M., 1991. Resolving double moral hazard problems with buyout agreements. RAND Journal of Economics 22, 232–240.

Edlin, A.S., 1997. Do guaranteed-low-price policies guarantee high prices, and can antitrust rise to the challenge?. Harvard Law Review 111, 528–575.

Edlin, A.S., Hermalin, B.E., 2000. Contract renegotiation and options in agency problems. Journal of Law, Economics, and Organization 16, 395–423.

Engers, M., 1987. Signalling with many signals. Econometrica 55, 663–674.

Fama, E.F., 1980. Agency problems and the theory of the firm. Journal of Political Economy 88, 288–307.

Fong, Y.-f., 2005. When do experts cheat and whom do they target?. RAND Journal of Economics 36, 113–130.

Fudenberg, D., Tirole, J., 1986. A 'signal-jamming' theory of predation. RAND Journal of Economics 17, 366–376.

Fudenberg, D., Tirole, J., 1990. Moral hazard and renegotiation in agency contracts. Econometrica 58, 1279–1320.

Fudenberg, D., Tirole, J., 1991. Game Theory. MIT Press, Cambridge, MA.

Gibbard, A., 1973. Manipulation of voting schemes. Econometrica 41, 587–601.

Gibbons, R.S., 1992. Game Theory for Applied Economists. Princeton University Press, Princeton, NJ.

González, P., 2004. Investment and screening under asymmetric endogenous information. RAND Journal of Economics 35, 502–519.

Green, J., Laffont, J.-J., 1977. Characterization of satisfactory mechanisms for the revelation of preferences for public goods. Econometrica 45, 427–438.

Grossman, S.J., 1981. The informational role of warranties and private disclosure about product quality. Journal of Law and Economics 21, 461–483.

Grossman, S.J., Hart, O.D., 1983. An analysis of the principal-agent problem. Econometrica 51, 7–46.

Grossman, S.J., Hart, O.D., 1986. The costs and benefits of ownership: a theory of vertical and lateral integration. Journal of Political Economy 94, 691–719.

Gul, F., 2001. Unobservable investment and the hold-up problem. Econometrica 69, 343–376.

Gul, F., Sonnenschein, H., Wilson, R.B., 1986. Foundations of dynamic monopoly and the coase conjecture. Journal of Economic Theory 39, 155–190.

Halac, M., 2012. Relational contracts and the value of relationships. American Economic Review 102, 750–779.

Hellwig, M., 1987. Some recent developments in the theory of competition in markets with adverse selection. European Economic Review 31, 319–325.

Hermalin, B.E., 2007. Leading for the long term. Journal of Economic Behavior and Organization 62, 1–19.

Hermalin, B.E., 2013. Unobserved investment, endogenous quality, and trade. RAND Journal of Economics 44, 33–55.

Hermalin, B.E., Katz, M.L., 1993. Judicial modification of contracts between sophisticated parties: a more complete view of incomplete contracts and their breach. Journal of Law, Economics, and Organization 9, 230–255.

Hermalin, B.E., Katz, M.L., 2004. Sender or receiver: who should pay to exchange an electronic message? RAND Journal of Economics 35, 423–448.

Hermalin, B.E., Katz, M.L., 2009. Information and the hold-up problem. RAND Journal of Economics 40, 405–423.

Hermalin, B.E., Katz, A.W., Craswell, R., 2007. Law & Economics of Contracts. In: Mitchell Polinsky, A., Shavell, S. (Eds.), Handbook of Law and, Economics, vol. 1

Holmstrom, B., 1979. Moral hazard and observability. Bell Journal of Economics 10, 74–91.

Holmstrom, B., 1999. Managerial incentive problems—a dynamic perspective. Review of Economic Studies 66, 169–182.

Huang, C.-f., Litzenberger, R.H., 1988. Foundations for Financial Economics. North-Holland, Amsterdam.

Katz, M.L., 1991. Game-playing agents: unobservable contracts as precommitments. RAND Journal of Economics 22, 307–328.

Katz, M.L., 2006. Observable contracts as commitments: interdependent contracts and moral hazard. Journal of Economics and Management Strategy 15, 685–706.

Klein, B., Leffler, K.B., 1981. The role of market forces in assuring contractual performance. Journal of Political Economy 89, 615–641.

Klemperer, P., 2004. Auctions: Theory and Practice. Princeton University Press, Princeton.

Krishna, V., 2002. Auction Theory. Academic Press, San Diego.

Laffont, J.-J., Martimort, D., 2002. The Theory of Incentives: The Principal-Agent Model. Princeton University Press, Princeton, NJ.

Larsen, B., 2012. The Efficiency of Dynamic, Post-Auction Bargaining: Evidence from Wholesale Used-Auto Auctions. MIT Working Paper.

Lau, S., 2008. Information and bargaining in the hold-up problem. RAND Journal of Economics 39, 266–282.

Lewis, T.R., Sappington, D.E.M., 1989. Countervailing incentives in agency problems. Journal of Economic Theory 49, 294–313.

MacLeod, W.B., 2007. Reputations, relationships, and contract enforcement. Journal of Economic Literature 45, 595–628.

Maggi, G., Rodriguez-Clare, A., 1995. On the countervailing incentives. Journal of Economic Theory 66, 238–263.

Mailath, G.J., 1987. Incentive compatibility in signaling games with a continuum of types. Econometrica 55, 1349–1365.

Mas-Colell, A., Whinston, M., Green, J., 1995. Microeconomic Theory. Oxford University Press, Oxford, UK.

McAfee, P.R., Reny, P.J., 1992. Correlated information and mechanism design. Econometrica 60, 395–421.

Mester, L.J., 1992. Perpetual signalling with imperfectly correlated costs. RAND Journal of Economics, Winter 23, 548–563.

Milgrom, P.R., 2004. Putting Auction Theory to Work. Cambridge University Press, Cambridge, UK.

Myerson, R.B., 1979. Incentive compability and the bargaining problem. Econometrica 47, 61–73.

Myerson, R.B., Satterthwaite, M.A., 1983. Efficient mechanisms for bilateral trading. Journal of Economic Theory 29, 265–281.

Nöldeke, G., Schmidt, K.M., 1995. Option contracts and renegotiation: a solution to the hold-up problem. RAND Journal of Economics 26, 163–179.

Nöldeke, G., Schmidt, K.M., 1998. Sequential investments and options to own. RAND Journal of Economics 29, 633–653.

Quinzii, M., Rochet, J.-C., 1985. Signalling multidimensional. Journal of Mathematical Economics 14, 261–284.

Riley, J.G., 1979. Informational equilibrium. Econometrica 47, 331–359.

Rochet, J.-C., 1985. The taxation principle and multi-time Hamilton-Jacobi equations. Journal of Mathematical Economics 14, 113–128.

Rochet, J.-C., Choné, P., 1998. Ironing, sweeping, and multidimensional screening. Econometrica 66, 783–826.

Rochet, J.-C., Tirole, Jean, 2006. Two-sided markets: a progress report. RAND Journal of Economics 37, 645–667.

Rothschild, M., Stiglitz, J., 1976. Equilibrium in competitive insurance markets: an essay on the economics of imperfect information. Quarterly Journal of Economics 90, 629–650.

Royden, H.L., 1968. Real Analysis, second edn. Macmillan Publishing, New York.

Rysman, M., 2009. The economics of two-sided markets. Journal of Economic Perspectives 23, 125–144.

Salanié, B., 1997. The Economics of Contracts: A Primer. MIT Press, Cambridge, MA.

Shapiro, C., 1982. Consumer information, product quality, and seller reputation. Bell Journal of Economics 13, 20–35.

Shapiro, C., 1983. Optimal pricing of experience goods. Bell Journal of Economics 14, 497–507.

Shavell, S., 1979. Risk sharing and incentives in the principal and agent relationship. Bell Journal of Economics 10, 55–73.

Spence, M.A., 1973. Job market signaling. Quarterly Journal of Economics 87, 355–374.

Stein, J.C., 1989. Efficient capital markets, inefficient firms: a model of myopic corporate behavior. Quarterly Journal of Economics 104, 655–669.

Stole, L.A., 2007. Price discrimination and competition. In: Armstrong, M., Porter, R.H. (Eds.), Handbook of Industrial Organization, vol. 3. North-Holland, Amsterdam.

Tirole, J., 1988. The Theory of Industrial Organization. MIT Press, Cambridge, MA.

van Tiel, J., 1984. Convex Analysis: An Introductory Text. John Wiley & Sons, New York.

Varian, H.R., 1989. Price discrimination. In: Schmalensee, R., Willig, R. (Eds.), Handbook of Industrial Organization, vol. 1. North-Holland, Amsterdam.

Williams, S.R., 1987. Efficient performance in two agent bargaining. Journal of Economic Theory 41, 154–172.

Williamson, O.E., 1976. Franchise bidding for natural monopolies—in general and with respect to CATV. The Bell Journal of Economics 7, 73–104.

Wilson, C., 1977. A Model of insurance markets with incomplete information. Journal of Economic Theory 16, 167–207.

Wilson, R.B., 1993. Nonlinear Pricing. Oxford University Press, Oxford.

Yeh, J., 2006. Real Analysis: Theory of Measure and Integration, second edn. World Scientific, Singapore.

CHAPTER 7

The Value of Individual and Societal Risks to Life and Health

W. Kip Viscusi
University Distinguished Professor of Law, Economics, and Management, Vanderbilt University, USA

Contents

Abstract

The value of risks to life as measured by the risk-money trade-off plays a fundamental role in economic analyses of health and safety risks and serves as the principal benefit measure for government risk regulation policies. The hedonic models that have been employed to generate empirical estimates of the value of statistical life (VSL) have produced a substantial literature on VSL based on market behavior. Segmentation of labor market opportunities requires that the hedonic approach be altered for disadvantaged labor market groups. Stated preference models often serve a beneficial function, particularly with respect to valuing risks other than acute accident risks and developing estimates of how utility functions depend on health status. The VSL varies with age, income, the cause of death (e.g., cancer), and other factors. This chapter also examines the risk-risk analysis approach and provides a comprehensive survey of the use of VSL by government agencies.

Handbook of the Economics of Risk and Uncertainty, Volume 1
ISSN 2211-7547, http://dx.doi.org/10.1016/B978-0-444-53685-3.00007-6

Keywords

Value of a Statistical Life, VSL, VSLY, Risk-Risk Analysis, Hedonic Model, Stated Preferences, CFOI

JEL Classification Codes

H51, I10, I18, J17, J31, K32

7.1 INTRODUCTION

The valuation of risks outside of the financial domain may pose greater challenges than the valuation of monetary lotteries, for which it is relatively straightforward to calculate the certainty equivalent as the pivotal valuation measure. For lotteries involving the simplest kinds of nonmonetary outcomes, the fact that the outcome does not involve money may pose few difficulties for valuation. In many instances, one can treat the outcome as being tantamount to adding a monetary equivalent to the utility function. The more challenging situation is that in which the outcome cannot be equated to a monetary gain or loss. Risks to life and health are often quite different from monetary effects in that these risks may alter the structure of the utility function in a fundamental manner, most typically by altering both the level of utility and the marginal utility for any given level of income. Fatalities and disabling personal injuries are two examples of such adverse health effects, as they entail effects on well-being for which money is not an effective substitute. The valuation of these fundamental risks has generated a substantial literature to deal with the distinctive effects that they create and the challenges that they pose for economic valuation.

In most economic contexts, such as market valuations and assessments of the benefits of government policies, the appropriate reference point is the sum of individuals' willingness to pay for small changes in the risk level, where these changes are perhaps the result of a safety-enhancing regulation. Consistent with this valuation objective, a principal focus of the economic literature has been on valuing these effects based on the rate of trade-off between risk and money. Thus, the emphasis for fatality risks has been on the *ex-ante* valuation of statistical lives because at the time of a decision the lives that will be saved are only known probabilistically. This emphasis is different from attempting to attach a dollar value to identified lives such as a trapped coal miner. The practical task is to assign dollar values to the endpoints of the health risk lottery.

That the proper focus for lifesaving activities should be on the valuation of risk rather than certain outcomes has been the emphasis of economic studies since the contribution by Schelling (1968), who addressed lifesaving activities from an individual choice perspective. Previously, the standard economic practice conceptualized the valuation approach in terms of human capital measures based on the present value of lost earnings. The human capital value and other wealth-related measures are related to people's risk-money trade-offs for small risks of death, but generate valuation amounts that are well below the valuations pertinent to assessments of reduced risk. Rather than focusing on such wealth measures, it is more appropriate to assess risk trade-off rates. Typically, the lives at risk are prospective statistical lives where the particular individuals who will die are not identified.[1] Even for risk-taking activities such as work on hazardous jobs, the worker exposed to these risks is a prospective possible fatality who does not become an identified victim until after the fatality. Schelling (1968) emphasized that the task is to establish values for statistical lives, not identified lives.

Developing an empirical methodology for assigning a monetary value to these expected lives is a quite different matter. Schelling was not optimistic about the prospects for developing an empirical measure for the value of fatality risk reductions either through surveys or analyses of market-based studies: "The main problem is that people have difficulty knowing what it is worth to themselves, cannot easily answer questions about it, and may object to being asked. Market evidence is unlikely to reveal much." A tremendous accomplishment of economic research since Schelling's seminal article is that empirical methods, available data, and survey techniques have developed considerably so that economists are now better able to address seemingly intractable matters such as valuing risks to life.

The most frequently used terminology to refer to the trade-off rate between fatality risks and money is the "value of statistical life," or the VSL. Unlike the earlier "value of life" terminology used in the literature, the value of statistical life terminology emphasizes the probabilistic aspect of the valuation to make it distinct from the amount we are willing to pay to save identified lives. The VSL remains controversial particularly among those who misinterpret what an economic valuation of health risks entails. Noneconomists continue to equate the VSL to a human capital measure. To reduce the confusion some have suggested that a less flamboyant terminology would generate less controversy.[2] However, given the nature of the VSL enterprise of monetizing risks to life, it is likely that the approach will remain controversial among noneconomists regardless of the label that is used. Indeed, some legal critics of the VSL approach argue, for example, that lives should be "priceless" and that any finite price demeans the value of the lives that are being saved irrespective of what terminology is used.[3]

For the most part, these critiques have been relegated to complaints outside of the economics literature, as the economic approach is well within the mainstream of current economic thought. Government agencies throughout the world have adopted the

---

[1] The role of identified versus statistical lives for policy analysis is reviewed by Hammitt and Treich (2007).

[2] To avoid misunderstanding of the VSL concept, Cameron (2008, 2010) advocates "euthanizing" the VSL terminology and in Cameron (2010) she advocates replacing it with 'willingness to swap' (WTS) alternative goods and services for a microrisk reduction in the chance of sudden death (or other types of risks to life and health)." This characterization is correct but more unwieldy than the VSL terminology. Shortening this alternative definition to WTS would not be appropriate since there is a counterpart to the risks to life WTS for a wide range of policy outcomes that do not involve the risk of death.

[3] Ackerman and Heinzerling (2004) provide an extended critique of the use of the VSL concept by government agencies.

methodology for valuing the health risk effects of government policies. Because the U.S. and other countries often do a benefit-cost analysis of policies and, in some cases, base the approval of policies on whether the effort passes a benefit-cost test, it is essential to be able to place a meaningful dollar value on fatality risks and other major health consequences of government policies. Despite the rhetorical appeal of designating such risk-related effects as being "priceless," failing to monetize them at all may make them worthless from the standpoint of benefit-cost analysis.

Moreover, in any meaningful economic sense, small reductions in fatality risks are not priceless. Due to society's limited economic resources, it is not possible to make an unbounded commitment to risk reduction, implying that eventually some trade-offs must be made. In the U.S., there are 128,000 accidental deaths per year so that devoting the entire GDP to accident prevention would only provide enough funds to allocate $115 million per accidental death. Even this amount overstates the available financial resources to promote health, as disabling injuries and illnesses are excluded, as are all other alternative expenditures that people might believe are worthwhile.

As a valuation measure, the VSL has attractive properties. It generates a cardinal measure for valuation rather than an ordinal index. The scale is also comparable across people, facilitating interpersonal comparisons. Doubling the VSL indicates that a person is twice as reluctant to incur fatality risks as measured by the amount needed to compensate the person for bearing the risk. The VSL methodology can also be applied to risk changes in both directions as well as estimates of willingness-to-pay values and willingness-to-accept values.

This chapter explores how to establish these economic values for trade-offs between health risks and money. After examining the basics of the risk-money trade-off approach in Section 7.2, Section 7.3 presents the hedonic model of market-based risks. This is the standard econometric approach to analyzing the implicit price for fatality risks as embodied in the prices for risky products and the wages for risky jobs. Unfortunately, the canonical hedonic model does not pertain to situations in which the market opportunities face different market participants. The Viscusi-Hersch segmented labor markets model presented in Section 7.4 presents an approach for testing the standard hedonic model assumption and for analyzing market data in which market opportunity curves differ.

While much of the literature has used market-based data to explore how people value fatality risks, there has also been substantial literature using stated preference approaches, as discussed in Section 7.5. Reliance on survey data based on stated rather than revealed preferences is often useful for specific health risks not adequately addressed by market evidence or for countries such as the U.K. where the market estimates do not appear to be stable. One can also use stated preference studies to ascertain the value of risks to the general public and to others, whereas the VSL literature focuses on privately born risks. Stated preference evidence also can provide greater detail on individual valuations of risk situations along a constant expected utility locus, making it possible to estimate health state-dependent utility functions, as discussed in Section 7.6.

The subsequent five sections provide detailed summaries of the empirical literature that has consisted of meta-analyses of the VSL literature (Section 7.7), new labor market estimates using more refined risk data (Section 7.8), estimates for market contexts outside the labor market such as housing markets (Section 7.9), life-cycle effects whereby VSL and the value of each life year vary over the individual's life cycle (Section 7.10), and variations in VSL by labor market groups that are at the heart of recent discussion of the heterogeneity of VSL (Section 7.11).

The discussion thus far assumes that fatalities are homogenous events, where a prototypical fatality is the result of an acute injury such as a motor-vehicle accident. However, fatalities may also be accompanied by sometimes lengthy periods of treatment and morbidity effects, as with cancer (Section 7.12). In addition, fatality risks may be associated with dread and other attributes, as in the case of terrorist attacks, that may alter the appropriate VSL amount (Section 7.13).

In practice, expenditures to reduce risks of death may be governed by concerns other than economic efficiency leading to costs per expected life saved that greatly exceed the VSL. This situation has given rise to risk-risk analysis whereby it is possible to determine the expenditure level that will lead to an expected life lost due to the opportunity cost of expenditures (Section 7.14). Section 7.15 provides an extensive review of the different practices of government agencies with respect to valuing health risks, and Section 7.16 concludes.

7.2 THE BASICS OF THE RISK-MONEY TRADE-OFF

The fundamentals of risk-money trade-offs can be illustrated using labor market decisions as the economic context. Most of the empirical work on the value of statistical life has utilized labor market data so that this framework is pertinent to much of the subsequent discussion.

The principal theoretical underpinning of the analysis can be traced back to Adam Smith's (1776) theory of compensating differentials, which is a theory of labor supply. Workers will require a higher wage for jobs that are unpleasant or otherwise unattractive, such as posing a greater risk of death or injury. Risky jobs consequently will command a compensating differential either in terms of higher wages or other offsetting advantages such as favorable job amenities. Otherwise, workers will not be willing to work on those dangerous jobs. Let p be the health risk and $w(p)$ be the market opportunities locus for the highest wage available for any given risk p, where $w'(p) > 0$. Workers will never select a job on any downward sloping part of $w(p)$ so that all observed market evidence will indicate a positive wage-risk trade-off. The locus $w(p)$ is the outer envelope of individual firms' market offer curves. Figure 7.1 illustrates one such curve of the choices available to the workers.

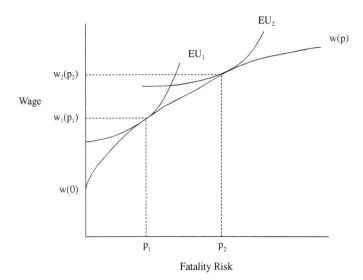

Figure 7.1 The standard hedonic labor market model.

The worker will choose the position that offers the highest expected utility (EU). Thus, the worker's preferences define a series of EU loci, and the point that is tangent to the highest EU curve is the optimal job choice. For the situation shown in Figure 7.1, worker 1 chooses risk p_1 with wage $w_1(p_1)$ while worker 2 chooses the higher risk p_2 with wage $w_2(p_2)$. Because these workers share the same market offer curve, the difference in risky decisions reflects a difference in willingness to bear risk.

These risk preferences can be traced to the workers' utility functions. Let $u(w(p))$ be the utility of income when healthy and $v(w(p))$ be the utility of income in the ill health state. In the case where the ill health state is death, $v(w(p))$ represents the bequest function. We make the assumption that the worker prefers higher wages, or u', $v' > 0$, and is either risk-neutral or risk-averse u'', $v'' \leq 0$. Then, following Viscusi (1978, 1979), the optimal job choice satisfies

$$w' = \frac{u - v}{(1 - p)u' + pv'}.$$

(7.1)

The left side of equation (7.1) is the wage-risk trade-off, or the slope of the market offer curve at the point in Figure 7.1 that has been selected by the worker. If p is the fatality risk, w' is the VSL. The right side of equation (7.1) is the difference in the utility levels in the two states divided by the expected marginal utility of income. Differences across workers in, for example, the relative values of u and v will affect their willingness to bear risk. The denominator for that term in effect normalizes the units for the expression. Or upon rearranging terms, one finds that the marginal increase in wages w' due to an increase in the risk p, multiplied by the expected marginal utility of income associated with that wage increase, $(1-p)u' + pv'$, equals the difference in the utility levels between the two states of the world, $u-v$. The formulation in equation (7.1) is so fundamental to the VSL literature that it has been "rediscovered" dozens of times.

Note that von Neumann-Morgenstern utility functions are only defined up to a positive linear transformation. Thus, the utility functions u and v are equivalent to $a+bu$ and $a+bv$ where a and b are positive constants. In the absence of some normalization as is provided by the denominator, $(1-p)u' + pv'$, the VSL corresponding to w' would be undefined both within and across people. The VSL is now unaffected by such transformations as

$$\frac{(a+bu)-(a+bv)}{(1-p)bu' + pbv'} = \frac{u-v}{(1-p)u' + pv'}. \tag{7.2}$$

An informative index of the economic import of the VSL is the extent to which it has played a central role in economic analysis of market risk decisions, where the VSL is the market price for safety. Consider the product safety model developed by Spence (1977). In that model, firms must select an optimal level of product safety, for which the firm must incur higher costs for safer products. If the consumer is injured, the firm is liable for some damages amount. The optimizing firm in a competitive market in which consumers are fully informed will set the marginal cost of safer products equal to the VSL term on the right side of equation (7.1) plus the value of producer liability for situations in which there is legal liability for a product failure.[4] In the absence of such liability payments, the marginal cost of safety is equated to the VSL. Although Spence (1977) did not specifically identify the presence of a VSL term or the broader economic significance of the expression, the relationship is consistent with what will be found below for the analysis of hedonic labor market models. In particular, the marginal costs of providing safety on the part of the firm equal the marginal valuation of safety (i.e., the VSL) by consumers in the product context and by workers in the job risk context.

7.3 HEDONIC MODELS OF MARKET-BASED RISKS

7.3.1 The Canonical Hedonic Model

The most common approach to estimating the VSL is to use labor market data to estimate the implicit wage-risk trade-off.[5] Risks to life are not traded explicitly in markets, but they are part of a bundled job attribute commodity. Estimating trade-offs based on individual choices focuses on the revealed preferences regarding actual risks, which are likely to be more informative than stated preferences regarding hypothetical risks.

---

[4] See in particular his equation 11.

[5] Another alternative is to use simulation methods to examine VSL within the context of workplace safety policies as in Kniesner and Leeth (1995) or with respect to individual life expectancy, as in Murphy and Topel (2006).

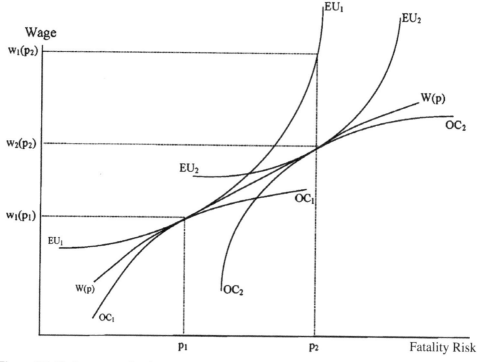

Figure 7.2 Market process for determining compensating differentials.

Figure 7.2 illustrates the underpinnings of the analysis that formed the basis for the market opportunities locus $w(p)$ in Figure 7.1. As described in the seminal work on hedonic models by Rosen (1974, 1986), the demand for labor by firms generates the market opportunities for workers.[6] In particular, firms select the number of workers, the quantity of capital, and the safety-related work environment equipment to maximize profits. Safety considerations enter the level of the firm's profits through the wage premium for unsafe jobs, workers' compensation costs, expected penalties for violations of job safety regulations, the costs of safety-related equipment, and possible effects of job safety on productivity and turnover.

Firms can obtain the same level of profits for different combinations of job risks and wages. Figure 7.2 illustrates the isoprofit curve OC_1 for firm 1, and OC_2 illustrates the isoprofit curve for firm 2. Firms differ in their technologies, and firm 2 has higher costs of reducing risks. To avoid excessive clutter in the diagram, the market opportunities locus that is tangent to the isoprofit curves in the market and shown in Figure 7.1 is

[6] The recent treatment by Kniesner and Leeth (2010) is comprehensive in its treatment as it includes influences such as job safety standards and workers' compensation. Also see Viscusi (1993) and Viscusi and Aldy (2003) for expositions of the hedonic wage model.

omitted. Firms would, of course, prefer to boost profits by choosing an isoprofit curve at higher risk and lower wages but such movements in the southeastern direction in the figure will no longer be tangent to the market opportunities locus. Workers will consider such jobs to be dominated by more attractive jobs offered by other firms.

As shown in the diagram, worker 1 with constant expected utility locus EU_1 selects firm 1 with risk p_1 and wage $w_1(p_1)$, while worker 2 selects the higher risk job at firm 2 with a fatality risk p_2 and wage $w_2(p_2)$. The hedonic labor market equilibrium curve $W(p)$ traces out these various points of tangency. Each point along the curve simultaneously reflects the joint tangency between labor supply and demand. Thus, at point $(p_1, w_1(p_1))$ the slope of $W(p)$ is worker 1's VSL and is also the firm's marginal cost of altering the fatality risk.

Note that the implications of the hedonic wage curve $W(p)$ only pertain locally. Thus, at a higher risk p_2 one cannot conclude that worker 1 will be willing to work at that risk level for wage $w_2(p_2)$. As indicated in Figure 7.2, to keep worker 1 on the same constant expected utility locus, the wage at firm 2 would have to be $w_1(p_2)$. This relationship is borne out empirically as willingness-to-accept values for increases in nonfatal job risks are up to almost twice as great as for the willingness-to-pay values for risk decreases, with market evidence on wage-job risk trade-offs yielding values between these two extremes (Viscusi and Evans, 1990).

7.3.2 Estimation of the Hedonic Wage Model

Attempts to jointly estimate the system of equations pertaining to labor demand and labor supply have been largely unsuccessful.[7] A variety of complications make this a challenging econometric task. Unlike prices for homogeneous goods, the VSL is an implicit price governed by the value of $w'(p)$. This implicit price in turn is an independent variable in the supply and demand equations. The job risk p is also endogenous, as decisions by both workers and firms affect the value. Workers with a strong preference for safety will also sort themselves into the safer firms, making it difficult to find exogenous instruments for the supply and demand equations.

A typical hedonic wage equation used to estimate $W(p)$ takes the form

$$w_i = \alpha + X_i'\beta + \gamma_1 p_i + \gamma_2 q_i + \gamma_3 q_i wc_i + \varepsilon_i, \tag{7.3}$$

where w_i is the worker's wage rate, X_i is a vector of worker and job characteristics, p_i is the fatality rate for workers i's job, q_i is the nonfatal injury rate for worker i's job, wc_i is the workers' compensation replacement rate for worker i, and α, β, γ_1, and γ_2 are parameters to be estimated. Equation (7.3) is more comprehensive than many analyses, which may omit the nonfatal injury rate variable because of a strong correlation with the p_i. Other authors omit the workers' compensation variable and instead include state indicators as workers' compensation benefits vary by state.

---

[7] See Brown and Rosen (1982), Epple (1987), Kahn and Lang (1988), and Kniesner and Leeth (2010) for discussion.

The dependent variable w_i is the worker's hourly wage rate. There is no theoretical basis for distinguishing between use of a linear or logarithmic form (Rosen, 1974), but the analysis in Moore and Viscusi (1988a) found that the semi-logarithmic form had a higher explanatory power than the linear wage equation based on a Box-Cox transformation. The log(wage) specification is the more common approach in the hedonic wage literature.

7.3.3 Fatality Rate Data Used in Hedonic Wage Models

The ideal measure of the fatality risk is a variable that reflects both worker and firm assessments of the risk of a particular job. In practice, the fatality risk variables have been much less precise, but the quality of the fatality risk data has improved markedly over time. Some studies have utilized measures of workers' subjective perceptions of job risk, such as Viscusi (1979), Viscusi and O'Connor (1984), Gerking et al. (1988), and Liu et al. (1997), but these measures are often fairly coarse and do not reflect the firm's risk assessment. For example, the subjective risk belief question in the University of Michigan Survey of Working Conditions asks workers if they believe their job exposes them to dangerous or unhealthy conditions. Such questions can be chained with objective fatality rate variables to, for example, correspond to the industry fatality rate if the worker considers the job to be dangerous in some respect. Precise elicitation of the magnitude of subjective risk beliefs for risks that currently are on the order of 1/25,000 annually poses practical problems because of the difficulties in eliciting and quantifying very small probabilities. Nevertheless, the similarity of the VSL estimates using subjective risk measures to those obtained using objective measures of job risks provides additional corroboration of the hedonic wage approach.

Some early studies used actuarial data on fatality rates for workers in different occupations (Thaler and Rosen, 1975; Brown, 1980; Leigh, 1981; Arnould and Nichols, 1983). These studies used risk measures based on the 1967 Society of Actuaries data. The fatality rates were derived from data used for life insurance policies and reflect total risks of death from all causes for people working in different occupations. The variable consequently confounded risks of the job with factors such as low income levels and lifestyle choices that were correlated with the characteristics of people in different occupations. As a result, the data suggest implausible risk relationships. For example, actors were among the highest risk workers based on this measure, which is attributable to their low earnings rather than on-the-job hazards. The average risk levels in the Society of Actuaries data also were implausibly large—on the order of 1/1,000 annually.

Comparisons of these risk data with industry risk averages for a comparable time period suggests that the occupational risk figures based on life insurance data exceed the average job-related risk during that time period by an order of magnitude (Viscusi, 1978). There are two possible implications of this relatively high risk value. First, the Society of Actuaries data may reflect workers who have self-selected into very risky jobs, which will lead to an underestimate of the VSL for workers generally. Second, the insurance-based measures may simply overstate the job-related risk component of the fatality rate. This systematic measurement error in the fatality rate variable will bias downward the VSL estimate. Perhaps for both of these reasons, VSL estimates based on Society of Actuaries data remain at the bottom end of the distribution of VSL estimates in the literature.

Although studies have utilized a variety of other fatality risk measures such as those based on workers' compensation data, the dominant approach has been to use national risk data that can be matched to workers in a sample based on their reported industry and possibly other characteristics, such as occupation. Mellow and Sider (1983) found that workers' reported industry is usually more accurate than their reported occupational category, and most studies have utilized industry level data. The degree of accuracy of the industry or occupational categorization depends on the level of refinement, e.g., whether it is at the 1-digit or 2-digit level. Categorizations based on broad occupation or industry groups tend to involve less misclassification.

There have been three principal waves of U.S. job fatality data, generated by U.S. government agencies. The first set of data compiled by the U.S. Bureau of Labor Statistics (BLS) was fatality risk data based on a survey of firms in different industries. The reliance on voluntary reports and a sampling approach led to possible measurement error and also limited the usefulness of the data to evaluate industry risk differences at levels more refined than 2-digit and 3-digit levels of industry code aggregation. The average U.S. fatality rates during the 1970s were on the order of 1/10,000 annually.

Beginning in 1980 the National Institute of Occupational Safety and Health (NIOSH) developed the National Traumatic Occupational Fatalities (NTOF) index. The NTOF fatality risk data are available by 1-digit industry code and by state. These data are based on death certificates and provide a more comprehensive measure than the sampling approach. However, there remained some questions about the accuracy of the job-related characterizations of the cause of death (Dorman and Hagstrom, 1998). There have always been controversies about health-related exposures, as the job-relatedness is often difficult to ascertain. But determining the fatality rates for acute accidents is more feasible so that improvements in such data should be able to eliminate the measurement error problem for accidental deaths.

The most comprehensive fatality data available are from the BLS Census of Fatal Occupational Injuries (CFOI), which became operational in 1992. The BLS utilizes multiple information sources to corroborate the job-related nature of the fatality. The BLS examines Occupational Safety and Health Administration accident reports, workers' compensation records, death certificates, newspaper articles, medical examiner reports, and other accident reports. The BLS verifies all deaths using at least two sources, and on average the BLS confirms each fatality using four sources (Loh and Richardson, 2004). The CFOI is available on an individual fatality basis, providing information about the cause of death and the deceased worker's industry, occupation, age, gender, race, immigrant status, location, and other characteristics. Using this information, economists have constructed a series of very refined fatality risk measures to reduce measurement error problems and to explore the labor market heterogeneity of the VSL. This heterogeneity has been a long-standing issue in labor economics and the subject of empirical analyses, as in Viscusi (1983, 2010) and Hersch and Pickton (1995), but the ability to estimate the heterogeneity has been enhanced by the availability of more refined fatality rate data.

The increased availability of more accurate fatality risk information also addresses many of the concerns with respect to measurement error in the fatality rate measure used in labor market studies. Moore and Viscusi (1988a) found that the reduction in measurement error in the fatality rate variable that was achieved by shifting to the NIOSH measure from the earlier Bureau of Labor Statistics fatality data led to a doubling of the estimated VSL so that the changes in data series can be quite consequential. The fatality risk variable has continued to attract considerable attention from the standpoint of potential measurement error (Black and Kniesner, 2003; Ashenfelter, 2006), but these critiques have all focused on the pre-CFOI data. In particular, the most recent wave of data considered by Black and Kniesner (2003) was the NIOSH fatality data, which they found was better than previous data but did not fully resolve the nonrandom measurement error problem. The Ashenfelter (2006) critique is less empirically based but also did not incorporate the CFOI data in the assessment of measurement error in the fatality rate measure.

Despite the advent of better fatality rate data, there are remaining econometric concerns. The fatality risk variable in a wage equation may be endogenous, as has been observed by Garen (1988) and others. The fatality rate is not determined solely by the firm's choice of technologies, but also hinges on the characteristics and safety-related behaviors of workers. This dependence will have a potential effect on observed VSL levels. Omitted variables such as person-specific skills in producing safety may affect estimated VSL and the degree to which the objective risk measure actually reflects the hazards to which the worker is exposed.

Various theoretical models have hypothesized how such complications pertaining to safety-related productivity influence the standard hedonic wage equation structure. One series of such contributions pertains to how workers' general risk-taking behaviors alter the riskiness in a particular type of job, which in turn will affect their wage. The predictions of the models by Hwang et al. (1992), Viscusi and Hersch (2001), and Shogren and Stamland (2002) differ depending on how individual safety-related productivity alters the results. In the case of productivity correlated with smoking status, Viscusi and Hersch (2001) found that smokers were paid less generally and were choosing jobs from a flatter hedonic wage locus than nonsmokers. Smokers appear to be riskier workers generally. Controlling for industry risk levels, they are injured more on the job. They also are subject to greater risk of injury off the job and engage in fewer protective health habits than nonsmokers. Recent studies discussed in Section 7.8 have used panel data to control for worker heterogeneity and instrumental variables to address endogeneity and measurement error (Kniesner et al., 2012).

7.4 THE VISCUSI-HERSCH SEGMENTED LABOR MARKET MODEL

The canonical hedonic labor market theory assumes that all workers face the same labor market opportunities locus as in Figure 7.1. A straightforward generalization is to allow for factors that may lead to different vertical intercepts for the wage offer curve. Thus, more years of education or a favorable local labor market could lead to a parallel upward shift in the $w(p)$ frontier. Including such factors in a standard hedonic wage equation will address these concerns by accounting for their influence on the base level wage rate.

What the standard theory must assume is that for any given risk p, the VSL given by dw/dp is the same irrespective of the level of the $w(p)$ curve, consistent with worker characteristics altering the intercept of the wage offer curve but not its shape. Similarly, the wage premium workers receive for a given risk as compared to a zero risk position is always identical. This assumption may not be borne out in practice as the slope and relative position of the $w(p)$ curve could be quite different across labor market groups. Viscusi and Hersch (2001) present a taxonomy of such possible shapes and a generalization of the hedonic model to account for such influences.

Suppose that workers' safety-related productivity depends on some characteristic or risky activity, which we define by s, which for concreteness one can view as the level of the person's cigarette smoking. Then the market opportunities locus may depend on s as well, or $w(p,s)$. If workers with the attribute s are riskier workers, the w_s will be negative, and at a zero risk level the wage offer curve for smokers will start at a lower level, or have a lower intercept. If s is related to the worker's safety-related productivity, then w_{ps} may be nonzero as well. If $w_{ps} > 0$ then smokers will face a steeper wage offer curve than nonsmokers. In that instance even if w_s is negative and the smokers' wage-offer curve starts lower, the curve may eventually cross that of nonsmokers. If, however, $w_{ps} < 0$, then the wage offer curve for smokers will always be below that of nonsmokers and increasingly so as the risk level increases, since the smoker curve is flatter.

An illustrative possible combination of labor market offer curves is shown in Figure 7.3. This is the case that was found in Viscusi and Hersch (2001) to accord with smokers and nonsmoking workers, as the smoker group faces an offer curve with a lower wage intercept value and a flatter offer curve slope. Worker 1 and worker 2 face the higher and steeper wage offer curve $w(p)$, while worker 3 faces the flatter wage offer curve $y(p)$ that also starts at a lower wage value. Thus, for any given fatality risk p, workers 1 and 2 will receive a higher wage rate and will have a higher VSL. The source of the difference in the slopes of the wage offer curves can be traced to difference in the isoprofit curves that give rise to the opportunities locus. For workers facing $y(p)$ the nature of the jobs

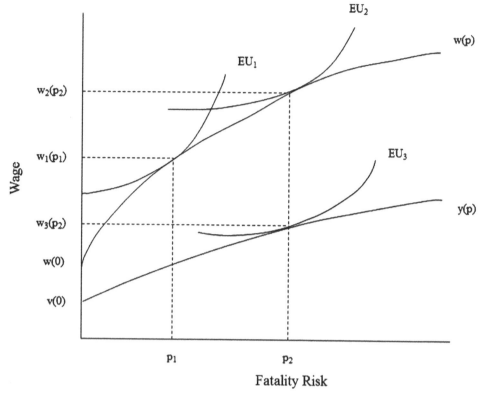

Figure 7.3 The Viscusi-Hersch hedonic labor market model.

is such that at any risk level the marginal costs of altering the safety level are less, giving rise to a flatter offer curve.

Although there are many possible variants of the segmented hedonic labor market model, for the situation in which there is a hypothesized relationship as in Figure 7.3, two conditions should be met. For any given fatality risk p, the VSL should be lower for workers facing $y(p)$ than that for workers facing $w(p)$ since $y(p)$ is flatter than $w(p)$. If workers facing offer curve $y(p)$ face greater risks but receive less hazard pay than other worker groups, than these workers cannot be facing the same market offer curves. Examination of overall wage levels indicates whether $w(p)$ is also higher than $y(p)$.

Suppose that group c workers earn some wage $w(p_1, c)$ at risk p_1 and wage $w(0, c)$ at zero risk. Thus, the total compensating differential for their position is $w(p_1, c) - w(0, c)$. Let worker group d earn a wage $w(p_2, d)$ for risk $p_2 < p_1$ and a wage $w(0, d)$ for a zero risk job. Thus, the group d workers receive a compensating differential $w(p_2, d) - w(0, d)$ for risk p_2. Workers c and d cannot be on the same offer curve if the compensating differential for the smaller risk p_2 is greater than that for p_1, or if

$$w(p_1, c) - w(0, c) < w(p_2, d) - w(0, d). \tag{7.4}$$

If workers in groups c and d were on the same offer curve, $w(0, c)$ and $w(0, d)$ would be equal so that inequality (7.4) reduces to

$$w(p_1, c) < w(p_2, d). \tag{7.5}$$

With identical offer curves,

$$w(p_1, c) = w(p_1, d). \tag{7.6}$$

Substituting this value of $w(p_1, d)$ based on equation (7.6) for $w(p_1, c)$ in inequality (7.5) yields

$$w(p_1, d) < w(p_2, d). \tag{7.7}$$

Since $p_1 > p_2$, this result contradicts the property of wage offer curves as upward sloping.

This model of segmented hedonic labor markets is applicable to a wide variety of situations, which are discussed in Section 7.11. As in the case of the basic hedonic wage model, differences on both sides of the market will affect the ultimate labor market outcome. However, if a worker group is at a higher risk level but has a lower VSL, that result cannot be because that group has a greater willingness to bear risk. There must also be a difference in the structure of that group's labor market opportunities.

7.5 STATED PREFERENCE MODELS

7.5.1 Rationales and Validity Tests for Stated Preference Models

An alternative to estimating implicit value of life and health based on market decisions is to use a stated preference survey methodology in which individuals are asked questions to elicit their risk-money trade-off. The initial attempts to ascertain VSL levels involved the use of survey techniques, but communicating the risks of eliciting meaningful valuations of hypothetical risks remains a challenging aspect of such studies. Despite these limitations, there are many potential benefits of such survey approaches. These studies can address levels of risk and types of risk outcomes, such as cancer, that are not captured in revealed preference studies. Such interview studies can also inform respondents of the risk level so that there is no need to match objective risk data to the individual and assume that these objective measures correspond to individual beliefs. In addition, stated preference studies can elicit preferences from different population groups such as those outside the labor market or groups who are not represented in the populations studied in implicit price studies of VSL, such as apartment dwellers for whom housing price studies may not reflect their valuation of safety. Stated preference studies also avoid the potential econometric problems associated with hedonic labor market studies. The principal drawback of stated preference studies is that there is no assurance that hypothetical choices reflect the trade-offs people would make in actual market situations.

In recognition of these potential shortcomings, a large environmental economics literature has specified various rationality and consistency tests that should be included as validity tests in stated preference studies.[8] Scope tests are the most common type of basic rationality test for stated preference studies. Respondents should value more of desirable commodities than less. In the context of risk reduction, a larger decrease in the probability of an adverse outcome should be preferred to a smaller decrease in that probability. Similarly, responses should satisfy reasonable behavioral tests so that there should be an increased value of safety in response to higher income levels or greater participation in the risky activity so that the risk exposure is greater.

Stated preference studies differ in terms of the commodity that is being valued. In some instances, the focus is the direct analog of market studies in that what is being elicited is the individual's trade-off between money and small risks to the individual, as with a study that asks the respondent the wage increase the person would require to incur an increased risk on the job. In other instances, the valuation task is directed at eliciting the value placed on risk reductions that affect the respondent as well as others, as in the case of the valuation of improved traffic safety. The valuation task also may eliminate purely altruistic values, such as how much a person is willing to pay to reduce risks to populations not including the respondent, which could be contemporaneous groups or may involve future generations. Even though risk-money trade-offs are being elicited in these various instances, what is being valued and the contexts in which these valuations constitute meaningful valuation measures may be quite different.

Stated preference studies and various experimental methods are also useful in exploring matters of interest to behavioral economists. Is there, for example, a certainty premium associated with the elimination of a risk? In the absence of market data that is associated with a zero risk level, it is not otherwise feasible to address that issue. Similarly, are the risk-money trade-offs different for risk increases as opposed to risk decreases, and are there similar kinds of reference point effects that alter the risk-money trade-offs when monetary amounts are increasing or decreasing?

Numerous survey approaches can be used to elicit valuations. The direct contingent valuation measure is to ask people how much compensation they would need to incur a particular risk. Such a question could be posed either in an open-ended fashion or through the use of payment cards. A second approach is for respondents to compare a pair of different money-risk packages, which could be manipulated until the respondent achieves indifference by, for example, increasing the monetary payment or decreasing the risk level of the less preferred option. Respondents also might consider alternative situations involving monetary costs and risks and indicate which option they prefer. One can use random utility models to estimate the rate of trade-off in this instance.

---

[8] Heberlein et al. (2005) outline a series of such tests.

7.5.2 Reference Risk Trade-off Methodology

Rather than directly valuing a particular commodity, another approach is to use a reference lottery to value utility functions. Viscusi et al. (1991) introduced a methodology in which the utility of different health states could be equated to some risk p of death, which could then be chained with VSL measures to establish the utility loss of adverse health outcomes. Thus, in their example,

$$u(\text{chronic bronchitis}) = (1 - p)u(\text{life}) + pv(\text{death}), \qquad (7.8)$$

where the survey task was to elicit the value of p that established this inequality. In other variants introduced by the authors, respondents equate two different lotteries where one lottery is a reference lottery on fatality risks and the other is a lottery involving risks with other dimensions such as morbidity effects or terrorism risks. The risk-risk trade-off approach has been adopted in numerous stated preference studies. For example, Chilton et al. (2002) utilize a similar survey structure in which respondents compare risks from car accidents with risks from rail accidents to examine the relative valuation of these different, but qualitatively similar, risks.

A primary focus of stated preference studies of VSL has been on transportation safety risks. Here we will focus on a series of studies with respect to a broad set of VSL issues undertaken using U.K. studies of transportation safety, but there have also been similar studies focusing more narrowly on VSL per se using data from other countries, including Sweden (Persson et al., 2001). Most of these transportation studies focus on the valuation of public risks rather than risks that affect a single individual. Thus, what is being elicited is often the value of a more general risk to society rather than a privately born risk. A series of studies of transportation safety in the U.K. have yielded estimates of VSL such as $3.8 million ($1990) in Jones-Lee (1989). A stated preference study of automobile accident risks in the U.S. by Viscusi et al. (1991) found a mean VSL of $9.7 million and a median value of $2.7 million ($1990), which reflects the fact that the distribution of VSL is substantially skewed across the population.

The key assumption of stated preference studies is that the risk values in these studies are meaningful and are used as the basis for expressed preferences. These risk values could either be probabilities given to respondents as part of the survey scenario or probabilities elicited from the respondent. In each instance, it may be the case that the stated probabilities either in the survey or indicated by the respondents do not correspond to the risk assessment that the individual used when making a particular choice in the survey. Because of the difficulties people have in processing probability information, studies generally focus on risks of at least 1/10,000 or more. There are also efforts to educate people regarding probabilities using pie charts, risk ladders, and grids. For example, a grid could include 1,000 squares where some are darkened to indicate the probability out of 1,000. For example, Corso et al. (2001) explore the use of visual aids in contingent valuation studies of mortality risk. Many other studies utilize visual aids as a component of the survey design.

7.5.3 Stated Risks versus Perceived Risks

Even if individuals are told the risk information, that may not be the risk level used in their valuations. Consider the situation in which survey respondents are presented with specific risk information as part of the survey. In Viscusi and Evans (1998), individuals considered household chemical products for which respondents were given the warning information and told an injury risk z associated with the product. However, in forming the risk beliefs regarding the product, the respondent can also draw on prior risk beliefs r and risk assessments p based on inspection of the product. If posterior risk beliefs q are governed by the beta distribution with informational weights ψ, λ, and ξ on r, p, and z, the posterior risk belief used in making the decision is

$$q = \frac{\psi r + \lambda p + \xi z}{\psi + \lambda + \xi}. \tag{7.9}$$

Studies that assume that respondents treat the stated risks z as the risk value for the study are focusing on a very special case. It is only in the situation in which $\psi = \lambda = 0$, or equivalently ξ has an infinite weight, that the probability values stated in the study are taken at face value. The empirical estimates for the data considered in Viscusi and Evans (1998) indicate that $q \neq z$, so that the standard assumption that people take survey probabilities at face value can be rejected. Viscusi's (1989) prospective reference theory model makes a similar point with respect to various lottery experiments in the behavioral economics field. In this case, the small stated probabilities z are associated with behavioral q values that overestimate the risk z, while large probabilities z are associated with q values that underestimate the risk. This formulation also provides a useful framework for estimating the more general relationship between risk beliefs and objective measures of mortality risk that can be applied to survey data such as that in Lichtenstein et al. (1978) and subsequent work that has estimated this relationship.

While these results pertain to the divergence between behavioral probabilities and probabilities presented to respondents, perhaps if respondents are asked to indicate their posterior risk assessment then this probability would equal the behavioral probability. Let the stated probability correspond to the assessed probability $z^{\star}$ indicated by the respondent, not the probability z included in the survey text. A similar analysis to that for stated survey probabilities yields the result that the behavioral probabilities do not correspond to the assessed probabilities, or $z \neq z^{\star}$.

Figure 7.4 illustrates the relationship. For low assessed probabilities, the behavioral probability exceeds the assessed probability, while for large probabilities the opposite is the case. In addition, the probabilities may not sum to 1.0, as they may be below 1.0 as reported in Viscusi and Evans (1998) and above 1.0 in some instances as reported in Viscusi and Evans (2006).

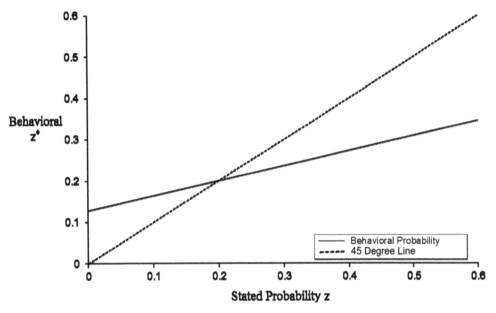

Figure 7.4 Relationship between behavioral and stated probabilities.

7.6 HEALTH-DEPENDENT UTILITY FUNCTIONS

7.6.1 The Structure of Utility Functions That Depend on Health Status

Individual well-being depends on one's health as well as income, goods, and personal activities. The assumption that utility functions are conditional on health status represents a simplification of a more general formulation in which health status enters the utility function directly. Thus, if there are n possible states of the world, expected utility EU is given by

$$EU = \sum_{j=1}^{n} p_j \, u(\text{health}_j, y_j) \tag{7.10}$$

defined across j health states with income y_j and health j in state j. Because we usually do not know how health status affects the utility function structure we instead use the health state-dependent formulation in which $u(\text{health}_j, y_j)$ is denoted $u_j(y_j)$. For the binary outcome case considered previously, $u(y)$ is the utility function of income y in the good health state, and $v(y)$ is the utility function in the ill health state. Although $v(y)$, and more generally $u_j(y)$, will continue to satisfy the general properties assumed above (i.e., $u_j' > 0, u_j'' \leq 0$), the shape of utility functions in different health states may vary in ways that affect the marginal utility of income as well as the overall utility level. How health status affects the structure of utility functions has a major influence on both the welfare effects of the health outcome as well as optimal levels of insurance.

One possibility is that the adverse health effect does not alter the structure of utility functions and is equivalent to a monetary loss l. Then in our binary outcome model, the utility function for the injured or ill health state is

$$v(y) = u(y - l). \tag{7.11}$$

In this instance, after the injury for any given income level y, the individual has a higher marginal utility of income than before the injury because the injury is equivalent to a drop in income. With this formulation, full insurance at actuarially fair rates is efficient. With that level of insurance, there is no difference in utility levels or the marginal utility of income across the two states.

If, however, the injury causes serious disability or death, it is likely to reduce the marginal utility of income so that $u'(y) > v'(y)$ for any given y. The plausibility of a reduction in the marginal utility of income after an injury is greater if medical expenses are covered by insurance or government programs so that the income amount is available for consumption purposes. If injuries reduce the marginal utility of income, the optimal level of insurance will not be the "make whole" amount that restores the person to the pre-injury level of welfare because money has diminished value. The intuition behind this result is reflected in the fact that few people provide bequests for which the anticipation of the bequest generates the same level of utility to them as they would have experienced had they been able to spend the money on personal consumption when alive.

7.6.2 Estimation of Utility Functions That Depend on Health Status

Efforts to resolve the effect of health status on the utility function have relied principally on the use of stated preference survey results. Viscusi and Evans (1990) utilize data drawn from a survey of chemical workers who were asked the pay increase that they required to work with different, possibly dangerous chemicals on the job. Thus, a worker with initial wage w for risk p_1 requires a wage $w(1+\delta)$ to be on the same constant expected utility locus EU when facing risk $p_2 > p_1$. The value of $w(1+\delta)$ exceeds the wage that would be predicted based on the rate of trade-off at point B along the market offer curve ABC in Figure 7.5. The survey provides information on two points B and D on EU shown in Figure 7.5, from which it is possible to estimate the state-dependent utility functions up to a positive linear transformation.[9]

Viscusi and Evans (1990) report two sets of results. Based on a first-order Taylor series approximation, the authors find that $u(y) - v(y) > 0$ so that workers prefer being healthy to being injured and $v'(y) < u'(y)$ so that injuries decrease the marginal utility of income. While this pattern of results was the case for three dangerous chemicals, such as

---

[9] With no loss of generality, the authors set $u'(y) = 1$.

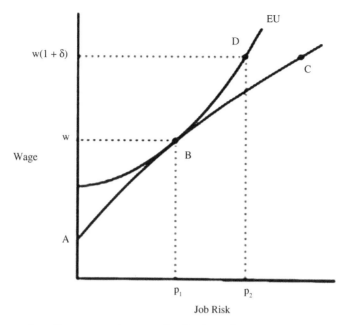

Figure 7.5 The market offer curve and expected utility locus for compensated risk changes.

asbestos, which is carcinogenic, there was one exception to the result that injuries lower the marginal utility of income. For the chemical chloroacetophenone, which is a chemical that causes only temporary irritation, the injury did not reduce the marginal utility of income. Given the temporary and minor nature of the injury, one would not have expected an effect on the structure of utility functions. A second estimation approach assuming logarithmic utility functions yielded similar results in terms of the utility levels and marginal utility in the two health states.

Knowledge of the structure of the utility functions provides much more information than the local wage-risk trade-offs used to compute VSL or, in this instance, the non-fatal analog which is the value of a statistical injury (VSI) at the initial risk-wage point. As the base risk level increases, the VSI rises. For nonincremental changes in risk, the VSI rises for large increases in risk and declines for large decreases in risk. This result is consistent with theoretical predictions that the trade-off rate embodied in the willingness to pay for risk decreases as the magnitude of the risk decrease becomes larger, with the opposite effect being observed for risk increases. Similarly, in a contingent valuation study by Gerking et al. (1988), the willingness-to-accept value for fatality risks had an associated VSL of $8.8 million ($1990) as compared to a willingness-to-pay estimate of VSL given by $3.4 million ($1990).

Estimates of utility functions also provide the empirical basis for ascertaining the income elasticity of the values people attach to reduce risks. The income elasticity of the VSI is around 1.0, with a value above 1.0 for the logarithmic utility case and a value below 1.0 for the Taylor's series case in Viscusi and Evans (1990).

A long-term concern in the literature has been how injuries affect the marginal utility of income and in turn influence the optimal income replacement amounts after an injury. If injuries lower the marginal utility of income, less than full earnings replacement by workers' compensation and similar insurance efforts will be desirable. Based on the utility function estimates, the optimal level of wage replacement 0.85 is substantial, but less than full insurance is desirable when injuries lower the marginal utility of income for the average job-related injury. This replacement rate is greater than the 0.64 average replacement rate that prevailed under U.S. workers' compensation programs at the time of the study, suggesting that benefit levels at the time were suboptimal. This result is corroborated based on the compensating differentials workers receive for higher levels of workers' compensation. The trade-off rate between wages and expected workers' compensation benefits estimated in Viscusi and Moore (1987) implied that the wage offset workers incurred exceeded the actuarial value of the workers' compensation coverage. Workers were willing to accept wage reductions in excess of the actuarial costs of the coverage. This result indicates that current benefits were suboptimal.

Utility functions for serious health outcomes were also the focus of the study by Sloan et al. (1998). Their contingent valuation study used a risk-risk comparison approach to value the effect of multiple sclerosis (MS) on utility. Severe health-related outcomes such as MS should reduce the marginal utility of income as most personal consumption activities are severely curtailed during advanced stages of MS. The survey consisted of two sample groups—patients who already had MS and healthy respondents for whom MS was a hypothetical disease for which they were asked questions based on the assumption that they contracted the disease. The survey provided respondents with detailed descriptions of the effects of MS. As expected, the estimates of the utility functions implied that respondents viewed MS as altering the structure of utility functions in a fundamental way. For the sample of healthy respondents, the perceived marginal utility of income was about an order of magnitude greater when the person is healthy than if they had MS. Interestingly, MS had a smaller effect on the marginal utility for people who had MS than for healthy respondents who were asked to envision the consequences of MS. For respondents in a sample that consisted of MS patients, the perceived marginal utility when healthy was only 50 percent greater than in the MS utility state. A comparison of this discrepancy to the greater marginal utility decline for people without MS suggests that people may have a tendency to overstate the health loss that will occur as the result of a serious disease. One reason for the possible overestimate of the utility loss is because healthy people may underestimate a person's ability to adapt to the adverse illness effects.

Minor health effects should not alter the marginal utility of income but should be tantamount to a monetary equivalent. Evans and Viscusi (1991a,b) considered the utility functions for minor consumer injuries from insecticide and toilet bowl cleaner, such as temporary hand burns. The general form of the utility functions estimated was

$$u(y) = \theta_i u(y - l_i) \qquad (7.12)$$

for injury type i, thus permitting the injury either to alter the marginal utility of income or to be equivalent to a monetary loss. As expected, the minor injuries had effects equivalent to a drop in income without altering the marginal utility by, for example, lowering θ_i in equation (7.12).[10]

The empirical results with respect to the effect of injuries on the structure of utility functions are mixed but are in no way inconsistent. Serious job-related injuries and illnesses reduce both the utility level and the marginal utility of income. Minor temporary injuries likewise reduce utility levels but are tantamount to monetary losses that do not reduce the ability to derive welfare-enhancing benefit from income. These effects are of broad policy significance as they affect the optimal insurance levels for these health effects that are provided through a variety of government policies such as workers' compensation and disability insurance.

Likewise, the pain and suffering awards provided as the result of tort awards in personal injury cases serve a potential insurance objective as well. Given this conceptualization, understanding how the injury has altered the structure of utility functions plays a fundamental role in ascertaining the optimal levels of pain and suffering compensation. If all injuries were tantamount to monetary losses, damages awards should be set at the "make whole" amount for efficient levels of insurance. But complete restoration of individual welfare levels will be quite expensive for catastrophic injuries such as paraplegia. Full compensation at the levels required to restore personal welfare to their pre-injury levels will exceed the insurance amount the victim would have chosen if permitted to purchase actuarially fair insurance before the injury.

To assess the pain and suffering component of health effects, researchers have sought to disentangle the valuations of the monetary and nonmonetary aspects of job injuries using the implications of wage equation estimates. Controlling for the income loss associated with job injuries makes it possible to isolate the valuation of the nonmonetary aspect of the injury. Viscusi and Moore (1987) found that the nonmonetary component of job injuries including pain and suffering as well as nonwork disability was $17,000 to $26,000 ($1977).

As with the job injury results, knowledge of the utility functions makes it possible to calculate the income elasticity of minor injuries associated with household chemicals. The income elasticity range of 0.17 to 0.38 estimated in Evans and Viscusi (1991b) is smaller than that estimated for serious job injuries.

[10] The empirical results indicated that the losses were tantamount to a monetary equivalent in seven of eight cases, with one result being a mixed case with both θ_i and l_i affected by the injury.

Other recent attempts to analyze dependence of utility functions on health states have utilized different empirical approaches than eliciting multiple risk-money combinations on a constant expected utility locus. Lillard and Weiss (1997) explore consumption profiles over time and find that the marginal utility of consumption in the healthy state exceeded that when ill. Such a result could occur either if sickness is equivalent to a loss of income or if the monetary costs of sickness are not borne by insurance, as they are in the workers' compensation case. Sojourner (2010) utilized statistical bounding techniques to explore the shape of worker indifference curves. Finkelstein et al. (2009, 2013) use variations in assessed personal happiness scores in response to health shocks to explore the effects on utility in different health states.

7.7 META-ANALYSES OF THE VALUE OF STATISTICAL LIFE

Several meta-analyses of the value of statistical life have sought to synthesize the implications of this line of research and to control for influences such as differences in empirical specifications across studies. These overview studies of the literature sometimes focus on evidence from the labor market, while others consider other market contexts, such as the housing market, as well as stated preference results. The review in Viscusi (1992, 1993) summarized the characteristics of the studies and the results of labor market analyses, evidence from other markets, and stated preference results. For example, this review documented how the VSL in labor market studies varies with the inclusion of a nonfatal risk variable in the analysis, the income level of the sample, and whether a workers' compensation variable is included. Many government agencies have used the sample and the results of this study in setting their VSL for valuing the risk reduction benefits of health, safety, and environmental regulations.[11]

More recent meta-analyses have included regressions in which the dependent variable is the VSL, which in turn is a function of the characteristics of the study, such as the variables included in the analysis, the risk levels being analyzed, and the econometric specification. Among the key differences across the studies are the selection of which studies are included in the analysis, whether the studies included must be published in peer reviewed outlets, whether the study includes all regressions reported in the study or only the authors' "best estimate," and whether there are any adjustments being made to the VSL because of tax rates or because the meta-analysis author made subjective adjustments for other reasons. Generally, such "adjustments" are best done by including

---

[11] The Viscusi (1993) article was based on an earlier report by the author to the Federal Aviation Administration, U.S. Department of Transportation. The estimates have also been used by the EPA in setting benefit levels for health risk reductions from environmental regulations. Among the EPA regulatory impact studies that cite Viscusi (1992,1993) are the 1996 proposed particulate matter national ambient air quality standard, the 1998 NOx SIP analysis, the 1999 regional haze rule, the 1999 Tier 2 sulfur control requirements, the 2000 Tier 2 motor vehicle emissions standards, the 2004 stationary internal combustion engine standard, and the 2004 nonroad diesel engine standard.

specific variables in the model to account for such differences. In situations in which multiple observations are included from the same study, it should be noted that these estimates are not independent VSL estimates. There is often an imbalance in the number of observations included in a particular study. For example, Viscusi (2004) reports 80 VSL estimates for different specifications so that including all these specifications gives substantial weight to that particular sample. Another difference across the different types of meta-analyses is that some meta-analyses focus not on VSL generally but on values pertinent to particular kinds of accidents such as road safety (de Blaeij et al., 2003).

The set of variables analyzed in the meta-analyses varies across studies, but there are many common concerns. Chief among these recurring issues is a set of variables characterizing the nature of the fatality risk variable used in the study. What is the magnitude of the fatality rate faced by the average worker in the sample? Is the reference population for the risk measure derived from industry averages or occupational averages? Did the study utilize a risk measure drawn from insurance data, employer accident reports, or workers' compensation data? The choices made with respect to the fatality rate variable affect the measurement error of the variable as well as the influence of possible selection effects if, for example, the sample is dominated by workers in very dangerous jobs.

Other than a common concern with the fatality rate variable, the scope and focus of the meta-analysis studies differ considerably. Liu et al. (1997) analyzed 17 wage-risk studies from Viscusi (1993), focusing primarily on the effect on the estimated VSL of income and the nature of the risk variable. Miller (2000) utilized an international sample of 60 studies of risk-money trade-offs involving wages, product prices, and contingent valuations studies. His study has a similar emphasis to that of Liu et al. (1997), along with an accounting for whether the study included occupation dummy variables. Bowland and Beghin's (2001) meta-analysis utilized 33 labor market and contingent valuation studies reported in Viscusi (1993) and Desvousges et al. (1995). They added additional variables such as union status and whether the data set used for the analysis was a blue-collar sample. Mrozek and Taylor (2002) used a sample of 203 observations including multiple observations from 33 wage-risk studies, resulting in 21 observations from one U.K. study, 28 observations from an unpublished Canadian consulting report, and a total of seven studies accounting for 10 or more observations. Mrozek and Taylor (2002) also included in their regression an extensive set of control variables, such as nonlinear risk variables and whether the study included a workers' compensation variable. Viscusi and Aldy (2003) updated and expanded the Viscusi (1993) labor market sample to have 49 published, peer-reviewed labor market VSL estimates. They replicated all the specifications used in the previous meta-analyses listed above, thus making it possible to distinguish the different implications of the meta-analyses based on the econometric specification rather than the studies in the sample. The Viscusi and Aldy (2003) meta-analysis also presented additional results based on sample characteristics including various job characteristic and regional variables. The estimates included robust and clustered standard errors, where the clustering is by wage data source, thus recognizing the lack of independence of the different estimates and the effect of multiple VSL estimates on the estimated standard errors.

Which adjustments should be taken into account when assessing an average VSL is not always clearcut. For example, it might be desirable to control for differences across industries, thus recognizing the difference in working conditions and job tasks across industries. However, if the worker fatality rate is matched to the workers in the sample based on their industry, then a complete set of industry controls that matches the level of aggregation used in the fatality rate data will eliminate the effect of the fatality risk variable. Such effects contribute to some of the differences across studies when the industry variables are included. The lower VSL estimates generated by Mrozek and Taylor (2002) as compared to those in Viscusi and Aldy (2003) are due in large part to the influence of the industry dummy variable set.[12] The studies in Mrozek and Taylor's (2002) sample that include a small set of industry dummy variables generate a VSL more similar to that in Viscusi and Aldy (2003). The Viscusi and Aldy (2003) meta-analysis generated a mean predicted VSL ($2000) ranging from $5.5 million to $7.6 million for the U.S. sample, and $5.0 million to $6.2 million including estimates from other countries as well where the ranges arise from using different specifications in the various meta-analyses.

A principal focus of these meta-analyses has been on the income elasticity of the VSL. It is instructive to compare the reported elasticity in the authors' meta-analyses with those that are obtained using a consistent sample in order to assess whether the difference in estimates derives from the variables included or the sample of studies analyzed. Here I report the authors' estimates followed by the replication of the study in Viscusi and Aldy (2003), where these estimates are in parentheses. The estimated income elasticities of VSL are 0.53 (0.51) based on Liu et al. (1997), 0.89 (0.53) based on Miller (2000), 0.46 (0.52) based on Mrozek and Taylor's Model 2 (2002), and 1.66 (0.61) based on Bowland and Beghin's (2001) linear model. As these comparisons indicate, the substantial variation in the estimated income elasticities of VSL is reduced if the studies utilize a consistent sample. Similarly, the income elasticity estimates reported by Viscusi and Aldy (2003) for six of their own specifications range from 0.46 to 0.60.

As the literature has evolved over time, there has also been a change in the estimation approach. Kochi et al. (2006) update the Viscusi (1992) sample and also include multiple observations from the studies, yielding a sample of 197 VSL estimates drawn from 40 studies. They find that using the empirical Bayes approach reduces the VSL variability, which has a mean of $5.4 million and a standard deviation of $2.4 million, in $2000. Bellavance et al. (2009) utilize a sample of 39 observations from 37 studies drawn from

---

[12] As discussed in Viscusi (2009b), there are additional differences in the studies as well, particularly in the treatment of the various eras of risk data.

nine countries. Using a mixed effects regression model, they conclude that much of the source of variability in the VSL studies can be traced to differences in the studies' econometric methodologies. Doucouliagos et al. (2012a) seek to control for publication selection effects and find that doing so lowers the estimated VSL.

7.8 VSL ESTIMATES USING CFOI DATA

7.8.1 Wage Equation Estimates Using Different CFOI Risk Measures

An alternative to expanding the sample or altering the estimation approach is to focus on a subset of the labor market studies using better and more accurate fatality risk data, thus avoiding the measurement error that served as the focus of the analyses in Black and Kniesner (2003) and Moore and Viscusi (1988a). Since the studies included in the meta-analyses discussed above were completed, the U.S. Bureau of Labor Statistics has compiled a detailed Census of Fatal Occupational Injuries, which provides information for every U.S. work-related fatality. Unlike some previous data series, the CFOI is not based on voluntary reporting by firms or a sample of the working population. Rather, it is a complete census of every occupational fatality. The BLS verifies the fatality and the job-relatedness of the death using data from multiple sources. The first policy-related article to advocate the use of CFOI estimates rather than a meta-analysis approach was that of Robinson (2008), who suggested the use of the estimates in Viscusi (2004) as the single best estimate to use in valuing homeland security policies. Since that time, the U.S. Department of Transportation (2013) has adopted the VSL estimates using the CFOI data as the agency-wide guidance.

While the hedonic labor market literature using the CFOI data is not as extensive as the earlier VSL literature using less refined risk measures, in many respects the studies are more comprehensive. In addition to providing an average estimate of the VSL across the labor force that is not subject to the same degree of measurement error as previous studies, the issues being addressed are much more refined in terms of isolating differences in the VSL across the population as well as addressing a variety of outstanding econometric issues.

Table 7.1 summarizes the results of all hedonic labor market estimates of the VSL using the CFOI data. The studies differ in terms of their substantive focus. In some instances, the main matter of concern is simply with respect to how the magnitude of the VSL estimate is affected by using more accurate fatality rate data. That is the emphasis of Viscusi (2004), who used three different CFOI fatality rate measures—industry, occupation, and industry-occupation. Due to greater measurement error in the worker's reported occupation than in the worker's reported industry, the industry measures based on 72 industry categories, and the 720 industry-occupation measures based on only 10 broad occupation groups combined with 72 industries, were preferable to the more detailed occupation-based measures. The study also employed six-year averages of the

Table 7.1 Labor Market VSL Estimates Using the Census of Fatal Occupational Injuries (CFOI) Data*

Study	CFOI Measure	Worker Sample	Representative VSL Estimates ($millions)
Viscusi (2003)	Industry-race, 6-year average	CPS (1997) 20 equations	21.5 white (full sample) 10.3 blacks (full sample)
Leeth and Ruser (2003)	Occupation-gender-race, 3-year average	CPS (1996–1998) 28 equations	6.0 (risks by occupation, men)
Viscusi (2004)	Industry, Occupation, Industry-occupation annual and 6-year averages	CPS (1997) 80 equations	6.7 (full sample) 10.0 (blue-collar males) 12.2 (blue-collar females)
Kniesner and Viscusi (2005)	Industry-occupation, 6-year average	CPS (1997) 6 equations	6.7 (full sample) 6.9 (male sample)
Kniesner et al. (2006)	Industry-occupation	PSID (1997) 10 equations	12.8 (base case with industry controls)
Viscusi and Aldy (2007)	Industry-age, 6-year average	CPS (1998) 20 equations	7.8 (age 55–62) to 16.4 (age 35–44)
Viscusi and Hersch (2008)	Industry-age-gender, 6-year average	CPS (1996) 4 equations	9.8 (nonsmokers) 9.7 (smokers)
Aldy and Viscusi (2008)	Industry-age	CPS (1993–2000) 8 equations	6.4 (full sample) 5.0 (age 18–24) 12.8 (age 35–44) 4.6 (age 55–62)
Kniesner et al. (2010)	Industry-occupation	PSID (1993–2001) 5 quantile equations	9.8 (median)
Evans and Schaur (2010)	Industry-age	HRS (1994–1998) 5 quantile equations, 1 OLS equation	20.7 (mean for 50 year olds)
Hersch and Viscusi (2010a)	Industry-occupation-age-immigrant status, 3-year average	New Immigrant Survey (2003); CPS (2003) 22 equations	11.0 (native U.S.), 6.6 (immigrants)
Kochi and Taylor (2011)	Accident or homicide by MSA for drivers	CPS (1996–2002) 13 equations	6.1–8.4 range
Scotton and Taylor (2011)	Industry-occupation, 6-year average	CPS (1996–1998) 9 equations	12.3 (undifferentiated deaths)
Kniesner et al. (2012)	Industry-occupation, annual and 3-year averages	PSID (1993–2001) 59 equations	11.4 (static first differences)
Kniesner et al. (2014)	Industry-occupation, annual and 3-year averages	PSID (1993–2001) 40 equations	13.0 (first difference for job changers, 3-year average risk)

All VSL estimates are in year 2012 dollars.

*Notes: CPS is Current Population Survey, and PSID is the Panel Study of Income Dynamics.

CFOI risk measures, reducing measurement error arising from year to year fluctuations in risk levels and decreasing the number of cells with zero risk levels. The 80 equations included in Viscusi (2004) spanned a comprehensive set of wage equations for different samples and with different sets of other job risk variables, such as the nonfatal injury rate and expected workers' compensation benefits.

Several studies have focused on variations in VSL for different discrete population groups defined based on race, gender, smoking status, and relative economic position. These studies have constructed fatality rate measures based on industry-race, industry-race-gender, occupation-race-gender, industry-age-gender, and industry-occupation. Workers who reported race as black have lower estimated VSL levels than those who reported race as white, as found in Viscusi (2003). Leeth and Ruser (2003) consider a variety of labor market groups and group-specific risk measures and only find significant compensation for fatality risks for white males and Hispanic males. Their risk measures were based on occupation rather than industry so that the potentially greater measurement error in occupational classifications than in industry classifications may have influenced their results. Perhaps because women are less likely to be killed on the job, gender differences in Leeth and Ruser (2003) proved to be difficult to estimate, but the VSL estimates for men and women are similar in Viscusi and Hersch (2008). In addition, Leeth and Ruser (2003) found large nonfatal risk premiums for women, which were over three times greater than for men. These results are consistent with the findings by Hersch (1998) that women experience frequent job injuries and receive significant compensating wage differentials, as do men.

The VSL for smokers and nonsmokers in Viscusi and Hersch (2008) were similar so that the differences in compensating differentials for nonfatal injury valuations that were found in Viscusi and Hersch (2001) were not apparent for fatalities. The smoker-specific VSL estimates provide a basis for calculating the private mortality costs of smoking which are on the order of $100–$200 per pack for men and women at a 3% discount rate, but are about an order of magnitude less than this amount using smokers' discount rates for remaining years of life (Scharff and Viscusi, 2011). Following the same general methodology, Cobacho Tornel et al. (2010) have developed mortality cost estimates of cigarettes smoking in Spain.

The most refined CFOI measure that has been used in these studies was conditional on immigrant status as well as industry-occupation-age, making it possible to estimate the VSL for risks specific to immigrant workers. Hersch and Viscusi (2010a) found that immigrants overall have a similar VSL to that of native workers, but Mexican immigrants and especially those who do not speak English have lower levels of compensation for risk.

Overall, the utilization of the potential refinements made possible by CFOI data has broadened our understanding of labor market performance and how different groups value risks. The VSL estimates across different demographic groups yield some striking comparative VSL levels. Workers who are black receive smaller compensating differentials than workers who are white despite facing greater fatality risks. Similarly, immigrant Mexican workers, and especially those who do not speak English, face higher fatality risks than native U.S. workers but receive lower hazard pay. These results, which take into account demographic differences in refined fatality rate measures and estimated levels of VSL, indicate that these different pairs of workers are noncompeting labor market groups. Consistent with the segmented market hedonic labor market theory of Viscusi and Hersch (2001), the market offer curves for workers who are black are lower and flatter than the curves for workers who are white, with similar differences being evident for workers who are Mexican immigrants as compared to native U.S. workers.

The greater refinement of the CFOI data also has facilitated estimation of wage premiums for more specialized studies. Kochi and Taylor (2011) estimated the wage premiums and associated VSL for the homicide risk incurred by taxicab drivers using a risk measure that accounted for the cause of death as well as the occupation. Kniesner and Viscusi (2005) explored the possibility that compensating differentials were influenced by relative economic position, but found no such relative position effect.

Refined CFOI data have also made possible more detailed econometric estimates of VSL that were not as feasible with the previously available, coarser measures. The quantile estimates of VSL in Kniesner et al. (2010) utilize industry-occupation risk measures that recognize the differences in the types of jobs and associated risks across the wage distribution. Their estimates indicate a substantial degree of heterogeneity in the VSL, with workers at the 90th percentile of the wage distribution having a VSL in excess of $20 million. Similarly, Evans and Schaur (2010) use fatality rates by industry-age and find very wide variation in the VSL across the labor force using quantile regression models, with a mean estimate of $14.7 million.

7.8.2 Use of CFOI Data in Panel Data Studies

The possibility of being able to construct precise risk measures by industry and occupation enabled Kniesner et al. (2012) to estimate the VSL exploiting the capabilities of panel data. The only previous panel data estimates using U.S. data were by Brown (1980) and relied on a cross-sectional risk measure. As a result, changes in risk levels over time were not included, leading to no risk variation for any worker who did not change jobs. The use of CFOI data on industry-occupation risks by year also facilitates the estimation of the VSL as well as isolating the principal labor market situations in which compensating differentials are generated. Most of the observed premiums for fatality rates are for workers who switched jobs. The within job variation in risk levels over time is not great, and much of this variation is due to statistical noise. Similarly, there is little evidence of compensating differentials for the within job sample as compared to job changes.

For the semilogarithmic wage equation, the first difference model for fatality risks takes the form for worker i in industry j, occupation k, and time t given by

$$\Delta \ln w_{ijkt} = \gamma \Delta p_{jkt} + \Delta X_{ijkt} \beta + \Delta \varepsilon_{ijkt}, \qquad (7.13)$$

where Δ is the first-difference operator. These estimates, which eliminate time-invariant effects, yield a VSL of $8.8 million when the fatality rate is calculated based on average hours and a 3-year average fatality rate, and $6.6 million based on annual fatality rates. The difference-in-difference version of the model takes the form

$$\Delta^2 \ln w_{ijkt} = \gamma \Delta p_{jkt} + \Delta^2 X_{ijkt} \beta + \Delta^2 \varepsilon_{ijkt}, \qquad (7.14)$$

where Δ^2 is the difference-in-difference operator $\Delta^2 = \Delta_t - \Delta_{t-1}$. The difference-in-difference VSL estimates control for differences in wage growth, not just wage levels, and yield a VSL of $13 million, but only $7.8 million using annual fatality rates.

By means of these and other specifications made possible through the use of CFOI risk data, it has been possible to address many of the long-standing issues in the hedonic wage literature. These include, among others, the role of worker heterogeneity and the endogeneity of the risk variable.

7.9 VSL ESTIMATES IN OTHER CHOICE CONTEXTS

Other situations in which risk-money trade-offs are estimated include hedonic price studies that are the product market analogs of the hedonic wage studies and assessments of the discrete decisions to buy safety-related products from which either a wage-risk trade-off or a lower bound on the VSL can be inferred, depending on the econometric structure of the analysis. Many of these studies have been of durable goods so that the temporal stream of risk effects enters the assessment, making the analysis less direct than labor market studies of within period wages and acute risks of death.

The first price studies involved housing prices, which consistent with economic theory are negatively related to adverse risk conditions. These price effects in turn have yielded estimates of the VSL. Mortality risks from air pollution reduced property values in Pennsylvania (Portney, 1981), yielding a VSL of $0.8 million ($1990). Similarly, the cancer risks from hazardous waste sites in the Great Grand Rapids, Michigan area, and publicity regarding these risks lowers housing prices. The VSL levels on the order of $3.2 million to $3.7 million ($2000) for cancer risks are similar to those in labor market studies (Hamilton and Viscusi, 1999; Gayer et al., 2000, 2002) after adjusting for the latency period associated with the risk.

There is also a substantial literature on the effect of automobile safety on automobiles. Safer cars command a higher price in the new car market, generating a VSL of $4.0 million ($1990) based on the estimates by Atkinson and Halvorsen (1990). The safety of the vehicle also is a principal determinant of the price of used cars (Dreyfus and Viscusi, 1995), as safer used cars command a higher price controlling for other attributes, implying a VSL range of $3.8–$5.4 million ($2000).

People reveal their implicit VSL levels through a variety of personal safety-related behaviors, which in turn have yielded estimates of the implicit VSL. The decision to buckle a seatbelt involves a trade-off between risk and the time involved in buckling, generating a VSL of $1.2 million ($1990) in Blomquist (1979) and a $1.9 million to $8.4 million range ($1998) in Hakes and Viscusi (2007). The set of transportation-related safety measures as embodied in seatbelts, car seats for infants, and motorcycle helmets have an associated VSL amount in the $1.7–$9.9 million range in the study by Blomquist et al. (1996). Studies in the same vein have found a VSL of $2.0 million ($1990) by Garbacz (1989) for the purchase of smoke detectors, $0.7 million ($1990) for responses to cigarette risk information by smokers in Ippolito and Ippolito (1984), $0.84 million ($2000) for purchase of car seats and buckling of children in those seats in Carlin and Sandy (1991), and values implied by bicycle helmet purchases of $1.4–$2.9 million for children age 5–9, $1.2–$2.8 million ($2000) for children age 10–14, and $2.1–$4.3 million for adults age 20–59 in the study by Jenkins et al. (2001). Broder (1990) found a peak stock market response of $50 million per fatality for accidental deaths such as airplane crashes and factory explosions.

It is also possible to estimate the VSL based on drivers' responses to changes in speed limits. In 1987, many states raised their speed limits on rural interstate roads from 55 mph to 65 mph. The faster driving that resulted from the increased speed limit reduced driving time but increased the fatality rate. Ashenfelter and Greenstone (2004) valued the reduction in the amount of driving time based on the average hourly wage rate. The trade-off rate between the value of time and fatality rates implied a VSL from $1 million to $10 million, with a value of $1.54 million ($1997) based on their preferred specification.

7.10 AGE, LIFE-CYCLE EFFECTS, AND THE VALUE OF A STATISTICAL LIFE YEAR (VSLY)

7.10.1 The VSL for Children

The analyses of age variations in the VSL generally focus on economic situations in which people are making choices on behalf of themselves. Thus, the situations are those in which there are market contexts in which the individual is making a decision that affects his or her risk of death. A notable exception to this situation is that involving children. Since children generally don't make decisions for themselves that affect their risk of death, economists have analyzed decisions on behalf of children made by parents and other adults. In some cases these are actual choices, as in the case of purchase of bicycle helmets, while in other cases the choices are hypothetical choices expressed in a stated preference survey.

The stated preference studies of the VSL for children by researchers such as Hammitt and Haninger (2010) and Blomquist et al. (2011) indicate that these valuations can be substantial, possibly even greater than the value the adults place on their own lives. The stated preference survey by Hammitt and Haninger (2010) focused on fatal disease risks from pesticide residues on produce and found that risks to the lives of children were valued twice as highly as risks to adults and had an associated VSL of $12 million to $15 million. Similarly, Blomquist et al. (2011) found that the valuation of reduced risks of asthma exhibited a peak value of VSL for young children that declined thereafter. Interestingly, these results also exhibited a nonmonotonic pattern over the life cycle.

7.10.2 The VSL over the Life Cycle

A substantial theoretical literature has analyzed the age variation in the VSL. Some models generate results consistent with greater expected future lifetime being more highly valued than less. Thus, with utility functions that are not dependent on age and total remaining lifetime being the key determinant of lifetime utility levels, the VSL peaks at birth and steadily diminishes. Models that generate the prediction that VSL steadily declines with age make the unrealistic assumption that capital markets and insurance markets are perfect and that you can draw on your lifetime resources without any moral hazard concerns. Under more realistic financial market assumptions with imperfect capital markets, models such as that of Shepard and Zeckhauser (1984) predict an inverted-U shaped pattern in which the VSL rises and then subsequently falls over the life cycle. Alternatively, models such as that of Rosen (1988) show that the VSL may increase with age.

Recognition of capital market imperfections is but one of many aspects of events over one's lifetime that may affect the VSL. Education, health status, marital status, the presence of children, and similar factors all may enter. Income and consumption levels vary over the life cycle, and one would expect spending on risk reduction to vary as well. Indeed, the theoretical model by Johansson (1996) focuses on the consumption-VSL relationship as being a principal determinant of the age-VSL relationship. A substantial literature has documented an empirical income-VSL linkage and a consumption-VSL linkage. To the extent that there is a life-cycle income trajectory and life-cycle consumption trajectory, each of which has an inverted-U shape, one would also expect there to be a similar relationship for VSL. Such a pattern also mirrors the predictions of theoretical models with imperfect capital markets.

Two principal sources of data have been used to analyze age variations in VSL—labor market evidence and stated preference studies. The implications of the stated preference studies tend to be mixed, as surveyed in Krupnick (2007). For example, there is some weak evidence based on Canadian survey data that the VSL declines with age for the very oldest respondents (Alberini et al., 2004; Krupnick et al., 2002).

The labor market evidence displays a more specific age-related pattern, but the shape of this age-VSL relationship varies with the era of fatality rate data that is used. The early labor market analyses were constrained by the available fatality rate data, which until recently could not be constructed to reflect age-specific risks. As a result, the studies generally imposed a rigid structure on the age-VSL relationship. However, the post-CFOI analyses make refinements in VSL-age relationship possible and will be the focus of the discussion below. The stated preference studies of age variations in VSL have an advantage over early labor market studies in that they can provide respondents with age-specific risk information so that the estimated VSL magnitudes do not confound differences in valuation and differences in risk.

The availability of the CFOI data has resulted in substantial advances in our understanding of VSL over the life cycle. Before the advent of the CFOI data, risk measures by industry assigned the same risk to all workers in an industry. As workers age, their occupation within an industry may change. In addition, the risk to the worker for any given job may be age-related. Older workers may be more experienced and exercise greater care, but they also may be more vulnerable to injury and death given that an accident has occurred.

There is an extensive literature that explored age-related variations in VSL without accounting for differences in risk because such data were not available. These include Moore and Viscusi (1988b, 1990a,b) and Viscusi and Moore (1989). Typically, such studies were based on the assumption that each year of life or each discounted life year had the same value because more refined estimates were not feasible. Imposition of this assumption leads to a declining VSL with age. The studies also yielded estimates of the implicit discount rate with respect to years of life, which were similar to prevailing market rates of interest.

As a result of the advent of the CFOI data, there has been an increase in interest in the age-VSL relationship as well as in the underlying pattern of age-related difference in fatality rates. Numerous studies have been concerned with VSL estimates over the life cycle, and these have utilized fatality rate measures by industry-occupation and industry-age. All of these studies have found an inverted U-shaped relation of VSL with respect to age, as will be discussed further in Section 7.10. In particular, the VSL tracks the life-cycle pattern of income and consumption, as shown in Kniesner et al. (2006). The VSL rises and then declines with age both overall (Viscusi and Aldy, 2007), conditional on smoking status (Viscusi and Hersch, 2008), and controlling for cohort effects (Aldy and Viscusi, 2008).

For analyses of labor market decisions involving risk to be instructive, there must be some risks that workers of different ages take. If, for example, only workers who are very young work on risky jobs, then no wage-risk trade-offs would be observed for older workers. However, the stylized view of all workplace fatalities being concentrated among young workers in very risky jobs is not borne out. Using age-specific mortality rates by worker industry constructed based on the CFOI data, Viscusi and Aldy (2007) show that, perhaps somewhat surprisingly, the fatality rate in most industries tends to exhibit an upward trend with respect to age. The fatality rate per 100,000 workers for different age groups in construction is 10.47 for ages 20–24 and 15.06 for ages 55–62, in manufacturing the rates are 3.00 for ages 20–24 and 4.83 for ages 55–64, in transportation the rates are 6.85 for ages 20–24 and 14.42 for ages 55–62, and with similar difference for other industry groups such as wholesale trade, retail trade, the financial industry, and services. The most common type of job-related fatality is due to a transportation accident, so it is not necessary for older workers to be assigned to the most demanding physical jobs to experience job injuries. Usage of various motor vehicles in job contexts creates a substantial risk of death.

Over the past several decades, there have been several levels of labor market analyses of the age-VSL relationship (Aldy and Viscusi, 2007). Most of the historical literature has used risk measures by industry or, in some cases, by occupation. Only a small group of recent studies have utilized fatality rates specific to different age groups. As a result, the previous literature confounds the influence of differences in the level of risk faced at different ages with the effect of differences in risk preferences at different ages. To make clear what effects each study is capturing, I indicate below whether the study incorporates CFOI risk measures by age group.

At the most basic level, authors have included an age-fatality rate interaction term and, in some cases, also a quadratic age term interacted with risk. A series of analyses undertaking this approach was the initial approach in the literature and has been incorporated in numerous studies. The review by Viscusi and Aldy (2003) of 11 sets of estimates of the age-risk interaction effect indicated that the age-fatality risk trade-off was either negative or not statistically significant. Thus, these results were consistent with the highly stylized theoretical models in which VSL always decreases with age. These estimates were not based on age-specific fatality rates and did not permit the shape of the age dependency of VSL to be as flexible as in some of the more recent studies. Even within this literature, questions began to be raised about whether VSL did in fact decline with age. In a study focusing on older workers, Smith et al. (2004) did not find the steady declining pattern that previous studies had imposed through their econometric specifications.

A variant on this approach is to analyze the age-fatality risk trade-off rate for different age groups without making the assumption that the age risk levels for an industry or occupation have a constant value independent of age. Thus, in the case of Viscusi and Aldy (2007) and Aldy and Viscusi (2008), the authors used CFOI fatality rates by industry and for the following five age groups: 18–24, 25–34, 35–44, 45–54, and 55–62. With this formulation, the coefficients for the fatality rate, nonfatal injury rate, and the workers' compensation variable are all permitted to vary with the age group.

Use of the age-specific industry risk measures has led to an inverted-U pattern in several different analyses. In Viscusi and Aldy (2007), the VSL rises over time, peaking for

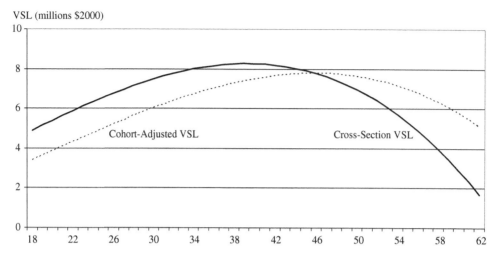

Figure 7.6 Cohort-adjusted and cross-section value of statistical life, 1993–2000 Aldy and Viscusi (2008).

the middle age group. The estimates in Aldy and Viscusi (2008) use a series of Current Population Survey (CPS) samples and control for cohort effects. As shown in Figure 7.6, the VSL for the cohort-adjusted results rises, reaching a peak around age 50 and declining thereafter. The inverted-U aspect of the pattern is not symmetric, as the VSL rises more steeply than the subsequent decline following the peak.

Recognition of the theoretical relationship between consumption and the life-cycle pattern of VSL leads to an inverted-U shaped relationship. Kniesner et al. (2006) find that the overall shape of the age-VSL relationship is closely patterned after the age-consumption relationship. They find that the VSL peaks in the 45–54 age group and does not drop off steeply on either side of the peak. The VSL for the most senior age group in the analysis is similar to the average VSL across the sample.

If each year of life has the same value, then an appropriate formulation is to analyze the discounted expected value of the life years at risk. This approach is a quantity-adjusted value of life analysis that was introduced in Moore and Viscusi (1988b). The econometric procedure yields both an estimate of the discount rate that workers apply to the value of each life year as well as the value of each life year. Studies using this approach constitute a separate literature that will be examined in greater detail later in this section.

A more complex type of model for incorporating quantity of life adjustments utilizes a structural hedonic model that reflects the utility maximization decision. A series of papers by Moore and Viscusi (1990a,b) and Viscusi and Moore (1989) estimate a variety of such models of discounted expected utility maximization over the life cycle.

7.10.3 The Value of a Statistical Life Year

Estimates of the VSL by age have also generated interest in the value of a statistical life year (VSLY) and how this value varies with age. The starting point for such analyses, as reflected in the review by Hammitt (2007), is the quantity-adjusted value of life formulation in Moore and Viscusi (1988b). Although their model is in continuous time, it has a direct discrete time analog. Let r be the rate of interest and L be the life expectancy. Then one can write the VSL in terms of the discounted value of the remaining years of life, given by the value of an infinite life minus the value of life years after one's life expectancy, or

$$VSL = \frac{VSLY}{r} - \frac{1}{(1+r)^L}\left[\frac{VSLY}{r}\right]. \tag{7.15}$$

This equation can be rewritten as

$$VSLY = \frac{rVSL}{[1-(1+r)^{-L}]}. \tag{7.16}$$

The implicit rate of discount with respect to years of life is one of the parameter estimates in the reduced form discounting model of Moore and Viscusi (1988b), who estimated an implicit rate of discount with respect to years of life to be 9.6–12.2%. Using various structural models in Viscusi and Moore (1989) and Moore and Viscusi (1990a,b), they estimate discount rates ranging from 1.0–14.2%. A similar approach can be used to estimate the implicit discount rate that purchasers of used cars have with respect to the mortality risks of cars. Using a hedonic price model that incorporated the discounted expected years of life lost due to risk from various cars, Dreyfus and Viscusi (1995) estimated a discounted range for years of life ranging from 11–17%.

These estimates imposed the constraint that the VSLY did not vary over the life cycle. Two more recent studies permit estimation of VSLY variations with age, making it possible to examine whether each year of life is valued identically. Using CFOI fatality measures incorporating variations in industry risks by age group, Aldy and Viscusi (2008) find that one can reject the hypothesis that the VSLY is time-invariant. In the late teens, the estimated VSLY is $125,000, after which it rises to a peak of $400,000 at age 54, and then declines to $350,000 at age 62. The VSLY peaks at a later age than does the VSL. The modest decline in VSLY is consistent with consumption patterns over the life cycle and also accounts for why the estimated VSL does not drop steeply with age.

In a comparison of the VSL and VSLY for smokers and nonsmokers at different ages using risk measures that account for age, Viscusi and Hersch (2008) found that VSLY amounts were similar for smokers and nonsmokers. Across the population, VSLY levels remained very high for older age groups. Even though smokers will tend to have poorer health than nonsmokers, there is remarkable similarity in the VSLY values for smokers and nonsmokers.

The implications of the age variations in VSL have two broader ramifications for valuing health risks. First, the search for a constant value per life year oversimplifies the pattern of valuations in risk valuations over the life cycle. Second, the common use of quality-adjusted life years to value health may not be warranted. Although health status generally declines with age and is worse for smokers than nonsmokers, the pattern of VSLY is quite different from what one would observe if all healthy years of life had the same value, and adjustments for declines in health status necessarily lowered this average value. The quantity and quality of life clearly matter, but they do so within the broader context of consumption over the life cycle.

Analysis of the role of discounted values of statistical lives also illuminates some fundamental differences in preferences that contribute to the different risks people are willing to incur. Viscusi and Moore (1989) found that the rate of time preference with respect to years of life decreased with the person's level of education, which is consistent with higher educated people being more forward looking. Such a difference is expected if lower discount rates lead a person to be more willing to invest in education. In Scharff and Viscusi (2011), smokers have a 14% rate of discount, which is significantly higher than that of nonsmokers. This greater discount rate may account for the smokers' greater present orientation than that of nonsmokers, in that smoking shortens individuals' expected lifetimes.

7.10.4 The Senior Discount Controversy

The utilization of age adjustments in policy analyses has generated substantial controversy. In 2003, the U.S. Environmental Protection Agency (EPA) assessed the benefits associated with its Clear Skies air pollution regulation using a lower VSL for those over age 65. This differential was potentially influential since there is substantial heterogeneity in the health effects of air pollution across the population. The U.S. EPA (2002, 2003) estimated that there would be three times as many fatalities prevented in the age 65 and over population as in the adult population aged 18 to 64. Whereas EPA used a VSL of $6.1 million for those aged 18 to 64, it reduced the VSL by 37% for those adults 65 and over based on the age adjustments implied by stated preference evidence for traffic safety by Jones-Lee et al. (1985) in the U.K. The senior discount adjustment led to a VSL for the benefits analysis of $3.8 million. Because of the concentration of the mortality risks in the older population, this "senior discount" consequently had a significant effect on the benefit values. The application of some form of a senior discount was not unprecedented as the European Commission (2001) recommends that the VSL decline with age, and Canada has used a VSL for older people that is 25% lower (Hara Associates, 2000).

Nevertheless, the EPA's use of a senior discount generated substantial controversy. Senior citizen groups waged protests against the "senior death discount."[13] While one can question the applicability of stated preference evidence from a different country to the U.S., it is likely that any downward age adjustment would have created controversy, however it was based. Notably, in labor market studies the age-VSL relationship eventually turns down but is relatively flat so that the VSL for those over the age of 60 remains above the population average. Application of the age-adjusted VSL estimates to the Clear Skies initiative benefits by Kniesner et al. (2006) indicates that application of their age-adjusted VSL estimates leads to a slightly higher total benefits estimate rather than a lower value. The controversy associated with age adjustments may exceed the practical importance of such adjustments depending on the policy context.

7.11 HETEROGENEITY OF ESTIMATES FOR OTHER LABOR MARKET GROUPS: INCOME, GENDER, AND UNIONS

Because the VSL is not a universal constant but varies with individual preferences, there has been a considerable focus on how the VSL varies with personal characteristics. It is instructive to begin with the influence of income, which along with the average VSL estimates themselves has played a central role in applications of VSL in policy contexts. The importance of VSL variations with income is also due to its role as the driving economic relationship in risk-risk analyses, which seek to ascertain the level of expenditures on risk reduction that will have the unintended effect of making society riskier because of the impact on health of the income loss associated with these expenditures.

Boosting one's income by earning compensating differentials for job risks is less attractive if a person already has substantial financial resources. The risk level in a worker's industry is negatively related to a worker's assets (Viscusi, 1978), as workers with higher asset levels sort themselves into safer occupations. Similarly, income differences over time and across countries are strongly correlated with societal risk levels (Viscusi, 1983), so that richer societies are in fact safer societies. That being richer is safer is also borne out in studies of mortality rates over the business cycle. Mortality rates tend to rise during periods of high unemployment. That there is a positive income elasticity for the valuation of health risks is well established. The principal outstanding issues pertain to what the value of the income elasticity of the VSL is, and whether and in what context such elasticities should be taken into account when applying the VSL for policy relevant purposes.

As safety is a normal good, there is a positive income elasticity of VSL. While health risks that create the chance that one will be in a less desirable health state are

---

[13] For representative coverage see "EPA to Stop 'Death Discount' to Value New Regulations," Wall Street Journal, May 8, 2003, and "What's a Granny Worth? Cost Benefits Must Be Based on Good Science and Sound Economics," Washington Times, July 7, 2003.

different in character from monetary risks, measures of risk aversion for financial risk are related to the VSL. Theoretical models by Eeckhoudt and Hammit (2001) and by Kaplow (2005) have established a linkage between the VSL and the coefficient of relative risk aversion (CRRA) in simple theoretical models. In particular, Kaplow (2005) found that the CRRA establishes a lower bound on the income elasticity of the VSL. However, the VSL-CRRA model by Evans and Smith (2010) found that this relationship in which CRRA establishes a lower bound on the income elasticity of VSL may no longer hold once one relaxes the assumptions to permit variable labor supply and to recognize the complementarity between consumption and labor supplied.

These theoretical analyses consequently do not pinpoint the level of VSL. There are various estimates of average CRRA values in the literature, such as 0.5 to 0.6, but as with the VSL one would expect there to be substantial heterogeneity in the CRRA level. In addition, preferences of student experimental subjects are valuable in providing insight into systematic anomalies in human behavior but are less instructive in providing empirical estimates of values such as CRRA that one would expect to vary with life-cycle income patterns and family commitments.

The empirical estimates of the income elasticity of VSL all indicate a substantial positive effect of income. As discussed above, the meta-analyses of the VSL literature imply an income elasticity in the 0.4 to 0.6 range in Viscusi and Aldy (2003) and their replication of four meta-analysis studies. These are estimates obtained across samples in which the average VSL for the different worker populations may not fully capture the extent of the heterogeneity of VSL. Doucouliagos et al. (2012b) present meta-analysis estimates of the income elasticity of VSL adjusting for publication bias and find estimates ranging from 0.25 to 0.63. The quantile estimates within a sample in Kniesner et al. (2010) indicate an elasticity of 1.6. Similarly, international evidence in terms of cross-country comparisons suggests that the VSL may be greater than 1.0 (Hammitt and Robinson, 2011).

Although labor unions earn economic rents for workers covered by collective bargaining agreements, they may also alter the structure of compensation. There are two principal roles of labor unions (Viscusi, 1979) with respect to compensating differentials for job risks. First, to the extent that they have an informational advantage over individual workers, they may be more cognizant of the risks and better able to strike a meaningful wage-risk trade-off. In some instances, unions are directly involved in the provision of safety information or ensuring that contracts include provision for employers to provide safety information. Second, while labor market estimates reflect the valuations of the marginal worker, unions can bargain on behalf of the infra-marginal workers. These less mobile workers tend to be more experienced, have higher wages, and place a greater value on safety due to their higher income and life-cycle effects. Econometric studies have examined the influence of unions through whether the worker is covered by a collective bargaining agreement or whether the worker is a union member, where the choice of variables depends on the available data.

Hedonic labor market estimates have estimated the effect of unions either using a union x fatality risk interaction term or by estimating separate equations for union and nonunion workers. Most of the 30 studies of unions' effects on compensation for job risks that are reviewed in Viscusi and Aldy (2003) find that unions boost the wage-fatality rate trade-off. The VSL and the implicit value of nonfatal injuries are greater in unionized contexts, as one would predict based on economic theory.

7.12 A POSSIBLE CANCER PREMIUM FOR VSL

7.12.1 The Rationale for a Cancer Premium

The VSL for different kinds of health outcomes varies with the associated characteristics of the ailments. Cancer risks differ from acute accident risks in three principal ways—the associated morbidity effects, possible fear and dread, and the latency period between the time of exposure and death. The role of morbidity effects is clearly pertinent from the standpoint of economic valuation of a risk as long periods of treatment and disease generate a utility loss in addition to the mortality loss. Even if people do not actually get cancer or die from cancer, they may experience a utility loss due to the fear associated with knowledge of being exposed to the risk and a latency period before the ailment becomes apparent. The role of fear and dread is discussed in the next section. The discussion in this section focuses on a possible VSL premium for the morbidity effects and cancer, which along with acute accidents is the most prominent cause of death addressed by government policies. For some government agencies, such as those responsible for environmental regulations, the reduction in cancer risks may account for the preponderance of all estimated benefits. Assessing the value of reductions in the rate of cancer is also an important input to broader policy assessments such as determining whether the war on cancer undertaken by medical researchers is worthwhile (Lakdawalla et al., 2010).

Government agencies charged with the regulation of cancer risks have begun to assess a cancer premium relative to the reduction of risks from acute accidents in recognition of the morbidity costs associated with the disease. The initial policy action to assign a cancer premium was taken in the U.K. as the U.K. Health and Safety Executive (2001) suggested as a placeholder value that the VSL for cancer should have twice the value as that for acute accidents. The more recent guidance from H.M. Treasury (2011) likewise continued this approach, which remains based on speculation rather than empirical evidence. After reviewing the existing literature on cancer risk valuation, the U.S. Environmental Protection Agency (2010) suggested that a 50% cancer VSL premium could be used as a placeholder value until the evidence on VSL is refined. Note that irrespective of the magnitude of any cancer premium that is used to value risks at the time of death, the benefit assessment should account for the cancer latency period in much the same manner as it would discount deferred cost and benefit effects.

7.12.2 Stated Preference Studies of Valuation of Cancer Risks

Most studies of the VSL for cancer risks have utilized stated preference approaches. These have been of two types. The most common approach has been to use acute accidental deaths in a reference lottery to establish the acute fatality risk p that is equivalent to some cancer risk probability q. This risk-risk trade-off methodology introduced in the context of valuing risks of chronic bronchitis in Viscusi et al. (1991) simplifies the valuation task and can be applied in straightforward fashion to a variety of risks that can be equated to the acute accident risk reference lottery. The results of such a risk-risk trade-off exercise can then be chained with estimates of the VSL for acute accidents to monetize the VSL for cancer. The alternative to the risk-risk approach is to use a stated preference methodology that elicits the monetary WTP value for a reduction in the risk of cancer.

As in the case of contingent valuation studies generally, it is essential that respondents have a good understanding of the good being valued. Thus, the survey should provide respondents with information regarding the symptoms and consequences of treatment of the particular form of cancer being studied. Some studies in the literature fail to do this and simply indicate that there is a risk of death from cancer, but such an approach permits respondents to imagine different scenarios associated with the disease. Open-ended survey questions that make vague allusions to cancer may evoke a general sense of dread but may be of little use in enabling people to value specific symptoms associated with particular types of cancer, many of which are not fatal. Thus, the scenarios being imagined may differ in nature and severity from the actual consequences of the cancer cases prevented by a particular government policy. All types of cancer do not have the same morbidity and mortality effects so that there is no general cancer risk value but rather there are different valuations for various cancer risks.

Consider the simplest risk-risk trade-off survey task in which the respondent must ascertain what lottery involving a risk of accidental death p in a motor-vehicle accident is equivalent to a risk q of death by a particular form of cancer, or

$$(1 - p)u(\text{healthy}) + pu(\text{auto death}) = (1 - q)u(\text{healthy}) + qu(\text{cancer}). \quad (7.17)$$

With no loss of generality, set $u(\text{healthy}) = 0$, so that

$$u(\text{cancer}) = (p/q)u(\text{auto death}). \quad (7.18)$$

If risks of cancer and auto deaths are equally unattractive and $p = q$, then the VSL for acute accidents can be applied to cancer cases. But if there is a cancer premium, then $(p/q) > 1$.

Magat et al. (1996) applied this approach to both terminal lymph cancer and curable lymph cancer. The risk-risk trade-off involved the choice to move to one of two regions, which were defined on two dimensions, cancer risk and automobile accident risk. Their stated preference study presented respondents with a detailed description of the disease and treatment but did not indicate any latency period. The terminal lymph cancer–auto death trade-off rate had a median ratio of 1.0. Respondents also considered a curable lymph cancer risk that had a 10% mortality risk contingent on having the disease. The curable lymph cancer–fatal lymph cancer trade-off rate was 0.75 so that fatal lymph cancer was more highly valued. But isolating the morbidity component of lymph cancer in the valuation implies that nonfatal lymphoma with no risk of death is tantamount to a 0.58 probability of death for the median respondent. Respondents were very averse to any serious form of cancer, even if potentially curable. These and other studies have not distinguished legitimate concerns with morbidity effects as opposed to fear and dread of cancer more generally.

Cancer is distinguished not only by its severity and importance in health risks policies but also by the presence of a latency period of a decade or more. Unlike acute accidents for which there are within period valuations for immediate risks, choices pertaining to cancer risks will have effects in future periods. The influence of a latency period from the time of exposure to the time of death can be easily taken into account in a benefit assessment if the latency period and discount rate are known or provided to the respondent as part of the study design. Matters get more complicated if the valuation task includes choices whereby the individual has to make choices to reveal the rate of discount with respect to years of life as well as the VSL for cancer at a point in time based on the assumption that the risk is immediate. A contingent valuation survey in the U.S. and Canada by Alberini et al. (2006) found that the latency period does affect valuations of health risks in the expected manner, with implicit discount rates in a reasonable range.

The risk-risk trade-off study by Van Houtven et al. (2008) introduced the influence of a latency period for cancer within the context of a cancer valuation study and used a similar risk-risk trade-off format to value fatal cases of stomach, liver, and brain cancer as compared to auto accident deaths. The complications introduced by a latency period and discounting may have made the estimates in Van Houtven et al. (2008) less stable. The study varied the latency period from 5 to 25 years and varied the morbidity period. Although the length of the morbidity period did not affect valuations, the VSL for cancer was affected by the latency period. With a 5-year latency period, cancer had a value 3 times that of the VSL for auto accidents, while for a 25-year latency period the premium is reduced to 1.5 times that of auto accidents. Chaining these results and estimating the implicit rate of discount implies that an immediate risk of cancer is equivalent to 3.56 times the risk of an immediate auto accident death.

Other evidence based on WTP studies indicates a smaller premium for cancer. Hammitt and Liu (2004) analyzed the preferences of a Taiwanese sample for environmental risks including cancer and other diseases. The study incorporated a latency period for which respondents' discount rate was about 1.5%. The study found that fatal lung cancer or liver cancer had a value of 1.33 times that of fatal chronic diseases that were not cancer-related. However, a lower cancer premium was found in a subsequent WTP study by Hammitt and Haninger (2010). Using a U.S. sample, the authors considered how much of a premium respondents would pay for reduced risks of pesticide exposures in food and the attendant diseases associated with these exposures. They found that the VSL was the same for motor-vehicle accidents, noncancer diseases, and cancer (brain, bladder, liver, or lymphocytes). Inability of respondents to adequately process the differences in the symptoms of these serious ailments may have accounted for the similarity of the valuations.

Valuing the risks of cancer due to exposure in arsenic has been the object of major policy controversy, as detailed by Burnett and Hahn (2001). Arsenic risks from drinking water have been the focus of very expensive and controversial U.S. regulations. If the costs exceed the benefits, as Burnett and Hahn (2001) suggest, then the regulation is not worthwhile. Sufficiently large benefit values for cancer would make the regulation attractive on economic grounds.

This controversy in turn has stimulated two studies to value the bladder cancer risks being prevented. Adamowicz et al. (2011) find that cancer death risks are viewed as several times more severe than cancer illnesses. The survey did not incorporate a specific latency period. Microbial deaths had a VSL ranging from $16 million to $20 million ($2004 Canada), while cancer deaths had a VSL ranging from $14 million to $17 million ($2004 Canada). These differences in values were not statistically significant. However, the magnitudes of the VSL estimates are quite large and suggest a major cancer and serious disease premium relative to acute job fatalities.

The study by Viscusi et al. (2013) analyzed how much people were willing to pay for water treatment efforts that would reduce the risk of fatal bladder cancer. Using a nationally representative U.S. sample, the authors obtained similar results using an iterative choice stated preference model as well as a random utility model of the initial stated preference choice. The study adopted a cancer latency period of a decade and informed respondents of the time period before the risks would have adverse health effects. Converted to current terms to correspond to an immediate risk of cancer, using a 3% discount rate, the VSL for cancer is $10.85 million ($2011), which is a premium of 21% if the median VSL for acute accidents is $9 million.

7.12.3 Revealed Preference Studies of the Valuation of Cancer Risks

It is also feasible to estimate the valuation of cancer using revealed preference data. Unfortunately, a major shortcoming of workplace fatality rate statistics is that they do not include cancer-related deaths. Whereas there is extensive market data pertaining to wage and price effects of acute accidents, the revealed preference estimates of the value of reduced risks of cancer from cancer risk exposures has been restricted to linking housing prices to cancer risks from hazardous waste sites using hedonic price models. The study by Gayer et al. (2000) of the housing price effects of cancer risks after EPA made public the information regarding the level of cancer risks indicated a VSL for cancer of $3.9 million to $4.6 million ($1996). Similarly, in an analysis of repeat sales of houses, Gayer et al. (2002) found a value of $4.3 million to $8.3 million ($1993) for cancer risks associated with the different hazardous waste sites. Adjusting for a 10-year latency period using a 3% discount rate leads to a VSL for cancer of $5.1 million to $9.7 million. A longer latency period would make the value of immediate cancer cases greater.

7.13 RISK ATTRIBUTES: RESPONSIBILITY, DREAD, AND TERRORISM

7.13.1 Multiple Risk Attributes

Fatality risks are a multiattribute commodity. How people are exposed to the risk and other aspects of the adverse risk outcome may be consequential as well. Even abstracting from the nature of the fatality risk, there are clear differences in valuations that people have for different types of deaths. Chilton et al. (2006) use the risk-risk trade-off methodology of Viscusi et al. (1991) to examine people's attitudes toward different kinds of deaths. They find that deaths from murder, rail accidents, and fires are particularly dreaded as compared to deaths from other causes, such as pedestrian accidents and home accidents.

Valuation of multiple deaths at any particular point in time may have a different value per fatality than valuation of individual risks of death. Whether the valuation per expected fatality should be greater or lower for cases of multiple deaths is not clear theoretically. Jones-Lee and Loomes (1995) examined individual valuations of fatalities for the London Underground Limited. Respondents did not find that 25–30 deaths in a single Underground accident would be worse than 25–30 fatalities in separate Underground accidents. Moreover, respondents on average believed that 27.5 fatalities occurring on a large scale were equivalent to 26.9 fatalities occurring individually so that there was an insignificant negative premium for large scale accidents. How such accidents would be valued in actual fatality situations also depends on media coverage and the extent to which it creates overestimation of the risks.

In terms of individual valuations, people who voluntarily choose to incur large risks on average have revealed that they place a lower value on risks to their lives than those who do not engage in such risk taking behavior. Societal altruism with respect to saving people's lives will likewise be dependent on the risk taking behaviors of those exposed to the risk. In part, such differences may arise because the decision to choose a risky pursuit provides information about the person's own valuation of the risk. If that personal valuation is low, others likewise may be willing to spend less to reduce those risks. Aspects of control, voluntariness, and responsibility affect the public's attitudes toward reducing the risks of Underground rail accidents (Jones-Lee and Loomes, 1995).

Exploration of these influences for a variety of specific situations indicates that public concerns with safety vary substantially depending on the context. To explore the influence of different kinds of fault with respect to fatal accident risks, the study of rail accidents by Covey et al. (2010) examined how irresponsible behavior on the part of the prospective accident victims affected society's willingness to pay for improved safety. The lowest priorities for public spending to reduce risks were for situations in which passengers committed suicide, drivers and workers deliberately violated safety standards, passengers under the influence of alcohol were accidentally killed, and trespassers were engaging in vandalism at the time of the accident. Similarly, influences such as blame and ease of avoiding the risk also influence the estimates of the valuations for policies addressing health risks and environmental hazards (Subramanian and Cropper, 2000).

The existence of dread and related responses to risk stems from how risk information is processed. One might view a "dread" risk as a hazard for which the fear of the risk exceeds what the person should experience based on the objective probability. While it may be convenient to summarize a lottery's value in terms of being the product of a probability p and a loss value L, with a summary value pL, how each of these components is processed will differ. Thus, the characteristics of the risk may be instrumental in determining whether a risk evokes a sense of dread.

Neuroimaging studies illuminate how different parts of the brain respond to different lottery components. Even if a risk is viewed as the product of a probability p and loss L, the brain may process and react to each of these components differently. Coaster et al. (2011) undertook an fMRI study to consider the responses to different degrees of physical harm, specified with different probabilities, where these risk probabilities have different formats. High levels of physical harm activate the region of the brain associated with anticipatory anxiety, the right bed nucleus of the stria terminalis and the cortical areas. Differences in the risk probability had a different effect in that high probabilities of harm activated the prefrontal regions. Presentation of the risk probabilities using a frequency response (e.g., 5 injuries out of a population of 1,000) rather than a numerical probability (e.g., 0.005) had a strong interactive effect with the magnitude of the harm so that format of the risk information influences how the brain processes and responds to the risk.

7.13.2 Valuing Risks from Terrorist Attacks

A prominent policy context involving risks that involve more than just the expected number of lives lost is that pertaining to terrorism. Preventing deaths from terrorist attacks may generate different valuations than preventing deaths from traffic accidents. Terrorist attacks may kill a large number of people at a single time. The events are highly publicized and generate substantial media attention. The people killed in these attacks generally have not selected to incur high levels of risk voluntarily, which may affect altruistic concerns for the victims as well as a belief that the risk may affect the broader population. Our general sense of national pride and national security is also threatened by these attacks.

Many of these aspects of terrorism risks have been the subject of studies of risk valuations. Terrorist attacks generally do not kill only a single person, as the 9/11 attack in the United States killed almost 3,000 victims.

Two contexts in which large numbers of people die from a single event are natural disasters and terrorist attacks. In each case there is also an involuntary aspect, particularly to the extent that natural disasters are viewed as "acts of God" rather than the person's decision to live in a hazard prone area, such as a flood plain. When confronted with an opportunity to reduce comparable risks from natural disasters and terrorist attacks using a series of risk-risk trade-offs, respondents rated 0.57 terrorism deaths as being equivalent to each natural disaster death so that terrorism deaths were valued almost twice as highly (Viscusi, 2009a). This greater valuation of terrorism risks is consistent with the additional dimensions associated with terrorism deaths. Consistent with this view is that the premium for terrorism deaths was greater for respondents who belonged to the political party most closely associated with support of national defense spending (Republican).

Terrorism risks did not, however, command a premium relative to traffic safety risks. Most respondents view terrorism risks as not being a great threat to themselves, whereas traffic safety risks are viewed as being pertinent to a larger proportion of the population. Despite the difference in the role of private versus public risk reductions, the terrorism fatalities have the same relative value as traffic safety deaths.

People are willing to make trade-offs involving risks of terrorism with respect to valued attributes other than money and comparable risks. A prominent antiterrorism strategy has been increased screening of airport passengers at airports. Some of this screening may involve profiling passengers based on personal characteristics such as race and ethnicity, which some may view as a violation of civil liberties. The trade-off dimensions considered by Viscusi and Zeckhauser (2003) consisted of increased time spent screening against preservation of civil liberties. Once the screening time reached 45 minutes, the policy of screening passengers based on personal characteristics so as to expedite the screening process received widespread support.

The role of death risks that threaten the population generally and create a sense of insecurity is the focus of the study by Smith et al. (2009). Their survey focused on reducing the risks to aircraft from shoulder mounted missiles through antimissile laser jamming countermeasures mounted on commercial aircraft. The survey text stressed the broader societal consequences of a terrorist attack: "One successful attack would affect everyone in the U.S. When people are killed in an attack it increases feelings of insecurity and reduces people's willingness to travel by air. The airline industry still suffers from the drop in air travel after 9/11. A 10% decline in airline travel reduces economic activity by about $40 billion a year. Another successful hijacking or missile attack would have serious impacts on our transportation system and on the whole U.S. economy." Respondents were willing to pay $100 to $220 per household for the measures that provided a general level of protection but did not reduce a specific expected number of deaths.

Studies of terrorist attacks and dread events generally have focused on valuations of risk reductions from policies that have broad societal effects. Thus, they combine valuations associated with a concern with personal safety and the valuation of risks to others. These valuations may differ across respondents because of a different perceived personal risk. Some studies have sought to control for these differences in risk belief and have attempted to develop estimates for those who perceive themselves to be at average risk. Other studies have not controlled for individual risk beliefs since the objective was to establish an average value across the population of different risk reduction policies rather than to disentangle the private and social valuations of risk.

7.14 RISK-RISK ANALYSIS

7.14.1 Types of Risk-Risk Analysis

A more conservative policy test than benefit-cost analysis that can be used to assess whether a risk policy is desirable is a risk-risk analysis test. Thus, wholly apart from whether a policy is efficient, does the policy on balance reduce the level of risk? This test has taken on potential practical importance because many legislative mandates require that agencies advance narrower objectives than those that also account for costs. For example, most U.S. environmental regulations have a cost per expected life saved above $100 million.

Two variants of risk-risk analysis have arisen. The first observes that government activity often generates risk effects. Thus, as noted by Lave (1981), a safety-related automobile recall could increase risks if more people are injured in car accidents when bringing their vehicles in for service than are protected by the repair. Similarly, regulations that mandate more fuel efficient cars reduce mortality risks through their effect on pollution levels but increase mortality risks by fostering reductions in vehicle weight. Government expenditures also stimulate economic activity and its associated risks. Such risk consequences can and should be taken into account when assessing the risk effects of a government policy. These impacts include direct effects as well as fatality costs resulting from activity that is stimulated by, for example, an increase in construction or manufacturing. Viscusi and Zeckhauser (1994) use an input-output analysis model to trace the fatality and nonfatal injury ramifications of different kinds of economic activity by 2-digit industry. Injury costs average about 3–4% of total financial costs.

The second, and more common, form of risk-risk analysis draws on the negative relationship between wealth and risk (Viscusi, 1978, 1983). Expenditures of all kinds have opportunity costs that reduce resources available for other purposes such as health-enhancing efforts. In the extreme case of an expenditure that has no positive beneficial consequences as the result of the activity, the expenditure will necessarily boost societal risk levels through the opportunity cost that is generated. This risk-risk concept can be incorporated in addition to being concerned with the net direct effects of a policy on risk apart from their effect on income levels.

7.14.2 The Relationship between VSL and Risk-Risk Analysis

Because expenditures can have a beneficial effect on safety as reflected in the VSL, there is a theoretical relationship between the expenditure level that leads to the loss of a statistical life and the VSL concept. The quest is to ascertain the level of expenditure after which additional expenditures have a counterproductive effect. As derived in Viscusi (1994a), expenditures have a positive effect on the survival probability if there is a net positive effect on survival due to the direct effect of the policy on safety, plus any effect of the policy on personal health expenditures due to the greater safety level, plus any effect of the policy through the financial opportunity costs that are involved.

After rearranging terms in this formulation, the condition can be rewritten with respect to the average cost per life saved at the point where expenditures become counterproductive:

$$\text{Average cost per life saved} < \frac{\text{VSL}}{\text{Marginal propensity to spend on health}}. \quad (7.19)$$

The marginal propensity to spend on health is the derivative of personal health-related expenditures with respect to income. Estimates of the marginal propensity to spend on health based on international data for the Organisation for Economic Co-Operation and Development (OECD) countries are about 0.09 (Viscusi, 1994b). The average U.S. propensity to spend on health was about 0.1 for that same period. Thus, for a marginal propensity value of 0.1 and a VSL of $9 million, risk policy expenditures that allocate more than $90 million per expected life saved have an adverse effect on personal mortality risks through the opportunity costs that are generated.

This framework assumes that higher levels of income are health-enhancing, which may not be the case. Health-related consumption activities and personal habits that are income-related sometimes increase life expectancy and sometimes decrease it. The chief examples linked to the risk-risk trade-off approach by Lutter et al. (1999) are smoking, excessive drinking, and diet and exercise. They provide empirical estimates of how income-related bad health habits affect the risk-risk analysis.

The initial empirical attempts to examine the risk-risk relationship did not account for the necessary linkage to the VSL but simply focused on empirical evidence linking mortality rates to income levels. As a result, the analyses sometimes generated internally inconsistent conclusions. Suppose that individual expenditures imply that people are willing to spend amounts to foster greater safety that imply a VSL of $10 million. Unless people are irrational and do not understand the safety-enhancing effects of their expenditures, it cannot also be the case that an expenditure of $10 million or less leads to the loss of one expected death. Otherwise, personal expenditures and related risk-taking behaviors, such as higher wages for dangerous jobs, would be counterproductive from a safety standpoint. Most of the early literature ignored the fundamental nature of this linkage and often yielded estimates of the cost levels that would lead to one expected death that were close to and sometimes below the VSL, which is a signal of the potential problems with the empirical estimates and methodology.

The early empirical studies also did not account for the endogeneity of income levels, as income affects one's health, but it is also the case that health impairments influence one's income. The first empirical estimate that specifically attempted to calculate the income loss that would lead to one statistical death was that of Keeney (1990), who used existing empirical evidence on the relationship of mortality rates to income and found that the income loss per statistical death was $12.5 million ($1992). His analysis in turn led to incorporation of the principle that expenditures could be counterproductive in legal analyses of government regulations (Williams, 1993).[14] Government economists Lutter and Morrall (1994) used international data on the mortality-income relationship from the World Bank and found a cost-per-life-saved cutoff value of $9.3 million ($1992). These international relationships have been controversial as the mortality-income relationship may stem from other international differences correlated with income. Among possible influential factors are differences in the structure of economies and markets captured through an economic freedom variable, which appears to be a contributory determinant of the income-mortality linkage (Smith et al., 1994). Numerous other estimates using a variety of empirical approaches have generated risk-risk cutoff values ranging from $1.9 million to $33.2 million ($1992) based on empirical relationships such as the effect of income differences on white males' longevity, the effect of income declines during recessions on mortality, and the mortality consequences of income differences for those who are retired. Unlike these studies, Chapman and Hariharan (1994) seek to account for the reverse causality in the income-mortality relationship by controlling for initial health status, generating a value of $12.2 million ($1990). However, as with other direct attempts to estimate the income-mortality relationship, these analyses have not fully addressed the reverse causality issues. In addition, other fundamental data issues remain as most studies have involved matching family income to individual mortality. The most promising approaches are those that are

---

[14] Use of the risk-risk analysis principle also was the subject of the letter from James B. MacRae, Jr., Acting Administrator, Office of Information and Regulatory Affairs, U.S. Office of Management and Budget, to Nancy Risque-Rohrbach, Assistant Secretary for Policy, U.S. Department of Labor, March 10, 1992, as well as his statement before the Senate Committee on Governmental Affairs, March 19, 1992.

grounded in economic theory and incorporate the linkage between VSL and the risk-risk cutoff value into the empirical analysis.

7.15 GOVERNMENT PRACTICES FOR USE OF VSL
7.15.1 The Evolution of VSL Benefit Assessment Practices

Over the past three decades the use of value of life or value of statistical life estimates has become the standard practice for government agencies valuing risk. Policy assessments utilizing VSL amounts continue to play a central role in government policy, especially those pertaining to risk and environmental regulations (Robinson, 2007; Graham, 2008). In the U.S., the primary source of these estimates is labor market estimates of VSL, either utilizing individual studies or meta-analyses of the literature. Perhaps because of the greater instability of econometric estimates of the VSL based on U.K. labor market studies, for policy analyses in the U.K., stated preference studies focusing on transport studies have had a more prominent role.

The adoption of VSL estimates for valuing mortality risks rather than the present value of lost earnings began in 1982, when I introduced the use of labor market estimates of the value of life after the pertinent government agencies drew me into the debate over the Occupational Safety and Health Administration (OSHA) proposed hazard communication regulation.[15] Use of the value-of-life statistics that at the time were on the order of $3 million, or over $7 million in current dollars, generated benefits in excess of the costs, leading to the issuance of the regulation.

The gradual evolution of the VSL estimates used by agencies as reflected in the VSL numbers employed in regulatory impact studies is shown in Table 7.2 for a variety of agencies and Table 7.3 for EPA. To make the values comparable, all estimates have been converted to 2012 dollars. Almost all the regulations listed in these tables are major regulations with costs of at least $100 million. The entire roster of such regulations indicates the tremendous impact VSL estimates have in the valuation of government policies. In almost all cases, the benefits associated with reducing mortality risks are a major source of the regulatory benefits.

Although the tallies in Tables 7.2 and 7.3 are incomplete, particularly before the late 1990s, they are comprehensive thereafter. There is clearly a daunting set of regulations for which agencies use the VSL to monetize benefits. Table 7.2 lists 48 regulatory analyses from agencies such as branches of the U.S. Department of Transportation and the Food and Drug Administration. Because of the very large number of regulations from EPA, Table 7.3 breaks this agency out separately and lists 50 regulatory analyses and one guidance document from EPA.

---

[15] I describe this policy effort and the results of my analysis in Viscusi (1992). Previously, OSHA valued the expected lives saved by the regulation using the present value of lost earnings, or what it called the "cost of death."

Table 7.2 Selected Values of Statistical Life Used by U.S. Regulatory Agencies*

Year	Agency	Regulation	Value of Statistical Life (millions, $2012)
1985	Federal Aviation Administration	Protective Breathing Equipment	$1.3
1988	Federal Aviation Administration	Improved Survival Equipment for Inadvertent Water Landings	$1.9
1990	Federal Aviation Administration	Proposed Establishment of the Harlingen Airport Radar Service Area, TX	$2.7
1994	Food and Nutrition Service (USDA)	National School Lunch Program and School Breakfast Program	$2.2, $4.6
1995	Consumer Product Safety Commission	Multiple Tube Mine and Shell Fireworks Devices	$7.4
1996	Food Safety Inspection Service (USDA)	Pathogen Reduction; Hazard Analysis and Critical Control Point Systems	$2.5
1996	Food and Drug Administration	Regulations Restricting the Sale and Distribution of Cigarettes and Smokeless Tobacco to Protect Children and Adolescents	$3.5
1996	Federal Aviation Administration	Aircraft Flight Simulator Use in Pilot Training, Testing, and Checking and at Training Centers	$4.0
1996	Food and Drug Administration	Medical Devices; Current Good Manufacturing Practice Final Rule; Quality System Regulation	$7.3
2000	Consumer Product Safety Commission	Portable Bed Rails; Advance Notice of Proposed Rulemaking	$6.6
2000	Department of Transportation	NPRM on Tire Pressure Monitoring System	$4.2–$6.6
2006	Food and Drug Administration	Recordkeeping Requirements for Human Food and Cosmetics Manufactured From, Processed With, Or Otherwise Containing, Material From Cattle	$5.7–$7.3
2007	Department of Homeland Security	Advance Information on Private Aircraft Arriving and Departing the United States	$3.3–$6.6
2008	Coast Guard	Vessel Requirements for Notices of Arrival and Departure, and Automatic Identification System	$6.7
2008	Consumer Product Safety Commission	Standard for the Flammability of Residential Upholstered Furniture	$5.4
2008	Department of Homeland Security	Documents Required for Travelers Departing From or Arriving in the United States at Sea and Land Ports-of-Entry From Within the Western Hemisphere	$3.2–$6.4

Continued

Table 7.2 (Continued)

Year	Agency	Regulation	Value of Statistical Life (millions, $2012)
2008	Federal Motor Carrier Safety Administration	New Entrant Safety Assurance Process	$6.2
2008	Pipeline and Hazardous Materials Safety Administration	Hazardous Materials: Improving the Safety of Railroad Tank Car Transportation of Hazardous Materials	$6.2 ($3.4, $9.0)
2008	U.S. Customs and Border Protection	Advance Information on Private Aircraft Arriving and Departing the United States	$3.2 & $6.4
2009	Food and Drug Administration	Prevention of Salmonella Enteritidis in Shell Eggs During Production, Storage, and Transportation	$5.4 & $7.0
2009	Food Safety & Inspection Service	Nutrition Labeling of Single-Ingredient Products and Ground or Chopped Meat and Poultry Products	$5.9
2009	NHTSA	Federal Motor Vehicle Safety Standards; Roof Crush Resistance; Phase-In Reporting Requirements	$6.2/$6.5
2009	Transportation Security Administration	Air Cargo Screening	$6.2
2009	Transportation Security Administration	Aircraft Repair Station Security	$6.2
2010	Coast Guard	Passenger Weight and Inspected Vessel Stability Requirements	$6.6
2010	Federal Aviation Administration	Flightcrew Member Duty and Rest Requirements	$6.3 & $9.0
2010	Federal Motor Carrier Safety Administration	Electronic On-Board Recorders for Hours-of-Service Compliance	$6.1
2010	Federal Motor Carrier Safety Administration	Limiting the Use of Wireless Communication Devices	$6.3
2010	Federal Railroad Administration	Positive Train Control Systems	$6.3
2010	Mining Safety and Health Administration	Maintenance of Incombustible Content of Rock Dust in Underground Coal Mines	$9.1
2010	Mining Safety and Health Administration	Lowering Miners' Exposure to Respirable Coal Mine Dust, Including Continuous Personal Dust Monitors	$9.1
2010	Mining Safety and Health Administration	Examinations of Work Areas in Underground Coal Mines for Violations of Mandatory Health or Safety Standards	$9.1
2010	NHTSA	Federal Motor Vehicle Safety Standards; Roof Crush Resistance	$6.1
2010	Occupational Safety and Health Administration	Walking-Working Surfaces and Personal Protective Equipment (Fall Protection Systems)	$7.6

Continued

Table 7.2 (Continued)

Year	Agency	Regulation	Value of Statistical Life (millions, $2012)
2010	Occupational Safety and Health Administration	Cranes and Derricks in Construction	$9.1
2011	Department of Homeland Security	Ammonium Nitrate Security Program	$6.1
2011	Federal Motor Carrier Safety Administration	Hours of Service of Drivers	$6.1
2011	Federal Railroad Administration	Hours of Service of Railroad Employees; Substantive Regulations for Train Employees Providing Commuter and Intercity Rail Passenger Transportation; Conforming Amendments to Recordkeeping Requirements	$6.1
2011	Federal Railroad Administration	Railroad Workplace Safety; Adjacent-Track On-Track Safety for Roadway Workers	$6.3
2011	Food and Drug Administration	Labeling and Effectiveness Testing; Sunscreen Drug Products for Over-the-Counter Human Use	$218,000 VSLY
2011	Food and Drug Administration	Labeling for Bronchodilators To Treat Asthma; Cold, Cough, Allergy, Bronchodilator, and Antiasthmatic Drug Products for Over-the-Counter Human Use	$8.06
2011	Food Safety & Inspection Service	Not Applying the Mark of Inspection Pending Certain Test Results	$6.8
2011	Mining Safety and Health Administration	Proximity Detection Systems for Continuous Mining Machines in Underground Coal Mines	$8.9
2011	Occupational Safety and Health Administration	General Working Conditions in Shipyard Employment	$8.9
2011	Transportation Security Administration	Air Cargo Screening	$6.1
2012	Federal Aviation Administration	Pilot Certification and Qualification Requirements for Air Carrier Operations	$6.0
2012	Federal Aviation Administration	Flightcrew Member Duty and Rest Requirements	$6.2
2012	Mining Safety and Health Administration	Examinations of Work Areas in Underground Coal Mines for Violations of Mandatory Health or Safety Standards	$8.7

When the published summaries of the regulatory impact analyses for these rules do not specify the year in which the reported dollars are denominated, the calculations assume that the dollar year corresponds to the date of rule publication for purposes of converting all values into 2012 dollars using the CPI-U. Note that the CPSC reported a VSL of $5 million in both its 1995 and 2000 regulations; the difference in values reflects the conversion to 2012 dollars.

Table 7.3 Values of Statistical Life Used by the U.S. Environmental Protection Agency*

Year	Regulation or Regulatory Impact Analysis (RIA)	Value of Statistical Life (millions, $2012)
1985	Regulation of Fuels and Fuel Additives; Gasoline Lead Content	$2.2
1988	Protection of Stratospheric Ozone	$6.3
1996	Requirements for Lead-Based Paint Activities in Target Housing and Child-Occupied Facilities	$8.2
1996	RIA: Proposed Particulate Matter National Ambient Air Quality Standard	$8.3
1996	RIA: Proposed Ozone National Ambient Air Quality Standard	$8.3
1997	Economic Analysis for the National Emission Standards for Hazardous Air Pollutants for Source Category: Pulp and Paper Production; Effluent Limitations Guidelines, Pretreatment Standards, and New Source Performance Standards: Pulp, Paper, and Paperboard Categories-Phase 1	$3.7–13.4
1997	National Ambient Air Quality Standards for Ozone	$8.2
1998	RIA: NOx SIP call, FIP, and Section 126 Petitions	$8.3
1999	RIA: Final Regional Haze Rule	$8.3
1999	Radon in Drinking Water Health Risk Reduction and Cost Analysis	$8.2
1999	RIA: Final Section 126 Petition Rule	$8.3
1999	RIA: Control of Air Pollution from New Motor Vehicles: Tier 2 Motor Vehicle Emissions Standards and Gasoline Sulfur Control Requirements	$8.3
2000	Control of Air Pollution from New Motor Vehicles: Tier 2 Motor Vehicle Emissions Standards and Gasoline Sulfur Control Requirements	$8.3
2000	Revised National Primary Drinking Water Standards for Radionuclides	$8.2
2000	Guidelines for Preparing Economic Analysis	$8.3
2000	Arsenic in Drinking Water Rule	$8.3
2004	RIA: Stationary Internal Combustion Engine (RICE) NESHAP	$8.2
2004	RIA: Industrial Boilers and Process Heaters NESHAP	$7.5
2004	Final Regulatory Analysis: Control of Emissions from Nonroad Diesel Engines	$8.2
2005	RIA: Final Clean Air Mercury Rule	$7.5
2005	RIA: Final Clean Air Interstate Rule	$7.5
2005	RIA: Final Clean Air Visibility Rule or the Guidelines for Best Available Retrofit Technology (BART) Determinations Under the Regional Haze Regulations	$7.5
2005	Economic Analysis for the Final State 2 Disinfectants and Disinfection Byproducts Rule	$9.6

Continued

Table 7.3 (Continued)

Year	Regulation or Regulatory Impact Analysis (RIA)	Value of Statistical Life (millions, $2012)
2006	RIA: Review of the Particulate Matter National Ambient Air Quality Standards	$7.5
2006	National Primary Drinking Water Regulations: Ground Water Rule; Final Rule	$9.1
2008	RIA: Final Ozone National Ambient Air Quality Standards	$7.4
2008	RIA: Control of Emissions of Air Pollution from Locomotive Engines and Marine Compression Ignition Engines Less than 30 Liters Per Cylinder	$7.3
2009	Reconsideration of the 2008 Ozone National Ambient Air Quality Standards (NAAQS)	$10.1
2009	Proposed SO_2 National Ambient Air Quality Standards (NAAQS)	$10.1
2009	Proposed NO_2 National Ambient Air Quality Standards (NAAQS)	$10.1
2010	Existing Stationary Spark Ignition (SI) RICE NESHAP	$9.7
2010	Proposed Federal Transport Rule	$8.9
2010	Guidelines for Economic Analysis	$8.4
2010	Proposed National Emission Standards for Hazardous Air Pollutants (NESHAP) for Mercury Emissions from Mercury Cell Chlor Alkali Plants	$10.1
2010	Existing Stationary Compression Ignition Engines NESHAP	$9.7
2010	NO_2 National Ambient Air Quality Standards	$10.1
2010	Amendments to the National Emission Standards for Hazardous Air Pollutants and New Source Performance Standards (NSPS) for the Portland Cement Manufacturing Industry	$9.8
2011	Standards of Performance for New Stationary Sources and Emission Guidelines for Existing Sources: Sewage Sludge Incineration Units	$9.7
2011	Final Mercury and Air Toxics Standard	$9.9
2011	Federal Implementation Plans to Reduce Interstate Transport of Fine Particulate Matter and Ozone in 27 States; Correction of SIP Approvals for 22 States	$8.9
2011	Proposed Manganese Ferroalloys RTR	$9.7
2011	Reconsideration Proposal for National Emissions Standards for Hazardous Air Pollutants for Industrial, Commercial, and Institutional Boilers and Process Heaters at Major Sources	$9.7
2011	Standards of Performance for New Stationary Sources and Emission Guidelines for Existing Sources: Commercial and Industrial Solid Waste Incineration Units	$9.7
2011	Proposed Toxics Rule	$8.9
2012	Proposed Reconsideration for Existing Stationary Spark Ignition RICE RESHAP	$9.7

Continued

Table 7.3 (Continued)

Year	Regulation or Regulatory Impact Analysis (RIA)	Value of Statistical Life (millions, $2012)
2012	Proposed Reconsideration of Existing Stationary Compression Ignition Engines NESHAP	$9.7
2012	Proposed Revisions to the National Ambient Air Quality Standards for Particulate Matter	$10.1
2012	Final Revisions to the National Ambient Air Quality Standards for Particulate Matter	$9.3
2012	Petroleum Refineries New Source Performance Standards	$9.7
2013	Reconsideration of Existing Stationary Compression Ignition (CI) Engines NESHAP	$9.7
2013	Reconsideration of Existing Stationary Spark Ignition (SI) RICE NESHAP	$9.7

*When the published summaries of the regulatory impact analyses for these rules do not specify the year in which the reported dollars are denominated, the calculations assume that the dollar year corresponds to the date of rule publication for purposes of converting all values into 2012 dollars using the CPI-U. Some minor differences in VSL levels are due to rounding effects rather than changes in the agency's valuation.

Because agencies such as the U.S. Department of Transportation previously remained anchored in the human capital approach, even after they adopted the VSL methodology, the department long utilized estimates from the lower end of the VSL spectrum. But beginning in 2008 it began using more mainstream VSL estimates (U.S. Department of Transportation, 2011).

As is apparent from Tables 7.2 and 7.3, over time the VSL estimates have increased so that they have become much more in line with the literature. The pattern shown for EPA likewise exhibits an upward trajectory, with several notable differences. First, the VSL levels used by EPA are greater than for other agencies because EPA has been especially vigilant in updating the estimates to reflect the current literature. Second, because EPA began operations in 1970 and did not have a long history of using human capital values for fatality risks, we do not see the same anchoring influence of a long-term historical use of human capital benefits measures. Third, it is possible that political factors and interest group pressures may enter as well.[16] Because EPA's legislative mandates often preclude that regulations be based on benefit-cost grounds, whereas U.S. Department of Transportation's legislation has no such prohibition, the role of economic

[16] The VSL survey by Viscusi (1993) was based on an earlier report to the Federal Aviation Administration, which sought to raise the value of life number used in policy assessments to reflect current labor market evidence. In the meeting where Viscusi presented a proposed increase in the VSL at the office of the Secretary of U.S. Department of Transportation, representatives of the U.S. auto industry advocated a number at the low end of the VSL estimates. The agency subsequently raised its VSL but to a level below labor market estimates.

assessments differs across the agencies, which in turn may affect their choice of the VSL. The U.S. auto industry also opposed many automobile regulations in the 1980s, which may have slowed the adoption of the VSL approach at the U.S. Department of Transportation since higher benefit estimates would lead to more stringent regulations.

Most of these VSL estimates used by U.S. government agencies have been based on labor market estimates of the value of statistical life or meta-analyses of the value of statistical life drawing on both labor market studies and stated preference studies.[17] For example, the U.S. Department of Transportation (2011) chose the mean value across five different studies, four of which were meta-analyses and a fifth (Viscusi, 2004) included 80 specifications from a single data set. In particular, the agency's set of valuations were a $5.2 million value from Miller (2000), a $2.6 million value from Mrozek and Taylor (2002), an $8.5 million value from Viscusi and Aldy (2003), a $6.1 million value from Viscusi (2004), and a $6.6 million value from Kochi et al. (2006). The U.S. Department of Transportation's procedure for selecting the VSL used in assessment after 2008 is noteworthy with respect to its transparency in that both the set of studies and the method for drawing on these estimates in choosing its VSL are indicated.

Other agencies have relied on similar sets of data and, in some instances, have also disclosed the set of studies considered and how the consensus estimate was reached. Notwithstanding the differences in samples and methodology, the range of VSL estimates across agencies is fairly similar. One would expect there to be some differences because of differences across studies in risk preferences of the sample and differences in methodology. The emergence of new and more accurate labor market data with the advent of the CFOI data reduces the measurement error associated with the labor market estimates and has led to somewhat higher estimates of the VSL.

Changes in the VSL that have accompanied the agencies' attempts to refine the VSL levels have been relatively uncontroversial, with two principal exceptions. First, the aforementioned controversy over the senior citizen discount created a firestorm because the EPA lowered the VSL for those over age 65 by 37%. Second, the EPA Air Office lowered the VSL it used in 2008, which also generated substantial adverse publicity. These events have an important common element. In each instance it was a reduction in the VSL rather than the absolute level of the VSL that created the controversy. There was an apparent anchoring effect that is closely related to various endowment effects, status quo effects, and reference dependence effects in the literature. People had a strong negative reaction to the lower VSL that was asymmetric in that an increase in the VSL would not have generated a comparable positive reaction.

The devaluation of life by the EPA Air Office, or more specifically the Office of Air and Radiation, was especially noteworthy in that it was not the result of a

---

[17] The principal studies utilized and cited by these agencies are Viscusi (1992, 1993, 2004), Mrozek and Taylor (2002), Viscusi and Aldy (2003), and Kochi et al. (2006).

department-wide policy decision, and the underlying rationale for the change remained opaque. Whereas the EPA Air Office previously used VSL levels of $7.7 million to $7.8 million, beginning in 2004 it used a value of $7.0 million for policies. The regulatory analyses using the lower estimate of VSL included assessment of the benefits of the 2004 standards for industrial boilers and process heaters, the 2005 mercury emissions rule, the 2005 final clean air visibility rule, the 2006 review of the standards for particulate matter, and the 2008 standards for controlling emissions from locomotive engines. This devaluation generated public attention beginning in 2008. The reduction in the VSL was puzzling in that it was inconsistent with general EPA guidance to use a VSL of $8.4 million ($2012), which was based on the series of labor market studies in Viscusi (2002) and supplemented by the agency. In contrast, the EPA Air Office relied on two meta-analyses by Mrozek and Taylor (2002) and Viscusi and Aldy (2003), but it does not discuss the rationale for combining the results of these meta-analyses in the manner that it did.[18]

While government agencies continue to grapple with issues regarding the proper treatment of age and life expectancy, there is a consensus that VSL based on revealed preferences and stated preferences provides a sound basis for policy evaluation. Even though the VSL methodology has been widely adopted for policy purposes, some conceptual issues remain. The fundamental principle for benefit assessment for risk reduction policies is society's willingness to pay for the risk reduction. The usual theoretical starting point for analyzing compensating differentials for risk is that the worker is choosing between a low risk job and a high risk job offering greater pay so that the estimated VSL is a willingness-to-accept (WTA) measure rather than a willingness-to-pay (WTP) measure. In a study of valuation of consumer safety risks, Viscusi et al. (1987) found a substantial gap between the WTA and WTP values, with the WTA values being greater. Across a broad set of studies pertaining primarily to environmental risks, Horowitz and McConnell (2002) found an average WTA/WTP ratio of 7.2. If a similar discrepancy exists for labor market estimates of VSL, and if these values reflect WTA, then the VSL estimates overstate the WTP amounts and will lead to an overestimate of benefit levels. To explore this possibility, Kniesner et al. (2014) used a sample of workers, focusing particularly on job changers. The study analyzed local trade-off rates for risk changes in each direction. Workers who experienced an increase in risk exhibited a WTA VSL, while workers who were decreasing their risk level had a WTP VSL. These estimated amounts were not significantly different.

---

[18] The EPA provided the following discussion but does not provide a rationale for the formula used. "Point estimate is the mean of a normal distribution with a 95 percent confidence interval between $1 and $10 million. Confidence interval is based on two meta-analyses of the wage-risk VSL literature. $1 million represents the lower end of the interquartile range from Mrozek and Taylor (2002) [sic] meta-analysis. $10 million represents the upper end of the interquartile range from the Viscusi and Aldy (2003) meta-analysis. The VSL represents the value of a small change in mortality risk aggregated over the affected population." See U.S. EPA (2004), Table 9.7, Unit Values Used for Economic Valuation of Endpoints ($2000).

There have also been efforts to use the VSL estimates as a compensation measure in wrongful death and personal injury cases. Although this approach has some advocates (Posner and Sunstein, 2005), the VSL is not well suited to serve as a compensatory damages measure. Use of the VSL for this purpose, known as the hedonic damages approach, employs a deterrence value for prevention of small risks of death as the compensatory damages amount, which will lead to compensation levels that exceed the optimal insurance amount. Nevertheless, the VSL could have two constructive functions in litigation contexts. First, it could provide a reference point for assessing whether a company's investments in product safety struck an efficient benefit-cost balance (Viscusi, 2007). In addition, if the function of the damages award is deterrence rather than insurance, as in the case in which punitive damages are awarded, then a total damages value linked to the VSL will establish efficient levels of incentives (Hersch and Viscusi, 2010b).

7.15.2 Current Revisions to the Use of VSL Estimates

Although agencies in the U.S. government traditionally estimated the VSL based on average values across many labor market studies, and in some cases included stated preference studies, in 2013 the U.S. Department of Transportation (2013) took a different approach. VSL estimates using the more refined CFOI fatality rate data entail less measurement error than previous studies using earlier eras of fatality rate data. As a result, the agency has chosen to base its VSL estimates on these data rather than a broader set of studies as embodied in meta-analyses.

More specifically, the current agency guidance document provides procedures for three specific concerns. First, the agency set the VSL equal to $9.1 million. It arrived at this figure by averaging the results for nine of the studies listed in Table 7.1 that pertained to broad population groups rather than population subgroups, such as smokers or immigrants. Second, the agency established a range of uncertainty for VSL from $5.2 million to $12.9 million based on the range reported in Kniesner et al. (2012). Third, the agency set the income elasticity of VSL equal to 1.0, reasoning that it was an intermediate value between the meta-analysis estimates in Viscusi and Aldy (2003) and the higher values in the quantile regression models of Kniesner et al. (2010) and the analysis of long-term trends in VSL by Costa and Kahn (2004).

7.16 CONCLUSION

Trade-off rates of various kinds play a fundamental role in economics generally. What is noteworthy about trade-offs involving risks to life is that the empirical challenges differ and the risk outcomes often affect utility functions in a manner that differs from standard economic goods. Risks to life and health are not traded explicitly in markets. As a consequence, economists had to develop more reliable survey methods to elicit these values as well as empirical techniques to reliably infer implicit prices for risk based on individual choices and market decisions. The fundamental focus on small risks of illness and death has remained unchanged, but there has been increased understanding of the way in which these health outcomes affect utility and how preferences differ by type of risk and across the population.

The dividends from this research span a wide range. Severe health outcomes and death affect both the level of utility and the marginal utility of income, whereas minor injuries and illnesses do not. This property influences not only the nature of the loss and its valuation, but also the optimal level of insurance after an injury. Serious injuries that reduce the marginal utility of income imply that less than full compensation for financial losses after a serious injury or death is not efficient. These results have implications for the structure of workers' compensation and the pain and suffering awards in tort law.

The dominant focus of the literature has been on the trade-off rate between money and fatality risks. Typically the focus is on private risks, or the VSL to the individual. In some instances, particularly in some stated preference studies, the focus is on broader risk reduction policies, which may or may not benefit the individual. The entire literature that has emerged on these issues indicates that the valuations are substantial, with VSL levels about an order of magnitude greater than the financial losses associated with a fatality. Consequently, shifting to the VSL approach does not make risks to life priceless, but it does increase their value by about an order of magnitude greater than the human capital methodology that was formerly used to value fatality risks.

In some instances in which agencies have mandates that do not permit benefit-cost balancing, risk–risk analysis illuminates the potential adverse health consequences of not basing policies on their economic merits. Inordinate expenditures on safety are not only wasteful but also may have counterproductive effects on health.

The substantial development in empirical methodologies has also greatly broadened the refinement of the VSL estimates. The early literature primarily focused on the VSL for general population groups, and this remains a continuing concern for broadly based government policies. But there has also been intense focus on the heterogeneity of VSL and the sources of this heterogeneity. This effort has been facilitated by the development of much more refined data than were available when this field of inquiry began. The quest for assessing the variations in VSL over the life cycle and for particular types of death, such as terrorist attacks and cancer, represent two such lines of research.

As much as any subfield within the economics of risk and uncertainty, estimates of VSL have played a pivotal role in policy contexts. Each year government agencies assess the benefits associated with risk and environmental policies that impose annual costs in the billions of dollars. The driving force in the justification of most of these efforts is the effect of the policies of mortality risks, which are monetized using estimates of the VSL.

ACKNOWLEDGMENTS

The author is indebted to Thomas Kniesner for valuable comments and to Jake Byl and Henri Rautonen for research assistance.

REFERENCES

Ackerman, F., Heinzerling, L., 2004. Priceless: On Knowing the Price of Everything and the Value of Nothing. The New Press, New York.

Adamowicz, W., Dupont, D., Krupnick, A., Zhang, J., 2011. Valuation of cancer and microbial disease risk reductions in municipal drinking water: an analysis of risk context using multiple valuation methods. Journal of Environmental Economics and Management 61, 213–226.

Alberini, A., Cropper, M., Krupnick, A., Simon, N., 2004. Does the value of a statistical life vary with age and health status? Evidence from the U.S. and Canada. Journal of Environmental Economics and Management 48, 769–792.

Alberini, A., Cropper, M., Krupnick, A., Simon, N.B., 2006. WTP for mortality risk reductions: does latency matter? Journal of Risk and Uncertainty 32, 231–245.

Aldy, J.E., Viscusi, W.K., 2007. Age differences in the value of statistical life: revealed preference evidence. Review of Environmental Economics and Policy 1, 241–260.

Aldy, J.E., Viscusi, W.K., 2008. Adjusting the value of a statistical life for age and cohort effects. Review of Economics and Statistics 90, 573–581.

Arnould, R.J., Nichols, L.M., 1983. Wage-risk premiums and workers' compensation: a refinement of estimates of compensating wage differential. Journal of Political Economy 91, 332–340.

Ashenfelter, O., 2006. Measuring the value of a statistical life: problems and prospects. Economic Journal 116, C10–C23.

Ashenfelter, O., Greenstone, M., 2004. Using mandated speed limits to measure the value of a statistical life. Journal of Political Economy 112, S226–S267.

Atkinson, S.E., Halvorsen, R., 1990. The valuation of risks to life: evidence from the market for automobiles. Review of Economics and Statistics 72, 133–136.

Bellavance, F., Dionne, G., Lebeau, M., 2009. The value of a statistical life: a meta-analysis with a mixed effects regression model. Journal of Health Economics 28, 444–464.

Black, D.A., Kniesner, T.J., 2003. On the measurement of job risk in hedonic wage models. Journal of Risk and Uncertainty 27, 205–220.

Blomquist, G., 1979. Value of life saving: implications of consumption activity. Journal of Political Economy 87, 540–558.

Blomquist, G.C., Dickie, M., O'Conor, R.M., 2011. Willingness to pay for improving fatality risks and asthma symptoms. Resource and Energy Economics 33, 410–425.

Blomquist, G.C., Miller, T.R., Levy, D.T., 1996. Values of risk reduction implied by motorist use of protection equipment. Journal of Transport Economics and Policy 30, 55–66.

Bowland, B.J., Beghin, J.C., 2001. Robust estimates of value of a statistical life for developing economies. Journal of Policy Modeling 23, 385–396.

Broder, I., 1990. The cost of accidental death: a capital market approach. Journal of Risk and Uncertainty 3, 51–63.

Brown, C., 1980. Equalizing differences in the labor market. Quarterly Journal of Economics 94, 113–134.

Brown, J.N., Rosen, H.S., 1982. On the estimation of structural hedonic price models. Econometrica 50, 765–768.

Burnett, J.K., Hahn, R.W., 2001. A costly benefit: economic analysis does not support EPA's new arsenic rule. Regulation 24, 44–49.

Cameron, T.A., 2008. The value of a statistical life: [they] do not think it means what [we] think it means. AERE Newsletter 28

Cameron, T.A., 2010. Euthanizing the value of a statistical life. Review of Environmental Economics and Policy 4, 161–178.

Carlin, P.S., Sandy, R., 1991. Estimating the implicit value of a young child's life. Southern Economic Journal 58, 186–202.

Chapman, K.S., Hariharan, G., 1994. Controlling for causality in the link from income to mortality. Journal of Risk and Uncertainty 8, 85–93.

Chilton, S., Covey, J., Hopkins, L., Jones-Lee, M.W., Loomes, G., Pidgeon, N., Spencer, A., 2002. Public perceptions of risk and preference-based values of safety. Journal of Risk and Uncertainty 25, 211–232.

Chilton, S., Jones-Lee, M., Kiraly, F., Metcalf, H., Pang, W., 2006. Dread risks. Journal of Risk and Uncertainty 33, 165–182.

Coaster, M., Rogers, B.P., Jones, O.D., Viscusi, W.K., Merkle, K.L., Zald, D.H., Gore, J.C., 2011. Variables influencing the neural correlates of perceived risk of physical harm. Cognitive, Affective, and Behavioral Neuroscience 11, 494–507.

Cobacho Tornel, M.B., López Nicolas, Á., Ramos Parreño, J.M., 2010. Mortality cost of smoking in Spain. Revista Española de Salud Pública 84, 271–280.

Corso, P.S., Hammitt, J.K., Graham, J.D., 2001. Valuing mortality-risk reduction: using visual aids to improve the validity of contingent valuation. Journal of Risk and Uncertainty 23, 165–184.

Costa, D.L., Kahn, M., 2004. Changes in the value of life, 1940–1980. Journal of Risk and Uncertainty 29, 159–180.

Covey, J., Robinson, A., Jones-Lee, M., Loomes, G., 2010. Responsibility, scale, and the valuation of rail safety. Journal of Risk and Uncertainty 40, 85–108.

De Blaeij, A., Florax, R.J.G.M., Rietveld, P., Verhoef, E., 2003. The value of a statistical life in road safety: a meta-analysis. Accident Analysis and Prevention 35, 973–986.

Desvousges, W.H., Johnson, F.R., Banzhaf, H.S., Russell, R.R., Fries, E.E., Dietz, K.J., Helms, S.C., 1995. Assessing the Environmental Externality Costs for Electricity Generation. Triangle Economic Research, Research Triangle Park, NC.

Dorman, P., Hagstrom, P., 1998. Wage compensation for dangerous work revisited. Industrial and Labor Relations Review 52, 116–135.

Doucouliagos, H., Stanley, T.D., Giles, M., 2012. Are estimates of the value of a statistical life exaggerated? Journal of Health Economics 31, 197–206.

Doucouliagos, H., Stanley, T.D., Viscusi, W.K., 2012b. Publication Selection and the Income Elasticity of the Value of a Statistical Life. Working Paper.

Dreyfus, M., Viscusi, W.K., 1995. Rates of time preference and consumer valuations of automobile safety and fuel efficiency. Journal of Law and Economics 38, 79–105.

Eeckhoudt, L.R., Hammitt, J.K., 2001. Background risk and the value of a statistical life. Journal of Risk and Uncertainty 23, 261–279.

Epple, D., 1987. Hedonic prices and implicit markets: estimating supply and demand functions for differentiated products. Journal of Political Economy 95, 59–80.

European Commission. 2001. Recommended Interim Values for the Value of Preventing a Fatality in DG Environment Cost Benefit Analysis. <http://ec.europa.eu/environment/enveco/others/pdf/recommended_interim_values.pdf>.

Evans, M.F., Schaur, G., 2010. A quantile estimation approach to identify income and age variation in the value of a statistical life. Journal of Environmental Economics and Management 59, 260–270.

Evans, M.F., Smith, V.K., 2010. Measuring how risk tradeoffs adjust with income. Journal of Risk and Uncertainty 40, 33–55.

Evans, W.N., Viscusi, W.K., 1991a. Estimation of state-dependent utility functions using survey data. Review of Economics and Statistics 73, 94–104.

Evans, W.N., Viscusi, W.K., 1991b. Utility-based measures of health. American Journal of Agricultural Economics 73, 1422–1427.

Finkelstein, A., Luttmer, E., Notowidigdo, M., 2009. Approaches to estimating the health state dependence of utility functions. American Economic Review 99, 116–121.

Finkelstein, A., Luttmer, E., Notowidigdo, M., 2013. What good is wealth without health? The effect of health on the marginal utility of consumption. Journal of the European Economic Association 11, 221–258.

Garbacz, C., 1989. Smoke detector effectiveness and the value of saving a life. Economic Letters 31, 281–286.

Garen, J.E., 1988. Compensating wage differentials and the endogeneity of job riskiness. Review of Economics and Statistics 70, 9–16.

Gayer, T., Hamilton, J., Viscusi, W.K., 2000. Private values of risk tradeoffs at Superfund sites: housing market evidence on learning about risk. Review of Economics and Statistics 32, 439–451.

Gayer, T., Hamilton, J., Viscusi, W.K., 2002. The market value of reducing cancer risk: hedonic housing prices with changing information. Southern Economic Journal 69, 266–289.

Gerking, S., DeHaan, M.H., Schulze, W., 1988. The marginal value of job safety: a contingent valuation study. Journal of Risk and Uncertainty 1, 185–199.

Graham, J.D., 2008. Saving lives through administrative law and economics. University of Pennsylvania Law Review 157, 395–540.

Hakes, J.K., Viscusi, W.K., 2007. Automobile seatbelt usage and the value of statistical life. Southern Economic Journal 73, 659–676.

Hamilton, J.T., Viscusi, W.K., 1999. Calculating Risks? The Spatial and Political Dimensions of Hazardous Waste Policy. MIT Press, Cambridge.

Hammitt, J.K., 2007. Valuing changes in mortality risk: lives saved versus life years saved. Review of Environmental Economics and Policy 1, 228–240.

Hammitt, J.K., Haninger, K., 2010. Valuing fatal risks to children and adults: effects of disease, latency, and risk aversion. Journal of Risk and Uncertainty 40, 57–83.

Hammitt, J.K., Liu, J., 2004. Effects of disease type and latency on the value of mortality risk. Journal of Risk and Uncertainty 28, 73–95.

Hammitt, J.K., Robinson, L.A., 2011. The income elasticity of the value per statistical life: transferring estimates between high and low income populations. Journal of Benefit-Cost Analysis 2, 1–27.

Hammitt, J.K., Treich, N., 2007. Statistical vs. identified lives in benefit-cost analysis. Journal of Risk and Uncertainty 35, 45–66.

Hara Associates, Inc. 2000. Benefit/Cost Analysis of Proposed Tobacco Products Information Regulations. Prepared for Health Canada and Consulting and Audit Canada, June 5, 2000, Ottawa, Ontario.

Heberlein, T.A., Wilson, M.A., Bishop, R.C., Schaeffer, N.C., 2005. Rethinking the scope test as a criterion for validity in contingent valuation. Journal of Environmental Economics and Management 50, 1–22.

Hersch, J., 1998. Compensating differentials for gender-specific job injury risks. American Economic Review 88, 598–607.

Hersch, J., Pickton, T.S., 1995. Risk-taking activities and heterogeneity of job-risk tradeoffs. Journal of Risk and Uncertainty 11, 205–217.

Hersch, J., Viscusi, W.K., 2010a. Immigrant status and the value of statistical life. Journal of Human Resources 45, 749–771.

Hersch, J., Viscusi, W.K., 2010b. Saving lives through punitive damages. Southern California Law Review 83, 229–262.

Horowitz, J.K., McConnell, K.E., 2002. A review of WTA/WTP studies. Journal of Environmental Economics and Management 40, 426–447.

Hwang, H.S., Reed, W.R., Hubbard, C., 1992. Compensating wage differentials and unobserved productivity. Journal of Political Economy 100, 835–858.

Ippolito, P.M., Ippolito, R.A., 1984. Measuring the value of life saving from consumer reactions to new information. Journal of Public Economics 25, 53–81.

Jenkins, R.R., Owens, N., Wiggins, L.B., 2001. Valuing reduced risks to children: the case of bicycle safety helmets. Contemporary Economic Policy 19, 397–408.

Johansson, P.O., 1996. On the value of changes in life expectancy. Journal of Health Economics 15, 105–113.

Jones-Lee, M.W., 1989. The Economics of Safety and Physical Risk. Basil Blackwell, Oxford.

Jones-Lee, M.W., Hammerton, M., Philips, P.R., 1985. The value of safety: results of a national sample survey. Economic Journal 95, 49–72.

Jones-Lee, M.W., Loomes, G., 1995. Scale and context effects in the valuation of transport safety. Journal of Risk and Uncertainty 11, 183–203.

Kahn, S., Lang, K., 1988. Efficient estimation of structural hedonic systems. International Economic Review 29, 157–166.

Kaplow, L., 2005. The value of statistical life and the coefficient of relative risk aversion. Journal of Risk and Uncertainty 31, 23–34.

Keeney, R.L., 1990. Mortality risks induced by economic expenditures. Risk Analysis 10, 147–159.

Kniesner, T.J., Leeth, J.D., 1995. Numerical simulation as a complement to econometric research on workplace safety. Journal of Risk and Uncertainty 12, 99–125.

Kniesner, T.J., Leeth, J.D., 2010. Hedonic wage equilibrium: theory, evidence and policy. Foundations and Trends in Microeconomics 5, 229–299.

Kniesner, T.J., Viscusi, W.K., 2005. Value of a statistical life: relative position vs. relative age. American Economic Review 95, 142–146.

Kniesner, T.J., Viscusi, W.K., Ziliak, J.P., 2006. Life-cycle consumption and the age-adjusted value of life. Contributions to Economic Analysis and Policy 5, 1–34.

Kniesner, T.J., Viscusi, W.K., Ziliak, J.P., 2010. Policy relevant heterogeneity in the value of statistical life: new evidence from panel data quantile regressions. Journal of Risk and Uncertainty 40, 15–31.

Kniesner, T.J., Viscusi, W.K., Ziliak, J.P., 2014. Willingness to accept equals willingness to pay for labor market estimates of the value of statistical life. Journal of Risk and Uncertainty., forthcoming

Kniesner, T.J., Viscusi, W.K., Woock, C., Ziliak, J.P., 2012. The value of statistical life: evidence from panel data. Review of Economics and Statistics 94, 19–44.

Kochi, I., Hubbell, B., Kramer, R., 2006. An empirical Bayes approach to combining and comparing estimates of the value of a statistical life for environmental policy analysis. Environmental and Resource Economics 34, 385–406.

Kochi, I., Taylor, L., 2011. Risk heterogeneity and the value of reducing fatal risks: further market-based evidence. Journal of Benefit-Cost Analysis 2, 1–26.

Krupnick, A., 2007. Mortality-risk valuation and age: stated preference evidence. Review of Environmental Economics and Policy 1, 261–282.

Krupnick, A., Alberini, A., Cropper, M., Simon, N., O'Brien, B., Goeree, R., Heintzelman, M., 2002. Age, health, and the willingness to pay for mortality risk reductions: a contingent valuation study of Ontario residents. Journal of Risk and Uncertainty 24, 161–186.

Lakdawalla, D.N., Sun, E.C., Jena, A.B., Reyes, C.M., Goldman, D.P., Philipson, T.J., 2010. An economic evaluation of the war on cancer. Journal of Health Economics 29, 333–346.

Lave, L., 1981. The Strategy for Social Regulation: Decision Frameworks for Policy. Brookings Institution, Washington, D.C.

Leeth, J.D., Ruser, J., 2003. Compensating wage differentials for fatal and nonfatal injury risk by gender and race. Journal of Risk and Uncertainty 27, 257–277.

Leigh, J.P., 1981. Compensating wages for occupational injuries and diseases. Social Science Quarterly 62, 772–778.

Lichtenstein, S., Slovic, P., Fischhoff, B., Layman, U., Combs, B., 1978. Judged frequency of lethal events. Journal of Experimental Psychology 4, 551–578.

Lillard, L., Weiss, Y., 1997. Uncertain health and survival: effects of end-of-life consumption. Journal of Business and Economic Statistics 15, 254–268.

Liu, J.T., Hammitt, J.K., Liu, J.L., 1997. Estimated hedonic wage function and value of life in a developing country. Economics Letters 57, 353–358.

Loh, K., Richardson, S., 2004. Foreign-born workers: trends in fatal occupational injuries, 1996–2001. Monthly Labor Review 127, 42–53.

Lutter, R., Morrall III, J.F., 1994. Health-health analysis: a new way to evaluate health and safety regulation. Journal of Risk and Uncertainty 8, 43–66.

Lutter, R., Morrall III, J.F., Viscusi, W.K., 1999. The cost-per-life saved cutoff for safety-enhancing regulations. Economic Inquiry 37, 599–608.

Magat, W.A., Viscusi, W.K., Huber, J., 1996. A reference lottery metric for valuing health. Management Science 42, 1118–1130.

Mellow, W., Sider, H., 1983. Accuracy of response in labor market surveys: evidence and duplications. Journal of Labor Economics 1, 331–344.

Miller, T.R., 2000. Variations between countries in values of statistical life. Journal of Transport Economics and Policy 34, 169–188.

Moore, M.J., Viscusi, W.K., 1988a. Doubling the estimated value of life: results using new occupational fatality data. Journal of Policy Analysis and Management 7, 476–490.

Moore, M.J., Viscusi, W.K., 1988b. The quantity-adjusted value of life. Economic Inquiry 26, 369–388.

Moore, M.J., Viscusi, W.K., 1990a. Discounting environmental health risks: new evidence and policy implications. Journal of Environmental Economics and Management 18, S51–S62.

Moore, M.J., Viscusi, W.K., 1990b. Models for estimating discount rates for long-term health risks using labor market data. Journal of Risk and Uncertainty 3, 381–401.

Mrozek, J.R., Taylor, L.O., 2002. What determines the value of life? a meta-analysis. Journal of Policy Analysis and Management 21, 253–270.

Murphy, K.M., Topel, R.H., 2006. The value of life and longevity. Journal of Political Economy 114, 811–904.

Persson, U., Norinder, A., Hjalte, K., Gralén, K., 2001. The value of statistical life in transport: findings from a new contingent valuation study in Sweden. Journal of Risk and Uncertainty 23, 121–134.

Portney, P.R., 1981. Housing prices, health effects, and valuing reductions in risk of death. Journal of Environmental Economics and Management 8, 72–78.

Posner, E.A., Sunstein, C.R., 2005. Dollars and death. University of Chicago Law Review 72, 537–598.

Robinson, L.A., 2007. How U.S. government agencies value mortality risk reductions. Review of Environmental Economics and Policy 1, 283–299.

Robinson, L.A., 2008. Valuing Mortality Risk Reductions in Homeland Security Analysis. Final Report to U.S. Customs and Border Protection. Department of Homeland Security, under contract to Industrial Economics.

Rosen, S., 1974. Hedonic prices and implicit markets: product differentiation in pure competition. Journal of Political Economy 82, 34–55.

Rosen, S., 1986. The theory of equalizing differences. In: Ashenfelter, O., Layard, R. (Eds.), Handbook of Labor Economics, vol. 1. North-Holland, Amsterdam.

Rosen, S., 1988. The value of changes in life expectancy. Journal of Risk and Uncertainty 1, 285–304.

Scharff, R.L., Viscusi, W.K., 2011. Heterogeneous rates of time preference and the decision to smoke. Economic Inquiry 49, 99–172.

Schelling, T.C., 1968. The life you save may be your own. In: Chase, S. (Ed.), Problems in Public Expenditure Analysis. Brookings, Washington, D.C.

Scotton, C.R., Taylor, L.O., 2011. Valuing risk reductions: incorporating risk heterogeneity into a revealed preference framework. Resource and Energy Economics 33, 381–397.

Shepard, D.S., Zeckhauser, R.J., 1984. Survival versus consumption. Management Science 30, 423–439.

Shogren, J.F., Stamland, T., 2002. Skill and the value of life. Journal of Political Economy 110, 1168–1173.

Sloan, F.A., Viscusi, W.K., Chesson, H.W., Conover, C.J., Whetten-Goldstein, K., 1998. Alternative approaches to valuing intangible health losses: the evidence for multiple sclerosis. Journal of Health Economics 17, 475–497.

Smith, A., 1776. Wealth of Nations, 1937 ed. Modern Library, New York.

Smith, V.K., Epp, D.J., Schwabe, K.A., 1994. Cross-country analyses don't estimate health-health responses. Journal of Risk and Uncertainty 8, 67–84.

Smith, V.K., Evans, M.F., Kim, H., Taylor Jr., D.H., 2004. Do the near-elderly value mortality risks differently? Review of Economics and Statistics 86, 423–429.

Smith, V.K., Mansfield, C., Clayton, L., 2009. Valuing a homeland security policy: countermeasures for the threats from shoulder mounted missiles. Journal of Risk and Uncertainty 38, 215–243.

Sojourner, A., 2010. Partial Identification of Willingness-to-Pay Using Shape Restrictions with an Application to the Value of a Statistical Life. Industrial Relations Center, University of Minnesota (Twin Cities Campus), Working Paper 0110.

Spence, M., 1977. Consumer misperceptions, product failure, and producer liability. Review of Economic Studies 44, 561–572.

Subramanian, U., Cropper, M., 2000. Public choices between life-saving programs: the tradeoff between qualitative factors and lives saved. Journal of Risk and Uncertainty 21, 117–149.

Thaler, R.H., Rosen, S., 1975. The value of saving a life: evidence from the labor market. In: Terleckyj, N.E. (Ed.), Household Production and Consumption. Columbia University Press, New York.

U.K. Health and Safety Executive, 2001. Reducing Risks, Protecting People: HSE's Decision-Making Process. <http://www.hse.gov.uk/risk/theory/r2p2.pdf>.

U.K. HM Treasury, 2011. The Green Book: Appraisal and Evaluation in Central Government: Treasury Guidance. TSO, London. <http://www.hm-treasury.gov.uk/d/green_book_complete.pdf>.

U.S. Department of Transportation, 2011. Office of the Assistant Secretary for Transportation Policy. Memorandum: Treatment of the Economic Value of Statistical Life in Departmental Analyses. <http://www.dot.gov/sites/dot.dev/files/docs/Value_of_Life_Guidance_2011_Update_07-29-2011.pdf>.

U.S. Department of Transportation, 2013. Office of the Secretary of Transportation. Memorandum: Guidance on the Treatment of the Economic Value of a Statistical Life in U.S. Department of Transportation Analyses. <http://www.dot.gov/office-policy/transportation-policy/guidance-treatment-economic-value-statistical-life>.

U.S. Environmental Protection Agency, 2002. Technical Addendum: Methodologies for the Benefit Analysis of the Clear Skies Initiative. <http://www.epa.gov/clearskies/tech_adden.pdf>.

U.S. Environmental Protection Agency, 2003. Technical Addendum: Methodologies for the Benefit Analysis of the Clear Skies Act of 2003. <http://www.epa.gov/clearskies/tech_addendum.pdf>.

U.S. Environmental Protection Agency, 2004. Regulatory Impact Analysis for the Industrial Boilers and Process Heaters NESHAP. Final Report.

U.S. Environmental Protection Agency, 2010. Valuing Mortality Risk Reductions for Environmental Policy: A White Paper. SAB Review Draft.

Van Houtven, G., Sullivan, M.B., Dockins, C., 2008. Cancer premiums and latency effects: a risk tradeoff approach for valuing reduction. Journal of Risk and Uncertainty 36, 179–200.

Viscusi, W.K., 1978. Wealth effects and earnings premiums for job hazards. Review of Economics and Statistics 60, 408–416.

Viscusi, W.K., 1979. Employment Hazards: An Investigation of Market Performance. Harvard University Press, Cambridge.

Viscusi, W.K., 1983. Risk by Choice: Regulating Health and Safety in the Workplace. Harvard University Press, Cambridge.

Viscusi, W.K., 1989. Prospective reference theory: toward an explanation of the paradoxes. Journal of Risk and Uncertainty 2, 235–264.

Viscusi, W.K., 1992. Fatal Tradeoffs: Public and Private Responsibilities for Risk. Oxford University Press, New York.

Viscusi, W.K., 1993. The value of risks to life and health. Journal of Economic Literature 31, 1912–1946.

Viscusi, W.K., 1994a. Mortality effects of regulatory costs and policy evaluation criteria. Rand Journal of Economics 25, 94–109.

Viscusi, W.K., 1994b. Risk-risk analysis. Journal of Risk and Uncertainty 8, 5–17.

Viscusi, W.K., 2002. Smoke-Filled Rooms: A Postmortem on the Tobacco Deal. University of Chicago Press, Chicago.

Viscusi, W.K., 2003. Racial differences in labor market values of a statistical life. Journal of Risk and Uncertainty 27, 239–256.

Viscusi, W.K., 2004. The value of life: estimates with risks by occupation and industry. Economic Inquiry 42, 29–48.

Viscusi, W.K., 2007. The flawed hedonic damages measure of compensation for wrongful death and personal injury. Journal of Forensic Economics 20, 113–135.

Viscusi, W.K., 2009a. Valuing risks of death from terrorism and natural disasters. Journal of Risk and Uncertainty 38, 191–213.

Viscusi, W.K., 2009b. The devaluation of life. Regulation and Governance 3, 103–127.

Viscusi, W.K., 2010. Policy challenges of the heterogeneity of the value of statistical life. Foundations and Trends in Microeconomics 6, 99–172.

Viscusi, W.K., Aldy, J.E., 2003. The value of a statistical life: a critical review of market estimates throughout the world. Journal of Risk and Uncertainty 27, 239–256.

Viscusi, W.K., Aldy, J.E., 2007. Labor market estimates of the senior discount for the value of statistical life. Journal of Environmental Economics and Management 53, 377–392.

Viscusi, W.K., Evans, W.N., 1990. Utility functions that depend on health status: estimates and economic implications. American Economic Review 80, 353–374.

Viscusi, W.K., Evans, W.N., 1998. Estimation of revealed probabilities and utility functions for product safety decisions. Review of Economics and Statistics 80, 28–33.

Viscusi, W.K., Evans, W.N., 2006. Behavioral probabilities. Journal of Risk and Uncertainty 32, 5–15.

Viscusi, W.K., Hersch, J., 2001. Cigarette smokers as job risk takers. Review of Economics and Statistics 83, 269–280.

Viscusi, W.K., Hersch, J., 2008. The mortality cost to smokers. Journal of Health Economics 27, 943–958.

Viscusi, W.K., Huber, J., Bell, J., 2013. Assessing Whether There Is a Cancer Premium for the Value of Statistical Life. Health Economics. http://dx.doi.org/10.1002/hec.2919.

Viscusi, W.K., Magat, W., Huber, J., 1987. An investigation of the rationality of consumer valuations of multiple health risks. RAND Journal of Economics 18, 465–479.

Viscusi, W.K., Magat, W., Huber, J., 1991. Pricing environmental risks: survey assessments of risk-risk and risk-dollar tradeoffs for chronic bronchitis. Journal of Environmental Economics and Management 21, 32–51.

Viscusi, W.K., Moore, M.J., 1987. Workers' compensation: wage effects, benefit inadequacies, and the value of health losses. Review of Economics and Statistics 69, 249–261.

Viscusi, W.K., Moore, M.J., 1989. Rates of time preference and valuations of the duration of life. Journal of Public Economics 38, 297–317.

Viscusi, W.K., O'Connor, C., 1984. Adaptive responses to chemical labeling: are workers Bayesian decision Makers? American Economic Review 74, 942–956.

Viscusi, W.K., Zeckhauser, R.J., 1994. The fatality and injury costs of expenditures. Journal of Risk and Uncertainty 8, 19–41.

Viscusi, W.K., Zeckhauser, R.J., 2003. Sacrificing civil liberties to reduce terrorism risks. Journal of Risk and Uncertainty 26, 99–120.

Williams, S.F., 1993. Second best: the soft underbelly of the deterrence theory in tort. Harvard Law Review 106, 932–944.

CHAPTER 8

Economic Analysis of Risk and Uncertainty Induced by Health Shocks: A Review and Extension

Tomas J. Philipson[a] and George Zanjani[b]

[a]Daniel Levin Professor of Public Policy, The University of Chicago, USA

[b]AAMGA Distinguished Chair in Risk Management and Insurance, Georgia State University, USA

Contents

Abstract

We review and extend the economic analysis of mitigating risks in the presence of health shocks. The existing literature is mainly focused on how shocks affect consumption, for example through their impact on medical spending. We argue that this focus is limited in that shocks to health itself, rather than consumption, may be more damaging. Since human capital is not transferrable, health risk—unlike medical spending risk—cannot be pooled through traditional insurance. Instead, medical innovation is the main method of achieving smoothing in health across disease states. We explore the welfare implications of this "health insurance" view of medical R&D . We also review the evidence on how FDA regulations affect overall health risk, as regulations lower health risks of products *ex post* but raise risk *ex ante* by discouraging medical innovation. More analysis seems warranted on the relative value of programs aimed at mitigating shocks to health itself by stimulating innovation versus health insurance reforms aimed mainly at consumption smoothing.

Keywords

Health Risk, Health Insurance, Medical Innovation, Health Human Capital, Health Care Spending

JEL Classification Codes

D80, G22, I1

Handbook of the Economics of Risk and Uncertainty, Volume 1
ISSN 2211-7547, http://dx.doi.org/10.1016/B978-0-444-53685-3.00008-8

8.1 INTRODUCTION

Dealing with uncertainties introduced by health shocks has generated much economic market and government activity, as well as intense policy debates, and has thus been the topic of much economic analysis. The problem of dealing with health shocks has led to private and public provision of insurance in a large number of areas including life insurance, annuities, workers compensation, health care insurance, long-term care insurance, and disability insurance, to name a few. A central feature of these insurance mechanisms is the pooling of financial risks, so that those who are lucky enough to avoid sickness pay for the losses of the unlucky ones that become sick. Accompanying the historical growth in insurance has been proliferation of economic literature on the prevalence, value, and desirability of insurance. In particular, there has been considerable debate on whether the public or private financing and production of insurance is more desirable.

In this paper we review some of the most commonly discussed results of this vast literature on dealing with health shocks. The goal of the paper is not an exhaustive review of various unrelated results, as a complete review of this economic field would indeed be impossible in a single chapter. Rather, the goal is to review the central aspects of this literature including the often discussed frictions associated with private health insurance markets, the value of public intervention, and the welfare effects induced by either form of provision.

Additionally, we call the reader's attention to what we regard as a critical gap in the literature on how to efficiently address future health shocks. Specifically, we argue that the existing literature is focused on the insurance of financial shocks and thus does not adequately address a more central and fundamental concern of dealing with health shocks—the restoration of health itself and the smoothing of health across various future disease states. Traditional analysis is almost exclusively focused on how to mitigate the impact of health shocks on consumption rather than the impact on health itself. For example, life-, annuity-, and health-care insurance arrangements all aim only to smooth the consumption uncertainty associated with health shocks. Even when utilized, however, these arrangements cannot fully smooth health across disease states. To illustrate, when an incurable cancer hits, consumption may be fully insured but what is not covered is the loss in health—and this is the real risk that may impose the largest loss in welfare.

It is important to recognize that because human capital cannot be traded, risk pooling arrangements in health itself, whether through private or public insurance, are often infeasible. For example, if an individual is hit by a deadly cancer, he cannot be made "whole" or fully healthy by getting health reallocated from someone else.[1] Thus, methods other than risk-pooling must be utilized to reduce risks to health itself. As medical

---

[1] A rare exception is when transplantations are feasible, but market mechanisms for such health transfers have been deemed unethical and are outlawed in many countries.

innovation is the primary method by which the real price of health is reduced over time, it can be viewed as serving the role of insuring future health. For example, the lower price of health enabled by innovation in treatments for breast cancer and HIV has smoothed health across such future disease states. Medical innovation is to health what health-care insurance is to health care; a certain payment for medical R&D lowers the price of future health while a certain health insurance premium lowers the price of future health care. Thus, medical R&D is "health insurance" in the literal sense of the phrase—as opposed to the colloquial usage where "health insurance" refers to insurance of medical expenditures. Both are certain investments for uncertain future price reductions, and we argue both may therefore be usefully analyzed and valued using similar methods. In a sense medical innovation acts like a "financial innovation" that completes a previously incomplete market by enabling a previously uninsurable shock to be insurable through traditional health care insurance.

While medical innovation is aimed at reducing risks associated with health shocks, the innovations themselves may involve additional health risks in terms of unsafe side effects. Indeed, the health risks associated with new medical innovations are regulated extensively by governments worldwide, such as the FDA in the US. However, regulations aimed at reducing the health risks associated with treatments impact real "health insurance" through their well-known adverse effects on medical innovation by raising R&D costs and delaying profits. We review the literature on assessing the health risks with medical products and discuss how it trades off *ex post* side effects of innovations with *ex ante* "health insurance" through medical innovation.

A brief outline of the review is as follows. Section 8.2 discusses some of the central aspects of the large literature on health care insurance. Section 8.3 discusses the role of medical innovation as a mechanism to smooth health risk given the infeasibility of pooling such risks. Section 8.4 reviews the literature on the health risks associated with new innovations and the public regulation of such risks by the FDA. Lastly Section 8.5 concludes with discussion of useful avenues for future research.

8.2 HEALTH CARE INSURANCE AND CONSUMPTION SMOOTHING

It is a well-known theoretical result that a risk-averse consumer prefers full insurance offered on actuarially fair terms under expected utility maximization without state dependence. For example, according to Arrow (1963, p. 961), "…[t]he welfare case for insurance policies of all sorts is overwhelming." Viewed in this light, it is not surprising that a state of being uninsured is often taken as *prima facie* evidence of a problem during economic analysis, and economists have devoted much attention to the theoretical and empirical examination of why people are not fully insured.

Health insurance is commonly viewed as the canonical example of an inefficient private insurance market, with unusually severe transactional complications that make the presence of the uninsured a pressing policy problem. Indeed, Arrow's endorsement of insurance's value quoted above came in the context of a lament about health insurance.

However, before examining the potential problems in the health insurance market, it is worth noting that, within the world of insurance generally, health insurance take-up is rather high. About 82% of the nonelderly population in the U.S. carried health insurance in 2010.[2] This is comparable to the rate of take-up of automobile liability insurance among motorists (86%)—which is currently compulsory in most states.[3] Insurance take-up rates from other markets where purchase is voluntary are often substantially lower than that for health insurance among the eligible populations facing the risks involved. For examples, only 11% of California homeowners carry earthquake insurance; 70% of US households carry life insurance; 43% of renters carry renter's insurance; and 1% of US properties outside high risk areas carry flood insurance (the take-up rate inside high-risk areas, where purchase is often mandated by lenders, is 49%).[4] While each market of course has its own idiosyncratic features, the general point is that health insurance penetration is fairly high when compared with other markets where purchase is not compulsory.

Nevertheless, the canonical model of insurance predicts full insurance under the assumption of actuarially fair pricing, and much economic analysis has been devoted to discussing the causes and consequences of factors disrupting this prediction. Most of this analysis has been under the assumption of the traditional rational choice framework, and our review will largely abide within this framework. It is worth noting, however, that a growing literature exists on the behavioral economics aspects of insurance choice and how relaxing the assumption of consumer rationality affects conclusions about insurance interventions and health policy generally (see, for example, Abaluck and Gruber (2011); Chernew and Fendrick (2008); Frank (2007); Frank and Lamiraud (2009); Liebman and Zeckhauser (2008); McFadden (2006)).

A natural place to start addressing the question of why people are not fully insured in a rational choice framework is with what is perhaps the simplest possible explanation—prices above costs of paying claims, which may be due to production costs in addition to claims (often called "administrative costs" in the context of insurance markets) or markups due to market power. Demand for insurance falls in price as for most other goods, so markups above expected claims costs may reduce or eliminate

---

[2] "Overview of the Uninsured in the United States: A Summary of the 2011 Current Populaion Survey," *ASPE Issue Brief*, US Department of Health and Human Services.

[3] Uninsured Motorists (2011), Insurance Research Council. Cited figure refers to estimates for 2009.

[4] *2011 California Earthquake Premium, Exposure and Policy Count Data Call Summary*, California Department of Insurance; *Trends in Life Insurance Ownership* (2010), LIMRA; 2006 Insurance Research Council survey on renters insurance; L. Dixon, N. Clancy, S. A. Seabury, and A. Overton, 2006, *The National Flood Insurance Program's Market Penetration Rate: Estimates and Policy Implications* (Santa Monica, CA: RAND Corporation).

equilibrium insurance coverage. Arrow's seminal work on insurance contemplated the situation where insurance prices would deviate from actuarially fair values due to production costs of various kinds, such as those relating to agent commissions and to company overhead. The impact on insurance purchase of course depends on the nature of the cost structure. Arrow showed that, in circumstances where the premium was determined by the expected loss times a proportional expense loading, the optimal insurance contract would feature full coverage beyond a deductible. Fixed costs could lead to other effects, including nonparticipation (e.g., Mulligan and Philipson (2004)). As a percentage of premiums, pricing above claims costs are substantial. Such pricing above costs (defined as any cost other than benefit payments to the insured or third-party service providers or claimants) can amount to 30% of the premium or more, depending on the line of insurance. This illustrates Arrow's (1963) observation that actuarial fairness may not be present in insurance markets generally. Additional markups may be generated by market power. Less work has been done on output restrictions due to market power in the insurance industry, although there is a literature estimating premium elasticities directly related to this issue.[5]

While it is possible that pricing above costs may explain certain patterns of limited coverage and nonparticipation in insurance markets, a lack of universal purchase is hardly unique to insurance products and not by itself necessarily indicative of market failure, even though perceived as such by many economists. Goods and services of course require resources for production. Thus, there is little hand-wringing among economists over production costs unless market imperfections are present. In the case of insurance, contracting costs are emphasized as market imperfections: In particular, moral hazard and adverse selection are often fingered as causes of insurance market failure.

8.2.1 Adverse Selection

Adverse selection commonly refers to a situation of asymmetric information between insurers and consumers, where insurers are unable to distinguish the underlying risk characteristics of consumers buying insurance. Consumers are aware of their own risk characteristics, which of course influence their demand for insurance. The two basic theoretical flavors of adverse selection are the "collapsing market" of Akerlof (1970) and the "separating equilibrium" of Rothschild and Stiglitz (1976).

To illustrate Akerlof's idea with an extreme version (adapted to the context of insurance), the only sustainable market price for contracts is the one corresponding to the expected costs of the worst risks in the consumer population. Any attempt by the insurer to offer a "pooling" contract—in which the price of the contract reflects the

---

[5] For estimates pertaining to individual health insurance, see Krueger and Kuziemko (2013), Strombom et al. (2002), and Gruber and Poterba (1994). For a partial survey of estimates in other markets, see Grace et al. (2004).

average cost in the consumer population—is doomed to failure, as the contract is only attractive to those risks who are "worse than average." As the better risks opt to go without coverage, those remaining in the pool are progressively riskier, so the price must rise—thus continuing the process of driving out the good risks along the margin. The unraveling of the market continues until only the worst risks (the "lemons") are left.

Rothschild and Stiglitz (1976), on the other hand, have a model similar in flavor but less gloomy in terms of predictions. In their model, the insurer still cannot identify individual risk characteristics but can effectively sort consumers by exploiting differences in their desire for coverage. This is accomplished by offering a menu of contracts ranging from high to low levels of coverage. The high levels of coverage feature high per unit prices (as these will be attractive to high risks) and the restricted levels of coverage feature low per unit prices (as these are attractive to low risks but scare off the high risks because of their greater need for coverage).

The economic burden of adverse selection thus falls on the shoulders of low-risk consumers, who, in one way or another, end up with less coverage in a second-best world with asymmetric information. And it is this theoretical observation that has driven much of the subsequent empirical literature. The key empirical test centers on the relationship between coverage and risk: Adverse selection models predict that high-risk individuals will purchase more coverage, and it is this connection which lies at the center of most tests.

Viewed across insurance markets—and even within insurance markets—the empirical evidence on adverse selection is mixed (see Cohen and Siegelman (2010) for a cross-market review, some of which is recapitulated here). In life insurance markets, most studies have found no evidence of adverse selection (Cawley and Philipson (1999); Hendel and Lizzeri (2003); McCarthy and Mitchell (2010)).[6] In annuity markets, on the other hand, the weight of the evidence points in the opposite direction, as most studies have found evidence consistent with adverse selection (Finkelstein and Poterba (2002, 2004); McCarthy and Mitchell (2010)). Recent work in auto insurance has tended toward negative findings (Richaudeau (1999); Chiappori and Salanié (2000); Dionne et al. (2001); Saito (2006)) although some researchers have found evidence in certain market segments or sublines (Cohen (2005); Kremslehner and Muermann (2013)).

Given the variety of findings in other insurance markets, it is not surprising that the findings in health insurance are similarly mixed. Cutler and Reber (1998) and Altman et al. (1998) both find evidence of significant adverse selection in the employer-based health insurance market. Like annuity markets (where adverse selection is also commonly found in empirical studies—see previous discussion), employer-based health insurance often features limited or no pricing differentials with respect to the risk characteristics

---

[6] He (2009) is an exception, finding a correlation between insurance purchase and subsequent death in HRS data.

of individual applicants. This suggests that the observed selection effects may owe more to the institutional arrangements in the market rather than the technical ability of the insurer to gather information. Indeed, Cardon and Hendel (2001) argue that much of the claims variation in health insurance can be explained by observable characteristics, and private information about health status seems to play only a small role.

In other circumstances, asymmetric information between consumers and insurers may be present, but adverse selection—in the sense that the insured population is of higher risk than the uninsured population—is not. This is found by Finkelstein and McGarry (2006) in the market for long-term care insurance and Fang et al. (2008) in the Medigap insurance market. In these circumstances, it is suggested that preference characteristics other than claims risk are influencing insurance demand. This can actually lead to circumstances of advantageous selection, where lower risk consumers have greater demand for insurance because of other unobservable characteristics. In aggregate, it is possible for the two influences to offset each other—even if there are consumers in the market who are exploiting private information.[7] Thus, asymmetric information is not necessarily *prima facie* evidence of serious inefficiency.

8.2.2 Moral Hazard

Moral hazard was suggested as being significant for the economic analysis of health insurance at least as early as Arrow (1963), who noted that the demand for medical services was influenced by the presence of insurance and that coinsurance provisions in insurance contracts were present to deal with this problem. The idea was extended by Pauly (1968), who clarified how consumer demand for medical services after a health shock varied according to the marginal cost of care; in the extreme case of full insurance, the consumer would face no marginal cost of care and would over-consume care relative to the economically optimal level when ill. This behavior was incorporated into the price of the insurance contract, and it was possible to imagine cases where the moral hazard problem would lead even a risk averse consumer to forego insurance because of his or her inability to commit to limiting care utilization after purchasing the contract. Zeckhauser (1970) extended this line of reasoning further by elucidating a key trade-off between correct incentives and risk-sharing in insurance contracting: cost sharing provisions such as coinsurance could limit moral hazard, but only at the cost of exposing the consumer to greater financial risk.

The theory has been generalized and extended. For example, Goldman and Philipson (2007) analyze moral hazard in the presence of multiple technologies, showing that the main predictions of the single treatment case break down when cross price

---

[7] For a striking example of such exploitation in the long-term care insurance market, see the influence of Huntington's Disease on demand revealed in Oster et al. (2010). Wolfe and Goddeeris (1991) also find adverse selection but conclude that it is unlikely to have serious welfare effects.

elasticities between treatments are nonzero. For example, even though drug demand may be highly elastic, it may be optimal to fully insure it (or even provide subsidies to consume it) to induce less hospital spending in the future. Another direction that seems useful is to extend the theory of insurance under moral hazard to incorporate altruism. This needs to recognize that low co-pays, in addition to raising moral hazard, act as beneficial Pigouvian subsidies from the rich to the poor if the rich care about expanding the care to the poor. The dual role played by copays is exemplified by the low Medicaid copays which, according to traditional theory, induce excessive moral hazard for the highly elastic care by the poor. This is clearly not inefficient if the rationale for the low co-pays is to stimulate demand of the poor. It seems that the effect of altruistic externalities on optimal insurance design is a useful area of future work.

Moral hazard is difficult to distinguish from adverse selection empirically since both effects work to produce insured populations with higher accident risk (*ex post*) than otherwise similar uninsured (or partially insured) populations. Thus, a positive statistical relationship between coverage and risk is consistent with both moral hazard and adverse selection. Abbring et al. (2003) show that it is technically possible to distinguish the two in an empirical setting, but panel data is required.

In a health insurance setting, consumer moral hazard could operate either through taking risks relating to health (for example, lifestyle choices) or through choice regarding the utilization of services once faced with a health shock. The latter effect has been well-documented in the literature, or at least inferred from studies of the price-elasticity of demand for medical services. The RAND Health Insurance Experiment featured the random assignment of families to health plans with different cost sharing provisions. The results clearly indicated that cost sharing provisions reduced overall usage of medical services (Manning et al. (1987)), and overall price-elasticity of demand in the experiment was estimated to be −0.2—a result echoed in Keeler and Rolph (1988). Though these figures are based on data from the 1970s, more recent work has produced similar findings (Chandra et al. (2010)).[8]

Moral hazard of a different ilk is present on the supply side of the market, as care decisions may be heavily influenced by physician recommendations. It follows that medical expenditure, in addition to depending on consumer incentives, will also depend on physician incentives if physician behavior is at all guided by financial incentives. The empirical evidence does indeed suggest that physician behavior is influenced by these incentives (e.g., Gaynor et al. (2004)).

Given the sensitivity of consumer expenditure to price, it is not surprising that coinsurance, co-payments, and deductibles are common features of health insurance

---

[8] These estimates are for overall medical expenditure, and much research has focused on components of medical expenditures. To give some sense of the breadth of research available, see Goldman et al. (2007) for a survey of price-elasticity of demand for prescription drugs; Kondo et al. (2009) for a study on the elasticity of demand for vaccinations; Connolly et al. (2009) for research on the elasticity of demand for Assisted Reproductive Technologies (ART).

plans. In addition, managed care organizations have introduced numerous cost-saving innovations aimed at the supply side of the market (see McGuire (2012) for a survey). These innovations generally may curb moral hazard and make insurance more attractive to consumers in an *ex ante* sense. Indeed, some might interpret the penetration rate of 82% mentioned above as evidence of the success of the private health insurance market in the US. However, the standards for success in the health insurance market are much higher. Many hold the ideal of universal coverage, and the failure of the private market to adequately address the needs of certain high risk segments of the population—such as the elderly and people with pre-existing conditions—has led to substantial government intervention in the health insurance market in developed countries.

8.3 HEALTH STOCK INSURANCE AND MEDICAL INNOVATION

In this section, we argue that the extensive policy focus on ensuring consumption smoothing in the face of health shocks ignores an important dimension of the welfare effects of such shocks. While it is true that financial shocks relating to health care are significant and deserve attention, much less attention is paid to policies aimed at smoothing health itself in response to shocks. To illustrate, when an individual is diagnosed with Parkinson's disease, there are two shocks to consider: One is the shock to wealth, since treatments are potentially costly and earnings may suffer; the second is the shock to health itself, since even the most advanced treatments are largely palliative and can only partially restore quality of life. For many people, the second shock may well be the more devastating one from a welfare perspective. Unfortunately, risk-pooling through insurance mechanisms in human capital is infeasible since human capital cannot be traded. This implies that risk reduction from health shocks must come through other means—the main one being medical innovation. Due to medical innovation, breast cancer and HIV today are shocks to health which are far more "smoothable" than previously.

More precisely, consider the following simple formalization of the full impact of health shocks and the *ex ante* insurance value of medical innovation. Let π_s be the probability of a bad disease state. If healthy, the consumer's health is H_0. If sick, the consumer's health is a function of medical spending, given the technology level x:

$$H_s(M; x) \leq H_0.$$

We consider a simple insurance contract with coinsurance $1 - i$ for any medical spending. For example, if the consumer spends M she is reimbursed $i_* M$ by insurance, with $0 \leq i \leq 1$. The premium is assumed to reflect the actuarial value times a loading factor $L(\tau) \geq 1$:

$$P(i, M) = (\pi_s * i * M)L(\tau)$$

where we assume that τ represents the technological efficiency of the insurance market so that $L' < 0$.

To focus on the central issues here, we assume away moral hazard. The consumer thus chooses both the coinsurance rate and medical care *ex ante* to maximize

$$V(Y, x, \tau) = max_{M,i}\{\pi_s U(Y - (1 - i)M - P(i, M), H_s(M; x)) + (1 - \pi_s)U(Y - P(i, M), H_0)\}.$$

The FOC for optimal *ex ante* care leads to:

$$\left(\pi_s \frac{\partial U_s}{\partial H_s}\right)\frac{\partial H_s}{\partial M} = \pi_s \frac{\partial U_s}{\partial C}(1 - i) + \left(\pi_s \frac{\partial U_s}{\partial C} + (1 - \pi_s)\frac{\partial U_0}{\partial C}\right)\frac{\partial P}{\partial M}$$

with the first term on the right-hand side representing the marginal cost associated with medical care copayment and the second term representing the marginal cost associated with premiums.

There are two key interrelated risks faced by the individual. The first is consumption risk, a risk which is created by uncertainty in the level of medical care spending. The second is health risk, which is mitigated by the utilization of medical care. The vast majority of the literature dealing with mitigating health risks is concerned with the former risk.

Improvements in the technological efficiency of the medical insurance market (represented in our simple model by increases in τ) enable better smoothing of consumption in the presence of health shocks and may improve health as well if optimal medical care spending increases in response to decreases in the effective price of care:

$$\frac{dH_s^*}{d\tau} = \frac{\partial H_s^*}{\partial M}\frac{\partial M^*}{\partial \tau} > 0$$

with an ultimate impact on welfare composed of an impact on consumption and an impact on health as in:

$$\frac{\partial V}{\partial \tau} = \left[\pi_s \frac{\partial U_s}{\partial C}\frac{dC_s^*}{d\tau} + (1 - \pi_s)\frac{\partial U_0}{\partial C}\frac{dC_0^*}{d\tau}\right] + \pi_s \frac{\partial U_s}{\partial H}\frac{dH_s^*}{d\tau}.$$

Through its influence on both consumption and health, the change in technology affects both consumption risk and health risk.

The second risk—risk to health itself—is less often addressed. As noted above, it is possible that improvements in the efficiency of insurance will improve health, and this has been analyzed extensively (for a review see Levy and Meltzer (2008)). However, the most important limitations on health risk mitigation will often concern medical technology. As it is impossible to have risk-pooling for human capital that is not tradable, limiting health risk will have to come from other means. The main one is medical innovation as represented by an increase in the productivity of producing health from medical care, the parameter x above. If we interpret increases in x as representing improvements in the productivity of medical care spending (i.e., $\frac{\partial^2 H_s}{\partial M \partial x} > 0$), then the first-order effect of increases in medical technology will be improvements in health. More productive health care raises the marginal product of care, and thereby raises the optimal health stock upon a health shock:

$$\frac{dH_s^*}{dx} = \frac{\partial H_s^*}{\partial M} \frac{\partial M^*}{\partial x} + \frac{\partial H_s^*}{\partial x}$$

and, more to the point, increases consumer welfare:

$$\frac{\partial V}{\partial x} = \left[\pi_s \frac{\partial U_s}{\partial C} \frac{dC_s^*}{dx} + (1 - \pi_s) \frac{\partial U_0}{\partial C} \frac{dC_0^*}{dx} \right] + \pi_s \frac{\partial U_s}{\partial H} \frac{dH_s^*}{dx}.$$

This simple analysis raises the key question of the relative value of improvements in medical technology (x) versus improvements in the efficiency of insurance (τ). At the margin, the consumer will value improvements in medical technology more than improvements in health insurance efficiency if:

$$\frac{\partial V}{\partial x} > \frac{\partial V}{\partial \tau}.$$

The value of improvements in medical technology to the consumer may often be much larger than the value of consumption smoothing. To illustrate, consider an incurable disease for which the current medical technology x is ineffective. In this extreme case:

$$\frac{\partial H_s}{\partial M} = 0.$$

Nothing is spent on care as it is unproductive, so expected utility is

$$V(Y, x, \tau) = sU(Y, H_s(0; x)) + (1 - s)U(Y, H_0).$$

Even though there is perfect consumption smoothing there is of course a loss in health induced by the health shock, and the value of traditional health care insurance is obviously zero. Moreover, gains in insurance market efficiency obviously yield no gains in welfare:

$$\frac{\partial V}{\partial \tau} = 0$$

since medical spending is unproductive under the current state of technology. Even if insurance were free, it would have no value. Gains in welfare in this scenario can come only from reducing the price of health through medical innovation.

Now consider the other extreme when medical innovation progresses in a way that more health can be obtained for successively lower amounts of medical care spending. This implies in the extreme there is no loss in health and there are minimal resources used to restore health upon a health shock. In this case, expected utility converges to $U(Y,H_0)$. With the most extreme form of perfect medical productivity, it is as if no health shock occurred in the first place. In this example, gains in medical innovation will eventually not only insure health smoothing but eliminate the need for consumption smoothing related to medical expenditure as medical technology reduces the cost of care. Put differently, there is no need for insuring consumption when faced with cheap care.

As a prelude to later analysis, consider the value of being relieved of health risk as illustrated by the willingness to pay W to transition between the two extreme forms of medical care productivity (completely unproductive to perfectly productive). In other words, how much income would one be willing to sacrifice in the high productivity world (where health risk is absent) to make one indifferent to the low productivity world, where the individual is still subject to health risk:

$$U(Y - W, H_0) = \pi_s U(Y, H_s(0; x)) + (1 - \pi_s)U(Y, H_0).$$

It measures how much money one would be willing to pay when healthy (high productivity case) to avoid facing the risk of disease (low productivity case), and is clearly greater than zero in this case—which is the value of smoothing consumption in the low productivity world.

More generally, it is important to note that the value of consumption smoothing evidently depends on the state of medical technology. In the extreme illustration above, there is no value to consumption smoothing when medical technology is completely ineffective. In addition, there also is no value when the medical technology is so effective that only minimal medical expenditure is required to restore health. However, intermediate states of medical technology, where improvements in health can be purchased at nonnegligible cost, will be associated with gains to insuring medical expenditures.

The reverse is also true: The value of medical technology improvements also will, in general, depend on the efficiency of the insurance market as represented by τ. As will be illustrated more formally in Section 8.3.2, access to an expensive medical technology may be possible only with insurance, meaning that the value of the technology depends on the existence of the insurance market.

8.3.1 Medical R&D as Insurance

Given the dual impact of health shocks on health and consumption, medical innovation serves the role of reducing adverse health events in future disease states and thus may be valued in a similar manner to other forms of risk reduction. Consider when there are two technologies that may be used to treat a disease, denoted by x_1 and x_2. The health outputs associated with these two technologies follow a Leontief production function requiring medical care inputs of M_1 and M_2 respectively. That is, for $k = 1,2$:

$$H_s(M; x_k) = H_s(0; x_k) < H_s(M_k; x_k) = H_s(\widehat{M}; x_k) \, \forall M < M_k, \widehat{M} \geq M_k.$$

The second technology is more effective in restoring health, so that:

$$H_s(M_1; x_1) < H_s(M_2; x_2) \leq H_0$$

but has not been developed. Suppose initially that R&D investment of size R per person is required to develop the second technology and is certain to succeed. In this case, the utility associated with undertaking the research and development effort (assuming the new technology is preferred to the previous one when developed) is:

$$V(Y - R, x_2, \tau) = max_i \{ \pi_s U(Y - (1 - i)M_2 - P(i, M_2) - R, H_s(M_2; x_2)) \\ + (1 - \pi_s) U(Y - P(i, M_2) - R, H_0) \}$$

while utility under the previous technology was

$$V(Y, x_1, \tau) = max_i \{ \pi_s U(Y - (1 - i)M_1 - P(i, M_1), H_s(M_1; x_1)) \\ + (1 - \pi_s) U(Y - P(i, M_1), H_0) \}.$$

Notice the parallel between the R&D effort and insurance. The R&D "premium" is simply the per person development cost R which is paid up front. The benefit is an in-kind "claim payment" in the form of improved health in the event that the consumer becomes sick. Although we have not modeled it as such, the claim payment could be uncertain in that the R&D effort might have uncertain prospects for success, but the overall impact is an expected improvement in health status in the sick state.

One can thus interpret R&D as a form of insurance of health itself—in which a payment of a development cost premium is made in exchange for a lower price of improved health in case of illness. Thus, medical R&D is "health insurance" in the literal sense of the phrase—as opposed to the colloquial usage where "health insurance" refers to insurance of medical expenditures.

This distinction between insuring health and insuring medical expenditures brings up an important trade-off between policies aimed at enabling better health and those aimed at consumption smoothing. Public resources can be spent on health insurance subsidies for *existing* technologies (for example, by granting tax breaks for health insurance purchase, or through public provision of existing medical technologies) or on R&D investment to generate *new* technologies. Medical expenditure insurance subsidies under the existing technology can be represented here as an increase in insurance market efficiency from τ to τ', with the total spent on the subsidy being:

$$[L(\tau) - L(\tau')] * \pi_s * M_1 * i^*(Y, \tau', x_1)$$

where $i^*(Y, \tau', x_1)$ is the co-insurance chosen by the consumer in the presence of the subsidy. To compare the relative efficiency of public subsidization of consumption smoothing versus health smoothing, we may consider τ' chosen so that the amount spent on the expenditure subsidy is the same as that spent on R&D investment:

$$[L(\tau) - L(\tau')] * \pi_s * M_1 * i^*(Y, \tau', x_1) = R.$$

The value of the expenditure subsidy in terms of willingness to pay can be defined as:

$$V(Y - W^E, \tau', x_1) = V(Y, \tau, x_1)$$

while the value of the R&D investment can similarly be defined as:

$$V(Y - W^R, \tau, x_2) = V(Y, \tau, x_1).$$

Thus, the value of buying the (perhaps uncertain) health restorations through medical R&D is larger than the value of buying consumption smoothing with health insurance subsidies whenever:

$$W^R > W^E.$$

An important determinant of the value of risk reductions through medical R&D is the value of the improved health from potential new medical innovation. There is a large literature on the "value of life" (see Viscusi and Aldy (2003) for a review) and the value of health more generally that relates to this issue. Of key concern is the value of the improvements in life expectancy or quality delivered by innovation, as it is these improvements that drive the value of risk reduction for the individual. Some evidence suggests that the gains can be quite large. For example, Murphy and Topel (2006) estimate that improvements from a 1% reduction in mortality from cancer would be worth about $500 billion a year *ex post* at the time of treatment. An important area of future research would be to estimate the insurance value of such gains and compare it to the value of consumption smoothing from health insurance.

8.3.2 Interactions Between Health Care Insurance and Health Insurance through Medical R&D

The foregoing analysis illustrates the potential value of "health insurance" provided by medical innovation as opposed to the consumption smoothing via traditional health care insurance. In this section we discuss existing papers and suggest new work on how the two types of insurance, medical innovation and health care insurance, interact in terms of how one affects the incentives for and value of the other.

8.3.2.1 *Health Care Insurance and Medical R&D Incentives*

As recognized as early as the patent clauses of the US Constitution, R&D in general and medical innovation in particular need to be supported by profits and adequate pricing. Weisbrod (1991) stressed the relationship between health care insurance or third-party pricing for the type of medical R&D undertaken.

Subsequent empirical work has found support for this idea. Danzon and Pauly (2002) argue that the rise of prescription drug coverage is likely to have spurred investment in R&D. Finkelstein (2004, 2007), and Clemens (2013) have documented a positive impact of insurance coverage on medical innovation. These papers stress the dynamic impact of coverage beyond the positive static incentive effects on utilization from lower demand prices or co-pays.

Hult and Philipson (2012) analyze explicitly how public insurance reforms affect the returns from medical innovation. Pioneered by the work of Newhouse (1992), research suggests that medical innovation is central to the growth in health care spending (see also Chernew and Newhouse (2012)). Moreover, public reforms are central to driving global innovative returns, as a large share of the world's care is publicly financed in rich countries. Therefore, public reforms have large effects on the uncertain future profits associated with medical innovation, which in turn drive spending growth in both the public and the private sector. The analysis considers cases in which the impact of government reforms on medical research and development (R&D) returns comes from three different sources: expected cash flows, the timing of the flows, and the risk adjustment of those cash flows. For the impact on expected cash flows, the analysis stresses the nonmonotonic effects of government expansions on innovative returns. In particular, government expansions often lower both demand prices (copays) and supply prices (reimbursements) through government monopsony power. This may imply that R&D returns rise when government expansions include poorer parts of the population by raising quantity more than lowering markups. For example, the recent Medicaid expansions in the Affordable Care Act of 2010 raise innovative returns in this manner. However, innovative returns fall when public insurance expansions include richer parts of the population if markups go down more than utilization goes up. For example, the single-payer European payment systems lower innovative returns in this manner. The nonmonotonic impact of government expansions across the income distribution implies that government cutbacks may raise R&D returns and pose upward pressure on future public liabilities. Likewise, government expansions may lower public liabilities.

Related to how reform affects innovative returns, Koijen et al. (2012) documented a large "medical innovation premium" that historically is paid to investors and the growth of the health care sector this premium implied. The paper provides an explicit analysis of the link between financial and real markets for health care by considering how the returns to medical R&D interact with the growth of the sector. The paper documents evidence of a "medical innovation premium," a large annual risk premium that is about 4–6% higher than predicted by benchmark asset pricing models for firms engaged in medical R&D. They interpret this premium as compensating investors for bearing risk with respect to public health insurance reforms, and the paper analyzes its quantitative implications for the growth of future health care spending. The calibration implies substantial effects of the premium on innovation and health care spending, on the order of magnitude of 4% of GDP, and therefore is argued to be important for future projections of the size of this sector.

8.3.2.2 Medical R&D for Rare Diseases

Many countries disproportionally subsidize medical innovation for rare or orphan diseases. For example, the Orphan Drug Act in the US provides R&D subsidies for diseases affecting less than 200,000 patients. Even private payers, moreover, often pay very high per-capita reimbursement rates under the rationale that per-capita revenues have to be larger in order to support R&D investment in diseases with few patients. This behavior seems puzzling since the same R&D spending could be used to help a larger set of patients; a small market size should lower efficient R&D according to traditional efficiency arguments. Indeed, a number of orphan drugs feature annual price tags well over $100,000 and are thus well beyond the means of the typical patient.[9] In the context of the usual model of financial insurance, it is hard to understand how this—the insurance of losses in excess of wealth, as well as investment in treatments that the affected consumers cannot afford—could possibly be efficient.

However, with the *ex ante* insurance role of medical innovation, rare disease R&D may well be efficient. This is because the R&D is essentially acting as an insurance against a low probability event that may often involve severe reductions to the health stock. Such insurance is similar to life insurance used to smooth consumption of beneficiaries: In both cases, the smoothing target is not simply the wealth or consumption of the purchaser. In the case of rare diseases, *ex post* per-capita pricing of treatments that are inversely related to prevalence to support R&D may be efficient when considering their value in terms of smoothing health.

The presence of risks to one's health stock, as distinguished from financial risk relating to medical care expenditures, complicates the analysis of optimal insurance of medical care expenditures by introducing a form of state dependence. Specifically, the marginal value of financial wealth can conceivably change dramatically according to whether one is in the "sick state" or the "healthy state," which can lead the optimal insurance contract to feature what appears to be "over insurance" or "under insurance" of financial shocks associated with the sick state as a consequence of state-dependent utility (e.g., Cook and Graham, 1977; Dionne, 1982; Nyman, 1999). This could in principle lead consumers either to transfer wealth into the sick state (Zeckhauser, 1973) or to underinsure the sick state (see Pauly, 1990). Viewed in this light, the optimal transfer

---

[9] "The World's Most Expensive Drugs" by Matthew Herper, Forbes.com 2/22/2010, accessed on 12/2/2012.

of wealth into a low-probability sick state could in principle be extreme—resulting in the expenditure of resources far beyond an individual's wealth in the sick state. Importantly, these effects may justify investment in very expensive treatments.

To illustrate, consider a case of a cure for an otherwise untreatable rare disease. Suppose the cure is costless to implement once developed but has a development cost of R (per diagnosis) that greatly exceeds typical wealth levels

$$R \gg Y.$$

This development cost must be recovered from each new diagnosis. This would seem at first glance to be an unviable treatment since the consumer cannot afford to pay for the cure. However, with a medical expenditure insurance market, the consumer would be able to buy insurance priced at

$$P = \pi_s * R * i * L(\tau).$$

And will do so if

$$\pi_s U(Y - (1 - i)R - P, H_0) + (1 - \pi_s)U(Y - P, H_0) > \pi_s U(Y, H_s)$$
$$+ (1 - \pi_s)U(Y, H_0).$$

Insurance in this case ensures "access" to an expensive treatment, an interpretation of the over-insurance of the sick state stressed by Nyman (1999). Insurance also enables *development* of the treatment, which would not otherwise be possible. Thus, medical expenditure insurance and R&D "insurance" can be complementary in the sense that the presence of one increases the demand for the other and vice versa.

Importantly, in this case the complementarity is efficiency-enhancing. From a health shock perspective, rare disease R&D may be efficient because it provides insurance against a small probability, but severe, health shock. In other words, rare disease R&D is a fixed payment today to potentially have a restoration of health in the case the small probability shock occurs. Even though there is a small market for the rare disease product once marketed, the *difference* in health across the two states is reduced *ex ante* by the medical R&D, and the *ex ante* effect on welfare may more than justify the expenditure of the "premium."

The foregoing argument is predicated on the notion that individual valuation of life may exceed financial resources. Yet the literature on the issue seems to support this. Existing estimates of the value of a statistical life (VSL) produce a wide range of answers, but a typical answer is well into the millions of dollars (see Kniesner et al. (2012) for a recent survey of the challenges in this literature and new estimates in the 4–10 million dollar range). Estimates are typically based on observed willingness-to-pay for mortality risk reductions (or willingness-to-accept risk increases). Estimates of the

VSL well into the millions, however, are paradoxical in the sense that the value of life is put far beyond the resources (e.g., the discounted present value of labor income) of the median individual. Such a finding, however, is consistent with the notion of health stock smoothing. As argued above, the willingness to pay for a mortality risk reduction in a fatal disease from a small probability π_s to zero (i.e., through some medical innovation) could well exceed $\pi_s \star Y$. Further suggestive evidence of the willingness of individuals to commit extreme resources to the preservation of health can be found in bankruptcy statistics. Recent evidence (Himmelstein et al., 2009) suggests that medical expenses are the major cause of more than half of all personal bankruptcies.

8.4 HEALTH RISKS OF TREATMENTS, THEIR REGULATION, AND THE IMPACT ON HEALTH SMOOTHING THROUGH MEDICAL INNOVATION

The discussion so far stressed the *ex ante* health insurance role of medical innovation. However, new innovations and treatments may introduce new risks to health in themselves, through unsafe products with side effects. In virtually all developed countries and many developing countries, governments provide regulatory oversight over the health risks of products generated by medical innovation. In the United States, this oversight is conducted by the Food and Drug Administration (FDA), which regulates drugs, medical devices, biologics (products made from living organisms, like vaccines and blood products), cosmetics, radiation-emitting electronic products, veterinary products, and food. According to the FDA, the products it regulates account for more than one-fifth of U.S. consumer spending in 2010.

The manner in which the FDA regulates the quality or health risks of medical products has a substantial impact on the cost of their development and thus on the speed at which medical innovation can ensure health smoothing when health shocks occur. The FDA requires that companies conduct clinical trials to demonstrate that their medical products are safe and effective. These trials account for a large portion of the total development costs of these products (DiMasi et al., 2003; Adams and Brantner, 2006). In addition, completion of trials does not guarantee that a product will be approved. This risk of nonapproval compounds the cost of product development (DiMasi et al., 2003).

Despite the central role of the FDA in regulating the quality and R&D costs of medical products, there has been relatively little theoretical or empirical research conducted by economists on the efficiency of FDA policies, particularly as they relate to the *ex ante* insurance role of medical innovation. Ironically, if a product application was presented to the FDA with the same scant amount of evidence that currently exists on the efficiency of the policies of the agency itself, such an application would likely be rejected on the basis of insufficient evidence.

Despite the lack of work on the *ex ante* or *ex post* efficiency of FDA policies, a substantial literature has emerged on descriptive aspects as well as the effects of various policies. We review some central features of this literature here. The FDA aims to economize on transaction costs in verifying product quality, a verification that would be very difficult for an average citizen to do. Early static analysis of FDA policies, starting with the papers by Wardell (1973) and Peltzman (1973), however, have raised concerns about the impact of FDA regulation on the expected profits of medical product companies and thus their incentive to innovate. Moreover, FDA regulation surely increases the cost of R&D by requiring the generation of extra information through costly clinical trials. Together these factors would reduce the return to, and thus the amount of, R&D investments intended to generate new medical products.

An important aspect of regulating the health risks of medical products is that in many countries including the United States, medical products are jointly regulated by agencies such as the FDA, which screens products to ensure they are safe and effective before they are sold, and the tort liability system, which allows patients to sue manufacturers after they have consumed these products. This "dual" aspect of product safety regulations for health risks has been analyzed by Philipson et al. (2009) who argue that one form of regulation may increase costs in the presence of the other. Work by Philipson et al. (2008) considers the dynamic welfare effects of FDA regulation by considering the present value of all future costs and benefits of the products being regulated.

Most of the literature on the FDA has to date been descriptive empirical analysis or analysis estimating the effects of various interventions. Empirical analysis of FDA regulation can be grouped into at least five categories

- The number of chemical entities introduced
- Development costs
- Development and review times
- Withdrawal rates
- Demand and supply curves for drugs in order to measure changes in consumer and producer surplus.[10]

There are two basic challenges to identifying how FDA regulation affects medical innovation and development. One is how to "quantify" FDA regulation. Researchers have taken two basic approaches. One is to look at adoption of any premarket clearance regulation, such as the 1962 amendments in the US (e.g., Peltzman, 1973). This treatment is coded as a dummy variable, set to 0 before 1962, and 1 after.[11] The other is to proxy for regulation by the time it takes for the FDA to review a new drug application

---

[10] Specifically, a proper welfare calculation requires separately estimating the lost surplus from products that are not approved by the FDA due to minimum quality regulations and the demand curve for products had the FDA not provided more accurate information on quality.

[11] Similarly, studies that examine the UK code the treatment dummy as 0 before 1973, when the UK adopted premarket screening for efficacy, and 1 after that (Grabowski et al., 1978).

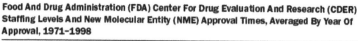

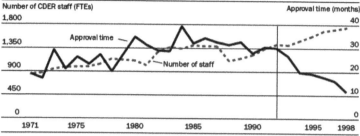

SOURCES: Number of full-time-equivalent (FTE) CDER staff (dashed line) is from the Food and Drug Administration. Approval times (solid line) are from Pharmaceutical Research and Manufacturers of America (PhRMA), based on FDA reports. NOTES: Data on approval times for 1979 were not available; the trend between 1978 and 1980 was provided by linear interpolation. The vertical line denotes the year in which the Prescription Drug User Fee Act (PDUFA) was passed, 1992.

Figure 8.1 Food and Drug Administration (FDA) Center for Drug Evaluation and Research (CDER) staffing levels and New Molecular Entity (NME) approval times averaged by year of approval, 1971–1998.

(NDA) (e.g., Wiggins, 1981; Jensen, 1987; Berndt et al., 2005a,b; Carpenter et al. 2008a; Philipson et al., 2008). This has varied substantially over time. In 1960, approval times were roughly 5 months. After the 1962 amendments, approval times rose dramatically, reaching 20 months in 1970. For most of the 1980s approval times hovered between 30 to 35 months. Approval times declined substantially after the passage of PDUFA in 1992. By 1998, approval times were approximately 12 months, which is roughly where they stand today. This rise and fall in approval times is illustrated in the Figure 8.1, which is reproduced from Olson (2004).

The second challenge is constructing a baseline against which to judge the effect of the FDA regulation. Because the FD&C Act is a national statute, researchers cannot use, for example, differences in outcomes across US states that regulate drugs and states that do not regulate drugs. This makes it difficult to separate effects of the statute from underlying time trends. Researchers have used two basic methods to overcome this problem. One is to assume a parametric structure for outcomes in the absence of the 1962 amendments. This could be as simple as including a time trend in the regression. Or it could involve something more elaborate. For example, Peltzman (1973) used pre-1962 data to estimate a model of new drug introductions and then predicted baseline new drug introductions after the amendments by inserting post-1962 data into his estimated model. When he plotted actual introductions of new chemical entities against his predicted introductions, the result was a striking plot that became popular among critics of the FDA. His figure is reproduced below as Figure 8.2.

The other approach researchers have used to construct a baseline is to examine the development of drug markets in countries that are similar to the US but either did not pass strict drug regulation in 1962 or took less time to review new drug applications. The primary candidate is the United Kingdom, which passed premarket clearance for

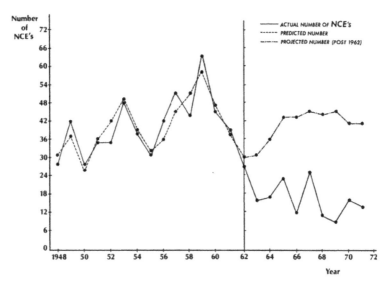

Figure 8.2 Actual versus Predicted New Chemical Entities, 1948–1972.

safety in 1963 but did not require proof of efficacy before sale until 1971 (Grabowski et al., 1978). The UK also had shorter review times than the US, at least until the passage of PDUFA in 2002. For example, in 1980, total development times (including preclinical testing, clinical testing and regulatory review times) were 145 months in the US versus just 70 months in the UK (Thomas, 1990).

Tables 8.1–8.3 summarize research on the effects of FDA regulation on three important sets of outcomes. Table 8.1 focuses on innovation and includes outcomes such as new drug introductions and the productivity of R&D expenditure (i.e., new drug introductions/R&D expenditures). Table 8.2 examines drug development and FDA approval times. Table 8.3 considers the effect of FDA regulations on safety. The main outcomes studied are involuntary drug withdrawals. The tables not only report findings, but also the data employed, how FDA regulation is measured (e.g., 1962 dummy or review time), and how the counterfactual or baseline is constructed (e.g., parametric time trend or international comparison).

8.4.1 Innovation

The initial papers studying the effect of FDA regulation on innovation used the 1962 amendments as a treatment and the number of new chemical entities (NCE) introduced each year as the outcome. Whether they used the UK (Wardell, 1973) or a model of introductions fitted to pre-1962 data (Peltzman, 1973) as the controls, they found large reductions in NCE introductions associated with the legislation. The chart from Peltzman (1973), reproduced above in Figure 8.2, is illustrative.

Table 8.1 Review of Literature Concerning the Effect of FDA Regulation on Innovation

Source	Data (Usually the Dependent Variable)	Measure of FDA Regulation	Baseline/Control	Finding
Wardell (1973)	NCE introductions, 1962–1971	1962 Amendments	UK	Annual NCE flow falls 54% due to 1962 amendments
Peltzman (1973)	NCE introductions, 1948–1971	1962 Amendments	Model of NCEs using pre-1962 data	Annual NCE flow falls 66% due to 1962 amendments
Grabowski et al. (1978)	NCE flow/R&D expenditures, 1960–1974	1962 Amendments and NDA approval times	UK	1962 amendments increased avg. cost of NCE by factor of 2.3 (using 1962 dummy) or 1.9 (using approval times)
Wiggins (1981)	NCE introductions, 1970–1976	NDA approval times	Therapeutic classes with shorter approval times	Increase in approval times due to 1962 amendments decrease NCE introductions 52%, holding R&D expenditures constant; accounting for effects of longer approval times on expenditures, reducing delay to pre-1962 levels would increase NCE introductions by 135%
Wiggins (1983)	R&D expenses (from PHRMA) by therapeutic class, 1965–1968, 1971–1976	NDA approval times	Therapeutic classes with shorter approval times	Approval times reduced R&D expenditures during 1971–1976, but not 1965–1968, possibly because it took time for drug companies to determine how stringent FDA regulation would be after 1962

Continued

Table 8.1 (Continued)

Source	Data (Usually the Dependent Variable)	Measure of FDA Regulation	Baseline/Control	Finding
May et al. (1983)	Number of NCEs tested on humans and NDA approvals, 1958–1979	1962 Amendments	Pre-1962 period	NCEs tested on humans fell from 89/year to 17/year in 1979; NDA approvals fell by 49%
Cullen (1983)	190 drug product launches across 18 countries during 1961–1976	Surveyed 6 companies for their views of "regulatory tightness" in different countries in 1982. Ratings from 1 (most stringent) to 5 (least stringent).	17 countries other than US	Countries rated as having tighter regulations had (1) a larger increase in lag between first introduction in any country and introduction in that country from the 1960s to the 1970s and (2) a smaller increase in the number of products introduced in that country from 1960s to 1970s
Jensen (1987)	NCE introductions by 26 firms 1969–1979	NDA approval times	Classes with shorter approval times, time trend	One month decrease in approval times increase annual NCE introductions by 15%
Thomas (1990)	NCE, sales and market cap of drug companies, 1960–1980	1962 Amendments and approval times	UK	FDA regulation did not affect NCEs at large firms, but did substantially reduce NCE introduced by small firms. Due to reduced competition from small firms, sales rose at large firms in the US

Table 8.2 Review of Literature Concerning the Effect of FDA Regulation on Approval Times

Source	Data (Usually the Dependent Variable)	Measure of FDA Regulation (or Other Treatment Variable)	Baseline/Control	Finding
OTA (1989)	Effective patent length of drugs	*Ex post* commercial importance of drug		Drugs with greater *ex post* commercial importance have longer effective patent length
Thomas (1990)	Preclinical testing, clinical testing, and NDA review times, 1960–1980	1962 Amendments	UK	US total development times grew from 35 months in 1960 to 120 months in 1970 to 145 months in 1980. The increases in preclinical testing, clinical, and NDA review times were 30, 60 and 20 months, respectively. In the UK, total development times increased from 30 to 70. Preclinical testing times were constant while the sum of clinical testing and review times increased by 40 months
Kaitin et al. (1991)	Approval times	FDA ratings novelty of drugs		FDA accelerated approval of more novel chemical entities
Dranove and Meltzer (1994)	Time from drug patent application to NDA approval for 564 NMEs between 1950–1986	Various measures of importance of drug (e.g., FDA rating, commercial value, citations, worldwide introductions)		Development and approval times are lower for more important drugs

Continued

Table 8.2 (Continued)

Source	Data (Usually the Dependent Variable)	Measure of FDA Regulation (or Other Treatment Variable)	Baseline/Control	Finding
Carpenter et al. (2003)	Approval times and FDA (CDER) staff, 1971–1998	PDUFA	Time trend	Funding for FDA staff has bigger influence on NDA review time than source of funding (user fees under PDFUA)
Olson (2004)	Approval times and FDA (CDER) staff, 1971–1998	PDUFA	Time trend	PDUFA reduced approval times by 34% by 1998. Different result than Carpenter et al. (2003) because Olson groups approvals by approval year rather than NDA submission year as Carpenter et al. do
Berndt et al. (2005a)	Clinical development and NDA review times, 1965–2003	PDUFA	Time trend	PDUFA reduced approval times by 7.6% per year during PDUFA I (1992–1996), and 3.6% per year during PDUFA II (1997–2001). PDUFA II may also have reduced clinical development times by 4.5%

Table 8.3 Review of Literature Concerning the Effect of FDA Regulation on Safety

Source	Data (Usually the Dependent Variable)	Measure of FDA Regulation	Baseline/Control	Finding
Bakke et al. (1984)	Drug discontinuations, 1964–1983	1962 Amendments	UK	Few discontinuations in either country so no significant differences in discontinuations in US vs. UK
Bakke et al. (1995)	Drug discontinuations, 1974–1993	1962 Amendments	UK, Spain	More drugs discontinued in UK (20) and Spain (16) than US (10). Normalizing by number of drugs approved shrinks the difference: 4% in UK vs. 3% in US
GAO (2002)	Drug withdrawals, 1986–2000	PDUFA	None	No significant effects of PDUFA on withdrawals. Withdrawals were 3.1% in 1986–1992 and 3.5% in 1993–2000
CDER (2004)	Drug withdrawals, 1971–2004	PDUFA	None	No significant effects of PDUFA on withdrawals. Withdrawals were 2.7% in 1971–1993, 2.3% in 1994–Apr. 2004
Berndt et al. (Nature, 2005b)	Drug or biologic withdrawals, 1980–2000	PDUFA	None	No significant effects of PDUFA on withdrawals. Withdrawals (including biologics) were 2.8% in 1980–1992, and 2.2% in 1993–2000
Carpenter et al. (2008a)	FDA withdrawals, blackbox warnings and voluntary withdrawals by drug companies, 1993–2004	PDUFA	Drugs approved well before or after PDUFA deadlines	PDUFA caused bunching of FDA approval during 2 months before deadlines. Drugs approved in 2 months before deadlines had higher odds of being withdrawn by the FDA (OR = 5.5), getting blackbox warnings (4.4) and of being voluntarily withdrawn (3.3) than drugs approved well before or after deadlines

The Peltzman paper was criticized, however, for overestimating the reduction in NCEs.[12] First, it examined only the quantity of drugs approved, not their quality. Perhaps only relatively unimportant drugs were held back in the 1960s. Second, drug companies may have voluntarily reduced NCE introductions even without the 1962 amendments. They may have interpreted the Thalidomide controversy as evidence of increased consumer demand for safety and stopped developing drugs that had substantial side effects. Coupled with the great advance in the ability of the pharmacological sciences to detect side effects from drugs, companies may have held back drugs for fear of losing goodwill or facing legal liability. Third, given the high value of drugs developed in the 1950s and 1960s, it is possible the returns to drug development had simply diminished by the 1960s (Grabowski et al., 1978).

A second round (Grabowski et al., 1978; Cullen, 1983; Thomas, 1990) of papers therefore focused on the UK as a control for the US. The UK experienced the same increase in demand for safety after the Thalidomide controversy and potentially diminishing returns in drug development. Yet the UK only introduced premarket testing for safety in 1963, and did not introduce testing for efficacy until 1973. Therefore, comparing the US and UK in the 1960s would highlight the effect of premarket screening for efficacy. These UK comparisons also showed significant reductions in research output associated with the increased US regulation.

One problem with studies that focused on the 1960s, according to Wiggins (1983), was that it took some time for the FDA to decide how to implement the 1962 amendments. Moreover, it also took drug companies some time to learn how cumbersome FDA regulation would ultimately be. Therefore, one can best assess the impact of the 1962 amendments by examining how innovation responded in the 1970s. The difficulty with studying the 1970s is that the US and UK regulatory systems eventually converged, so the UK was no longer obviously a valid control.[13] Therefore, investigators (Grabowski et al. 1978; Wiggins, 1981, 1983; Jensen, 1987; Thomas, 1990) began quantifying FDA regulation by the amount of time it took for the FDA to review new drug applications (NDA).

Another issue that concerned economists was that, although NCE introductions fell in the 1960s, research expenditures rose. One interpretation was that the Peltzman finding underestimated the effect of FDA regulation because it focused on output rather than the productivity of research expenditures. A number of studies investigated this possibility by using NCE introductions/R&D expenditures as an outcome variable. For example, Grabowski et al. (1978) estimated that the 1962 amendments increased the average cost of each NCE by a factor of 1.86 to 2.3. In addition, Wiggins (1981, 1983) examined whether FDA regulations reduced the amount companies invested in R&D

---

[12] Wardell's papers, e.g., Wardell (1973), were widely cited but did not receive serious attention in the economics literature. This may be because the papers did not employ any serious statistical analysis to probe the findings.

[13] Because the UK still had shorter approval times, Grabowski et al. (1978) were still able to use the UK as a control, although they used approval times as a measure of FDA regulatory rigor.

and found that delays in FDA approval due to the 1962 amendments reduced R&D expenditures in the 1970s. Holding these expenditures constant, NCE introductions fell 52%. Accounting for these reductions in R&D expenditures, NCE introductions fell a total of 135% after 1962.

While various studies have introduced other improvements to the analysis of the effects of FDA regulation on innovation,[14] the most important of these is Thomas (1990), which observed that FDA regulation might have had different effects on different companies. Specifically, regulation may have had a larger effect on small companies that were unable to afford the clinical testing required by the FDA and had less experience with the FDA process than larger companies.[15] In addition, FDA regulation may have provided an indirect benefit to large companies by eliminating competition from smaller companies. As support, Thomas finds that FDA regulation did not affect NCE introductions by large firms, but did dramatically reduce NCE introduction by small firms. Moreover, due to reduced competition, sales (and market valuations) at large firms actually rose after FDA regulation.

8.4.2 Approval Times

A second important parameter in evaluating FDA regulation is its effects on approval time. Early work by Wardell demonstrated that the US drug development times grew versus the UK after the 1962 amendments (Wardell, 1973). This gap became known as the "drug lag." Thomas (1990) showed that the lag grew fastest in the 1960s, but still grew in the 1970s, despite the fact that formally the UK and US regulatory systems had converged by 1973. For example, the lag between the US and UK grew from 5 months in 1960 to 70 months in 1970, and then to 75 months by 1980.

The remaining papers that examine approval times fall into two categories. One examines heterogeneity in approval times for different drugs and the other examines the role of PDUFA in lowering approval times. One criticism of the early literature on drug lag was that it may overestimate the cost of FDA delay because the delay might only affect less valuable drugs. Of the studies that examine this issue, the best is Dranove and Meltzer (1994), which shows that drug approval times are lower for more important drugs, where importance is measured by FDA ranking of a drug's novelty, its commercial value once approved, its citations in the academic literature and in subsequent patents.[16]

---

[14] For example, May et al.(1983) examined the number of NCEs that reached the stage of clinical testing. Cullen (1983) used companies' ratings of different countries' regulatory systems so countries other than UK might be used as controls.

[15] Carpenter et al. (2008b) provides another form of disparate impact from FDA regulation. That paper shows that the FDA takes longer to approve later drugs, giving early entrants a regulatory advantage. They find that a standard deviation increase in the log order of entry increases FDA approval time by 3.6 months. This gradient was increased by the 1962 amendments, but unaffected by PDUFA.

[16] Another important insight in the Dranove and Meltzer study is that FDA regulation might affect not only approval times but the amount of time required for drug development. The higher the FDA standard, the more time companies have to spend investigating a drug to see if, or prove, it meets the higher standard. Therefore, Dranove and Melzer look at the total time from patent filing to approval for more and less important drugs.

In 1992 Congress took note of the drug lag and passed PDUFA, which imposed deadlines on the FDA's review of NDAs and provided the FDA with more resources—from user fees imposed on NDA applicants—to evaluate NDA applications more quickly. The question academics asked was whether PDUFA actually lowered approval times and, if so, whether this was due to deadlines and/or the resources provided by Congress.[17] Carpenter et al. (2003) and Olson (2004) come out on opposite sides of this debate. The difference is that Carpenter and colleagues assigned a drug to the year that its NDA application was filed,[18] while Olson assigned it to the year its NDA was approved. Since PDUFA was a national (rather than state) law, studies have used a dummy for the period after 1992 to code the treatment variable. Thus, year of assignment is critical to one's findings. Olson's filings are confirmed and extended by Berndt et al. (2005a), which shows that PDUFA I (1992–2006) reduced the approval times by 7.6% annually while PDUFA II only reduced approval times by 3.6% annually. That paper also shows that, whereas PDUFA I had no effect on clinical development times, PDUFA II did lower these times by 4.5%. This is not surprising as one of the goals of subsequent versions of PDUFA was to streamline the regulatory process between the IND application and the NDA application (Hutt et al., 2007).

8.4.3 Withdrawals

Early work on how FDA regulations affect the rate or time at which drugs were withdrawn from the market focused on comparing the US to the UK. They implicitly used the 1962 amendments as the treatment variable. Bakke et al. (1984) looked at withdrawals from 1963 to 1983 and found no difference between the two countries. But this can largely be explained by the small number of withdrawals in each country and thus low power to detect any differences in withdrawal rates. Bakke et al. (1995) revisited the question with data from 1974 to 1993 and found a larger difference between the US and UK. As predicted, the US, which had relatively strict regulation (at least as measured by approval times) had both fewer drug withdrawals (10 vs. 20 in the UK) as well as lower withdrawal rate (2% vs. 3% in the UK).

More recent work on withdrawal rates has focused on approval times as a measure for FDA regulatory intensity. Some relatively simple papers by the GAO (2002), CDER (2004) and Berndt et al. (2005b) compared the probability a drug was withdrawn during the period prior to PDUFA to the period after the statute's adoption. They uniformly found somewhat lower, but not significantly lower, withdrawal rates prior to PDUFA.

Carpenter et al. (2008a) used a more sophisticated approach to identify the effect of PDUFA. Instead of conducting a before-after PDUFA comparison, that study

---

[17] Hutt et al. (2007) report, however, that Congress reduced its funding for the FDA as user fees grew so that total funding did not grow as fast as user fees.

[18] The deadline clearly had some effect. Carpenter et al. (2008a, 2008b) show that PDUFA caused the FDA to make many more judgments on drugs in the two months before statutory deadlines.

demonstrated that PDUFA caused the agency to compress the timing of decisions on drugs to the two months just before PDUFA deadlines (months 11 and 12 for standard review drugs, and months 9 and 10 for priority review drugs). The study then compared drugs approved close to the deadline to drugs approved well before or after deadlines. They found that drugs approved near deadlines had higher odds of being withdrawn (odds ratio = 5.5). Moreover, these drugs also had higher odds of having a black box warning (OR = 4.4) and of being voluntarily withdrawn by drug companies (OR = 3.3). Of course, these estimates only show that earlier deadlines increase withdrawal rates. They must be divided by the change in approval times implied by the early deadline in order to generate a regulatory dose-response curve. In effect, they need to compare the timing of decisions (and withdrawals) during PDUFA to the timing of decisions (and withdrawals) prior to PDUFA.

8.4.4 Development Costs

There have been a number of studies since the early 1970s that estimate the cost of drug development. These studies are spaced roughly a decade apart and generally cover the period between studies. DiMasi and Grabowski (2010) review this literature in Chapter 2. In early years, these studies relied on a small sample of drugs from a single firm (Sarett, 1974) or aggregate data (Mund, 1970; Baily, 1972). More recent studies have relied on drug-level data from a sample of drug companies (e.g., Hansen, 1979; DiMasi et al., 1991; Adams and Brantner, 2006).[19] The latter studies attempt, on the one hand, to separate the cost of preclinical testing from clinical testing and, on the other hand, the direct out-of-pocket costs of research from the opportunity costs of that research. The last component—opportunity costs—is driven largely by delay and the real cost of capital. In order to account for the fact that many drugs ultimately fail to demonstrate value in trials, or are not approved by the FDA, the studies divide total costs by the number of drugs that are approved, resulting in an estimate of the cost per approved drug rather than, say, the cost per drug ever tested.

Together, these studies paint a picture of steadily increasing drug development costs. This is illustrated in Figure 8.3 (reproduced from DiMasi et al., 2003), which reports estimates from Hansen (1979) and DiMasi et al. (1991, 2003) that roughly cover the 1970s, 1980s and 1990, respectively. Total costs per approved drug have risen from $138 million in the 1970s to $802 million in the 1990s. More recent estimates suggest the costs might now be over $1 billion per drug.

An important limitation of the literature on development costs is that it only demonstrates that costs have grown. The studies do not show that FDA regulation is responsible for this growth. While the dramatic increase in development costs after the 1962 amendments and during the run up in approval times through the 1980s suggests

---

[19] The two major sources of data are The Tufts Center on Drug Development and Pharmaprojects.

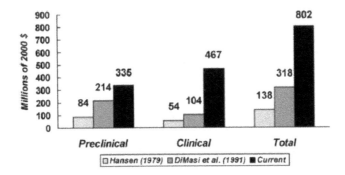

Figure 8.3 Drug Development Costs.

that the FDA is responsible, the continued growth of development costs even after the decline of approval times in the 1990s raises some questions. Has drug development hit diminishing returns and is that the main driver of cost growth in recent decades? Are approval times an adequate measure of FDA regulation or does the FDA offset lower approval times with a higher standard for minimum quality or more rigorous screening of IND applications?

8.4.5 Consumer and Producer Surplus

The final parameters required to evaluate FDA policies are consumer and producer surplus effects, ultimately driving social surplus effects. As Table 8.4 shows, there are only three papers that have attempted to estimate these.

The first paper is Peltzman (1973), which estimates the demand curve for new drugs by regressing the market share of newly introduced drugs in a therapeutic class on the ratio of new and old drug prices in that class. Peltzman included a dummy for the 1962 amendments as a demand shifter. Peltzman uses his estimate of the demand for new drugs only to estimate the value of information provided by the FDA minus the reduction in innovation due to FDA regulation. Peltzman's static framework for valuing the information produced by the FDA (see Section II.A.2 and Figure 5.2) suggests that the pre-1962 demand curve may not identify the "true" demand for new drugs because the FDA was not yet producing information about the quality of drugs. However, Peltzman argues that before 1962 consumers learned about the true quality of drugs through experience, and thus demand during that period was still "true" demand. He estimates that the 1962 amendments reduced demand for new drugs and thus the surplus from these drugs by roughly $420 million per year through 1970. He concludes that the loss of innovation due to the 1962 amendments offset the value of any information they provided.

Table 8.4 Literature Concerning the Social Surplus from FDA Regulation

Source	Data	Measure of FDA Regulation	Methodology	Finding
Peltzman (1973)	Quantity and price of prescriptions of newly introduced and old drugs, by therapeutic class and year, 1960–1962, 1964–1970	1962 Amendments	Regress market share of new drugs on ratio of new and old drug prices Surplus is $0.5^*(a\text{–}p)q$, where a is the y-intercept of the demand curve estimated above	Consumer surplus for each year's NCEs was $51.9 million/year before the 1962 amendments, $9.9 million per year after the amendments. Assuming 10 percent rate of return, discounted loss from amendments was $420 million per year
Philipson et al. (2008)	Sales for all drugs, 1998–2002; PDUFA fees	PDUFA	Regress sales on age of drug to construct age-profile of sales Producer surplus is PV of sales − user fees − variable costs, which are 1/4 to 1/2 of sales. Social surplus calculated as different fractions of sales (before patent expiration: all sales, 1/2 sales, 0; after expiration: all sales)	Additional producer surplus from PDUFA was $8–13 billion and additional total surplus from PDUFA is $13–30 billion, assuming a 9% rate of return

Continued

Table 8.4 (Continued)

Source	Data	Measure of FDA Regulation	Methodology	Finding
			Change in surplus from PDUFA is benefit of starting sales earlier	
Philipson et al. (2009)	Survival probabilities for HIV, certain cancer patients by year; annual patient expenditures on key HIV, cancer drugs	N/A	Use Murphy-Topel framework to estimate willingness to pay for improved survival. WTP minus patient expenditures is measure of consumer surplus. Producer surplus is 80% of patient expenditures (assuming marginal costs are 20% of expenditures)	Consumer (producer) surplus from introduction of HAART in 1996 was $364 ($38) billion. Entry 1 year earlier would have increased consumer (producer) surplus by $19 ($4) billion
			Examine effect of 1 year acceleration of drug entry on social surplus	Consumer (producer) surplus from introduction of Rituxan in 1998 was $12 ($4) billion. Entry 1 year earlier would have increased consumer (producer) surplus $310 ($330) million
				Consumer (producer) surplus from introduction of Receptin in 1999 was $149 ($12) billion. Entry 1 year earlier would have increased consumer (producer) surplus $8 ($1) billion

The second paper to examine the FDA's impact on social surplus is Philipson et al. (2008). This differs from Peltzman (1973) in a number of respects. Instead of studying the effect of the 1962 amendments, this paper examines PDUFA and the value of reducing FDA approval times. Moreover, the paper uses a substantially different methodology to identify surplus. Instead of estimating demand curves, the paper simply uses sales data to bound the annual social surplus from all drugs on the market during 1998–2002. It then uses drugs of different ages to estimate the stream of social surplus from a new drug over its life cycle. Finally, it uses prior estimates of how much PDUFA accelerated drug introductions to estimate the value of accelerating these streams of social surpluses. It concludes that PDUFA, by accelerating drug approvals, increased social surplus by $13–30 billion assuming a 9% cost of capital.

The last paper is Philipson et al. (2009). Like Philipson et al. (2008), the focus is identifying the value of accelerated introduction of drugs. The main difference is that the paper uses the effect of new drug introductions on survival probabilities of patients (combined with a value of life-years) to estimate a willingness to pay for a drug. Subtracting the price of the drug from this willingness to pay yields the individual patient's consumer surplus. Producer surplus is estimated as 80% of sales revenue (assuming marginal costs of 20% of revenue). After estimating the stream of aggregate social welfare from three drugs (HAART for HIV patients, Rituxan for Hodgkin's lymphoma patients, and Herceptin for breast cancer patients), the authors calculate the value of accelerating this stream by 1 year. At a 9% cost of capital, the authors estimate, for example, that introducing HAART one year earlier would have increased consumer and producer surplus by $19 and $4 billion, respectively.

8.5 CONCLUDING REMARKS AND AVENUES OF FUTURE RESEARCH

We have reviewed some of the central aspects of the vast positive and normative literature on the role of markets and public policies in mitigating the effects of health shocks. The literature has been primarily concerned with various forms of insurance that attempt to smooth consumption across health shocks by insuring financial effects on health care spending or wealth. We stressed that this literature has been primarily concerned with the impediments to full consumption insurance and the role of the government in addressing these impediments as well as any negative impacts due to the lack of universal purchase of these products. This large literature has focused almost exclusively on consumption smoothing rather than smoothing of the stock of health itself, although we argue the latter may be more important for welfare. Because human capital cannot be traded, risk pooling of health shocks is infeasible beyond the existing medical care that treats them, necessitating other forms of lowering health risk. We argued that medical innovation can be interpreted as an insurance mechanism of a population's health. We explored the positive and normative implications of this population insurance view of medical R&D and stressed the *ex-ante* insurance value of medical innovations.

There are several avenues of future research raised by considering the role of medical innovation in insuring health. One is in assessing the relative value of public subsidies for medical innovation versus health insurance reforms. Much of the debate and legislation concerning health reforms has been under the rationale of reducing market inefficiencies in shocks to consumption induced by health shocks. Our analysis may suggest that, given the potentially large value of smoothing health itself rather than consumption, more explicit analysis is needed on the relative value of public programs stimulating medical innovation versus health reforms aimed at enabling consumption-smoothing.

A second area concerns the role of rare disease R&D that eliminates small risks with severe health impacts. Public subsidies towards rare disease R&D are common, such as the Orphan Drug Act in the US. Our analysis suggests that small disease RD may be efficient when it is interpreted as an insurance mechanism for a low probability but severe event. For the same reasons life insurance is valuable to the vast majority of people with coverage who do not die, small disease R&D is valuable for the vast majority of people who never get the disease.

A third area concerns the exact risk-properties of medical treatments and how FDA regulations affect them. In particular, clinical trials only estimate mean effectiveness or side effects levels, and not variance or covariance between them. The net benefit of a treatment—the value of health it generates net of side effects and price—has very different risk properties depending on whether side effects are positively or negatively correlated with effectiveness; if a side effect only occurs when a treatment is successful it is a more tolerable treatment than if it only occurs when it is unsuccessful. But FDA policies based on mean levels do not capture this difference in value induced by the covariance of efficacy and side effects.

In general, it seems plausible that, given the large value of health estimated by economists (see e.g., Murphy and Topel, 2006), that the current preoccupation with policies aimed at consumption smoothing across disease states may have lower marginal returns than policies aimed at smoothing health itself across those same disease states.

ACKNOWLEDGMENTS

We are thankful to the editors for comments that improved the chapter.

REFERENCES

Abaluck, J., Gruber, J., 2011. Choice inconsistencies among the elderly: evidence from plan choice in the medicare part D program. American Economic Review 101, 1180–1210.
Abbring, J.H., Chiappori, P.A., Heckman, J.J., Pinquet, J., 2003. Adverse selection and moral hazard: can dynamic data help to distinguish?. Journal of the European Economic Association 1, 512–521.
Adams, C.P., Brantner, V.V., 2006. Estimating the cost of new drug development: is it really $802 million?. Health Affairs 25, 420–428.

Akerlof, G.A., 1970. The market for "lemons": quality uncertainty and the market mechanism. Quarterly Journal of Economics 84, 488–500.

Altman, D., Cutler, D.M., Zeckhauser, R.J., 1998. Adverse selection and adverse retention. American Economic Review 88, 122–136.

Arrow, K.J., 1963. Uncertainty and the welfare economics of medical care. American Economic Review 53, 942–973.

Baily, M.N., 1972. Research and development costs and returns: The U.S. pharmaceutical industry. Journal of Political Economy 80, 70–85.

Bakke, O.M., Wardell, W.M., Lasagna, L., 1984. Drug discontinuations in the United Kingdom and the United States, 1964 to 1983: issues of safety. Clinical Pharmacology & Therapeutics 35, 559–567.

Bakke, O.M., Manocchia, M., de Abajo, F., Kaitin, K.I., Lasagna, L., 1995. Drug safety discontinuations in the United Kingdon, the United States, and Spain from 1974 through 1993: a regulatory perspective. Clinical Pharmacology & Therapeutics 58, 108–117.

Berndt, E.R., Gottschalk, A.H.B., Philipson, T.J., Strobeck, M.W., 2005a. Assessing the impacts of the prescription drug user fee acts (PDUFA) on the FDA approval process. Forum for Health Economics & Policy 8. Article 2.

Berndt, Ernst.R., Gottschalk, A.H.B., Philipson, T.J., Strobeck, M.W., 2005b. Industry funding of the FDA: effects of PDUFA on approval times and withdrawal rates. Nature Reviews Drug Discovery 4, 545–554.

Cardon, J.H., Hendel, I., 2001. Asymmetric information in health insurance: evidence from the national medical expenditure survey. RAND Journal of Economics 32, 408–427.

Carpenter, D., Chernew, M., Smith, D.G., Fendrick, A.M., 2003. Approval times for new drugs: does the source of funding for FDA staff matter?. Health Affairs, http://dx.doi.org/10.1377/hlthaff.w3.618.

Carpenter, D., Zucker, E.J., Avorn, J., 2008a. Drug-review deadlines and safety problems. New England Journal of Medicine 358, 1354–1361.

Carpenter, D., Zucker, E.J., Avorn, J., 2008b. Drug-review deadlines and safety problems: author's reply. New England Journal of Medicine 359, 96–98.

Cawley, J., Philipson, T.J., 1999. An empirical examination of information barriers to trade in insurance. American Economic Review 89, 827–846.

Center for Drug Evaluation and Research (CDER), 2004. 2003 Report to the Nation: Improving Public Health through Human Drugs. US Dept. of Health and Human Services, Food and Drug Administration.

Chandra, A., Gruber, J., McKnight, R., 2010. Patient cost-sharing and hospitalization offsets in the elderly. American Economic Review 100, 193–213.

Chernew, M.E., Fendrick, A.M., 2008. Value and increased cost sharing in the American health care system. Health Services Research 43, 251–257.

Chernew, M.E., Newhouse, J.P., 2012. Health care spending growth. In: Pauly, M.V., McGuire, T.G., Barros, P.P. (Eds.), Handbook of Health Care Economic. Elsevier, Amsterdam, pp. 1–44.

Chiappori, P.-A., Salanié, B., 2000. Testing for asymmetric information in insurance markets. Journal of Political Economy 108, 56–78.

Clemens, J.P., 2013. The Effect of US Health Insurance Expansions on Medical Innovation. SIEPR Discussion Paper No. 11-016. Available at SSRN: <http://ssrn.com/abstract=2101246> or http://dx.doi.org/10.2139/ssrn.2101246.

Cohen, A., 2005. Asymmetric information and learning in the automobile insurance market. Review of Economics and Statistics 87, 197–207.

Cohen, A., Siegelman, P., 2010. Testing for adverse selection in insurance markets. Journal of Risk and Insurance 77, 39–84.

Congressional Budget Office (CBO), January 2008. Technological Change and the Growth of Health Care Spending.

Connolly, M.P., Griesinger, G., Ledger, W., Postma, M.J., 2009. The impact of introducing patient co-payments in Germany on the use of IVF and ICSI: a price-elasticity of demand assessment. Human Reproduction 24, 2796–2800.

Cook, P.J., Graham, D.A., 1977. The demand for insurance and protection: the case of irreplaceable commodities. Quarterly Journal of Economics 91, 143–156.

Cullen, R., 1983. Pharmaceuticals inter-country diffusion. Managerial & Decision Economics 4, 73–82.

Cutler, D.M., Reber, S.J., 1998. Paying for health insurance: the trade-off between competition and adverse selection. Quarterly Journal of Economics 113, 433–466.

Danzon, P.M., Pauly, M.V., 2002. Health insurance and the growth in pharmaceutical expenditures. Journal of Law and Economics 45, 587–613.

Dimasi, J.A., Grabowski, H.G., 2012. R&D costs and the returns to new drug development: a review of the evidence. In: Danzon, P.M., Nicholson, S. (Eds.), The Oxford Handbook of the Economics of the Pharmaceutical Industry. Oxford University Press, New York, pp. 21–46.

Dimasi, J.A., Bryant, N.R., Lasagna, L., 1991. New drug development in the united-states from 1963 to 1990. Clinical Pharmacology & Therapeutics 50, 471–486.

Dimasi, J.A., Hansen, R.W., Grabowski, H.G., 2003. The price of innovation: new estimates of drug development costs. Journal of Health Economics 22, 151–185.

Dionne, G., 1982. Moral hazard and state-dependent utility function. Journal of Risk and Insurance 49, 405–422.

Dionne, G., Gouriéroux, C., Vanasse, C., 2001. Testing for evidence of adverse selection in the automobile insurance market: a comment. Journal of Political Economy 109, 444–453.

Dranove, D., Meltzer, D., 1994. Do important drugs reach the market sooner?. RAND Journal of Economics 25, 402–423.

Fang, H., Keane, M.P., Silverman, D., 2008. Sources of advantageous selection: evidence from the Medigap insurance market. Journal of Political Economy 116, 303–350.

Finkelstein, A., 2004. Static and dynamic effects of health policy: evidence from the vaccine industry. Quarterly Journal of Economics 119, 527–564.

Finkelstein, A., 2007. The aggregate effects of health insurance: evidence from the introduction of medicare. Quarterly Journal of Economics 122, 1–37.

Finkelstein, A., McGarry, K., 2006. Multiple dimensions of private information: evidence from the long term care insurance market. American Economic Review 96, 938–958.

Finkelstein, A., Poterba, J., 2002. Selection effects in the United Kingdom individual annuities market. Economic Journal 112, 28–50.

Finkelstein, A., Poterba, J., 2004. Adverse selection in insurance markets: policyholder evidence from the U.K. annuity market. Journal of Political Economy 112, 183–208.

Frank, R., 2007. Behavior economics and health economics. In: Diamond, P., Vartiainen, H. (Eds.), Behavior Economics and its Applications. Princeton University Press, Princeton, NJ.

Frank, R., Lamiraud, K., 2009. Choice, price competition, and complexity in markets for health insurance. Journal of Economic Behavior and Organization 71, 550–562.

Gaynor, M., Rebitzer, J.B., Taylor, L.J., 2004. Physician incentives in health maintenance organizations. Journal of Political Economy 112, 915–931.

General Accounting Office (GAO), 2002. Effect of User Fees on Drug Approval Times, Withdrawals, and Other Agency Activities.

Goldman, D., Joyce, G., Zheng, Y., 2007a. Prescription drug cost sharing: associations with medication and medical utilization and spending and health. Journal of the American Medical Association 298, 61–69.

Goldman, D., Philipson, T., 2007b. Integrated insurance design with multiple medical technologies. American Economic Review 97, 427–432.

Grabowski, H.G., Vernon, J.M., Thomas, L.G., 1978. Estimating the effect of regulation on innovation: an international comparative analysis of the pharmaceutical industry. Journal of Law and Economics 21, 133–163.

Grace, M.F., Klein, R.W., Kleindorfer, P.R., 2004. Homeowners insurance with bundled catastrophe coverage. Journal of Risk and Insurance 71, 351–379.

Gruber, J., Poterba, J., 1994. Tax incentives and the decision to purchase health insurance: evidence from the self-employed. Quarterly Journal of Economics 109, 701–733.

Hansen, R.W., 1979. The pharmaceutical development process: estimates of current development costs and times and the effects of regulatory changes. In: Chien, R.I. (Ed.), Issues in Pharmaceutical Economics. Lexington Books, Lexington, MA, pp. 151–187.

He, D., 2009. The life insurance market: asymmetric information revisited. Journal of Public Economics 93, 1090–1097.

Hendel, I., Lizzeri, A., 2003. The role of commitment in dynamic contracts: evidence from life insurance. Quarterly Journal of Economics 188, 299–327.

Himmelstein, D.U., Thorne, D., Warren, E., Woolhandler, S., 2009. Medical bankruptcy in the United States, 2007: results from a national study. The American Journal of Medicine, 741–746.

Hult, K., Philipson, T., 2012. Health Care Reforms and the Value of Future Public Liabilities. NBER Working Paper 18571.

Hutt, P.B., Merrill, R.A., Grossman, L.A., 2007. Food and drug law: cases and materials, third ed. Foundation Press, NY.

Jensen, E.J., 1987. Research expenditures and the discovery of new drugs. Journal of Industrial Economics 36, 83–95.

Kaitin, K.I., DiCerbo, P.A., Lasagna, L., 1991. The new drug approvals of 1987, 1988, and 1989: trends in drug development. The Journal of Clinical Pharmacology 31, 116–122.

Keeler, E.B., Rolph, J.E., 1988. The demand for episodes of treatment in the health insurance experiment. Journal of Health Economics, 337–367.

Kniesner, T.J., Viscusi, W.K., Woock, C., Ziliak, J.P., 2012. The value of a statistical life: evidence from panel data. Review of Economics and Statistics 94, 74–87.

Koijen, R., Philipson, T., Uhlig, H., 2012. Financial Health Economics. Working Paper, Department of Economics, University of Chicago.

Kondo, M., Hoshi, S., Okubo, I., 2009. Does subsidy work? Price elasticity of demand for influenza vaccination among elderly in Japan. Health Policy 91, 269–276.

Kremslehner, D., Muermann, A., 2013. Asymmetric Information in Automobile Insurance: New Evidence from Telematic Data. Working Paper. Available at SSRN: <http://ssrn.com/abstract=2048478> or http://dx.doi.org/10.2139/ssrn.2048478.

Krueger, A.B., Kuziemko, I., 2013. The demand for health insurance among uninsured Americans: results of a survey experiment and implications for policy. Journal of Health Economics 32, 780–793.

Levy, H., Meltzer, D., 2008. The impact of health insurance on health. Annual Review of Public Health 29, 399–409.

Liebman, J., Zeckhauser, R., 2008. Simple Humans, Complex Insurance, Subtle Subsidies. NBER Working Paper 14330.

Manning, W.G., Newhouse, J.P., Duan, N., Keeler, E.B., Leibowitz, A., Marquis, M.S., 1987. Health insurance and the demand for medical care: evidence from a randomized experiment. American Economic Review 77, 251–277.

May, M.S., Wardell, W.M., Lasagna, L., 1983. New drug development during and after a period of regulatory change: clinical research activity of major United States pharmaceutical firms, 1958–1979. Clinical Pharmacology and Therapeutics 33, 691–700.

McCarthy, D., Mitchell, O.S., 2010. International adverse selection in life insurance and annuities. In: Tuljapurkar, S., Ogawa, N., Gauthier, A.H. (Eds.), Ageing in Advanced Industrial States: Riding the Age Waves, vol. 3. Springer, pp. 119–135.

McFadden, D., 2006. Free markets and fettered consumers. American Economic Review 96, 5–29.

McGuire, T.G., 2012. Demand for health insurance. In: Pauly, M.V., McGuire, T.G., Barros, P.P. (Eds.), Handbook of Health Economics, vol. 2. Elsevier.

Mulligan, C., Philipson, T.J., 2004. Insurance Market Participation under Symmetric Information. Working Paper.

Mund, V.F., 1970. The return on investment of the innovative pharmaceutical firm. In: Cooper, J.D. (Ed.), The Economics of Drug Innovation. American University, Washington, DC, pp. 125–138.

Murphy, K.M., Topel, R.H., 2006. The value of health and longevity. Journal of Political Economy 114, 871–904.

Newhouse, J., 1992. Medical care costs: how much welfare loss?. Journal of Economic Perspectives 6, 3–21.

Nyman, J.A., 1999. The value of health insurance: the access motive. Journal of Health Economics 18, 141–152.

Olson, M.K., 2004. Explaining reductions in FDA drug review times: PDUFA matters. Health Affairs, http://dx.doi.org/10.1377/hlthaff.w4.s1.

Oster, E., Shoulson, I., Quaid, K.A., Dorsey, E.R., 2010. Genetic adverse selection: evidence from long-term care insurance and Huntington's disease. Journal of Public Economics 94, 1041–1050.

Pauly, M.V., 1968. The economics of moral hazard: comment. American Economic Review 58, 531–537.

Pauly, M.V., 1990. The rational nonpurchase of long term care insurance. Journal of Political Economy 98, 153–168.

Peltzman, S., 1973. An evaluation of consumer safety protection legislation: the 1962 drug amendments. Journal of Political Economy 81, 1049–1091.

Philipson, T.J., Berndt, E.R., Gottschalk, A.H.B., Sun, E., 2008. Cost-benefit analysis of the FDA: the case of the prescription drug user fee acts. Journal of Public Economics, 92, 1306–1325.

Philipson, T.J., Sun, E., Goldman, D., 2009. The Effects of Product Liability Exemption in the Presence of the FDA. NBER Working Paper 15603.

Philipson, T., Sun, E., Sun, A. Jena., Goldman, D., 2009. A Re-examination of the Costs of Medical R&D. Working Paper.

Richaudeau, D., 1999. Automobile insurance contracts and risk of accident: an empirical test using French individual data. The Geneva Papers on Risk and Insurance - Theory 24, 97–114.

Rothschild, M., Stiglitz, J., 1976. Equilibrium in competitive insurance markets: an essay on the economics of imperfect information. Quarterly Journal of Economics 90, 629–649.

Saito, K., 2006. Testing for asymmetric information in the automobile insurance market under rate regulation. Journal of Risk and Insurance 73, 335–356.

Sarett, L.H., 1974. FDA regulations and their influence on future research and development. Research Management 17, 18–20.

Strombom, B.A., Buchmueller, T.C., Feldstein, P.J., 2002. Switching costs, price sensitivity and health plan choice. Journal of Health Economics 21, 89–116.

Thomas, L.G., 1990. Regulaton and firm size: FDA impacts on innovation. RAND Journal of Economics 21, 497–517.

Viscusi, W.K., Aldy, J.E., 2003. The value of a statistical life: a critical review of market estimates throughout the world. Journal of Risk and Uncertainty 27, 5–76.

Wardell, W., 1973. Introduction of new therapeutic drugs in the United States and Great Britain: an international comparison. Clinical Pharmacology and Therapeutics 14, 773–790.

Weisbrod, B., 1991. The health care quadrilemma: an essay on technological change, insurance, quality of care, and cost containment. Journal of Economic Literature 29, 523–552.

Wiggins, S.N., 1981. Product quality regulation and new drug introductions: some new evidence from the 1970s. Review of Economics and Statistics 63, 615–619.

Wiggins, S.N., 1983. The impact of regulation on pharmaceutical research expenditures: a dynamic approach. Economic Inquiry 21, 115–128.

Wolfe, J.R., Goddeeris, J.H., 1991. Adverse selection, moral hazard, and wealth effects in the Medigap insurance market. Journal of Health Economics 10, 433–459.

Zeckhauser, R.J., 1970. Medical insurance: a case study of the tradeoff between risk spreading and appropriate incentives. Journal of Economic Theory 2, 10–26.

Zeckhauser, R.J., 1973. Coverage for Catastrophic illness. Public Policy 21, 149–172.

CHAPTER *9*

Regulating Occupational and Product Risks

Thomas J. Kniesner[a,b,c] and John D. Leeth[d]

[a]Claremont Graduate University, Claremont, CA, USA
[b]Syracuse University, Syracuse, NY, USA
[c]IZA, Bonn, Germany
[d]Bentley University, Waltham, MA, USA

Contents

Abstract

Market forces, supplemented by government policy, affect how firms and households jointly determine product and workplace safety levels. After developing the economic theory of how labor and product markets pair prices and health risks we then explain the effects of the relevant government policies, including information, tort liability laws, direct regulation of job and product attributes, and mandatory no-fault insurance to compensate injured parties. Each theoretical development is followed by econometric evidence concerning policy induced outcomes. An important finding is that the most influential economic incentives for product and job safety stem from the fact that people tend not to buy hazardous products or accept employment in hazardous jobs unless the price they pay or the wages they are paid compensate for health risks and safety risks. We conclude with policies of future interest, including greater attention to how one is injured or killed and the distributional impacts of policy.

Keywords

Workplace Safety, Product Safety, Auto Safety, Hedonic Equilibrium, OSHA, MSHA, Workers' Compensation Insurance, Tort Liability, CPSC, NHTSA

JEL Classification Codes

D61, D82, H75, I18, J28, J81, J88, K13, K32

Handbook of the Economics of Risk and Uncertainty, Volume 1
ISSN 2211-7547, http://dx.doi.org/10.1016/B978-0-444-53685-3.00009-X

9.1 INTRODUCTION TO REGULATORY ISSUES

Consumers and workers value safety and health. Knowledgeable people will not buy hazardous products or accept employment in hazardous work sites unless the product prices they pay or the wages they receive compensate for dangers. The positive relationship between wages and risk and the negative relationship between product price and risk means that markets reward firms for improving workplace safety via lower labor costs and for improving product (both goods and services) safety via higher revenues. Eliminating hazards may be expensive, but the wage reduction or the price increase may more than pay for the costs of additional safety efforts. The chapter to follow examines both theoretically and empirically how private market forces as supplemented by government policy affect how firms operate and in turn jointly produce product and work site safety levels.

The oldest government policy in force is the court system, which through the application of tort liability laws, encourages firms to consider safety and health. Companies producing more dangerous products or having more hazardous worksites are more likely to be sued by their customers or workers for damages. Even if companies insure against possible lawsuits the pricing of insurance creates incentives for firms to consider occupational and consumer safety and health. At a minimum, the price of insurance must equal the expected loss of the event, meaning firms with better safety records face lower premiums for product liability (malpractice) and workers' compensation insurance.[1]

Supplementing the existing tort law system, additional government involvement in the area of workplace safety began in the United States in the 1910s when states began passing workers' compensation insurance legislation. Workers' compensation laws made firms strictly liable for industrial injuries. Regardless of fault, employers must pay all of injured workers' medical bills and a portion of lost income. In return for no fault insurance coverage workers cannot sue employers for damages due to work-related injuries. Proponents of workers' compensation legislation argued that courts' *ex post* negligence determination left too many workers uncompensated for injury and created too much uncertainty regarding payment of damages. By 1920 most states had passed workers' compensation laws and by 1948, with passage in Mississippi, all states had enacted legislation.

The exclusive remedy clause of workers' compensation prevents workers from suing their employers for damages from industrial accidents and diseases, but workers may bypass the limitation by suing other parties under product liability law. The ability of workers to prevail in product liability suits skyrocketed beginning in the 1960s when the courts moved to a strict liability standard wherein manufacturers are legally responsible for damages if the products they produce are unreasonably dangerous or if they

---

[1] Malpractice liability insurance is dealt with elsewhere and not considered here. (See Sloan and Chepke, 2010; Dionne and Harrington, Chapter 5).

fail to warn their customers of the potential hazards. The success of product liability suits spills over into occupational safety by expanding the incentives of manufacturers to produce safe equipment and products for industrial use and to warn workers of possible dangers.

From 1958 to 1970 the average manufacturing injury rate grew by about two percent per year. The dramatic rise in workplace injuries led to passage of the Occupational Safety and Health Act of 1970 (Viscusi, 1983, p. 29). The Act created two federal agencies: the Occupational Safety and Health Administration (OSHA), which establishes and enforces workplace safety and health standards, and the National Institute for Occupational Safety and Health (NIOSH), which conducts research into the causes and possible remedies of occupational injuries and illnesses.

In the area of consumer safety, the tort system of product liability has been augmented several times by federal agencies charged with creating and enforcing safety and health standards. The first federal involvement began in the early 1900s in reaction to Upton Sinclair's *The Jungle*, detailing unsanitary conditions in meat-packing plants, and a series of articles by Harvey Wiley, investigating unhealthy food additives (Williams, 2010). The Meat Inspection Act of 1906 directed the U.S. Department of Agriculture to inspect meat and meat products to ensure that animals are slaughtered and processed under sanitary conditions, and the Pure Food and Drug Act of 1906 created the Food and Drug Administration (FDA). Continuing concerns with safety and health, as exemplified by Nader (1965), led to legislation in the early 1970s creating the National Highway Traffic Safety Administration (NHTSA), the Consumer Product Safety Commission (CPSC), and the Environmental Protection Agency (EPA).

The FDA now regulates most food products for safety and health, except for meat and poultry, which are regulated by U.S. Department of Agriculture. In addition, the FDA regulates cosmetics, drugs, medical devices, biologics (medical products created biologically, not chemically, such as vaccines and gene therapies), veterinary products, and radiation-emitting electronic products. The NHTSA sets design standards for all new cars, trucks, and motorcycles sold in the U.S., investigates vehicles for safety defects, and issues recall and repair orders to manufacturers for serious design, construction, or performance defects. The CPSC fulfills similar functions to the NHTSA but with respect to thousands of other consumer products. It too issues mandatory design standards, investigates products for defects, and issues recall and repair orders. If no feasible standard would adequately protect the public, the CPSC can take action to ban the sale of the product. Consumer products not regulated by the CPSC for safety and health concerns include pesticides and fungicides, which are regulated by the EPA, and tobacco, alcohol, and firearms.[2]

---

[2] EPA and FDA regulatory efforts are topics considered in Aldy and Viscusi (2014), Chapter 10 and Philipson and Zanjani (2014), Chapter 8 and are not a component of what follows.

To summarize our chapter, we begin by developing the economic theory of market wages for jobs that involve health risks and market prices for products that may injure the consumers who use them. Once we explain how labor and product markets allocate and implicitly price jointly produced risks to health, we explicate how various forms of government interventions, information, tort liability laws, direct regulation of job and product attributes, and mandatory no-fault insurance to compensate injured parties affect safety outcomes and individuals' economic well-being. We then consider available econometric evidence for the absolute and relative effectiveness of the various pillars of safety policy in the United States. We conclude with the likely issues of future interest to economists and policymakers.

9.2 RISK CHOICES AND HEDONIC EQUILIBRIUM

Before determining where society may use government involvement to improve occupational and consumer safety and health further, we first need to examine how workers, consumers, and firms make decisions regarding safety and health risks. One might be tempted to claim that ideally no one would gamble with his or her health. Workers would demand a completely safe workplace and consumers would demand totally safe products. Even in such ideal situations people would still have to make trade-offs, though. Large heavy cars are safer than small light cars, but because big cars are more expensive and less fuel-efficient than small cars, many people choose the riskier small cars. People ski, bike, hang-glide, rock climb, and engage in other risky activities because the enjoyment compensates for the high chance of injury or death. In the area of workplace safety and health, for a worker to choose a more hazardous workplace he or she must get something in return, such as a higher wage (inclusive of fringe benefits) to offset the greater chance of an injury or illness. In the area of product safety, for one to purchase a more dangerous product the consumer must be offered something in return, such as a lower price. Improving workplace and product safety is expensive and firms may be willing to pay higher wages to their workers or reduce prices to their customers to avoid the added costs of greater safety.

9.2.1 Labor Markets

We begin by examining occupational safety and health in some detail and then show how the framework can be modified when examining product markets. One way to conceptualize a firm's provision of safety is to view safety as an input into the production process, similar to capital and labor. To ease the presentation that follows, we examine the simplified case where employers offer identical hours of work, and workers accept employment in one firm only. Further, we will focus on a single job characteristic, π, which is the probability of a standard workplace injury or illness that is known to both workers and firms. Finally, we will assume that both labor and product markets are competitive.

In the context of such a basic economic case, expected profit can be represented algebraically as

$$\bar{g} = R(p_O, S(\pi), n, k; \mu) - W(\pi)(1 - \pi)n - p_s S(\pi) \\ -p_k k - P_b(\pi)bn - V(\pi, e) - d\pi, \tag{9.1}$$

where $\bar{g} \equiv$ expected profit,

$R(\cdot) \equiv$ the expected revenue function,

$p_O \equiv$ the per-unit price of output,

$s \equiv$ the quantity of safety measures with $s = S(\pi)$ such that $S(\cdot)$ is the (inverse) safety production function with $S' < 0$,

$n \equiv$ the number of workers,

$k \equiv$ the quantity of capital,

$\mu \equiv$ a parameter representing the efficiency of safety equipment in the production of output ($\partial^2 R / \partial s \partial \mu > 0$),

$W(\pi) \equiv$ the market wage function, observable to workers and firms, with $W' > 0$,

$p_s \equiv$ the price per-unit of safety measures (equipment),

$p_k \equiv$ the price per-unit of capital,

$P_b(\pi) \equiv$ the price per-unit (of the benefits) of workers' compensation insurance, $P_b' > 0$,

$b \equiv$ insurance benefits provided to workers if injured,

$V(\pi, e) \equiv$ the expected fine for violating safety and health standards with $\partial V / \partial \pi > 0$, $\partial V / \partial e \geq 0$, and $\partial^2 V / \partial \pi \partial e \geq 0$,

$e \equiv$ the level of government enforcement of safety and health regulations, and

$d \equiv$ the expected court award to a worker if injured.

By differentiating equation (9.1) with respect to n, k, and π and rearranging terms, we can show that the optimal usage of each input occurs when

$$\frac{\partial R}{\partial n} = W(\pi)(1 - \pi) + P_b(\pi)b, \tag{9.2}$$

$$\frac{\partial R}{\partial k} = p_k, \tag{9.3}$$

$$\frac{\partial R}{\partial S} \frac{\partial S}{\partial \pi} - \left(\frac{\partial W}{\partial \pi}(1 - \pi) - w \right)n - \frac{\partial P_b}{\partial \pi}bn - \frac{\partial V}{\partial \pi} - d = p_s \frac{\partial S}{\partial \pi}. \tag{9.4}$$

Firms increase their use of labor and capital until the expected marginal revenue product of each input equals its expected marginal cost. In addition, firms reduce workplace hazards until the marginal benefits of greater safety–higher output,[3] lower wages,[4] lower insurance costs, lower government fines for workplace hazards, and lower court awards for damages from worker injuries–equal the marginal costs of supplying greater safety. Because the output effects of safety programs vary among workplaces the marginal benefits of reducing work-related health hazards differ among firms, in turn causing the optimum level of safety to vary. Firms where safety equipment is highly productive reduce hazards more than firms where safety equipment is less productive.

Notice that, even in the absence of government programs geared toward improving workplace safety, equations (9.2–9.4) indicate that managers still have incentives to engage in safety efforts as a result of the reduction in wages associated with greater worker safety.[5] The government can augment these incentives by mandating insurance coverage for workplace injuries (b), clarifying the relationship between the price of workers' compensation insurance coverage and risk ($\frac{\partial P_b}{\partial \pi}$), establishing and enforcing workplace safety and health standards ($\frac{\partial V}{\partial \pi}$), and allowing workers to sue for work related illnesses and injuries (d).

Figure 9.1 provides another way to think about firms' decisions regarding workplace safety. The figure shows the market wage function (W) and the offer wage functions (Φ) for two companies. Graphically, a firm's offer wage function (isoprofit curve) shows the trade-off between wages and workplace safety at a constant level of expected profit with capital and labor used in optimal quantities. To keep the same level of profit, wages must fall as workplace safety rises to compensate for the added cost of purchasing safety equipment. Offer wage functions slope upward. Firms with greater costs of producing a safe workplace require a greater wage reduction to improve safety than firms with smaller costs of producing a safe work environment, all else equal. The firm with the higher marginal cost of producing a safer workplace will have a more steeply sloped offer wage function at a given wage and injury rate than a firm with a lower marginal cost. Finally, profits rise as wages fall, implying that the lower the offer wage function, the higher the profit.

The $W(\pi)$ depicted in Figure 9.1 need not be an equilibrium wage function as yet; firms and workers need only observe and make their decisions based on the relationship

---

[3] Safety enhancing programs may increase or decrease production. Viscusi (1979b) argues that safety equipment increases output by diminishing the disruptive effects of injuries and by increasing the stability of the workforce. In the other direction, programs such as slowing the pace of the assembly line or installing cumbersome machine guards can interfere with the work process and decrease output. On net, which effect dominates is an unresolved empirical question. For purposes of discussion, we assume that safety equipment is a productive factor. None of the conclusions we present change if safety equipment reduces output.

[4] Although wages fall for all workers when the safety level increases, a reduction in the number of injuries means that a greater proportion of workers are paid for the full period. We focus on the case where the wage reduction from greater safety swamps the wage bill increase from fewer accidents.

[5] A more complete model would consider the firm's decision to purchase disability insurance in the absence of a government mandate. To simplify the discussion we consider the situation where any required level of workers' compensation insurance coverage exceeds the level that would be chosen for profit maximization.

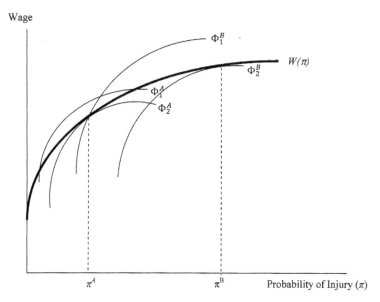

Figure 9.1 Firm equilibrium.

between wages and workplace risk. As can be seen, company A maximizes profit by offering workers job risk equal to π^A, the level where the offer wage function is just tangent to the market wage function. Because its costs of providing a safe work environment are greater, company B maximizes profit by offering a less agreeable job, π^B, but paying higher wages than company A to compensate workers for the less pleasant working conditions. With a sufficiently large number of diverse firms, each point on the market wage function represents a point of tangency for some company or companies. The market wage function represents an upper envelope of a family of offer wage curves that differ because of the variation in the technical abilities of firms to produce workplace safety. It slopes upward because firms are willing to pay higher wages to avoid bearing the added expenses of providing better working conditions.

The problem confronting a worker is to find the level of consumption and workplace safety that maximizes expected utility subject to the overall budget constraint. Algebraically, after substituting the income constraint into the utility functions for consumption goods, a worker's expected utility becomes

$$\bar{u} = (1 - \pi)U(W(\pi) + y; \xi) + \pi\widetilde{U}(b + d + y; \xi), \tag{9.5}$$

where $\bar{u} \equiv$ expected utility,

$U(\cdot) \equiv$ the worker's utility function if uninjured,

$\widetilde{U}(\cdot) \equiv$ the worker's utility function if injured, $U > \widetilde{U}$ and $U' > \widetilde{U}'$,

$y \equiv$ nonlabor income, and

$\xi \equiv$ a parameter determining an individual's aversion to risk.

Expected utility is a weighted average of the utility if uninjured and the utility if injured with the weights equaling the probabilities of the two states. The formulation in equation (9.5) explicitly considers both monetary and nonmonetary losses from workplace injuries. The difference between $U(\cdot)$ and $\widetilde{U}(\cdot)$, income held constant, represents the pain and suffering resulting from an injury or illness.

By differentiating expected utility with respect to π, setting the result equal to 0, and then rearranging, a worker's optimal level of risk (safety) occurs when

$$(1 - \pi)U' \frac{\partial W}{\partial \pi} = U(W(\pi) + y; \xi) - \widetilde{U}(b + d + y; \xi). \qquad (9.6)$$

The story here is the standard one: a worker weighs the marginal benefit of increased risk against the marginal cost. The left-hand side of equation (9.6) represents the marginal benefit, the expected added pay from a more risky job, while the right-hand side represents the marginal cost, the greater likelihood of an injury that lowers both income and the utility from income. Because people differ in their degrees of risk aversion, the perceived marginal gain and cost differ among people, in turn causing the optimal level of safety to vary. Workers with low risk aversion sort into high risk jobs, and workers with high risk aversion sort into low risk jobs.

Similar to the situation for firms, workers' decisions regarding risk can also be depicted graphically. A worker's acceptance wage function (indifference curve) illustrates the trade-off between wages and π at a constant level of utility. Because risk reduces expected utility, wages must rise to compensate for bearing more risk. Acceptance wage functions slope upward. Additionally, more risk averse workers require greater wage compensation for a given increase in π than less risk averse workers, all else equal, so the worker with the steeper acceptance wage function at a given (W, π) is the more risk averse. Lastly, workers prefer higher wages to lower wages at any level of risk, so the higher the acceptance wage function the higher the utility. The choice of the optimal level of π can be viewed similarly to the choice of the optimal purchase of commodities with the market wage function replacing the standard income constraint.

Figure 9.2 portrays acceptance wage functions (Θ) for two workers in relation to a market wage function. We see worker C maximizing utility by selecting a job with the level of risk equal to π^C. The highest level of utility the worker can achieve occurs where the acceptance wage function is just tangent to the market wage curve. Although π^C maximizes worker C's utility, it does not maximize worker D's utility; worker D requires a smaller increase in wages to accept a slight rise in workplace risk, utility held constant. Worker D maximizes utility by choosing a slightly more dangerous job, characterized by π^D, and earning a higher wage. With a sufficiently large number of

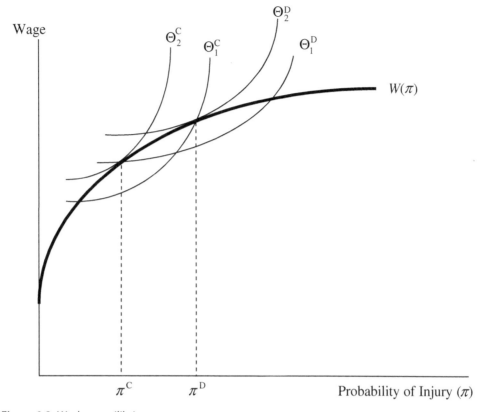

Figure 9.2 Worker equilibrium.

diverse workers, each point on the hedonic wage function is a point of tangency for some group of workers. In technical language, the wage function represents the lower envelope of a family of acceptance wage curves, which differ because workers vary in their attitudes regarding π.

Firms supply a given type of workplace based on the market wage function and their ability to produce a safe work environment. Workers sort into particular job risks based on the market wage function and their preferences regarding safety. The market wage function equilibrates the supply and demand for labor along the entire job risk spectrum. A shortage of workers in high-risk establishments, for instance, will drive up wages, thereby enticing some workers away from safer employment. At the same time, the wage hike will encourage some firms to expand their expenditures on workplace safety to reduce labor costs. With workers moving toward greater π and firms moving toward lower π, wages must rise in relatively safer workplaces. An excess demand for labor at any point along the job risk spectrum alters the delicate balancing of labor supply and demand everywhere. Wages adjust until the supply of labor equals the demand

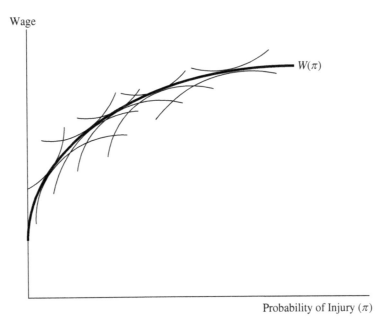

Figure 9.3 Hedonic labor market equilibrium.

for labor along the entire spectrum. Because in equilibrium wages must rise to compensate workers for undesirable job characteristics such as poor workplace safety, the market wage function is referred to as a hedonic wage function (Rosen, 1974).

The slope of the acceptance wage function measures the wage a worker is willing to sacrifice to reduce job disamenities by a small amount and, therefore, provides a dollar figure of a worker's willingness to pay for workplace safety implicitly. At the same time, the slope of the isoprofit curve measures the reduction in wages required by a firm to compensate for the higher costs of improving the work environment. As can be seen in Figure 9.3 the hedonic wage function maps out a set of tangencies between workers' acceptance wage functions and firms' isoprofit curves or offer wage functions. The equality between the slope of the hedonic wage function and the slope of workers' indifference curves means that estimates of the wage function provide dollar estimates of workers' willingness to pay for safety, which we will discuss in more detail soon.

9.2.2 Product Markets

The thought process of hedonic equilibrium is the same in product markets as in labor markets (Spence, 1977), except the end result is a negative relationship between price and risk. The added cost of producing safer products implies that the firms' isoprofit curves would be downward sloping. As risk expands output price must fall to keep profits constant. At the same time, consumers value both more safety and more goods and services, meaning that they would only purchase a riskier product if it were cheaper. Indifference curves must also be downward sloping. Similar to labor markets, the interaction of firms and consumers generates a price function where consumers sort along the function based on their valuations of safety and firms sort along the function based on their abilities to produce safe products. In equilibrium, the hedonic price function represents an upper envelope of isoprofit curves and a lower envelope of indifference curves (profit expands and utility falls as price rises), meaning the slope of the price function provides an estimate of consumers' willingness to pay for added safety and firms' cost of providing added safety. Assuming consumers have good information about risks and process the information properly, a freely functioning competitive market will generate the economically optimal level of product market safety.

9.2.3 Information

Proponents of government involvement in the area of consumer and occupational safety and health argue that people lack the basic information necessary to make the trade-offs between safety and higher product prices or between safety and lower wages. If people do not understand the hazards they face, then they cannot choose between a safe and a risky product or between a safe and a risky job (Hermalin, forthcoming). In the absence of information about hazards, consumer and labor markets will not establish compensating price and wage differentials for risk and firms will lack incentives to improve safety. Even if consumers and workers realize hazards exist but they underestimate the risks they face, then compensating price and wage differentials will be too small and safety incentives will be too low.

Evidence indicates consumers and workers consider risk when purchasing products and accepting employment. Many labor market studies show wages rising as the chance of a fatal or nonfatal injury or disease at work expands. All else equal, the typical U.S. worker in a job with a likelihood of injury at about the labor market average earns about 1 to 2 percent more than a person working in a totally safe job (Viscusi and Aldy, 2003, p. 29). The positive relationship between wages and risk has been found in the U.S. and other industrial countries and also in less developed countries. Wages rise not only for accident risks but also for the risks of long-term illnesses such as cancer (Lott and Manning, 2000; Sandy and Elliott, 2005). In the product sphere, house prices drop the closer they are to environmental hazards such as Superfund hazardous waste sites, earthquake faults, landfills, and interstate gas pipelines and car prices fall as the risk of a fatal accident rises (Andersson, 2005; Brookshire et al., 1985; Dreyfus and Viscusi, 1995; Farber, 1998; Hansen et al., 2006; Viscusi and Aldy, 2003).

Even when consumers and workers do not understand the risks they face initially, they reevaluate their beliefs relatively quickly. Evidence indicates that workers quit hazardous jobs more frequently than relatively safe jobs (Viscusi, 1992). Increases in the probability of an accident also raise quit intentions and job searching, and reduce job tenure. Learning about job risks after accepting employment may be responsible for about one-third of all workers' quits (Viscusi, 1979a).

Viscusi and O'Connor (1984) directly examine how workers incorporate new information into risk assessments. When a group of chemical workers were told that they would soon be working with sodium bicarbonate, a safe chemical, they reduced their assessment of workplace hazards by 50 percent. When told that they would be working with either asbestos or TNT they increased their assessment of workplace hazards by 200 percent. No worker required extra compensation to handle the safe sodium bicarbonate but they did demand an extra $7,000 to $12,000 per year to handle the dangerous asbestos or TNT.[6] No workers said they would quit their jobs because they would be handling sodium bicarbonate but a majority of workers said they would quit because they would be handling asbestos or TNT.

Consumers also react to new information concerning safety and health aspects of products. When told about the possible risks of using two products, insecticide and toilet bowl cleaner, surveyed consumers replied that they were willing to pay more for both products if the risks, which were largely temporary, were eliminated. As would be expected, consumers with young children were willing to pay more for these risk reductions than were consumers without young children (Evans and Viscusi, 1991). In a similar context, when 400 consumers were presented with information on the risks of liquid bleach (vomiting and stomach aches from drinking, chloramine gas poisoning if mixed with ammonia) and a liquid drain opener (burns to the mouth and throat if ingested, burns to the hand if spilled), the decision to engage in precautionary behavior rose (Viscusi et al., 1986).

Although consumers and workers do react to information concerning safety and health risks, the public goods aspect of basic research means that the private market will underprovide safety and health information. The government must play a role in trying to uncover and disseminate information on the causes and consequences of safety and health hazards. The explicit purpose of NIOSH is to gather information and conduct scientific research about workplace injuries and illnesses. On the consumer side, the FDA, CPSC, NHTSA, and EPA all engage in research examining safety and health issues ranging from general hazards of a product to specific design or production defects of a single manufacturer of a product.

Research on occupational and consumer hazards is used in three ways. First, the information helps determine product or workplace characteristics required to eliminate or minimize a newly discovered hazard. OSHA requires safety guards to prevent injury from moving machine parts, the NHTSA requires seat belts and air bags to be included in all new cars, and the CPSC requires new lawnmowers sold in the U.S. to include a dead-man control to stop the blade from moving within three seconds of releasing the

---

[6] All dollar figures appearing throughout our entry have been adjusted for inflation to 2011 using the CPI-U.

control. Second, decision makers can use information to institute a ban on a product or production technology or to institute a recall of a product found to be defective. The FDA prevents the sale of pharmaceuticals in the U.S. found not to be safe and effective, and the CPSC can ban products if no feasible standard can assure consumer safety. The FDA, NHTSA, and CPSC monitor products for safety defects such as *E. coli* contamination of food products, sudden acceleration of motor vehicles, and fire and burn hazards from lamps. Finally, information can be conveyed to consumers and workers via a hazard warning. The FDA requires risk labeling of pharmaceutical products and the EPA mandates that pesticides include information on appropriate usage. Perhaps the best-known hazard warning is the one imposed by Congress in 1965 requiring that each pack of cigarettes include the warning that smoking may be dangerous to one's health.

By clarifying job or product hazards, warnings increase the likelihood that workers and consumers demand compensating wage and price differentials for their exposure to risk. In the case of jobs, equation (9.4) illustrates that an expansion in the compensation for risk $(\frac{\partial W}{\partial \pi})$ raises managerial incentives to improve worker safety. Firms will likewise expand safety efforts to reduce labor turnover and the associated costs of recruitment and training.

A benefit of hazard warnings over safety and health standards or product bans is that warnings allow consumers to make the cost/benefit calculations for possible precautions to take based on their own circumstances and preferences. Requiring child resistant packaging may be appropriate for families with young children but may not be suitable for people with arthritis. Mandating motorcycle helmet use may lower motorcycle fatalities but for some riders the joy of riding without a helmet exceeds the value of greater safety. Accidents also generally do not happen in a vacuum, but instead are the result of the interaction of the user and the technological characteristics of the product. Simply specifying product or workplace characteristics may not address all of the contributors to deteriorating safety and health. Additionally, in many situations, usage of a product is so decentralized that government monitoring of regulations dictating appropriate precautions is difficult, if not impossible, so that hazard warnings may be the only way to encourage consumers and workers to take suitable precautions (Viscusi, 1991b, 2014).

For hazard warnings to be effective they need to explain the degree of danger the person is facing, describe the appropriate precautions that should be taken, and indicate the particular risks that will be reduced by taking the specified precautions (Viscusi, 1991b, 2014). Information overload can occur if precautionary labels present too much information or if too many products have precautionary labels. Warnings about small risks such as the risk of cancer from silica (sand) may actually reduce safety by convincing people that warning labels are irrelevant. A proliferation of hazard warnings may also prove counterproductive if people are led to view all activities or products as equally dangerous.

9.3 VALUING SAFETY AND HEALTH

Because of the difficulty of conveying and processing information on hazards the government frequently augments market incentives to produce the appropriate level of safety with regulations specifying product or workplace characteristics. To create the efficient level of safety, regulations should be imposed only if the benefits of improved safety outweigh the costs. Cost estimates of proposed safety and health standards are usually generated through accounting or engineering studies. Determining the benefits of improved safety requires estimating a monetary value of injuries, illnesses, and fatalities avoided. Although several approaches exist to determine life-saving benefits, economists most often rely on estimates of an hedonic wage function as shown in Figure 9.3.

The theory of hedonic wage and product price equilibrium provides the basis for the economic approach to evaluating the benefits of programs aimed at improving safety and health, which requires placing a monetary value on the potential lives saved or injuries avoided. The slope of the acceptance wage function measures the portion of his or her wage a worker is willing to sacrifice to lower the chance of injury by a small amount and, therefore, provides an implicit dollar estimate of a worker's willingness to pay for workplace safety. In equilibrium, the slope of the hedonic wage function equals the slope of the indifference curves, so for small improvements in safety, the drop in the market wage reflects the value workers place on the improvement. Say wages in Figure 9.4 fall by $80 when the chance of a workplace fatality drops from 5 in 100,000 to 4 in 100,000. A typical worker is willing to sacrifice $80 to reduce his or her chance of death by 1 in 100,000, meaning that, collectively, 100,000 workers would sacrifice $8 million and, on average, one life would be saved. The saved life is not known beforehand, but in a sense is drawn randomly from the 100,000 workers at risk, so the $8 million represents the value of a statistical life (VSL). In Section 9.6 we demonstrate similar calculations based on drivers' willingness to pay for safer cars. An implicit value of injury can be found in a similar manner by dividing a market wage change for a small reduction in the probability of a workplace nonfatal injury or illness by the change in the probability of occurrence. The resulting calculation is known as the value of a statistical injury (VSI). (We refer readers interested in a more extensive treatment of VSL and VSI to Viscusi, 2014.)

To elaborate, let W' represent the first derivative of the hedonic wage function with respect to risk. For small changes in π, $W'd\pi$ reasonably approximates the reduction in wage along the indifference curve, which represents the worker's willingness to pay for safety improvements. The $80 wage reduction moving down the tangent line in Figure 9.4 from 5 in 100,000 to 4 in 100,000 (a VSL of $8 million) is only slightly larger than the wage reduction along the indifference curve. For large reductions in π the approximation substantially overstates the value workers place on safety. The first derivative approach suggests workers would be willing to pay $400 to move from their current level of risk to complete safety, when in actuality the movement along the indifference

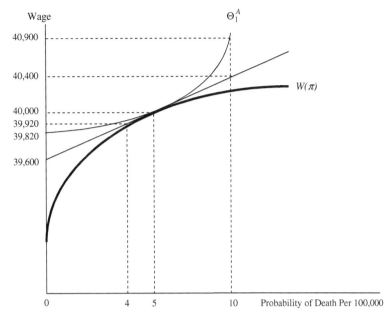

Figure 9.4 VSLs, Willingness to pay, and Willingness to accept.

curve suggests they value the improvement by only $180. In the other direction, the slope of the tangent line underestimates the costs of serious deteriorations in safety. The rise in wage necessary to maintain worker welfare moving to the right along the indifference curve, referred to as the willingness to accept, is considerably greater than the movement along the tangent line for large changes in risk. The true VSL as measured by the willingness to accept is $18 million for a doubling of risk from 5 in 100,000 to 10 in 100,000, and not $8 million, as would be calculated using estimates of the hedonic wage equation.

As should be clear from Figure 9.4, VSLs do not measure the amount of money people would pay to avoid certain death. A risk reduction from 100,000 in 100,000 to 0 in 100,000 represents the largest possible change in risk, so that the willingness to pay would fall considerably below the value implied by the slope of the tangent line along the hedonic wage or price function. As we will discuss later, the range of VSLs is considerable, but even at the lower end of the spectrum few people would have the financial resources to pay the amount of money implied by an estimated VSL to save their own life. Income constraints become binding.

In the opposite direction, VSLs underestimate the value society places on saving known lives. Once the identities of the people who will be saved by some action are known, feelings of altruism become paramount. On August 5, 2010, part of an underground copper mine collapsed in Chile trapping 33 miners 2000 feet below ground. For 69 days the world focused on freeing the 33 miners and no expense was avoided in the effort. VSLs are a useful guide for determining the value of efforts aimed at preventing or limiting the impact of a mine collapse, such as requiring more costly roof supports or mandating escape ladders in ventilation systems, but once a mine shaft has collapsed trapping individuals VSLs serve no policy role in determining the extent of rescue efforts.

An additional issue in evaluating policies geared at reducing workplace disamenities (or increasing amenities) is the impact of the policy on hedonic equilibrium. As noted, equations (9.2–9.4) indicate that the government can expand on market safety incentives by establishing and enforcing workplace safety and health standards. Specifically, by totally differentiating the three first-order conditions, one can show that the impact of greater safety enforcement, e, on the firm's optimal level of safety is

$$\frac{\partial \pi}{\partial e} = \frac{\frac{\partial^2 V}{\partial \pi \partial e}\left[\left(\frac{\partial^2 R}{\partial n^2}\right)\left(\frac{\partial^2 R}{\partial k^2}\right) - \frac{\partial^2 R}{\partial n \partial k}\right]}{H}. \tag{9.7}$$

To assure an interior maximization, the Hessian determinant of the system, $\boldsymbol{H}$, must be negative and the term in brackets must be positive, meaning that if $\frac{\partial^2 V}{\partial \pi \partial e} > 0$, then $\frac{\partial \pi}{\partial e} < 0$. Expected fines for violating safety and health standards, v, can be represented as the product of the probability of inspection, the number of violations per inspection, and the average penalty per violation (Viscusi, 2007). As long as OSHA more frequently inspects riskier workplaces for possible violations of safety and health standards, finds more violations of standards in riskier workplaces, or assesses a higher penalty per violation in riskier workplaces the cross-partial derivative $\frac{\partial^2 V}{\partial \pi \partial e}$ will be positive and greater enforcement efforts will lower a firm's optimal level of workplace risk.[7]

If the policy affects only a few workers or a few firms the change is unlikely to alter market conditions markedly, leaving the hedonic equilibrium locus constant. If the policy affects many workers and firms, however, the relocation of workers and firms alters the balancing of supply and demand resulting in a new locus, which may reinforce or mitigate the initial welfare effects.

The impact on the hedonic equilibrium locus is frequently ignored in policy evaluations. In their discussions of OSHA both Borjas (2010) and Ehrenberg and Smith (2009), for example, show fully informed workers harmed by safety and health standards that eliminate extremely risky jobs without considering any feedback effects of the regulations on hedonic equilibrium. In Figure 9.5, the hedonic wage function maps out the relationship between wages and the probability of an accident or disease on the

---

[7] Viscusi (1979b) develops a more complete model of OSHA enforcement where worker safety efforts are negatively related to the level of safety within the firm. In such a model, greater enforcement of safety and health standards expands firms' safety inputs but reduces workers' safety efforts with a possible reduction in overall safety. Viscusi argues that for OSHA to have a counterproductive effect on safety, expected fines would need to be quite high and considerably higher than currently observed.

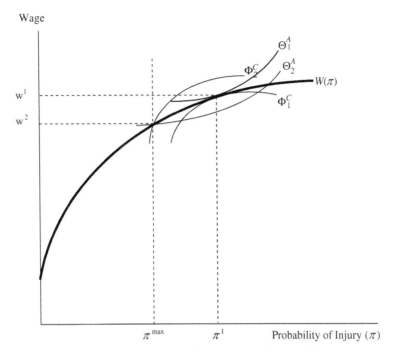

Figure 9.5 The welfare impact of OSHA with no changes in hedonic equilibrium.

job. In the absence of OSHA, the highest indifference curve worker A can reach is the one just tangent to the hedonic function at the probability of injury (π^1) and wage (w^1). On the other side of the market the lowest isoprofit curve (the highest level of profit) firm C can reach is the one just tangent to the wage curve at the probability of injury (π^1) and wage (w^1). Assume OSHA regulations require all firms to install enough safety equipment so the chance of injury is no greater than π^{max}. All firms originally offering higher risk jobs, such as firm C, will install additional safety equipment reducing the chance of injury to π^{max}. Although the improvement in safety allows the firm to lower wages to w^2, the lower labor expenses fail to outweigh the higher costs of safety equipment and profits fall from Φ_1 to Φ_2. With the high-risk jobs eliminated workers, like A, accept employment at the safer worksites but earn lower wages. The reduction in wage more than offsets the improvement in safety and utility falls from Θ_1 to Θ_2. OSHA reduces both firm profits and worker welfare initially.

Based on the above discussion, OSHA, or any policy mandating minimum workplace standards, lowers profits for firms originally offering a less agreeable workplace, lowers the welfare of workers who chose work in the less agreeable workplaces, and leaves everyone else equally well off. The difficulty with the conclusion thus far is that it ignores the impact of the policy on hedonic wage function. Improving working conditions reduces profits causing some firms to shut down and fire their workers. In the other direction, the improvement in working conditions means other firms can pay a lower wage, which causes them to expand hiring. The improvements may also directly affect labor productivity. If productivity rises, then the firms moving to $\pi^{\max}$ will expand hiring even more. On the worker side, the loss of welfare from working may cause some workers to exit the labor market. The drop in wage also creates income and substitution effects that alter the number of hours that workers are willing to supply. With the demand for labor and the supply of labor changing it is very unlikely the wage will remain constant at $\pi^{\max}$, and any wage change at $\pi^{\max}$ will disequilibrate the entire balancing of supply and demand along the entire characteristic spectrum.

In numerical simulations Kniesner and Leeth (1988, 1989a) examine the impact of OSHA in a more complete equilibrium context. In their simulations OSHA regulations raise and flatten the hedonic wage function. Regulations and associated penalties for noncompliance encourage firms to expand safety efforts and move to the left along the hedonic wage function. To restore equilibrium workers must also move to the left. Safety is a normal good so the increase in income from the hedonic function rising causes workers to desire safer employment. The flattening of the hedonic function also means the added compensation for accepting job hazards is lower, causing workers to desire safer jobs.

As can be seen in Figure 9.6, prior to OSHA worker A accepts employment with a high chance of injury (π^1). OSHA regulations increase firms' costs of accidents and

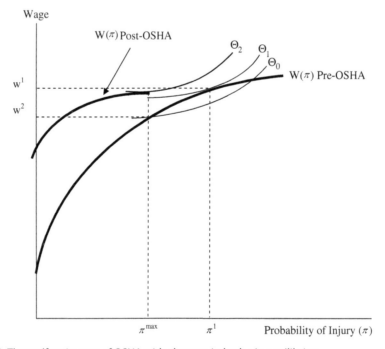

Figure 9.6 The welfare impact of OSHA with changes in hedonic equilibrium.

diseases and reduce the maximum observed chance of injury on the job to $\pi^{\max}$. If the hedonic wage function remained the same then worker A's welfare would fall from Θ_1 to Θ_0, but the function rises and becomes flatter, allowing the worker to reach a higher indifference curve, Θ_2. Additionally, workers originally employed in relatively safe employment also receive wage increases as the wage function rises so their welfare improves. The higher labor costs reduce firm profitability, not only for high-risk workplaces but also for low-risk workplaces. Firms in turn cut back on production resulting in higher output prices and a loss of consumer surplus. Workers ultimately gain, and firms and consumers lose.

To summarize the effect of job safety regulation as depicted in the hedonic equilibrium loci in Figure 9.6, the regulations eliminate the most dangerous jobs and raise wages on the remaining jobs.[8]

9.4 EVIDENCE ON THE IMPACT OF OSHA ON WORKER SAFETY AND HEALTH

Congress passed the Occupational Safety and Health Act in 1970 (OSH Act) "to assure safe and healthful working conditions for working men and women." To achieve its goal the Act created the Occupational Safety and Health Administration (OSHA) and directed it to promulgate occupational safety and health standards, conduct worker education programs about workplace hazards, inspect worksites under its jurisdiction, investigate worker complaints about safety and health, and cite and fine employers for noncompliance with safety and health standards.[9] If a worksite is so hazardous that workers are in "imminent danger" of death or serious physical harm, the Secretary of OSHA can petition in U.S. district court to shut down the worksite until the danger has been removed.

The law encouraged states to develop and operate their own workplace safety and health systems. State standards must be as effective at promoting worker safety and health as federal standards and most states with their own programs establish workplace standards identical to the federal standards. Currently, 27 states and jurisdictions operate their own plans, but five cover only public sector workers.

OSHA safety and health standards come in a variety of forms. The best known are specification standards that mandate specific types of safety programs. Examples of specification standards include requirements that guards be affixed to machinery to prevent injuries from moving parts, engineering and work practice controls to eliminate or minimize employee exposure to blood-borne pathogens, and requirements that machinery be shut down and locked/tagged to prevent restart during servicing. Less

---

[8] A similar graph describes the effect of product safety regulations on product prices and safety levels.

[9] It is important to note that there is some concern among legal scholars that Congress has delegated an unconstitutionally excessive amount of regulatory decision-making power under the Act (Sunstein, 2008).

well-known are performance standards that set maximum levels of exposures to particular hazards such as noise or dust but allow employers to decide how best to achieve the desired levels of exposure. Performance standards provide employers with the flexibility to reduce hazards in the most cost-efficient manner and to accommodate changing circumstances or technological breakthroughs. The General Duty Clause of the OSH Act is the most wide-ranging performance standard. It requires an employer to "furnish to each of his employees employment and a place of employment which are free from recognized hazards that are causing or are likely to cause death or serious physical harm to his employees." Besides specification and performance standards, OSHA can also require employers to post warnings specifying potential dangers from operating equipment or using a product and detailing the appropriate precautions or procedures workers need to take to avoid the dangers.

The OSH Act establishes three violation categories: (1) nonserious, (2) serious, and (3) willful and repeated. OSHA inspectors need not penalize companies for nonserious violations of safety and health standards, but must levy fines for serious violations (infractions substantially increasing the likelihood of a worker fatality or serious injury) and willful or repeated violations. Inspectors can fine firms up to $7,000 for each serious or other than serious violation of a safety and health standard, $70,000 for each willful or repeated violation, and $7,000 per day for each failure to comply with a previously cited standard within the specified abatement period.[10] The OSH Act also established criminal sanctions for willful violations of OSHA standards resulting in a death of a worker, unauthorized notice of upcoming inspections, or falsifying business records required by OSHA.

Initial penalties are generally much lower than the statutory maximums established by the OSH Act because OSHA uses a penalty structure based on the gravity of the offense. Inspectors evaluate each violation based on both the likely severity of the injury/illness that could result from the unabated hazard and the probability that an injury could occur. Hazards with a high chance of generating a severe injury/illness receive the statutory maximum fine of $7,000, while hazards with a small chance of producing a fairly minor injury/illness receive a fine of $3,000. The penalties are further modified based on the employer's history of compliance with OSHA standards within the previous 5 years, the number of employees, the good faith efforts by the employer to implement an effective workplace safety and health program, and the immediate abatement of cited hazards. The modifications cannot raise penalties above the statutory maximum of $7,000 or lower them below $500. Currently the average penalty is around $1,000 (Michaels, 2010). Although the average is small, proposed OSHA penalties can become substantial as the number of violations escalates. OSHA issued BP Products

---

[10] In the original OSH Act maximum fines were $1,000 for each serious violation, $10,000 for each willful and repeated violation, and $1,000 per day for failure to comply. The 1990 Omnibus Budget Reconciliation Act raised the maximums to the levels listed.

North America Inc. an $87.4 million penalty in 2009 for multiple failures to abate previously cited hazards (US Department of Labor, OSHA, 2009).

Finally, OSHA is responsible for monitoring the safety and health conditions of about 130 million workers employed across 8 million different worksites. The federal budget for OSHA in 2011 was $573 million, about $1/18^{th}$ the size of the Environmental Protection Agency and $1/4^{th}$ the size of the Fish and Wildlife Service, but more than four times larger than the National Highway Traffic Safety Administration and the Consumer Product Safety Commission. In 2011, the federal and state programs employed about 2,200 inspectors and conducted 92,704 inspections (US Department of Labor, OSHA, 2012). At the recent inspection rate, a typical establishment has slightly more than a 1 in 100 chance of being inspected in a given year.

9.4.1 The Historical Record

According to OSHA, federal and state regulatory efforts have had a dramatic effect on worker safety over the last 40 years, "coupled with the efforts of employers, safety and health professionals, unions and advocates," (US Department of Labor, OSHA, 2012). Workplace fatalities and nonfatal injuries and illnesses have dropped precipitously since its creation in 1970.

Figure 9.7 puts the 40-year improvement in workplace safety in the U.S. into historical context. The figure displays two worker fatality rate series: the first is from the National Safety Council (1994) and runs from 1933 to 1991 and the second is from the Bureau of Labor Statistics (BLS) and runs from 1992 to 2010. The pre-1992 data are generated from a sampling of establishments and are considered to be less reliable than the newer data, which are generated from a census of workplace fatalities. The National Safety Council data end at 1991 because the Council quit independently calculating workplace fatalities, instead relying on the estimates from the annual Census of Fatal Occupational Injuries (http://www.bls.gov/iif/oshcfoi1.htm) conducted by the BLS.[11]

As shown in Figure 9.7 the frequency of workplace deaths in the U.S. has declined dramatically over the past 77 years. Workplace fatalities dropped from 37 per 100,000 workers in 1933 to 8 per 100,000 workers in 1992, a 78 percent reduction, and from 5 per 100,000 workers in 1993 to 3.6 per 100,000 workers in 2010, a 28 percent reduction. As points of reference, in 2010 the chance of dying in a motor vehicle accident was over three times greater (11.5 per 100,000 persons) and the chance of dying in an accident at home was almost six times greater (20.3 per 100,000 population) than the chance of dying in an accident at work (National Safety Council, 2012). Workplace

---

[11] The BLS determines work relatedness for the yearly CFOI by examining death certificates, medical examiner reports, OSHA reports, and workers' compensation records. Because workplace fatalities are relatively infrequent, the previous BLS statistics derived from a sampling of firms are subject to considerable measurement error.

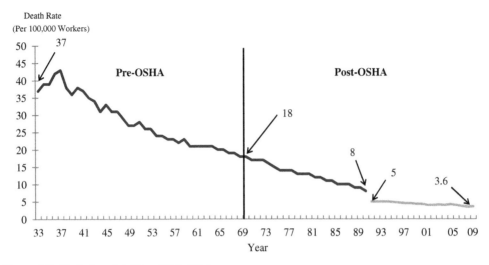

Figure 9.7 Workplace fatalities, 1933–2010.

fatalities were highest in agriculture, forestry, fishing, and hunting (27.9 per 100,000 workers) and lowest in financial activities (0.9 per 100,000 workers).

OSHA may be responsible for some of the post-1970 drop in workplace fatalities, but the decline began well before 1970, suggesting other factors also played contributing roles. Using National Safety Council data, in the 33 years before OSHA the fatality rate dropped from 37 per 100,000 workers to 18 per 100,000 workers, a yearly decline of about 2.2 percent and in the 23 years after OSHA the fatality rate dropped from 18 per 100,000 workers to 8 per 100,000, a yearly decline of about 3.5 percent. From 1993 to 2010 the yearly decline falls to about 1.9 percent using BLS data.

Figure 9.8 shows the frequency of all nonfatal workplace injuries and illnesses and the frequency of lost workday nonfatal injuries and illnesses since 1973, the first year of available data. The BLS altered its collection of nonfatal injury and illnesses data shortly after passage of the OSH Act. Until 1990 the pattern of nonfatal workplace injuries and illnesses in Figure 9.8 followed the business cycle closely, as might be expected. Injuries rise with worker inexperience and fatigue and as employers cut corners to maintain the pace of production. The two measures of nonfatal injuries and illnesses rose slightly during the business upturn of the late 1970s, fell during the recession of the early 1980s, rose again during 1980s expansion, and then fell during the recession of the early 1990s. After the early 1990s the rate of nonfatal workplace injuries steadily declined although business activity accelerated in the late 1990s and the mid-2000s.

As with fatalities, OSHA may be responsible for the downward trend in nonfatal workplace injuries and illnesses seen in Figure 9.8, but other factors may also be responsible. Skeptics of OSHA's effectiveness note that the improvement in safety began

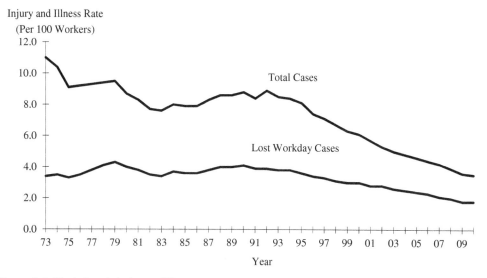

Figure 9.8 Workplace injuries and illnesses, 1973–2010.

20 years after passage of the OSH Act and the timing of the improvement appears largely unrelated to any changes in OSHA enforcement efforts. To determine OSHA's impact on worker safety and health, one must control for other factors that also influence worker safety and health.

9.4.2 Empirical Studies of OSHA's Impact on Safety

As shown by equation (9.7), more active monitoring of safety and health standards should expand firm efforts to reduce workplace hazards resulting in fewer worker injuries and illnesses. Table 9.1 summarizes the major empirical studies of OSHA's impact on worker safety. The studies vary widely in terms of samples used, risk measurements investigated, and OSHA enforcement activities examined. In broad terms, economists have explored three aspects of OSHA: (1) program effects: safety improvements caused by introducing safety and health standards, (2) deterrence effects: safety improvements caused by firms facing higher probabilities of inspections or higher expected fines for violations, and (3) abatement effects: safety improvements caused by actual inspections.

9.4.2.1 Program Effects

The most straightforward way to determine the impact of OSHA is to compare injury rates before and after passage of the OSH Act, controlling for contributing factors such as the unemployment rate and the gender composition of the labor force. Unfortunately, the BLS changed its method of monitoring worker safety at the same time that OSHA was established making this direct comparison using national injury rate data problematic. Mendeloff (1979) tries to overcome this difficulty by

Table 9.1 Empirical Estimates of OSHA's Impact on Safety and Health

I. Program Effects

Study	Time Period	Sample	Risk Measurement	OSHA Enforcement Measurement	Impact
Mendeloff (1979)	1971–1975	U.S. manufacturing, 1948–1975	BLS Lost workday injury rate	A comparison of the actual year-to-year change in the injury rate and the predicted year-to year change	No impact
		California manufacturing, 1948–1975	California Department of Industrial Relations Frequency of: (1) Caught in or between injuries (2) Struck by injuries (3) Strains (4) Falls and slips	A comparison of actual and predicted injury rates Predicted injury rates and injury rate changes are derived from regression estimates using pre-OSHA data	(1) 19%–27% decrease 1974–75 (2) No impact (3) 8%–14% increase 1972–75 (4) 31%–34% decrease 1974–75
Curington (1986)	1971–1976	Time-series/cross section of 18 New York manufacturing industries, 1964–1976	New York Workmen's Compensation Board Frequency of workers' compensation claims and days of impairment for all injuries, caught in machine injuries, and struck by machine injuries	Passage of OSH Act (1 = post-OSH Act, 0 = pre-OSH Act)	Pooled sample: OSHA reduced struck by machine injuries 13.1%. By industry: OSHA decreased the severity of injury in 5 industries, the frequency of struck by machine injuries in 9 industries, and the severity of caught in machine injuries in 6 industries. It increased the frequency of injury in 5 industries, the severity of injury in 3 industries, and the frequency of caught in machine injuries in 1 industry.

Continued

Table 9.1 (Continued)

	Time Period	Sample	Risk measurement	OSHA Enforcement Measurement	Impact
Butler (1994)	1970–1990	U.S. employment, 1947–1990	National Safety Council Aggregate worker fatality rate	Passage of OSH Act (1 = post-OSH Act, 0 = pre-OSH Act)	No impact

II. Deterrence Effects

Study	Time Period	Sample	Risk measurement	OSHA Enforcement Measurement	Impact
Viscusi (1979b)	1972–1975	Time-series/cross section of 2-digit manufacturing industries	BLS Injuries and illnesses per full-time worker	Inspections per 100,000 workers in years t, $t-1$, $t-2$, and $t-3$ Proposed penalties per 1,000 workers in years t, $t-1$, $t-2$, and $t-3$	Individually and jointly insignificant Individually and jointly insignificant
Bartel and Thomas (1985)	1974–1978	Time-series/cross section of 3-digit industries in 22 states	BLS Log of lost workdays per 100 workers	Inspections per worker	A doubling of inspections would increase compliance by 25.8% but lower injuries by only 2.5%. The impact of compliance on injuries is significant at only the 10% level, 1-tail test
Viscusi (1986)	1973–1983	Time-series/cross section of 2- and 3-digit manufacturing industries	BLS (1) Frequency of injuries and illnesses (2) Frequency of lost workday injuries and illnesses (3) Rate of lost workdays	Inspections per production worker in year t and $t-1$ Assessed penalties per production worker in year t and $t-1$	(1) no impact (combined) 2.6% reduction (year $t-1$) (2) 1.5% reduction (combined) 3.6% reduction (year $t-1$) (3) 4.7% reduction (combined) 6.1% reduction (year $t-1$) Insignificant across all three risk measures

Continued

Table 9.1 (Continued)

Study	Time Period	Sample	Risk Measurement	OSHA Enforcement Measurement	Impact
Scholz and Gray (1990)	1979–1985	Time-series/cross section of manufacturing plants	BLS (1) Percentage change in lost workday injuries (2) Percentage change in lost workdays	Change in the expected probability of an inspection with penalty years t, t−1, and t−2	A 10% increase in inspections reduces lost workday injuries by 1.61% and lost workdays by 0.88%
				Change in the expected penalty given an inspection with penalty in years t, t−1, t−2 Inspection with penalty in years t, t−1, and, t−3	A 10% increase in average penalties reduces lost workday injuries by 0.93% and lost workdays by 0.50%
Ruser and Smith (1991)	1979–1985	Time-series/cross section of manufacturing plants	BLS Frequency of lost workday injuries	Frequency of inspections per establishment by state, 2-digit industry, and 9 establishment size classes year t and t−1	No impact individually or jointly

III. Abatement Effects

Study	Time Period	Sample	Risk Measurement	OSHA Enforcement Measurement	Impact
Smith (1979)	1972–1974	Cross section of plants	BLS Frequency of lost workday injuries	Inspections (1 = inspected early in the year, 0 = inspected late in the year)	Plants inspected in 1973: Injuries fell 7% in 1973 and 11.6% in 1974. Plants inspected in 1974: No impact
Cooke and Gautschi (1981)	1970–1976	Time-series/cross section of Maine manufacturing plants	Maine Industrial Accident Commission Change in average days lost from injury	Citations per plant	Citations reduced average days lost by 23% in plants with 200 or more workers and 37% in plants with more than 300 workers. Citations had no impact on average days lost in plants with fewer than 200 workers.

Continued

Table 9.1 (Continued)

McCaffrey (1983)	1976–1978	Cross section of plants	BLS Frequency of lost workday injuries	Inspections (1=inspected early in the year, 0=inspected late in the year)	No impact 1976, 1977, and 1978
Ruser and Smith (1991)	1979–1985	Time-series/cross section of manufacturing plants	BLS Frequency of lost workday injuries	Inspections (1=inspected early in the year, 0=inspected late in the year)	No impact
Gray and Scholz (1993)	1979–1985	Time-series/cross section of manufacturing plants	BLS (1) Percentage change in lost workday injuries (2) Percentage change in lost workdays	Inspection with penalty years t, $t-1$, $t-2$, $t-3$	An inspection with penalty reduces injuries by 22% and lost workdays by 20% over four years
Gray and Mendeloff (2005)	1979–1998	Time-series/cross section of manufacturing plants	BLS Frequency of lost workday injuries	Inspection in the previous 4 years Inspections with penalty in previous 4 year	1979–85: 10.4% reduction 1987–91: 4.4% reduction 1992–98: No impact 1979–85: 19.2% reduction 1987–91: 11.6% reduction 1992–98: No impact
Mendeloff and Gray (2005)	1992–1998	Time-series/cross section of manufacturing plants with fewer than 250 workers	BLS (1) Percentage change in injuries with days away from work related to OSHA standards (2) Percentage change in injuries with days away from work unrelated to OSHA standards	Inspections with penalties in previous 4 years	(1) 7.2% reduction (2) 11.2% reduction

Continued

Table 9.1 (Continued)

Haviland et al. (2010)	1998–2005	Time-series/cross section of single-establishment manufacturing firms in Pennsylvania with 20 to 250 workers	Pennsylvania Workers' Compensation (1) Change in the log number of injuries with days away from work related to OSHA standards (2) Change in the log number of injuries with days away from work unrelated to OSHA standards	Inspections with penalty in year t or t−1	(1) 8.2% reduction over 2 years (2) 14.4% reduction over 2 years
Haviland et al. (2012)	1998–2005	Time-series/cross section of single-establishment manufacturing firms in Pennsylvania with more than 10 workers	Pennsylvania Workers' Compensation Change in the log number of injuries with days away from work	Inspections with penalty in year t or t−1 Inspection with penalty year t, t−1, t−2, t−3	19.3% annual reduction in injuries over 2 years for firms with 21–250 workers. No impact for firms with 11–20 workers or more than 250 workers. Firms with 21–250 workers: t no impact t−1 reduction t−2 no impact t−3 no impact
Levine et al. (2012)	1996–2006	Time-series/cross section of 409 randomly selected inspected establishments with 409 eligible, but not inspected match-control establishments. All firms were single-establishment firms with 10 or more workers.	Workers' Compensation Insurance Rating Board Number of injuries	Inspection in year t or any previous year Inspection in year t, t−1, t−2, t−3, and t−4	9.4% annual reduction in injuries t reduction t−1 no impact t−2 no impact t−3 reduction t−4 reduction

regressing year-to-year changes in the manufacturing injury rate against changes in several explanatory variables (such as the new hire rate and percentage of young men employed) using pre-OSHA data. He then multiples the coefficient estimates from the regression by the actual changes in the explanatory variables post-OSHA to form injury rate change predictions absent OSHA. He finds no statistical differences between the predicted changes and the actual changes in injury rates from 1970 to 1975, leading him to assert, "we cannot reject the conclusion that OSHA has had no effect on the overall injury rate" (p. 105).

Another way to circumvent the absence of a consistent national injury rate series spanning OSHA's creation is to use data not subject to the method changes instituted by the BLS in 1970. Butler (1994) examines the National Safety Council data on worker fatalities to see if the downward trend shown in Figure 9.7 accelerated post-OSHA. He finds an absence of an OSHA effect both in the overall decline and in the decline after controlling for other factors. In the four empirical specifications he uses, the estimated impact of OSHA is generally positive (although statistically insignificant), meaning the fatality rate decline slowed post-OSHA.

Two studies examine another source of unchanged information on worker safety, data drawn from state records of claims for workers' compensation insurance benefits. Both find the creation of OSHA caused some types of injuries to fall, but other types of injuries to rise. Based on California data from 1948 to 1975, Mendeloff (1979) finds that OSHA reduced "caught in or between" injuries and falls and slips; had no impact on "struck by" injuries or all disabling injuries; and raised the number of strains. Based on New York data from 1964 to 1976, Curington (1986) finds that overall OSHA reduced only "struck by machine" injuries. On a more disaggregated basis, he finds OSHA lowering the severity of injury in five industries, the frequency of "struck by machine" injuries in nine industries, and the severity of "caught in machine" injuries in six industries. He also discovers OSHA raising the total frequency of injury in five industries (only one industry experiences a reduction in total injuries), raising the severity of injury in three industries, and raising the frequency of "caught in machine" injuries in two industries.

In reconciling the differences across injury types, Mendeloff argues that early OSHA standards were largely directed at preventing workers from being caught in or between equipment or being struck by equipment. The standards did not address strains and overexertion injuries and could only marginally prevent falls and slips. Further, the rise in workers' compensation indemnity benefits in the early 1970s enticed some workers to file fraudulent claims for benefits, which resulted in an increase in difficult to diagnose injuries such as strains. He finds that OSHA reduced caught in or between injuries by 19% in 1974 and 27% in 1975, but had no impact on struck by injuries. With caught in or between injuries representing about 10% of all worker injuries, Mendeloff contends that OSHA reduced worker injuries overall by about 2%, an impact that was masked by the rise in strains and the general randomness of injuries unaddressed by OSHA standards.

9.4.2.2 Deterrence Effects

Another approach to determine if OSHA is effective in improving worker safety is to examine the relationship between enforcement activities and injuries. Firms in industries targeted by OSHA for more frequent inspections or higher fines for violations are more likely to comply with the standards and have fewer injuries.

The two studies by Viscusi (1979b, 1986) included in Table 9.1 use essentially the same empirical method and data on manufacturing industries, but examine different time periods. In the first study, which spans from 1972 to 1975, Viscusi finds no impact of OSHA enforcement activities on worker safety, but in the second study, which spans from 1973 to 1983, he finds the rate of inspections within an industry reducing lost-workday injuries by 1.5 to 3.6 percent. In neither study does the frequency of inspections or the rate of proposed penalties within an industry have an effect on the severity of injuries nor does the rate of proposed penalties have an impact on the frequency of injury. Because the results show no evidence of increasing OSHA effectiveness over time, Viscusi credits the varying level of statistical significance of inspections on the frequency of injury in the second study to the differing sample sizes. With more years to examine, his later study is able to detect a statistically significant, but fairly small, impact from OSHA enforcement efforts.

In another study using industry data, Bartel and Thomas (1985) conclude based on the experience from 1974 to 1978 that OSHA enforcement activities expanded compliance with safety and health standards but compliance had only a small, and statistically fragile, impact on worker safety. They argue that their results demonstrate that OSHA standards do not address the underlying causes of workplace injuries and diseases. The standards mandate the physical characteristics of acceptable plant and equipment "when most accidents in fact are caused by complex epidemiological interactions of labor, equipment, and the workplace environment." OSHA can force firms to comply with their dictates but their dictates can have little to do with safety.

The final two studies examining the deterrence effect of OSHA use individual plant level data and come to quite different conclusions concerning OSHA's effectiveness in improving worker safety. Scholz and Gray (1990) examine data from 1979 to 1985 and find that a 10 percent increase in the frequency of OSHA inspections decreased lost workday injuries in manufacturing by 1.61 percent and that a 10 percent increase in the average OSHA penalty lowered lost workday injuries in manufacturing by 0.93 percent. Based on their estimates (and ignoring the econometric issue of forecasting out of the range of the underlying data), overall OSHA enforcement efforts reduced injuries by 10 to 16 percent. Alternatively, Ruser and Smith (1991) examine another cross section of plants from the same period and find no evidence that more frequent inspections within an industry reduced worker injuries.

The Scholz and Gray study is unique in that their data and empirical procedure allow them to examine both the deterrence and abatement effects simultaneously. They find that over 90 percent of the overall improvement in safety from more frequent inspections is from the threat of inspection and fines deterring firms not yet inspected by OSHA from violating safety standards in the first place, and less than 10 percent of the improvement in safety is from firms eliminating safety hazards after they have been inspected. The authors suggest that their results may not be representative across all firms. The sample they investigate is composed of larger, more hazardous, and more frequently inspected plants than typically found in manufacturing, and managers in such plants may be more responsive to OSHA enforcement efforts.

Considering the conflicting econometric results, it is difficult to come to a solid conclusion regarding OSHA's general deterrence effect. Of the five studies just discussed only Scholz and Gray find OSHA enforcement efforts reducing injuries dramatically. Smith (1992) argues that their results are not credible because a 16 percent reduction in the aggregate injury rate would be readily observable in the aggregate data. Moreover, he believes that the very low overall frequency of inspection and level of penalties existing in the 1980s make it unlikely that the pre-inspection deterrence effect of OSHA would be so large, more than 90 percent of the total improvement in safety. More likely, their results are driven by the unique nature of their sample or the estimating technique they use. The other four studies find, at best, only a small deterrence effect from OSHA enforcement activities, a 1.5 to 3.6 percent reduction in worker injuries and illnesses.

9.4.2.3 Abatement Effects

The final method for estimating OSHA's effectiveness is to examine the impact of inspections on the change in worker safety within a plant or a firm. The approach will underestimate OSHA's impact if firms largely comply with safety and health standards before they are inspected and will overestimate OSHA's impact if inspections are geared toward more dangerous worksites or worksites with deteriorating safety records. To control for the possibility of selection effects three studies examine the impact of inspections by comparing lost workday injuries in plants inspected early in the year to lost workday injuries in plants inspected late in the year. The factors causing OSHA to inspect the firms should be the same regardless of the time of year they were inspected, but firms inspected first have more time to eliminate workplace hazards and, therefore, should have fewer injuries if inspectors correctly identify hazards. Smith (1979) discovers inspections in 1973 reduced injuries but inspections in 1974 did not. McCaffrey (1983) finds no impact of inspections on lost workday injuries from 1976 to 1978 and Ruser and Smith (1991) find no impact of inspections on lost workday injuries from 1979 to 1985.

Cooke and Gautschi (1981) examine the impact of OSHA inspections by relating injury rate changes to the number of citations issued during an inspection. Using a sample of Maine manufacturing plants from 1970 to 1976 they estimate OSHA citations lowered the number of days lost from injury by 23 percent in plants with more than 200 workers and by 37 percent in plants with more than 300 workers. Citations had no statistical impact on the number of days lost from injury in plants with fewer than 200 workers. The sizable impact Cooke and Gautschi find may reflect their somewhat limited sample or a type of regression to the mean. Ruser (1995) shows that unexplained high injury rates decline over time even in the absence of OSHA inspections. In their sample of Maine manufacturing plants, average days lost were considerably higher for plants visited by OSHA than plants not visited, meaning the drop in injuries after inspection may simply reflect a decline unrelated to OSHA.

Several studies separate inspections into those with and without penalties arguing that an abatement effect can only occur if OSHA inspectors actually uncover and cite safety hazards. Gray and Scholz (1993), using a large national cross section of establishments from 1979 to 1985, find that an OSHA inspection with penalty on average lowered injuries in the plant the year of the inspection and in each of the following three years. Cumulated over the entire four years, OSHA inspections with penalties reduced injuries by 22 percent.

Gray and Mendeloff (2005) extend the Gray and Scholz research by another 13 years to determine if OSHA inspections have become more or less effective over time. They find that inspections with penalties reduced lost-workday injuries by about 19 percent in 1979–1985 (a result very close to the original estimate by Gray and Scholz), but by only 11 percent in 1987–1991, and by a statistically insignificant 1 percent in 1992–1998.

Haviland et al. (2012) use the same approach as the previous two studies but use data for 1998–2005 drawn from a single state, Pennsylvania. The authors find no impact of OSHA inspections with penalties on firms with fewer than 20 workers or with more than 250 workers, but for single-establishment firms with 20 to 250 workers, an OSHA inspection with penalty on average reduced injuries by a cumulative 19.3 percent over two years. The authors then argue that the decline in the effectiveness of OSHA penalty inspections from the late 1970s to the late 1990s documented by Gray and Mendeloff (2005) reversed in the early 2000s. One can disagree with their approach as the results from a single state may not represent national trends and differences between the two studies make a direct comparison problematic. Most notably, the Haviland, et al. estimates are for inspections with penalties in the current or previous year, whereas the Gray and Mendeloff estimates are for inspections with penalties in the current or any of the previous three years. With a four-year window, Haviland et al. find the impact of an inspection with penalty from 1998 to 2005 fell to a cumulative 3.9 percent.

Another set of studies narrow the focus of penalty inspections to determine their impact on specific categories of injuries. Mendeloff and Gray (2005) argue that OSHA standards attempt to control hazards that are likely to result in certain types of injuries such as "struck by objects and equipment" and "caught in or compressed by objects or equipment," but not other types of injuries such as "bodily reaction and exertion" and "falls on same level." For companies employing fewer than 250 workers, they find statistically significant declines from an inspection with penalty in 2 of the 5 injury categories they believe are controllable by safety standards and in 2 of the 3 injury categories they believe are not controllable by safety standards. Aggregating over the two broad classes of injuries, an OSHA inspection with penalty reduced controllable injuries by 7.2 percent and uncontrollable injuries by 11.2 percent through the three years following the inspection. They also find that citations for violating standards on personal protective equipment not only reduced caught-in injuries and eye abrasions, as might be expected, but also reduced exertion injuries, which seem unrelated to the use of personal protective equipment. Surprisingly, citations for machine guarding had no impact on caught-in injuries, but did reduce injuries from high falls. Mendeloff and Gray argue OSHA citations force managers to pay more attention to worker safety and this general attention spills over into areas not directly related to OSHA standards.

Haviland et al. (2010) updates Mendeloff and Gray (2005) using data drawn from Pennsylvania single-establishment firms employing 20–250 workers from 1998 to 2005, the same data used in Haviland et al. (2012). Similar to the earlier study they find that OSHA inspections with citations reduced injuries, with the impact largest for injuries seemingly unrelated to OSHA standards and smallest for injuries related to OSHA standards, 14.4 percent versus 8.2 percent cumulated over two years. As expected, citations for violating the personal protective equipment standard reduced caught-in and eye-abrasion injuries, but unexpectedly reduced exertion injuries that have little to do with using personal protective equipment. Also unexpectedly, electrical wiring citations reduced high-fall injuries, fire extinguisher citations raised eye-abrasion injuries, and struck-against injuries and forklift truck citations raised high-fall injuries. Similar to Mendeloff and Gray, the authors argue that citations cause managers to be more concerned with safety overall, thereby explaining the reduction in injuries unrelated to OSHA standards. The authors do not explain the positive impact of citations on some categories of injuries.

Levine et al. (2012) examine the effectiveness of OSHA inspections by comparing injury rates from a sample of 409 single-establishment firms in California that were randomly chosen by OSHA for a programmed inspection from 1996 to 2006 with a matched sample of 409 firms eligible for inspection but not chosen. They find an OSHA inspection in the current year or any of the previous 4 years reduced annual injuries by 9.4 percent and workers' compensation outlays by 26 percent. Based on their estimates, an OSHA inspection reduces injuries by a whopping 47 percent over the five years after an inspection and creates a $355,000 (2011 dollars) savings in workers' compensation expenses, roughly 14 percent of average annual payroll of the sample of firms included in the study. The authors find no evidence that the improvement in safety came at the expense of employment, payroll, sales, credit ratings, or firm survival.

The Levine et al. study is the only one finding OSHA inspections in general having a large impact on worker safety. Their results are difficult to reconcile with previous studies finding much smaller safety improvements from inspections with penalties. The results may also not pertain across all worksites. During the time of the study programmed inspections in California were restricted to firms in high-hazard industries. Inspections may be less effective in improving worker safety in less hazardous environments or other states.

9.4.3 Why has OSHA had a Comparatively Small Impact on Worker Safety?

OSHA's efforts to inspect firms for violations of safety and health standards and fine them for noncompliance can improve worker safety in two ways: the threat of fines may deter firms from violating safety and health standards in the first place and an actual inspection may cause inspected firms to abate existing hazards. Based on existing evidence OSHA's deterrence effect is fairly small, a 1.5 to 3.6 percent reduction in worker injuries, at best (Viscusi, 1986). The current abatement effect appears much larger, but given the small fraction of firms inspected by OSHA, the overall impact is quite small. The two most recent studies included in Table 9.1 find inspections with penalties reduce worker injuries in small establishments by about 20 percent over two years (Haviland et al., 2012) and inspections in general reduce injuries by about 50 percent over 5 years (Levine et al., 2012). With only about 1 in 100 worksites inspected by OSHA each year, the abatement effect on worker safety using the 50 percent reduction is less than 0.5 percent over all firms. Giving OSHA the benefit of the doubt, its inspection efforts in total have reduced worker injuries by a modest 4 percent. By way of comparison, Moore and Viscusi (1989) estimate workers' compensation insurance has reduced workplace fatalities by 22 percent.

No estimates exist on the safety impacts of the market incentives created by compensating wage differentials for workplace risk or legal incentives created by the court system. Still, the financial incentives of the other three pillars of the U.S. safety policy system dwarf the financial incentives created by OSHA. In 2010, initial proposed OSHA penalties for safety and health violations totaled less than $150 million (Jung and Makowsky, 2012). Employers' costs for providing workers' compensation insurance coverage totaled nearly $72 billion and using 2 percent as the wage premium for accepting the average level of workplace risk, the total value of compensating wage differentials paid by firms in the U.S. is around $100 billion (Sengupta et al., 2012; Viscusi and Aldy, 2003). Estimating legal liability for worker accidents and illnesses in a given year is difficult but is likely to be high, particularly for producers of products used by workers. Estimates place the eventual cost of asbestos litigation in the $200–$265 billion range (as reported in White, 2004).

In passing the OSH Act, Congress believed American worker safety and health would improve by creating an agency that would generate workplace safety and health standards, inspect employers for violations, and then fine them for noncompliance. Why has the approach not created the vast improvements in worker safety proponents of the agency had predicted? The reason is that the regulatory approach can fail at each stage of the process. Worker safety and health will not improve if standards do not address the underlying causes of workplace injuries and diseases; if inspectors fail to uncover violations related to worker safety and health; or if the frequency of inspections and level of assessed fines are too low to get firms to comply with the standards. OSHA's record in all three areas is not strong.

Mendeloff (1984) directly examines the question of the effectiveness of OSHA standards in reducing workplace fatalities. He finds only 13–19 percent of the 645 workplace fatalities reported to workers' compensation in California in 1976 resulted from violations of standards, and only half of the violations could have been detected before the accident. Another study finds little evidence linking firm compliance with mandated worker training in safety and health and tangible improvements in worker safety (Cohen and Colligan, 1998). In a more indirect route, Bartel and Thomas (1985) examine industry data and find OSHA enforcement activities having a sizable impact on compliance with OSHA standards but compliance having only a small, and statistically fragile, impact on worker safety. They argue their results support the view "that the Act itself is flawed because it emphasizes standards for capital equipment when most accidents in fact are caused by complex epidemiological interactions of labor, equipment, and the workplace environment."

Workplace accidents are rare events. Using the rates for 2010, a workplace fatality occurs less than once every 50,000,000 work hours and a lost-workday injury occurs about once every 100,000 work hours. Standardizing across all hours of the day, a workplace fatality occurs once every 139 minutes and a workplace injury once every 6 seconds (National Safety Council, 2012). Although such rates may seem high, by way of comparison a motor vehicle death and a motor vehicle injury occurs once every 15 minutes and once every 9 seconds, while an accidental death and an accidental injury in the home occurs once every 8 minutes and once every 2 seconds (National Safety Council, 2012). Based on the National Health Interview Survey, 52.6 percent of the recorded medically consulted injury and poisoning episodes in 2009 were inside or outside the home; only 3.1 percent of the episodes occurred in areas of industry, construction, or farming (National Safety Council, 2012). Workplace fatalities and workplace injuries are generally a combination of unusual events. In a probability framework, they represent the simultaneous occurrence of multiple events, with each event residing in the tail of its respective probability distribution, making the likelihood of the joint event extremely rare. It is debatable whether a regulatory approach can effectively identify and control the largely random and momentary hazards that result in workplace fatalities and injuries.

Studies finding no impact of OSHA inspections on worker safety in the inspected establishments suggest inspectors may not uncover the true causes of worker accidents. A study by Weil (2001) examines the relationship between the distribution of cited violations and the distributions of the causes of fatalities and nonfatal injuries within the construction industry from 1987 to 1993, one of the most hazardous industries for American workers and an industry targeted by OSHA for expanded inspection efforts. He finds OSHA violations were not closely related to the causes of either fatalities or nonfatal injuries. For instance, 4 percent of the violations cited during the time were for standards addressing accidents that are categorized as "struck by hazards" and yet 31 percent of the injuries and 9 percent of the fatalities were caused by "struck by hazards." The single largest category of citations by number was for falls, 42 percent of all violations, and yet falls resulted in only about 19 percent of the nonfatal injuries and 28 percent of the fatal injuries. OSHA has no standards addressing overexertion injuries but cumulative trauma and musculoskeletal injuries accounted for about 25 percent of the reported nonfatal injuries in construction. Finally, although 10 percent of all fatalities were from machine injuries, only 3 percent of all violations were for machine hazards.

Most experienced OSHA inspectors are well acquainted with the dangers that confront workers in construction and the safety and health standards that apply. They may be less familiar with the dangers facing workers in other, less frequently inspected, industries and the relationship between compliance and worker safety and health may be even lower. Given the variety of different worksites and production technologies OSHA inspectors are asked to investigate, the lack of specific knowledge of the risks confronting workers in a given situation is certainly understandable. Although understandable, the lack of knowledge certainly reduces an inspector's effectiveness in uncovering potential dangers.[12]

9.4.4 Is OSHA Cost Effective?

Although OSHA may have reduced worker injuries and deaths by only a small amount, the benefit of this small improvement may more than outweigh the compliance and enforcement costs of OSHA, resulting in a net gain in social welfare. Does OSHA, as currently designed, pass such a cost/benefit test? As one might anticipate, evaluating the benefits of safety improvements from any program can be quite controversial. Some believe that life has infinite value and so the benefits of improving safety always exceed the costs. But people do not live as if their lives had infinite value. No one lives

---

[12] As an addendum we note that in mining the Mine Safety and Health Administration (MSHA) has effected inspection rates that are much more frequent and financial penalties for safety violations that are much higher than under OSHA, with few if any estimable effects on miner safety (Kniesner and Leeth, 2004).

a risk-free life and everyone makes trade-offs between safety and other things they like, such as the lower expense of driving a small car, the joy of skiing, the time saved from jaywalking, or the pleasure of smoking.

Economists argue the best way to evaluate the benefits of safety improvements is to use the monetary value that people place on small improvements in their own safety. Workers maximize their expected welfare by choosing the level of safety where the benefit of slightly greater safety just equals the cost of slightly greater safety. The slope of the wage curve in Figure 9.3 measures the drop in wage that workers must sacrifice to get additional safety and through the equality of benefits and costs it also equals the value workers place on a small reduction in the chance of a fatal workplace injury.

Suppose that based on an estimated wage equation, wages fall by $80 when the chance of a workplace fatality drops from 5 in 100,000 to 4 in 100,000, all else equal. If a typical person would pay $80 to reduce his or her chance of death by 1 in 100,000, then collectively 100,000 people would pay $8 million and, on average, one life would be saved. The saved life is not known beforehand, but in a sense is drawn randomly from the 100,000 so the $8 million represents the value of a statistical life. An implicit value of injury can be found in a similar manner by dividing an estimated wage change for a small reduction in the probability of a workplace nonfatal injury or illness by the change in the probability. The resulting calculation is known as the value of a statistical injury.

The value of a statistical life or the value of statistical injury does not represent the amount people would pay to avoid their own certain death or injury or society would pay to rescue individuals from certain death or injury. Instead, the values allow policy-makers to determine the benefits of actions that reduce risk by small amounts.

Viscusi and Aldy (2003) review the evidence and find across U.S. labor market studies estimates of the value of a statistical life range from $6.3 million to $15.2 million, with a median value of $8.9 million, and the estimates of the value of a statistical injury range from $25,000 to $89,000 (all values have been converted to 2010 dollars using the CPI).[13] There were 4,690 fatalities and 933,200 lost-work day accidents and illnesses in 2010, so if OSHA improved safety on average by 4 percent, it prevented 38,883 lost-workday injuries and 195 fatalities (US Department of Labor and Bureau of Labour Statistics, 2011a,b). Using the median estimate for the value of a statistical life and the midpoint of the estimated range for the value of a statistical injury, the monetary benefit of OSHA is $4.0 billion.

Only a few studies attempt to estimate the total yearly cost of all OSHA regulations on business. Using changes in input productivity and expenditures on OSHA mandated capital equipment, Hahn and Hird (1991) place the cost of OSHA's safety and health standards that existed in 1988 at $15.7 billion (2010 dollars). They argue their estimate probably overstates OSHA's true cost because firms would have instituted some of the

---

[13] For additional support for the values used in the cost-effectiveness calculations to follow, see Viscusi (2014) and Kniesner et al. (2012).

safety features in response to labor market pressures in the absence of OSHA. James (1998) examines the regulatory impact analyses commissioned by OSHA on 25 major rules. The 25 rules were issued from 1980 to 1993 with expected compliance costs in excess of $100 million per year so as to generate a yearly compliance estimate for all affected firms of $9.1 billion (2010 dollars). Using data from the National Association of Manufacturers of the compliance costs of regulations issued in the 1970s, James argues that it is reasonable to assume that total compliance costs are at least 5.55 times higher per-firm than the costs of the 25 rules he examines, for a total compliance cost of $50.5 billion. Using a similar method, Johnson (2001) estimates that the yearly compliance costs of the major rules issued by OSHA from 1980 to 2000 were $9.4 billion (2010 dollars), and the total cost of complying with all regulations was $51.9 billion. Crain and Crain (2010) update Johnson's work to incorporate the major rules issued by OSHA from 2001 to 2008. They find the new rules added another $447 million in annual compliance costs to generate a total cost of complying with all OSHA regulations of $65.6 billion.

Eisenbrey and Shapiro (2011) take issue with the approach of estimating OSHA's total compliance costs by multiplying the yearly compliance costs of major regulations by a factor of 5.55, a number generated by an unpublished, and now dated, study by the National Association of Manufacturers. They further contend the cost estimates from the regulatory impact analyses are themselves outdated. The cost figures reflect production practices and technologies that existed prior to the adoption of the standards. With the passage of time and the adoption of new work practices and technologies, the costs of complying with OSHA standards likely have fallen. For at least two of the more costly standards issued by OSHA, actual compliance costs were lower than the costs predicted in the regulatory impact analyses, consistent with the belief that costs fall over time.

If one ignores the 5.55 adjustment factor, the yearly cost of complying with the major standards issued by OSHA since 1980 based on the regulatory impact analyses is $9.9 billion. On top of the $9.9 billion one must also include the yearly federal expenditure on OSHA, which in 2010 was $560 million for a total cost of $10.5 billion (US Department of Labor, 2010). Based on the most optimistic empirical studies of OSHA's impact on worker safety, the monetary benefit of OSHA is $4.0 billion, meaning the agency fails the cost/benefit test for improving social welfare. For OSHA to pass the test, the regulatory impact analyses would have to have overestimated compliance costs on average by more than 250 percent, which seems unlikely. Moreover, the yearly cost figure of $10.5 billion excludes the cost of complying with pre-1980 regulations, all regulations expected to generate compliance costs under $100 million per year, and state expenditures on state-operated OSHA programs, which means the total compliance and enforcement cost of OSHA may far exceed $10.5 billion.

In the other direction, however, there is much about OSHA's impact on safety and health that we still do not know. Most empirical studies examining OSHA's effectiveness at reducing worker injuries have focused on the manufacturing sector.[14] Our knowledge of the safety impacts of OSHA outside of manufacturing is limited. The long latency period for many industrial diseases makes estimating the impact of regulatory efforts on reducing their incidence difficult. No empirical studies have examined the impact of OSHA's consultation programs or individual standards such as the Hazard Communication standard, the process safety standard, or the respiratory protection standard.

Given our gaps in knowledge of the overall impact of OSHA and its overall costs, a more fruitful way to evaluate OSHA's effectiveness may be to examine specific safety and health regulations to see if these regulations themselves individually pass a cost/benefit test. To maximize social welfare, OSHA should establish a new safety and health standard only if the standard generates more benefits in terms of injuries, illnesses, and deaths avoided than it imposes costs on firms, workers, and others.

Morrall (2003) examines the cost effectiveness of 76 final regulatory actions aimed at improving safety and health that were imposed by the Federal government from 1967 to 2001, including 25 regulatory actions by OSHA. To be able to compare across the various regulations, he divides the total yearly compliance cost of the regulation by the expected number of lives saved per year to generate the opportunity costs per statistical life saved (OCSLS). An effective OSHA regulation would be one where the life-saving benefits of the regulation, as measured by workers' willingness to pay for reductions in mortality risk, exceed the opportunity costs per statistical life saved. The work of Viscusi and Aldy suggest that $8.9 million is a reasonable dollar figure to use to value a statistical life saved and so serves as a dividing line between cost-effective regulations and cost-ineffective regulations.

Table 9.2 reproduces Morrall's Table 2 for the 25 OSHA regulatory actions with the dollar amounts adjusted to reflect the impact of inflation to 2010. Of the 25 regulatory actions, 13 have costs per statistical life saved below $8.9 million and are cost effective. Of the 12 regulatory actions failing the cost-effectiveness standard, the range of cost per life saved is enormous. The Grain Dust standard saves a statistical life at a cost of about $13.3 million, just moderately above the value of a statistical life as indicated by U.S. labor market studies, while the Formaldehyde standard saves a statistical life at a cost exceeding $9.4 billion. The extremely large costs per life saved shown in Table 9.2 suggest that at least some of OSHA's regulatory actions are misguided and enforcement resources could be better allocated in other directions.

The difficulty with Table 9.2 is that it ignores any benefits from reducing the frequency or severity of nonfatal workplace accidents and diseases. Viscusi (1985b) considers both aspects in his investigation of OSHA's 1978 health standard limiting worker exposure to cotton dust. Based on Viscusi's estimates, with full compliance the

---

[14] An exception is Kniesner and Leeth (2004) who do similar cost-effectiveness calculations for MSHA enforcement efforts and find similarly cost-ineffective results for the mining industry.

Table 9.2 Opportunity Costs Per Statistical Life Saved (OCSLS)

Regulation	Year Issued	Type of Standard	OCSLS (millions of 2010 $)
Respiratory Protection	1998	Health	0.12
Logging Operations	1994	Safety	0.12
Electrical Safety	1990	Safety	0.12
Safety Standards for Scaffolds	1996	Safety	0.24
Electrical Power Generation	1994	Safety	0.48
Underground Construction	1983	Safety	0.61
Servicing Wheel Rims	1984	Safety	1.09
Crane Suspended Personnel Platform	1984	Safety	1.82
Trenching and Excavation	1989	Safety	2.55
Concrete & Masonry Construction	1985	Safety	2.91
Confined Spaces	1993	Safety	3.03
Hazard Communication	1983	Safety	3.76
Asbestos	1972	Health	6.67
Grain Dust	1988	Safety	13.33
Methylene Chloride	1997	Health	15.76
Benzene	1987	Health	26.67
Acrylonitrile	1978	Health	37.57
4.4 Methylenedianiline	1992	Health	43.64
Coke Ovens	1976	Health	61.82
Asbestos	1986	Health	80.00
Asbestos/Construction	1994		86.06
Arsenic	1978	Health	93.33
Ethylene Oxide	1984	Health	96.97
Lockout/Tagout	1989	Safety	118.79
Formaldehyde	1987	Health	94,543.46

Source: Morrall (2003).

standard would reduce over 9,000 cases of byssinosis per year, but most of the cases prevented would be quite minor, resulting in occasional chest tightness or breathing difficulties on the first day of the workweek. The symptoms from such minor forms of byssinosis can be eliminated by simply transferring the worker to an area free of cotton dust. The standard would only prevent 1,210 illnesses resulting in partial disability and 487 illnesses resulting in total disability. By severity, the standard imposed costs on firms of $33,400 (2010$) per year per case of the least serious forms of the illness; $1.26 million per year per case resulting in partial disability; and over $3.3 million per year per case resulting in total disability. With labor market studies suggesting that workers are only willing to forgo $25,000 to $89,000 to avoid the possibility of a serious accident, Viscusi concludes that, "the costs seem somewhat disproportionate to the benefits."

Viscusi raises another very important issue: regulations should be designed to achieve the desired results at the least cost. OSHA's Cotton Dust Standard required that firms install engineering controls to limit worker exposure to cotton dust, monitor workers' health for signs of byssinosis, and mandate that their workers wear respirators in conditions of high cotton dust exposure. Similar reductions in the rate of byssinosis could have been achieved by requiring workers to wear cotton dust masks for a few hours a day in high-exposure situations and by rotating workers around the plant to limit their cumulative exposure to cotton dust, which is much cheaper than the engineering controls chosen by OSHA.

On the positive side for OSHA, an early estimate placed the capital cost of fully complying with the Cotton Dust Standard at $599 million: $171 million for ventilation equipment and $428 million for new production equipment. Viscusi finds that firms would have purchased most of the new production equipment even if the standard had not been imposed to improve productivity. When such purchases are excluded, the capital costs of complying with the standard drops by more than half to $246 million. Nevertheless, even with the much lower capital costs, the total costs of complying with the Cotton Dust Standard far exceed "any value that can be reasonably placed upon its achievements" (Viscusi, 1985b).

9.5 WORKERS' COMPENSATION INSURANCE AND WORKER SAFETY AND HEALTH

As noted, equations (9.2–9.4) indicate that the government can also expand on market safety incentives by mandating insurance coverage for workplace injuries (b) and by clarifying the relationship between the price of workers' compensation insurance coverage and risk ($\frac{\partial P_b}{\partial \pi}$).

9.5.1 Institutional Details of Workers' Compensation Insurance

Workers' compensation is primarily a state-operated disability insurance program covering workers against losses caused by industrial accidents and some diseases. (Most industrial diseases are covered by Social Security Disability Insurance.) At the federal level, two programs cover federal employees and long shore and harbor workers. Federal legislation also provides benefits similar to workers' compensation to coal mine, railroad, and maritime employees.

Regardless of who is at fault, employers must fully compensate employees for medical expenses and partially compensate them for lost wages caused by work-related injuries. Although standards for replacing lost wages vary, most states require employers replace two-thirds of weekly wages up to a maximum benefit of two-thirds of the state's average weekly wage for more serious injuries. The cap on cash benefits means that workers' compensation insurance replaces less than two-thirds of the income loss from injury for high-wage workers and, in some cases, far less. Most states also impose a minimum cash benefit for low wage workers. For some states, the minimum benefit is an absolute dollar amount so that very-low-wage workers receive more than a 100 percent of their lost income when injured (even in a before-tax basis), while in other states workers earning less than some fixed amount receive indemnity payments equal to their post-injury earnings. As proceeds from an insurance policy, cash benefits are nontaxable, which means workers' compensation typically replaces more than two-thirds of an injured workers' after-tax income. In the other direction, employers or their insurance providers do not reimburse workers for lost fringe benefits and so the two-thirds figure understates the fraction of total labor earnings replaced. In return for full coverage of medical expenses and partial coverage of income loss, workers forgo their rights to sue employers for damages, including damages related to pain and suffering, even when the employer is negligent.

Not all injured workers receive disability benefits. To receive benefits for lost income the injury must be sufficiently severe so as to keep the worker off the job for some minimum number of days. In some states, the minimum is three days and in others seven days. The waiting period acts as a type of deductible that workers must pay before they can receive income benefits and, thereby, serves to shift more of the costs of low-severity injuries from employers to workers. In some states, a worker whose recovery extends beyond a certain number of days, referred to as the retroactive period, is reimbursed for the lost income during the waiting period.

Most workers' compensation cases do not involve income benefits. In 2007, 76 percent of the claims for workers' compensation insurance were for the payment of medical benefits only (Sengupta et al., 2012). When paying indemnity benefits to workers or their families, insurance companies classify injuries as: (1) temporary total disabilities, (2) temporary partial disabilities, (3) permanent partial disabilities, (4) permanent total disabilities, and fatalities. Less than 1 percent of workers' compensation claims for indemnity benefits in 2007 were for fatalities or permanent total disabilities and these two types of injuries in total comprised only 10.0 percent of the cash benefits paid. In terms of both cases and benefits, the most prevalent types of injuries were for temporary total disabilities (61% of cases; 17% of benefits) and for permanent partial disabilities (38% of cases; 72% of benefits) (Sengupta et al., 2012).

Equations (9.2–9.4) describing the behavior of firms also show that the government can expand on market safety incentives by allowing workers to sue for work-related illnesses and injuries (d). Before workers' compensation insurance was introduced, workers who sued had to prove that an injury was caused by the employer's negligence before they could recover damages. An employer could avoid a negligence ruling in court by demonstrating that the worker's injury resulted at least partially from his or her own actions (contributory negligence), was an ordinary hazard of employment (assumption of risk), or resulted from the carelessness of a coworker (the fellow-servant doctrine).

Because legal defenses made damage recovery uncertain the negligence system was viewed as providing insufficient compensation for injured workers and inadequate incentives for employers to provide reasonably safe work environments (Darling-Hammond and Kniesner, 1980; Fishback, 1987; Fishback and Kantor, 1998). In contrast, workers' compensation insurance provides certain benefits for injured workers regardless of fault and, by shifting financial costs of accidents to the employer, provides an economic incentive for employers to reduce workplace hazards.

Most states allow employers to provide workers' compensation coverage by either purchasing insurance with a private provider or by self-insuring after proof of financial ability to pay. The price of workers' compensation insurance coverage consists of a manual rate and an experience rating modification factor. Insurance providers combine the injury experience of a group of workers within an industrial class to determine the manual rate for that class. The manual premium is higher for industrial classes with more accidents and lower for industrial classes with fewer accidents. For small employers, insurance companies take the product of each worker's wage rate and the manual rate for his or her industrial class and then sum over all workers to determine the total workers' compensation insurance premium for the firm. As employer size rises, insurance companies modify the manual rate to reflect the firm's injury experience. Firms with worse safety records pay more than the manual rate and firms with better safety records pay less. Excluding firms that self-insure, only the very largest firms have workers' compensation premiums that are completely experience rated. The process is very similar to the pricing of car insurance. The so-called manual rate is higher for people living in urban areas than in rural areas, and within each area the rate will rise for people with worse driving records and fall for people with better driving records.

9.5.2 The Theoretical Impact of Workers' Compensation Insurance

By examining the first-order conditions for profit and utility maximization, one can see the various avenues that workers' compensation insurance can take to influence firms' and workers' safety decisions. As can be seen in equation (9.4), one of the benefits to the firm from expanding safety is the reduction in costs of purchasing workers' compensation insurance. The size of the reduction is directly related to the responsiveness of insurance prices to changes in workplace hazards ($\frac{\partial P_b}{\partial \pi}$), the size of the income benefits mandated by state law (b), and the number of workers the firm employs (n). As long as insurance prices are sufficiently experience-rated, passage of workers' compensation legislation or an expansion in disability payments will increase the marginal benefit of safety and cause firms to expand their safety efforts, all else equal.

On the other side of the market, one of the costs of accepting a high-risk job is the possible loss of income if injured. By reducing the economic loss from an accident or disease, higher workers' compensation benefits lowers the marginal cost from injury and encourages workers to be less concerned with safety. Workers may take less care to avoid hazards on the job or may accept higher risk employment. As can be seen in equation (9.6), the size of the reduction in accident costs from rising workers' compensation insurance benefits is tempered by the utility drop from injury holding income constant, the alternative sources of income available to the worker, and the initial level of benefits. With diminishing marginal utility of income, the higher is nonlabor income or the initial level of workers' compensation benefits, the smaller is the decline in the marginal costs of injury and the smaller the increase in risk. Likewise, the greater the health consequences from injury as measured by the utility loss holding income constant, the smaller is the decline in the marginal cost of injury and the smaller the increase in risk. More generous workers' compensation benefits may reduce worker efforts to avoid injuries, but the impact is likely larger for less severe injuries where the utility loss is less than for more severe injuries where the utility loss is far greater.

As depicted in Figure 9.9, by altering firm and worker decisions regarding safety, the introduction of workers' compensation insurance or an increase in the level of disability benefits alter the demand for and supply of labor along the risk spectrum, causing changes to the hedonic wage function. Wages adjust not only for undesirable job characteristics, such as a high likelihood of injury, but also for desirable ones, such as generous insurance coverage. Employers pass along some of the costs of higher insurance benefits through lower wages (Fishback and Kantor, 1998; Moore and Viscusi, 1989; Viscusi, 2004). Additionally, by reducing income losses from injury, more generous

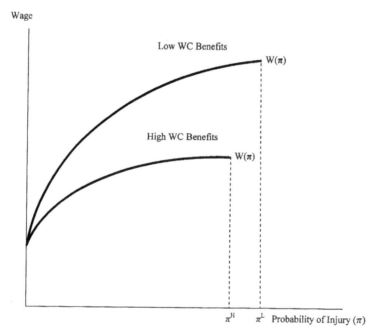

Figure 9.9 The impact of workers' compensation benefits on the hedonic wage function.

workers' compensation benefits reduce the wage premium demanded by workers for accepting a more dangerous job. Greater *ex post* compensation for an injury lowers the *ex ante* compensation required for accepting higher job risk, which flattens the market wage function and reduces firms' incentives to provide a safe work environment.

On a theoretical basis, one cannot determine the impact on overall worker safety from the introduction of workers' compensation insurance or an expansion of benefits.[15] Firms choose more safety at the same time workers choose less safety. If the impact on workers is sufficiently great, then changes to the hedonic wage function counteract firm incentives to provide greater safety and the frequency of injury rises. If the impact on workers is small, then changes to the hedonic wage function counteract worker desires to choose higher risk jobs, and the frequency of injury falls. Improvements to safety are more likely the more closely workers' compensation insurance premiums reflect the level of safety within a firm, the higher the initial level of disability benefits, the greater nonlabor income including other sources of disability income such as SSDI, and the larger the health consequences from a work-related injury or disease.

Besides exploring the impact on worker safety, one could also examine the effect of workers' compensation insurance on worker decisions on filing for workers' compensation benefits and returning to work after injury. More generous indemnity benefits expand worker incentives to exaggerate the extent of their injuries, to falsify an injury, or to claim a non-work-related injury as occurring on the job. The impact of this type of moral hazard would be greatest for more subjective and more difficult to verify injuries, such as sprains and strains, and least for more objective and easier to verify injuries, such as cuts and lacerations. Worker desires to claim off-the-job injuries as work-related should also cause injuries to spike on Mondays or after three-day weekends, particularly for injuries that are difficult to verify and where treatment can be delayed. Because of the incentive of workers to exaggerate or to falsify an injury, claims for workers' compensation insurance might rise as income benefits expanded even if injuries, properly measured, fell. Once a worker receives workers' compensation benefits, the cost of remaining off the job after an injury falls as the level of benefits rises, which should result in a positive relationship between injury duration and benefits, all else equal, even if injury severity remained constant. Once again, the impact on worker incentives may create a false picture of workers' compensation's true impact on safety.

---

[15] Passage of state workers' compensation laws not only increased insurance payments to injured workers, but also reduced the likelihood that workers could sue their employers for damages. If expected damage awards pre-workers' compensation were greater than insurance benefits post-workers' compensation, then passage of workers' compensation legislation would reduce firm incentives to provide a safe working environment and raise worker incentives to demand a safe working environment. Fishback (1987) and Fishback and Kantor (1995) provide evidence that both the fraction of workers receiving compensation for injuries and the average amount of compensation they received rose, meaning workers' compensation benefits far exceeded expected damage awards pre-workers' compensation.

9.5.3 Empirical Studies of Workers' Compensation's Impact on Safety

Table 9.3 summarizes the major studies exploring the safety effects of workers' compensation. The table examines four major questions: (1) Did passage of state workers' compensation laws affect worker safety? (2) Does benefit generosity raise or lower the number or the frequency of workplace injuries? (3) Does experience rating or other program changes that raise employer costs of workers' compensation claims improve worker safety? and (4) Does the provision of insurance or the expansion of benefits cause workers to exaggerate or to falsify reports of difficult-to-verify injuries or spend more time off the job to recover from injury?

9.5.3.1 Passage of State Workers Compensation Laws

Three studies examine the safety effects from introducing workers' compensation insurance. Unlike the situation with the introduction of OSHA, workers' compensation legislation did not change how firms were required to report injuries so program effects can be identified over time within a state. Additionally, the introduction of workers compensation varied by state so that program effects can also be identified across states at a point in time, at least until 1948 when Mississippi became the last state to pass a workers' compensation law. Still, getting a clear-cut measure of the safety effects of moving from a negligence liability system to a strict, but partial employer liability system of workers' compensation is difficult. No consistent measure of workplace injuries exists over the almost 40 years between when the first state and the last state passed a workers' compensation law, and limited information is available on intervening factors affecting worker safety.

The three studies summarized in Table 9.3 that examine the safety effects of introducing workers' compensation come to quite different conclusions. Chelius (1976) measures the impact of workers' compensation using data on non-motor vehicle machinery deaths per worker by state from 1900 to 1940. Although not all machinery deaths are work-related and not all workplace fatalities are caused by machinery, Chelius argues that the machinery death rate is the best available overall measure of industrial safety over the 30 years. Besides workers' compensation, Chelius also examines the impact of changing liability laws and safety regulations on worker safety. Before passing workers' compensation, some states had modified or abolished employer common law defenses such as the fellow-servant rule, thereby making it more likely that workers could sue and recover damages for work-related injuries. Chelius finds that both expanded employer liability for injuries and passage of workers' compensation strongly lowered machinery deaths, but that state safety regulation had no impact.

Fishback (1987) examines the frequency of coal-mining fatalities in 23 leading coal-mining states from 1903–1930. Similar to Chelius, he also tconsiders changes in liability laws that made it easier for workers to recover damages from their employers

Table 9.3 The Impact of Workers' Compensation Insurance (WC) on Safety and Health

I. Passage of State Workers' Compensation Laws

Study	Time Period	Sample	Risk Measurement	Workers' Compensation Benefit Variable	Impact
Chelius (1976)	1900–1940	Time-series/cross section of 26 states	US Bureau of the Census Non-motor vehicle machinery death rate by year and state relative to national average by year	WC law (1 = law, 0 otherwise) Employer liability law (1 = law, 0 otherwise)	Both WC and employer liability lowered the machinery death rate relative to the national average
Fishback (1987)	1903–1930	Time-series/cross section of 23 leading coal mining states	US Bureau of Mines Frequency of coal mining fatalities	Employer liability laws (1 = laws present no WC, 0 otherwise) Exclusive state WC insurance fund (1 = yes, 0 otherwise) Nonexclusive state WC insurance fund (1 = yes, 0 otherwise) WC without a state insurance fund (1 = yes, 0 otherwise) Excluded category, no WC and no employer liability laws	Percentage change: Liability law = 17.3 Exclusive WC = 23.0 Nonexclusive WC = 20.2 WC no state fund insignificant
Butler and Worrall (2008)	1900–1916	Time-series/cross section of occupations employed in the 4 largest steam railroads in New Jersey	New Jersey Department of Labor and Industries Injuries per day (injuries per year/days worked per year)	Federal Employers Liability Act (1 = after passage but before WC, 0 otherwise); WC law (1 = law, 0 otherwise)	Expanded employer liability and expanded employer liability with WC reduced injuries for outside workers but raised them for indoor workers

Continued

Table 9.3 (Continued)

II. Expansion of Benefits: Non-fatal Injuries

Study	Time Period	Sample	Risk Measurement	Workers' Compensation Benefit Variable	Impact
Chelius (1974)	1967	Cross section of 2,627 manufacturing establishments across 13 states	BLS Frequency of disabling injuries	Instrumental variable representing an index of WC benefits by state and 2-digit industry Length of waiting period	Positive Insignificant
Chelius (1982)	1972–1975	Time-series/cross section of 2-digit manufacturing industries in 36 states	OSHA (1) Lost Workdays (2) Frequency of lost workdays (3) Days lost per case (1)–(3) relative to industry average in other states	(B) Income replacement rate (W) Length of waiting period (B) and (W) relative to industry average in other states	Coefficient estimates |	1	2	3
---	---	---	---
B		0.14	−0.09
W	−0.02	−0.03		
Butler and Worrall (1983)	1972–1978	Time-series/cross section of 35 states	National Council on Compensation Insurance (NCCI) Log of claim frequency: (1) temporary total (2) minor permanent partial (3) major permanent partial	Log of expected weekly benefits for: (a) temporary total (b) minor permanent partial (c) major permanent partial (W) length of the waiting period	Elasticities |	1	2	3
---	---	---	---
a		0.60	1.71
b		0.26	
c		−0.45	
W	−0.33	−0.17		
Chelius (1983)	1972–1978	Time-series/cross section of 2-digit manufacturing industries in 28 states	OSHA (1) lost workdays (2) frequency of lost workday cases (3) days lost per case (1)–(3) relative to industry average in other states	(B) Income replacement rate for temporary total disabilities (W) length of the waiting period (B) and (W) relative to industry average in other states	Coefficient estimates |	1	2	3
---	---	---	---
B		0.16	0.22
W				

Continued

Table 9.3 (Continued)

Leigh (1985)	1977–1979	Time-series/cross section of workers	Panel Study of Income Dynamics (PSID) Receipt of WC benefits (1 = receipt, 0 otherwise)	Potential temporary total weekly benefits	Sample mean elasticity controlling for time and state effects = 0.3 (insignificant)
Chelius and Kavanaugh (1988)	1978–1984	Maintenance workers in 2 community colleges	WC Injury Reports (1) lost-time injuries per worker (2) severe lost-time injuries per worker (>7 days) (3) lost workdays per worker (4) lost workdays from severe injuries	Low WC benefits (1 = 70% wage replacement and a 7 day waiting period, 0 = 100% wage replacement and no waiting period)	(1) negative (2) negative (3) insignificant (4) insignificant The switch to self-insurance lowered (1), (2), and (4)
Krueger (1990)	1983/1984; 1984/1985	Time-series/cross section of workers	Current Population Survey Initial receipt of WC benefits (1 = receipt, 0 otherwise)	Log of expected temporary total benefits; Length of the waiting period; Retroactive Period	Elasticities: 0.454–0.741 (all) 0.428–0.993 (men) Insignificant (women); Increase from 3 to 7 days lowers recipiency rate by 38.7% (all workers); Insignificant
Kaestner and Carroll (1997)	1983–1988	Cross section/time-series of 1-digit industries by state	BLS Frequency of lost-work-day injuries	Maximum income benefit for temporary total disability relative to wage; Medical and income benefits for temporary total disability; Rate regulation of WC premiums	Maximum benefits raise injuries but total benefits (medical + income) lower injuries. The absolute decline in injuries from total benefits is lower in states with deregulated (lower) insurance pricing.

Continued

Table 9.3 (Continued)

III. Program Changes: Nonfatal Injuries

Study	Time Period	Sample	Risk Measurement	Workers' Compensation Benefit Variable	Impact
Shields et al. (1999)	1991–1994	Time-series/cross section of Texas firms with 50 or more workers	Texas Workers' Compensation Claims Database WC claims per 100 employees Indemnity claims per 100 employees Average cost of high-dollar claims	Purchase of a high-deductible WC insurance policy (1 = high deductible, 0 otherwise)	Purchase of a high-deductible policy lowered total claims by 16.4 percent and indemnity claims by 39.8 percent by the third year. Purchase of a high deductible policy reduced the average cost of high-dollar claims the following year.
Boden and Ruser (2003)	1987–1997	Time-series/cross section of cells by year, state, 2-digit industry, and 4 establishment size classes	BLS Number of injury cases per 100 full-time workers for: (1) non-lost workday injuries (2) restricted-workday injuries (3) lost workday injuries	Average weekly benefit for temporary total disability Laws requiring objective medical findings Laws eliminating claims for aggravating non-work conditions Laws restricting medical provider choice	Higher benefits raise all three classes of injuries Laws requiring objective evidence of disability lower (3) but raise (2). Laws eliminating claims for aggravating non-work conditions have a similar, but smaller impact.
Guo and Burton (2010)	1975–1999	Time-series/cross section of 45 states and DC by year	BLS Frequency of lost workday injuries Published study by Blum and Burton	Expected cash benefits per claim Changes in compensability rules for WC benefits Share of claims for permanent partial disabilities	Benefits had no significant impact on injuries 1975–1989 or 1990–1999. Tightening compensability rules raised injuries 1990–1999.
Bronchetti and McInerney (2012)	1977–2004	Time-series/cross section of workers	Current Population Survey Initial receipt of WC benefits (1 = receipt, 0 otherwise)	Potential weekly benefit for a temporary total disability	Using typical controls for past labor earnings WC receipt/benefit elasticity = 0.4. Using more flexible controls for past earnings, WC receipt/benefit elasticity = 0.1. WC receipt/benefit elasticity fell post-1990.

Continued

Table 9.3 (Continued)

IV. Experience Rating

Study	Time Period	Sample	Risk Measurement	Workers' Compensation Benefit Variable	Impact
Chelius and Smith (1983)	1979	15 2-digit manufacturing industries in 37 states	BLS Frequency of lost work-day cases in large firms versus small firms	Temporary total benefits for the average worker	Across the 60 industry/size comparisons 32 estimates are negative indicating fewer injuries in experience-rated companies; only 5 statistically significant
Ruser (1985)	1972–1979	Time-series/cross section of 25 3-digit industries in a maximum of 41 states	BLS (1) frequency of injuries (2) frequency of lost workday injuries, excluding fatalities	(B) Average weekly benefits for temporary total disabilities (P) Average proportion of compensable lost workdays (B) and (P) interacted with firm size (average number of workers per establishment)	Elasticities (table below). Interaction of (B) and firm size was negative and significant for (1) and (2) and interaction of (P) and firm size was negative and significant for (1)
Ruser (1991)	1979–1984	Time-series/cross section of manufacturing establishments	BLS Frequency of lost workday injuries	Average weekly benefits for temporary total disabilities interacted with establishment size	Elasticities for negative binomial specification: 0.53 (1–99 employees) 0.21 (100–249) 0.21 (250–499) 0.12 (500+)
Bruce and Atkins (1993)	1951–1989	Annual time-series data on two industries in Ontario province: forestry and construction	Unspecified Fatalities per employed worker	Income replacement rate Presence of experience rating (present=1, 0 otherwise)	Introduction of experience rating led to a 40 percent reduction in the fatality rate in forestry relative to the sample mean and 20 percent reduction in the fatality rate in construction relative to the sample mean.

Elasticities (Ruser 1985):

	1	2
B	0.275	0.313
P		

Continued

Table 9.3 (Continued)

Study	Time Period	Sample	Risk Measurement	Workers' Compensation Benefit Variable	Impact
Thomason and Pozzebon (2002)	1996	Survey of manufacturers with more than 50 employees in Quebec	Measures related to firm efforts to improve workplace safety Measures related to aggressively managing WC claims by workers Number of injuries per 100 workers	Retrospective WC insurance pricing (full experience rating=1, 0 otherwise) Personalized WC insurance pricing (partial experience rating=1, 0 otherwise) Degree of personalized pricing (experience rating factor)	Experience rating expanded measures to both improve safety and manage WC claims. Injury rates rise by 8.7 per 100 in firms with personalized pricing relative to retrospective pricing.

V. Expansion of Benefits: Fatalities

Study	Time Period	Sample	Risk Measurement	Workers' Compensation Benefit Variable	Impact
Butler (1983)	1940–1971	Time-series/cross section of 15 industries in South Carolina	South Carolina Industrial Commission Frequency of: (1) fatalities (2) permanent dismemberment or disfigurement (3) permanent partial (4) temporary total (5) index of injuries	Log of average annual benefits for (1)–(4) Log of a benefit index Log of expected weekly benefits for an average worker	
Moore and Viscusi (1989, 1990)	1982	National cross section of workers from the PSID	National Institute of Occupational Safety and Health Frequency of fatalities by 1-digit industry and state	Maximum weekly benefits for temporary total disabilities Expected weekly benefits for temporary total disabilities	Maximum weekly benefits for Elasticities: Maximum benefit =−0.22 Expected benefit=−0.48 Benefit/firm size interactions are negative and significant

Impact (Butler 1983):

	Elasticities	
	Benefit Index	Expected Benefits
1		5.20
2	0.36	
3	0.33	
4		
5		

Continued

Table 9.3 (Continued)

Study	Time Period	Sample	Risk Measurement	Workers' Compensation Benefit Variable	Impact
Ruser (1993)	1979–1984	Time-series/cross section of manufacturing establishments	BLS Per establishment: (1) Non-lost-workday injuries (2) Restricted workday injuries (3) Lost-workday injuries (4) Fatalities	Average weekly benefits for temporary total disabilities interacted with establishment size (a) 0–99 workers (b) 100–249 workers (c) 250–499 workers (d) 500+ workers	Elasticities mixed fixed effect negative binomial-multinomial logit

Elasticities mixed fixed effect negative binomial-multinomial logit:

logit	1	2	3	4
a			0.62	
b	0.35		0.55	−1.30
c	0.29		0.53	
d		0.48	0.31	−1.33

VI. Claims-Reporting Moral Hazard

Study	Time Period	Sample	Risk Measurement	Workers' Compensation Benefit Variable	Impact
Worrall and Appel (1982)	1958–1977	Workers' compensation claims	NCCI (1) Temporary total indemnity claims (all indemnity claims) to medical only claims (2) Cost of temporary total indemnity claims (all indemnity claims) to the costs of medical only claims	Income replacement rate for temporary total disabilities	Elasticities (1) temporary total = 0.614 all indemnity = 0.465 (2) temporary total = 0.990 all indemnity = 0.960

Continued

Table 9.3 (Continued)

Smith (1990)	1978–1979	Individual injury reports in 4 states	BLS Supplemental Data System **(1)** Cuts and lacerations **(2)** Fractures **(3)** Sprains and strains		The percentage of (3) reported on Mondays exceed the percentages of (1) and (2). The mix of injuries is more heavily weighted toward (3) on Mondays and after 3-day weekends. A greater fraction of (3) are reported earlier in the workday than (1) and (2) and the fraction of (3) reported earlier in the workday expands on Mondays and after 3-day weekends.
Krueger and Burton (1990)	1972–1983	Time-series/cross section of 29 states in 1972, 1975, 1978, and 1983	NCCI **(1)** Log of adjusted manual rates (WC premiums) per $100 of payroll **(2)** Log of net WC costs per worker	Log of weighted weekly benefits for temporary total, permanent partial, and fatal injuries	Elasticity of (1) or (2) to benefits exceeds 1.0 instrumenting for WC benefits (indicating a rise in the number of claims). No evidence either elasticity differs from 1.0 using OLS.
Butler and Worrall (1991)	1954–1983	Time-series/cross section of 33 states	NCCI **(1)** log of expected indemnity costs per worker **(2)** Log expected medical costs per worker	Log of temporary total benefits for a typical worker	**(1)** claims reporting moral hazard = 0.68 **(2)** risk bearing moral hazard = −0.36

Continued

Table 9.3 (Continued)

Card and McCall (1996)	1985–1989	Individual WC injury reports	Minnesota Department of Labor and Industry (1) All injuries (2) Back injuries (3) Strains	Probability of off-the-job medical insurance coverage. Income replacement rate	No higher fraction of Monday injuries for workers less likely to have medical insurance coverage or with a higher income replacement rate. No higher fraction of denials for WC benefits on Monday for workers less likely to have medical coverage or with a higher income replacement rate. Workers with a higher income replacement rate were more likely to be denied coverage regardless of day of injury.
Hirsch et al. (1997)	1977–1992	Time-series/cross section of workers	Current Population Survey Initial receipt of WC benefits (1 = receipt, 0 otherwise)	Temporary total benefits as a fraction of pre-injury earnings Length of the waiting period	Temporary total benefits have an insignificant positive impact on initial receipt of WC after including individual characteristics and union status. Length of the waiting period lowers the WC recipiency rate in non-state fixed effect specifications. Union workers are about 60 percent more likely to receive WC benefits than nonunion workers.

Continued

Table 9.3 (Continued)

Ruser (1998)	1992	Individual injury reports of a nation-ally representative cross section of lost-workday cases	BLS Relative probabilities of back sprains, car-pal tunnel syndrome (CTS), cuts and lacera-tions, and fractures.	Higher (1) raises the fraction of CTS relative to cuts and frac-tures. Modest impact on back sprains relative to cuts and lac-erations and fractures. Increases the reporting of injuries of all types on Monday. Lower (2) raises CTS relative to cuts and fractures and increases sprains relative to fractures. Neither (1) nor (2) affect the likelihood of reporting a hard-to-diagnose injury on Monday. Higher (1) raises the probability that an injury of any type will be reported on Monday.
			(1) Income replacement rate	
			(2) Length of the waiting period	
			(3) Workers can freely choose their own doctor	
Bolduc et al. (2002)	1976–1986	Time-series/cross section of Québec construction workers	Québec Workers' Composition Board Easy-to-diagnose injury; difficult-to-diagnose injury; no injury	A 1 percent increase in the replacement rate causes a 0.13–0.40 percent rise in the pro-portion of difficult-to-diagnose to easy-to-diagnose injuries. Probability of a difficult-to-diagnose injury rises during the winter.
			Income replacement rate	
Biddle and Roberts (2003)	1996–1997	Survey of workers in Michigan identified by physicians as having work-related back, wrist, hand, or shoulder pain from repetitive trauma injuries.	Michigan's Bureau of Workers' Disability Compensation and sur-vey data A claim for WC benefits	The elasticity of reporting a time-loss claim and the income replacement rate is near unity.
			Income replacement rate	

Continued

Table 9.3 (Continued)

Study	Time Period	Sample	Risk Measurement	Workers' Compensation Benefit Variable	Impact
Campolieti and Hyatt (2006)	1992	Random sample of lost-time claims in Ontario	Workers' Compensation Board of Ontario All injuries, back, sprains and strains, lacerations, dislocations, burns, contusions, and fractures.		Back and strain and sprain injuries more likely to be reported on Monday, but not other types of injuries.

VII. Expansion of Benefits: Duration

Study	Time Period	Sample	Risk Measurement	Workers' Compensation Benefit Variable	Impact
Worrall and Butler (1985); Butler and Worrall (1985)	1979–1983	Claims filed by men for low back injuries in Illinois	NCCI Duration of temporary total disability	Log of income replacement rate for temporary total disabilities	Elasticities: 0.187 0.374 correcting for duration dependence 0.183 correcting for unobserved heterogeneity
Johnson and Ondrich (1990)	1970	1,040 permanently partially impaired workers from Florida, New York, and Wisconsin injured during the year	Survey Data Duration of absence away from work	Log of temporary total benefits	Elasticities 1.114–1.161
Krueger (1990b)	1986	Claims filed in Minnesota for injuries occurring during the year	Administrative Records Log duration of temporary total disability	Log weekly temporary total benefits	Elasticity = 1.67
Dionne and St-Michael (1991)	1978–1982	Closed cases of workers with a total temporary disability in Québec Province	Commission des accidents du travail du Québec Days of compensation	Program change raising income coverage for low-income workers and lowering it for high-income workers	Greater income replacement rate raised recovery time for all injuries with biggest impact on difficult-to-diagnose injuries.

Continued

Table 9.3 (Continued)

Study	Years	Sample	Dependent variable	Benefit measure	Results
Curington (1994)	1964–1983	Scheduled permanent partial cases closed in New York	New York Workers' Compensation Board Log duration: (1) Severe Impairments (2) Minor Impairments	Workers affected by legislative changes in benefits (1=yes, 0 otherwise)	Varies by year of change Elasticities for 1968 (1) 1.08 (2) insignificant
Meyer et al. (1995)	1979–1984 Kentucky 1981–1986 Michigan	Temporary total disability claims in Kentucky and Michigan	NCCI Log duration of temporary total disability	High wage workers affected by increased maximum; low wage workers unaffected by program change	Elasticities: 0.3–0.4
Ohsfeldt and Morrisey (1997)	1975–1985	Time-series/cross section of 2-digit industries by state	Unspecified Lost workdays due to injuries per 100 workers	Maximum benefit relative to average industry wage Minimum benefit relative to average industry wage Length of the waiting period	Maximum benefits have a positive impact on lost workdays; minimum benefits and length of the waiting period have negative impacts.
Butler et al. (2001)	1973–1990	Workers in Ontario, Canada with serious back injuries	Survey of Ontario Workers with Permanent Impairments Days away from work	Expected wage replacement rate for a temporary total disability	Elasticities allowing for variable duration dependence and unobserved heterogeneity: Men = 0.400 Women = 1.426
Galizzi and Boden (2003)	1989–1990	Wisconsin workers with a nonfatal and nonpermanent-total lost-time injury in 1989 or 1990	Wisconsin Workers' Compensation Division Days until return to work	Log weekly temporary total disability benefits	Elasticities: 0.06–0.36 short-term injuries 0.23–0.35 long-term injuries
Neuhauser and Raphael (2004)	1993–1996	WC claims for medical and/or income benefits	California Workers' Compensation Institute Days of income payment for a temporary total disability Frequency of income benefits to all claims	Two natural experiments: a 1994 and a 1995 increase in temporary total indemnity benefits for high wage workers	A frequency-benefit elasticity of 0.5, 1994; insignificant, 1995 A duration-benefit elasticity of 0.3. Correcting for sample selection bias, 0.8.

when injured and the level of state regulation of safety standards, specifically the state budget for mine inspectors' salaries. Unlike Chelius, Fishback finds the movement to a more liberal liability system and the adoption of workers' compensation lowered worker safety. Coal mining fatalities increased by 17 percent with state passage of more liberal liability standards and by another 15 to 23 percent with state passage of workers' compensation insurance. State safety regulation had no impact on fatalities.

Fishback argues that the conflict between his and Chelius' results is perfectly consistent with a broader based theoretical model of worker safety. From the Coase theorem, the assignment of liability for industrial injuries should have no impact on safety in a world of perfect information and zero bargaining and transaction costs. In such a world, if the low-cost producer of safety is assigned the liability from injury then he will take the appropriate actions. On the other hand, if the high-cost producer of safety is assigned the liability from injury then he will bribe the low-cost producer to take the necessary actions and the same level of safety will be produced.

In a world of costly bargaining and enforcement, the assignment of liability matters. More lenient employer liability laws improve worker safety if employers are the low-cost providers of safety, but they lower worker safety if workers are the low-cost providers. Given the high cost of supervising miners during the period examined, Fishback argues that miners were the low-cost providers of safety and the movement to greater employer liability shifted the costs of injury from workers who could best avoid hazards to employers who lacked the ability to monitor worker actions easily. Over the broad class of workers Chelius examines, employer monitoring costs might have been far lower than in mining, meaning the change in liability from workers' compensation insurance shifted injury costs to the low-cost provider generally, but to the high-cost provider in the specific instance of mining.

Butler and Worrall (2008) revisit the question of a possible diversity of reactions among workers to changing liability standards by examining four classes of railroad workers employed in the four largest steam railroads in New Jersey from 1900 to 1916. They find that the move to greater employer liability after passage of the Federal Employers' Liability Act in 1908 and workers' compensation in 1911 lowered the rate of injury for depot workers, trainmen, and linemen, but raised them for craft workers. The three occupations with a drop in injuries from expanded employer liability worked outside and under circumstances where railroads might have been the low-cost provider of safety through their choices regarding equipment and the establishment of proper safety procedures. Craft workers, who worked inside, and experienced a rise in accidents, were similar to the miners studied by Fishback: they were the low-cost providers of safety. By reducing the monetary costs of injury, employer liability standards and workers' compensation insurance shifted accident costs from the low-cost to the high-cost provider, resulting in more accidents for this group of workers.

9.5.3.2 The Impact of Benefits on Nonfatal Injuries

The second panel in Table 9.3 presents the empirical evidence regarding the impact of benefit generosity on the frequency of nonfatal injuries. The results are clear-cut: workplace accidents and illnesses rise as workers' compensation indemnity benefits expand. Chelius (1974, 1982, 1983), Butler and Worrall (1983), Leigh (1985), Chelius and Kavanaugh (1988), and Krueger (1990a), all find higher workers' compensation benefits increasing injuries after controlling for other factors also affecting worker safety. Most of the studies exploring other aspects of workers' compensation insurance that we will discuss later also find a positive relationship between nonfatal workplace injuries and workers' compensation disability payments (Butler, 1983; Ruser, 1985, 1991, 1993; Krueger and Burton, 1990; Kaestner and Carroll, 1997; Boden and Ruser, 2003). The positive relationship is robust to sample composition, injury definition, or benefit measurement. The studies in Table 9.3 examine samples composed of states, industries, establishments, and individuals. They investigate all injuries, lost-workday injuries, disabling injuries, and injuries by workers' compensation classification. They evaluate benefit generosity either at the state level by including cash payments for a typical injury, all injuries, or for a specific class of injuries such as a temporary total disability or at the individual level by calculating expected benefits for each worker.

The study by Butler and Worrall (1983) is a good example of the early efforts to determine the impact of cash indemnity benefits on workplace safety using state level data. Based on information provided by the National Council on Compensation Insurance (a private, not-for-profit provider of workers' compensation data to insurance companies and government agencies), they calculate the frequency of temporary total, minor permanent partial, and major permanent partial disabilities in 35 states from 1972 to 1978. To measure the generosity of the state workers' compensation programs they use the state's waiting period for temporary total benefits and construct what they refer to as expected workers' compensation benefits for each of the three types of disabilities. For each state, year, and disability category, they multiply the fraction of workers earning below the minimum benefit level by the minimum income payment, the fraction of workers earning above the maximum benefit level by the maximum income payment, and the fraction of workers earning between the two levels by the average expected income payment paid within the range, and then sum the three amounts. In each case the benefit payment is for a worker with a spouse and two dependent children.

Because the relevant measure of workers' compensation generosity is the replacement of income, Butler and Worrall include as an explanatory variable in their frequency of claims/injury rate equations the state average wage. Other explanatory variables include average work hours, fraction of manufacturing workers, the new-hire rate, the fraction of unionized workers, and dummy variables for state and year fixed effects and the South. They then incorporate the injury rate equation into a simultaneous system of three equations that explain the injury rate, hours of work, and wage and estimate the system separately for each injury rate.

For temporary total disabilities, the three expected workers' compensation benefit variables are statistically insignificant individually and jointly. For minor permanent partial disabilities, benefits for temporary total disabilities and minor permanent partial disabilities raise the frequency of claims but benefits for major permanent partial disabilities lower the frequency of claims. Jointly a 10 percent rise in all three types of benefits would expand the rate of minor permanent partial disabilities by 4.1 percent, significant at the 5 percent level. For major permanent partial disabilities, only an increase in the benefits for temporary total disabilities is statistically significant individually. Jointly the three benefit levels are significant at the 10 percent level and imply that a 10 percent increase in benefits would generate a whopping 22 percent rise in the rate of major permanent partial disabilities. The other measure of workers' compensation generosity, the length of the waiting period, lowered the frequency of temporary total and minor permanent partial disabilities, but had an insignificant impact on the frequency of major permanent partial disabilities.

Krueger (1990a) finds very similar results to Butler and Worrall using individual worker data drawn from the Current Population Survey (CPS). The Census Bureau collects the CPS micro data by interviewing a household for four months, waiting eight months, interviewing the same household again for four months, and then dropping the household from the sample. Although the CPS is not a longitudinal data set, the re-interviewing of the same household one year later allows researchers to generate observations for most individuals across two years. The CPS contains no direct information on workplace injuries, but the March survey does include detailed information about sources of income earned by each worker the previous year, including receipt of workers' compensation benefits, which allows creation of a proxy variable for a workplace accident or disease. Specifically, workers who receive workers compensation benefits in year t, but not in $t-1$ have been injured in year t, whereas workers receiving no benefits in either year are uninjured. Kruger uses information from the March surveys in 1983 and 1984 and 1984 and 1985 to develop two panels of data.

For each worker, Krueger calculates the income benefits from workers' compensation insurance a worker would receive for a temporary total disability using information on the workers' predisability weekly wage, number of dependents, and the parameters of the state workers' compensation law in effect. He includes two other measures of workers' compensation insurance generosity: (1) the length of the waiting period and (2) the length of the retroactive period. As further control variables he includes in all specifications the worker's wage, marginal tax rate, demographic characteristics, and year and in some specifications fixed effects for occupation, industry, and state.

Krueger finds injury/benefit elasticities ranging from 0.454 to 0.741 for all workers and from 0.428 to 0.993 for male workers. Workers' compensation benefits had a negative, but statistically insignificant, impact on the probability of an injury for female workers. Expanding the length of the waiting period from three to seven days reduces the probability of receiving income benefits by 38.7 percent for all workers. Krueger argues this large impact from the lengthening of the waiting period is not a true measure of improving safety, but merely the truncating of injuries eligible to receive benefits. The length of the retroactive period, the number of days a worker must remain off the job before being reimbursed for lost wages during the waiting period, is small and statistically insignificant across all specifications.[16]

Chelius and Kavanaugh (1988) document an interesting natural experiment that sheds light on the relationship between benefit generosity and workplace injury. A special statute in New Jersey specifies that employees working in public institutions of higher learning receive workers' compensation benefits equal to 100 percent of wages with no dollar maximum and no waiting period to receive benefits. In preparing for labor negotiations with their unionized maintenance workers, the administrators of one state community college decided after a careful reading of the legislation that the special provisions applied only to the faculty and the administration and not to maintenance workers. After negotiating with the union, benefits to the maintenance workers were lowered to the rate for most workers in the state (70 percent of wages) and subject to the same waiting period (seven days). Other community colleges continued to interpret the special statute as applying to all workers, meaning injured maintenance workers at other schools received 100 percent of lost wages and were not subject to a waiting period.

Using workers' compensation injury reports, Chelius and Kavanaugh calculate injury rates and severity rates (lost workdays per worker) by quarter from 1978 to 1984 for maintenance workers at the community college with reduced benefits and another community college within the same metropolitan area and with similar characteristics, which acts as a control in the estimations. The change in benefits for the first community college occurred approximately at the midpoint of the seven years of data. At different points during the seven years, both community colleges shifted from purchasing workers' compensation coverage from an outside provider to self-insuring against losses. Because the move to self-insurance could cause the community colleges to expand their safety efforts or monitor workers' compensation claims more aggressively, Chelius and Kavanaugh include a dummy variable in their regressions to reflect the shift. The other independent variables are binary variables for the period of reduced

---

[16] In an earlier paper, Leigh (1985) uses the Panel Study of Income Dynamics to measure the transition into the workers' compensation system. He finds an injury/benefit elasticity only slightly smaller than Krueger (1990a) but statistically insignificant (two-tailed test) after correcting for time and state fixed effects.

workers' compensation benefits, the comparison community college, and the interaction of reduced workers' compensation benefits and self-insurance.

Chelius and Kavanaugh find that the lowering of workers compensation benefits and the move to a seven-day waiting period reduced both the frequency of all lost-time injuries and the frequency of injuries where workers were away from their jobs for more than seven days. Hence, the natural experiment corresponds to the same positive injury/benefit relationship seen in the two previous studies and the other empirical studies summarized in Table 9.3. The lowering of benefits had no statistically significant impact on the number of lost workdays per worker, which might reflect the more random nature of injury severity than injury frequency or a changing composition of injuries as accidents fall.

The positive relationship between nonfatal injuries and benefits found in the empirical studies summarized in Table 9.3 may simply reflect the differing incentives facing employers and workers as insurance benefits expand. Kaestner and Carroll (1997) examine these conflicting incentives by investigating the impact of cash benefits and total benefits (cash and medical) on the frequency of lost workday cases separately. They argue that a rise in the cost of purchasing workers' compensation coverage regardless of whether from more generous cash benefits or from expanding medical care costs would cause firms to expand their safety efforts, whereas only higher cash benefits would lower workers' desires to avoid injuries. By including both cash and total benefits into a standard injury rate regression, controlling for other influences on risk, they are able to separate the impact of higher benefits on workers from the impact on firms. As expected, income benefits raise nonfatal injuries, but total benefits lower them. Overall, the impact on workers from higher benefits exceeds the impact on firms and lost workday injuries rise.

9.5.3.3 The Impact of Other Program Changes on Nonfatal Injuries

Employer costs of providing workers' compensation insurance coverage skyrocketed in the 1980s and, in reaction, many states introduced changes in the 1990s to reduce costs. A dozen states passed legislation limiting the types of injuries covered by workers' compensation insurance. Before the legislative change, workers' compensation covered all injuries arising "out of and in the course of employment." After the change, workers' compensation covered only injuries where the workplace was the major or the predominant cause of the disability. Firms or their insurance providers no longer needed to pay benefits to workers who had aggravated a preexisting condition or a condition related to the aging process. The legislation also required workers to demonstrate the extent of their disability using objective medical evidence. Additionally, ten states moved from allowing injured workers complete freedom in choosing their health care provider to requiring them to seek care from managed care organizations contracted by their employer (Boden and Ruser, 2003). In an effort to revive lagging profitability, insurance providers began writing policies for workers' compensation insurance with large deductibles, thereby shifting more of the costs of injuries to firms.

The third panel of Table 9.3 summarizes the studies investigating the impact of the 1990 program changes on nonfatal injuries. Boden and Ruser (2003) examine the impact of laws making it more difficult or less beneficial for workers to file claims for workers' compensation benefits and restricting workers' choice of medical care provider on the frequency of reported workplace injuries. Using establishment data collected by the BLS, they calculate the frequency per 100 workers of non-lost-workday, restricted-workday only, and days-away-from work injuries by year, state, two-digit SIC industry, and four establishment size classes. Employing a difference-in-difference empirical approach, they determine the impact of these legal changes on the three injury frequencies, allowing for the possibility that the impact might occur with a multi-year lag. To account for the chance that a rise in injuries might cause legislators to enact the changes in the first place, they also include two binary variables to measure the two years before passage of the act. The two lead variables control for a possible reversion to the mean that would bias the legislative change variables downward. Finally, to control for other confounding factors they include as independent variables, average weekly workers' compensation benefits for a temporary total disability, the average wage, the state unemployment rate, and fixed effects for industry, establishment size, state, and year.

The data Boden and Ruser examine provide little evidence that restricting worker choice of health care provider impacts the frequency of any type of injury, but strongly suggest that laws making it more difficult for workers to file a workers' compensation claim does. Four or more years after passage, an objective-evidence requirement reduced the rate of days-away-from-work injuries by 14 percent relative to a sample mean of 2.93 injuries per 100 workers. Legislation restricting the payment of benefits to injuries where work was the predominate cause of disability also reduced days-away-from-work injuries, but the impact was smaller, and less-clear cut. Both of these legislative changes making it more difficult to file for workers' compensation benefits raised the rate of restricted-workday-only cases. The conflicting results for the two types of injuries indicates that legislation aimed at reducing worker incentives to file claims for benefits may cause some work injuries to go unreported and may induce some injured workers to remain on the job.

Shields et al. (1999) examine the safety effects of large deductible insurance policies. By eliminating payments for some losses, insurance deductibles shift accident costs away from insurance providers and back to individual firms. A large deductible acts like self-insurance for smaller losses, raising the marginal benefit of safety, and boosting firm expenditures on safety programs. To determine the impact of large deductibles on worker safety, the authors examine a sample of Texas firms from 1991 to 1994. Of the 4,394 firms they examine, 220 had purchased a large deductible workers' compensation insurance policy in 1992, the first year such policies were available in Texas. They find, after controlling for other factors including selecting into the treatment group, the purchase of a high-deductible workers' compensation insurance policy lowers the rate of all workers' compensation claims by 16.4 percent and the rate of indemnity claims by 39.8 percent after the third year. Although the purchase of a high-deductible policy has no statistically significant impact on the filing of claims after only a single year, the cost of high-dollar claims falls immediately, indicating a better ability of firms to manage accident costs quickly through early return-to-work programs or through more aggressive supervision of medical and indemnity payments than to prevent accidents in the first place.

Guo and Burton (2010) and Bronchetti and McInerney (2012) revisit the issue of the relationship between workers' compensation generosity and nonfatal injuries in light of legislative and other program changes in the 1990s. Guo and Burton follow an approach similar to Butler and Worrall (1983), using as their measure of nonfatal injuries the BLS frequency of lost-workday injuries by state and year. To capture benefit generosity, they calculate the average expected benefit per claim: a weighted average of the benefits paid for temporary total disabilities, permanent partial disabilities, permanent total disabilities, and fatalities. With this measure and controlling for the usual set of influences on injury rates, they find no statistically significant relationship between benefits and injuries either in the period before the legislative changes made to control costs (1975–1989) or in the period after (1990–1990).

Bronchetti and McInerney (2012) follow along the lines of Krueger (1990a) by considering the impact of benefits on the receipt of workers' compensation payments using information drawn from consecutive CPS samples. For each worker, they construct potential workers' compensation payments for a temporary total disability using the worker's actual wage and the parameters of the workers' compensation program. The injury/benefit elasticities they estimate using data from 1977 to 2004 and standard controls for wages, taxes, demographic characteristics, and time fixed effects range from 0.4 to 0.5. The elasticities are statistically significant, in the range of other estimated elasticities for nonfatal injuries, but smaller than Krueger finds for 1983–1985. Bronchetti and McInerney find similar elasticities to Krueger when they limit their sample to the same years, indicating the years were somewhat anomalous.

When Bronchetti and McInerney allow for the impact of wages on workers' compensation recipiency to vary across the distribution of earnings (holding workers' compensation benefits constant, a rise in the wage for a lower income worker might have a stronger impact on receiving workers' compensation benefits than for a higher income worker) the injury/benefit elasticities become quite small and statistically insignificant. They find no change in injury/benefit elasticities before and after 1990 using the standard set of controls, but do find significant differences allowing for the impact of wages to vary across the earnings distribution. When they control for past wages using a 4-piece spline, the injury/benefit elasticity before 1990 is positive, statistically significant, and at 0.310, well within the range of other estimates in Table 9.3, but the elasticity after 1990 is near zero and statistically insignificant.

9.5.3.4 Experience Rating

Theoretically, the relationship between injuries and workers' compensation benefit generosity cannot be determined. Expanding indemnity benefits raises the cost of accidents to firms, but lowers the cost of accidents to workers. If worker incentives dominate, then workplace accidents rise. If firm incentives dominate, then accidents fall. And if the two forces counteract each other, accidents remain constant.

As can be seen from the first-order conditions for profit maximization, firm incentives to expand safety efforts as benefits (b) rise are tempered by how closely the price of workers' compensation insurance mirrors changes in the frequency of injury, ($\frac{\partial P_b}{\partial \pi}$), and the number of workers the firm employs. For firms that self-insure the "price" of workers' compensation coverage automatically and perfectly reflects the firms' safety efforts. For other firms, the relationship between safety and the price of workers' compensation insurance depends on the degree that insurance prices are experienced rated.

In practice, insurance providers combine injury statistics for all workers in an industrial class to determine the so-called manual rate for workers' compensation coverage. For small firms, insurance companies multiply each worker's wage by the manual rate for the worker's industrial class and then sum across all workers to determine the firm's cost of insurance. As the number of workers expands, insurers pay less attention to the average experience of the industrial class (the manual rate) and more attention to the safety record of the individual firm. Experience rating refers to this process of adjusting insurance prices to reflect individual versus group experience. Workers' compensation premiums are fully experience-rated only for very large firms.

For small firms, expanding safety efforts will reduce injuries but the reduction will have only a minimal impact on the price they must pay for workers' compensation coverage. In terms of equation (9.4), $\frac{\partial P_b}{\partial \pi} \approx 0$, which means that raising workers' compensation benefits will influence small firms' decisions regarding safety programs minimally. As firm size expands, the degree of experience rating rises and insurance prices better reflect individual safety efforts. In terms of equation (9.4), $\frac{\partial P_b}{\partial \pi} > 0$, and firm efforts to reduce worker injuries should rise as benefits expand.

The fourth panel of Table 9.3 presents the results of the major studies that examine the impact of experience rating of workers' compensation insurance premiums on workers safety. Chelius and Smith (1983) were the first to examine the relationship between experience-rating, as proxied by firm size, and the safety effects of expanding workers' compensation generosity. Specifically, they regress the relative frequency of lost-workday cases in large firms versus small firms in 15 2-digit industries across 37 states against the income benefits paid the average worker in the state for a temporary total disability. They examine four size comparisons (very large/very small, very large/small, very large/small, and large/small) for a total of 60 estimates. Only 32 of the 60 benefit coefficients are negative, as would be expected if larger firms expanded their safety efforts more than smaller firms as benefits rose, and only five are statistically significant.

Two papers by Ruser (1985, 1991) provide much stronger evidence of a positive impact of experience rating on worker safety. In the first paper, he measures risk using the yearly rate per 100 workers of all injuries and the yearly rate per 100 workers of lost workday injuries, excluding fatalities, in 25 3-digit industries in 41 states from 1972 to 1979. Similar to other studies, he finds at sample means higher workers' compensation income benefits raise the frequency of all injuries and the frequency of lost-workday injuries after controlling for other factors, with injury/benefit elasticities of around 0.30. More importantly, he finds a statistically significant negative interaction between benefits and firm size, indicating a smaller increase in injuries in industries with more workers per establishment.

In the second paper, Ruser examines both the annual frequency and the annual number of lost-workday injuries within 2,788 manufacturing establishments from 1979 to 1984. He creates four binary variables to reflect firm size, which he interacts with the weekly workers' compensation benefit for an average production worker with a temporary total disability. The injury-rate regressions provide strong support that injuries rise less in larger, experience-rated establishments, than in smaller, nonexperience rated establishments. The injury/benefit elasticities monotonically decline from near 0.8 for the smallest establishments to 0.20 for the largest establishments. The results are only slightly less robust for the various count-data models Ruser uses to estimate the relationship between the number of lost-workday injuries and workers' compensation benefits. Injury/benefit elasticities are largest in the smallest establishments and smallest in the largest establishments across all of the estimates, but they do not decline monotonically as establishment size rises. In the preferred fixed-effect negative binomial estimation, the injury/benefit elasticity is 0.38 and statistically significant for establishments with fewer than 100 workers and -0.02, but statistically insignificant, for establishments with more than 500 workers.

A more direct estimate of the effect of experience rating of workers' compensation coverage on workplace safety comes from a type of "natural experiment" in Canada. The Canadian workers' compensation program is very similar to most state programs in the U.S., but with one important difference. In the U.S. most states permit private insurance carriers to write insurance coverage. In Canada, workers' compensation coverage is provided by an agency within each province. For most industries, the workers' compensation board in the province sets a flat rate for insurance coverage for all firms in the industry. In 1984, the province of Ontario introduced experience rating in two major industries: forestry and construction. Bruce and Atkins (1993) examine the impact of this change on worker fatality rates in the two industries using yearly data from 1951 to 1989. They find the introduction of experience rating reduced the rate of fatalities in forestry and construction by 40 percent and 20 percent relative to the sample means, respectively.

Thomason and Pozzebon (2002) delve behind the injury rate statistics to determine if experience rating of workers' compensation coverage changes safety practices within the firm. Using survey data from 450 Quebec firms in 1995 they find that, all else equal, compared to firms paying only a flat or a manual rate for workers' compensation coverage, firms with a fully experience-rated insurance policy are more likely to have staff dedicated to accident prevention and to have employed a safety consultant. Fully experience-rated firms engaged in more safety promoting activities such as distributing safety pamphlets to workers and establishing worker incentive programs to encourage safety. Their staff performed more activities related to accident investigation and prevention and their worker-management safety committees met more frequently. They spent more time training their workers on safety protocols and they purchased more personal protective equipment. In short, the results correspond well with the prediction that greater experience-rating of workers' compensation insurance coverage expands firm efforts to produce a safe working environment.

9.5.3.5 The Impact of Benefits on Fatalities

Another way to assess the safety effects of workers' compensation insurance is to examine the impact of rising benefits on the most severe category of injury, workplace fatalities. Although more generous benefits might expand the frequency of nonfatal workplace accidents and diseases, they are unlikely to increase the frequency of workplace fatalities. As can be seen in equation (9.6), workers consider both the monetary and the nonmonetary costs of injury when deciding on the level of risk to accept. Because the nonmonetary costs of fatalities are so large, higher workers' compensation death benefits will have only a minimal impact on workers' decisions to accept greater fatal injury risk. The rise in post-accident utility from additional income will be slight. But, the same rise in benefits might encourage workers to be willing to accept more nonfatal injury risk if the pain and suffering from these less severe injuries is sufficiently small. For both types of risks, the expanding cost of purchasing workers' compensation coverage entices firms to expand their safety efforts. With fatal injuries the impact on firms should dominate the limited impact on workers causing deaths to fall, while with nonfatal injuries the impact on workers may dominate the impact on firms causing injuries to rise.

Nonfatal injuries may also rise as workers' compensation benefits expand because higher benefits entice workers to report injuries, either legitimate or fictitious, that they otherwise would not have reported. Injured workers must decide if it is worthwhile to apply for benefits. The application process is costly. To receive benefits workers must remain out of work for longer than the waiting period, losing labor income or drawing down their sick leave. Remaining out of work longer than necessary to recover from injury is also costly. Human capital and productivity declines the longer a worker remains off the job. Employers may also view the length of time to recover as a signal of future permanent impairment and weak labor force attachment. Workers denied disability payments under Social Security Disability Insurance (SSDI) suffer a 10 percent reduction in wages when they later reentered the labor force compared to similarly injured workers who never applied for benefits (Halpern and Hausman, 1986). Exaggerating or falsifying a claim may also generate feelings of guilt, similar to welfare stigma described by Moffitt (1983).

Against the costs, workers must weigh the expected benefits of receiving workers' compensation disability income. If medical personnel could perfectly categorize the cause and extent of injury then workers would have no incentive to exaggerate or falsify claims for benefits. Unfortunately, the process, particularly for workplace diseases, which includes repetitive motion disorders, is far from clear-cut. One-fifth of eligibility rulings for SSDI would have been reclassified by a second evaluation team (Parsons, 1984). Providers of workers' compensation insurance face a more daunting problem. Not only must they determine the extent of a worker's disability, similar to SSDI, but they must also verify that the worker's injury arose "out of and in the course of employment."

In insurance jargon, workers' compensation creates two types of moral hazards for workers. The provision of insurance or the expansion of indemnity benefits lowers the costs of injuries to workers, reducing their incentives to avoid job hazards. Butler and Worrall (1991) refer to this type of moral hazard as risk bearing moral hazard. To the extent that fatal injury risks are separate from nonfatal injury risks, the provision of workers' compensation insurance or the expansion of benefits should have a minimal impact on workers' incentives to avoid such severe job hazards. Risk bearing moral hazard may cause nonfatal injuries to rise, but is unlikely to cause fatal injuries to expand.

The second type of moral hazard created by workers' compensation revolves around the reporting of work injuries. As cash benefits increase, more workers find the expected benefit of reporting an injury to exceed the costs, raising the frequency of injury even in situations where the real level of safety remains unchanged. Butler and Worrall refer to the second type of moral hazard as claims reporting moral hazard. The difficulty of disputing or exaggerating a claim for a workplace fatality makes it less likely data on fatal injuries suffers from this reporting effect, meaning fatal injury risk will more accurately reflect true changes in safety from rising workers' compensation payments than nonfatal injury risk.

Three of the four studies summarized in the fifth panel of Table 9.3 indicate a negative and sizable impact of higher cash benefits on workplace fatalities. The two studies by Moore and Viscusi (1989, 1990) use the 1982 Panel Study of Income Dynamics (PSID) for information on individual workers and NIOSH's National Traumatic Occupational Fatality (NTOF) data on workplace fatalities. The NTOF data are a particularly good source of information to determine the safety impacts of workers' compensation insurance. NIOSH determines work–relatedness based on information from a census of death certificates, meaning the data are unlikely to be contaminated by a reporting effect even if higher workers' compensation benefits entice more families to file for survivorship benefits. By relying on a census, the data also do not suffer from sampling error, expanding the reliability of the estimates. Finally, the data are reported by state and 1-digit industry. By disaggregating by state, the injury data mirror state differences in workers' compensation generosity, which better permits identifying the impact of workers' compensation benefits on safety.

In the first study, Moore and Viscusi examine the impact on fatal injury risk of a state's maximum weekly benefit for a temporary total disability after controlling for firm size and industry. They separately analyze workers subject and not subject to the state cap on benefits, after adjusting for selectivity into the two groups. In the second study, they examine the impact on fatal injury risk of a worker's expected cash payment from a temporary total disability based on the worker's actual wage, again controlling for firm size and industry. To eliminate simultaneity bias they estimate the risk equation using two-stage least squares. The results of the two approaches are very similar in terms of direction and statistical significance with only the magnitudes of the injury/benefit elasticities varying. Both show more generous workers' compensation benefits improve worker safety with the first finding a 10 percent increase in benefits reduces fatalities by 2.2 percent and the second finding a 10 percent increase in benefits reduces fatalities by 4.8 percent. The fatal injury rate data also indicate a significant negative interaction between workers' compensation benefits and firm size, consistent with greater experience-rating of large firms' insurance premiums causing them to expand their safety efforts more as benefits rise than small firms.

Ruser (1993) uses the manufacturing establishment data he developed for his earlier paper (Ruser, 1991) to analyze the impact of workers' compensation benefits on four classes of injuries: non-lost workday injuries, restricted workday injuries, lost workday injuries, and fatalities. Ruser models the generation of worker injuries as a combination of two random processes. The first process determines if an injury occurs and, given that an injury occurs, the second process determines the type of injury. Similar to his earlier paper, expanding workers' compensation benefits raises the number of lost workday injuries with the biggest increase occurring in the smallest establishments. The lost workday injury/benefit elasticity with establishment fixed effects monotonically declines from 0.62 for establishments with fewer than 100 workers to 0.31 for establishments with 500 or more workers. The results for non-lost workday injuries and restricted workday injuries are far less robust with many estimates statistically insignificant and a few changing direction depending on the inclusion/exclusion of establishment fixed effects.

The results for fatalities are clear-cut: higher workers' compensation benefits reduce the number of worker deaths. Across the four employment size classes, the fatality/benefit elasticity ranges from -1.47 to -0.96 without establishment fixed effects and from -1.33 to -0.69 with establishment fixed effects. Some of the elasticities are not statistically significant and they do not monotonically decline as employment size rises. Still, with or without establishment fixed effects the smallest reduction in fatalities occurs in establishments with fewer than 100 workers and the biggest reduction occurs in establishments with 500 or more workers—establishments likely to purchase experience-rated workers' compensation insurance policies or self-insure against losses. Both of the fatality/benefit elasticities for the largest employment size class are statistically significant at the 1 percent level or higher.

Butler (1983) is the sole study finding a positive relationship between fatalities and workers' compensation benefits. He examines injury rate data drawn from workers' compensation claims in 15 industries in South Carolina from 1940 to 1971 and measures workers' compensation benefits as the real payments paid per case for each of the four types of injuries he examines, a benefit index composed of the principle components of the real payments paid per case, and expected workers' compensation benefits for the average worker in the industry. In the fatality rate equation that includes actual payments made for all four types of injuries, the coefficient on death benefits is positive, statistically significant and fairly large implying a fatality/benefit elasticity of 1.9. In the fatality rate regression measuring workers' compensation benefits using an index of benefits, the coefficient on benefits fails to reach statistical significance, but is also positive. In the final regression using expected workers' compensation benefits, the benefit coefficient is once again statistically significant and large, implying a fatality/benefit elasticity of 5.2. During the time period Butler examines, the parameters of the workers' compensation system changed only slightly, which prevents him from including both expected workers' compensation benefits and the average industry wage in the estimating equation because of multi-collinearity. The inability to control for the level of preinjury income and, therefore, measure the fraction of income replaced by workers' compensation benefits may explain the extremely large estimated elasticities.

By limiting the investigation to a single state, Butler eliminates the institutional variation among states that may contaminate estimates of the relationship between fatalities and benefits. Still, a single state's experience may not represent the general experience across all states and the limited exogenous variation in a single state's payment of benefits makes the estimates somewhat questionable. To the extent that work-related deaths are difficult, but not impossible to dispute, Butler's use of closed workers' compensation claims to determine workplace fatalities may also suffer from a reporting effect. Families may more frequently and forcefully contest the denial of death benefits as benefit generosity expands, causing a positive relationship between successful (closed) workers' compensation death claims and workers' compensation benefits.

The three studies finding a negative relationship between fatalities and benefits rely on broad national cross sections of workers or establishments. They measure fatalities using information unrelated to the receipt of workers' compensation payments, a census of death certificates for Moore and Viscusi and employer reports to the BLS for Ruser. Moreover, the three use a variety of techniques to generate truly exogenous variation in workers' compensation benefits including using the state's maximum indemnity payment, the expected payment for the average worker, and the expected payment for an individual worker but then estimating the injury/benefit relationship using two-stage least squares. The results may not be universal but the three more persuasive studies find a strong negative relationship between fatalities and benefits and seem to show workers' compensation insurance strongly improving worker safety. Based on Moore and Viscusi's estimates, eliminating workers' compensation insurance would raise worker deaths by 22 to 48 percent.

9.5.3.6 Claims-Reporting Moral Hazard

Two types of moral hazard can explain the seemingly conflicting results of more generous workers' compensation benefits raising nonfatal injuries but lowering fatalities. Events generating nonfatal injuries may in some sense be separable from the events generating fatalities. By reducing the monetary costs of injuries, higher workers' compensation benefits reduce workers' incentives to avoid hazards in situations where the post-accident utility of income is likely to be high—the pain and suffering from the accident small. With respect to less severe injuries, risk bearing moral hazard causes workers to reduce their safety efforts and their actions trump firm efforts to expand safety. With respect to fatalities, the dire consequence of an accident minimizes risk bearing moral hazard and firm efforts trump worker actions.

Alternatively, workers' compensation benefits might reduce both nonfatal and fatal injuries, if nonfatal accidents and diseases were properly measured. The rise in benefits encourages workers to report an injury and file a claim for benefits. This incentive to report more accidents, either legitimate or illegitimate, may cause reported injuries to rise even when actual injuries fall. If fatalities are freer of a reporting effect, then the drop in fatalities from rising benefits measures the actual improvement in safety from workers' compensation insurance and the growth of nonfatal injuries reflects merely the expanded reporting of injuries to collect benefits.

To see if it is possible for reported injuries to rise as actual injuries fall, Kniesner and Leeth (1989b) develop an economic model with three types of injuries: injuries with no lasting consequences, injuries with permanent partial impairments, and injuries with permanent total impairments. In the model, workers must determine the appropriate level of risk to accept and firms must determine the appropriate level of risk to offer, conditioned on the parameters of the workers' compensation system. Additionally, injured workers must decide if the expected benefits of applying for workers' compensation when injured or filing an exaggerated claim for damages exceed the expected costs, which include a drop in future labor income if denied coverage. The inability of insurance providers to determine the cause or extent of injury perfectly means some workers filing false claims will receive benefits, while some workers filing legitimate claims will be denied. Based on simulations of the full hedonic equilibrium model, they show that it is quite easy for reported injuries to rise as actual injuries fall. Increasing workers' compensation benefits by 10 percent reduces actual injuries by 0.3 percent, but raises reported injuries by 2.3 percent, consistent with most empirical estimates of the impact of benefits on nonfatal injuries. The expansion of benefits also alters the mix of injuries as the incentive to exaggerate damages as disability payments rise causes a decline in reported permanent partial disabilities and a rise in permanent total disabilities.

The sixth panel of Table 9.3 summarizes the major studies examining various aspects of claims-reporting moral hazard. Butler and Worall (1991) investigate the question of reported versus actual injuries directly by using insurance data on indemnity (income) payments and medical costs. In the absence of any change in safety or incentive to report injuries, workers' compensation indemnity payments should mirror differences in benefit generosity either across states or over time: a one percent rise in benefits should expand indemnity payments by one percent, all else equal. Holding safety constant, if more generous benefits produce a reporting effect than a one percent rise in workers' compensation benefits will cause indemnity payments to rise by more than one percent. A change in actual injuries as a result of higher benefits will cause both medical and indemnity payments to rise, meaning the difference between the growth of indemnity payments and the growth of medical payments arises from claims reporting moral hazard. After controlling for sample selection (the data exclude self-insured firms), the mix of employment in manufacturing and construction, time (post-1971), and state fixed effects, Butler and Worrall find a 10 percent increase in workers' compensation benefits reduces medical claims by 3.6 percent, indicating a fall in accidents. The reduction in accidents should lower indemnity payments by the same percent, but instead indemnity payments rise by 3.2 percent, implying an increase in reported injuries of 6.8 percent. In short, Butler and Worrall find a real safety improvement from workers' compensation that is masked by worker incentives to report injuries as disability payments expand.[17]

The inability to dispute or exaggerate some types of injuries makes it unlikely workers or their families will file false claims for damages. Claims reporting moral hazard should be concentrated in situations where it is difficult to determine the cause and extent of injury and where the economic advantages of falsifying a claim are high. Besides encouraging possible fictitious injuries, higher workers' compensation benefits might cause a growth in reported workplace injuries if higher benefits encourage workers to report off-the-job injuries as occurring on-the-job. Workers may not be able to delay treatment for some types of injuries, such as for cuts or lacerations, but might for

---

[17] Worrall and Appel (1982) also find a much stronger impact of workers' compensation benefits on claims for indemnity payments than on medical only claims, indicating a sizable reporting effect.

other types of injuries, such as for sprains and strains. The ability to delay treatment and the difficulty of verifying the cause and extent of injury makes sprains and strains likely candidates for misreporting. Because workers are actually injured, they would wish to report these off-the-job injuries as quickly as possible once they returned to work to expedite medical treatment. Based on this reasoning, reported sprains and strains should skyrocket relative to cuts and lacerations after a weekend or a three-day holiday and a greater fraction of sprains and strains should be reported earlier in the work day relative to cuts and lacerations.

Smith (1990) was the first to examine what is now referred to as the Monday effect as evidence of claims reporting moral hazard. Using data from the BLS drawn from seven states in 1978 and 1979, he finds a greater fraction of all sprains and strains are reported on Monday or after a three-day holiday weekend than the fraction of all cuts and lacerations. Also consistent with workers reporting hard to verify, off-the-job injuries as job-related, the mix of injuries on Monday is more heavily weighted toward sprains and strains than on the other four days of the week. All types of injuries occur earlier in the workday on Monday or after a three-day holiday than on Tuesday through Friday, but the jump in sprains and strains far exceed the jump in cuts and lacerations. Workers may be more prone to injury after a prolonged absence from work, but the much larger increase in sprains and strains during the early hours of the workday on Monday seems to be more in keeping with a reporting effect than a real reduction in safety.

Card and McCall (1996) re-examine the so-called Monday effect in light of another aspect of workers' compensation insurance: workers' compensation pays all of the medical bills arising from a workplace injury. For workers not covered by a standard medical plan, falsifying a workers' compensation claim for a non-work-related injury provides a way to cover medical expenses. All else equal, the Monday effect for hard-to-verify injuries should be greatest for workers unlikely to be covered by health insurance. Card and McCall estimate a medical insurance coverage predictor using data from the March 1987 CPS, which they tie to a 10 percent random sample of first injury reports to the Minnesota Department of Labor and Industry, 1985–1989. They find no relationship between the fraction of all injuries reported on Monday or the fraction of back injuries reported on Monday and the probability of medical coverage. Even after controlling for demographic, industry, and occupation effects and nature and cause of injury, they find no evidence that the likelihood of health coverage or the percent of wages replaced when injured reduces the fraction of all injuries, back injuries, or strains reported on Monday. Also inconsistent with a Monday effect, employers are no more likely to contest a workers' compensation claim for a Monday injury than a claim for an injury occurring on any other day of the week, as would be expected if a higher fraction of Monday claims are fraudulent. Even for workers unlikely to be covered by medical insurance, employers are no more likely to fight a Monday claim than any other type of claim. Card and McCall suggest the greater fraction of strains, sprains, and back injuries reported on Monday results not from a reporting effect but from a true rise in injuries as a result of a return to work after a prolonged period of inactivity.[18]

Following along similar lines to Card and McCall, Ruser (1998) uses a nationally representative cross section of lost-workday injury reports collected by the BLS in 1992 to determine the relationship between the reporting of hard-to-verify versus easy-to-verify injuries and workers' compensation indemnity payments. Consistent with a reporting effect, a higher wage replacement rate or a shorter waiting period raises the fraction of hard-to-verify carpel tunnel syndrome cases relative to cuts and fractures, while a decrease in the length of the waiting period increases hard-to-verify back sprains relative to fractures.[19] Inconsistent with a reporting effect, a higher wage replacement rate does not expand the fraction of back-sprains relative to cuts or fractures that are reported on Monday, but does increase the likelihood that an injury of any type will be reported on a Monday versus any other workday.

Biddle and Roberts (2003) take a different tack on examining a possible reporting effect from higher workers' compensation benefits. In Michigan, health care workers are required to report "known or suspected" cases of occupational diseases to the state's Department of Consumer and Industry Services. State health authorities consider repetitive trauma injuries to be a type of occupational illness. As their universe of actual injuries, Biddle and Roberts limit their investigation to repetitive trauma injuries to the shoulder, back, wrist, or hand. About 40 percent of nonfatal occupational illnesses and injuries in Michigan with days away from work affect the shoulder, back, wrist, or hand. Although health care providers considered all of these workers to be injured in the course of employment, many did not file claims for workers' compensation coverage. Of the workers in their sample who missed more than seven days of work, more than 40 percent report that they filed no insurance claim to receive compensation for lost wages, and 28 percent report that they filed no insurance claim at all, even for medical expenses.

Biddle and Roberts tie these health care reports of injuries to data from Michigan's Bureau of Workers' Disability Compensation on claims for disability benefits to determine if the wage replacement rate expands the propensity to file a claim. Based on a survey of the injured workers, the two have detailed information on the extent of a worker's injury, the workers' general health, individual characteristics, job characteristics, wage, and family income. Not surprisingly they find, after controlling for a host of other factors, the propensity to file a claim for workers' compensation is strongly related to the

[18] Campolieti and Hyatt (2006) provide further evidence that a Monday effect is not caused by workers trying to cover medical expenses from off-the-job injuries. They investigate the timing of workers' compensation claims in Canada, which has nationalized health insurance. They discover that claims for easier to conceal injuries, such as back injuries and strains and sprains, occur more frequently on Mondays, after controlling for demographic, occupation, and industry factors, but not claims for other types of injuries. The data are insufficient to determine if the rise in hard-to-verify injuries on Mondays represents a reporting effect or a real impact from time away from work.

[19] Bolduc et al. (2002) also find workers' compensation benefits increasing the proportion of hard-to-verify injuries in Canada.

workers' general level of health and the severity of the injury itself. Although of a smaller magnitude workers' compensation benefits positively impact workers' decisions to file a claim. With the standard set of controls, a 10 percent rise in the wage replacement rate expands the likelihood of reporting a time-loss claim for benefits by about 10 percent. The claim/benefit elasticity falls when family income is included as an explanatory variable and nearly doubles using an instrumented wage replacement rate.

The results of Biddle and Roberts indicate workers have wide latitude in the reporting of actual injuries through the workers' compensation system that is influenced by economic considerations. The positive relationship between claims and benefits is clearly a reporting effect and not a safety effect. More injured workers find it worthwhile to file for workers' compensation as benefits expand. To the extent that the first step in filing a workers' compensation claim is for a worker to report an injury to his employer, the same economic incentives are likely to not only bias nonfatal injury statistics based on claims for workers' compensation insurance but also BLS statistics derived from employer reports.

The work of Hirsch et al. (1997) also suggests a wide worker latitude in the filing of workers' compensation claims. Using matched March CPS files from 1977 to 1992, they determine the relationship between the receipt of workers' compensation benefits and workers' compensation generosity for union and nonunion workers. Based on their results, union workers are much more likely to receive workers' compensation benefits than similar nonunion workers, and they are much more sensitive to variation in indemnity payments and waiting periods than similar nonunion workers. Differences between union and nonunion workers may arise because unions provide information to their injured members about the availability of benefits and they prevent employers from discouraging workers from applying for benefits or penalizing them if they do. Alternatively, union members might be exploiting the workers' compensation program by filing and receiving compensation for marginal or nonexistent injuries, knowing the union will prevent employers from too closely monitoring worker claims. Although the authors are unable to differentiate between the two theories, they do suggest that the positive injury/benefit elasticity and the larger elasticity for union than for nonunion workers indicates "a large scope for moral hazard" (p. 233).

9.5.3.7 *The Impact of Benefits on Injury Duration*
The final panel of Table 9.3 examines another moral hazard created by providing workers cash payments when injured. By reducing the amount of lost income, higher insurance benefits lower the opportunity cost of recuperating, lengthening observed recovery times. In the most basic theoretical framework, a worker returns to work after an injury when the utility of working is greater than the utility of not working. The utility of working is conditioned on wages, work hours (lost leisure), and possible residual pain

from injury that may be intensified by working, while the utility of remaining off the job is conditioned on cash payments received from workers' compensation insurance. Any increase in these payments raises workers utility from remaining off the job, making it less likely at any point in time that the worker will return to work, thereby expanding the length of time the worker stays off the job and collects workers' compensation benefits. A more complete model would also consider the full costs of remaining away from work, including possible job loss, deterioration of human capital, and decreased ability to find new employment as employers view a prolonged absence from work as a signal of low labor force attachment.

Just as with injuries, a rise in benefits produces opposing influences on employers. The cost to the employer of workers remaining off the job expands as cash benefits rise, meaning firms should more aggressively monitor workers' compensation claims and encourage early return to work. The pricing of workers' compensation insurance premiums mitigates these incentives to some extent. The standard formula for the experience rating of workers' compensation insurance puts far greater weight on the frequency of injuries than on the severity of injuries. Except for self-insuring firms, the economic incentive for a firm to monitor its claims more closely as benefits expand is fairly small.

The results presented in the last panel of Table 9.3 indicate the impact of higher benefits on workers desires to delay a return to work far exceed firm desires to expedite a return to work. All studies summarized in the panel find a positive duration of injury/benefit elasticity with estimates ranging from 0.18 to 1.7. Several of the studies identify the impact of benefits by relying on the variation in the income replacement rates across workers within a single state (Worrall and Butler, 1985; Butler and Worrall, 1985; Butler et al., 2001; Galizzi and Boden, 2003) or across multiple states (Johnson and Ondrich, 1990; Ohsfeldt and Morrisey, 1997), while others rely on changing state laws to create a natural experiment (Krueger, 1990b; Dionne and St-Michael, 1991; Curington, 1994; Meyer et al., 1995; Neuhauser and Raphael, 2004).

The study by Meyer et al. (1995) is a good example of using a natural experiment to identify the impact of benefit generosity on the duration of work injuries. In 1980, Kentucky raised its maximum workers' compensation indemnity payment from $131 to $217 per week, an increase of 66 percent. The minimum payment remained roughly unchanged, falling by 60 cents from $44.00 to $43.40, and payments for workers earning more than necessary to receive the minimum, but less than enough to reach the maximum, continued to receive two-thirds of pre-injury weekly earnings. Figure 9.10 provides a depiction of the change ignoring the 60 cent reduction in the minimum weekly payment. Workers injured before the effective date of the mandated change, earning more than $325.50 per week, received weekly benefits of $131, while workers injured after the effective date received $217. Hence, the impact of benefits on injury duration can be estimated by examining differences in duration before and after the legislated change for these high-income earners. In particular, the 66 percent jump in

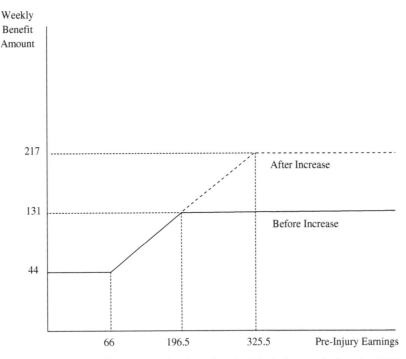

Figure 9.10 Kentucky workers' compensation benefit schedule before and after the 1980 changes (based on Figure 1, Meyer et al. (1995)).

benefits for all workers earning more than $325.50 makes these workers a natural treatment group and the workers totally unaffected by the legislative changes, all workers earning more than $66 per week but less than $196.50, makes them a natural control for purposes of comparison.

Michigan instituted similar, although slightly more complicated changes in 1982. The state raised its maximum benefit from $181 to $307, a 70 percent increase, and instituted major changes in how it compensated low-wage workers. The state abolished the previous minimum benefit level of $144 and changed the replacement rate from two-thirds of pre-tax wages to 80 percent of after-tax wages. The law stipulated, however, that a worker could continue to be paid under the old standard if his calculated benefits were higher under that standard. Workers who would have received more than the previous minimum but less than the previous maximum were better off receiving two-thirds of pretax wages than 80 percent of after-tax wages and so the legislative change did not impact them. Ignoring changes to the very lowest paid workers, the Michigan changes look very similar to the changes in Kentucky, but with different income thresholds. Workers earning more than $460.50 received a 70 percent increase in benefits after the legislative change ($325.50 in Kentucky), while workers earning less than $216 per week but more than $271.50 are not affected ($66 and $196.50 in Kentucky). Once again, the highest wage workers act as the treatment group to determine the impact of higher benefits on the duration of injury, while the lower wage workers who are unaffected by the changes serve as a control.

The authors examine the impact of higher benefits in the two states on injury duration using detailed claim information from the National Council on Compensation Insurance. The data contains longitudinal information on a random sample of injured workers, including workers from Kentucky and Michigan. As their measure of duration they use the number of weeks of temporary total benefits paid for cases closed 42 weeks after injury. For cases still open, they set duration to 42 weeks (less than 0.5 percent of all cases) to prevent outliers from biasing the estimates. For their comparison groups, they use injuries that occurred one year before and one year after the legislative changes in the two states.

In both Kentucky and Michigan, the expansion of benefits raises the mean logarithm of the duration of temporary total benefits for high-income earners, but produces no statistically significant impact on lower-wage workers not affected by the legislative changes. The authors generate a difference-in-difference estimate of claim duration by subtracting the impact on low-wage workers from the impact on high-wage workers. Events occurring over time that influence injury rate duration unrelated to legislative changes should affect both groups, a potential bias that a difference-in-difference estimator eliminates. Compared to lower-wage workers, the increase in benefits increases the difference-in-difference mean logarithm of claim duration in both Kentucky and Michigan by roughly the same magnitude, although the difference is statistically significant only in Kentucky. Not surprisingly, medical costs rise over time for both high- and lower-wage injured workers, but the pre- and post-legislative changes in costs are roughly the same for both groups, indicating no expansion of injury rate severity. The rise in duration from more generous benefits is from workers reacting to economic incentives to remain away from work, not from their needing more time to recuperate from more severe injuries. The difference-in-difference estimates imply a duration elasticity of 0.34 in Kentucky and 0.40 in Michigan. More sophisticated regression estimates employing a difference-in-difference framework but controlling for worker, job, and injury characteristics generate roughly similar elasticity estimates for the two states.

The duration elasticities the authors estimate are near the lower end of the range of estimates presented in Table 9.3. All of the studies summarized in the last panel show a positive duration of injury/benefit elasticity, indicating higher benefits delay the return to work after injury. The elasticity estimates in the table appear to be unrelated to the empirical approach taken or the composition of injuries examined. Krueger (1990b) uses a type of natural experiment in Minnesota similar to Meyer et al., but finds an elasticity more than four times larger. Johnson and Ondrich (1990) take an alternative tack to identify the impact of benefits on duration by using the variability of benefits across workers and find an elasticity near the top of the range of estimates, while Worrall and Butler (1985), Butler and Worrall (1985), and Galizzi and Boden (2003) who also use the variability of benefits across workers, find elasticities closer to Meyer et al.

The evidence on differences in duration/benefit elasticity by injury type is equally conflicting. Curington (1994) finds no statistically significant impact of benefits on claims duration for minor impairments, but a significant and sizable impact on severe impairments, whereas Galizzi and Boden (2003) find a range of estimates for short-term and long-term injuries that largely overlap. Dionne and St-Michael (1991) find a bigger impact on recovery time from an increase in benefits for difficult-to-diagnose injuries than easier-to-diagnose injuries, but Worrall and Butler (1985) and Butler and Worrall (1985) who limit their investigation to workers with low back injuries, perhaps the most difficult-to-diagnose workplace injury, find elasticities at the low end of the spectrum.

9.6 EVIDENCE ON GOVERNMENT REGULATION OF PRODUCT SAFETY

The four pillars of government policy also apply to safety and health attributes of goods and services. Earlier we discussed government efforts to improve consumers' information. The largest product liability lawsuit in the U.S. concerns cigarettes, which are regulated by the FDA, and not considered here (see Philipson and Zanjani, 2014, Chapter 8 of this handbook; Viscusi, 2002b). Where the product markets are concerned, liability insurance most applicable is medical malpractice insurance, which is also covered elsewhere (Sloan and Chepke, 2010; Dionne and Harrington, 2014, Chapter 5 of this handbook). What remains then is regulation of products not related to health directly which we now discuss. In light of the overwhelming importance of auto-related accidents as the leading source of accidental deaths in the United States, we close with results of a recent case study of the safety effects of airbags in automobiles.

9.6.1 Consumer Product Safety

The economic model of product safety is quite similar to the economic model of workplace safety presented earlier, except the end result is a negative relationship between product price and risk. Consumers value both more safety and more goods and services, meaning everything else the same they will only purchase a riskier product if it is cheaper than a safer product. At the same time, the higher cost of producing safer products implies that the price of the product must rise as the probability of injury falls to compensate producers for the added costs. Similar to labor markets, the interaction of firms and consumers generates a price function where firms sort along the function based on their abilities to produce safe products and consumers sort along the function based on their valuations of safety.

Rodgers (1993) provides a simple example of hedonic product market equilibrium from the standpoint of consumers. Assume two products: a generic composite product, q, and a risky product, x, with two possible grades, $i=1, 2$. Suppose the market price of grade i is p_i. The full price considers the likelihood of a product defect, π_i, and the resulting harm from the defect, h_i, and is $\hat{p}_i = p_i + \pi_i h_i$. Oi (1973) demonstrates that with the availability of actuarially fair insurance or when consumers sequentially purchase the product over an extended period and can borrow and lend funds to cover shortfalls and surpluses, consumer demand for either product grade will be driven by its full price. In such a situation, consumers will maximize utility $U(q, x_1, x_2)$ subject to an income constraint, $y = p_q q + x_1(p_1 + \pi_1 h_1) + x_2(p_2 + \pi_2 h_2)$.

Constrained maximization generates the usual first-order conditions and the resulting requirement that the marginal rate of substitution equals the ratio of product prices. The relevant product price is then the full price that includes expected damages from possible defects and $U_1/U_2 = (p_1 + \pi_1 h_1)/(p_2 + \pi_2 h_2)$, where $U_i = \partial U/\partial x_i$. When the two product grades are close substitutes, the relationship can be rearranged to become:

$$p_1 - p_2 = \pi_2 h_2 - \pi_1 h_1. \tag{9.8}$$

Equation (9.8) implies that the difference in prices between the two product grades equals the difference in expected damages. If product grade 1 has fewer defects or results in lower damages when defective then it will sell at a premium to product grade 2. Just as wages must rise to compensate for unfavorable job conditions, product prices must fall to compensate for undesirable attributes such as a higher likelihood of harm from use.

The court system provides a backup to the market process generating compensating price differentials, particularly in the case of unsuspected hazards. Under common law, people injured by products can sue manufacturers for damages. The original standard was one of negligence, where a company was liable for a product-related injury only if it failed to exercise the care of a reasonable person. Starting in the 1960s strict liability increasingly became the norm and producers became liable for product-related injuries regardless of negligence. The ability of consumers to win damage awards for design or manufacturing defects increases the costs of producing risky products either directly through expanded court judgments or indirectly through higher prices for product liability insurance. In moving to a strict liability standard, the courts believed that manufacturers could assume product risks and spread the resulting damages across all consumers through higher prices (Viscusi, 1991a).

As noted, in a world of perfect information and zero bargaining and transaction costs, the assignment of liability generates no change in safety. But, if bargaining and transaction costs are substantial or information poor then expanding manufacturing liability for harm reduces injuries when manufacturers are the low-cost providers of safety, as might be expected in the case of design defects, but raises injuries when consumers are the low-cost providers of safety, as might be expected when injuries result from inappropriate care in using the product.

The tort system of product liability has been augmented several times by federal agencies charged with creating and enforcing safety and health standards. The first federal involvement began in the early 1900s with passage of the Meat Inspection Act of 1906, which directed the U.S. Department of Agriculture to inspect meat and meat products to ensure that animals are slaughtered and processed under sanitary conditions, and the Pure Food and Drug Act of 1906, which created the Food and Drug Administration (FDA). Additional concerns with safety and health led to creation of the National Highway Traffic Safety Administration (NHTSA), the Consumer Product Safety Commission (CPSC), and the Environmental Protection Agency (EPA) in the early 1970s.

9.6.2 Consumer Product Safety Commission

Beginning in the mid-1960s, Congress passed a series of narrowly drawn laws addressing safety issues affecting specific consumer products such as automobiles, toys, flammable fabrics, lead-based paints, refrigerators, and poisonous and toxic substances (Pittle, 1976; Grabowski and Vernon, 1978). At roughly the same time, President Nixon established the National Commission on Product Safety to study the adequacy of existing measures to protect consumers against unreasonable risks of injury and provide recommendations for improvements. The final report of the Commission released in 1970 noted that 20 million Americans were injured at home each year from using consumer products (30,000 resulting in death and 110,000 in permanent disability) with an annual cost to the nation of $5.5 billion. The Commission argued that product-liability suits for damages were insufficient to compensate injured victims adequately or provide manufacturers the necessary incentives to produce safe products. Further, the Commission believed that efforts to educate or to inform consumers on the safe usage of potentially dangerous products would reduce the frequency of product-related injuries only slightly. Consequently, the Commission recommended federal regulation of product design and manufacture to eliminate "unreasonable" product market hazards (Oi, 1973).

In 1972, Congress passed the Consumer Product Safety Act creating the CPSC. The CPSC is an independent regulatory agency tasked with reducing injuries from consumer products sold in the U.S. Besides the thousands of products normally viewed as consumer-related, the CPSC also has jurisdiction over structural items found in the home, such as stairs, ramps, landings, windowsills, and retaining walls, and home fixtures, such as doors, architectural glass, and electrical wiring (Pittle, 1976). Consumer products outside of the scope of the CPSC include food, drugs, cosmetics, automobiles, aircraft, boats, tobacco, alcohol, firearms, pesticides, and fungicides, which are regulated by other federal agencies.

The Consumer Product Safety Act allows the CPSC to issue mandatory design standards, investigate products for manufacturing or design defects, and issue recall and repair orders if necessary. If no feasible standard would adequately protect the public, the CPSC can take action to ban the sale of the product.

Although by law manufacturers must notify the CPSC within 24 hours of learning of product defects that may potentially cause an injury or death, the CPSC's primary source of information for determining if an unreasonable hazard exists is its hospital reporting system. The CPSC collects data from a national probability sample of hospitals from across the U.S. on product-related injuries treated in their emergency rooms. The data, which are entered into the National Electronic Injury Surveillance System (NEISS) database within 72 hours of treatment, include information on the nature and extent of injury, cause of injury, and demographic characteristics of the injured party. The NEISS data contain no information on the underlying population at risk, meaning the data are insufficient to determine the frequency of injury. Outside estimates of product usage must be combined with the NEISS data on injury counts to determine the probability of being injured from a specific product or class of products. The CPSC also discovers potential product-related hazards through newspaper stories, coroner reports, insurance investigations, lawsuits, and complaints from competing manufacturers (Felcher, 2003).

The Consumer Product Safety Improvement Act of 2008 increased the funding of the CPSC and provided it with expanded enforcement tools, including expedited rulemaking and product recall authority. Further, it lowered allowable lead levels in children's products, required third-party testing of certain children's products for conformity with CPSC standards, banned the use of phthalates above 0.1 percent in children's toys and child care products, and mandated that the CPSC establish new safety standards for a number of products. The 2008 Act was later amended in 2011 to allow products with lead levels exceeding the newly established standards to be resold if they were manufactured before the effective date of the standards. The amendments also excluded some products from the lead-level requirements.

9.6.2.1 Impact on Safety

Table 9.4 summarizes the major studies of the CPSC's impact on product safety. Viscusi (1985a) is the only one that attempts to determine CPSC's overall impact. The others examine the impact of CPSC actions more narrowly by examining a specific type of injury or injuries from a specific product. Rodgers (1993) examines the ban on the sale of three-wheeled all-terrain vehicles (ATVs) on the prices of used ATVs and Freedman et al. (2012) consider the impact of CPSC toy recalls on sales of similar products. Both studies demonstrate consumers rationally making product choices using newly available information on product risks and thereby provide an indirect measure of the CPSC's potential to affect safety.

To determine the overall impact of the CPSC on consumer safety, Viscusi (1985a) investigates data on the unintentional injury death rate in the home compiled by the

Table 9.4 Empirical Estimates of the CPSC's Impact on Safety and Health

Study	Sample Period	Product	Outcome Measurement	Enforcement Measurement	Impact
Viscusi (1985a)	1933–1981; 1949–1981	Consumer products:	National Safety Council Accidental death rate: (1) in the home (2) poisonings (3) burns (4) ingestions	Creation of the CPSC (1 = post-CPSC, 0 = pre-CPSC)	(1) No impact either period (2) No impact either period (3) No impact either period (4) No impact either period
	1963–1980	Aspirin	Poison Control Center: Poisoning death rate children under 5	Safety Cap required (1 = post standard, 0 = pre-standard)	No impact on deaths or poisonings
	1963–1980	Analgesics	Poisoning rate children under 5	Fraction of bottles sold with safety caps	No impact on deaths or poisonings
			Poisoning rate children under 5	SC: Safety Cap required (1 = post standard, 0 = pre-standard)	No impact
				UNREG: Safety Cap required in similar products, but not product in question (1 = yes, 0 otherwise)	Positive

Continued

Table 9.4 (Continued)

Study	Sample Period	Product	Outcome Measurement	Enforcement Measurement	Impact
	1968–1980	Prescription drugs	Poisoning Rate	SC, UNREG	No impact, positive
		Unregulated internal medicines,		UNREG	positive
		Baby Aspirin,		SC	No impact
		Adult Aspirin,		SC	No impact
		Aspirin unspecified		SC	No impact
		Analgesics		SC, UNREG	No impact, positive
		Barbiturate sedatives		SC, UNREG	No impact, no impact
		Nonbarbiturate sedatives		SC, UNREG	No impact, positive
		Internal antibiotics		SC, UNREG	No impact, positive
		Psychopharmacological agents			
		Iron preparation		SC, UNREG	No impact, no impact
		Hormones		SC, UNREG	No impact, no impact
		Cardiovascular drugs		SC, UNREG	No impact, no impact
		Amphetamines		SC, UNREG	No impact, no impact
		Misc. internal medicines		SC, UNREG	No impact, positive
		Liquid polish or wax		SC	Positive
		Turpentine		SC	No impact
		Solvents and thinners		SC	No impact
		Unregulated cleaning and polishing products		UNREG	Positive

Continued

Table 9.4 (Continued)

Study	Sample Period	Product	Outcome Measurement	Enforcement Measurement	Impact
	1974–1978	Mattresses/bedding	National Electronic Injury Surveillance System (NEISS)		Regulated period average per year:
			Death rate per 100,000	Actual Predicted	−0.13
		Matches	Injuries per 100,000	Actual Predicted	0.07
		Carpets and rugs	Injuries per 100,000	Actual Predicted	7.30
		Cribs	Injuries per 1,000 births	Actual Predicted	0.15
		Bicycles	Injuries per 1,000 bicycles in use	Actual Predicted	1.83
Magat and Moore (1996)	12/1972– 9/1978	Bicycles	NEISS Monthly accident rate per million bicycles in use	Fraction of bicycles in use complying with CPSC standards	By age: 0–4: −3.24 5–9: −4.906 10–14: −4.265 15–19: no impact A 1% increase in compliance decreases the accident rate by 0.5%
Moore and Magat (1996)	12/1972– 10/1990	Lawn Mowers	NEISS Month with a lawnmower accident	Fraction of lawn mowers in use complying with laceration warning	No impact
				Fraction of lawn mowers in use with required deadman control	Negative
			Log of the monthly injury rate for months with injuries	Fraction of lawn mowers in use complying with laceration warning	No impact
				Fraction of lawn mowers in use with required deadman control	No impact

Continued

Table 9.4 (Continued)

Study	Sample Period	Product	Outcome Measurement	Enforcement Measurement	Impact
Rodgers (1993)	9–12/1987; 1–4/1988	Used ATVs manufac- tured during the 1985–1987 model years	National Automobile Dealer Association appraisal guides for ATVs Prices of used ATVs	Sold post-consent decree ban on the sale of new 3-wheeled ATVs (yes = 1, 0 oth- erwise) × 4-wheels (yes = 1, 0 otherwise)	Price of used 4-wheel ATVs rose $186 relative to equiv- alent 3-wheel models post- consent decree. Price of used 4-wheel ATVs rose $223 relative to equiv- alent 3-wheel models post- consent decree.
	9–12/1987; 1–4/1989				
Freedman et al. (2012)	1/2005– 12/2007	Toy sales	NPD Group Log of unit toy sales in 4th quarter by manufacturer- category (grouping of similar toys)	Manufacturer had a recall in 2007 in catego- ry (yes=1, 0 otherwise)	A recall in 2007 reduces a manufacturer's unit sales of similar toys by 38.9%. 4th quarter unit sales of similar toys to recalled toys of manufacturers with no recalls fell 30.9% in 2007 compared to 2005.

National Safety Council. Deaths due to unintentional home injuries include deaths from falls, poisons, fires and burns, suffocations, firearms, drownings, electrocutions, explosions or involving hot substances, corrosive liquids, and steam. Not all of the injuries just mentioned are from consumer products or consumer products covered by CPSC standards, but the series is the only one encompassing injuries largely resulting from the use of consumer products that extends from before to after the creation of the CPSC. He also examines poisonings, burns, and ingestions in the home separately, which are largely product-related and influenced by CPSC actions.

Figure 9.11 presents the data per 100,000 population from 1928 to 2010. Revisions in the categorization of diseases in 1948 and the adoption of the Census of Fatal Occupational Injuries in 1992 required the National Safety Council adjust the classification of home injuries in those two years, creating the two gaps in the home fatality rate series. Viscusi uses the data to examine two time periods: 1933–1981 and 1949–1981. He excludes the very early years to avoid the onset of the Great Depression and to generate a consistent starting point for the four categories of injuries he examines. The second series excludes the war years and provides a more current pre-CPSC time period for comparison purposes. One should notice that home fatalities fell slightly

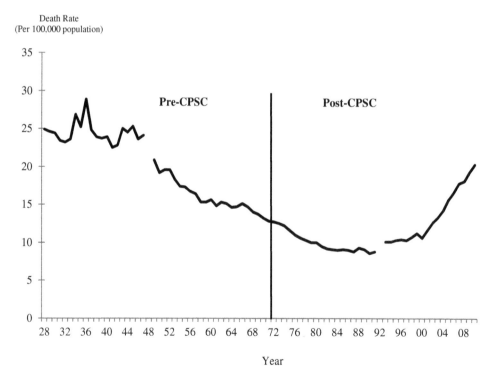

Figure 9.11 Unintentional injury death rates in the home, 1928–2010. *Source*: National Safety Council (2012).

until the Great Depression, rose until 1936, dropped until the start of World War II, rose slightly until shortly after the war, and then steadily declined until 1992. The post-1992 period shows a sizable growth in the rate of home fatalities.

Over the two time periods Viscusi examines, home fatality rates are largely declining, meaning for the CPSC to have improved consumer safety it would have had to have strengthened the already existing downward trend in fatalities. Viscusi examines this possibility by regressing the annual home fatality rate against a binary variable that equals 1 in the period post-CPSC (1973–1981) and 0 otherwise. He controls for other possible influences on the annual rate of home fatalities by including in the regression the fatality rate lagged one year, real per capita consumption, the percentage of the population under the age of five, and four binary variables to capture time period effects. The CPSC coefficient is slightly positive in the 1933–1981 period and negative in the 1949–1981 period, but not statistically significant in either period.

Viscusi uses the same general framework to examine the CPSC's impact on poisonings, burns, and ingestions for the entire population and for the population under the age of five. Instead of reflecting the creation of the CPSC, the CPSC variables in the regressions capture the impact from the introduction of standards likely to affect the relevant category of injuries. With two time periods, two populations, and three types of fatalities there are a total of 12 estimated CPSC effects. None of the estimated CPSC coefficients are statistically significant and only three are negative, as would be expected if the standards generally improved safety.

Viscusi narrows the focus even more greatly by examining the impact of CPSC standards on specific product-related injuries or deaths. Before the creation of the CPSC, Congress passed the Poison Prevention Packaging Act to address concerns with accidental poisonings of young children, primarily children under the age of five. The FDA, which administered the original legislation, introduced regulations in 1972 requiring protective bottle caps on aspirin, furniture polishes, methyl salicylate, and some controlled drugs. Packaging regulations were later expanded to other products including turpentine, oral prescription drugs, and acetaminophen. The Consumer Product Safety Act transferred regulatory authority from the FDA to the newly created CPSC.

Using a slightly modified regression framework, Viscusi examines the impact of the new standards on the aspirin poisoning death rate of children under the age of five and the overall poisoning rate of children under the age of five. He measures the impact of the standards using alternatively: a binary variable that equals one for the years after the protective bottle cap requirement (1972 and later) or the fraction of aspirin sold with safety caps. The regulation allowed manufactures to market one bottle size without a child-protective cap and, generally, they chose their most popular size (the 100-tablet bottle). As in his other regressions he controls for confounding influences using the lagged dependent variable and real per capita consumption. He also includes in the regressions one of three possible measures of total aspirin sales to capture the impact on poisonings from the declining popularity and use of aspirin as a pain reliever. Neither of the two regulatory variables reaches statistical significance in any of the 12 specifications and in 5 of the specifications the regulatory coefficient is positive.

Viscusi also examines the impact of protective bottle cap standards on a variety of other drugs and products and finds no statistical evidence that the standards had any impact on the associated rate of poisonings. He does find some evidence that the CPSC mattress flammability standard imposed in 1975 reduced the rate of mattress/bedding deaths by about 12 percent, but argues that the decline may simply reflect the decline in cigarette smoking that was occurring at roughly the same time. He finds no evidence the CPSC standards on matchbooks, carpets, cribs, or bicycles improved safety. Instead of a decline, as would be expected, the new standards raised the frequency of injury for all four products relative to pre-CPSC trends.

The absence of an overall safety impact from the CPSC may be perfectly understandable. The CPSC is tasked with establishing safety standards and monitoring the safety of thousands of consumer products. Given limited resources, the Commission is forced to target only a few areas, meaning its overall impact across all products may be slight. Additionally, many injuries are not the result of technologically related hazards or product defects, but simply the outcome of user carelessness. With the overall improvement in safety from CPSC standards and safety enforcement likely to be small, its impact could easily be concealed statistically by the randomness of injuries in general. More troubling is the absence of safety improvements from specific CPSC standards on the products in question. As Viscusi notes, the CPSC does not suffer from the same problem facing OSHA. To assure compliance with its standards, OSHA must visit thousands of employers, whereas the CPSC can generally visit a single retail establishment to determine if a product meets established guidelines.

Viscusi (1984, 1985a) provides a possible explanation for CPSC ineffectiveness, at least in the case of the protective bottle cap standard. The introduction of protective caps could create a type of moral hazard where consumers reduce their safety efforts with respect to the product in question. Parents may be less concerned with keeping aspirin safely away from their young children knowing the cap provides another layer of protection. Alternatively, the difficulty of removing the cap may cause some parents to leave the cap off the bottle entirely, raising the likelihood of a poisoning. Parents may also misinterpret the standard as providing more protection than the standard actually generates. The protective caps are more difficult for children to open, but they are not, as many still call them, "child-proof" caps. Believing children are unable to open bottles with "child-proof" caps, parents might be unconcerned with leaving these types of bottles in plain sight of their children or even giving them to their children to play with as a type of rattle. Finally, the reduction in care of the product in question might spill over to other products not directly regulated. Parents may make decisions on where to store drugs or other hazardous products collectively and the improvement in the safety of aspirin could lead some of them to relocate all drugs away from a fairly safe place, such as an out-of-the way bathroom cabinet, to a less safe place, such as a low-lying kitchen cabinet. Parents might also simply get out of the habit of taking safety precautions and so a mother who normally carries aspirin with a protective cap in her purse might not think about carrying another drug lacking a child-resistant cap in her purse. Viscusi refers to the possible impact on unregulated products the lulling effect of safety regulation.

Viscusi (1985a) finds no direct impact of protective bottle cap regulations on aspirin poisonings or poisonings from other drugs as these drugs became subject to the regulations. In the case of aspirin, although the proportion of aspirin sold in child-protective bottles remained constant, the proportion of poisonings from child-protective bottles rose from 40 percent in 1972 (the first year of the regulation) to 73 percent in 1978. The disproportionate rise in the rate of child poisonings from child-protective bottles is consistent with parents taking fewer precautions. Equally notable, the share of poisonings from open bottles (both child and non-child protected) rose from 41 percent in 1972 to 49 percent in 1978, a rise consistent with consumers replacing bottle caps less frequently after opening because of the difficulty of opening and closing bottles with child-protective caps.

In the regressions examining the impact of safety cap regulations on poisonings from other drugs and products, Viscusi includes both a variable to reflect the period when the product became subject to the standard and a variable reflecting the period when the drug was not subject to the standard but some products within the same product class were. For instance, manufacturers of analgesics were required to provide child-resistant packaging in 1980, but aspirin manufacturers were required to do so in 1972, so the second variable (UNREG) takes on a value of 1 from 1972–1979, and 0 in all other years. The coefficient on UNREG measures the possible spillover of higher safety in one area causing consumers to take less care elsewhere. Viscusi finds significant spill-over effects that raise the rate of poisonings from analgesics, internal antibiotics, psychopharmacological agents, miscellaneous internal medicines, and unregulated cleaning and polishing agents. In short, Viscusi finds no evidence safety cap standards reduce poisonings from directly regulated products, but does find evidence that the standards raise the rate of poisonings in unregulated products for a net reduction in consumer safety.

Offsetting behavior has been discovered in other situations. Peltzman (1975) examines the impact of NHTSA requirements to install safety devices in new cars and finds no impact on the highway death rate, although engineering studies suggest highway deaths should be 20 percent lower. He argues that drivers compensate for the decreased risk of death from an accident by taking greater accident risks. Rodgers (1996a) examines bicycle and helmet usage and finds similar offsetting behavior: an increased risk of an accident raises the rate of helmet usage and a decreased risk of an accident reduces the rate of helmet usage. In this instance, the behavioral response is not large enough to offset the direct protection that helmets provide and the overall chance of a head injury falls.

Viscusi and Cavallo (1996) examine consumer survey data to determine the likely offsetting response to the introduction of child-resistant mechanisms on cigarette lighters. The overwhelming majority of parents would continue to exercise the same level of care keeping the newly equipped lighters away from their children and educating them on their dangers, but about 12 percent of the sample indicated they would reduce precautionary behavior as a result of diminished risk expectations. Similar to helmet usage, the behavioral response of parents' reducing their precautions seems insufficient to outweigh the direct effective of the child-resistant mechanism lowering children's abilities to start fires and overall safety would likely improve. Nevertheless, the survey data indicate a fairly large behavioral response to the introduction of child-resistant lighters and if young children learn how to use these mechanisms more quickly or if parents' reduce their precautions more dramatically than initial estimates indicate, overall safety could fall.

The CPSC used the likelihood of offsetting behavior to modify its flammability standards on children's sleepwear in 1996. Since the 1970s, the CPSC had regulated sleepwear for children under the age of 15 to prevent death or serious burn injury from small open-flame sources. The original CPSC standards required garments self-extinguish after exposure for three seconds to a small open-flame ignition source. Several synthetic fabrics could pass the flammability test, but untreated cotton fabrics usually could not. After one of the chemicals used to treat cotton to reduce flammability, tris (2,3-dibromopropl) phosphate, generally referred to as Tris, was found to cause cancer in test animals and could be absorbed by children, garments treated by any chemical process largely disappeared from the market leaving synthetic fabrics as the only "sleepwear" option available to parents. Yet, many parents preferred sleepwear made from cotton or cotton blends to sleepwear made from synthetic fabrics and so they dressed their children for sleep in underwear, shirts, adult-sized t-shirts, or other cotton garments not subject to the flammability standards. Besides not passing the three-second standard, many of these garments were loose fitting and, therefore, children were more likely to expose them to flame and once exposed to flame the garment is more likely to ignite. With a tight garment, the close proximity of the skin dissipates the heat needed for a fire to spread (Rodgers and Adair, 2009).

The 1996 amendments to the flammability standard exempted all garments sized for infants nine months of age or younger and all children's tight-fitting sleepwear garments. The Commission felt that babies lacked the mobility to come in contact with open flames on their own and by exempting tight-fitting garments, parents would substitute away from unregulated loose-fitting, non-sleepwear garments to safer tight-fitting garments. The changes were not universally applauded, with some groups arguing that relaxing the nonflammability requirements would lead to more sleepwear burn injuries.

To analyze the impact of their standards' changes better, the CPSC developed in 2003 a new comprehensive data reporting system from U.S. burn center hospitals on clothing-related burn injuries. Rodgers and Adair (2009) examine the injury reports collected from the 92 participating burn centers from March 2003 to December 2005. Over the three years they study, none of the 475 reported burn injuries involved exempted tight-fitting cotton sleepwear garments, although 33 percent to 40 percent of sleepwear garments sold during the three years were exempted cotton garments. Excluding clothing for infants also appears to have not reduced safety at all. There were only seven burn victims under the age of one year and of these seven, only one was burned as a result of a small-open flame igniting his clothing. In this case, the infant was wearing a snapsuit, a nonsleepwear garment that had never been subject to CPSC flammability standards. Verifying the CPSC's initial concerns that the original standards might have been counterproductive, 17 of the 25 instances where a small open flame ignited garments used for sleeping, the garments were nonsleepwear apparel, such as t-shirts, not subject to the sleepwear standard.

Studies by Magat and Moore (1996) and Moore and Magat (1996) paint a far more favorable impact of CPSC effectiveness. Magat and Moore examine the impact on the rate of bicycle injuries from a series of bicycle performance requirements established by the CPSC in 1976 covering areas such as braking, steering, wheels, sharp edges, protrusions, and reflectorization. The standards were primarily aimed at children, although they also applied to bicycles ridden by adults. Using data from the NEISS on bicycle injuries and industry sales data and product-life assumptions determined by the CPSC, Magat and Moore construct monthly injury rates (per million bicycles in use) across various age groups. As their measure of compliance they use the fraction of bicycles in use manufactured after the date the regulations became effective. Based on regressions that control for seasonal effects, autocorrelation, and a time trend, the CPSC standards strongly reduce the frequency of injury for children four and under, five to nine, and ten to fourteen, but have limited impact on children over the age of fourteen or on adults. For the three affected age groups, evaluated at sample means, a 1 percent increase in the fraction of bicycles in use complying with CPSC standards reduces bicycle-related injuries by about 0.5 percent.[20]

The United Kingdom instituted bicycle safety regulations in 1984 and Magat and Moore (1996) find the standards significantly reducing bicycle injuries for children five to nine and 15 to 19, but having no statistically significant impact on any other age group. The impact of the British regulations is also much smaller, about one-seventh the size of the estimate for the U.S.

In 1980, the CPSC established a requirement that all new power lawn mowers display a label showing a hand with a bladelike object cutting into it as a warning to

---

[20] The Moore-Magat results should be treated with some caution, however, because they focused on the cases where risk went down over time.

consumers to not reach into the blade housing when the motor is running. In 1982, the Commission further required that every new power lawn mower come equipped with a deadman control that stops the mower blade from rotating within three seconds of releasing the control. Using much the same empirical procedure as in their bicycle study, Moore and Magat (1996) examine the impact of the two standards on power lawn mower injuries and find deadman controls significantly lowering injuries, but warning labels having no impact.

During the 1980s one of the major issues facing the CPSC was the supposed dangers to consumers posed by all-terrain vehicles (ATVs), vehicles intended to be used on trails or unpaved surfaces. The popularity of ATVs had grown dramatically in the 1980s, along with the injuries associated with their use. The CPSC viewed the three-wheel version as particularly dangerous and filed a complaint to have them declared "imminently hazardous" under Section 12 of the Consumer Product Safety Act (Heiden and Lenard, 1995). The case was settled in 1988 when the major producers of ATVs agreed to stop selling three-wheeled ATVs in the U.S.

Controversy exists over whether the CPSC had sufficient justification to ban the sale of three-wheeled ATVs. Rubinfeld and Rodgers (1992) use data drawn from the NEISS on injuries and survey data on ATV usage to calculate ATV injury rates and relate these rates to rider and ATV characteristics. They find, all else equal, the probability of injury is higher for three-wheeled ATVs than for four-wheeled ATVs, lending support to the CPSC action. Heiden and Lenard (1995) argue a mutatis mutandis comparison is more appropriate. Three-wheel models have smaller engines and are more likely to have been modified by the purchaser than four-wheeled models and these factors also influence risk. Using regression results that allow for some interactions among vehicle characteristics and evaluating the injury rate relationship at the respective means for each model, they find injury rates to be roughly the same. Rodgers (1996b) argues Heiden and Lenard's use of data compiled after the ban on the sale of new three-wheeled ATVs lowers estimates of their hazardousness because the publicity around their ban alerted users to their dangers, causing riders to take greater care when operating them. He further disagrees that the risk of the two models should be evaluated at different mean engine sizes. Under almost all assumptions, including allowing mean engine size to vary, he finds strong support for the CPSC ban on the sale of new three-wheeled ATVs.

A central question facing public policy makers in the area of consumer safety is the responsiveness of consumers to new information on product risks. Rodgers (1996b) study on three-wheel ATV risk provides indirect evidence that consumers do process information on newly publicized hazards and alter their behavior accordingly. In 1985, the year the CPSC first began studying the issue, the risk of injury from riding a three-wheeled ATV was 2.3 times the risk of riding a four-wheeled ATV, all else equal. By 1989, the year following the ban on the sale of new three-wheeled ATVs, the risk of injury from a three-wheeled ATV had fallen to 1.5 times the risk of a four-wheeled

ATV. Rodgers credits the drop to precautions taken by three-wheeled ATV drivers after learning of the potential hazards from the publicity surrounding the CPSC ban.

Rodgers (1993) provides additional evidence that consumers react to new product hazard information in his study of used ATV prices from before and after the ban on the sale of new three-wheeled ATVs. The ban did not prevent the buying and selling of used three-wheeled ATVs. From equation (9.8), the difference in the prices of two product grades should equal the difference in the expected damages of each grade (the probability of an accident or defect multiplied by the size of the loss). According to equation (9.8) the lower risk of four-wheeled ATVs (grade 1) should cause them to sell for a premium compared to three-wheeled ATVs (grade 2) and the premium should expand as the perceived expected damages from the three-wheel model rises. Rodgers finds four-wheel ATVs selling for $275 more than equivalent three-wheel ATVs before the ban and for $461 after the ban, consistent with the arrival of new information causing consumers to update their risk expectations. The Commission had released the findings of their analysis of the relative risks of the two types of ATVs earlier, but some consumers may have been unaware or skeptical of the Commission's conclusions. The publicity surrounding the consent decree banning the sale of new three-wheel ATVs expanded consumer awareness of potential hazards and made the Commission's results more credible. The price differential also appears to reflect accurately the actual differences in damages between the two models, indicating a reasonably efficient market. The difference in expected accidents costs between three-wheel and four-wheel ATVs is $120 per year. With an average life span of seven years and a 5 percent discount rate, the present value of this yearly difference is $560, which is only slightly greater than the estimated price differential.

Freedman et al. (2012) also address the issue of consumer reaction to new product risk information by examining the response of toy sales to the dramatic rise of CPSC toy recalls in 2007. From 2006 to 2007, recalls of toys rose from 38 to 82 and recalls of other children's products rose from 56 to 130, jumps of 116 percent and 132 percent, respectively. Recalls of household items, outdoor products, and sports and recreation products remained fairly constant over the same two years. The nature of the recalls also changed. Almost 49 percent of the toy recalls in 2006 were for choking hazards, only 11 percent for possible lead paint exposure, while in 2007, 52 percent of the toy recalls were for lead paint exposure, only 20 percent for choking hazards. In 2006, 76 percent of the toys recalled by the CPSC were toys manufactured in China, while in 2007 over 95 percent of the toy recalls were toys manufactured in China. The publicity surrounding the 2007 recalls and the resulting public concerns with safety ultimately led to passage of the Consumer Product Safety Improvement Act in 2008.

Using monthly sales data from January 2005 to December 2007, the authors find that product recalls have significant spillover effects on the sales of toys similar to those that have been recalled. Toy manufacturers with recalled products experience about a 30 percent decline in unit sales of toys similar to those recalled, relative to the other toys they produce. The result is consistent with consumers using the information of a recall to update their expectations about the safety of similar toys produced by the same manufacturer and suggests recalls impose significant costs on producers. The recalls do not appear to affect the sales of other toys produced by the same manufacturer. Consumers either do not believe that the recall provides new information about the safety of unrelated toys or because of the prevalence of licensing and branding in the industry, they do not realize that these other toys are produced by the same manufacturer. Recalls also affect the sales of uninvolved manufacturers that produce similar types of toys to those having been recalled. Consumers appear to update their assessment of the hazards for the entire product line, not just simply the products produced by a single manufacturer involved in a recall.

The studies by Rodgers and Freedman et al. demonstrate that consumers react to new information about product risks as expected. When consumers learn a product is more hazardous than originally believed, they update their assessments of expected damages causing the market price and sales of the product to fall. Moreover, as shown by Viscusi and Hersch (1990) and Freedman et al. (2012) the resulting drop in revenue from a product recall reduces the market value of a company. In short, market forces reinforce CPSC actions, which should magnify firm incentives to produce safe products. The results also suggest that new information about potential hazards would reduce the firm's revenue from the product-line in question and, perhaps, across all of the firm's product lines. Lost revenue and reduced stock price in combination with potentially large liability losses are powerful motivators for firms to be concerned with product safety, even in the absence of regulatory efforts.

9.6.3 Case Study: Auto Airbag Regulations

The automobile air bag was invented in the early 1950s as a means of protecting drivers and passengers when serious accidents occur. Driver's side versions were first introduced into some models of consumer automobiles in the mid-1970s. Automobile manufacturers in the 1970s and early 1980s, however, were reluctant to integrate wide scale use of air bags in their vehicle lines until the technology became more advanced and consumer demand increased for the product. Government requirements for air bags began when the 1984 amendments to the Federal Motor Vehicle Safety Standard 208 (FMVSS 208, U.S. Department of Transportation, 1985, 2005) stated that, by the 1990 model year, all new cars produced for sale in the U.S. must have a "passive restraint"—either a driver's side air bag or automatic safety belts.[21] Federal regulations became more stringent in 1991, with the passage of the Intermodal Surface Transportation Efficiency Act (ISTEA,

---

[21] FMVSS 208 also mandated a phase-in schedule that specified the fractions of each manufacturer's vehicles that had to meet the standard in the years preceding the deadlines. A similar FMVSS 208 regulation applied to light trucks and sport utility vehicles (SUVs) with a later deadline of 1998 for full compliance; however, that regulation was superseded by the earlier ISTEA air bags deadlines.

U.S. 102nd Congress, 1991), which required that all new cars sold in the U.S. have driver's side air bags by model year 1996 and passenger's side air bags by model year 1997. The law also required new light trucks and SUVs to have driver's side air bags by 1997 and passenger's side air bags by 1998.

The prevalence of drivers' and passenger' side automobile air bags over time appears in Figure 9.12 taken from Rohlfs et al. (2012). As all four curves in Panel A show, use of air bags was rare until the FMVSS 208 regulation became effective in 1990. After 1990, all four fractions increase sharply until reaching 100% at their respective 1996, 1997, and 1998 deadlines. In practice, the phase-in schedules and deadlines for total compliance were not binding for many auto manufacturers. Although automatic seatbelts remained an option until the 1996, 1997, and 1998 deadlines, focus group results consistently show that consumers strongly preferred air bags (Kramer, 1978). Air bags were primarily restricted to luxury cars until 1988, when Chrysler announced that it would phase in air bags for its entire fleet by 1990, a decision that it reported was primarily driven by regulations. The models for which air bags were adopted prior to the deadlines tended to be higher end vehicles (due to higher demand for air bags in higher end vehicles) and vehicles with higher production volume (due to diminishing marginal costs). Ford and General Motors lagged behind Chrysler, claiming that consumers were not willing to pay the higher costs. The Japanese manufacturers (who tended to target a lower-end market) lagged further behind.

Panels B and C in Figure 9.12 show steady increases in the fractions of purchased and registered vehicles with air bags over the entire sample period. The increases are slower and later than those seen in panel A due to the gradual introduction of newer automobiles into the population of vehicles. Hence, although 100% of vehicles produced in 1998 and later had dual air bags, the corresponding fractions were only about 61% of cars and 49% of light trucks and SUVs sold that year. By 2005, the latest year in the sample, about 66% of cars and 64% of light trucks and SUVs that were registered had dual air bags.

9.6.3.1 Safety Effects

To summarize the research framework of Rohlfs et al. (2012), let P_{iyt} denote the year t price of automobile model i from model year y, and let F_{iy}^{p} denote the rate of deaths in position p (driver's or passenger's side) per vehicle in a typical year for model i from model year y. $Airbag_{iy}^{Driver}$ and $Airbag_{iy}^{Psngr}$ are indicator variables for whether model i automobiles included air bags in the driver's and passenger's side production year y. Rohlfs et al. (2012) describe an automobile's fatality rate and price by the following two equations:

$$F_{piy} = \phi_{p}^{Driver} * Airbag_{iy}^{Driver} + \phi_{p}^{Psngr} * Airbag_{iy}^{Psngr} + \mathbf{x}'_{1iy}\delta_{\mathbf{p}} + u_{piy}, \qquad (9.9)$$

$$P_{iyt} = \alpha_{t}^{Driver} * Airbag_{iy}^{Driver} + \alpha_{t}^{Psngr} * Airbag_{iy}^{Psngr} + \mathbf{x}'_{2iyt}\boldsymbol{\beta} + \varepsilon_{iyt}. \qquad (9.10)$$

Panel A: Fraction of Vehicles with Air Bags by Model Year

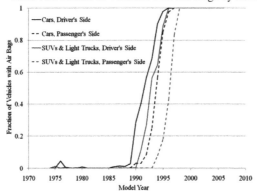

Panel B: Fraction of New and Used Vehicles with Air Bags by Year Purchased

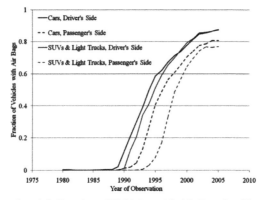

Panel C: Fraction of Vehicles with Air Bags by Observation Year

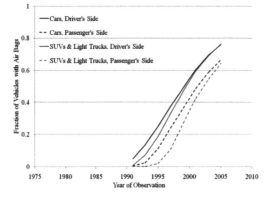

Figure 9.12 Fraction of vehicles with air bags by model year and observation year. *Source*: Rohlfs et al. (2012).

The parameters ϕ_p^{Driver} and ϕ_p^{Psngr} represent the effects of drivers' and passengers' side air bags on a vehicle's annual rate of fatalities in position p. Both ϕ_{Driver}^{Driver} and ϕ_{Psngr}^{Psngr} should be negative, because having an air bag in a given position reduces fatalities among those seated in that position. The parameters α_t^{Driver} and α_t^{Psngr} represent the increases in automobile prices associated with driver's side and passenger's side air bags, respectively. The t subscript indicates that these effects are likely to vary over time. The fatalities equation includes a vector of controls $\mathbf{x}_{1iy}'$ to capture other characteristics about the vehicle and typical drivers of that vehicle. The price equation includes a different vector $\mathbf{x}_{2iyt}'$ to capture other vehicle characteristics and observation year trends.

One concern when estimating $\phi_{Driver}^{Driver}, \phi_{Psngr}^{Psngr}, \alpha_t^{Driver}$, and α_t^{Psngr} is omitted variables bias. Because luxury automobiles were first and low-cost imports were last to adopt air bags, cars with driver's and passenger's side air bags probably had other features that made them safer and more comfortable than other cars. Additionally, individuals who buy automobiles with air bags may be more careful than average drivers are. To adjust for such potential sources of bias, Rohlfs et al. (2012) use a regression discontinuity strategy based upon model year. For each vehicle model in the data, there are specific model years in which the driver's and the passenger's side air bags were first available. By restricting the data to the model years just before and just after that year for each model it is possible to limit the sample to vehicles that are essentially identical except for the presence of air bags. The direct effects of vintage are controlled for with a quadratic in model year or fixed model year effects, depending on the specification. Additionally, many of the specifications control for model fixed effects. After controlling for the factors just listed, all of the variation in air bag availability is caused by some vehicles having been made just before the switch for that model and others having been made just after the switch.

Including $Airbag_{iy}^{Psngr}$ in the driver's side and $Airbag_{iy}^{Driver}$ in the passenger's side fatalities regressions allows for an over-identifying test of the validity of the authors' regression discontinuity strategy. The true values of ϕ_{Driver}^{Psngr} and ϕ_{Psngr}^{Driver} should be zero because an air bag does not affect fatalities in the adjacent seat. Estimating the parameters in the regressions in (9.9) and (9.10) makes it possible to determine whether the estimated coefficients of the two air bag variables are equal to the known values of zero.[22]

As noted, Rohlfs et al. (2012) recognize that air bags are generally correlated with other design features and that vehicles with air bags may be purchased by particularly safe or careful drivers. However, controlling for fixed effects corrects for much of the problem, and including fixed effects in the discontinuity sample appears to address the problem satisfactorily.

---

[22] Another requirement of the discontinuity strategy is that having an air bag does not affect the degree to which one drives safely. A preliminary analysis of the fatality data indicated that, when controls were included, having an air bag had no systematic effect on being the cause of deaths in other vehicles.

The authors' estimated coefficient on driver's side air bags range from −11.61 to −30.26, indicating that a driver's side air bag reduces the likelihood of a driver's side death in a given year by 11 to 30 per million. Estimated passenger's side air bag coefficients range from −2.482 to −5.601. Both the driver's side and passenger's side air bags' effects on "own position" fatalities are fairly stable across specifications, and neither changes in a systematic way between the full sample and the discontinuity sample or as controls and fixed effects are added to the regressions.

9.6.3.2 Willingness to Pay for Auto Safety

Given that air bags are effective at decreasing fatalities, it was also informative to measure how much consumers valued the reductions. Rohlfs et al. (2012) also estimate equation (9.10). Their estimates indicate that, in 1991, the premiums on driver's and passenger's side air bags were both large and positive, and the premium on passenger's side air bags was larger than that on driver's side air bags—possibly because passenger's side air bags were relatively rare. Estimated coefficients on $Airbag_{iy}^{Driver}$ range across specifications from \$2,020 to \$7,840, and all estimated coefficients on $Airbag_{iy}^{Psngr}$ are positive and significant, with values ranging from \$4,315 to \$7,700. The estimated changes in the premiums over time confirm that the premiums on air bags were large and positive in the early years of the technology when air bags were rare, and they declined in successive years as air bags became more common.

An air bag increases the value of a vehicle by reducing the likelihood of death over the remaining life of the vehicle. The authors let $\tilde{\phi}_{piyt}^{p}$ denote the effect of having an air bag in position p on the probability of death for the remaining years that the vehicle is used. While the regression coefficients ϕ_{p}^{Driver} and ϕ_{p}^{Psngr} measure reductions in deaths per year of usage, the parameters $\tilde{\phi}_{piyt}^{Driver}$ and $\tilde{\phi}_{piyt}^{Psngr}$ measure the reductions in deaths over the multiple years of remaining vehicle life. The two parameters are specific to the model (which influences life expectancy), model year, and the year in which the vehicle is being observed. For model i from model year y in observation year t, the cost per life saved by purchasing an air bag in position p can be expressed as $-\alpha_{t}^{p}/\tilde{\phi}_{piyt}^{p}$. Let VSL_i denote the VSL for consumer i, let $f(.)$ denote its population density function (pdf), and let $F(.)$ denote the Cumulative Distribution Function (CDF) of VSL_i. Both distributions are unknown, and the aim of the Rohlfs et al. (2012) study is to estimate the shape of the CDF, $F(.)$. In year t, the fraction selecting vehicles with air bags in side p can be expressed as $1 - F(-\alpha_{t}^{p}/\tilde{\phi}_{piyt}^{p})$. Hence, $-\alpha_{t}^{p}/\tilde{\phi}_{piyt}^{p}$ can be interpreted as the VSL for the buyer at the $(1 - Q_{t}^{p})$th point in the Marginal Willingness to Pay (MWTP) distribution.

In their main specifications, the point estimates of the VSLs implied by the hedonic prices on driver's side air bags range from \$13.0 million to \$18.5 million at the 75th percentile of the MWTP distribution, \$8.9 million to \$10.8 million at the 50th percentile, and from −\$9.6 million to −\$5.2 million at the 25th percentile. The value of auto safety, as revealed by the implied VSL in the middle of the distribution, is similar to the value of job safety, which is expected given that a frequent source of work-related accidental deaths is via motor vehicle accidents while driving at work.

9.7 CONCLUSION

Here we have discussed the forces conditioning how managers may guide the firm's safety and health determining decisions for jobs and products. The problem of achieving a safer society is fundamentally an economic one in that good safety policy decisions avoid waste as tempered by political realities of the regulatory process (See Viscusi et al., 2005, Chapter 2). It is also the case that safety regulation can effectively occur via optimally complementary litigation of damage claims for injuries from products such as asbestos, tobacco, firearms, or lead paint (Shavell, 1984; Viscusi, 2002a, b).

Programs or policies that overtly influence managers' decisions here are (1) information (product labeling) requirements, (2) workers' compensation or product liability (malpractice) insurance, (3) product or job safety regulations, and (4) tort lawsuits. Insurance, regulation, and lawsuits are direct economic influences on job or product safety because injury insurance premiums are designed to rise with injury claims and penalize hazardous firms, as do fines on firms found not to be in compliance with safety regulations. To the extent that workers successfully sue employers and the firms who make products or design processes that their employers purchase for the workplace that harm workers, then liability lawsuits encourage workplace safety too. We have seen, though, that workers' compensation premiums do not fully reflect the injury experiences of all firms purchasing the insurance and that it is not always possible to attribute diseases and illnesses to the workplace or product, so that they are not reflected in insurance premiums. Similarly, fines for noncompliance with regulations may be small or irregularly imposed and the regulations themselves may have little to do with removing what causes workers or consumers to become ill or injured. Although tort liability suits have come into play, they run counter to the desire to make injured or sickened workers or consumers whole without regard to fault and also run counter to the trend away from large damage claims in U.S. liability cases more generally.

The economic evidence is that the most important financial incentive for workplace or product safety and health improvements is implicit, operating through the matching of workers and workplaces or customers and products. The incentives for firms to adjust the safety and health aspects of the worksite or product will be made evident by a difficulty in hiring new or replacing separated workers or in selling theirs goods or services. A firm with too little safety will discover that spending to make a safer and healthier workplace (product) will lower wage costs (raise its selling price). Although managers will confront the costs of insurance, regulation, and lawsuits directly they must also pay attention to the implicit voice of the labor and product markets and the opportunities to trade off expenditures on safety and health against lower wage costs (higher selling prices) and, in turn, achieve greater profitability.

In looking to the future, new regulation will effectively occur via litigation of future damage claims for injuries from products and services such has been the case already for tobacco, firearms or lead paint (Viscusi, 2002a, b). Ideally, regulations will be proposed that consider the benefits and inevitable opportunity costs. Even if we ignore the benefit side of a regulation on the workplace or product market for any reason, including the emotional objection to valuing life extension, there is the reality that a dollar spent on safety in one area is not being spent in another area. (For a numerical example, see Kniesner and Leeth, 2004). This is an aspect of so-called risk-risk trade-offs (Graham and Wiener, 1995), which should take on greater importance over time as part of a continuing push to make government policy not excessively economically onerous on firms. The differences in lives saved across possible regulations is, for want of a better word, astonishing. Tengs et al. (1995) document 500 programs and how some regulations save a life at the cost of virtually $0, while others have astronomical costs.

In considering a portfolio of future regulatory efforts, policymakers will confront several issues related to interpersonal differences. Does it matter what type of death is prevented or is a death a death? Is it better for society to prevent a death from a terrorist attack versus a natural disaster or to prevent an automobile accident versus a terrorist attack (Viscusi, 2009)? Another interpersonal issue that will appear more in the future is that of forming regulations that take account of fairness, psychological, or macroeconomic concerns. For example, a bill introduced in Congress during 2012, "The Regulatory Freeze for Jobs Act" (HR 4078), would prohibit any agency from significant regulatory action until the national unemployment rate was no larger than 6.0 percent. The field of behavioral economics, which considers the empirical findings of social psychology as they relate to how individuals process information and make economic decisions, has had a growing influence in regulatory initiatives (Sunstein, 2001, 2011). Finally, an executive order by President Obama (Executive Order 13,563) reaffirms President Clinton's Executive Order 12,866 that agencies consider the values of equity and distributive impacts when developing new regulations, which will be the likely area of most immediate future interest to regulation scholars and policymakers.

REFERENCES

Aldy, J.E., Viscusi, W.K., 2014. Environmental risk and uncertainty. In: Machina, M., Viscusi, W.K. (Eds.), Handbook of the Economics of Risk and Uncertainty. Elsevier, Amsterdam. pp. 609–649.

Andersson, H., 2005. The value of safety as revealed in the Swedish car market: an application of the hedonic pricing approach. Journal of Risk and Uncertainty 30, 211–239.

Bartel, A.P., Thomas, L.G., 1985. Direct and indirect effects of regulation: a new look at OSHA's impact. Journal of Law and Economics 28, 1–26.

Biddle, J., Roberts, K., 2003. Claiming behavior in workers' compensation. Journal of Risk and Insurance 70, 759–780.

Boden, Leslie I., Ruser, John W., 2003. Workers' compensation 'reforms', choice of medical care provider, and reported workplace injuries. Review of Economics and Statistics 85 (4), 923–929.

Bolduc, Dennis, Fortin, Bernard, Labrecque, France, Lanoie, Paul, 2002. Workers' compensation, moral hazard, and the composition of workplace injuries. Journal of Human Resources 37 (3), 623–652.

Borjas, George J., 2010. Labor Economics, fifth ed. McGraw-Hill/Irwin, New York, NY.

Bronchetti, Erin Todd, McInerney, Melissa, 2012. Revisiting incentive effects in workers' compensation: do higher benefits really induce more claims? Industrial and Labor Relations Review 65 (2), 286–315.

Brookshire, David S., Thayer, Mark A., Tschirhart, John, Schulze, William D., 1985. A test of the expected utility model: evidence from earthquake risks. Journal of Political Economy 93 (2), 369–389.

Bruce, Christopher J., Atkins, Frank J., 1993. Efficiency effects of premium-setting regimes under workers' compensation: Canada and the United States. Journal of Labor Economics 11 (1), S38–S69.

Butler, Richard J., 1983. Wage and injury rate response to shifting levels of workers' compensation. In: Worrall, John.D. (Ed.), Safety and the Work Force: Incentives and Disincentive in Workers' Compensation. ILR Press, Ithaca, NY, pp. 61–86.

Butler, Richard J., 1994. Safety Through Experience Rating: A Review of the Evidence and Some New Findings. Industrial Relations Center, University of Minnesota: Mimeo.

Butler, Richard J., Baldwin, Marjorie L., Johnson, William G., 2001. The effects of worker heterogeneity on duration dependence: low-back claims in workers' compensation. Review of Economics and Statistics 88 (4), 708–716.

Butler, Richard J., Worrall, John D., 1983. Workers' compensation: benefit and injury claims rates in the seventies. Review of Economics and Statistics 65 (4), 580–589.

Butler, Richard J., Worrall, John D., 1985. Work injury compensation and the duration of nonwork spells. Economic Journal 95 (3), 714–724.

Butler, Richard J., Worrall, John D., 1991. Claims reporting and risk bearing moral hazard in workers' compensation. Journal of Risk and Insurance 53 (2), 191–204.

Butler, Richard J., Worrall, John D., 2008. Wage and injury response to shifts in workplace liability. Industrial and Labor Relations Review 61 (2), 181–200.

Campolieti, Michele, Hyatt, Douglas E., 2006. Further evidence on the 'Monday effect' in workers' compensation. Industrial and Labor Relations Review 59, 438–450.

Card, David, McCall, Brian P., 1996. Is workers' compensation covering uninsured medical costs? Evidence from the 'Monday effect'. Industrial and Labor Relations Review 49 (4), 690–706.

Chelius, James R., 1974. The control of industrial accidents: economic theory and empirical evidence. Law and Contemporary Problems 38 (4), 700–729.

Chelius, James R., 1976. Liability for industrial accidents: a comparison of negligence and strict liability systems. Journal of Legal Studies 52 (2), 293–309.

Chelius, James R., 1982. The influence of workers' compensation on safety incentives. Industrial and Labor Relations Review 35 (2), 235–242.

Chelius, James R., 1983. The incentive to prevent injuries. In: Worrall, John.D. (Ed.), Safety and the Work Force: Incentives and Disincentive in Workers' Compensation. ILR Press, Ithaca, NY, pp. 154–160.

Chelius, James R., Kavanaugh, Karen, 1988. Workers' compensation and the level of occupational injuries. Journal of Risk and Insurance 55 (2), 315–323.

Chelius, James R., Smith, Robert S., 1983. Experience-rating and injury prevention. In: Worrall, John.D. (Ed.), Safety and the Work Force: Incentives and Disincentive in Workers' Compensation. ILR Press, Ithaca, NY, pp. 128–137.

Cohen, Alexander, Colligan, Michael J., 1998. Assessing Occupational Safety and Health Training: A Literature Review. DHHS (NIOSH) Publication No. 98–145. <http://www.cdc.gov/niosh/pdfs/98-145.pdf>.

Cooke, William N., Gautschi III, Frederick H., 1981. OSHA, plant safety programs, and injury reduction. Industrial Relations 20 (3), 245–257.

Crain, Nicole V., Mark, Crain W., 2010. The Impact of Regulatory Costs on Small Firms. Washington, DC: Small Business Administration Office of Advocacy. <http://archive.sba.gov/advo/research/rs371tot.pdf>.

Curington, William P., 1986. Safety regulation and workplace injuries. Southern Economic Journal 53 (1), 51–72.

Curington, William P., 1994. Compensation for permanent impairment and the duration of work absence. Journal of Human Resources 29 (3), 888–910.

Darling-Hammond, Linda, Kniesner, Thomas J., 1980. The Law and Economics of Workers' Compensation. Rand, The Institute for Civil Justice, Santa Monica, CA.

Dionne, Georges, Scott, Harrington, 2014. Insurance markets. In: Machina, M., Viscusi, W.K. (Eds.), Handbook of the Economics of Risk and Uncertainty. Elsevier, Amsterdam. pp 203–261.

Dionne, Georges, St-Michael, Pierre, 1991. Workers' compensation and moral hazard. Review of Economics and Statistics 73 (2), 236–244.

Dreyfus, Mark K., Viscusi, W. Kip, 1995. Rates of time preference and consumer valuations of automobile safety and fuel efficiency. Journal of Law and Economics 38 (1), 79–105.

Ehrenberg, Ronald G., Smith, Robert S., 2009. Modern Labor Economics, Theory and Public Policy, 10th ed. Pearson Education, Inc, Boston, MA.

Eisenbrey, Ross, Shapiro, Isaac, 2011. Deconstructing Crain and Crain: Estimated Cost of OSHA Regulations Is Way Off Base. Economic Policy Institute, Issue Brief #312. <http://www.epi.org/publication/crain_and_crains_osha_cost_estimates_are_way_off_base/>.

Evans, William N., Viscusi, W. Kip, 1991. Estimation of state-dependent utility functions using survey data. Review of Economics and Statistics 73 (1), 94–104.

Farber, Stephen, 1998. Undesirable facilities and property values: a summary of empirical studies. Ecological Economics 24, 1–14.

Felcher, Marla E., 2003. Product recalls: gaping holes in the nation's product safety net. Journal of Consumer Affairs 37 (1), 170–179.

Fishback, Price V., 1987. Liability rules and accident prevention in the workplace: empirical evidence from the early twentieth century. Journal of Legal Studies XVI, 305–328.

Fishback, Price V., Kantor, Shawn E., 1995. Did workers pay for the passage of workers' compensation laws? Quarterly Journal of Economics 110 (3), 713–742.

Fishback, Price V., Kantor, Shawn E., 1998. The adoption of workers' compensation in the United States, 1900–1930. Journal of Law and Economics XLI, 305–341.

Freedman, Seth, Kearney, Melissa, Lederman, Mara, 2012. Product recalls, imperfect information, and spillover effects: lessons from the consumer response to the 2007 toy recalls. Review of Economics and Statistics 94 (2), 499–516.

Galizzi, Monica, Boden, Leslie I., 2003. The return to work of injured workers: evidence from matched unemployment insurance and workers' compensation data. Labour Economics 10 (3), 311–337.

Grabowski, Henry G., Vernon, John M., 1978. Consumer product safety regulation. American Economic Review 68 (2), 284–289.

Graham, John D., Wiener, Jonathan Baert (Eds.), 1995. Risk vs. Risk, Tradeoffs in Protecting Health and the Environment. Harvard University Press, Cambridge, MA.

Gray, Wayne B., Mendeloff, John M., 2005. The declining effects of OSHA inspections on manufacturing injuries, 1979–1998. Industrial and Labor Relations Review 58 (4), 571–587.

Gray, Wayne B., Scholz, John T., 1993. Does regulatory enforcement work? A longitudinal study of OSHA enforcement. Law and Society Review 27 (1), 177–213.

Guo, Xuguang (Steve), Burton Jr., John F., 2010. Workers' compensation: recent developments in moral hazard and benefit payments. Industrial and Labor Relations 63 (2), 340–355.

Hahn, Robert W., Hird, John A., 1991. The costs and benefits of regulation: review and synthesis. Yale Journal on Regulation 8 (1), 233–278.

Halpern, Janice, Hausman, Jerry A., 1986. Choice under uncertainty: labor supply and the decision to apply for disability insurance. In: Blundell, Richard W., Walker, Ian (Eds.), Unemployment and Labor Supply. Cambridge University Press, Cambridge, UK, pp. 294–302.

Hansen, Julia L., Benson, Earl D., Hagen, Daniel A., 2006. Environmental hazards and residential property values: evidence from a major pipeline event. Land Economics 82 (4), 529–541.

Haviland, Amelia, Burns, Rachel, Gray, Wayne, Ruder, Teague, Mendeloff, John, 2010. What kinds of injuries do OSHA inspections prevent? Journal of Safety Research 41 (4), 339–345.

Haviland, Amelia, Rachel, Burns, Wayne, Gray, Teague, Ruder, John, Mendeloff, 2012. A new estimate of the impact of OSHA inspections on manufacturing injury rates, 1998–2005. American Journal of Industrial Medicine 55, 964–975.

Heiden, Edward J., Lenard, Thomas M., 1995. The CPSC's ATV risk model. Journal of Regulatory Economics 7 (2), 145–160.

Hermalin, Benjamin, 2014. Uncertainty and imperfect information in markets. In: Machina, M., Viscusi, W.K. (Eds.), Handbook of the Economics of Risk and Uncertainty. Elsevier, Amsterdam. pp. 263–384

Hirsch, Barry T., Macpherson, David A., Michael Dumond, J., 1997. Workers' compensation recipiency in union and nonunion workplaces. Industrial and Labor Relations Review 50 (2), 213–236.

James, Harvey S., 1998. Estimating OSHA's compliance costs. Policy Sciences 31 (4), 321–341.

Johnson, Joseph M., 2001. A review and synthesis of the cost of workplace regulations. Mercatus Center, George Mason University, Working Papers in Regulatory Studies. <http://mercatus.org/sites/default/files/publication/MC_RSP_RA-SynthesisofWorkplaceCost_010830.pdf>.

Johnson, William G., Ondrich, Jan, 1990. The duration of post-injury absences from work. Review of Economics and Statistics 72 (4), 578–586.

Jung, Juergen, Makowsky, Michael D., 2012. Regulatory enforcement, politics, and institutional distance: OSHA inspections 1990–2010. Towson University Working Paper No. 2012-02.

Kaestner, Robert, Carroll, Anne, 1997. New estimates of the labor market effects of workers' compensation insurance. Southern Economic Journal 63 (3), 635–651.

Kniesner, Thomas J., Leeth, John D., 1988. Simulating hedonic labor market models: computational issues and policy applications. International Economic Review 29 (4), 755–789.

Kniesner, Thomas J., Leeth, John D., 1989a. Can we make OSHA and workers' compensation insurance interact more effectively in promoting workplace safety: a numerical simulation analysis of hedonic labor market equilibrium. Research in Labor Economics 10, 1–51.

Kniesner, Thomas J., Leeth, John D., 1989b. Separating the reporting effects from the injury rate effects of workers' compensation insurance: a hedonic simulation. Industrial and Labor Relations Review 42 (2), 280–293.

Kniesner, Thomas J., Leeth, John D., 2004. Data mining mining data: MSHA enforcement efforts, underground coal mine safety, and new health policy implications. Journal of Risk and Uncertainty 29 (2), 83–111.

Kniesner, Thomas J., Viscusi, W. Kip, Woock, Christopher, Ziliak, James P., 2012. The value of a statistical life: evidence from panel data. Review of Economics and Statistics 94 (1), 74–87.

Kramer, Larry, 1978. 58% Favor Passive Restraints; Seatbelts Ignored by Public; DOT Finds Public Ignores Seatbelts. The Washington Post, Business and, Finance; D1. (August 31).

Krueger, Alan B., 1990a. Incentive effects of workers' compensation insurance. Journal of Public Economics 41 (1), 73–99.

Krueger, Alan B., 1990b. Workers' Compensation Insurance and the Duration of Workplace Injuries: National Bureau of Economic Research, Cambridge, MA, Working Paper No. 3253 (February).

Krueger, Alan B., Burton Jr., John. F., 1990. The employers' costs of workers' compensation insurance: magnitudes, determinants, and public policy. Review of Economics and Statistics 72 (2), 228–240.

Leigh, J. Paul, 1985. Analysis of workers' compensation using data on individuals. Industrial Relations 24 (2), 247–256.

Levine, David I., Toffel, Michael W., Johnson, Matthew S., 2012. Randomized government safety inspections reduce worker injuries with no detectable job loss. Science 336 (May), 907–911.

Lott, John R., Manning, Richard L., 2000. Have changing liability rules compensated workers twice for occupational hazards? Earnings premiums and cancer risks. Journal of Legal Studies 29 (1), 99–130.

Magat, Wesley A., Moore, Michael J., 1996. Consumer product safety regulation in the United States and the United Kingdom: the case of bicycles. Rand Journal of Economics 27 (1), 148–164.

McCaffrey, David P., 1983. An assessment of OSHA's recent effects on injury rates. Journal of Human Resources 18 (1), 131–146.

Mendeloff, John, 1979. Regulating Safety: An Economic and Political Analysis of Occupational Safety and Health Policy. MIT Press, Cambridge, MA.

Mendeloff, John, 1984. The role of OSHA violations in serious workplace accidents. Journal of Occupational Medicine 26 (5), 353–360.

Mendeloff, John, Gray, Wayne B., 2005. Inside the black box: how do OSHA inspections lead to reductions in workplace injuries? Law and Policy 27 (2), 229–237.

Meyer, Bruce D., Viscusi, W. Kip, Durbin, David L., 1995. Workers' compensation and injury duration: evidence from a natural experiment. American Economic Review 85 (3), 322–340.

Michaels, David, 2010. Testimony of David Michaels, Assistant Secretary for Occupational Safety and Heath, US Department of Labor, Before the Subcommittee on Workforce Protections, The Committee on Education and Labor, US House of Representatives, March 16, 2010. <https://www.osha.gov/pls/oshaweb/owadisp.show_document?p_table=TESTIMONIES&p_id=1062>.

Moffitt, Robert, 1983. An economic model of welfare stigma. American Economic Review 73 (5), 1023–1035.

Moore, Michael J., Viscusi, W. Kip, 1989. Promoting safety through workers' compensation: the efficacy and net wage costs of injury insurance. Rand Journal of Economics 20 (4), 499–515.

Moore, Michael J., Viscusi, W. Kip, 1990. Compensation Mechanisms for Job Risks: Wages, Workers' Compensation, and Product Liability. Princeton University Press, Princeton, NJ.

Moore, Michael J., Magat, Wesley A., 1996. Labeling and performance standards for product safety: The case of CPSC's Lawn Mower standards. Managerial and Decision Economics 17 (5), 509–516.

Morrall III, John F., 2003. Saving lives: a review of the record. Journal of Risk and Uncertainty 27 (3), 221–237.

Nader, Ralph, 1965. Unsafe at Any Speed. Grossman Publishers, New York, NY.

National Safety Council, 1994. Accident Facts, 1994 Edition. Itasca, IL: Author.

National Safety Council, 2012. Injury Facts, 2012 Edition. Itasca, IL: Author.

Neuhauser, Frank, Raphael, Steven, 2004. The effect of an increase in worker's compensation benefits on the duration and frequency of benefit receipt. Review of Economics and Statistics 86 (1), 288–302.

Ohsfeldt, Robert L., Morrisey, Michael A., 1997. Beer taxes, workers' compensation, and industrial injury. Review of Economics and Statistics 79 (1), 155–160.

Oi, Walter Y., 1973. The economics of product safety. Bell Journal of Economics and Management 4 (1), 3–28.

Parsons, Donald O., 1984. Social Insurance with Imperfect State Verification: Income Insurance for the Disabled. The Ohio State University, Department of Economics, Working Paper No. 84–27 (July).

Peltzman, Sam, 1975. The effects of automobile safety regulation. Journal of Political Economy 83 (4), 677–725.

Philipson, Tomas, Zanjani, George, 2014. Health risks. In: Machina, M., Viscusi, W.K. (Eds.), Handbook of the Economics of Risk and Uncertainty. Elsevier, Amsterdam. pp. 453–491.

Pittle, David R., 1976. The consumer product safety commission. California Management Review 18 (4), 105–109.

Regulatory Freeze for Jobs Act of 2012. H.R. 4078, 112th Congress, 2nd Session (2012).

Rodgers, Gregory B., 1993. All-terrain vehicles: market reaction to risk information. Economic Inquiry 31 (1), 29–38.

Rodgers, Gregory B., 1996a. Bicyclist risks and helmet usage patterns: an analysis of compensatory behavior in a risky recreational activity. Managerial and Decision Economics 17 (5), 493–507.

Rodgers, Gregory B., 1996b. Revisiting all-terrain vehicle injury risks: response to critique. Journal of Regulatory Economics 10 (2), 201–216.

Rodgers, Gregory B., Adair, Patricia K., 2009. Exemptions to the children's sleepwear flammability standards: a description of policy considerations and an evaluation of the effects on burn injuries to children. Journal of Consumer Policy 32 (1), 59–71.

Rohlfs, Chris, Sullivan, Ryan, Kniesner, Thomas J., 2012. New Estimates of the Value of a Statistical Life Using Airbag Regulations as a Quasi Experiment, IZA Working Paper, No. 6994.

Rosen, Sherwin, 1974. Hedonic prices and implicit markets: product differentiation in pure competition. Journal of Political Economy 82 (1), 34–55.

Rubinfeld, Daniel L., Rodgers, Gregory B., 1992. Evaluating the injury risk associated with all-terrain vehicles: an application of Bayes' rule. Journal of Risk and Uncertainty 5 (2), 145–158.

Ruser, John W., 1985. Workers' compensation insurance, experience rating, and occupational injuries. Rand Journal of Economics 16 (4), 487–503.

Ruser, John W., 1991. Workers' compensation and occupational injuries and illnesses. Journal of Labor Economics 9 (4), 325–350.

Ruser, John W., 1993. Workers' compensation and the distribution of occupational injuries. Journal of Human Resources 28 (3), 593–617.

Ruser, John W., 1995. Self-correction versus persistence of establishment injury rates. Journal of Risk and Insurance 62 (1), 67–93.

Ruser, John W., 1998. Does workers' compensation encourage hard to diagnose injuries? Journal of Risk and Insurance 65 (1), 101–124.

Ruser, John W., Smith, Robert S., 1991. Re-estimating OSHA's effects: have the data changed? Journal of Human Resources 26 (2), 212–235.

Sandy, Robert, Elliott, Robert F., 2005. Long-term illness and wages: the impact of the risk of occupationally related long-term illness on earnings. Journal of Human Resources 40 (3), 744–768.

Scholz, John T., Gray, Wayne B., 1990. OSHA enforcement and workplace injuries: a behavioral approach to risk assessment. Journal of Risk and Uncertainty 3 (3), 283–305.

Sengupta, Ishita, Reno, Virginia, Burton Jr., John F., Marjorie, Baldwin, 2012. Workers' Compensation: Benefits, Coverage, and Costs, 2010. National Academy of Social Insurance, Washington, DC.

Shavell, Steven, 1984. A model of the optimal use of liability and safety regulation. RAND Journal of Economics 15 (2), 271–280.

Shields, Joseph, Xiaohua, Lu, Oswalt, Gaylon, 1999. Workers' compensation deductibles and employers' costs. Journal of Risk and Insurance 66 (2), 207–218.

Sloan, Frank A., Chepke, Lindsey M., 2010. Medical Malpractice. MIT Press, Cambridge, MA.

Smith, Robert S., 1979. The impact of OSHA inspections on manufacturing injury rates. Journal of Human Resources 14 (2), 145–170.

Smith, Robert S., 1990. Mostly on Mondays: is workers' compensation covering off-the-job injuries? In: Borba, Philip S., Appel, David (Eds.), Benefits, Costs, and Cycles in Workers' Compensation. Kluwer Academic Publishers, Boston, pp. 115–128.

Smith, Robert S., 1992. Have OSHA and workers' compensation made the workplace safer? In: Lewin, D., Mitchell, O.S., Sherer P.D., (Eds.), Research Frontiers in Industrial Relations and Human Resources. Madison, WI: Industrial Relations Research Association, University of Wisconsin, pp. 557–586.

Spence, Michael, 1977. Consumer misperceptions, product failure, and producer liability. Review of Economic Studies 44, 561–572.

Sunstein, Cass R., 2001. Human behavior and the law of work. Virginia Law Review 87 (2), 205–276.

Sunstein, Cass R., 2008. Is OSHA unconstitutional? Virginia Law Review 94 (6), 1407–1449.

Sunstein, Cass R., 2011. Empirically informed regulation. University of Chicago Law Review 78 (4), 1349–1429.

Tengs, Tammy O., Adams, Miriam E., Pliskin, Joseph S., Safran, Dana Gelb, Siegel, Joanna E., Weinstein, Milton C., Graham, John D., 1995. Five-hundred life-saving interventions and their cost-effectiveness. Risk Analysis 15 (3), 369–390.

Thomason, Terry, Pozzebon, Silvana, 2002. Determinants of firm workplace health and safety claims management practices. Industrial and Labor Relations Review 55 (2), 286–307.

US Department of Labor, 2010. FY 2010 Detailed Budget Documentation. <http://www.dol.gov/dol/budget/index-2010.htm>.

US Department of Labor and Bureau of Labor Statistics, 2011a. Revisions to the 2010 Census of Fatal Occupational Injuries (CFOI) counts. <http://stats.bls.gov/iif/oshwc/cfoi/cfoi_revised10.pdf>.

US Department of Labor and Bureau of Labor Statistics, 2011b. Nonfatal Occupational Injuries and Illnesses Requiring Days Away From Work, (2010). <http://www.bls.gov/news.release/osh2.nr0.htm>.

US Department of Labor, OSHA, 2009. US Department of Labor Issues Record Breaking Fines to BP. <http://www.osha.gov/pls/oshaweb/owadisp.show_document?p_table=NEWS_RELEASES&p_id=16674>.

US Department of Labor, OSHA, 2012. Commonly Used Statistics. Accessed (July 12, 2012). <http://osha.gov/oshstats/commonstats.html>.

Viscusi, W. Kip, 1979a. Job hazards and worker quit rates: an analysis of adaptive worker behavior. International Economic Review 20 (1), 29–58.

Viscusi, W. Kip, 1979b. The impact of occupational safety and health regulation. Bell Journal of Economics 10 (1), 117–140.

Viscusi, W. Kip, 1983. Risk by Choice: Regulating Health and Safety in the Workplace. Harvard University Press, Cambridge, MA.

Viscusi, W. Kip, 1984. The lulling effect: the impact of child-resistant packaging on aspirin and analgesic ingestions. American Economic Review 74 (2), 324–327.

Viscusi, W. Kip, 1985a. Consumer behavior and the safety effects of product safety regulation. Journal of Law and Economics 28 (3), 527–553.

Viscusi, W. Kip, 1985b. Cotton dust regulation: an OSHA success story? Journal of Policy Analysis and Management 4 (3), 325–343.

Viscusi, W. Kip, 1986. The impact of occupational safety and health regulation, 1973–1983. Rand Journal of Economics 17 (4), 567–580.

Viscusi, W. Kip, 1991a. Product and occupational liability. Journal of Economic Perspectives 5 (3), 71–91.

Viscusi, W. Kip, 1991b. Reforming Products Liability. Harvard University Press, Cambridge, MA.

Viscusi, W. Kip, 1992. Fatal Tradeoffs: Public & Private Responsibilities for Risk. Oxford University Press, New York.

Viscusi, W. Kip (Ed.), 2002a. Regulation through Litigation. Brookings Institution Press, Washington, DC.

Viscusi, W. Kip, 2002b. Smoke-filled rooms: a postmortem on the tobacco deal. University of Chicago Press, Chicago, IL.

Viscusi, W. Kip, 2004. The value of life: estimates with risks by occupation and industry. Economic Inquiry 42 (1), 29–48.

Viscusi, W. Kip, 2007. Regulation of health, safety, and environmental risks. In: Polinsky, A.M., Shavell, S. (Eds.), Handbook of Law and Economics. Elsevier Publishing, Amsterdam. Chapter 9.

Viscusi, W. Kip, 2009. Valuing risks of death from terrorism and natural disasters. Journal of Risk and Uncertainty 38 (3), 191–213.

Viscusi, W.Kip., 2014. The value of individual and societal risks to life and health. In: Machina, M., Viscusi, W.K. (Eds.), Handbook of the Economics of Risk and Uncertainty. Elsevier, Amsterdam. pp.385–452.

Viscusi, W. Kip, Aldy, Joseph E., 2003. The value of a statistical life: a critical review of market estimates throughout the world. Journal of Risk and Uncertainty 27 (1), 5–76.

Viscusi, W. Kip, Cavallo, Gerald, 1996. Safety behavior and consumer responses to cigarette lighter safety mechanisms. Managerial and Decision Economics 17 (5), 441–457.

Viscusi, W. Kip, Hersch, Joni, 1990. The market response to product safety litigation. Journal of Regulatory Economics 2 (3), 215–230.

Viscusi, W. Kip, O'Connor, Charles, 1984. Adaptive responses to chemical labeling: are workers Bayesian decision makers? American Economic Review 74 (5), 942–956.

Viscusi, W. Kip, Harrington Jr., Joseph E., Vernon, John M., 2005. Economics of Regulation and Antitrust, Fourth ed. The MIT Press, Cambridge, MA.

Viscusi, W. Kip, Magat, Wesley A., Huber, Joel, 1986. Informational regulation of consumer health risks: an empirical evaluation of hazard warnings. RAND Journal of Economics 17 (3), 351–365.

Weil, David, 2001. Assessing OSHA Performance: New Evidence from the Construction Industry. Journal of Policy Analysis and Management 20 (4), 651–674.

White, Michelle J., 2004. Asbestos and the future of mass torts. Journal of Economic Perspectives 18 (2), 183–204.

Williams, Richard, 2010. A New Role for the FDA in Food Safety. Mercatus Center, George Mason University, Working Paper, No. 10-69, <http://mercatus.org/sites/default/files/publication/wp1069-a-new-role-for-the-fda.pdf>.

Worrall, John D., Appel, David, 1982. The wage replacement rate and benefit utilization in workers' compensation insurance. Journal of Risk and Insurance 49 (3), 361–371.

Worrall, John D., Butler, Richard J., 1985. Benefits and claim duration. In: Worrall, John D., Appel, David (Eds.), Workers' Compensation Benefits: Adequacy, Equity, and Efficiency. ILR Press, Ithaca, NY, pp. 57–70.

CHAPTER *10*

Environmental Risk and Uncertainty

Joseph E. Aldy[a] and W. Kip Viscusi[b]

[a]Assistant Professor of Public Policy, Harvard University, John F. Kennedy School of Government, USA
[b]University Distinguished Professor of Law, Economics, and Management, Vanderbilt University, USA

Contents

Abstract

Environmental risks may comprise the most important policy-related application of the economics of risk and uncertainty. Many biases in risk assessment and regulation, such as the conservatism bias in risk assessment and the stringent regulation of synthetic chemicals, reflect a form of ambiguity aversion. Nevertheless, there is evidence that people can learn from warnings and risk information, such as Toxics Release Inventory data, consistent with Bayesian models. The fundamental uncertainties with respect to environmental risks are coupled with irreversibilities, making sequential decisions and adaptive behavior desirable. Uncertainties over the benefits and costs of mitigating environmental risks pose challenges for any regulator, but insights drawn from the instrument choice literature can inform the design and implementation of welfare-maximizing environmental pollution control policies. The problem of mitigating climate change risks motivates a series of illustrations of how uncertainty affects policy.

Keywords

Environment, Toxic, Warnings, Irreversibility, Climate Change, Discount Rates, Risk, Dose-Response, Hazardous Wastes

JEL Classification Codes

Q0, D8

Handbook of the Economics of Risk and Uncertainty, Volume 1
ISSN 2211-7547, http://dx.doi.org/10.1016/B978-0-444-53685-3.00010-6

10.1 INTRODUCTION

Perhaps the most important policy area in which risk and uncertainty come into play is with respect to environmental risks. Health and safety hazards of course arise with respect to products and jobs as well, and financial risks pose potentially large welfare losses also. However, in these contexts there is usually some kind of functioning market that will foster incentives for safety and efficient outcomes. These market operations may be imperfect, and the incentives they engender may be inadequate, but the risk is nevertheless the result of some kind of market transaction. In instances in which these transactions are flawed, there are often ex post remedies in the form of legal liability for injuries, such as when the injurer is negligent.

The characterization of environmental risks is quite different. These hazards typically are the result of public exposures to risks, not voluntary market-based transactions. Even in situations in which market forces come into play, as in the case of a person who purchases a less expensive house in a polluted area, there is usually no transmittal of an incentive to the polluter, who generally is not a party to the transaction. Similarly, in the absence of specific laws or regulations prohibiting pollution, there is no duty on behalf of the polluter that would lead to legal liability for the pollution. It is, of course, possible to purchase insurance for many environmental hazards such as floods and earthquakes, but doing so does not affect the probability of the event since nature has no financial stake in the outcome. As a result, the range and scope of environmental risks for which there is some form of government regulation is quite broad. Indeed, as the review of environmental regulations utilizing the value of statistical life methodology in Chapter 7 indicates, there is more regulatory activity with respect to environmental risks than all other health and safety hazards addressed through U.S. government regulations.

Our focus here is not on cataloging the entire range of environmental policies but on articulating some of the key economic principles as they relate to the risk and uncertainty aspects of policies. We begin in Section 10.2 with a review of the general manner in which environmental agencies assess risks, followed by a detailed examination of risk assessment practices in the U.S. The methodologies examined in detail in Section 10.3 are quite general, though the institutional biases vary internationally. Though risk assessment practices would appear to be outside the domain of economic analysis, current risk assessment procedures embody policy-related decisions and implicit economic judgments. Situations involving risk are often characterized by differences in risk information. As a result, various forms of risk communication can also be useful, as explored in Section 10.4. Many of the most daunting environmental risks, such as climate change, are coupled with substantial uncertainties about the risk. Many environmental risks involve a latency period and, in some cases, such as climate change, also have effects that extend for many decades and even centuries, which influences the consideration of the benefits of mitigating climate change risks. Section 10.5 examines the uncertainties characterizing the benefits of mitigating environmental damages. Section 10.6 turns to the uncertainties in the costs of mitigating environmental damage, with particular attention to policy-related uncertainties. Uncertainties over benefits and costs pose potentially severe challenges when coupled with the irreversible aspects of environmental damages. Section 10.7 examines the economic frameworks that have been developed to address these issues. Section 10.8 explores the nature of policy instrument choice under uncertainty, beginning with fundamental concerns of the choice between regulating prices or quantities. Section 10.9 concludes by highlighting some open, pressing economic concerns.

10.2 GENERAL RISK ASSESSMENT METHODOLOGY

10.2.1 Hazard Identification

Much of the impetus for risk assessment stemmed from the 1983 report of the National Research Council, *Risk Assessment in the Federal Government: Managing the Process*. The report recognized that a key component of assessing environmental policies is "the reliability and objectivity of scientific assessment that forms the basis for federal regulatory policies applicable to carcinogens and other public health hazards." Such concerns clearly require the input of natural scientists. However, ascertaining how risks should be assessed is not an inherently neutral exercise and has a fundamental impact on how risks enter an economic analysis of an environmental policy. Our fundamental assumption is that government policies should be risk-neutral and that the policy objective should be to maximize the difference between expected benefits and expected costs. Individual risk aversion of those affected by the policies may of course affect the assessment of the expected benefit levels. Actual policy practices may be quite different than one would expect in an unbiased assessment. One cannot necessarily assume that the risk values used in policy analyses, such as the estimated probability of cancer from exposures to pollution, correspond to actual probabilities since often there are many judgments incorporated in these assessments. In effect, in much the same way that people may exhibit various types of irrationality, such as ambiguity aversion, the risk analysis process itself may incorporate policy perspectives that incorporate biases that distort the actual risk levels. Government practices consequently may institutionalize individual irrationalities (Viscusi, 1998).

Examination of the underlying components of the analysis is essential for making unbiased assessments of the merits of policies. If the economic analysis is confined to monetizing the endpoints, such as assigning a dollar value to the costs and the expected lives saved, the estimation of the expected benefits and costs will not reflect the overall benefits and costs to society unless the underlying risk estimates are derived from an unbiased evaluation of the probabilities and outcomes.

Because government regulators often assumed that regulation could make lives risk-free, a frequent starting point for risk assessments is to determine risk at the no-observed-effect levels (NOELs) and the no-observed-adverse-effect levels (NOAELs) of exposure to chemicals, where these levels are based on short-term, acute animal studies. To extrapolate these NOEL and NOAEL results to humans and to ensure a reasonable certainty of no harm, analysts then assumed that the safe exposure level for humans required that the threshold animal risk exposure levels had to be divided by 100. This factor is based on the unsupported assumption that people are 10 times as sensitive to risks as animals and that the heterogeneity in susceptibility to risk across the population may differ by a factor of 10. Conservative assumptions such as these will tend to systematically bias risk estimates upwards.

Hazard identification is the initial step before a substance is regulated. If a hazard is found to pose a nonzero risk, such as a risk of cancer, then it is pertinent to ascertain the magnitude of the risk, the expected benefits associated with reducing the risk, and the costs associated with such a reduction. To determine whether a substance is hazardous, environmental regulators rely on animal bioassay studies and, in less frequent instances, on epidemiological studies. Such epidemiological studies are less frequent because of the difficulty of accounting for the correlation of the risk exposure with unobservable characteristics and the complications induced by the long latency period for cancer. When combining the results of the studies, the U.S. Environmental Protection Agency (EPA) (1987) procedures give greater weight to studies that show a carcinogenic effect than those that do not, even if the studies are equally credible and based on the same sample size. Thus, the informational weight placed on the results is not independent of the implied risk value. Interestingly, this inequality of weighting of the results in which a greater weight is placed on the high risk estimate mirrors a common behavioral bias noted below in which individuals place a disproportionate weight on high risk estimates when the results of different studies conflict.

The categories of risk used for environmental carcinogens follow the National Research Council (1994) guidelines for risk assessment. Substances categorized as human carcinogens or probable human carcinogens are possible candidates for quantitative risk assessment. An intermediate category of possible human carcinogens, for which there is limited evidence of carcinogenicity based on animal data but no human data, are considered on a case-by-case basis. The categories for which no risk assessment is undertaken are those that are not classifiable with respect to human carcinogenicity, as when there are no data, or for which there is no evidence of carcinogenicity based on either animal or human studies.

10.2.2 Assessment of Dose-Response Relationships and Exposures

If a substance is carcinogenic, the next task is to ascertain the risk level associated with the exposure to the chemical, or the dose of the particular agent. As with the evidence determining carcinogenicity, there is heavy reliance on the results of animal studies for which adjustments must be made both with respect to extrapolating to humans and the variation in the risk for different dosage amounts. More typically, a study determines a maximum tolerated dose, after which scientists fit curves to the observed positive risk level and associated dose based on assumptions about the shape of the relationship. This curve could be linear starting at the origin, or it could have a threshold exposure amount below which the risk is zero, or there could be a nonzero background risk and consequently a positive intercept. The dose–response relationships are usually taken as given components in the economic analysis of a policy's benefits, but should not necessarily be regarded as unbiased assessments of the risk.

The pertinent dose amount depends on the estimated risk exposure (EPA, 1992). Determining the risk exposure involves multiple components. Consider the risk exposure assessment for a particular individual. How is the person exposed to the risk? In the case of hazardous waste sites, the exposure could be through the air that the person breathes, water that the person drinks or that comes in contact with the skin such as while bathing, dirt that has dermal contact or is eaten, or food such as fish that has been contaminated by the pollutant. These different means of exposure to risk are generally characterized as risk pathways. For any given risk pathway, the next task is to determine how much exposure the person has to the chemical and how often the exposure occurs. What is the concentration of the chemical? What is the frequency and duration of the exposure? What is the body uptake from these exposures? These amounts will vary across the population and possibly with respect to different environmental conditions, such as what part of the hazardous waste site is associated with the risk exposure.

10.2.3 Risk Estimation

In some environmental contexts, the key risk value of policy purposes is the probability of an adverse outcome, such as the probability of cancer (EPA, 1996; European Commission, 1996). In the case of EPA hazardous waste policies, the probability of cancer alone is a trigger for policy remedies (Hamilton and Viscusi, 1999). In particular, if the hazardous waste site poses a lifetime excess cancer risk above 10e-4, then cleanup of the site is warranted. In the case of sites for which the cumulative lifetime excess cancer risk is in the range of 10e-6 to 10e-4 or the site poses a relatively great noncancer risk value (i.e., a noncarcinogenic hazard quotient, or relative risk level, above 1), then remedial action is discretionary. For sites posing cancer risks below 10e-6 and relative noncancer risk levels below 1, cleanup action is not warranted. Thus, a cleanup decision can be dictated by risk probability levels wholly apart from estimation of the expected benefits and costs of cleanup.

In regulatory contexts subject to more formal policy tests of economic attractiveness, such as those associated with major new rulemakings, the assessed probabilities are coupled with outcomes associated with these probabilities. The correct calculation of the risk amount for valuation purposes is straightforward. Multiplying the probabilities of different possible outcomes by the associated outcome, such as the number of lives saved in that state of the world, produces the expected risk level. What is reported in practice may not, however, correspond to the expected risk but more often pertains to an upper bound value on the risk that is characterized as the risk estimation.

The incorporation of upward biases in risk estimation poses challenges both for policy evaluation but also for risk communication. If the analysis yields an overestimate of the risk, then communicating that information to the public will not foster more accurate risk beliefs. In situations where it is possible for the public to assess the accuracy of the information, overstatements of the risk may jeopardize the long-run credibility of the government agency.

10.3 RISK ASSESSMENT POLICY ISSUES

10.3.1 Risk Assessment for Hazardous Waste Sites Case Study

It is frequently noted that government risk practices incorporate a variety of conservatism assumptions that may affect policy assessments (Nichols and Zeckhauser, 1986). Such assumptions distort policymaking so that there is typically no way to ascertain how a precisely estimated risk compares to an uncertain risk that has been the subject of various conservatism biases. Understanding how these conservatism assumptions arise and the extent of the biases resulting from these assumptions is exemplified by considering hazardous waste cleanup policies as a case study. For concreteness consider the pathway involving ingestion of contaminated dirt. Because the risk calculation includes multiple components, there are multiple ways in which distortions in risk assessment can be introduced.

The lifetime excess cancer risk (LECR) is given by the product of five variables divided by the product of two variables:

$$LECR = (ED \times EF \times IR \times CC \times TOX)/(BW \times AT), \qquad (10.1)$$

where
    ED = exposure duration,
    EF = exposure frequency,
    IR = ingestion rate,
    CC = contaminant concentration,
    TOX = toxicity,
    BW = body weight and
    AT = averaging time.

The two numbers in the denominator are unbiased estimates, or population means. However, each of the five numbers in the numerator is some kind of upper bound value. The particular nature of the upper bound varies. In some instances in which the distribution of the variable across the population can be determined from the literature, the upper bound of the 95th percentile is often used in the calculation. In other cases, such as contaminant concentration, the worst-case concentration at the site serves as the value of the variable. Note too that the toxicity assumption, or the dose-response relationship, is an upper bound value as well, but by no means the only upper bound value in the analysis.

The result is that the conservatism biases are compounded. Suppose that the risk level is the product of a series of independent and identically distributed lognormal parameters (Burmaster and Harris, 1993; Cullen, 1994). Even with only three such variables for which the 95th percentile is used in the calculation, the risk estimate would not be at the 95th percentile but at the 99.78^{th} percentile of the risk distribution. With four parameters, the risk estimate is at the 99.95^{th} percentile of the risk distribution. Using Monte Carlo techniques to analyze 85 hazardous waste sites, and assuming both independence of the parameters and adjusting for all components other than the toxicity value, for over two-thirds of the sites the risk estimates were at the 99th percentile or higher (Viscusi et al., 1997). The extent of the overestimation of the risk is roughly two orders of magnitude without also accounting for the upward bias in the dose-response relationships.

10.3.2 Precautionary Principles

The types of conservatism biases incorporated in risk assessment practices are consistent with various formulations of precautionary principles. There are many manifestations of precautionary principles that have been suggested for environmental regulations. In the extreme case, the precautionary principle could take the form of requiring that a product or technology be proven to be safe before it can be introduced. Such a formulation creates a bias against new technologies and is also inconsistent with the nature of classical statistical hypothesis testing in which it is possible not to reject the null hypothesis of zero risk at some given level of confidence, but it is not possible to prove that a particular risk exposure entails zero risk.

Sound economic formulations of the precautionary principle, such as those in Gollier and Treich (2003), draw on the option value literature in their conceptualizations. The precautionary principle embodies an approach in which decisions are viewed as sequential decisions rather than single period optimizations. In such contexts, information acquisition and adjustment is feasible. Following Arrow and Fisher (1974) and Henry (1974), investing with no chance of dis-investing is often undesirable, as preserving flexibility for future decisions is often preferable to undertaking an irreversible decision now.

A particularly useful distinction drawn by Gollier and Treich (2003) is between prevention and precaution. Actions that serve as a form of prevention decrease the risk at any given time, where the analyst assumes that there is a stable probability distribution.

In contrast, precautions are temporary, flexible measures designed to take advantage of learning about the scientific uncertainties. Their general result is that a precautionary approach will tend to leave open the option of reconsidering development and will favor flexibility in the policy.

While there is a well-developed economic literature consistent with applications of the precautionary principle, in practice the precautionary principle has been viewed as an alternative to applying an economic analysis approach that recognizes trade-offs between benefits and costs. Lofstedt (2004) reviews the policies in Europe, where Sweden instituted the most stringent precautionary principle in 1969. In short, the precautionary principle reversed the burden of proof for environmentally hazardous activities. Thus, a producer would have to demonstrate that the technology was safe before it could undertake production of the product. Other countries and the European Union have developed approaches that are less stringent and are more in line with Germany's less stringent "cautionary principle." The general cautionary principle guideline is "to prevent the development of harmful effects" rather than to certify the safety of an undertaking in advance.

Notwithstanding the softening of the precautionary principle, which occurred in part because of the threat that strict application of the precautionary principle posed to economic development, there has been a continued shift away from this approach. As Lofstedt (2004) chronicles, the principal alternative that has gained credibility is that of regulatory impact analysis. Such an application of benefit-cost analysis to regulatory policies need not be inconsistent with economic frameworks that recognize potential benefits from precaution, but they do not take a rigid, risk-based approach that is independent of the other consequences of a policy.

10.3.3 Synthetic and Natural Chemicals

A related form of conservatism bias is linked to the source of the risk. A prominent example is the treatment of natural chemicals as compared to synthetic chemicals. Because synthetic chemicals tend to be often new and natural chemicals are not, people may have tighter prior beliefs concerning natural chemicals than synthetic chemicals. Thus, aversion to synthetic chemicals can be viewed as a manifestation of ambiguity aversion (Ellsberg, 1961; Camerer and Weber, 1992) applied to situations involving losses. Such beliefs may not always be unwarranted if there is in fact learning that has taken place with respect to natural chemicals based on past experiences. However, such learning is often highly impressionistic, and it may be that the perceptions regarding synthetic chemicals are based on a form of ambiguity aversion rather than substantive beliefs. Alternatively, one might be able to de-bias people with respect to ambiguity aversion by indicating that an ambiguous lottery often can be converted into an equivalent reference lottery involving hard probabilities (Raiffa, 1961). Other types of persuasion may also be effective in overcoming ambiguity aversion (Charness et al., 2013).

The nature and extent of any biases in treatment can be examined by considering the results of tests of natural chemicals and synthetic chemicals for carcinogenicity. For each of these classes of chemicals, government agencies use the results of animal studies to ascertain the maximum tolerated dose of the chemical. Based on such tests, about half of all tested natural chemicals and half of all synthetic chemicals have been found to be rodent carcinogens (Ames and Gold, 1990; Ames et al., 1990). Such carcinogens are present in widely consumed products that would be judged to be very safe based on the absolute value of the risks that are posed. Roasted coffee contains more than 1,000 chemicals, and 19 of the first 26 that were tested were found to be carcinogenic (Ames and Gold, 1996). The risks that natural chemicals pose to humans are not less than those posed by synthetic chemicals, as the body's defenses against the risks posed by synthetic chemicals are similar to those posed by natural chemicals (Ames et al., 1990; Jakoby, 1980).

The potential for biases against synthetic chemicals is also borne out in regulatory policies. Viscusi and Hakes (1998) constructed a sample of 350 chemicals that had been tested for cancer potency. Using this sample, it was possible to control for the carcinogenicity of the chemical in terms of the dose that led to 50% of the deaths of the tested animals. Agencies varied in their bias against synthetic chemicals. For EPA and the Occupational Safety and Health Administration, the effect of cancer potency on the probability of regulation was equivalent for synthetic and natural carcinogens. However, the Food and Drug Administration placed disproportionate weight on cancer potency for synthetic carcinogens, which is consistent with the agency's approach to food additives under the so-called Delaney Clause, or the Food Additives Amendment to the Federal Food, Drug, and Cosmetics Act.

For this sample, it is also possible to estimate the role of risk potency on the likelihood of regulation. Other aspects of the regulatory context being equal, a higher risk potency score should increase the expected benefits of regulation. The principal measure of risk potency is the TD_{50} value for male and female rats, which is the quantity of the chemical when administered chronically that causes half of the rats in the sample to develop tumors. Lower TD_{50} values are associated with greater riskiness. EPA regulations are responsive to the risk level in the expected direction, whereas the opposite effect is observed for FDA regulations, which target risks that are less serious threats and involve synthetic chemicals.

10.3.4 Real Versus Perceived Risks

The analysis thus far has focused on objective measure of the risk. Thus, in the case of policies that affect individual mortality risks, the benefits consist of the value of the expected number of lives saved given objective estimates of the change in mortality risks. An alternative approach is to value the policy effects in terms of the public's perceptions of the expected risk reduction. Thus, the policies that would garner the most attention would be those that the public believed posed the greatest threats, irrespective of the level of the actual threat. Political pressures to regulate are more likely to be based on perceived rather than actual risks so that the political impetus for regulation may not be aligned with the actual risk threat. In much the same manner, government policy makers may be subject to the same kinds of biases and heuristics that have led to the public's misperception of the risk. Public opinion polls have long indicated a mismatch between environmental risks that the public views as the most pressing concerns and the risks that the scientific community views to be greatest.

Consider the following example, inspired in part by Portney's (1992) Happyville parable. Suppose that there are two equally costly policy options to reduce different risks. Suppose that there are differences in risk judgments. For concreteness assume that the scientific experts have perfect information, but the public relies on their subjective risk beliefs. Both risk experts and the public agree that option A will save 10 expected lives. For option B there is a divergence of judgments, as experts believe that the policy is relatively ineffective and will save only one expected life, whereas the public believes that option B will save 100 expected lives. The clear political favorite will be option B even though option A will generate more risk reduction benefits.

The policy choice ultimately involves a choice between addressing real risks or enacting policies that reflect the political will and consequently abide by the revealed preferences of the general public. According to the advocates of option B, choosing option B is consistent with respecting citizen sovereignty in much the same manner as economists believe that respect for the efficiency properties of markets respects consumer sovereignty. This analogy does not seem compelling since even in the case of market behavior consumer sovereignty is not absolute. If consumers underestimate the risk of a product, then there is a potential rationale for the government to regulate the product as risk levels in the market will be above their efficient level. Similarly, government policies can be misdirected by inaccurate beliefs.

A potentially sounder rationale for the perceived risk emphasis of option B is that there may be real economic benefits associated with addressing people's fears irrespective of whether they have a sound basis. The resolution of lotteries over time may entail worry and anxiety effects. Even if a risk is not real or substantial, those exposed to the fear of that risk may suffer a welfare loss. In addition, fear of a hazard may generate actual economic costs. If a person sells a house near a hazardous waste site because of an irrational fear of contamination from the site, then there will be transactions costs as well as possible actual welfare loss associated with the move.

One potential policy alternative to being restricted to option A and option B as perceived by the public is to address the fundamental source of the inefficiency, which are the inaccurate beliefs of the public. Doing so requires that the government undertake an effective risk communication effort to provide accurate information in a convincing manner.

The economic consequences of biases in risk beliefs and the potential for over-coming such biases are manifested by consumer responses to risks posed by hazardous wastes. Public opinion polls consistently place hazardous waste exposures among the most salient environmental risks. Similarly, there is evidence that the public tends to overestimate these risks (McClelland et al., 1990). This overestimation in turn leads to inordinately large housing price effects whereby the implicit value per expected case of cancer exceeds the usual range of estimates of the value of a statistical life. However, after the EPA releases its remedial investigation of the hazardous waste site, which summarizes scientists' estimates of the risk, this information generates a hous-ing market response whereby the implicit value of expected cases of cancer is of the same general magnitude as estimates of the value of a statistical life in labor markets (Gayer et al., 2000). Other studies likewise indicate that toxic waste sites (Michaels and Smith, 1990; Kolhase, 1991) and other environmental disamenities such as pol-lution levels and incinerators generate housing price effects (Portney, 1981; Kiel and McClain, 1995).

The appropriate cleanup of hazardous wastes should be based on efficiency concerns and reflect society's willingness to pay for risk reduction rather than distributive con-cerns (Hird, 1990; Caputo and Wilen, 1995). However, only a minority of hazardous waste sites reduce risks with a cost per case of cancer prevented of under $100 million, so that the cost-effectiveness of these policies is out of line with market valuations of risk (Hamilton and Viscusi, 1999). The disposal of low-level radioactive wastes is subject to similar inefficiencies (Cohen, 1981; Coates et al., 1994).

10.4 RISK COMMUNICATION

10.4.1 A Bayesian Model of Risk Information Processing

Information about risks can often foster better decisions. Better information improves public policy decisions, private firms' decisions, and individual consumer decisions. Information provision and disclosure comprises a large class of potentially effective environmental policies (Tietenberg, 1998). Policies in the environmental context may use information in different ways. Pesticides and chemicals may bear hazard warnings because the use of the product by consumers cannot be monitored, so that providing information may foster appropriate precautionary behavior. Some of these precau-tions may affect the individual's well-being, as in averting potential injury from using a dangerous product, while other warnings may be designed to protect the environment by, for example, fostering safe use and disposal of chemicals. Labels indicating the fuel efficiency and environmental impacts of new automobiles serve such a dual function, as they seek to convey information about the private fuel economy savings of more fuel efficient vehicles as well as the societal benefits that certain vehicles offer in terms of reduced emissions of carbon and other pollutants.

To analyze how information affects risk beliefs, consider the following Bayesian learning model. We assume the priors can be characterized by a Beta distribution (Pratt et al., 1995). Suppose the person underestimates the level of the risk and has prior risk beliefs p of the adverse outcome, where $p < p^*$, which is the true probability of the adverse outcome. The associated precision of the prior is γ. Thus, the prior is tantamount to having drawn γ balls from a Bernoulli urn, where a fraction p indicates that the adverse outcome has occurred. Similarly, let there be an informational policy that conveys a probability q with informational content ξ. Then, for a rational Bayesian, the posterior risk belief p' after seeing the new information is given by

$$p' = \frac{\gamma p + \xi q}{\gamma + \xi}. \tag{10.2}$$

There are several results pertaining to the effectiveness of warnings that are borne out in this equation. If the communicated risk q is the same as p, then the level of risk beliefs will not change after receiving the information, but the precision of the risk beliefs will increase, thus reducing the degree of uncertainty around the prior belief. Reminder warnings that do not convey new information have generally not been effective in altering behavior because they do not affect risk beliefs (Adler and Pittle, 1984). The credibility of the warning depends on the relative weight accorded to the information, or the ratio of ξ to γ. The information has greater effect on risk beliefs as the relative credibility increases. Situations in which people have very tight prior beliefs, or in this notation, very large values of γ, are less susceptible to being influenced by informational policies.

Application of this framework to patterns of risk beliefs also predicts the observed biases in mortality risk beliefs. Suppose people have prior risk beliefs p that are the same for all different kinds of death. Thus, in the absence of information, the risk belief is p, which would be the vertical intercept on a curve linking perceived risks to actual risks. Suppose that for each cause of death people receive the same amount of information about the pertinent risk q. Then the slope of the linear relationship between perceived and actual risks will be given by $\xi/(\gamma + \xi) < 1$. In contrast, the 45-degree line for which perceived risks equal actual risks has a slope of 1.0 so that Bayesian beliefs with respect to risks will generate the established pattern of overestimation of small risks and underestimation of large risks.

The Bayesian model can be modified to incorporate ambiguity aversion. Suppose the risk p' is that of an adverse outcome. Thus, for income y, there are two possible outcomes, being healthy with utility $u(y)$ and being injured or dead with utility function $v(y)$. With standard expected utility models, the expected utility after receiving the information is $(1-p')u(y) + p'v(y)$. However, suppose that with ambiguity aversion there is an ambiguity aversion effect $a(p, \gamma, q, \xi)$ that reduces the assessed probability of a favorable outcome but does not affect the assessed probability of an unfavorable outcome. Thus, expected utility EU with ambiguity aversion is consistent with both the aversion to ambiguous chances of winning a prize in the Ellsberg experiment and ambiguity aversion in situations in which there is the chance of a loss. Then EU is given by

$$EU = (1 - p' - a(p, \gamma, q, \xi)) \, u(\gamma) + p' v(\gamma). \tag{10.3}$$

Estimates of this model for ambiguous environmental risks by Viscusi and Magat (1992) found that ambiguity aversion increased with the spread of the risk range, or the difference between p and q, but at a diminishing rate.

Whether behavior is ambiguity averse or ambiguity seeking with respect to losses depends on the characteristics of the ambiguous lottery. In a study of business owners and managers, Viscusi and Chesson (1999) found that for low probabilities of catastrophic storm damage, subjects were ambiguity averse, but for extremely high probabilities, they were ambiguity seeking. To the extent that most environmental risks tend to involve low probabilities, one would expect ambiguity aversion to be the more common phenomenon.

These formulations utilizing Bayesian models to analyze the formation of risk beliefs in the presence of risk information generalize to situations of multiple information sources as well. Suppose that q_i is the risk implied by information source i, and ξ_i is the associated information content of source i, $i = 1, 2$. Then the posterior risk belief p' after seeing both forms of risk information is given by

$$p' = \frac{\gamma p + \xi_1 q_1 + \xi_2 q_2}{\gamma + \xi_1 + \xi_2}. \tag{10.4}$$

Thus, posterior risk beliefs can be viewed as a weighted average of prior risk beliefs and each source of information, where each different information source is weighted by the fraction of the total informational content associated with that information source.

The potential influence of multiple sources of information is often complex. Suppose that there are different information sources, such as government and industry. If equally credible government studies are the source of the risk information, then let the informational weight ξ_1 pertain to both studies. Similarly, if both studies are by industry, then let information weights be given by ξ_2 for both studies. However, if the parties disagree, then the information weight accorded to each source should be ξ_1 for government studies and ξ_2 for industry studies. However, the experimental results reported in Viscusi (1997) are inconsistent with this formulation. When two parties disagree, as in the context of a risk debate, people place a very high weight on the worst-case estimate and gravitate to this value when forming their posterior beliefs. This result is an extreme case of ambiguity aversion. When there are two divergent risk estimates, but from the same source, respondents tend to report posterior values just above the midpoint of the range, consistent with ambiguity aversion. Interestingly, the public risk debate over nuclear power in Taiwan did not reduce the public's alarmist assessment of the risk (Liu and Smith, 1990), which also is consistent with people focusing on worst-case estimates in the presence of a risk debate.

10.4.2 Warnings Policies

A well-established form of information provision is the use of warnings policies. Informational efforts of this type are particularly valuable for dealing with environmental risks, many of which involve low probabilities that are not well understood (Camerer and Kunreuther, 1989). In many cases, the warnings are on-product warnings. Linking the warning to the product, as done for warnings on containers for household chemicals and pesticides, facilitates the receipt and processing of the warning message in conjunction with use of the product. In other contexts, such as warnings of impending natural disasters, the warning may be through the media. Because responses to warnings are voluntary, they are sometimes accompanied by mandatory requirements, such as those with respect to evacuating areas if there is a catastrophic hurricane that is threatening.

Such mandates may be desirable since the evidence with respect to people's ability to adapt to information about natural disasters is mixed. There is some experimental evidence that people fail to learn adequately from their experience with respect to low-probability, high-consequence events (Meyer, 2012). Similarly, people seem to be better able to learn from experimentation with high-probability risks than low-probability risks (Shafran, 2011), which is problematic since many catastrophic events involve low probabilities. However, there is also evidence of responses to experiences with natural disasters that are more consistent with rational learning. In the case of risks from tornadoes there is evidence of housing demand effects with respect to variations in tornado risks across different areas in tornado-prone states (Sutter and Poitras, 2010). Tornadoes and hurricanes also induce both the expected housing responses as well as responses by insurers to perceived changes in the risk level (Smith et al., 2006; Born and Viscusi, 2006).

Although warnings are now an accepted part of the informational landscape, they have not always been the norm. In the U.S. the first law requiring the imposition of warnings was the Federal Caustic Poison Control Act in 1927. This Act required on-product "Poison" warnings for 12 very dangerous chemicals, including hydrochloric acid and sulfuric acid. The next major warnings policy was the Federal Food, Drug, and Cosmetic Act in 1938. This Act imposed warnings on prescription drugs to indicate any adverse reactions and possible drug interactions.

The first specifically environmental warnings followed the passage of the Federal Insecticide, Fungicide, and Rodenticide Act in 1947. After the passage of this law, insecticides and herbicides were required to have hazard warning labeling. These warnings requirements have continued to the current time. Firms submit draft warning labels to EPA for approval so that all labels are reviewed by the agency but there is no required standardization of formats. The passage of the Federal Hazardous Substance Labeling Act in 1960 extended the domain of warnings policies to include substances that are flammable or radioactive. The law also specifies the use of human hazard signal words, "Danger," "Warning," and "Caution."

In 1966, cigarettes became the first consumer product to bear a warning for risks that arise from a product even if used in the manner that the manufacturer intended. There have been changes in cigarette warnings over time, as they now include warnings about risks to others with respect to environmental tobacco smoke and risks to the baby if the mother smokes during pregnancy.

The 1980s marked a major shift in warnings efforts with the emergence of various "right-to-know" efforts. In 1983 the Occupational Safety and Health Administration issued its hazard communication regulation that for the first time required the labeling of dangerous chemicals in the workplace, other than the aforementioned 12 most dangerous chemicals. EPA began disseminating information regarding toxic exposures, so that broadly based environmental hazards also became the focus of the informational efforts.

A general economic purpose of such warnings efforts is to foster more accurate risk beliefs. Particularly for hazards that are not well known, people may underestimate the risk, so that $p < p^*$. However, for many risks that are known and highly publicized, people may exhibit a tendency to overestimate the risk. In the case of mortality risks of death, empirical evidence suggests that people overestimate small risks of death, such as risks from being killed by a tornado or a hurricane, and underestimate the much more serious risks of death, such as the chance of dying due to a stroke or heart disease (Lichtenstein et al., 1978). A similar characterization of risk beliefs in which small probabilities are overestimated and large probabilities are underestimated is incorporated as an assumption in Kahneman and Tversky's (1979) prospect theory.

Such a pattern of biases in risk beliefs has two additional consequences. First, if people overestimate small probabilities, then reducing the probability to zero will have an effect on the risk belief that is greater than the actual reduction of the risk. Thus, there is a certainty premium for the elimination of a risk. Second, to the extent that the risk belief function flattens the relationship between the perceived probability and the actual probability, the incremental benefits of taking precautionary actions will be reduced.

The accuracy of risk beliefs also varies with different environmental contexts. Kunreuther et al. (1978) found that people underestimated the risk of many natural disasters and failed to purchase adequate insurance. In contrast, the discovery that the bottled water Perrier contained benzene led to a recall of the product and a dramatic reduction in Perrier's market position. Highly publicized risks associated with hazardous waste sites may have an inordinate effect on house prices (McClelland et al., 1990) that is far out of proportion with the actual extent of the risk.

Whether warnings foster more accurate risk beliefs depends in part on the nature of the warnings message. Few warnings convey probabilistic information, and the provision of any quantitative information remains fairly unusual. When quantitative information is provided, it is often only partial. Thus, people may be informed that m people in a population of n people are killed by an environmental exposure, but unless they know the denominator n, or the number of people exposed to the risk, it is not feasible to construct the risk probability m/n that corresponds to the risk probability.

It is common for public risk information efforts to communicate only the numerator, such as the number of people killed due to a specific class of risks. However, doing so creates the potential for highly distorted risk beliefs. In situations in which the denominator is not communicated, there tend to be biases in subsequent risk beliefs. When the exposed population is small, people may underestimate the risk when presented with information about the numerator alone, but when the exposed population is very large there is a well-established tendency of denominator blindness whereby people subsequently overestimate the risk level (Viscusi and Zeckhauser, 2004). Accomplishing the ultimate objective of leading people to have accurate beliefs is often difficult given the challenges that communicating and processing risk information often present.

10.4.3 Cognitive Factors and Information Processing

The manner and extent to which a person processes warning information is dependent on the person's cognitive abilities. Even if the warning is received and read, it nevertheless may not be understood and may not affect the person's risk beliefs. If there were no cognitive limits, one could provide people with estimates of carcinogenicity from the scientific literature and let them make their own risk assessments. Wholly apart from issues pertaining to lacking the requisite scientific background, such a risk communication approach would exceed the person's ability and willingness to process the warning information. As a result, most effective warnings are fairly concise and easily understood.

Experimental structures in which consumers gave responses to different warnings for chemicals and pesticides yield evidence of such limitations (Viscusi and Magat, 1987; Magat and Viscusi, 1992). The first form of limitation is that of label clutter. If there is too much crowding of the information with respect to the dimensions of the labeling space, the warning will be difficult to process. Once a warning is relatively uncluttered and in legible print size it will be possible to read and understand the warning. A second potential limitation of warnings is that of information overload. People generally are able to process up to four to five pieces of information from a warning. Very extensive warnings are less effective as people are unable to process the overall message. Appropriately designed warnings that provide new information can and do affect behavior, both for household chemicals and pesticides as well as for other environmental risks such as radon (Smith et al., 1988).

One can apply these considerations to the recently enacted EPA warning label to promote fuel economy and the environment. The motor-vehicle label is intended to inform consumers at the time of purchase of the characteristics of the car. For fuel efficiency concerns, the label provides redundant information in terms of the miles per gallon and fuel costs for trips. This information is targeted primarily at the consumer's financial self-interest. The environmental information is less concrete as there are relative ratings of performance with respect to conventional pollutants and the carbon footprint, though the relative weights and absolute impacts on the environment are unclear. Conveying the environmental information is more challenging because the consequences are societal benefits, not private monetary benefits. Moreover, it may be intrinsically difficult to quantify or compare the multidimensional environmental consequences of vehicle use.

10.4.4 Toxics Release Inventory

A large scale information dissemination effort is EPA's Toxics Release Inventory (TRI). As a result of the Emergency Planning and Community Right-to-Know Act of 1986, beginning in 1989 EPA made available information on chemicals firms discharged into the environment, where this information was generated by the TRI system's reporting requirements. The congressional voting in favor of this program was consistent with the district-level incidence of the effects of the program (Hamilton, 1997). The TRI policy served as an integral component of community right-to-know efforts that had emerged in the 1980s. Toxic releases do not, however, necessarily imply human exposures so the presence of releases is not tantamount to a hazard warning.

Whether making information about toxic releases available will be useful depends on the accuracy of the information. The reporting of emissions may be incomplete or inaccurate, but these do not appear to be serious problems with the TRI. Most of the failures to comply with the reporting requirements appear to be due to ignorance with respect to the program requirements and procedures rather than deliberate attempts to be evasive (Brehm and Hamilton, 1996). However, there is evidence that firms did not accurately report their chemical levels based on Benford's Law, whereby the first digits of the TRI data should follow a monotonically decreasing distribution (de Marchi and Hamilton, 2006).

Notwithstanding some inaccuracies in the data, the program generated informational content that was found to be valuable. As documented by Hamilton (1995, 2005), the main audience for the information often was not the general public but was journalists and investors. But for this audience, the TRI program provided new information as evidenced by its effects. There was considerable variation in both the coverage and consequences of the toxic release information. Overall, the stock market events associated with publication of information on a firm's toxic releases has led to significant negative abnormal returns. Worsening performance over time strengthens these negative effects (Khanna et al., 1998; Khanna and Anton, 2002).

Konar and Cohen (1997) observe that several different influences could account for this stock market effect. Firms with large toxic releases per firm revenue amount could have inefficient technologies. The large emissions also may trigger opposition to the firm by local environmental groups and may make the firm a more likely target of future government regulation.

A principal objective of the information dissemination is not only to promote awareness but also is to create incentives for firms to reduce their emissions, and to reduce the associated risks as well. That emissions might change in response to incentives generated by the market is not surprising. For example, Sigman (1996) found that waste management was sensitive to state tax levels. If an environmental disclosure program can create similar financial incentives, then one likewise would expect there to be an effect on toxic wastes.

In analysis of emissions in the form of air carcinogens, Hamilton (1999, 2005) found that as the pollution data became public, firms reduced their emissions, with the largest reductions being for emissions that posed the greatest health risks. The effects of TRI on voluntary emissions reductions also are more substantial in states with large environmental group membership, as these states pose a greater threat of mandatory regulation (Maxwell et al., 2000). If, however, the emissions pose threats to neighboring states rather than the state in which the plant is located, the political pressures are reduced and there is a weaker effect observed in such border locations (Helland and Whitford, 2003).

One component of the TRI effort is its 33/50 Program, in which EPA announced a goal of reducing releases and transfers of 17 target chemicals by 33% by 1992 and by 50% by 1995. Arora and Cason (1995) found that firms were more likely to join this program if they were large firms with substantial consumer contact. Participation is subject to selection effects so that conceivably only firms with low emissions or that were planning emissions reductions would join. However, Khanna and Damon (1999) found that the program did indeed lead to reductions in toxic releases.

Whereas studies of hazardous waste sites have indicated often substantial housing price effects based on individual home sales, analysis by Bui and Mayer (2003) of repeat sales did not find an effect of TRI reporting on housing prices at the zip code level. The housing price effects of listings in the TRI may be more localized and more directly linked to human health threats than is apparent at a broad level of aggregation. That there might be such effects is borne out in the analysis by Currie et al. (2013) of 1,600 openings and closings of plants that emit toxic pollutants. They find that housing prices drop by 1.5% when plants are opened, rise by 1.5% when plants close, and that effects are more concentrated close to the plant, such as within a one-half mile radius.

Other publicly available environmental information efforts likewise could induce a policy effect. For example, information about violations of drinking water standards will enable consumers to switch from community tap water to bottled water (Bennear and Olmstead, 2008). This information may be particularly valuable to the elderly and groups at high risk from contaminated water.

10.5 UNCERTAINTY IN ESTIMATING THE BENEFITS OF MITIGATING ENVIRONMENTAL DAMAGES

Uncertainty over environmental damages can take several forms, but can be simply described as unknown uncertainties and known uncertainties. In the former case, some environmental pollutants are not known to cause adverse health or environmental harm. Scientific research—on the properties of potential pollutants and on the relevant epidemiology—can reduce some of these unknown uncertainties. In some cases, environmental policy progresses without full resolution of such uncertainties. For example, the 1990 Clean Air Act Amendments established a sulfur dioxide emission trading program intended to reduce the adverse impacts of acid rain. Subsequent analyses that included more recent epidemiological scholarship show that while the program has helped reduce acidification of waterways and forests in the eastern United States, the economic benefits from reduced premature mortality, which were not considered in the design of the program, amount to as much as $100 billion annually (Schmalensee and Stavins, 2013). Other environmental policy interventions, however, represent cases in which the monetized health benefits are much smaller than the costs (failing on efficiency grounds) and smaller than the benefits of other, similar health policy interventions (failing on cost-effectiveness grounds) (Viscusi and Gayer, 2002).

Once an uncertainty, such as premature mortality risk, is known, then the question becomes one of precision in estimating the benefit of reducing the risk. This will reflect the distributions over key parameters in mortality risk reduction, in particular, the estimated dose-response relationship and the estimated value of statistical life. As the discussion in sections 10.2 and 10.3 illustrates, the dose-response relationships that represent the chain of events from emission of an environmental pollutant to a change in an outcome valued by an individual involve meaningful uncertainty. Efforts to estimate the benefits of combating climate change illustrate the significant uncertainty that characterizes the problem.

10.5.1 Uncertainty over the Benefits of Mitigating Climate Change

Consider an example of the various elements of uncertainty associated with the risks posed by global climate change. Billions of decisions made each day—driving a car to work, charging a mobile phone, manufacturing steel, harvesting crops, etc.—have an impact on greenhouse gas emissions. Over time, the flow of carbon dioxide (CO_2) and other greenhouse gas emissions may change due to population growth, technological change, and economic development. These emissions accumulate in the atmosphere, although some molecules will dissolve in the ocean or be sequestered in biomass relatively quickly and some molecules will reside in the atmosphere for thousands of years. The resulting increase in the atmospheric concentration of carbon dioxide will then drive changes in temperature, with a "*likely*" range of 1.1 to 6.4 degrees Celsius by 2100 (Solomon et al., 2007, p. 13; italics in original). The increase in temperatures will affect a myriad of outcomes, such as sea level rise, extreme weather events (such as droughts, floods, typhoons, etc.), agricultural productivity (with some gains and some losses around the world), the range of infectious diseases, ecosystem services, etc. over decades and centuries. The severity of these impacts will depend on the extent of adaptation (and perhaps geoengineering to offset the atmospheric accumulation of greenhouse gases), and the economic magnitude of the damages will also depend on the characteristics of economic development over long time horizons. Uncertainty characterizes each step in this process, and in aggregate, for at least some potential states of the world, it may not be possible to precisely *sign* the economic damages associated with climate change (Tol, 2009).

Economists have employed integrated assessment models in an effort to estimate the potential economic damages associated with global climate change. These models integrate information along each one of the points in the process from economic activity to greenhouse gas emissions to a change in the global climate to economic damages. A common output of such models is the social cost of carbon: the present value economic damage from the emission of another ton of carbon dioxide. It can also serve as the estimate of the marginal benefit of avoiding the emission of another ton of carbon dioxide, and standard benefit-cost analysis would suggest setting a Pigouvian tax on greenhouse gas emissions equal to the social cost of carbon.

In its recent review of the externality costs of energy production, the National Research Council (2010) reported that the economic damage associated with an incremental ton of carbon dioxide emissions could be on the order of $1 to $100. The NRC noted that about one order of magnitude reflects uncertainty in estimating climate change damages and about one order of magnitude reflects the choice of discount rate.

Tol's (2009) review of the social cost of carbon literature drew from 232 published estimates and found that the average social cost of carbon is $105 per ton CO_2 (1995US$) with a standard deviation of $243. The median social cost of carbon is $29 per ton CO_2, revealing the significant impact that large, adverse impacts have in estimating the mean measure. The 95th percentile in the sample of social cost of carbon estimates compiled by Tol is $360 per ton CO_2. The average social cost of carbon for those analyses employing a 3 percent discount rate is $18 per ton CO_2, about one-fifth the magnitude of the social cost of carbon for those analyses employing a 1 percent discount rate.

The U.S. government published estimates of the social cost of carbon for use in economic evaluations of regulatory proposals that affect carbon dioxide emissions (Interagency Working Group on the Social Cost of Carbon, 2010, 2013; Greenstone et al., 2013). This effort involved Monte Carlo analysis employing three prominent integrated assessment models used frequently in this literature, the DICE model (Nordhaus, 2013), the FUND model (Anthoff and Tol, 2013), and the PAGE model (Hope, 2011). A given model run (1) draws from a set of economic, energy, and population trajectories to forecast economic growth and greenhouse gas emissions; (2) draws from a distribution for the climate sensitivity parameter, which represents the extent of warming for a doubling of atmospheric carbon dioxide concentrations; and (3) draws from one of three discount rates, 2.5 percent, 3.0 percent, and 5.0 percent. Each model runs out to a distant time horizon, ranging between 2200 and 3000 depending on the model.

The U.S. government issued new estimates for the social cost of carbon in the spring of 2013. These revisions reflect only changes in the underlying damage functions in the DICE, FUND, and HOPE models made by the original model developers when updating their models to the latest understanding of climate impacts. There were no changes in the assumptions about economic growth, climate sensitivity, discount rates, or any of the other factors accounted for in the 450,000 Monte Carlo simulations undertaken in this updated guidance. With the updated climate damage functions, the average social cost of carbon for 2020 increased by nearly two-thirds from \$26 per ton CO_2 to \$43 per ton CO_2 (Interagency Working Group on the Social Cost of Carbon, 2013). This is more than double the median social cost of carbon of about \$20 per ton CO_2 for 2020. In this revision, the average social cost of carbon for scenarios based on a 2.5 percent discount rate is \$65 per ton CO_2, more than five times the average social cost of carbon for scenarios based on the 5 percent discount rate. Figure 10.1 illustrates the uncertainty in these estimates by presenting a censored histogram of the 450,000 model simulations; the full distribution of estimates extends into the tens of thousands of dollars, negative and positive, for the estimated social cost of carbon.

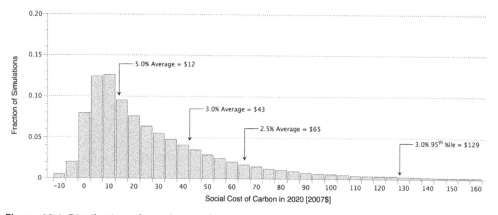

Figure 10.1 Distribution of social cost of carbon estimates for 2020. *Source:* Interagency Working Group on the Social Cost of Carbon (2013).

The Tol survey of the literature and these two U.S. government analyses, based on three of the most prominent models in the economics of climate change literature, illustrate much of the uncertainty that characterizes efforts to estimate the benefits of mitigating climate change. First, the estimated benefits vary significantly depending on the choice of discount rate (see section 10.5.2 for further discussion of this issue). Second, the estimated benefits vary significantly depending on the trajectory of future economic growth, which affects the extent of warming, the economic magnitude of damages, and the capacity for adaptation. Third, the estimated benefits vary significantly with the scientific relationship between increased atmospheric concentrations of greenhouse gases and warming. The representation of catastrophic climate change in integrated assessment models remains a challenge. Pindyck (2013) claims that a major flaw in the U.S. government's estimated social cost of carbon and in most academic estimates of the social cost of carbon is the failure to account for catastrophic climate change outcomes.

Indeed, it is uncertainty about climate sensitivity that has motivated much of the so-called "fat tails" and catastrophic climate change debate (Weitzman, 2009, 2011; Nordhaus, 2011; Pindyck, 2011). Weitzman's (2009) so-called dismal theorem suggests that the structural uncertainty that characterizes catastrophic climate change risks is "capable of swamping the outcome of any benefit-cost analysis that disregards this uncertainty" (Weitzman, 2011, p. 288). The risk of catastrophic climate change can be represented as the product of the magnitude of the potential welfare loss from catastrophe and the probability of the catastrophe. Weitzman notes that the critical question is whether this product goes to zero, implying that the probability declines faster than the growth in welfare loss, or if it goes to some large and potentially unbounded welfare loss.

Using Bayesian analysis, Weitzman posits an uninformative, scale-invariant prior distribution for the "diswelfare" of climate change, effectively a measure that accounts for climate sensitivity, the temperature increase associated with a doubling of preindustrial CO_2 concentrations, and the welfare losses associated with warming. Based on 22 distributions of climate sensitivity published in the scientific literature, Weitzman uses this information to update prior to produce a posterior distribution that is a so-called fat tail distribution (i.e., a distribution that has power-law tails).[1] The underlying uncertainty about extreme warming—in part because of the very limited statistical record about the historic relationship between atmospheric greenhouse gas concentrations and warming—effectively drives a "fattening" of the tail of the distribution in the Weitzman model.

Weitzman describes some potential states of the world with such high levels of climate sensitivity that the warming, on the order of 10 °C or more globally, could cause

---

[1] Nordhaus (2011, 2012) critiques Weitzman's construction of his posterior distribution by noting that it is inappropriate to assume independence across each published distribution in the literature given the correlations across studies in terms of underlying data and models.

some places in the world to become uninhabitable and cause consumption to decline to zero. In the standard constant relative risk aversion utility model, employed in several models in the integrated assessment literature, consumption declining to zero causes utility to go to negative infinity (for risk-averse agents with elasticities of the marginal utility of consumption bounded from below at one). As a result, the gist of Weitzman's dismal theorem is that the probability of a catastrophic climate event declines to zero at a slower rate than utility declines to negative infinity, and expected marginal utility effectively explodes.

Newbold and Daigneault (2009) and Nordhaus (2011, 2012) note that Weitzman's dismal theorem is not robust to variations in the functional forms employed to represent utility, consumption, and climate sensitivity. Nordhaus (2012) illustrates that the dismal theorem only holds when distributions are very fat-tailed and utility functions show very high risk aversion. Moreover, Nordhaus (2012) critiques the dismal theorem for lacking actionable policy content. Consider the Nordhaus classification scheme for tail dominance. First, a problem could be characterized by tail irrelevance: the distribution of a random variable that describes a problem does not influence policy or its outcome. Second, a problem could be characterized by weak tail dominance: the tails of the distribution matter, but a close examination of the tails results in an identification of optimal policy and outcomes (i.e., convergence). Third, a problem could be characterized by strong tail dominance: as one goes further and further out into the tail of the distribution, the preferred policy continues to change, and as a result there is no optimal policy (i.e., unbounded outcomes). In effect, the dismal theorem represents the problem of climate change as displaying strong tail dominance, without policy. Nordhaus argues that efforts to trim the tail of the distribution in order to avoid catastrophe, such as through geoengineering options that limit warming via the stratospheric injection of aerosols to reflect incoming solar radiation, converts the problem of strong tail dominance without policy to one of weak tail dominance with policy. Aldy et al. (2010) describe in further detail the potential trade-offs between very ambitious emission abatement and deployment of a portfolio of last-resort technologies, such as geoengineering and air capture to remove greenhouse gases from the atmosphere, as means to address catastrophic climate change risks.

Setting aside the issues associated with construction of the posterior distribution and the choice of utility function, the debate around the dismal theorem including the Nordhaus policy critique raises important questions about how society should approach low-probability catastrophic outcomes. How does society identify potential catastrophic events? More specifically in the context of climate change, what additional research could better inform our understanding of catastrophic outcomes (Pindyck, 2013)? Given the ambiguity in the climate science, do insights about individual ambiguity aversion inform consideration of societal ambiguity aversion? What are the implications for benefit-cost analysis and in operationalizing the precautionary principle of low-probability, large-magnitude events? How would alternative decision-making frameworks approach these questions (Millner, 2013)? How should society consider weighting the foregoing of current consumption to avoid uncertain, presumably low, but unknown probabilities of future catastrophic climate change (Summers and Zeckhauser, 2008)?

10.5.2 Long-term Damages and the Discount Rate

Damages over decades and even centuries characterize an array of environmental problems. The emission of ozone-depleting substances, such as chlorofluorocarbons, degraded the stratospheric ozone layer, which absorbs some incoming ultraviolet radiation and effectively reduces the incidence of skin cancer, cataracts, and various kinds of harm to crops and natural vegetation. Efforts to phase-out ozone-depleting substances represent some of the most impressive success stories in international environmental policy coordination (Barrett, 2003). Significant reductions in ozone-depleting substances occurred over the 1990s and 2000s and will deliver environmental and health benefits over more than a century given the long time that it takes for stratospheric ozone concentrations to return to preperturbation levels. Likewise, the management of radioactive waste from civilian nuclear power plants involves planning on the order of millennia given the long half-lives for some of the radioactive elements produced through the power-production process.

The challenge of global climate change also involves consideration of the very long term. Some greenhouse gases, such as methane, reside in the atmosphere for a little more than a decade, while some synthetic perfluorocarbons may reside in the atmosphere for millennia. The most common greenhouse gas, carbon dioxide, decays over a long period of time, with as much as 35 percent of CO_2 emissions today likely to remain in the atmosphere for 200–2,000 years (Archer et al., 2009). The very long time horizon over which greenhouse gas emissions accumulate in the atmosphere and affect the global climate has important implications for the estimation of the damages associated with global climate change. Indeed, this issue has motivated an extensive literature on the question of how to appropriately account for economic damages occurring generations in the future in any evaluation of contemporary climate change mitigation policy. While a full review of the issues in intertemporal welfare economics is beyond the scope of this chapter, we focus on how uncertainty about future states of the world affects how an analyst may calculate the present value benefits associated with mitigating distant-future climate change.[2]

A stylized example illustrates how uncertainty about the discount rate affects the estimated present value of a distant, future event. Suppose that a project yields $100 of

---

[2] For a review of the broader literature on discounting, refer to Heal (2005, 2007), Arrow et al. (2012), and Arrow et al. (1996). For discussions of discounting in the context of climate change, refer to the September 2007 symposium on the economics of climate change in the *Journal of Economic Literature*.

benefits in 100 years. Consider two equally plausible states of the world in 100 years' time, state A with a discount rate of 1 percent and state B with a discount rate of 5 percent. The present value of benefits in state A is about $37 and the present value of benefits in state B is about 75 cents. The average present value is about $18.50, taking these states as equally likely, but the present value of the average discount rate of 3 percent would be much smaller, about $5.20. The certainty-equivalent discount rate that yields the average present value of these two states is about 1.7 percent.

This example shows how uncertainty over the discount rate effectively reduces the discount rate over longer and longer time horizons (Weitzman, 2001). Over time, the high-discount rate state of the world carries less weight in calculating the expected present value because it effectively discounts itself toward zero faster than low-discount rate states of the world. Modifying this example for a project yielding $100 benefits in 200 years with the same states of the world would produce a certainty-equivalent discount rate of about 1.35 percent. As the time horizon extends to infinity, the certainty-equivalent discount rate will converge to the lowest possible discount rate among the states of the world under consideration (1 percent in this example). Thus, a benefit-cost analysis that accounts for uncertainty in the discount rate should average discount rate factors (e^{-rt}), which enter linearly in expectations, not discount rates (r), since discounted values are a convex function of the discount rate (Newell and Pizer, 2003b).[3]

Newell and Pizer (2003b) analyze historic interest rates to present an illustration of the effect of uncertainty over future discount rates on the present value of distant future events. The starting point for their analysis is that the discount rate is generally understood today (e.g., based on market rates for government bonds), but that the discount rate could change over time. They employ data for about 200 years on U.S. government bonds and assume that the historical pattern of changes in the interest rates on these bonds can inform and perhaps reveal likely patterns of future changes in discount rates. The estimated statistical models show persistence and uncertainty in historic interest rates. Based on the estimated statistical models, they undertake 100,000 simulations of three scenarios: a constant 4 percent discount rate (which corresponds to the average rate in their sample); a mean-reverting model that starts at 4 percent; and a random-walk model that starts at 4 percent. In each simulation, they estimate the present value of $100 at various points of time in the future. If the historic pattern over the past 200 years holds for the next 200 years, then the random walk model certainty-equivalent discount rate falls from 4 percent to 1 percent. Groom et al. (2007) extend on this work with a

---

[3] Gollier (2010), Gollier and Weitzman (2010), and Weitzman (2010) address the so-called Weitzman-Gollier puzzle: use the lowest possible discount rate for estimating present value benefits for very distant events (Weitzman) and use the highest possible discount rate to estimate the very distant future value of an investment made today (Gollier). They find that their two approaches are identical when adjusting probabilities for risk and allowing for agents to optimize their consumption plans. As a result, the general intuition in the example holds: the appropriate long-run discount rate declines toward its lowest possible value over time.

broader set of statistical models and find similar results. A recent panel of leading experts on discounting advised consideration of such reduced-form estimates of certainty-equivalent discount rates in setting a declining discount rate schedule for long-term environmental policy (Arrow et al., 2012).

10.6 UNCERTAINTY IN THE COSTS OF MITIGATING ENVIRONMENTAL DAMAGES

Mitigating environmental damages typically involves real resource costs characterized by significant uncertainty. Uncertainty about markets may affect the supply and/or demand for pollution-intensive goods, and the potential necessary scope and form of environmental policy. In some cases, the novelty of the environmental problem may raise questions about the costs and efficacy of new pollution control strategies under consideration by firms. The prospect of technological innovation, albeit uncertain, may identify opportunities to mitigate environmental damage. Substantial uncertainties associated with public policy intended to reduce pollution—on the timing, form, and impact of such policies—also affect the costs borne by the private sector.

10.6.1 Market and Technology Uncertainty

Firms and individuals make decisions in markets in the face of uncertainty about the returns to those decisions. The underlying source of the uncertainty could be related to uncertainty about technological innovation, uncertainty about the limitations and opportunities under public policy (whether it's environmental regulation, changes in the tax code, monetary policy, etc.), or uncertainty about the decisions of the myriad of market participants that impose pecuniary externalities on other participants in the market. A few illustrations can convey the gist of this point, and section 10.7 provides a more rigorous discussion of how uncertainty affects investment.

In 2008, world crude oil prices increased to all-time nominal and real highs, resulting in higher prices for gasoline and diesel. This increase in fuel prices reflected, in large part, an unexpected increase in demand in Asian emerging economies. The run-up in gasoline prices drove a shift in the composition of new cars and trucks sold toward more fuel-efficient vehicles (Ramey and Vine, 2010), adversely impacting auto manufacturers with a sales fleet oriented toward sport utility vehicles, light trucks, and minivans (such as GM and Chrysler). The higher gasoline prices also reduced vehicle miles traveled and fuel consumption by the existing fleet, adversely affecting the returns to oil refineries.

The so-called shale gas revolution in the United States has significantly affected the power sector as well as many local communities. As a result of the expansion of hydraulic fracturing techniques to extract natural gas from shale formations, the United States has reached an all-time high in gas production that has pushed down natural gas prices dramatically since 2008. Electric utilities responded to the dramatic decline in natural gas prices (and decline in the relative gas-coal price) by dispatching more electricity from gas plants that resulted in lower carbon dioxide (CO_2) emissions and the lowest share of U.S. power generation by coal in some four decades (Aldy, 2012). While this expansion of shale gas has changed the U.S. power market, it has also affected many of the local communities where production takes place, including impacts on local labor markets, infrastructure, and air and water quality.

Volatile energy prices may inhibit energy-related innovation, but higher prices typically induce innovation. Empirical evaluations of the impacts of energy prices on markets over the long run have found that higher prices induce more innovation, measured by frequency and importance of patents (Popp, 2002). In response to higher energy prices, manufacturers increase the commercial availability of more energy-efficient products, especially among energy-intensive goods such as air conditioners and water heaters (Newell et al., 1999).

10.6.2 Policy and Regulatory Uncertainty

Firms may face uncertain environmental policy compliance costs given uncertainty about the form and stringency a public policy intervention may take. Will the government employ conventional command-and-control regulatory mandates? Or an emission tax? Or cap-and-trade? For that matter, will the government pursue subsidies for pollution control equipment in lieu of regulation? Will the government delay action to learn more about the environmental problem and the prospects for technology to address the problem? Will industry preempt government action through voluntary initiatives to mitigate pollution? How do business cycles and political cycles affect the timing of government regulatory action?

Firms often have to form some kind of expectation about future policy and regulatory actions to inform current investment decisions (Dixit and Pindyck, 1994; Bernanke, 1983). For example, the U.S. Energy Information Administration undertakes an energy forecast for the United States through its *Annual Energy Outlook*, which includes details on expected investment in new energy infrastructure. Based on its outreach to firms making investment decisions in the energy sector, the U.S. EIA (2013) assumes a higher cost of capital for greenhouse gas emission-intensive projects, such as coal-fired power plants and coal-to-liquids plants, roughly commensurate with a $15 per ton carbon price. This reflects what the forecasters learned from the market participants: the prospect of some kind of future greenhouse gas regulatory regime—cap-and-trade, carbon tax, or command-and-control mandates—suggests that only those emission-intensive projects that are likely to be profitable in such a regulatory environment will go forward. This represents a way in which the forecaster accounts for the industry's expectation of a regulatory regime in its deterministic model to forecast the energy economy. It recognizes that heterogeneity in subjective probabilities from one firm's management to another, as well as updating as new information comes along, suggests that firm- and date-specific expected regulatory burden could vary from this value.

Moreover, uncertainty due to the implementation of environmental policy can also affect expected and realized costs of controlling pollution. Consider a few lessons from the sulfur dioxide (SO_2) cap-and-trade program. First, some firms made investments in SO_2 emission control technology that may have appeared optimal *ex ante*, but were more costly than necessary given the clearing price of emission allowances in the early years of trading. The irreversibility of these technology investments and expectation errors—i.e., individual firms expecting higher emission allowance prices than were realized—contributed to lower than expected allowance prices (Montero and Ellerman, 1998). Second, the empirical evaluations of the cap-and-trade program show that it delivered lower compliance costs than conventional command-and-control mandates, but it did not realize the least-cost potential (Carlson et al., 2000; Ellerman et al., 2000). Firms realized significantly different marginal abatement costs (Carlson et al., 2000), in contrast to the theory that suggests that firms' marginal abatement costs would converge on the emission allowance price. This may reflect the irreversibility of investments and the volatility in allowance prices evident in Figure 10.2. The high frequency of changes in allowance prices may make it challenging for a power plant operator to modify capital in a way to ensure that its marginal abatement cost equals the tradable allowance price at every point in time.

$/tSO_2

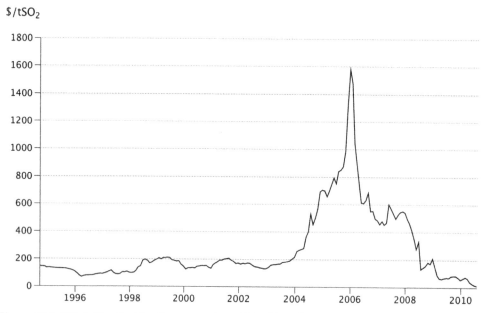

Figure 10.2 U.S. Sulfur dioxide allowance prices, 1994–2010. *Source:* Cantor Fitzgerald Market Price Index for current year vintages.

While these first two lessons reflect the uncertainty that may be expected under any cap-and-trade program, because of the uncertainties associated with any new market that requires irreversible investment (more on this in sections 10.7 and 10.8), a third lesson reflects the explicit actions of the government to modify the environmental regulatory regime. The sharp run-up in allowance prices over 2004–2006 was driven in large part by a proposed air quality regulation that would have effectively reduced the value of banked emission allowances and thus increased the price of allowances. The dramatic decline in allowance prices occurred after a Federal court ruling rejected the air quality regulation, which was then followed by different air quality rules that would have the intent of significantly limiting trading (Schmalensee and Stavins, 2013). As a result, the prospect of changes in the rules of a cap-and-trade program, especially one that allows for the banking of allowances for future use, can influence current allowance prices and hence the costs of compliance to regulated firms.

In 2012–2013, the European Union (EU) debated a variety of proposals to address concerns about low allowance prices in the Emission Trading Scheme (ETS). These low prices are a function of the recessionary economy characterizing much of the EU as well as other policies, such as subsidies for renewable power, that reduce demand for emission allowances under the ETS. The EU has considered making future emission caps more stringent in order to increase the allowance price. The spot market for allowances has moved with every piece of news as market participants update their subjective probabilities over the potential for tighter emission caps in the future.

Nordhaus (2007) noted the significant volatility in the prices for sulfur dioxide emission allowances and remarked that comparable volatility in a U.S. economy-wide carbon dioxide cap-and-trade program could adversely affect energy markets and investment planning. This volatility is evident in an array of emission allowance markets, including the U.S. nitrogen oxide (NO_X) cap-and-trade program and the EU Emission Trading Scheme for carbon dioxide emissions, as well as the SO_2 cap-and-trade program (Figures 10.2 to 10.4). Annual volatility—measured by the annualized absolute logarithmic month-to-month change in allowance prices—ranged from about 130 to nearly 300 percent for these three allowance markets, significantly exceeding the volatility in crude oil prices over contemporary periods of time.

Consider the evolution of emission allowance prices in the EU Emission Trading Scheme over 2006–2007. In April 2006, allowance prices exceeded €30 per ton CO_2, fell to less than €13 per ton CO_2 the following month, and traded for less than €1 per ton CO_2 a year later. To put these allowance prices in the context of U.S. energy markets, the effective carbon price would have been about 200 percent of the cost of coal delivered to U.S. power plants in April 2006, less than 75 percent of the cost of coal a month later, and about 5 percent the cost of coal delivered in May 2007.

The costs of complying with an environmental policy may depend in part on regulatory determinations made by other jurisdictions, which can affect environmental

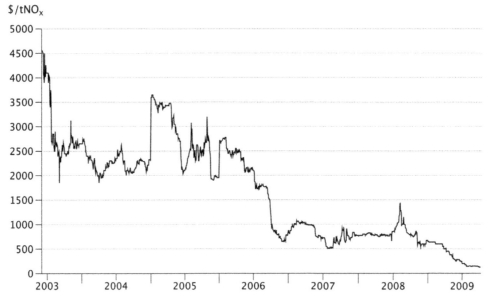

Figure 10.3 U.S. Nitrogen oxide allowance prices, 2003–2009. *Source:* ICAP Energy.

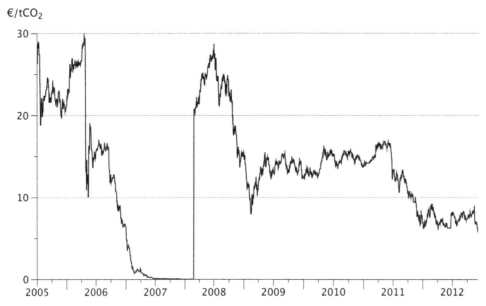

Figure 10.4 EU emission trading scheme allowance prices, 2005–2012. *Source:* Datastream International (BlueNext Series).

regulatory costs indirectly through private markets or directly through linked tradable emission allowance markets (in those cases in which cap-and-trade is the means of implementation). For example, the U.S. Environmental Protection Agency implemented the Reformulated Gasoline rule in 1995, intended to reduce emissions of local air pollutants in the combustion of gasoline. Some states had discretion on whether they could require filling stations to carry the so-called RFG gasoline. In the months leading up to the implementation for the 1995 summer driving season, several state governments that had initially announced their intent to mandate RFG gasoline changed their decisions out of concerns of higher costs for the RFG gasoline (Mayer et al., 1995). Removing this demand for RFG effectively pushed down the retail price for RFG and thus lowered costs for those states and cities that were required by the U.S. EPA to use RFG. This also lowered the returns to refiners that had invested in RFG refining capacity.

The cost of complying with an environmental policy may depend on whether foreign trading partners engage in similar domestic environmental regulations. For example, manufacturers of goods that face extensive international competition may find it challenging to pass along environmental compliance costs if their foreign competitors do not face similar costs. This issue of competitiveness has become prominent in the debate over climate change policy, although the estimated impacts in several studies suggest that political rhetoric overestimates the likely magnitude of costs borne by firms covered by greenhouse gas emission mitigation policies (Aldy and Pizer, 2009; Aldy et al., 2010).

In the context of global climate change policy, uncertainty in domestic abatement costs reflects in part the ultimate structure of an international climate policy architecture, especially the extent of participation in linked emission trading markets (Jaffe and Stavins, 2010). For example, estimates by the U.S. government showed that a Kyoto Protocol expanded to include China, India, Brazil, and Mexico with unfettered international emission trading would lower the marginal abatement cost in the United States by about 80 percent relative to autarky (AEA, 1998). Such uncertainty in abatement costs may further weaken the incentive for countries to participate in an international climate agreement in the first place (Kolstad, 2007).

10.7 UNCERTAINTY AND IRREVERSIBILITY

Environmental policy almost always involves irreversibilities on both the benefits and the costs sides of the ledger. Environmental damage may be irreversible: clearing a forest, increasing atmospheric concentrations of long-lived greenhouse gases, or radioactive contamination of water are all permanent, at least over fairly long (if not infinite) timescales. As noted in section 10.6, pollution control investments—such as installing pollution scrubbers, engaging in long-term contracts for lower-polluting inputs, training personnel to better manage a pollution source—are typically sunk costs. Uncertainty about the benefits of forestalling irreversible environmental damage or uncertainty about the costs and returns to undertaking pollution control can alter the standard net present value decision rule for projects and public policy if information can reduce uncertainty over time.

10.7.1 Arrow-Fisher Quasi-Option Value Model

Arrow and Fisher (1974) present a simple two-period model of a decision to develop an unspoiled, natural area.[4] In the model, the decision maker may choose to develop the land in the first period, delay development until the second period, or choose not to develop the land in either period. Once developed, the land cannot be restored to its natural state (i.e., irreversibility).

The decision maker is initially uncertain about the second period benefits associated with the land in the undeveloped state. This uncertainty is resolved after the first period.

They show that the decision maker aiming to maximize social welfare may decide to delay development at least until after uncertainty about the benefits of preserving the land in its natural state is resolved. If the decision maker expects no new information during the decision-making time frame (or if the problem is not characterized by uncertainty), then a simple comparison of expected benefits and costs could inform the decision to develop. The prospect of new information—and the value associated with this information—alters the decision calculus. There will be some cases in which development in the first period would be optimal if there is no new information expected after the first period but for which preservation in the first period becomes optimal if information is expected after the first period.

This so-called quasi-option value represents the value of information about future environmental benefits conditional on the decision not to irreversibly degrade the environment. Arrow and Fisher succinctly summarize their key finding at the close of their article: "Essentially, the point is that the expected benefits of an irreversible decision should be adjusted to reflect the loss of option it entails" (p. 319).

10.7.2 Dixit-Pindyck Real Options Model

Dixit and Pindyck (1994) develop many-period discrete and continuous time models to characterize investment decisions under uncertainty. They characterize the decision to invest as akin to the decision to execute an option. As long as a decision maker holds an option, she can decide to execute it any time, but once executed, she cannot reverse that decision. As in the Arrow-Fisher model, a decision maker may opt to delay the decision to execute an option, i.e., invest, if postponement may provide for the opportunity for uncertainty to be resolved or reduced. To be clear, postponing a decision to invest has value only insomuch as new information will become available, and

---

[4] Refer to Maler and Fisher (2005) for a technical review of the Arrow-Fisher and Dixit-Pindyck models.

this information only has value if the decision maker has the opportunity to postpone investment.

Fisher (2000) illustrates the equivalence of the Arrow-Fisher and Dixit-Pindyck approaches to investment decisions characterized by irreversibility and uncertainty. Maler and Fisher (2005) provide a rigorous review of this modeling approach. Pindyck (2002) provides an application of the continuous time framework to an environmental problem with many of the same properties as climate change.

10.7.3 Integrating Arrow-Fisher and Dixit-Pindyck to Inform Climate Change Policy

Arrow and Fisher's 1974 paper is one of the first economics papers to acknowledge the potential risks posed by climate change by noting that increasing atmospheric carbon dioxide concentrations could yield irreversible environmental impacts. Kolstad (1996a,b) undertook simulations to evaluate the impacts of the "dueling" irreversibilities of the climate change problem: what Pindyck (2007) describes as the sunk benefits of climate preservation versus the sunk costs of pollution control. Kolstad's theoretical and simulation models find that the irreversibility effect associated with pollution control likely dominates the irreversibility effect of increasing atmospheric greenhouse gas concentrations. Thus, the socially optimal emission mitigation policy would require less mitigation in the early years if learning can reduce uncertainty over time than under a no-learning scenario. Likewise, Fisher and Narain (2003) find that the effect of sunk capital in pollution control dominates the effect of the climate change irreversibility effect, thereby supporting lower early-period emission mitigation than what an analysis that ignored irreversibility would deliver. Ulph and Ulph (1997) find ambiguous results in their analysis of climate change; under-control or over-control relative to the no-learning scenario could be socially optimal depending on the parameterization of utility and production.

To be fair, the Kolstad finding results from the fact that in his model of damages, the irreversibility effect for climate change occurs only if there is the potential that future decision makers will want to undertake "negative emissions." In his model calibrated to the state of knowledge in the early 1990s, this appeared to be quite unlikely. Given the rapid growth in global greenhouse gas emissions over the past two decades and some scientists' calls for reducing atmospheric greenhouse concentrations below today's levels, the climate irreversibility effect would likely have a greater impact if Kolstad were to replicate his analysis with updated information. In addition, Kolstad (1996b) notes that risk aversion could motivate even greater emission abatement today to avoid the potential for catastrophic impacts in the future.

Manne and Richels (1992) describe how climate change policy can be thought of as a hedging strategy against potential severe climate change impacts. In particular, they address how the optimal hedging strategy varies with the quality and timing of new information about climate impacts, i.e., the resolution of at least some of the uncertainty characterizing the benefits of climate change mitigation. As a result, they call for a sequential process of taking action to mitigate emissions, then a process of learning about the efficacy of the action, followed by an informed, revised action to further mitigate climate change. Webster et al. (2008) show that the optimal amount of hedging depends on the extent of uncertainty and the degree to which the uncertainty can be reduced. Pindyck (2000) finds that the greater the uncertainty over benefits and/or costs, the stronger the incentive to delay taking action until the uncertainty is reduced. This effect is mitigated by a small decay rate, such as what characterizes the long atmospheric lifetimes of greenhouse gases.

More recently, Pindyck (2013) has called for a similar hedging strategy to impose a modest carbon price on greenhouse gas emissions now and to undertake research to better understand the potential abrupt and catastrophic impacts of climate change. The learning from this research could inform revisions to the climate change risk mitigation policy.

10.8 INSTRUMENT CHOICE UNDER UNCERTAINTY

Uncertainty and heterogeneity are the primary rationales for employing market-based instruments in environmental policy. The regulator does not have perfect information on firm- or source-specific emission abatement costs. Moreover, differences across firms in abatement opportunities indicate that one-size-fits-all command-and-control regulatory mandates would result in higher social costs for given environmental benefits. Thus, policy instruments that account for the regulator's information deficit, such as emission taxes and cap-and-trade, can deliver cost-effective attainment of environmental goals, at least in theory. While a tax and a cap-and-trade program can be designed to be equivalent in an abstract world of certainty, a rich literature has evolved since Weitzman's 1974 "Prices vs. Quantities" article that explores the effect of uncertainty on the welfare implications of choosing a tax or cap-and-trade.

10.8.1 Prices vs. Quantities

Weitzman (1974) developed a simple model to illustrate the relative costs and benefits of choosing a price instrument or a quantity instrument to allocate resources in an economy in the presence of uncertainty. He notes the policy question of emission taxes or pollution quotas (i.e., cap-and-trade) as one of the motivating rationales, and several other authors explored this instrument choice question in the environmental context (Roberts and Spence, 1976; Yohe, 1978). Weitzman employs quadratic benefit and cost functions for an arbitrary commodity and introduces uncertainty that is resolved only after a regulator chooses an instrument to allocate the commodity. The relative welfare advantage of a price instrument over a quantity instrument can be represented by the following equation based on Weitzman's model:

$$\Delta = \frac{\sigma_c^2}{2c^2}(c - b)$$ (10.5)

where

$\Delta =$ the relative welfare advantage of prices over quantities,

$\sigma_c^2 =$ the variance of the shocks to the marginal cost function,

$c =$ the slope of the marginal cost function, and

$b =$ the slope of the marginal benefit function.[5]

This yields the so-called relative slopes rule. If the absolute value of the slope of the marginal cost function is greater than the absolute value of the slope of the marginal benefit function, then $\Delta > 0$, and a price instrument, such as an emission tax, would deliver greater expected net social benefits. If the absolute value of the slope of the marginal benefit function is greater than the absolute value of the slope of the marginal cost function, then $\Delta < 0$, and a quantity instrument, such as a cap-and-trade program, would deliver greater expected net social benefits.[6]

Figures 10.5 and 10.6 illustrate the cases when a price instrument is preferred to a quantity instrument and when a quantity instrument is preferred to a price instrument, respectively, in the presence of uncertainty over marginal cost. Suppose that the regulator has one of two policy instruments at her disposal: she can choose to set a tax on each unit of emissions (denoted by T) or she can set a cap on emissions, which yields a quantity of emission abatement (denoted by $Q^{C\&T}$). Assume that the regulator knows the marginal benefits of abating pollution (denoted MB; this also holds if the regulator had an estimate of the expected marginal benefit function), which reflect diminishing marginal returns to emission abatement, and she has estimated an expected marginal cost function (denoted EMC), which reflects a convex total cost function. Since the regulator does not know marginal costs with certainty, she can choose an emission tax T or an abatement quantity $Q^{C\&T}$ to equate marginal benefits and expected marginal costs.

Consider the case when the absolute value of the slope of marginal cost exceeds the absolute value of marginal benefit, as shown in Figure 10.5. If uncertainty over marginal costs is resolved after choosing an instrument, and the realized marginal costs (denoted by MC_H) are higher than expected marginal costs, then neither the emission tax nor the cap-and-trade program would deliver the efficient level of emission abatement (denoted

[5] Technically, Weitzman derived an expression that would represent an accurate local approximation. Subsequent work, such as in Adar and Griffin (1978), assumed linearity in the marginal benefit and cost functions, which delivers the exact equality presented here.

[6] Kelly (2005) argues that, in general equilibrium, more than just the relative slopes matter for determining the relative welfare advantage of prices over quantities. In particular, the risk aversion of consumers and the relative impacts of these instruments on the variation in production and hence consumption can dominate the relative slopes contribution to the welfare determination.

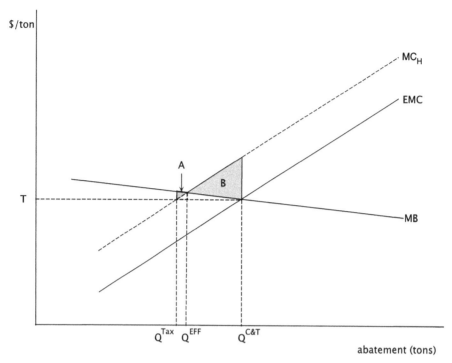

Figure 10.5 Prices versus quantities I.

by Q^{EFF}). The tax yields too little abatement (denoted by Q^{Tax}), while the cap-and-trade program yields too much abatement (denoted by $Q^{C\&T}$). The deadweight loss associated with choosing a policy instrument before uncertainty over marginal costs is represented by triangle A for the price instrument and triangle B for the quantity instrument. In this case, deadweight loss B significantly exceeds deadweight loss A.

Now consider the case when the absolute value of the slope of marginal benefit exceeds the absolute value of marginal cost, as shown in Figure 10.6. If uncertainty over marginal costs is resolved after choosing an instrument, and the realized marginal costs are again higher than expected marginal costs, then neither the emission tax nor the cap-and-trade program would deliver the efficient level of emission abatement. As in Figure 10.5, the tax yields too little abatement, while the cap-and-trade program yields too much abatement. In this case, the deadweight loss of the tax, triangle A, significantly exceeds the deadweight loss of cap-and-trade, triangle B. These figures show that if the regulator aims to minimize the social welfare losses of choosing an instrument under uncertainty, then she should choose cap-and-trade if the change in environmental benefit is greater than the change in abatement cost for any deviation from what would be *ex post* efficient, and she should choose a tax if the change in abatement cost is greater than the change in environmental benefit for any likewise deviation from what would be *ex post* efficient.

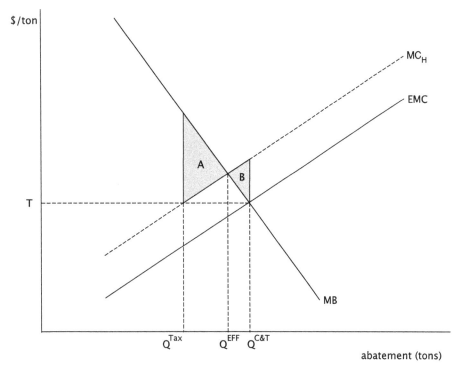

Figure 10.6 Prices versus quantities II.

This result illustrates how the greater the uncertainty over marginal costs, represented by the variance of the shocks to the marginal cost function, the greater the welfare advantage for a price instrument if $(c - b) > 0$, or for a quantity instrument if $(c - b) < 0$. In this stylized model, the uncertainty in the benefit function does not matter for instrument choice; only the uncertainty in the cost function affects the calculation of the welfare advantage of the preferred policy instrument (Adar and Griffin, 1976). Suppose that the MB function is replaced with an expected marginal benefits function in Figures 10.5 and 10.6. In addition, assume that these figures include a MB^{H} function representing realized marginal benefit function higher than expected after resolution of uncertainty, akin to the MC_{H} function. A quick assessment of the graphical analysis shows how this would have no bearing on the amount abated or the relative deadweight losses of the instruments in these figures. Under cap-and-trade, the quantity abated is determined by the regulator through the setting of the cap. The cap does not change if realized marginal benefits differ from what was expected. The price to abate is determined by the intersection of the realized marginal cost function and the quantity required under the cap. Under the emission tax, the price is by design set by the tax and the quantity abated is determined by the intersection of the tax and the realized marginal cost function.

To illustrate the potential implications of this prices versus quantities analysis for climate change policy, Pizer (2002) employs a stochastic version of Nordhaus's DICE model that allows for uncertainty in costs and benefits and finds that the optimal price policy delivers about five times the expected gain of the optimal quantity policy. Pizer finds that the expected marginal benefits function is nearly horizontal, reflecting the fact that annual contributions of emissions to the atmosphere are small relative to the current stock (also see Aldy and Pizer, 2009). This relatively flat marginal benefits schedule for mitigating greenhouse gas emissions is consistent in other studies, such as Kolstad (1996b). Aldy et al. (2010) posit that a global carbon tax rising at the rate of interest would likely incur lower costs than equivalently set annual emission caps for a policy objective to stabilize the global climate at any arbitrary concentration level.

10.8.2 Correlated Benefit and Cost Uncertainty

Stavins (1996) noted an often-overlooked footnote in Weitzman (1974) on how correlation in benefits and costs can affect the relative welfare determination of price and quantity instruments. In particular, benefit uncertainty matters in the cases in which benefits and costs are correlated. A positive correlation improves the comparative advantage of quantity instruments, while a negative correlation improves the comparative advantage of price instruments. This is evident in the expanded expression for relative welfare advantage to account for benefit and cost correlation:

$$\Delta = \frac{\sigma_c^2}{2c^2}(c - b) - \frac{\rho_{bc}\sigma_b\sigma_c}{c} \tag{10.6}$$

where
  ρ_{bc} = the correlation between benefits and costs,
  σ_b = the standard deviation of benefits,
  σ_c = the standard deviation of costs, and all other terms are the same as above.
If costs and benefits are positively correlated, and if marginal costs are higher than expected, then firms facing a tax would abate less but would do so at a time when marginal benefits of emission abatement are also higher than expected. If the correlation is negative and if marginal costs are again higher than expected, then firms facing cap-and-trade would incur greater costs of compliance at a time when marginal benefits are lower than expected.

Significant uncertainty in either benefits or costs magnifies the impact of the correlation on the relative welfare determination. The steeper the slope of marginal cost, however, the weaker is the effect of benefit-cost correlation on the welfare determination. Theoretically, the impact of correlation could dominate the impact of the relative slopes in identifying the policy instrument that maximizes expected net social benefits.

Stavins identifies several environmental examples in which benefits and costs are positively correlated, and thus would suggest that cap-and-trade would dominate a tax.

For example, a sunny day may increase the production of ground-level ozone (incident ultraviolet radiation transforms ozone precursors, nitrogen oxides and volatile organic compounds, into ozone) and thus increase the costs necessary to reduce ambient ozone concentrations. At the same time, a sunny day may attract more people outdoors, thereby increasing their exposure to ozone and the benefits of lowering ozone concentrations.

The implications of this correlation analysis are likely mixed in the context of climate change: there are potential cases of negative, positive, and zero correlation. Severe climate change may dramatically alter precipitation patterns that could reduce the power generation from some existing hydroelectric dams, and thus increase the cost of generating low- and zero-carbon electricity. Other dams, however, may benefit from the change in precipitation patterns and produce even more electricity, delivering lower costs for abating emissions in the power sector. Some regions of the world could benefit from warming in terms of longer growing seasons and enjoy an increase in biological sequestration, thereby lowering marginal (net) abatement costs, while other regions could experience such high temperatures that biomass and vegetation growth suffer. Clearly the spatial heterogeneity in the impacts of climate change could yield positive and negative correlations in benefits and costs. This may also be complicated by the temporal element—how are distant future benefits correlated with the costs of mitigating climate change today? Finally, some climate change risk mitigation strategies, such as geoengineering, may involve costs that are independent of the benefits of combating climate change.

10.8.3 Stock Pollutants and Dynamics

Newell and Pizer (2003a) evaluate the instrument choice problem in the context of a stock pollution problem and present an evaluation in the context of climate change. They derive a modified version of the Weitzman relative welfare advantage expression that includes a persistence factor for benefits and a correlated costs factor. The relative slopes rule generally holds, with the caveats that: (1) lower discount rates, lower stock decay rates, and greater rates of growth in benefits tend to favor quantity instruments; and (2) greater positive correlation in costs over time tends to favor quantity instruments. They simulate the impacts of persistence and serial cost correlation in a modified version of the DICE model and, like Pizer (2002), find that price instruments dominate quantity instruments in mitigating greenhouse gas emissions.

Hoel and Karp (2002) also investigate the instrument choice problem for a stock pollutant and in their climate change simulations they find that prices dominate quantities. Karp and Zhang (2006) permit learning over time in their model, and again the analysis suggests that prices are preferred to quantities. Fell et al. (2012) investigate the properties of cap-and-trade when firms may bank current emission allowances for future use or borrow future allowances for current use. Banking and borrowing effectively reduces price volatility, and in simulations of climate change policy, they find that a cap-and-trade program with full intertemporal flexibility can closely approximate the welfare advantages of an emission tax over relatively short time horizons (e.g., a decade), but over forty or more years, intertemporal trading yields about half the welfare gain over conventional cap-and-trade that an emission tax achieves.

10.8.4 Hybrid Instruments

Roberts and Spence (1976) proposed a hybrid price-quantity approach to control pollution (also see Yohe, 1978). In effect, the regulator could set an emission cap and allocate emission allowances to the economy. At the start of the cap-and-trade program, the regulator could also announce that she stands prepared to sell an unlimited number of additional allowances at a preset price. As long as allowance prices trade below this regulator's preset price, then the policy operates as cap-and-trade. If the prices for allowances rise to the preset price, then firms may minimize their compliance costs by purchasing additional allowances from the regulator at that price. The policy then operates effectively as an emission tax. Pizer (2002) evaluates the welfare properties of such a hybrid approach and finds that it can generate significant gains over only a cap-and-trade program to address climate change. Depending on the level of the trigger price set by the regulator, this hybrid could closely approximate the gains of a tax policy. Of course, an ambitious emission cap coupled with a low trigger price would likely result in such a hybrid operating like a tax most of the time. Such an approach may hold some political appeal by providing the opportunity to cap emissions that is favored by environmentalists while also providing an assurance to industry that marginal compliance costs are effectively subjected to a ceiling.

Over the past decade, several legislative proposals for U.S. greenhouse gas emission cap-and-trade programs have included a so-called "safety valve"—the sale of additional allowances at a preset price (Aldy and Pizer, 2009). In addition, about 30 states have implemented renewable portfolio standards—quantity-based policies that require a specified share of power to come from qualifying renewable energy sources. Some states have implemented safety valves in their renewable mandates to ensure that the costs of compliance are not unexpectedly high (Aldy, 2012). For example, the Massachusetts renewable portfolio standard has had a binding safety valve price for one class of renewable power covered under state law. As a result, utilities choose to pay into a state fund in lieu of incurring greater costs to deliver higher cost renewable power.

An alternative modification to cap-and-trade with the same aim of mitigating concerns about abatement cost uncertainty is the idea of indexing emission caps to a measure that is correlated with cost drivers. For example, the Council of Economic Advisers (2000) described an approach to setting national greenhouse gas emission caps as a function of economic growth, given the strong historical correlation between economic and carbon dioxide emission growth rates. In the context of international climate negotiations, such an approach could address the concerns of developing countries that an emission cap could limit economic development and potentially impose significant costs if their economies grew more quickly than anticipated and address the concerns of some developed countries that an emission cap could require no meaningful emission abatement by developing countries if their economies grew more slowly than anticipated (Lutter, 2000; Aldy, 2004). In recent years, China and India have proposed national carbon intensity goals that would require the reduction in the carbon dioxide emissions to GDP ratio by as much as 45 percent over fifteen years in China and as much as 25 percent over fifteen years in India.

Newell and Pizer (2008) formally evaluate the idea of indexed targets within the traditional Weitzman framework. They derive expressions for the relative welfare advantage of prices, quantities, and indexed quantities and apply them to the problem of climate change. Given the variation in the correlation of GDP and carbon dioxide emissions across countries, an emission intensity cap (a type of indexed quantity policy) dominates a traditional, fixed emission cap for some countries but not others. Webster et al. (2010) also derive formal expressions to compare intensity targets with the safety valve hybrid. They find that the correlation between GDP and emissions necessary to justify an intensity target over a safety valve is implausibly high. They illustrate the dominance of the safety valve numerically through a Monte Carlo simulation using a computable general equilibrium model of the U.S. economy.

10.8.5 Uncertainty, Irreversibility, and Quantity Instruments

Baldursson and von der Fehr (2004) develop two-period and multiperiod dynamic models that incorporate elements of the real options framework and the prices versus quantities framework. They find that accounting for the irreversibility of investment in the presence of uncertainty yields modestly more support for the choice of a price instrument. They also find that under cap-and-trade, investment occurs later and allowance prices are more volatile in the presence of irreversibility.

While cap-and-trade programs deliver cost-effective abatement and can deliver the socially optimal level of abatement, in theory, the practice suggests that cap-and-trade falls short on both dimensions. The experience with the SO_2 cap-and-trade program shows that firms did not bear common marginal abatement costs (Carlson et al., 2000), the necessary condition for cost-effectiveness. In addition, the volatility in allowance prices (see Figure 10.2) suggests that the marginal cost of compliance, even if equated across firms, did not equal the marginal benefit of abatement over most of the life of the program, thereby failing on efficiency grounds.[7] Despite the significant uncertainty over the "right" estimate of the social cost of carbon, it is evident in the volatility of the EU ETS allowance prices (see Figure 10.4) that the marginal cost of abating carbon dioxide emissions rarely equals the marginal benefit of emission abatement.

---

[7] If anything, the allowance prices were below the marginal benefit of abatement for most if not all of the period of operation of the SO_2 cap-and-trade program, in part because of the lack of understanding of the reduced mortality risk benefits associated with sulfur dioxide abatement at the time Congress created the program (Schmalensee and Stavins, 2013).

Consider an explanation of these empirical findings that is generally consistent with the Baldursson and von der Fehr theory work. Suppose a regulator can choose between an emission tax or cap-and-trade. Under either instrument, the regulated firm would need to identify its own abatement cost function in order to minimize compliance costs. If the regulator sets a tax, then the firm chooses the abatement technologies identified in its abatement cost function that minimizes compliance costs with the tax (i.e., minimizes the tax payment plus abatement costs or, alternatively, maximizes profits subject to compliance with the tax). If the regulator implements cap-and-trade, then the firm must also form an expectation about the clearing price for emission allowances that could determine which abatement options available to the firm would be economic. Since this is a new market, firms may differ about their expectations of allowance prices. The modeling work of the SO_2 cap-and-trade program in the late 1980s and early 1990s provides some dispersion in estimated allowance prices (Ellerman et al., 2000), and more significantly in the context of climate change, there is significant dispersion in estimated allowance prices even within a single study using a single model with a variety of assumptions about economic growth and technological change (e.g., refer to U.S. EIA 2010).

If there are no sunk costs associated with the abatement options, i.e. no irreversibility, then firms can costlessly adjust abatement as allowance prices evolve over time. In practice, however, irreversibility characterizes many kinds of emission abatement investments (Kolstad, 1996a; Dixit and Pindyck, 1994; Montero and Ellerman, 1998). In the context of the SO_2 cap-and-trade program, some of the most prominent irreversible investments included the purchase and installation of SO_2 scrubbers and long-term low-sulfur coal contracts. As a result, under cap-and-trade, firms may lock in some irreversible abatement options that, given their expectations of the allowance market, may appear *ex ante* to be optimal but which would be *ex post* suboptimal once the uncertainty over allowance prices is resolved. This could deliver the heterogeneity in marginal abatement costs across firms that undermines cost-effectiveness and efficiency and could contribute to the price volatility predicted in Baldursson and von der Fehr (2004) and evident in the SO_2, NO_X, and CO_2 cap-and-trade programs. Given the less extensive policy experimentation with emission taxes, it is difficult to provide a fair, real-world comparison of performance under taxes. Nonetheless, the uncertainty associated with the start-up and operation of cap-and-trade programs and the irreversibility of many pollution control investments suggests that, *ceteris paribus*, the choice of an emission tax could dominate cap-and-trade.

10.9 CONCLUSION

Virtually every aspect of environmental policy involves risks. Economic tools provide a framework for structuring analyses of environmental policy that accounts for such risks in a rational manner. Sound economic analysis also helps avert suboptimal outcomes, such as over-reacting to negligible risks or dismissing truly major risks simply because they are uncertain or deferred. The risk analysis practices and targeting of environmental policies are sometimes flawed in ways that can be ameliorated by grounding policies in proper assessment of the expected benefits and costs.

The presence of risk and uncertainty creates a potential role for informational policies that assist in indicating the magnitude of the environmental risks. Warnings and various right-to-know efforts are often effective, low-cost ways of mitigating risk exposure. Economic studies have also illuminated the characteristics of informational efforts that have made certain information programs particularly effective.

As our understanding of environmental hazards has evolved over time, one might have expected policies to be more concerned about risk than uncertainty. There have, of course, been advances in knowledge that make it feasible to estimate some risks with greater precision. Yet, uncertainties continue to characterize the benefits and costs of policy efforts to mitigate environmental risk, and failing to account for these uncertainties could lead to socially inefficient public policies. Many environmental policies require irreversible investments in pollution abatement, and some policies do so in order to avoid irreversible environmental and public health harms. The prospect to learn about environmental risks and reduce uncertainty with respect to benefits and costs can affect the decision calculus for those cases that involve such irreversibilities. For example, if the prospect of irreversible, catastrophic climate change dominates the irreversible, sunk costs of investing in pollution abatement, then ignoring uncertainty and the opportunity to learn over time would result in less emission abatement than is socially optimal.

While taxes and cap-and-trade programs generally deliver more cost-effective and higher net social welfare outcomes than conventional command-and-control regulatory mandates, understanding the potential impacts of uncertainty on welfare outcomes can inform the choice of a price instrument, such as emission taxes, or a quantity instrument, such as cap-and-trade. Most analyses of climate change suggest that a price instrument would deliver greater expected social welfare than a quantity instrument, and the uncertainty endogenous to the operation of cap-and-trade could inhibit investment and increase costs of mitigating risk. The potential welfare gains from improved environmental risk management illustrate the increasing importance that sound economic analysis can have in the design of environmental policy.

ACKNOWLEDGMENTS

Thanks to Jisung Park and Napat Jatusripitak for excellent research assistance and to Dallas Burtraw, Gary Hart, Alex Marten, Billy Pizer, Sam Stolper, and Ann Wolverton for providing data used in the figures.

REFERENCES

Adar, Z., Griffin, J.M., 1976. Uncertainty and the choice of pollution control instruments. Journal of Environmental Economics and Management 3, 178–188.
Adler, R., Pittle, D., 1984. Cajolery and command: are education campaigns an adequate substitute for regulation? Yale Journal of Regulation 2, 159–194.

Administration Economic Analysis (AEA), 1998. The Kyoto Protocol and the President's Policies to Address Climate Change: Administration Economic Analysis: The White House, Washington, DC.

Aldy, J.E., 2004. Saving the planet cost-effectively: the role of economic analysis in climate change mitigation policy. In: Lutter, R., Shogren, J.F. (Eds.), Painting the White House Green: Rationalizing Environmental Policy Inside the Executive Office of the President. Resources for the Future Press, Washington.

Aldy, J.E., 2012. Promoting clean energy in the American power sector: a proposal for a national clean energy standard. Environmental Law Reporter 42, 10131–10149.

Aldy, J.E., Krupnick, A.J., Newell, R.G., Parry, I.W.H., Pizer, W.A., 2010. Designing climate mitigation policy. Journal of Economic Literature 48, 903–934.

Aldy, J.E., Pizer, W.A., 2009. Issues in designing U.S. climate change policy. Energy Journal 30, 179–210.

Ames, B.N., Gold, L.S., 1990. Chemical carcinogenesis: too many rodent carcinogens. Proceedings of the National Academy of Sciences 87, 7772–7776.

Ames, B.N., Gold, L.S., 1996. The causes and prevention of cancer. In: Hahn, R.W. (Ed.), Risks, Costs, and Lives Saved: Getting Better Results from Regulation. Oxford University Press, Oxford.

Ames, B.N., Profet, M., Gold, L.S., 1990. Nature's chemicals and synthetic chemicals: comparative toxicology. Proceedings of the National Academy of Sciences 87, 7782–7786.

Anthoff, D., Tol, R.S.J., 2013. The uncertainty about the social cost of carbon: a decomposition analysis using FUND. Climatic Change 117, 515–530.

Archer, D., Eby, M., Brovkin, V., Ridgwell, A., Cao, L., Mikolajewicz, U., Caldeira, K., Matsumoto, K., Munhoven, G., Montenegro, A., Tokos, K., 2009. Atmospheric lifetime of fossil fuel carbon dioxide. Annual Review of Earth and Planetary Science 37, 117–134.

Arora, S., Cason, T., 1995. An experiment in voluntary environmental regulation: participation in EPA's 33/50 program. Journal of Environmental Economics and Management 28, 271–286.

Arrow, K.J., Cline, W.R., Maler, K.-G., Munasinghe, M., Squitieri, R., Stiglitz, J.E., 1996. Intertemporal equity, discounting, and economic efficiency. In: Bruce, J.P., Lee, H., Haites, E.F. (Eds.), Climate Change 1995: Economic and Social Dimensions of Climate Change. Cambridge University Press, Cambridge.

Arrow, K.J., Cropper, M.L., Gollier, C., Groom, B., Heal, G.M., Newell, R.G., Nordhaus, W.D., Pindyck, R.S., Pizer, W.A., Portney, P.R., Sterner, T., Tol, R.S.J., Weitzman, M.L., 2012. "How Should Benefits and Costs Be Discounted in an Intergenerational Context? The Views of an Expert Panel". Resources for the Future Discussion Paper 12–53.

Arrow, K.J., Fisher, A.C., 1974. Environmental preservation, uncertainty, and irreversibility. Quarterly Journal of Economics 88, 312–319.

Baldursson, F.M., von der Fehr, N.-H., 2004. Prices versus quantities: the irrelevance of irreversibility. Scandinavian Journal of Economics 106, 805–821.

Barrett, S., 2003. Environment and Statecraft: The Strategy of Environmental Treaty-Making. Oxford University Press, Oxford.

Bennear, L., Olmstead, S.M., 2008. The impact of the right to know: information disclosure and the violation of drinking water standards. Journal of Environmental Economics and Management 56, 117–130.

Bernanke, B.S., 1983. Irreversibility, uncertainty, and cyclical investment. Quarterly Journal of Economics 98, 85–106.

Born, P.B., Viscusi, W.K., 2006. The catastrophic effects of natural disasters on insurance markets. Journal of Risk and Uncertainty 33, 55–72.

Brehm, J., Hamilton, J.T., 1996. Noncompliance in environmental reporting: are violators ignorant, or evasive, of the law? American Journal of Political Science 40, 444–477.

Bui, L.T.M., Mayer, C.J., 2003. Regulation and capitalization of environmental amenities: evidence from the Toxics Release Inventory in Massachusetts. Review of Economics and Statistics 85, 693–708.

Burmaster, D.E., Harris, R.N., 1993. The magnitude of compounding conservatism in Superfund risk assessments. Risk Analysis 13, 131–134.

Camerer, C., Kunreuther, H., 1989. Decision processes for low probability events: policy implications. Journal of Policy Analysis and Management 8, 565–592.

Camerer, C., Weber, M., 1992. Recent developments in modeling preferences: uncertainty and ambiguity. Journal of Risk and Uncertainty 5, 325–370.

Caputo, M.R., Wilen, J.E., 1995. Optimal cleanup of hazardous wastes. International Economics Review 36, 217–243.

Carlson, C., Burtraw, D., Cropper, M., Palmer, K., 2000. Sulfur dioxide control by electric utilities: what are the gains from trade? Journal of Political Economy 108, 1292–1326.

Charness, G., Karni, E., Levin, D., 2013. Ambiguity attitudes and social interactions: an experimental investigation. Journal of Risk and Uncertainty 46, 1–25.

Coates, D., Heid, V., Munger, M., 1994. Not equitable, not efficient: U.S. policy on low-level radioactive waste disposal. Journal of Policy Analysis and Management 13, 526–538.

Cohen, L., 1981. Who pays the bill: insuring against the risks from low level nuclear waste disposal. Natural Resources Journal 21, 773–787.

Council of Economic Advisers, 2000. The Economic Report of the President. Government Printing Office, Washington.

Cullen, A.C., 1994. Measures of compounding conservatism in probabilistic risk assessment. Risk Analysis 14, 389–393.

Currie, J., Davis, L., Greenstone, M., Walker, R., 2013. Do Housing Prices Reflect Environmental Health Risks? Evidence from More than 1600 Toxic Plant Openings and Closings. NBER Working Paper 18700.

de Marchi, S., Hamilton, J.T., 2006. Assessing the accuracy of self-reported data: an evaluation of the Toxics Release Inventory. Journal of Risk and Uncertainty 32, 57–76.

Dixit, A.K., Pindyck, R.S., 1994. Investment under Uncertainty. Princeton University Press, Princeton.

Ellerman, A.D., Joskow, P.L., Schmalensee, R., Montero, J.-P., Bailey, E.M., 2000. Markets for Clean Air: The U.S. Acid Rain Program. Cambridge University Press, Cambridge.

Ellsberg, D., 1961. Risk, ambiguity, and the savage axioms. Quarterly Journal of Economics 75, 643–669.

Environmental Protection Agency (EPA), 1987. The Risk Assessment Guidelines of 1986. EPA-600/8-87/045. (Guidelines for carcinogen risk assessment; Guidelines for mutagenicity risk assessment; Guidelines for the health risk assessment of chemical mixtures; Guidelines for the health assessment of suspect developmental toxicants; Guidelines for estimating exposures.) U.S. EPA, Office of Health and Environmental Assessment, Washington.

Environmental Protection Agency (EPA), 1992. Guidelines for Exposure Assessment. Federal Register 57, 22888–22938.

Environmental Protection Agency (EPA), 1996. Proposed Guidelines for Carcinogen Risk Assessment. Federal Register 61, 17960–18011.

European Commission, 1996. Technical Guidance Document in Support of Commission Directive 93/67/EEC on Risk Assessment for New Notified Substances and Commission Regulation No. 1488/94 on Risk Assessment for Existing Substances. Office for Official Publications of the European Communities, Luxembourg.

Fell, H., MacKenzie, I.A., Pizer, W.A., 2012. Prices versus Quantities versus Bankable Quantities. NBER Working Paper 17878.

Fisher, A.C., 2000. Investment under uncertainty and option value in environmental economics. Resource and Energy Economics 22, 197–204.

Fisher, A.C., Narain, U., 2003. Global warming, endogenous risk, and irreversibility. Environmental and Resource Economics 25, 395–416.

Gayer, T., Hamilton, J.T., Viscusi, W.K., 2000. Private values of risk tradeoffs at Superfund sites: housing market evidence on learning about risk. Review of Economics and Statistics 82, 439–451.

Gollier, C., 2010. Expected net present value, expected net future value, and the Ramsey rule. Journal of Environmental Economics and Management 59, 142–148.

Gollier, C., Treich, N., 2003. Decision-making under scientific uncertainty: the economics of the precautionary principle. Journal of Risk and Uncertainty 27, 77–103.

Gollier, C., Weitzman, M.L., 2010. How should the distant future be discounted when discount rates are uncertain? Economic Letters 107, 350–353.

Greenstone, M., Kopits, E., Wolverton, A., 2013. Developing a social cost of carbon for US regulatory analysis: a methodology and interpretation. Review of Environmental Economics and Policy 7, 23–46.

Groom, B., Koundouri, P., Panopoulou, E., Pantelidis, T., 2007. Discounting the distant future: how much does model selection affect the certainty equivalent rate? Journal of Applied Econometrics 22, 641–656.

Hamilton, J.T., 1995. Pollution as news: media and stock market reactions to the Toxics Release Inventory data. Journal of Environmental Economics and Management 28, 98–113.

Hamilton, J.T., 1997. Taxes, torts, and the Toxics Release Inventory: congressional voting on instruments to control pollution. Economic Inquiry 35, 745–762.

Hamilton, J.T., 1999. Exercising property rights to pollute: do cancer risks and politics affect plant emission reductions? Journal of Risk and Uncertainty 18, 105–124.

Hamilton, J.T., 2005. Regulation through Revelation: The Origin, Politics, and Impacts of the Toxics Release Inventory Program. Cambridge University Press, New York.

Hamilton, J.T., Viscusi, W.K., 1999. Calculating Risks?: The Spatial and Political Dimensions of Hazardous Waste Policy. MIT Press, Cambridge, MA.

Heal, G., 2005. Intertemporal welfare economics and the environment. In: Maler, K.-G., Vincent, J.R. (Eds.), Handbook of Environmental Economics. Elsevier B.V.

Heal, G., 2007. Discounting: a review of the basic economics. University of Chicago Law Review 74, 59–77.

Helland, E., Whitford, A.B., 2003. Pollution incidence and political jurisdiction: evidence from the TRI. Journal of Environmental Economics and Management 46, 403–424.

Henry, C., 1974. Investment decisions under uncertainty: the irreversibility effect. American Economic Review 64, 1006–1012.

Hird, J., 1990. Superfund expenditures and cleanup priorities: distributive politics or the public interest? Journal of Policy Analysis and Management 9, 455–483.

Hoel, M., Karp, L., 2002. Taxes versus quotas for a stock pollutant. Resource and Energy Economics 24, 367–384.

Hope, C., 2011. The Social Cost of CO_2 from the PAGE09 Model. Cambridge Judge Business School Working Paper No. 4/2011.

Interagency Working Group on the Social Cost of Carbon, 2010. Technical Support Document: Social Cost of Carbon for Regulatory Impact Analysis under Executive Order 12866. United States Government, February.

Interagency Working Group on the Social Cost of Carbon, 2013. Technical Support Document: Technical Update of the Social Cost of Carbon for Regulatory Impact Analysis under Executive Order 12866. United States Government, May.

Jaffe, J., Stavins, R.N., 2010. Linkage of tradable permit systems in international climate policy architecture. In: Aldy, J.E., Stavins, R.N. (Eds.), Post-Kyoto International Climate Policy: Implementing Architectures for Agreement. Cambridge University Press, Cambridge.

Jakoby, W.B. (Ed.), 1980. Enzymatic Basis of Detoxification. Academic Press, New York.

Kahneman, D., Tversky, A., 1979. Prospect theory: an analysis of decisions under risk. Econometrica 47, 263–291.

Karp, L., Zhang, J., 2006. Regulation with anticipated learning about environmental damages. Journal of Environmental Economics and Management 51, 259–279.

Kelly, D., 2005. Price and quantity regulation in general equilibrium. Journal of Economic Theory 125, 36–60.

Khanna, M., Anton, W.R.Q., 2002. Corporate environmental management: regulatory and market-based incentives. Land Economics 78, 539–558.

Khanna, M., Damon, L.A., 1999. EPA's voluntary 33/50 program: impact on toxic releases and economic performance of firms. Journal of Environmental Economics and Management 37, 1–25.

Khanna, M., Quimio, W.R.H., Bojilova, D., 1998. Toxic release information: a policy tool for environmental protection. Journal of Environmental Economics and Management 36, 243–266.

Kiel, K.A., McClain, K.T., 1995. House prices during siting decision stages: the case of an incinerator from rumor through operation. Journal of Environmental Economics and Management 28, 241–255.

Kolhase, J.E., 1991. The impact of toxic waste sites on housing values. Journal of Urban Economics 30, 1–26.

Kolstad, C.D., 1996a. Fundamental irreversibilities in stock externalities. Journal of Public Economics 60, 221–233.

Kolstad, C.D., 1996b. Learning and stock effects in environmental regulation: the case of greenhouse gas emissions. Journal of Environmental Economics and Management 31, 1–18.

Kolstad, C.D., 2007. Systematic uncertainty in self-enforcing international environmental agreements. Journal of Environmental Economics and Management 53, 68–79.

Konar, S., Cohen, M.A., 1997. Information as regulation: the effect of community right to know laws on toxic emissions. Journal of Environmental Economics and Management 32, 109–124.

Kunreuther, H., Ginsberg, R., Miller, L., Sagi, P., Slovic, P., Borkan, B., Katz, N., 1978. Disaster Insurance Protection: Public Policy Lessons. Wiley, New York.

Lichtenstein, S., Slovic, P., Fischhoff, B., Layman, U., Combs, B., 1978. Judged frequency of lethal events. Journal of Experimental Psychology 4, 551–578.

Liu, J.T., Smith, V.K., 1990. Risk communication and attitude change: Taiwan's national debate over nuclear power. Journal of Risk and Uncertainty 3, 331–349.

Lofstedt, R.E., 2004. The swing of the regulatory pendulum in Europe: from precautionary principle to (regulatory) impact analysis. Journal of Risk and Uncertainty 28, 237–260.

Lutter, R., 2000. Developing countries' greenhouse gas emissions: uncertainty and implications for participation in the Kyoto protocol. Energy Journal 21, 93–120.

Magat, W.A., Viscusi, W.K., 1992. Informational Approaches to Regulation. MIT Press, Cambridge, MA.

Maler, K.-G., Fisher, A., 2005. Environment, uncertainty, and option values. In: Maler, K.-G., Vincent, J.R. (Eds.), Handbook of Environmental Economics. Elsevier B.V.

Manne, A.S., Richels, R.G., 1992. Buying Greenhouse Insurance: The Economic Costs of CO_2 Emission Limits. MIT Press, Cambridge.

Maxwell, J.W., Lyon, T.P., Hackett, S.C., 2000. Self-regulation and social welfare: the political economy of corporate environmentalism. Journal of Law and Economics 43, 583–617.

Mayer, S.L., Kumins, L., Segal, M., 1995. Implementation of the Reformulated Gasoline Program. Congressional Research Service Report 95–850, Washington.

McClelland, G.H., Schulze, W.D., Hurd, B., 1990. The effects of risk beliefs on property values: a case study of hazardous waste site. Risk Analysis 10, 485–497.

Meyer, R.J., 2012. Failing to learn from experience about catastrophes: the case of hurricane preparedness. Journal of Risk and Uncertainty 45, 25–50.

Michaels, R.G., Smith, V.K., 1990. Market segmentation and valuing amenities with Hedonic models: the case of hazardous waste sites. Journal of Urban Economics 28, 223–242.

Millner, A., 2013. On welfare frameworks and catastrophic climate risks. Journal of Environmental Economics and Management 65, 310–325.

Montero, J.-P., Ellerman, A.D., 1998. "Explaining Low Sulfur Dioxide Allowance Prices: The Effect of Expectation Errors and Irreversibility". Center for Energy and Environmental Policy Research Working Paper 98-011, Massachusetts Institute of Technology.

National Research Council, 1994. Science and Judgment in Risk Assessment. National Academy Press, Washington.

National Research Council, 2010. The Hidden Costs of Energy. National Academy Press, Washington.

Newbold, S., Daigneault, A., 2009. Climate response uncertainty and the benefits of greenhouse gas emissions reductions. Environmental and Resource Economics 44, 351–377.

Newell, R.G., Jaffe, A.B., Stavins, R.N., 1999. The induced innovation hypothesis and energy-saving technological change. Quarterly Journal of Economics 114, 941–975.

Newell, R.G., Pizer, W.A., 2003a. Regulating stock externalities under uncertainty. Journal of Environmental Economics and Management 45, 416–432.

Newell, R.G., Pizer, W.A., 2003b. Discounting the distant future: how much do uncertain rates increase valuations? Journal of Environmental Economics and Management 46, 52–71.

Newell, R.G., Pizer, W.A., 2008. Indexed regulation. Journal of Environmental Economics and Management 56, 221–233.

Nichols, A.L., Zeckhauser, R.J., 1986. The perils of prudence: how conservative risk assessments distort regulation. Regulation 10, 13–24.

Nordhaus, W.D., 2007. To tax or not to tax: alternative approaches to slowing global warming. Review of Environmental Economics and Policy 1, 26–44.

Nordhaus, W.D., 2011. The economics of tail events with an application to climate change. Review of Environmental Economics and Policy 5, 240–257.

Nordhaus, W.D., 2012. Economic policy in the face of severe tail events. Journal of Public Economic Theory 14, 197–219.

Nordhaus, W.D., 2013. The Climate Casino. Yale University Press, New Haven.

Pindyck, R.S., 2000. Irreversibilities and the timing of environmental policy. Resource and Energy Economics 22, 233–259.

Pindyck, R.S., 2002. Optimal timing problems in environmental economics. Journal of Economic Dynamics and Control 26, 1677–1697.

Pindyck, R.S., 2007. Uncertainty in environmental economics. Review of Environmental Economics and Policy 1, 45–65.

Pindyck, R.S., 2011. Fat tails, thin tails, and climate change policy. Review of Environmental Economics and Policy 5, 258–274.

Pindyck, R.S., 2013. Pricing carbon when we don't know the right price. Regulation, 43–46.

Pizer, W.A., 2002. Combining price and quantity controls to mitigate global climate change. Journal of Public Economics 85, 409–434.

Popp, D., 2002. Induced innovation and energy prices. American Economic Review 92, 160–180.

Portney, P., 1981. Housing prices, health effects, and valuing reductions in risk of death. Journal of Environmental Economics and Management 8, 72–78.

Portney, P., 1992. Trouble in Happyville. Journal of Policy Analysis and Management 11, 131–132.

Pratt, J., Raiffa, H., Schlaifer, R., 1995. Introduction to Statistical Decision Theory. MIT Press, Cambridge.

Raiffa, H., 1961. Risk, ambiguity, and the savage axioms: comment. Quarterly Journal of Economics 75, 690–694.

Ramey, V.A., Vine, D.J., 2010. Oil, Automobiles, and the U.S. Economy: How Much Have Things Really Changed? NBER Working Paper 16067.

Roberts, M.J., Spence, M., 1976. Effluent charges and licenses under uncertainty. Journal of Public Economics 5, 193–208.

Schmalensee, R., Stavins, R.N., 2013. The SO_2 allowance trading system: the ironic history of a grand policy experiment. Journal of Economic Perspectives 27, 103–122.

Shafran, A.P., 2011. Self-protection against repeated low probability risks. Journal of Risk and Uncertainty 42, 263–285.

Sigman, H., 1996. The effect of hazardous waste taxes on waste generation and disposal. Journal of Environmental Economics and Management 30, 199–217.

Smith, V.K., Carbone, J.C., Pope, J.C., Hallstrom, D.G., Darden, M.E., 2006. Adjusting to natural disasters. Journal of Risk and Uncertainty 33, 37–54.

Smith, V.K., Desvousges, W.H., Fisher, A., Johnson, F.R., 1988. Learning about Radon's risk. Journal of Risk and Uncertainty 1, 233–258.

Solomon, S., Qin, D., Manning, M., Chen, Z., Marquis, M., Averyt, K.B., Tignor, M., Miller, H.L. (Eds.), 2007. Summary for Policymakers, Climate Change 2007: The Physical Science Basis. Cambridge University Press, Cambridge.

Stavins, R.N., 1996. Correlated uncertainty and policy instrument choice. Journal of Environmental Economics and Management 30, 218–232.

Summers, L., Zeckhauser, R., 2008. Policymaking for posterity. Journal of Risk and Uncertainty 37, 115–140.

Sutter, D., Poitras, M., 2010. Do people respond to low probability risks? Evidence from tornado risk and manufactured homes. Journal of Risk and Uncertainty 40, 181–196.

Tietenberg, T., 1998. Disclosure strategies for pollution control. Environmental and Resource Economics 11, 587–602.

Tol, R.S.J., 2009. The economic effects of climate change. Journal of Economic Perspectives 23, 29–51.

Ulph, A., Ulph, D., 1997. Global warming, irreversibility and learning. Economic Journal 107, 636–650.

U.S. Energy Information Administration (U.S. EIA), 2010. Energy Market and Economic Impacts of the American Power Act of 2010. Department of Energy, Washington.

U.S. Energy Information Administration (U.S. EIA), 2013. Annual Energy Outlook 2013. Department of Energy, Washington.

Viscusi, W.K., 1997. Alarmist decisions with divergent risk information. Economic Journal 107, 1657–1670.

Viscusi, W.K., 1998. Rational Risk Policy. Oxford University Press, Oxford.

Viscusi, W.K., Chesson, H., 1999. Hopes and fears: the conflicting effects of risk ambiguity. Theory and Decision 47, 153–178.

Viscusi, W.K., Gayer, T., 2002. Safety at any price? Regulation 25, 54–63.

Viscusi, W.K., Hakes, J.K., 1998. Synthetic risks, risk potency, and carcinogen regulation. Journal of Policy Analysis and Management 17, 52–73.

Viscusi, W.K., Hamilton, J.T., Dockins, P.C., 1997. Conservative versus mean risk assessments: implications for Superfund policies. Journal of Environmental Economics and Management 34, 187–206.

Viscusi, W.K., Magat, W.A., 1987. Learning about Risk: Consumer and Worker Responses to Hazard Information. Harvard University Press, Cambridge, MA.

Viscusi, W.K., Magat, W.A., 1992. Bayesian decisions with ambiguous belief aversion. Journal of Risk and Uncertainty 5, 371–387.

Viscusi, W.K., Zeckhauser, R.J., 2004. The denominator blindness effect: accident frequencies and the misjudgment of recklessness. American Law and Economics Review 6, 72–94.

Webster, M., Jakobovits, L., Norton, J., 2008. Learning about climate change and implications for near-term policy. Climatic Change 89, 67–85.

Webster, M., Sue Wing, I., Jakobovits, L., 2010. Second-best instruments for near-term climate policy: intensity targets vs. the safety valve. Journal of Environmental Economics and Management 59, 250–259.

Weitzman, M.L., 1974. Prices versus quantities. Review of Economic Studies 41, 477–491.

Weitzman, M.L., 2001. Gamma discounting. American Economic Review 91, 260–271.

Weitzman, M.L., 2009. On modeling and interpreting the economics of catastrophic climate change. Review of Economics and Statistics 91, 1–19.

Weitzman, M.L., 2010. Risk-adjusted gamma discounting. Journal of Environmental Economics and Management 60, 1–13.

Weitzman, M.L., 2011. Fat-tailed uncertainty in the economics of catastrophic climate change. Review of Environmental Economics and Policy 5, 275–292.

Yohe, G.W., 1978. Towards a general comparison of price controls and quantity controls under uncertainty. Review of Economic Studies 45, 229–238.

CHAPTER *11*

Economics of Natural Catastrophe Risk Insurance

Howard Kunreuther and Erwann Michel-Kerjan
Center for Risk Management and Decision Processes, The Wharton School, University of Pennsylvania, USA

Contents

Abstract

Economic and insured losses from natural catastrophes have increased significantly in recent years and are challenging the way catastrophe risk insurance markets operate today. This chapter focuses on how insurance in combination with other policy tools can reduce losses from natural disasters and provide funds to aid the recovery process following catastrophic events. To address this issue we discuss conditions of insurability and how insurers have behaved with respect to extreme events in the United States. We then examine the demand for homeowners insurance and why there is limited interest by many individuals in voluntarily purchasing and maintaining coverage against catastrophe losses. We introduce two guiding principles for insurance: *Premiums should reflect risk* and *Dealing with equity and affordability issues,* and discuss several options for providing coverage against large-scale risks that embrace these principles including offering fixed-price multi-year insurance contracts as a complement to annual policies.

Keywords

Catastrophes, Insurance Markets, Behavioral Economics, Multi-year Insurance

JEL Classification Codes

G22 – Insurance, Insurance Companies, Q54 – Climate, Natural Disasters, Global Warming, H84 - Disaster Aid

Handbook of the Economics of Risk and Uncertainty, Volume 1
ISSN 2211-7547, http://dx.doi.org/10.1016/B978-0-444-53685-3.00011-8

11.1 INTRODUCTION

The recent unprecedented series of large-scale disasters and crises, ranging from terrorist attacks and cyber-attacks to massive earthquakes, hurricanes, floods, droughts, oil spills and financial and fiscal crises, has triggered growing interest in the economics of catastrophe risks from academia as well as the private and public sectors in the United States and abroad.[1]

For instance, in December 2010, the Council of the Organization for Economic Development and Cooperation (OECD) that comprises 34 member countries, adopted a recommendation titled "*Good practices for mitigating and financing catastrophic risks*".[2] It provides governments and relevant public and private institutions with a framework for identifying disaster risks, promoting risk awareness, enhancing prevention and loss mitigation strategies, and designing of compensation arrangements (OECD, 2010). And in 2012 for the first time the G20, under the Mexican Presidency, has officially recognized disaster risk management as a top priority (Michel-Kerjan, 2012a).

This chapter focuses primarily on the role that insurance has played in financing catastrophic losses from natural disasters and the role it can play in the future in combination with other policy tools. More specifically, we examine how catastrophic risks are shared between those exposed, the private sectors of insurance, reinsurance and financial markets, and the public sphere. We then address the question "Who should pay for future losses?" and suggest a role that insurance can play in this regard.

We will use the United States as our base case throughout the chapter as it has the largest insurance market in the world and provides us with a benchmark for assessing the changing nature of catastrophe risk insurance.

The year 2011 was the most costly year in the history of insurance worldwide, due primarily to the massive earthquake and tsunami in Japan and thousands of tornadoes that hit the United States. The year 2011 also had the highest number of Presidential disaster declarations in the United States (99 declarations), reinforcing an increasing trend over the past 50 years. The year 2012 was another very costly year on the natural disaster front: the year-long drought cost $30 billion (2012 was the hottest year on record of the past 50 years in the U.S.) and Hurricane Sandy cost another $68 billion in the continental United States.

We believe this trend toward more costly catastrophes is likely to continue, given that more people are residing in high-risk areas across the planet. A fuller understanding of how people make decisions under risk and uncertainty is becoming more important, and this information needs to be widely disseminated to businesses and elected

---

[1] For recent work on *macro*-economic disasters (e.g., wars), see Barro (2009), Barro and Ursua (2008), Gourio (2008), Martin (2008), and Gabaix (2008).

[2] This document was proposed by the OECD Secretary-General Board on Financial Management of Catastrophes that has been advising the head of the organization and the governments of member countries since its inception in 2006.

government officials so they can make more informed decisions as to ways to reduce catastrophic losses in the future (Michel-Kerjan and Slovic, 2010; Kunreuther et al., 2013).

This chapter addresses the above points. Section 11.2 provides evidence of the growing concerns regarding catastrophe losses worldwide and the significant increase in insured losses. We also show that in the United States, the federal government has been increasingly generous in providing devastated areas with historical amounts of post-disaster relief.

Section 11.3 discusses a simple model of insurance supply to be used as a benchmark for evaluating actual behavior by insurers. We show that catastrophe risks pose very specific challenges for insurers who do not necessarily act according to the benchmark model of choice. We illustrate this by discussing how insurers have behaved vis-à-vis terrorism, earthquake, hurricane and flood risks in the United States. Recent catastrophes have prompted many insurers to leave these markets or seriously reconsider their involvement, leading to an increased role for state and federal government in catastrophe risk financing. Section 11.4 turns to the demand side of the insurance market where there is limited interest by many individuals in voluntarily purchasing and maintaining coverage against catastrophe losses. We examine why this is the case.

In this context, Section 11.5 proposes two guiding principles to use insurance mechanisms more effectively: (1) insurance premiums should be risk-based, and (2) attention needs to be given to issues of equity and affordability. We then discuss several proposals for providing coverage against catastrophic risks that embrace these principles, including a proposal that public and private insurers should consider offering fixed-price multi-year insurance (MYI) contracts as a way of ensuring stable coverage over time and guaranteeing price stability to their policyholders. Section 11.6 provides conclusions and suggestions for future research.

11.2 A NEW ERA OF CATASTROPHES

11.2.1 Natural and Man-Made Disasters Are Becoming More Costly

Economic and insured losses from natural catastrophes such as hurricanes, earthquakes, and floods have increased significantly in recent years. Hurricane Katrina, which severely struck Louisiana and Mississippi in the United States in August 2005, resulted in massive flooding after the inadequate levee system in New Orleans failed. Over 1,300 people died, millions were displaced, and many saw the response by the U.S. Federal Emergency Management Agency as insufficient. Hurricane Katrina was "only" a Category 3 hurricane when it made landfall but its strength, combined with the failure of the flood protection system, led to economic losses in the range of $150 to $200 billion—an historical record in the United States for a natural disaster. Hurricane Sandy, which hit the Northeastern part of the United States at the end of October 2012, caused an estimated

$68 billion in economic losses to residences, business owners, and infrastructure owners (Aon Benfield, 2013). It is the second most costly natural disaster in the United States after Hurricane Katrina.

Conventional wisdom holds that major accidents and disasters are low-probability events. But when you look at a whole state or country, as insurers normally do, such events have a relatively high chance of occurring somewhere during a short time period. It is somewhat sobering, for instance, to learn that the probability is 1 in 6 that at least $10 billion dollars of insured property will be destroyed by hurricanes somewhere in Florida next year. This is equivalent to the chance of getting the number 3 in one toss of a die—hardly a low probability. If we extend the time horizon from one year to 10 years while keeping the population of Florida constant, the likelihood of at least one hurricane causing damage exceeding this amount is greater than 5 in 6. With economic development in coastal areas of this state and the apparent increased intensity of hurricanes due to global warming, we are almost certain to experience a disaster with losses exceeding $10 billion in Florida in the next decade (Kunreuther and Michel-Kerjan, 2011).

Worldwide, economic losses from natural catastrophes increased from $528 billion in the decade 1981–1990, to $1,197 billion during 1991–2000, and $1,213 billion during 2001–2010. In 2011 alone, economic losses amounted to over $400 billion, in large part due to the March 2011 Japan earthquake and resulting tsunami; 2012 brought another $170 billion in economic losses (Munich Re, 2013). Figure 11.1 depicts the evolution

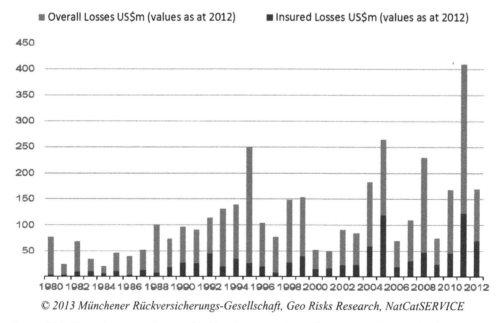

© 2013 Münchener Rückversicherungs-Gesellschaft, Geo Risks Research, NatCatSERVICE

Figure 11.1 Natural catastrophes worldwide 1980–2012: Overall and insured losses ($ billion).

of the direct economic losses and the insured portion from great natural disasters over the period 1980–2012.[3]

Insured losses have dramatically increased as well. Between 1970 and the mid-1980s, annual insured losses from natural disasters worldwide (including forest fires) were only in the $3 billion to $4 billion range. Hurricane Hugo, which made landfall in Charleston, South Carolina, on September 22, 1989, was the first natural disaster in the United States to inflict more than $1 billion of insured losses, with insured losses of $4.2 billion (1989 prices). During the period 2001 to 2010, insured losses from weather-related disasters alone averaged $30 billion annually (Swiss Re, 2011).

Table 11.1 ranks the 25 most costly *insured* catastrophes that occurred in the world over the period 1970–2012. With the exception of insured losses from the 9/11 terrorist attacks, all of the events were natural disasters. The data reveals that eighteen of these disasters occurred since 2001, with almost two-thirds in the United States, due in part to the high concentration of value at risk and the high degree of insurance penetration compared to less developed countries.

11.2.1.1 Impact on Gross Domestic Product (GDP)

At an aggregate level, one can estimate the economic impact of disasters by determining the losses in relation to the country's annual GDP. A major flood in the United States or a large European country will have much less impact on GDP than a similar event occurring in a developing country. In the United States where the GDP is nearly US$15 trillion, even a US$250 billion loss will have an impact on GDP that is less than 2 percent. By contrast, in Myanmar, a 2 percent GDP loss would be associated with damages in the range of US$1.8 billion. Smaller countries like island nations also often have a limited geographical spread of their economic assets relative to the spatial impact of disasters, and are subject to more direct, indirect, and downstream losses (UNDP, 2004).

However, using annual GDP to measure the relative economic impact of a disaster does not necessarily reveal the impact of the catastrophe on the affected region; property damage, business interruption, real estate prices and tax revenues could have a severe local impact. The long-term effects of disasters on a country's GDP can also vary based on the state of development of the country, the size of the event, and the overall economic vulnerability of the country. Potentially negative long-term economic effects after a disaster include an increase in the public deficit and the worsening of the trade balance (demand for imports increase and exports decrease). For example, after Hurricane Mitch in 1998, Honduras experienced total direct and indirect losses that were 80 percent of its GDP (Mechler, 2003).

---

[3] Catastrophes are classified as "great" if the ability of the region to help itself is overtaxed, making inter-regional or international assistance necessary. This is normally the case when thousands of people are killed, hundreds of thousands made homeless or when a country suffers substantial economic losses.

Table 11.1 The 25 Most Costly Insured Catastrophes in the World, 1970–2012

$ Billion	Event	Victims (Dead and Missing)	Year	Area of Primary Damage
76.3*	Hurricane Katrina; floods	1,836	**2005**	USA, Gulf of Mexico
39	9/11 terrorist attacks	3,025	**2001**	USA
35.7	Earthquake (M 9.0) and tsunami	19,135	**2011**	Japan
35.0*	Hurricane Sandy; floods	237	**2012**	USA
26.2	Hurricane Andrew	43	1992	USA, Bahamas
21.7	Northridge Earthquake (M 6.6)	61	1994	USA
21.6	Hurricane Ike; floods	136	**2008**	USA, Caribbean
15.7	Hurricane Ivan	124	**2004**	USA, Caribbean
15.3	Floods; heavy monsoon rains	815	**2011**	Thailand
15.3	Earthquake (M 6.3); aftershocks	181	**2011**	New Zealand
14.7	Hurricane Wilma; floods	35	**2005**	USA, Gulf of Mexico
11.9	Hurricane Rita	34	**2005**	USA, Gulf of Mexico, et al.
11.0	Drought in the Corn Belt	123	**2012**	USA
9.8	Hurricane Charley	24	**2004**	USA, Caribbean, et al.
9.5	Typhoon Mireille	51	1991	Japan
8.5	Hurricane Hugo	71	1989	Puerto Rico, USA, et al.
8.4	Earthquake (M 8.8); tsunami	562	**2010**	Chile
8.2	Winter Storm Daria	95	1990	France, UK, et al.
8.0	Winter Storm Lothar	110	1999	France, Switzerland, et al.
7.4	Storms; over 350 tornadoes	350	**2011**	USA (Alabama et al.)
7.2	Major tornado outbreak	155	**2011**	USA (Missouri et al.)
6.7	Winter Storm Kyrill	54	**2007**	Germany, UK, NL, France
6.2	Storms and floods	22	1987	France, UK, et al.
6.2	Hurricane Frances	38	**2004**	USA, Bahamas
6.0	Hurricane Irene	55	**2011**	USA, Caribbean

*Including payment by the U.S. federal National Flood Insurance Program.

Sources: Authors' calculation. Data from Swiss Re and Insurance Information Institute (in 2011 prices).

Note: Years from 2001–2012 are in bold.

11.2.1.2 Fatalities

Natural disasters also have a much more devastating human impact in low-income countries than in the developed world. The Bhola cyclone in the Ganges Delta in 1970 killed an estimated 500,000 in East Pakistan (now Bangladesh) and is classified as one of the deadliest natural disasters in history. In recent years, the 2004 tsunami in Southeast Asia killed between 225,000 and 275,000; the earthquake in Haiti in 2010 killed approximately 230,000 (CBC News, 2010). The historic floods in Pakistan in the summer of 2010 killed 2,000 and affected 20 million people. These fatalities have a long-term impact on the country's development potential. A population weakened by a natural disaster may lack the organizational capacity to maintain social assets, thus making communities more likely to experience catastrophes in the future. Losses in sanitation facilities, schools, health services and housing can further cripple an already affected nation (UNISDR/World Bank, 2011).

11.2.2 The Question of Attribution

The increased costs of disasters in recent years is primarily due to a higher degree of urbanization and an increase in the value at risk. In 1950, approximately 30 percent of the world's population lived in cities. In 2000, about 50 percent of the world's population (6 billion) resided in urban areas. Projections by the United Nations (2008) show that by 2025, this figure will have increased to 60 percent based on a world population estimate of 8.3 billion people.

In the United States in 2003, 53 percent of the nation's population (153 million people), lived in the 673 U.S. coastal counties, an increase of 33 million people since 1980, according to the National Oceanic Atmospheric Administration (Crossett et al., 2004). Yet coastal counties, excluding Alaska, account for only 17 percent of land area in the United States. In hazard-prone areas, this urbanization and increase in population translate into greater concentration of exposure and hence a higher likelihood of catastrophic losses from future disasters.

This new vulnerability is best understood in an historical context. It is possible to calculate the total direct economic cost of catastrophes in the past century adjusted for inflation, population, and wealth normalization. For example, a study by Pielke et al. (2008) normalizes mainland U.S. hurricane damage for the period 1900–2005. They show that the hurricane that hit Miami in 1926 would have been almost twice as costly as Hurricane Katrina had it occurred in 2005, and the Galveston hurricane of 1900 would have had total direct economic costs as high as those from Katrina. We are very likely to see even more devastating disasters in the coming years because of the ongoing growth in values located in risk-prone areas.

There is another element to consider in determining how to adequately manage and finance catastrophe risks: the possible impact of a change in climate on future weather-related catastrophes. Between 1970 and 2004, storms and floods were responsible for over 90 percent of the total economic costs of weather-related extreme events worldwide. Storms (hurricanes in the U.S. region, typhoons in Asia, and windstorms in Europe) contributed to over 75 percent of insured losses. In constant prices (2004), insured losses from weather-related events averaged $3 billion annually between 1970 and 1990 and then increased significantly to $16 billion annually between 1990 and 2004 (Association of British Insurers, 2005). In 2005, 99.7 percent of all catastrophic losses worldwide were due to weather-related events (Mills and Lecomte, 2006).

There have been numerous scientific debates as to whether the series of hurricanes that occurred in 2004 and 2005 and 2012 might be partially attributable to the impact of a change in climate. One of the expected effects of global warming will be an increase in hurricane intensity. This increase has been predicted by theory and modeling, and substantiated by empirical data on climate change. Higher ocean temperatures lead to an exponentially higher evaporation rate in the atmosphere, which increases the intensity of cyclones and precipitation (IPCC, 2011). An increase in the number of major hurricanes over a shorter period of time is likely to translate into a greater number hitting the coasts, with a greater likelihood of damage to residences and commercial buildings today than in the 1940s—a trend that raises questions about the insurability of weather-related catastrophes.

11.2.3 Increasing Governmental Disaster Relief

The upward trend in losses has had an impact on post-disaster relief to assist the affected communities in rebuilding destroyed infrastructure[4] and providing temporary housing to displaced victims. In the United States, federal and state governments have played an increasingly important role in providing such relief. Under the current U.S. system, the governor of the state(s) can request that the president declare a "major disaster" and offer special assistance if the damage is severe enough, with the amount of aid determined by Congress. A look at the number of U.S. presidential disaster declarations since 1953 clearly reveals an upward trend (see Figure 11.2).

Overall, the number of presidential disaster declarations has dramatically increased over time, from 191 declarations over the decade 1961–1970 to 597 for the period 2001–2010 (Michel-Kerjan and Kunreuther, 2011). As Figure 11.2 also reveals, many of the peak years correspond to presidential election years. This is consistent with research that reveals that presidential election years spur disaster assistance.[5] Four salient examples are the Alaska earthquake (March 1964), Tropical Storm Agnes (June 1972), Hurricane Andrew (September 1992), and the four Florida hurricanes (August–September 2004). In 1996 and 2008 (both presidential election years) there were 75 presidential declarations. This record number was exceeded in 2010 when there were 81 major disaster declarations, and again in 2011 with 99 declarations.

Increasing relief also creates a spiral of increasing expectations of relief which may account for the significant growth in government disaster relief in the United States during the past 75 years. As David Moss (2010) states:

"Congress provided assistance to the victims of a major fire in New Hampshire as early as 1803, and historians have counted 128 specific acts of Congress providing ad hoc relief for the victims of various disasters over the years 1803 to 1947. Nevertheless, disaster relief was not generally viewed as an ongoing federal responsibility in the United States until well into the twentieth century" (p. 152).

---

[4] On the question of protection of critical infrastructures, see Auerswald et al. (2006).

[5] Reeves (2004, 2005) shows that a battleground state with 20 electoral votes received more than twice as many presidential disaster declarations as a state with only three electoral votes.

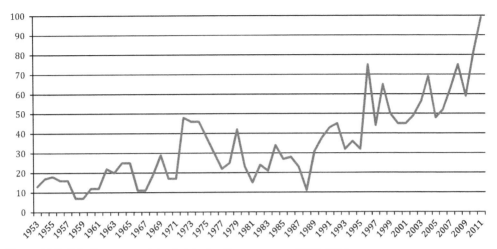

Figure 11.2 U.S. disaster presidential declarations per year, 1953–2011.

This view was also shared by Kunreuther and Miller (1985) who noted more than 25 years ago:

"The role of the federal government with respect to hazards has been changing over the past 30 years. Although Congressmen and federal agencies have become more concerned with finding ways to help communities struck by severe disasters, there has also been a realization that government has been viewed as the protector of risks in ways that would have been unthinkable 50 years ago" (p. 148).

The more pronounced role of the federal government in assisting disaster victims can also be seen by examining several major disasters occurring in the past 50 years as shown in Table 11.2.[6] For example, the total economic cost of Hurricane Sandy was estimated to be $68 billion. Congress voted a $55.5 billion relief package in early 2013 (in addition to the $9.7 billion provided to the National Flood Insurance Program (NFIP)[7] so it could meet its claims): an historically high 88 percent.

Media coverage in the immediate aftermath of catastrophes often raises compassion for victims of the tragedy.[8] The magnitude of the destruction often leads governmental agencies to provide disaster relief to victims. The expectation of governmental funding results in economic disincentives for people and businesses to reduce their own

---

[6] See Cummins et al. (2010) for a more systematic analysis of government exposure to extreme events.

[7] A discussion of the NFIP is provided in Section 11.3.4.4.

[8] Moss (2002, 2010) and Eisensee and Stromberg (2007) have shown the critical role played by increasing media coverage of disasters in increasing government relief in the United States. See Kunreuther and Miller (1985) for a discussion on the evolution of disaster relief in the 1980s. See also Raschky and Schwindt (2009) and Jaffee and Russell (2012).

Table 11.2 Role of the U.S. Federal Government in National Disaster Relief

Disaster	Federal Aid as % of Total Damage
Hurricane Sandy (2012)	77%
Hurricane Ike (2008)	69%
Hurricane Katrina (2005)	50%
Hurricane Hugo (1989)	23%
Hurricane Diane (1955)	6%

Sources: Michel-Kerjan and Volkman Wise (2011).

exposure and/or purchase proper insurance coverage (Michel-Kerjan and Volkman Wise, 2011).[9]

If individuals assume that they will be bailed out after a disaster, why should they purchase insurance or avoid locating in high-risk areas?[10] The reality is that governmental disaster relief is usually earmarked to rebuild destroyed infrastructure, not as direct aid to the victims. To the extent that a large portion of such disaster relief goes to the states, post-disaster assistance also distorts the incentives of state and local governments to prefinance their disaster losses through insurance and other mechanisms.

In summary, the occurrence of numerous very devastating catastrophes over a short period of time is challenging the way catastrophe risk insurance markets operate today. In the next two sections we will discuss the supply and demand side of this market.

11.3 SUPPLY OF INSURANCE AGAINST CATASTROPHIC EVENTS

This section outlines a benchmark model of choice for suppliers of insurance against catastrophic risk. It then highlights challenges that insurers face in providing coverage against terrorism and natural disasters where the probability of a loss occurring is low but where claims payments are likely to be high if the event occurs.

11.3.1 A Benchmark Model of Insurance Supply[11]

Insurance is said to be priced at an actuarially fair rate when the premium charged to cover a risk of losing L with a probability p equals the expected loss (i.e., pL). An insurer will normally charge an additional administrative cost to cover its own expenses and generate a profit. A risk neutral party would thus not be interested in purchasing

---

[9] It is surprising how little data is publicly available on the amount that victims of disaster actually receive as direct aid. The Federal Emergency Management Agency (FEMA) has a series of disaster relief programs, but most of them are loan-based (e.g. Small Business Administration's program). This can address the liquidity issues that victims and their families face after a disaster, but does not transfer the loss to a third party, as insurance does.

[10] See Browne and Hoyt (2000) for a discussion of the notion of "charity hazard."

[11] For more details on key concepts in the benchmark model of supply see Chapter 7 by Dionne and Harrington (this volume) and Chapter 2 in Kunreuther et al. (2013).

coverage unless required to do so. On the other hand, a risk–averse party would be willing to pay a higher price than the expected loss to avoid the negative consequences of a large loss.

An insurer normally relies on risk pooling and the law of large numbers when providing coverage against a specific risk. If the risks are independent and there are a significant number of policyholders, then the variance in the expected loss is very small so the insurer can estimate with some degree of accuracy how large its annual claims payments will be *on average*.

A benchmark model of insurance supply assumes that insurance companies are maximizing long-run expected profits for their owners in a competitive insurance market. In this environment there are many insurance firms, each of whom is free to charge any premium for a prespecified amount of coverage. The assumption of competition implies that their premiums will be just enough to allow the insurers to cover their costs and make a reasonable profit.

Potential customers and the insurers are assumed to have accurate information on the likelihood of a loss and its consequences. In this idealized world, virtually every uncertain event of concern would be insured to some extent if the administrative cost of furnishing coverage was not high and consumers were sufficiently risk averse and maximized their expected utility (Arrow, 1963).

11.3.2 The Practice of Insurance

As indicated above, insurers need to make a profit and generate a sufficient return to their owners to make this an attractive investment. An important element in this regard is the concept of *insurability*.[12] To understand this concept, consider a standard policy whereby premiums are paid at the start of a given time period to cover losses during this interval (usually a year). Two conditions must be met before insurance providers are willing to offer coverage against an uncertain event. The first is the ability to identify and quantify, or estimate at least partially, the chances of the event occurring and the extent of losses likely to be incurred. The second condition is the ability to set premiums for each potential customer or class of customers at prices that provide a competitive return at the assumed level of risk.

If both conditions are satisfied, a risk is considered to be *insurable*. But it still may not be profitable. In other words, it may be impossible to specify a premium for which there is sufficient demand and incoming revenue to cover the development, marketing, operating, cost of holding capital (see discussion below) and costs of claims processing, and yield a net positive profit over a prespecified time horizon. In such cases, the insurer will not want to offer coverage against this risk. In addition, as discussed below, state regulations often limit insurers in their premium-setting process. Competition

---

[12] This subsection is based on Kunreuther and Michel-Kerjan (2011).

can also play a role in determining what premium can be charged. Even in the absence of these influences, an insurer must consider problems associated with asymmetry of information (*adverse selection* and *moral hazard*), and degree of *correlation of the risk* in determining what premium to charge. We briefly examine each of these factors in the following subsections.

11.3.2.1 Adverse Selection

If the insurer cannot differentiate the risks facing two groups of potential insurance buyers and if all buyers know their own risk, then the insurer is likely to suffer greater losses if it sets the same premium for both groups by using the entire population as a basis for this estimate. If only the highest risk group is likely to purchase coverage for that hazard and the premium is below its expected loss, the insurer will have a portfolio of "bad" risks. This situation, referred to as *adverse selection*, can be rectified by the insurer charging a high enough premium to cover the losses from the bad risks. In so doing, the good risks might purchase only partial protection or no insurance at all, because they consider the price of coverage to be too expensive relative to their risk.[13]

This was the argument made by private insurers regarding the noninsurability of flood risk that led to the creation of the National Flood Insurance Program (NFIP) in 1968. Indeed, insurers thought that families who had lived in a specific flood-prone area for many years had a much better knowledge of the risk than any insurer would have gained unless it undertook costly risk assessments. Likewise, certain businesses may have a much better knowledge about the risk they are exposed to, and their degree of preparedness for a loss than will the insurer.

11.3.2.2 Moral Hazard

Moral hazard refers to an increase in the expected loss (probability or amount of loss conditional on an event occurring) due to individuals and firms behaving more carelessly as a result of purchasing insurance. A firm with insurance protection may alter its behavior in ways that increase the expected loss relative to what it would have been without coverage. If the insurer cannot predict this behavior and relies on past loss data from uninsured firms to estimate the distribution of claim payments, the resulting premium is likely to be too low to cover expected losses. The introduction of deductibles, coinsurance or upper limits on coverage can be useful tools in reducing moral hazard, by encouraging insureds to engage in less risky behavior, as they know they will incur part of the losses from an adverse event.

---

[13] For a survey of adverse selection issues, see Dionne et al. (2000).

11.3.2.3 Correlated Risks

The potential for highly correlated losses from extreme events has an impact on the tail of the distribution and normally requires the insurer to hold additional capital in liquid form to protect itself against large losses. Insurers normally face spatially correlated losses from large-scale natural disasters. State Farm and Allstate paid $3.6 billion and $2.3 billion in claims, respectively, in the wake of Hurricane Andrew in 1992 due to their high concentration of homeowners' policies in the Miami-Dade County area of Florida. Given this unexpectedly high loss, both companies began to reassess their strategies of providing coverage against wind damage in hurricane-prone areas (Lecomte and Gahagan, 1998).

Hurricanes Katrina and Rita, which devastated the U.S. Gulf Coast in August and September 2005, had dramatic impacts on several lines of insurance, notably property damage and business interruption. Edward Liddy, chairman of Allstate, which provided insurance coverage to 350,000 homeowners in Louisiana, Mississippi and Alabama, shortly after Katrina declared:

> "… extensive flooding has complicated disaster planning … and the higher water has essentially altered efforts to assess damage. We now have 1,100 adjusters on the ground. We have another 500 who are ready to go as soon as we can get into some of the most-devastated areas. It will be many weeks, probably months, before there is anything approaching reliable estimates" (Francis, 2005).

11.3.2.4 Importance of the Cost of Capital

The importance of the *cost of capital*[14] as a requisite for insurers to secure an adequate rate of return to their shareholders is often not sufficiently understood. In particular, the prices charged for disaster insurance must be sufficiently high not only to cover the expected claims costs and other expenses, but also the costs of allocating capital to underwrite this risk. Moreover, because large amounts of risk capital are needed to underwrite catastrophe risk, the resulting premium will be high relative to its loss expenses, simply to earn a fair rate of return on equity and thereby maintain the insurer's credit rating.

Much of the public debate surrounding a fair price of catastrophe insurance uses the concept of "actuarially fair" premiums. However, while *actuarially fair* is a useful statistical concept, the implied premiums are not economically sustainable; insurers must cover all their costs (not only expected claims) in order to survive and attract capital.

---

[14] "Cost of capital" is the opportunity cost of an investment; that is, the rate of return that an investor in a given insurance company would otherwise be able to earn at the same risk level if the money had been invested elsewhere. For example, when an investor purchases stock in an insurance company, s/he expects to see a return on that investment. Since the individual expects to receive more than his/her initial investment, the cost of capital is equal to this return that the investor receives.

The price of insurance is thus very sensitive to the ratio of the amount of capital to expected liability, needed to preserve one's credit rating. A ratio of 1 is normal for the combined books of business of many property liability insurers. However, for catastrophic risk, with its very large tail risk (which severely affects the insurer's credit risk), the capital to liability ratio needs to be higher. Indeed, the capital-to-liability ratio depends on volatility of the catastrophe liability and its correlation with the insurer's remaining portfolio. For the catastrophe risk premium for individual homeowners, this may translate into a loading factor λ—on top of the expected loss $E(L)$—perhaps approximating 0.5 to 1.0; that is premium $= (1 + \lambda)E(L)$. Thus the premium would be 150 or 200 percent of the expected loss. This does not reflect undue profitability, but simply that insurers need considerable capital to supply this insurance and the cost of that capital is included in the premium.

When it comes to reinsurance of catastrophic risk, the relative capital cost is much higher. For higher layers of catastrophe reinsurance, the expected loss is often quite low and the volatility very high.

At these layers, the required capital-to-liability ratio will increase the premium required to generate a fair return on equity.

A second issue with respect to catastrophic risk is that it can be expensive to underwrite since it requires extensive modeling. Many companies buy commercial models and/or use their own in-house modeling capability, which adds to their administrative cost.

There are other considerations that can dramatically increase the capital cost, notably the impact of double taxation. Harrington and Niehaus (2001) have simulated the tax burden over many parameters and show that tax costs alone can reasonably be as much as the claim cost and lead to further increases in premiums. When we account for all these factors (i.e., high capital inputs, transaction costs and taxes), catastrophe insurance premiums often are several multiples of expected claims costs.

11.3.3 Behavioral Characteristics of Insurers

There is growing evidence in the literature that insurance firms often deviate from the ideal benchmark supply model for several reasons stemming from behavioral factors.

Risk aversion by managers. Managers will be risk averse if they are rewarded when profits rise, but fear that they may become unemployed or suffer a loss to their reputation if the firm becomes insolvent (Greenwald and Stiglitz, 1990). Managers will behave in this way because losing a job at a firm that goes bankrupt is likely to create anxiety and worry as well as involve search costs in finding new employment. By extension, this causes the firm itself to behave as if it were risk averse. In this case, the firm will fail to maximize expected profits because managers set reserves at higher levels than stockholders would prefer.

Such deviations between the objectives of owners and managers become more important as an insurer's portfolio becomes more highly correlated. A more highly correlated portfolio of risks increases the likelihood that the firm will suffer a large loss and perhaps become insolvent. To reduce the likelihood of this outcome, insurance firm managers will want to increase the level of capital reserves that they hold. These actions are likely to increase the cost of coverage as well as drive down average profits.

Ambiguity aversion by insurers. The ambiguities associated both with the probability of an extreme event occurring and the resulting outcomes raise a number of challenges for insurers with respect to pricing their policies. Actuaries and underwriters both utilize rules of thumb that reflect their concern about those risks where past data do not indicate with precision what the loss probability is. Consider estimating the premium for wind damage to homes in New Orleans from future hurricanes. Actuaries first use their best estimates of the likelihood of hurricanes of different intensities to determine an expected annual loss to the property and contents of a particular residence. When recommending a premium that the underwriter should charge, they increase this figure to reflect the amount of perceived ambiguity in the probability of the hurricanes or the uncertainty in the resulting losses. More specifically, if the premium for a nonambiguous risk is given by z, then an actuary will recommend a premium of $z' = z(1+\alpha)$ where α reflects the degree of ambiguity regarding the risk (Kunreuther, 1989).

Underwriters then utilize the actuary's recommended premium as a reference point and focus on the impact of a major disaster, on the probability of insolvency, or on some prespecified loss of surplus to determine an appropriate premium to charge. In 1973, Insurance Commissioner James Stone of Massachusetts suggested that an underwriter who wants to determine the conditions for a specific risk to be insurable will focus on keeping the probability of insolvency below some threshold level ($q*$) rather than trying to maximize expected profits (Stone, 1973). From discussions with insurance underwriters today, this safety-first model still characterizes their behavior.

The safety-first model proposed by Commissioner Stone explicitly concerns itself with the likelihood of insolvency when determining whether to provide insurance against a particular risk and, if so, how much coverage to offer and what premiums to charge. Suppose that the insurer sets $q* = 1/250$. This implies that it will want to set premiums so that the likelihood of the insurer suffering a catastrophic loss is no greater than 1/250. The safety-first model also implies that insurers may not pay attention to events whose likelihood of causing insolvency to the insurer is below $q*$.

Actual insurer behavior often seems to follow a safety-first type model rather than the benchmark model of maximizing expected profit. The empirical evidence based on surveys of underwriters supports the hypothesis that insurers will set higher premiums when faced with ambiguous probabilities and uncertain losses for a well-specified risk. Underwriters of primary insurance companies and reinsurance firms were surveyed about the prices they would charge to insure a factory against property damage from a severe earthquake under the following four different cases:

- Case One: well-specified probabilities (p) and known losses (L);
- Case Two: ambiguous probabilities (Ap) and known losses (L);
- Case Three: well-specified probabilities (p) and uncertain losses (UL);
- Case Four: ambiguous probabilities (Ap) and uncertain losses (UL).

For the nonambiguous cases, the probability (p) of the earthquake was set at either 1 percent or 0.1 percent and the loss (L) should the event occur was specified at either \$1 million or \$10 million. For the highly ambiguous case (Ap, UL), the premiums were between 1.43 to 1.77 times higher than if underwriters priced a nonambiguous risk. The ratios for the other two cases were always above 1, but less than the (Ap, UL) case (Kunreuther et al., 1993).

Recent research reveals that when seeking advice from multiple advisors, insurers are sensitive to whether these experts agree or disagree with each other with respect to a specific forecast and/or in their recommendations for actions (Cabantous et al., 2011). A web-based experiment provided actuaries and underwriters in insurance companies with scenarios in which they seek advice and request probability forecasts from different groups of experts and then must determine what price to charge for coverage. The data revealed that insurers charge higher premiums when faced with ambiguity than when the probability of a loss is well specified (risk). More specifically, across three hazards (floods, hurricanes, house fires), we find that on average insurers report they would charge premiums that are between 21 percent and 30 percent higher for ambiguous damages than the premiums they would charge for damages under a risk situation. Furthermore, they would likely charge more for conflict ambiguity (that is, experts disagree on point estimates) than imprecise ambiguity (that is, experts agree on a range of probability, recognizing that they cannot estimate the probability of the event precisely) for flood and hurricane hazards (8.5 percent and 14 percent more for a one-year contract, respectively) but less in the case of fire (9 percent less for a one-year contract).

11.3.4 A Change in Catastrophe Risk Sharing between Markets and Governments

We now discuss several examples of insurer and manager behavior specific to catastrophe risk that do not adhere to the benchmark supply model.

These behaviors have led to a more active public sector role in providing protection against risks, as illustrated with the market for terrorism risk insurance, hurricane and earthquake insurance.

11.3.4.1 Terrorism Risk Insurance Market Before and After 9/11

Before the terrorist attacks of September 11, 2001 (9/11 hereafter), terrorism risk was included as an unnamed peril in most commercial insurance contracts in the United States (outside of transportation insurance) and hence the cost for providing such coverage to firms was never calculated.

One of the first attacks to significantly impact the insurance industry occurred in the UK in 1992 and cost insurers nearly $700 million (indexed to 2001) (Swiss Re, 2002). In 1993, three other major terrorist attacks occurred. The first was the bombing of the World Trade Center in New York City in February 1993, perpetrated in one of the garages of the Towers; the bombing killed six people and injured 1,000, and caused $725 million in insured damages. The second was a series of 13 bomb attacks in India that killed 300 and injured 1,100 others. Given the lack of insurance coverage, these attacks had no major impact on insurers, though. The third major attack occurred with a bomb exploding near NatWest Tower in April 1993 in London. This attack triggered $900 million in insured losses.

British insurers recognized the significance of these earlier attacks for the future of their industry and created a dedicated terrorism insurance program shortly after the attack in 1993, Pool Re. Surprisingly, insurers in the United Kingdom continued to cover this peril without explicitly pricing it in their commercial insurance policies. Two years later, the Oklahoma City bombing killed 168 people, but the largest losses were to federal property and employees, and were covered by the government. In 1998, bomb attacks on the U.S. embassy complex in Nairobi, Kenya killed more than 250 people and injured 5,000 others. Still, U.S. insurers and international reinsurers operating there continued to cover terrorism as they had done before. As Berkshire Chairman Warren Buffett said in his 2001 letter to shareholders, "We, and the rest of the industry, included coverage for terrorist acts in policies covering other risks, and received no additional premium for doing so."

Things radically changed after September 11, 2001. The Al Qaeda attacks killed more than 3,000 people[15] from over 90 countries and injured more than 2,250 others. The attacks also inflicted damage estimated at nearly $80 billion, about $32.5 billion (2001 prices) of which was covered by nearly 150 insurers and reinsurers worldwide (including $21 billion for damage and business interruption alone) (U.S. Treasury et al., 2006). Private reinsurers, who covered a majority of these losses, then decided to exit this market, leaving insurers without protection. A few months after 9/11, insurers had excluded terrorism from their policies in most states. In fact, by early 2002, 45 states permitted insurance companies to exclude terrorism from their corporate policies.[16]

---

[15] This number represents victims of the attacks in New York City, Washington, DC, and aboard Flight 93, which crashed in Stony Creek Township, Pennsylvania, as well as among teams of those providing emergency service.

[16] Workers' compensation insurance policies cover occupational injuries without regard to the peril that caused the injury.

Commercial enterprises thus found themselves in a very difficult situation, with insurance capacity extremely limited and priced very high.

For instance, prior to 9/11, Chicago's O'Hare Airport carried $750 million of terrorism insurance at an annual premium of $125,000; after the terrorist attacks, insurers offered only $150 million of coverage at an annual premium of $6.9 million (Jaffee and Russell, 2003). This new premium, if actuarially fair, implies the likelihood of a terrorist attack in the coming year on O'Hare Airport to be approximately 1 in 22 ($6.9 million/$150 million), an extremely high probability.

A principal reason that U.S. insurers refused to offer terrorism coverage after 9/11 was that global reinsurers, who are unconstrained by premium regulation and U.S. taxes, refused to provide protection to insurers against losses from another attack.

This led the U.S. Congress to pass the Terrorism Risk Insurance Act (TRIA) at the end of 2002, which provided a federal backstop of up to $100 billion for private insurance claims related to terrorism. Under TRIA, the U.S. federal government provides free reinsurance upfront, but would recoup part of its claims payment following a terrorist attack. This policy thus overcomes the liquidity problem that private insurers face after a severe loss (Wharton Risk Management Center, 2005). Today, nearly 60 percent of large firms in the United States have purchased some type of terrorism insurance (Michel-Kerjan and Raschky, 2011). TRIA is now set to expire in December 2014. It is not clear, however, what will happen if this happens, since insurers would not benefit from federal reinsurance anymore nor will they be required to offer terrorism insurance to all their clients as is currently the case under TRIA (Michel-Kerjan, 2012b).

11.3.4.2 Changes in Property Insurance Markets in Florida

Rate regulation has had more impact on property insurance than on any other line of coverage, particularly in states that are subject to potentially catastrophic losses from natural disasters. Consider the case of Florida. After Hurricane Andrew (August 1992), nine insurers became insolvent as a result of losses from the disaster. Insurers requested that state regulators give them permission to increase premiums, pointing to their large losses following Hurricane Andrew as a basis for those requests, without considering the likelihood of another disaster of this magnitude occurring. Insurers assumed that regulators would agree to the requested rate increases. They were not quite right.

Florida regulators resisted this recommendation and allowed insurers to only gradually raise rates over the decade. Moreover, they restricted insurers' ability to cancel existing homeowners' policies. Specifically, in May 1993 the state imposed a moratorium for six months on the cancellation and nonrenewal of residential property for the upcoming hurricane season for insurers that wanted to continue to do any business in Florida. In November 1993, the legislature enacted a bill preventing insurers from canceling more than 10 percent of their homeowners' policies in Florida in the next year and canceling more than 5 percent of their homeowners' policies statewide for each of the next three years. During the 1996 legislative session, this phase-out provision was extended until June 1, 1999 (Lecomte and Gahagan, 1998).

Following guidelines based only on recent loss history, not on analytic models, insurers concluded that those regulated premiums were inadequate (Grace et al., 2004). Insurers responded by reducing the supply of new homeowners' policies.

Then came the 2004 and 2005 hurricane seasons. As a result of unprecedented levels of insured losses, the price of catastrophe reinsurance in the U.S. increased significantly, rising 76 percent between July 1, 2005 and June 30, 2006 and 150 percent for Florida-only insurers over the same time period. Between July 1, 2006 and January 2008, prices fell slightly but increased again at the January 2009 renewals; they remain considerably higher than in January 2005 (Kunreuther and Michel-Kerjan, 2011).

In addition to this hard reinsurance market, insurers also faced increases in catastrophe risk estimates by modeling firms[17] and more stringent criteria by rating agencies for measuring the financial strength of companies (*Insurance Journal*, 2006). Insurers responded to these changes by filing for significant rate increases in states subject to hurricanes. While only a portion of these increases were granted, the average home-owner's premium in Florida more than doubled, increasing from $723 at the start of 2002, to $1,465 in the first quarter of 2007 (Klein, 2007; Kunreuther and Michel-Kerjan, 2011).

Early in 2007, Florida enacted legislation that sought to increase regulatory control over rates and roll them back. The new legislation also expanded the reinsurance coverage provided by the Florida Hurricane Catastrophe Fund (FHCF).[18] Insurers were required to reduce their rates to reflect this expansion of coverage, which was priced below private reinsurance market rates. This requirement applies to every licensed insurer even if an insurer did not purchase reinsurance from the FHCF.

Florida's residual market mechanism for property insurance, the Citizens Property Insurance Corporation, was established in 2002 but experienced a significant increase in market share of the Florida residential property market with legislative changes in 2007 accelerating that growth. Consumers are allowed to purchase a policy from Citizens if a comparable policy would cost 25 percent more in the private market; this was reduced to 15 percent in 2008 legislation. Citizens has ballooned to become the state's largest insurer, with about 1.4 million policies at the beginning of 2013 (Kunreuther et al.,

---

[17] Risk Management Solutions, one of the leading catastrophe modeling firms, announced in March 2006 that changes in hurricane landfall frequencies increased its estimates of average annual insurance losses by 45 percent across the Gulf Coast, Florida and the Southeast. Their previous model used long-term 1900–2005 historical average hurricane frequencies to estimate annual expected insurance losses (RMS, 2006).

[18] The FHCF was established after Hurricane Andrew as a result of the increased cost of reinsurance. Under its state mandatory coverage program, the FHCF will reimburse a fixed percentage of a participating insurer's losses from each covered event in excess of a per event retention and subject to a maximum aggregate limit for all events. The fixed percentage can be 45 percent, 75 percent, or 90 percent at the option of the insurer.

2013). In the ideal world of the benchmark supply model, a residual mechanism should be a source of last resort.

The transformation of the insurance market in Florida following the severe hurricanes of 2004 and 2005 can be viewed as a failure of the private insurance market to provide affordable coverage against wind damage from hurricanes. Insurers appear to have overreacted to the large losses they incurred, regulators resisted proposed rate increases, and the state-funded company, Citizens, filled the gap by providing relatively inexpensive insurance (Kunreuther and Michel-Kerjan, 2011).

The growth of Citizens, combined with the expansion of the Florida Hurricane Catastrophe Fund, is effectively socializing a large portion of the catastrophe risk in the state. Several other coastal states (Louisiana, Mississippi, and Texas) have now followed the Florida example and expanded the reach of their state-run wind pools. The main problem here is that these are artificial disaster financial solutions in that they do not collect enough premiums and send the wrong signal to individuals and businesses that they can purchase cheap insurance (some might think, "it might not be that risky after all").

11.3.4.3 The California Earthquake Authority

The marketing of earthquake insurance in California provides another example of how insurers who suffered large losses from a disaster are reluctant to continue offering coverage against this risk. In 1985, the California legislature passed a law requiring insurers writing homeowners' insurance on one- to four-family units to offer earthquake coverage on these structures. While insurers were free to set whatever rates they wanted, typical premiums were moderate (e.g., $400 per year for a $200,000 house with a $10,000 deductible, which was based on 5 percent of the value of the property). There was no requirement by the state that the owners had to buy earthquake insurance, only that the insurers had to offer it. Lenders required homeowners' or commercial coverage against the usual perils, but not the purchase of earthquake insurance.

The Northridge earthquake of 1994 caused insured losses of $21.7 billion (in 2012 prices) and led to a significant demand for earthquake insurance. For example, in Cupertino County, more than two-thirds of the homeowners surveyed in the county had purchased earthquake insurance in 1995 (Palm, 1995). In that same year, private insurance companies in California reevaluated their earthquake exposures, and decided that they could not risk selling any more policies on residential property. As with terrorism insurance and coverage against hurricanes, insurers were concerned about the impact of another catastrophic event on their balance sheet, almost without regard to the likelihood of it occurring. Fixating on the worst-case outcome, they decided not to offer coverage at any price. Based on the benchmark model of supply, where insurers are expected to utilize both the likelihood of specific events and the resulting losses to determine premiums, this behavior must be viewed as anomalous.

In view of the law requiring inclusion of earthquake coverage in homeowners' policies, the only legal response to their fear of high losses was for insurers to stop offering new homeowners' policies. The California Insurance Department surveyed insurers and found that up to 90 percent of them had either stopped or had placed restrictions on the selling of new homeowners' policies. After extended discussions between the California Insurance Department and the large insurers in 1996, an advisory group of insurers and actuaries proposed the formation of a state-run earthquake insurance company—the California Earthquake Authority (CEA) (Roth, 1998).

In many parts of the state, the CEA set the premiums, which had to be approved in advance by the California Insurance Department, at higher levels than insurers had used prior to the Northridge earthquake of 1994. The minimum deductible for policies, offered through the CEA, was raised from 10 percent to 15 percent of the insured value of the property. This price-coverage combination was not especially attractive to homeowners in the state. A 15 percent deductible based on the amount of coverage in place is actually quite high relative to damages that typically occur. Most homes in California are wood-frame structures that would likely suffer relatively small losses in a severe earthquake, although there is still a chance that the house could be seriously damaged or totally destroyed. For example, if a house was insured at $200,000, a 15 percent deductible implies that the damage from the earthquake would have to exceed $30,000 before the homeowner could collect a penny from the insurer.

Today, the CEA writes 70 percent of all residential earthquake policies sold in California and has almost $10 billion in overall claim-paying capacity. But the higher rates and the perceived small chance of collecting on a claim (due to the high deductible) prompted many homeowners to drop their coverage as the last damaging earthquake receded from memory. As of the end of 2010, only 12 percent of homeowners in California had earthquake coverage, considerably below the 30 percent of homeowners with coverage at the end of 1994, presumably because the homeowners think that expected benefits above the deductible are not large enough to offset the high premium. If a major earthquake were to occur in California next year, it is likely that the uninsured losses would be very large.

11.3.4.4 The National Flood Insurance Program

Following the Mississippi floods of 1927 and continuing through the 1960s there developed a widespread belief among private insurance companies that the flood peril was uninsurable. It was argued that floods could not be insured by the private sector alone because: (1) only particular areas are subject to the risk, and as such, adverse selection would be a problem; (2) risk-based premiums would be so high that no one would be willing to pay them; and (3) flood losses could be catastrophic and cause insolvencies of some insurers (Overman, 1957; Gerdes, 1963; Anderson, 1974). Moreover, the level of sophistication in hazard assessment was quite limited back in the 1960s compared to what it is today (Czajkowski et al., 2013).

This lack of coverage by the private sector led the federal government to provide significant relief to victims of Hurricane Betsy in 1965. Discussion took place about the role that the federal government could play in developing some form of public insurance coverage, which led to the creation of the National Flood Insurance Program (NFIP) in 1968 (Kunreuther et al., 1978). It was thought that a government program could potentially be successful because it would have funds to initiate the program, pool risks more broadly, subsidize existing building owners to maintain their property values while charging actuarial rates to new construction, and tie insurance to land-use changes that might lower risks. The program would also have the capacity to spread losses over time by borrowing money from the federal government to compensate for a deficit, something private insurers cannot do. Thus, the main goal of the NFIP was to provide flood insurance to those in hazard-prone areas with the understanding that there might still be truly exceptional events for which the program would have to borrow money from the federal government.

The Federal Emergency Management Agency (FEMA) runs the program under the U.S. Department of Homeland Security. In communities where local governments enact floodplain management regulations that follow FEMA requirements, property owners are eligible to buy flood insurance from the NFIP.

To encourage further mitigation, the NFIP has established the Community Rating System (CRS), a voluntary program that rewards communities undertaking mitigating activities with lower premiums. The cost of flood insurance is determined by the federal government, which manages the program. The length of the contract is also determined by the government; it is currently one year.

The majority of NFIP policies are written through the Write-Your-Own (WYO) Program, which allows participating property/casualty insurance companies to write and service NFIP's standard one-year flood insurance policy.

The insurance companies bear no risk and are compensated for writing policies and settling claims.[19] FEMA benefits from the private industry's marketing channels and the presence of private insurers in participating communities. Nearly all flood policies issued today by the NFIP are written by 90 companies through the WYO program.

The NFIP provides insurance up to a maximum limit for residential property damage, now set at $250,000 for building coverage and $100,000 for contents coverage. Note that some additional coverage is offered by private insurers above the current $250,000 maximum building-coverage limit covered by the NFIP for residential property owners, even though this represents a relatively small portion of the market today. For commercial entities (including small businesses), the building and content limits are

---

[19] Over the period 1984–2008, participating insurers and agents received nearly $10 billion in fees (Michel-Kerjan, 2010).

both $500,000, totaling $1 million.[20] Here too, commercial firms can purchase additional coverage from insurers.

The NFIP has grown significantly since 1968. The total property value insured was $174 billion in 1978, $367 billion in 1990, and $740 billion in 2000 (in 2011 prices). Between 2001 and 2012, total exposure increased by another 76 percent, reaching nearly $1.3 trillion as of December 2012.[21]

It should be clear from our discussions of these different U.S. catastrophe risk insurance markets that while private insurers continue to play a critical role in providing financial coverage to victims of such disasters, governments are becoming more actively involved, too, changing the business model of insurance supply.

11.3.5 Alternative Risk Instruments

Capital markets emerged in the 1990s to complement reinsurance in covering large losses from natural disasters through new financial instruments, such as industry loss warranties, catastrophe bonds, sidecar reinsurers, and contingent loans (see Kunreuther and Michel-Kerjan, 2011 for more details, and Cummins and Weiss, 2009 for a technical review).

Several forces combined to make these new instruments attractive. The shortage of reinsurance following Hurricane Andrew in 1992 and the Northridge earthquake in 1994 led to higher reinsurance prices and made it feasible for insurers to offer catastrophe bonds with high enough interest rates to attract capital from investors. In addition, the prospect of an investment that is uncorrelated with the stock market or general economic conditions is also attractive to capital market investors. Finally, catastrophe models emerged as a tool to more rigorously estimate loss probabilities, so that disaster risk could be more accurately quantified and priced than in the past.

Following Hurricane Katrina, there has been a significant increase in the number and volume of catastrophe bond issuances and the creation of sidecars, but the total volume of financial protection remains somewhat limited compared to what is currently provided by traditional reinsurance.

Still, nearly 200 transactions were realized between 1996 and 2011 and in recent years, several firms (Disney, Universal Studios, Electricity de France, Dominion) and governments (Thailand, Mexico, and more recently several states in the U.S.) are using these tools to hedge some of their exposure to disasters (Michel-Kerjan et al., 2011). More transactions could mean a more liquid market, which in turn will attract more sponsors and investors, providing the much needed capital to finance future catastrophes. Over $40 billion in cat bonds have been issued between 2003 and 2013, with $19 billion outstanding in 2013 alone.

---

[20] Commercial: occupied or vacant commercial buildings; Commercial Real Estate Owned (REO); residential dwellings of more than four families; apartment buildings, office buildings, farms, and other commercial properties.

[21] The NFIP is one of the largest flood insurance programs in the world. It is interesting to note that, contrary to what is done in the United States, flood insurance is sold mainly by the private market in the UK, Germany and France.

11.4 DEMAND FOR INSURANCE AGAINST CATASTROPHIC EVENTS

This section outlines a benchmark model of demand for insurance by consumers using the concepts of expected utility [E(U)] theory and compares this normative theory with two descriptive models. The section concludes by examining actual behavior by insurers that does not conform to the E(U) and explains these anomalies using concepts from behavioral economics.

11.4.1 A Benchmark Model of Demand[22]

The benchmark model of demand is based on the assumption that insurance buyers maximize their expected utility. Individuals purchase insurance because they are willing to pay a certain small premium to avoid an uncertain large loss. Expected utility theory tells us that risk-averse individuals are willing to purchase insurance at premiums that exceed their expected loss. A hypothetical example is the consumer who is willing to pay $12 annually to insure against a loss of $100 that has a 1 in 10 chance of occurring. The expected loss under that scenario is $10. The additional $2—the risk premium—reflects the extra amount above the expected loss the person is willing to pay for insurance. For the same expected loss, the risk premium will increase should the gamble involve a potentially larger loss and a smaller probability (for example, 1 in 100 chance of losing $1,000) because of the diminishing marginal utility of money—a way of characterizing their attitude toward financial risk. In other words, the 1,000[th] dollar of loss reduces utility more than the 100th dollar of loss for a risk-averse individual.

The above example assumes that the consumer is considering a choice between purchasing insurance that will cover the entire loss should the untoward event occur, or remaining uninsured. A more realistic example would give the consumer a choice as to how much insurance to purchase, for example, whether to cover 100 percent of a possible loss or only 70 percent. The premiums for lower amounts of coverage obviously will be less than if one is fully protected. An individual decides how much insurance to purchase by trading off the higher expected loss for less than full coverage with the cost of paying higher premiums for more protection.

The next two subsections discuss models of demand for insurance that may make different predictions regarding consumer behavior than the expected utility model: prospect theory and a goal-based model of choice.

11.4.2 Prospect Theory[23]

Daniel Kahneman and Amos Tversky (1979) developed prospect theory as a model to describe how individuals make choices in the face of uncertainty. One of its central

---

[22] For more details on the benchmark model of demand see Chapter 5 by Dionne and Harrington (this volume) and Chapter 2 in Kunreuther et al. (2013).

[23] For more details on prospect theory and other nonexpected utility models see Chapter 12 by Quiggin (this volume).

features is the concept of a reference point that normally reflects the individual's current status when approaching a specific decision. Insurance decisions usually are made when a policy expires and one has to decide on whether to renew it, or when an insured individual is considering purchasing coverage, as in the case when a homeowner buys a house in California and is considering whether to purchase earthquake insurance. In either case, the reference point is likely to be the status quo at the time one makes the decision: having insurance and deciding to renew or cancel a policy, or not having insurance and deciding whether to buy coverage or remain uninsured.

The value function. In analyzing the decision to buy insurance, prospect theory emphasizes the changes in wealth from a given reference point, rather than the final wealth level that forms the basis for choices using the benchmark expected utility model. Prospect theory also values losses differently than it values gains. Empirical investigations show that individuals tend to experience the pain of a loss approximately twice as strongly as they enjoy gains of the same magnitude (Tversky and Kahneman, 1991). In other words, a certain loss of $20 will be viewed as considerably more painful than the positive feeling from a gain of $20. Stated simply, people tend to be loss-averse.

The shape of the value function, on the other hand, holds that the desire to avoid losses drives consumers to treat the risk of experiencing a loss differently than obtaining a positive return. In the gain domain, the value function implies that a person will be averse to gambles involving positive outcomes, while in the loss domain an individual is assumed to be risk-taking when it comes to uncertain losses.

The weighting function. To explain consumer interest in purchasing insurance, we turn to the use of the weighting function postulated by prospect theory to characterize how individuals perceive probabilities. Empirical studies suggest that individuals overweight the chances of low-probability events where the likelihood is below 30–40 percent—risks that are most relevant to insurance—and underweight the chances of higher probability events occurring (Camerer and Ho, 1994; Wu and Gonzalez, 1996). According to prospect theory, highly unlikely events are either ignored or overweighted. Hence, the discontinuity of the weighting function is near zero.

For a low-probability event that is not ignored, a person who is risk-taking in the loss domain may still be willing to purchase insurance if his decision weight implied by the weighting function reflects an overestimation of the probability of a loss. In other words, a high enough perceived chance of incurring a loss makes insurance attractive, even with premiums that reflect a 30–40 percent premium loading factor. This explanation has some intuitive psychological plausibility: some people worry (sometimes excessively) about low-probability, high-negative-impact events, and hence assign them high weights when considering their likelihood.

But there is a fundamental empirical difficulty with prospect theory's account of insurance purchase using decision weights that also applies to the expected utility model. Empirical research suggests that the loss probability often does not play a role in people's decision processes (Camerer and Kunreuther, 1989; Hogarth and Kunreuther, 1995; Huber et al., 1997). When loss probability is in fact considered, it is derived from experience, not from actuarial tables. Ralph Hertwig and his colleagues showed that when the probabilities are based on experience rather than on statistical summaries, people underweight low probabilities in making risky decisions except when there has been a very recent occurrence of the event class in question (Hertwig et al., 2004).

Preference for low deductibles and rebates. One of the best examples of how prospect theory can explain actual insurance behavior better than the benchmark model of demand is the choice of low deductibles and the purchase of insurance policies that offer rebates if one doesn't suffer a loss, even though such policies are generally not as financially attractive as those without such dividends.

As shown in Figure 11.3, the negative value of the additional premium caused by eliminating the deductible is very small relative to the very large reduction in the negative value caused by reducing the deductible to zero. A better inducement than a deductible to get individuals to avoid making claims would be to offer them a rebate from which claims are deducted. Figure 11.3 reveals that insurance with a rebate should be more attractive than an equivalent and less expensive policy with a deductible, since the negative value of the deductible is much greater than the positive value of the rebate even if one did not have any claims on the policy and thus was able to collect the entire

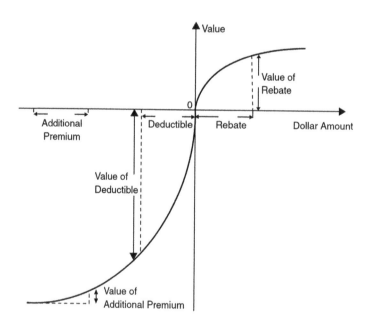

Figure 11.3 Deductible and rebate frames. *Source: Johnson et al., 1993.*

rebate. Insurance policies with rebates may satisfy a person's need to collect something on her insurance policy when she has not suffered a loss.

11.4.3 A Goal-based Model of Choice

Both expected utility theory and prospect theory assume that financial considerations determine a person's decisions regarding insurance purchase. But people often construct or select insurance plans designed to achieve multiple goals, not all of which are purely financial (Krantz and Kunreuther, 2007). The relative importance of these goals varies with the decision maker as well as the context in which the decision to purchase insurance may be triggered. For example, an insurance purchaser may think chiefly about the goals of satisfying the requirements of the bank that holds the mortgage loan. But when that same person reflects on her valuable works of art, she may think chiefly about reducing anxiety and avoiding regret.

To illustrate how the plan/goal representation captures the insurance decision-making process, consider behavior that is often observed: people purchase flood insurance after suffering damage in a flood, but then cancel their policies when several consecutive years pass with no flood. One explanation is that avoiding anxiety and feeling justified are both important goals. Following flood damage, anxiety is high, and reducing it is a salient goal; it is also easy to justify buying the insurance because a flood has just occurred and the experience is deeply etched in the purchaser's recent memory. But a couple of years later, many people may find that the prospect of a flood no longer intrudes on their peace of mind, so anxiety avoidance takes on less importance.

In a similar spirit, insured individuals do not feel justified in continuing to pay premiums when they do not collect on their policy. The differential weighting of these goals at the time one suffers a flood and several years without experiencing another loss can lead to a decision to cancel the existing policy. These individuals view insurance as a poor investment rather than celebrating the fact that they have not suffered any losses for the past few years.

Four of the main goal categories that may influence insurance purchase using the plans/goals model are (1) investment goals, (2) satisfying legal or other official requirements, (3) worry or regret, and (4) satisfying social and/or cognitive norms. Two other goals—maintaining a relationship with a trusted agent/advisor and affording insurance protection—may also play a role. These goal categories do not themselves constitute a complete theory of demand for insurance, but do seem to capture some aspects of behavior inconsistent with expected utility theory.

Investment goals. Many homeowners view insurance through an investment lens rather than as a protective measure. These individuals purchase coverage with the expectation that they will collect on their policy often enough so that it is considered to be a worthwhile expenditure. It is difficult for them to appreciate the maxim that "the best return on one's insurance policy is no return at all," meaning that one was spared damage from an event for which one was insured. At one level, everyone agrees that a person is better off not suffering a loss than experiencing one. But for those who treat insurance as an investment, each year that they do not collect on their policy, they regret having bought coverage.

Satisfying requirements. Insurance coverage is often mandatory: Automobile liability insurance is required by most states; homeowners' insurance is normally required by mortgage lenders; flood insurance must be purchased as a condition for a federally insured mortgage in special flood hazard areas; and malpractice insurance is needed for several different professions. In these cases, purchase of insurance may be viewed as a subgoal for meeting end goals, such as owning a car or a home or practicing one's profession. The amount of coverage and size of the deductible are often discretionary so that the relative importance of specific goals will play a key role in these decisions.

Emotion-related goals: worry or regret. There is an established literature on how affect and emotional goals influence an individual's decisions under risk (Lowenstein et al., 2001; Finucane et al., 2000). Three goals in this category with relevance to insurance are reduction of anxiety (i.e., peace of mind), avoidance of anticipated regret, and consolation. Because emotions —even anticipation of anxiety or regret—have considerable immediate presence, individuals sometimes purchase an insurance policy that has a high loading cost if doing so satisfies emotional goals, even if it leads to a shortage of funds to pursue other goals in the more distant future. Long-term care insurance is a good example. Elderly households of modest means can more frequently become financially stressed by trying to keep up high nursing home insurance payments than by paying for nursing home care—which will eventually be covered by Medicaid. But still some people buy the private insurance.

For low-probability, high-impact events, individuals may buy coverage to reduce their anxiety about experiencing a large financial loss. It is important to separate the following two goals: financial protection from the loss, and reduction of anxiety about the loss. Situations vary in the degree to which financial losses are made vivid and to which they provoke or relieve anxiety. Hence, the relative importance of these goals may change over time.

One may also anticipate anxiety and take measures to avoid it. For example, some people claim that they refuse to fly, not because they fear a crash, but because they anticipate and dislike feeling anxious about a crash while they are on the plane. But if one cannot avoid anxiety about a loss, one may still find opportunities to reduce this emotion by taking protective measures, including insurance, where appropriate. This feeling may partially explain the demand by the few who purchase flight insurance.

Regret (Bell, 1982; Loomes and Sugden, 1982; Braun and Muermann, 2004) and disappointment (Bell, 1985) are quite different from anxiety, in that they are primarily experienced after a loss occurs rather than before. Consider the example of mailing a package worth $50. If you do not purchase insurance, then if the package is lost or badly damaged, you likely wish that you had purchased the coverage. If, at the time of mailing, you anticipate unpleasant regret or disappointment if an uninsured loss occurs, then you may decide to purchase insurance as a way of avoiding the possibility of such emotions.

Individuals may also purchase insurance as a form of consolation should they suffer a loss. In particular, if you have special affection for an item, such as a piece of art, then the knowledge that you can make a claim should the item be destroyed or stolen has special meaning. Hsee and Kunreuther (2000) attribute the need for consolation as the reason individuals are willing to pay higher premiums for the same amount of coverage for objects they love than for those for which they have no special feeling.

With respect to negative feelings about a situation, experimental findings indicate that people focus on how severe the outcome will be rather than on its probability when they have strong emotional feelings attached to the event (Rottenstreich and Hsee, 2001; Sunstein, 2003). In the case of terrorism, a national field survey conducted in November 2001 revealed that Americans living within 100 miles of the World Trade Center felt a greater personal risk from terror than if they lived farther away (Fischhoff et al., 2003). This may explain the large New York area demand for terrorism insurance coverage immediately after 9/11 even at extremely high premiums (U.S. Government Accountability Office, 2002; Wharton Risk Management Center, 2005).

Satisfying social and/or cognitive norms. Many insurance decisions are based on what other people are doing, or on what those whom one respects believe is an appropriate action to take. For example, a new parent may purchase life insurance because his or her own parent, partner, or financial adviser thinks that it is important to provide protection for the spouse and child. The amount purchased might follow some standard guideline (e.g., three times annual income) regardless of the loading on the insurance or the buyer's risk-aversion. Once again, multiple goals may come into play: the new parent may be trying to achieve the goal of financial protection for the family against a low-probability, high-impact event, but trying as well to satisfy what others expect or wish them to do.

There is also empirical evidence that purchase of insurance, like adoption of new products, is based on knowledge of what friends and neighbors have done, even if the purchaser's own beliefs about the probabilities or consequences of a loss event have not changed. Someone who purchases insurance soon after suffering damage from a disaster may do so in part because it is easy to justify the expenditure to others by pointing to the event that just occurred. Similarly, some may cancel their insurance coverage after being protected for some years because it is hard to justify an expenditure that has not paid off. The importance of justification as part of the decision process has been demonstrated in experiments that suggest social norms are an important determinant of choice (Shafir et al., 1993). In the process, people often use arguments that have little to do with the trade-offs between the cost of insurance and the expected loss that forms the basis of economic analyses of insurance or warranty transactions (Hogarth and Kunreuther, 1995).

11.4.4 Other Behavioral Explanations

In addition to the above factors characterizing behavior, individuals may process information in ways that are not assumed in the benchmark model of demand. Some examples of this misprocessing behavior include a bias toward maintaining the *status quo* and hence a reluctance to consider new alternatives, an *availability bias* which leads to an overweighting of recent events in the decision process, and *budget constraints*.

Status quo bias. There is considerable empirical evidence that some individuals are reluctant to depart from the status quo even though there may be substantial benefits to them from doing so (Samuelson and Zeckhauser, 1988). This behavior can be partially explained by loss aversion associated with the value function where the disadvantages of moving from the status quo loom larger than the advantages of doing so (Tversky and Kahneman, 1991).

Availability bias. There are situations in which people assess the probability of an event by the ease with which instances of occurrence can be brought to mind. For example, a homeowner is likely to estimate the chances of a future flood as much higher right after experiencing water damage from a hurricane than four or five years later should there not have been another disaster during this interval (Tversky and Kahneman, 1973).

Short-run budget constraints. Another reason that some individuals may not purchase insurance is that they believe they are constrained by their current finances, and that they do not have easy access to funds for investment in protection against low-probability events. Individuals may not buy insurance because they mentally allocate their planned expenditures of income into different accounts so that they feel constrained in what they are willing to spend on certain activities (Thaler, 1985). If a family is already committed to spending considerable funds on required insurance (e.g., homeowners', automobile, life, medical), it may feel that it has exhausted its insurance budget and will not want to buy coverage for events such as earthquakes or floods. Or people may respond to an increase in insurance premiums caused by higher expected losses by seeking to reduce coverage in order to keep the premium within the bounds of the mental account.

The idea of borrowing small amounts today to expand one's budget in order to pay the annual premium for insurance that will avoid a large loss tomorrow may not be part of some consumers' mental accounting procedures. For example, many people who do not have health insurance appear to have sufficient income and assets that they could buy insurance and still have enough left over to pay other expenses (Bundorf and Pauly, 2006). They may be using this budgeting heuristic as the basis for not purchasing insurance.

11.4.5 (Lack of) Demand for Catastrophe Insurance

Individuals are often reluctant to purchase catastrophe risk insurance voluntarily and keep that coverage over time for reasons that can be partially explained by features of the descriptive models outlined in the previous subsection.

Failure to protect against low-probability, high-consequence events. As discussed in section 11.3.4.3, only 12 percent of Californians have earthquake insurance. This level has remained surprisingly stable even after the series of massive earthquakes that occurred in Haiti, Chile, New Zealand and Japan.[24] Should a devastating earthquake hit California tomorrow it is not clear how those 88 percent of residents will recover financially, except to hope that the federal government will help them.

Flood presents another case of underinsurance. Consider the flood in August 1998 that damaged property in northern Vermont. Of the 1,549 victims of this disaster, FEMA found that 84 percent of the homeowners in flood-prone areas did not have insurance, even though 45 percent of these individuals were required to purchase this coverage (Tobin and Calfee, 2005). In the Louisiana parishes affected by Katrina, the percentage of homeowners with flood insurance ranged from 57.7 percent in St. Bernard Parish to 7.3 percent in Tangipahoa when the hurricane hit. Only 40 percent of the residents in Orleans Parish had flood insurance (Bayot, 2005).

At the corporate level, 40 percent of large American corporations do not have terrorism risk insurance coverage, and it is unclear if these firms have enough resources to recover should they suffer losses from another major attack and whether they will be able to raise enough external capital in the aftermath of such a disaster (Michel-Kerjan and Raschky, 2011). Arguably, those enterprises are more diversified in the United States and internationally than a family whose chief asset is typically its main residence.

Status quo bias. Changes in the automobile insurance laws in New Jersey in 1988 and Pennsylvania in 1990 provided an opportunity to examine the impact of the status quo bias on the choice of auto insurance policies. Both states introduced the option of a limited right to sue with accompanying lower insurance rates, but the default option for drivers varied by state. In New Jersey, motorists had to actively acquire a right to sue at a more expensive price. In Pennsylvania, however, the status quo was the full right to sue, with motorists now having an opportunity to reduce their insurance costs by giving up some of their right to sue.

When offered the choice, only about 20 percent of New Jersey drivers chose to acquire the full right to sue, with 80 percent maintaining the status quo of no right to sue. In Pennsylvania, 75 percent of the insured population retained the full right to sue. Similar results were obtained in a hypothetical study of 136 university employees. Interestingly, the effect was even larger in the real world than in the controlled experiment (Johnson et al., 1993).

---

[24] We thank Glenn Pomeroy, CEO of the California Earthquake Authority, for insight on this point; personal communication in September 2012.

Purchasing insurance after a disaster occurs. Individuals are often more interested in buying insurance coverage after a disaster occurs, rather than prior to the event. This is true even though premiums are usually increased after the catastrophe. A prime example of this behavior is the purchase of earthquake insurance following a major seismic event. Surveys of owner-occupied homes in counties in California affected by the 1989 Loma Prieta earthquake showed a significant increase in coverage. Just prior to the disaster, only 22.4 percent of the homes had earthquake coverage. Four years later, 36.6 percent had purchased earthquake insurance—a 72 percent increase in coverage (Palm, 1995).

There are at least two explanations for this behavior. The event may have been more salient in people's minds due to the availability bias, so residents in quake-prone areas perceived the likelihood of a loss from a future disaster to be much higher than before the quake occurred. People may also focus on emotion-related goals because they were concerned about the consequences of a future disaster. They then would decide to purchase insurance to gain peace of mind. This latter form of behavior is consistent with the studies in California following the 1989 earthquake in which "worry that an earthquake will destroy my house or cause major damage in the future" was the most important determinant in a homeowner's decision to buy earthquake insurance (Palm, 1995).

Cancelling insurance after a few years. Recent empirical research has shown that many people who first purchased catastrophe insurance let their coverage lapse after a few years. The flood insurance market offers striking evidence. To further analyze the cancellation of NFIP policies, we examined the entire portfolio of the NFIP over the period 2000–2009. We looked at the number of new policies issued by the program and their respective durations through 2009 for those residing in Special Flood Hazard Areas (SFHAs; high flood risk) and non-SFHAs (Michel-Kerjan et al., 2012). Our results, presented in Table 11.3 can be interpreted as follows: of the 841,000 new policies in 2001, only 73 percent were still in force one year later. After two years, only 49 percent of the original 2001 policies were still in place. Eight years later, in 2009, only 20 percent of them were still in place. Similar patterns were found for each of the other years between 2002 and 2008 in which a flood insurance policy was first purchased.

Although some of these individuals may have sold their homes and cancelled their policies because they moved, the large percentage decrease in the insured policies-in-force over time can only be partially explained by migration patterns. Data from the annual American Community Survey over the period covered by the flood insurance dataset revealed that the median length of residence was between 5 and 6 years—somewhat higher than the 2 to 4 year median tenure of flood insurance. All new homeowners in SFHAs are required to purchase flood insurance as a condition for obtaining a federally insured mortgage; however, some let their policy lapse if the financial institution holding their mortgage did not enforce that regulation.

Table 11.3 Tenure Results: Duration of New NFIP Policies by Year after Purchase, 2001–2009

	2001	2002	2003	2004	2005	2006	2007	2008	2009
New flood policies-in-force (000s)									
All	841	876	1,186	986	849	1,299	974	894	1,051
SFHA/Non-SFHA	542 299	613 264	880 306	696 291	529 320	635 664	542 432	487 407	595 456
Tenure longer than:									
1 year	**73%**	**67%**	**77%**	**78%**	**76%**	**73%**	**74%**	**73%**	
SFHA/Non-SFHA	74% 71%	67% 67%	78% 76%	77% 80%	75% 78%	74% 72%	74% 74%	75% 70%	
2 years	**49%**	**52%**	**65%**	**65%**	**63%**	**59%**	**58%**		
SFHA/Non-SFHA	48% 52%	52% 50%	66% 64%	64% 67%	62% 64%	59% 60%	58% 59%		
3 years	**39%**	**44%**	**57%**	**55%**	**53%**	**48%**			
SFHA/Non-SFHA	37% 41%	44% 43%	57% 56%	54% 57%	53% 54%	47% 49%			
4 years	**33%**	**38%**	**50%**	**48%**	**44%**				
SFHA/Non-SFHA	32% 36%	39% 38%	50% 48%	47% 49%	43% 44%				
5 years	**29%**	**33%**	**44%**	**38%**					
SFHA/Non-SFHA	28% 31%	34% 33%	44% 42%	38% 38%					
6 years	**25%**	**30%**	**33%**						
SFHA/Non-SFHA	24% 28%	30% 29%	34% 32%						
7 years	**22%**	**26%**							
SFHA/Non-SFHA	21% 25%	26% 25%							
8 years	**20%**								
SFHA/Non-SFHA	18% 22%								

Source: Michel-Kerjan et al. (2012) (original data from NFIP).

11.5 PROPOSALS TO IMPROVE INSURANCE COVERAGE AGAINST CATASTROPHES

To improve the level of protection against catastrophe risks, we propose that instead of the standard one-year contracts, disaster insurance should be offered as multi-year insurance (MYI) contracts. For MYI policies to be viable from the insurers' vantage point, two principles must be adhered to which we will discuss in the next subsection. We then provide a rationale for MYI policies and suggest ways that it could be implemented by the National Flood Insurance Program as an illustrative example. This section also discusses several complementary proposals to improve insurance coverage against future natural disasters.

11.5.1 Principles for Designing Insurance Policies

For insurance to play a key role in the management and financing of catastrophic risks, we propose the following two guiding principles that are discussed in greater detail in Kunreuther and Michel-Kerjan, 2011:

Principle 1 – Premiums Should Reflect Risk: Insurance premiums should be based on risk to provide signals to individuals as to the hazards they face and to encourage them to engage in cost-effective mitigation measures to reduce their vulnerability to catastrophes. Risk-based premiums should also reflect the cost of capital insurers' need to integrate into their pricing to assure adequate return to their investors.

Principle 1 provides a clear signal of the expected damage to those currently residing in areas subject to natural disasters and those who are considering moving into these regions. Moreover, insurers will have an economic incentive to reduce premiums to homeowners and businesses who invest in cost-effective loss-reduction mitigation measures. If Principle 1 is applied in hazard-prone areas where premiums are currently subsidized, some residents will be faced with large price increases. This concern leads to the second guiding principle.

Principle 2 – Dealing with Equity and Affordability Issues: Any financial assistance given to residents currently residing in hazard-prone areas (e.g., low-income homeowners) should come from general public funding and not through insurance premium subsidies.

It is important to note that Principle 2 applies only to those individuals who currently reside in hazard-prone areas. Those who decide to buy property in the area in the future should be charged premiums that reflect the risk.

11.5.2 A Proposal for MYI Contracts Combined with Means-tested Insurance Vouchers[25]

Given the recent increase in catastrophic losses there is now an opportunity to institute new programs for encouraging long-term thinking while at the same time recognizing that homeowners, insurers and elected officials tend to be myopic. Multi-year insurance (MYI) contracts could be one such solution.

A MYI contract would increase the likelihood that consumers at risk stay protected longer. Combining MYI with long-term loans for investments in risk reduction measures would encourage cost-effective mitigation by spreading the upfront costs of mitigation measures over time. If insurance rates are actuarially based, then the premium reduction from adopting a risk-reduction measure will be greater than the annual loan cost. Well-enforced building codes could ensure that structures are designed to withstand damages from future disasters. Given the multi-year insurance contract, the insurer would have a greater incentive to inspect the property over time, something it would not be as likely

---

[25] This section draws on Jaffee et al. (2010).

to do with annual contracts, knowing its policyholders could switch to a competitor in the coming year. Insurance regulators might also be more willing to permit insurers to charge prices that reflect risk, knowing that policies were long-term so homeowners in their state would not face a huge price increase or availability challenge after a disaster that would occur during the length of time covered by those longer contracts.

11.5.2.1 Why MYI Does Not Exist Today

In his seminal work on uncertainty and welfare economics, Kenneth Arrow defined "the absence of marketability for an action which is identifiable, technologically possible and capable of influencing some individuals' welfare (…) as a failure of the existing market to provide a means whereby the services can be both offered and demanded upon the payment of a price." (Arrow, 1963).

Several factors have contributed to the nonmarketability of MYI for protecting homeowners' properties against losses from fire, theft and large-scale natural disasters. Today, insurance premiums in many states are restricted to be artificially low in hazard-prone areas. A related second stumbling block for marketing MYI policies is that insurers are unclear as to how much they will be allowed to charge for premiums in the future due to price regulations at the state level. Uncertainty regarding costs of capital and changes in risk over time may also deter insurers from providing MYI.

Although catastrophe models have considerably improved in recent years, there is still significant ambiguity as to the likelihood and consequences of flood risk. As noted earlier, controlled experiments with underwriters and actuaries reveal that insurers would want to charge more if there is considerable ambiguity with respect to the risk (Kunreuther et al., 1995; Cabantous et al., 2011). For this reason, insurers want financial protection against catastrophic losses over the length of the MYI policy in the form of multi-year reinsurance policies, catastrophe bonds or other risk transfer instruments.

On the demand side, homeowners may be concerned with the financial solvency of their insurer over a long period, particularly if they feel they would be locked in if they sign a MYI contract. Consumers might also fear being overcharged if insurers set premiums that reflect the uncertainty associated with longer term risks.

11.5.2.2 Demand for MYI Policies

Jaffee et al. (2010) have developed a two-period model where premiums reflect risk in a competitive market setting to compare the expected benefits of annual contracts versus MYI. They show that a MYI policy reduces the marketing costs for insurers over one-period policies and also reduces the search costs to the consumer that would occur if their insurer decides to cancel its one-period policy at the end of period 1. If the policyholder is permitted to cancel a MYI policy at the end of period 1 should she learn that the cost of a 1-period policy is sufficiently low to justify paying a cancellation cost (C), then it is always optimal for the insurer to market a MYI policy and for a consumer to purchase one. The insurer will set C at a level that enables it to break even on those policies that are canceled before the maturity date.

To empirically test the demand for multi-year insurance, we recently undertook a web-based experiment in the United States, offering individuals a choice between one-year and two-year contracts against losses from hurricane-related damage (Kunreuther and Michel-Kerjan, 2012). A large majority of the responders preferred the two-year contract over the one-year contract (five times as many did), even when the two-year contract was priced at a higher level than the actuarially fair price. Introducing a two-year insurance policy into the menu of contracts also increased the aggregate demand for disaster insurance (Kunreuther and Michel-Kerjan, 2012).

11.5.2.3 Combining MYI with Means-tested Insurance Vouchers to Address the Affordability Challenge

There is growing economic analysis examining the problem of affordability of insurance. A study using data from the American Housing Survey on eight cities in four states exposed to hurricane risks (Florida, New York, South Carolina and Texas), found that between 16 percent (Dallas) and 31 percent (Tampa) of owner-occupied homes are owned by households that cannot afford insurance using 200 percent of the federal poverty line as the threshold level. At 125 percent of the federal poverty line, the percentage varies from nearly 7 percent in Dallas to 17 percent in Tampa. Among low-income households judged unable to afford insurance, a large percentage of homes are nevertheless insured, even when there is no mortgage requiring coverage. Fewer than 27 percent of low-income homeowners in San Antonio fail to purchase insurance coverage. Any plan that directs subsidies to all low-income homeowners will allocate much of the payment to those who are already insured. In summary, these data reveal that many homeowners whose income is below the 100 or 200 percent of poverty level do purchase homeowners' insurance while some individuals above this level do not buy this coverage (Kunreuther and Michel-Kerjan, 2011, Chapter 11).

Equity issues also come into play here. If some homeowners see their premiums jump by thousands of dollars in a single year, they may feel treated unjustly relative to others with similar homes whose premiums remain unchanged. To deal with issues of equity and affordability we recommend that residents be given an insurance voucher. This type of in-kind assistance assures that the recipients use the funds for obtaining insurance rather than having the freedom to spend the money on goods and services of their own choosing.

A low-income family in a hazard-prone area would pay a risk-based insurance premium and then be provided with an insurance voucher to cover some fraction of the increased cost of insurance. The amount of the insurance voucher would be determined by the family's income and the magnitude of the increase in the insurance premium. Several existing programs could serve as models for developing such a voucher system: the Food Stamp Program, the Low Income Home Energy Assistance Program

(LIHEAP) and Universal Service Fund (USF); we discuss them briefly in Appendix 11.1. Although a voucher can be justified on equity grounds and can serve as a basis for risk-based premiums, there still may be resistance to this concept by real estate developers and builders and middle- and upper-income households who would prefer the current program of subsidized premiums.

There are several different ways that funds for these vouchers could be obtained that address the general question as to who should pay for the risks faced by those currently residing in hazard-prone areas that deserve special treatment:

General taxpayer. If one takes the position that everyone in society is responsible for assisting those residing in hazard-prone areas, then one could utilize general taxpayer revenue from the federal government to cover the costs of insurance vouchers. The Food Stamp and the Low Income Home Energy Assistance Programs operate in this manner.

State government. An alternative (or complementary) source of funding would be to tax residents and/or commercial enterprises in the state exposed to natural disaster. States obtain significant financial benefits from economic development in their jurisdictions through the collection of property taxes or other revenue such as gasoline taxes, state income taxes or sales taxes. If residents in coastal areas receive greater benefits from the economic development in these regions than others in the state, they should be taxed proportionately more than those residing inland.

Insurance policyholders. A tax could be levied on all insurance policyholders to provide vouchers to those currently residing in hazard-prone areas who require special treatment. The rationale for this type of tax would be that all homeowners (as opposed to all taxpayers) should be responsible for helping to protect those who cannot afford protection, a rationale that is the basis for the Universal Service Fund that provides affordable telephone service to all residents in the country.

The above risk-sharing programs reflect different views as to who should pay for losses from natural disasters. By examining who bears the costs and who reaps the benefits from each of these proposed risk-sharing arrangements, political leaders could make more informed decisions.

11.5.3 Developing Multi-Year Flood Insurance Through the NFIP

Given current premium rate regulation at the state level, it might be difficult for private insurers to develop MYI for homeowners' coverage. However, the National Flood Insurance Program (NFIP), a federal insurance program, provides an excellent framework for developing this type of contract, particularly with the passage of the Biggert-Waters Flood Insurance Reform Act of 2012 in July 2012.

The Biggert–Waters Act renewed the NFIP for five years as a part of a comprehensive and very significant piece of legislation that reflects the two guiding principles discussed above (*Premiums Should Reflect Risk* and *Dealing with Equity and Affordability Issues*). The legislation contains several features that will impact a large number of households in the United States:

- The Federal Emergency Management Agency (FEMA) will improve flood maps so that they more accurately reflect the risks that households face with respect to flood damage.
- Flood insurance rate subsidies will be phased out for second homes and residences subject to repetitive flooding. Beginning in January 1, 2013 those premiums will increase 25 percent each year, so that by the beginning of 2016 they will reflect risk.
- For primary residences, including nonsubsidized properties, assessed at higher risk levels as a result of updated flood mapping, premiums will increase over time to reflect risk. The increase will be phased in over a five-year period at an annual rate of 20 percent of the differential between the current premium and the risk-based premium.
- The Act authorizes a FEMA / National Academy of Sciences study for establishing an affordability framework for flood insurance, including targeted assistance such as means-tested vouchers. The Government Accountability Office (GAO) is undertaking complementary studies on these issues as well.

The new legislation provides an opportunity for our MYI proposal to be implemented since, as discussed in section 11.4.5, the median tenure of flood insurance from 2001 to 2009 was 2 to 4 years only, leaving thousands of homes unprotected. To ensure that exposed properties remain insured, the NFIP could introduce multi-year flood insurance into its current menu of contracts with the policy tied to the structure rather than the homeowner. The insurance could be required on all residences in flood-prone areas for the same reason that automobile insurance is required in all states today: providing financial protection in the case of a loss. Should the homeowner move to another location, the flood insurance policy would remain with the property.

Premiums on the flood insurance policy would be fixed for a prespecified time period (for example, 5 years) and would reflect risk based on updated flood maps. Some homeowners currently residing in flood-prone areas whose premiums increased would be given a means-tested insurance voucher to reflect the difference. Homeowners who invest in loss reduction measures would be given a premium discount to reflect the reduction in expected losses from floods whether or not they had an insurance voucher. Long-term loans for mitigation would encourage investments in cost-effective mitigation measures. Well-enforced building codes and seals of approval would provide an additional rationale for undertaking these loss reduction measures (Michel-Kerjan and Kunreuther, 2011).[26]

A multi-year flood insurance policy has many advantages over the current annual policies from the perspective of the many relevant stakeholders: homeowners, FEMA, banks and financial institutions, and the general taxpayer. Such multi-year contracts would prevent millions of individuals from cancelling their policies after just a few years—a major issue for the NFIP. Multi-year flood insurance would also ensure the spread of risk within the program. Requiring flood insurance for all homeowners

---

[26] This proposal for means-tested flood insurance vouchers is now integrated in the 2012 Flood Insurance Reform Act.

residing in hazard-prone areas would provide much needed financial revenue for the program over time by increasing the size of the policy base.

As a complement to MYI, we suggest that banks provide mitigation loans to homeowners for the purposes of investing in cost-effective risk-reduction measures. A bank would have a financial incentive to provide this type of loan, since it is now better protected against a catastrophic loss to the property. The general public will also benefit, because it will be less likely to have large amounts of their tax dollars going for disaster relief.

11.5.4 All-Hazards Insurance[27]

Currently, insurance programs for residents in hazard-prone areas in the United States are segmented across perils. Standard homeowners and commercial insurance policies, normally required as a condition for a mortgage, cover damage from fire, wind, hail, lightning, winter storms and volcanic eruption. Earthquake insurance can be purchased for an additional premium. Flood insurance is offered through the National Flood Insurance Program. This can be very confusing for many homeowners, especially with regard to coverage against damage from flooding due to hurricanes.

11.5.4.1 Features of the Program

An all-hazards insurance policy, if developed, should adhere to the two guiding principles of rates reflecting risk and affordability. The idea of an insurance program where all natural disasters are covered by a single policy has been adopted in several countries. In 1954, Spain formed a public corporation, the Consorcio de Compensation de Seguros that today provides mandatory insurance for so-called "extraordinary risks," including natural disasters and political and social events such as terrorism, riots and civil commotion. Such coverage is an add-on to property insurance policies that are marketed by the private sector (Freeman and Scott, 2005).

In France, a mandatory homeowners policy covers a number of different natural disasters, along with terrorism risk where a publicly owned reinsurer, the Caisse Centrale de Reassurance, provides protection for flood, earthquakes, and droughts, and an insurance pool, Gareat, provides unlimited government guaranteed coverage for terrorism losses. There is no public reinsurance for storms (Michel-Kerjan and de Marcellis-Warin, 2006).

11.5.4.2 Advantages of All-Hazards Insurance

Consider an insurer who wishes to market homeowners' coverage in different parts of the country. With risk-based rates, it would collect premiums that reflect the earthquake risk in California, hurricane risk on the Gulf Coast, tornado damage in the Great Plains states, and flood risk in the Mississippi Valley. Each of these disaster risks is independent

---

[27] This section draws on Kunreuther (2007).

of the others. This higher premium base and the diversification of risk across many hazards reduce the likelihood that the insurer would suffer a loss that exceeds its surplus in any given year for a given book of business.

An all-hazards homeowners policy should be attractive to both insurers and policyholders in hurricane-prone areas, because it avoids the costly process of having an adjuster determine whether the damage was caused by wind (today, covered by private insurers and state-run companies in certain states) or water (today, covered by the National Flood Insurance Program). This problem of differentiating wind damage from water damage was a particularly challenging one following Hurricane Katrina. Across large portions of the coast, all that remained of demolished buildings were foundations and stairs, making it difficult to determine the cause of damage.

An all-hazards policy would also deal with the problem that insurers currently face with respect to fire damage caused by earthquakes. Even if a homeowner has not purchased an earthquake insurance policy, it will be able to collect reimbursements for damages from a fire caused by an earthquake. In the case of the 1906 San Francisco earthquake, most of the damage was caused by fire, and insurers were obligated to cover these losses. In this sense, homeowners insurance actually covers a portion of earthquake losses even though this coverage is excluded from the policy.

Another reason for having an insurance policy that covers all hazards is that there will be no ambiguity by the homeowner as to whether or not she has coverage. Many residing in the Gulf Coast believed they were covered for water damage from hurricanes by their homeowners' policies. The attractiveness of insurance that guarantees that the policyholder will have coverage against all losses from disasters independent of cause has been demonstrated experimentally by Kahneman and Tversky (1979).

They showed that 80 percent of their responders preferred such coverage to what they termed "probabilistic insurance," where there was some chance that a loss was not covered. What matters to an individual is the knowledge that she will be covered if her property is damaged or destroyed, not the cause of the loss.

An all-hazards insurance policy will be more expensive than the standard homeowners' policy because it is more comprehensive. If premiums are based on risk, however, then policyholders would be charged only for hazards that they face. Thus, a homeowner in the Gulf Coast would theoretically be covered for earthquake damage but would not be charged anything for this additional protection if the area in which she resides is not a seismically active area. In promoting this all-hazard coverage, one needs to highlight this point to the general public, who may otherwise feel that they are paying for risks that they do not face.

11.5.4.3 Disadvantages of All-Hazards Insurance

The major disadvantage of an all-hazards insurance program with premiums reflecting risk (*Principle 1*) is that it will force insurers to raise their prices considerably to cover the potential damage in hazard-prone areas. A large increase in premium could be viewed by homeowners as unjustified and there would be significant resistance to paying for this coverage. For high-income residents who have second homes on the coast, there is an economic rationale for them to pay the cost of their insurance. For lower-income residents, some type of insurance voucher may have to be provided so that these home-owners can afford coverage (*Principle 2*).

Many insurers are likely to resist all-hazards insurance because they may fear the pos-sibility of even larger losses than they have suffered to date, due to the increase of their exposure. Some rightly note that if both wind and water damage were to be included in homeowners policies, the losses from Hurricane Katrina to private insurers would be considerably higher. Other might argue that insurers would have also collected more premiums over the years. To assume the additional risk, there would be a need for a substantial increase in insurers' surplus and/or increased capacity through reinsurance, insurance-linked securities, state funds or federal reinsurance.

There will also be special needs facing small insurers operating in a single state who have smaller surplus than larger firms and are limited in their ability to diversify their risk. These insurers may find that the variance in their losses increases by incorporating the flood and earthquake risks as part of a homeowners' policy. For example, a Louisiana insur-ance company providing protection against hurricane damage might find the variance in losses to be higher than it is today if both wind and water damage were covered under a homeowners policy. For these companies to compete with larger firms, they would have to be able to protect themselves against catastrophic losses through either private- or public-based risk transfer instruments that would not price them out of the market.

Insurers who market an all-hazards insurance policy face an additional challenge in trying to convince homeowners that they will pay only for risks that they actually face. One way for insurance companies to do this is to itemize the cost of different types of coverage on the policy itself in much the way current homeowners or automobile insurance breaks up the cost for different types of protection. If a family living on the Gulf Coast knew that it would be paying $3,000 for wind coverage, $1,500 for water coverage, $500 for fire coverage and $0 for earthquake coverage, it would not com-plain about covering damage from seismic risk facing California homeowners. Such an itemized list of coverage would also highlight the magnitude of risks of living in that particular area, another role that insurance can play—a signal as to how hazardous a particular place is likely to be.

11.5.5 Creation of a Coastal Hurricane Zone[28]

One way to address the challenge of lack of liquidity to cover catastrophic losses from hurricanes is to establish a multistate zone in which risks are diversified and the market

[28] This section is based on Fishman, 2007a; Fishman, 2007b (Jay Fishman is CEO of Travelers Companies).

regulated at a federal level. Travelers Companies recently proposed the creation of a federally regulated *Coastal Hurricane Zone* from Texas to Maine. Private insurers would still market policies covering wind damage from hurricanes, and the federal government would regulate and oversee most aspects of wind underwriting by private insurers including pricing.

The rationale for this proposal is that the current system, wherein each state regulates and oversees its own insurance market, has led to regulatory inconsistency and unpredictability with respect to rates for insurers and customers alike following major hurricanes. A properly designed and executed Coastal Hurricane Zone would provide a more stable set of rules that would allow insurers to make long-term commitments of capital to those areas for wind risks, increasing the availability of insurance. Federal oversight would ensure that rates are actuarially sound, so that premiums reflect the risk (*Principle 1*). States would continue their regulatory oversight, including monitoring insurer insolvency and administering markets of last resort (i.e., residual markets).

Beyond this regulatory innovation, the proposed Coastal Hurricane Zone would also include a mechanism to equitably adjust premiums after periods of significant weather-related profits or losses. If actual hurricane-related damage and loss over a predefined multi-year period were less than anticipated, a portion of premiums would be returned to the policyholders; if actual losses were more than anticipated, the price of insurance would be increased so that policyholders' rates were actuarially fair. A rolling five- or ten-year time period might be appropriate for determining whether a portion of insurer profits would be returned or an assessment be made, thus constituting a type of mutual organization.

To deal with affordability problems (*Principle 2*), temporary federal tax credits would be offered to low-income residents with homes along the Atlantic and Gulf Coasts to purchase insurance to cover their wind exposure. The tax credit would be based upon need (as determined by income and asset level), property value and cost of wind insurance. The tax credits would be funded by increases in taxes of those residing in the Coastal Hurricane Zone who can afford it.

To reduce losses from inevitable hurricanes, federal, state and local governments have another critical role to play in promoting risk-mitigation programs. Foremost in this regard is the adoption and enforcement of similar multistate building codes for both new construction and renovations. The use of storm shutters and impact-resistant windows should be encouraged through economic incentives. Coastal states would be entitled to federal grants if they adopt a proposed federal building code and related mitigation measures. Other loss-mitigation plans include prudent land use management, such as acknowledging the importance of coastal wetlands in minimizing a hurricane's impact upon landfall.

11.5.6 Auctions for Federal Reinsurance Contracts

In the aftermath of Hurricane Andrew in 1992 and the Northridge earthquake in 1994, Lewis and Murdock (1996) developed a proposal that the federal government offer catastrophe reinsurance contracts that would be auctioned annually in order to provide the private sector with more capacity to handle truly extreme events. The U.S. Treasury Department would auction a limited number of contracts indexed on the aggregate direct insured losses occurring as a result of a catastrophic natural disaster. Originally, they proposed contracts covering losses between $25 billion and $50 billion but then modified this so that private insurers, reinsurers and/or state pools could select any trigger level that did not crowd out coverage available in the private market (Cummins et al., 1999). The design of such contracts would have to be specified, and a more detailed analysis would have to be undertaken to determine the potential impact of such an auction mechanism on the relevant stakeholders.

11.5.7 Creation of a Data Collection and Information Sharing Entity

Another proposal to consider is the development of more granular data collection on insurance coverage and claims payment over time: the evolution of different lines of coverage in specific locations. With the increased population in coastal regions, we need to better understand and quantify who has insurance coverage and the amount of protection they have. We propose the creation of a data collection entity to determine the degree of insurance penetration in different parts of the country.

The implementation of this concept could be achieved at a very small cost via the Internal Revenue Service (IRS), with homeowners answering a few questions about their property insurance coverage for flood, earthquake and wind on their annual tax returns. The IRS could collect this information and make it available on an aggregate level (e.g., postal zone) so that individuals cannot be identified. By providing more detailed data on the degree of insurance protection of homeowners, it should be possible to develop strategies for reducing losses and aiding recovery from future natural disasters.

11.6 CONCLUSIONS AND SUGGESTIONS FOR FUTURE RESEARCH

Since the 1990s, we have witnessed a series of large-scale catastrophes that have inflicted historical economic and insured losses. The growing concentration of population and structures in high-risk areas, combined with the potential consequences of global warming, are likely to lead to even more devastating catastrophes in the coming years unless cost-effective risk reduction measures are put in place.

In this chapter we suggested ways to reduce the catastrophic losses from natural disasters by encouraging long-term thinking and recognizing behavioral biases that affect both the supply and demand side of the catastrophe risk insurance market. Our two guiding principles—*risk-based insurance premiums* and *addressing affordability issues*—are likely to be the two pillars of any sustainable answer to the challenges posed by extreme events. The concept of multi-year insurance attached to the property at risk in the case of natural hazard insurance, combined with multi-year mitigation loans, has a much broader potential if premiums can reflect risk and means-tested insurance vouchers are used to address equity and affordability issues. The National Flood Insurance Program offers an opportunity to design these policies; the new Flood Insurance Reform Act includes several of the ideas discussed in this chapter.

Additional research is needed to design multi-year alternative risk transfer instruments for protecting insurers against catastrophic losses that occur over several years. Additional studies are also needed to integrate insurance with other policy tools such as well-enforced building codes, zoning regulations, tax incentives and seals of approval. Given the difficulty many have in processing information about risk and uncertainty, risk and financial education is likely to be even more critical in the coming years.

Note also that we have seen a shift towards more involvement of the states and federal government in catastrophe risk insurance markets. The U.S. public debt ($16 trillion as of September 2012) triggers an important question: how much more exposure to future disasters will the American taxpayers want to assume? This question is not specific to the United States: it was discussed extensively during the latest annual meeting of the World Economic Forum in Davos, a reflection that catastrophe risk financing is rising to the agenda of top decision makers around the world.

APPENDIX

Government Program to Address Affordability Issues

Food Stamp Program. Under the Food Stamp Program, a family is given vouchers to purchase food based on its annual income and size of the family. This program concept originated in the late 1930s, was initiated as a pilot program in 1961 and extended nationwide in 1974. The current program structure was implemented in 1977 with a goal of alleviating hunger and malnutrition by permitting low-income households to obtain a more nutritious diet through normal purchasing of food from grocery stores. Food stamps are available to most low-income households with limited resources regardless of age, disability status or family structure. Households, except those with elderly or disabled members, must have gross incomes below 130 percent of the poverty line. All households must have net incomes below 100 percent of poverty to be eligible.[29] The program is funded entirely by the federal government. Federal and state governments share administrative costs (with the federal government contributing nearly 50 percent). In 2003, total federal food stamp costs were nearly $24 billion.

Low Income Home Energy Assistance Program (LIHEAP). The mission of this program is to assist low-income households that pay a high proportion of their income for home

---

[29] More details on this program can be found at http://www.frac.org/html/federal_food_programs/programs/fsp.html.

energy in meeting their immediate energy needs. The funding is provided by the federal government but is administered by the states and federally recognized tribes or insular areas (e.g., Guam, Puerto Rico, Virgin Islands) to help eligible low-income homeowners and renters meet their heating or cooling needs (eligibility based on similar criteria to the food stamp program).[30] The federal government became involved in awarding energy assistance funds to low-income households program as a result of the increase in oil prices resulting from the Organization of Petroleum Exporting Countries (OPEC) oil embargo in 1973. Over the past few years, the annual appropriation of this program has averaged $2 billion.[31]

Universal Service Fund (USF).[32] The USF was created by the Federal Communications Commission in 1997 to ensure that consumers in all regions of the nation have access to and pay rates for telecommunications services that are reasonably comparable to those in urban areas. To achieve this goal, the program first provides discounts to all households living in a particular high cost area (e.g., rural areas) so they all pay the same subsidized rate regardless of income. There are also universal service programs that are strictly for low-income households, regardless of whether they live in high- or low-cost areas.

REFERENCES

Anderson, D.R., 1974. The national flood insurance program: problems and potential. Journal of Risk and Insurance 41, 579–599.

Aon Benfield, 2013. Annual Global Climate and Catastrophe Report: 2012. Aon Benfield Impact Forecasting, Chicago, IL.

Arrow, K., 1963. Uncertainty and the welfare economics of medical care. American Economic Review 53, 941–973.

Association of British Insurers, 2005. Financial Risks of Climate Change. Association of British Insurers, London.

Auerswald, P., Branscomb, L., La Porte, T., Michel-Kerjan, E., 2006. Seeds of Disasters, Roots of Response. How Private Action Can Reduce Public Vulnerability. Cambridge University Press, New York.

Barro, R., 2009. Rare disasters, asset prices, and welfare costs. American Economic Review 99, 243–264.

Barro, R., Ursua, J., 2008. Consumption disasters in the twentieth century. American Economic Review 98, 58–63.

Bayot, J., 2005. Payouts hinge on the cause of damage. New York Times, August 31.

Bell, D., 1982. Regret in decision making under uncertainty. Operations Research 30, 961–981.

Bell, D., 1985. Disappointment in decision making under uncertainty. Operations Research 33, 1–27.

---

[30] For instance, at the end of August 2007, Secretary of Health and Human Services (HHS) Mike Leavitt announced that $50 million in emergency energy assistance would be given to 12 states that experienced much hotter than normal conditions during the summer.

[31] For more details on this program, see U.S. Department of Health and Human Services at http://www.acf.hhs.gov/programs/liheap/.

[32] For more details on this program see http://www.usac.org/about/universal-service as of October 2011.

Braun, M., Muermann, A., 2004. The impact of regret on the demand for insurance. Journal of Risk and Insurance 71, 737–767.

Browne, M.J., Hoyt, R.E., 2000. The demand for flood insurance: empirical evidence. Journal of Risk and Uncertainty 20, 291–306.

Bundorf, M.K., Pauly, M.V., 2006. Is health insurance affordable for the uninsured? Journal of Health Economics 25, 650–673.

Cabantous, L., Hilton, D., Kunreuther, H., Michel-Kerjan, E., 2011. Is imprecise knowledge better than conflicting expertise? Evidence from insurers' decisions in the United States. Journal of Risk and Uncertainty 42, 211–232.

Camerer, C., Ho, T., 1994. Violations of the betweenness axiom and nonlinearity in probabilities. Journal of Risk and Uncertainty 8, 167–196.

Camerer, C., Kunreuther, H., 1989. Decision processes for low probability events: policy implications. Journal of Policy Analysis and Management 8, 565–592.

CBC News, 2010. The world's worst natural disasters. Calamities of the 20th and 21st centuries. August 30.

Crossett, K.M., Culliton, T.J., Wiley, P.C., Goodspeed, T.R., 2004. Population Trends Along the Coastal United States: 1980–2008. National Oceanic and Atmospheric Administration, Silver Spring, MD.

Cummins, J.D., Lewis, C., Phillips, R., 1999. Pricing excess-of-loss reinsurance contracts against catastrophe loss. In: Froot, K. (Ed.), The Financing of Catastrophe Risk. University of Chicago, Chicago (Chapter 3).

Cummins, D., Suher, M., Zanjani, G., 2010. Federal financial exposure to natural catastrophe risk. In: Lucas, D. (Ed.), Measuring and Managing Federal Financial Risk. University of Chicago Press (National Bureau of Economic Research).

Cummins, D., Weiss, M., 2009. Convergence of insurance and financial markets: hybrid and securitized risk-transfer solutions. Journal of Risk and Insurance 76, 493–545.

Czajkowski, J., Kunreuther, H., Michel-Kerjan, E., 2013. Quantifying riverine and storm-surge flood risk by single-family residence: application to Texas. Risk Analysis http://dx.doi.org/10.1111/risa.12068.

Dionne, G., Doherty, N., Fombaron, N., 2000. Adverse selection in insurance markets. In: Dionne, G. (Ed.), Handbook of Insurance. Kluwer, Boston.

Eisensee, T., Stromberg, D., 2007. News floods, news droughts, and US disaster relief. Quarterly Journal of Economics 122, 693–728.

Finucane, M.L., Alhakami, A., Slovic, P., Johnson, S.M., 2000. The affect heuristic in judgments of risks and benefits. Journal of Behavioral Decision Making 13, 1–17.

Fischhoff, B., Gonzalez, R.M., Small, D.A., Lerner, J.S., 2003. Judged terror risk and proximity to the World Trade Center. Journal of Risk and Uncertainty 26, 137–151.

Fishman, J., 2007a. Something's Gotta Give: a private market-based hurricane wind concept. Paper presented at the American Risk and Insurance Association Annual Meeting, August 6th, Quebec City, Canada.

Fishman, J., 2007b. Before the next 'Big One' hits. Wall Street Journal. August 27.

Francis, T., 2005. CEO Says allstate adjusts storm plan: interview of Edward Liddy. Wall Street Journal, C1–C3. September 5.

Freeman, P., Scott, K., 2005. Comparative analysis of large scale catastrophe compensation schemes. In: Catastrophic Risks and Insurance. Organization for Economic Cooperation and Development (OECD), Paris. July.

Gabaix, X., 2008. Variable rare disasters: a tractable theory of ten puzzles in macro-finance. American Economic Review 98, 64–67.

Gerdes, V., 1963. Insuring against flood peril. Journal of Insurance 30, 547–553.

Gourio, F., 2008. Disasters and recoveries. American Economic Review 98, 68–73.

Grace, M.F., Klein, R.W., Kleindorfer, P.R., 2004. Homeowners insurance with bundled catastrophe coverage. Journal of Risk and Insurance 71, 351–379.

Greenwald, B.C., Stiglitz, J.E., 1990. Asymmetric information and the new theory of the firm: financial constraints and risk behavior. American Economic Review 80, 160–165.

Harrington, S.E., Niehaus, G., 2001. Government insurance, tax policy, and the affordability and availability of catastrophe insurance. Journal of Insurance Regulation 19, 591–612.

Hertwig, R., Barron, G., Weber, E.U., Erev, I., 2004. Decisions from experience and the effect of rare events in risky choice. Psychological Science 15, 534.

Hogarth, R., Kunreuther, H., 1995. Decision making under ignorance: arguing with yourself. Journal of Risk and Uncertainty 10, 15–36.

Hsee, C.K., Kunreuther, H., 2000. The affection effect in insurance decisions. Journal of Risk and Uncertainty 20, 149–159.

Huber, O., Wider, R., Huber, O., 1997. Active information search and complete information presentation in naturalistic risky decision tasks. Acta Psychologica 95, 15–29.

Insurance Journal, 2006. S&P to Implement New Way to Assess Insurer Cat Risk. March 31.

Intergovernmental Panel on Climate Change (IPCC), 2011. Special Report on Managing the Risks of Extreme Events and Disasters to Advance Climate Change Adaptation (SREX) <http://ipcc-wg2.gov/SREX/report/>.

Jaffee, D., Kunreuther, H., Michel-Kerjan, E., 2010. Long term property insurance (LTI) for addressing catastrophe risk. Journal of Insurance Regulation 29, 167–187.

Jaffee, D., Russell, T., 2003. Markets under stress: the case of extreme event insurance. In: Arnott, R., Greenwald, B., Kanbur, R., Nalebuff, B. (Eds.), Economics for an Imperfect World: Essays in Honor of Joseph E. Stiglitz. MIT Press, Cambridge, MA.

Jaffee, D., Russell, T., 2012. The welfare economics of catastrophic loss. Presented at NBER Universities-Research Conference on Insurance Markets and Catastrophe Risk, May 11–12, 2012

Johnson, E., Hershey, J., Meszaros, J., Kunreuther, H., 1993. Framing, probability distortions, and insurance decisions. Journal of Risk and Uncertainty 7, 35–51.

Kahneman, D., Tversky, A., 1979. Prospect theory: an analysis of decision under risk. Econometrica 47, 263–291.

Klein, R.W., 2007. Catastrophe Risk and the Regulation of Property Insurance: A Comparative Analysis of Five States. Working paper. Georgia State University, December.

Krantz, D., Kunreuther, H., 2007. Goals and plans in decision-making. Judgment and Decision Making 2, 137–168.

Kunreuther, H., 1989. The role of actuaries and underwriters in insuring ambiguous risks. Risk Analysis 9, 319–328.

Kunreuther, H., 2007. Reflections on U.S. disaster insurance policy for the 21st century. In: Quigley, J., Rosenthal, L. (Eds.), Risking House and Home: Disasters, Cities, Public Policy. Berkeley Public Policy Press, Berkeley.

Kunreuther, H., Ginsberg, R., Miller, L., Sagi, P., Slovic, P., Borkan, B., Katz, N., 1978. Disaster Insurance Protection: Public Policy Lessons. John Wiley and Sons, New York.

Kunreuther, H., Hogarth, R., Meszaros, J., 1993. Insurer ambiguity and market failure. Journal of Risk and Uncertainty 7, 71–87.

Kunreuther, H., Meszaros, J., Hogarth, R.M., Spranca, M., 1995. Ambiguity and underwriter decision processes. Journal of Economic Behavior & Organization 26, 337–352.

Kunreuther, H., Michel-Kerjan, E., 2011. At War with the Weather: Managing Large-Scale Risks in a New Era of Catastrophes. MIT Press.

Kunreuther, H., Michel-Kerjan, E., 2012. Demand for Multi-Year Insurance: Experimental Evidence. Working paper. Center for Risk Management and Decision Processes, The Wharton School, University of Pennsylvania.

Kunreuther, H., Michel-Kerjan, E., Pauly, M., 2013. Making America more resilient toward natural disasters: a Call for action. Environment Magazine. July/August.

Kunreuther, H., Miller, L., 1985. Insurance versus disaster relief: an analysis of interactive modeling for disaster policy planning. Public Administration Review 45, 147–154.

Kunreuther, H., Pauly, M., McMorrow, S., 2013. Behavioral Economics and Insurance: Improving Decisions in the Most Misunderstood Industry. Cambridge University Press, New York.

Lecomte, E., Gahagan, K., 1998. Hurricane insurance protection in Florida. In: Kunreuther, H., Roth, R., Sr. (Eds.), Paying the Price: The Status and Role of Insurance against Natural Disasters in the United States. Joseph Henry Press, Washington, DC, pp. 97–124.

Lewis, C., Murdock, L., 1996. The role of government contracts in discretionary reinsurance markets for natural disasters. Journal of Risk and Insurance 63, 567–597.

Loomes, G., Sugden, R., 1982. Regret theory: an alternative theory of rational choice under uncertainty. The Economic Journal 92, 805–824.

Lowenstein, G.F., Weber, E.U., Hsee, C.K., Welch, N., 2001. Risk as feelings. Psychological Bulletin 127, 267–286.

Martin, I., 2008. Disasters and the welfare cost of uncertainty. American Economic Review 98, 74–78.

Mechler, R., 2003. Macroeconomic Impacts of Natural Disasters. <http://info.worldbank.org/etools/docs/library/114715/istanbul03/docs/istanbul03/03mechler3-n%5B1%5D.pdf>.

Michel-Kerjan, E., 2010. Catastrophe economics: The U.S. national flood insurance program. Journal of Economic Perspectives 24, 165–186.

Michel-Kerjan, E., 2012a. How resilient is your country? Nature 491, 497.

Michel-Kerjan, E., 2012b. TRIA at 10 years: the future of terrorism risk insurance. Testimony before the House Financial Committee, Subcommittee on Insurance. September 11. Washington, DC.

Michel-Kerjan, E., de Marcellis-Warin, N., 2006. Public-private programs for covering extreme events: the impact of information distribution on risk-sharing. Asia-Pacific Journal of Risk and Insurance 1, 21–49.

Michel-Kerjan, E., Kunreuther, H., 2011. Reforming flood insurance. Science 333. July 22.

Michel-Kerjan, E., Lemoyne de Forges, S., Kunreuther, H., 2012. Policy tenure under the U.S. national flood insurance program. Risk Analysis 32, 644–658.

Michel-Kerjan, E., Raschky, P., 2011. The effects of government intervention in the market for corporate terrorism insurance. European Journal of Political Economy 27, 122–132.

Michel-Kerjan, E., Slovic, P. (Eds.), 2010. The Irrational Economist. Public Affairs Press, New York.

Michel-Kerjan, E., Volkman Wise, J., 2011. The Risk of Ever-Growing Disaster Relief Expectations. Paper presented at the annual NBER Insurance Group conference, Cambridge, MA, September 2011. Accessible at: <http://nber.org/confer/2011/INSf11/Michel-Kerjan_Volkman_Wise.pdf>.

Michel-Kerjan, E., Zelenko, I., Cárdenas, V., Turgel, D., 2011. Catastrophe Financing for Governments: Learning from the 2009–2012 MultiCat Program in Mexico. OECD Working Papers on Finance, Insurance and Private Pensions, No. 9.

Mills, E., Lecomte, E., 2006. From Risk to Opportunity: How Insurers Can Proactively and Profitably Manage Climate Change. Ceres Report, August.

Moss, D., 2002. When All Else Fails. The Government as the Ultimate Risk Manager. Harvard University Press.

Moss, D., 2010. The peculiar politics of American disaster policy: how television has changed federal relief. In: Michel-Kerjan, E., Slovic, P. (Eds.), The Irrational Economist. Public Affairs Books, New York, pp. 151–160 (Chapter 18).

Munich Re, 2013. Topics geo, Natural catastrophes 2012, Report, Munich Re, Munich.

OECD, 2010. OECD Recommendation: Good practices for mitigating and financing catastrophic risks. Organization for Economic Cooperation and Development, Paris.

Overman, E.S., 1957. The flood peril and the federal flood insurance act of 1956. Annals of the American Academy of Political and Social Science 309, 98–106.

Palm, R., 1995. Earthquake Insurance: A Longitudinal Study of California Homeowners. Westview Press, Boulder.

Pielke Jr, R., Gratz, J., Landsea, C., Collins, D., Saunders, M., Musulin, R., 2008. Normalized hurricane damage in the United States: 1900–2005. Natural Hazards Review 9, 29–42.

Raschky, P., Schwindt, M., 2009. Aid, Natural Disasters and the Samaritan's Dilemma. Policy Research Working Paper 4952, The World Bank, Washington, DC.

Reeves, A., 2004. Plucking Votes from Disasters. Los Angeles Times, May 12.

Reeves, A., 2005. Political Disaster? Electoral Politics and Presidential Disaster Declarations, Work in progress, Kennedy School of Government, Harvard University, Cambridge, MA.

Risk Management Solutions (RMS), 2006. New RMS View of U.S. Hurricane Activity Rates Increases Losses by 40% in Florida and Gulf Coast, Press release, March 22, California.

Roth Jr., R.J., 1998. Earthquake insurance protection in California. In: Kunreuther, H., Roth, R., Sr. (Eds.), Paying the Price: The Status and Role of Insurance Against Natural Disasters in the United States. Joseph Henry Press, Washington, DC, pp. 67–95.

Rottenstreich, Y., Hsee, C.K., 2001. Money, kisses, and electric shocks: on the affective psychology of risk. Psychological Science 12, 185–190.

Samuelson, W., Zeckhauser, R., 1988. Status quo bias in decision making. Journal of Risk and Uncertainty 1, 7–59.

Shafir, E., Simonson, I., Tversky, A., 1993. Reason-based choice. Cognition 49, 11–36.

Stone, J., 1973. A theory of capacity and the insurance of catastrophic risks: Part I and Part II. Journal of Risk and Insurance 40, 339–355.

Sunstein, C., 2003. Terrorism and probability neglect. Journal of Risk and Uncertainty 26, 121–136.

Swiss Re, 2002. Terrorism: Dealing With the New Spectre. Focus Report, Zurich.

Swiss Re, 2011. Sigma No 1/2011: Natural Catastrophes and Man-Made Disasters in 2010.

Thaler, R., 1985. Mental accounting and consumer choice. Marketing Science 4, 199–214.

Tobin, R., Calfee, C., 2005. The National Flood Insurance Program's Mandatory Purchase Requirement: Policies, Processes, and Stakeholders. American Institutes for Research, Washington, DC.

Tversky, A., Kahneman, D., 1973. Availability: a heuristic for judging frequency and probability. Cognitive Psychology 5, 207–232.

Tversky, A., Kahneman, D., 1991. Loss aversion in riskless choice: a reference-dependent model. Quarterly Journal of Economics, 1039–1061.

U.S. Department of the Treasury, Board of Governors of the Federal Reserve System, U.S. Securities and Exchange Commission, Commodity Futures Trading Commission, 2006. Terrorism Risk Insurance: Report of the President's Working Group on Financial Markets. Washington, DC, September.

U.S. Government Accountability Office, 2002. Terrorism Insurance: Rising uninsured exposure to attacks heightens potential economic vulnerabilities. Testimony of Richard J. Hillman Before the Subcommittee on Oversight and Investigations, Committee on Financial Services, House of Representatives, February 27.

United Nations, 2008. World population prospects: the 2008 revision. United Nations Department of Economic and Social Affairs.

United Nations Development Programme (UNDP), 2004. Bureau for Crisis Prevention and Recovery. A Global Report: Reducing Disaster Risk, A Challenge for Development <http://www.undp.org/cpr/whats_new/rdr_english.pdf>.

United Nations International Strategy for Disaster Reduction (UNISDR)/World Bank, 2011. Global Assessment Report on Disaster Risk Reduction. Rogers, D., Tsirkunov V., 2010. Costs and Benefits of Early Warning Systems. In: UNISDR/World Bank (2011). Global Assessment Report on Disaster Risk Reduction. <http://www.preventionweb.net/english/hyogo/gar/report/index.php?id=9413>.

Wharton Risk Management Center, 2005. TRIA and Beyond. Philadelphia, PA.

Wu, G., Gonzalez, R., 1996. Curvature of the probability weighting function. Management Science 42, 1676–1690.

CHAPTER 12

Non-Expected Utility Models Under Objective Uncertainty

John Quiggin
School of Economics, University of Queensland, Australia

Contents

Abstract

Although expected utility (EU) theory is a powerful tool for the analysis of decision under risk, it has long been known that individual behavior, in both experimental and market settings, deviates from the predictions of simple EU models. These violations of EU predictions were largely disregarded until the late 1970s, when a variety of alternatives to, and generalizations of, EU theory began to appear, most notably prospect theory of Kahneman and Tversky. Dozens of generalized EU models appeared in the 1980s and early 1990s. Of these, the most prominent classes were rank-dependent models, betweenness models and regret-theoretic approaches.

Keywords

Risk, Generalized Expected Utility Theory

JEL Classification Code

D81

12.1 INTRODUCTION

Formal study of decision under uncertainty began with the study of gambling games by Pascal, Fermat and others in the 17th century.[1] Provided the rules are observed, such

---

[1] In view of the benefits to be obtained by understanding betting odds, and the simplicity of the associated mathematics, it is surprising that theories of probability took so long to emerge.

Handbook of the Economics of Risk and Uncertainty, Volume 1
ISSN 2211-7547, http://dx.doi.org/10.1016/B978-0-444-53685-3.00012-X

games involve bets with known probabilities or, more precisely, objective probabilities that can be computed by anyone with an understanding of the relevant theory. Expected utility theory can be traced back to the work of Bernoulli (1738, 1954), in the context of the St Petersburg paradox, a hypothetical gambling game with an unbounded expected value

As with the pioneering work of Pascal and Fermat, the modern theory of economic behavior under uncertainty began with the study of games. Von Neumann and Morgenstern (1944) established modern game theory, now understood more generally to encompass any strategic interaction between agents. Once again, it was natural to consider the problem as one involving known probabilities. Optimal play in the two-person zero-sum games considered by von Neumann and Morgenstern typically involves the adoption of mixed strategies. Equilibrium requires that players should know what mixed strategies their opponent is playing, and it is natural to express this awareness in terms of known probabilities. Hence, von Neumann and Morgenstern expressed the objective of the players in terms of the expected utility (EU) received for a given combination of mixed strategies. Similar arguments apply to the Nash equilibrium concept and its generalizations.

The assumption of known probabilities is more problematic in decision theory. Decision problems may be considered games with Nature, conceptualized as a player with a known mixed strategy. However, this interpretation raises the difficulty that there is no concept of game-theoretic equilibrium on which to base the premise that the probabilities of different acts of Nature are known. Nevertheless, there are many decision problems in which the assumption of given objective probabilities seems reasonable, on the basis of considerations of symmetry (as in the case of coins and other gambling devices) or of known relative frequencies.

Problems of this kind are commonly referred to as decisions under risk, as opposed to the more general class of decisions under uncertainty. The distinction is commonly stated as that between known and unknown probabilities. However, this distinction is problematic. The class of decisions under risk clearly involves the case of known objective probabilities, but it is unclear where to draw the line between risk and uncertainty. The distinction was first drawn by Knight (1921) who wrote at a time when the only well developed theory of probability was the frequentist approach in which the probability of an event was the limiting frequency in repeated trials. In his discussion of risk, Knight appears to consider only examples of this kind (for example, the actuarial calculations of insurance companies) and to use the term uncertainty to cover all other decisions. The development of the theory of subjective probability by de Finetti (1931) laid the basis for a subjective expected utility theory based entirely on preferences (Savage, 1954; Anscombe and Aumann, 1963). The term *uncertainty* was then used to distinguish between subjective and objective probabilities. The work of

Ellsberg (1961), who used the term *ambiguity* to refer to problems in which choices were inconsistent with any well-defined set of probabilities, further complicated the picture.

Despite these complexities, the majority of economic analysis of choice under uncertainty focuses on the case of risk: that is, the case in which the probability distribution of variables of interest is commonly known by all agents and observable by modellers. EU theory has been applied to the analysis of a vast range of decisions under risk including health care (Arrow, 1963), the theory of the firm under uncertainty (Sandmo, 1971), and the theory of crime and punishment (Becker, 1968).

Although EU theory has been a powerful tool, it has long been known that individual behavior, in both experimental and market settings, deviates from the predictions of simple EU models. These violations of EU predictions were largely disregarded until the late 1970s, when a variety of alternatives to, and generalizations of, EU theory began to appear, most notably the prospect theory of Kahneman and Tversky (1979). The trickle of alternative models turned into a flood in the 1980s and early 1990s, when dozens of generalized EU models appeared, almost all of which dealt with the case of decision under risk. Of these, the most prominent classes were rank-dependent models, beginning with Quiggin (1981, 1982), betweenness models (Chew, 1983) and regret-theoretic approaches (Loomes and Sugden, 1982).

Subsequent work integrated some of these developments The cumulative prospect theory of Tversky and Kahneman (1992, see also Wakker and Tversky, 1993) integrated prospect theory and rank-dependent EU. Gul (1991) presented a betweenness model, referred to as disappointment theory, that captured some of the intuition behind earlier regret-theoretic models.

Since the 1990s, theoretical attention has shifted to problems involving uncertainty and ambiguity, stimulated by the work of Schmeidler (1989) and Gilboa and Schmeidler (1989), but work on the estimation, application and characterization of generalized EU models for risk continued apace. Crucial issues included the significance of *first-order* aversion to small risks, and the capacity of generalized EU models to incorporate mixtures of risk

This chapter presents a summary of the development, and some of the applications of generalized models of decision under risk. The chapter is organized as follows. Section 12.2 presents a summary of the standard EU model. Section 12.3 describes some of the experimental and market evidence of violations of EU predictions, beginning with the famous Allais "paradox". Section 12.4 describes the idea of probability weighting and the development of rank-dependent probability weighting models. Section 12.5 describes betweenness and regret models, and Section 12.6 more general treatments of the problem, not involving a specific functional form. Section 12.7 deals with risk attitudes and concepts of increasing risk in generalized EU models. Section

12.8 considers the economic implications of generalized EU theories. Finally, some concluding comments are presented.

12.2 THE EU MODEL

In a standard problem of choice under risk, the objects of choice are simple lotteries $\mathbf{p} = \left(x_1 \dots x_N; p_1 \dots p_N\right)$ over some finite set of prizes $x_n \in X, n = 1 \dots N$ for some output space X. The probability of receiving x_n is given by the probability $p_n, 0 \leq p_n \leq 1, \sum_n p_n = 1$. The set of all such lotteries is denoted P and preferences over P are represented by an ordering $\succeq$ with associated indifference relation $\sim$ and strict ordering. More generally, we may consider cumulative probability distribution functions F over some compact set of outcomes, such as the interval $[0, M]$.

From its first presentation by von Neumann and Morgenstern (1944) the dominant model of choice under risk has been expected utility (EU) theory. Von Neumann and Morgenstern proposed the following axioms:

A.1 Completeness. For all $\mathbf{p}, \mathbf{p}'$ either $\mathbf{p} \succeq \mathbf{p}'$ or $\mathbf{p}' \succeq \mathbf{p}$.

A.2 Transitivity. If $\mathbf{p} \succeq \mathbf{p}'$ and $\mathbf{p}' \succeq \mathbf{p}''$ then $\mathbf{p} \succeq \mathbf{p}''$.

A.3 Archimedean (Continuity) axiom. For any $\mathbf{p}, \mathbf{p}', \mathbf{p}''$ such that $\mathbf{p} \succ \mathbf{p}' \succ \mathbf{p}''$, there exist $\lambda, \lambda' \in (0, 1)$ such that

$$\alpha \mathbf{p} + (1 - \alpha) \mathbf{p}'' \succeq \mathbf{p}'$$
$$\mathbf{p}' \succeq \lambda' \mathbf{p} + \left(1 - \lambda'\right) \mathbf{p}''.$$

All of these axioms have analogs in models of consumer preference, where the objects of choice are consumption bundles. The crucial additional axiom giving rise to expected utility was presented by von Neumann and Morgenstern in terms of an "algebra of combining" applied to indifference classes of lotteries. In our notation, the key assumption may be stated as

A.4 Independence axiom (substitution form). If $\mathbf{p} \sim \mathbf{p}'$, then for any $\lambda \in [0, 1]$ and any $\mathbf{p}''$

$$\lambda \mathbf{p} + (1 - \lambda) \mathbf{p}'' \sim \lambda \mathbf{p}' + (1 - \lambda) \mathbf{p}''.$$

From these axioms von Neumann and Morgenstern derived the expected utility representation result:

Proposition 12.1 *Preferences satisfy A.1–4 if and only if there exists a function* $u : X \to \Re$, *unique up to affine transformations such that* $\mathbf{p} \succeq \mathbf{p}'$ *if and only if* $V(\mathbf{p}) \geq V\left(\mathbf{p}'\right)$ *where*

$$V(\mathbf{p}) = \sum_n p_n U\left(x_n\right). \tag{12.1}$$

For general cumulative distribution functions, a slightly stronger version of the continuity axioms yields

$$V(F) = \int U(x)\, dF(x). \tag{12.2}$$

The interpretation of the von Neumann–Morgenstern utility function U has been the subject of some controversy, particularly for the case when outcomes x are wealth levels. It is natural to interpret concavity of U in terms of diminishing marginal utility of wealth which, in turn, implies that U should be regarded as a cardinal utility function. Von Neumann and Morgenstern rejected this view, but did not provide convincing arguments for doing so.

The crucial feature of the EU representation is that it is "linear in the probabilities". This simple feature, derived from A.4, has a wide variety of implications. It means, for example, that the utility function over an entire interval $[0, M]$ can be elicited using only lotteries with 0 and M as prizes. In extensive-form decision problems, it ensures a range of attractive properties as dynamic consistency, a non-negative value for information and the capacity to "roll back the decision tree." The presentation of the axioms by von Neumann and Morgenstern tended to obscure the crucial role of A.4. Appreciation of this crucial role, and the use of the term *independence axiom* came with the subsequent work of Dalkey (1949), Malinvaud (1952), Samuelson (1952) and others. A detailed discussion of this piece of intellectual history is given by Fishburn and Wakker (1995).

Although the implications of A.4 are appealing, its normative basis is far less obvious than that of the other substantive axiom, transitivity.[2] The most convincing presentation is based on the Sure-Thing principle, due to Savage (1954). Savage presented the Sure-Thing principle in the context of decision under uncertainty, where subjective probabilities of states of nature are derived from preferences over acts. But the argument is applicable to the case of objectively known probabilities, assuming that any two states with equal probability may be treated interchangeably.

Informally, the argument may be illustrated by considering a pair of two-stage lotteries. The first stage is the toss of a coin (not necessarily fair), which determines which of two lotteries are to be offered. Prospect A yields lottery $\mathbf{p}_H^A$ if the coin toss yields heads, and $\mathbf{p}_T^A$ if it yields tails. Prospect B yields lottery $\mathbf{p}_H^B$ if the coin toss yields heads, and $\mathbf{p}_T^B$ if it yields tails. Suppose that $\mathbf{p}_H^A \succeq \mathbf{p}_H^B$ and $\mathbf{p}_T^A \succeq \mathbf{p}_T^B$. Then, choosing A over B yields a "sure thing." Whichever way the coin flip turns out, the resulting lottery is preferred. We may state the general principle as

---

[2] The Archimedean axiom is a matter of mathematical convenience. Further, given transitivity, completeness is essentially a consistency condition. If an individual consistently chooses $\mathbf{p}$ over $\mathbf{p}'$, we may infer $\mathbf{p} \succeq \mathbf{p}'$. If sometimes one is chosen and sometimes the other, then $\mathbf{p} \sim \mathbf{p}'$. As long as there is no violation of transitivity, incompleteness can only refer to choices that have not been observed.

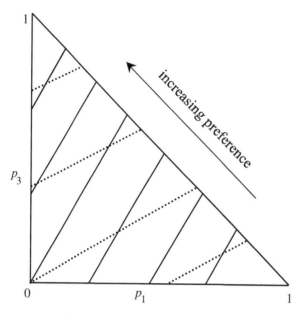

Figure 12.1 Expected utility indifference curves in the probability triangle.

A.4* Independence axiom (sure-thing form) For any $\mathbf{p}, \mathbf{p}', \mathbf{p}'', \mathbf{p}'''$ such that $\mathbf{p} \succeq \mathbf{p}'$ and $\mathbf{p}'' \succeq \mathbf{p}'''$, and any $\lambda \in [0, 1]$,

$$\lambda \mathbf{p} + (1 - \lambda)\mathbf{p}'' \succeq \lambda \mathbf{p}' + (1 - \lambda)\mathbf{p}'''.$$

It is obvious that A.4* implies A.4. The simplest way to prove the converse is via Proposition 12.1.

The EU model presented in equation (12.1) displays two crucial properties. First, the probability and utility components are multiplicatively separable. Second, by virtue of the independence property, EU preferences are linear in the probabilities. This point may be illustrated by the Marschak-Machina triangle, first developed by Marschak (1950) and popularized by Machina (1982) (see Figure 12.1).

The triangle represents possible preferences for the case $N = 3$. We will assume $x_1 < x_2 < x_3$. Points (p_1, p_2, p_3) in the unit simplex are represented by the corresponding point (p_1, p_3) in the triangle, with p_2 implicit in the requirement $\sum_n p_n = 1$. It follows that the least preferred outcome is the lower right vertex, corresponding to $(1, 0, 0)$ and the preferences increase with movement in a generally north-westerly direction.

All of these properties follow from a simple dominance requirement, that decision makers should prefer a higher probability of a better outcome.[3] The independence

---

[3] For the case of a fixed and finite set of outcomes, this is the first-order stochastic dominance requirement (Hadar and Russell, 1969; Hanoch and Levy, 1969).

property corresponds to the requirement that indifference curves should be linear and parallel. This may be seen from the fact that a movement $(\Delta p_1, \beta \Delta p_1)$ along the indifference curve, where β is the slope of the curve, corresponds to a shift of $(\Delta p_1, -(1 + \beta) \Delta p_1, \beta \Delta p_1)$ in the probability distribution $\mathbf{p}$. Under EU, the resulting change in V is given by

$$\Delta V = \Delta p_1 \left(u(x_1) + \beta u(x_3) - (1 + \beta) u(x_2) \right)$$

and $\Delta V = 0$ if and only if

$$\beta = \frac{u(x_2) - u(x_1)}{u(x_3) - u(x_2)}$$

which is independent of $\mathbf{p}$.

12.3 PROBLEMS WITH EU

In the decade following the publication of von Neumann and Morgenstern, both the normative validity of the EU model and its adequacy as a description of behavior were much debated. The crucial criticism came from Allais (1953), a lifelong critic of the EU model. Although the issues raised by Allais remained unresolved, they were largely ignored for the following quarter century, re-emerging in the late 1970s. The main criticism of EU during this period came from advocates of the mean-variance approach pioneered by Markowitz (1952) and Tobin (1958), among others, and focused on the practical question of whether EU was useful in deriving "the kind of comparative static results economists are interested in" (Tobin, 1969). The development of tools such as the theory of stochastic dominance (Hadar and Russell, 1969; Hanoch and Levy, 1969) and the coefficients of relative and absolute risk aversion (Arrow, 1965; Pratt, 1964) answered this question in the affirmative, as was shown by the work of Sandmo (1971), Leland (1972) and Rothschild and Stiglitz (1970, 1971) in the early 1970s.

From the late 1970s onwards, however, the earlier concerns about EU theory re-emerged. One major contribution to this revival of interest was the work of Allais and Hagen (1979) which led to the establishment of a biennial international conference on Foundations and Applications of Utility, Risk and Decision Theory (FUR), from 1982 onwards. Another was the work of Tversky and Kahneman (1974) which demonstrated a range of behavior patterns inconsistent with the EU axioms.

This section gives a brief summary of the main evidence against the EU model. More detailed surveys are given by Machina (1987) and Starmer (2000).

12.3.1 The Allais Problem

Almost as soon as it was introduced, EU theory came under attack, most notably from a (defiantly) French economist, Maurice Allais. Isolated from developments in the United States by World War II and by his insistence on publishing in French, Allais undertook extensive work on decision theory independently of von Neumann and Morgenstern, and had developed his own theory of cardinal utility[4]. On this basis, he argued that rational decision makers would be concerned about the dispersion of utility, as well as its mean value. This view led Allais to reject the axioms of von Neumann and Morgenstern. Although it is not fully spelled out in Allais (1953), Allais clearly accepts the existence of a representation consistent with Axioms A1–A3, as well as the requirement for statewise dominance.

Allais sought to refute A.4 by offering a counter-example, which became known as the "Allais paradox," or, for those not convinced of the validity of the EU axioms, the Allais problem. The Allais problem involves prizes $x_1 = 0, x_2 = 100$ million francs, $x_3 = 500$ million francs[5]. Allais proposed two choices, first between $A = (x_2, 1)$ and $B = (x_1, x_2, x_3; 0.01, 0.89, 0.10)$ and then between $C = (x_1, x_2; 0.89, 0.11)$ and $D = (x_1, x_3; 0.90, 0.10)$.[6]

Most subjects preferred A to B and C to D, but this violates independence. This may be seen by rewriting all the prospects to have three outcomes, not all distinct, with probabilities $(0.01, 0.89, 0.10)$, so that we have $A = (x_2, x_2, x_2; 0.01, 0.89, 0.10)$, $B = (x_1, x_1, x_3; 0.01, 0.89, 0.10)$, $C = (x_2, x_1, x_3; 0.01, 0.89, 0.10)$ and $D = (x_1, x_1, x_3; 0.90, 0.10)$. So, the two pairs of gambles are the same, except that the "common consequence," x_2 occurring with probability 0.89 in gambles A and B has been replaced by x_1 in gambles C and D.[7]

---

[5] For reference, 100 million francs were worth approximately $US300 000 in 1953, which in turn converts to about $US2.5 million in current (2012) values.

[4] In fact, in his later work, he argued that utility was a cardinal function of wealth, the same for all individuals.

[6] Presented in the original French, to provide the flavor:

1) Préférez-vous la situation à la situation B?

SITUATION A: Certitude de recevoir 100 millions.

SITUATION B

89 chances sur 100 de gagner 100 millions.

10 chances sur 100 de gagner 500 millions.

1 chance sur 100 de ne rien gagner.

(2) Préférez-vous la situation C à la situation D?

SITUATION C 11 chances sur 100 de gagner 100 millions. 89 chances sur 100 de ne rien gagner.

SITUATION D 10 chances sur 100 de gagner 500 millions. 89 chances sur 100 de ne rien gagner.

Si le postulat de M. Savage était justifié, la préférence A>B devrait entrainer la préférenceC > D. Or, et precisement pour la plupart des gens tres prudents, dont la courbure de la satisfaction n'est pas trop grande et que l'opinion commune considere comme tres rationnels, ont observe les reponses

A > B, C <D.

Elles sont donc en opposition avec le cinqueume axiome de M. Savage.

The reference is to Savage (1952), where the fifth axiom corresponds to Axiom S2 in Savage (1954), the Sure-Thing principle.

[7] Note that the ordering of the outcomes, which was monotonic in the original presentation, now differs between gambles. This is irrelevant in the context of expected utility theory, but crucial in the context of the rank-dependent models discussed later.

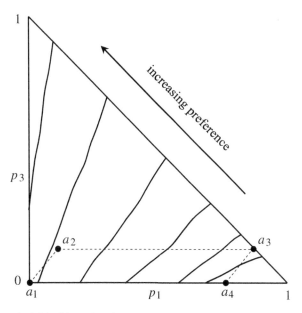

Figure 12.2 The Marschak-Machina triangle.

The violation of the independence axiom may be seen using the Marschak-Machina triangle, in Figure 12.2, from Machina (1982), where the Allais choices (A, B, C, D) are labelled as (a_1, a_2, a_3, a_4). The shift from the pair (A, B) to (C, D) is represented by a parallel movement of 0.89 along the horizontal axis corresponding to the probability of prize x_1, so that the four prizes form a parallelogram. Since the EU indifference curves are also parallel, EU requires that the preference ranking must remain unchanged. On the other hand, with general indifference curves, such as those in the figure, there is no such requirement. Machina described the pattern of indifference curves shown in Figure 12.2 as "fanning out".[8]

Allais presented his criticisms at a meeting held in Paris in 1952. The subsequent discussion was vigorous but eventually ended without any agreement. EU advocates thought that Allais had not understood the point that concave utility captures risk aversion with respect to income/consumption. Allais presented a variety of arguments which may be interpreted, in retrospect, as referring to probability weighting, but which were not formalized in a way that made his point clear.

After decades of neglect, Allais' critique of expected utility theory enjoyed a revival in the 1970s. Allais himself returned to the field, supported by Ole Hagen. Their edited volume (Allais and Hagen, 1979) stimulated new interest in the topic, and a search for generalized models consistent with Allais-type behavior.

[8] The local utility function model used by Machina to characterize "fanning out" is discussed further in Section 12.7.

12.3.2 Gambling and Insurance

In applications of the EU framework to economic choices, the assumption that the von Neumann–Morgenstern utility function is concave is standard. Within the EU framework, this assumption is equivalent to risk aversion. However, a large proportion of the population engages in gambling, which appears to suggest risk preference. Moreover, most people who gamble also engage in various forms of risk reducing behavior, such as the purchase of insurance.

Beginning with Friedman and Savage (1948), a variety of attempts have been made to resolve this contradiction. Friedman and Savage propose the idea that a large increase in wealth may permit a qualitative shift in social class. This implies the possibility of a convex segment in the utility function. Most subsequent attempts to resolve the insurance–gambling problem within the EU framework involve some similar approach, such as the desire to finance a "lumpy" purchase.

All such models imply that, if possible, individuals should gamble only once, seeking the best possible odds for a gamble which will deliver a gain sufficient to move wealth out of the convex segment of the utility function. In the case where actuarially fair gambles are available these strategies yield a final wealth distribution of the form concentrated on the two local maxima of $u'(w)$. This is consistent with the broader class of results derived by Dubins and Savage (1965), who show the optimality of "bold" strategies for EU maximizers seeking to maximize the chance of achieving a target wealth level.

In reality, however, gambling and insurance preferences are typically quite stable over time, and rarely involve "bold" strategies. Thus, it does not appear that the EU framework can explain this phenomenon.

12.3.3 Common Ratio Effect

The long-neglected and much-misinterpreted criticisms of Allais (1953) were reinforced by new empirical evidence, which demonstrated the robustness of the "Allais paradox" and other violations of expected utility, such as the common ratio effect. The common ratio effect may be illustrated by the following example, cited by Kahneman and Tversky (1979).

Choice 1
A: (0,6,000;0.55 0.45) [14], B: (0, 3,000; 0.1,0.90). [86]★
Choice 2
C: (0, 6,000;0.999, .001), D: (0,3,000;0.998 .002). [73]★ [27]

The modal choices are B over A (86 percent) and C over D (73 percent). A majority of subjects in this study choose the inconsistent pair (B, C).

If we normalize by setting $u(0) = 0$, it is evident that these preferences are inconsistent with EU. Preference for B implies that

$$0.9 * u(3000) > 0.45 * u(6000)$$

so,

$$u(6000) < 2u(3000)$$

which is consistent with a concave utility function.

On the other hand, preference for C over D implies that

$$0.002 * u(3000) < 0.001 * u(6000)$$

One possible explanation is that the low probability event "win 6000 with probability 0.001" is "overweighted" relative to its objective probability. This idea has proved both fruitful and problematic, as we will now discuss.

12.4 PROBABILITY WEIGHTING

A number of attempts were made to develop generalizations of expected utility theory that could account for the Allais paradox and related phenomena such as the common ratio effect. The central idea was that decision makers tend to overweight low-probability events. This idea had made occasional appearances in the psychological literature on choice under uncertainty (Preston and Baratta, 1948; Edwards, 1954), where it was interpreted as an instance of the more general phenomenon of diminishing responsiveness to stimuli.

The central idea was to replace probabilities p with weights $w(p)$ where it was normally assumed that w mapped the unit interval onto itself in such a way that $w(p) > p$ for small p, while $w(p) < p$ for p near 1. The graph of w is therefore an inverse S-shape, as illustrated in Figure 12.3.

A formal model of probability weighting was presented by Handa (1977), who proposed a model based on the idea of probability weighting, which he referred to as 'certainty equivalence', with the functional form

$$CE(\mathbf{p}) = \sum_n w(p_n) x_n, \tag{12.3}$$

where w is a monotone mapping of the unit interval onto itself.

There are two critical problems with this formulation, which may be traced to the fact that probabilities are not simple objects of perception but are measures of the likelihood of events. This means that the weights associated with the prizes in any lottery must sum to 1. In addition, if the outcome space includes two identical prizes, the weight associated with the two prizes must be equal to the sum of the weights on the individual prizes.

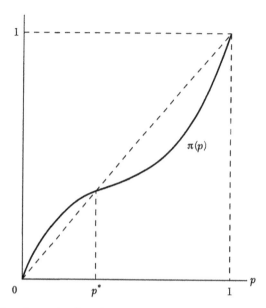

Figure 12.3 S-shaped transformation function.

The probability weighting approach will, in general, not satisfy these conditions. One implication is that representations based on probability weighting will, in general, violate dominance requirements, in that a lottery may be rejected in favor of one that gives lower prizes with probability one. In addition, preferences over lotteries will typically violate continuity.

To see the first problem, suppose that, for some N, $w\left(\frac{1}{N}\right) > \frac{1}{N}$, as is required for the standard inverse S weighting function, so that, $Nw\left(\frac{1}{N}\right) > 1$. Hence, for suitable values of $\delta_1 \ldots \delta_N$ a lottery $\mathbf{p}$ yielding prizes $1 - \delta_n$, $n = 1..N$, each with probability $\frac{1}{N}$ will have $CE\left(\mathbf{p}\right) > 1$. As a concrete example, consider $w\left(p\right) = p^{\alpha}$ for $\alpha < 1$, and suppose that there are two distinct prizes, $1 - \delta_1$ and $1 - \delta_2$, each occurring with probability $\frac{1}{2}$. Then provided $1 - \delta_n > 2^{\frac{1}{1-\alpha}}$, $n = 1, 2$, we have $CE\left(\mathbf{p}\right) > 1$.

To see the second problem, observe that, whenever $w\left(p_1 + p_2\right) \neq w(p_1) + w\left(p_2\right)$ there will be a discontinuity whenever a series with two slightly different prizes, x_1 with probability p_1 and x_2 with probability p_2 converges to a lottery such that $x_1 = x_2$. This argument assumes the property of coalescing, that is that there is no difference between a lottery with two payoffs, both equal to x, occurring with probabilities p_1 and p_2 and one with a single payoff x occurring with probability $p_1 + p_2$. Birnbaum (2007) argues that this property is not in fact satisfied by observed preferences, but it is hard to see how such a distinction could be consistent with any kind of coherent choice behavior.

Although Handa's approach was unsuccessful, it played a significant role in stimulating interest in the field. The *Journal of Political Economy* (JPE) was deluged with comments pointing out the violation of stochastic dominance. The most elegant, and the only one published, was that of Fishburn (1978). Among the unpublished responses to Handa was one contributed by Mark Machina, then a graduate student at MIT. Another response, not submitted to JPE, formed the starting point for the development of rank-dependent expected utility in an undergraduate Honors thesis (Quiggin, 1979).

12.4.1 Prospect Theory

A more durable contribution to the literature on probability weighting was the prospect theory of Kahneman and Tversky (1979). As well as providing experimental evidence that formed the basis of much subsequent research, Kahneman and Tversky presented a theoretical model, named prospect theory, in which they sought to encompass a range of empirically observed phenomena, notably including probability weighting and reference point effects. The evaluation proposed in prospect theory was similar to that of earlier models using weighting functions, namely

$$V(\mathbf{p}) = \sum_n \pi(p_n) v(x_n).$$

(12.4)

However, the value function is defined in terms of deviations from a reference level of wealth, and is defined to be concave for positive values, and convex for negative values. This captures the idea that, while individuals are generally risk averse, they display "risk seeking in the domain of losses."

In addition to the formal valuation, the editing phase consists of a preliminary analysis of the offered prospects, which often yields a simpler representation of these prospects. Proposed editing operations included coalescing probabilities associated with identical outcomes, and coding, which determines the reference point for the evaluation of gains and losses. Perhaps the most significant editing operation, though one that is mentioned only briefly, is described as 'the scanning of offered prospects to detect dominated alternatives, which are rejected without further evaluation'. As Kahneman and Tversky note (p. 284), this process rules out direct violations of dominance, but admits 'indirect' violations, that is, intransitivities. The need for this editing operation was eliminated by the development of cumulative prospect theory (see below). Kahneman and Tversky (1979) did not give a formal treatment, or even a systematic discussion, of the editing process as a whole. This aspect of decision making, along with the closely related concept of "framing" has yet to receive any complete treatment, though various insights have emerged over the years.

12.4.2 Rank-Dependent EU and Cumulative Prospect Theory

The central problem of prospect theory, as with other probability weighting theories, was that, since probability weights did not sum to one, the theory naturally gave rise to widespread violations of dominance, in the strong sense that one prospect might be preferred to another, even though the second prospect yielded a better outcome with probability one.

Quiggin (1981, 1982), originally motivated by an independent discovery of the dominance violation problem in the work of Handa (1977), proposed an alternative approach to probability weighting which resolved the problem. The model was originally referred to as "anticipated utility" [9], but is now generally referred to as Rank-Dependent Expected Utility (RDEU) or Rank-Dependent Utility (RDU). The key idea was to make probability weighting dependent on the rank-order of the outcomes. Intuitively, the central point was that arguments for overweighting of low-probability events were mainly applicable to low-probability extreme events.

The crucial technical innovation was to apply probability weighting to the cumulative probability distribution, rather than to individual probabilities. For the discrete case, the functional form may therefore be written as

$$V\left(\mathbf{p}\right) = \sum_{n=1}^{N} w_n\left(\mathbf{p}\right) U\left(x_n\right),$$

where $x_1 \leq x_2 \ldots \leq x_N$. The requirement for rank-ordering of the outcomes gives the model its name.

$$w_n\left(\mathbf{p}\right) = q\left(\sum_{j=1}^{n} p_j\right) - q\left(\sum_{j=1}^{n-1} p_j\right)$$

and $q : [0, 1] \rightarrow [0, 1]$ is a probability transformation function, such that $q\left(0\right) = 0, q\left(1\right) = 1$.

Some observations:

1. For the case of a two-outcome bet, RDEU corresponds with the standard probability weighting approach, with the additional constraint that $w\left(p\right) + w\left(1 - p\right) = 1$.
2. There is an immediate extension to the case where the state space is an interval with Lebesgue measure, so that a prospect may be represented by its cumulative distribution function F. We have

$$V\left(F\right) = \int U\left(x\right) d\left(q \circ F\left(x\right)\right).$$

3. We have

$$\sum_{n} w_n\left(\mathbf{p}\right) = q\left(1\right) - q\left(0\right) = 1.$$

---

[9] The name was intended to convey the idea of a generalized expectation.

That is, the vector of rank-dependent probability weights $w_n(\mathbf{p})$ has the standard properties of a probability distribution. More generally, $q \circ F$ has all the standard properties of a cumulative distribution function. It follows that, for any choice set where all prospects yield the same rank-ordering of states (that is, in the terminology introduced by Schmeidler (1989), all prospects are comonotonic), RDEU "looks like" EU with respect to a transformed probability distribution.

4. Provided q is monotonic, RDEU preserves first-order stochastic dominance.

Tversky and Kahneman (1992) combined the rank-dependent weighting function of RDEU with the reference point model of prospect theory to produce cumulative prospect theory. The significance of this work was recognized by the award of the 2002 Nobel Memorial Prize in Economic Sciences to Kahneman, with a special posthumous mention of Tversky.

12.4.3 Independent Discoveries of RDEU

Quiggin (1981, 1982) attracted little attention initially. Contemporaneously, Weymark (1981) proposed the same functional form, in the context of social welfare theory, as the basis for a generalization of the Gini index. However, as with Quiggin (1981, 1982) this work was not noticed by researchers working on uncertainty until the idea of rank-dependent probability weighting had become more widely known. Partly as a result, and partly because it is the only modification of EU with desirable properties such as separation between outcomes and (transformed) probabilities, versions of the RDEU functional form were developed independently by a number of authors. Thus, the model represents an interesting example of the theory of multiple discoveries, put forward by Merton (1973) and discussed in an economic context by Stigler (1982).

Lopes (1984, 1987) used the idea of a Lorenz curve to represent transformation of probabilities. Her focus was on representing experimental data and although she cited Allais (1953) she did not develop applications to the Allais problem or other violations of EU predictions. Segal (1990) took an axiomatic approach, arguing that apparent violations of the EU Independence Axiom could be explained if preferences did not satisfy Reduction of Compound Lotteries. The "dual model" of Yaari (1987), developed further by Roell (1987) was also based mainly on axiomatic considerations. Yaari exploited a number of formal symmetries between EU and a special case of RDEU in which the utility function is linear. The linearity of the utility function implied that, in the dual model, risk attitudes are entirely divorced from declining marginal utility of wealth.

Another rediscovery, also based on the notion of risk aversion as a phenomenon distinct from declining marginal utility of wealth, was made by Allais (1988) whose work had provided the starting point for the whole field. Allais (1953) had observed that "Sensitivity to the dispersion of monetary values due to the curvature of the utility function is likely quite distinct from the sensibility to the dispersion of psychological values. It does not involve what we think is the fundamental feature characterizing the psychology of risk, sensitivity to the dispersion of psychological values."

All of these models were developed for the case of decision under risk, that is, of given objective probabilities. An analogous development, for the case of subjective probability, is Choquet expected utility [Schmeidler (1989), Gilboa (1989)] based on the notion of nonadditive measures or capacities, originally developed in the work of Choquet (1953).

12.5 WEIGHTED UTILITY AND BETWEENNESS

Whereas most previous attempts at generalizing expected utility had focused on probability weights, Chew (1983) used a weighting function based on outcomes. The motivation for weighted utility theory was primarily technical rather than intuitive. Weighted utility satisfies the property of betweenness, which is a natural weakening of the "linear-in-probabilities" character of expected utility theory. Betweenness requires:

if $\mathbf{p} \succ \mathbf{p}'$, then $\mathbf{p} \succ \lambda\mathbf{p} + (1 - \lambda)\mathbf{p}'$, for $\lambda \in [0, 1)$.

and may be characterized as the intersection of quasiconcavity:

for every $\mathbf{p} \neq \mathbf{p}'$, and $\lambda \in [0, 1)$, $V\left(\lambda\mathbf{p} + (1 - \lambda)\mathbf{p}'\right) \geq \min\left[V(\mathbf{p}), V(\mathbf{p}')\right]$ and quasiconvexity:

for every $\mathbf{p} \neq \mathbf{p}'$, and $\lambda \in [0, 1)$, $V\left(\lambda\mathbf{p} + (1 - \lambda)\mathbf{p}'\right) \leq \min\left[V(\mathbf{p}), V(\mathbf{p}')\right]$.

Quasiconcavity implies preference for randomization over similarly valued prospects, quasiconvexity implies aversion for randomization, and betweenness implies indifference. Chew relaxed the Independence Axiom to betweenness. In combination with a quasilinearity property, this yields the "generalized mean" representation of the certainty equivalent

$$M(\mathbf{p}) = u^{-1}\left(\frac{\sum_n p_n U\left(x_n\right)\phi\left(x_n\right)}{\sum_n p_n \phi\left(x_n\right)}\right),$$

where $\phi : X \rightarrow \mathbb{R}_+$ is a weighting function.

For the case of general cumulative distribution functions F, this becomes

$$M(F) = \phi^{-1}\left(\int \phi(x)\, dF(x)\right).$$

A wide variety of models satisfying betweenness have been proposed (Dekel, 1986; Neilson, 1992). The most prominent is the disappointment theory model of Gul (1991).

Gul's idea is to define elation and disappointment for a prospect $\mathbf{p}$ relative to a certainty equivalent c with utility v, which is, itself, implicitly defined by preferences. Disappointment outcomes (those worse than the certainty equivalent) are evaluated with a utility function $u(x)$ while elation outcomes (those better than the certainty equivalent) are evaluated with respect to a weighted utility function $\frac{u(x)+\beta v}{1+\beta}$. Thus we may define

$$\phi(x, v) = \begin{array}{ll} u(x) & u(x) > v \\ \frac{u(x)+\beta v}{1+\beta} & u(x) \leq v. \end{array}$$

It is easy to see that, if $u(c) = v, \phi(c, v) = v$. So the certainty equivalent $c(\mathbf{p})$ may be defined consistently by the requirement

$$u(c) = \sum \phi\left(x_n, u(c)\right) p_n.$$

12.6 REGRET THEORY

Regret theory (Loomes and Sugden, 1982, see also Bell, 1982) was based on the same intuition that later gave rise to Gul's disappointment theory. The key technical idea is that rather than evaluating prospects in terms of a summary statistic like expected utility or a certainty equivalent, decision makers base choices between prospects on a comparison of their state-contingent payoffs and are concerned to minimize the regret that arises if their choice leads to a low payoff in the realized state of nature when an alternative choice might have led to a much higher payoff, or, conversely, to maximize the rejoicing that arises when a choice turns out well.

The basic approach proposed by Loomes and Sugden may be traced back to Savage's (1951) work on statistical decision theory. Savage proposed the adoption of a minimax loss criterion for statistical decisions, which he attempted (not entirely successfully) to reconcile with the EU approach. The regret theory model explicitly involves intransitivity in preferences and they attempt to refute the standard arguments used to support the claim that intransitivity is irrational.

Less attention is given to the question of stochastic dominance. Loomes and Sugden (1982) note that regret-theoretic preferences do not preserve first-order stochastic dominance in the sense of Hadar and Russell, but that statewise stochastic dominance is preserved. Quiggin (1990, 1994) shows that violations of stochastic dominance are pervasive in regret theory, in the sense that for any prospect with more than two distinct outcomes, there exists a preferred prospect which is first-order stochastically dominated by the initial one.

Formally, Loomes and Sugden compare state-contingent acts with known probabilities. That is, given a set of states $S = \{1, \ldots S\}$ with probabilities $p_1 \cdots p_S$ an act is a mapping $A : S \to X$ where X is an outcome set. Denote by x_{is} the outcome of act i in state s. Considering a choice of A_i over A_j and supposing that state s is realized, the decision maker receives outcome x_{is} when the alternative choice would have yielded x_{js}.

Loomes and Sugden (1982) define the modified utility $M\left(x_{is}, x_{js}\right)$ where M is increasing in its first argument and decreasing in its second, capturing the idea that the choice of A_i gives rise to less regret, or more rejoicing, the better is x_{is} relative to the foregone alternative. Action i will be preferred over j if

$$E_j^i = \sum p_s M\left(x_{is}, x_{js}\right) \geq \sum p_s M\left(x_{js}, x_{is}\right) = E_i^j.$$

The way the model works may be illustrated by considering the resolution of the common ratio effect proposed under regret theory. Loomes and Sugden begin by assuming that the bets are independent. In this case, with prize probabilities of 0.05 and 0.04, the likelihood that both bets will pay off in a given state is 0.002. So, if the low-payoff bet is chosen, there is a probability of 0.038 of receiving nothing when the high-payoff bet would have yielded a prize. Conversely, if the high-payoff bet is chosen, there is a probability of 0.048 of receiving nothing when the low-payoff bet would have yielded a prize. Given a suitably convex regret function, the first of these effects will dominate, so decision makers will prefer the lower-probability high-payoff bet. Now consider the case when the probabilities are 1 and 0.8. In this case, the probability of receiving nothing from the low-payoff bet when the high-payoff bet would have yielded a prize is zero, while the probability of receiving nothing from the low-payoff bet when the low-payoff bet would have yielded a prize is 0.2. So, if regret considerations are important, the low-payoff bet will be chosen.

12.7 GENERALIZED MODELS

All of the approaches discussed above involve replacing EU with a more general functional form, derived by relaxing the independence assumption in some way. An alternative is to impose minimal restrictions on preferences and to consider properties that do not rely on any special characteristics of the functional form.

12.7.1 Machina and Local Utility Functions

The first such generalization was that of Machina (1982), who considered the general class of preference functionals over probability distributions. He showed that, provided preferences were appropriately smooth, they can be represented by a Frechet differentiable function, and that the Frechet derivative at any point is linear in the probabilities. That is, the Frechet derivative has the standard properties of an EU functional, and may be interpreted as the expectation of a "local utility function."

More precisely, given a preference mapping $V :\to \mathbb{R}$, the Frechet derivative $\Psi\left(\bullet; F\right) :\to \mathbb{R}$ is a continuous linear functional that satisfies

$$V\left(F^{*}\right) - V\left(F\right) = \Psi\left(F^{*} - F; F\right) + o\left\|F^{*} - F\right\|,$$

where $o\left\|F^{*} - F\right\|$ is second-order small.

Using the Riesz representation theorem, Machina shows that, for each F there exists a local utility function $U\left(\cdot; F\right)$ such that, for any F^{*}

$$V\left(F^{*}\right) - V\left(F\right) = \int U\left(x; F\right)\left(dF\left(x\right) - dF^{*}\left(x\right)\right) + o\left\|F^{*} - F\right\|.$$

Using path integrals, Machina showed that whenever all the local utility functions display properties such as monotonicity and concavity, the corresponding property is shared by the global preference functional. Thus, if all local utility functions preserve some stochastic order, such as first-order or second-order stochastic dominance, the same is true of preferences globally. For any of the standard forms of stochastic dominance, if F dominates F^{*}, F also dominates $\lambda F + (1 - \lambda)F^{*}$, for $\lambda \in [0, 1]$. If all local utility functions preserve the relevant stochastic dominance relationship, then V must decline monotonically along the path from $\lambda = 0$ to $\lambda = 1$.

Many of the functional forms proposed as generalizations of expected utility, are not Frechet differentiable. Fortunately, the path integration argument used by Machina requires only that the local utility function be well defined in any direction, which is true whenever V satisfies the weaker condition of Gateau differentiability (Chew et al., 1987). For the case of RDEU, the local utility function is:

$$U_F\left(x\right) = \int_{-\infty}^{x} U'\left(\gamma\right) q'\left(F\left(\gamma\right)\right) d\gamma. \tag{12.5}$$

Machina also reintroduced Marschak's expository device of representing the set of probability distributions over three given outcomes by a triangle. He showed that the behavior observed in Allais' common consequence and common ratio effects could be explained by a pattern he referred to as "fanning out." This pattern is illustrated in Figure 12.2.

12.8 RISK ATTITUDES AND GENERALIZED EU

The relationship between generalized EU models and preservation of second-order stochastic dominance may be characterized using Machina's local utility function. Machina shows that Frechet-differentiable preferences preserve second-order stochastic dominance (that is, are averse to increases in risk in the sense of Rothschild and Stiglitz, 1970) if and only if the local utility function $U\left(x; F\right)$ is globally concave for all F. As shown by Chew et al. (1987), the same result holds for Gateau differentiable functions. For the case of RDEU, differentiating (12.5) yields:

$$U_F'(x) = U'(\gamma)\, q'(F(\gamma))$$
$$U_F''(x) = U''(\gamma)\, q'(F(\gamma)) + U'(\gamma)\, q''(F(\gamma))$$

which is globally concave if and only if U and q are concave.

Dual results may be obtained for comparisons of risk aversion. The standard result for expected utility is that if U_A is a concave transformation of U_B, then any compensated increase in risk for U_A will be acceptable to a decision maker whose preferences are given by U_B. Machina shows that the same result holds if, for each F, the local utility function $U_A(\cdot; F)$ is a concave transformation of $U_B(\cdot; F)$. Hence for the RDEU case, the result holds if and only if U_A is a concave transformation of U_B and q_A is a concave transformation of q_B.

Not all the standard results from EU theory carry over to the generalized EU preferences. Consider the most basic definition of risk-aversion, namely that an individual should always prefer a fixed sum of money to a risky prospect with the same mean (we will call this weak risk-aversion). In EU theory, Jensen's inequality shows that this is true if and only if U is concave. In EU theory, this basic definition may be extended to a stronger risk ordering.

As shown by the Rothschild and Stiglitz (1970) analysis of increases in risk, and the theory of second-order stochastic dominance (Hadar and Russell, 1969; Hanoch and Levy, 1969), the class of risk orderings preferred by all EU maximizers with concave U contains all pairs that may be derived using a sequence of elementary reductions in risk, raising return in a bad state of nature and reducing returns in a good state, while holding the mean constant.

Machina (1982) observes that this equivalence is not preserved in the general case. Consider, for example, the Yaari (1987) model of RDEU with linear utility. Provided $q(p) \geq p, \forall p, V(F) \leq V(\mu_F)$. More generally, provided u is concave, $q(p) \geq p \Leftrightarrow \forall p, V(F) \leq V(\mu_F)$. For the case of general u, the situation is more complicated (Ryan, 2006; Chateauneuf et al., 2004a). Rather than detail the partial results on this topic, it is more useful to consider the question analogous to that of the stochastic dominance literature under EU, namely 'Under what conditions will F be preferred to F' for all RDEU preferences satisfying weak risk-aversion?'

The answer, derived by Quiggin (1991a) is that F must be related to F' by a monotone spread. The simplest characterization of a monotone spread is in terms of random variables, which may be considered as measurable mappings $\gamma : \Omega \to \mathbb{R}$, where Ω is a state space. Two variables γ, γ' with cumulative distribution functions F and F' are related by a monotone spread if

$$\gamma' = \gamma + \varepsilon,$$

where γ and ε are, in the terminology of Schmeidler (1989), comonotonic. That is, for any $\omega, \omega' \in \Omega$

$$\left(\gamma\left(\omega\right) - \gamma\left(\omega'\right) \right) \left(\varepsilon\left(\omega\right) - \varepsilon\left(\omega'\right) \right) \geq 0$$

if $E\left[\varepsilon\right] = 0$, the monotone-spread is mean-preserving.

Closely related concepts include that of a deterministic transformation (Meyer and Ormiston, 1989) and a Bickel and Lehmann (1976) increase in dispersion. A variety of generalizations of the concept are considered by Chateauneuf et al. (2004b).

Quiggin (1991a) shows that, given concave u, the following conditions on preferences are equivalent:

(i) $q\left(p\right) \geq p, \forall p$
(ii) $V\left(F\right) \leq V\left(\mu_F\right), \forall p$
(iii) If F and F' are related by a mean-preserving monotone spread, $V\left(F\right) \geq V\left(F'\right)$.

Increases in risk in the sense of second-order stochastic dominance can be derived as the limit of a sequence of elementary increases in risk, in which the outcome in an initially favorable state of nature is increased by one unit, while that in an equally probably unfavorable state is reduced by one unit[10]. For monotone spreads, the corresponding notion of an elementary increase in risk is that, for some $\gamma^\star$, the outcome for all ω with $\gamma\left(\omega\right) \leq \gamma^*$ is uniformly reduced, while that for all ω with $\gamma\left(\omega\right) \leq \gamma^*$ is uniformly increased, in a mean-preserving fashion. Grant and Quiggin (2005) observe that, if the mean-preservingness requirement is dropped, the monotone spread concept provides the basis for a model-free notion of increasing uncertainty, even in the absence of well-defined probabilities.

12.9 ECONOMICS WITHOUT EU

The literature on generalized EU has been focused primarily on decision-theoretic issues, such as the derivation of representation theorems, and has paid relatively little attention to the economic implications of non-EU preferences. Conversely, despite the large body of empirical evidence inconsistent with EU preferences, and the development of a wide range of alternatives to, and generalizations of EU, most economic analysis of choice under uncertainty remains restricted to the case of EU preferences.

There are at least two reasons why the use of non-EU models may be of interest in the analysis of economic decisions under uncertainty. First, non-EU models may provide explanations of observed market behavior inconsistent with the EU axioms.

---

[10] In the context of income distribution, the reverse of this process is called a Dalton transfer.

Second, it is useful to consider the robustness of results derived under the assumption of EU preferences. Examples in the first category include attitudes to extreme risk, and the phenomenon of first-order risk aversion. In the second category, it may be shown that much of the standard comparative static analysis derived for EU preferences carries over to the generalized case.

Most economic analysis using generalized expected utility models has focused on rank-dependent models, such as RDEU and CPT. On the one hand, as shown previously, these models allow a relaxation of the standard EU assumptions of global risk aversion and local risk-neutrality, which appear unrealistic in many contexts. On the other hand, a wide variety of EU comparative static results may be generalized to the case of rank-dependent preferences. For this reason, the primary focus of this section will be on the rank-dependent case.

12.9.1 Attitudes to Extreme Risks

The standard S-shaped weighting function implies overweighting the probabilities of extreme events. At the bottom tail, overweighting of extreme adverse outcomes reinforces the risk aversion associated with a concave utility function. At the upper tail, overweighting of extreme favorable outcomes means that individuals with generally risk-averse attitudes will be willing to make bets which offer high returns with low probabilities. Services such as lotteries arise in response to this demand. It follows that RDEU can explain the problem, first raised by Friedman and Savage (1948), of explaining the behavior of individuals who simultaneously buy insurance and participate in lotteries. Quiggin (1991b) shows that for RDEU preferences with an S-shaped weighting function, the optimal design of lotteries includes a few large prizes and a large number of small prizes, consistent with actual observation.

A similar analysis may be applied to portfolio theory. Whereas risk-averse EU investors will always prefer to minimize variance, investors with RDEU preferences will place a positive value on right-skewed payoff distributions similar to those yielded by lotteries. Shefrin and Statman (2000) present a behavioral portfolio theory, based on prospect theory, incorporating probability weighting and reference point effects.

12.9.2 First-Order and Second-Order Risk Aversion

For the case of a differentiable utility function[11], expected utility displays the property of local risk-neutrality or, in the terminology of Segal and Spivak (1990), second-order risk aversion. Rabin (2000) illustrates the stringency of the requirement for local risk-neutrality in EU, by showing even modest risk aversion for small risks implies an unwillingness to accept what appear to be highly attractive prospects with moderate stakes. He notes:

---

[11] Since any monotone increasing function is differentiable except at countably many points, this assumption involves no loss of generality.

Suppose that, from any initial wealth level, a person turns down gambles where she loses $100 or gains $110, each with 50% probability. Then she will turn down 50–50 bets of losing $1,000 or gaining any sum of money.

The underlying argument is simple. Given the preferences described above, and assuming EU, the marginal utility of money must be declining in such a way that, for any w, $U'(w + 110) < (10/11)U'(w - 1000)$. It is then easy to show that the series

$$\sum_{k=1}^{\infty} U(w + 110(k+1)) - U(w + 110(k))$$

is convergent, and bounded above by

$$U(w) - U(w - 1000)$$

which yields Rabin's conclusion. Rabin's analysis is consistent with preferences that display first-order risk-aversion, including RDEU. However, RDEU does imply local risk neutrality in the presence of large background risks (Quiggin, 2003), so that a calibration exercise similar to Rabin's might be performed (Safra and Segal, 2008), though it is not clear what the results might be.

In economic terms, local risk neutrality implies that individuals will always be willing to accept some exposure to an actuarially favorable risk, provided that it is independent of their base wealth. In particular, therefore, individuals with different subjective probabilities about an event will always be willing to bet with each other on that event. Except on a set of measure zero, when their estimated value for an asset exactly equals its market price, the optimal portfolio will always include a non zero long or short position for every asset. This need not be true in the presence of first-order risk aversion (Dow and Werlang, 1992). More generally, first-order risk aversion may help to explain the inconsistency between risk preference and time preference apparent in the well-known equity premium puzzle (Epstein and Zin, 1990).

Individuals subject to risk will never seek full insurance against that risk if the contract is actuarially unfair, which will always be true if the insurance premium is required to cover administrative costs as well as expected payouts.

12.9.3 Comparative Statics

Most comparative static analysis using generalized expected utility models has focused on rank-dependent models, such as RDEU and CPT. On the one hand, as shown above, these models allow a relaxation of the standard EU assumptions of global risk aversion and local risk-neutrality, which appear unrealistic in many contexts. On the other hand, a wide variety of EU comparative static results may be generalized to the case of rank-dependent preferences.

The robustness of EU comparative static results under rank-dependent preferences reflects the fact the RDEU may be interpreted as maximizing Expected Utility with respect to a transformed cumulative distribution function $q°F$. Hence if the function q preserves a partial ordering, such as first or second stochastic dominance, on the space $\mathcal{F}$ of cumulative distribution functions, then any EU results concerning that ordering will carry over to the RDEU context.

More precisely, consider a choice problem of the form

$$\max_{\alpha} E_F \left[U \left(\gamma \left(\theta, \alpha \right) \right) \right]$$

where U is a utility function, θ is a random variable with cumulative distribution function F, α is a scalar control variable and $\gamma : \mathbb{R}^2 \to \mathbb{R}$. The archetypal example is the two-asset portfolio problem where θ is the return on a risky asset and θ is investment in the risky asset, with remaining wealth earning a non-stochastic return r. If, as is typically the case, the values of the random variable of interest θ may be ordered unambiguously from worst to best, regardless of the choice of action, we may write the problem for an RDEU-maximizer, with probability transformation function q as

$$\max_{\alpha} E_{q°F} \left[U \left(\gamma \left(\theta, \alpha \right) \right) \right].$$

That is, this is the same as the EU problem for the transformed distribution $q \circ F$.

Now consider comparative statics. Let $\mathcal{R}$ be a relation on $\mathcal{F}$, the class of cumulative distribution functions on $\mathbb{R}$ and let $\mathcal{U}$ be a family of von Neumann–Morgenstern utility functions. Consider a shift from θ to θ', with associated cumulative distribution functions F and F'. Then a typical comparative static result states that if $F'\mathcal{R}F$, all Expected Utility maximizers with $U \in \mathcal{U}$ will choose a higher value of α. It follows immediately that if $q \circ F' \mathcal{R} q \circ F$, all RDEU maximizers with transformation function q and $U \in \mathcal{U}$ will also choose a higher value of α. Let

$$Q^*(R) = \{ q : [0,1] \to [0,1] : F'\mathcal{R}F \implies q°F'\mathcal{R}q°F' \}$$

Then, provided the outcomes from every action are better, the higher is the realization of the relevant random variable θ; a shift in the distribution of θ that produces an increase in α for all EU-maximizers with $U \in \mathcal{U}$ will also produce an increase in α for all EU-maximizers with $U \in \mathcal{U}$ and $q \in Q^*(R)$.

For example, a standard result in the portfolio problem is that, provided preferences satisfy decreasing absolute risk-aversion, a uniform upward shift in the distribution of θ will produce an increase in the optimal investment in the risky asset. This result carries over directly to RDEU.

Quiggin (1991c) presents the general argument in more detail and discusses applications such as the problem of the competitive firm under price uncertainty, first analyzed by Sandmo (1971). Applications to insurance include Ryan and Vaithianathan (2003), Jeleva (2000), Schmidt and Zank (2007), Segal (1986), and Wakker et al. (1997), along with an independent development of the rank-dependent model by Wang (1997). Rank-dependent models have been used to generalize the concept of Quality Adjusted Life Years (QALYs) widely used in health economics (Bleichrodt and Quiggin, 1997; Bleichrodt and Pinto, 2000; Bleichrodt et al., 2004). Neilson and Winter (1997 see also Neilson, 1998) examine risk attitudes in relation to crime. Neilson and Winter examine Becker's (1968) observation that criminals are more sensitive to changes in the probability of punishment than to changes in severity, and show that this pattern is consistent with risk-aversion under rank-dependent preferences, but not under EU. Further discussion of the relationship between crime and risk attitudes is given by Lattimore et al. (1992). There also is a large literature on applications of rank-dependent models to tax evasion and compliance, summarized by Hashimzade et al. (2012).

12.10 CONCLUDING COMMENTS

The expected utility model for decision plays a central role in fields ranging from finance theory to macroeconomics, as well as almost all areas of microeconomics. Yet it has long been known that the model does not give an accurate representation of individual behavior, either in experimental studies or in market decisions. Generalized expected utility theories have shown that, for the case of decisions under risk, it is possible to encompass a less restrictive representation of economic behavior, while maintaining the capacity to generate sharp analytical results.

Although the basic properties of generalized EU models, such as stochastic dominance, are now well understood, a great deal of work remains to be done, particularly as regards applications to problems involving intertemporal choices, health risks and problems of portfolio choice for agents who are not globally risk averse. The generalized theory of decision under risk remains a fruitful field for theoretical and empirical investigation.

ACKNOWLEDGMENTS

I thank Edi Karni and Nancy Wallace for helpful comments and criticism.

REFERENCES

Allais, M., 1953. Le comportement de l'homme rationnel devant le risque: critique des postulats et axiomes de l'École Americaine. Econometrica 21, 503–546.
Allais, M., 1988. The general theory of random choices in relation to the invariant cardinal utility function and the specific probability function. In: Munier, B. (Ed.), Risk, Decision and Rationality. Reidel, Dordrecht, pp. 233–289.

Allais, M., Hagen, O., 1979. Expected Utility Hypotheses and the Allais Paradox. Reidel, Dordrecht, Holland.

Anscombe, F., Aumann, R., 1963. A definition of subjective probability. Annals of Mathematical Statistics 49, 453–467.

Arrow, K., 1963. Uncertainty and the welfare economics of medical care. American Economic Review 53, 941–973.

Arrow, K., 1965. Aspects of the Theory of Risk-Bearing. In: Yrjo Jahnsson Lecture, Helsinki.

Becker, G., 1968. Crime and punishment: an economic approach. Journal of Political Economy 76, 169–217.

Bell, D., 1982. Regret in decision making under uncertainty. Operations Research 20, 961–981.

Bernoulli, D., 1954. Exposition of a new theory of the measurement of risk. Econometrica 22, 23–36.

Bickel, P.J., Lehmann, E.L., 1976. Descriptive statistics for nonparametric models. III. Dispersion. Annals of Statistics 4, 1139–1158.

Birnbaum, M., 2007. Tests of branch splitting and branch-splitting independence in Allais paradoxes with positive and mixed consequences. Organizational Behavior and Human Decision Processes 102, 154–173.

Bleichrodt, H., Diecidue, E., Quiggin, J., 2004. Equity weights in the allocation of health care: the rank-dependent QALY model. Journal of Health Economics 23, 157–171.

Bleichrodt, H., Pinto, J., 2000. A parameter-free elicitation of the probability weighting function in medical decision analysis. Management Science 46, 1485–1496.

Bleichrodt, H., Quiggin, J., 1997. Characterizing QALYs under a general rank dependent utility model. Journal of Risk and Uncertainty 15, 151–160.

Chateauneuf, A., Cohen, M. and Meilijson, I., 2004a. Four notions of mean preserving increase in risk, risk attitudes and applications to the Rank-Dependent Expected Utility model. HAL – CCSD, <http://hal.ccsd.cnrs.fr/oai/oai.php>.

Chateauneuf, A., Cohen, M., Meilijson, I., 2004b. More pessimism than greediness: a characterization of monotone risk aversion in the rank-dependent expected utility model. Economic Theory 25, 649–667.

Chew, S., 1983. A generalization of the quasilinear mean with applications to the measurement of income inequality and decision theory resolving the Allais paradox. Econometrica 51, 1065–1092.

Chew, S.H., Karni, E., Safra, Z., 1987. Risk aversion in the theory of expected utility with rank-dependent preferences. Journal of Economic Theory 42, 370–381.

Choquet, G., 1953. Theory of capacities. Annales Institut Fourier 5, 131–295.

Dalkey, N., 1949. A numerical scale for partially ordered utilities. RAND Memo 296, Santa Monica, CA.

Dalton, H., 1920. The measurement of the inequality of incomes. Economic Journal 30, 348–361.

de Finetti, B., 1931. Sul significato soggettivo della probabilita. Fundamenta Mathematicae 17, 298–329.

Dekel, E., 1986. An axiomatic characterization of preferences under uncertainty: weakening the independence axiom. Journal of Economic Theory 40, 304–318.

Dow, J., Werlang, S., 1992. Uncertainty aversion, risk aversion, and the optimal choice of portfolio. Econometrica 60, 197–204.

Dubins, L., Savage, L., 1965. Inequalities for Stochastic Processes: How to Gamble if You Must. Dover Publications, New York.

Edwards, W., 1954. Probability preferences among bets with differing expected values. American Journal of Psychology 67, 56–67.

Ellsberg, D., 1961. Risk, ambiguity and the savage axioms. Quarterly Journal of Economics 75, 643–669.

Epstein, L., Zin, S., 1990. 'First-order' risk aversion and the equity premium puzzle. Journal of Monetary Economics 26, 387–407.

Fishburn, P., 1978. On Handa's 'new theory of cardinal utility' and the maximization of expected return. Journal of Political Economy 86, 321–324.

Fishburn, P., Wakker, P., 1995. The invention of the independence condition for preferences. Management Science 41, 1130–1144.

Friedman, M., Savage, L.J., 1948. The utility analysis of choices involving risk. Journal of Political Economy 56, 279–304.

Gilboa, I., 1989. Additivizations of nonadditive measures. Mathematics of Operations Research 14, 1–17.

Gilboa, I., Schmeidler, D., 1989. Maxmin expected utility with non-unique prior. Journal of Mathematical Economics 18, 141–153.

Grant, S., Quiggin, J., 2005. Increasing uncertainty: a definition. Mathematical Social Sciences 49, 117–141.

Gul, F., 1991. A theory of disappointment aversion. Econometrica 59, 667–686.

Hadar, J., Russell, W., 1969. Rules for ordering uncertain prospects. American Economic Review 59, 25–34.

Handa, J., 1977. Risk, probabilities and a new theory of cardinal utility. Journal of Political Economy 85, 97–122.

Hanoch, G., Levy, H., 1969. The efficiency analysis of choices involving risk. Review of Economic Studies 36, 335–346.

Hashimzade, N., Myles, G.D., Tran-Nam, B., 2012. Applications of behavioral economics to tax evasion. Journal of Economic Surveys (Online preview), <http://dx.doi.org/org/10.1111/j.1467–6419.2012.00733.x>.

Jeleva, M., 2000. Background risk, demand for insurance, and Choquet expected utility preferences. The Geneva Papers on Risk and Insurance 25, 7–28.

Kahneman, D., Tversky, A., 1979. Prospect theory: an analysis of decision under risk. Econometrica 47, 263–291.

Knight, F., 1921. Risk, Uncertainty and Profit. Houghton Mifflin, New York.

Lattimore, P., Baker, J., Witte, A., 1992. The influence of probability on risky choice: a parametric examination. Journal of Economic Behavior and Organization 17, 377–400.

Leland, H.E., 1972. Theory of the firm facing uncertain demand. American Economic Review 62, 278–291.

Loomes, G., Sugden, R., 1982. Regret theory: an alternative theory of rational choice under uncertainty. Economic Journal 92, 805–824.

Lopes, L.L., 1984. Risk and distributional inequality. Journal of Experimental Psychology: Human Perception and Performance 10, 465–485.

Lopes, L.L., 1987. Between hope and fear: the psychology of risk. Advances in Experimental Social Psychology 20, 255–295.

Machina, M., 1982. 'Expected utility' analysis without the independence axiom. Econometrica 50, 277–323.

Machina, M., 1987. Choice under uncertainty: problems solved and unsolved. Journal of Economic Perspectives 1, 121–154.

Malinvaud, E., 1952. Note on von Neumann–Morgenstern's strong independence axiom. Econometrica 20, 679.

Marschak, J., 1950. Rational behavior, uncertain prospects and measurable utility. Econometrica 18, 111–141.

Markowitz, H., 1952. Portfolio selection. Journal of Finance 7, 77–91.

Merton, R., 1973. The Sociology of Science. University of Chicago Press, Chicago.

Meyer, J., Ormiston, M., 1989. Deterministic transformation of random variables and the comparative statics of risk. Journal of Risk and Uncertainty 2, 179–188.

Neilson, W.S., 1992. A mixed fan hypothesis and its implications for behavior toward risk. Journal of Economic Behavior and Organization 19, 197–211.

Neilson, W.S., 1998. Optimal punishment schemes with state-dependent preferences. Economic Inquiry 36, 266–271.

Neilson, W.S., Winter, H., 1997. On criminals' risk attitudes. Economics Letters 55, 97–102.

Pratt, J., 1964. Risk aversion in the small and in the large. Econometrica 32, 122–136.

Preston, M., Baratta, P., 1948. An experimental study of the auction value of an uncertain outcome. American Journal of Psychology 61, 183–193.

Quiggin, J., 1979. The multi-product firm under price uncertainty. Unpublished Honours Thesis, Australian National University.

Quiggin, J., 1981. Risk perception and risk aversion among Australian farmers. Australian Journal of Agricultural Economics 25, 160–169.

Quiggin, J., 1982. A theory of anticipated utility. Journal of Economic Behavior and Organization 3, 323–343.

Quiggin, J., 1991a. Increasing risk: another definition. In: Chikan, A. (Ed.), Progress in Decision, Utility and Risk Theory. Kluwer, Amsterdam.

Quiggin, J., 1991b. On the optimal design of lotteries. Economica 58, 1–16.

Quiggin, J., 1994. Regret theory with general choice sets. Journal of Risk and Uncertainty 8, 153–165.

Quiggin, J., 1991c. Comparative statics for rank-dependent expected utility theory. Journal of Risk and Uncertainty 4, 339–350.

Quiggin, J., 2003. Background risk in generalized expected utility theory. Economic Theory 22, 607–611.

Rabin, M., 2000. Risk aversion and expected-utility theory: a calibration theorem. Econometrica 68, 1281–1292.

Roell, A., 1987. Risk-aversion in Quiggin and Yaari's rank-order model of choice under uncertainty. Economic Journal 97, 143–159.

Rothschild, M., Stiglitz, J., 1970. Increasing risk: I. A definition. Journal of Economic Theory 2, 225–243.

Rothschild, M., Stiglitz, J., 1971. Increasing risk: II. Its economic consequences. Journal of Economic Theory 3, 66–84.

Ryan, M.J., 2006. Risk aversion in RDEU. Journal of Mathematical Economics 42, 675–697.

Ryan, M.J., Vaithianathan, R., 2003. Medical insurance with rank-dependent utility. Economic Theory 22, 689–698.

Safra, Z., Segal, U., 2008. Calibration results for non-expected utility theories. Econometrica 76, 1143–1166.

Samuelson, P.A., 1952. Probability, utility, and the independence axiom. Econometrica 20, 670–678.

Sandmo, A., 1971. On the theory of the competitive firm under price uncertainty. American Economic Review 61, 65–73.

Savage, L.J., 1951. The theory of statistical decision. Journal of the American Statistical Association 46, 55–67.

Savage, L., 1952. Une axiomatisation de comportement raisonnable face a l'incertitude. Colloques internationaux du Centre National de la Recherche Scientifique XL, 29–40.

Savage, L.J., 1954. Foundations of Statistics. Wiley, New York.

Schmeidler, D., 1989. Subjective probability and expected utility without additivity. Econometrica 57, 571–587.

Schmidt, U., Zank, H., 2007. Linear cumulative prospect theory with applications to portfolio selection and insurance demand. Decisions in Economics and Finance 30, 1–18.

Segal, U., 1986. Probabilistic insurance and anticipated utility. Unpublished working paper.

Segal, U., 1990. Two-stage lotteries without the independence axiom. Econometrica 58, 349–377.

Segal, U., Spivak, A., 1990. First-order versus second-order risk-aversion. Journal of Economic Theory 51, 111–125.

Shefrin, H., Statman, M., 2000. Behavioral portfolio theory. Journal of Financial and Quantitative Analysis 35, 127–151.

Starmer, C., 2000. Developments in non-expected utility theory: the hunt for a descriptive theory of choice under risk. Journal of Economic Literature 38, 332–382.

Stigler, G., 1982. Merton on multiples, denied and affirmed. In: Stigler, G. (Ed.), The Economist as Preacher and other Essays. University of Chicago Press, Chicago, pp. 98–106.

Tobin, J., 1958. Liquidity preference as behavior toward risk. Review of Economic Studies 25, 65–86.

Tobin, J., 1969. Comment on Borch and Feldstein. Review of Economic Studies 36, 13–14.

Tversky, A., Kahneman, D., 1992. Cumulative prospect theory: an analysis of attitudes towards uncertainty and value. Journal of Risk and Uncertainty 5, 297–323.

Tversky, A., Kahneman, D., 1974. Judgment under uncertainty: heuristics and biases. Science 185, 1124–1131.

Von Neumann, J., Morgenstern, O., 1944. Theory of Games and Economic Behavior. Princeton University Press, Princeton.

Wakker, P., Tversky, A., 1993. An axiomatization of cumulative prospect theory. Journal of Risk and Uncertainty 7, 147–175.

Wakker, P., Thaler, R., Tversky, A., 1997. Probabilistic insurance. Journal of Risk and Uncertainty 15, 7–28.

Wang, S., 1997. Insurance pricing and increased limits ratemaking by proportional hazards transforms. Insurance Mathematics and Economics 17, 43–54.

Weymark, J., 1981. Generalized Gini inequality indices. Mathematical Social Sciences 1, 409–430.

Yaari, M., 1987. The dual theory of choice under risk. Econometrica 55, 95–115.

CHAPTER 13

Ambiguity and Ambiguity Aversion

Mark J. Machina[a], and Marciano Siniscalchi[b]

[a]Distinguished Professor of Economics, University of California, San Diego, CA, USA
[b]Department of Economics, Northwestern University, Evanston, IL, USA

Contents

Abstract

The phenomena of *ambiguity* and *ambiguity aversion*, introduced in Daniel Ellsberg's seminal 1961 article, are ubiquitous in the real world and violate both the key rationality axioms and classic models of choice under uncertainty. In particular, they violate the hypothesis that individuals' uncertain beliefs can be represented by *subjective probabilities* (sometimes called *personal probabilities* or *priors*). This chapter begins with a review of early notions of subjective probability and Leonard Savage's joint axiomatic formalization of expected utility and subjective probability. It goes on to describe Ellsberg's classic urn paradoxes and the extensive experimental literature they have inspired. It continues with analytical descriptions of the numerous (primarily axiomatic) models of ambiguity aversion which have been developed by economic theorists, and concludes with a discussion of some current theoretical topics and newer examples of ambiguity aversion.

Keywords

Ambiguity, Ambiguity Aversion, Subjective Probability, Subjective Expected Utility, Ellsberg Paradox, Ellsberg Urns

JEL Classification Codes

D81 - Criteria for Decision-Making under Risk and Uncertainty, D80 - Information, Knowledge and Uncertainty, D01 - Microeconomic Behavior: Underlying

Handbook of the Economics of Risk and Uncertainty, Volume 1
ISSN 2211-7547, http://dx.doi.org/10.1016/B978-0-444-53685-3.00013-1

13.1 INTRODUCTION

Almost by its very nature, the phenomenon of uncertainty is ill-defined. Economists (and many others) agree that the uncertainty inherent in the flip of a fair coin, the uncertainty inherent in a one-shot horse race, and even the uncertainty inherent in the lack of knowledge of a deterministic fact (such as the $1,000,000^{\text{th}}$ digit of π) are different notions, which may have different economic implications. Of the different forms of uncertainty, the phenomenon of *ambiguity*, and agents' attitudes toward it, is the most ill-defined.

The use of the term "ambiguity" to describe a particular type of uncertainty is due to Daniel Ellsberg in his classic 1961 article and 1962 PhD thesis,[1] who informally described it as:

"the nature of one's information concerning the relative likelihood of events... a quality depending on the amount, type, reliability and 'unanimity' of information, and giving rise to one's degree of 'confidence' in an estimation of relative likelihoods." (1961, p.657)

As his primary examples, Ellsberg offered two thought-experiment decision problems, which remain the primary motivating factors of research on ambiguity and ambiguity aversion to the present day.[2] The most frequently cited of these, known as the *Three-Color Ellsberg Paradox*,[3] consists of an urn containing 90 balls. Exactly 30 of these balls are known to be red, and each of the other 60 is either black or yellow, but the exact numbers of black versus yellow balls are unknown, and could be anywhere from 0:60 to 60:0. A ball will be drawn from the urn, and the decision maker is presented with two pairs of bets based on the color of the drawn ball.

	THREE-COLOR ELLSBERG PARADOX (single urn)				TWO-URN ELLSBERG PARADOX URN I		URN II	
	30 balls	60 balls			100 balls		50 balls	50 balls
	red	black	yellow		red	black	red	black
a_1	$100	$0	$0	b_1	$100	$0		
a_2	$0	$100	$0	b_2			$100	$0
a_3	$100	$0	$100	b_3	$0	$100		
a_4	$0	$100	$100	b_4			$0	$100

---

[1] Ellsberg (1961,1962). Ellsberg's thesis has since been published as Ellsberg (2001).

[2] In (1961, p.653) and (1961, p.651, n.9) Ellsberg refers to Frank Knight's (1921) "identical comparison" and to John Chipman's (1958, 1960) "almost identical experiment" of the Two-Color Paradox, and in (1961, p.659, n.8) describes Nicholas Georgescu-Roegen's (1954, 1958) notion of "credibility" as "a concept identical" to his own notion of ambiguity.

[3] Ellsberg (1961, pp.653–656; 2001, pp. 155–158). Ellsberg (2001, pp. 137–142) discusses an essentially equivalent version with the payoffs $100:$0 replaced by $-$100:$0.

Ellsberg posited, and experimenters have confirmed,[4] that decision makers would typically prefer bet a_1 over bet a_2, and bet a_4 over bet a_3, which can be termed *Ellsberg preferences* in this choice problem. Such preferences are termed "paradoxical" since they directly contradict the subjective probability hypothesis—if an individual did assign subjective probabilities to the events {red,black,yellow}, then the strict preference ranking $a_1 \succ a_2$ would reveal the strict subjective probability ranking prob(red) > prob(black), but the strict ranking $a_3 \prec a_4$ would reveal the strict ranking prob(red) < prob(black).

The widely accepted reason for these rankings is that while the bet a_1 guarantees a known probability 1/3 of winning the $100 prize, the probability of winning offered by a_2 is unknown, and could be anywhere from 0 to 2/3. Although the range [0, 2/3] has 1/3 as its midpoint, and there is no reason to expect any asymmetry, individuals seem to prefer the known to the unknown probability. Similarly, bet a_4 offers a guaranteed 2/3 chance of winning, whereas the probability offered by a_3 could be anywhere from 1/3 to 1. Again, individuals prefer the known-probability bet. Ellsberg described bets a_2 and a_3 as involving *ambiguity*, and a preference for known-probability over ambiguous bets is now known as *ambiguity aversion*.[5]

Ellsberg presented a second problem known as the *Two-Urn Paradox*, which posits a pair of urns, the first contains 100 black and red balls in unknown proportions, and the second contains exactly 50 black and 50 red balls.[6] The decision maker is asked to rank the four bets shown in the Two-Urn Paradox table, where bet b_1 consists of drawing a ball from the first urn, and winning $100 if it is black, etc. Agents are typically indifferent between b_1 and b_3, and indifferent between b_2 and b_4, but prefer the latter two bets over the former two, on the grounds that the latter two offer known probabilities of winning whereas the former two do not. Again, such preferences are incompatible with the existence of subjective probabilities—the ranking $b_1 \prec b_2$ would imply prob(red in Urn I) < 1/2, but the ranking $b_3 \prec b_4$ would imply prob(black in Urn I) < 1/2.

In this chapter we consider how economists have responded to these and similar examples of such "ambiguity averse" preferences. Section 13.2 gives an overview of early discussions of what has now come to be known as subjective uncertainty and the phenomenon of ambiguity. Section 13.3 reviews the classical approach to uncertainty, subjective probability and preferences over uncertain prospects. Section 13.4 presents the experimental and empirical evidence on attitudes toward ambiguity motivated by Ellsberg's and similar examples. Section 13.5 gives analytical presentations of the most

---

[4] See Section 13.4 of this chapter.

[5] Individuals who would be indifferent between a_1 and a_2, and between a_3 and a_4, would be termed *ambiguity neutral*, and individuals who would prefer a_2 over a_1 and a_3 over a_4 would be termed *ambiguity loving*.

[6] Ellsberg (1961,pp.650–651,653; 2001, pp.131–137). It is unfortunate that Fellner's (1961) independent discovery, extensive discussion, and early experimental examination of the Two-Urn phenomenon has gone largely unrecognized.

important models of ambiguity and ambiguity aversion. Sections 13.6 and 13.7 present some recent developments in the field, and Section 13.8 concludes.

13.2 EARLY NOTIONS OF SUBJECTIVE UNCERTAINTY AND AMBIGUITY

13.2.1 Knight's Distinction

It is often asserted that the distinction between situations of probabilistic and nonprobabilistic beliefs was first made by Frank Knight (1921), in his use of the terms "risk" versus "uncertainty." However, as LeRoy and Singell (1987) have convincingly demonstrated, Knight's distinction between "risk" and "uncertainty" did *not* refer to the existence/absence of personal probabilistic beliefs, but rather, to the existence/absence of *objective probabilities* in the standard sense. In other words, Knight used "risk" to refer to situations where probabilities could either be theoretically deduced ("*a priori* probabilities") or determined from empirical frequencies ("statistical probabilities"), and "uncertainty" to refer to situations that did not provide any such basis for objective probability measurement. However, Knight postulated that even under "uncertainty," agents would still form *subjective* probabilities:"it is true, and the fact can hardly be over-emphasized, that a judgment of probability is actually made in such cases" (p.226) (Knight termed such probabilities "estimates"). Indeed, it is hard to find any more explicit adoption of the hypothesis of probabilistic sophistication under conditions of subjective uncertainty than Knight's assertion that

> *"we must observe at the outset that when an individual instance [i.e., a one-time event] only is at issue, there is no difference for conduct between a measurable risk and an unmeasurable uncertainty. The individual, as already observed, throws his estimate of the value of an opinion into the probability form of 'a successes in b trials' (a/b being a proper fraction) and 'feels' toward it as toward any other probability situation."[7]*

Although Knight provided a verbal formulation of the concept of "subjective uncertainty," the notion that agents in such situations might reject the standard probability calculus is due to his contemporary, John Maynard Keynes.

13.2.2 Keynes' "Probabilities"

The fundamental concept in Keynes' (1921) theory is a "probability," which he defined as the "logical relation" between one proposition and another in situations where the

---

[7] Knight (1921, p.234). Since he assumed that individuals always represented their beliefs by well-defined probabilities, what was the significance of the risk/uncertainty distinction for Knight? The answer is that under risk, probabilities are subject to independent measurement and hence are amenable to insurance, whereas under uncertainty they are not. Accordingly, only returns for bearing *uncertainty* should be attributed to a firm's profits, since returns for bearing *risk* should be treated as costs (namely, the imputed cost of the firm's decision to "self-insure" rather than purchase market insurance). See LeRoy and Singell (1987) for more complete discussion of this and other points.

first proposition neither logically assures nor logically excludes the second.[8] For a given set of premises, therefore, the probability of a proposition is defined as the "rational degree of belief" that should be attached to it. Keynes did not consider "degree of belief" to be a personal or subjective notion, any more than its extreme cases of logical necessity or logical impossibility (say, of geometric propositions) are personal or subjective:

> "The Theory of Probability is logical, therefore, because it is concerned with the degree of belief which it is rational to entertain in given conditions, and not merely with the actual beliefs of particular individuals, which may or may not be rational." (p.4).

Keynes did allow some of his probabilities to take on numerical values, although

> "the cases in which exact numerical measurement is possible are a very limited class, generally dependent on evidence which warrants a judgement of equiprobability by an application of the Principle of Indifference"[9] (p.160).

Other probabilities, though not numerically measurable, can still be ranked:

> "In these instances we can, perhaps, arrange the probabilities in an order of magnitude … although there is no basis for an estimate how much stronger or weaker the [one probability] is than the [other]" (p.29).

However, some probabilities will not even be *ordinally* comparable:

> "Is our expectation of rain, when we start out for a walk, always more likely than not, or less likely than not, or as likely as not? I am prepared to argue that on some of these occasions none of these alternatives hold…" (p.30).

Thus, a given pair of Keynesian probabilities can be related in one of three ways:

> "I maintain … that there are some pairs of probabilities between the members of which no comparison of magnitude is possible; that we can say, nevertheless, of some pairs of relations of probability that the one is greater and the other less, although it is not possible to measure the difference between them; and that in a very special type of case … a meaning can be given to numerical comparisons of magnitude. I think that the results of observation, of which examples have been given earlier in this chapter, are consistent with this account." (p.34).

In light of this, Keynes formally modeled his probabilities as a partial order (that is, transitive but not complete) with the following properties: all probabilities run from impossibility to certainty, certain subsets of probabilities form "ordered series" of mutually comparable elements, a probability may be a member of more than one ordered series, and all numerically measurable probabilities belong to a common ordered series. Since it allows for structures of belief which cannot be represented by numerical

---

[8] Since propositions can take the form such as "the event A has occurred" and "the event B will occur," this notion can also represent the relationship between a pair of events.

[9] This was Keynes' term for the Principle of Insufficient Reason (Section 13.2.5).

probabilities,[10] Keynes' theory is the earliest example of a formal statement of non-probabilistic beliefs.[11]

13.2.3 Shackle's "Potential Surprise"

The other early model of nonprobabilistic beliefs and preferences is that of George Shackle (1949a,b). The fundamental concept in Shackle's theory of belief is the "potential surprise" we would expect to experience upon learning that a particular event has occurred, or that a particular hypothesis is true. To distinguish this concept from standard probability, Shackle (1949a, p.113) gives the example of four equally qualified candidates for some appointment. A probabilistic representation of this situation may well assign each candidate a probability of 1/4, and hence view Candidate A's appointment as "unlikely." But given this symmetric uncertainty, we would hardly exhibit any "surprise" upon learning that Candidate A has received the position—nor, of course, would we be surprised to learn that it had gone to someone other than Candidate A. Moreover, these two surprise levels would remain at zero even if the number of equally qualified candidates rose from four to eight. On the other hand, if the pool were enlarged by the addition of clearly unqualified candidates, these new contenders would each be assigned a positive potential surprise.

The notion of potential surprise is geared toward the world *outside* of the gambling house, where our ignorance is not just in the relative likelihoods of a known set of alternatives, but in the very set of alternatives that might occur: "we need a measure of acceptance by which the individual can give to new rival hypotheses, which did not at first occur to him, some degree, and even the highest degree, of acceptance without reducing the degrees of acceptance accorded to any of those already in his mind" (1949b, p. 70)

Of course, by its very nature, such a measure of uncertainty will be nonadditive—as we have seen, the potential surprises of each member of an exhaustive set of events *could* all be zero, although according to Shackle, they *could not* all be positive. Shackle (1949a, App. E) gives their formal properties, including rules for their combination (e.g., the potential surprise of the union or the intersection of two events, of one event conditional upon another, etc.).

Just as his theory of beliefs departs from the traditional additive probability calculus, Shackle's theory of *preferences* over uncertain prospects departs from the additive expected value/expected utility approach. Consider an individual confronted with a set of alternative actions: "In order to assess the merits of any given course of action, a man must find some way of reducing the great array of hypotheses about the relevant consequences of this course … to some compact and vivid statement" (1949a, p. 14).

---

[10] Among other reasons, all likelihood relations represented by true numerical probabilities must be complete.
[11] See, however, Ramsey's (1926,§2) positive and normative criticisms of Keynes' theory.

To make this reduction, the individual will begin by determining the ability of each possible gain in an action to "stimulate him agreeably," where this level of stimulation is an increasing function of the value of the gain and a decreasing function of its potential surprise. However, "the power of *mutually exclusive* hypotheses of success [alternative possible gains in a given action] to afford enjoyment by imagination is *not additive*" (1949a, p. 16). In fact, the entire positive stimulation of an action is defined to be that of its most stimulating possible gain:

> "amongst all the hypotheses of success [potential gains] which the individual could entertain in regard to any venture, one alone is accountable in full for the enjoyment which he derives from the thought of this venture, and by itself determined the intensity of this enjoyment" (1949a, p.16)

Similarly, the entire negative stimulation of an action is defined to be that of its most stimulating possible loss. Actions are then evaluated and ranked on the basis of "indifference maps" defined over such (stimulation of gain, stimulation of loss) pairs. Both the stimulation function and these indifference maps are amenable to theoretical analysis and empirical fitting, and Shackle applies his model to issues of gambling, investment, taxation and bargaining.

Although several writers[12] have criticized the unrealistic nature of some of his assumptions, Shackle's work represents an admirable attempt to develop *and apply* a new mathematical theory of belief and decision under uncertainty, at a time when the expected utility model had not yet taken over the profession.

13.2.4 Ramsey's "Degrees of Belief"

The earliest actual characterization of probabilistically sophisticated beliefs, in the sense of a set of assumptions on choice behavior which imply the existence of a classical probability measure over events, is that of Frank Ramsey (1926). Although he was probably not the first to observe that probabilistic beliefs could be measured by betting odds, he was the first to accomplish this without having to assume actual risk neutrality.

Since he was interested in the measurement of subjective probabilities—termed "degrees of belief"—rather than attitudes toward risk, Ramsey imposed the Bernoullian principle of expected utility maximization upon his agents, and indeed, worked directly in terms of the utilities, or as he called them, the "values," of various outcomes. Accordingly, he assumed that "behaviour is governed by what is called the mathematical expectation [of utility or value]; that is to say, if $\mathcal{P}$ is a proposition about which [the agent] is doubtful, any goods or bads for whose realization $\mathcal{P}$ is in his view a necessary and sufficient condition enter into his calculations multiplied by the same fraction,

---

[12] E.g., Turvey (1949), Graaf and Baumol (1949), Carter (1950), Arrow (1951) and Ellsberg (1961).

which is called the 'degree of his belief in P.' We thus define degree of belief in a way which presupposes the use of the mathematical expectation." (1926, §3).

Ramsey defined a proposition P to be *ethically neutral* if, holding all other aspects of the world constant, the individual is indifferent between its truth or falsity. The individual is said to have a "degree of belief 1/2" in such a proposition if the prospects

$$\{\alpha \text{ if } P \text{ is true; } \beta \text{ if } P \text{ is false}\} \quad \text{and} \quad \{\beta \text{ if } P \text{ is true; } \alpha \text{ if } P \text{ is false}\}$$

are indifferent for all values α and β. Ramsey's main assumptions are:

1. There exists at least one ethically neutral proposition with degree of belief 1/2
2. If P and Q are both ethically neutral propositions with degree of belief 1/2, and the individual is indifferent between the prospects

$$\{\alpha \text{ if } P \text{ is true; } \beta \text{ if } P \text{ is false}\} \quad \text{and} \quad \{\gamma \text{ if } P \text{ is true; } \delta \text{ if } P \text{ is false}\}$$

then he or she will be indifferent between the prospects

$$\{\alpha \text{ if } Q \text{ is true; } \beta \text{ if } Q \text{ is false}\} \quad \text{and} \quad \{\gamma \text{ if } Q \text{ is true; } \delta \text{ if } Q \text{ is false}\}$$

for all values α, β, γ and δ.

These assumptions, along with some technical ones, allowed Ramsey to identify the set of values with the real numbers, with the above preferences implying $\alpha + \beta = \gamma + \delta$. Having defined a way of measuring value/utility, he then invoked the principle of expectation to derive the individual's beliefs, that is, their subjective probabilities of propositions or events: If the individual was indifferent between receiving α with certainty or the prospect $\{\beta \text{ if } R \text{ is true; } \gamma \text{ if } R \text{ is false}\}$, Ramsey defined their degree of belief in R as $(\alpha - \gamma)/(\beta - \gamma)$, and assumed that this ratio would be the same for any other triple of values $\{\alpha', \beta', \gamma'\}$ that satisfy the same preference relation. Ramsey went on to derive notions such as the "conditional degree of belief in P given Q" and to show that this concept of "degrees of belief" indeed satisfies the basic laws of probability theory.

Ramsey's approach is limited (i) in that it imposes the property of expected utility maximization rather than jointly axiomatizes it, and (ii) in its dependence upon an essentially objective 50:50 randomization device (Assumption 1. above). (Both of these limitations are overcome by the approach of Savage (1954) described in Section 13.3.3.) However, since Ramsey was the first to characterize probabilistically sophisticated beliefs in terms of choice behavior, his insightful article deserves a prominent place in the literature.

13.2.5 Principle of Insufficient Reason

The earliest hypothesis concerning belief under subjective uncertainty is the so-called *Principle of Insufficient Reason*, which states that in situations where there is no logical or empirical reason to favor any one of a set of mutually exclusive events or hypotheses over any other, we should assign them all equal probability.[13] This principle is generally attributed to James (also known as "Jacob") Bernoulli (1738). It was invoked by Bayes (1763) in his development of the binomial theorem (Stigler, 1986, pp.122–129) and by Laplace (1814) in his developments the Law of Succession and what is now called the Laplace distribution (Stigler, 1986, pp.109–113).[14]

Keynes (1921, Ch. IV), who also cites von Kries (1886), raised several objections to the Principle. The first relates to its implication that, in conditions of complete ignorance, we should assign equal probably to the validity of a hypothesis "this book is red" or to its complement. The problem of course is that the complement may consist of more than one mutually exclusive hypothesis ("this book is black," "this book is blue," etc.), and it is clearly impossible to assign a probability of 1/2 to *each* of these mutually exclusive hypotheses. A related objection also concerns multiple choice of partitions. If we have no information whatsoever as to the area or population of the regions of the world, then we would say that (i) a man is as likely to be an inhabitant of Great Britain as of France, and (ii) a man is as likely to be an inhabitant of *England* as of France. This, of course, would imply that Scotland and Wales are barren.

Another objection pertains to the application of the Principle to physical variables. Say we do know that the volume of a one-pound weight lies between 1 and 3 cubic inches, but have no further information on that value. This means that there is a 50:50 chance that its volume is greater than two cubic inches. On the other hand, our original information implies that the *density* of the object is between 1/3 and 1 pound/cubic inch, implying that there is a 50:50 chance that its density is greater than 2/3 pounds/cubic inch, which is inconsistent with the first conclusion.[15]

The most sophisticated of Keynes' objections pertained to a situation identical to Urn I in Ellsberg's Two-Urn example. In an urn with 100 black or red balls, does the Principle instruct us to treat all *ratios* of black to red balls (i.e., 0:100, 1:99, 2:98, …) as equally likely, or does it instruct us to treat the color of each *individual* ball as equally likely to be black or red? Although the implications for betting on a single draw would be identical, the two conclusions have quite different implications for bets involving multiple draws.[16]

Formal axiomatic developments of the Principle of Insufficient Reason have been provided by researchers such as Chernoff (1954), Milnor (1954) and Sinn (1980).

---

[13] Since this implies a uniform probability distribution over the events or hypotheses, it accordingly qualifies as a probabilistically sophisticated model of beliefs.

[14] See also Keynes (1921, p.372) on Venn's (1866) use of the Principle of Insufficient Reason in the Rule of Succession. On the other hand, see Shafer (1978) for arguments that at least some of James Bernoulli's notions of "probability" were nonadditive.

[15] A more economically-based example is that bond prices and interest rates cannot *both* have uniform probability densities.

[16] See Savage (1954, pp. 63–67) for additional critical discussion of the Principle of Insufficient Reason.

13.3 THE CLASSICAL MODEL OF SUBJECTIVE PROBABILITY

13.3.1 Objective versus Subjective Uncertainty

Uncertain prospects can take different forms. A simple example of an *objectively uncertain prospect*—often called a *lottery* or a *roulette lottery*—is the gamble $\mathbf{P} = (x_1, p_1; \ldots; x_n, p_n)$ yielding *outcome* x_i with a well-specified *objective probability* p_i. The outcomes in an objective lottery needn't be monetary; an objective lottery can be defined over any space of outcomes, such as standard consumption bundles, intertemporal time streams of monetary payments, vacations in different locales, etc. Nor need they be finite in number; the vector of probabilities $(p_1, \ldots, p_n)$ could be replaced by an arbitrary objective probability measure over outcome spaces in $\mathbb{R}^1$ or $\mathbb{R}^n$. The most general form of an objective lottery is that of an arbitrary probability measure $\pi(\cdot)$ over an arbitrary outcome space $\mathcal{X}$.

As mentioned, the uncertainty inherent in a fair coin or fair roulette wheel is distinct from the uncertainty inherent in a horse race or the weather. A *subjectively uncertain prospect*—often called an *act* or a *horse lottery*—is the bet $f(\cdot) = (x_1$ if $E_1; \ldots; x_n$ if $E_n)$ (or simply $(x_1, E_1; \ldots; x_n, E_n)$) yielding x_j should the *event* E_j occur, for some mutually exclusive and exhaustive partition $\{E_1, \ldots, E_n\}$ of all possible unfolding of the world, such as the partition $\{$horse 1 wins,$\ldots$,horse n wins$\}$. Partitions $\{E_1, \ldots, E_n\}$ may in turn be thought of as alternative partitions (of varying coarseness) of an underlying space $\mathcal{S} = \{\ldots, s, \ldots\}$ of *states of nature,* which represents the subjective uncertainty at its finest and most basic level. Again, a subjective act needn't be finite-outcome; most generally, it consists of an arbitrary mapping $f(\cdot)$ from an arbitrary state space $\mathcal{S}$ to an arbitrary outcome space $\mathcal{X}$. It is fair to say that, outside of gambling halls, most real-world uncertainty is subjective rather than objective.[17]

Uncertainty, be it objective or subjective, might well be resolved in two or more stages. A *two-stage* (or *compound*) *objective lottery* takes the form $(\ldots; \mathbf{P}_i, p_i; \ldots)$, yielding the objective lottery $\mathbf{P}_i = (\ldots; x_{ik}, p_{ik}; \ldots)$ with probability p_i, where for each i the probabilities $(\ldots, p_{ik}, \ldots)$ sum to unity. A *two-stage subjective act* takes the form $(\ldots; f_j(\cdot)$ if $E_j; \ldots)$, yielding *subact* $f_j(\cdot) = (\ldots; x_{jk}$ if $E_{jk}; \ldots)$, where for each j the collection of *subevents* $\{\ldots, E_{jk}, \ldots\}$ is a partition of the event E_j. A two-stage *mixed* or *objective-subjective* prospect—termed a *horse-roulette act*, or sometimes an *Anscombe-Aumann act*—consists of a subjective act whose prizes are objective lotteries, and takes the form $(\ldots; \mathbf{P}_j$ if $E_j; \ldots) = (\ldots; (\ldots; x_{ij}, p_{ij}; \ldots)$ if $E_j; \ldots)$. Such prospects play an important role in the theory of ambiguity and ambiguity aversion. We analyze these in detail in Section 13.5.

Each two-stage objective lottery $(\ldots; \mathbf{P}_i, p_i; \ldots) = (\ldots; (\ldots; x_{ik}, p_{ik}; \ldots), p_i; \ldots)$ has a corresponding single-stage *reduced form lottery* $(\ldots; x_{ik}, p_{ik} \cdot p_i; \ldots)$, obtained by compounding

---

[17] Although the first occurrence of this framework in its full generality seems to be Savage (1950) (in his review of Wald (1950)), it comes as a natural outgrowth of the statistical literature on hypothesis testing (Neyman and Pearson (1933), Wald (1939, 1950)), where the "states" were alternative hypotheses, "acts" were decisions to accept/reject the various hypotheses, and "consequences" were the (expected) values of the loss function.

the probabilities p_{ik} and p_i for each i,k.[18] A decision maker may or may not be indifferent between a two-stage objective lottery and its corresponding reduced form—the hypothesis that they are in fact indifferent is known as the *Reduction of Compound Lotteries Axiom*.

Given a pair of objective lotteries $\mathbf{P}=(x_1,p_1;\ldots;x_n,p_n)$ and $\mathbf{P}^*=(x_1^*,p_1^*;\ldots;x_n^*,p_{n^*}^*)$ and some *mixture probability* $\alpha \in [0,1]$, the $\alpha{:}(1-\alpha)$ *probability mixture* of $\mathbf{P}$ and $\mathbf{P}^*$ is the single-stage objective lottery $\alpha{\cdot}\mathbf{P}+(1-\alpha){\cdot}\mathbf{P}^*=(x_1,\alpha{\cdot}p_1;\ldots;x_n,\alpha{\cdot}p_n;x_1^*,(1-\alpha){\cdot}p_1^*;\ldots;x_{n^*}^*,(1-\alpha){\cdot}p_{n^*}^*)$. The probability mixture $\alpha{\cdot}\mathbf{P}+(1-\alpha){\cdot}\mathbf{P}^*$ of two lotteries is seen to be the single-stage reduced form of the two-stage compound lottery $(\mathbf{P},\alpha;\mathbf{P}^*,(1-\alpha))$. A corresponding definition holds for probability mixtures $\alpha{\cdot}\pi(\cdot)+(1-\alpha){\cdot}\pi^*(\cdot)$ of general objective lotteries.

Similarly, given two subjective acts $(x_1,E_1;\ldots;x_n,E_n)$ and $(x_1^*,E_1;\ldots;x_n^*,E_n)$ over a common partition[19] $\{E_1,\ldots,E_n\}$ of $\mathcal{S}$ and a subset $\{E_1,\ldots,E_m\}$ of these events, the $\{E_1,\ldots,E_m\}{:}\{E_{m+1},\ldots,E_n\}$ *event mixture* of $(x_1,E_1;\ldots;x_n,E_n)$ and $(x_1^*,E_1;\ldots;x_n^*,E_n)$ is the (single-stage) act $(x_1,E_1;\ldots;x_m,E_m;x_{m+1}^*,E_{m+1};\ldots;x_n^*,E_n)$ yielding outcome x_j if one of the events $E_1,\ldots,E_m$ should occur and x_j^* if one of $E_{m+1},\ldots,E_n$ occurs. Given a pair of general subjective acts $f(\cdot)$ and $f^*(\cdot)$ and event $E \subseteq \mathcal{S}$, the $E{:}{\sim}E$ event mixture of $f(\cdot)$ and $f^*(\cdot)$ is the act $(f(\cdot),E;f^*(\cdot),{\sim}E)$ which yields outcome $f(s)$ for each state s in E and the outcome $f^*(s)$ for each state s in ${\sim}E$.

Although both objective lotteries and subjective acts can be defined more generally, from this point we restrict our attention to finite-outcome lotteries and acts.

13.3.2 Objective Expected Utility

The earliest and most basic model of preferences over uncertain prospects is the *objective expected utility* model, proposed by Bernoulli (1738) and formalized by von Neumann and Morgenstern (1944), Marschak (1950), Samuelson (1952) and others. In this model, preferences over objective lotteries can be represented by an ordinal *preference function* of the form $V(x_1,p_1;\ldots;x_n,p_n)=\sum_{i=1}^{n}U(x_i){\cdot}p_i$ or $V(\pi(\cdot))=\int_{\mathscr{X}}U(x){\cdot}d\pi(x)$, for some cardinal *von Neumann-Morgenstern utility function* $U(\cdot)$ over outcomes. Researchers such as Arrow (1963), Pratt (1964) and others have demonstrated how properties of the utility function $U(\cdot)$ correspond to features of attitudes toward objective uncertainty,[20] and the objective expected utility model has formed the cornerstone of the economic analysis of choice under uncertainty.

In addition to the usual properties corresponding to the existence of a preference ranking $\succcurlyeq$ with a numerical representation $V(\cdot)$, the key feature of objective expected utility preferences, known as the *Independence Axiom*, is the property

---

[18] Thus, the single-stage reduced form of the two-stage lottery $(($\$$10,1/3;$\$$20,2/3),1/2;($\$$0,1/2;$\$$10,1/6;$\$$30,1/3),1/2)$ is the single-stage lottery $($\$$0,1/4;$\$$10,1/4;$\$$20,1/3;$\$$30,1/6)$.

[19] This partition could consist of any common refinement of the two acts' original partitions.

[20] See Chapter 3 of this Handbook.

Independence Axiom: For all lotteries $\mathbf{P}, \mathbf{P}^*, \hat{\mathbf{P}}$ and all $\alpha \in (0,1]$, $\mathbf{P}^* \succcurlyeq \mathbf{P}$ if and only if $\alpha \cdot \mathbf{P}^* + (1 - \alpha) \cdot \hat{\mathbf{P}} \succcurlyeq \alpha \cdot \mathbf{P} + (1-\alpha) \cdot \hat{\mathbf{P}}$.[21]

The intuition behind this property of preferences is most clearly revealed by thinking of the probability mixtures $\alpha \cdot \mathbf{P}^* + (1-\alpha) \cdot \hat{\mathbf{P}}$ and $\alpha \cdot \mathbf{P} + (1-\alpha) \cdot \hat{\mathbf{P}}$ in terms of their corresponding two-stage lotteries $(\mathbf{P}^*, \alpha; \hat{\mathbf{P}}, (1 - \alpha))$ and $(\mathbf{P}, \alpha; \hat{\mathbf{P}}, (1 - \alpha))$, where the first stage consists of the flip of a coin with objective probabilities $\alpha{:}(1-\alpha)$ of landing heads:tails. Choosing between the two prospects essentially consists of choosing whether to receive $\mathbf{P}^*$ or $\mathbf{P}$ if it lands heads; if it lands tails two prospects will yield the same thing (namely $\hat{\mathbf{P}}$) anyway, so the decision maker should rank these two prospects in the same way he or she ranks $\mathbf{P}^*$ and $\mathbf{P}$.

Paradoxes such as those of Allais (1953) have revealed systematic violations of the Independence Axiom, and have led to the development of *non-expected utility* models of preferences over objective lotteries. Such preferences are typically represented by functions $V(x_1, p_1; \ldots; x_n, p_n)$, and several specific forms of such functions have been proposed.[22]

13.3.3 Savage's Characterization of Subjective Expected Utility and Subjective Probability

As noted above, virtually all real-world uncertainty is subjective rather than objective, which led to the development of the corresponding *subjective expected utility* (*SEU*) model of Savage (1954). In this model, preferences over subjective acts are represented by an ordinal preference function of the form $W(x_1, E_1; \ldots; x_n, E_n) = \sum_{j=1}^n U(x_j) \cdot \mu(E_j)$ or $W(f(\cdot)) = \int_{\mathscr{S}} U(f(s)) \cdot d\mu(s)$, for utility function $U(\cdot)$ and unique, additive *subjective probability measure*[23] $\mu(\cdot)$ over states. Just as the utility function $U(\cdot)$ represents an expected utility maximizer's attitudes toward risk, the subjective probability measure $\mu(\cdot)$ represents their beliefs of the likelihoods of the various states of nature and hence of the events based on them. Different decision makers can, and typically do, have different subjective probability measures (this, after all, is what makes for bets on horse races).

Savage obtained his characterization of subjective expected utility and subjective probability by means of the following axioms on a decision maker's preferences over subjective acts:[24]

P1 Ordering: The preference relation $\succcurlyeq$ is complete, reflexive and transitive.

---

[21] Although implicitly invoked by von Neumann and Morgenstern in their formalization of the expected utility hypothesis (Malinvaud (1952)), the first formal statements of this property seem to be those of Marschak (1950) and Samuelson (1952).

[22] See the Machina (1987) as well as Chapters 12 and 14 of this Handbook.

[23] Savage (1954) used the term *personal probabilities*.

[24] Axiom numbers are Savage's. Except for the Sure-Thing Principle, axiom names are our own. Savage (1954) provides an additional axiom, P7, used to extend his characterization to the case of infinite-outcome acts.

P2 Sure-Thing Principle: For all events E and all acts $f^*(\cdot), f(\cdot), f'(\cdot)$ and $f''(\cdot), (f^*(\cdot), E; f'(\cdot), \sim E) \succsim (f(\cdot), E; f'(\cdot), \sim E)$ if and only if $(f^*(\cdot), E; f''(\cdot), \sim E) \succsim (f(\cdot), E; f''(\cdot), \sim E)$.

P3 Eventwise Monotonicity: For all outcomes x^*, x, all nonnull[25] events E and all acts $f(\cdot), (x^*, E; f(\cdot), \sim E) \succsim (x, E; f(\cdot), \sim E)$ if and only if $x^* \succsim x$.

P4 Weak Comparative Probability: For all events E^*, E and all outcomes $x^* \succ x, \hat{x}^* \succ \hat{x}, (x^*, E^*; x, \sim E^*) \succsim (x^*, E; x, \sim E)$ if and only if $(\hat{x}^*, E^*; \hat{x}, \sim E^*) \succsim (\hat{x}^*, E; \hat{x}, \sim E)$.

P5 Non-Degeneracy: There exist outcomes x^* and x such that $x^* \succ x$.

P6 Small Event Continuity: For all acts $f^*(\cdot) \succ f(\cdot)$ and outcomes x, there exists a partition $\{E_1, \ldots, E_n\}$ of $\mathcal{S}$ such that both $f^*(\cdot) \succ (x, E_j; f(\cdot), \sim E_j)$ for all j and $(x, E_j; f^*(\cdot), \sim E_j) \succ f(\cdot)$ for all j.

Chapter 1 of this volume covers the axiomatic characterization of both objective and subjective expected utility. The axioms most relevant to the study of ambiguity and ambiguity aversion will turn out to be P2 (Sure-Thing Principle), P4 (Weak Comparative Probability) and a stronger version of P4 described in Section 13.3.5.

The intuition behind the Sure-Thing Principle is virtually identical to that of the Independence Axiom, with the coin replaced by an event E which may or may not occur. If two acts $(f^*(\cdot), E; f'(\cdot), \sim E)$ and $(f(\cdot), E; f'(\cdot), \sim E)$ yield the same outcome $f'(s)$ for each state s in the event $\sim E$, it should not matter what those statewise common outcomes are. Thus, replacing the common outcome $f'(s)$ with some different common outcome $f''(s)$ for each state s in $\sim E$ will not affect the preference ranking over the prospects. In the language of modern consumer theory, the Sure-Thing Principle states that preferences over subjective acts are *separable* across mutually exclusive events.

However, event-separability is only one of two distinguishing features of the subjective expected utility model, and by itself does not ensure the existence of well-defined subjective probabilities.[26] To P2 we must also add P4 (Weak Comparative Probability), which states that for any pair of events, the event on which the individual would prefer to stake the better of two prizes will not depend upon the prizes themselves. In other words, the decision maker has a well-defined *comparative likelihood ranking* over events. Together, the Sure-Thing Principle and Weak Comparative Probability Axiom form the heart of the subjective expected utility model.

13.3.4 Anscombe and Aumann's Joint Objective-Subjective Approach

The contribution of Anscombe and Aumann's (1963) joint objective-subjective approach is twofold. First, it provides a framework for representing uncertain prospects

---

[25] An event E is said to be *null* if, for all acts $f(\cdot)$ and $g(\cdot)$ such that $f(s) = g(s)$ for all $s \in \sim E$, it is the case that $f(\cdot) \sim g(\cdot)$ — that is, payoffs received on the event E do not matter.

[26] A decision maker with a "state-dependent" expected utility preference function $\int_s U(f(s)|s) \cdot d\mu(s)$ will be event-separable and hence satisfies the Sure-Thing Principle, but will not necessarily reveal well-defined likelihood rankings over events.

which involve both objective and subjective uncertainty. Such prospects play a key role in the field of ambiguity and ambiguity aversion—the key feature of Ellsberg urns is precisely that they involve both types of uncertainty. The second contribution is that by introducing objective prospects into the subjective framework, their approach allows for an axiomatic derivation of subjective probability which is considerably simpler than that of Savage (1954).

In addition to horse-roulette acts $(\ldots;\mathbf{P}_j \text{ if } E_j;\ldots)=(\ldots;(\ldots;x_{ij},p_{ij};\ldots) \text{ if } E_j;\ldots)$, Anscombe and Aumann consider three-stage compound prospects. These are objective lotteries $(\ldots;f_k,p_k;\ldots)$ whose "prizes" consist of horse-roulette acts $f_k(\cdot)=(\ldots;\mathbf{P}_{jk} \text{ if } E_j;\ldots)=(\ldots;(\ldots;x_{ijk},p_{ijk};\ldots) \text{ if } E_{jk};\ldots)$. Such prospects can be termed *roulette-horse-roulette acts*. (A two-stage, horse-roulette act is thus a special case of a three-stage, roulette-horse-roulette act in which the first stage roulette lottery is degenerate.) It is important to note that, whereas horse-roulette acts $f_k(\cdot)=(\ldots;\mathbf{P}_{jk} \text{ if } E_j;\ldots)$ can involve different payoffs $\ldots,x_{ijk},\ldots$, they are all defined over the same partition $\{\ldots,E_j,\ldots\}$. In other words, a roulette-horse-roulette act is a roulette wheel whose respective prizes are different bets on the same horse race (where the prizes can themselves be roulette lotteries). We note that, in the recent literature, the term "Anscombe-Aumann act" is usually reserved for two-stage, horse-roulette acts: see Section 13.5.

Because they are interested in deriving subjective probability, Anscombe and Aumann preassume that the individual has expected utility preferences over primitive objective lotteries $\mathbf{P}=(\ldots;x_i,p_i;\ldots)$, i.e., that there exists a von Neumann-Morgenstern utility function $U(\cdot)$ over final payoffs such that the expected utility of any primitive lottery is given by $U(\mathbf{P})=\cdots+p_i\cdot U(x_i)+\cdots$. Furthermore, they assume that the individual also has expected-utility preferences over roulette-horse-roulette acts: there exists a von Neumann-Morgenstern utility function $W(\cdot)$ over horse-roulette acts such that the expected utility of the roulette-horse-roulette act $(\ldots;f_k,p_k;\ldots)$ is given by $\cdots+p_k\cdot W(f_k)+\cdots$. Note that the horse-roulette acts f_k are treated simply as prizes. Of course, these expected-utility preferences over primitive lotteries and roulette-horse-roulette acts satisfy the von Neumann-Morgenstern Independence axiom on the respective domains.

Their first assumption, which they term "Monotonicity in the Prizes," is that if a pure roulette lottery $\hat{\mathbf{P}}_j$ is weakly preferred to $\mathbf{P}_j$, then the horse-roulette act $(\ldots;\mathbf{P}_{j-1} \text{ if } E_{j-1};\hat{\mathbf{P}}_j \text{ if } E_j;\mathbf{P}_{j+1} \text{ if } E_{j+1};\ldots)$ is weakly preferred to $(\ldots;\mathbf{P}_{j-1} \text{ if } E_{j-1};\mathbf{P}_j \text{ if } E_j;\mathbf{P}_{j+1} \text{ if } E_{j+1};\ldots)$, or in the author's words, "if two horse lotteries are identical except for the prizes associated with one [horse], then your preference between the lotteries is governed by your preference between the prizes associated with that [horse]."

Their second assumption, "Reversal of Order in Compound Lotteries," is that, for a given horse race $\{\ldots,E_j,\ldots\}$, given probability vector $(\ldots,p_k,\ldots)$ and given collection of primitive objective lotteries $\{\mathbf{P}_{ij}\}_{i,j}$ to serve as prizes, the individual is indifferent between the roulette-horse-roulette acts

$$(\ldots; (\ldots; \mathbf{P}_{ij} \text{ if } E_j; \ldots), p_i; \ldots) \quad \text{and} \quad (\ldots; (\ldots; \mathbf{P}_{ij}, p_i; \ldots) \text{ if } E_j; \ldots)$$

(note that the first prospect is a nondegenerate roulette-horse-roulette act, but the second is actually a horse-roulette act). In Anscombe and Aumann's words, "if the prize you receive is to be determined by both a horse race and the spin of a roulette wheel, then it is immaterial whether the wheel is spun before or after the race" (1963, p. 201).

These authors demonstrate how their mixed objective-subjective framework and set of assumptions imply the existence of well-defined subjective probabilities $(\ldots, q_j, \ldots)$ over the states (in their setting, the horses), in the sense that the individual's expected utility $W(f)$ of any horse-roulette act $f = (\ldots; \mathbf{P}_j \text{ if } E_j; \ldots)$ is given by $\ldots + q_j \cdot U(\mathbf{P}_j) + \ldots$[27]

13.3.5 Probabilistic Sophistication

Although the Savage axioms imply both properties, it is possible for a decision maker to exhibit well-defined probabilistic beliefs without necessarily having expected utility risk preferences. A preference function $W(\cdot)$ over subjective acts is said to be *probabilistically sophisticated* (or satisfy the *Hypothesis of Probabilistic Sophistication*) if it takes the form $W(x_1, E_1; \ldots; x_n, E_n) = V(x_1, \mu(E_1); \ldots; x_n, \mu(E_n))$ for some probability measure $\mu(\cdot)$ over events and preference function $V(\cdot)$ over objective lotteries. Such a decision maker is accordingly indifferent between any subjective act $(x_1 \text{ on } E_1; \ldots; x_n \text{ on } E_n)$ and its associated objective lottery $(x_1, \mu(E_1); \ldots; x_n, \mu(E_n))$. Since the preference function $V(\cdot)$ needn't take the expected utility form, such individuals are not necessarily subject to *Allais-type* violations of the Independence Axiom. However, since they retain the property of probabilistic beliefs, they are precisely the target of the *Ellsberg-type* effects—that is, the paradoxes of Section 13.1 and the additional effects reported in Section 13.4.

Machina and Schmeidler (1992, Thm.2)[28] have shown how the property of probabilistic sophistication can be characterized by dropping Savage's Sure-Thing Principle P2 and strengthening his Weak Comparative Probability Axiom P4 to the following:

P4* Strong Comparative Probability: For all pairs of disjoint events E^*, E, all outcomes $x^* \succ x$ and $\hat{x}^* \succ \hat{x}$, and all acts $f^*(\cdot)$ and $f(\cdot)$, if $(x^*, E^*; x, E; f^*(\cdot), \sim(E^* \cup E)) \succcurlyeq (x, E^*(\cdot); x^*, E; f^*(\cdot), \sim(E^* \cup E))$ then $(\hat{x}^*, E^*; \hat{x}, E; f(\cdot), \sim(E^* \cup E)) \succcurlyeq (\hat{x}, E^*; \hat{x}^*, E; f(\cdot), \sim(E^* \cup E))$.

Since the Sure-Thing Principle P2 and the Strong Comparative Probability Axiom P4* are independent properties of preferences, a decision maker could satisfy either one without the other—the probabilistically sophisticated form $W(x_1, E_1; \ldots; x_n, E_n) = V(x_1, \mu(E_1); \ldots; x_n, \mu(E_n))$ will satisfy P4* but generally not P2, whereas the

---

[27] Other joint axiomatizations of expected utility and subjective probability by means of an extraneous randomization device include those of Davidson and Suppes (1956), Pratt et al. (1964), DeGroot (1970, Ch.6), Fishburn (1970, Ch.6).

[28] See also Machina and Schmeidler (1995). Derivations of probabilistic sophistication under weaker assumptions have also been provided by Grant (1995) and Chew and Sagi (2006).

state-dependent expected utility form $W(\ldots;x_j,s_j;\ldots)=\sum_j U(x_j|s_j)\cdot\mu(s_j)$ will satisfy P2 but generally not P4*.[29]

While most Ellsberg urn examples illustrate violations of both P2 and P4*, not all do, and it is departures from probabilistic sophistication (i.e., violations of P4*) which constitute the phenomena of ambiguity aversion or ambiguity preference.

13.4 ELLSBERG URNS

The examples of Section 13.1 are two of many proposed by Ellsberg and others of what have come to be known as *Ellsberg Urns*. Ellsberg's (1961) article contained another example, suggested to him by Kenneth Arrow, similar in spirit to the Two-Urn example but involving a single urn.[30] Again, the conjectured response is that decision makers would prefer the unambiguous bet c_1 over the ambiguous c_2 (which would imply prob(red) > prob(green)), and prefer the unambiguous c_4 over the ambiguous c_3 (which would imply prob(red) < prob(green)).

FOUR-COLOR ELLSBERG PARADOX

	100 balls		50 balls	50 balls
	black	red	green	yellow
c_1	$100	$100	$0	$0
c_2	$100	$0	$100	$0
c_3	$0	$100	$0	$100
c_4	$0	$0	$100	$100

13.4.1 Initial Reactions and Discussion

Because they struck at the heart of what many considered to be basic principles of rationality—the Sure-Thing Principle and probabilistic beliefs—Ellsberg's examples spawned a lot of discussion among the decision theory establishment. Ellsberg summarized some of their initial reactions as follows:[31]

> *"Responses do vary. There are those who do **not** violate the axioms, or say they won't, even in these situations (e.g., G. Debreu, R. Schlaifer, P. Samuelson); such subjects tend to apply the axioms rather than their intuition, and when in doubt, to apply some form of the Principle of Insufficient Reason. Some violate the axioms cheerfully, even with gusto (J. Marschak, N. Dalkey); others sadly but persistently…. Still others (H. Raiffa) tend, intuitively, to violate the axioms but feel guilty about it and go back into further analysis."*

---

[29] This is essentially the point of footnote 26.
[30] Ellsberg (1961, p.654, n.4). See also (1961, p.651, n.1).
[31] Ellsberg (1961, pp. 655–656).

Ellsberg's report of a wide range of views on these issues played out in the subsequent literature. Whether or not he had any intuitive tendency for violation, Raiffa (1961) offered what has come to be the standard argument to an individual who would make the typical choices in the Three-Color Urn: If you really prefer a_1 over a_2 and a_4 over a_3, then you presumably prefer a 50:50 coin flip of a_1:a_4 versus a 50:50 coin flip of a_2:a_3. But both coin flips reduce to a purely objective 50:50 coin flip of \$100:\$0. In Raiffa's view, "Something must give!" (1961, p.694)

Others have expressed a variety of views. Although Fellner (1961) largely supported a decision maker's right to possess Ellsberg-like preferences, he also asked whether a decision maker "is or is not likely gradually to lose this trait *as he gets used to the uncertainty with which he is faced.*"[32] Brewer (1963) argued that the rationality/irrationality of Ellsberg-type "slanting down of subjective probabilities" depends on whether or not a decision maker is allowed a free choice to bet on either an event or its complement—if not, he argues, Raiffa's comparison with a 50:50 coin flip won't apply (discussion of these issues continued in Fellner (1963) and Brewer and Fellner (1965)). Roberts (1963) reported, but did not accept, the argument that losing in either bet b_2 or bet b_4 on the 50:50 urn is somehow different from losing in either bet b_1 or bet b_3 on the unknown urn.[33] Smith (1969) and Sarin and Winkler (1992), however, suggest that a decision maker indeed does have distinct (and measurable) utility of money functions for prizes won from the two different urns. Finally, historians of economic thought are directed to the interesting 1961–1963 correspondence between Ellsberg and Leonard Savage (Savage (1963)).

13.4.2 Experiments on Ellsberg Urns and Ambiguity Aversion

Although Ellsberg himself only offered his examples as thought experiments, he recognized the need for formal experimentation from the very start.[34] The earliest reported experiments of this form seem to be those of Chipman (1958,1960).[35] Fellner (1961) offered various versions of the Two-Urn problem to a group of Yale undergraduates, and found an overall tendency to prefer the 50:50 rather than the unknown odds. Subsequent experiments by Becker and Brownson (1964), MacCrimmon (1968), Slovic and Tversky (1974), Curley and Yates (1989) and others also confirmed Ellsberg's conjecture of widespread ambiguity aversion. Although most of these experiments use students as subjects, researchers such as MacCrimmon (1965), Hogarth and Kunreuther (1989), Einhorn and Hogarth (1986), Viscusi and Chesson (1999), Ho et al. (2002) and

[32] Fellner (1961, pp.678–679), original emphasis.
[33] "If I pick [bet b_1], I would be completely out of luck if there were no red balls in the urn." (p. 333). See also the discussion of Roberts (1963) and Ellsberg (1963) on Roberts' notion of "vagueness" in decision making and its implications for Ellsberg-type choice situations.
[34] "To test the predictive effectiveness of the axioms … controlled experimentation is in order." (1961, p.655, n.6).
[35] See footnote 2.

Maffioletti and Santori (2005) have examined the ambiguity preferences of business owners, trade union leaders, actuaries, managers and executives, with the same overall findings.

In their own series of experiments, MacCrimmon and Larsson (1979) recognized that the interesting parameter in Ellsberg's examples was not the winning prize level, but rather, the amount of objective versus subjective uncertainty, which in the Three-Outcome Urn is given by the (known) proportion of red balls in the urn. MacCrimmon and Larsson's sequence of experiments accordingly set out to examine how subjects' choices depended on this proportion. In the standard specification of the Three-Color Urn, the proportion of red balls is $1/3$ (30 out of 90). Of course, if the proportion of red balls were actually zero, all subjects would prefer option a_2 in the first pair and a_4 in the second pair, which is consistent with the Sure-Thing Principle, and if this proportion were unity, all would now prefer a_1 in the first pair and a_3 in the second (also consistent with the Sure-Thing Principle). As the proportion increased from zero toward unity, the percentage of a_1 choices and a_3 choices should both rise, and under the hypothesis of ambiguity aversion, there would be some intermediate interval of probabilities within which a subject's choice would have flipped from a_2 to a_1, but not yet flipped from a_4 to a_3, yielding the classic Ellsberg-type violation of the Sure-Thing Principle for this urn. Using 100-ball urns, MacCrimmon and Larsson were able to present subjects with urns whose red-ball proportions took the values 0.20, 0.25, 0.30, 0.33, 0.34, 0.40, and 0.50. They indeed found such an intermediate interval of probabilities, and perhaps not surprisingly, the percentage of such violations was the greatest at $p = .33$.

Although each of Ellsberg's own examples pits a purely objective urn against an ambiguous urn with a fixed probability range,[36] researchers have also explored attitudes toward changes in the size of this range (holding the center constant). Becker and Brownson (1964), Larson (1980) and Viscusi and Magat (1992) did find an aversion to increases in the size of the range; Curley and Yates (1985) and Yates and Zukowski (1976) did not. In a reversal of Ellsberg's original specification of a fixed prize and ambiguous probability, Eliaz and Ortolevaz (2011) also found ambiguity aversion in the case of a fixed objective probability but an ambiguous prize level.[37] Du and Budescu (2005) found that subjects were willing to pay more to reduce the range ("vagueness") of outcome uncertainty than probability uncertainty.[38]

While the phenomena of Reduction of Compound Lotteries and ambiguity neutrality are distinct properties, many researchers consider them to be closely related, and some of the rationality arguments against ambiguity aversion (such as Raiffa's (1961)) explicitly or implicitly invoke the reduction principle. In an experimental examination

---

[36] In the Three-Color Paradox the unknown probability of a black ball ranges from 0 to 2/3; in the Two-Urn Paradox it ranges from 0 to 1; in the Four-Color Paradox it ranges from 0 to 1/2.

[37] See these authors' further results in the case of joint outcome/probability ambiguity.

[38] Outcome and probability ranges were each classified into "low," "medium," or "high" levels of vagueness.

of this, Halevy (2007) appended two urns to the original two-color urns: one urn where the proportion of black balls satisfied a uniform objective distribution, and one urn which was either all black, or all red, with objective 50:50 probabilities. The two urns, together with Ellsberg's Urn I, are all purely objective, and each reduces to a 50:50 objective lottery over the best:worst monetary prize.[39] However, in Halevy's second urn all uncertainty is resolved in the first stage, whereas in Ellsberg's urn I all uncertainty is resolved in the second stage (Halevy's first urn involves both first stage and second stage uncertainty). Using this framework, Halevy found that subjects who satisfied the Reduction of Compound Lotteries Axiom under objective uncertainty were typically ambiguity neutral. Ozdenoren and Peck (2008) also took a dynamic approach, framing a two-stage Ellsberg urn problem as a "game against nature" and exploring various implications for ambiguity aversion and dynamic consistency.

Another systematic feature of attitudes toward ambiguity—reported in Ellsberg (1962, 2001) but not in Ellsberg (1961)—emerges from what he termed his *n-Color Example*.[40] Each of two urns contains 100 balls, from among 10 different colors. Urn I contains exactly 10 balls of each color, whereas Urn II contains the colors (and perhaps not all of them) in unknown quantities. Ellsberg naturally conjectured that most would prefer bet d_1 over d_3, preferring d_1's fixed 10% chance of getting \$0 to d_3's unknown chance, which might be much higher. But he also felt that "a significant number" would *disprefer* bet d_2 to d_4, dispreferring d_2's fixed (but mere) 10% chance of winning \$100 to d_4's unknown chance, which might also be much higher. As with the Two-Urn Paradox, the ranking $d_1 \succ d_3$ violates the hypothesis of probabilistic beliefs in the direction of ambiguity aversion.[41] But by a similar argument, the ranking $d_2 \prec d_4$ violates probabilistic beliefs in the direction of *ambiguity preference*. In the language of Viscusi and Chesson (1999), the ambiguity in d_4's small chance of winning the \$100 payoff allows for "hopes" that it might be much higher, whereas the ambiguity in d_3's small chance of getting \$0 makes for "fears" that *it* might be much higher. A similar phenomenon occurs in bets involving losses: Kahn and Sarin (1988) found that subjects tended to be averse ("fearful") toward ambiguity in small chances of having to suffer a given loss, but prefer (be "hopeful" toward) ambiguity in small chances of not having to suffer it.[42] Similar results were also obtained by Becker and Brownson (1964), Yates and Zukowski (1976), Curley and Yates (1985, 1989), Einhorn and Hogarth (1986), and Hogarth and Einhorn (1990). Cohen et al. (1985, 1987), however, found no correlation between subjects' *overall* levels of ambiguity aversion toward gains versus ambiguity aversion toward losses.

---

[39] Halevy used the prizes \$2:\$0 and \$20:\$0 for both his own and those of Ellsberg's urns used in his experiments.

[40] Ellsberg (1962, pp. 268–281; 2001, pp. 199–209). In his discussion, Ellsberg chooses $n = 10$, but feels that the effect would be more pronounced for $n = 100$.

[41] $d_1 \succ d_3$ would imply prob(red in Urn II) > 1/10, which under the natural conjecture that prob(red in Urn II) = ... = prob(mauve in Urn II), would imply prob(red in Urn II) + ... + prob(mauve in Urn II) > 1. Similarly for $d_2 \prec d_4$.

[42] Viscusi and Chesson (1999) found that for a potential loss, the threshold probability "at which ambiguity shifts from being a negatively valued fear to a positively valued hope" was about 1/2.

n-COLOR ELLSBERG PARADOX

URN I

	10 balls red	10 balls yellow	10 balls black	10 balls green	10 balls blue	10 balls purple	10 balls white	10 balls grey	10 balls orange	10 balls mauve
d_1	$0	$100	$100	$100	$100	$100	$100	$100	$100	$100
d_2	$100	$0	$0	$0	$0	$0	$0	$0	$0	$0

URN II

100 balls

	red	yellow	black	green	blue	purple	white	grey	orange	mauve
d_3	$0	$100	$100	$100	$100	$100	$100	$100	$100	$100
d_4	$100	$0	$0	$0	$0	$0	$0	$0	$0	$0

13.4.2.1 Forms of Preference Elicitation

One methodological issue, present throughout experimental work on choice and decision making, concerns exactly how preferences over Ellsberg-type prospects "should" be elicited. Ellsberg's original presentations, and the great preponderance of subsequent experiments, simply presented subjects with pairs of alternatives, and asked for a direct choice within each pair. But standard consumer theory posits that the same ranking would be revealed if a subject's preferences were instead assessed via an independent monetary valuation of each prospect,[43] with the valuations then compared. Fox and Tversky (1995), Chow and Sarin (2001) and Du and Budescu (2005) found that ambiguity aversion was reduced substantially (though not completely) when subjects were asked for separate monetary evaluations of ambiguous and unambiguous prospects (via their willingness to pay or willingness to accept) rather than asked for direct comparisons.

In another alternative to simple pairwise choice, MacCrimmon and Larsson (1979) presented subjects with sets of 11 prospects each, and asked them for a complete ranking of all prospects within each set (indifference was allowed). By including bets on stock index prices along with classic Ellsberg urns in their menus, these researchers were able to explore another question related to ambiguity, namely how subjects treated ambiguity in unknown urns with ambiguity outside of the laboratory.[44] MacCrimmon and Larsson found no net effect in either direction.

---

[43] Such as the procedure of Becker et al. (1964).

[44] Selten has suggested that many subjects may feel they can make "a very good estimate" of stock market events, and suggests investment in developing counties as better for such experiments (MacCrimmon (1968, p.28)).

13.4.2.2 Experimental Studies of Insurance and Medical Decisions Under Ambiguity

Other experimenters have also elicited subjects' ambiguity preferences in choices more relevant and realistic than simply drawing balls from urns. An obvious domain is that of insurance. Experiments on insurance decisions under ambiguity typically place subjects in the role of either consumers or suppliers of contracts such as flood or earthquake insurance, product warranties, etc. Although subjects are typically students, experiments and surveys by Einhorn and Hogarth (1986), Hogarth and Kunreuther (1992), Kunreuther (1989) and others have also found ambiguity aversion in hypothetical decisions by both professional actuaries and experienced insurance underwriters. Kunreuther et al. (1995) found ambiguity aversion in a field survey of primary-insurance underwriters in commercial property and casualty insurance companies. In experiments which included professional actuaries, and where subjects were asked to price insurance both as consumers and firms, Hogarth and Kunreuther (1989) found results which paralleled those of Kahn and Sarin (1988), Viscusi and Chesson (1999) and others as reported above, namely that both consumers and firms revealed ambiguity aversion toward low likelihood losses, which decreased as the likelihood of the loss increased. In an experiment involving real losses, Koch and Shunk (2013) found that ambiguity aversion was higher under unlimited liability than limited liability. Market and policy implication of ambiguity aversion are examined in Hogarth (1989), Camerer and Kunreuther (1989a,b), Hogarth and Kunreuther (1985) and Kunreuther and Hogarth (1992). Baillon et al. (2012) explore how different ambiguity attitudes play out in group belief aggregation.

Medical decisions by both patients and doctors, which also inherently involve ambiguity, have also been proposed to experimental subjects. Such experiments include decisions regarding vaccination of children (Ritov and Baron (1990)), heart disease (Curley et al. (1989)), residential location based on health risks (Viscusi et al. (1991), Viscusi and Magat (1992)) and others (e.g., Curley et al. (1984)). Gerrity et al. (1990) developed a multivariate measure of physicians' reactions to uncertainty, and used the results of an extensive survey to develop two "reliable and readily interpretable subscales" which they term "stress from uncertainty" and "reluctance to disclose uncertainty to others."

13.4.2.3 Additional Experiments on Ambiguity and Ambiguity Aversion

In other experiments involving real-world scenarios, Hogarth (1989) and Willham and Christensen-Szalanski (1993) gave subjects actual medical liability cases and manipulated ambiguity about the probability of winning in a legal scenario where hypothetical plaintiffs and defendants had to decide whether to go to court or settle out of court. In direct comparisons across contexts, Kahn and Sarin (1988) found that consumers' ambiguity attitudes differed across choices involving radio warranties, pharmaceutical decisions and restaurant food quality. Maffioletti and Santori (2005) examined subjects' attitudes toward bets on real-world election results, and Baillon and Bleichrodt (2011) used bets on the temperature and on stock index prices. And while initially solely the realm of economists and psychologists, experimental work on decisions under ambiguity has now extended to the realm of neurology.[45]

Ambiguity aversion has been and continues to be one of the most intensively experimentally explored phenomena in decision theory. Further discussion of this literature is provided in the surveys listed in Section 13.8.

13.5 MODELS AND DEFINITIONS OF AMBIGUITY AVERSION

Unlike the economic concepts of "risk" and "risk aversion,"[46] there is not unanimous agreement on what "ambiguity aversion," or even "ambiguity" itself, exactly is. However several models and definitions have been proposed.

Most (though not all) of these models take as their starting point the following formalization of the objective/subjective uncertainty framework of Sections 13.3.1 and 13.3.4. Preferences are defined over the domain of horse-roulette acts—henceforth called *acts*—namely maps $f = (\ldots;\mathbf{P}_j \text{ if } E_j;\ldots) = (\ldots;(\ldots;x_{ij},p_{ij};\ldots),E_j;\ldots)$ from a (finite or infinite) state space $\mathcal{S}$ to roulette lotteries $\mathbf{P}_j$ over a set of prizes $\mathcal{X}$. The Independence property over this richer domain is identical to the Independence Axiom of objective expected utility, except for the more general notion of probability mixing it entails. Probability mixtures of horse-roulette acts are defined statewise: given acts $f = (\ldots;\mathbf{P}_j \text{ if } E_j;\ldots)$ and $g = (\ldots;\mathbf{Q}_j \text{ if } E_j;\ldots)$ over a common[47] partition $\{E_1,\ldots,E_n\}$ of the state space $\mathcal{S}$, and probability $\alpha \in [0,1]$, the mixture $\alpha \cdot f + (1-\alpha) \cdot g$ is defined as the act

$$\alpha \cdot f + (1 - \alpha) \cdot g = (\ldots; \alpha \cdot \mathbf{P}_j + (1 - \alpha) \cdot \mathbf{Q}_j; \ldots)$$

The axioms that characterize subjective expected utility in this framework are accordingly[48]

Weak Order: $\succeq$ is complete and transitive.

Non-Degeneracy: There exist acts f and g for which $f \succ g$.

Continuity: For all acts f, g, h, if $f \succ g$ and $g \succ h$, there exist $\alpha, \beta \in (0,1)$ such that $\alpha \cdot f + (1-\alpha) \cdot h \succ g$ and $g \succ \beta \cdot f + (1-\beta) \cdot h$.

Independence: For all acts f, g, h and all $\alpha \in (0,1]$, $f \succeq g$ if and only if $\alpha \cdot f + (1-\alpha) \cdot h \succeq \alpha \cdot g + (1-\alpha) \cdot h$.

---

[45] See Hsu et al. (2005), Chew et al. (2008), Huettel et al. (2006), as well as the survey of Weber and Johnson (2008).

[46] E.g., Rothschild and Stiglitz (1970), Pratt (1964).

[47] As before, $\{E_1,\ldots,E_n\}$ could be any common refinement of the two acts' original partitions.

[48] These versions of the expected utility axioms, due to Fishburn (1970), are referred to in the literature as the *Anscombe-Aumann axioms*. See also Schmeidler (1989).

Monotonicity: For all acts f, g, if the roulette lottery $f(s)$ is weakly preferred to the roulette lottery $g(s)$ for every state s, then $f \succeq g$.

The expected utility representation of preferences over horse-roulette acts $f = (\ldots;\mathbf{P}_j$ if $E_j; \ldots) = (\ldots;(\ldots;x_{ij},p_{ij}; \ldots),E_j; \ldots)$ implied by these axioms takes the form

$$W(f) = \int_{\mathscr{S}} U(f(s))d\mu(s) = \sum_{j=1}^{n} U(\mathbf{P}_j) \cdot \mu(E_j) = \sum_{j=1}^{n} \left[\sum_i U(x_{ij})p_{ij} \right] \cdot \mu(E_j)$$

where $U(\cdot)$ is a von Neumann-Morgenstern utility function and μ is a finitely additive probability measure ("*prior*"), which is uniquely identified as in Savage's axiomatization. As seen in the above equation, the term $U(f(s))$ in the integral $\int_{S} U(f(s))d\mu(s)$ is the *expected* utility of the roulette lottery $f(s)$. This is also the case for many of the models that we consider in this section, and that are axiomatized in the horse-roulette framework.

The above Independence axiom[49] turns out to imply the Sure-Thing Principle,[50] which implies that any Ellsberg-type violation of the Sure-Thing Principle is also a violation of Independence. It follows that any model of ambiguity aversion in the horse-roulette act framework must relax Independence.

Versions of the above axioms can also be stated in a setting closer to that of Savage, where acts are purely subjective horse lotteries. This requires that the set of prizes be suitably rich (for instance, an interval of the real line), with a suitable notion of "subjective mixture" on prizes. Nakamura (1990), Gul (1992) and Wakker (1989) take this approach, and Ghirardato et al. (2003) introduce a general notion of subjective mixture of prizes which allows a direct translation of the above axioms, and many of their relaxations are discussed in this section.

13.5.1 Maxmin Expected Utility / Expected Utility with Multiple-Priors

Gilboa and Schmeidler (1989, p.142) suggest the following explanation of the modal behavior in the Ellsberg Paradox:

"One conceivable explanation of this phenomenon which we adopt here is as follows: [...] the subject has too little information to form a prior. Hence (s)he considers a set of priors as possible. Being uncertainty averse, (s)he takes into account the minimal expected utility (over all priors in the set) while evaluating a bet." (original emphasis)

---

[49] We distinguish between the two identically named conditions by the capitalization "Independence Axiom" for the Marschak/Samuelson axiom of Section 13.3.2 and "Independence axiom" for the current Independence property.

[50] Defining event mixtures as in Section 13.3.1, suppose $(f^*, E; f', \sim E) \succeq (f, E; f', \sim E)$. By Independence, $1/2 \cdot (f^*, E; f', \sim E) + 1/2 \cdot (f^*, E; f'', \sim E) \succeq 1/2 \cdot (f, E; f', \sim E) + 1/2 \cdot (f^*, E; f'', \sim E)$, which can be equivalently written as $\cdot 1/2 \cdot (f^*, E; f'', \sim E) + 1/2 \cdot (f^*, E; f', \sim E) \succeq 1/2 \cdot (f, E; f'', \sim E) + 1/2 \cdot (f^*, E; f', \sim E)$. Invoking Independence once again yields $(f^*, E; f'', \sim E) \succeq (f, E; f'', \sim E)$.

The resulting model is called *Maxmin Expected Utility* (*MEU*) or sometimes the *Multiple-Priors* (*MP*) model.[51] Formally, consider a closed,[52] convex set $\mathcal{C}$ of probability measures—priors—on the state space $\mathcal{S}$, and a von Neumann-Morgenstern utility function $U(\cdot)$. An act $f(\cdot)$ is evaluated according to

$$W(f(\cdot)) = \min_{\mu \in \mathcal{C}} \int U(f(\cdot))d\mu. \tag{13.1}$$

To see how this model allows for the typical preferences in Ellsberg's examples, consider the Three-Color Paradox of Section 13.1 (the analysis of the Two-Urn Paradox is similar). Let the state space be $\mathcal{S} = \{s_r, s_b, s_y\}$, where s_r denotes the draw of a red ball, etc., let the set of prizes be $\mathcal{X} = \{\$0, \$100\}$, and set $U(\$100) = 1$ and $U(\$0) = 0$. To reflect the assumption that 30 out of the 90 balls in the urn are red, but that the number of black and yellow balls is not known, consider the set of priors[53]

$$\mathcal{C} = \{\mu \in \Delta(\mathcal{S}) : \mu(s_r)\} = 1/3. \tag{13.2}$$

Under this set of priors, the four acts in the Three-Color Paradox are evaluated as

$$W(a_1) = 1/3 \qquad W(a_2) = 0 \qquad W(a_3) = 1/3 \qquad W(a_4) = 2/3$$

which implies the Ellsberg rankings $a_1 \succ a_2$ and $a_3 \prec a_4$.[54] To derive these values, observe that every prior $\mu \in \mathcal{C}$ assigns probability $1/3$ to the state s_r, so that $W(a_1) = 1/3$. Similarly, every prior $\mu \in \mathcal{C}$ assigns probability $2/3$ to the event $\{s_b, s_y\}$, so that $W(a_4) = 2/3$. Act a_2 yields \$100 on state s_b and \$0 otherwise; in other words, it is a bet on black. The prior in $\mathcal{C}$ that assigns zero probability to s_b is the one that minimizes expected utility, and will accordingly be the one selected by the *MEU* criterion, so that $W(a_2) = 0$. In other words, the individual evaluates a bet on black as if *none* of the 60 unknown balls in the urn were black. Act a_3 yields \$100 on the event $\{s_r, s_y\}$ and zero otherwise; in other words, it is a bet *against* black. This time, the prior in $\mathcal{C}$ that assigns unit probability to s_b (thus zero probability to s_y) is the one that minimizes expected utility and hence is the one selected, so that $W(a_3) = 1/3$. That is, the individual evaluates a bet *against* black as if *all* of the 60 unknown balls were black. This is a (stark) example of the "worst-case scenario" thinking embodied in equation (13.1). While the set $\mathcal{C}$ used here is extreme, it is not the only one that generates the standard Ellsberg preferences: any set of priors where the probability

---

[51] The expression "multiple-priors" is potentially ambiguous, because there are several well-known models which also employ sets of priors (for instance, the Variational and Smooth Ambiguity Preferences models).

[52] If the state space is finite, the set $\mathcal{C}$ is closed in the usual Euclidean topology. If it is infinite, it is closed in the weak* topology.

[53] $\Delta(\cdot)$ denotes the family of probability measures over a set. When no confusion can arise, to simplify notation, we write $\mu(\{s_r\}), \mu(\{s_r, s_b\}), \nu(\{s_r\}), \ldots$ as $\mu(s_r), \mu(s_r, s_b), \nu(s_r), \ldots$ for measures (and later capacities) over singletons or finite sets.

[54] Note this also implies that a_3 is considered no better than a_1, in spite of the fact that it yield a higher payoff on s_y.

of s_r is constant at $1/3$ and the probability of s_b ranges from less than $1/3$ to greater than $1/3$ will yield the above rankings.

As a historical note, Ellsberg himself proposed a decision criterion that is effectively a special case of *MEU*. He proposes that, by careful deliberation, an individual faced with an ambiguous situation may nevertheless "arrive at a composite 'estimated' distribution μ_0 that represents all his available information on relative likelihoods"; however, due to ambiguity, "[o]ut of the set $\Delta(\mathcal{S})$ of possible distributions there remains a set $\mathcal{D}$ of distributions that still seem 'reasonable,' reflecting judgments that he 'might almost as well' have made, or that his information... does not permit him confidently to rule out."[55] He then suggested (p.664) that individuals may evaluate acts according to the criterion

$$W\left(f(\cdot)\right) = \rho \cdot \int U\left(f(\cdot)\right) d\mu_0 + (1-\rho) \cdot \min_{\mu \in \mathcal{D}} \int U\left(f(\cdot)\right) d\mu$$

where $\rho \in (0,1)$ represents the individual's "degree of confidence" in the estimate μ_0 and $\mathcal{C} = \rho \cdot \mu_0 + (1-\rho) \cdot \mathcal{D}$ is seen to be the set of priors. Kopylov (2006) analyzes this model when the set $\mathcal{D}$ equals the set $\Delta(\mathcal{S})$ of all possible probability distributions—a specification which also appears in the literature on robust Bayesian analysis.

Gilboa and Schmeidler (1989) axiomatize the *MEU* decision criterion via axioms on horse-roulette acts. They retain the Weak Order, Monotonicity, Continuity and Non-Degeneracy axioms stated above, but weaken Independence, replacing it with

Certainty Independence: For all acts f,g, all constant acts x, and all $\alpha \in (0,1]$: $f \succcurlyeq g$ if and only if $\alpha \cdot f + (1-\alpha) \cdot x \succcurlyeq \alpha \cdot g + (1-\alpha) \cdot x$.

Uncertainty Aversion: For all acts f,g and all $\alpha \in (0,1]$: $f \succcurlyeq g$ implies $\alpha \cdot f + (1-\alpha) \cdot g \succcurlyeq g$.

That Independence must be relaxed follows from the fact that, as noted above, Independence implies Savage's Postulate P2, and hence must be violated by Ellsberg-type preferences. The key question is to what extent Independence should be weakened. To gain some intuition, it is useful to add to the four acts $a_1,...,a_4$ of the Three-Color Paradox a fifth act a_5 representing a bet on yellow: specifically, a_5 yields $100 if a yellow ball is drawn and $0 otherwise. An individual with *MEU* preferences characterized by the set $\mathcal{C}$ in equation (13.2) will be indifferent between betting on black or on yellow, that is, $a_2 \sim a_5$. However the mixture $1/2 \cdot a_2 + 1/2 \cdot a_5$ is strictly preferred to a_2, which would not be possible with *EU* preferences. How should this be interpreted, and what is its relationship to ambiguity?

Act a_2 will yield $100 if the ambiguous color black is drawn and $0 if the ambiguous color yellow is drawn. Act a_5 instead yields $100 if yellow and $0 if black. Thus, whether

---

[55] Ellsberg (1961, p.661); notation in this paragraph adapted to the present chapter.

or not the better prize \$100 is obtained—if it is obtained at all—hinges crucially on which of the two ambiguous colors is drawn. (Both acts yield \$0 under the unambiguous color red.) By way of contrast, a 50:50 mixture of the two acts provides *hedging*: it removes the dependence of the prize on which of the two ambiguous colors is drawn. Specifically, the mixture $1/2 \cdot a_2 + 1/2 \cdot a_5$ yields the same objective roulette lottery (\$100,1/2;\$0,1/2) for *both* of the ambiguous colors yellow and black. The Uncertainty Aversion Axiom thus reflects a *preference for hedging*.[56] Mathematically, Uncertainty Aversion corresponds to *quasiconcavity* of the functional representation of preferences—an analytically convenient property.

On the other hand, mixing an act with a constant act (a constant prize or a constant objective lottery) does not provide such hedging, and there is less of an argument that such mixtures should necessarily be preferred (or dispreferred) by an ambiguity averter. The Certainty Independence Axiom accordingly requires that mixtures with *constant* acts do *not* affect preferences. While *MEU* preferences do satisfy Certainty Independence, there are reasons to relax or drop this axiom: see Sections 13.5.6–13.5.9.

Gilboa and Schmeidler (1989) show that the above axioms are necessary and sufficient for the existence of the *MEU* representation (13.1), with affine utility function $U(\cdot)$ and convex set of priors C which is "identified up to convex closure"—that is, any other set of priors which represents preferences will have C as its convex closure (the closure of its convex hull).

A generalization of the *MEU* model is the so-called α-maxmin, or α-*MEU* model

$$W\left(f(\cdot)\right) \equiv \alpha \cdot \min_{\mu \in C} \int U\left(f(\cdot)\right) d\mu + (1 - \alpha) \cdot \max_{\mu \in C} \int U\left(f(\cdot)\right) d\mu. \quad (13.3)$$

For $\alpha = 1$, this representation reduces to *MEU*, and for $\alpha = 0$ it reduces to what is termed max*max* expected utility $\max \int_C U(f(s)) d\mu$ and it allows for a whole range of intermediate attitudes toward ambiguity. Unfortunately, a general, behavioral characterization of this class of preferences is not available.[57] Furthermore, the intuitive interpretation of α as an ambiguity-aversion parameter is not warranted in general: Siniscalchi (2006) demonstrates that an α-*MEU* decision maker with $\alpha = 2/3$ and set of priors specified in (13.2) will have preferences in the Three-Color problem that are indistinguishable from one with $\alpha = 1$ (i.e., *MEU*) and set of priors $\{\mu \in \Delta(S) : \mu(s_r) = 1/3, \mu(s_b) \geq 2/9\}$. The elements α and C of the representation are not separately identified.

---

[56] The condition "$f \succcurlyeq g$ implies $f \succcurlyeq \alpha \cdot f + (1-\alpha) \cdot g$," known as the *Uncertainty Loving* condition, captures the opposite intuition, and corresponds to the max*max* preference function defined below.

[57] Ghirardato et al. (2004) provide an axiomatization, but it turns out (Eichberger et al. (2011)) that their axioms can only hold for the cases $\alpha = 1$ and $\alpha = 0$. (Klibanoff et al. (2011)) provide a non-degenerate axiomatization of α-*MEU* when the state space describes the realizations of an exchangeable sequence of experiments.

Lehrer (2012) axiomatizes a special class of *MEU* preferences in which the set C is generated by a partially specified probability. Axiomatizations of *MEU* which do not rely on horse-roulette acts, but require a rich outcome space, have been provided by Casadesus-Masanell et al. (2000a,b) and Ghirardato et al. (2003).

13.5.2 Choquet Expected Utility/Rank-Dependent Expected Utility

Another important model of ambiguity aversion, proposed by Schmeidler (1989), is the *Rank-Dependent* or *Choquet* model. Rather than capturing the individual's perception of ambiguity by means of a family of priors as in the *MEU* model, it does so by means of a single *non-additive* probability measure ("*capacity*") $v(\cdot)$. For example, in the Three-Color problem, the individual may have the beliefs

$$v(s_r) = 1/3, \quad v(s_b, s_y) = 2/3, \quad v(s_b) = v(s_y) = \varepsilon \tag{13.4}$$

for some $\varepsilon \in [0, 1/3]$. The fact that $v(s_b, s_y) > v(s_b) + v(s_y)$ indicates that there is ambiguity about the relative likelihood of a black vs. yellow draw: there is a residual probability mass equal to $v(s_b, s_y) - v(s_b) + v(s_y)$ that the individual, so to speak, does not know how to allocate between s_b and s_y. On the other hand, $v(s_b s_y) + v(s_r) = 1 = v(\mathcal{S})$, which indicates that there is no ambiguity about the probability of drawing a red vs. a non-red ball. A nonadditive probability measure can encode both the individual's assessment of relative likelihoods and the confidence attached to such assessment in a single function. Formally, a capacity is defined as a nonnegative real function $v(\cdot)$ defined over an algebra or σ-algebra of subsets of the state space $\mathcal{S}$ that satisfies the normalization $v(\phi) = 0$ and $v(\mathcal{S}) = 1$, and the monotonicity property that $E \subseteq F$ implies $v(E) \leq v(F)$ (a standard probability measure is a capacity since additivity implies monotonicity). Capacities need not be additive, but they still retain the property that the weight assigned to a set is not smaller than the weight assigned to any subset.

Note that given this departure from additivity, specifying the capacity of the individual states in a finite state space does *not* fully characterize the capacity. For example, equations (13.4) do not pin down a unique capacity, because they leave $v(s_r, s_b)$ and $v(s_r, s_y)$ unspecified.

A key issue is how to compute the integral/expected value of a function with respect to a capacity. Consider a finitely-ranged function $g : \mathcal{S} \to \mathbb{R}$ that takes values $\alpha_1, \ldots, \alpha_n$. The problem is that what might seem like the natural definition, namely

$$\int g(s) dv(s) = \sum_i \alpha_i \cdot v\left(\{s : g(s) = \alpha_i\}\right)$$

can lead to failures of monotonicity, even in simple cases.[58]

---

[58] For any capacity with $v(s_r) = v(s_b) = v(s_y) = 1/2$ and $v(s_r, s_b, s_y) = 1$, the act $\{7$ if $s_r; 8$ if $s_b; 9$ if $s_y\}$ will be assigned the value $(1/2) \cdot 7 + (1/2) \cdot 8 + (1/2) \cdot 9 = 12$, which exceeds the value of 10 assigned to the dominating act $\{10$ if $s_r; 10$ if $s_b; 10$ if $s_y\}$. A similar candidate, namely the formula $\Sigma_s g(s) \cdot v(s)$, is subject to the same difficulties.

To resolve this problem, Schmeidler (1986,1989) proposes the use of the *Choquet Integral*. Given a function $g : \mathcal{S} \rightarrow \mathbb{R}$ which takes values $\alpha_1 \geq \ldots \geq \alpha_n$, the Choquet integral of g with respect to a capacity v is defined as

$$\int g(s)dv \equiv \alpha_1 \cdot v(\{s:g(s)=\alpha_1\}) + \Sigma_{i=2}^{n}\alpha_i \cdot \left[v(\{s : g(s) \geq \alpha_i\}) - v(\{s : g(s) \geq \alpha_{i-1}\})\right].$$

(13.5)

The telescoping property of the respective weights

$$v(\{s : g(s) = \alpha_1\}), \ldots, \left[v\left(\{s : g(s) \geq \alpha_i\}\right) - v\left(\{s : g(s) \geq \alpha_{i-1}\}\right)\right], \ldots,$$
$$\left[1 - v\left(\{s : g(s) \geq \alpha_{n-1}\}\right)\right]$$

in this formula ensures that they sum to one, avoiding the difficulties noted in footnote 58. If the capacity v is additive, and hence a probability measure, equation (13.5) reduces to the standard integral of g with respect to v. For a general, bounded measurable function g, the Choquet integral is defined as

$$\int g \, dv = \int_{-\infty}^{0} \left[v\left(\{s : g(s) \geq \alpha\}\right) - 1\right]d\alpha + \int_{0}^{\infty} v\left(\{s : g(s) \geq \alpha\}\right)d\alpha$$

where the integrals on the right side are in the sense of Riemann.

The *Choquet Expected Utility* (or *CEU*) representation of preferences over acts f is thus

$$W(f(\cdot)) \equiv \int U(f(\cdot))dv$$

(13.6)

where $U(\cdot)$ is a von Neumann-Morgenstern utility, $v(\cdot)$ is a capacity, and the integral is in the sense of Choquet. This representation is sometimes also called *Rank-Dependent Expected Utility*, with reference to the analogous model of preferences under objective uncertainty.[59]

To see that the *CEU* model can accommodate Ellsberg in the Three-Color example, consider the capacity v defined by

$$v(s_r) = 1/3 \quad v(s_b, s_y) = 2/3 \quad v(s_b) = v(s_y) = 1/6 \quad v(s_r, s_b) = v(s_r, s_y) = 1/2$$

and set $U(\$100) = 1$ and $U(\$0) = 0$. Applying equation (13.5) yields $V(a_1) = 1/3$, $V(a_2) = 1/6$, $V(a_3) = 1/2$ and $V(a_4) = 2/3$, giving the Ellsberg rankings $a_1 \succ a_2$ and $a_3 \prec a_4$.

[59] E.g. Quiggin (1982), Yaari (1987), Segal (1987b). See also Section 13.5.3 below.

CEU preferences capture ambiguity aversion (or preference) by allowing the individual to exhibit a preference (or aversion) for *hedging*. Observe that a 50:50 probability mixture of the ambiguous acts b_1 and b_3 in the Two-Color problem yields the completely objective (and to an ambiguity averter, strictly preferred) lottery (\$100;1/2;\$0,1/2). This occurs, of course, because b_1 yields its best prize \$100 for a red draw, whereas b_3 yields its best prize for a black draw—the two acts are, in a sense, "negatively correlated," so that mixing them in this way reduces the variability of outcomes (or more generally, utility) across states. Given a pair of multiple-state acts $f = [x_1 \text{ if } s_1;\ldots;x_n \text{ if } s_n]$ and $g = [y_1 \text{ if } s_1;\ldots;y_n \text{ if } s_n]$, this effect will occur, in part, for any a pair of states s_i, s_j for which $x_i > x_j$ and $y_i < y_j$. When two acts are *comonotonic*, that is, when $x_i \geq x_j \Leftrightarrow y_i \geq y_j$ for all i, j, probability mixing cannot lead to any hedging.

The Choquet model captures ambiguity aversion/preference by weakening the Sure-Thing Principle just enough to allow such a preference/aversion for hedging— that is, preferences are allowed to violate the key mixture property of the axiom so long as, but *only* so long as, there is actually some potential for hedging. Whenever there is *no* such potential, that is, whenever the acts being mixed are comonotonic, the mixture property must continue to hold:

Comonotonic Independence: For every triple of pairwise comonotonic acts f, g, h, and every $\alpha \in (0,1]$: $f \succeq g$ if and only if $\alpha \cdot f + (1-\alpha) \cdot h \succeq \alpha \cdot g + (1-\alpha) \cdot h$.

Schmeidler (1986) shows that a function defined on simple (or bounded) measurable functions is monotonic, as well as both monotonic and additive with respect to comonotonic functions, if and only if it is a Choquet integral. Building on this, Schmeidler (1989) shows that *CEU* preferences are characterized by Weak Order, Continuity, Monotonicity, Non-Degeneracy, and the Comonotonic Independence Axiom. The uniqueness properties of *CEU* are the same as those for *SEU*: the capacity v is unique, and utility is unique up to a positive affine transformation.

As noted, *CEU* preferences needn't be uncertainty-averse. Schmeidler (1989) demonstrates that a *CEU* preference function will satisfy the Uncertainty Aversion Axiom of Section 13.5.1 if and only if its capacity v is *convex*: that is, if for every pair of events E, F, $v(E \cup F) + v(E \cap F) \geq v(E) + v(F)$. Uncertainty-averse *CEU* preferences are thus also a (strict) special case of *MEU* preferences, where the set $\mathcal{C}$ of priors coincides with the *core* of the capacity v:

$$\mathcal{C} = core(v) = \{\mu \in \Delta(\mathcal{S}) : \forall E, \mu(E) \geq v(E)\}.$$

Gilboa (1987) and Sarin and Wakker (1992) provide axiomatizations of *CEU* in the original Savage framework. Nakamura (1990) provides another, in a setting where the state space can be finite, provided the set of prizes is suitably rich. Another axiomatization of *CEU* in a fully subjective setting with rich outcomes can be found in Ghirardato et al. (2003). The most complete exposition of the rank-dependent model is that of

Wakker (2010). Lehrer (2009) proposes an integral for capacities that coincides with the Choquet integral if the capacity is convex, but is different in general.

13.5.3 Segal's Recursive Model

The *Recursive Model* of Segal (1987a) is the earliest of a group of models which can be described as "two-stage." Ambiguity is modeled by assuming that the probability distribution μ over the state space $\mathcal{S}$ is not known, but random with probability measure M over $\Delta(\mathcal{S})$. In the first stage, one particular probability measure $\mu \in \Delta(\mathcal{S})$ is realized. In the second stage, the state s is drawn according to the distribution μ. The first stage may be only an idealization, a fictitious construct that is helpful to describe a particular way to evaluate acts; the second stage is real. Here we assume that all measures have finite-support.

Under this model, an individual treats a basic act $(\ldots;x_j \text{ if } E_j;\ldots)$ as the two-stage prospect $(\ldots;(\ldots;x_j,E_j; \ldots),\mu_k; \ldots)$, where μ_k, the probability distribution (prior) over states, is the realization of the first-stage uncertainty, and E_j, the realized event under distribution μ_k, is the realization of second stage uncertainty.[60] Each such act has a corresponding two-stage objective lottery of the form $(\ldots;(\ldots;x_j,\mu^{-1}(x_j); \ldots),M(\mu_k); \ldots)$. The key question is how to evaluate such two-stage acts and lotteries.

An individual who applies the Reduction of Compound Lotteries (*ROCL*) axiom of Section 13.3.1 to collapse this two-stage objective lottery to a single-stage one cannot exhibit Ellsberg-type preferences: such an individual will be probabilistically sophisticated, with statewise subjective probabilities $\sum_k \mu_k(s_i) \cdot M(\mu_k)$. Segal, however, argues that it is appropriate to drop *ROCL* in such a setting:

> "...if a sufficiently long time passes between the two stages of the lottery, then there is no reason to make this reduction assumption... It is my belief that decision makers consider the Ellsberg urn as a real two-stage lottery, in which the first, imaginary stage and the second, real stage are clearly distinguishable. Therefore, they do not feel themselves obliged to obey the reduction of compound lotteries axiom..." (1987a, p.178)

Segal begins by assuming the individual has a preference function $V(\cdot)$ defined over single-stage lotteries. Given an act $f(\cdot) = (\ldots;x_j,E_j; \ldots)$, each measure μ over $\mathcal{S}$ induces a simple lottery of the form $(\ldots;x_j,\mu(E_j); \ldots)$ and the individual uses $V(\cdot)$ to determine the *certainty equivalent* $CE(f,\mu)$ of this lottery, that is, the value for which

$$V(CE(f, \mu), 1) = V(\ldots; x_j, \mu(E_j); \ldots).$$

The individual's uncertainty over the measure $\mu(\cdot)$, as represented by the measure $M(\cdot)$ over the space $\Delta(\mathcal{S})$, generates the real-valued lottery $(\ldots;CE(f,\mu_k),M(\mu_k); \ldots)$.[61]

---

[60] Since it involves the orthogonal state spaces $\mathcal{S}$ and $\Delta(\mathcal{S})$, the mixture $(\ldots;(\ldots;x_j,E_j; \ldots),\mu_k; \ldots)$ is to be distinguished from a *two-stage subjective act* $(\ldots;f_j(\cdot) \text{ if } E_j; \ldots)$ as defined in Section 13.3.1, which involves subpartitions of $(\ldots;\{\ldots,E_{jk}, \ldots\};\ldots)$ of a common state space $\mathcal{S}$.

[61] For simplicity, we assume that the measure M over $\Delta(\mathcal{S})$ has finite support.

The individual evaluates this lottery again using the function $V(\cdot)$, which yields the preference function

$$W(f(\cdot)) \equiv V(\ldots; CE(f, \mu_k), M(\mu_k); \ldots) \tag{13.7}$$

Together, this implies the chain of indifferences

$$f(\cdot) \sim (\ldots; f(\cdot), \mu_k; \ldots) \sim (\ldots; CE(f(\cdot), \mu_k), \mu_k; \ldots) \sim$$
$$(\ldots; CE(f(\cdot), \mu_k), M(\mu_k); \ldots)$$

or equivalently

$$(\ldots; x_j, E_j; \ldots) \sim (\ldots; (\ldots; x_j, E_j; \ldots), \mu_k; \ldots)$$
$$\sim (\ldots; CE((\ldots; x_j, E_j; \ldots), \mu_k), \mu_k; \ldots)$$
$$\sim (\ldots; CE((\ldots; x_j, E_j; \ldots), \mu_k), M(\mu_k); \ldots)$$

where the first object is the subjective act $f(\cdot)$ from states to payoffs which is being evaluated, the second is the representation of this act as a map from the set of measures $\mu_k \in \Delta(\mathcal{S})$ to subjective acts which takes the value $f(\cdot)$ for all μ_k, the third is the map from this set of measures to the act's certainty equivalent under each measure, and the fourth is the objective lottery over these certainty equivalents values implied by the probability measure $M(\cdot)$ over the measures.

If the preference function $V(\cdot)$ over objective lotteries is expected utility, then the final evaluation reduces to subjective expected utility. However, Segal suggests using *anticipated utility*, or *rank-dependent expected utility* form (Quiggin (1982), Yaari (1987), Segal (1987b)). For a lottery $\mathbf{P} = (\ldots; \alpha_i, p_i; \ldots)$, with $\alpha_1 > \cdots > \alpha_n$, this preference function takes the form

$$V(\mathbf{P}) = U(\alpha_1) \cdot \delta(p_1) + \sum_{i=2}^{n} U(\alpha_i) \cdot \left[\delta(p_1 + \cdots + p_i) - \delta(p_1 + \cdots + p_{i-1}) \right].$$

As such, it is analogous to the Choquet expected utility form (13.5) over subjective acts, with the nonadditive capacity v replaced by a nonlinear (and typically convex) *distortion function* $\delta : [0,1] \to [0,1]$ for which $\delta(0) = 0$ and $\delta(1) = 1$. When $\delta(\cdot)$ is linear, this form reduces to objective expected utility.

Labeling the induced lotteries $\mathbf{P}_k = (\ldots; x_j, \mu_k(E_j); \ldots)$ so that $V(\mathbf{P}_1) \geq \cdots \geq V(\mathbf{P}_n)$, and observing that the certainty equivalent of a lottery $\mathbf{P}$ is given by $U^{-1}(V(\mathbf{P}))$, the Recursive preference function over subjective acts takes the form

$$W(f(\cdot)) = V(\mathbf{P}_1) \cdot \delta(M(\mu_1)) + \sum_{i=2}^{n} V(\mathbf{P}_i) \cdot \left[\delta \left(M(\{\mu_1, \ldots, \mu_i\}) \right) \right.$$
$$\left. - \delta \left(M(\{\mu_1, \ldots, \mu_{i-1}\}) \right) \right].$$

To illustrate how this model can accommodate Ellsberg preferences in the Three-Color Urn, keep the normalization $U(\$100) = 1$ and $U(\$0) = 0$, and suppose that the decision-maker assigns probability $1/2$ to each of the distributions

$$\mu_1(s_r, s_b, s_y) = (1/3, 2/3, 0) \qquad \mu_2(s_r, s_b, s_y) = (1/3, 0, 2/3). \qquad (13.8)$$

Then bet a_1 on red induces the same lottery $\mathbf{P} = \{\$100; 1/3; \$0, 2/3\}$ under either measure, so we can identify it with the degenerate two-stage lottery $\{\mathbf{P}, 1\}$ to obtain $W(\alpha_1) = V(\mathbf{P}) = \delta(1/3)$. A similar argument establishes $W(a_4) = V(\mathbf{P}) = \delta(2/3)$.

Consider now the bet a_2 on black. Under distribution μ_1 it yields the lottery $\mathbf{P}_1 = \{\$100, 2/3, \$0, 1/3\}$, while under μ_2 it yields $\mathbf{P}_2 = \{\$100, 0; \$0, 1\}$. We have $V(\mathbf{P}_1) = \delta(2/3)$ and $V(\mathbf{P}_2) = 0$, so from equation (13.7), $W(a_2) = V(\mathbf{P}_1) \cdot \delta(M(\mu_1)) = \delta(2/3) \cdot \delta(1/2)$. A similar argument establishes $W(a_3) = 1 \cdot \delta(1/2) + \delta(1/3)[1 - \delta(1/3)]$. For distortion function $\delta(p) = (e^p - 1)/(e - 1)$ these values become[62] $W(a_1) = 0.2302 > 0.2082 = W(a_2)$ and $W(a_3) = 0.5208 < 0.5516 = W(a_4)$, which yield the Ellsberg rankings.

While Segal (1987a) utilizes the same preference function to evaluate single-stage lotteries as well as lotteries over certainty equivalents, Segal (1990) considers the possibility of using different preference functions in the two stages.

13.5.4 Klibanoff, Marinacci and Mukerji's Smooth Ambiguity Preferences Model

The *Smooth Ambiguity Preferences Model* Klibanoff et al. (2005) (*KMM*) follows a similar two-stage approach. The main differences with Segal's Recursive Model are that the primitives are preferences over horse lotteries, i.e., subjective acts, rather than objective roulette lotteries, and that different preference functions are used in the different stages. In particular, these are each expected utility functions, with different utility functions. This is related to Example 2 in Segal (1990).

In applications, the smooth representation typically takes the following form: for any act (horse lottery) $f : \mathcal{S} \to \mathcal{X}$, the smooth ambiguity index is

$$W(f(\cdot)) = \int_{\Delta(s)} \phi \left(\int U(f(\cdot) d\mu \right) dM(\mu) \qquad (13.9)$$

where $U(\cdot)$ is the von Neumann-Morgenstern utility function, M is the individual's *second-order prior*, that is, a probability measure over the set $\Delta(\mathcal{S})$ of measures μ on the state

---

[62] Segal (1987a, p.185), see also his Theorem 4.2 for a general result along the lines of this example.

space S, and $\varphi(\cdot)$ is the individual's *second-order utility function*. As in Segal's Recursive model, the interpretation is that the individual is uncertain about which probability measure μ describes the likelihood of realizations of the state; this second-order uncertainty is modeled using the second-order prior M. Each measure μ determines a different expected utility $\int U(f(\cdot))d\mu$ or the act f. If the individual simply averaged these expected utilities using M, and hence evaluated f according to

$$\int_{\Delta(S)} \int_S U\left(f(\cdot)\right) d\mu \ dM(\mu)$$

this would yield expected utility preferences, where the subjective probability measure is the "average measure" that assigns to each event E the probability $\int \mu(E)dM(\mu)$. Instead, the individual "distorts" the expected utilities $\int U(f(\cdot))d\mu$ using the second-order utility function $\varphi(\cdot)$. As we shall see momentarily, concavity of $\varphi(\cdot)$ corresponds to a notion of ambiguity aversion. (Similarly, convexity of $\varphi(\cdot)$ corresponds to ambiguity preference, and linearity of $\varphi(\cdot)$ corresponds to expected utility and hence ambiguity neutrality.)

To see how this representation can accommodate the modal preferences in the Three-Color Paradox, suppose that, as in the preceding subsection, the individual assigns equal second-order probabilities to the distributions in equation (13.8). Continue to assume that $U(\$100) = 1$ and $U(\$0) = 0$, and let $\varphi(r) = \sqrt{r}$. Then $W(a_1) = \varphi(1/3) = 0.5773 > 0.4082 = 1/3 \cdot \varphi(1/3) + 1/2 \cdot \varphi(0) = W(a_2)$ and similarly $W(a_3) = 1/2 \cdot \varphi(1/3) + 1/2 \cdot \varphi(1) = 0.7887 < 0.8165 = \varphi(2/3) = W(a_4)$, as required.

We now show how *KMM* obtain the representation in equation (13.9); in so doing, we also illustrate the formal connection with Segal's approach.

KMM adopt a decision framework in which, loosely speaking, the realizations of objective roulette wheels are modeled as part of the state space; preferences over acts that depend *only* on the roulette-wheel component of the state space are assumed consistent with *EU* with a uniform prior probability measure. Formally, the state space S is the Cartesian product of a set Ω of interest and the interval $[0,1]$ (the roulette wheel). The set of prizes is an interval of real numbers. The individual is endowed with not one, but two preference relations. The first, denoted $\succcurlyeq$, is a preference over (standard) acts $f : S \to \mathcal{X}$. Its restriction to the set of acts that only depend on the roulette-wheel component $[0,1]$ of the state space S is assumed to admit an expected utility representation, with a continuous, strictly increasing utility U and a prior λ which is the Lebesgue measure on $[0,1]$. It is clear that, for every roulette lottery $\mathbf{P} = (\ldots;x_i,p_i;\ldots)$ with prizes in the set $\mathcal{X}$, there exists an act $f_\mathbf{P}$ that depends only on the roulette-wheel component of the state space and which generates the same probability distribution as $\mathbf{P}$, in the sense that $\lambda(\{r: f_\mathbf{P}(\omega,r) = x_i \text{ for all } \omega\}) = p_i$ for all i. For this reason, call such acts *lottery acts*.

The second preference relation, denoted $\succcurlyeq^{(2)}$, is defined over *second-order acts*, i.e., maps $f^{(2)} : \Delta(\mathcal{S}) \rightarrow \mathcal{X}$. We return to the interpretation of this relation below. The relation $\succcurlyeq^{(2)}$ is assumed to have an expected utility representation, with continuous, strictly increasing utility v (not necessarily equal to U) and probability measure $M \in \Delta(\Delta(\mathcal{S}))$.

The key axiom, *Consistency*, connects the preferences $\succcurlyeq$ on standard acts and $\succcurlyeq^{(2)}$ on second-order acts. It also indicates how the Smooth Ambiguity Preferences model is related to Segal's Recursive approach. The Consistency axiom formalizes Segal's analysis of the Three-Color Urn in the previous subsection (and is also consistent with Segal's own intended use of the model). We assumed that each act a_1, a_2, a_3, a_4 was associated with a collection of single-stage lotteries, corresponding to the probability distributions over states that the individual contemplates; then, we evaluated the act by evaluating the two-stage lottery obtained by attaching probabilities to each such single-stage lottery. *KMM*'s Consistency axiom makes this process explicit: they associate with each standard act f the second-order act $f^{(2)}$ such that, for every $\mu \in \Delta(\mathcal{S})$, $f^{(2)}(\mu)$ is a certainty equivalent of the lottery act that yields each outcome x in the range of f with probability measure $\mu(f^{-1}(x))$. Given the assumption that preferences over lottery acts are consistent with expected utility, with a continuous and strictly increasing (hence, invertible) utility function $U(\cdot)$, this means that

$$f^{(2)}(\mu) = U^{-1}\left(\int U\left(f(\cdot)\right) d\mu \right)$$

for every $\mu \in \Delta(\mathcal{S})$. The key assumption is then

Consistency: For all acts $f, g, f \succcurlyeq g$ iff $f^{(2)} \succcurlyeq^{(2)} g^{(2)}$.

That is: the ranking of f and g is precisely the ranking of the corresponding second-order acts $f^{(2)}$ and $g^{(2)}$.

Consistency and the assumption that preferences over second-order acts admit an expected utility representation then immediately imply that standard, first-order acts f can be ranked according to

$$W\left(f(\cdot)\right) = \int_{\Delta(S)} v\left(f^{(2)}(\mu)\right) dM(\mu) = \int_{\Delta(S)} \phi\left(\int U\left(f(\cdot)\right) d\mu \right) dM(\mu)$$

where $\varphi(\cdot) = v(U^{-1}(\cdot))$ is the *second-order utility* and M the *second-order probability measure,* or *second-order prior.* This is the representation in equation (13.9). (In *KMM*, each measure μ in the support of the second-order prior is an independent product of Lebesgue measure λ on $[0,1]$ and a suitable probability measure on the coordinate of actual interest, namely Ω. In applications, the Lebesgue component is simply omitted.) Notice that, while this model is commonly referred to as the *Smooth Ambiguity Preferences* model, the function φ is not necessarily smooth (though it can be, and typically is, in applications).

The interpretation of second-order acts requires some elaboration. *KMM* acknowledge that a direct interpretation of them as bets on different elements in $\Delta(\mathcal{S})$ is not straightforward:

> *"there is a question whether preferences with respect to these acts are observable. The mapping from observable events to events in $\Delta(\mathcal{S})$ may not always be evident. When it is not evident we may need something richer than behavioral data, perhaps cognitive data or thought experiments" (p. 1854).*

If second-order acts are not directly observable, then the second-order utility v and second-order probability measure M should be thought of solely as a way to provide a numerical representation of preferences over *first*-order, standard acts. The question is then whether these objects can be identified on the basis of preferences over standard acts alone. In general, the answer is negative: for a trivial example, observe that if the second-order utility $\phi(\cdot)$ is linear (equivalently, if $v = U$), one can equivalently replace a given second-order probability measure M with one that is concentrated on the "average probability measure" $\int \mu \, dM(\mu)$ without changing first-order preferences at all. As *KMM* indicate, it is an open question to what extent and under what conditions $\phi(\cdot)$ and M can be identified from first-order preferences alone. For an environment in which uncertainty concerns infinitely many repetitions of an experiment, a positive answer is provided by Klibanoff et al. (2011) under a "symmetry" restriction on preferences. A related result can be found in Al-Najjar and De Castro (2013).

On the other hand, there are settings in which second-order acts are observable. An obvious example are experiments involving physical devices: one can resolve bets on the composition of an urn by simply opening the urn and examining its contents. Bets on long-run averages can also be thought of as observable second-order acts, though arguably only as idealizations or approximations. However, in these cases, first- and second-order acts only differ because they depend on different "coordinates" of the state space; the model in equation (13.9) essentially allows the individual to be differently risk-averse, depending on the *source* of uncertainty. In other words, rather than ambiguity attitudes, the smooth model reflects *issue preference*, which we consider in the following section.

An alternative axiomatization of the Smooth Ambiguity Preferences model is provided by Seo (2009). That paper takes a different approach. The individual is assumed to have preferences over roulette-horse-roulette acts (see Section 13.3.4). The key assumption is that individuals do *not* reduce compound lotteries, though they satisfy a suitable "dominance" property. Seo obtains an extension of the representation in equation (13.9) to lotteries over horse-roulette acts; the function $\phi(\cdot)$ captures both attitudes towards ambiguity and violations of reduction. Thus, one implication of his model is that an agent who reduces compound *objective* lotteries must be ambiguity-neutral. There is some evidence that attitudes toward reduction and ambiguity are correlated (Halevy (2007)); however, one may wish for a model that does not impose perfect correlation between these distinct behavioral traits.

The main attraction of the Smooth Ambiguity Preferences model is its tractability. The numerical example above suggests that calculations may involve simple adaptations of familiar expected utility analysis. As further evidence, *KMM* show that concavity of the second-order utility function $\phi(\cdot)$ corresponds to a notion of "ambiguity aversion" which implies Schmeidler's Uncertainty Aversion Axiom (although their notion is defined in terms of second-order beliefs, and hence subject to the preceding qualifications).

13.5.5 Ergin and Gul's Issue-Preference Model

Ergin and Gul (2009) propose a variant of Segal's two-stage approach, and provide an elegant axiomatization in a Savage-style environment. Their model highlights a different interpretation of the Ellsberg Paradoxes.

To illustrate, it is useful to rephrase the Three-Color Paradox slightly. Imagine that the balls in the urn are numbered from 1 to 90. Balls numbered 1–30 are known to be red. Balls numbered 31–90 may be either black or yellow: the color of each of these balls is not known. Thus, the experiment involves two *sources of uncertainty*, or *issues*: the number of the ball drawn, and the colors of balls 31–90. Importantly, these issues are *independent*: if you learn the number of the ball drawn, that does not tell you anything about the colors of balls 31–90, or conversely.

This richer description can be modeled using a two-coordinate state space, for example

$$S = \{1, \ldots, 90\} \times \{c = (c_{31}, \ldots, c_{90}) : \forall i, c_i \in \{b, y\}\}.$$

Denote an arbitrary state in S by $s = (n,c)$, where n is the number of the drawn ball and c is a color assignment, i.e., the vector $(c_{31}, \ldots, c_{90})$. The bets in the Three-Color Paradox can then be modeled as follows (with some abuse of notation, we use the same letters as in Section 13.1): the bets on "red" and "black or yellow" correspond respectively to

$$a_1((n,c)) = \begin{cases} \$100 & n = 1, \ldots, 30 \\ \$0 & n \geq 31 \end{cases} \quad \text{and} \quad a_4((n,c)) = \begin{cases} \$0 & n = 1, \ldots, 30 \\ \$100 & n \geq 31 \end{cases}.$$

The bets on "black" and "red or yellow," on the other hand, correspond to

$$a_2((n,c)) = \begin{cases} \$0 & n = 1, \ldots, 30 \\ \$100 & n \geq 31 \text{ and } c_n = b \\ \$0 & n \geq 31 \text{ and } c_n = y \end{cases} \quad \text{and} \quad a_3((n,c)) = \begin{cases} \$100 & n = 1, \ldots, 30 \\ \$0 & n \geq 31 \text{ and } c_n = b \\ \$100 & n \geq 31 \text{ and } c_n = y. \end{cases}$$

An obvious difference between a_1 and a_4 on one hand, and a_2 and a_3 on the other, is that the former only depend upon the number of the ball drawn, whereas the latter depend upon both the number of the ball drawn and the color assignment to balls 31...90 (in particular, the color of the ball drawn). Now suppose that the individual has *probabilistic beliefs*, and in particular believes that every ball is equally likely to be drawn, and also that, independently, every color assignment is equally likely to have occurred. This implies that, for both acts a_1 and a_2, the probability of receiving \$100 is 1/3; similarly, the probability of winning is 2/3 for both acts a_3 and a_4. The Ellsberg preferences $a_1 \succ a_2$ and $a_3 \prec a_4$ can then interpreted as follows: despite the fact that the winning probabilities in each comparison are the same, the individual prefers bets that only depend upon the first issue (here, the number of the ball drawn) to bets that depend upon both issues (the number as well as the color assignment).

Recall that an individual is probabilistically sophisticated if he or she evaluates an act $f = (\ldots;x_j,E_j;\ldots)$ by first reducing it to a lottery $\mathbf{P}_f = (\ldots;x_j,\mu(E_j);\ldots)$ where μ is their subjective probability over the state space $\mathcal{S}$, and then applying a suitable preference function over lotteries. Even in the above modified formulation of the Three-Color Urn bets, Ellsberg preferences are not probabilistically sophisticated—acts that induce the same probability distribution over prizes are strictly ranked. However, Ergin and Gul note that they are *second-order probabilistically sophisticated*, in the sense that each act is evaluated by first reducing it to a *compound* lottery, in which the first stage corresponds to the assignment of colors to balls 31,...,90 and the second stage corresponds to the draw of a numbered ball from the urn, and then applying a suitable *compound-lottery* preference function. This reduction of acts to compound lottery is essentially what was done in order to apply Segal's two-stage model to the Three-Color Paradox. Ergin and Gul point out that this form of reduction is a higher-order version of probabilistic sophistication and, more importantly, provide a complete axiomatization of the resulting preferences.

Their axiomatization builds upon that of Machina and Schmeidler (1992) for probabilistically sophisticated preferences in a Savage framework (Section 3). To provide some detail, assume that the state space is a Cartesian product, $\mathcal{S} = \mathcal{S}_a \times \mathcal{S}_b$, where the two coordinates correspond to *issue a* and *issue b*. In the Three-Color Urn, issue a is the number of the ball drawn, and issue b is the color assignment. The Machina-Schmeidler Strong Comparative Probability axiom is applied only to acts that depend solely on issue a. Ergin and Gul's key novel axiom, $a|b$ *Strong Comparative Probability*, serves three purposes. First, it implies that Strong Comparative Probability also holds for acts that depend solely on issue b. Second, it implies that the two issues are statistically independent, as in the example. Third, it implies, loosely speaking, that the individual is concerned with second-order risk related to issue b, and not second-order risk related to issue a (Ergin and Gul (2009, p.906) provide an illustration).

To formally describe the Ergin-Gul representation, note that exploiting the product structure of the state space allows an act f to be represented as

$$f = \begin{pmatrix} x_{11} & \cdots & x_{1m} & A_1 \\ \vdots & \ddots & \vdots & \vdots \\ x_{n1} & \cdots & x_{nm} & A_n \\ B_1 & \cdots & B_m & \end{pmatrix}$$

where $\{A_1,\ldots,A_n\}$ is a partition of $\mathscr{S}_a$, $\{B_1,\ldots,B_m\}$ is a partition of $\mathscr{S}_b$, and x_{ij} is the prize delivered by f at all states $s \in A_i \times B_j$. Given a product measure $\mu = \mu_a \times \mu_b$ on $\mathcal{S}$, associate with f the two-stage compound lottery

$$\mathbf{P}_f^* = \left(\ldots; \left(\ldots; x_{ij}, \mu_a(A_i)\right), \mu_b(B_j); \ldots\right).$$

Under Ergin and Gul's axioms, there exists a unique product measure $\mu = \mu_a \times \mu_b$ on $\mathcal{S}$ such that every act f is evaluated according to $W(f(\cdot)) = V^*(\mathbf{P}_f^*)$, where $\mathbf{P}_f^*$ is the compound lottery associated with f and V^* is a suitably continuous preference function on two-stage lotteries that satisfies stochastic dominance; again, see the original paper for details. If a version of Savage's Sure-Thing Principle is imposed, this function reduces to two-stage expected utility with different utility functions, as in the Smooth Ambiguity Preferences model of Section 13.5.3. If instead a *Comonotonic Sure-Thing Principle* axiom is imposed, the first-stage lottery is evaluated using a Choquet integral. Ergin and Gul also draw a formal connection between uncertainty aversion and issue preference.

Nau (2006) proposes a related model, which allows for state-dependent preferences but restricts attention to additive representations in both stages. Different perspectives on source preference are suggested by Chew and Sagi (2008) and Abdellaoui et al. (2011). Finally, Skiadas (2013) assumes that prizes are monetary and preferences over acts are scale-invariant: $(\ldots; x_j, E_j; \ldots) \succ (\ldots; y_j, F_j; \ldots)$ if and only if, for every real number $\alpha > 0$, $(\ldots; \alpha \cdot x_j, E_j; \ldots) \succ (\ldots; \alpha \cdot y_j, F_j; \ldots)$. This yields a two-stage expected utility representation *a la* Ergin and Gul, with different constant relative risk averse utility functions for the two stages.

13.5.6 Vector Expected Utility

Siniscalchi (2009a) proposes a different approach to modeling ambiguity-sensitive preferences. There are three key ingredients in this approach. First, the individual evaluates acts by a process reminiscent of "anchoring and adjustment" (Tversky and Kahneman (1974)). Second, the *anchor* is a standard expected utility evaluation, where expectations are taken with respect to a *baseline* subjective probability measure. Third, the *adjustment* depends upon a measure of statistical similarity of the act under consideration with "examples" or "models" of ambiguous acts.

The proposed representation is called *vector expected utility* (*VEU*) because a key role is played by a vector of expectations. Specifically, the *VEU* representation evaluates acts according to

$$W(f(\cdot)) = \int U(f(\cdot)) \cdot d\mu + A\left(cov\left(U\left(f(\cdot)\right), \zeta_1\right), \dots, cov\left(U(f(\cdot)), \zeta_n\right)\right)$$
(13.10)

where μ is the baseline prior, $\zeta_1, \dots, \zeta_n$ are *adjustment factors*, i.e., real-valued functions on the state space S that satisfy $\int \zeta_i \, d\mu = 0$, $cov(\cdot, \cdot)$ denotes covariance (computed with respect to μ), and $A(\cdot)$ is the *adjustment function*, which satisfies $A(0, \dots, 0) = 0$ and $A(\varphi) = A(-\varphi)$ for every vector φ. Notice that, due to the normalization of the adjustment factors $\zeta_1, \dots, \zeta_n$,

$$cov\left(U\left(f(\cdot)\right), \zeta_i\right) = \int U\left(f(\cdot)\right) \cdot \zeta_i \cdot d\mu.$$

To see how the *VEU* model accommodates Ellsberg preferences, consider a simple specification with a single adjustment factor ζ_1, defined by

$$\zeta_1(s_r) = 0 \quad \zeta_1(s_b) = 1 \quad \zeta_1(s_y) = -1$$

a uniform baseline prior, and the adjustment function

$$A(\varphi) = -|\varphi|.$$

The adjustment factor ζ_1 can be interpreted as a bet whereby the individual wins or loses one util, depending on which of the two ambiguous colors is drawn, but nothing happens if the unambiguous color red is drawn.[63] Intuitively, this suggests that ζ_1 is a "purely ambiguous" bet, and indeed a model of the kind of bets that are ambiguous in this problem.[64]

A related interpretation of the adjustment factor ζ_1 formalizes the following intuition, proposed by Epstein and Zhang (2001) for the modal preferences in the Ellsberg Paradox:

> *"The intuition for this reversal is the* **complementarity** *between s_b and s_y—there is imprecision regarding the likelihood of s_b, whereas {s_b, s_g} has precise probability 2/3" (p. 271;* **boldface** *added for emphasis, and notation adapted to this chapter).*

---

[63] For the sake of this interpretation, assume that initial utility is constant and normalized to zero.
[64] This intuitive interpretation corresponds closely to the way adjustment factors are formally identified from preferences: see Section 4.1 in Siniscalchi (2009a).

The fact that $\zeta_1(s_b) = 1$ whereas $\zeta_1(s_r) = 0$ reflects the perception that s_b is ambiguous but s_r is not; setting $\zeta_1(s_y) = -1$ indicates that ambiguity about s_b and s_y "cancels out." In this sense, s_b and s_y are *complementary* in the *VEU* representation; this formalizes the Epstein-Zhang interpretation. (The relationship with the previous interpretation is that, in order for ζ_1 to be a purely ambiguous bet in this example, it *must* reflect the complementarity between s_b and s_y.)

We now verify that the *VEU* representation proposed here induces the Ellsberg rankings.

$$W(a_1) = 1/3 - |0| = 1/3$$
$$W(a_2) = 1/3 - |1/3| = 0$$
$$W(a_3) = 2/3 - |-1/3| = 1/3$$
$$W(a_4) = 2/3 - |0| = 2/3$$

In the calculation of $W(a_4)$, the covariance term is zero precisely because ambiguity about s_b and s_y cancels out: $cov(U(a_4), \zeta_1) = 1/3 \cdot \sum_s \zeta_1(s)a_4(s) = 1/3 \cdot (0 \cdot 0 + 1 \cdot 1 + 1 \cdot (-1)) = 0$.

The key axiom in the characterization of *VEU* preferences is *Complementary Independence*. A preliminary definition: two acts f, f^c are *complementary* if the mixture $1/2 \cdot f + 1/2 \cdot f^c$ is a constant act. Intuitively, complementary acts are the "negative" of each other, up to a constant. An important feature is that they share the same *prize variability*, or volatility: if the (utility of the) prizes delivered by f at different states varies a lot, the same is true of prizes delivered by f^c, except that prizes vary in opposite directions. The main axiom for *VEU* preferences is then

Complementary Independence: For all acts f, g, f^c, g^c such that f, f^c and respectively g, g^c are complementary: if $f \succcurlyeq f^c$ and $g \succcurlyeq g^c$, then $1/2 \cdot f + 1/2 \cdot g \succcurlyeq 1/2 \cdot f^c + 1/2 \cdot g^c$.

When comparing complementary acts, variability cannot play a role because, as just noted, any two complementary acts have the same volatility. The axiom requires that, absent volatility considerations, a form of Independence must hold. This implies that any departures from expected utility must be determined by *attitudes toward variability*. For further interpretation, the reader is referred to the Siniscalchi (2009a).

VEU preferences can accommodate a wide range of ambiguity attitudes. If the Uncertainty Aversion Axiom is imposed, the function A must be negative and concave. It turns out that a negative, but not necessarily concave function A also captures a notion of ambiguity aversion; we discuss this further in Section 13.6.

Chambers et al. (2013) consider preferences that admit a representation similar to that of equation (13.10), but with an arbitrary aggregator to combine the baseline expectation and adjustment terms. They adopt the Complementary Independence axiom, and also require a form of uncertainty aversion. See also Grant and Polak (2013).

13.5.7 Variational and Multiplier Preferences

The Uncertainty Aversion Axiom of Section 13.5.1 is common to a broad class of preference models. In addition to *MEU* preferences, suitable parameterizations of smooth ambiguity, Ergin-Gul, and *VEU* preferences also satisfy it. As we will discuss in Section 13.6, its interpretation is not entirely straightforward, or uncontroversial; on the other hand, the fact that it is a familiar and analytically convenient quasiconcavity assumption has made it an obvious reference point in the theoretical and applied literature on ambiguity-sensitive preferences. This subsection and the next two discuss other preference models that satisfy Uncertainty Aversion, and can be thought of as direct generalizations of the *MEU* specification.

To introduce these models, recall that the characterization of *MEU* preferences also involves Certainty Independence. Unlike the Uncertainty Aversion Axiom, Certainty Independence is seen to be quite restrictive. We noted in Section 13.5.1 that, when an act such as a_2 (bet on black) in the Three-Color-Urn is mixed with a constant act, no hedging occurs: like the act a_2, the mixture yields a strictly better prize in case a black ball is drawn than if a yellow or red ball is drawn. By way of contrast, mixing a_2 with a bet on yellow results in an act which delivers a good prize if either of the ambiguous colors is drawn. However, mixing a_2 with a constant act does have two potentially important effects. First, it reduces the *utility variability* across the two ambiguous states s_b and s_y: for instance, a_2 yields utility $U(\$100)$ and $U(\$0)$ in case a black or, respectively, nonblack ball is drawn, whereas a 50:50 mixture of a_2 with the constant act \$0 yields $1/2 \cdot U(\$100) + 1/2 \cdot U(\$0)$ and $U(\$0)$ respectively. Second, mixing with a constant act also shifts utilities up or down: to see this, compare the utilities delivered by a 50:50 mixture of a_2 with \$0 to those delivered by a 50:50 mixture of a_2 with \$100, namely $U(\$100)$ for a black ball and $1/2 \cdot U(\$100) + 1/2 \cdot U(\$0)$ for a nonblack ball.

Both of these changes may potentially affect preferences. After all, in choice under risk, changes in the *scale* (i.e., outcome variability) and *location* (upward/downward shifts) of *monetary prizes* can affect preferences. For instance, if preferences exhibit decreasing absolute risk aversion, an individual becomes more willing to take bets as their initial (nonrandom) wealth increases, i.e., shifts upward. Similarly, unless preferences display constant relative risk aversion, an individual with constant initial wealth may accept a given bet, but turn it down if both their wealth and the stakes in the bet are doubled (or vice versa). Arguably, it would be desirable to allow for similar behavior in the context of ambiguity: changing the scale and/or location of utilities may influence preferences.

However, Certainty Independence is a location- and scale-invariance assumption, so such phenomena are ruled out.

13.5.7.1 Variational Preferences

Motivated in part by these considerations, Maccheroni et al. (2006a) propose a weakening of Certainty Independence:

Weak Certainty Independence: For all acts f, g, constant acts x, y and all $\alpha \in (0,1]$: if $\alpha \cdot f + (1-\alpha) \cdot x \succcurlyeq \alpha \cdot g + (1-\alpha) \cdot x$, then $\alpha \cdot f + (1-\alpha) \cdot y \succcurlyeq \alpha \cdot g + (1-\alpha) \cdot y$.

This axiom assumes invariance to changes in the location, but *not* the scale, of utilities. In the Three-Color Urn problem, it allows for the following pattern of preferences:

$$a_1 > a_2 \quad \text{and} \quad 1/2 \cdot a_1 + 1/2 \cdot 0 < 1/2 \cdot a_2 + 1/2 \cdot 0.$$

A possible interpretation might be that, by scaling down the utilities of the acts involved in the comparison, the individual becomes less sensitive to the fact that black is an ambiguous color but red is not. (We do not claim that such preferences would be reasonable or natural, merely that they are allowed by Weak Certainty Independence.) At the same time, Maccheroni et al.'s axiom still requires that, since the 50:50 mixture of a_1 with \$0 is considered worse than the 50:50 mixture of a_2 with \$0, the same must be true if \$0 is replaced with \$100.

Maccheroni et al. show that the Weak Order, Non-Degeneracy, Monotonicity, Continuity, Uncertainty Aversion and Weak Certainty Independence Axioms are necessary and sufficient for the existence of a representation of the form

$$W\left(f(\cdot)\right) \equiv \min_{\mu \in \Delta(\mathcal{S})} \int U\left(f(\cdot)\right) d\mu + c(\mu) \tag{13.11}$$

where $c : \Delta(\mathcal{S}) \rightarrow [0, \infty]$ is a lower semicontinuous, convex *cost function* that satisfies $\inf_\mu c(\mu) = 0$. They call equation (13.11) the *variational representation* of preferences.

The cost function $c(\cdot)$ is the key ingredient of the representation. Once a utility function has been fixed, a "canonical" or "minimal" cost function is uniquely identified (refer to Maccheroni et al. for details). If the utility function U is replaced with a positive affine transformation $\alpha \cdot U + \beta$, the cost function c must be replaced with $\alpha \cdot c$.

Observe that the minimization in equation (13.11) is over all priors over the state space S. However, one can obtain *MEU* preferences as a special case as follows: fix a compact, convex set C of priors, and define

$$c(\mu) = \begin{cases} 0 & \mu \in C \\ \infty & \mu \notin C \end{cases}$$

(such a function is often called an "indicator function" in convex analysis). With this specification of the cost function, it is clear that a prior $\mu \notin C$ will never be a solution of the minimization problem in equation (13.11) whereas priors in $\mathcal{C}$ are costless, so the minimization problem reduces to that in equation (13.1).

Maccheroni et al. propose the following "malevolent Nature" interpretation. When the individual contemplates choosing an act f, Nature tries to minimize its expected utility. To do so, she can choose any prior $\mu \in \Delta(\mathcal{S})$; however, to choose μ, Nature must pay a cost $c(\mu)$. In the case of *MEU* preferences, priors in C are costless, and all other priors are infinitely costly; however, the variational representation allows for intermediate cases as well—that is, for priors that have a nonzero but finite cost. Nature's problem is thus to minimize the sum of the individual's expected utility and the cost of priors.

Skiadas (2013) also axiomatizes a version of Variational Preferences with constant relative risk averse utility.

13.5.7.2 Multiplier Preferences

Another special parameterization of Variational Preferences deserves special mention. Hansen and Sargent (2001) and Hansen et al. (1999) consider the following specification:

$$W\left(f(\cdot)\right) \equiv \min_{\mu \in \Delta(\mathcal{S})} \int U\left(f(\cdot)\right) d\mu + \theta \cdot R(\mu||\mu^*) \qquad (13.12)$$

where attention is restricted to countably additive probability measures when the state space is infinite, $\theta \geq 0$ is a parameter, and $R(\mu||\mu^*)$ denotes the *relative entropy* of the prior μ with respect to a *reference prior* μ^*. The latter is defined as

$$R\left(\mu||\mu^*\right) = \int \left(\log \frac{d\mu}{d\mu^*}\right) d\mu$$

if μ is absolutely continuous with respect to μ^*, and $R(\mu^*||\mu^*) = \infty$ otherwise. This defines the so-called *Multiplier Preferences* preference function. Equation (13.12) is a special case of equation (13.11), yielding tractability since the explicit solution to the problem in equation (13.12) is known, and indeed one can show that

$$W\left(f(\cdot)\right) = -\theta \cdot \log \left\{-\int - \exp\left(-\frac{U\left(f(\cdot)\right)}{\theta}\right) d\mu^*\right\}$$

(the reason for the two consecutive minus signs will be clear momentarily). An exact characterization of Multiplier Preferences within the class of Variational Preferences is provided by Strzalecki (2011).

The above equation indicates that, if one restricts attention to horse lotteries, i.e. acts that map states to prizes (rather than to roulette lotteries over prizes), Multiplier Preferences are ordinally equivalent to *SEU* preferences with utility function $-\exp(-\theta^{-1} \cdot U(\cdot))$. To see this, note that $W(f(\cdot))$ is the composition of the function $f - \exp(-\theta^{-1} \cdot U(\cdot)) \, d\mu$

which takes on strictly negative values, with the function $x \rightarrow -\theta \log(-x)$, which is strictly increasing when restricted to the negative reals. On the other hand, if one restricts attention to roulette lotteries, the individual's risk preferences are represented by $U(\cdot)$. In other words, one can interpret the multiplier-preferences model as postulating that the individual is more risk-averse toward *subjective* risk than toward *objective* risk. The idea that risk attitudes may be *source-dependent* was discussed in Section 13.5.5.

13.5.8 Confidence-Function Preferences

Chateauneuf and Faro (2009) propose a model that is "dual" to Variational Preferences: whereas the latter relax the scale-invariance requirement of Certainty Independence but preserve location-invariance, Chateauneuf and Faro's *Confidence-Function Preferences* retain scale invariance but drop translation invariance. More precisely, these authors assume that the set $\mathcal{X}$ of prizes contains a worst element x^*, and impose

Worst Independence: For all acts f, g and all $\alpha \in (0,1]$: $f \sim g$ implies $\alpha \cdot f + (1-\alpha) \cdot x^* \sim \alpha \cdot g + (1-\alpha) \cdot x^*$.

Together with Weak Order, Continuity, Monotonicity, Ambiguity Aversion and other axioms, Worst Independence characterizes the following representation:

$$W\left(f(\cdot)\right) = \min_{\mu : \varphi(\mu) \geq \alpha} \frac{1}{\varphi(\mu)} \int U\left(f(\cdot)\right) d\mu \qquad (13.13)$$

where the utility function $U(\cdot)$ satisfies $U(x^*) = 0$, α is a parameter in $(0,1]$, and $\varphi(\cdot)$ is an upper semicontinuous, quasiconcave function on $\Delta(\mathcal{S})$ that satisfies $\varphi(\mu) = 1$ for some prior μ.

The proposed interpretation is that $\varphi(\cdot)$ measures the "degree of confidence" that the individual assigns to the different measures. Nature is malevolent, and wants to minimize the individual's expected utility. However, she must choose only priors to which the individual assigns a high enough level of confidence. Furthermore, Nature must pay a multiplicative cost $\varphi(\mu)^{-1}$ to choose the prior μ.

Confidence-function preferences are positively homogeneous: if all utility values are multiplied by some constant $\beta > 0$, the function in equation (13.13) is also multiplied by β. If utility is also positively homogeneous, i.e., if it displays constant relative risk aversion, then the overall representation of preferences is also positively homogeneous. This is convenient in certain applications, especially in financial economics. Furthermore, it makes it possible to invoke standard results on the existence of a representative agent.

13.5.9 Uncertainty-Averse Preferences

Cerreia-Vioglio et al. (2011a) characterize the class of preferences that satisfy Continuity, Monotonicity and Uncertainty Aversion, in addition to Independence on lotteries and certain other technical assumptions. In other words, they drop both location and scale invariance. Their powerful result unifies all the models that generalize *MEU*, as well as many other specifications, such as the Smooth Ambiguity Preferences model. The general *Uncertainty-Averse Preferences* representation is

$$W(f(\cdot)) \equiv \min_{\mu \in \Delta(\mathcal{S})} G\left(\int U(f(\cdot))d\mu, \mu\right) \tag{13.14}$$

where the function $G : \mathbb{R} \times \Delta(\mathcal{S}) \to (-\infty, +\infty]$ is quasiconvex, increasing in the first variable, and satisfies $\inf_{\mu \in \Delta(\mathcal{S})} G(t, \mu) = t$ for all t.

Due to their generality, Uncertainty-Averse Preferences representations are only unique in a weak sense. For a fixed utility function, there is a minimal function $G(\cdot, \cdot)$. If a positive affine transformation of U is taken, G must be suitably rescaled.

MEU preferences are, of course, also Uncertainty-Averse Preferences, with

$$G(t, \mu) = \begin{cases} t & \mu \in C \\ \infty & \mu \notin C \end{cases}.$$

Variational Preferences correspond to the special case

$$G(t, \mu) = t + c(\mu)$$

whereas Confidence-Function Preferences obtain if

$$G(t, \mu) = \begin{cases} \frac{t}{\varphi(\mu)} & \varphi(\mu) \geq \alpha \\ \infty & \varphi(\mu) < \alpha \end{cases}.$$

Finally, recall that Smooth Ambiguity Preferences also satisfy Uncertainty Aversion, provided the second-order utility function $\varphi(\cdot)$ is concave. Under additional technical assumptions, Cerreia-Vioglio et al. (2011a) show that the Smooth Ambiguity Preference representation can be written as in equation (13.14), with

$$G(t, \mu) = t + \min_{M' \in \Gamma(\mu)} I_t\left(M'|M\right)$$

where M' is the second-order probability measure in the Smooth Ambiguity Preferences representation, $\Gamma(\mu)$ is the set of second-order measures $N' \in \Delta(\Delta(\mathcal{S}))$ that reduce to μ, in the sense that

$$\int_{\Delta(\mathcal{S})} \pi(E)dM'(\pi) = \mu(E)$$

for every event $E \subseteq \mathcal{S}$, and $I_t(M'|M)$ is a so-called *statistical distance function,* i.e., a nonnegative, lower semicontinuous, quasiconvex function that satisfies $I_t(M|M) = 0$ (a specific formula is provided by Cerreia-Vioglio et al., 2011a). In other words, Nature attempts to minimize the expected utility of the act under consideration by choosing a probability distribution μ, at a cost given by the result of the minimization problem above. The latter has an interesting "prior uncertainty" interpretation: out of all second-order probability measures M' whose reduction equals μ, Nature chooses the one closest to M. As for Multiplier Preferences, the intuition is that, while M is the individual's "preferred" second-order belief, measures M' close to it are also plausible.

13.5.10 Gul and Pesendorfer's Expected Uncertain Utility

Gul and Pesendorfer (2013) introduce a new model that can accommodate Ellsberg preferences, as well as source preference. Their model applies to a setting *a la* Savage, with an infinite state space S and outcomes in some real interval $[l,m]$. The key intuition is that the individual is able to assign probabilities to a (suitably rich) collection of events, but displays complete ignorance with respect to all other events.

Formally, the proposed representation, *Expected Uncertain Utility* (EUU) starts with a σ-algebra Σ, which comprises the events whose likelihood the individual can confidently assess. A countably additive and nonatomic measure μ represents beliefs on Σ. The *EUU* model ranks Σ-measurable acts according to expected utility; these acts are "unambiguous." The question is how to rank an arbitrary Savage act $f : \mathcal{S} \rightarrow [l, m]$ that is not Σ-measurable. To do so, according to *EUU*, the individual *brackets* any act f between a lower Σ-measurable approximation f_1 and an upper Σ-measurable approximation f_2, in the sense that

$$\mu(\{s : f_1(s) \leq f(s) \leq f_2(s)\}) = 1$$

and furthermore such pair (f_1, f_2) is the "tightest" approximation of f: if there is another pair (g_1, g_2) with the same property, then $\mu(\{s : g_1(s) \leq f_1(s) \leq f_2(s) \leq g_2(s)\}) = 1$. The last ingredient of the *EUU* representation is a continuous, increasing *interval utility function,* that is, a map $U(\cdot, \cdot)$ from the set $I = \{(x, y) : x \leq y\}$ to $\mathbb{R}$. The interpretation is that $U(x, y)$ is the utility of receiving a prize somewhere in the interval $[x, y]$, when the individual is completely ignorant as to which prize in this interval he or she will actually receive. The representing function is then

$$W(f(\cdot)) \equiv \int U(f_1(\cdot), f_2(\cdot)) d\mu. \tag{13.15}$$

To see how this representation works, consider a bet on an event A, i.e., an act $f = (x, A; y, \sim A)$ with $x > y$ (which implies that x is strictly preferred to y). If the event

A is not in Σ, the measure μ does not assign a probability to it; however, we can consider the quantity sup $\{\mu(E) : E \in \Sigma, E \subseteq A\}$. There will be an event $E_1 \in \Sigma$ that attains this supremum. Similarly, there is an event $E_2 \in \Sigma$ that attains sup $\{\mu(E) : E \in \Sigma, E \subseteq \sim A\}$. A bracketing of the binary act f is then given by $f_1 = (x, E_1; y, \sim E_1)$ and $f_2(x, \sim E_2; y, E_2)$. Then

$$W(f(\cdot)) = U(x, x) \cdot \mu(E_1) + U(y, y) \cdot \mu(E_2) + U(y, x) \cdot \mu(\sim (E_1 \cup E_2)).$$

This has an intuitive interpretation. On the unambiguous event $E_1 \subseteq A$, the individual receives x for sure. Similarly, he or she receives y on $E_2 \subseteq \sim A$. How about states that belong to neither E_1 nor E_2? Some of these states are in A, and some are in $\sim A$, but the individual is unable to rank the relative likelihood of $A \backslash E_1$ and $(\sim A) \backslash E_2$. Thus, according to EUU, he or she assigns to all such states the interval utility value $U(y,x)$—by definition, the utility assigned to receiving some prize between y and x.

The authors provide an elegant, Savage-style axiomatization of EUU. The events in Σ are identified as those events for which Savage's Sure-Thing Principle P2 holds, provided it holds for their complement as well. An axiom in the spirit of Savage's P6 ensures the existence of a rich collection of such events. Furthermore, a rich collection of events similar to $\sim(E_1 \cup E_2)$ in the above example is also assumed. The reader is referred to the original paper for further details.

13.5.11 Bewley's Incomplete-Preference Model

A common feature of all the preceding models is that, despite the presence of ambiguity, the individual was assumed to be able to rank all acts, or all suitably measurable acts. Bewley (2002, 2011) proposes a different approach: he assumes that, due to ambiguity, some acts may simply not be comparable. For example, Bewley's take on the Three-Color Paradox is that, quite simply, the individual is unable to compare a bet on red to a bet on black, or a bet on red or yellow to a bet on black or yellow.

He proposes a representation of incomplete preferences that features a set $\mathcal{C}$ of probability distributions, as in MEU. According to his model, for any two acts f, g, f is preferred to g if and only if

$$\int U(f(\cdot)) d\mu \geq \int U(g(\cdot)) d\mu \quad \forall \mu \in \mathcal{C}.$$

This is sometimes called the *unanimity rule*: all priors in $\mathcal{C}$ must "agree" that f is better than g. This representation plays a role in recent developments on the definition of ambiguous beliefs, as in Section 13.6.

To complement this incomplete decision criterion, Bewley suggests an *inertia assumption*, which is essentially a form of status-quo bias: if an act f describes the individual's initial endowment, or default option, and there is no act g that is strictly better than f according to the above criterion, the individual retains f.

The connection between inertia and the status-quo bias is formalized in Ortoleva (2010). This paper takes as primitive a collection of preferences over acts, of which one is an "unconditional" preference, and the others are preferences "conditional" upon an exogenously given status-quo act. Under suitable axioms, the joint representation of these preferences identifies an underlying incomplete, Bewley-style preference, and involves inertia.

13.5.12 Models with "Objective Ambiguity"

Ambiguity and ambiguity attitudes have also been modeled by extending von Neumann and Morgenstern's analysis of expected utility under objective uncertainty rather than Savage's axiomatization of expected utility under subjective uncertainty.

One approach in this strand of the literature identifies ambiguous bets and acts with *sets of lotteries*. For instance, a bet on the ambiguous color black in the Three-Color Paradox can be identified with the set $\{(\$100, \alpha; \$0, 1-\alpha): \alpha \in [0, 2/3]\}$. An unambiguous act such as a bet on red is instead identified with the singleton set $\{(\$100, 1/3; \$0, 2/3)\}$. These sets of lotteries are *not* part of a parametric representation: in this model, they are the objects of choice. A state space is *not* specified. The individual is characterized by a preference ordering $\succcurlyeq$ over sets of objective lotteries. Preferences over singleton sets obey the von Neumann-Morgenstern axioms; the interest is chiefly in the way nonsingleton sets are evaluated.

Olszewski (2007) characterizes the α-MEU criterion, with α strictly between 0 and 1. Ahn (2008) proposes the criterion

$$V(A) = \frac{\int \phi\left(U(\mathbf{P})\right) d\mu}{\mu(A)}$$

where μ is a measure over all lotteries that is "conditioned" on each menu A, U is a von Neumann-Morgenstern utility, and φ is an increasing function. Dumav and Stinchcombe (2013) provide a general analysis of linear representations of preferences over sets of lotteries, and investigate the connection with models that do employ a state space, such as the ones described in Sections 13.5.1–13.5.11.

A related literature considers preferences over tuples consisting of a set of probability distributions on a state space, an act, and possibly a reference probability. Sets of probability distributions can be interpreted as representing *imprecise information*, perhaps obtained by econometric techniques. The issue of interest is how to model the individual's attitudes toward such imprecise information.

Gajdos et al. (2008) consider preferences over pairs (P, f) of probability sets and acts (note that it is assumed that comparisons with different sets of probability distributions are also observed). A first, general representation evaluates such a pair by a maxmin criterion applied to a suitably selected subset of P. Under additional assumption, an elegant representation is obtained for finite state spaces, in which (P, f) is evaluated according to a weighted average of the minimum expected utility over P and the expected utility with respect to the *Steiner point* of P (a construct which generalizes the notion of center of gravity). Wang (2003) instead considers preferences over tuples (P, p, f), where P is a set of probability distributions, p is a reference prior (a distinguished element of P) and f is an act. He axiomatizes a *MEU* criterion in this set, as well as an analog of the Multiplier Preferences representation of Hansen and Sargent (2001).

Viscusi (1989) proposes a different approach within the von Neumann-Morgenstern framework, termed *Prospective Reference Theory*. He suggests that "stated" probabilities in a lottery are not necessarily taken at face value by the individual. Rather, they are interpreted as signals about the "true" probabilities. Individuals then behave according to a weighted average of the stated probability and a prior, or baseline, probability; importantly, they may attribute different weights to the stated probabilities of different events. In particular, they may assign greater weight to the stated probability of a red draw from the Three-Color Ellsberg urn than to the stated probability of a black draw; correspondingly, they may assign a greater weight to the stated probability of a yellow or black draw than to the stated probability of a red or black draw. This allows the Prospective Reference Theory model to match the modal preferences in the Three-Color Paradox.

13.6 RECENT DEFINITIONS AND EXAMPLES

13.6.1 Recent Definitions of Ambiguity and Ambiguous Events

The parametric representations of preferences discussed in Section 13.5 suggest conditions under which an event E may be deemed "ambiguous." For instance:

- The intuitive interpretation of the Maxmin Expected Utility model is that the individual may be unable to assign a unique probability to certain events; thus, an event E may be called "ambiguous" if $\min_{\mu \in \mathcal{C}} \mu(E) < \max_{\mu \in \mathcal{C}} \mu(E)$.
- A similar interpretation applies to the Smooth Ambiguity Preferences model: E is ambiguous if $\min_{\mu \in \mathrm{supp} M} \mu(E) < \max_{\mu \in \mathrm{supp} M} \mu(E)$, where M is the second-order prior and "supp" denotes the support of a measure.
- The suggested interpretation of the Choquet Expected Utility model is that the individual expresses his or her lack of confidence in likelihood assessments by violating additivity. Thus, E may be called "ambiguous" if the capacity v satisfies $v(E) + v(\sim E) < 1$.
- In the Vector Expected Utility model, the adjustment function captures departures from expected utility, so E may be called "ambiguous" if $A(cov(1_E, \zeta_1), \ldots, cov(1_E, \zeta_n)) \neq 0$.

However, these definitions are all closely tied to specific functional forms. Several authors have proposed definitions of ambiguous and unambiguous events that are stated solely in terms of a decision-maker's preferences. We now review two that are, in a sense, polar opposites.

13.6.1.1 The Epstein-Zhang (2001) Definition

Epstein and Zhang (2001) propose a definition of ambiguous and unambiguous events that generalizes the preference pattern in the Three-Color Paradox. Recall that, loosely speaking, the modal preferences in that paradox exhibit a kind of *preference reversal*: the individual prefers to bet on red rather than on black, but once yellow is added to the event on which the favorable prize $100 is delivered, the decision maker prefers to bet on black or yellow rather than on red or yellow. As noted in Section 13.5.2, this indicates that there is a "complementarity" between yellow and black, but not between red and black. The basic idea behind the approach is to take the fact that yellow is "complementary" to another color (in this case, black) as the *defining feature* of an ambiguous event. More generally, an event T is an *un*ambiguous event if it is not "complementary" to some other, disjoint event, in the sense that a preference reversal similar to that in the Three-Color Paradox never obtains.

The Epstein-Zhang definition adds two "robustness checks" to the above intuition. To motivate the first, consider a five-color version of the Three-Color Paradox, and allow for a set of prizes that contains $0 and $100, but other elements as well. The acts under consideration are

	30 balls	60 balls		60 balls	
	red	black	yellow	white	green
a_1	$100	$0	$0	w'	w''
a_2	$0	$100	$0	w'	w''
a_3	$100	$0	$100	w'	w''
a_4	$0	$100	$100	w'	w''

We have added two colors, white and green, and assigned arbitrary prizes to all four acts at the corresponding states; importantly though, the prize in case a white ball is drawn is the same (namely w' for all four acts, and similarly (w'') if a green ball is drawn. Regardless of information available regarding the number of white or green balls, the intuition in the Three-Color Paradox should still apply: yellow should still be "complementary" to black, regardless of the number of white or green balls. Conversely, if we observed the preference pattern $a_1 \succ a_2$ and $a_3 \prec a_4$ for *some* choice of prizes w', w'', we should still conclude that yellow is an ambiguous color.

For the second robustness check, consider the following variation on the previous one:

| | 30 balls | 60 balls | | 60 balls | |
	red	black	yellow	white	green
a_1	\$100	\$0	z'	w'	w''
a_2	\$0	\$100	z'	w'	w''
a_3	\$100	\$0	z'	w'	w''
a_4	\$0	\$100	z'	w'	w''

The prizes \$0 and \$100 have been replaced with arbitrary prizes z and z' respectively. One may argue that if z is close to \$0 and z' is close to \$100, the rankings $a_1 \succ a_2$ and $a_3 \prec a_4$ should still be plausible. Conversely, if we observed such rankings, we might say that the individual likes acts that deliver *similarly good* prizes in case of a black or yellow draw: this, too is a form of complementarity between yellow and black, so we can take it as indication that yellow is an ambiguous color. Indeed, Epstein and Zhang suggest that this conclusion would be warranted so long as a preference reversal occurs for *some* choice of z and z', even if it does not obtain with $z = \$0$ and $z' = \$100$. Accordingly, an event T is defined to be *unambiguous* if (a) for all disjoint subevents A, B of $\sim T$, all prizes x, y, z, z' with $x \succ y$ and all acts h,

$$(x, A; y, B; z, T; h, (\sim T)\backslash(A \cup B)) \succcurlyeq (y, A; x, B; z, T; h, (\sim T)\backslash(A \cup B))$$

implies

$$(x, A; y, B; z', T; h, (\sim T)\backslash(A \cup B)) \succcurlyeq (y, A; x, B; z', T; h, (\sim T)\backslash(A \cup B))$$

and furthermore (b) the same is true if T is replaced everywhere with $\sim T$. An event is *ambiguous* if it is not unambiguous.

Epstein and Zhang observe that, in general, the collection of unambiguous events is *not* an algebra. In particular, the intersection of two unambiguous events may be ambiguous. Zhang (2002) proposes the following examples: an urn contains white, red, green and blue balls. It is known that there are 50 red and blue balls, and 50 green and blue balls; the total number of balls is 100. Intuitively, the events "red or blue" and "green or blue" are unambiguous, but their intersection, "blue," is ambiguous.[65] However, under suitable assumptions (see below), the collection of unambiguous events contains the state space $\mathcal{S}$ and is closed under complements and countable *disjoint* unions; in other words, it is a λ-system.

Epstein and Zhang consider preferences over Savage acts, and assume that preferences satisfy Savage's postulate P3 (Monotonicity). They then consider the family of *unambiguous acts*, that is, acts measurable with respect to unambiguous events, and show that, under suitable axioms, there exists a unique, convex-ranged and countably additive

[65] To clarify, this is *not* a consequence of the above definition, because we have not specified preferences. However, if we did so (for instance, by considering *MEU* preferences with $\mathcal{C} = \{p \in \Delta(\mathcal{S}) : p(s_r, s_b) = p(s_g, s_b)\}$ in the obvious notation), the definition would indeed lead to the intuitive conclusions in the text.

probability measure μ such that preferences over unambiguous acts are *probabilistically sophisticated* with respect to μ.

The interpretation is as follows: Recall that the Ellsberg Paradoxes contradict not just expected utility theory, but the more general assumption of probabilistic sophistication. Conversely, a probabilistically sophisticated individual does not exhibit Ellsberg preferences. Since the definition of unambiguous events was *motivated* by analogy with the Three-Color Paradox, it is almost a tautology that preferences over acts measurable with respect to unambiguous events cannot exhibit Ellsberg-type behavior. But the Epstein-Zhang result says much more: preferences over such acts uniquely pin down a probability measure over unambiguous events, and indeed they are probabilistically sophisticated.

If the decision-maker is probabilistically sophisticated in the sense of Machina and Schmeidler (1992), then the above definition deems *all* events to be unambiguous, and the Epstein-Zhang axioms hold; thus, their result is consistent with Machina and Schmeidler's. The Epstein-Zhang result is mainly of interest when the overall preferences are *not* probabilistically sophisticated; in such cases, it identifies a subset of events and preferences for which probabilistic sophistication holds.

Underlying the terminology employed by Epstein and Zhang is the implicit assumption that *ambiguity means a violation of probabilistic sophistication*. As we shall see, the approach we discuss next makes a different implicit assumption.

13.6.1.2 The Ghirardato-Maccheroni-Marinacci/Nehring Definition

An alternative approach has been suggested by Ghirardato et al. (2004) and Nehring (2001). We follow the exposition in the former paper.

Ghirardato et al. consider preferences over horse-roulette acts. Their starting point is the observation that Ellsberg preferences violate the Independence axiom, as noted in Section 13.5. They then propose to examine *unambiguous* preference rankings—that is, rankings that are preserved by *all* mixtures, or equivalently, for which there is no preference reversal. Formally, they define the unambiguous preference relation $\succcurlyeq^*$ by

$$f \succcurlyeq^* g \quad \text{iff} \quad \forall \lambda \in (0, 1], \quad \forall h : \lambda \cdot f + (1 - \lambda) \cdot h \succcurlyeq \lambda \cdot g + (1 - \lambda) \cdot h. \quad (13.16)$$

An equivalent definition is that $\succcurlyeq^*$ is the maximal subrelation of $\succcurlyeq$ that satisfies Independence.

If the primitive preference relation $\succcurlyeq$ satisfies a minimal set of axioms (Monotonicity, Continuity and *Risk Independence*—that is, the Independence axiom restricted to constant acts only), it will follow that $\succcurlyeq^*$ is a *Bewley preference* (Section 13.5.11).[66] Therefore, there is a set $\mathcal{C}$ of probability measures, or *relevant priors*, such that, for all acts $f, g, f \succcurlyeq^* g$

---

[66] Ghirardato et al. show that this is the case under the stronger assumption of Certainty Independence. Siniscalchi (2009a, Lemma 2) proves it under the weaker assumption of Weak Certainty Independence. Cerreia-Vioglio et al. (2011) establish the general result cited in the text.

if and only if $\int U(f(\cdot))d\mu \geq \int U(g(\cdot))d\mu$ for all $\mu \in \mathcal{C}$, where U is the utility function that represents the primitive preference relation when restricted to constants.

Ghirardato et al. call an act f *crisp* if it is unambiguously indifferent to a constant roulette lottery: that is, there is a prize (roulette lottery) x such that $f \sim^* x$.[67] The intuition is straightforward: preferences over roulette lotteries are consistent with expected utility, and hence not subject to ambiguity; thus, an act that is treated just like a lottery, even when mixing with other acts, is also not affected by ambiguity. It can be shown that an act is crisp if and only if its expected utility $\int U(f(\cdot))d\mu$ is the same for all relevant priors $\mu \in \mathcal{C}$. Thus, effectively, preferences over crisp acts are consistent with expected utility.

Finally, an event E is deemed *unambiguous* if every bet on E, that is, any binary act of the form $(x, E; y, \sim E)$ with $x \succ y$, is crisp. From the characterization of crisp acts, it is immediate that this is equivalent to the property that $\mu(E)$ is constant for all relevant priors $\mu \in \mathcal{C}$: that is, the probability measures in the set $\mathcal{C}$ "collapse" at E. Conversely, E is ambiguous if and only if $\min_{\mu \in \mathcal{C}} \mu(E) < \max_{\mu \in \mathcal{C}} \mu(E)$. Recall that this is the "intuitive" notion of ambiguity for events in the *MEU* representation. However, in the approach advocated by Ghirardato et al./Nehring, this notion applies to a broad class of preferences that includes virtually all the models of Section 13.5, and it is fully characterized by a behavioral condition (the assertion that bets on E are crisp).

There are several formal differences with the Epstein–Zhang approach. Epstein and Zhang adopt the Savage framework, start from a definition of unambiguous events, and derive a definition and characterization of unambiguous acts. Ghirardato et al. adopt the horse-roulette act framework, start from a definition of crisp (i.e., unambiguous) acts, and derive a characterization of unambiguous events. Conceptually, however, the key difference is that Epstein and Zhang regard any probabilistically sophisticated preference relation (or restriction thereof) as unambiguous; Ghirardato et al./Nehring, on the other hand, only deem expected utility preferences to be unambiguous. Both approaches classify Ellsberg preferences as ambiguity-sensitive, and expected utility preferences as unambiguous, but the Epstein–Zhang notion of ambiguity is seen to be more demanding.

For instance, consider a *MEU* preference on acts defined over a three-point state space, with $\mathcal{C} = \{p : p(s) \geq 1/9 \text{ for all } s\}$. These preferences can be equivalently described as rank-dependent, with distortion function $\delta(x) = x^2$ and a uniform prior. According to Ghirardato et al./Nehring, the only unambiguous events are the empty set and the entire space; Epstein and Zhang consider all events unambiguous. Ultimately, it may be difficult to decide which interpretation is correct.

One advantage of the Ghirardato et al./Nehring approach is that computing the set $\mathcal{C}$ of priors in the Bewley representation of unambiguous preferences, and hence

---

[67] Ghirardato et al. actually use a different definition that relies on Certainty Independence. We use here the more general definition in Cerreia-Vioglio et al. (2011).

determining which events are unambiguous, is relatively straightforward for many parametric models of preferences. For preferences that satisfy Certainty Independence (e.g., *CEU* and *MEU*), Ghirardato et al. show that $\mathcal{C}$ is the Clarke (1983) differential of the function that represents preferences, evaluated at 0. For instance, an expected utility preference with prior μ has a single relevant prior, namely μ—a basic check that indicates the soundness of the definition; a *MEU* preference with priors $\mathcal{C}$ has precisely $\mathcal{C}$ as the set of relevant priors. Ghirardato and Siniscalchi (2012) provide a general characterization that does not require Certainty Independence, and thus covers virtually all the models in Section 13.5 (see Ghirardato and Siniscalchi (2010) for explicit calculations of the relevant priors for Variational, Multiplier, Uncertainty-Averse, Smooth Ambiguity and *VEU* Preferences).

Ghirardato and Siniscalchi (2012) also propose a local notion of unambiguous preference, provide a differential characterization, and relate it to the global definition of unambiguous preference described above. They also relate local unambiguous preferences to optimizing behavior.

13.6.2 Recent Definitions of Ambiguity Aversion

The Uncertainty Aversion Axiom of Schmeidler (1989) represents the first attempt to formalize the notion that individuals dislike ambiguity. As discussed in Section 13.5, the intuition is that, by mixing two acts, the individual may be able to hedge against variation in utilities, much like, by forming a portfolio consisting of two or more assets, one can hedge against variation in monetary payoffs.

However, other attempts to characterize a dislike for ambiguity have been proposed in the literature.

13.6.2.1 Epstein's Comparative Definition

Epstein (1999) critiques the Uncertainty Aversion Axiom, focusing on the case of *CEU* preferences. Recall from Section 13.5.2 that a *CEU* preference satisfies Uncertainty Aversion if and only if the representing capacity v is convex: that is, if and only if, for every pair of events E,F, $v(E \cup F) + v(E \cap F) \geq v(E) + v(F)$. Epstein (p. 582) observes that this condition is "neither necessary nor sufficient" for *CEU* preferences to reproduce the modal choices in the Three-Color Paradox. For example, if $v(\{s_r\}) = 8/24$, $v(\{s_b\}) = v(\{s_y\}) = 7/24, v(\{s_b,s_y\}) = 13/24$ and $v(\{s_r,s_y\}) = v(\{s_r,s_b\}) = 1/2$, then the modal rankings $a_1 \succ a_2$ and $a_4 \succ a_3$ are obtained, but the capacity thus defined is not convex: for instance, $13/24 = v(\{s_b,s_y\}) = v(\{s_b\} \cup \{s_y\}) + v(\{s_b\} \cap \{s_y\}) < v(\{s_b\}) + v(\{s_y\}) = 14/24$. Accordingly, convexity of the capacity is not necessary. Suppose instead that $v(\{s_r\}) = 1/12$, $v(\{s_b\}) = v(\{s_y\}) = 1/6$, $v(\{s_b,s_y\}) = 1/3$ and $v(\{s_r,s_y\}) = v(\{s_r,s_b\}) = 1/2$; this capacity is convex, but the corresponding *CEU* preference generates the uncertainty-*loving* rankings $a_2 \succ a_1$ and $a_3 \succ a_4$! This shows that convexity of the capacity is not sufficient—it does not even prevent uncertainty-loving patterns of behavior.

The fact that the Uncertainty Aversion Axiom is neither necessary nor sufficient for the *CEU* model to exhibit Ellsberg Preferences naturally casts doubts on the implications for this axiom in other decision models. With this motivation, Epstein sets out to provide an alternative definition of ambiguity aversion. The approach introduced in his 1999 paper is refined and, in a sense, brought to completion in Epstein and Zhang (2001) as discussed in Section 13.6.1. We thus follow the exposition in the latter paper.

The decision setting is that of Savage, so in particular, acts map states to prizes rather than lotteries over prizes. The starting point of Epstein's analysis is Yaari's (1969) notion of *comparative risk aversion*, namely that a preference relation $\succcurlyeq^2$ is *more risk-averse* than another preference relation $\succcurlyeq^1$ if, for all acts h and prizes x

$$h \succcurlyeq^2 x \Rightarrow h \succcurlyeq^1 x \quad \text{and} \quad h \succ^2 x \Rightarrow h \succ^1 x. \tag{13.17}$$

That is, whenever $\succcurlyeq^2$ prefers an (intuitively, risky) act h to a (riskless) prize x, so does $\succcurlyeq^1$; this leaves open the possibility that some act h', which $\succcurlyeq^2$ may rank inferior to a prize x', may instead be ranked above x' by $\succcurlyeq^1$. With monetary prizes and expected utility preferences, this definition is equivalent to the usual characterizations in terms of the relative concavity of the von Neumann-Morgenstern utility functions. (The advantage of this definition is that it applies to non-*EU* models just as well, and hence provides a sort of "neutral testing ground" for comparing risk attitudes.)

To define a notion of risk aversion *per se,* as opposed to comparative risk aversion, one needs to fix a *benchmark*—that is, to decide which preferences to declare "risk-neutral." With monetary prizes, we can take this benchmark or reference to be *expected-value preferences*. In the general case, we say that a preference $\succcurlyeq$ is risk-averse if it is more risk-averse than *some* expected-value preference $\succcurlyeq^m$. Again, with expected utility preferences, this coincides with the usual characterization in terms of concavity of the utility function; however, the same definition can be usefully applied to non-*EU* preferences as well.

Epstein's suggestion is to define ambiguity aversion in an analogous fashion. Recall that Epstein and Zhang (2001) identify a class (a λ–system) of unambiguous events: acts measurable with respect to this class are thus unambiguous acts. First, say that $\succcurlyeq^2$ is *more ambiguity-averse* than $\succcurlyeq^1$ if, for every arbitrary act f and unambiguous act h,

$$f \succcurlyeq^2 h \Rightarrow f \succcurlyeq^1 h \quad \text{and} \quad f \succ^2 h \Rightarrow f \succ^1 h. \tag{13.18}$$

As a consequence of equation (13.18), $\succcurlyeq^2$ and $\succcurlyeq^1$ rank unambiguous acts the same way. However, $\succcurlyeq^1$ may prefer some arbitrary act f to an unambiguous act h, when $\succcurlyeq^2$ instead prefers the unambiguous act; on the other hand, the opposite never happens. In this sense, $\succcurlyeq^2$ is more ambiguity-averse than $\succcurlyeq^1$.

To define ambiguity aversion *per se*, a benchmark must be selected. Consistently with the approach discussed in Section 13.6.1, Epstein and Zhang adopt probabilistically sophisticated preferences as the benchmark. Thus, they propose that *a preference relation is ambiguity-averse if it is more ambiguity-averse than some probabilistically sophisticated preference relation.*

Epstein and Zhang (2001, Corollary 7.4) characterize *CEU* preferences that are ambiguity-averse in this sense. For *MEU* preferences, Epstein (1999, Thm. 3.3) shows that, if all priors in the set $\mathcal{C}$ coincide on unambiguous events, then ambiguity aversion holds (the next subsection indicates why a qualification is required). Epstein (1999, Sect. 3.4) shows that the Ellsberg choices in the Three-Color Paradox imply ambiguity aversion, and that, conversely, ambiguity aversion rules out the behavioral pattern that is intuitively associated with an attraction to ambiguity.

13.6.2.2 Ghirardato and Marinacci's Comparative Definition

An alternative approach is proposed by Ghirardato and Marinacci (2002), and then further developed by Ghirardato et al. (2004) and Cerreia-Vioglio et al. (2011b). Ghirardato and Marinacci consider both the Savage setting, with acts mapping to prizes, and the horse-roulette act framework, with acts mapping to objective probability distributions over prizes. They restrict attention to preferences that admit a *CEU* representation on *binary* acts, but are otherwise arbitrary (for instance, all *MEU* preferences satisfy this restriction). In the Savage environment, they further restrict comparisons to preferences that satisfy a *cardinal symmetry* requirement, which implies that a common von Neumann-Morgenstern utility can be used in the *CEU* representation on binary acts.

The starting point is again Yaari's (1969) approach, but these authors focus on comparisons between acts and constant prizes. Formally, Ghirardato and Marinacci deem a preference $\succeq^2$ *more ambiguity-averse* than $\succeq^1$ if, for all acts f and prizes x,

$$f \succeq^2 x \Rightarrow f \succeq^1 x \quad \text{and} \quad f \succ^2 x \Rightarrow f \succ^1 x. \tag{13.19}$$

The interpretation is analogous to that provided in the previous subsection for Epstein's definition: whenever $\succeq^2$ prefers an (intuitively, potentially ambiguous) act f to a (clearly unambiguous) constant x, so does $\succeq^1$; the opposite, however, need not hold.

To define ambiguity aversion per se, Ghirardato and Marinacci take as benchmark *expected utility* preferences. Thus, according to these authors, *a preference is ambiguity-averse if it is more ambiguity averse than some EU preference.*

Cerreia-Vioglio et al. (2011b) provide a characterization for a general class of preferences that satisfy Monotonicity, Continuity and Risk independence in a horse-roulette act framework (or in environments with subjective mixtures, as discussed at the beginning of Section 13.5). This is also the class of preferences for which a Bewley characterization of unambiguous preferences can be provided (Section 13.5.11). Any such preference relation is ambiguity-averse in the sense of Ghirardato and Marinacci if and only if there exists a probability measure μ such that

$$\int U\left(f(\cdot)\right)d\mu \geq V\left(f(\cdot)\right)$$

where $V(\cdot)$ as usual denotes the utility index assigned to acts. In other words, there must exist an expected utility representation, with utility function U, which dominates $V(\cdot)$ pointwise. Some immediate consequences of this characterization (and of earlier ones provided by Ghirardato and Marinacci (2002) and Ghirardato, et al.) are as follows:

- All Maxmin Expected Utility preferences are ambiguity-averse.
- Choquet Expected Utility preferences are ambiguity-averse if and only if the capacity v has a *non-empty core*: that is, if there exists a probability measure p such that $p(E) \geq v(E)$ for every event E.
- Vector Expected Utility preferences are ambiguity-averse if and only if the adjustment function A is nonpositive.
- Smooth Ambiguity Preferences with a concave second-order utility function φ are ambiguity averse.

As will be seen in Section 13.6.3 (in particular footnote 69), there are interesting and experimentally verified preference patterns that are inconsistent with Schmeidler's Uncertainty Aversion Axiom, but are consistent with Ghirardato and Marinacci's notion of ambiguity aversion. On the other hand, Cerreia-Vioglio et al. (2011b, Example 2) show that Schmeidler's Uncertainty Aversion Axiom is in general not stronger than Ghirardato and Marinacci's notion of ambiguity aversion.

A comparison with the Epstein/Epstein-Zhang approach is in order. The main conceptual difference is that—as was the case for the Epstein vs. Ghirardato et al./ Nehring notions of ambiguity—the choice of the ambiguity-neutral benchmark is different. Epstein adopts probabilistic sophistication; Ghirardato and Marinacci choose expected utility. Epstein (1999) observes that using *EU* as benchmark implies that, for instance, the modal preferences in Savage's restatement of the Allais paradox (Savage (1954, p.103)) are classified as ambiguity averse. There is, of course, nothing that evokes ambiguity or ambiguity attitudes in the Allais bets, even when translated in a Savage framework: the composition of the urn is known to the individual, who presumably trusts the experimenter, etc. But the force of this argument derives in part from the particular example it considers. One can easily imagine choice situations in which ruling out ambiguity aversion on the basis of available information is not straightforward. Suppose for instance that an individual is asked to bet on which of three cities in an unfamiliar foreign country has the highest average temperature in the month of May. Suppose that this individual's preferences admit the *MEU* representation of Section 13.5.1, with $\mathcal{C} = \{p : p(s) \geq 1/9 \text{ for all } s\}$. We noted above that these preferences can equivalently be described as rank-dependent (*CEU*), with distortion function $\delta(x) = x^2$ and a uniform prior. Since these preferences are probabilistically sophisticated, Epstein classifies them as ambiguity-neutral; Ghirardato and Marinacci instead classify them as ambiguity averse.

This alternative example does not provide clear indications as to whether or not ambiguity plays a role.[68]

The Epstein definition is accordingly more "conservative": if a pattern of behavior is deemed "ambiguity-averse," it *surely* has features that are inconsistent with probabilistic beliefs. Thus, for instance, if one was interested in demonstrating the presence and relevance of ambiguity in a given economic environment, applying the Epstein definition would provide more convincing evidence. On the other hand, the Ghirardato-Marinacci definition captures a broader range of behavioral patterns that *may* be influenced by ambiguity, and is easily characterized in a variety of parametric preference models.

13.6.2.3 Smooth Ambiguity Aversion

As anticipated in Section 13.5.4, Klibanoff et al. (2005) propose a notion of ambiguity aversion that is specific to the Smooth Ambiguity Preferences model.

These authors identify an individual with a collection $\{\succsim_K, \succsim_K^{(2)}\}$ of first- and second-order preferences, indexed by the *support K* of the second-order probability measure M representing each pair. They assume that all first-order preferences in any such collection exhibit the same risk attitudes, and hence pin down the same utility $U(\cdot)$; similarly, they assume that risk preferences are the same for all second-order preferences, which pins down the utility function $v(\cdot)$ in the *EU* representation of second-order acts, and consequently also the second-order utility $\varphi(\cdot)$. The objective is to provide a condition on all elements of the collection $\{\succsim_K, \succsim_K^{(2)}\}$ that characterizes second-order risk aversion, i.e., concavity of the function $\varphi(\cdot)$.

Their construction is as follows: Recall that any act f and any first-order probability measure μ induce a lottery over prizes, $(\ldots;x_i,\mu(f^{-1}(x_i));\ldots)$. This lottery has expected utility $\int U(f(\cdot))d\mu$. Since the second-order measure M is defined over first-order probabilities μ, it induces a *lottery over expected utilities*, which in the case of a finite support $K=\{\ldots,\mu_j,\ldots\}$ can be expressed as

$$\mathbf{P}_f^* \equiv \left(\ldots; \int U(f(\cdot))d\mu_j, M(\mu_j); \ldots\right).$$

The smooth ambiguity evaluation of the act f corresponds to computing the "expected utility" of the lottery $\mathbf{P}_f^*$ with respect to the second-order utility $\varphi(\cdot)$. Hence, to characterize concavity of the latter, we need to compare f with a prize $x_f(M)$ whose utility is precisely the expected value of $\mathbf{P}_f^*$—equivalently, the *average* expected utility of f. Such a prize exists because U has a convex range. Klibanoff et al. then show that the

---

[68] Epstein and Zhang's characterization of ambiguous and unambiguous events, and hence their definition of ambiguity aversion, requires a rich state space. However, Epstein's original definition does not restrict the state space, and classifies any probabilistically sophisticated preference as ambiguity neutral. Thus, our discussion of the temperature example is indeed consistent with Epstein (1999).

second-order utility $\varphi(\cdot)$ is concave if and only if the individual is *smooth ambiguity averse*, in the sense that for every support K with associated second-order measure M, and for every act f, the individual prefers the prize $x_f(M)$ to f— formally, $x_f(M) \succcurlyeq_K f$. A similar construction can be used to characterize comparative smooth ambiguity aversion.

It should be noted that, due to the way $x_f(M)$ is defined, smooth ambiguity aversion depends crucially on the representation of second-order preferences. Thus, the qualifications on second-order preferences, and on the interpretation of the smooth representation noted in Section 5.4, similarly apply here. Furthermore, again because its definition involves elements of the functional representation, smooth ambiguity aversion cannot be directly compared with the Epstein and Ghirardato-Marinacci definitions (though of course one can ask whether specific parameterizations satisfy one of these definitions, as we did in the previous section).

13.6.3 Recent Examples of Ambiguity Aversion

The models of ambiguity aversion reviewed in Section 13.5 were designed to capture aspects of ambiguity aversion revealed in Ellsberg's original examples, each of which only involved two possible outcome values (Ellsberg used \$0 and \$100). However, additional aspects of ambiguity aversion, which can only reveal themselves in choices involving three or more outcome values, have since come to light, and pose challenges to some of these models.

A simple example of this is illustrated in the following table, based on an urn containing 50 red or black balls, and 51 green or yellow balls.[69] In the first pair of bets, it is likely that ambiguity aversion would outweigh bet a_1's slight 50:51 disadvantage, causing it to be preferred over a_2. In the second pair, the difference in the bets' amounts ambiguity is not as stark, and this same 50:51 disadvantage may cause an individual to rank a_4 over a_3. Such preferences clearly violate the Sure-Thing Principle as well as Machina and Schmeidler's (1992) Strong Comparative Probability Axiom, and are accordingly not compatible with probabilistically sophisticated beliefs. But in addition, they are seen to violate the Comonotonicity Axiom of the Choquet Expected Utility model.

	50 balls		51 balls	
	red	black	green	yellow
a_1	\$45	\$45	\$40	\$40
a_2	\$45	\$40	\$45	\$40
a_3	\$1,000	\$45	\$40	\$0
a_4	\$1,000	\$40	\$45	\$0

[69] This is based on an example of Machina (2009). Baillon et al. (2011) demonstrate that similar examples can also violate standard specifications of the Multiple-Priors, Smooth Ambiguity Preferences (with concave ϕ) and Variational Preferences models, though not the Vector Expected Utility model. (See also Siniscalchi (2008b) as well as the experimental results of L'Haridon and Placido (2010).) Lehrer (2007) demonstrates that they do not violate the models of Lehrer (2009,2012) and Dillenberger and Segal (2012) demonstrate that they do not violate the model of Segal (1987a).

Three particular aspects of ambiguity and ambiguity aversion can arise once three or more outcomes are allowed, each of which poses problems for at least some of the models reviewed in Section 13.5. The first is that some of the models' preferences over *purely subjective* (i.e., not mixed) prospects can inherit the same Allais-type difficulties[70] faced by expected utility preferences over purely objective prospects. The reason for this is that some purely subjective prospects can be said to be "more objective" than others, and some of the models' preferences over such "almost-objective" prospects converge to expected utility preferences.

To construct such prospects, partition a continuum state space $\mathcal{S} = [0,1)$ into m equal intervals $\{[0,1/m),\ldots,[i/m,(i+1)/m),\ldots,[(m-1)/m,1)\}$, and for each $\alpha \in [0,1]$ define $[0,\alpha \underset{m}{\times} \mathcal{S}$ as the union of the left α portions of these intervals, so that $[0,\alpha) \underset{m}{\times} \mathcal{S} = \sim_{i=0}^{m-1} [i/m, (i+\alpha)/m)$. As shown by Poincaré (1912) and others,[71] such events will satisfy $\lim_{m\to\infty} \pi([0,\alpha) \underset{m}{\times} \mathcal{S}) = \alpha$ for any measure $\pi(\cdot)$ over $[0,1)$ with a sufficiently regular density. More generally, for any set $\wp \subseteq [0,1)$ consisting of a finite union of intervals, and any positive integer m, define event $\wp \underset{m}{\times} \mathcal{S}$ by

$$\wp \underset{m}{\times} \mathcal{S} = \bigcup_{i=0}^{m-1} \{ (i+\omega)/m \,|\, \omega \in \wp \}$$

that is, as the union of the natural images of $\wp$ into each of $\mathcal{S}$'s equal-length intervals. Events with this type of periodic structure are termed *almost-objective events,* and satisfy $\lim_{m\to\infty} \pi(\wp \underset{m}{\times} \mathcal{S}) = \lambda(\wp)$ where $\lambda(\cdot)$ is the uniform Lebesgue measure over $[0,1)$. Bets of the form $(x_1 \text{ on } \wp_1 \underset{m}{\times} \mathcal{S}; \ldots; x_n \text{ on } \wp_n \underset{m}{\times} \mathcal{S})$ are termed *almost-objective bets,* and are seen to be purely subjective.

As shown in Machina (2013), under natural smoothness conditions, Multiple-Priors,[72] Smooth Ambiguity Preferences and Variational Preferences preferences over almost-objective bets will converge to expected utility, that is

$$\lim_{m\to\infty} W_{MP}(x_1 \text{ on } \wp_1 \underset{m}{\times} \mathcal{S}; \ldots; x_n \text{ on } \wp_n \underset{m}{\times} \mathcal{S}) = \sum_{i=1}^{n} U(x_i) \cdot \lambda(\wp_i)$$

$$\lim_{m\to\infty} W_{SM}(x_1 \text{ on } \wp_1 \underset{m}{\times} \mathcal{S}; \ldots; x_n \text{ on } \wp_n \underset{m}{\times} \mathcal{S}) = \phi\left(\sum_{i=1}^{n} U(x_i) \cdot \lambda(\wp_i) \right)$$

$$\lim_{m\to\infty} W_{VP}(x_1 \text{ on } \wp_1 \underset{m}{\times} \mathcal{S}; \ldots; x_n \text{ on } \wp_n \underset{m}{\times} \mathcal{S}) = \sum_{i=1}^{n} U(x_i) \cdot \lambda(\wp_i) + \min_{\pi(\cdot) \in P} c(\pi(\cdot)).$$

---

[70] Such as the classic Allais Paradox, Common Consequence Effect and Common Ratio Effect (e.g., Allais (1953), MacCrimmon and Larsson (1968)).

[71] See Machina (2004, p.9).

[72] For the Multiple-Priors result, the set $\mathcal{C}$ is also assumed to be a convex polytope (the convex hull of a finite number of probability distributions).

Thus, if an individual is asymptotically indifferent between the almost-objective bets

$$a_1 = (\$1M, 1)$$

$$a_2 = (\$5M \text{ on } [0, .10] \times S; \$1M \text{ on } [.10, .99] \times S; \$0 \text{ on } [.99, 1) \times S)$$

$$a_3 = (\$5M \text{ on } [0, .10] \underset{m}{\times} S; \$0 \text{ on } [.11, 1) \underset{m}{\times} S)$$

$$a_4 = (\$1M \text{ on } [0, .11] \underset{m}{\times} S; \$0 \text{ on } [.11, 1) \underset{m}{\times} S)$$

and their respective purely objective counterparts

$$\hat{a}_1 = (\$1M, 1) \qquad\qquad \hat{a}_2 = (\$5M, .10; \$1M, .89; \$; 0, .01)$$

$$\hat{a}_3 = (\$5M, .10; \$0, .90) \qquad\qquad \hat{a}_4 = (\$1M, .11; \$0, .89)$$

the standard Allais-type preferences $\hat{a}_1 \succ \hat{a}_2$ and $\hat{a}_3 \succ \hat{a}_4$ over these objective bets induce the corresponding preferences $a_1 \succ a_2$ and $a_3 \succ a_4$ over these purely subjective acts, violating Multiple-Priors Preferences, Smooth Ambiguity Preferences and Variational Preferences over purely subjective uncertainty.

A second aspect concerns the Choquet Expected Utility model's ability to capture attitudes toward different sources, with different amounts, of ambiguity. Take an urn with a single ball, which is either black or white, as well as a coin which has been slightly (but only slightly) bent, and consider the following bets, where the coin is flipped and the ball is drawn simultaneously. Bet I spreads the uncertainty of receiving +$8,000 versus −$8,000 across the only slightly ambiguous coin whereas Bet II spreads this uncertainty across the more ambiguous urn, so that ambiguity averter would presumably prefer Bet I.

	Bet I				Bet II	
	black	white			black	white
heads	+$8,000	$0		heads	$0	$0
			vs.			
tails	−$8,000	$0		tails	−$8,000	+$8,000

To see that the Choquet model is incapable of exhibiting such a preference, observe that the model evaluates the bets according to the respective formulas[73]

Bet I : $U(\$8,000) \cdot C(HB) + U(-\$8,000) \cdot [1 - C((HB) \cup C(HW) \cup C(TW)]$

Bet II : $U(\$8,000) \cdot C(TW) + U(-\$8,000) \cdot [1 - C((HB) \cup C(HW) \cup C(TW)]$

On the assumption that the capacity $C(\cdot)$ evaluates the informationally symmetric events HB and TW equally, these values are equal, so the Choquet model must rank the

---

[73] Where HB denotes a heads and a black ball, etc., and we set $U(0) = 0$.

two bets as indifferent, and cannot allow a strict preference over these different sources and amounts of ambiguity.[74]

A final aspect which arises once three or more outcomes are allowed concerns how ambiguity attitudes are allowed to vary with wealth. Defining \$c as the individual's certainty equivalent of an objective 50:50 lottery over \$0:\$100, the bets on Urns I and II below are each seen to differ from the purely objective bet b_0 by the introduction of ambiguity across some pair of its events. Urn I is obtained from bet b_0 by introducing ambiguity across its middle and lower outcome, whereas Urn II is obtained from b_0 by introducing ambiguity across its middle and upper outcome.

	1 ball	1 ball	1 ball
b_0	\$0	\$c	\$100

URN I				URN II		
2 balls		1 ball		1 ball	2 balls	
black	white	red		red	black	white
\$0	\$c	\$100	VS.	\$0	\$c	\$100

For the same reason that individuals might be less risk averse over higher than lower outcomes, they may exhibit less ambiguity aversion over higher than lower outcomes, which would lead to a preference for Urn II. However, the Multiple-Priors, Rank-Dependent, Smooth and Variational Preferences models evaluate the acts via the respective formulas

$$W_{RD}(\text{URN I}) = 2/3 \cdot C(WW) + 1/2 \cdot [C(WW \cup BW \cup WB) - C(WW)]$$
$$+ 1/3 \cdot [1 - C(WW \cup BW \cup WB)] = W_{RD}(\text{URN II})$$

$$W_{MP}(\text{URN I}) = \min_{(p_{BB}, p_{BW}, p_{WB}, p_{WW}) \in P_0} [1/3 \cdot p_{BB} + 1/2 \cdot p_{BW}$$
$$+ 1/2 \cdot p_{WB} + 2/3 \cdot p_{WW}]$$
$$= W_{MP}(\text{URN II})$$

$$W_{SM}(\text{URN I}) = \int \phi \left(1/3 \cdot p_{BB} + 1/2 \cdot p_{BW} + 1/2 \cdot p_{WB} + 2/3 \cdot p_{WW}\right)$$
$$\cdot d\mu(p_{BB}, p_{BW}, p_{WB}, p_{WW}) = W_{SM}(\text{URN II})$$

$$W_{VP}(\text{URN I}) = \min_{(p_{BB}, p_{BW}, p_{WB}, p_{WW}) \in P}$$
$$[1/3 \cdot p_{BB} + 1/2 \cdot p_{BW} + 1/2 \cdot p_{WB} + 2/3 \cdot p_{WW} + c(p_{BB}, p_{BW}, p_{WB}, p_{WW})]$$
$$= W_{VP}(\text{URN II})$$

---

[74] Although not related to the present example, attitudes toward different sources of uncertainty have been experimentally examined by Abdellaoui et al. (2011).

Accordingly, none of the four models can allow attitudes toward ambiguity to depend upon the wealth level at which it occurs.

The reason for this incompatibility comes out when the two bets are expressed in the Anscombe-Aumann format of Section 13.3.4, that is, as mappings from each urn's four possible states $\{BB,BW,WB,WW\}$[75] to their implied objective lotteries. Setting $U(\$100)=1$ and $U(\$0)=0$ so that $U(\$c)=1/2$, the statewise expected utilities of the two urns are seen to be identical. Since the four models evaluate Anscombe-Aumann acts via their statewise expected utilities, they cannot discriminate between the two urns' bets.

	BB	*BW*	*WB*	*WW*
URN I	($0,2/3;$100,1/3)	($0, 1/3; $c, 1/3; $100, 1/3)	($0, 1/3; $c, 1/3; $100, 1/3)	($c,2/3;$100,1/3)
URN II	($0, 1/3; $c, 2/3)	($0, 1/3; $c, 1/3; $100, 1/3)	($0, 1/3; $c, 1/3; $100, 1/3)	($0,1/3;$100,2/3)
expected utility	1/3	1/2	1/2	2/3

A similar example[76] establishes that the four models cannot express a preference or aversion to ambiguity in losses versus gains:

Ambiguity in Losses versus Gains

	URN I				vs.		URN II		
	1 ball		1 ball			1 ball		1 ball	
	black	white	red	green		red	green	black	white
	−3	−1	+2	+2		−2	−2	+1	+3

Another recent variation on Ellsberg's standard form was examined by Yang and Yao (2011), who allowed subjects to draw twice with replacement from the same urn, with a different color winning each time, again finding a substantial number of violations of the major theories of ambiguity aversion.

---

[75] Where *BW* denotes that the first ball in the urn is black and the second is white, etc.

[76] With outcomes already expressed in utils.

13.7 UPDATING AND DYNAMIC CHOICE

Savage's axiomatization of expected utility is atemporal—time is not an explicit consideration or an input to the theory. Alternatively, one can view Savage's theory as dealing with one-period decision problems: the individual chooses an act, then the state is realized, which determines the prize accruing to the decision maker. However, Postulate P2, the Sure-Thing Principle, provides a way to extend the theory to *dynamic decision problems*, in which the individual may acquire partial information about the state of nature over time, and take actions at several decision points, until all uncertainty is resolved and a final prize is obtained. A formal analysis of the extension of Savage's atemporal theory to dynamic choice is beyond the scope of this chapter; instead, we emphasize two key ingredients of this extension.

The first is *updating*. The notion of updating a prior probability measure μ so as to reflect information the individual has acquired is familiar. If one assumes that the individual is an expected utility maximizer, and that his or her risk attitudes and tastes do not change, the probabilistic conditioning operator determines a *conditional preference*. Savage (1954, p.22) suggested the converse approach: one can start with a *definition* of conditional preference, and show that it characterizes probabilistic updating. Specifically, Savage stipulates that act f is weakly preferred to act g given event E, written $f \succcurlyeq_E g$, if and only if, for *some* act h,

$$(f, E; h, \sim E) \succcurlyeq (g, E; h, \sim E). \tag{13.20}$$

It is easy to see that, if the *ex-ante* preference $\succcurlyeq$ is an EU preference, with subjective prior μ, then the updated preference $\succcurlyeq_E$ is also consistent with EU. Then, if the event E is nonnull,[77] one has $\mu(E) > 0$, and the probability measure associated with the updated preference $\succcurlyeq_E$ is the usual update $\mu(\cdot|E)$ of μ. We emphasize that Postulate P2 is essential to ensure that this definition is well-posed: if P2 is violated, then different choices of acts h may lead to contradictory rankings of f and g conditional on E.

The second key ingredient in the extension of Savage's theory to dynamic choice is *dynamic consistency*. One possible formulation of this property is as follows: if act f is weakly preferred to act g conditional on E, and also conditional on $\sim E$, then f is unconditionally preferred to g; also, if one of the conditional preferences is strict, so is the unconditional preference. Formally:

$$f \succcurlyeq_E g, f \succcurlyeq_{\sim E} g \;\Rightarrow\; f \succcurlyeq g \quad \text{and} \quad f \succ_E g, f \succcurlyeq_{\sim E} g \;\Rightarrow\; f \succ g \tag{13.21}$$

(The second part of the definition requires that the event E be nonnull.) Dynamic consistency is essential to ensure that, if a multiperiod choice problem is solved by *backward*

---

[77] See footnote 25.

induction or *recursion*, one obtains a solution that is also optimal *ex ante*. It turns out that Savage's Postulate P2 also ensures that conditional preferences as defined above satisfy dynamic consistency. (Indeed, the connection between P2 and dynamic consistency is tight: see Epstein and Le Breton (1993), Ghirardato (2002) and Siniscalchi (2011, Sect. 4.2).)

Since ambiguity-sensitive preferences violate Postulate P2, it should come as no surprise that updating and consistent dynamic choice pose challenges. As we shall see, there is no unique way to define conditional preferences or—in any given parametric model—conditional "beliefs." Furthermore, no matter how we define conditional preferences, we can construct examples in which dynamic consistency is violated. Different approaches have been proposed to deal with these issues. We now briefly discuss some of the relevant contributions.

Lack of space prevents us from discussing two other broadly related issues which have seen recent work. The first is learning under ambiguity: see Epstein and Schneider (2007). The second is the notion of exchangeability, or symmetry: Epstein and Seo (2010, 2012) extend the classic results of de Finetti (1937) and Hewitt and Savage (1955) to ambiguity-sensitive preferences. See also Al Najjar and De Castro (2013).

13.7.1 Updating Ambiguous Beliefs

Early contributions focus on updating rules for capacities in the Choquet Expected Utility model. Two rules have received particular attention: the *Dempster-Shafer Rule* and the *Full Bayesian Rule*. Both essentially originate in the work of Dempster (1967), who considers the following scenario: An individual has a probabilistic belief μ on a set Ω; furthermore, there is a correspondence (a multivalued map) $\Gamma : \Omega \rightarrow S$, where S is the state space of interest, which for simplicity we assume to be finite. Intuitively, the map Γ describes the individual's partial information about the relationship between elements of Ω, whose likelihood the individual can assess with confidence, and the events in S. The individual's beliefs on S are represented by the capacity v defined by

$$v(A) = \frac{\mu\left(\{\omega : \emptyset \neq \Gamma(\omega) \subseteq A\}\right)}{\mu\left(\{\omega : \Gamma(\omega) \neq \emptyset\}\right)}.$$

Intuitively, this embodies a conservative stance: the individual assigns to each A only the probability of those elements of Ω that he or she knows for sure to correspond to elements in A. The capacity thus defined is convex, and indeed satisfies a stronger property that characterizes so-called "belief functions" (e.g., Shafer (1976) and Jaffray (1992)). The reason why Γ is allowed to take on an empty value will be clear momentarily.

Dempster describes the following updating rule. Suppose the individual learns that event $E \subseteq S$ has occurred. The initial information, as encoded by Γ, was that element ω of Ω applied to states s in $\Gamma(\omega)$: but since he or she now knows that the state s must also lie in E, he or she associates ω with $\Gamma(\omega) \cap E$. We can then define $\Gamma_E(\omega) = \Gamma(\omega) \cap E$ and construct the capacity $v_{DS}(\cdot|E)$ derived from Γ_E as above (we explain the superscript below). Dempster shows that

$$v_{DS}(A|E) = \frac{v([A \cap E] \cup [\sim E]) - v(\sim E)}{1 - v(\sim E)}.$$

While this expression may seem a bit mysterious, the above construction clarifies its origin. The subsequent literature has mostly taken the above formula (or alternative, equivalent formulae) as the *definition* of a particular updating rule; since it also plays a prominent role in the work of Shafer (1976), it is commonly referred to as the *Dempster-Shafer* updating rule (hence the subscript in $v_{DS}(\cdot|E)$).

An alternative updating rule for capacities is related to sets of priors. It is known that, if a capacity v is a "belief function," then it satisfies the following duality relation: letting $\mathcal{C}_v$ be the set of probability distributions μ such that $\mu(A) \geq v(A)$ for all events A, it is the case that, for every event A, $v(A) = \inf\{\mu(A) : \mu \in \mathcal{C}_v\}$ (this is *not* true for arbitrary convex capacities). Thus, a possible updating rule is as follows: first, assuming $v(E) > 0$, update all probability distributions in $\mathcal{C}_v$ according to the usual probabilistic conditioning formula; then, consider the lower envelope of the resulting set. That is, we define the so-called *Full Bayesian updating rule* for the belief function v by $v_{FB}(A|E) = \inf\{\mu(A|E) : \mu \in \mathcal{C}_v\}$. Jaffray (1992) shows that $v_{FB}(\cdot|E)$ is indeed a belief function, and furthermore that

$$v_{FB}(A|E) = \frac{v(A)}{v(A) + 1 - v(A \cup \sim E)}.$$

An alternative approach leading to the above definition of Full Bayesian updating can be found in Fagin and Halpern (1991).

Gilboa and Schmeidler (1993) are the first to provide an axiomatic treatment of updating rules in a decision setting; in particular, they adopt the horse-roulette act environment discussed in Section 13.5, and assume that there exist a best and a worst prize. They consider uncertainty-averse Choquet Expected Utility preferences (which are thus also Maxmin Expected Utility preferences) and consider the class of *h-Bayesian update rules*, where h is an arbitrary act. Given an unconditional preference $\succeq$, the h-Bayesian update given E, denoted $\succeq_{E,h}$, is defined by

$$f \succeq_{E,h} g \quad \Leftrightarrow \quad (f, E; h, \sim E) \succeq (g, E; h, \sim E).$$

Under Savage's Postulate P2, all h-Bayesian update rules coincide with Savage's update rule; however, for more general preferences, different choices of h induce different conditional preferences. In particular, Gilboa and Schmeidler show that, if one takes *h* to be the constant act that yields the *best possible prize*, the resulting conditional preference is *CEU*, with capacity given by the Dempster-Shafer update of the prior capacity (the utility function is unchanged relative to the prior preference). They interpret this as a form of "pessimistic updating": when receiving the information that *E* has occurred, the individual ranks acts as if, in the counterfactual event, he or she would have received the best possible prize.

Eichberger et al. (2007) and Horie (2007) characterize Full Bayesian updating for arbitrary capacities. Their main axiom is adopted from Pires (2002), a paper we discuss below; thus, we defer the discussion of their contribution.

Two main updating rules have been proposed for maxmin expected utility (*MEU*) preferences. The first stipulates that, given a set $\mathcal{C}$ of priors on the state space $\mathcal{S}$, all priors $\mu \in \mathcal{C}$ with $\mu(\cdot|E) > 0$ be updated upon learning that *E* has occurred; this is called the *Full* or *Generalized Bayesian updating rule* for the set $\mathcal{C}$. It is related to Full Bayesian updating for belief functions, in the sense that (i) a *CEU* preference for which the capacity is a belief function, and hence convex, is also a *MEU* preference, and (ii) by the result stated above, the *CEU* preference characterized by the full Bayesian update of the capacity is the same as the *MEU* preference characterized by the full Bayesian update of the set $\mathcal{C}$. However, it is important to emphasize that full Bayesian updating of sets of priors is well-defined for arbitrary sets $\mathcal{C}$, not just those that consist of probability distributions that dominate a given belief function.

Full Bayesian updating of priors has been axiomatized by Pires (2002) in the horse-roulette act setup; related results can be found in Walley (1991, pp. 632–638) and Jaffray (1994). The key axiom establishes a connection between the conditional certainty equivalent *x* of an act *f* and unconditional ranking of *x* *vis-à-vis* a suitable composite act: formally, for every (nonnull) event *E*, act *f* and prize *x*, it requires that $f \sim_E x$ if and only if $(f, E; x, \sim E) \sim x$. One implication of this axiom is that conditional preferences can be elicited from prior preferences: this is done by determining, for each act *f*, the prize *x* that solves the preference equation $(f, E; x, \sim E) \sim x$.[78]

Eichberger et al. (2007) use the same axiom to characterize Full Bayesian Updating for capacities; however, Horie (2007) points out that, while Pires's axiom is sufficient to deliver full Bayesian updating, it is too strong. Horie shows that the appropriate necessary and sufficient condition is a version of Pires's axiom that is restricted to binary acts *f*.

An alternative updating rule was proposed and characterized by Gilboa and Schmeidler (1993). Recall that they characterize Dempster-Shafer updating for uncertainty averse *CEU* preferences, which are thus also *MEU* preferences. Hence, their result necessarily also pins down a procedure to update sets of priors. The procedure

---

[78] Siniscalchi (2011) shows that Pires's axiom is equivalent to a weakening of the standard dynamic consistency property discussed above.

works as follows: out of the set $\mathcal{C}$ of priors characterizing the *ex-ante* preference, select the measures assigning the maximum probability to the event E that has occurred, and only update those. Gilboa and Schmeidler call this the *maximum-likelihood update rule*. Note that their characterization result only covers preferences that are both *MEU* and *CEU*; a characterization of maximum-likelihood updating for general *MEU* preferences is not known.

Finally, Siniscalchi (2009a) defines and axiomatizes an updating rule for *VEU* preferences, which entails (i) updating the baseline prior in the usual way, and (ii) replacing the covariances in equation (13.10) with suitably rescaled conditional covariances.

13.7.2 Dynamic Choice under Ambiguity

Regardless of the preference model and updating rule one adopts, the potential for dynamic inconsistency of preferences arises as soon as one relaxes Savage's Postulate P2. This is easy to see from the following decision tree, which can be thought of as a dynamic version of the Three-Color Paradox. There are two decision points, identified by filled circles; in the first, *ex-ante*, stage, the individual chooses whether to stop (S) and get a 50% chance to receive \$100, or continue (C) with the bet. Then, the individual learns whether the ball drawn is yellow or not; if it is yellow, the individual receives \$x. If instead the ball is not yellow, the individual can choose to bet on red or black. The composition of the urn, and the individual's information about it, is as in the (static) Three-Color Paradox.

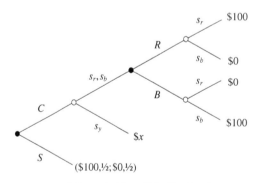

A Dynamic Three-Color Urn Paradox

The objects of choice in this problem are not, strictly speaking, acts: rather, they are *actions* (such as R and B, C and S) at different nodes. The individual can also formulate *plans*, such as "choose C, then choose R if the second decision node is reached" (denoted CR). The atemporal models discussed in Section 13.5 do not directly induce preferences over actions or plans. However, one can adopt a standard *reduction* assumption, and evaluate a plan or action according to the act that it induces. For instance, the plan CR induces the act ($\$100,s_r;\$0,s_b;\$x,s_y$); this can be evaluated by any one of the functional representations of Section 13.5. Similarly, the action R at the second decision node induces a "partial" act ($100,$s_r$;$0,s_b); any one of the updating rules discussed in the previous subsection can be used to evaluate such acts, as prizes assigned on the event s_y are irrelevant when conditioning on $\{s_r, s_b\}$.

To see that dynamic consistency may fail, suppose *ex-ante* preferences are *MEU*, with priors as in equation (13.2). Consider the case $x = \$100$, and observe that then the plans CR and CB correspond to the Three-Color urn's bets a_3 and a_4 respectively. As noted in Section 13.5.1, letting $U(\$100) = 1$ and $U(\$0) = 0$, bet a_4, and therefore CB yield utility 2/3, whereas a_3 and hence CR yield utility 1/3; on the other hand, choosing S yields utility 1/2. Therefore, the *ex-ante* optimal plan for this decision maker is CB. Now suppose that this individual uses the Full Bayesian updating rule. The updated set of probability distributions is

$$C_{\{s_r,s_b\}} = \left\{ \mu : \mu(\{s_r\}) \geq 1/3, \ \mu(\{s_y\}) = 0 \right\}.$$

Therefore, upon reaching the second decision node, the individual will strictly prefer R, which yields $100 with probability at least 1/3, to B, which may yield $100 with probability 0. This means that, *although CR is the ex-ante optimal plan, the individual will not actually want to carry it out.* Furthermore, if we analyze the problem according to backward induction, we conclude that the individual will choose R at the second node. Hence, from the perspective of the first node, choosing C is "just as good" as committing to plan CB, which—as noted above—has an *ex-ante* utility of only 1/3. Therefore, the individual will prefer to choose S at the initial node, according to backward induction. Thus, *backward induction yields a different solution than ex-ante optimization.* Both these issues can be traced back to a violation of dynamic consistency: the acts a_4 and a_3 (equivalently, the plans CR and CB) are indifferent conditional on $\{s_y\}$ because they both yield $x = \$100$, the individual strictly prefers a_3 to a_4 conditional on $\{s_r, s_b\}$, but strictly prefers a_4 to a_3 unconditionally.

Similar examples can be constructed for different preference representations and updating rules; the issues highlighted are not unique to *MEU* or full Bayesian updating.

There are three ways to address this failure of dynamic consistency.[79] The first was introduced by Epstein and Schneider (2003) in the context of *MEU* preferences, and extended to Variational Preferences by Maccheroni et al. (2006b), to Smooth Ambiguity Preferences by Klibanoff et al. (2009), and to Vector Expected Utility preferences by Siniscalchi (2010). This approach has also been broadly adopted in applications, especially in financial economics. The basic observation is that the noted tight connection

---

[79] A fourth way is to drop the reduction assumption. In the example, one could argue that the individual may prefer plan CR to plan CB in the tree of the figure, even though he or she prefers act a_4 to act a_3 in the static Three-Color Paradox. This is explored in Li (2011).

between Savage's Postulate P2 and dynamic consistency does *not* prevent the coexistence of *some* departures from P2 and *some* form of dynamic consistency. More precisely, if for a given state space one wishes to ensure dynamic consistency in *every possible decision tree*, then Postulate P2 must hold for *all* events, and therefore there is no scope for Ellsberg behavior. However, one can fix *one* particular decision tree, and require dynamic consistency only for that particular tree. This implies that P2 will hold only for *some* events, but there will still be scope for Ellsberg-type behavior.

For a simple example, suppose that a fair coin is tossed; if it comes up heads, the individual is confronted with the Three-Color Ellsberg urn and must choose to bet on red vs. black; if it comes up tails, the individual faces the same urn but must choose whether to bet on red or yellow vs. black or yellow. Letting the space be $\mathcal{S} = \{H,T\} \times \{r,b,y\}$ to simplify notation, a plausible set of priors for this problem is

$$\mathcal{C} = \left\{ \mu : \mu(\{H_r\}) = \mu(\{T_r\}) = 1/6, \mu(\{H_b\}) = \mu(\{T_b\}), \mu(\{H_y\}) = \mu(\{T_y\}) \right\}.$$

For this set of priors, the modal Ellsberg preferences obtain, both *ex ante* and after each realization of the coin toss. Dynamic consistency also holds in this tree. Note that this set of priors is obtained by taking the product of the uniform probability on $\{H,T\}$ with the priors in the set $\mathcal{C}$ of equation (13.2). Epstein and Schneider show that dynamic consistency of *MEU* preferences in a particular tree characterizes a generalization of this property of the representing set of priors, called *rectangularity*. Furthermore, they show that dynamic *MEU* preferences with a rectangular set of priors admit a *recursive* representation; this accounts for the popularity of this approach in applications.

Rectangularity does rule out, for example, the set of priors in equation (13.2) from Section 13.5.1, which we used to analyze the dynamic version of the Three-Color Paradox in the above figure. Intuitively, conditioning on the event $\{s_r, s_b\}$ "breaks" the *complementarity* between the states s_b and s_y (cf. Sections 13.5.6 and 13.6.1) and this leads to a violation of dynamic consistency. Loosely speaking, rectangularity rules out precisely these complementarities across different conditioning events. Of course, in some contexts, such complementarities may be the main object of interest—as is the case in the stylized problem of the figure. In such cases, alternatives to the Epstein-Schneider approach can be pursued.

One such alternative was advocated by Hanany and Klibanoff (2007, 2009), who adapt arguments first proposed by Machina (1989) in the context of risky choice. The basic intuition is that the preceding arguments implicitly made the assumption that, when the individual is evaluating choices at a node in a decision tree, *bygones are bygones*: the only relevant considerations are the residual uncertainty, and the prizes delivered at terminal nodes that can still be reached. Machina, as well as Hanany and Klibanoff, argues that this need not be the case. For example, in the choice problem of the figure, when the individual faces a choice between R and B, he or she may take into account that this choice occurs "in the context" of a given decision tree. In particular, he or she may take into account *the prize $x that would have been delivered if a yellow ball had been drawn*. Formally, this allows the individual to express a *conditional* preference for R over B if $x = \$0$, and for B over R if $x = \$100$. Hence, in particular, with $x = \$100$ there no longer is any dynamic inconsistency: *ex ante*, the individual prefers CB to CR, and upon reaching the second decision node, prefers B to R.

Formally, Hanany and Klibanoff (2007) focus on *MEU* preferences, and impose a (weak) form of dynamic consistency. They consider a class of two-period decision problems and a class of updating rules, i.e., mappings that associate a second-period conditional preference to every prior preference, decision problem and *ex-ante* optimal act. Within this class, they characterize the ones that are dynamically consistent in the sense that the *ex-ante* optimal act remains conditionally optimal. Their 2009 paper extends the results to arbitrary Uncertainty-Averse Preferences.

One consequence of this approach is that the resulting conditional preferences may display either uncertainty aversion or uncertainty neutrality, depending on the prizes assigned at counterfactual terminal nodes; an example is provided in Siniscalchi (2009b). This seems at odds with the usual interpretation of ambiguity, which concerns information rather than prizes.

The final approach we discuss can be traced back to Strotz (1956), and was advocated in the context of ambiguity by Siniscalchi (2011). The basic idea is to assume that individuals are *sophisticated:* that is, even though they may be dynamically inconsistent, they correctly anticipate their future behavior, and respond accordingly. Strotz argues that a sophisticated individual should engage in a *strategy of consistent planning*: at each decision point, they should choose the plan that is best according to their *current* preferences, among all those plans that, in view of their future preferences, they will *actually* be able to carry out. Consistent planning is thus a "refinement" of backward induction, in the sense that, whenever two or more plans are optimal from the perspective of future preferences, the one that is optimal for the current preferences is selected.

In the tree of the figure with $x = \$100$, consistent planning implies that, at the initial node, the individual will anticipate their preference for R over B upon learning that a yellow ball was not drawn; hence, they will realize that choosing C is tantamount to committing to the plan CR, and will therefore choose S instead. In other words, consistent planning coincides with backward induction in this example.

Siniscalchi provides an axiomatization of consistent planning. The key insight is that, to formulate the sophistication principle (and other assumptions implicit in consistent planning), preferences need to be defined over *decision trees*, rather than acts, or even plans. This is analogous to the use of preferences over *menus* in the literature on

preference for flexibility, or temptation and self-control. One advantage of this approach is that it yields insight into the issue of the *value of information* under ambiguity. The reader is referred to the original paper for detail.

13.8 CONCLUSION

In recent decades the theoretical and experimental literature on the economics of ambiguity and ambiguity aversion spawned by Ellsberg (1961,1962) has exploded to the point where it is much too extensive to be covered in a single chapter of this form. For additional discussion, the reader is referred to the surveys of Sugden (1986), Camerer and Weber (1992), Kelsey and Quiggin (1992), Kischka and Puppe (1992), Camerer (1995), Mukerji (2000), Starmer (2000), Siniscalchi (2008a), Gilboa et al. (2008), Al-Najjar and Weinstein (2009), Hey et al. (2010), Etner et al. (2012) and Gilboa and Marinacci (2012), the journal symposium issues of Bonanno et al. (2009) and Ellsberg et al. (2011), and the extensive annotated bibliography of Wakker (2013).

REFERENCES

Abdellaoui, M., Baillon, A., Placido, L., Wakker, P., 2011. The rich domain of uncertainty: source functions and their experimental implementation. American Economic Review 101, 695–723.

Ahn, D.S., 2008. Ambiguity without a state space. Review of Economic Studies 75, 3–28.

Al Najjar, N., De Castro, L., 2013. Parametric Representation of Preferences. manuscript., Kellogg Graduate School of Management, Northwestern University.

Al-Najjar, N., Weinstein, J., 2009. The ambiguity aversion literature: a critical assessment. Economics and Philosophy 25, 249–284.

Allais, M., 1953. Le comportement de l'homme rationnel devant le risque, critique des postulats et axiomes de l'ecole Américaine. Econometrica 21, 503–546.

Anscombe, F., Aumann, R., 1963. A definition of subjective probability. Annals of Mathematical Statistics 34, 199–205.

Arrow, K., 1951. Alternative approaches to the theory of choice in risk-taking situations. Econometrica 19, 404–437.

Arrow, K., 1963. Comment. Review of Economics and Statistics 45 (Supplement), 24–27.

Baillon, A., Bleichrodt, H., 2011. Testing Ambiguity Models Through the Measurement of Probabilities for Gains and Losses. manuscript. Erasmus University Rotterdam.

Baillon, A., Cabantous, L., Wakker, P., 2012. Aggregating imprecise or conflicting beliefs: an experimental investigation using modern ambiguity theories. Journal of Risk and Uncertainty 44, 115–147.

Baillon, A., l'Haridon, O., Placido, L., 2011. Ambiguity models and the machina paradoxes. American Economic Review 101, 1547–1560.

Bayes, T., 1763. An essay toward solving a problem in the doctrine of chances. Philosophical Transactions of the Royal Society of London 53, 370–418.

Becker, S., Brownson, F., 1964. What price ambiguity? or the role of ambiguity in decision-making. Journal of Political Economy 72, 62–73.

Becker, G., DeGroot, M., Marschak, J., 1964. Measuring utility by a single-response sequential method. Behavioral Science 9, 226–232.

Bernoulli, D., 1738. Specimen Theoriae Novae De Mensura Sortis, Commentarii Academiae Scientiarum Imperialis Petropolitanae (Papers of the Imperial Academy of Sciences in Petersburg V, 175–192. English Translation: Exposition of a New Theory on the Measurement of Risk. Econometrica 22 (1954), 23–36).

Bewley, T., 2002. Knightian decision theory. Part 1. Decisions in Economics and Finance 25, 79–110.

Bewley, T., 2011. Market innovation and entrepreneurship: a Knightian view. In: Debreu, G., Neuefeind, W., Trockel, W. (Eds.), Economics Essays: A Festschrift for Werner Hildenbrand. Springer.

Bonanno, G., Van Hees, M., List, C., Tungodden, B., 2009. Special issue on ambiguity aversion. Economics and Philosophy 25, 247–369.

Brewer, K., 1963. Decisions under uncertainty: comment. Quarterly Journal of Economics 77, 159–161.

Brewer, K., Fellner, W., 1965. The slanting of subjective probabilities—agreement on some essentials. Quarterly Journal of Economics 79, 657–663.

Camerer, C., 1995. Individual decision making. In: Kagel, J., Roth, A. (Eds.), Handbook of Experimental Economics. University Press, Princeton.

Camerer, C., Kunreuther, H., 1989a. Decision processes for low probability events: policy implications. Journal of Policy Analysis and Management 8, 565–592.

Camerer, C., Kunreuther, H., 1989b. Experimental markets for insurance. Journal of Risk and Uncertainty 2, 265–300.

Camerer, C., Weber, M., 1992. Recent developments in modeling preferences: uncertainty and ambiguity. Journal of Risk and Uncertainty 5, 325–370.

Carter, C., 1950. Expectation in Economics (Review of Shackle (1949a)). Economic Journal 60, 92–105.

Casadesus-Masanell, R., Klibanoff, P., Ozdenoren, E., 2000a. Maxmin expected utility over savage acts with a set of priors. Journal of Economic Theory 92, 33–65.

Casadesus-Masanell, R., Klibanoff, P., Ozdenoren, E., 2000b. Maxmin expected utility through statewise combinations. Economics Letters 66, 49–54.

Cerreia-Vioglio, S., Maccheroni, F., Marinacci, M., Montrucchio, L., 2011a. Uncertainty averse preferences. Journal of Economic Theory 146, 1275–1330.

Cerreia-Vioglio, S., Ghirardato, P., Maccheroni, F., Marinacci, M., Siniscalchi, M., 2011b. Rational preferences under ambiguity. Economic Theory 48, 341–375.

Chambers, R., Grant, S., Polak, B., Quiggin, J., 2013. A Two-Parameter Model of Dispersion Aversion. manuscript, University of Queensland.

Chateauneuf, A., Faro, J., 2009. Ambiguity through confidence functions. Journal of Mathematical Economics 45, 535–558.

Chernoff, H., 1954. Rational selection of decision functions. Econometrica 22, 422–443.

Chew, S., Li, K., Chark, R., Zhong, S., 2008. Source preference and ambiguity aversion: models and evidence from behavioral and neuroimaging experiments in neuroeconomics. Advances in Health Economics and Health Services Research 20, 179–201.

Chew, S.H., Sagi, J., 2006. Event exchangeability: probabilistic sophistication without continuity or monotonicity. Econometrica 74, 771–786.

Chew, S.H., Sagi, J., 2008. Small worlds: modeling attitudes toward sources of uncertainty. Journal of Economic Theory 139, 1–24.

Chipman, J., 1958. Stochastic choice and subjective probability (abstract). Econometrica 26, 613.

Chipman, J., 1960. Stochastic choice and subjective probability. In: Willner, D. (Ed.), Decisions Values and Groups. Pergamon Press, New York.

Chow, C., Sarin, R., 2001. Comparative ignorance and the Ellsberg paradox. Journal of Risk and Uncertainty 22, 129–139.

Clarke, F.H., 1983. Optimization and Nonsmooth Analysis. Wiley-Interscience, New York.

Cohen, M., Jaffray, J.-Y., Said, T., 1985. Individual behavior under risk and under uncertainty: an experimental study. Theory and Decision 18, 203–228.

Cohen, M., Jaffray, J.-Y., Said, T., 1987. Individual behavior under risk and under uncertainty for gains and losses. Organizational Behavior and Human Decision Processes 39, 1–22.

Curley, S., Eraker, S., Yates, F., 1984. An investigation of patient's reactions to therapeutic uncertainty. Medical Decision Making 4, 501–511.

Curley, S., Yates, F., 1985. The center and range of the probability interval as factors affecting ambiguity preferences. Organizational Behavior and Human Decision Processes 36, 272–287.

Curley, S., Yates, F., 1989. An empirical evaluation of descriptive models of ambiguity reactions in choice situations. Journal of Mathematical Psychology 33, 397–427.

Curley, S., Young, M., Yates, F., 1989. Characterizing physicians' perceptions of ambiguity. Medical Decision Making 9, 116–124.

Davidson, D., Suppes, P., 1956. A finitistic axiomatization of utility and subjective probability. Econometrica 24, 264–275.

de Finetti, B., 1937. La prévision: ses lois logiques, ses sources subjectives. Annales De L'institut Henri Poincaré 7, 1–68.

DeGroot, M., 1970. Optimal Statistical Decisions. McGraw-Hill Book Co, New York.

Dempster, A., 1967. Upper and lower probabilities induced by a multivalued mapping. Annals of Mathematical Statistics 38, 325–339.

Dillenberger, D., Segal, U., 2012. Recursive Ambiguity and Machina's Examples. manuscript, University of Pennsylvania.

Du, N., Budescu, D., 2005. The effects of imprecise probabilities and outcomes in evaluating investment options. Management Science 51, 1791–1803.

Dumav, M., Stinchcombe, M., 2013. The von Neumann-Morgenstern Approach To Ambiguity. manuscript, University of Texas at Austin.

Eichberger, J., Grant, S., Kelsey, D., 2007. Updating choquet beliefs. Journal of Mathematical Economics 43, 888–899.

Eichberger, J., Grant, S., Kelsey, D., Koshevoy, G.A., 2011. The meu model: a comment. Journal of Economic Theory 146, 1684–1698.

Einhorn, H., Hogarth, R., 1986. Decision making under ambiguity. Journal of Business 59 (Supplement), S225–S250.

Eliaz, K., Ortoleva, P., 2011. A Variation on Ellsberg. manuscript, Brown University.

Ellsberg, D., 1961. Risk, ambiguity, and the savage axioms. Quarterly Journal of Economics 75, 643–669.

Ellsberg, D., 1962. Risk, Ambiguity and Decision. Ph.D. thesis, Harvard University.

Ellsberg, D., 1963. Risk, ambiguity, and the savage axioms: reply. Quarterly Journal of Economics 77, 336–342.

Ellsberg, D., 2001. Risk, Ambiguity and Decision. Garland Publishing, Inc., New York & London (Published version of Ellsberg (1962)).

Ellsberg, D., Machina, M., Ritzberger, K., Yannelis, N. (Eds.), 2011. Economic Theory 48, 219–548. Symposium on the 50th Anniversary of the Ellsberg Paradox.

Epstein, L., 1999. A definition of uncertainty aversion. Review of Economic Studies 66, 579–608.

Epstein, L., Le Breton, M., 1993. Dynamically consistent beliefs must be Bayesian. Journal of Economic Theory 61, 1–22.

Epstein, L., Schneider, M., 2003. Recursive multiple-priors. Journal of Economic Theory 113, 1–31.

Epstein, L.G., Schneider, M., 2007. Learning under ambiguity. The Review of Economic Studies 74, 1275–1303.

Epstein, L., Seo, K., 2010. Symmetry of evidence without evidence of symmetry. Theoretical Economics 5, 313–368.

Epstein, L., Seo, K., 2012. Ambiguity with Repeated Experiments. manuscript, Boston University.

Epstein, L., Zhang, J., 2001. Subjective probabilities on subjectively unambiguous events. Econometrica 69, 265–306.

Ergin, H., Gul, F., 2009. A theory of subjective compound lotteries. Journal of Economic Theory 144, 899–929.

Etner, J., Jaleva, M., Tallon, J.-M., 2012. Decision theory under ambiguity. Journal of Economic Surveys 26, 234–270.

Fagin, R., Halpern, J., 1991. A new approach to updating beliefs. In: Uncertainty in Artificial Intelligence, , 6, pp. 347–374.

Fellner, W., 1961. Distortion of subjective probabilities as a reaction to uncertainty. Quarterly Journal of Economics 75, 670–689.

Fellner, W., 1963. Slanted subjective probabilities and randomization: reply to Howard Raiffa and K.R.W. Brewer. Quarterly Journal of Economics 77, 676–690.

Fishburn, P., 1970. Utility Theory for Decision Making. John Wiley & Sons, New York.

Fox, C.R., Tversky, A., 1995. Ambiguity aversion and comparative ignorance. Quarterly Journal of Economics 110, 585–603.

Gajdos, T., Hayashi, T., Tallon, J.M., Vergnaud, J.C., 2008. Attitude toward imprecise information. Journal of Economic Theory 140, 27–65.

Georgescu-Roegen, N., 1954. Choice, expectations and measurability. Quarterly Journal of Economics 58, 527–530.

Georgescu-Roegen, N., 1958. The nature of expectation and uncertainty. In: Bowman, M. (Ed.), Expectations, Uncertainty, and Business Behavior. Social Science Research Council, New York.

Gerrity, M., Devellis, R., Earp, J., 1990. Physicians' reactions to uncertainty in patient care: a new measure and new insights. Medical Care 28, 724–736.

Ghirardato, P., 2002. Revisiting savage in a conditional world. Economic Theory 20, 83–92.

Ghirardato, P., Maccheroni, F., Marinacci, M., 2004. Differentiating ambiguity and ambiguity attitude. Journal of Economic Theory 118, 133–173.

Ghirardato, P., Maccheroni, F., Marinacci, M., Siniscalchi, M., 2003. A subjective spin on roulette wheels. Econometrica 71, 1897–1908.

Ghirardato, P., Marinacci, M., 2002. Ambiguity made precise: a comparative foundation. Journal of Economic Theory 102, 251–289.

Ghirardato, P., Siniscalchi, M., 2010. A More Robust Definition of Multiple Priors. Carlo Alberto Notebook N. 144.

Ghirardato, P., Siniscalchi, M., 2012. Ambiguity in the small and in the large. Econometrica 80, 2827–2847.

Gilboa, I., 1987. Expected utility with purely subjective non-additive probabilities. Journal of Mathematical Economics 16, 65–88.

Gilboa, I., Marinacci, M., 2012. Ambiguity and the Bayesian paradigm. In: Advances in Economics and Econometrics: Theory and Applications, Tenth World Congress of the Econometric Society.

Gilboa, I., Postlewaite, A., Schmeidler, D., 2008. Probability and uncertainty in economic modeling. Journal of Economic Perspectives 22, 173–188.

Gilboa, I., Schmeidler, D., 1989. Maxmin expected utility with a non-unique prior. Journal of Mathematical Economics 18, 141–153.

Gilboa, I., Schmeidler, D., 1993. Updating ambiguous beliefs. Journal of Economic Theory 59, 33–49.

Graaf, J., Baumol, W., 1949. Note on expectation in economics. Economica 16, 338–342.

Grant, S., 1995. Subjective probability without monotonicity: or how Machina's mom may also be probabilistically sophisticated. Econometrica 63, 159–189.

Grant, S., Polak, B., 2013. Mean-dispersion preferences and constant absolute uncertainty aversion. Journal of Economic Theory 148, 1361–1398.

Gul, F., 1992. Savage's theorem with a finite number of states. Journal of Economic Theory 57, 99–110.

Gul, F., Pesendorfer, W., 2013. Expected Uncertainty Utility Theory. manuscript, Princeton University.

Halevy, Y., 2007. Ellsberg revisited: an experimental study. Econometrica 75, 503–536.

Hanany, E., Klibanoff, P., 2007. Updating preferences with multiple priors. Theoretical Economics 2, 261–298.

Hanany, E., Klibanoff, P., 2009. Updating ambiguity averse preferences. In: BE Journal of Theoretical Economics 9.

Hansen, L., Sargent, T., 2001. Robust control and model uncertainty. American Economic Review 91, 60–66.

Hansen, L., Sargent, T., Tallarini, T., 1999. Robust permanent income and pricing. Review of Economic Studies 66, 873–907.

Hewitt, E., Savage, L., 1955. Symmetric measures on Cartesian products. Transactions of the American Mathematical Society 80, 470–501.

Hey, J., Lotito, G., Maffioletti, A., 2010. The descriptive and predictive adequacy of theories of decision making under uncertainty/ambiguity. Journal of Risk and Uncertainty 41, 81–111.

Ho, J., Keller, L.R., Keltyka, P., 2002. Effects of outcome and probabilistic ambiguity on managerial choices. Journal of Risk and Uncertainty 24, 47–74.

Hogarth, R., 1989. Ambiguity and competitive decision making: some implications and tests. Annals of Operations Research 19, 31–50.

Hogarth, R., Einhorn, H., 1990. Venture theory: a model of decision weights. Management Science 36, 780–803.

Hogarth, R., Kunreuther, H., 1985. Ambiguity and insurance decisions. American Economic Review Papers and Proceedings 75, 386–390.

Hogarth, R., Kunreuther, H., 1989. Risk ambiguity and insurance. Journal of Risk and Uncertainty 2, 5–35.

Hogarth, R., Kunreuther, H., 1992. Pricing insurance and warranties: ambiguity and correlated risk. Geneva Papers on Risk and Insurance Theory 17, 35–60.

Horie, M., 2007. A General Update Rule for Convex Capacities. Working Papers 644, Kyoto University, Institute of Economic Research, November 2007.

Hsu, M., Bhatt, M., Adolphs, R., Tranel, D., Camerer, C., 2005. Neural systems responding to degrees of uncertainty in human decision-making. Science 310, 1680–1683.

Huettel, S.A., Stowe, C., Gordon, E., Warner, B., Platt, M., 2006. Neural signatures of economic preferences for risk and ambiguity. Neuron 49, 765–775.

Jaffray, J.-Y., 1992. Bayesian updating and belief functions. IEEE Transactions on Systems, Man and Cybernetics 22, 1144–1152.

Jaffray, J.-Y., 1994. Dynamic decision making with belief functions. In: Yaeger, R.R., et al. (Eds.), Advances in the Dempster-Shafer Theory of Evidence. Wiley.

Kahn, B., Sarin, R., 1988. Modeling ambiguity in decisions under uncertainty. Journal of Consumer Research 15, 265–272.

Kelsey, D., Quiggin, J., 1992. Theories of choice under ignorance and uncertainty. Journal of Economic Surveys 6, 133–153.

Keynes, J., 1921. A Treatise on Probability. Macmillan and Co, London.

Kischka, P., Puppe, C., 1992. Decisions under risk and uncertainty: a survey of recent developments. Mathematical Methods of Operations Research 36, 125–147.

Klibanoff, P., Marinacci, M., Mukerji, S., 2005. A smooth model of decision making under ambiguity. Econometrica 73, 1849–1892.

Klibanoff, P., Marinacci, M., Mukerji, S., 2009. Recursive smooth ambiguity preferences. Journal of Economic Theory 144, 930–976.

Klibanoff, P., Mukerji, S., Seo, K., 2011. Relevance and Symmetry. Discussion Paper N.539, Oxford University.

Knight, F., 1921. Risk, Uncertainty, and Profit. Houghton, Mifflin, New York.

Koch, C., Shunk, D., 2013. Limiting liability? – Risk and ambiguity attitudes under real losses. SBR 65, 54–75.

Kopylov, I., 2006. A Parametric Model of Ambiguity Hedging. manuscript, University of California At Irvine.

Kunreuther, H., 1989. The role of actuaries and underwriters in insuring ambiguous risks. Risk Analysis 9, 319–328.

Kunreuther, H., Hogarth, R., 1992. How does ambiguity affect insurance decisions? In: Dionne, G. (Ed.), Contributions To Insurance Economics. Springer, New York.

Kunreuther, H., Meszaros, J., Hogarth, R., Spranca, M., 1995. Ambiguity and underwriter decision processes. Journal of Economic Behavior and Organization 26, 337–352.

Laplace, P., 1814. Théorie analytique des probabilités. Courcier, Paris.

Larson, J., 1980. Exploring the external validity of a subjectively weighted utility model of decision making. Organizational Behavior and Human Performance 26, 293–304.

Lehrer, E., 2007. A Comment on an Example of Machina. manuscript, Tel-Aviv University.

Lehrer, E., 2009. A new integral for capacities. Economic Theory 39, 157–176.

Lehrer, E., 2012. Partially-specified probabilities: decisions and games. American Economic Journal: Microeconomics 4, 70–100.

LeRoy, S., Singell, L., 1987. Knight on risk and uncertainty. Journal of Political Economy 95, 394–406.

L'Haridon, O., Placido, L., 2010. Betting on Machina's reflection example: an experiment on ambiguity. Theory and Decision 69, 375–393.

Li, J., 2011. Preferences for Information and Ambiguity. manuscript, University of California, Berkeley.

Maccheroni, F., Marinacci, M., Rustichini, A., 2006a. Ambiguity aversion, robustness, and the variational representation of preferences. Econometrica 74, 1447–1498.

Maccheroni, F., Marinacci, M., Rustichini, A., 2006b. Dynamic variational preferences. Journal of Economic Theory 128, 4–44.

MacCrimmon, K., 1965. An Experimental Study of the Decision Making Behavior of Business Executives. University of California, Los Angeles, Doctoral Dissertation.

MacCrimmon, K., 1968. Descriptive and normative implications of the decision-theory postulates. In: Borch, K., Mossin, J. (Eds.), Risk and Uncertainty: Proceedings of a Conference Held by the International Economic Association. Macmillan and Co, London.

MacCrimmon, K., Larsson, S., 1979. Utility theory: axioms versus 'paradoxes'. In: Allais, M., Hagen, G.M., (Eds.), Expected Utility Hypotheses and the Allais Paradox. D. Reidel., Dordrecht.

Machina, M., 1987. Choice under uncertainty: problems solved and unsolved. Journal of Economic Perspectives 1, 121–154.

Machina, M., 1989. Dynamic consistency and non-expected utility models of choice under uncertainty. Journal of Economic Literature 27, 1622–1668.

Machina, M., 2004. Almost-objective uncertainty. Economic Theory 24, 1–54.

Machina, M., 2009. Risk, ambiguity, and the rank-dependence axioms. American Economic Review 99, 385–392.

Machina, M., 2013. Ambiguity Aversion with Three or More Outcomes. manuscript, University of California, San Diego.

Machina, M., Schmeidler, D., 1992. A more robust definition of subjective probability. Econometrica 60, 745–780.

Machina, M., Schmeidler, D., 1995. Bayes without Bernoulli: simple conditions for probabilistically sophisticated choice. Journal of Economic Theory 67, 106–128.

Maffioletti, A., Santori, M., 2005. Do trade union leaders violate subjective expected utility? Some insights from experimental data. Theory and Decision 59, 207–253.

Malinvaud, E., 1952. Note on von Neumann-Morgenstern's strong independence axiom. Econometrica 20, 679.

Marschak, J., 1950. Rational behavior, uncertain prospects, and measurable utility. Econometrica 18, 111–141 (Errata, Econometrica 18, 312).

Milnor, J., 1954. Games against nature. In: Thrall, R., Coombs, C., Davis, R. (Eds.), Decision Processes. John Wiley & Sons, New York.

Mukerji, S., 2000. A survey of some applications of the idea of ambiguity aversion in economics. International Journal of Approximate Reasoning 24, 221–234.

Nakamura, N., 1990. Subjective expected utility with non-additive probabilities on finite state spaces. Journal of Economic Theory 51, 346–366.

Nau, R., 2006. Uncertainty aversion with second-order utilities and probabilities. Management Science 52, 136–145.

Nehring, K., 2001. Ambiguity in the Context of Probabilistic Beliefs. manuscript, University of California, Davis.

Neyman, J., Pearson, E., 1933. On the problem of the most efficient tests of statistical hypotheses. Philosophical Transactions of the Royal Society, Series A 231, 289–337.

Olszewski, W., 2007. Preferences over sets of lotteries. Review of Economic Studies 74, 567–595.

Ortoleva, P., 2010. Status quo bias, multiple priors and uncertainty aversion. Games and Economic Behavior 69, 411–424.

Ozdenoren, E., Peck, J., 2008. Ambiguity aversion, games against nature, and dynamic consistency. Games and Economic Behavior 62, 106–115.

Pires, C., 2002. A rule for updating ambiguous beliefs. Theory and Decision 53, 137–152.

Poincaré, H., 1912. Calcul des Probabilités, second edn. Gauthiers-Villars, Paris.

Pratt, J., 1964. Risk aversion in the small and in the large. Econometrica 32, 122–136.

Pratt, J., Raiffa, H., Schlaifer, R., 1964. The foundations of decisions under uncertainty: an elementary exposition. Journal of the American Statistical Association 59, 353–375.

Quiggin, J., 1982. A theory of anticipated utility. Journal of Economic Behavior and Organization 3, 323–343.

Raiffa, H., 1961. Risk, ambiguity, and the savage axioms: comment. Quarterly Journal of Economics 75, 690–694.

Ramsey, F., 1926. Truth and probability. In: Ramsey, F. (Ed.), Foundations of Mathematics and other Logical Essays. K. Paul, Trench, Trubner and Co, London (1931).

Ritov, I., Baron, J., 1990. Reluctance to vaccinate: omission bias and ambiguity. Journal of Behavioral Decision Making 3, 263–277.

Roberts, H., 1963. Risk, ambiguity, and the savage axioms: comment. Quarterly Journal of Economics 77, 327–336.

Rothschild, M., Stiglitz, J., 1970. Increasing risk: I. a definition. Journal of Economic Theory 2, 225–243.

Samuelson, P., 1952. Probability, utility, and the independence axiom. Econometrica 20, 670–678.

Sarin, R., Wakker, P., 1992. A Simple axiomatization of nonadditive expected utility. Econometrica, 1255–1272.

Sarin, R., Winkler, R., 1992. Ambiguity and decision modeling: a preference-based approach. Journal of Risk and Uncertainty 5, 389–407.

Savage, L.J., 1950. The role of personal probability in statistics. Econometrica 18, 183–184.

Savage, L., 1954. The Foundations of Statistics. John Wiley & Sons, New York. Revised and Enlarged Edition, New York: Dover Publications, 1972..

Savage, L., 1963. Leonard J. Savage Papers. Yale University Library Manuscripts and Archives, Collection Number 695.

Schmeidler, D., 1986. Integral representation without additivity. Proceedings of the American Mathematical Society 97, 255–261.

Schmeidler, D., 1989. Subjective probability and expected utility without additivity. Econometrica 57, 571–587.

Segal, U., 1987a. The ellsberg paradox and risk aversion: an anticipated utility approach. International Economic Review 28, 175–202.

Segal, U., 1987b. Some remarks on quiggin's anticipated utility. Journal of Economic Behavior and Organization 8, 145–154.

Segal, U., 1990. Two-stage lotteries without the reduction axiom. Econometrica 58, 349–377.

Seo, K., 2009. Ambiguity and second-order belief. Econometrica 77, 1575–1605.

Shackle, G., 1949a. Expectation in Economics. Cambridge University Press, Cambridge.

Shackle, G., 1949b. A non-additive measure of uncertainty. Review of Economic Studies 17, 70–74.

Shafer, G., 1976. A Mathematical Theory of Evidence, vol. 1. Princeton University Press, Princeton.

Shafer, G., 1978. Non-additive probabilities in the work of Bernoulli and Lambert. Archive for History of the Exact Sciences 19, 309–370.

Siniscalchi, M., 2006. A behavioral characterization of plausible priors. Journal of Economic Theory 128, 91–135.

Siniscalchi, M., 2008a. Ambiguity and ambiguity aversion. In: Durlauf, S., Blume, L. (Eds.), The New Palgrave Dictionary of Economics, second edn. Macmillan, London.

Siniscalchi, M., 2008b. Machina's Reflection Example and VEU Preferences: A Very Short Note. manuscript, Northwestern University.

Siniscalchi, M., 2009a. Vector expected utility and attitudes toward variation. Econometrica 77, 801–855.

Siniscalchi, M., 2009b. Two out of three ain't bad: a comment on 'the ambiguity aversion literature: a critical assessment'. Economics and Philosophy 25, 335–356.

Siniscalchi, M., 2010. Recursive Vector Expected Utility, manuscript. Northwestern University.

Siniscalchi, M., 2011. Dynamic choice under ambiguity. Theoretical Economics 6, 379–421.

Sinn, H.-W., 1980. A rehabilitation of the principle of sufficient reason. Quarterly Journal of Economics 94, 493–506.

Skiadas, C., 2013. Scale-invariant uncertainty-averse preferences and source-dependent constant relative risk aversion. Theoretical Economics 8, 59–93.

Slovic, P., Tversky, A., 1974. Who accepts savage's axiom? Behavioral Science 19, 368–373.

Smith, V., 1969. Measuring nonmonetary utilities in uncertain choices: the Ellsberg urn. Quarterly Journal of Economics 83, 324–329.

Starmer, C., 2000. Developments in non-expected utility theory: the hunt for a descriptive theory of choice under risk. Journal of Economic Literature 38, 332–382.

Stigler, S., 1986. The History of Statistics: The Measurement of Uncertainty Before 1900. Harvard University Press, Cambridge, MA.

Strotz, R.H., 1956. Myopia and inconsistency in dynamic utility maximization. Review of Economic Studies 23, 165–180.

Strzalecki, T., 2011. Axiomatic foundations of multiplier preferences. Econometrica 79, 47–73.

Sugden, R., 1986. New developments in the theory of choice under uncertainty. Bulletin of Economic Research 38, 1–24.

Turvey, R., 1949. Note on 'expectation in economics'. Economica 16, 336–338.

Tversky, A., Kahneman, D., 1974. Judgment under uncertainty: heuristics and biases. Science 185, 1124–1131.

Venn, J., 1866. The Logic of Chance. Macmillan and Co, London. 2nd Ed. 1876. 3rd Ed. 1888.

Viscusi, W., 1989. Prospective reference theory: toward an explanation of the paradoxes. Journal of Risk and Uncertainty 2, 235–264.

Viscusi, W.K., Chesson, H., 1999. Hopes and fears: the conflicting effects of risk ambiguity. Journal of Risk and Uncertainty 47, 153–178.

Viscusi, W., Magat, W., 1992. Bayesian decisions with ambiguous belief aversion. Journal of Risk and Uncertainty 5, 371–387.

Viscusi, W., Magat, W., Huber, J., 1991. Communication of ambiguous risk information. Theory and Decision 31, 159–173.

von Kries, J., 1886. Die Principien der Wahrscheinlichkeits-Rechnung: Eine logische Untersuchung. Mohr, Tübingen.

von Neumann, J., Morgenstern, O., 1944. Theory of Games and Economic Behavior. Princeton University Press, Princeton (2nd Ed. 1947; 3rd Ed. 1953).

Wakker, P., 1989. Additive Representations of Preferences: A New Foundation of Decision Analysis. Kluwer Academic Publishers, Dordrecht, Holland.

Wakker, P., 2010. Prospect Theory: For Risk and Ambiguity. Cambridge University Press, Cambridge, UK.

Wakker, P., 2013. Annotated Bibliography. Available from: <http://people.few.eur.nl/wakker/refs/webr-frncs.doc>.

Wald, A., 1939. Contributions to the theory of statistical estimation and testing hypotheses. Annals of Mathematical Statistics 10, 299–326.

Wald, A., 1950. Some recent results in the theory of statistical decision functions. Econometrica 18, 182–183.

Walley, P., 1991. Statistical Reasoning with Imprecise Probabilities. Chapman and Hall, London.

Wang, T., 2003. A Class of Multi-Prior Preferences. manuscript, Sauder School of Business, University of British Columbia.

Weber, E.U., Johnson, E., 2008. Decisions under uncertainty: psychological, economic, and neuroeconomic explanations of risk preference. In: Glimcher, P., Camerer, C., Fehr, E., Poldrack, R. (Eds.), Neuroeconomics: Decision Making and the Brain. Elsevier, New York.

Willham, C., Christensen-Szalanski, J., 1993. Ambiguity and liability negotiations: the effects of the negotiators' role and the sensitivity zone. Organizational Behavior and Human Decision Processes 54, 277–298.

Yaari, M.E., 1969. Some remarks on measures of risk aversion and on their uses. Journal of Economic Theory 1, 315–329.

Yaari, M.E., 1987. The dual theory of choice under risk. Econometrica 55, 95–115.

Yang, C.-L., Yao, L., 2011. Ellsberg Paradox and Second-order Preference Theories on Ambiguity: Some New Experimental Evidence. manuscript, Academia Sinica.

Yates, F.J., Zukowski, L.G., 1976. Characterization of ambiguity in decision making. Behavioral Science 21, 19–25.

Zhang, J., 2002. Subjective ambiguity, expected utility and choquet expected utility. Economic Theory 20, 159–181.

CHAPTER 14

Choice Under Uncertainty: Empirical Methods and Experimental Results

John D. Hey
Department of Economics and Related Studies, University of York, UK

Contents

Abstract

This chapter is concerned with the empirical exploration and experimental investigation of the numerous theories of decision making under uncertainty proposed in the earlier chapters of this handbook. This chapter begins with *static* theories of behavior under *risk*; then we look at *dynamic* theories under risk; and finally look at decision making under *ambiguity* (the theory of which is largely static at this point in time). As we proceed through the chapter we will come across a number of methodological issues concerning the conduct of experiments, and relating to the econometric analysis of the data. These issues will be elaborated further in the concluding subsections of the appropriate sections and in a concluding section at the end of the chapter.

Keywords

Experiments, Risk, Ambiguity, Static, Dynamic, Econometrics

JEL Classification Codes

D81, D99

14.1 STATIC DECISION MODELS UNDER RISK[1]

14.1.1 The First SEU-Testing Experiments

The natural starting point is (Subjective) Expected Utility (SEU), and with Maurice Allais' sustained attack on it (see, in particular Allais (1953)). We do not need to extol the

---

[1] We follow the literature in describing a decision problem under risk as a situation in which the outcome is not known with certainty but each possible outcome has an (objective) probability associated with it, and the decision maker takes these probabilities as known and given; or at least he or she acts as if he or she does.

Handbook of the Economics of Risk and Uncertainty, Volume 1
ISSN 2211-7547, http://dx.doi.org/10.1016/B978-0-444-53685-3.00014-3

theoretical virtues of SEU—its simplicity, elegance and coherence—as these have been well-evidenced throughout this handbook. We concentrate here on its empirical robustness, particularly in experimental settings. We start with Allais' experiment, not only because it was one of the earliest, but also because it set the tone for the style of many subsequent experiments. From a modern perspective, there is much to criticize in what he did: he ran an experiment without incentives; with absurd amounts of (hypothetical) money; with a small number of problems; with carefully selected problems; and with a wholly unrepresentative set of subjects (economists at an international conference). But the basic idea is interesting. Let us take one of his more famous examples: he asked subjects to choose between A and B in problem 1 following, and then to choose between C and D in problem 2 following. The currency is former French francs.

Problem 1: choose between A and B
A: getting 100 million for sure;
B: getting 500 million with probability 0.10, or 100 million with probability 0.89, or 0 with probability 0.01.
Problem 2: choose between C and D
C: getting 100 million with probability 0.11, or 0 with probability 0.89;
D: getting 500 million with probability 0.10, or 0 with probability 0.90.

These are examples of what are termed *pairwise-choice* problems. Subsequent experiments would typically ask a whole series of carefully chosen such problems ("carefully chosen" being a term that we shall discuss later) and, for those experiments where monetary incentives were provided (which has become the norm in experimental economics), the *random lottery incentive mechanism* would be used. This mechanism involves choosing, after the subject has answered all the questions, one of them at random, and subsequently playing out the chosen gamble and paying the subject according to the outcome.

This particularly famous pair of problems was chosen by Allais because it provides a test of SEU[2]: if a subject's behavior is consistent with SEU, then he or she will choose A over B if and only if he or she chooses C over D. Allais reported that this was not the case: many of the subjects chose A in problem 1 and D in problem 2.

14.1.2 The First non-SEU-Theory-Testing Experiments

Similar evidence was reported in the seminal paper by Kahneman and Tversky (1979). They too carried out an experiment in which subjects were asked a series of pairwise-choice questions. They too did not provide appropriate incentives to

---

[2] Normalize the utility function with $u(0)=0$ and $u(500\ million)=1$. Put $u(100\ million)=u$. Then we have $EU_A=u$, $EU_B=0.10+0.89u$, $EU_C=0.11u$, and $EU_D=0.10$. Then A is preferred to B if and only if $EU_A \geq EU_B$; that is, if and only if $u \geq 0.10+0.89u$; that is, if and only if $0.11u \geq 0.10$. Similarly C is preferred to D if and only if $EU_C \geq EU_D$; that is, if and only if $0.11u \geq 0.10$, which is the same condition.

the subjects; all questions were hypothetical. Kahneman and Tversky wrote: "The respondents were asked to imagine that they were actually faced with the choice described in the problem, and to indicate the decision they would have made in such a case." Such practices would not be entertained in experimental economics nowadays, though they remain acceptable in some parts of experimental psychology. Kahneman and Tversky asked questions similar to those asked by Allais, with the same intention. For example,

Problem 1: choose between A and B:
A: getting 2,500 with probability 0.33; 2,400 with probability 0.66; 0 with probability 0.01;
B: getting 2,400 with certainty.
Problem 2: choose between C and D:
C: getting 2,500 with probability 0.33; 0 with probability 0.67;
D: getting 2,400 with probability 0.34; 0 with probability 0.66.

Here the (hypothetical) amounts are Israeli pounds. This is a scaled-down version of the Allais problem; once again it is a test of SEU. Kahneman and Tversky write[3] "the data show that 82 per cent of the subjects chose B in Problem 1, and 83 per cent of the subjects chose C in Problem 2. *Each of these preferences is significant at the .01 level… ".* It is instructive to ask what they mean by this latter statement. It could mean either that the null hypothesis that the subjects were answering at random is rejected at the 1% level; or that the hypothesis that the proportion of the population from which the par-ticular subjects on this experiment were selected who preferred B to A (or C to D) was equal to 50% is rejected at the 1% level. In a sense, however, these two interpretations are not relevant for the key hypothesis that one might want to test: namely that the proportion preferring A in the first problem is significantly different from the propor-tion preferring C in the second. If this hypothesis is rejected then it is evidence against SEU. Clearly with 18% preferring A in the first and 83% preferring C in the second, on the basis of the usual test (of the difference between two proportions) carried out by that generation of experimental economists or experimental psychologists, SEU is rejected.

We have to be careful how we interpret this result and indeed Allais' similar test result. If we ignore, for the time being, the possible presence of *noise* in subjects' responses, we can clearly reject the null hypothesis that **all** subjects' preferences are SEU. We could go further and make the inferences subject specific. Those subjects who chose A and C, or who chose B and D, demonstrated preferences consistent with SEU; those that report other choices did not; unless of course if subjects were indiffer-ent between A and B on Problem 1 and between C and D on Problem 2 and simply answered at random.

---

[3] Our added italics.

14.1.3 Noise

But we have to take into account that responses are *noisy*. By this we mean that subjects do not always report their true preferences, or that they state different preferences when asked the same question on different occasions. This is true in all kinds of experiments, and the noise has to be taken into account in the design of the experiment and in the analysis of the data. Towards the end of this section we will talk a lot about how we might specify the noise, but for the time being we will start simple. To illustrate the procedures and implications we use the seminal paper by Colin Camerer (1989) who was one of the earliest experimentalists to do a more rigorous test of the adequacy of SEU using experimental data. He also used a series of pairwise-choice problems, all involving at most three payoffs (like Allais' questions)—in total he had 14 of such questions, and three levels of payoffs (large hypothetical gains, like Allais, small real gains and small real losses), though not all subjects were presented with all 14 questions on each set of payoffs. Indeed each subject "made choices for four pairs of problems for each of the payoff levels, and a single repetition of one of the twelve pairs, a total of 13 choices." We will later discuss the adequacy of this number; this clearly depends on the noisiness of the data and what we plan to do with it. In each pair of problems, one of the two choices/prospects was less risky than the other. The 14 pairs of questions were chosen in such a way that if the prospects were plotted in a Marschak-Machina Triangle (MMT) and the prospects in any pair were joined by a straight line, then the resulting 14 lines spanned the triangle and *all had the same slope*. The motive for this can be gleaned from the discussion of the MMT earlier in the book: if a subject has SEU preferences then his indifference curves in the MMT are parallel straight lines. So if he or she prefers the riskier (less risky) prospect in one pair then he or she should also prefer the riskier (less risky) prospect in all the other pairs. So, if we do a between-subjects analysis of the data then it must be the case that the proportion of subjects choosing the less risky prospect *is the same on all pairs*. Manifestly it was not—varying from 20% to 76% across the triangle. While intuitively such differences are not explicable by random error, Camerer carried out a formal test and concluded that "we can strongly reject the hypothesis that the fractions [proportions] in each triangle are all equal." It is interesting, and useful for our future discussion, to reflect on the nature of this test. While the formalities are relegated to a footnote, it can be inferred that he is doing a standard test for the difference in two proportions. If p_1 and p_2 are the two observed proportions, then he is using the result that p_i is normally distributed with mean π_i and variance $\pi_i(1-\pi_i)/n$ where n is the number of observations (subjects answering that problem) and π_i is the true or population proportion. The SEU hypothesis is that $\pi_i = \pi_j$ for all problem pairs i and j. But we should note the statistical assumptions behind this. The result that p_i is $N[\pi_i, \pi_i(1-\pi_i)/n]$ comes from assuming that each observation is a random draw where the probability of choosing the riskier (less risky) choice is equal to π_i. However, if each subject has SEU preferences, but different SEU preferences—so that the risk-aversion varies across the subjects—then this assumption is rather dubious. Suppose that all subjects had been presented with all 14 questions on each payoff set; then it would simply not be true that "each observation is a random draw where the probability of choosing the riskier (less risky) choice is equal to π_i". Indeed the observations for those with risk aversion sufficiently low would be *always* to choose the most risky option and for those with risk aversion sufficiently high would be *always* to choose the least risky option. The thing that partially supports the hypothesis is that there was randomness in the questions allocated to subjects—but even so, this does not generate the randomness necessary for the correct implementation of the test. However, it is important to be clear about the stochastic assumption that is implicit in this between-subjects test. The assumption is that risk aversion is distributed over the population from which the subjects were drawn, *but that subjects do not make errors when they state their preferred option.* This means that, for any one question, and for any one subject drawn at random from the population, there is a certain probability that subject will choose the riskier option.

Camerer also carries out what he calls *within-subjects analyses.* An example of this is when he tests *betweenness.* He takes two pairwise-choices along the same line in the MMT; call these Pairwise Choice 1 and Pairwise Choice 2. If a subject's preferences are SEU then if he or she chooses the riskier option in Pairwise Choice 1, then he or she should also choose the riskier option in Pairwise Choice 2. Taking a particular pair he notes that 83% of the subjects chose in accordance with this, while 14% chose the less risky option in Pairwise Choice 1 and the riskier option in Pairwise Choice 2, while just 3% did the contrary. He writes "… if the betweenness violations are random, then the percentage of same choices …" (the 83% reported above) "… should equal the percentage of same choices when the same gamble was presented twice … 86.7%". He carries out a standard z-test. Notwithstanding whether this test is appropriate, or implemented correctly, he invokes a different assumption as to where the noise/randomness is coming from: note his words "*if betweenness violations are random,*" which now indicates that subjects are noisy in their responses. This is different from the noise assumption in the between-subjects analysis—in which the noise comes from the fact that subjects are different.

This is an important difference, and the within-subjects' assumption adopted by Camerer incorporates the fact that subjects are noisy in their responses: given the same question twice, they may well give different answers. The key question now is how one should model this noise. This is something to which we will return on many occasions. We shall shortly turn to the paper by Harless and Camerer (1994), who consider this in more detail. But first let us summarize Camerer's analyses and findings. In essence he was testing the SEU implication that indifference curves in the MMT are parallel straight lines; other theories imply different shaped indifference curves: possibly nonlinear and maybe fanning-in or fanning-out across the MMT. Many of his statistical tests were looking for evidence of fanning-in and fanning-out in different parts of the MMT.

It is interesting to note that, at that time, his methodology was *not* to assess theories in their entirety, but theories in different parts of the evidence-space. In this respect it is useful to quote Camerer's conclusions: "The important empirical question is whether any theory that generalizes EU can explain the violations. The results of our test and other recent tests are decidedly mixed: Each theory can account for some of the violations, but not all." This was at a time when his list of generalizations of SEU consisted of Weighted Utility, Implicit Expected Utility, "The Fanning-out Hypothesis", Lottery-Dependent Utility, Prospect Theory (PT) and Rank-Dependent Utility (RDU). By 1997 a list published in Hey (1997) contained some 20 generalizations of SEU.

14.1.4 Fitting as Distinct from Testing

We now turn to Harless and Camerer (1994); they do more than Camerer in that they not only see if the data is consistent with SEU, but they also consider other preference functionals, and explore their goodness of fit, and see if they explain the data "significantly better" (in some sense) than SEU. So rather than considering "bits" of the experimental data in separate analyses and applying different statistical procedures to different parts of the data, they consider the data as a whole. Indeed, they not only consider the data for each subject as a whole, but also all the data from all the subjects in an experiment as a whole. This is a significant advance in the use of the data from experiments.[4] They begin their analysis with data from a particularly simple experiment (that of Battalio et al. (1990)) in which subjects were asked just three pairwise-choice questions, in each of which one prospect was less risky than the other. As with Camerer (1989) the pairs were such that the lines joining the two prospects in each pair in the MMT were parallel. As a consequence, for a subject to be consistent with SEU, if that subject chose the safer option on one pairwise-choice, he or should do the same on the other two. So, for example, for a subject to be consistent with SEU his or her three answers have to be either SSS or RRR (where "S" denotes the safer option and "R" the riskier one); any other pattern is a violation of SEU. Harless and Camerer thought that this was too harsh a judgment (indeed with enough data all behavior violates virtually all theories—with the exception of the vacuous theory that people do anything), and they looked for a way of reporting "how close" observed choices were to the various theories. To model this they assumed that in reporting their preferences, subjects did so *with error*. Their specific assumption, which looks nowadays very strong, is that all subjects on all problems made a mistake in reporting their true preference with a *constant* probability ε; moreover committing an error is independent across problems. This appears strong in two respects: that all subjects are equally noisy in their responses; and that all subjects

---

[4] If one carries out N tests independently of N hypothesis H_n $(n = 1, \ldots, N)$ against some appropriately specified alternative using an $x\%$ significance level, this is not the same as testing the union of H_n over $n = 1, \ldots, N$ using an $x\%$ significance level (except under very strict and unusual circumstances).

are equally noisy on all problems. Moreover the across-question independence assumption might be criticized (though recent evidence does suggest that subjects do separate one question from another).

The advantage of this noise assumption is that it enabled Harless and Camerer to proceed to (maximum likelihood) estimation of the implied parameters of the various functionals, and hence to a measure of goodness of fit of the different models to the data. Take for example SEU; here the parameters are the proportion of subjects who truly prefer SSS (and hence the proportion who truly prefer RRR) and the noise parameter ε. In the subsequent literature, this parameter has become known as a *tremble*. To take a second example, that of PT, where RRS and RRR are the possible consistent responses (under certain assumptions), the parameters are the proportion of subjects who truly prefer RRS (and hence the proportion who truly prefer RRR) and the tremble parameter ε. It will be noted that SEU and PT are equally parsimonious in their parameterization though other theories are more profligate (for example Rank Dependent Expected Utility Theory). Harless and Camerer discuss various ways of measuring and testing the goodness of fit of the various theories. One possibility that they discuss, and reject on the grounds that it is rather weak, is to carry out a test of whether the observations could have been generated by simply random choice everywhere. They prefer measures based on the maximized log-likelihood, following the procedure discussed above and elaborated below.

First they carried out a chi-squared test, using the maximized log-likelihoods, for each preference functional individually, against the null hypothesis of purely random behavior. Using the Battalio et al. Real-Losses-Series-1 data set, they showed that three variants of Rank Dependent and Fanning Out all were significant under this test. They then carried out a test of whether the more general theories (all have SEU nested within them) fitted significantly better than SEU. Using the same data set, it was clear that three variants of Rank Dependent and Fanning Out fitted the data much better than SEU. This latter test takes into account the different number of estimated parameters for the different models (clearly more general models—those with more parameters—are bound to fit no worse than less general models and the tests used take into account the number of extra parameters).

In the analysis reported above, the number of questions asked to each subject was just three. However, Harless and Camerer got more observations by aggregating the responses over all 33 subjects in the experiment. Notice that individual differences between the subjects are less than the number of subjects. Take SEU for example in the context of the experiment reported above: even if they all differ in their SEU preferences, all that matters is whether they prefer the Safe option on any one pairwise-choice question. So rather than there being 33 individual risk-aversion parameters to estimate, there is just the proportion that prefer the safer option. Notice that this "trick" means that the experimentalist does not have to assume that all subjects are identical. However, this reduction in the number of parameters to estimate is achieved at a cost: all the pairwise-choice questions must imply the same slope, in the MMT, of the line joining the two options. It will be noted that Camerer (1989) also used this method. Clearly the *positions* of the lines in the triangle can be varied—so that one can explore, for example, whether there are fewer violations of SEU *properly within the triangle* (which is one of the analyses reported in Harless and Camerer (1994)), or whether it is *betweenness* or *independence* that is being violated—but one is losing information about the SEU-consistency or otherwise of those subjects whose degree of risk aversion is a lot higher or a lot lower than that implied by the slopes of these lines in the MMT.

There are obviously ways round this problem—and we shall turn to these shortly. Before we do so, it would probably be useful to summarize the message that emerged from Harless and Camerer's paper. While we have just mentioned one application of their approach above (to the data of Battalio et al. (1990)), they studied 23 different data sets, containing nearly 8,000 choices and 2,000 choice patterns, and used the same technique throughout. Obviously if subjects were presented with many choice problems, then the number of parameters to fit for any given model (the population proportions with different choice patterns) inevitably increases and the method becomes less parsimonious. But, depending upon the experiment, if the number of choice problems is low, their technique for "explaining" the data seems an appropriate one; if the number is high, then different techniques are more appropriate.

Their conclusions include: (1) all the theories that they consider are rejected on the basis of a chi-squared test; (2) some theories are too lean, others are too fat; (3) there are large differences in explanatory power depending upon the nature of the questions; (4) there are some winners among the competing theories and some losers: "Losers include general theories that rely on betweenness rather than independence, and theories which assume fanning-in throughout the triangle; those theories are dominated by other theories which use fewer free parameters and are more accurate." We should note, rather obviously, that in all these statistical analyses, the null hypothesis is that *all* the subjects in a particular experiment have the same *type* of preferences. By this is meant that they are all SEU, or all Rank Dependent, or whatever, though they do allow preferences *within* the type (for example, the level of risk aversion) to vary across subjects. This seems a very strong assumption—though one necessitated by the type of statistical analyses carried out on the data. If one wants to allow different subjects to have different *types* of preferences, then one needs to estimate subject-by-subject *and* have lots of data, or to employ some kind of *mixture model*. We shall talk about these alternatives later.

At this stage we should recall two restrictions on the experimental questions used by Harless and Camerer: all the questions were pairwise-choice questions; and all the lines joining the two lotteries in each pair had the same slope in the MMT. We have already pointed out that this gives very little information about subjects who are very risk-averse or very risk-loving (with respect to the common slope). The obvious way round this problem is to vary the slopes of the lines implied by the pairwise-choice questions. Ideally one would tailor the slopes to the risk-aversion of individual subjects, but this requires some prior information about their risk-aversion—and this might lead to possible manipulation, rather than truth-telling, by the subjects. We will talk more later about experimental designs that are possibly manipulable, but, in the meantime, we will look at the paper by Hey and Orme (1994) which had pairs of questions that implied different sloped lines in the MMT.

Because of this design feature, and because of the fact that the researchers were convinced that subjects were different, it was deemed desirable to analyze the data subject by subject; as a consequence, it was necessary to ask more questions to each subject. Indeed, Hey and Orme asked, in each of two separate experimental sessions, 100 questions to the subjects. These questions were over four amounts of money, and were asked in four different (but intermingled) sets, each over three of the four amounts of money. So the experiment involved four different MMTs, with the slopes of the lines varying over the triangles. The usual incentive mechanism—the *random lottery incentive mechanism*—was used: after all 200 questions were answered, one of them was chosen at random, the preferred option played out, and the subject paid accordingly. A total of 80 subjects completed the experiment.

For reasons implied by our earlier discussion, and for other reasons that we will describe shortly, Hey and Orme adopted an error story different from that used by Harless and Camerer. The latter assumed that the subjects had some true preference over the pair, but that expressed preferences were reported with error, with the properties reported above. While the independence hypothesis was kept, Hey and Orme wanted to change the assumption that the error rate was the same independently of the question being asked. This seemed unattractive in that, in some questions, the two options might be close together in terms of the preferences of the subject (and therefore likely to lead to a higher error rate), while in other questions the two options might be far apart (leading to a lower error rate). To model this, it was necessary to introduce (and estimate) the preference functional of the subject. Let us denote by p and q the probabilities in the two options in a particular pairwise-choice problem, and let us denote by $V(p)$ and $V(q)$ the *true* preferences for p and q. So the subject *truly* strictly prefers p to q if and only if $V(p) - V(q) > 0$; the subject *truly* strictly prefers q to p if and only if $V(p) - V(q) < 0$; and is indifferent otherwise. The model of error adopted by Hey and Orme was that this true preference was perceived and acted on with error. So the decision was based, *not* on the value of $V(p) - V(q)$, but on the value of $V(p) - V(q) + \varepsilon$, where ε is some error associated with evaluating the difference. Clearly some stochastic assumption has to be made about ε. The natural thing (certainly as perceived at that time) was to assume that ε was normally distributed with mean 0 and standard deviation σ. Note that this assumes that the stochastic specification is the same for all questions—though also note that this is **not** the same as assuming the error is the same on all questions.

Hey and Orme fitted 11 preference functionals to the data—subject by subject—using maximum likelihood techniques. Parameters had to be stated and estimated. For example, for SEU, there is the utility "function" of the individual subjects to estimate, but seeing as there were just four possible outcomes (amounts of money), x_1, x_2, x_3, and x_4 in the experiment, rather than specifying a particular functional form (for example, CARA or CRRA) and estimating the parameters of that form, it was decided to simply estimate $u(x_2)$ and $u(x_3)$; normalizing[5] by putting $u(x_1)$ equal to 0 and $u(x_4)$ equal to 1. This gives the maximum flexibility to the fitting process. For some preference functionals, functional forms had to be specified for some components; for example, the probability weighting function in Rank Dependent had to be given a functional form as there were too many probabilities (9 in total) for the values of the weighting function for each of the possible probability values to be separately estimated; additionally it was feared that monotonicity might be violated unless constraints were imposed on the form of the function.

As we have noted above, the 11 preference functionals (see Appendix 14.1 for details, references and functional specifications) were fitted by maximum likelihood to the data obtained from the experiment. The preference functionals included many of the alternatives to SEU popular[6] at that time: Disappointment Aversion Theory, Prospective Reference Theory, Quadratic Utility, Regret Theory, Rank Dependent EU Theory, Yaari's Dual Model and Weighted EU. The stochastic specification has already been mentioned above, and we will comment on this later. We should note at this stage one complication—caused by Hey and Orme giving the subjects the possibility of expressing indifference on any and all pairwise-choice question. It is not clear why they did so: if subjects are truly indifferent then *any* answer is consistent with the preferences and with the incentive scheme (the random lottery incentive mechanism). Worse, given the stochastic assumption made by Hey and Orme, the probability of a subject being *exactly* indifferent between any two prospects p and q is $Prob[V(p) - V(q) + \varepsilon = 0]$ which is equal to $Prob[\varepsilon = -V(p) + V(q)]$ where ε by assumption is N(0,1). This probability is, unfortunately, zero (as indeed is the probability that any normally distributed random variable is exactly equal to *any* value). But there were statements of indifference by some subjects on some questions. To include such questions, Hey and Orme were forced to assume that indifference was expressed when $V(p) - V(q) + \varepsilon$ is in some small range $[-\tau, \tau]$ around zero. Here the parameter τ is a *threshold* and was assumed to be subject-specific; it was estimated along with the other parameters.

In summary, the 11 preference functionals (those mentioned above with two variants of Rank Dependent and two variants of Regret plus SEU plus Risk Neutrality) were fitted by maximum likelihood methods to the answers to the 200 pairwise-choice

[5] Actually Hey and Orme used a different (but equivalent) normalization—putting the standard deviation of the error term equal to 1 and estimating $u(x_4)$.
[6] It is interesting to note their popularity today!

questions individually for 80 subjects. Thus, for each subject and for each preference functional, we have the estimated parameters of the models plus the maximized log-likelihood. The latter can be used to measure the goodness-of-fit of the various preference functionals. Obviously the more general models fit better and we can test (using a likelihood ratio test) whether a more general model fits *significantly* better than a less general model. Risk Neutrality is nested inside both SEU and Yaari's Dual Model: the results roundly reject the less general model for virtually all subjects. Of the remaining models SEU is nested inside them all: here the results of the likelihood ratio tests are less emphatic, but for more than half the 80 subjects SEU is rejected in favor of one or more of the more general models at 5%, and for slightly less than half of them at the 1% level. One can get a sort of "average" picture of how well the various models do by looking at rankings based on the Akaike Information Criterion (Akaike, 1974). This criterion is the maximized log-likelihood punished for the number of parameters/ degrees of freedom involved in the functional. Using all the data from all 200 questions, the functional with the lowest (best) average ranking is Rank Dependent (with the Quiggin weighting function) followed by Prospective Reference Theory[7]; Risk Neutrality does worst. However, this information is misleading (or indeed useless) if one believes that people are different and that one should find the best functional subject by subject rather than search for something which might be termed the "best average" functional.

One might be also interested in measuring the *economic* rather than *statistical* significance of the differences between the various models. One simple way to compute this is to ask what would be the magnitude of the error in prediction if we used the wrong model: overall, if we used SEU to predict rather than the best-fitting model, we would make a mistake 8.2% of the time; using Risk Neutrality instead of SEU we would make a mistake 22.8% of the time. So moving to SEU improves things considerably but does not eliminate error completely.

In conclusion Hey and Orme (1994) wrote:

> "… we are tempted to conclude by saying that our study indicates that behavior can be reasonably well modelled … as 'EU plus noise'. Perhaps we should now spend some time on thinking about the noise, rather than about even more alternatives to EU?"

This call has been listened to. We shall explain how soon, but first we must fill in some more details of other experimental studies of decision making under risk. We intend to discuss the *type* of decision task posed to the subjects; the way that the data has been analyzed with respect to the stochastic specification of the data-generating process; the way that the data has been analyzed in terms of its *aggregation*; the way that the data has been analyzed in terms of *fitting versus prediction*; and then we intend to conclude

---

[7] This is effectively SEU *within* the MMT but there are discontinuities in the indifference curves around the circumference.

on various methodological issues concerned with the running of experiments. We start with an examination of the *type* of decision problem.

14.1.5 Different Kinds of Experiments

All the experiments that we have discussed so far have involved a set of pairwise-choice questions (with the random lottery incentive mechanism used to furnish an appropriate incentive). Such questions are easy for subjects to understand. They are also easy to use in an experimental session. However, they are not particularly informative: if the subject states that they prefer L to R, that is all you know—and you do not know *how much* they prefer L to R. Two other ways of getting more informative data are giving subjects a *complete ranking* problem or an *allocation* problem. We discuss these in turn.

A *complete ranking* experiment was implemented by Carbone and Hey (1994). In their experiment subjects were presented with 44 different lotteries, and were asked to rank them in order from the most preferred to the least preferred. Note that the nature of the information obtained is different from that from a pairwise-choice experiment; and that in principle asking for a complete ranking seems potentially more informative. But then it depends on the errors made by subjects. Putting 44 lotteries in order is not a particular easy task, and whether subjects made the effort depended upon the incentive mechanism. This involved two of the 44 lotteries being picked at random at the end of the experiment, checking the subject's ranking to see which was the highest in the ranking, playing out that highest-ranking lottery and paying the subject the outcome. Is this a sufficient incentive? The authors note that reporting the true ranking implied an expected extra payment from the experiment of £3.38 in one treatment, and of £10.27 in a second treatment, compared to the expected payment just reporting a complete ranking at random. This was in 1994, so the incentive was modest in the first treatment and more striking in the second; whether it was sufficient depended on the effort involved in making the complete ranking.

It is illuminating to note that Carbone and Hey used a different error specification than previous authors: they assumed that the preference, $V(p)$, for a lottery p was perceived by the subject with error; that is the perception was $V(p) + \varepsilon$. However, rather than assume that ε was N(0,1), they assumed that it followed an Extreme Value distribution with unit variance. This has the advantage (compared to the normal distribution) that the distribution function can be explicitly stated—$P(\varepsilon \leq t) = exp\{-exp(-t)\}$—and, more importantly, that one can state explicitly the likelihood of any ranking of the n (=44) lotteries, so that the maximum likelihood method could be used to estimate the parameters of the various preference functionals. These latter included SEU, Prospective Reference theory, Disappointment Aversion theory, Weighted Utility theory and Rank Dependent Expected Utility theory. The results showed that for about one-half of the subjects, SEU "appears to fit the data no worse than the other models, while for the other half Rank Dependent seems to fit better." Interestingly this seems to be the conclusion of history: "SEU is not bad, and where it is, then it is Rank Dependent that is better."

A radical new experimental approach was implemented in an *allocation* experiment by Choi et al. (2007), which followed an original idea contained in Loomes (1991). In principle this provides much more informative data since the choices of the subjects are the result of *optimization* and not just simple pairwise-choice: so one knows (if we ignore errors for the time being) that the chosen allocation was preferred to *all other* possible allocations and not just to *one* other. In Choi et al. (2007)[8] there were just two risky states, 1 and 2; their probabilities, π_1 and π_2 ($\pi_1 + \pi_2 = 1$), were told to the subjects[9]. Subjects were given in each problem a given number of tokens t and were asked to allocate these tokens between the two states, t_1 and t_2, such that $t_1 + t_2 = t$. For each problem there was an *exchange rate* e_i between tokens allocated to state i and *money*. There were 50 such allocation problems in total. To incentivize the subjects the following mechanism was used: at the end of the experiment one of the 50 problems was chosen at random; then one of the two states was chosen randomly using the prespecified probabilities. The subject was then paid the money equivalent to the tokens allocated to that state. This mechanism induces the following optimization problem: max $U(e_1 t_1, e_2 t_2; \pi_1, \pi_2)$ subject to $t_1 + t_2 = t$, where $U(.)$ is the subject's preference functional. Clearly the optimal allocation depends upon this preference function. As written, we have put no restrictions on it: utility simply depends upon the amounts of money implied by the allocation to the two states, and their probabilities. If the preference function was SEU we could write $U(.)$ as $\pi_1 u(e_1 t_1) + \pi_2 u(e_2 t_2)$, where $u(.)$ is the subjects' (SEU) utility function. Choi et al. worked with a more general preference functional (for which SEU is a special case) namely that of *Disappointment Aversion theory* (Gul, 1991)—specifically

$$\min\{\alpha\pi_1 u(e_1 t_1) + \pi_2 u(e_2 t_2), \pi_1 u(e_1 t_1) + \alpha\pi_2 u(e_2 t_2)\}.$$

Note that when the parameter α takes the value 1 the functional form reduces to that of SEU.

They fit this preference functional to the choices of the subjects; they do so subject by subject. Because of the fact that the experiment is an allocation problem, and hence that the payoff to the subject could take almost a continuous range of values, they need to make some assumption about the utility functions $u(.)$ of the subjects; estimating it at all possible outcomes would involve the loss of too many degrees of freedom. They estimate both the CRRA and the CARA forms. In order to estimate the parameters of the preference functional they use two methods: Non-Linear Least Squares (NLLS) and Maximum Likelihood (ML). The latter is that which Harless and Camerer (1994) and Hey and Orme (1994) used, and makes explicit what stochastic assumptions are being

---

[8] We will use our words to describe the experiment, so that our description uses the same words as those that we will use later in the chapter.

[9] In different treatments π_1 took values $\{1/2\}$, $\{1/3\}$ and $\{2/3\}$.

made; with NLLS it is somewhat obscure—even though the method can be interpreted as ML with some kind of stochastic specification. Let us start with Non-Linear Least Squares: when using the CRRA specification they estimated the parameters by minimizing the sum of squared differences between the observed values of $\ln(e_1t_1/e_2t_2)$ and those predicted by the theory; when using the CARA specification they estimated the parameters by minimizing the sum of squared differences between the observed values of $(e_1t_1 - e_2t_2)$ and those predicted by the theory. These can be interpreted as ML with a normality assumption for $\ln(e_1t_1/e_2t_2)$ in the CRRA case, and with a normality assumption for $(e_1t_1 - e_2t_2)$ in the CARA case. When they use the ML approach the specification again differs from the CRRA to the CARA case. In both cases they start with the DA preference function given above $\min\{\alpha\pi_1u(e_1t_1)+\pi_2u(e_2t_2), \pi_1u(e_1t_1)+\alpha\pi_2u(e_2t_2)\}$. In the CRRA case, where $u(x)=x^{1-\rho}/(1-\rho)$, they first of all use this to state the objective function as

$$\min\left[\frac{\alpha(e_1t_1)^{1-\rho}}{1-\rho} + \frac{(e_2t_2)^{1-\rho}}{1-\rho}, \frac{(e_1t_1)^{1-\rho}}{1-\rho} + \frac{\alpha(e_2t_2)^{1-\rho}}{1-\rho}\right]$$

and then they include two error terms ε_1 and ε_2 to get the "perceived" objective function

$$\min\left[\frac{\alpha(e_1t_1)^{1-\rho}}{1-\rho}\varepsilon_1 + \frac{(e_2t_2)^{1-\rho}}{1-\rho}\varepsilon_2, \frac{(e_1t_1)^{1-\rho}}{1-\rho}\varepsilon_1 + \frac{\alpha(e_2t_2)^{1-\rho}}{1-\rho}\varepsilon_2\right].$$

They then show that the perceived optimal allocation depends on the magnitude of $\varepsilon_1 - \varepsilon_2$. They need to make some assumption about the distribution of this error term; they assume that it is normally distributed with mean 0 and variance σ^2—which they estimate along with the other parameters. Interestingly they have to make some "adjustments" for boundary allocations as the CRRA model does not allow allocations at the extremes.

In the CARA case, where $u(x)=-e^{-Ax}$, they first of all use this to state the objective function as

$$\min\left[-\alpha\pi_1e^{-Ae_1t_1} - \pi_2e^{-Ae_2t_2}, -\pi_1e^{-Ae_1t_1} - \alpha\pi_2e^{-Ae_2t_2}\right]$$

and then they include[10] two error terms ε_1 and ε_2 to get the "perceived" objective function

$$\min\left[-\alpha\pi_1e^{-Ae_1t_1-\varepsilon_1} - \pi_2e^{-Ae_2t_2-\varepsilon_2}, -\pi_1e^{-Ae_1t_1-\varepsilon_1} - \alpha\pi_2e^{-Ae_2t_2-\varepsilon_2}\right].$$

---

[10] Note that they follow the same procedure in the two cases, though the precise way that the error enters differs in the two cases.

Again they assume that the distribution of $\varepsilon_1 - \varepsilon_2$ is normal with mean 0 and variance σ^2.

Interestingly their NLLS estimates are quite different from their ML estimates: on the former, for just 6 of the 93 subjects is the estimated α parameter significantly different from 1 (the value for which Disappointment Aversion reduces to SEU) at the 5% level; while on the latter, for 44 of the 93 subjects α is significantly greater than 1 at the 5% level. This shows how crucial the stochastic specification is to the inferences one can draw. Unfortunately, for this study we do not have information to work out which is the correct stochastic specification.

14.1.6 Mixture Models

So far we have seen two different ways of analyzing the data from experiments: first, like Harless and Camerer, putting all the data for all the subjects together; second, like Hey and Orme, analyzing different subjects separately. The former, at least in the studies that we have discussed so far, has had the drawback that we have been forced to investigate whether one model is better than some other model *over all subjects*. However, as we have very clearly seen from the second approach, subjects are different, and hence it follows that there can be no one "best model" for all subjects. Ideally one wants a way of using all the data on all the subjects together without imposing the constraint that subjects are identical (either in terms of their preference function or their parameters). Mixture Models provide a way to do this, as illustrated in Conte et al. (2011) and Harrison and Rutstrom (2009). We begin with the former.

Conte et al. (2011) work with the data from Hey (2001) in which 53 subjects were asked on five separate occasions to make 100 pairwise-choice decisions, each over a subset of the outcomes £0, £50, £100 and £150. Conte et al. assumed that each subject had either SEU preferences or RDEU preferences. For both sets of preferences the utility function was assumed to be either CARA, $u(x) = (1 - e^{-rx})/(1 - e^{-150r})$, or CRRA, $u(x) = (x/150)^r$; while the weighting function was assumed to be either the "Quiggin" function, $w(p) = p^{\gamma}/[p^{\gamma} + (1 - p)^{\gamma}]^{1/\gamma}$, or the power function, $w(p) = p^{\gamma}$. The parameter r measures risk aversion, while the parameter γ indicates the shape of the weighting function. All four combinations—CARA with Quiggin, CARA with Power, CRRA with Quiggin and CRRA with Power—were estimated so that the robustness of the results could be tested. It was assumed that a proportion of the subjects had SEU preferences and that the residual proportion had RDEU preferences. For the SEU subjects it was assumed that the parameter r was distributed across the subjects and the parameters of this distribution were estimated; for the RDEU subjects it was assumed that the parameters r and γ were jointly distributed across the subjects and the parameters of this distribution were estimated. Maximum likelihood methods were used to estimate the various parameters of the overall model. The stochastic specification combined that of Hey and Orme (an additive normally distributed zero mean addition to the preference function) with that of Harless and Camerer (a simple, constant probability, tremble).

It was found that the best-fitting combination (by some distance) was CRRA with Quiggin; that a little over 80% of the subjects were clearly RDEU while a little under 20% were clearly SEU; and there was one rather confused subject who could not be classified. The Harless and Camerer tremble occurred with probability of a little over 1.0%. Crucially the mixture specification fitted significantly better than either, assuming that all subjects were SEU or that all were RDEU.

Harrison and Rutstrom (2009) also estimate a Mixture Model in a similar context, using data from an experiment with 60 pairwise-choice questions. They too chose two models in their mixture, SEU and Prospect Theory, though not the original theory of Kahneman and Tversky (1979) but rather what is called elsewhere Cumulative Prospect Theory and which eliminates the possible violation of dominance in the original. It might also be called Rank Dependent EU with a reference point. So the RDEU we discussed in the previous paragraph is nested within what Harrison and Rutstrom call Prospect Theory (though if the reference point is exogenous the two models are identical). In many ways this paper is similar to Conte et al. except that demographic variables are used to describe variations in the parameters across subjects (rather than through stochastic variations as in Conte et al.). So the former has some demographic explanatory power, but lacks a genuinely random component to the explanation of the behavioral parameters (r and γ). The stochastic specification is an additive error term, but unlike some authors, this is assumed to follow the logistic/extreme value distribution rather than the normal. The former is similar to the latter but has less fat tails. Harrison and Rutstrom find that around one-half of the subjects seem to have SEU preferences and the other half Prospect Theory preferences.

14.1.7 Noise Again

We have commented a number of times on the importance of the stochastic assumptions explicitly or implicitly employed in any econometric analysis. We should now be more systematic in our treatment. Let us begin with Wilcox (2008) who provides an analysis of five different stochastic stories each combined with one of two preference functionals. To motivate the material in this section we can do no better than quote from Wilcox's abstract:

> *"Econometric comparisons suggest that … choices of stochastic models may be far more conse-quential than choices of structures such as expected utility or rank-dependent utility."*

In other words, the stochastic specification may be more important than the preference functional.

We have already encountered two of the stochastic specifications explored by Wilcox: the *tremble* specification of Harless and Camerer (1994) and the Fechner error specification (termed by Wilcox *strong utility*) of Hey and Orme (1994). Two of his other specifications—*strict utility* and *moderate utility*—can be considered variations on the strong utility theme, but the fifth, *random preferences,* stands apart. In this fifth, the randomness in behavior comes not from error in the implementation of preferences, but from the preferences themselves. So the decision maker is assumed not to know his or her true preferences with certainty, but with some random component. Thus, for example, the decision maker may know that he or she has CARA SEU preferences—$u(x) = a - b\ e^{-rx}$—but does not know the precise value of *r,* the risk-aversion parameter. Randomness in behavior comes from the fact that *r* is random, coming from some distribution. The story here is that, on each pairwise choice question, a drawing is made from this distribution, and the question answered using that value of *r.* Different questions would have different drawings, and hence answers have a random component.

All the other stories assume that preferences are known with certainty but implemented with error. So with the *strong utility* story (which we have already encountered), when asked whether *p* or *q* is preferred, subjects answer on the basis of the value of $V(p) - V(q) + \varepsilon$ where ε is normally[11] distributed with mean 0 and variance σ^2. In the *strict utility* story,[12] it is assumed that subjects answer on the basis of $\ln(V(p)) - \ln(V(q)) + \varepsilon/\sigma^2$ where ε has a logistic distribution; in a sense this is a sort of logarithmic transformation of the strong utility specification.

Note crucially that the variance is constant in the strong (and strict) utility model, and one may well want to query this assumption: some pairwise choice questions may be easier than others and lead to smaller errors. This is the line followed by the *moderate utility* approach. Wilcox (2008) notes that this can be subdivided into two broad strands: the first that he calls the *wandering vector* approach; and the second *contextual utility.* This is not the place to go into detail but we can describe the first strand as requiring that ε is distributed with mean 0 and variance $\sigma^2 d$ where *d* is question specific. There are various ways of specifying *d*: one is that it is a measure of the *d*istance between the probability vectors *p* and *q*. With this, the closer together are the two lotteries in the pairwise choice, the more noise will be evident in the subjects' responses. In contrast, in the *contextual utility* approach, *d* is defined as $[V(x_{max}) - V(x_{min})]/\sigma^2$, where x_{max} and x_{min} are respectively the highest and lowest payoffs in the two lotteries in the pairwise choice. This is a kind of measure of the "distance" between the best and the worst things that could happen to the subject on that particular pairwise choice question.

Wilcox carries out a comparison of five different noise specifications combined with two different preference functional specifications. The results are instructive and we copy his table[13] here. This shows the log-likelihoods of the various fitted models over the subjects in Hey and Orme (1994).

---

[11] Or logistically distributed, though the logic of this approach only requires that ε has some distribution function $F(.)$ which satisfies $F(0) = 0.5$ and $F(x) = 1 - F(-x)$.

[12] Note that this requires that all utilities are positive.

[13] Wilcox (2008), page 271, Table 7.

Stochastic Model	Estimated on all Three Contexts	Estimated on Two of the Three Contexts
	Log-Likelihoods on all Three Contexts (In-Sample Fit)	Log-Likelihoods on Third Context (Out-of-Sample Fit)
EU structure		
Strong utility	−5311.44	−2409.38
Strict utility	−5448.50	−2373.12
Contextual utility	−5297.08	−2302.55
Wandering vector	−5362.61	−2417.76
Random preferences	−5348.36	−2356.60
RDEU structure		
Strong utility	−5207.81	−2394.75
Strict utility	−5306.48	−2450.41
Contextual utility	−5190.43	−2281.36
Wandering vector	−5251.82	−2397.91
Random preferences	−5218.00	−2335.55

As a rather over-simplifying (but not distorting) generalization, the differences between the different error specifications seem more important than the differences between the two functional forms. As Wilcox concludes (page 272) "perhaps ... we ought to be paying more attention to stochastic models."

There are two final stochastic specifications that we ought to mention before finishing this section: Blavatskyy's (2011) *truncated error model* and Busemeyer and Townsend's (1993) *decision field theory*. The motivation for Blavatskyy's specification starts from the fact that strong utility (and indeed strict and contextual utility) may violate first degree stochastic dominance. Indeed, even if both p and q are deterministic, and p is better than q, the subject may end up choosing q. The reason for this is that the random variable ε is unbounded: it has tails going off to infinity in both directions. Blavatskyy *truncates* the distribution, in a rather clever way. Without going into too much detail, let us give a flavor of his approach. Start with two lotteries p and q. Construct two new lotteries $p \cup q$ and $p \cap q$, which can respectively be described as the least upper bound and greatest lower bound on the lotteries p and q in terms of first-order stochastic dominance. By this is meant that $p \cup q$ first-order dominates both p and q, and there is no other distribution which $p \cup q$ dominates that has the same property. *Mutatis mutandis*, both p and q first-order dominate $p \cap q$, and there is no other distribution that has the same property and which $p \cap q$ dominates. So, loosely, $p \cup q$ can be described as the worst possible lottery that is better than both p and q, while $p \cap q$ can be described as the best possible lottery that both p and q are better than. So, in a rather obvious sense, $p \cup q$ and $p \cap q$ are the tightest *bounds* on p and q. He now makes the following stochastic specification:

$[V(\mathbf{p}) - V(\mathbf{q})]/[V(\mathbf{p} \cup \mathbf{q}) - V(\mathbf{p} \cap \mathbf{q})]$ is symmetrically random about zero on the interval $[-1, 1]$.

Note the bounds on the distribution. This specification has lots of nice properties, including that first-order dominance cannot be violated, and that weak stochastic transitivity is respected. Unfortunately, from time to time with experimental data, first-order dominance *is* violated; in order to accommodate such violations, Blavatskyy has to include *trembles* in his empirical analyses. This rather distracts from the attraction of his specification.

Decision Field Theory was introduced by psychologists Busemeyer and Townsend back in 1993 and has largely been ignored by economists. This is described by them as "Random EU Theory." In the absence of measurement error it is exactly the same as deterministic SEU theory. With error, it follows in the spirit of contextual utility by prescribing a heteroscedastic error. We give a brief description of DFT here though we refer the reader to Busemeyer and Townsend (1993) for the details. Consider a choice problem between two lotteries with three possible outcomes, 1, 2 and 3: suppose that lottery $\mathbf{x}$ leads to outcomes x_1, x_2 and x_3 in these three states; similarly suppose that lottery $\mathbf{y}$ leads to outcomes y_1, y_2 and y_3 in these three states. To save notational clutter, let us use $v_1, v_2, v_3, w_1, w_2,$ and w_3 (just in this paragraph) to refer to the associated utilities. According to DFT, the *attention weight* (similar to a probability) for any state is a random variable, and the associated (Subjective) Expected Utility for each lottery is therefore a random variable. To distinguish DFT from SEU, Busemeyer and Townsend use the expression *valence* instead of (Subjective) Expected Utility. The valence for lottery $\mathbf{x}$ is given by $V = P_1 v_1 + P_2 v_2 + P_3 v_3$ and that of lottery $\mathbf{y}$ by $W = P_1 w_1 + P_2 w_2 + P_3 w_3$ where the "attention weights" P_1, P_2 and P_3 are random variables centered on the individual's subjective probabilities p_1, p_2 and p_3 for the three states. So the key variable on which the decision will be taken, $V-W$, is a random variable with mean $d = (p_1 v_1 + p_2 v_2 + p_3 v_3) - (p_1 w_1 + p_2 w_2 + p_3 w_3)$ and variance σ^2. This variance is crucially not constant, but, in the theory expounded by Busemeyer and Townsend, is given by the expression $s^2 \{ p_1 (v_1 - w_1)^2 + p_2 (v_2 - w_2)^2 + p_3 (v_3 - w_3)^2 - (V-W)^2 \}$. It can be interpreted as the weighted variance of the difference between the utilities of the outcomes conditional on the states. Busemeyer and Townsend call it the variance of the valence difference. An interesting special case is when both lotteries are certainties and one dominates the other. In this case, we have that $v_1 = v_2 = v_3 = v$, that $w_1 = w_2 = w_3 = w$, and that $v = w + d$. In this case it follows that the variance σ^2 is zero, so that the subject never makes an error and always chooses the dominating lottery; Stronger Utility also has this property. Another nice property is that the theory implies that the more dispersed are the outcomes for particular states, then the more likely it is that the subject makes a mistake. The explanation for this property is based on the stochastic modeling of computational processes, which are discussed in detail in the Busemeyer and Townsend paper.

14.1.8 Testing vs. Prediction

This subsection contains a brief discussion on methodology which is not restricted to the context of the first part of this chapter (decision making under risk) but is more general, and applies to the chapter as a whole. Indeed, we think that it applies to the whole of economics. So in one sense this present subsection is irrelevant from the specific point of view of the overall aim of this chapter; though in our opinion it is crucial. It concerns what it is that we are trying to do with our theories and our empirics.

We have argued strongly above that testing is not interesting from an economist's point of view and that we should be more interested in which theory *best explains* the data. We have used the log-likelihood as a measure of goodness of fit of the data to a theory, and we have suggested that one should use the log-likelihood (or the corrected log-likelihood where theories differ in their degrees of freedom) as the way of choosing the "best" theory.

But we feel that we should go further. We believe that what economists should be trying to do is to *predict* behavior, not simply *explain* it. So we believe that we should examine theories from the perspective of their *predictive*, not solely *explanatory*, power. This is a view that has been proposed also in Wilcox (2007), which is a masterful, though unpublished, contribution to the literature. He recommends using part of the data from an experiment for fitting models, and then using the fitted models to predict behavior on the rest of the data; using the goodness-of-fit on the prediction part to compare theories. This has the advantage that one does not need to worry about degrees of freedom: more general models may well "penalize" themselves by *over-fitting* the model to the data.

If one agrees with this line of argument, then Wilcox (2007) is obligatory reading, though one should be clear that his analysis is confined to pairwise choice experiments in a risky context, and to prediction *out-of-context*. By this latter is meant prediction in a different context from that in which the fitting was done. With pairwise choice questions, this is easy to illustrate: suppose that there are four possible outcomes in an experiment: x_1, x_2, x_3 and x_4. Suppose that the pairwise choice questions were selected from four different subsets of these outcomes: $S_{-1} = (x_2, x_3, x_4)$, $S_{-2} = (x_1, x_3, x_4)$, $S_{-3} = (x_1, x_2, x_4)$, and $S_{-4} = (x_1, x_2, x_3)$. Then what he means by out-of-context prediction is that the prediction was done on one or more of these subsets that were *not* used for fitting; for example, fitting using S_{-4}, S_{-3} and S_{-2} and prediction using S_{-1}. What Wilcox found was that even with as many 100 pairwise choice questions used for fitting (and 50 for prediction), the predictive ability of most of the models[14] he considered was hardly better than totally unsophisticated predictors such as the Pratt covariate[15].

---

[14] Two structural models (SEU and RDEU) each combined with three stochastic specifications (Strong Utility, Contextual Utility and Random Preferences).

[15] This is a term introduced by Wilcox (2007) to give "a rough and ready approximation of the difference between the certainty equivalents of the lotteries in any pair."

This finding seems to be another reason to use questions other than pairwise choice questions when trying to assess theories of decision making under risk (and indeed other theories). We have advocated above the use of *allocation* questions and one should see if Wilcox's pessimistic conclusions also apply with this type of experiment.

14.1.9 Some Methodological Points

Before concluding our examination of experiments investigating static theories of decision making under risk, we should group together in this subsection a number of methodological points concerning the design and implementation of experiments that we have touched upon during this section. These points include: (1) instructions; (2) whether there should be some test to see if the subjects have understood the instructions; (3) the number and type of questions to ask the subjects; (4) the presentation of questions in the experiments; (5) whether subjects should be subject to minimum and maximum times for answering questions; (6) whether some kind of questionnaire should be administered to the subjects at the end of the experiment; (7) the incentive mechanism to be used in the experiment, and, in particular, the use of the Random Lottery Incentive Mechanism; (8) how should the data be analyzed; including (9) functional form restrictions.

Instructions are vital and are usually provided in written form, supplemented by a PowerPoint presentation that plays at a predetermined speed; subjects are more likely to concentrate on the latter than the former. Many experimentalists now include some kind of *test* of understanding of the instructions; the problem with this is in deciding what to do if subjects "fail" the test.

We have already discussed both the *number* and the *type* of questions to ask; one should do extensive simulation prior to the experiment to ensure that both of these are adequate. The *presentation* is important: it is becoming increasingly the norm for experiments to be computerized (many using the purpose-built z-Tree software) and a variety of different displays have been used. Computerized experiments have many advantages, not least that *all* relevant data can be stored, that all subjects get exactly the same treatment, and, particularly recently, that the time for each stage of the experiment can be controlled—with perhaps a minimum time imposed for answering each question (to stop subjects from just clicking quickly and randomly, under the belief that this behavior will make little difference to how much they get paid), and perhaps also a maximum (more relevant in interactive experiments where slow subjects hold up faster subjects). Increasingly experimentalists are including an end-of-experiment *questionnaire*, seeking information on the subjects' demographic, sociological, perhaps political, and perhaps other characteristics; the problem with this kind of data is that it is self-reported and difficult to incentivate properly. The experiment proper, however, can be given an appropriate incentive, possibly using the *random lottery incentive* mechanism or even paying them off on all questions[16]. As far as post-experimental data analysis is concerned, we have already stated our prejudices: we believe that experiments should be used to find the "best" theory of behavior, best in terms of explanation and prediction.

14.2 DYNAMIC DECISION MAKING UNDER RISK[17]

Much of economic theory assumes a *static* decision problem: the decision maker takes a decision; a move by Nature occurs; the decision maker receives a payoff; end of story. However, in real life most decisions are dynamic: there is a sequence of decisions and subsequent moves by Nature, and the payoffs could be obtained at any point in the sequence or at the end. The decision maker could find the optimal strategy in one of two obvious ways: (1) by working backwards from the end-point (assuming that there is one)[18] and hence proceed by *backward induction*; (2) by turning the problem into one of choosing an optimal *strategy*—which is a set of conditional decisions. There is a nice result that these two ways lead to the same solution—*as long as the preferences of the decision maker are Expected Utility preferences.*

This result can be illustrated with a simple example, in which there are two decisions to be taken each with subsequent moves by Nature. The problem is illustrated in Figure 14.1. In this figure the box on the left and the four in the middle are decision nodes at which the decision maker must decide whether to move Up or Down. The two boxes towards the left and the eight towards the right are chance nodes where Nature moves. Let us assume for simplicity that Nature moves up with probabilities p_1 and p_2 at the first chance nodes (numbering from the top) and with probabilities $q_{i,}$ $i = 1, \ldots, 8$ at the second chance nodes (again numbering from the top)[19]. The boxes at the right-hand side are the payoffs to the subject if they get to that box. To keep our discussion general, let us denote these payoffs x_i where i goes from 1 at the top to 16 at the bottom, and, to save space in what follows, let us denote by u_i the utility obtained from x_i. Let us also use the notation U_1 (D_1) to denote the decision to move Up (Down) at the first decision node, and U_{2j} (D_{2j}) to denote the decision to move Up (Down) at the j'th (numbering from the top) second decision node. We note the following: if the decision maker is using *backward induction*, then he or she considers first what he or she would do at each of the second decision nodes. If the decision maker has EU preferences then he or she would choose U_{2j} (D_{2j}) at the j'th second decision node if

---

[16] Though this introduces possible wealth effects.

[17] We should note that we are ignoring problems with *discounting* as these are entirely separate from (though similar in nature to) problems under risk.

[18] We shall ignore the complications caused by an infinite sequence, largely on the grounds that none of us live an infinite amount of time, but also because taking this into account does not affect the *spirit* of the arguments that we are about to propound.

[19] In the experiment reported in Bone et al. (2009) from which this figure was taken, all these probabilities were one-half.

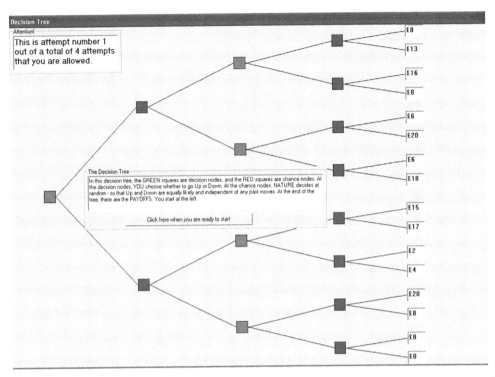

Figure 14.1 A dynamic decision problem. Green boxes: far left and second from left columns; red boxes far right and second from right columns.

$$\mathbf{q}_{2(j-1)+1}\mathbf{u}_{4(j-1)+1} + (1 - \mathbf{q}_{2(j-1)+1})\mathbf{u}_{4(j-1)+2} \geq (\leq)\mathbf{q}_{2(j-1)+2}\mathbf{u}_{4(j-1)+3}$$
$$+ (1 - \mathbf{q}_{2(j-1)+2})\mathbf{u}_{4(j-1)+4}.$$

Working backwards, conditional on this anticipated decision, he or she will choose $U_1 (D_1)$ at the first decision node if

$$p_1 max[q_1 u_1 + (1 - q_1)u_2, q_2 u_3 + (1 - q_2)u_4] + (1 - p_1)max[q_3 u_5$$
$$+ (1 - q_3)u_6, q_4 u_7 + (1 - q_4)u_8] \geq (\leq)p_2 max[q_5 u_9 + (1 - q_5)u_{10}, q_5 u_{11}$$
$$+ (1 - q_5)u_{12}] + (1 - p_2)max[q_7 u_{13} + (1 - q_7)u_{14}, q_8 u_{15} + (1 - q_8)u_{16}].$$

Notice that this can be written

$$max[p_1 q_1 u_1 + p_1(1 - q_1)u_2, p_1 q_2 u_3 + p_1(1 - q_2)u_4] + max[(1 - p_1)q_3 u_5$$
$$+ (1 - p_1)(1 - q_3)u_6, q_4 u_7 + (1 - p_1)(1 - q_4)u_8] \geq (\leq)max[p_2 q_5 u_9$$
$$+ p_2(1 - q_5)u_{10}, p_2 q_5 u_{11} + p_2(1 - q_5)u_{12}] + max[(1 - p_2)q_7 u_{13}$$
$$+ (1 - p_2)(1 - q_7)u_{14}, q_8 u_{15} + (1 - p_2)(1 - q_8)u_{16}].$$

Now consider someone who works by the *strategy method*. Such a person works out all the possible strategies, which set consists of both moves at the first decision node and all conditional (conditional on the move by Nature) at the second node. The expected utility following each strategy is given in Table 14.1. It is clear from this that the best strategy is the one that gives the maximum of the second column elements in this table. It is also immediately clear that the optimal strategy is also the one that would be followed by an Expected Utility maximizer using backward induction. The reason for this is that expected utility is *linear in the probabilities*.

However, if the preference functional is *not* linear in the probabilities, then this result does not go through, and thus the decision maker gets a different solution to the optimization problem depending on whether he or she is using backward induction or the strategy method. This can be shown in a very simple fashion using Prospect Theory, where there is a *weighting function* on the probabilities. So in the backward induction method each probability p or q would be replaced by $w(p)$ or $w(q)$, while using the strategy method each pq would be replaced by $w(pq)$. Unless $w(.)$ is linear (or has very special properties) it is *not* the case that $w(pq) = w(p)w(q)$.

The interesting question then is: what do they do? Perhaps this could be informed by the answer to the question: what should they do? However, this question is a difficult one, as the fact that they have non-expected utility preferences says that they will come up with different strategies depending upon their preferences and the way that they process dynamic problems. If you like they are *dynamically inconsistent*. This is a very important problem for economic theory—much theorising depends upon agents being dynamically consistent.

Table 14.1 The Set of Strategies Relevant for the Decision Problem of Figure 14.1

Strategy	Expected Utility Following the Strategy
U_1U_{21}	$p_1q_1u_1 + p_1(1-q_1)u_2 + (1-p_1)q_3u_5 + (1-p_1)(1-q_3)u_6$
U_1D_{21}	$p_1q_1u_1 + p_1(1-q_1)u_2 + (1-p_1)q_4u_7 + (1-p_1)(1-q_4)u_8$
U_1U_{22}	$p_1q_2u_3 + p_1(1-q_2)u_4 + (1-p_1)q_3u_5 + (1-p_1)(1-q_3)u_6$
U_1D_{22}	$p_1q_2u_3 + p_1(1-q_2)u_4 + (1-p_1)q_4u_7 + (1-p_1)(1-q_4)u_8$
D_1U_{23}	$p_2q_5u_9 + p_2(1-q_5)u_{10} + (1-p_2)q_7u_{13} + (1-p_2)(1-q_7)u_{14}$
D_1D_{23}	$p_2q_5u_9 + p_2(1-q_5)u_{10} + (1-p_2)q_8u_{15} + (1-p_2)(1-q_8)u_{16}$
D_1U_{24}	$p_2q_6u_{11} + p_2(1-q_6)u_{12} + (1-p_2)q_7u_{13} + (1-p_2)(1-q_7)u_{14}$
D_1D_{24}	$p_2q_6u_{11} + p_2(1-q_6)u_{12} + (1-p_2)q_8u_{15} + (1-p_2)(1-q_8)u_{16}$

There are two ways that have been adopted to experimentally investigate this inconsistency: first to see which particular principles underlying dynamic consistency are being violated; second to see whether subjects are aware of it and what they do about it. We shall consider these in turn.

The first approach is followed in particular by Cubitt et al. (1998), who test which principles of dynamic choice are involved in common ratio type violations of the Independence Axiom. Indeed, their strategy is based on the observation that, since the Independence Axiom can be shown to follow[20] from specific principles of dynamic choice, when it is violated, at least one of those principles must be violated as well. Following this approach, they implement a between-subject experimental design and find evidence of failure of the *time independence* principle, and therefore those theories of choice which are based on it.[21,22] A similar approach is followed by Cubitt and Sugden (2001), who are, however, particularly interested in controlling for the role affective experiences have in dynamic choice under risk. They propose evidence that the time independence and the separability principles are jointly rejected by the data. Finally, a related paper by Busemeyer et al. (2000) uses a within-subject design to investigate violations of a set of consistency principles in a dynamic choice problem. They find robust evidence of violation of dynamic and strategic consistency but not of consequential consistency.

One important implication of dynamic inconsistency is that the *framing* of a decision problem quite clearly affects decision making. Consider someone who does not have Expected Utility preferences, realizes that they are dynamically inconsistent and decides to use backward induction in a dynamic decision problem with the payoffs at the end (as in Figure 14.1). Now suppose that the problem is rephrased as a single-stage strategy problem (without telling the decision maker anything about the reframing). What will he or she do? Possibly take different decisions. This suggests that he or she might be sensitive to the *framing* of the problem. This possibility—that people may have preferences over the frame—was investigated by Hey and Paradiso (2006). They presented exactly the same dynamic decision problem to subjects in three different formats. They found that many subjects were consistent with EU and hence were dynamically consistent, and they found a significant number that were resolute—in the sense that they took a decision at the beginning and stuck with it throughout the decision problem, despite being tempted to change their minds. Indeed there were subjects who were happy to pay for precommitment, perhaps fearing that they might change their minds later.

---

[20] But does not necessarily *have* to follow.

[21] As explained by Cubitt et al., this is the principle "according to which an agent, if required to pre-commit to an action to be taken conditional on a prior act of nature, pre-commits to the action which would be chosen if the moment of choice was delayed until after that act of nature". See Cubitt et al. (1998, p. 1366).

[22] Recent unpublished work by Dubois and Nebout (2009) extends the previous analysis by using a within-subject experimental design and essentially confirms the main findings.

Expanding on these findings, Hey and Lotito (2009) implemented an experiment where both behavior and preferences are investigated. They use data on tree evaluations together with data on choices and find evidence that the strategy method, as opposed to that of backward induction, is followed by the majority of subjects.

Central to both the strategy method and backward induction to all such theories is the concept of a plan: in order to decide what to do today, rational economic agents should first consider what they will do in the future. This is so whether the agents solve the dynamic decision problem by turning it into a strategy problem, or whether they use some form of backward induction. It is also so whether the agents' preferences are Expected Utility or whether they are not, though in this latter case the potential problem of dynamic inconsistency may arise. As this idea of planning is central to economic theorizing, many economists have sought to test whether it appears to be valid or not. Economists typically have fought shy of simply asking people—on the methodological grounds that it is difficult or impossible to appropriately motivate an honest answer. If one simply asks the agent, but the agent is not forced to implement the stated plan, then there appears to be no motive for answering honestly. If instead agents are forced to implement the stated plan, then the problem is transformed into one of precommitment. Moreover, asking the subjects what they are planning to do suggests to subjects that they might want to plan—if subjects had never thought about doing so then the design of the experiment at least brings the idea to their mind—and hence, perhaps, defeats the very purpose of the experiment. These issues are discussed with great clarity in the papers of Cubitt et al. (1998, 2004). Psychologists, however, have been less reluctant to simply ask subjects. Prominent among such psychologists are Jerome R. Busemeyer and his co-workers who have done a series of experiments on dynamic decision making, two good examples being Barkan and Busemeyer (1999) and Busemeyer et al. (2000).[23] These experiments suggest that planning by subjects is not as economists imagine it to be. However, economists remain suspicious of these results—for the methodological reasons outlined above. One experiment in economics which attempted to identify the plan (if any) being made by subjects was Hey (2002) but this relied on the assumption that the subjects had Expected Utility preferences. This assumption is too strong for most economists. Bone et al. (2009) evaded this problem by having a decision problem whose solution was driven by *dominance*—thus avoiding the thorny issue of preferences. Figure 14.1 is one of the decision trees that subjects were faced with. Note the payoffs. If one examines the tree and works backwards, it can be seen that all decisions can be taken just using dominance. Each move by Nature has probability one-half, so the decision at the top second decision node is between a prospect that gives a 50–50 chance of £8 or £13 and a prospect that gives a 50–50 chance

---

[23] We should note that the work of Busemeyer and his colleagues is far-reaching and goes far beyond our current concerns. Here we refer only to issues concerned specifically with planning.

of £16 or £8. So Down is optimal irrespective of the preferences of the subject (as long as they respect dominance). Dominance drives all the second decision node decisions. Working back and eliminating choices that will not be made at the second nodes, the decision at the first stage is between playing Up which yields a prospect that pays £16 or £8 or £6 or £20 (all with probability one-quarter) and Down which yields a prospect that pays £15 or £17 or £20 or £8 (all with probability one-quarter). Clearly choosing Down at the first decision node dominates playing Up. All the decision trees in this experiment had this dominance property. Bone et al. had three treatments: two Individual Treatments (differentiated by whether subjects were asked to precommit to their future decision or not) and one Pairs Treatment (in which one subject took the decision at the first decision node and a second the decision at the second node—no communication was allowed between the members of any Pair). The precommitment treatment was suggested by a referee and was originally disputed by the authors on the grounds that it effectively forced the subjects to think ahead. The Pairs treatment had a similar intent—as the first player should think about what the second player might do. However the experiment revealed that many subjects took the "wrong" (by which we mean the non-backward induction decision) decision at the first node—and hence were not thinking about the second decision node, even in the Pre-Commitment treatment. Bone et al.'s interpretation was that, while the subjects were being forced to think about their second move *along their chosen path*, we had not forced them to think about the implications if they had chosen differently at the first stage.

A more complicated design, with different objectives, though with a similar dominance-supported optimal strategy, was implemented by Hey and Knoll (2011). This involved a three-decision three-moves-by-Nature design, and the software was so designed that the experimenters could replay (to themselves, not to the subjects) the way that the subject had tackled the problem. Some subjects were using backward induction (the strategy method would have been too difficult to implement) and a number of simplifying heuristics were identified.

Most of the above experiments involved pairwise choice decisions. In contrast, Hey and Panaccione (2011) implemented an experiment with allocation problems. The authors extended the experimental method pioneered by Loomes (1991) to a dynamic decision problem. Again a two-decision, two-chance-moves framework was involved. In the first stage, each subject allocated money between two alternatives; then Nature moved and selected at random one of them. In the second stage, each subject had to allocate the money that Nature's move implied between two further risky alternatives. After a final move by Nature, the subject earned the money that Nature's move implied (on a randomly selected one of the tasks). In the experiment, 71 subjects were asked to repeat this decision task on 27 problems with different probabilities for Nature's moves.

Of course, as we have already noted, while allocation questions are potentially more informative than pairwise choice questions, the downside is that many more payoffs are possible and one is forced to assume some preference functional and to estimate its parameters. Hey and Panaccione assumed the Rank Dependent form with a CRRA utility function and a Quiggin weighting function. Their methodology was to fit such a preference functional to each of the subject's responses, making four different assumptions as to how the subjects resolved the potential dynamic inconsistency, and to see which fitted the behavior the best. These four were: Resolute (deciding a conditional plan at the beginning and implementing it come what may); Sophisticated (using backward induction); Naive (starting out thinking that they would implement a plan but changing their minds when they got to the second stage); and Myopic (forgetting that there was a second state till they got to it). Interestingly, it was found that the majority of the subjects appeared to be Resolute, a significant few appeared to be Sophisticated, rather few appeared to be Naive and similarly few appeared to be Myopic. These results seem to conflict rather starkly with some other findings.

One thing is clear from these experiments: that it is difficult to design a dynamic decision-making experiment that is sufficiently easy for subjects to understand yet sufficiently rich to enable strong inferences to be drawn. It seems to me that the field is still wide open.

14.3 DECISION MAKING UNDER AMBIGUITY

14.3.1 Overview

Ambiguity differs from risk in that the events are uncertain but the probabilities (if they exist) are not known to the decision maker. Most of the experimental work on ambiguity has been confined to the static case and we shall restrict our attention largely to that, though dynamic decision making under ambiguity is likely to become an increasingly studied, though difficult, field of research in the future. Our discussion starts with Ellsberg (1961), who sets the scene, and then we refer to an early survey by Camerer and Weber (1992) of theoretical contributions to the study of decision making under ambiguity and (largely experimental) tests of those theories. We then note that the later stages of the twentieth century and the early stages of the twenty-first were marked by rapid expanses in theoretical contributions (see Chapter 13 in this handbook), leading to ever more sophisticated stories of behavior. We conclude this section with a subsection examining experimental tests of these new theories.

14.3.2 Ellsberg

We have to start with Ellsberg (1961) which many think of as the defining article on the inability of SEU to explain behavior in an ambiguous situation: the Ellsberg Paradox is well-known in the literature. However, his "experiment" was hypothetical. He wrote:

Let us suppose that you confront two urns containing red and black balls, from one of which a ball will be drawn at random. To "bet on Red I" will mean that you choose to draw from Urn I; and that *you will receive a prize a (say $100) if you draw a red ball ("if Red I occurs") and a smaller amount b (say, $0) if you draw a black ("if not-Red I occurs"). You have the following information. Urn I contains 100 red and black balls, but in a ratio entirely unknown to you; there may be from 0 to 100 red balls. In Urn II, you confirm that there are exactly 50 red and 50 black balls. An observer—who, let us say, is ignorant of the state of your information about the urns—sets out to measure your subjective probabilities by interrogating you as to your preferences in the following pairs of gambles:*

1. "Which do you prefer to bet on, Red I or Black I: or are you indifferent?" That is, drawing a ball from Urn I, on which "event" do you prefer the $100 stake, red or black: or do you care?
2. "Which would you prefer to bet on, Red II or Black II?"
3. "Which do you prefer to bet on, Red I or Red II?"
4. "Which do you prefer to bet on, Black I or Black II?"

Ellsberg noted that "…if you prefer to bet on Red II rather than Red I, and Black II rather than Black I … or if you prefer to bet on Red I rather than Red II, and Black I rather than Black II … you are now in trouble with the Savage axioms." After introspecting about the likely results from conducting an experiment of this type, Ellsberg concluded that many people would be in "trouble with the Savage Axioms."

It is important and instructive to note his form of words when describing what has now come to be called the "Ellsberg Urn": namely "Urn I contains 100 red and black balls, but in a ratio entirely unknown to you; there may be from 0 to 100 red balls." Such terminology should be unacceptable in modern laboratory practice, though I note that it is still in use. Problems arise for a number of reasons, not least when the experimenter has chosen the 'winning color': subjects are naturally suspicious that the experimenter is manipulating the experiment to save money. Even when the subject can choose the winning color, suspicion may remain: the experimenter should be explicit as to how the ambiguous urn was composed and how it will be played out. We discuss these issues later.

14.3.3 The Early Literature

This is well summarized in Camerer and Weber (1992). Their paper is partly a survey of theoretical developments and partly a review of experimental investigations of them. The theories they discuss are partly motivated by concern about experimental implementations of ambiguity as we shall explain. Camerer and Weber (1992) start with SEU and then devote a section to "ambiguity as second-order probability". So for example, each of the possible 101 configurations of Ellsberg's Uncertain Urn (0 red 100 black, 1 red 99 black,…,100 red 0 black) have some probability (perhaps 1/101) of occurring. Of course, an individual obeying the axioms of SEU would simply use the reduction principle and consider Urns I and II as identical. An alternative scenario is that the decision maker could list the various possibilities concerning the composition of the Uncertain Urn but not be able to attach probabilities to them. There is clearly a close connection between the experimental implementation of the ambiguity and the theoretical account of behavior. We will comment further on this below.

14.3.4 Recent Experimental Research into Behavior Under Ambiguity

After the flurry of activity reported in Camerer and Weber (1992) and Camerer (1995) there was a pause of some 15 years before serious largely theoretical research on behavior under ambiguity restarted. There followed a revival of experimental work—mainly caused by the spate of new theories of behavior under ambiguity. These theories are well surveyed in Etner et al. (2012).

We note an important distinction between two types of theory which currently exist in the literature: part of the recent literature envisages the decision maker as realizing that he or she does not know the values of the relevant probabilities (even when they exist), or is not prepared to make subjective judgments about the possible probabilities; while another part envisages the decision maker as being able to list the various possibilities for the various probabilities and, moreover, as being able to attach probabilities to the various possibilities. This second part therefore models ambiguity through the use of second-order probabilities, or probabilities of probabilities. Models of this type are sometimes referred to as *multiple prior models* (Conte and Hey, 2013), and include the Smooth Model of Klibanoff et al. (2005). We remain agnostic as to whether these can be really considered as models of ambiguity.

Halevy (2007) marks the start of new experimental work investigating the recent theories; subsequent contributions are those of Andersen et al. (2009), Ahn et al. (2010), Hey et al. (2010), Hey and Pace (2011), Abdellaoui et al. (2011) and Conte and Hey (2013). In this section, we first survey these papers one by one, and then turn to a discussion of the design considerations of the experiments. We start with an overview.

Halevy (2007) implemented ambiguity in the laboratory using traditional Ellsberg Urns and asked reservation price questions. Because of the way that his "Ellsberg Urns" were implemented, his set of models includes models of both types that we discussed earlier, in particularly two-stage-probability models such as Recursive Nonexpected Utility and Recursive Expected Utility, as well as nonmultiple-prior models. He used *reservation price* questions; we will discuss these later—as they are an alternative to pairwise choice questions and to allocation questions. Halevy did not use his data to estimate preference functionals and hence did not compare their descriptive and predictive power; instead he carried out an extensive set of tests of the various theories. Unfortunately this econometric procedure does not help to draw unique conclusions about the "best" preference functional, even for individual subjects. However Halevy concludes that his "…findings indicate that currently there is no unique theoretical model that universally captures ambiguity preferences."

Andersen et al. (2009) use a technique similar to that used by Ahn et al. (2010) in estimating two parameters (one a measure of risk aversion and the other a measure of ambiguity) in a minimalist non-EU model. They comment that this minimalist model comes either from the Source-Dependent Risk Attitude model or the Uncertain Priors model; in our terminology it is a two-stage-probability model[24] that looks exactly like Recursive Expected Utility. The bottom line is the following: suppose that there are I possible outcomes $i = 1, \ldots, I$ with unknown probabilities. The decision maker has a set of J possible values for these probabilities; we denote the j'th possible value $p_{1j}, p_{2j}, \ldots, p_{Ij}$, and the decision maker considers that the probability that this is the correct set is π_j. The preference functional is the maximization of

$$\Sigma_{j=1}^{J} \pi_j v [\Sigma_{i=1}^{I} p_{ij} u(x_{ij})].$$

Note that there are two functions here: $u(.)$ which can be considered as a normal utility function, capturing attitude to risk; and $v(.)$ which can be considered as an ambiguity function capturing attitude to ambiguity; note that if $v(y) = y$ then this model reduces to Expected Utility theory—it is the nonlinearity of $v(.)$ that captures aversion to ambiguity. Andersen et al. (2009) assumed that both these functions are power functions—so that $u(x) = x^\alpha$ and $v(y) = y^\beta$. They estimated the two parameters α and β using maximum likelihood techniques (with careful attention paid to the stochastic specification) and assumptions[25] about the π's and the p's.

Hey et al. (2010) employed an experimental design with three possible outcomes (thus avoiding having to parameterize the utility function), and asked a large number (162) of pairwise choice questions; they examined the descriptive and predictive ability of 12 theories of behavior under ambiguity: some very old and not using a preference functional (proceeding directly to a decision rule) such as the original MaxMin and MaxMax; and some very recent, such as the Alpha Expected Utility model. The findings were that the very old simple models (those without a preference function) were largely discredited, but that more modern and rather sophisticated models (such as Choquet) did not perform sufficiently better than simple theories such as Subjective Expected Utility theory. Estimation of the preference functions was done using maximum likelihood techniques with the stochastic specification determined by a model of how subjects made errors in their pairwise choices.

Ahn et al. (2010) used allocation questions, but implemented ambiguity by not telling the subjects the true objective probabilities of two of the three possible outcomes of the experiment. They did not look at the predictive ability of any models; neither did they examine the descriptive performance of any specific theory. Instead they examined two broad classes of functionals, smooth and kinked, which are special cases of

---

[24] Chambers et al. (2010) also investigate a generic Multiple Priors model.
[25] The authors admit that the assumptions were quite strong and discuss the serious identification problems with two-stage-probability models.

various theoretical models that we specifically estimate. Econometrically, they estimated, subject by subject, the risk-aversion parameter of an assumed Constant Absolute Risk Aversion utility function, and a second parameter measuring ambiguity aversion, using Non Linear Least Squares (NLLS), that is by minimizing the sum of squared differences between actual allocations and the theoretically optimal allocations for those risk and ambiguity aversion coefficients. They comment in a footnote that "…for simplicity, the estimation technique for both specifications is NLLS, rather than a structural model using maximum likelihood (ML). We favor the NLLS approach, because it provides a good fit and offers straightforward interpretation." They do not provide a formal justification to the choice of NLLS instead of ML.

Hey and Pace (2011) instead, although using a Bingo Blower to implement ambiguity in the laboratory, used *allocation* questions, which necessitated the parameterization, and hence estimation, of the utility function. They fitted five different preference functionals, each combined with three different stochastic/utility function specifications, and compared the descriptive and predictive validity of the different preference functionals/specifications. They concluded that the more general models do not predict significantly better than Subjective Expected Utility theory.

Abdellaoui et al. (2011) investigated only Rank Dependent Expected Utility theory. They did not explicitly examine its descriptive (nor predictive) ability, being more concerned with the effect on the estimated utility and weighting functions of different *sources* of ambiguity. As we have already noted, they implemented ambiguity in the laboratory in two ways: in one part of the experiment, using 8-color "Ellsberg Urns"; and in the other part using "natural" events. They elicited certainty equivalents (or reservation prices) in order to infer preferences, not using the BDM mechanism (presumably because of the problems we will allude to below), but instead using Holt-Laury price lists[26]. This mechanism seems to be a better way of eliciting certainty equivalents, even though the outcome does appear to be sensitive to the elements in the list—the number of them and their range. The resulting certainty equivalents are a valuation, just as Halevy's reservation prices, even though they come from a set of pairwise choice questions. However, econometrically it must be the case that the valuation resulting from an ordered list with n elements is less informative than n independent pairwise choice questions. They estimated utility functions (assumed to be power or CRRA) "using nonlinear least squares estimation with the certainty equivalent as dependent variable"; similarly they estimated the weighting function by "minimising the quadratic distance". They do not explain why.

---

[26] In which subjects are presented with a set of pairwise choices arranged in a list. In each pair subjects are asked to choose between some ambiguous lottery and some certain amount of money. As one goes down the list, the certain amount increases. The subject's certainty equivalent is revealed by the point at which the subject switches from choosing the lottery to choosing the certain amount. See Holt and Laury (2002).

Conte and Hey (2013) set up an experiment to explore the empirical validity of a subset of the multiple prior models of ambiguity by having a design in which choices were explicitly expressed in a multiple prior format. They estimated a mixture model, involving five models: Expected Utility (EU), the Smooth Model (SM) of Klibanoff et al. (2005), Rank Dependent (RD) model and Alpha Model (AM) of Ghirardato et al. (2004). The mixture model enabled the authors to classify subjects to models with a high degree of accuracy, with posterior probabilities of subjects being of one type or another being over 0.90 for around 90% of our subjects. These posterior probabilities suggest that around 22% of the subjects follow EU, 53% SM, some 22% RD and around 3% AM. Interestingly the assignments based on the estimated data do not differ very much from those based on prediction data—unlike in Wilcox (2007).

We now turn to design considerations, in particular: the kinds of questions asked to the subjects; the way that ambiguity was implemented in the laboratory; and information about the theories (or class of theories) under test. Table 14.2 gives an overview.

Table 14.2 Recent Experimental Work on Behavior Under Ambiguity

Paper	Type of questions	Implementation of Ambiguity	Theories Being Investigated
Halevy (2007)	Certainty equivalents/Reservation prices (using BDM Mechanism)	Ellsberg-type urns	SEU, Maximin, Anticipated Utility[a,c], Smooth[d]
Andersen et al. (2009)	Pairwise Choices	Bingo cage and real events	Minimalist non-EU model (a special case of Smooth[d])
Ahn et al. (2010)	Allocations	Probabilities of two of the three states not stated	Two broad classes: smooth and kinked; special cases of more general models
Hey et al. (2010)	Pairwise choices	Bingo Blower	EV, SEU, Choquet, Prospect, Cumulative Prospect, Decision Field Theory, Alpha[b] plus some older theories
Hey and Pace (2011)	Allocations	Bingo Blower	SEU, Choquet, Alpha[b], Vector EU, Contraction[e]
Abdellaoui et al. (2011)	Certainty equivalents /Reservation prices (using Holt-Laury price lists)	8-color Ellsberg type urns	RDEU
Conte and Hey (2013)	Pairwise choices	Multiple priors	SEU, Smooth, Alpha[b], Anticipated Utility

Notes: [a]Referred to as Recursive Nonexpected Utility.[b]Ghirardato et al. (2004) (Including the special cases Maxmin and Maxmax.).[c]It is not clear which weighting function (Quiggin or Power.) is used.[d]Klibanoff et al. (2005).[e]Gajdos et al. (2008).

In these experiments, there were three different *types of questions* asked to the subjects: (1) reservation price questions; (2) pairwise choice questions; (3) allocation questions. The advantage of the first and last types is that there is more information contained in the answer to each question than in the second type; the disadvantage is that it becomes necessary to estimate a utility function. Conte and Hey (2013) used pairwise choice questions since they wanted to reduce the number of parameters that were needed to be estimated. They therefore took the decision not to estimate a utility function and hence restricted the payments to the subjects to one of two values. This implied immediately that they could not ask allocation questions nor ask reservation price questions; and thus were restricted to pairwise choice questions. They compensated by having relatively many questions: 49 tasks and 256 pairwise choice questions in total; this is many more questions than is usually the case.

In contrast, the papers by Ahn et al. (2010) and Hey and Pace (2011) used allocation questions, in which subjects were asked, in each of a series of questions, to allocate a given sum of tokens to various events, with given exchange rates between tokens and money for each of the events. If a particular question was selected to determine the payment to the subject, then the question was played out and the resulting event, combined with the allocation that the subject had made to that event and the prespecified exchange rate between tokens and money for that question and that event, determined the payment that the subject received for his or her participation (plus any given participation fee). As a result the actual payment might take one of a range of values, and hence a utility function over this range would have to be inferred from the subject's answers. This was also the case in the experiments of Halevy (2007) and Abdellaoui et al. (2011), though both of these papers asked subjects to state *certainty equivalents* for certain events. In the first of these papers, the Becker-Degroot-Marschak (BDM) method (see Becker et al., 1964) was used to get subjects to state their certainty equivalents; in the second Holt-Laury (see Holt and Laury, 2002) price lists were used. Both of these mechanisms have their problems: the BDM, in that it appears to be the case that subjects find it difficult to understand what the mechanism entails; and the Holt-Laury, in that it appears that the answers given by subjects are sensitive to the bounds on the lists.

Let us discuss the issues concerned with Halevy's use of the BDM mechanism to measure certainty equivalents in more detail. Essentially he wants to know how much subjects value bets on various events. Let us consider a particular Ellsberg Urn and a particular color. The subject is asked to imagine that he or she owns a bet which pays a certain amount of money ($2) if that colored ball is drawn from that particular urn. Halevy wanted to elicit the subject's reservation price for this bet, this reservation price telling us about the subject's preferences. Halevy used the Becker-DeGroot-Marschak mechanism: "the subject was asked to state a minimal price at which she was willing to sell the bet… The subject set the selling price by moving a lever on a scale between $0 and $2. Then a random number between $0 and $2 was generated by the computer. The random number was the "buying price" for the bet. If the buying price was higher than the reservation price that the subject stated, she was paid the buying price (and her pay-off did not depend on the outcome of her bet). However, if the buying price was lower than the minimal selling price, the actual payment depended on the outcome of her bet. This BDM technique is well-known in the literature, but is complicated to describe and difficult for subjects to understand. Moreover there are well-known problems, see Karni and Safra (1987), with using this technique when preferences are *not* expected utility preferences—which, of course, is precisely the concern of the paper.

The *implementation of ambiguity* in the laboratory also varies from paper to paper. Hey et al. (2010) and Hey and Pace (2011) used a Bingo Blower[27] in which balls of differing colors (which define the events) are blown around inside the Blower in such a way that the balls can be seen but not counted. Andersen et al. (2009) used a Bingo Cage, which is similar to a Bingo Blower in that the balls cannot be counted, but differs from it in that the balls are stationary and not being blown about continuously. In addition, Andersen et al. used bets on natural events (for example, the temperature in Paris at a precise time in the future; see Baillon (2008) for more detail). Halevy (2007) used Ellsberg-type urns, described in much the same way as Ellsberg did:

"Urn 2: The number of red and black balls is unknown, it could be any number between 0 red balls (and 10 black balls) to 10 red balls (and 0 black balls)"

as well as urns which would be better described as two-stage lotteries:

"Urn 3: The number of red and black balls is determined as follows: one ticket is drawn from a bag containing 11 tickets with the numbers 0 to 10 written on them. The number written on the drawn ticket will determine the number of red balls in the third urn. For example, if the ticket drawn is 3, then there will be 3 red balls and 7 black balls."

Abdellaoui et al. (2011) also used Ellsberg-like urns, but with 8 colors:

*"The known urn **K** contained eight balls of different colours: red, blue, yellow, black, green, purple, brown, cyan. The unknown urn contained eight balls with the same eight colours, but the composition was unknown in the sense that some colours might appear several times and others might be absent."*

This has the same feature as the original unknown Ellsberg urn—subjects were not informed about the process of the formation of this urn. It might therefore be the case that they regard this as the "suspicious urn."

In contrast, and particularly because the Conte and Hey (2013) experiment was specifically designed to test multiple-prior models of ambiguity, Conte and Hey used two-stage lotteries (like Halevy's Urns 2 and 3). Thus, the problem facing the subjects is exactly of the type of ambiguity referred to in the theories under test—which were multiple prior models. Moreover, and in contrast to Halevy, they specified the probabilities

---

[27] See http://www.york.ac.uk/media/economics/images/exec/heyandpace/3rd.avi.

of the various possibilities, and hence the probabilities are therefore immune to subjects' subjective interpretation and assessment.

Partly because of the different types of questions and the different implementations of ambiguity, the *theories under test* also differ from paper to paper. But there is a second key difference between the theories under test. Three of the papers do not investigate *specific* models but rather "generic classes" of models. This is particularly true of Ahn et al. (2010) who investigate special cases of two classes: smooth and kinked. The kinked class essentially consists of those theories that are rank dependent in some sense: obviously Choquet EU (see Schmeidler, 1989) is in this set, as is Rank Dependent Expected Utility. There is a kink in the preference function when the ranking of the outcomes changes. In contrast there is no kink in the members of the smooth set, because ranking has no explicit role in this model. A key member of this latter set is Klibanoff et al.'s Smooth Model (Klibanoff et al., 2005). So, in a sense, the Ahn et al. paper investigates two *generic* classes, though it should be noted that it does not investigate any *specific* model in either class. Andersen et al. do a similar investigation of the smooth class, while Abdellaoui et al. do the same for the kinked class. It follows that none of these theories investigate specific theories. This is in contrast to the other papers in the table.

One key remaining difference between these various papers is their objectives. The Hey et al., Hey and Pace, and Conte and Hey papers *estimate* preference functionals and see how well the data fits the various theories. So does Andersen et al. In contrast Halevy *tests* between the various theories. Abdellaoui et al., by design, do not compare different theories but instead describe the way that ambiguity and risk enter the decision process. While Ahn et al. adopt a different methodological approach to that of Abdellaoui et al., their interest is similar; they too are interested in how attitude to ambiguity can be characterized and how it enters into the decision-making process. We feel that the correct objective of this line of research is to discover which of these is "best" and hence worth pursuing. Moreover, we would go further and follow Wilcox (2007) in arguing that the true test of a good theory is in its ability to *predict*. This is what Hey et al., Conte and Hey, and Hey and Pace do.

Some recurring issues have come out of the above. We first list them and then discuss them in detail. We should note that they are experimental issues, but only those relating to static and dynamic decision-making under risk and ambiguity.

1. What is the objective of the experiment?
2. What type of decision problems should you use and how many of them should you have?
3. How many subjects should you use?
4. How long should subjects be in the laboratory and how should you determine your incentive mechanism?
5. How should you analyze the data and what stochastic assumptions should you make? We now discuss these in turn.

14.3.5 What is the Objective of the Experiment?

This is a crucial first question to ask yourself. There are three main types of experiment: (1) to test some theory (presumably against some other); (2) to see how well a theory (or several) explains the data and how good it (or they) is at prediction; (3) just to get some ideas about how people behave.

Usually experiments of the first type use a *statistical* test. We have great scepticism about the value of this. We can illustrate this scepticism with a simple example. Suppose we want to test the hypothesis that some variable x in some large population has mean μ and we want to test it against the rather bland hypothesis that the mean is not equal to μ. Suppose that the real mean is $\mu + \varepsilon$. Then, irrespective of the value of ε (as long as it is not exactly zero), if we have a large enough sample we will end up rejecting the hypothesis that the mean is μ at any level of significance. This is irrespective of the *economic* significance of the departure of the mean from μ. So, for example, μ could be £50,000.00 and the true mean £50,000.01 and sooner or later (if you have enough data) you will reject the null that the true mean is £50,000.00. Well, of course this is true, but *is it important*? As an economist you will answer "no." So why carry out a statistical test when you are interested in *economic* significance/importance?

The other procedure is to *estimate* theories. This is obviously less parsimonious than testing theories or testing *bits* of theories, particular axioms, for example. It depends what one wants to do: if you know that a particular theory does not work, you might be interested in knowing which particular axioms of the theory are the faulty ones—with a view to building a new theory with changed axioms. But if you are interested in looking at the empirical validity of whole theories then estimating the whole theory and looking at its goodness of fit seems the appropriate way to go. The problem with this is that it is necessarily less parsimonious than simply testing bits of theories. One will normally have to specify particular functional forms of the theory and estimating particular parameters. It may be the case that the theory does not fit very well because one has chosen wrong functional forms. But if one wants to use the theory, either for prediction or for policy purposes, then one has to do this. This brings me to another point: I strongly believe that one needs theories in order to be able to *predict*, and therefore the true test of a theory is its (comparative) ability to predict. It is common knowledge that if one has two theories and one is nested inside the other, then the first is bound to fit better than the second. There are indeed statistical ways of correcting for the extra parameters (such as the Bayesian or Akaike Information Criteria), but once again these are statistical, not economic. Moreover it is common knowledge that an over-fitted model is bound to fit better but it may well predict worse. So prediction seems to us to be the true test of a model's ability to explain the data. Some (for example, Wilcox) suggest predicting *out-of-sample* but it is not always obvious what that means.

The third objective of an experiment—simply observing what subjects do—seems an eminently sensible objective, if the experiment is well designed. Unfortunately, the chances of such research getting published are slim!

14.3.6 What Type of Decision Problems Should You Use and How Many of Them Should you Have?

We have mentioned several times the different kinds of decisions that subjects could be asked to make. In the literature we see (1) pairwise choice questions, (2) allocation questions and (3) certainty equivalent questions. We have already noted that (1) is less informative than (2) and (3) but is easier for subjects to understand, but (1) usually requires less parameterization and hence fewer parameters to estimate. Clearly the more parameters you need to estimate, the more data that you need, and this brings us to the second question. The answer depends upon the amount of noise in subjects' responses, and this can only be determined by pilot studies. Once the typical level of noise is known, one can do extensive simulations to determine how many questions you need and what they should be. The answer to these questions may also depend on whether you are planning to do subject-by-subject estimation or whether you are planning to do a Mixture Model.

14.3.7 How Many Subjects Should You Use?

The answer to this question is related to the final sentence in the subsection preceding. If you are doing a subject-by-subject of the data, then it depends upon the variation between subjects. Once you have done a pilot study you will have some idea of this variation, and hence be able to choose your sample size appropriately. If, however, you are planning to do a mixture model (in which all the subjects' responses are pooled together) you might need fewer questions per subject and more subjects. Again, a pilot and extensive simulation will help you determine how many subjects you will need.

14.3.8 How Long Should Subjects be in the Laboratory and How Should You Determine Your Incentive Mechanism?

Clearly the (expected) payment to subjects should depend on how long they are required to stay in the laboratory. We suggest something over the relevant wage rate per hour should be the expected payment. We also suggest slowing subjects down—as some have realized that they make more money per hour spent in the lab if they simply answer at random. Perfectly rational behavior—which can be partially rectified by making them all stay the same time. However, this does not make them think more! It goes without saying that their payment must be related to their decisions in the experiment.

14.3.9 How Should You Analyze the Data and What Stochastic Assumptions Should You Make?

Inevitably, if one is going to do more than simply *describe* what subjects do, then one has to make some assumptions about stochastics when analyzing the data. Some experimentalists simply use standard statistical tests without thinking of the behavioral implications, but, as we have already seen several times in this chapter, stochastic assumptions are important and can change significantly the inferences one can draw. Indeed, Wilcox (2008) has argued that the stochastic assumptions are more important than behavioral assumptions. We cannot but agree, though this is not a message that has been received and understood by all experimentalists.

14.4 CONCLUSIONS

We have come a long way in this chapter and have covered a lot of ground. Rather than survey what we have done, we conclude with a warning: the inferences one can draw from an experiment depend heavily on the way that the experiment was designed (including the number and types of decision problems posed to the subjects); extensive pre-experimental simulations (informed by pilot experiments) are crucial for getting a good design. If one has a bad design then one will only get bad inferences.

APPENDIX

The preference functionals estimated by Hey and Orme (1994)

We confine attention to gambles with at most four outcomes, denoted by x_i, $i = 1, \ldots, 4$, where we put $x_1 = 0$, where $x_1 < x_2 < x_3 < x_4$, and we normalize the utility function $u(.)$ so that $u(x_1) = 0$. We denote by u_i the value of $u(x_i)$. Outcome i has probability p_i and the set of probabilities (p_1, p_2, p_3, p_4) is denoted by $\boldsymbol{p}$. We denote the value of the gamble by U.

All the references can be found in Hey and Orme (1994).

- Risk Neutrality:

$$U = p_2 x_2 + p_3 x_3 + p_4 x_4.$$

- (Subjective) Expected Utility theory:

$$U = p_2 u_2 + p_3 u_3 + p_4 u_4.$$

- Disappointment Aversion theory (Gul, 1991)

$$U = min(U_1, U_2, U_3) \text{where}$$

$$U_1 = [(1+\beta)p_2 u_2 + (1+\beta)p_3 u_3 + p_4 u_4]/(1 + \beta p_1 + \beta p_2 + \beta p_3)$$

$$U_2 = [(1+\beta)p_2 u_2 + p_3 u_3 + p_4 u_4]/(1 + \beta p_1 + \beta p_2)$$

$$U_3 = [p_2 u_2 + p_3 u_3 + p_4 u_4]/(1 + \beta p_1).$$

- Prospective Reference theory (Viscusi, 1989)

$$U = \lambda(p_2 u_2 + p_3 u_3 + p_4 u_4) + (1 - \lambda)(c_2 u_2 + c_3 u_3 + c_4 u_4)$$

where $c_i = 1/n(p)$ if $p_i > 0$ and 0 otherwise, and $n(p)$ is the number of nonzero elements in p.
- Quadratic Utility (Chew et al., 1991)

$$U = \Sigma_i \Sigma_j \psi(x_i, x_j)$$

where $\psi(x_i, x_j) = \psi(x_j, x_i)$ for all i, j and we normalize so that $\psi(x_1, x_1) = 0$.
- Regret theory with dependence (Loomes and Sugden, 1982).

This can only be used to compare two gambles p and q. The preferred gamble is indicated by the value of the expression below:

$$W = z_1 \psi_{21} + z_2 \psi_{32} + z_3 \psi_{43} + z_4 \psi_{31} + z_5 \psi_{42} + z_6 \psi_{41}$$

where z is a rather complicated function of p and q and $\psi_{ij} = \psi(x_i, x_j)$. For details see Hey and Orme (1994).
- Regret theory with independence (Loomes and Sugden, 1982).

This is where the z takes a particular form and we get:

$$W = (p_1 q_2 - p_2 q_1)\psi_{21} + (p_2 q_2 - p_3 q_2)\psi_{32} + (p_3 q_4 - p_4 q_3)\psi_{43} + (p_1 q_3 - p_3 q_1)\psi_{31}$$
$$+ (p_2 q_4 - p_4 q_2)\psi_{42} + (p_1 q_4 - p_4 q_1)\psi_{41}.$$

The same restrictions on ψ apply as in Regret theory with dependence.
- Rank Dependence (Quiggin, 1982; Yaari, 1987 and Chew et al., 1987)

$$U = [w(p_2 + p_3 + p_4) - w(p_3 + p_4)]u_2 + [w(p_3 + p_4) - w(p_4)]u_3 + [w(p_4)]u_4$$

where $w(.)$ is some *weighting function*.
- Weighted Utility theory (Chew, 1983 and Dekel, 1986)

$$U = [w_2 p_2 u_2 + w_3 p_3 u_3 + p_4 u_4]/(p_1 + w_2 p_2 + w_3 p_3 + p_4)$$

where w_2 and w_3 are weights attached to x_2 and x_3.
- Yaari's Dual Model (Yaari, 1987) This can be considered as a special case of Rank Dependence, though it was developed independently.

$$U = [w(p_2 + p_3 + p_4) - w(p_3 + p_4)]x_2 + [w(p_3 + p_4) - w(p_4)]x_3 + [w(p_4)]x_4.$$

REFERENCES

Abdellaoui, M., Baillon, A., Placido, L., Wakker, P., 2011. The rich domain of uncertainty: source functions and their experimental implementation. American Economic Review 101, 695–723.
Ahn, D., Choi, S., Gale, D., Kariv, S., 2010, Estimating ambiguity aversion in a portfolio choice experiment. Working Paper, UCL.
Akaike, H., 1974. A new look at the statistical model identification. IEEE Transactions on Automatic Control 19, 716–723.

Allais, M., 1953. Le comportement de l'Homme Rationnel devant le Risque: Critique des Postulats et Axiomes de l'Ecole Americaine. Econometrica 21, 503–546.

Andersen, S., Fountain, J., Harrison, G.W., Rutström, E.E., 2009. Estimating Aversion to Uncertainty. Working Paper.

Baillon, A., 2008. Eliciting subjective probabilities through exchangeable events: an advantage and a limitation. Decision Analysis 5, 76–87.

Barkan, R., Busemeyer, J.R., 1999. Changing plans: dynamic inconsistency and the effect of experience on the reference point. Psychonomic Bulletin and Review 6, 547–554.

Battalio, R.C., Kagel, J.H., Jiranyakul, K., 1990. Testing between different models of choice under uncertainty: some initial results. Journal of Risk and Uncertainty 3, 25–50.

Becker, G.M., DeGroot, M.H., Marschak, J., 1964. Measuring utility by a single-response sequential method. Behavioral Science 9, 226–232.

Blavatskyy, P.R., 2011. Stronger utility. unpublished manuscript.

Bone, J., Hey, J.D., Suckling, J., 2009. Do people plan? Experimental Economics 12, 12–25.

Busemeyer, J.R., Townsend, J.T., 1993. Decision field theory: a dynamic-cognitive approach to decision making in an uncertain environment. Psychological Review 100, 432–459.

Busemeyer, J.R., Weg, E., Barkan, R., Li, X., Ma, Z., 2000. Dynamic and consequential consistency of choices between paths of decision trees. Journal of Experimental Psychology: General 129, 530–545.

Camerer, C., 1989. An experimental test of several generalized expected utility theories. Journal of Risk and Uncertainty 2, 61–104.

Camerer, C., 1995. Individual decision making. In: Kagel, J., Roth, A. (Eds.), Handbook of Experimental Economics. Princeton University Press., pp. 587–703.

Camerer, C., Weber, M., 1992. Recent development in modeling preferences: uncertainty and ambiguity. Journal of Risk and Uncertainty 5, 325–370.

Carbone, E., Hey, J.D., 1994. Estimation of expected utility and non-expected utility preference functionals using complete ranking data. In: Munier, B., Machina, M.J. (Eds.), Models and Experiments on Risk and Rationality. Kluwer Academic Publishers, pp. 119–139.

Chambers, R.G., Melkonyan, T., Pick, D., 2010. Experimental Evidence on Multiple Prior Models in the Presence of Uncertainty. Working Paper.

Chew, C.S., 1983. A generalization of the quasilinear mean with applications to the measurement of inequality and decision theory resolving the Allais Paradox. Econometrica 51, 1065–1092.

Chew, C.S., Epstein, L.G., Segal, U., 1991. Mixture symmetry and the independence axiom. Econometrica 59, 139–164.

Choi, S., Fishman, R., Gale, D., Kariv, S., 2007. Consistency and heterogeneity of individual choice under uncertainty. American Economic Review 97, 1921–1938.

Conte, A., Hey, J.D., 2013. Assessing multiple prior models of behaviour under ambiguity. Journal of Risk and Uncertainty 46, 113–132.

Conte, A., Hey, J.D., Moffat, P., 2011. Mixture models of choice under risk. Journal of Econometrics 162, 79–88.

Cubitt, R.P., Starmer, C., Sugden, R., 1998. Dynamic choice and the common ratio effect: and experimental investigation. Economic Journal 108, 1362–1380.

Cubitt, R.P., Starmer, C., Sugden, R., 2004. Dynamic decisions under uncertainty: some recent evidence from economics and psychology. In: Brocas, I., Carrillo, J.D. (Eds.), The psychology of economic decisions. Reasons and choices, vol. 2. Oxford University Press, London.

Cubitt, R.P., Sugden, R., 2001. Dynamic decision making under uncertainty: an experimental investigation of choices between accumulator gambles. Journal of Risk and Uncertainty 22, 103–128.

Dekel, E., 1986. An axiomatic characterization of preferences under uncertainty: weakening the independence axiom. Journal of Economic Theory 40, 304–318.

Dubois, D., Nebout, A., 2009, When Allais meets Ulysses: Dynamic consistency and the Certainty Effect, LAMETA DR 2009-2030.

Ellsberg, D., 1961. Risk, ambiguity and the savage axiom. Quarterly Journal of Economics 75, 643–669.

Etner, J., Jeleva, M., Tallon, J.M., 2012. Decision theory under ambiguity. Journal of Economic Surveys 26, 234–270.

Gajdos, T., Hayashi, T., Tallon, J.-M., Vergnaud, J.-C., 2008. Attitude toward imprecise information. Journal of Economic Theory 140, 27–65.

Ghirardato, P., Maccheroni, F., Marinacci, M., Differentiating Ambiguity and Ambiguity Attitude, 2004. Journal of Economic Theory 118 (2), 133–173.

Gul, F., 1991. A theory of disappointment in decision making under uncertainty. Econometrica 59, 667–686.

Halevy, Y., 2007. Ellsberg revisited: an experimental study. Econometrica 75, 503–536.

Harless, D.W., Camerer, C.F., 1994. The predictive utility of generalized expected utility theories. Econometrica 62, 1251–1289.

Harrison, G.W., Rutstrom, E.E., 2009. Expected utility theory and prospect theory: one wedding and a decent funeral. Experimental Economics 12, 133–158.

Hey, J.D., 1997. Experiments and the economics of individual decision making under risk and uncertainty. In: Kreps, D.M., Wallis, K.F. (Eds.), Advances in Economics and Econometrics: Theory and Applications, vol. V 1. Cambridge University Press., pp. 173–205.

Hey, J.D., 2001. Does repetition improve consistency? Experimental Economics 4, 5–54.

Hey, J.D., 2002. Experimental economics and the Theory of Decision Making Under Risk and Uncertainty. Geneva Papers on Risk and Insurance Theory 27, 5–21.

Hey, J.D., Knoll, J.A., 2011. Strategies in dynamic decision making—an experimental investigation of the rationality of decision behaviour. Journal of Economic Psychology 32, 399–409.

Hey, J.D., Lotito, G., 2009. Naïve, resolute or sophisticated? A study of dynamic decision making. Journal of Risk and Uncertainty 38, 1–25.

Hey, J.D., Lotito, G., Maffioletti, A., 2010. The descriptive and predictive adequacy of theories of decision making under uncertainty/ambiguity. Journal of Risk and Uncertainty 41, 81–111.

Hey, J.D., Orme, C.D., 1994. Investigating generalisations of expected utility theory using experimental data. Econometrica 62, 1291–1326.

Hey, J.D., Pace, N., 2011. The Explanatory and Predictive Power of Non Two-Stage-Probability Theories of Decision Making Under Ambiguity. University of York, Department of Economics and Related Studies Discussion Paper 11/22.

Hey, J.D., Panaccione, L., 2011. Dynamic decision making: what do people do? Journal of Risk and Uncertainty 42, 85–123.

Hey, J.D., Paradiso, M., 2006. Preferences over temporal frames in dynamic decision problems: an experimental investigation. Manchester School 74, 123–137.

Holt, C.A., Laury, S.K., 2002. Risk aversion and incentive effects. American Economic Review 92, 1644–1655.

Kahneman, D., Tversky, A., 1979. Prospect theory: an analysis of decision under risk. Econometrica 47, 263–292.

Karni, E., Safra, Z., 1987. Preference reversals and the observability of preferences by experimental methods. Econometrica 55, 675–685.

Klibanoff, P., Marinaci, M., Mukerji, S., 2005. A smooth model of decision making under ambiguity. Econometrica 73, 1849–1892.

Loomes, G.C., 1991. Evidence of a new violation of the independence axiom. Journal of Risk and Uncertainty 4, 91–108.

Loomes, G., Sugden, R., 1982. Regret theory: an alternative theory of rational choice under uncertainty. Economic Journal 92, 805–824.

Quiggin, J., 1982. A theory of anticipated utility. Journal of Economic Behavior and Organization 3, 323–343.

Schmeidler, D., 1989. Subjective Probability and Expected Utility without Additivity. Econometrica 57, 571–587.

Viscusi, W.K., 1989. Prospective reference theory: towards a resolution of the paradoxes. Journal of Risk and Uncertainty 2, 235–264.

Wilcox, N., 2007. Predicting risky choices out-of-context: a monte carlo study. University of Houston Department of Economics. Working Paper.

Wilcox, N., 2008. Stochastic models for binary discrete choice under risk: a critical primer and econometric comparison. In: Isaac, R.M., Norton, D.A. (Eds.), Research in Experimental Economics. Emerald Group Publishing Limited.

Yaari, M.E., 1987. The dual theory of choice under risk. Econometrica 55, 95–115.

INDEX